British Colonial Rule

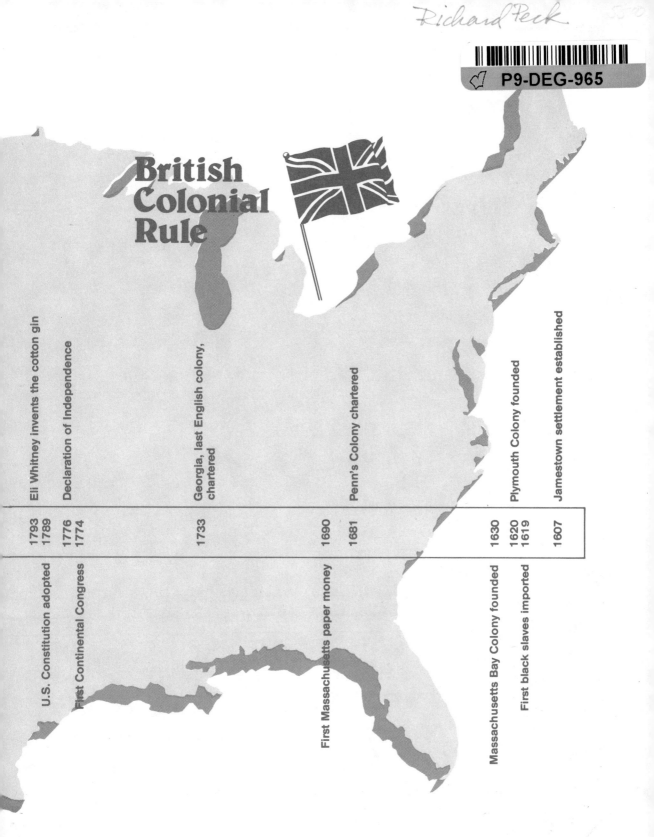

1793	Eli Whitney invents the cotton gin
1789	U.S. Constitution adopted
1776	Declaration of Independence
1774	First Continental Congress
1733	Georgia, last English colony, chartered
1690	First Massachusetts paper money
1681	Penn's Colony chartered
1630	Massachusetts Bay Colony founded
1620	Plymouth Colony founded
1619	First black slaves imported
1607	Jamestown settlement established

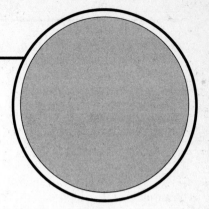

American Economic History

Fourth Edition

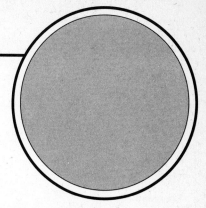

American Economic History

Fourth Edition

Jonathan Hughes
Late, Northwestern University

Louis P. Cain
Northwestern University

HarperCollins*CollegePublishers*

Executive Editor: John Greenman
Project Coordination and Text Design:
    Proof Positive/Farrowlyne Associates, Inc.
Cover Design: Kay Petronio
Photo Researcher: Nina Page
Production Manager: Kewal Sharma
Compositor: Weimer Graphics, Inc.
Printer and Binder: R. R. Donnelley & Sons Company
Cover Printer: The Lehigh Press, Inc.

For permission to use copyrighted material, grateful acknowledgment is made
to the copyright holders on pp. 589–92, which are hereby made part of this
copyright page.

American Economic History, Fourth Edition

Library of Congress Cataloging-in-Publication Data

Hughes, Jonathan R. T.
    American economic history / Jonathan Hughes, Louis P. Cain.—4th ed.
        p.   cm.
    Includes bibliographical references and indexes.
    ISBN 0-673-46868-2
    1. United States—Economic conditions.   I. Cain, Louis P.
    II. Title.
    HC103.H75   1993
    330.973—dc20   93-11768
                                                             CIP

93 94 95 96   9 8 7 6 5 4 3 2 1

CONTENTS

PART 1

P A R T

2

The National Period and Constitutional Crisis: 1791–1861

P A R T   **3**

Extended Growth and Development: Achievements and Problems, 1861–1914   233

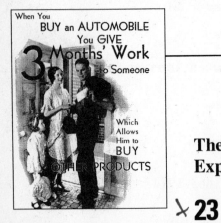

P A R T  **4**

The Climacteric of American Capitalism: Expansion of the Federal Power, 1914–45   **407**

P A R T 5

For more than three decades, research in American economic history, the "Cliometric Revolution," has caused considerable modifications in our view of the nation's past. A key reason for writing *American Economic History,* Fourth Edition, is to integrate these continuing contributions into a general picture of economic development and change. We have no intention of "throwing the baby out with the bath water"; large parts of our economic biography have not been modified by cliometric revisions. The ideal, as Douglass C. North writes, is to "explain the structure and performance of economies through time."[1]

A second motivation for writing this book is the set of modern problems faced by the United States. For the most part, our present is explained by our past. A textbook of American economic history should take us from the earliest beginnings to the present. The story of U.S. economic achievement in per capita income, technological leadership, and dynamic entrepreneurship—a thriving free-market economy, together with a generous welfare state securely anchored in a growing economy—is the picture one finds in the textbooks circa 1960. It is now the 1990s, and the situation is not as it was. The roots of the changes of the past three decades lie before 1960, and we must find those roots and explore them.

It is most unlikely, after all, that an entire society could produce one result and then turn in its track and, using the same institutional technology, produce an entirely different outcome. The country's current fiscal woes are as much the product of its past as the seeming fiscal policy triumphs of the early 1960s. The perspective of American economic history from the 1970s and '80s is different from what it was when an earlier generation chronicled the victorious march through the troubles of the 1930s to the apex of American world prestige at the end of Eisenhower's presidency. As the twentieth century draws to a close, it is important to understand what has happened in the context of economic history; and we devote relatively more space to it than has been true of similar texts in the past. We have also included a more extensive treatment of the law and of institutional developments.

Since cliometrics has produced massive and fascinating revisions of our economic history, we have endeavored to include the major conclusions, while not emphasizing the background economic analysis. In doing this, we are trying to make cliometric findings accessible to students and to instructors who are not specialists in economics.

ORGANIZATION OF THE TEXT

The history of America's economy, presented here in mainly chronological order, has been divided into five major parts: The Colonial period (1607–1780); the National period (1781–1861); the Civil War and post–Civil War period (1861–1914); World War I to World War II (1914–45); and the post–World War II period (1945–present). Each part begins with a short "Main Currents" essay in which relevant political and social themes are introduced to give the reader some background into the time period.

Four Special Topics chapters are included, one at the end of each of the first four parts of the text, in order to deal in greater depth with certain tangential subjects—tangential either because their material is more theoretical and speculative than that in the more "traditional" chapters, or because the topics are still unsettled and being debated in the professional literature. We believe this material should not "crowd out" other parts of the narrative. Some instructors will prefer to linger over these chapters; others may ignore them.

Although the text is structured chronologically, there is necessarily some overlap. For example, the second agricultural chapter (Chapter 15) contains a discussion that terminates near the outbreak of World War I. Included in this chapter is a brief account of the giant water conservation projects the United States has undertaken. These projects began in the nineteenth century as part of the primary occupation of the land for agricultural development, but, in the fullness of time, have produced "habitat" for great cities and large urban populations in the high plains, the Southwest, and the Northwest. They are mainly twentieth-century achievements, but, in historical perspective, they are direct outcomes of the initial occupation of the land. To preserve continuity in cases such as this, the discussion runs ahead of the straight chronological sequence.

NEW IN THIS EDITION

It is our hope that this edition adequately illustrates the vigor and originality of the new research by economic historians. In several cases, important work that was reported in earlier editions has now appeared in book form. The references to Claudia Goldin on the gender gap, Herbert Hovenkamp on business and the law, Martha Olney on consumer credit, and Winifred Rothenberg on the emergence of markets are now references to their books rather than to their research. New books referenced in the Fourth Edition include the Carr, Menard, and Walsh book on Maryland, William Cronon's on the Midwest, Barry Eichengreen's on the gold standard, Diane Lindstrom's on Philadelphia, and Peter Temin's on the lessons from the Great Depression. Among the new articles that the Fourth Edition takes account of are those of Bruce Smith and Charles Calomiris on colonial money, Douglas Allen on homesteading, Ronald Bailey on the financing of the slave trade, Gavin Wright on the development of America's technological leadership, Thomas Weiss on the nineteenth-century labor force estimates, Charles Calomiris on deposit insurance, Christina Romer on the ending of the Great Depression, and Robert Higgs on prosperity during World War II. In addition, with

few exceptions, the references to the *Historical Statistics of the United States* are now to the Bicentennial Edition.

New research findings can only be surveyed briefly in a textbook such as this. A textbook can never be the same as a thorough reading of the original material itself. We expect the instructors who have adopted this book to direct interested students toward the sources listed in the notes and suggested readings that accompany each chapter. As in earlier editions, we have not been able to include some new research on specialized topics that are fascinating, and for these cases we can only plead space considerations. It is our hope that students' comprehension of the development of the American economy will benefit greatly from the new material and that it will spark stimulating classroom discussion.

BENEFITS FOR THE STUDENTS

There is an additional reason for the chronological organization of this text. We have become increasingly aware of the need to re-emphasize chronology, since many students have only sketchy memories of their high-school American history classes. The chronological approach gives students a sense of the evolution of events, of how the economic and historical changes have been intertwined throughout the more than three and a half centuries of America's development. We have included a "time line" on the front inside cover of the book as a visual reference for students, to get them thinking in terms of the sequence in which these changes occurred.

Important economic terms have been emphasized in the text in boldface or italic type and are defined as they are introduced to help the student with a limited economic background grasp more readily their significance in the discussion. All of the boldfaced terms appear in the glossary at the end of the text. Students may wish to scan this glossary before beginning to read the text and to revisit it as need dictates when the terms appear in later chapters. As noted, there are lists of Suggested Readings at the conclusion of each chapter, both articles and books. These readings are closely tied to the topics discussed in the chapter and can be assigned as additional readings for class discussions. They provide the bibliographical foundation for research papers. These readings also offer the student whose curiosity is piqued the opportunity to pursue a particular issue in the original sources.

American economic history is our "clinical experience" in the effort by theorists and policymakers to continue the work of improving the national economic performance and the welfare of Americans. The experience of the past is a vital part of our knowledge of the economy—how it works and how its functioning can usefully be improved as new problems arise. As some-one once said, "You can't know where you're going until you know what road you're on."

J. R. T. H.
Evanston, Illinois
L. P. C.
Glenview, Illinois

1. Douglass C. North, *Structure and Change in Economic History* (New York: Norton, 1981), p. 3.

ACKNOWLEDGMENTS

Before Jonathan Hughes' untimely death, he asked me to collaborate with him on the Fourth Edition. We discussed at length what was to be done, and the revisions reflect mutually agreed intentions. John was my teacher, my colleague, and my friend. I wish we could have done more of the work together; I hope my execution is consistent with his intent.

I want to thank several people who assisted me in putting together the Fourth Edition. I am grateful to Daniel Shiman and Martha Olney and her students for their many comments on the previous edition and to Thomas Weiss for his detailed comments on how best to integrate his revised estimates of the nineteenth-century U.S. labor force. John Greenman and Nina Page of HarperCollins and the staff of Proof Positive/ Farrowlyne Associates, Inc. helped navigate the manuscript through publication. Sonali Thakkar and, particularly, Joyce Burnette provided excellent bibliographical research. Gina Germane double-checked each table, updating each reference to the *Historical Statistics of the United States* to the Bicentennial Edition. The contribution of these three individuals is invaluable.

I wish to join John in thanking the many instructors who have written and offered suggestions on how to improve this book, and I would invite any instructor to forward his or her comments and criticisms of this edition to me. As before, mention must be made of the singular critical contribution of Professor Stanley Engerman. Martin Bronfenbrenner, Robert Higgs, and John Wallis all took the time to give John their criticisms of the first edition in extraordinary detail. Yang Xinzhong, who came to Northwestern from Sichuan University in 1982–84 to work with John, caused him to go through the book with great care. John always attributed his association with her as helping to clarify the text.

I wish to add my gratitude to those who assisted John over the first three editions:

Hugh Aitken, Amherst College
John Altazen, University of New Orleans
Hank Ammerpohl, Central Piedmont Community College, N.C.
Terry Anderson, Montana State University
Jeremy Atack, Vanderbilt University
Peter Balash, University of Texas at Austin
Fred Bateman, University of Georgia
Jack Blicksilver, Georgia State University
Robert T. Bray, California State Polytechnic University, Pomona
Stuart Bruchey, Columbia University
Luvonia Casperson, Louisiana State University, Shreveport
Barry Eichengreen, University of California, Berkeley
Robert Fogel, University of Chicago
Robert Gallman, University of North Carolina, Chapel Hill
Robert C. Graham, University of North Carolina, Chapel Hill
John R. Hansen, Texas A & M
James Keenen, Montclair State College
James Livingston, North Central College, Illinois
James McLain, University of New Orleans
Lee Melton, Louisiana State University, Baton Rouge
Douglass C. North, Washington University, St. Louis
Stanley B. Parsons, University of Missouri, Kansas City
Roger Ransom, University of California, Riverside
Hugh Rockoff, Rutgers University

Morton Rothstein, University of California, Davis
Lester Saft, California State University, Northridge
Dana Stevens, New College, University of
    South Florida
Lea Templer, College of the Canyons
Thomas Ulen, University of Illinois, Urbana
Samuel Williamson, Miami University, Ohio
Gavin Wright, Stanford University

I want to thank my colleagues and students at Loyola, Northwestern, and U.B.C. for their help in shaping my views. A special thank-you goes to our colleagues, past and present, in the economic history group at Northwestern: Joel Mokyr, Joe Ferrie, Charlie Calomiris (University of Illinois, Urbana), Betsy Hoffman (Iowa State University), and Eric Jones (LaTrobe University). Without their longstanding support and encouragement, without their criticism, without their friendship, writing this text would have been a far more difficult and even more lonely task.

Lastly, my wife and daughter were always supportive in spite of the fact that I spent far too much time with the computer and far too little time with them.

L. P. C.
Glenview, Illinois

The subject matter of American economic history is the growth and development of a giant economy from very small, inconsequential beginnings. In quantitative measurements, that economic history is largely a "success story." The result is an economy that provides its present population with one of the highest living standards known in history.

It is also an economy with problems. But all economies this side of utopia have problems; ours are mainly the ones we have created for ourselves, very largely as a result of solving earlier problems. For example, our growing population needed an industrialized economy with its huge payoff of manufactured goods. To solve that problem, we built our giant infrastructure of basic metals, chemicals, and energy distribution systems. The resulting standard of life, with its proliferation of employments and consumer options, also produced, as an unwanted side effect, pollution of the air, water, and, in some locations, the earth itself.

The internal-combustion engine—in cars, trucks, and tractors—was a solution to the desire for more flexible and dependable power sources for transportation and other work needs. Better highways, serving the need for stable surfaces on which to move cars and trucks, stimulated suburban living. Convenient neighborhood shopping malls eliminated the need to drive to "downtown" for family provisioning. All this further stimulated the demand for cars and trucks. More efficient farm machinery was developed to better utilize the mobile power source in the farm tractor, and some self-propelled equipment appeared. Coal-fired boilers were replaced by gas- and oil-fired burners to improve the quality of urban air. Such increased demand for petroleum helped oil producers limit output and raise oil prices. Now we struggle to find solutions to those problems. American economic history provides a continuous record of such problem-solving, problem-producing solutions to the challenges of economic development. It is a study of the down-to-earth processes that lie beneath our larger cultural and political life.

Some who study economic history's gentle art complain of its pedestrian flavor, of its tendency toward dullness compared to other kinds of history. Now, admittedly, there is a certain scarcity of the sublime in economic history. Its great figures, like Josiah Wedgwood and Henry Ford, lack the dramatic flavor. Those who have labored in Mammon's vineyard inspire only small admiration in us compared, say, to the adoration given military heroes like Napoleon or to political figures like FDR. The subject matter of economic history, individuals apart, includes mainly topics like historical demography, technological change, institutional development—pale stuff compared to the movements of armies, the fall of empires, the rhetoric of political campaigns, or the romance of great love affairs. Moreover, the connecting logic of economic history is economic analysis, which can seem like dry stuff.

A tree, standing alone upon a windswept ridge, may inspire the poet to supreme flights of creative genius. To a biologist, though, that same tree invokes a more lowly muse. Yet, the biologist's knowledge is perhaps more important than the poet's if what we desire is an understanding of forest ecology. So it is with economic history, our plain subject. Its relatively everyday facts tell us why economies flourish, why they stagnate, why they die. So, if a flourishing economy is the object of public policy, that economy's history is of vital importance. Where we will go depends a great deal upon what road we have taken in the past.

The existing economy, after all, is an artifact. It is the debris of the past. The distribution of incomes, location of industry, dispersion of cities, networks of transport and communications, age structure and ethnic composition of population, balance of private and collective economic interest—all these things and more are, as they stand in our time, the consequences of decisions made in the past. The vast majority of those decisions were made by populations now long dead. If we want to preserve our present, or even to change the course of our future economic affairs intelligently, it is best that we understand why the present relationships came into existence. These relationships are the survivors of history's grinding mill; they were not easily achieved and probably should not be altered without a thorough understanding of why they exist in their present forms. Such knowledge is the meat of economic history, and its importance can scarcely be overvalued. We have an economic past, and a long one.

Oddly enough, though, Americans tend to think of their country as somehow young. Partly this conception is due to a fundamental reality, and that reality is incessant economic and social change. We have been a nation of dramatic change during all our history. Population increase alone has been so powerful a force that every fifty years have produced fundamental alterations in the way we live.

In 1991, we had more than 250 million people; in 1930, 123 million; in 1880, 50 million. In 1988, we worried about the ecology and the continuing energy crisis. In 1930, such problems were only on the horizon; in 1880, they were unthinkable. From 1776 to our bicentenary in 1976, our population increased by an astounding factor of 85, while Europe's population grew only by a factor of 4. We also have undergone an industrial revolution in the past century and become a predominantly urban people. We now have only about 3 percent of our labor force working on farms, but that number was as high as 25 percent in 1920. Today, more than two thirds of our labor force is no longer employed directly in the making of either food or goods but is, instead, engaged in services and professions.

As a nation we are lovers of gadgets, so we continually make and buy new things. We move about within the country as much as ever we did during the pioneering epoch, and we have no coherent class structure that can be passed on from generation to generation. Instead, we are a society of socially mobile people, both upward and downward. Such constant change motivates us to emphasize how new everything seems to be.

Yet, American economic history actually is the study of a largely European society, continuous on this continent for more than three hundred fifty years in the English-speaking part (Jamestown, Virginia, was settled in 1607), at least as long among French speakers (Quebec City was founded in 1608), and longer still among those who are descended from the Spanish (St. Augustine, Florida, was founded in 1565 and Santa Fe, New Mexico, has been continuously occupied since 1610). For those of Native American descent, an even older North American history can be reached through archaeology. Our federal Constitution (1789) is the oldest document of its kind in continuous use by any major nation, and much of our law, descending directly from its English ancestors, still bears the recognizable stamp of the Magna Carta (A.D. 1215).

So we are a paradox as a nation, as a living society; old in origin, long-lived in continuous institutions, yet continually renewed in structure and spirit. The study of this complex society's economic evolution will necessarily be a taxing one, and we shall come across remote and archaic origins of vital contemporary realities in our study—strange words and ideas transformed into the rules of daily life in the 1990s. To really understand our modern American economy, we need to study almost four centuries of continuous social evolution.

Every economy has a history, of course, and to some extent, the knowledge gained in studying any single economy's development is helpful in understanding the history of others. In part, therefore, the study of economic history is of general use, like the study of basic economic theory. But even the more general economic theory has its limits: Supply and demand may not explain price determination in a planned economy; the theory of the firm in competition will not explain output in a regulated industry. Similarly, there are characteristics special to each society that must be learned, by way of background information, before we can understand why that society's economy grows at rates and in structural forms different from others.

When one considers the radically different economies of the United States and Mexico, side by side in North America, the need for such background information is painfully obvious. The same is true even of cross sections in American history itself. Land settlement in seventeenth-century New England and Virginia and land settlement in nineteenth-century Iowa were so different in character that we will need to seek out knowledge of legal history as well as of changes in population and technology. Similarly, the labor force participation rates of white females are now so different from those that prevailed even fifty years ago that deep-seated economic and social changes must be considered. The role played by government in the modern economy is so much greater than it was half a century ago that we must ask penetrating questions about political change. Even "high culture" must fall into focus if we are to comprehend fully the great increase during this century in formal education among the American population.

Other topics—geology, geography, climatology, agronomy, plant and animal genetics, fundamental changes in science and technology—must also be considered. Over the long history of the American economy, the labor contract has changed radically, the form of business organization has been fundamentally altered, and even the relationship between the individual and the state has changed incredibly, despite the continuous use of the same Constitution as the basic law of the land. So, even if economic history may seem to be a relatively narrow subject, in reality it is not.

Finally, we must keep in mind that we use history to understand ourselves. Since we are, in the broadest sense, the product of our past, we should reasonably expect the study of that past to lead to the present, *as it is,* and not as someone might wish it to be. This point is very important. Many who study and write about history try to pull it this way and that to fit preconceived ideas about how it ought to have come out. For example, leftist writers have hoped again and again in our history—in the late nineteenth century, in the 1930s, during the upheavals of the Vietnam War—that our response to the problems of twentieth-century American capitalism would lead to socialism. It did not happen. If logic really were on the side of the development of American socialism, why have we been so bull-headed? American economic history should answer such a question.

Similarly, the developing mixed economy, or "welfare state," of the last forty years has dismayed free-market theorists who believe that the expanding role of government is both wasteful and illogical. So why have Americans persisted in their construction of an economy that so runs against the principles of the free-enterprise economy? We hope to answer such questions. If the mixed economy was supposed to solve our problems, why do we still have those problems? Why, after forty years of progressive taxation and redistribution of income, are wealth and income so unevenly distributed in this country? Why, after electing seven fearless inflation fighters in a row to the White House, do we still have inflation? Our study should provide some answers to those questions, too. All such problems are history's consequences, and it is in the study of history that we will understand those problems. There is no other way.

We begin our journey in the distant past, when the first group of people, complete with their laws and institutions, were transplanted from England. William Penn, the founder of Pennsylvania, wrote about government in 1682 something that could be said of all societies:

> Governments, like clocks, go from the motion men give them; and as governments are made and moved by men, so by them are they ruined too. Wherefore governments rather depend upon men, than men upon governments. Let men be good, and the government cannot be bad; if it be ill, they will cure it. But if men be bad let the government be [ever] so good, they will endeavor to warp and spoil it to their turn. . . .[1]

Three centuries after Penn launched his "Holy Experiment," the government and colony of Pennsylvania, we are still testing the wisdom of those propositions, in economics, in law, in morals and justice. In the processes of American economic history we will see the dialectical play, to and fro, of people and their institutions in the unending search for justice and equity.

Notes

1. Francis Newton Thorpe (ed.), *The Federal and State Constitutions, Colonial Charters, and Other Organic Laws* (Washington, D.C.: Government Printing Office, 1909), p. 3054.

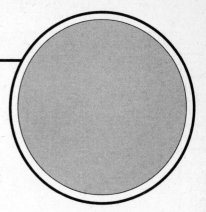

American Economic History
Fourth Edition

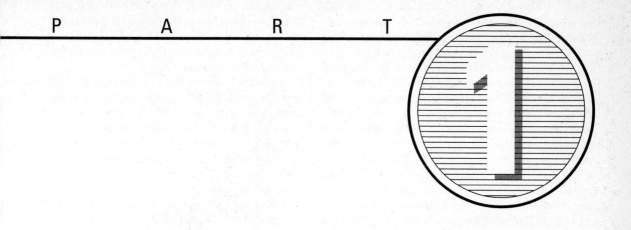

The Colonial Period
1607–1780

Main Currents 1607–1780

I n this section our discussion will concentrate upon three major topics:

1. The character of the initial institutions and the economic behavior that would shape the future of American development
2. The regional and occupational specializations enabling the colonial economy to grow internally and to fit into the world economy that nurtured it in its infancy
3. The forces of growth that pushed the colonial economy into independence from England, its original founder and sponsor

The discovery and colonization of the American continents by the North Atlantic European powers were part of the processes of population growth and nation-building that gripped Europe from the latter part of the fifteenth century onwards. For the future American economy, it was the history of England, from Elizabeth I to George III, that mattered most. The policies of those sovereigns determined the nature of the laws in this country governing land acquisition and ownership, commercial practices, and population growth through immigration (free and unfree). Major characteristics of the American economy to this day derive from those remote origins. This was the institutional "gene pool" that would determine future economic evolution. Few important foreign—non-Anglo-American—elements would enter into the legal and constitutional future of the United States after the end of the colonial era. The population increases and economic growth that followed would develop mainly along lines first established in the colonial era.

Natural endowments necessarily determined patterns of growth from the beginning. The Eastern Seaboard and its immediate hinterland (the site of the original colonies) made up an area having a variety of soils, minerals, and climate. Adaptation to those natural realities caused the colonies to become specialized in economic activity in different ways, which produced long-lasting regional characteristics that sharply distinguished the New England, Middle Atlantic, and Southern economies from each other. In part, these regional economies were internally complementary; they were advantageous to each other. But the initial differentiations depended greatly for success upon the participation of the regional economies in the larger international economy. In trade, the regions depended more on the world outside than upon their neighbors on the North American continent. The colonies were on the fringe of the Atlantic basin, and their ships, once at sea, were very nearly as close to Europe as to each other.

By the mid-eighteenth century, the perceived economic needs of the rapidly growing colonial populations increasingly came into conflict with the larger imperial designs of England. Conflicts over Western lands (i.e., west of the Appalachian Mountains), internal economic specialization, and shipping and international commerce added to and supported the political motivations of those who agitated against the administration of the Empire after 1763, the end of the Seven Years' War. By the mid-1770s, with 2.5 million people, the 13 colonies were a third as populous as England and Wales and had more population than did countries such as Sweden, Denmark, Switzerland, and Portugal. The westward movement was already beginning; land companies were formed to settle beyond the Alleghenies, and settlers streamed over the mountains. That is why the Quebec Act of 1774, which reserved the Western lands to the government of Quebec and, hence, imperial control, was itself considered an act of war, as was the closing of the port of Boston that year. The Revolution came, and the British had created, by design and accident, the first of the independent overseas nations forever cast in England's mold by language, law, and custom.

American economic history is the story of economic growth. What is it? Economists define **economic growth** as an increase in the real output of goods and services measured relative to the increase in population. Economic growth does not necessarily measure an improvement in life, but it does initiate the potential for improvement. There are many ways to describe the good life, depending upon one's viewpoint.

The great French Postimpressionist painter, Paul Gauguin (1848–1903), traded the comforts and amenities of Western civilization in 1891 for the simplicity of Tahiti. For him words like *well-being, progress,* and *welfare* meant something far different from the definitions usually found in the literature of economic development. We have come to measure progress as economic growth. It is a convention. Total output divided by total population—per capita output—usually is taken to indicate how economically rewarding life is in a given society for the average person. By either measure, *increase* in per capita output or *average* output per capita, we would consider an employed man or woman living in the pollution and congestion of modern Tokyo to be "better off" than a suntanned artist watching yet another glorious sunset on the beach in Tahiti. That is the peculiarity of the modern mind.

This frame of mind is reflected in American economic history. Until very recently, no one questioned that trees cut down, prairies plowed up, rivers dammed, and suburbs extended were measures of progress, and certainly that kind of thinking was characteristic of early Americans. Well-being was not measured by the number of standing available trees per head of population, but by the number cut down or the amount of forest cleared per family. American economic history is written in that tradition: Cutting railroads through virgin prairies is considered progress. The net market value of all activity directed at "taming the continent," divided by the population, is national income per capita, and the rate at which the output (income to those who produce it) expands is economic growth.

Basically, we will be studying the application of all grades of human labor, together with the capital tools that made it effective, to this continent's natural resources. What is produced in aggregate is the national output, which is equal in value to the incomes of all participating factors of production. Economists generally indicate that there are three **factors of production:** labor, capital, and natural resources.

Viewed as the price of output, the sum of all activity at market prices in a given year is called the **Gross National Product (GNP).** As GNP expands relative to population, we have a conventional measure of economic growth. For most of American history, this convenient number can only be roughly estimated because our information is too incomplete; GNP must be inferred from our best judgment of the evidence we have.

Now let us continue the process at the simplest level. All output comes from applications of inputs of labor and materials in given production processes. Consider an example: A man mows a lawn. The mowed grass is the output of the production process, a man pushing a mower. The amount mowed per hour is the output per labor hour. We call the latter **labor-hour productivity.** The man's work is labor, the lawn mower is our capital, and the uncut grass is our natural resource; all three are our inputs. The amount of grass mowed, to repeat, is the output. Changes that raise the amount of grass mowed per hour—that is, that raise productivity—are changes that will bring about economic growth. Add up all lawns mowed, consider all economic activity as lawns mowed, and you have the "GNP." All improvements in productive activity—whether in the quality of the machine inputs (the addition of a motor to the lawn mower), the quality of the human inputs (a better diet for the man), or the quality of materials—will tend to raise output per labor hour and thus raise GNP. For that reason any such innovations—changes in economic processes—in our economic history will interest us.

American economic history is something like our simple example, if you consider the process involved as mowing lawns from 1607 to the present. Populations came to this continent from Europe, bringing with them the technology of the Europeans. Settlements were established, and the colonists turned to the task of finding a way to live in the new environment. Over time as the population grew, the colonists succeeded in raising their output, trading some of it with Europe, and acquiring in return the necessary supplies to raise their output even more. Economic growth, once begun, was sustained generation after generation, despite some temporary setbacks. Growth occurred slowly at first, accelerating by the late nineteenth century, with successive improvements in technology and incomes high enough to finance investment as well as to raise consumption. The modern American economy is the outcome. Of course, as we shall see, the real world was far more complex than our simple model of productivity and growth. But the simple model is a guide and reference to which we may turn to assess the real-world information with which history provides us. One fact rules: Economic growth comes from increases in productivity.

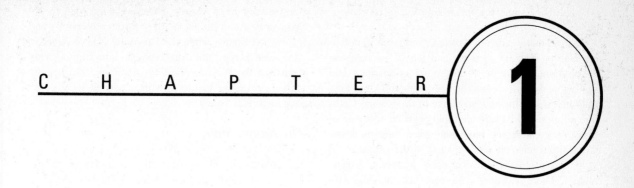

Overseas Empire

Our story begins with a fast, and necessarily superficial, tour of European history to gain a necessary perspective on our European roots and their subsequent importance.

EUROPEAN EXPANSION AND COLONIZATION

Historians customarily end the epoch known as "antiquity" in Europe with the overthrow of Romulus Augustus in A.D. 476 by the barbarian leader, Odoacer, who proclaimed himself king of Italy. This act ended the Roman Empire in the West. For nearly three centuries of swirling and bloody history, the peoples of western Europe survived in the cultural and legal ruin of Rome, while the Roman Empire in the East, based on Constantinople, flourished in even greater glory. Then, in the seventh century, most of the old Roman Empire was overturned by the relentless force of Islam, and the Eastern or Byzantine Roman Empire was boxed in. The Muslim armies swept the world, from the Atlantic to Asia, wiping out the cultures and dynastic structures of preceding millennia.

The Response to Islam

Mohammed died in A.D. 632, and in less than a century, from Persia to Spain, the armies of the Prophet triumphed. The old Persian Empire was conquered in A.D. 634. In Spain, Cadiz fell to the Muslims in A.D. 711. The next step was France, the old Roman province of Gaul. It was here, according to the great Belgian historian, Henri Pirenne, that the tide of history changed. The victory of Charles Martel at the Battle of Tours, A.D. 732, marked the end of the Muslim expansion into western Europe. The Muslims were left in control of Spain and the Mediterranean's southern shore, all the way to Byzantium and south to the Indian Ocean and beyond. The Caliph of Baghdad ruled the greatest empire in history.

To Pirenne, it was the European response to Islam that created modern Western civilization. Beginning with Charlemagne (A.D. 742–814), the thousand-year process of uniting European peoples into *nation states*—political and economic groupings of similar language, custom, culture, and dynastic linkages—ensued. Charlemagne ruled over many peoples and multinational empires combined, while, one by one, the various European languages and nations emerged.

At first, the organization of land and labor in northern Europe became what we call *feudal*—a complex and pyramidal hierarchy of mutual obligations and rights that extended from the peasant to the king. Surrounding it was the spiritual force of the Roman Catholic religion and its supranational organization, one of history's greatest and most long-lived bureaucracies. Its spiritual mission was adjusted to the centuries of kings and queens, of Holy Roman Emperors, of Viking raiders. There was even a Roman Catholic establishment for the Viking settlement of Greenland—the Bishop of Bergen, Norway. When the Norman descendants of the Viking raiders of northern France conquered England in 1066, they came with priests. The Saxons, too, were long-time Christians by then, and in 1492, when Queen Isabella of Spain granted Christopher Columbus his patent to work his will on "some islands and a continent in the ocean," it was the right of conquest of a Christian sovereign that was invoked—together with a promise to indemnify any Christian prince injured by the forceful actions of Isabella's agent, Columbus.

The late fourteenth century saw the beginning of the movement toward the modern European nation state. The Renaissance bloomed in the fifteenth century as Europe surged ahead in so many humanistic, political, and military areas. Christian Spain increased its victories against Muslim Spain, and finally, in 1492, Ferdinand and Isabella captured Granada from the Moors, ending more than 700 years of Muslim rule in Spain. During the centuries European sovereigns had developed certain rules of the game, and foremost among them was disdain for all non-Christian societies. This attitude was to be revived in the Americas.

Right of Conquest

The right of conquest of any Christian prince looms large in early American history, for it was that power, recognized among the sovereigns of Europe, that legitimized the European colonial acquisitions in the Americas. The Europeans might fight among themselves, sometimes appealing to Rome for arbitration and mediation, more often making (secular) treaties among themselves, but the European right to subdue and rule the American "savages" was not in ques-

tion—not in 1521 when Cortez subjected Mexico to Spanish rule and not in the late nineteenth century in the United States, when the surviving Native Americans were herded onto reservations. The military response of the West to non-Christian conquest, begun with its response to the Muslims, had an incredibly long historical legacy.

The Nation State

The counterplay of Roman Catholicism and Islam reflects, in the broadest possible brush strokes, the historical transformation of the early modern European world. For the peoples of Europe, the centuries from the fall of Rome to the voyages of discovery numbered ten. By the end of that period, the feudal age passed. The culture of European peoples had emerged as a blend of old and new—the Roman alphabet and Arabic numerals. The nation state was now emerging in Europe: National rulers appeared in Sweden, England, Russia, France, and Spain, together with groupings of German-speaking peoples under their own kings and nobles. The movement was accelerated by the Protestant Reformation, beginning in 1519, which underpinned the independent power of the English, Dutch, Swedes, and major German principalities.

The power of the city state, dominant in Italy and in the Hanseatic League, was fading, as was that of the great supranational rulers. Charles V, Hapsburg Holy Roman Emperor from 1519 to 1556, was the last European sovereign to realistically campaign for a universal Christian empire, the medieval ideal since Charlemagne. Charles was the son of Philip I of Castile and was born in 1500, just eight years after the discovery of America. By then, the Wars of the Roses had ended in England, and that nation had been reunited under Tudor rule. It was Charles' son, Philip, who wed Bloody Mary, Queen of England and daughter of Henry VIII, and who, as Philip II of Spain, failed to staunch the Protestant flood across northern Europe when Elizabeth's navy defeated the Spanish Armada in 1588. The history of western Europe after that dealt mainly with national states and their formation. With the feudal age ended, the power of the papacy and the Catholic monarchies waned, and Protestant Europe came into its ascendancy.

Northern Europe by the end of the fifteenth century had already become a center of commercial growth.

Greater security of persons and property at home and abroad had resulted from the centuries-long legal evolution of the more stable governments into recognized political configurations. Long-distance trade was growing at sea and along the rivers, especially in the North Sea and Baltic, under the laws of the Hanse cities. These commercial rules, replacing even more ancient laws of the Mediterranean area, were concentrated in the *laws of Oleron and Wisbuy*. The laws of Oleron were meant for traders along the coasts of France; the laws of Wisbuy governed in the Baltic and Rhine trades. Subsequent compilations of international merchant legal codes descended from these two (for example, the *Jus Hanseaticum Maritimum* of 1667 and the maritime law of 1681 promulgated by Louis XIV of France). These laws were rules for insurance, negotiable instruments, property rights, and salvage.

Security of persons and property, embodied in well-understood law, is a necessary foundation of economic investment and development. Stable law makes the world less uncertain. The evolution of such law enhanced the economic development of western Europe. Other necessary institutions developed with it. The Italian merchant bankers, such as the Bardi, Peruzzi, and Frescobaldi families, had branches all over western Europe as early as the fourteenth century, including some in England. They financed manufacturing as well as trade, and they loaned money to kings and commoners alike. They utilized the **bill of exchange,** a dated order to pay against the shipment of goods, to cut down on the need for shipping coin and bullion to make payments, thus greatly simplifying the conduct of foreign trade. The names of these resourceful Italian merchant bankers were joined in the late fourteenth and early fifteenth centuries by the aggressive and brilliant Medici of Florence and in the fifteenth and sixteenth centuries by the Fugger family of Augsburg. Jakob Fugger is reputedly the man whose gold bought the Holy Roman Empire for Charles V in 1519. These few famous names represent scores of merchant bankers, allied to kings and nobles, whose wealth and skills financed trade expansion.

Population Patterns

The growth of commerce implies the growth of cities and population. Despite its agrarian base, the organization of feudal Europe, before the time of the nation state, contained suitable provision for urban growth. Late medieval Europe was alive with cities. Bologna in the early thirteenth century may have numbered 64,000 persons; Florence in 1347, 55,000; Cologne in the early fourteenth century had 50,000; Hamburg, 30,000; Strasbourg, 30,000. Late-fourteenth-century Ghent had as many as 60,000; London 35,000; and Paris at the beginning of the fourteenth century may have numbered 60,000 people. In addition, there were hundreds of smaller towns and thousands of market towns and villages that were the sites of production—food processing, milling, wood and metal fabrication—and the accumulation of tradable goods, such as textiles. From these towns and cities trade spread into the hinterland and down the rivers to the oceans and more distant markets.

The development of towns and trade was uneven, though, in part because of the uneven fate of population. The story of European population growth is complex, and it is not a story of steady growth. Evidence shows that the population of western Europe declined from the fifth century A.D. to a low point in perhaps the ninth or tenth century A.D. From the middle of the tenth century to the early fourteenth century, there was strong growth, which nourished the brilliant civilization of the late Middle Ages. This was a time of massive growth and permanent investment, shown not only in urban growth and new, enlarged city boundaries but also in the great Gothic cathedrals of the time. This brilliant episode ended relatively suddenly because of famine and then the plague in the early to middle fourteenth century. The most famous disaster was the Black Death of 1347–8, which may have killed half of Europe's population. Estimates of the death count run from 30 percent to 50 percent. Recovery took generations. It was said that as many as 200,000 of the smaller medieval towns and villages were completely depopulated. Estimates of English population show a total of about 3.7 million in 1348, a loss of 600,000 by 1350, and only 2.25 million remaining by 1374 (one estimate shows only 2.1 million alive by then). France lost perhaps 40 percent of its total population.

Recovery from that catastrophe provided a rising base for renewed commercial and productive development in the fifteenth to eighteenth centuries, just at the time that the new nation states were engaged in active overseas expansion. By 1545, Britain had 3.2 million people and had not yet recovered entirely from the plague. France is thought to have recovered its pre-plague population completely by the late sixteenth century. With minor setbacks, primarily due to the incredible destruction of life caused by the religious wars of the late sixteenth century, European population increase provided the strength for the commercial expansion that would characterize the years of discovery and colonial settlement of the Americas.[1]

The Discoveries

European expansion here in the Americas was part of the nation-building process at home. Although the Portuguese had driven the Muslims out of Portugal as early as the twelfth century, conflict was recurrent. The Portuguese crossed over to North Africa in 1415 and captured Cuenta—this marks the beginning of permanent European expansion overseas—reaching Madeira in 1419, the Canaries shortly afterwards. The Azores were colonized in 1439–53. The Portuguese worked their way down the west coast of Africa; the Muslim domination of the eastern Mediterranean blocked European access to trade with Asia by land. Voyages around the horn of Africa would bypass the Muslim blockade. In 1488, Bartholomeu Diaz rounded the Cape of Good Hope, the event that would launch the long Portuguese career in East Africa, the Persian Gulf, the Indian Ocean, China, and islands beyond. In 1493 Columbus was back in Spain from his first voyage. An arrangement was made with the Portuguese, the Treaty of Tordezillas (1494), in which Spain was granted all lands discovered more than 370 leagues west of the Cape Verde islands, a measurement that in time gave Portugal claim to Brazil.

Discoveries continued. Vasco da Gama, under the flag of Portugal, reached India in 1498. Then, Alfonso de Albuquerque conquered Goa in 1510. A few years later, the Portuguese reached China and by 1557 had founded Macao. The Spanish followed up their Caribbean discoveries in due course and then shifted to the mainland. Diego Velázquez conquered Venezuela in 1499–50 and Cuba in 1511.

Between 1517 and 1524, Hernan Cortez accomplished the total conquest of Mexico. Vasco de Balboa sighted the Pacific after marching across the Isthmus of Panama in 1513. Ferdinand Magellan, a Portuguese under the flag of Spain, pursued this discovery to the Philippines, died there on his epic voyage around the world in 1521, but claimed those islands for Spain. In 1528 De Soto landed in Florida. More land was added. Before dying in what is now Arkansas, De Soto discovered the Mississippi River. Working up from Mexico by land, the Spanish crossed the Southwest, going as far as modern Kansas. One of the Spanish officers under Francisco Coronado discovered the Grand Canyon in 1540. These discoveries established Spanish claims to large portions of what is now the United States. Buenos Aires was founded in 1535, and in 1543 Francisco Pizarro ended his long campaign in Peru with victory over the Incan Empire.

Thus, in 50 years, primarily due to the Spanish and Portuguese, the dimensions of the world in European eyes had completely changed. Other European monarchs followed suit.

The English were the first to organize. In 1496 penny-pinching Henry VII issued a patent to the Genoese adventurer Giovanni Caboto (John Cabot) "to seeke out, discover and finde whatsoever isles, countries, regions or provinces of the heathen and infidels, which before this time had been unknown to all Christians."[2] On 24 June 1497 Cabot reached Cape Breton (Nova Scotia), which he claimed for Henry VII. He was rewarded with a pension of £10 a year when he got back to England with the news. However, his discovery (and later voyages by him and his sons) established the initial English claim to the New World and again altered the course of history. But not for another century. The English long continued to hope that a northwest passage, a shortcut to Asia, could be found in the continent's northern waters. After several futile attempts by Henry's son and his granddaughter, Elizabeth, to find this shortcut, the first permanent English settlement was made in Virginia in 1607 by a company with a charter from James I.

England was not the only European nation with designs on North America. In 1608 the French founded Quebec. The Pilgrims (the major English dissenters) landed in 1620 at Plymouth, and the Dutch, long in the Hudson River for trade purposes, established what became New York City in 1624. A Swedish colony, established in 1643 in what became Pennsylvania, was passed to the Dutch in 1655 and, then, to the English.

End Results

By 1650 the Spanish, English, Dutch, and French were all established in what would become the United States and Canada. All four powers were nation states in the modern sense (the Dutch had a republic). The Spanish and French represented European military prowess, actually their main interest. The Dutch and English represented the commercial revolution that was sweeping northern Europe (in part fueled by Spanish gold from America), as its populations recovered from the ravages of the Black Death and then grew apace. England would have the most impact on our history.

ENGLAND OVERSEAS: EXPORT OF INSTITUTIONS

Early English Enterprises

By the time the English followed Cabot's discoveries with actual colonization, the riches of the New World had become legendary. Gold and silver shipped to Spain (some of it intercepted by English privateers) had found its way into circulation all over Europe. The English had good information regarding the American potential for supplying ship timbers, masts, and naval stores, and for settlement locations north of the Spanish colony in Florida. In addition, they still had some hope of finding a northwest passage to the Orient. The English had picked up furs from trade with the Indians at temporary fishing camps and aborted settlements along the northeast coast, while furs from French trading in Canada also were available in Europe. Many English ship captains had visited the mainland for trading, and, in 1605, Sir George Weymouth had brought back five Indians who were shown about in London by Sir Ferdinando Gorges, a promoter of New World ventures.

The maps and writings of Richard Hakluyt and others had familiarized English leaders with the prospects of North American colonies. English adventurers by the early seventeenth century had at least a superficial knowledge of the area they were hoping to colonize, and despite earlier failures, there were merchants and other capitalists ready to risk money on colonizing ventures. Furs, fish, timber, and the hope of finding precious metals were sufficient to induce some to bet their money on the hope of great gain. The Spanish, Dutch, and Portuguese were finding profits in foreign ventures, and some English magnates were hoping for similar successes. In addition, there was usually the advantage of some governmental participation, if only in the form of military protection, which reduced risks.

In 1606, the Virginia Company was chartered, with two sections, one in London and the other in Plymouth, to launch colonization ventures. The method used, the **joint-stock company** with a royal charter, was a form of partnership in which shares were issued to each partner up to the amount of the partner's investment.[3] The English organized their overseas ventures in several ways. A joint-stock company like that in Virginia began with a royal charter, but private capital and initiative motivated it. Later in Virginia and elsewhere, the government of the colony was taken over and operated directly by the crown, making each a crown or **royal colony.** In some cases extensive rights and great tracts of land were granted as personal favors by the king to individual grant proprietors such as Sir Ferdinando Gorges, Lord Baltimore, and William Penn. These colonies, **proprietary colonies,** were in some respects like little kingdoms, but their citizens enjoyed all the rights of other Englishmen, including institutions of representative government. Thus, capital for the Virginia venture was raised in corporate style, from many sources, with the risks spread. The first Virginia colonists set out in high hopes.

Those who signed up to come to America came originally from many walks of life, and they came with very different motives. Some came for religious reasons, seeking freedom to practice faiths that were frowned upon in Europe. The English Puritans, French Protestants, and Catholics, Quakers, and Mennonites from Germany were examples of these. Some came as independent settlers with sufficient capital to buy land, set up as merchants, or followed other professions. Most whites came as indentured servants, working off debts by their labor in the New World. Africans came as slaves. Also, some thousands of prisoners of the crown—debtors, condemned criminals, and prisoners of war—came under bonds of indenture, gaining freedom by their labor. We will deal with them all in due course.

Let's take a moment to note the remote origins of the original diversity of laws in the colonies since this diversity was enhanced afterwards by legislation and practice and, of course, continues among the American states to this day. The years of permanent English settlement of the American colonies before the American Revolution run from the Jamestown settlement, begun precariously in 1607, to the founding of Savannah, Georgia, in 1733. Halifax, Nova Scotia, was settled in 1749, but that colony stayed with the crown after 1776 and became a province of Canada. So, we are talking about a historical process of transplanting English society that continued for about 150 years. Constitutionally, the England that launched the Virginia and New England settlements in 1607–30 was different from the one whose king was to sign the first charter for Georgia. England had in the interim passed through the Puritan Civil War, the restoration of the Stuarts, and finally, to its Protestant monarchy, much reduced in its power by an ever more dominant Parliament. In 1607 James I was ruling by divine right (an idea that brought his son, Charles I, to the axeman), while in 1733 George II was ruling in the age of parliamentary supremacy. In 1606, when James I granted the first Virginia charter, Queen Elizabeth had been dead only a short three years. It was still Elizabethan England, and the early laws and experiences of Virginia and Massachusetts show that influence.

English Law in America

From the outset the colonies were considered English land and the colonists English subjects. James was perfectly clear about this in the charter of 1606. He said that the colonists departing for Virginia "shall have and enjoy all Liberties, Franchises and Immunities, within any of our other Dominions . . . as if they had been abiding and born, within this our Realm of England."[4] As the decades passed and more colonies were added, the accepted rule was that all English **common law** (the string of rules made from court decisions), plus all **statute law** (enactments of Parliament), up to the time of settlement was the basic law of each colony. Since each colony was founded at a different time, each colony had slightly different background laws to begin with.

Besides that small difference, we can say that there was a common body of laws among the colonies. Laws made by Parliament for the colonies, or extended to them, were their laws, too. For example, in 1645 during the Puritan Revolution, the Massachusetts colonists passed a law inviting foreign ships into Massachusetts harbors: "All ships which come for Trading onely, from other parts, shall have free access to our Harbours, and quiet Riding there, and free Liberty to depart without any Molestation by us."[5] This was essentially what we now would call **free trade,** a concept that appeared two centuries before its time in the

Massachusetts law. But when Charles II was restored in 1660, the Cromwellian Navigation Act of 1651, which restricted colonial trade, was repassed by Parliament. One year later, the Massachusetts law was changed so that the English navigation law could be enforced.

The rights of English citizens in the seventeenth century comprised those of legislative power and taxation by the representatives of the people themselves. By the seventeenth century, the English had evolved a *bicameral legislature,* one made up of two parts—the House of Commons and the House of Lords. With different names substituted for the legislative bodies in each colony, the tradition came straight over the Atlantic. Each colony had an appointed governor and council and developed an elected lower house. Taxation measures began in the lower house, as they did in England and the successor governments, and as they do in the present-day 50 state capitals and the federal government in Washington. The parliamentary tradition was destined to pass right through the Revolution at the state level to be established at the national level by the federal Constitution. An independent judiciary was added because the new Senate would not have judicial powers, as did its English ancestor, the House of Lords.

Origins of Judicial Review

As we have seen, the original charters gave the colonists the right to legislate as long as their laws remained within the general boundaries of English law. This requirement not only maintained the forms of English government but protected the colonists from potential infringements of their rights in daily proceedings in a land so distant from the home government. In 1621, the Virginia colony's government was taken over by the crown. A new system with a bicameral legislature was established: the Council of State, whose members were appointed in England, and the General Assembly, made up of "Burgesses" of every town "to be respectively chosen by the inhabitants."[6] Article V of the new royal charter was specific about the form the new system was to take. "We require the said General Assembly, as also the said Council of State, to imitate and follow the Policy of the Form of Government, Laws, Customs, and Manner of Trial, and other Administration of Justice, used in the Realm of *England.* . . ." And in Article VI, what we now call *judicial review* was imposed upon the colonists. No legislation passed by the assembly was to become law unless "[it was] ratified and confirmed, in a General Quarter Court of the said company here in England and so ratified to them under our Seal. . . ." In short, all American law was officially nonoperative until reviewed in England. The General Quarter Court represented the English stockholders in England, and its powers also were restricted. Its orders, once sent to Virginia, were not to go into effect unless ratified there by the General Assembly. Given the circumstances and the slow communications of the time between London and Virginia, government was to be a formal and well-organized affair. Such was true also of the other British colonies, and it formed a basis of settled law to reduce risk for all "adventurers"—those who invested and those who went as settlers to Virginia.

The idea was to bind "England" together by law, since England was about to create a worldwide empire, and yet to try to remain a single nation wherever the population was predominantly English—a peculiar idea. When Maryland was chartered as a proprietary colony in 1632, the owner, the Lord Baltimore (and his heirs), was granted extraordinary powers by the king. Yet, it was required that the colony remain forever English. Lord Baltimore and his heirs would owe the crown "the Faith and Allegiance and Sovereign Dominion due to Us, our Heirs, and Successors."[7] Baltimore and his heirs were free to make their own laws "of what kind soever, according to their sound Discretion," but with a proviso: "So, nevertheless, that the Laws aforesaid be consonant to Reason, and be not repugnant or contrary, but (so far as conveniently may be) agreeable to the Laws, Statutes, Customs, and Rights of this Our Kingdom of England."

Such limitations held in all the colonies. From 1696 onwards, all laws passed by the colonial assemblies were reviewed in England by Board of Trade lawyers, and those acts found repugnant to the laws of England were disallowed (about 5.4 percent of the total).[8]

Individual Colonies

The sequence of colonization was more or less a matter of chance, depending upon events in Europe as well as in America. However, there is a problem with the founding dates of the individual colonies. The question is whether the year of the charter or that of the first

permanent settlement should be considered. We will follow the custom of dating by the settlement (see Figure 1.1). Virginia, in 1607, was supposed to be a profit-making enterprise for a joint-stock company. The Plymouth Colony (1620) and the Massachusetts Bay Colony (1630) were of religious origins, created by the flight of Puritans from the persecution of the established church in England. Maryland (1634) was partly

Figure 1.1   Colonial Cities and Their Founding Dates

St. Augustine was a Spanish settlement. The English towns began with Jamestown in 1607, then Richmond, followed by Plymouth, Salem, and Boston. The final English colony was Savannah, founded in 1733. The earliest colonial cities were either seaports or on water routes leading to the sea.

motivated by Lord Baltimore's desire to find a haven for Roman Catholics, but it also was meant to be profitable, the profits to come from land sales, feudal taxes, and fees of all sorts. The flight of Roger Williams from Puritan Massachusetts (he was banished) to Rhode Island (1644, a charter granted in 1663) was again motivated in part by religious difference, this time in the New World exclusively.

Connecticut was an offshoot of the Puritan Massachusetts Bay Colony. In 1639 settlers in New Haven organized themselves into a permanent government. Then, in an amended constitution of 1643, only "members of some or other of the approved churches of New England" were allowed to vote and hold office. In 1662, Connecticut was granted a more liberal charter by Charles II.

Religion again was the major force behind the proprietary colony of Pennsylvania, founded in 1681. The year is that of Penn's takeover; the Swedes and Dutch had already been there some four decades. Pennsylvania began as a huge land grant awarded to William Penn by Charles II in payment of an old debt owed to Penn's father, Admiral Sir William Penn. The Quaker leader dreamed of a haven for his persecuted coreligionists and other Protestant groups. Penn also hoped, vainly, that he would make a profit from land sales and rents.

Delaware came into existence in 1702 (the Charter was signed in 1701) after separation from Pennsylvania, in part due to a boundary dispute between Penn and Lord Baltimore's heir. Georgia (1773) began as a mainly charitable enterprise, with both slavery and rum forbidden, but ended up as a royal colony with a more lowly end, such as money, on everyone's mind. That was clear when black slavery was introduced in order to make the colony pay. To make life there more bearable, rum imports and consumption also came to be allowed.

New York was settled by charter from the Dutch West India Company. The charter was granted in 1621; the settlement at Albany dates from 1624, and permanent settlement on Manhattan is dated from a fort built there in 1626. The British took the New York Colony in 1664. It continued as a proprietary colony of James, Duke of York, until he became King of England in 1685.

New Jersey began with Dutch and Swedish settlers. Then, for a short time, it had several English proprietary owners. Part of the colony went with Penn's grant in 1681. In 1702 the remainder became a royal colony.

South and North Carolina came from the original grants to a group of proprietors for Carolina in a charter of 1663. A permanent settlement was made in 1670. By 1719 South Carolina had a royal charter, and ten years later, the same was true of the mainly backwoods settlements that would become North Carolina.

The Colonial Empire in Retrospect

Not one of the original colonies began as a royal colony. All were private ventures, either proprietary or joint-stock. But the problems of colonization led to crown takeovers in all but Rhode Island, Connecticut, Pennsylvania, Delaware, and Maryland by the time of the Revolution. The colonies, for the most part, had existed as so many separate appendages of England, all governed from London. The scheme to unite the Northern colonies under Governor Edmund Andros in 1686–89 died when James II was driven from the throne of England. The earlier Confederation of New England (1643–84) had come to nothing, and Benjamin Franklin's later plan to unite the colonies in 1754 at the beginning of new troubles with the French and Indians was overturned by the Board of Trade.

The British did not want a separate union on the North American continent, even a union of loyal British subjects. The sugar-producing plantation colonies of the Caribbean isles long seemed more valuable to the crown than the backwoods settlements on the mainland. Sugar and rum were cash-earning commodities in great demand. But by the mid-eighteenth century, much had changed. What was of fundamental importance at the beginning was the mutual tie of the separate colonies to England. This would give the Americans a common pool of language, laws, customs, and business morality and practice—mutually understood foundations upon which to build their own constitutions and laws when the time came. English institutions, transplanted overseas, would continue to grow, for the most part, changed over time by new challenges met in the American environment.

LAND ACQUISITION AND TENURE

As we noted, Europeans considered conquest, if it was from non-Christian occupiers of land, a legitimate

THE STADTHUYS OF NEW YORK IN 1679
Corner of Pearl St. and Coentijs Slip.

G. Hayward & Co. 171 Pearl St. N.Y.

The Stadthuys of New Amsterdam (New York City) in 1679 reflects the cultural and economic endowment of the Dutch.

transfer of ownership to Christians. If no non-Christian owner could be identified, then discovery alone was sufficient. Such was as true of the English as of any other Europeans. For example, the English claimed New York by right of discovery and considered the Dutch settlement there usurpation. They eventually took New York from the Dutch by war and treaty. As for the Native Americans living in New York at the time, either they received land back from the English (and some, like the Iroquois, did), or they simply were killed or driven off.

Property Rights

In theory, all English land belonged to the king. He was the sole and absolute owner. All Englishmen were the king's tenants on their land. Only he, as the Lord Paramount, was beholden to no one save God for his property rights. Such was the theory of English feudalism. In the United States today, the position of the king has evolved in some sense to that of the state. Thus if you do not pay your property taxes, your rights are annulled for the amount of the taxes. In other countries, land can be owned *allodially*—that is, by absolute right—but not in the United States. This is an uncelebrated part of our "English heritage." To these authors' knowledge, the American people were never asked by what right they wanted to own their land.

According to English feudalism, all land ownership was a grant for services from the king. He was the "donor," and without his authority, no land ownership rights could exist for his subjects. His tenants, all others who owned rights in real property, were his liege men. William Blackstone, the great English legal writer, said in his *Commentaries on the Laws of England* (1765) that the ownership right in real property, land, could come to no Englishman, either by purchase or inheritance, "unless accompanied by those feudal clogs which were laid upon the first feudatory when it was originally granted." The English developed elaborate techniques for transfers of such rights, including written deeds of ownership after passage of *The Statute of Frauds* in 1677.

Indian Land

Those techniques of land transfer were of crucial importance in the dispossession of the American Indians since they had no written evidence of ownership. They might obtain land (their own, or someone else's) from the king (or his agents, including colonial governments) by grant or purchase or treaty, but they had no recognized natural rights to the land they had long hunted over except the right of "occupancy," which was feeble indeed. The long and the short of it is that their territorial claims were doomed the moment the Europeans stepped ashore, except to the land that the Europeans allowed them to keep. All colonial governments attempted (with uneven success) to restrict purchases from the Indians by private settlers. This policy was necessary because claims of Indian tribes could not be shown by any written instruments except those acquired from the whites themselves. When an Indian, chief or other, took money for land, what was being sold? The answer is, the patrimony of all Indians. Here was a classic example of a communal property right, unrecognized in law, that could be exploited for profit by individual Indians (and whites) at the expense of all other Indians.

Every land-selling Indian was a free rider in these circumstances. (A **free rider** is someone who gains, at little or no cost, the benefits of the efforts of others.)

Any Indian seller who could find a white buyer could sell out the communal rights of his fellows by selling all the land of the tribe. Restrictions might prevent the worst abuses, but it might also pay both parties to violate the restrictions, and, of course, many did, giving rise to violence, illegal entry into land, Indian wars, disputed claims, and uncertainty. What was involved was a primitive process in which a migratory and largely hunting-and-gathering people were being dispossessed of those rights by whites who intended to settle and farm permanently on the land. What can be said of it? What was justice? One of our greatest jurists, Chancellor James Kent of the Supreme Court of New York, wrote hopefully of the outcome in 1826 in his *Commentaries on American Law:* "The settlement of that part of America now composing the United States has been attended with as little violence and aggression, on the part of the whites . . . as is compatible with the fact of the entry of a race of civilized men into the territory of savages."[9]

The Battle of the Little Big Horn was just one half-century later. After that, violent conflict with the Indians became rare, then stopped, as the Indians were confined to reservations. Now that these Native Americans are full citizens and so many of their ancestors' dealings with the whites were of uncertain legality, interesting lawsuits have in recent years enlivened the newspapers from Maine to Oregon. In some cases, remnants and descendants of Indian tribes have been awarded sizable compensation.

Land Acquisition by Individuals

Apart from the acquisition of Indian land, white Europeans acquired original titles to land in America in essentially five ways: by ownership shares in the founding colonization companies; by headright grants; by purchase from governments; by preemption ("squatters' rights"); and by special purpose grants of governments.

1. *Ownership shares.* In the cases of Virginia and Plymouth, some land rights were assigned on a per share basis. In Virginia, also, land was granted in large blocs in consideration for subscriptions in cash that did not entitle the subscribers to full membership in the company. Thousands of acres originally were assigned in this manner.

2. *Headright grants.* In the case of headright land grants, commonly 50 acres were given to, or for, each person who crossed the ocean. (There was considerable variation, especially in Virginia.) If the grant was 50 acres, and one man came, he got 50 acres. If he brought over four other people, he would acquire 250 acres by headright. Such was the policy in Virginia, New York, New Jersey, the Carolinas, to some extent in Maryland, Pennsylvania, and also Georgia. In Virginia, at first there were few limits on the amount of headright land granted, and great abuses of the privilege were charged. In a country that needed both land settlement and people, the headright system was a powerful stimulus for colonization.

3. *Purchase from governments.* All colonies finally developed techniques for outright sales of land by the colonial governments. The first of the colonies to attempt to transfer nearly all of its land by sale alone was Pennsylvania. Penn had a grant of 47 million acres and hoped to sell most of it. By the mid-eighteenth century, all the colonies had developed the practice of land disposal for cash payment only.

4. *Preemption.* Attitudes regarding preemption, or land transfers to individuals for actual settlement, varied. In the Southern and Middle colonies, preemption came to be encouraged, but not in New England. The issue of "squatters' rights" came to the fore by the third quarter of the eighteenth century, when a rapidly growing population faced a largely empty wilderness to the west. This produced a number of settlers who, for lack of money or knowledge of the law, or because of indifference to law, began moving into empty lands. By the end of the Revolutionary period, the trickle became a flood.

There had always been some squatters. In fact, there were squatters in Massachusetts before 1630. The original settlers of Connecticut were technically squatters—they had moved into that territory without leave. Vermont, as early as 1752, had a large population of squatters. The famous armed militia, the "Green Mountain boys," was a band of armed squatters prepared to defend their cleared lands. In New England, squatter settlements were resisted by government, but in the Middle colonies and the South, especially in Virginia, squatters were desired as pioneers, and land-rich governments were generous with preemption land transfers. During the Revolution, both Virginia and North Carolina passed laws granting preemption rights to *all* frontier settlers. The Middle and especially the Southern colonies were far more generous with frontier squatters than the federal government would be after it took over the public domain.

5. *Special-purpose grants.* Colonial governments also granted lands for various special purposes— to encourage settlement or industry or bridges or ferries or whatever. In Massachusetts grants were made to form new congregations in frontier townships. Land, called a *glebe,* was granted to help support churches. Soldiers were commonly awarded land in payment for their services. Land was given to encourage special trades or services: Colonel Williams, founder of Williams College, received 200 acres to build a fort and grist mill; in Massachusetts an Indian, named Hobbamock, received land in payment for his services as an interpreter.

By all such means, the colonial land was slowly filled with people. Their rights in that land are of crucial importance as a background to subsequent American economic development. Colonial land ownership contained the seeds of the American capitalism that was to come.

American Land Tenure

It is customary to think of individual ownership in real property as a "bundle of rights." A buyer has a different bundle than a landlord or sharecropper. In England, during the centuries after the Norman Conquest, a complex net of feudal relationships based upon mutual obligations produced an intricate set of rights in real property. Those rights, the content of ownership, are called the **tenure.** No one could transfer more rights, that is, a stronger tenure, than he himself owned. The question of how much *less* a seller could transfer to a buyer, how much he could "reserve" for himself, was a complex matter. A feudal lord, for example, might grant tenures that required labor to be performed, that restricted the "right of waste"—such as cutting trees or digging mines. Land might pass in the market that was "dirtied" with lingering feudal obligations, even if bought by a free man. Such land had labor servitudes attached to it.

Fortunately, colonial land laws were relatively simple because, from Virginia to Georgia, the crown had permitted only one tenure to be established in America—**free and common socage.** The main distinguishing characteristics of this tenure were the following:

1. It was perpetual (not limited to any term of years).
2. It was directly heritable by heirs (did not need to be regranted by the donor).
3. It could be passed by will.
4. All the obligations on it had to be "fixed and certain."
5. The *fruits of chivalry* (e.g., the rights to wardship and marriage of minor heirs) did not accrue to the guardian. Nor did other uncertain obligations, like the requirement to contribute to marriage of the donor's children, or *heriot,* which is a tax upon the death of the owner.
6. The right of waste existed fully.
7. Socage land was freely *alienable* (it could be sold) by its owner.

Socage tenure's origins in English history are vague. It seems originally to have been a *base tenure* (one that involved obligatory labor), and one form of it, *villein socage,* long existed with labor services required. However, free and common socage came to carry no base or uncertain obligations, or "incidents." Unlike the major tenure in English feudal landowning, in socage tenure, no military service was due. Indeed, all of the colonial charters forbade military tenures, or tenure by knight service. The incidents, the running costs of the tenure of free and common socage, generally included fixed payments on the land alone, known as *reserved ground rents,* which were perpetually due to the donor. In colonial America, the bundle of fixed incidents was combined into singular periodic payments called **quit rents,** which meant that the owner who paid them was "quit and free" of all other obligations. These rents eventually became the local property taxes of modern America, and, as in colonial America and feudal England, payment of the obligation is an absolute right of the donor (now the state government and its local units) or the tenure simply vanishes. In colonial America, apart from Massachusetts, which did not encumber its land with quit rents, as now, land taxes were obligatory—at least in theory. These days, taxes tend to be collected on real property. In colonial America proprietors often had difficulty collecting quit rents. The colonists resisted paying these taxes because they were burdensome. In some colonies the isolation of settlements made collections difficult. Eventually, the very idea of such perpetual obligations came to be considered "foreign" and unjust.

These are the basic elements of American land ownership. They were shared by military tenures in fee simple (which means the "simple feud"—direct inheritance) in England, and Americans in time came to call their tenure **fee simple.** The word *socage* vanished from common use.

Certain antique words from this past linger on. Those who held this tenure had the right to be *seated* on the land (others, only to squat), and were considered *seised* of the property. The owner was the *fee holder.* This quaint language may still be found on legal documents in land transfers; the seller or mortgagor represents that he or she is "fully seised" of the property or of the fee and can thereby transfer rights to it.

We need not go further into the complex topic of land law to get the gist of it for our purposes.[10] Americans who bought land could sell it if they wished; buyers had the same rights as the sellers. The land could be divided up or its nature changed (trees cut, fields planted, ores mined, wells drilled, ponds constructed). All that was due the seller was the sale price. He could, and still can, reserve certain rights for himself or others—for example, mineral rights. Servitudes still exist, for example, such as those for rights of way for roads, power lines, and utilities. Since taxes are due in order for the tenure to be maintained, the tenure imposes a cost for holding land idle, and there would be an inducement to keep only as much land as would yield more than the taxes on it. This force was commonly thought to have favored the development of family farms as the main vehicle of land settlement unless there were sufficient amounts of other exploitable resources on the land—such as timber, minerals, water—or unless the land could be rented, leased, or sharecropped at rates that exceeded the taxes.

Long-Run Implications

Socage tenure made American land a commodity almost from the beginning, one unencumbered by other rights and obligations to it. Active land markets became characteristic of American economic history, and land speculation at times came close to being the main national industry. The freedom of the tenure also defined the freedom of its owners, causing Americans early on to view land ownership and personal freedom as linked to each other. This relationship would be a powerful tradition in American economic history, to be eroded slowly in the twentieth century as land became encumbered by the larger needs of society. Today, instead of the military services and obligatory labor of feudal England, landowners find themselves faced with rights of land ownership and sale limited by zoning, land use, and environmental impact laws. For the most part, though, from colonial times until the mid-twentieth century, the land itself would be a major commodity in the developing market economy and the base for exploitation of its natural resources on an individual-enterprise basis. At the time of colonization, a fifth of all newly discovered precious metals had been reserved for the crown, but few such reservations remained for the state when coal, oil, iron, and other minerals began to be extracted and refined by private owners in the years of American industrialization.

To cover a vast topic in a small space, we have omitted many details. For the record, we should add that the restrictions on socage tenure could be eased by the crown; some occurred originally in the Carolinas. Throughout the colonial period in the proprietary colonies of Maryland, Delaware, and Pennsylvania, the "lifting" of a medieval statute (*Quia Emptores Terrarum*, 1290) restricting the right to create new feudal obligations provided the possibility of New World feudalism. A few backwoods manors were created, and some *courts of view-of-Frankpledge* (manorial courts) were held. But such antiquities had no future here. Also, in Georgia all land was originally nonalienable and could only be inherited by males. This practice, along with the restrictions against rum and slaves, soon was abandoned.

In short, land in America came to individuals from the king of England in the tenure of free and common socage. American land policies and practices for the succeeding centuries are best understood against that simple statement of the original conditions.

POPULATION SOURCES AND GROWTH

You could conquer the land, but it had to be settled. Empty land was no asset. The owners of the colonies—the king, proprietors, and colonial governments—had to find people, primarily Europeans. Where did the colonial people originate? One way to answer this question is to examine the population at the end of the colonial period. Table 1.1 shows the composition of the population (excluding Indians) in 1790, the year of the first national census.

Slave Origins

In 1790, just under one-fifth of the population was of identifiable African origin, and just over four-fifths was of European origin. The blacks mainly were shipped from West Africa, but there was also a slave trade from Madagascar and Zanzibar to the New World. Most slave-trading ports were on the west coast of Africa, but it is known that slaves sold there for transport to the New World came also from distant parts of the interior. So, African ancestors of modern Americans may well have come from most parts of that continent below the Sahara Desert. It is estimated that 10 million, perhaps 15 million, African slaves were transported to the Americas from 1501 to 1865. How many came to what became the United States? Robert Fogel and Stanley Engerman report that 6 percent of the Atlantic slave trade was with the 13 colonies. That would indicate total imports of more than 600,000 individuals, possibly too high a figure. Others estimate that, by 1700, there were about 28,000 blacks in the colonies and that 250,000 were imported in 1700–1790. Fogel and Engerman think that between 1780 and 1807 many more slaves were brought in. If this is correct, we might conservatively say that

Table 1.1   U.S. Population in 1790

	Nonwhites		Whites		Totals	
Year	Count	Percentage	Count	Percentage	Count	Percentage
1790	757,000	19.3	3,172,000	80.7	3,929,000	100.0

Source: *Historical Statistics of the United States* (Washington, D.C.: United States Government Printing Office, 1975), series A91–104.

at least half a million, possibly more, were brought in by 1807, which would be less than the number imported (but how much less?) in the colonial years. Efforts to be precise about these figures are doomed to failure.

White Origins

White immigration data are at least as vague as those for black slaves. However, because of the white use of surnames, it is possible for scholars to say something about the remote European origins of the existing population in 1790. Assuming that an O'Hara was of Irish origin; a McDougall, Scottish; a von Schlieben, German; a van Ryswick, Dutch; and a Westwick, English, the estimates are that 60.9 percent of the population had English surnames. Of the others, 8.3 percent were Scottish, 9.7 percent were Irish, 8.7 percent were German, 3.4 percent were Dutch, 1.7 percent were French, and 0.7 percent were Spanish. The rest, 6.6 percent, were not assigned. One suspects that since common names like Hughes and Smith could be English, Irish, or Scottish, it would be safer to have one category for the British (all from the British Isles). Grouped in this way, the British made up 78.9 percent of the total. Considering the territories, we find that in the Northwest Territory (now the Upper Midwest), surnames were 57.1 percent French, and in Louisiana, surnames were 64 percent French. In those areas to be acquired from the defunct Spanish Empire, about 96 percent of the names were Spanish. Among the original colonies, Pennsylvania surnames were 33 percent German, compared to 35 percent English. New York still had 17 percent Dutch names in 1790, and New Jersey had nearly as many with 16.6 percent. English names were highest in New England and Virginia—82 percent in Massachusetts, 76 percent in what is now Vermont, 71 percent in Rhode Island, and 68.5 percent in Virginia.

Thus, of the whites, the remote origins of just under three-fourths of the 1790 population represented immigration from the British Isles. For the most part, English institutions were utilized for colonial economic development by people who were already familiar with them. The blacks, mostly slaves (59 percent of those blacks in the North and 95 percent of those in the South), had no say in the matter. So far as we can tell, the other Europeans, naturalized by conquest or voluntarily by immigration, adapted well to English laws and practices.

Population Growth

Since immigration records were irregular or non-existent, figures for the total colonial white immigration must be taken with a grain of salt, especially in the early years. Edmund Morgan, for example, reports that records of the Virginia Company show some 15,000 souls shipped to Virginia between 1607 and 1640. But in the latter year, the colony numbered only about 7000, including the natural increase.

We know that the Puritan immigration to New England was perhaps 35,000 persons. Estimates of total white immigration between 1700 and 1775 center on the number 300,000. It seems fair to suppose that as many whites as blacks immigrated—altogether, perhaps half a million would be a conservative estimate. David Galenson has estimated total white immigration between 1650 and 1780 to have been about 600,000.[11] If that figure is correct, then Fogel and Engerman's estimate of 600,000 for black immigration is more reasonable. The white immigration was much larger than the black immigration in the seventeenth century. So, with natural increases, the proportion of whites in the total population remained overwhelming.[12]

Since death rates among immigrants in the seventeenth century were so stupendous in each colony, it is difficult to say what is meant by *immigrant*. If a person were dead before he or she could make any meaningful contribution, was that person an immigrant in an economic sense? In Virginia, supposing that 15,000 really did step ashore in the fifteen years between 1625 and 1640 and there were only about 7000 alive in 1640, were those who died so quickly immigrants in the sense that they added to population or to colonial economic growth? Earlier immigration was equally luckless. For example, 143 left London for Virginia in December 1606. In the fall of 1607, only 50 were still alive. There were 490 alive in Virginia in the fall of 1609. When Lord Delaware arrived in June 1610, there were 60 left, and he intercepted them as they were fleeing the place. At Plymouth Colony, as many as half the colonists died the first winter. Accepted population estimates for the colonies are shown in Table 1.2 on page 22.

Birth and Death Rates

Despite the early mortality history, population grew prodigiously. By the end of the colonial period, only one white in ten had been born abroad. Blacks born abroad were two in ten, which shows that the slave trade was still more important to black population growth than immigration was to white population growth. It is generally agreed that once populations were firmly established, relatively low mortality and high birth rates, rather than immigration, accounted for the remarkable increase of colonial population. From 1700 to 1780, the rate of population increase was about 30 persons per 1000 (3 percent per annum compounded). This population growth rate is not much lower than those typical of modern Third World countries such as Mexico, Ghana, and Libya. The colonial growth rates were sufficient to double the population about every 25 years.

In early decades the rate of increase was much higher, of course, high mortality or not, since it started from zero in each colony. The birth rate ranged from about 35 births to as high as 50 births per 1000 of population per year in some areas; 40 per 1000 per annum seems an acceptable figure on the average. These were very high rates, a third or more higher than such rates in Europe at that time. (In 1990, the American birth rate per 1000 was 16.7, which illustrates dramatically colonial demographic vitality.) Colonial death rates in the eighteenth century were 20 to 25 per 1000 per annum, below those of contemporary Europe.[13] As Billy Smith and others have shown, though, death rates in colonial cities like Philadelphia and Boston could well have been twice as high as the average, which included mostly farmers living in relative isolation.[14]

Given the primitive medicine of the time, the population growth must be attributed to a better climate, better food and water, and less damage from epidemic diseases such as influenza, smallpox, malaria, and diphtheria. Survival rates were about the same for blacks and whites, but if you were destined to be a slave, you were better off in the Southern colonies than you were in the Caribbean. Fogel and Engerman found, for example, that if mortality rates among mainland black slaves had equaled the terrible rates of the West Indies, the surviving black population of 1 million in 1800 would have been only 186,000. In addition

to lower death rates, fertility rates among mainland black slaves exceeded those on the Caribbean islands.

Marriage and Fertility

Although it was long assumed by historians that high colonial birth rates were due to younger marriages in America than prevailed in Europe, the work of Robert Higgs and Louis Stettler has shown that, at least in New England, women married on the average at age 21 and men at age 24. These ages are just about the same as now. Fertility in colonial marriages, on the other hand, was very high compared to either contemporary Europe or modern America. Women died more often than now in childbirth, and men remarried. Families were large; as Higgs and Stettler laconically put the matter, "the number of children born to a man in all his marriages being about seven on the average."[15]

The vital data are very rough, but the population aggregates are solid and are justified when compared with the first American census, which was taken in 1790. So, we see the colonial population growth as very powerful. This natural vitality in the United States continued into the nineteenth century before it began to slow down.

Regional Distribution

Note in Table 1.2 the relative sizes of Virginia, Massachusetts, and New York by 1780, a comparison that explains a lot about this country's early political history and the powerful contribution of rural Virginia, even with more than a third of its population still enslaved. Pennsylvania's growth from 1681 was very strong, so that even though it was founded later than New York, Massachusetts, Maryland, and Virginia, by 1780 it had overtaken all but Virginia. Note also the movement of population by the end of the period into Vermont and across the Appalachians into Kentucky and Tennessee. The westward movement was already underway.

New England as a whole had fallen behind the Middle colonies in population by the end of the colonial period, but the Southern population growth continued to dominate, led by Virginia and North and South Carolina, which together comprised some 40 percent of the total colonial population growth in the last two decades before American independence was gained by the

Peace of Paris (1783). Nearly half the total colonial population lay in the five Southern colonies at the end of the colonial period, a point of considerable economic importance, as we shall see when we discuss the colonial trade balance with Europe in the next chapter.

THE COLONIAL LABOR CONTRACT

Especially at the beginning, the English were hard put to find sufficient colonists for their American enterprise. Early reports home from Virginia and Plymouth cannot have been very optimistic. Nevertheless, partly because of political upheavals and religious persecution, some free immigrants came. As we discussed earlier in this chapter, possibly half, or more, of the whites who came over during the colonial period came unfree,

as indentured servants, and virtually all the blacks came as slaves.

Free Population

Of those who came to America on their own funds, just coming across the Atlantic made them eligible for headright land grants in most colonies, and land could be purchased from most colonial governments. Not only farmers came, of course; there was from the beginning (the first Virginia settlement apart) an immigration of artisans of all sorts—merchants, sailors, carters and draymen, scholars—the entire array of developed English commercial life appeared on the colonial scene, especially in the seaports. Those who came independently were free, as in England, to contract for their services, although, following English law

Table 1.2   Estimated Population of the American Colonies 1610–1780

Colonies	1610	1630	1650	1680	1700
New England Colonies					
Maine	—	400	1,000	(———————	included
New Hampshire	—	500	1,305	2,047	4,958
Vermont	—	—	—	—	—
Massachusetts	—	506	14,037	39,752	55,941
Plymouth	—	390	1,566	6,400	(——
Rhode Island	—	—	785	3,017	5,894
Connecticut	—	—	4,139	17,246	25,970
Total New England Colonies	0	1,796	22,833	68,462	92,763
Middle Colonies					
New York	—	350	4,116	9,830	19,107
New Jersey	—	—	—	3,400	14,010
Pennsylvania	—	—	—	680	17,950
Delaware	—	—	185	1,005	2,470
Total Middle Colonies	0	350	4,301	14,915	53,537
Southern Colonies					
Maryland	—	—	4,504	17,904	29,604
Virginia	350	2,500	18,731	43,596	58,560
North Carolina	—	—	—	5,430	10,720
South Carolina	—	—	—	1,200	5,704
Georgia	—	—	—	—	—
Kentucky	—	—	—	—	—
Tennessee	—	—	—	—	—
Total Southern Colonies	350	2,500	23,235	68,130	104,588
Total Colonial Population	350	4,646	50,368	151,507	250,888
Total Black	—	60	1,600	6,971	27,817
Percentage Black	—	1.3	3.2	4.6	11.1

Source: *Historical Statistics of the United States* (Washington, D.C.: United States Government Printing Office, 1975), series Z1–19.

and custom, there were extensive controls over prices, wages, business licensing, and quality of production (to be discussed in the next chapter). To have economic development in the seventeenth and eighteenth centuries, those who owned property and organized it were necessary. The colonial governments were not planning boards. By the eighteenth century, there seems to have been a sufficient number of such entrepreneurial types in the colonies.

Indentured Servitude

To do laboring work, especially in the beginning decades in the colonies, reliance was placed upon **indentured servitudes** of various sorts—contracts whereby individuals agreed to do certain work for a term of years in return for specified payments, mainly food,

1720	1750	1760	1780
in Massachusetts ——————————)			49,133
9,375	27,505	39,093	87,802
—	—	—	47,620
91,008	188,000	202,600	268,627
—— included in Massachusetts ———————————)			
11,680	33,226	45,471	52,946
58,830	111,280	142,470	206,701
170,893	360,011	449,634	712,829
36,919	76,696	117,138	210,541
29,818	71,393	93,813	139,627
30,962	119,666	183,703	327,305
5,385	28,704	33,250	45,385
103,084	296,459	427,904	722,858
66,133	141,073	162,267	245,474
87,757	231,033	339,726	538,004
21,270	72,984	110,442	270,133
17,048	64,000	94,074	180,000
—	5,200	9,578	56,071
—	—	—	45,000
—	—	—	10,000
192,208	514,290	716,087	1,344,682
466,185	1,170,760	1,593,625	2,780,369
68,839	236,420	325,806	575,420
14.8	20.2	20.4	20.7

clothing, housing, or perhaps some education or training in a craft or skill. Thousands came over this way. It was a highly organized affair. Those who signed such contracts of their own free will could do so in England with sea captains or regular merchants in the servant trade. The cost of passage was paid by the holder of the indenture contract in England, and, upon arrival in American ports, the contracts (and the people) were sold, usually on the ships before the servants disembarked. The purchase price paid was for the cost of passage plus whatever profit the seller could squeeze out, which depended upon the labor market in the colonies. The buyer received the labor of the indentured servant for the stated term of years.

Recent work by David Galenson and Robert Heavener shows in some detail the extent of the organized markets available for this species of unfree labor.[16] Contracts of from four to seven years were the most common. By the mid-eighteenth century, the evidence indicates that the supply of those selling themselves into servitude in England was declining. Generally, the price fetched by a servant depended upon the age, sex, and skills of the servant, given the market conditions in the colonies. The contracts of indenture had status in courts of law, and servants could appeal to the courts for violations of their rights. The servitudes were viewed essentially as apprenticeships, with an agreement that a trade would be learned during the term of the indenture being common.

At the end of the stated term (if it had not been legally extended because of violations by the servant, such as excessive absenteeism or malingering), the servant was free and might receive tools, a year's supplies, and, in Pennsylvania at least, perhaps a land grant. Children born of indentured servants during servitude were born free, but it was customary, especially in New England, to place teenagers into apprenticeships to learn trades. Edmund Morgan, in *The Puritan Family,* suggested this was done in part to relieve parents of the problems of coping with their own teenagers!

Redemptioners

Immigrants from the European continent, especially Germans, came with a different status from the English immigrants. Known as **redemptioners,** they were brought over by ship captains who then allowed them time to arrange to pay for their passage after arrival.

Payment was often made by placing one or more of their children into indenture to raise the money. Whereas English servants usually came over alone, the Germans came in families, bringing their own supplies and movable property with them.[17]

Prisoners

A less common, but perhaps more widely known (thanks to Hollywood), method of getting labor to the colonies was to send convicted felons. These cases, called "His Majesty's seven-year passengers," were men and women, convicted of one of the 300-odd crimes punishable by death in England, who were allowed to live on condition that they would transport themselves out of England.

These convict shipments, which may have amounted to 35,000 persons over the entire colonial period, were unpopular in the colonies, but efforts there to legislate against them were thrown out repeatedly by the Board of Trade lawyers. The shipments stopped during the Revolution, but following the Treaty of Paris (1783; sometimes called the Treaty of Versailles, confusingly), British courts, oblivious to the meaning of American independence, resumed shipments. Finally, in 1788, Congress, by resolution, forbade further convict transports from England, and the British turned to Australia as a dumping ground for their undesirable populations.

The convicts were sold as indentured servants at dockside, just as were other kinds of indentured servants. It might be added that, in the early years, press gangs (official parties of soldiers seizing ordinary citizens off the streets for military service) and kidnappers added to the colonial labor supply by direct action. Children were valuable because they might yield the longest service; the Virginia Company paid £5 a head for them, and, in 1627 alone, from 1400 to 1500 children were shipped. In 1655 the Venetian ambassador in London reported a sweep by His Majesty's soldiers through the brothels that netted 400 "women of loose life" who were shipped out. When labor was scarce in the colonies, servants were acquired by whatever means worked.

Finally, there were the special categories of rebels and prisoners of war. The Irish and Scots were especially prominent among these, and there were many occasions for such prisoners to be taken until the Battle of Culloden Moor in 1746, when the Stuart claim to the English throne was finally lost. Nearly a century earlier, Cromwell's march into Scotland in 1650 and the crushing defeat of the Scots at Dunbar had netted some 10,000 prisoners. Through a letter written by the Massachusetts Bay Colony Puritan leader, John Cotton, to his friend Cromwell, we gain a glimpse of this particular phase of the early colonial labor supply. Unlike convicts, military prisoners, mainly young males, were particularly desirable:

> The Scots, whom God delivered into your hands at Dunbarre, and whereof sundry were sent hither, we have been desirous (as we could) to make their yoke easy. Such as were sick of scurvy or other diseases have not wanted physick and Chyurgery. They have not been sold for slaves to perpetuall servitude, but for 6 or 7 or 8 years, as we do our owne; and he that bought the most of them (I heare) buildeth houses for them, for every 4 an house, layeth some acres of ground thereto, which he giveth them as their owne, requiering 3 dayes in the weeke to worke for him (by turnes) and 4 dayes for themselves, and promiseth, assone as they can repay him the money he layed out for them, he will set them at liberty.[18]

Ship captains wanted servants and prisoners as cargo and no doubt traded them directly for colonial produce to take back on their return voyage. The trade was profitable for all. Later on, by the mid-eighteenth century, improved conditions at home, natural population growth in the colonies, increasing colonial demand for shipments of European goods, and an increasing abundance of black slaves made white indentured servants less desirable than in earlier times. Black slaves cost more than white servants, on the average, but that was because their "contract" to the buyer was superior to that of white servants—slaves tended to be more profitable.

Slavery

African slaves were not protected as British subjects. Their term of service soon came to be for life, and children, if born to a slave mother, were slaves for life—no matter who was the father. This idea of children following the condition of the mother was of Biblical origin. So, the purchaser of a female slave's "life contract" also received the natural increase if the slave was a woman. This rule lasted until the American Civil War ended slavery.

African slaves had no status at all in court. There were no British laws governing them, and the colonials developed laws of their own that did not allow slaves redress of grievances. The laws did allow, however, dismembering, disfiguring, and, occasionally, death to slaves who "disobeyed." In classical Roman slavery, a master might put to death a disobedient slave, and although in colonial America this extreme was not usually forbidden, it was assumed that no man would do such a thing, "destroy his own estate," without sufficient cause.

Much has been written in recent years about American slavery, and we will discuss it at length in later chapters. It is enough to say here that it was deemed absolutely necessary to colonial economic development. It began in Virginia in 1619, and, as Edmund Morgan says, developed hand-in-hand with colonial American ideas of freedom. Farming in the North tended to be based upon smaller, family-sized plots of land, and labor was mainly supplied by the families themselves. Slavery existed in all the colonies but was on a larger scale in the South. Although no doubt fueled by inherent racism from the beginning, labor was needed, especially on the Southern tobacco, rice, and indigo plantations. African slavery was a response to that need.

In Virginia, both land and labor could be had with a single purchase. An imported slave was also good for a headright grant, as in the case of imported servants. The net yield from a slave purchase being far superior to that of an indentured servant, slave prices were accordingly higher. Transportation costs for slaves were minimal, food and clothing outlays by owners were not subject to a legal oversight, and the term, expiring at death, cost no freedom payments beyond simple graves.

James Kent, the great American jurist, was embarrassed by the persistence of American slavery when he wrote his *Commentaries* in 1826, but there is probably no more illuminating description, even in the most lurid writings, of the legal status of the American slave than in Kent's spare lines.

> Slaves are considered . . . though not in criminal prosecutions as things or property, rather than persons, and are vendible as personal estate. They cannot take property by descent or purchase, and all they find, and all they hold, belongs to the master. They cannot make lawful contracts, and they are deprived of civil rights. They are assets in the hands of executors, for the payment of debts, and cannot be emancipated by will or otherwise, to the prejudice of creditors. Their condition is more analogous to that of the slaves of the ancients than to that of villeins of feudal times, both in respect to the degradation of the slaves and the full dominion and power of the master.[19]

The laws of the colonies, until 1776, could not be repugnant to the laws of England. In 1772, in the Sommersett case heard in London, it was held by Chief Justice Lord William Mansfield that slavery did not exist in the English constitution and, hence, could not exist in England. The ruling led ultimately to compensated emancipation in the British Caribbean islands in the 1830s and to the peaceful extinction of African slavery in the British Empire. But it came too late for the Americans. Slavery passed through the Revolution, was recognized in the federal Constitution (each slave was worth three-fifths of a man for congressional apportionment), and nine decades after the Sommersett case, in a blending of slavery with states' rights, the Americans solved their own problem by a bloody civil war. The international slave trade had been prohibited by the Constitution since 1808, but statesmanship and jurisprudence could not find a peaceful way to root the institution out of American society.

THE LEGACY

The lack of freedom in the initial conditions of American labor is reflected by the fact that, under common law, organized labor was considered a criminal conspiracy. This meant that workers faced a long, uphill battle from colonial times onward to gain social status, recognition, and rights to bargain collectively. We will return to these issues later.

Notes

1. Francis Newton Thorpe, ed., *The Federal and State Constitutions, Colonial Charters and Other Organic Laws* (Washington: Government Printing Office, 1909), p. 46.
2. Thorpe, p. 46.
3. Sir Francis Drake's famous voyage around the world, lasting three years and landing him back in England in 1580, was a joint-stock enterprise. Queen Elizabeth was a shareholder in the venture.
4. Thorpe, p. 3788.
5. William Whitmore, ed., *The Colonial Laws of Massachusetts* (Boston: Boston City Printers, 1889), p. 192.
6. Thorpe, *The Federal and State Constitutions, Colonial Charters and Other Organic Laws,* p. 3812.
7. Thorpe, p. 1680.
8. The principle of judicial review was revived in our Constitution, especially when, in 1803, Chief Justice John Marshall affirmed in *Marbury* v *Madison* that an act of Congress might be overturned by the courts. The Constitution, in place of king and Parliament, now ruled. Marshall wrote: "It is a proposition too plain to be contested, that the Constitution controls any legislative act repugnant to it." Thus was established the American doctrine of judicial review, a practice that would have profound effects upon the political, social, and economic life of the United States. The seed of it was planted in Virginia, the first colony, and the practice was maintained right through the colonial period of our history.
9. James Kent, *Commentaries on American Law* (Boston: Little, Brown, 1884), vol. III, p. 516.
10. For an analysis of the differences in inheritance practices across all the colonies, see Lee J. Alston and Morton Owen Shapiro, "Inheritance Laws Across the Colonies: Causes and Consequences," *JEH,* June 1984.
11. David W. Galenson, *White Servitude in Colonial America: An Economic Analysis* (1981), p. 18.
12. Most whites had the option of returning to the countries they had left; many exercised that option.
13. Colonial death rates rose to perhaps as high as 24 per 1000 in the seventeenth century. Robert Paul Thomas and Terry Anderson, "White Population, Labor Force and Extensive Growth of the New England Economy in the Seventeenth Century," *JEH,* December 1977.
14. Billy G. Smith, "Death and Life in a Colonial Immigrant City: A Demographic Analysis of Philadelphia," *JEH,* December 1977.
15. Robert Higgs and Louis Stettler, "Colonial New England Demography: A Sampling Approach," *William and Mary Quarterly,* April 1970, p. 291.
16. David Galenson, "Immigration and the Colonial Labor System: An Analysis of Length of Indenture," *EEH,* October 1977; Robert Heavener, "Indentured Servitude: The Philadelphia Market, 1771–1773," *JEH,* September 1978.
17. There is a recent study of this "market" in population: Farley Grubb, "The Auction of Redemptioner Servants, Philadelphia, 1771–1805," *JEH,* September 1988.
18. Thomas Hutchinson, *The Hutchinson Papers* (Albany, NY: The Prince Society, 1865), vol. 1, p. 264.
19. James Kent, *Commentaries of American Law,* vol. II, p. 253.

Suggested Readings

Articles

Alston, Lee J., and Shapiro, Morton Owen. "Inheritance Laws Across the Colonies: Causes and Consequences." *Journal of Economic History,* vol. XLIV, no. 2, June 1984.

Galenson, David. "The Rise and Fall of Indentured Servitude in the Americas: An Economic Analysis." *Journal of Economic History,* vol. XLIV, no. 1, March 1984.

———. "Immigration and the Colonial Labor System: An Analysis of Length of Indenture." *Explorations in Economic History,* vol. 14, no. 4, October 1977.

Gray, Ralph, and Wood, Betty. "The Transition from Indentured Servant to Involuntary Servitude in Colonial Georgia." *Explorations in Economic History,* vol. 13, no. 4, October 1976.

Grubb, Farley. "The Auction of Redemptioner Servants, Philadelphia, 1771–1804," *Journal of Economic History,* vol. XLVIII, no. 3, September 1988.

Heavener, Robert. "Indentured Servitude: The Philadelphia Market, 1771–1773." *Journal of Economic History,* vol. XXXVIII, no. 3, September 1978.

Higgs, Robert, and Stettler, Louis. "Colonial New England

Demography: A Sampling Approach." *William and Mary Quarterly,* vol. XXVII, no. 2, April 1970.

Morgan, Edmund. "The First American Boom: Virginia 1618 to 1630." *William and Mary Quarterly,* vol. XXVIII, no. 2, April 1971.

Potter, Jim. "The Growth of Population in America, 1700–1860." In D. V. Glass and B. E. C. Eaversley, eds. *Population in History: Essays in Historical Demography.* Chicago: Aldine, 1960.

Russell, J. C. "Late Ancient and Medieval Population." *Transactions of the American Philosophical Society,* new series, vol. 48, part 3, June 1958.

Smith, Billy G. "Death and Life in a Colonial Immigrant City: A Demographic Analysis of Philadelphia." *Journal of Economic History,* vol. XXXVIII, no. 4, December 1977.

Thomas, Robert Paul, and Anderson, Terry. "White Population, Labor Force and Extensive Growth of the New England Economy in the Seventeenth Century." *Journal of Economic History,* vol. XXXIII, no. 3, September 1973.

Books

Abernethy, Thomas Perkins. *Western Lands and the American Revolution.* New York: Appleton-Century, 1937.

Bancroft, George. *History of the United States of America from the Discovery of the Continent.* Boston: Little, Brown, 1879, 6 vols.

Boorstin, Daniel. *The Americans: The Colonial Experience.* New York: Vintage Books, 1958.

Curtin, Philip. *The Atlantic Slave Trade: A Census.* Madison: University of Wisconsin Press, 1969.

Fogel, Robert William, and Engerman, Stanley. *Time on the Cross: The Economics of American Negro Slavery.* Boston: Little, Brown, 1974.

Ford, Amelia Clewly. *Colonial Precedents of Our National Land System as It Existed in 1800.* Philadelphia: Porcupine Press, 1976.

Galenson, David. *White Servitude in Colonial America: An Economic Analysis.* New York: Cambridge University Press, 1981.

Harris, Marshall. *Origin of the Land Tenure System in the United States.* Westport, CT: Greenwood Press, 1970.

Hughes, Jonathan. *Social Control in the Colonial Economy.* Charlottesville: University Press of Virginia, 1976.

Jones, E. L. *The European Miracle.* Cambridge: Cambridge University Press, 1981.

Morgan, Edmund. *American Slavery, American Freedom: The Ordeal of Colonial Virginia.* New York: Norton, 1975.

———. *The Puritan Family: Religion and Domestic Relations in Seventeenth-Century New England.* New York: Harper & Row, 1966.

Morison, Samuel Eliot. *The Oxford History of the American People.* New York: Oxford University Press, 1964.

Morris, Richard. *Government and Labor in Early America.* New York: Columbia University Press, 1946.

North, Douglass, and Thomas, Robert Paul. *The Rise of the Western World.* New York: Cambridge University Press, 1973.

Notestein, Wallace. *The English People on the Eve of Colonization.* New York: Harper & Bros., 1954.

Pirenne, Henri. *A History of Europe from the Invasions to the XVI Century.* New York: University Books, 1956.

Powell, Sumner Chilton. *Puritan Village: The Formation of a New England Town.* Middletown, CT: Wesleyan University Press, 1963.

Smith, Abbot Emerson. *Colonists in Bondage: White Servitude and Convict Labor in America, 1607–1776.* Chapel Hill: University of North Carolina Press, 1947.

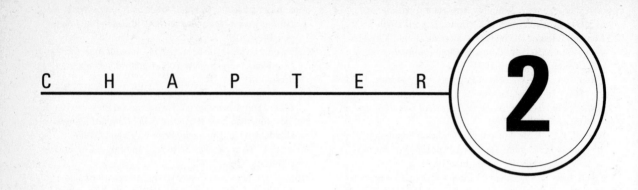

C H A P T E R   2

Colonial Development

To understand colonial economic history, we must comprehend the pattern of initial settlement. Even though most colonists did not live in towns (except during the first few decades), the concentration of certain activities in villages and towns was vital for sustained economic life.

SEAPORTS AND TOWNS

The simplest conceivable placement of population is an *undifferentiated plain*—a place where people are distributed homogeneously like salt sprinkled upon a kitchen table. But human population is rarely distributed spatially in equal portions. People build communities, villages, towns, and cities to take advantage of commerce, government, and medical care. Even in an area such as rural Iowa that, to an Easterner, seems featureless and completely homogeneous, towns and villages are not distributed spatially like the salt. Why are they located where they are? What are the determinants that influence the placement of population?

Location Determinants

Economists have found that a primary determinant for the location of seaports and towns is the presence of a **break-in-transport**—essentially a place of loading and unloading. Since the original English access to this continent was by water, it is no surprise that the earliest settlements—Jamestown, Plymouth, New Amsterdam, Albany—occurred at the water's edge, either along the ocean shore or on lakes or rivers. But they did not occur at *random* points along the shore, for two reasons: (a) There would be several possible ports in any location, depending upon the topography. (b) Some surrounding terrains, or *hinterlands*, had access to more local produce than others. Those breaks-in-transport with hinterlands best able to support a two-way commerce, imports *and* exports, would be favored.

At first, such commerce was Indian-white—that is, furs for European goods; thus, towns grew up where Indian trails came through the forest to the water's edge, although even the trails through the forest were limited in number, following the line of least resistance (e.g., along creek beds, across saddle points between mountains, and between Indian villages).

Apart from early Indian trade, the colonists soon engaged in primary economic activity—farming, timbering, fishing, and mining—wherever possible. So, the areas surrounding those harbors with exploitable hinterlands were dominated by primary activities at first. Even an **entrepôt** location (i.e., a town serving basically as a trading point) like Newport, Rhode Island, would be capable of considerable growth since its port was excellent and so were its seaborn connections to other entrepôts. Road-building to the interior was an arduous task, and it developed only as population grew and labor was found. For this reason, water transport dominated at first.

Now let us return for a moment to the undifferentiated plain, just to emphasize that it *did not exist* on the eastern shore of the American continent. Due to irregularities in terrain, such as rivers and mountains, the ocean (bays, inlets) and the rivers had to be the highways. Once colonists were ashore and an economic hinterland began to develop, the two-way movement of goods at the break-in-transport would justify the establishment of substantial distribution and collection facilities, such as docks, warehouses, and stores. Such *nodal points* (or concentrations) of economic activity might also require some governmental managerial activity, such as a military establishment of some sort (e.g., a fort with supplies) or a place where regular courts of law could meet and the civil activity of government could be transacted. At a seaport there might soon be some sort of customs control and facilities for naval stores. The fact that the American colonies were offshoots of imperial England would guarantee those kinds of activities. Wherever they were located would add to the volume of transactions at that site, compared to other locations.

The location of a break-in-transport in a differentiated topography, together with a rich hinterland and its developmental capabilities, reduced the number of possible sites for early settlements. Some locations were favored over others, such as waterside locations on the east coast. But consider that Virginia, with the largest colonial population of all (and by that measure, the richest hinterland), had the fewest towns of any note. If the land were effectively homogeneous, in an economic sense, so that populations could be sup-

ported at scattered points, but if we alter the model slightly to allow for *many* possible breaks-in-transport due to an abundance of rivers, bays, coves, and inlets serving that scattered population, then there would be no particular tendency, administration apart, for particular nodal points to grow more than others. This is what happened in Virginia for the most part.

The other major colonial settlements do tend to fit our model. Their hinterlands were diverse, with fewer potential breaks-in-transport, and major nodal points therefore developed: Boston in its bay, Hartford on its river, New York and Philadelphia near the meeting of rivers and ocean, Charleston with its excellent harbor and several rivers stretching into its hinterland.

Production from the hinterland, whether it came merely to a trading post or to a collection point for more substantial activities, such as facilities to handle agricultural and timber products, in turn created the conditions for a market. Given the established property rights of colonial America (which we outlined in the previous chapter), landowners had items to sell, and it was profitable for sellers and buyers to concentrate those activities at the nodal points where marketing would naturally arise. If an activity enhanced the value of traded goods (weight reduction by processing or dressing or packaging) or provided services for traders or others, it paid a merchant to locate such activities, in most cases, at the nodal points; the search and transactions costs (looking for custom or recording change in ownership, for example) of doing such business would be reduced by the concentration of potential customers and suppliers at those points. Such cost-reducing elements in economic life are called **external economies.** Their presence enhanced the possibilities that nodal points would grow—the greater the external economies, the greater the growth possibilities.[1]

Townships and Counties

Soon after primary economic activities were established, villages and towns grew. Their density helped determine the legal and political organization of everyday life. Economics determined many locations, but also there were important noneconomic forces at work that had lasting effects. The New England Puritans for many decades established new settlements only when there was sufficient demand to create new congregations. Religious conflicts as well as population growth helped this process along. When new congregations applied to the colony government, they were granted enough land for a new town. For a long time, as a result, New England expanded in chunks; new towns were seen as copies of the old ones, and a New England town was not only the nodal point (in New England called the "center") but it included the supporting land around it. The result was a miniature form of government below that of the colony, yet larger than that of the village or borough.

In other colonies, however, expansion into the interior tended to be more continuous, but piecemeal, so that population was thinly settled. For administrative purposes, and for protection as well as for trading, there would be some sort of nodal point established, but it would encompass a larger and more heterogeneous area, the county. Since both township- and county-size units existed in England (the "hundred" and the county), these developments were not new inventions, just institutional applications to differing circumstances. One long-term result, though, was that, as the Americans moved into the interior, township government prevailed where New England influence was strongest, and county government prevailed elsewhere. In states such as Illinois and Indiana, settled in their northern parts by New Englanders and in their southern parts by transplants from old Virginia, there exists a dizzying mixture of overlapping political and taxing jurisdictions to this day. Farther west, county government prevails for the same reason it did originally in Virginia: Political life began with population spread thinly over large areas.

The tendency to lay things out in rectangles of curious dimensions came from colonial practice. The rectangular township covering 36 square miles began in New England in the eighteenth century (Bennington, Vermont, was apparently the first one), and the idea of the 640-acre section (one square mile) seems to have had its origins in North Carolina. These early beginnings were to have lasting organizational consequences when, in the Northwest Ordinances of 1785 and 1787, the Americans determined the future layout of the continent on the basis of the colonial experiences.[2] The townships were squares 6 miles by 6 miles, and the sections were 640 acres, whereas a quarter section, 160 acres, became a typical farm. The tradition continued with both squatter and homesteader receiving 160 acres in the Homestead Act of 1862.

The Major Towns

When the first national census was taken in 1790, there were only 24 places with population in excess of 2500 persons. Out of a total population of 3,929,000, only 202,000 (a mere 5 percent) could be classified as "urban" residents. Fifteen years earlier, the proportion was even smaller. If we consider the 20 largest towns just at the end of the 150 colonial years, it is pretty clear how important the role of water transport had been in the establishment of nodal points.

The interior cities were all located on major navigable rivers, but most urban locations were still seaports. Note also (Figure 2.1) the predominance of urban centers in the Middle and New England colonies. Philadelphia, with its rich hinterland and solid base of fabrication and primitive manufacturing, was founded late, in 1681 (survivors of previous Dutch and Swedish groups were living in caves along the river), and, yet, by the Revolution, it had overtaken all. In fact, in 1776, Philadelphia was second in population only to London

Table 2.1   Town and City Colonial Populations

Town/City	Year	Population
Philadelphia	1775	40,000
New York City	1775	25,000
Boston	1775	16,000
Charleston	1775	12,000
Newport	1775	11,000
New Haven	1771	8,300
Norwich	1774	7,000
Norfolk	1775	6,200
Baltimore	1775	6,000
New London	1774	5,400
Salem	1776	5,300
Lancaster	1776	5–6,000
Hartford	1774	4,900
Middletown	1775	4,700
Portsmouth	1775	4,600
Marblehead	1776	4,400
Providence	1774	4,400
Albany	1776	4,000
Annapolis	1775	3,700
Savannah	1775	3,200

Source: Carl Bridenbaugh, *Cities in Revolt* (New York: Oxford University Press, 1971), pp. 216–17.

Figure 2.1   Twenty Colonial Cities

The Colonial cities were trading centers primarily. Of the 20 largest, note the concentration in New England, where domestic manufacturing, processing of fish and wood products, shipbuilding, and equipping predominated. Providence was a center of the slave trade. Production of naval stores and distilling were also prominent New England economic activities.

itself, the "great wen" among English cities. Williamsburg, Virginia's capital and second city, contained only 1500 inhabitants, while Norfolk, the seaport at the mouth of the James River, had more than 6000. Already, the institutional wherewithal of urban life—fire departments and fire regulations, a night watch for protection against crime, almshouses for poor relief, and attention to the provision of water supplies—were developing. The colonial cities, as Carl Bridenbaugh

shows in his two books, *Cities in the Wilderness* and *Cities in Revolt,* were well developed as places of urban civilization by the end of the colonial period. Later in this chapter, we will examine this developing institutional structure in some detail.

Early Manufacturing

Serving primarily as points of exchange between the mainly agricultural colonies and the external world, the centers of urban life also were developing into centers of fabrication—manufacturing with the technology of the time: handwork, waterpower, and animal power. As the work of Diane Lindstrom and John Sharpless suggests, the colonial heritage, spilling over into the early national period, was one of mixed commercial manufacturing enterprises in these cities.[3] Merchant activity, because of the break-in-transport feature of their locations, had been joined by artisans of all sorts. (The existence of external economies would lead us to expect this clustering.) Both sectors served each other and developed together; milling, leather tooling and woodworking, distilling, sugar refining, shipbuilding, spinning, hatmaking—such activities characterized the larger colonial cities. Exceptions were trades like iron-working (to some extent) and timbering, where transportation costs dictated that weight-reducing activities take place at the sites of initial extraction. Smaller villages and farmsteads also were locations for manufacturing, especially in the Middle colonies and New England. For both local needs and for export, American colonists were well along the road to industrial development, even according to European standards of the time. Carl Bridenbaugh estimates that "in the four commercial cities of the North [Boston, New York, Newport, and Philadelphia] between one third and one half of the gainfully employed—thousands of citizens—were artisans."[4]

Future urban growth would depend upon both commerce and manufacturing. Centers like Newport, whose hinterland would not support an urban manufacturing center, were destined to lag behind. Ultimately, in the later nineteenth century, when the industrial revolution came to America, it would be mainly an urban phenomenon. Even in colonial times, though, the attractiveness of external economies served to concentrate primitive manufacturing in and around the commercial nodal points. A crucial consequence was that British efforts in the late 1760s and early 1770s to suppress and control manufacturing fell upon these *concentrations* of artisans, craftsmen, and shop and forge workers. The close contact of the aggrieved parties produced a powerful response— thousands of angry workers joined the radicals and contributed to a revolution.

REGIONAL SPECIALIZATION

As we discussed, the little cities and towns of colonial America served as nodal points for the main event of the colonial economy. *Primary production,* which employed more than nine-tenths of the population, were the major occupations of agriculture, fishing, timbering, and mining (together with the processing and shipping of the surplus for export).

Comparative Advantage

The boundaries of the original colonies were set in England by men who had never been to America and who did not even have adequate maps of the lands they granted. The basis of their decisions was political expediency, not economics. Within those boundaries, however established, the nodal points appeared at breaks-in-transport. The question is, "What was being transported?" That would be determined by economic realities. The *natural endowment*—the climate, distribution of soil, topography, kinds and quantities of trees and minerals—was located by nature. Its development, using the knowledge, techniques, and machinery of the time, would determine the direction of primary development.

Since private profit was the main object of most colonial economic activity—the exploitation of those property rights vested in the charters—maximum profits were most desirable. Development proceeded on the basis of trial and error at first. Trial and error were necessary. The first English settlers faced a new environment and a different climate and, therefore, many unknowns. The only way to learn which strain of wheat could be grown; which native crops, such as maize, potatoes (native to South America, introduced to North America by the colonists), and squashes, could be used for human food; where the great native weed, tobacco, could best be grown; what could be used as fodder for animals; and which animals could best suit colonial

uses was to try everything, learn from failure, and try again. The English were anxious to find ways to eliminate their dependence upon their European rivals, so efforts were made by subsidy and protective measures to cultivate such exotics as mulberry trees (for the silkworm) and ginger. In the South there was great success with two exotic imports, rice and indigo, that were much desired by the British. There also was continuing hope for gold and silver discoveries, and small amounts of gold were found intermittently, along with abundant supplies of the ores of baser metals.

Gradually, when it was learned what could be produced profitably, the next question became, "Which of those products are the *most* profitable?" If a field in Virginia or Maryland grew both wheat and tobacco successfully, profit maximization still required the determination of which crop paid the most. Most Virginia tobacco growers could be wheat growers on the same land, but, given the relative costs of production and the state of the markets for wheat and tobacco, the Virginia growers opted for tobacco, even at the risk of starvation. Early governors of Virginia had to order the cultivation of wheat rather than tobacco; in 1616 no man was allowed to plant tobacco until he had planted two acres of wheat. Tobacco was tried in all colonies, but in most places outside the South, its yields were poor compared to other field crops. The English, seized hard and early by Lady Nicotine, tried growing it in England, but the colonies were protected from this unlikely source of competition by appropriate legislation.

Tobacco continued to be grown in the Middle colonies and even in New England, especially in the valley of the Connecticut River, where the long, sweltering summer days rival the Congo. The choice of tobacco over wheat in Virginia, even when wheat was profitable, showed that the **comparative advantage**—what Virginians could produce relatively more efficiently than others—was in tobacco. When prices changed, so did the choice of crops. When tobacco prices fell relative to wheat in the mid-eighteenth century, the Virginians shifted crops and surpassed Pennsylvania in wheat exports. The market changed, and with it the comparative advantage at work. In some places, sheep grazed instead of cattle. In some places, farmers abandoned agriculture to follow trades; in others, such as the Yankee hill farms, activities were diversified so that trades could be followed *on the farm*. If nothing could be done competently and families were still determined to remain on their land, then it paid to specialize in those things that were done *least incompetently*.

Given the other factors we have discussed and the climates, colonial development based on comparative advantage produced a fairly distinct regional specialization. It must be added that such specialization was also due to the "empire connection." The colonists traded more with England, with the rest of the empire, with foreign islands in the Caribbean, and with Europe than they did with each other. So, the specialization that developed (e.g., tobacco, rice, and indigo in the South; wheat and animals in the Middle colonies; shipbuilding and fishing in New England) did so from the very beginning largely in response to the international market. The early Virginians needed some way to reimburse the Company in London. The Plymouth colonists reorganized their company internally so that furs and other products could be sent to England to pay their debts. It would be many decades after independence before purely domestic demand dictated the output patterns of the American economy. In the colonial era the colonies grew as part of the world market, and to some extent, then, the needs of that world market dictated the way they grew. New Englanders exported fish products, small manufactures, ships and shipping services, and imported food. Southerners exported rice, tobacco, indigo, forest products, and imported manufactures.

New England

At first the colonial settlement had only one concern: simply finding the means of existence. For all the colonists, this meant acquiring food through farming, fishing, and hunting. After the bare requirements of life were found, the forces of the market and comparative advantage began to work. In New England, which had very little agricultural land of good quality, expansion of the economy quickly focused on other gifts of nature. New England's lack of quality farmland was unique. Rocks and mountains made farming a subsistence occupation at best. The Yankee farmer had to find subsidiary occupations, such as lumbering in winter; gathering and refining maple syrup in earliest spring; running a forge, a distillery, a woodworking or farm shop, perhaps a small foundry or grist mill. The New England farmer had to use his wits to stay on his land. Corn and summer vegetables were the main field crops

there. The inhospitable climate with late frosts in spring, early frosts in the fall, and rocky soil made New England agriculture a difficult, marginal activity. When land across the mountains became available in the early nineteenth century, much of New England was simply abandoned by the backwoods Yankees who gave up the uneven struggle and fled west. Lonely stone walls and foundations, deep in the woods and now overgrown, stand as mute witnesses to the long effort to grow crops on stones. Among those who stayed behind, livestock raising (sheep), dairying, and lumbering kept rural New England from being totally abandoned.

Those Yankees living on the sea were quickly drawn into fishing, which had, after all, attracted Europeans to the New England shores long before there were any permanent settlements. As early as 1700 the New England fishing fleet produced 10 million pounds of fish for export, surpassing England itself. By 1775 the New England cod fishery alone employed 4400 men and had 665 vessels. The shore stations—for salting, drying, smoking, and packing—employed many more. Whaling also became a major New England industry, with 360 ships by the 1770s. Whale oil, used for candles and lighting fuel for lamps, was the product of an industry destined for a long nineteenth-century life.

With an abundance of timber for ships and barrels, the Yankees quickly became skilled at making barrelstaves, cooperage (binding barrels), and shipbuilding. The other products of the forests, tar and pinepitch, used to caulk and line ship hulls, added to the strength of the New England shipping industry. Sawmills were placed along streams and rivers. Shipyards in New England appeared in places such as Newburyport, Salem, Marblehead, and New Haven as well as in larger centers such as Boston, Portsmouth, and Newport. The native white pine was unrivalled for masts. Bog iron ore in abundant supply, along with woods for charcoal, supported an iron industry. That industry, together with a host of other trades related to shipbuilding such as wagon-making, ships stores, brewing, and distilling, gave New England a base for manufacturing that supported its abundance of small towns and seaports. Farm wives spun wool, mixed it with linen threads, and wove cloth for sale in New England markets. Sheep, cattle, and hogs provided meat; cattle also supported leather tanning and shoemaking. Even before an elementary factory system appeared at the end of the

A century after the early colonization, there was an "American economy" based on the export of domestic produce and the import of commodities from Europe and the Caribbean. New York was a leading center of such commerce.

eighteenth century, these town and cottage industries laid the groundwork for the industrial, commercial, and sea-going Yankee nation to come. New England's misfortune, its poor land endowment, led its colonial settlers to an adaptation that would be New England's fortune by the early nineteenth century.[5] Winifred Rothenberg's studies of developing New England farm labor markets lead her to argue that the increased productivity that came, finally, from market utilization and better farm management, even without significant technological change, freed New England farm labor for other uses, including factories, when they came. Lack of technological advance did not necessarily impair productivity increases due to more intelligent uses of the resources available.[6]

The Middle Colonies

New York, New Jersey, Pennsylvania, and Delaware did contain good land. The first three had sufficient agricultural land to make a large and expanding agricultural base possible. Pennsylvania's liberal rules for land acquisition encouraged a flood of immigration. As agriculture expanded, augmented by mining, immigration swelled. There were, in addition, essentially the same trades as in New England, including shipbuilding. These, together with an abundance of land for diversified farming, supported the rapidly growing population. The two largest seaports, New York and Philadelphia, did a thriving commercial and entrepôt trade.[7] During the eighteenth century, ironmaking in

Pennsylvania and New Jersey began in earnest. Trades such as shoemaking, pottery, glassmaking, woodworking, leather tanning, and the like served the bustling interior. German immigrants came in the tens of thousands to settle the rich valleys of Pennsylvania, contributing their language, architecture (the great stone barns), cuisine, and culture to Penn's colony.

The Middle colonies were especially important for the wheat grains and flour they produced in mills along the splendid millrace rivers and creeks like the Schuylkill and the Brandywine. They were known as the "breadbasket" of the colonies.[8] The Middle colonies also were the major colonial sources of the cattle, hogs, and sheep used for export to Europe and the Caribbean and also of dressed and salted meats. By the end of the colonial period, these colonies already had surpassed New England in population, and their growth, rooted in a diversified and expanding agricultural sector and characterized by family farming, would provide a powerful internal market for growing commerce and industry in the future.

The South

Colonial Maryland shared many of the characteristics of the Middle colonies, but one statistic, the slave population, marked it as a Southern colony.[9] In 1770, Pennsylvania, with a population of 240,000, had 5761 slaves; the adjacent colony, Maryland, with 203,000 people, had a slave population of 64,000. To understand the Southern economy, even in the eighteenth century, we must come to grips with the uses of black slavery there.

Consider the data in Table 2.2. The great difference in black slaves between the South and the other colonies set off not only the Southern labor force from that of the others, but also the economy in which that labor force was employed. Overall, as we saw in our discussion earlier in this chapter, the South was even more rural than the other colonies, with few urban settlements of note. Yet, Virginia and Maryland were heavily populated. Even though these two states had been major destinations for indentured servants in the seventeenth century, in the eighteenth century, when servants had more choice and a greater proportion of those coming in were free, the South, apart from the Chesapeake region, was not a favored destination. Southern landowners faced this situation and perhaps encour-

aged it by adapting the Atlantic slave trade to their needs. The relative efficiency of slavery, once laws to control it sufficiently were in place, made the Southern colonies predominantly slave colonies.

Why the European immigrants avoided the Southern colonies is not entirely clear. Pennsylvania, the main destination of white immigrants in the eighteenth century, had developed relatively liberal institutions, and land was readily and easily available. But Virginia was no different in these respects. Jefferson's famous comment in *Notes on the State of Virginia,* "In a warm climate, no man will labour for himself who can make another labour for him," is hardly to be taken seriously.[10] In the first place, it is true of cold climates, too, and, in any case, the fact that the South is warmer than the North from November through May should have been an attraction to Europeans. The summertime temperature-humidity indexes of Maryland, Virginia, North Carolina, and Pennsylvania are as abominable as those in the South, not to mention, after all, New York City and the entire Hudson Valley. Also, wages paid could be used to "make" others labor, if the wages were high enough.

The growing dependency upon slave labor in the Southern colonies seems to have been a more complicated matter. First, the prevalence of large-scale landholding required labor beyond that of the immediate family. Large holdings in Maryland, and especially Virginia, originated in headright land grants (slaves were counted as "servants" for this purpose, making

Table 2.2 Percentage of Black Slaves in Total Population of 1770

Colonies	Percentage
New Hampshire	1.0
Massachusetts	2.0
Connecticut	3.1
Rhode Island	6.5
New York	11.7
New Jersey	7.0
Pennsylvania	2.4
Delaware	5.2
Maryland	31.5
Virginia	42.0
North Carolina	35.3
South Carolina	60.5
Georgia	45.5

Source: *Historical Statistics,* Series Z 1–19.

an imported slave bought at dockside worth 50 acres). Second, adherence in the South to the common-law rule of descent, called **primogeniture** (the land going to the oldest son), meant that estates were not automatically broken up upon the deaths of the landholders. In the Middle colonies and New England, on the other hand, equal division with a double portion to the oldest son was generally followed.

Comparatively, primogeniture would tend to produce larger landed estates, other things being equal, than would the double portion method. We would expect, a priori, larger concentration of landed wealth (and other wealth, too, since land was its ultimate source) in the South than elsewhere after the lapse of several generations, and, indeed, such is the finding of Alice Hanson Jones, the leading modern student of the subject. She found that by 1774 the private nonhuman wealth per *free* wealth holder in the South was 46 percent greater than in the Middle colonies and 63 percent greater than in New England.[11] About one quarter of Southern wealth was the estimated value of slaves, and a quarter of it was land. However, since nearly half the population of the South was slave, these comparative wealth figures should not be exaggerated.

On a strict per capita basis, the South was still wealthier than the rest of the colonies, even if slaves are excluded as countable wealth. Slave-produced wealth in these figures accrued to the slave owners, and primogeniture ensured that estates would not be automatically broken apart and easily squandered by heirs.

Wealth is the net of nonconsumption from income over time, inherited and earned currently, and any institutional device to hold it together over the generations helps it accumulate. In the other colonies, half of the value of wealth in 1774 was land. With respect to other evidences of wealth (such as livestock, farm tools and implements, crops, and consumer durables) the Southern colonies were also slightly higher per white capita. These data show what the planters knew: that slavery paid, at least for them.

The colonial South had an abundance of rich, arable land; raw materials; and timber. These the colonies worked not only to provide a self-sufficiency in food staples and animal husbandry but also to produce a rich export trade in tobacco (primarily Maryland and Virginia) and rice (primarily South Carolina). There was indigo, introduced into South Carolina in 1743 by Eliza Lucas and after 1748 supported by an English bounty,

and there were pitch, turpentine, tar, and resin from Southern pine forests. The cash export crops were most effectively worked by relatively unskilled labor in groups, or "gangs," due to **scale economies:** Within the limits of the land, large groups of workers produce more per worker by cooperative effort than would be true if the land and work were divided and each worker produced only from the worker's own portion. Most agricultural field work using animal power and appropriate tools and machinery is subject to scale economies.

The South was a region with extensive land resources, and the needed labor to exploit them, utilizing scale economies, could most readily be found in the Atlantic slave trade. European immigrants would have wanted land for themselves. There were not sufficient indentured servants available to make up the massive labor force Southern expansion required.

Georgia was a good example of the presence of scale economies in slave labor. The Georgia planters were originally prohibited from using slaves. After some years of failure in nearly every crop, the British finally acceded to their agitation for slavery in 1749. Then Georgia colonists reported immediate agricultural success. In 1753, only four years later, there were 1066 slaves in Georgia and 2381 whites. Rice production thrived. By 1770 Georgia's population was 23,400, growth by a factor of 10 in less than a generation, and 45 percent of that population was slave.

Slave codes were developed to control this labor input and to direct it specifically to those places where known scale economies existed. The colonial Georgia slave code read:

> No Artificer shall be suffer'd to take any Negro as an Apprentice, nor shall any planter lend or let out a Negro or Negroes to another planter, to be employ'd otherwise than in manuring and cultivating the Plantations of the Country.[12]

It is obvious that slaves could be profitably employed at *all* employments (hence the restriction), but the most powerful interest in Georgia was agricultural. Then, as now, vested interests manipulated governments to gain their own ends at others' expense.

To explain the Southern preference for slaves, we must seek *general* arguments that point out characteristics of the Southern colonies that made them different from the others. The combination of headright land acquisition, inheritance rules, the nature of main-crop cultivation, and, finally, institutional adaptation to these over time seem to be sufficient. Tobacco cultivation required constant clearing of new lands, and rice cultivation needed much labor. Slaves were the answer. The argument that the Southern climate directly encouraged slavery, favored by Jefferson and by generations of succeeding historians, can be abandoned.

In the Constitutional Convention discussions in 1787, it was held that slavery was not a moral issue but a matter of "interest" only. After all, in 1787 there were slaves in every state. The discussion shows that some delegates believed then that slavery was going to die out. Virginia had several times attempted unilaterally to end the Atlantic slave trade to Virginia ports but had been overruled by the Board of Trade lawyers in London, who followed the early-eighteenth-century dictum of Chief Justice Holt: "Negroes are merchandise and within the Navigation acts." Virginia could not annul the Navigation Acts except in the way it finally did it, by force of arms. By then, the die was cast. Within a decade of the Constitutional Convention, a Yankee visiting in Georgia, Eli Whitney, made an invention—the cotton gin—that changed everything. Because of their colonial development, the Southern states already had a labor system whose efficiency in cotton production would come to astound the world and to produce a rupture in the 1787 constitutional agreements that only a bloody civil war would close.

The Legacy

It is interesting that the general economic characteristics of the country in 1776 would continue. By 1860 these descriptions of the three sets of colonies would still largely apply to the United States on the eve of the War Between the States, but now they would move westward.

THE COMMON-LAW HERITAGE

An important part of economic development in the colonial era was the use and consequences of the background of English common law. The common law was the law in all of the colonies for customary relations between persons and government and for disputes between private persons. Quite an astonishing amount

of the modern American economy is still powerfully influenced by this remote source; for example, the "police power" of government to regulate and control everything from the issuance of licenses to barbershops to the Environmental Protection Agency. It is a tradition well worth a few pages in any American history book and some considerable thought by any student of American economics.

Markets and Caveat Emptor

We saw in the previous chapter how our land tenure fit into the English land-ownership system, with the feudal chain of property rights secured at first by delivery—"livery and seisin," in the old language.[13] After the *Statute of Frauds* of 1677, the use of land conveyances by written deeds became the standard English method of securing titles. But what about chattel goods, movable property? When was property in commodities or livestock legally transferred from one person to another? There could never be extensive commercial development without secure titles to chattels, providing protection for both buyer and seller.

In England, the problem had been solved by the system of established markets, or the **market overt.** Certain towns were designated market towns, and certain days were fixed as market days in those towns. In London alone, every day was a market day, and every shop a market overt. In the rest of the kingdom, market days and market towns were the only places chattels could be legally sold—secure titles transferred—without each transaction being observed by three witnesses. In addition, larger marketing areas were merged occasionally by the appointment of fairs at specific times and places. All transfers at those times and places were considered in law to have been witnessed, and the property rights, negotiated by sale or trade, were secure.

In a largely static society, most of whose population was illiterate, the system of market overt was a satisfactory solution. Since professional merchants and occasional sellers (e.g., peasants bringing their own produce to market) were largely itinerant, a special set of courts was established to render justice when disputes arose. These courts, called *courts of Pie Powder* (*pied poudre,* "dusty foot"), were courts of record with rights of appeal. A law of Edward III in 1353 set the system on a formal basis: "[Because] the merchants cannot often tarry in one place in hindrance of their business, we will and grant, that speedy right be to them done from day to day and from hour to hour."[14] These adjustments were the early beginnings of equity proceedings in courts of law.

The entire English system was initially transferred to American shores. When the colonists first began to organize their settlements as going concerns, it was natural that they would try to reestablish a system whose workings they understood. Accordingly, we find market overt and fair days set up in all the colonies. In Massachusetts in the 1630s and 1640s, the laws read: "There shall henceforth be a market kept at Boston . . . upon the fifth day of the week . . . at Salem . . . upon the fourth day . . . And at Linn upon the third day. . . ." Boston was to have two fairs a year "on the first third day of the third month, and on the first third day of the eighth month from year to year to continue for two or three days together."[15] Similar fairs were provided for Salem, Watertown, and Dorchester.

In New York, Pennsylvania, Maryland, Virginia, South Carolina, and the other colonies, similar markets overt were established. Georgia forbade efforts to corner the markets in the classic medieval language, forbidding "forestalling, engrossing, and unjust exactions therein."[16]

A place in each town was selected for the market, and an official (variously called the "clerk of the market," the "market master," or the "warden") was empowered to settle disputes, to serve as judge, and to prevent the sale of shoddy goods. There were ordinances against adulterated foods, rigged prices, false weights, and poor workmanship. William Penn's concessions to his colonists of 1681 stated, "There shall be no buying or selling, be it with an Indian, or one another, of any goods to be exported, but what shall be performed in public market . . . where they shall pass the public stamp or mark."[17] The clerk of the market could also fix prices where needed to assure that "justice" was done between buyer and seller.

The colonial economy became one of vast physical expansion. Transactions took place wherever buyers and sellers met in a frontier society. The ruling that only chattel property rights exchanged in established markets were of guaranteed legality was unrealistic in the evolving American circumstances. Farmers objected, saying that market days glutted the towns with produce, placing sellers at a disadvantage, forcing them to sacrifice their perishable goods in order to sell them all before the end of the market day.

By the close of the seventeenth century, New England farmers were allowed to sell directly to customers on their farms on whatever days the customers appeared. Slowly, intermediary merchants, wholesalers, and then retailers appeared on the scene to profit from such market imperfections and, thus, to eliminate them. Colonial towns became places where regular sales of country produce could take place on a wholesale or retail basis. Artisans in the town also objected to marketing requirements. They developed a "bespoke" trade, doing agreed-upon amounts of work for specific customers. This, too, developed into retailing from shops. In 1789, for example, the master shoemakers of Philadelphia refused membership to any who sold shoes "in the public market of this city."

By then Penn's rule was an impediment to regular and expanding trade. Part of the English rule of markets had always been *caveat emptor*, "let the buyer beware." In open market, if the buyer had a fair chance to examine the goods (and there were rules to ensure that such was the case), then the buyer assumed responsibility for the quality of the commodity once the property right in it had been transferred by sale. This principle could be applied anywhere, without the protective cover of market overt. By late colonial times, the requirements of sales in market overt had proved to be excessively restrictive of expanding commerce, and because the rule of *caveat emptor* protected both buyer and seller, had been largely abandoned; *caveat emptor* was never meant to be a cover for fraud, and aggrieved buyers could always sue sellers in civil courts for damages.

Towns and cities continued to pass quality-control ordinances and to control the times and days when trade could take place, as they still do: So-called blue laws, preventing many types of trade on Sundays, exist in many towns and states. The "police powers" of government to control business never lapsed; the wide extent of *caveat emptor* until recent decades would allow an expanding economy greater freedom to "do business" wherever the opportunity arose—in the countryside, with traveling salespeople, by mail order—as time and technologies changed. Market overt still exists in public and farmers' markets all across the country. The states, and now the federal government, have replaced the colonial officials of the markets, imposing safety and quality standards upon manufacturers and sellers of services and commodities. The Occupational Safety and Health Administration, Consumer Product Safety Commission, and Environmental Protection Agency, to name a few, are modern clerks of the market in this respect. *Caveat emptor* still exists, but only where there are no other regulations.

Licensing and Other Controls

In colonial times, as today, access to business opportunities was restricted by licensing. Today, a butcher shop, barbershop, and bank all require official permission, a license, to do business. Why not just "let'er rip," and let anyone who can find customers do business of any sort? This is not allowed now and never has been in American history. Since antiquity, there seem to have been four primary motives to prohibit by force of law such runaway *laissez-faire* (freedom). These restrictions of free trade are (a) monopoly power; (b) quality controls; (c) morals; and (d) taxes.

Monopoly Power. It was, and is, in the interests of persons in trades and services to gain monopoly power for themselves whenever possible. The most effective form of monopoly is that created by government itself, prohibiting competition. With competition eliminated, higher prices may be charged. Typical restrictions of this sort in colonial towns were to prevent "outsiders" from moving in or local residents from entering protected businesses. Such restrictions were commonly achieved by organized trade groups. These obvious prohibitions could be re-enforced by restricting access to trades with rules of apprenticeship imposed by law. Entry was then controlled by those already established. Apprenticeship requirements were easily achieved because of concern with quality.

Quality Control. Colonial governments were genuinely concerned that colonial exports achieve a reputation for quality. Governments routinely passed ordinances to guarantee quality by imposing not only apprenticeships but also viewers, reeves, gaugers, searchers, and inspectors to examine merchandise for sale to ensure its quality—to be sure that it gained "the public mark," as Penn put it. The public commonly was enlisted in the enforcement effort by splitting the fines of those convicted between informers and

the courts. This tactic sharply reduced enforcement costs.[18]

Morals. Then, as now, certain goods, services, and actions were deemed offensive to public morals, and laws restricted those trades. Nowadays, we restrict the sale and smoking of marijuana, for example. In those days, things forbidden were unlicensed preaching, sales of spirits to minors, lending money to seamen, wearing luxurious clothing if you were poor (sumptuary laws), keeping "disorderly" houses, riotous behavior, and "lewd dancing." Americans have always believed that morals can be legislated.

Taxes. Whenever a license can be issued, a fee can be collected. Such a fee is a tax on that business. Then, as now, governments found license fees a steady source of revenue.[19]

In addition to these sorts of routine controls, the kind of government intervention we now call *public utility regulation* was universally engaged in by colonial governments. Again, the custom was ancient in England and was begun immediately in the colonies. Draymen, porters, carters, coachmen, and innkeepers were licensed, and their rates were controlled by public bodies. Similarly, where competition was limited by nature—at docks and wharves or toll bridges or ferries—charges and services were restricted by the ancient English rule that service must be supplied to all who apply, competently and at reasonable rates. As Jefferson reported in his *Notes on the State of Virginia*, "Ferries are admitted only at such places as are appointed by law, and the rates of ferriage are fixed." When, in later years, canals, railroads, telegraphs, telephones, airplanes, central power and water sources, and gas facilities were created by the processes of technological change, no new concepts of control were needed. The modern Interstate Commerce Commission, Civil Aeronautics Board, Federal Communications Commission, and Federal Power Commission are merely modern versions of the seventeenth-century selectmen of colonial Massachusetts who "shall have power to regulate" because there was found to be "a very great abuse in the Townes of Boston and Charleston, by Porters, who many times do require and exact more than is just and righteous."[20] Nowadays, we have public service commissions to exact a "reasonable" rate of profit from the consuming public in such cases.

Rightly or wrongly, such rates were not left to the impersonal determination of the market—nor are they now.

Employment, Wages, and Income Supports

Captain John Smith is reported to have laid down the rule at the beginning of the Virginia settlement, "He that will not work shall not eat." In colonial America, work, at least for the lower classes, was required, even for whites not bound in servitude. The background law was Queen Elizabeth's *Statute of Artificers and Apprentices* (1562) containing "divers orders for artificers, labourers, servants of husbandry and apprentices." This law, by requiring all to have some means of support, was designed to prevent pauperism and civil unrest. In the statute, after a long enumeration of those who were exempt (e.g., persons of noble origin, persons with specified wealth and income, military people, clergy, scholars, mariners, miners, fishermen, persons in trades, masters, journeymen or apprentices in cities and corporate or market towns), all others could be compelled to labor in agriculture. Men from the age of 12 to 60, and single women between the ages of 12 and 40, could be so compelled. Hours of daily labor were prescribed, as were conditions of job mobility. Agricultural laborers could not leave employment without prescribed exit papers (as in the former U.S.S.R.). In the harvest weeks, artisans could be compelled to go into the country and work. Wages were to be set by local authority. Those offering higher than legal wages were to be fined, the fines being split between the courts and the informers. Those refusing such work could be adjudged vagabonds. Under the "charitable alms" law of Henry VIII (1535), as amended by Elizabethan statutes, penalties for vagabonds were whipping, branding, ear lopping, and hanging for the third offense. Merrie olde England.

In colonial America, many of these early English laws were in force. Jefferson pointed out in *Notes on the State of Virginia,* "I never saw a native American begging in the streets or highways." In Virginia, he wrote, ". . . vagabonds, without visible property or vocation, are placed in work houses, where they are well clothed, fed, lodged and made to labor."[21] In Massachusetts, the laws stated that idle persons were to be committed to prison, with ten lashes, and put to work to earn "necessary bread and water, or other mean food." The prison officials were empowered to whip and starve the prisoners until they were brought to "some meet order." Apprenticeships were prescribed for those whose parents were lax in their duties. The selectmen of each township could judge which children were not being suitably instructed "in some honest lawful calling, labour, or employment, either in husbandry or some other trade, profitable to themselves or the commonwealth."[22] Such children could be taken from their parents and bound by the courts "with some masters for years," the girls to age 18, the boys to age 21.

For all others, each colony had its almshouses, workhouses (Philadelphia's was called the "house of industry"), or, failing all else, prisons for the poor. Compulsory labor was provided for those who could find nothing of their own. Penn wanted all children bound out in Pennsylvania at the age of 12 and taught a trade "to the end none may be idle, but the poor may work to live and the rich, if they become poor, may not want."[23]

On Saturday afternoons, it was the custom at places of incarceration to offer the imprisoned poor up for servitude to those needing labor. (Samuel Slater, an English immigrant and the founder of the American textile industry, when congratulated by General Jackson on his success in America, is reported to have quipped that it was a good thing to succeed in a country where the poor were sold every Saturday afternoon.)

Compulsory labor at wages fixed by courts, selectmen, or local magistrates was, by law, the fate of those who had no other place in society. We should not judge an underdeveloped country too harshly. In an economy very close to subsistence, such rules seemed to make sense. Subsidized unemployment, whether by charity or by unemployment insurance, is in some sense a luxury, either of the rich or of a rich society. Colonial society could hardly afford drones. It provided for its aged and sick poor; others had to work. These ideas and laws lasted for centuries. Within living memory, as late as the 1930s, idle persons were still being jailed in this country for the crime of having "no visible means of support." The idea of the work ethic, given renewed fame by President Reagan, had such origins. Many Americans doubtless believe, as did Henry Ford, that "work is our salvation." But for the doubters, there was always compulsion.

Such rules, when enforced, could surely reduce the amount of charity required of society. That was important because, from Henry VIII onward, English communities (originally parishes) were compelled to tax themselves to provide for the poor and destitute. This was also true in the colonies. If the freedom to starve is considered of little value, then the theory behind compulsory labor in colonial America is difficult to condemn on economic grounds. There was guaranteed employment then, although modern liberal politicians might not approve of either its motivations or its spirit.

Note that such a scheme robbed the work force of the right to withhold its labor to gain higher wages. Compulsory labor laws tend to keep wages down; however, balanced against this was the colonial need for people and labor. The colonial labor supply was kept in check in a given region by the ability of free labor to acquire cheap land out west.

The colonial years (as under Nixon's phases and Carter's guidelines) were strewn with efforts to control wages and prices by governmental authority. Labor organizations were considered, by law, criminal conspiracies against society, and so strikes for higher wages were both rare and generally unsuccessful. We already have noted the element of compulsion in the vast unfree labor force of indentured servants and slaves. The element of compulsory labor for those who were neither slaves nor in servitude must be added. The poor did not starve in colonial America when it was unnecessary, nor were they idle when work could be found or created by authorities, if necessary, in jails. These lowly and semicriminal beginnings for labor in this country are not what we celebrate each year on Labor Day, but perhaps ought to be.

EXPANSION AND THE WESTERN LANDS

If one were asked to argue that, for economic reasons, the American Revolution was inevitable, the easiest place to begin would be the question of the land beyond the Appalachians. The original grant to the Virginia Company had been "from sea to sea." This grant of King James, by his Majesty's "merest motion," no doubt reflected his, and his advisors', vast ignorance of what the North American continent might be or contain. This ignorance would come back to haunt the descendants of all concerned. The claims of Virginia, and

those whose original patents came from the Virginia charter, Massachusetts and Connecticut, were abruptly restricted by the royal *Proclamation of 1763,* limiting trans-Appalachian settlement to lands attained by crown approval, and the Quebec Act of 1774, which gave to that province all the land west of the Ohio River. The Quebec Act, along with the Port of Boston Act (closing it) issued in the same year, were considered acts of war by the colonists, pure and simple.

As we saw in Table 1.1 in the previous chapter, by the end of the colonial period, there were already permanent populations in Kentucky, Tennessee, and Vermont (a temporary escape hatch for land-hungry settlers fleeing out of Massachusetts, New Hampshire, and the Hudson Valley to escape politics, Indians, land scarcity, and overlapping claims). It had taken a century for Americans to begin a serious movement from the early seacoast settlements, across the Appalachian barrier, into the continental interior. The Spanish and French were already established in the Mississippi basin and in the Southwest by the mid-eighteenth century. English fur traders were aware of the interior's riches, too. But until population increase made good settlement lands scarce in the Atlantic coastal areas, there was not sufficient incentive to provoke settlement of the interior: There was, in addition, the matter of legal jurisdiction. As we have seen, colonial land settlement was not the disorderly affair suggested by Hollywood epics. Secure land titles had to come from established authority, and authority was not always easy to establish beyond the Appalachians. Before the end of the Seven Years' War (also called the French and Indian War) in 1763, the French laid claim to most of the Mississippi watershed. Unfortunately, it was already occupied by Native Americans.

West of the Ohio

Interior settlement was a political, legal, and of necessity, a military matter. George Washington's experience in the Pittsburgh area was a case in point. By the 1740s the Virginians had become interested in their trans-Appalachian lands. Thomas Lee, president of the Virginia Council of State, had organized an Ohio Company in 1747 with the object of trading with the Indians there and exerting Virginia's territorial claims. A year later this company received a royal grant of 200,000 acres in the Ohio Valley, on condition that it be settled.

Fur Trappers and Traders. These entrepreneurs were the economic link between the Europeans and the Indians. Once a year trappers brought their furs overland by horseback or downriver in boats (above right) to rendezvous with traders and Indians (above). The furs would pass through frontier outposts such as "Bellevue," the present day Omaha (below), and then to a major city such as St. Louis (below right).

The French responded by occupying and fortifying various strong points. It was in the interests of the proposed Virginia settlement that Governor Dinwiddie sent 21-year-old George Washington to discuss with the French in October 1753 their occupation of Virginia territory. Washington was treated hospitably and sent home. A few months later he returned with a small force, started building a fort, attacked the French, was beaten, and then surrendered his fort, his men, and himself in July 1754. Again, he was sent home, as were the Virginia soldiers. The fort he built, renamed Fort Duquesne, was completed and staffed by the French. A year later, Washington was back in the area as an aide to General Braddock, only to meet defeat once more. The survivors escaped back into Virginia. Pennsylvania settlers pulled back to a line of forts in the mountains, planned and partly built under the personal direction of an unlikely military engineer, Benjamin Franklin. In 1758 Fort Duquesne was taken by General John Forbes and renamed Pittsburgh. Montreal fell to the English in 1760; then came the great Indian uprising led by Pontiac. Only after peace was settled in 1763 was colonizing on any scale reasonably safe in the area. However, Washington reported attempting (unsuccessful) conversations with German-speaking settlers in 1754 in this backcountry. Already the movement west was evident.

Kentucky and the Southern Expansion

Farther south, the problems impeding westward movement were Indians, the Appalachian Mountains, and the unknown. Virginia's claim was the relevant one again. In 1750 Thomas Walker found the Cumberland Gap, which provided an accessible passage through the Appalachians. In 1752 John Finley reached the present site of Louisville, going down the Ohio River by canoe. His description inspired Daniel Boone's trek in 1769 (he had been a wagoner with Braddock and Washington). In 1774 the town of Harrodsburg was established. By then Pittsburgh was a going concern. In 1775 Richard Harrison and a company of North Carolinians made a treaty with the Cherokee (declared void by the government of Virginia) for a colony they called Transylvania. The way west was open at the same time that the American Revolution was underway. The two events became indissolubly linked, because those western lands were a reason for the war and were the occasion for acceptance of the Articles of Confederation by the warring colonists.

Land Companies and Speculation

After the Seven Years' War, it was clearly time to rethink imperial policy regarding the western lands. In addition to Lee's Ohio Company, other private companies were forming to exploit the interior. The Loyal Company and the Greenbrier Company were organized in Virginia in the early 1750s for colonization. The Loyal Company had been granted 800,000 acres across the Appalachians. With abundant land and few settlers, the problem would be to *attract* colonists, and conditions of land acquisition would have to be more favorable than they had become in the older settled areas. In Pennsylvania, the Indiana Company was formed, hoping to gain land in Virginia's western territories. Ben Franklin was involved in its management, and it opened a land office in Pittsburgh. It is significant that its principles of settlement were made to exclude quit rents altogether. It intended to sell land in blocks of 400 acres per settler. Such liberalization was in the wind. In 1754 the British government had seriously considered a scheme to open the western lands with grants of 1000 acres per settler, but the war had stopped its implementation. Virginia's terms were liberalized for settlers. In 1773 the Council of Virginia issued an order granting preemption rights to frontier squatters on condition that they pay £3 per 100 acres to whatever land company had been granted rights in the territory or else the squatters would be holding their lands from soldiers given rights to them by the Royal Proclamation of 1763. Also, in 1773 the Council of Virginia abolished quit rents throughout the colony (except in the Northern Neck, where semifeudal magnates with huge estates ruled).

Once the fighting started, Virginia seized the reins without further regard for the crown's rights. There would be no further review of its laws by the English. Virginia settlers were now pouring into lands granted to the land companies, and on 14 May 1776 the Virginia assembly passed a law granting *preemption rights* (the right to first bid and purchase) to all squatters on private company lands. This was a complete break with previous policy. The settler could claim the land, sell it, and move on to more. A pattern was set, heralding more than a century of American history during which land speculation seemed almost the main national industry at times. In fact, Virginia was more generous with settlers' preemption rights than the federal government would prove to be once it acquired the "public domain." Virginia also put no upper limit on individual acquisitions.

Virginia's Land Act of 1779 really opened the continent for purchase, sale, and resale. It was a headlong rush. By 1780 Virginia had granted nearly 2 million acres to the Loyal and Greenbrier companies and nearly 5 million acres to its Revolutionary soldiers. It had sold Treasury Warrants for an immense 38 million acres of its domain, from "sea to sea." In January 1787 Virginia opened its land north of the Ohio River to its Revolutionary veterans. By then other forces were about to take over. The Northwest Ordinance of 1785 laid down the principles of prior survey, and the Northwest Ordinance of 1787 outlined the conditions of tenure, sale, inheritance, and political organization (including prohibition of slavery). In 1789 Governor Arthur St. Clair organized his territorial government, and settlement commenced—under private companies. Congress had granted a new Ohio Company 1.5 million acres in 1786, while another 1 million acres had gone to a New Jersey group. Individuals purchased vast tracts with depreciated Revolutionary currency or with military claims. Once the western lands were open and land acquisition was put strictly on a market basis, populations rushed into them. Thirty years after the first census was taken in 1790, the old Northwest (Ohio, Michigan, Indiana, and Illinois) contained nearly 800,000 people, perhaps as many as Virginia and Pennsylvania combined at the outbreak of the Revolution.[24]

British Policy

Once we see what was unleashed in 1763, it is clear that British policy was doomed. The sudden reality of British possession of the Northwest Territories presented the crown in 1763 with new responsibilities and with opportunities undreamed of under the old land grants, which had not been acted upon until the Virginia colonists themselves moved against the French and Indians. The Proclamation of 1763 had been a holding effort, an attempt to restrict entry to property rights granted directly by the crown, to protect the newly acquired fur trade (in the interest of an old English chartered company, Hudson's Bay), and to keep peace with the Indian tribes. The colonists, wanting the land, cared nothing for the Hudson's Bay Company or for peace with the Indians, now by far the weaker population contending for the land. The Quebec Act of 1774, an "intolerable" act, was an effort, once and for all, to separate the Americans from their ancient claims. What did George III and his ministers care about promises made to the colonists by James I more than a century and a half earlier? But the Quebec Act robbed Virginians of millions of acres. George Washington (himself an owner of western lands) said in 1774 that he was prepared to outfit 1000 men at his own expense and lead them personally to Boston to fight the British. He did more than that. British land policy after 1763 must be counted a disaster. The colonial governments had successfully granted land and settled populations for a century and a half. The old system might have been adapted to post-1763 conditions. It was not. The British tried to change it; the Americans changed it even more and changed history in the bargain.

What was true of the land was also true of trade and commerce. By the 1770s British policy had become insupportable after a long period of relative success. But, unlike the issue of land policy, it is not so easy to argue that colonial objection to the British trade policies of the 1770s was simply a matter of economics. These policies did not take away American rights so much as they attempted to tax the exercise of them.

Notes

1. Consider that although there are more pleasant locations for the wholesale diamond business today than New York City, that is where it is centered. Historically, the American diamond business grew there; it was the largest retail market. Once jobbing and cutting started in New York, other dealers and cutters located there to take advantage of labor, communications, buyers, and sellers, and finally the trade was there because it was there.

Battle Mountain, Nevada, offers lower rents and lower crime rates but lacks external economies. External economies tend to make cities.

2. For a fascinating essay on the colonial experience and its consequences, see Amelia Clewly Ford, *Colonial Precedents of Our National Land System as It Existed in 1800* (1976).

3. Diane Lindstrom and John Sharpless, "Urban Growth and Economic Structure in Antebellum America," in *REH*, 1978, vol. 3.

4. Carl Bridenbaugh, *Cities in Revolt: Urban Life in America, 1743–1776* (1955), p. 272.

5. New England's shortage of good arable land did not induce a decline in per capita wealth in the 18th century as population increased, as some scholars have believed. Adaptations were made soon enough to avoid impoverishment imposed by poor farmlands. Gloria L. Main, "The Standard of Living in Colonial Massachusetts," *JEH,* March 1983. There is also evidence, fragmentary at first, of a developing market in farm labor, a good indicator of developing specialization among the farm population. Winifred B. Rothenberg, *From Market-Places to a Market Economy* (1992), ch. 6.

6. Rothenberg, pp. 166–174.

7. Thomas M. Doerflinger, *A Vigorous Spirit of Enterprise: Merchants and Economic Development in Revolutionary America* (1986). This book, slightly mistitled, is a close examination of merchants, especially in Philadelphia, and the world they made.

8. The evidence indicates a modest growth of agricultural productivity, even in the seventeenth century. Duane E. Bell and Gary Walton, "Agricultural Productivity Changes in Eighteenth Century Pennsylvania," *JEH,* March 1976.

9. For an interesting view of a family living on the Maryland frontier in the mid-seventeenth century, one that examines the connections between agriculture and societal development, see Lois Green Carr, Russell R. Menard, and Lorena S. Walsh, *Robert Cole's World: Agriculture and Society in Early Maryland* (1991).

10. Thomas Jefferson, *Notes on the State of Virginia* (London: John Stockdale, 1788), pp. 271–2.

11. Alice Hanson Jones, *Wealth of a Nation to Be: The American Colonies on the Eve of the Revolution* (1980), p. 58, Table 3.7. On a strict per capita basis, in 1774 total wealth in the 13 colonies averaged £46.5; in New England, £36.6; in the Middle colonies, £41.9; and in the South, £54.7, including slaves (Jones, p. 54, Table 3.5).

12. Charles C. Jones, *The History of Georgia* (Boston: Houghton Mifflin, 1883), p. 423.

13. Delivery was usually affected by the donor handing over a piece of turf and a twig to the buyer, the person making "entry," before witnesses, usually the neighbors. It was also the *only* method of land transfer recognized by common law. In A.D. 937 the men of Malmsbury received 500 acres of land to be held in common from King Athelstan for assistance at the legendary Battle of Brunanburh. To this day the young men of Malmsbury receive this property right by delivery at a ceremony when they are 21. The representative of the donor recites the lines "Turf and twig I give to thee, as King Athelstan gave to me." In 1687 Samuel Sewall of Massachusetts got into a dispute over his rights on Hog Island, near Boston. In his diary he wrote: "May 2. I go to Hog Island. Mr. Moodey, Oakes, Capt. Townsend and Seth Perry in one column; Capt. Hill, Mr. Parson and Mr. Addington in the other, witness my taking Livery and seised of the Island by Turf and Twigg and the House." Michael G. Hall, Lawrence H. Leder, and Michael G. Kammen, eds., *The Glorious Revolution in America: Documents on the Colonial Crisis of 1689* (1964), p. 27. Even if one considers law as custom, the continuity of English common law is quite astonishing. So is it when we consider that our own land tenure is still that of medieval England.

14. Edward A. Adler, "Business Jurisprudence," *Harvard Law Review,* vol. 28, 1914–15, p. 139.

15. William Whitmore, ed., *Colonial Laws of Massachusetts* (Boston: Boston City Printers, 1889), p. 150.

16. Charles C. Jones, *The History of Georgia,* pp. 479–85.

17. Jonathan Hughes, *The Vital Few* (New York: Oxford University Press, 1986), p. 54.

18. In colonial times, both Virginia and Maryland introduced schemes to restrict tobacco output and to control the quality of the marketed product. Mary McKinney Schweitzer, "Economic Regulation and the Colonial Economy: The Maryland Tobacco Inspection Act of 1747," *JEH,* September 1980.

19. For examples of all such colonial regulation see Jonathan Hughes, *Social Control in the Colonial Economy* (1976), ch. 9.

20. William Whitmore, *Colonial Laws of Massachusetts,* p. 185.

21. Jefferson, *Notes on the State of Virginia,* p. 220.

22. Hughes, pp. 96–111 and footnotes there.

23. Hughes, *The Vital Few,* p. 55.

24. The best survey of the western lands issue in colonial America is still Thomas P. Abernathy, *Western Lands and the American Revolution* (1937). It is the main source for the discussion presented here.

Suggested Readings

Articles

Adler, Edward A. "Business Jurisprudence." *Harvard Law Review,* vol. 28, 1914–15.

Anderson, Terry. "Wealth Estimates for the New England Colonies, 1650–1709." *Explorations in Economic History,* vol. 14, no. 4, October 1977.

Bell, Duane, and Walton, Gary. "Agricultural Productivity Change in Eighteenth Century Pennsylvania." *Journal of Economic History,* vol. XXXVI, no. 1, March 1976.

Henretta, James. "Economic Development and Social Structure in Colonial Boston." *William and Mary Quarterly,* vol. XXII, no. 1, January 1965.

Hughes, Jonathan. "William Penn and the Holy Experiment." *The Vital Few: American Economic History and Its Protagonists.* New York: Oxford University Press, 1986, chapter 2.

Jones, Alice Hanson. "Wealth Estimates for the New England Colonies About 1770." *Journal of Economic History,* vol. XXXII, no. 1, March 1972.

Lindstrom, Diane, and Sharpless, John. "Urban Growth and Economic Structure in Antebellum America." In Paul Uselding, ed., *Research in Economic History.* Greenwich, Conn.: JAI Press, 1978, vol. 3.

Main, Gloria L., "The Standard of Living in Colonial Massachusetts," *Journal of Economic History,* vol. XLIII, no. 1, March 1983.

Shepherd, James, and Williamson, Samuel. "The Coastal Trade of the British North American Colonies 1768–1772." *Journal of Economic History,* vol. XXXVII, no. 4, December 1972.

Walton, Gary M. "New Evidence on Colonial Commerce." *Journal of Economic History,* vol. XXVIII, no. 3, September 1968.

Books

Abernathy, Thomas Perkins. *Western Lands and the American Revolution.* New York: Appleton-Century, 1937.

Bridenbaugh, Carl. *Cities in the Wilderness.* New York: Oxford University Press, 1971 (reprint).

———. *Cities in Revolt.* New York: Oxford University Press, 1971 (reprint).

Bruchey, Stuart, ed. *The Colonial Merchant: Sources and Readings.* New York: Harcourt, Brace, Jovanovich, 1966.

———. *The Roots of American Economic Growth.* London: Hutchinson University Library, 1965.

Carr, Lois Green, Menard, Russell R., and Walsh, Lorena S. *Robert Cole's World: Agriculture and Society in Early Maryland.* Chapel Hill: University of North Carolina Press for the Institute of Early American History and Culture, 1991.

Doerflinger, Thomas M. *A Vigorous Spirit of Enterprise: Merchants and Economic Development in Revolutionary America.* Chapel Hill: University of North Carolina Press, 1986.

Ford, Amelia Clewly. *Colonial Precedents of Our National Land System As It Existed in 1800.* Philadelphia: Porcupine Press, 1976.

Hall, Michael G., Leder, Lawrence H., and Kammen, Michael G., eds. *The Glorious Revolution in America: Documents on the Colonial Crisis of 1689.* Chapel Hill: University of North Carolina Press, 1964.

Hodges, Graham Russell. *New York Cartmen, 1667–1850.* New York: New York University Press, 1985.

Hughes, Jonathan. *Social Control in the Colonial Economy.* Charlottesville: University Press of Virginia, 1976.

Jones, Alice Hanson. *American Colonial Wealth: Documents and Methods.* New York: Arno Press, 1977.

———. *Wealth of a Nation to Be: The American Colonies on the Eve of the Revolution.* New York: Columbia University Press, 1980.

Katz, Michael B. *In the Shadow of the Poorhouse: A Social History of Welfare in America.* New York: Basic Books, 1986.

Kulikoff, Allan. *Tobacco and Slaves: The Development of Southern Cultures in the Chesapeake, 1680–1800.* Chapel Hill: University of North Carolina Press, 1986.

McCusker, John J., and Menard, Russell R. *The Economy of British America, 1606–1789: Needs and Opportunities for Study.* Chapel Hill: University of North Carolina Press, 1986.

Rothenberg, Winifred B. *From Market-Places to a Market Economy: The Transformation of Rural Massachusetts, 1750–1850.* Chicago: University of Chicago Press, 1992.

Walton, Gary M., and Shepherd, James F. *The Economic Rise of Early America.* New York: Cambridge University Press, 1979.

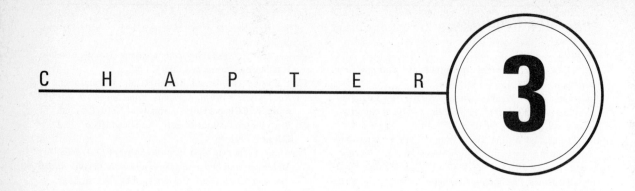

The End of British Rule

We are accustomed to viewing our Revolutionary ancestors as quaint picture-book figures in homespun knee breeches, seeing them as rough frontier types who tossed out the rich and effete English. However, the evidence, using a modern frame of reference, suggests that colonial life was far more than just the bare essentials; it was a life that was more comfortable.

ON THE EVE OF REVOLUTION

When we look at structures dating to the colonial period that have survived to modern times, we see evidence of past solidity and wealth in Portsmouth, Newburyport, Boston, Philadelphia, Georgetown, and Charleston. We suppose that only the best buildings survived. Yet these solid structures were places of everyday business and the houses of common persons who were not princes or feudal lords. There was a surrounding social and economic infrastructure that had voluntarily supported such opulence. Common sense alone would suggest that colonial society, by the end of the period, must have been prosperous.

Growth Again

Modern scholarship has thrown some light on the issue of growth, but the questions are by no means all resolved. Let us return for a moment to our growth model. We defined growth as increases in real output per head of population. The money value of output is income to the owners of the factors of production. Incomes received are either consumed or saved. Net saving over time adds up to a stock of something we call *wealth*. Whether it is in solid structures, livestock, or money claims, it is society's wealth. It is a certain stock at a given moment of time. It can also be called **capital.** Colonial wealth has been roughly estimated in various ways. One method is to use the surviving probate records of estates.

Probably the leading modern student of such data is Alice Hanson Jones, and her estimates of colonial wealth are astonishingly large.[1] She found that the average free person in colonial America owned perhaps £76 in real wealth. Now, if we accept that amount as the best number available, some interesting information emerges with a little arithmetic. Walton and Shepherd point out that £76, in 1973 prices (which would exclude, therefore, ownership of slaves!), was $2860.[2] A tidy sum! If we consider this figure a measure of capital per head, then dividing it by various capital/output ratios produces a result that is a measure of output (income) per head in 1774. Historic capital/output ratios fall somewhere between the boundaries 3 to 1 and 5 to 1.[3] At the former figure, income per capita in 1774 was £25, at the latter, £15. Using Shepherd and Walton's conversion to "modern values," colonial Americans had incomes per capita in 1774 in the range of $995 to $573 per head; again, these are converted to 1973 prices. These amounts would have given colonial Americans a possible standard of life something like that of 1973 Mexico, Brazil, or Greece with the lower figure and like that of 1973 U.S.S.R. with the higher one. Of course, the colonists would have had the consumer goods and capital goods of 1774, not those of 1973, to absorb their incomes.

If we take such estimates at all seriously, several important generalizations present themselves about colonial America just before the Revolution. First, on the average, Americans already had achieved greater affluence than had their British cousins. This was especially true of the Southern colonies, which by these measures had three times the wealth per capita of the Middle and Northern colonies.[4] The eighteenth-century population was growing at mean annual rates of more than 3 percent (Table 1.2, Chapter 1). Estimates of per capita growth are in the neighborhood of 0.4 to 0.5 percent per annum in the eighteenth century, slightly above the contemporary English growth rates.[5]

The Standard of Life

The numbers indicate that the colonists, deploying European technology, *very quickly* raised per capita output to English levels in whatever enterprises they formed and developed in new areas of settlement. Then growth *slowed down* to levels justified by the state of existing technology and its gradual improvement. Such a pattern explains both high apparent income levels and relatively slow growth once initial settlements were made. It is not an unreasonable pattern of growth. If a large body of modern Americans were transplanted to a Third World country, one would expect strong immediate improvements in economic development to occur since the Americans would employ their own technology and not that of the Third World. Such a

pattern of growth would explain testimony quoted by Stuart Bruchey in *The Colonial Merchant: Sources and Readings.* In 1663 Reverend John Higginson of Boston said, just three decades after landing, "We live in a more plentiful and comfortable manner than ever we did expect."[6] And Ben Franklin observed in 1740, while he was clerk of the Pennsylvania legislature, and only 60 years after Penn's charter for the colony, "The first drudgery of settling new colonies, which confines the attention of people to mere necessaries, is now pretty well over: and there are many in every province in circumstances that set them at ease."[7]

In another book, Bruchey, dealing with the historical evidence available in the early 1960s, concludes in what was then a somewhat risky statement, "Probably in few societies in history have the means of subsistence been so widely distributed among the mass of the people as in colonial America."[8] As we shall see at the end of this chapter, he was not describing an equal distribution, but an abundant and largely sufficient one. Since the British were paying most of the administrative costs of the colonies, domestic resources were free to pursue economic growth until the Revolution.

How were these resources deployed? Evidence of the technology available shows that Americans were abreast of Europe. Colonial agriculture, once European methods were adapted to American climate and soils, was very productive. But the colonists also fabricated products of the farm, forests, mines, and fisheries. They made iron and iron products; they built ships; they made bricks; they wove cloth in abundance of wool and linen on the farmsteads; and they made weapons. They built mills and ground flour and converted timber into lumber; they fished and maintained a large export industry in that product as well as in hides; and they dried and salted meat for export. They had tanneries and salteries; they made shoes; they printed newspapers; and they made their own glassware and pewter ware. Wherever they settled, the Americans quickly replicated their civilization economically, just as they carried with them their relations, property laws, levels of education, and moral code.[9]

In short, the American Revolution was not a conflict between a "Third World–type" colonial dependency and "the metropolis." It was a conflict between two

An English artist's view of colonial people and manners portrays colonial women agreeing to give up tea drinking in protest of the Tea Tax.

nations on a roughly equal level in terms of per capita incomes, with the insurgents having some 40 percent of England's population and total income. Of course, England was much better organized for war, but this was much like the American effort in Vietnam: It was far away and fought among a hostile population. The results were about the same for the British in North America as they were for the Americans in Southeast Asia in the twentieth century.

Location in 1776

Even though colonial eyes were fixed on lands west of the Alleghenies by 1776, there was still very little settlement beyond the Atlantic fall line. In 150 years the colonists had managed to settle in the great bays north of Spanish Florida. Because the major occupation was farming and transport was limited to water or animal-drawn wagons on poor roads, the flat Atlantic coastal lands and the valleys of major rivers up to the fall line contained most of the farms and towns—from the Savannah River in the south to the Penobscot in Maine. Beyond the mountains, populations were mainly strung in isolated settlements down river valleys, with scattered settlements in what are now West Virginia, Kentucky, and Tennessee. Even more isolated were the settlements north of New Orleans up the Mississippi, Wabash, and Ohio rivers. Detroit lay virtually alone on the Great Lakes. From the British viewpoint, a war against the colonists would involve ships and control of major river basins along the Atlantic coast. What were the causes of the conflict?

CONFLICT AND REVOLUTION

We noted in Chapter 1 the theory of British colonization: that the colonists were, and their descendants would remain, the king's subjects under the laws of

England and with the rights of English citizens. It must be emphasized again how well the scheme worked for a very long time. But in trade, as in land policy, the French defeat and the end of Pontiac's rebellion meant that after 1763, the English were free to change their policies drastically, and that the colonials, no longer in danger from the French in Canada and the interior, were free to resist that change if they so desired. Both things happened.

The Navigation Acts

In 1651 Oliver Cromwell, The Lord Protector, was building an empire overseas. The Navigation Act of that year defined that empire, restricting shipping and trade between it and the external world. In 1660, with Cromwell dead, the English decided that they were a monarchy after all, sent a fleet to Holland for Charles II, and brought him home. That year was counted as the twelfth year in the reign of Charles II (his father was executed in 1648). Parliament was busy repassing the Commonwealth laws it wanted retained since the laws of Cromwell and the Commonwealth were now in limbo and no longer regarded as law. The eighteenth law of 1660 was the 1651 Navigation Act again, ''An Act for the Encouraging and Increasing of Shipping and Navigation.''

The Navigation Act's immediate object was to reserve the trade in commodities originating inside the empire to the shipowners, mariners, and merchants who owed allegiance to the King of England. More narrowly, they were to enlarge and protect his income derived from customs, fines, confiscations, and taxes. The ships and sailors of the colonies were treated as English under the act. Until 1707 Scotland was a separate kingdom (with Charles as its king), so only one port serving Scotland, Berwick on Tweed, was included in the Act's provisions. Of its several parts, the Act's main injunctions relating to the colonies were the following:

1. No commodities originating from the empire were to be shipped in any but British (including colonial) ships, under a British captain, with at least three fourths of the crew to be His Majesty's subjects.
2. The same provisions held for imported commodities from Asia, Africa, or parts of America other than the British colonies.

3. None but British subjects were allowed to be merchants or factors in the colonies.
4. None but British ships with their three-fourths British crews were to carry commodities from one English port to another.

Penalties were provided for violations of these provisions. In addition, several enumerated commodities exported from the ''plantations'' of America, Asia, and Africa could be landed *only* in England. The commodities listed were sugar, tobacco, cotton, indigo, ginger, and fustick or other wood products used for dying cloth. There was a restriction on the carrying trade that no goods could be carried from foreign countries into the empire in English ships except directly from their place of origin. The latter would be greatly restricted in 1663. The Act included special customs duties for fish and whale products usually caught by English fishermen that were imported into England in other than English ships, and customs surcharges were placed against French ships entering English ports. The first provision was for the protection of the English fishing industry; the second was in retaliation for the policies of Louis XIV of France against the English.

In 1662 and 1663 the Act was amended to include further enumerated commodities and more rules for shipping and customs. In the amendment of 1663, imports from Europe into the colonial empire were prohibited except in English vessels ''laden and shipped'' in England. This stringent amendment was to protect English manufacturers and to encourage

> . . . vent for English woolen and other manufacturers and commodities, rendering the navigation to and from the same [colonies] more safe and cheap, and making this kingdom a staple, not only of the commodities of those plantations, but also of the commodities of other countries and places, for the supplying of them, it being the usage of other nations to keep their plantations trade to themselves.

Amendments in subsequent years were true to the spirit of these laws. Essentially, the empire was treated as if it were the domestic coastal trade, the waters connecting the empire as if they were British coastal or inland waters. That such laws invited smuggling is obvious enough. How much, we will never know. In 1733 the Molasses Act imposed high duties on foreign sugar, molasses, and rum imported into the colonies to protect West Indies planters. Colonial sea captains flagrantly ignored that law because (a) they had to trade their goods in the Caribbean, (b) there was insufficient production in the British plantations there, and (c) the Americans traded where they could, which meant that Spanish, French, and Dutch sugar and molasses were traded for American commodities. The English preferred to ignore this trade until 1764 when a new Sugar Act was enforced, and the Americans resisted. The navigation laws were the "rules of the road" for the growing trade of an expanding empire, and until 1763 they worked well enough, defining and binding together the English world, mother country, and overseas colonies.

Mercantilism

Was there any profound logic to the navigation laws? Writers have considered them part of the contemporary European commercial policy theory called, collectively, **mercantilism.** Business enterprises had grown up, some of them trading abroad. Governments licensed, regulated, and taxed all such activity to raise money for governmental activity. Some industries were favored by light taxes, some were even subsidized for reasons of state. It is the sum of all such government action that is called mercantilism. Probably far too much has been made of this issue.

By modern standards, there is nothing extraordinary about the navigation laws or about English mercantilism: As the 1663 Navigation Act put it, "It being the usage of other nations to keep their plantations trade to themselves." The use of subsidies, tax rebates, tariffs, and quotas to attempt to protect and encourage American industries at the expense of the rest of the world is standard modern practice. If every member of Congress and every president had the economic backgrounds and viewpoints of Adam Smith and David Ricardo (the great theorists of classical economics), we would not pursue such policies. But they do not, and we do pursue them, *as do all other governments in the world today and as they did throughout the seventeenth and eighteenth centuries.* Europeans, and the English, used governmental power to create industries, fleets of ships, and employment for their own nationals that the world market would not have created if market forces alone had decided what would be produced, where, how, and for whom. The prodigious writing on European mercantilism by historians was an attempt

to explain why governments did not act according to the precepts of competitive market theory and free trade. Governments almost never do. World production was (and is) less than it otherwise might have been (or can be) as a result. Trade and commerce in the mercantilist age grew more to governmental liking, or so government leaders believed at the time and continue to believe today as they vigorously pursue such policies.

One item of special note in so-called mercantilist theory is the emphasis upon export surpluses—"beggar-thy-neighbor policy." In the days before our own Federal Reserve System learned to circulate its notes backed only by holdings of government securities, Americans thought that a "favorable" balance of trade was a good thing. We used gold for money, and one way to get gold was to sell more to foreigners than they sold to you. That way, they shipped you more gold in payment than you shipped to them. This would increase your own supply of gold, and therefore money, and business people knew that more money meant brisk trade and higher prices, which was good for them. Governments knew that brisk trade yielded higher taxes than did slack trade, so governments favored export surpluses, too (and laid on tariffs, embargoes, and quotas to help out). The mercantilist theory made sense to mercantilists. Trade surpluses made your kingdom rich and powerful; if they made your enemies (almost everyone else in the seventeenth and eighteenth centuries) poor and weak, so much the better.

The Direction of Colonial Trade

In Figure 3.1 we see the overall direction of colonial commodity trade flows in 1768–72. In the 1730s the navigation laws were amended to allow some direct colonial trade with Europe south of Cape Finisterre (near the northern tip of the Spanish Peninsula). Some 56 percent of colonial exports went to the United Kingdom, 18 percent to southern Europe, 26 percent to the West Indies, and less than 1 percent directly to Africa. In return, four fifths of colonial imports came from the United Kingdom, 18 percent from the West Indies, and only much smaller proportions from southern Europe and Africa. The work of economic historians James Shepherd and Gary Walton enables us to get a more refined look at these trade patterns and to grasp their

Figure 3.1   Percentage Distribution of Total Colonial Trade

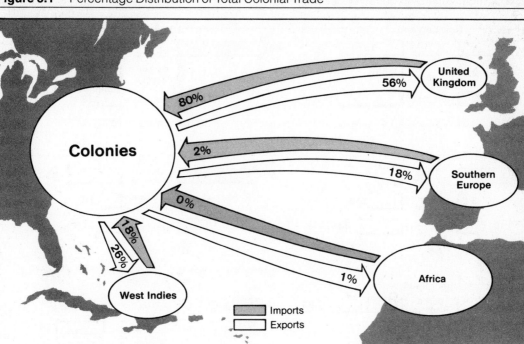

Source: James F. Shepherd and Gary M. Walton, *Shipping, Maritime Trade, and the Economic Development of North America* (Cambridge: Cambridge University Press, 1972), pp. 160–61.

The United Kingdom was colonial America's dominant trading partner in exports and imports, followed by the West Indies and southern Europe.

larger implications. In Figure 3.2 we see the regional trading breakdowns.

The regional differences in overseas trading patterns were mainly determined by economic development on the basis of comparative advantage, as we discussed in Chapter 2. New England's largest customer for exports was the West Indies. There the products of New England lumbering, woodworking, fishing, small manufacturing, and naval stores and supplies found their readiest markets. Direct shipments to the United Kingdom and southern Europe were far smaller. Yet fully two thirds of New England's imports came from the United Kingdom, and nearly a third from the West Indies.

Middle colony exports—grains, hides, flour, livestock, and small manufactures—were more nearly balanced between the United Kingdom, southern Europe, and the West Indies, but fully 76 percent of Middle colony imports came from the mother country. Twenty-one percent of imports were the products of the West Indies.

Southern exports, more exotic (especially tobacco, which was largely reexported to the Continent), went in overwhelming proportions to the mother country, and, in return, the United Kingdom supplied more than 80 percent of Southern imports.

The fact that New England and the Middle colonies were more hard-pressed to find markets outside the empire through the sieve of the navigation laws led to more commercial conflicts between them and the Crown than was the case of the Southern colonies. British restrictions on trade after 1763 would be more immediately felt in the North. But, as we already have noted, there would be a major source of conflict

Figure 3.2   Percentage Distribution of Colonial Trade, 1768–72

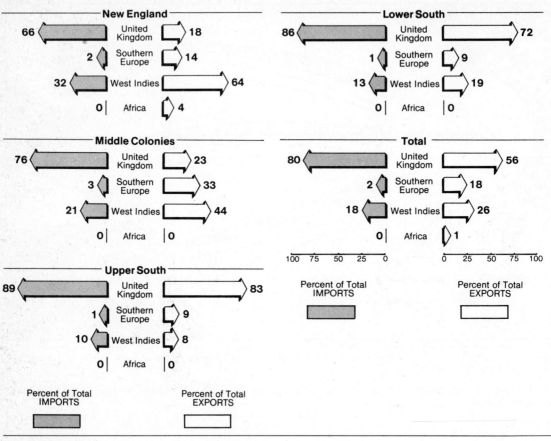

Source: Figure 3.1

The United Kingdom's dominance as an importer/exporter in the colonial trade market holds for all regions except New England, where the West Indies had a sizable share of the market.

between Virginia and England over the western lands. Walton's work indicates that our previous ideas about trading "triangles" were too restrictive.[10] There were such triangular routes, as we know (e.g., New England rum taken to Africa and traded for slaves that were shipped to the West Indies and traded for sugar and molasses to be imported into New England to make rum), but the evidence shows that colonial shipmasters mainly were itinerant voyagers, like modern "tramp" steamers, who picked up and discharged cargoes where and when opportunities allowed, given the navigation laws and ship captains' calculations

about the probability of getting caught with contraband.

The colonies had a large trade deficit in commodity trade alone. They imported more visible commodities from the external world than they exported to it, but by far the greater portion of commodity–trade deficit grew out of their trade with the United Kingdom. Within the navigation laws, colonial trade in commodities left them in a deficit position. The annual regional deficits during the years 1768–72, together with the totals, are shown in Figure 3.3. Of total deficits in those years, three-fourths occurred in bilat-

Figure 3.3   Average Annual Trade Balances in the Colonies, 1768–72

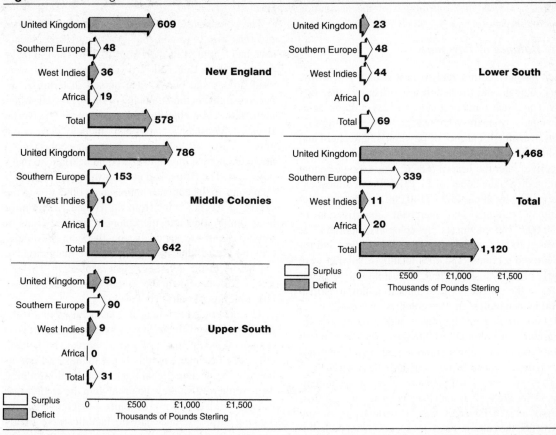

Source: James F. Shepherd and Gary M. Walton, *Shipping, Maritime Trade, and the Economic Development of North America* (Cambridge University Press, 1972), p. 115.

The deficit in commodity trade was mainly incurred in bilateral trade with the United Kingdom, primarily by New England and the Middle colonies. The Southern colonies had small net surpluses in their trade with southern Europe. Three-fourths of the net overall deficit in commodity trade alone came from trade with the United Kingdom.

eral trade with the United Kingdom. The largest area of surplus came from trade with Europe. It is fair to assume that the surplus arose because of the prohibitions within the navigation laws against imports of northern European goods directly into the colonies and that part of the deficit with the United Kingdom was due to the extra costs of transshipping those goods through the United Kingdom.

The evidence of colonial smuggling in the *Reports* of the Admiralty Courts by the 1760s indicates that efforts by Americans to "run" cargoes of contraband into colonial ports had become systematic, frequent,

and increasingly bold. British ships and customs officers were hard put to stop it. One judge acidly accused the Americans of trying to "rid themselves of the Navigation Act" after hearing the evidence.[11] The Americans knew that their commodities, transshipped through the United Kingdom to Europe because of the navigation laws, could be sold there directly at more favorable prices and that American demand for European products was strong. Commodity trade with the West Indies also yielded a small surplus, but the major features of commodity trade by the colonial era were simply a huge deficit with the United Kingdom and a surplus with the Continent. This was obvious to the colonists, as was the contribution of the navigation laws to this pattern.

The Balance of Payments

Then, as now, commodity trade was only part of the story, though, and the deficit was offset by other factors. The actual annual net indebtedness of the colonies was relatively small. What was the sum of all transactions, the overall **balance of payments?** Shepherd and Walton have made this calculation, and it is most instructive.[12] For the years 1768–72, this average annual commodity–trade deficit of £1,121,000 was almost entirely offset by ship sales of £140,000 together with net shipping earnings and merchant commissions of £880,000. Net payments by colonial importers for slaves (£200,000 mainly from the West Indies) and for indentured servants (£80,000) totaling £280,000 were nearly offset by a single item, British military expenditures in the colonies of £230,000. In addition, British naval expenditures in the colonies averaged a net £70,000. Adding up the pluses and minuses, the increase in net colonial indebtedness was only about £40,000 annually, a figure representing mainly mercantile credits extended by the British to the Americans.

The figure for annual net increase of foreign indebtedness in 1768–72 is nowhere near as large as historians once believed it was. Obviously, in overall payments, the colonies were prospering from their empire connection.

Money

One reason the colonials complained about the navigation laws was the "shortage" of money—by which they meant a shortage of gold and silver coins—in the colonies. They believed, as have generations of historians, that the scarcity of English coin was because the trade deficit was steadily bleeding the colonies of **specie,** gold and silver in coin form.

It is clear that, had the colonies paid out coins for every import of a good or service and received coins for every export, they would have been experiencing a net drain of coins—say, of £40,000 a year if there were no credit and no other means of payment. There is no doubt that coins were viewed as being in short supply in the colonies, but the extent of this aggravation varied by region. The Southern colonies had a surplus and

would be, other things being equal, a net receiver of specie.[13]

The colonies did not produce enough of their own precious metals to coin money (although Massachusetts had a mint of its own from 1652 to 1684 to make underweight silver coins). Various expedients were used. Prices and wages were quoted in terms of tobacco weights in the South and in skins, powder, wampum, shot, corn, chickens, and whatever in the North. Because Gresham's law—bad money drives out good—was at work then, as now, existing coins tended not to circulate if *anything* else could be found to make payments. The British did not allow the export of their own coins to the colonies but made no objection to the export of foreign coins from the United Kingdom or their importation into the colonies. So, the coins of foreign countries, especially from the Spanish colonies (via the West Indies trade), became the main circulating media in the colonies: "pieces of eight", whose legacy still survives in the American language—"two bits, four bits, six bits, a dollar."

The colonies, beginning in Massachusetts in 1690, found money substitutes in issues of certificates of governmental indebtedness of various sorts. The British, obviously fascinated by this paper money, did not allow it to be declared legal tender but did not prohibit its use either. What they did prohibit in the colonies, as in England, was the use of joint-stock companies for banking purposes. Since banking facilities were greatly needed in the colonies, this prohibition aroused colonial antagonism. In 1781 the Revolutionary Congress chartered The Bank of North America, a joint-stock bank of deposit and discount, ending one era and beginning another in American economic history.

1763–74: THE FINAL DRAMA

After 1763 the British began what they hoped would be a new phase in their colonial enterprises on the North American continent. What was needed, they believed, was a revision of the old (in part, individual) settlements between the Crown and the colonies. With an expensive war just ended, they wanted a system of colonial revenues that would make colonial government more self-supporting and less costly to England. There followed a series of laws that produced the American Revolution. Lance E. Davis and Robert Huttenback show that the American colonists were among the most lightly taxed people in the European world in the 1770s.[14] Therefore, we must deal with more than merely the amount of the taxation if we are to understand the breakup of the British North American Empire.

Viewed from London, the American Revolution was an outcome of political troubles as well as fiscal problems. Evolution toward parliamentary rule was not quite complete, and the king, now the stubborn, 25-year-old George III (grandson of George II, who died in 1760), was determined to rule, not just reign. Old William Pitt had resigned as Prime Minister in 1761. George tried, by interference in parliamentary affairs, to get his way and finally succeeded. There followed a period of bungling and incompetence at the top almost without precedent in English history. Worse luck, the United Kingdom was entering a period of general upheaval in European history that only ended with the Congress of Vienna in 1815. It was an era of war, revolution, and more war.

The American Revolution marked the beginning of this era. The United Kingdom, so lately victorious over France, now had its own system disrupted from within, and France and Spain joined with the colonials. The war was fought worldwide. By 1782 when Lord Rodney sent the French fleet to the bottom in the West Indies, the Americans were exhausted, and so were the British. The Americans gained their independence, the French were bankrupted by the expense, and in six years the French monarchy was overthrown by the revolution.

What went wrong in America? In part it can be viewed as a case of managerial failure. The technique of British rule in North America had become outdated. By the 1760s, there was no unified colonial government on the ground in America. Each colony had its own separate arrangement, its own charter. Ben Franklin's plan to unify the colonial administration, presented in 1754, had been unwisely rejected. The English Privy Council (a formless and long-lasting jumble of English eminences derived from the *curia regis* of the Normans), with the Board of Trade, ruled the Isle of Man, the Channel Islands off the coast of France, the American colonies, the West Indies, and other holdings spread around the world.

The Board of Trade had been established in a general reorganization in 1696, and its conservative management of colonial affairs produced some notable long-term results: its delineation of the Hudson Bay Company's southern limits in 1719 became the ultimate U.S.-Canada boundary; its review of colonial laws was the origin of our own judicial review; its practice of forbidding the colonies to discriminate in trade *against each other* was the origin of the commerce clause in the federal Constitution.

But the Board was merely a bureaucracy and had no control over political evolution. As it was, the Board's administration was obsolete in the 1770s. By then, under George III's influence, British political life was chaotic, and in America the colonial assemblies had evolved into a competence and power undreamed of in 1696. They raised taxes; they appointed officials; they granted Western lands; they dealt with the Indians. How could they be ruled by an English bureaucracy? Parliament ruled England, Wales, Scotland, and Ireland by the 1760s. The overseas colonies had lobbyists in Westminster (e.g., Ben Franklin), but there could be no question of direct colonial representation, as members of Parliament, under the English constitution. Administratively, then, the British were incompetent to cope with the consequences of their own actions—as events soon proved.

Eighteenth-century British government, like most governments now, was one of organized special interests gaining advantages for themselves at the expense of the unorganized. Subsidies here, taxes there, prohibitions, special grants of privilege, year after year, decade after decade, had produced the "British government."[15] Prohibitions in the 1750s against colonial iron-goods manufacturing while colonial pig and bar iron were admitted into England duty-free is a typical example—alienating colonial iron workers and owners, together with British pig and bar iron producers, for the benefit of British manufacturers.

From the British viewpoint, nothing made more sense than colonial tax reform. Before 1767, customs revenues in the colonies annually yielded about £2,000 and cost £9,000 a year to collect. What was needed was a set of taxes that could be collected and a new bureaucracy to collect them. The British, after a long and costly war to protect the colonists from the French, now wanted to garrison 10,000 troops in the colonies for their own protection and wanted the colonists to contribute to their support.

The Proclamation of 1763 was meant to move control of Indian affairs away from colonial governments to the crown. The colonists rightly saw their own governmental powers thus reduced. The Currency Act of 1764 was designed to make colonial paper money issues self-limiting by establishing *sinking fund obligations* (reserves that could redeem the notes in coin or English money), a financially sound move that, however, placed restrictions upon colonial fiscal powers. The Sugar Act of 1764 was meant to protect West Indian interests by placing taxes on foreign sugar and molasses, thus restricting colonial sources of supply and providing officials to enforce the law. The Stamp Tax of 1765 was a minor measure to gain revenues from legal documents and newspapers. Colonial officials were to collect the tax. This was viewed in the colonies as more "taxation without representation." A Stamp Tax Congress met in New York, a nonimportation agreement was reached (it was not honored in the Lower South), and British exports to the colonies fell by two-thirds. Stamp tax collectors were harassed.

The Stamp Tax could not be collected. The British backed down and repealed the tax, but an outraged Parliament passed the Declaratory Act in 1766, which, they believed, established legal authority once and for all for them to tax and legislate for the colonies. That added more fuel to the fire. In 1767 Chancellor of the Exchequer Charles Townshend pushed legislation through Parliament placing taxes on tea, glass, and paper and establishing in America a Customs Board with rights of general search and seizure—*writs of assistance*. By 1768 these measures produced serious disorders in the colonial ports; by 1770 they resulted in the Boston Massacre.

Lord North, George III's favorite statesman, "a good-natured, indolent man, of limited intelligence, but shrewd and businesslike," became Prime Minister in 1770.[16] Until 1782 his hand, guided by George III, piloted the British government from disaster to disaster. In 1773 the Tea Act reduced the price of tea to the colonists but threatened colonial merchants with extinction by granting the East India Company the right to sell its tea directly to the colonies, bypassing the chain of jobbers and merchants the company had formerly supported. The result was the Boston Tea Party.

At this point, in 1774, Lord North and Parliament committed those famous acts of tyranny—the passage of the Port of Boston Act, the Massachusetts Government Act (making Massachusetts a crown colony), and the Quebec Act—that broke the ties that had bound the colonies and England together for a century and a half. To the British government, the colonists were children who wanted punishment. To the colonists, the British government had become "intolerable." The First Continental Congress met in Philadelphia in September 1774, and on 14 October 1774 listed in plain language its complaints against the British government.

1. Taxes had been imposed upon the colonies by the "British" Parliament.
2. Parliament had claimed the right to legislate for the colonies.
3. Commissioners were set up in the colonies to collect taxes.
4. Admiralty court jurisdictions had been extended into the interior.
5. Judges' tenures had been put at the pleasure of the crown.
6. A standing army had been imposed upon the colonies.
7. Persons could be transported out of the colonies for trials.
8. The Port of Boston had been closed.
9. Martial law had been imposed upon Boston.
10. The Quebec Act had confiscated the colonists' western lands.

These complaints were followed by resolutions restating the legal position of the colonies.

> That our ancestors, who first settled these colonies, were at the time of their emigration from the mother country, entitled to all the rights, liberties and immunities of free and natural-born subjects, within the realm of England.
>
> That by such emigration they by no means forfeited, surrendered, or lost any of those rights, but they were, and their descendants now are, entitled to the exercise and enjoyment . . . of them. . . .

The colonists did not object to the laws of navigation "for the purpose of securing the commercial advantages of the whole empire to the mother country, and the commercial benefits of its respective members," but they rejected "every idea of taxation, internal or external, for raising a revenue on the subjects, in America, without their consent."

They further resolved—

That the respective colonies are entitled to the common law of England, and more especially to the great and inestimable privilege of being tried by their peers of the vicinage, according to the course of that law.

There were more resolutions and then a listing of eight laws whose repeal the colonists demanded—these laws amounted to virtually all changes in British government in America since 1763.[17]

On 6 July 1775, the Congress published the "Declaration of the Causes and Necessity of Taking Up Arms." One year later, 4 July 1776, independence was declared. In September of 1783, after another long war, the Treaty of Versailles was signed, granting the Americans complete independence, together with the western lands they claimed by ancient right. The British ceded Minorca and Florida (gotten from the French in 1763, who had gotten it earlier from the Spanish) to Spain and St. Lucia, Tobago, Senegal (West Africa), and an island off its coast, Goree, to France.

RETROSPECT: WEALTH AND INCOME AGAIN

As we have seen, Americans in 1774 (excluding slaves) enjoyed per capita incomes estimated by Alice Hanson Jones to have been in the neighborhood of $573–$955 in the prices of 1973, or, at the highest figure, at about the level of per capita income in the Soviet Union in the mid-1970s. The lower estimate would have given the colonists modern Mexico's real income per capita. Admitting, as one must, the large margin of error in such calculations, it still must be the case that Americans two centuries ago enjoyed real incomes far higher than those of two-thirds of people in the world today.

The colonists had come to a new land with the technology and commercial institutions of contemporary England, and what they did with their available resources represented the "best practice" of that time. Defense and administration had been mainly supplied by English taxpayers, leaving colonial resources, accordingly, free for narrowly economic pursuits. The long colonial years had been an epoch of economic achievement, measured in per capita income increases from the "starving time" in Virginia and Plymouth. The handful of survivors from those early settlements, their descendants, and new immigrants, both slave and free, had grown to a population of some 2.5 million.

For a free white with property, it was one of the most bountiful economic lives in the world. In 1782 Hector Saint-John de Crevecoeur, who had served as a French officer under Montcalm at Quebec and stayed on to farm in New York until 1780, published 12 essays addressed to Europeans called *Letters from an American Farmer.*

> A hundred families barely existing in some parts of Scotland, will here in six years, cause an annual exportation of 10,000 bushels of wheat; 100 bushels being but a common quantity for an industrious family to sell, if they cultivate good land . . . [a hired man would be] well fed at the table of his employer, and paid four or five times more than he can get in Europe.[18]

Modern research supports Crevecoeur's eyewitness account. Indeed, Terry Anderson found that wealth in New England in the late seventeenth century was already growing at a robust 1.6 percent per annum.[19] It would be left for the United States after independence to improve upon what the English started.

The distribution of wealth and income in colonial America by the end of the period was uneven. Unequal income distribution is the case in most societies today, even in Red China. Depending upon tastes and social choices, together with the distribution of resources, skills, and talents, and the demand for them, almost any economy will produce differential rewards to participants. When the residues of unequal incomes and different consumption habits—wealth—are inherited, wealth holdings are also, obviously, going to be unequal. James Henretta found that in 1771 the top 10 percent of wealthholders in Boston owned 57 percent of the wealth.[20] Alice Hanson Jones found that in 1774 the top 10 percent in New England owned 40 percent of the wealth, and in the Middle colonies 32 percent of the wealth belonged to the top 10 percent.[21] In a study of American wealth holdings in modern times, Robert Lampman found that in 1953 the top 10.8 percent of the "top" wealth holders had 46.4 percent of the estates subject to wealth taxes.[22] It is a vexing question among economists whether such inequality helps, hinders, or is generated by the processes of economic growth.[23] We will return to this question in later chapters.

It is perhaps worth a few more lines here to illustrate more completely colonial experiences regarding inequality. As we already noted, in early Virginia, attempts at equal distribution of the social product were unsatisfactory. When Captain Smith said that the individual colonists must work to eat, he was expressing a present social need. In Plymouth colony, early attempts to distribute work assignments and rewards equally resulted in a deficient agricultural output. Governor Bradford recorded in his journal the changes they made and the results. The year was 1623.

> So they begane to think how they might raise as much corne as they could, and obtaine a beter crope then they had done, that they might not still thus languish in miserie. At length, aftermuch debate of things, the Governor . . . gave way that they should set corne every man for his owne perticuler, and in that regard trust to them selves; in all other things to goe on in the generall way as before. And so assigned to every faniily a parcell of land, according to the proportion of their number for that end, only for present use (but made no devission for inheritance), and ranged all boys & youth under some familie. This had very good success; for it made all hands very industrious, so as much more corne was planted then other waise would have bene by any means the Governor or any other could use, and saved him a great deall of trouble, and gave farr better contente. The women now wente willingly into the feild, and tooke their litle-ons with them to set corne, which before would aledg weaknes, and inabilitie; whom to have compelled would have bene thought great tiranie and oppression.
>
> The experience that was had in this commone course and condition, tried sundrie years, and that amongst godly

and sober men, may well evince the vanitie of that conceite of Platos & other ancients, applauded by some of later times;—that the taking away of propertie, and bringing in communitie into a comone wealth, would make them happy and flourishing; as if they were wiser then God. For this comunitie (so farr as it was) was found to breed much confusion & discontent. . . . For the yong-men that were most able and fitte for labour & service did repine that they should spend their time & striength to worke for other mens wives and children, with out any recompence. The strong, or man of parts, had no more in devission of victails & cloaths, then he that was weake and not able to doe a quarter the other could; this was thought injueste. . . . Let none objecte this is men's corruption, and nothing to the course it selfe. I answer, seeing all men have this corruption in them, God in his wisdome saw another course fiter for them.[24]

Bradford might have noted God's injunction to Adam when he and Eve were tossed out of Paradise: "In the sweat of thy face shalt thou eat bread." From Plymouth Colony until now, apart from a few utopian experiments like Brook Farm and the later Mormon United Orders (and perhaps a few modern Vermont communes), the dream of Plato and the other ancients has been confounded by the superior economic achievement of distribution according to individual contribution. An unending question has been, and is, "Where does justice lie in income distribution?"[25] Is justice equality, payment for work done, risks taken, or what? Americans have never settled on this problem.

Notes

1. Alice Hanson Jones, *American Colonial Wealth: Documents and Methods* (1977). Shorter essays by Jones are utilized later in this chapter.
2. Gary M. Walton and James F. Shepherd, *The Economic Rise of Early America* (1979). See their Chapter 7 for an excellent survey and analysis of the data and issues on this subject. This paragraph states only their major conclusions. It also should be noted that not all scholars have made estimates as high as those of Dr. Jones. Yet she has made a most thorough and careful search of the records, and her conclusions must be given primary attention, as the issue stands now.
3. The capital/output ratio purports to show the amount of net savings over time—the stock of capital—a society uses to produce income. If it is 3/1, then $3.00 of "capi-

tal" in a given period produces $1.00 of output. It is a very crude and questionable analytical device, but useful for some purposes. Even using modern data, one must be careful with it. The selected boundaries are very conservative.
4. Data from Jones, quoted by Shepherd and Walton, pp. 11–12.
5. See Shepherd and Walton, pp. 140–2, for a survey of modern estimates.
6. Stuart Bruchey, ed., *The Colonial Merchant: Sources and Readings* (1966), p. 1.
7. Bruchey, p. 1.
8. Stuart Bruchey, *The Roots of American Economic Growth* (1965), p. 65.
9. Carl Bridenbaugh, *Cities in the Wilderness: The First*

Century of Urban Life in America, 1625–1742 (1971) and *Cities in Revolt: Urban Life in America 1743–1776* (1971), together provide a wide range of evidence on this issue.

10. Gary M. Walton, "New Evidence on Colonial Commerce," *JEH,* September 1968.

11. Jonathan Hughes, *Social Control in the Colonial Economy* (1976), pp. 155–6.

12. Shepherd and Walton, *The Economic Rise of Early America,* p. 101.

13. Which they were not. The lack of internal roads meant that Southern trade with the Northern colonies was by ship, and that trade was, in volume, equal to about one third of overseas trade. Earnings to Northern shipowners from this trade should have siphoned off a good deal of Southern coin. James F. Shepherd and Samuel Williamson, "The Coastal Trade of the British North American Colonies 1768–1772," *JEH,* December 1972.

14. Lance E. Davis and Robert A. Huttenback, "The Cost of Empire," in Richard Sutch, Roger Ransom, and Gary M. Walton, eds., *Explorations in the New Economic History: Essays in Honor of Douglas C. North* (1982), p. 44, Table 3.2.

15. Nearly two decades ago, economic historians conducted a vigorous debate over this issue: Did the Navigation Acts place an excessive burden on the American colonies? It was an old issue among historians. In 1943 Lawrence Harper's study, "Mercantilism and the American Revolution," *Canadian Historical Review,* March 1942, showed that British policies overall probably aided colonial economic growth although restrictions on trade between the colonies and Europe may have imposed a small net tax burden. The issue was rekindled into a bright flame. The first spark was Robert Paul Thomas, "A Quantitative Approach to the Study of the Effects of British Imperial Policy upon Colonial Welfare: Some Preliminary Findings," *JEH,* December 1965. Others soon added both fuel and water. Peter D. McClelland, "The Cost to America of British Imperial Policy," with discussions by Jonathan Hughes and Herman Krooss, *AER,* May 1969. Discussion ranged far and wide: Gary M. Walton, "The New Economic History and the Burdens of the Navigation Acts," *EHR,* November 1971; Peter McClelland, "The New Economic History and the Burdens of the Navigation Acts: A Comment," *EHR,* November 1973; Gary M. Walton, "The Burdens of the Navigation Acts: A Reply," *EHR,* November 1973. A broadening of the range from purely economic arguments to politics was achieved by Joseph D. Reid, Jr., "Economic Burdens: Spark to the American Revolution?" *JEH,* March 1978. Reid shows in a beneficially subtle way how the issues surrounding the Navigation Acts fueled political debate and motivated *some* colonists into action, and that lowered the cost of Revolution to the rest.

16. Charles Oman, *A History of England* (London: Edward Arnold, 1895), p. 544.

17. *Documents Illustrative of the Formation of the American States* (Washington: Government Printing Office, 1927), pp. 1–4.

18. Henry Steele Commager, ed., *America in Perspective* (New York: Mentor Books, 1964), pp. 34–35.

19. Terry L. Anderson, "Wealth Estimates for the New England Colonies, 1650–1709," *EEH,* April 1975. The land, relatively poor for agriculture, still produced a capital gain, on average, as population increased. Land, it has been shown, was the main source of increase in heritable wealth in southern New England. Main, Gloria L. and Jackson T., "Economic Growth and the Standard of Living in Southern New England," *JEH,* March 1988. The increase in inheritable wealth was relatively quick. Walsh, Lorena S., "Urban Amenities and Rural Self Sufficiency: Living Standards and Consumer Behavior in the Colonial Chesapeake, 1643–1777," *JEH,* March 1983. Evidence of estates shows that by mid-eighteenth century rural households in the Chesapeake area enjoyed physical appurtenances like furniture and kitchen equipment at a level indicating a life-style about equal to those of urban populations of the same period. A high standard of consumerism was apparent in rural households.

20. James Henretta, "Economic Development and Social Structure in Colonial Boston," *William and Mary Quarterly,* January 1965.

21. Alice Hanson Jones, "Wealth Estimates for the American Middle Colonies," *EDCC,* July 1970; "Wealth Estimates for the New England Colonies After 1770," *JEH,* March 1972.

22. Robert Lampman, *The Share of Top Wealth-Holders in National Wealth 1922–56* (New York: National Bureau of Economic Research, 1962), p. 109.

23. Bruce C. Daniels, for example, found that among the upper strata of the colonial wealth distribution, concentration (inequality) *increased* from 1700 to 1776. As the economy expanded, the inequality grew. "Long Range Trends of Wealth Distribution in 18th Century New England," *EEH,* Winter 1973–4.

24. William Bradford, *Of Plymouth Plantation* (New York: Capricorn Books, 1962), pp. 90–91.

25. In recent years American philosophers have taken up this question in earnest once more. John Rawls, *A Theory of Justice* (Cambridge: Harvard University Press, 1971); Robert Nozick, *Anarchy, State and Utopia* (New York: Basic Books, 1974). Rawls would disapprove of the Pilgrims' solution; Nozick would approve of it.

Suggested Readings

Articles

Anderson, Terry L. "Wealth Estimates for the New England Colonies 1650–1709." *Explorations in Economic History,* vol. 14, no. 4, October 1977.

Cole, Arthur H. "Trends in Eighteenth-Century New England." *Economic History Review,* 2nd series, vol. X, no. 3, April 1958.

Daniels, Bruce D. "Long-Range Trends in Wealth Distribution in Eighteenth-Century New England." *Explorations in Economic History,* vol. XI, no. 2, Winter 1973–4.

Davis, Lance E., and Huttenback, Robert A. "The Cost of Empire," in Richard Sutch, Roger Ransom, and Gary M. Walton, eds., *Explorations in the New Economic History: Essays in Honor of Douglas C. North* (New York: Academic Press, 1982).

Gilbert, Geoffrey. "The Role of Breadstuffs in American Trade, 1770–1790." *Explorations in Economic History,* vol. 14, no. 4, October 1977.

Gray, Ralph, and Wood, Betty. "The Transition from Involuntary to Indentured Servitude, in Colonial Georgia." *Explorations in Economic History,* vol. 13, no. 4, October 1976.

Hacker, Louis M. "The First American Revolution." *Columbia University Quarterly,* vol. XXXVII, 1935.

Henretta, James. "Economic Development and Social Structure in Colonial Boston." *William and Mary Quarterly,* vol. XXVII, no. 1, January 1965.

Jones, Alice Hanson. "Wealth Estimates for the New England Colonies About 1770." *Journal of Economic History,* vol. XXXII, no. 1, March 1972.

———. "Wealth Estimates for the American Middle Colonies," *Economic Development and Cultural Change,* vol. XVII, no. 4, July 1970.

Land, Aubrey C. "The Tobacco Staple and the Planter's Problems: Technology, Labor and Crops." *Agricultural History,* vol. 43, no. 2, January 1969.

Main, Gloria L., and Jackson, T. "Economic Growth and the Standard of Living in Southern New England, 1640–1774," *Journal of Economic History,* vol. XVIII, no. 1, March 1988.

McClelland, Peter D. "The Cost to America of British Imperial Policy" and discussions by Jonathan Hughes and Herman Krooss. *American Economic Review,* vol. LIX, no. 2, May 1969.

Nettels, Curtis P. "British Mercantilism and the Economic Development of the Thirteen Colonies." *Journal of Economic History,* vol. XII, no. 2, Spring 1952.

Ostrander, Gilman M. "The Colonial Molasses Trade." *Agricultural History,* vol. XXX, no. 1, January 1956.

Price, Jacob. "Note on the Value of Colonial Exports of Shipping." *Journal of Economic History,* vol. XXXVI, no. 3, September 1976.

Reid, Joseph D., Jr. "Economic Burdens: Spark to the American Revolution?" *Journal of Economic History,* vol. XXXVIII, no. 1, March 1978.

Schweitzer, Mary McKinney. "Economic Regulation and the Colonial Economy: The Maryland Tobacco Inspection Act of 1747." *Journal of Economic History,* vol. XL, no. 3, September 1980.

Shepherd, James F. "Commodity Exports from the British North American Colonies to Overseas Areas, 1768–1772: Magnitudes and Patterns of Trade." *Explorations in Economic History,* vol. 8, no. 1, Fall 1970.

Shepherd, James, and Williamson, Samuel. "The Coastal Trade of the British North American Colonies, 1768–1772." *Journal of Economic History,* vol. XXXVII, no. 4, December 1972.

Sheridan, Richard B. "The Molasses Act and the Market Strategy of the British Sugar Planters." *Journal of Economic History,* vol. XVII, no. 1, March 1957.

Thomas, Robert Paul. "A Quantitative Approach to the Study of the Effects of British Imperial Policy upon Colonial Welfare: Some Preliminary Findings." *Journal of Economic History,* vol. XXV, no. 4, December 1965.

Walsh, Lorena S. "Urban Amenities and Rural Self Sufficiency: Living Standards and Consumer Behavior in the Colonial Chesapeake, 1643–1777," *Journal of Economic History,* vol. XLIII, no. 1, March 1983.

Walton, Gary M. "The Burdens of the Navigation Acts, A Reply." *Economic History Review,* vol. XXVI, no. 4, November 1973.

———. "The New Economic History and the Burdens of the Navigation Acts." *Economic History Review,* vol. XXIV, no. 4, November 1971.

———. "New Evidence on Colonial Commerce." *Journal of Economic History,* vol. XXVII, no. 3, September 1968.

———. "Sources of Productivity Change in American Colonial Shipping, 1675–1775." *Economic History Review,* 2nd series, vol. XX, no. 1, April 1967.

Weiss, Roger. "The Issue of Paper Money in the American Colonies, 1720–1774." *Journal of Economic History,* vol. XXX, no. 4, December 1970.

Books

Andrews, Charles M. *The Colonial Period of American History.* New Haven: Yale University Press, 1934, 4 vols.

Bailyn, Bernard. *The New England Merchants in the Seventeenth Century.* Cambridge: Harvard University Press, 1955.

Beer, George Louis. *The Old Colonial System 1660–1754.* New York: Macmillan, 1912.

Boorstin, Daniel J. *The Americans: The Colonial Experience.* New York: Vintage Books, 1958.

Bridenbaugh, Carl. *Cities in the Wilderness: The First Century of Urban Life in America 1625–1742.* New York: Oxford University Press, 1971 (reprint).

———. *Cities in Revolt: Urban Life in America 1743–1776.* New York: Oxford University Press, 1971 (reprint).

Bruce, Philip A. *Economic History of Virginia in the Seventeenth Century.* New York: Macmillan, 1896, 2 vols.

Bruchey, Stuart. *The Colonial Merchant: Sources and Readings.* New York: Harcourt Brace, 1966.

———. *The Roots of American Economic Growth 1607–1861: An Essay in Social Causation.* London: Hutchinson University Library, 1965.

Coleman, D. C., ed. *Revisions in Mercantilism.* London: Methuen, 1969.

Dickerson, Oliver Morton. *American Colonial Government 1696–1765.* Cleveland: Arthur H. Clark, 1912.

Goodwin, John A. *The Pilgrim Republic.* Boston: Ticknow, 1888.

Greene, Jack P., and Pole, J. R., eds. *Colonial British America: Essays in the New History of the Early Modern Era.* Baltimore, The Johns Hopkins University Press, 1984.

Hughes, J. R. T. *Social Control in the Colonial Economy.* Charlottesville: University Press of Virginia, 1976.

Jones, Alice Hanson. *American Colonial Wealth: Documents and Methods.* New York: Arno Press, 1977.

Schlesinger, A. M. *The Colonial Merchants and the American Revolution.* New York: Frederick Unger, 1964.

Ver Steeg, Clarence. *The Formative Years, 1606–1763.* New York: Hill & Wang, 1964.

Walton, Gary M., and Shepherd, James F. *The Economic Rise of Early America.* New York: Cambridge University Press, 1979.

———. *Shipping, Maritime Trade, and the Economic Development of Colonial North America.* New York: Cambridge University Press, 1972.

Weeden, William B. *Economic and Social History of New England, 1620–1789.* Boston: Houghton Mifflin, 1890, 2 vols.

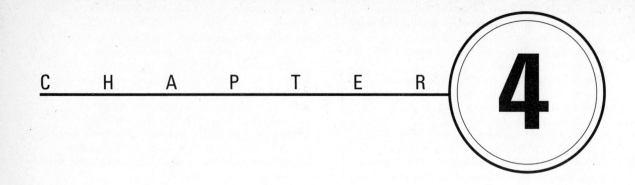

Special Topics in American Colonial History

In this chapter, we will take up in more detail special-interest subjects that were treated only briefly in the previous chapters. We will ask three questions: Did Britain stifle American economic growth? How much did it cost America to be a colony instead of an independent country? Did colonial America suffer from a money shortage? We have reserved these questions until now because (a) they are quite controversial and have no clear-cut answers, and (b) the responses are somewhat involved, requiring a bit more analysis than has been presented in the core chapters.

HOW DID BRITAIN AFFECT AMERICAN ECONOMIC GROWTH?

The colonial experience becomes more understandable if we pull back a bit and look at it in a very general way.

Perspectives

Did Britain aid American economic growth in the eighteenth century, or did it, as the colonists charged, hamper our growth? This controversial question, which has occupied historians since the Revolution, has no "right" answer. Still, it is an issue having important implications that we should examine. Let's start with a little thought experiment.

Suppose that a giant spaceship were created by the United Nations, containing the population and the necessary resources to support permanent interplanetary life. The ship shadows the Earth's orbit, using solar energy for power and exchanging its specialized products with Earth. What sorts of institutions would the vehicle be given for self-government and development? What would our expectations for its future be? What would we expect the space colony's relations with us to be like five generations from now? Would we try to control its social and political evolution, placing safeguards against the growth of such political excesses as military dictatorships and ideological totalitarianism? Would we try to control its economic evolution so that the colony would remain congenial and mutually interdependent with us and not develop a rival economy? Would we believe that we had a "right" to do that, and that the colony would benefit throughout time from our guiding hand and steadying influence?

Perhaps one can see the parallel with colonial America, but with one important difference. Because transatlantic travel was by sailing ship, it could take a month to send a message from London to Philadelphia. Irregular internal communications made matters worse. There is a record of a complaint sent from the Privy Council to the Governor of backwoods North Carolina in the eighteenth century, reprimanding him for not communicating for two years. His answer, written a year later, professed surprise and protested that he had been a regular correspondent.

Britain expected the American colonies to produce and grow and yet to remain loyal, as we have seen. The British supplied the necessary provisions in part, sent over people, provided administration and military protection, and hoped to benefit from the enterprise. The colonies were launched with English institutions but were allowed to modify them to meet local needs, with the proviso that they "be not repugnant" to the laws of England. After only 150 years, there was a violent separation of the two systems—the American Revolution. Scholars have studied that upheaval ever since to identify what parts of its origins came from economic life and what parts from flaws in the arrangements between England and the colonies. In this section, we will examine some of the main issues in colonial economic growth commonly associated with our revolutionary separation from Britain.

"Full Employment" in the Colonies

The original necessity of the colonists was work; a subsistence had to be wrested from the wilderness. The colonies, to be self-sustaining, had to earn at least the amount of the flow of British investment (plus interest) of manpower, provisions, transportation costs, and the like. Ultimately, they yielded far more, as we have seen, and attracted not only continued British investment and immigration but domestic wealth accumulations and rising per capita income as well. What were the possible effects of this foreign (British) induced growth upon economic structure, and what difference might the American Revolution have made?

In Figure 4.1, panel (a), we depict the initial situation, measuring units of primary production (agriculture, timbering, and naval stores) along the horizontal axis and units of all other production (trades, crafts, "manufacturing," services, essentially town life) on the vertical axis. The curved line Y_1 represents all possible combinations of output (which can be considered

in market prices as income). If all output was produced in towns, that is, production is "all other," the amount would be ow_1, and primary production would be zero. If all output, on the other hand, were primary production, we would have output oz_1, and zero output of "all other." No such extreme conditions existed, of course. More than 90 percent of the population labored in primary occupations, but a proportion, less than 10 percent, lived in towns, implying a similar (perhaps slightly larger) proportion of output coming from urban occupations. We assume, perhaps unrealistically, that the proportions of "unproductive" populations—the young, aged, and disabled—would be the same in both sectors.

The purpose of the severe labor regulations, discussed earlier, was to maintain employment on, or near, the full employment curve Y_1, producing as much as possible. This would be **full employment,** and slavery and servitude with severe punishments for vagrancy (unemployment) would help to achieve that. Suppose that point e on the output curve was the initial selection of occupations, producing primary output of oj and output of all other product at oa. If significant malingering (employment at point d) were allowed, less of primary output, perhaps oh, would be achieved. Malingering would not raise the output of anything else, so town output would remain at oa; society would lose production amounting to hj. Unemployment was costly, and in the early stages of colonization the laws and agencies of government were stringently employed to prevent it.

Growth in Fixed Proportions

If there were essentially no technical improvements, then increased population (men and women injected into the economy at first by forced emigration from Britain, then by voluntary emigration, by slave imports into the colonies, and by the natural growth of all colonial population) would simply move the possible output combinations, curves Y_2 and Y_3, outward parallel to each other.[1] The concavity of the curves from the origin implies the existence of diminishing returns; to get more of "all other" products, the colonists had to sacrifice increasing amounts of primary production.

Maintaining the initial proportional combination of total output would produce point f on curve Y_2, yielding ob of "all other" output and ok of primary production.

Figure 4.1 Trade-Offs Between Primary Production and All Other Production

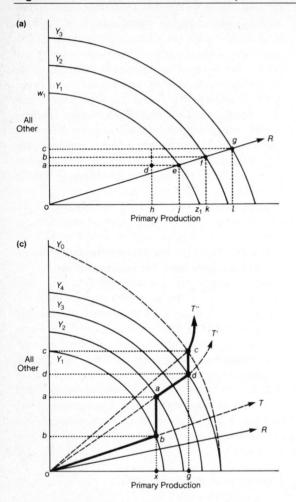

(a)

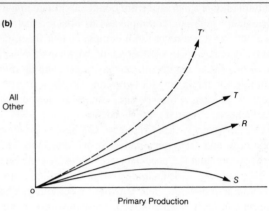

(b)

Panel (a) shows the balance of economic activity between primary and all other production. Y_1, Y_2, and Y_3 are production possibility curves. If the initial balance between primary and all other production never changed from the starting balance at point e on Y_1, then R would be the fixed-proportion growth path through time. In panel (b) alternate growth paths are shown. S is the increasingly agricultural economy; R and T are fixed-proportion paths (T having more of an urban mix than R at every point). T' is the case of an increasingly urban mix through time. In panel (c), if growth path T were operative but constrained by British mercantilist policies, the revolution presumably would produce movement to T' once previously forbidden nonprimary output appeared. Actually, the jump was to T'' and an ever-increasing proportion of "all other," thanks to the industrial revolution.

More population, shifting the output possibility curve to Y_3, would yield oc of "all other" and ol of primary product. Since there was no change in the proportions of output selection, a straight line, R, projected out of the origin, would connect all the production-choice points. Colonial economic life, in that hypothetical situation, would have remained in fixed proportions even though income (output) expanded. With technological improvements of any kind, the Y curves would have moved outward over time by greater proportions than population increased, and there would have been per capita economic growth.

Alternative Types of Growth

In Figure 4.1, panel (b), we illustrate other possibilities. Line R, as before, describes a growth path of fixed proportions. Had British policy aimed at *increasing* the proportion of primary output at the expense of all other output, line S would have been the policy. Colonial America would have become increasingly rural as it grew. This result, in the view of some scholars, would have been the logical outcome of British mercantilism: Allow the colonies to grow only as congenial economic supplements to the domestic British economy, to the output choices made there. By forbidding all output in the colonies that would compete with British domestic production, say, of manufactured goods, the British would have forced the colonies to become increasingly specialized primary producers, not because of comparative advantage but because of the law. A more reasonable British policy would have been to allow growth path T to occur: The colonies develop proportionately more urban-style output as time passes than was true with growth path R. This was apparently the reality since, as we have seen, urbanization was proceeding and urban-style productions were expanding accordingly.

It was, however, the contention of some colonials (and some later historians) that growth path T was a constrained one forced upon them by British laws. Prohibitions such as these against the development of banking, manufacture of wrought iron, and export of colonial woolen goods held down the growth of colonial urban-style industry. Hence, they kept the growth path off its natural course T', in which, as output expanded, there would have been accelerated growth of nonprimary outputs and employments compared to growth path T. If the latter were in fact the case, then the effect of the Revolution would have been a shift, fairly quickly, to growth path T'. The Revolution would produce, say, a rise of b to a on the vertical axis in Figure 4.1, panel (c), a relatively sudden shift from T to T' and an acceleration of urban and manufacturing growth compared to expansion of primary production. There would no longer have been a foreign constraint upon the pace of the shift from primary production to manufacturing.

The American and Industrial Revolutions

Dramatic acceleration of manufacturing of all kinds did, in fact, occur within half a century after 1776 and has continued ever since. But we cannot say with confidence that the American Revolution initiated that shift because of the technological changes associated with another, mainly English, and contemporaneous development, the industrial revolution. The total output curves did *not* shift in parallel fashion. With improved technology and heightened productivity in manufacturing, the trade-offs between primary production and

"all other" shifted not to Y_4 in Figure 4.1, panel (c), but to Y_0, so that with any output of primary production, *og,* instead of *od* of all other output, *oc* was achieved, and the growth path jumped to T''.

British inventiveness began to result in machine production run by prime movers (water power, then steam), and those changes quickly appeared in America. James Watt's steam engine was patented in Britain in 1769. By 1783, it was used to work a hammer at John "Iron Master" Wilkinson's works, and he already was using it to "blow" his blast furnaces. When Richard Arkwright, the great English textile innovator, bought Watt's steam engines to run his machinery in 1790, he already had been preceded by at least two other textile magnates, Robert Peel and Peter Drinkwater. By 1800, hundreds of steam engines were at work in British factories. Those factories, grouped together to gain external economies, were producing the first true industrial cities. The industrial revolution was on, and Britain would soon achieve a power and influence out of all proportion to her relative size in the world. The lost American empire would be replaced by one of vast dimensions—"a third of the earth"—in Asia, Africa, Australia, and New Zealand.

The Americans were quick to follow their British cousins where comparative advantage dictated the profitability of such imitation. Samuel Slater, one of the Arkwright's English workers, arrived in America in 1789 with Arkwright's machinery designs memorized. By 1790, with American backers, Slater built the machines and launched the spinning factory of Almy and Brown at Pawtucket, Rhode Island. At that point, the industrial revolution in America can be said to have begun. In 1793, Eli Whitney's invention of the cotton gin created the supply side of a major American cotton textile industry and, incidentally, fastened slavery onto the South again. Cotton made black slavery a long-lasting success because it was a crop that needed many hands to harvest it. It gave the Southern states a very profitable commodity that was best cultivated by slave gangs, given the technology of the time. Cotton quickly became the South's staple product, supplying the textile industries of both Britain and the United States.

The industrial revolution accelerated the urbanization process on both sides of the Atlantic, and it came so quickly on the heels of the political and military

American Revolution that we will never know whether *T* was the natural growth rate in colonial America—forbidden by British mercantilism and only achieved by violent separation. The evidence is that this was extremely unlikely. In any case, even if the American Revolution had not occurred, the British could not have stopped the industrial revolution in America, nor, most likely, would they have wanted to. Considering their persistent heavy investment of money in this country *after* the Revolution, they probably would have spread the industrial revolution here themselves. As we shall see in the next section, scholars, in any case, have not been able even to agree about the extent to which the British policies were financially burdensome, let alone technologically restricting.

HOW MUCH DID IT COST TO BELONG TO BRITAIN?

Was "membership" in the British Empire a good or a bad idea, economically speaking? It is clear that the colonists saw, correctly, that independence *with* access to the western lands would mean a great future for them and their descendants. But could they justify their revolution on the basis of current economic burdens imposed by the British? Actually, they did not need to do so. Revolutions are violent and bloody upheavals, usually between competing evils. If a gang of militant radicals overturns an oppressive dictator and then installs a monstrous regime of firing squads and economic chaos or "planned" economic stagnation or worse, what "good" was served? Measuring the degree of improvement in the quality of life would not be easy. The American Revolution had shades of such a monster in it, but level heads usually prevailed. Assuming that the revolutionaries believed the British were oppressing them economically on a current basis, were they correct? Would income per capita be higher, on the information available to would-be revolutionaries in 1774, without Empire membership? The answer is not easy to produce.

Regional Specialization Revisited

We discussed earlier the effects of comparative advantage on the location of specialized primary and other productions in the colonies. Producers in each region discovered, mainly by trial and error, those commodities that were best suited to the climate, soil, topography, nature of the available labor force, and institutions that gradually adapted to these activities. In time, fairly distinct economic regionalization developed; generally speaking, for export purposes, the South specialized in tobacco, rice, indigo, and naval stores; the Middle colonies in grain, animals (and hides), and fabricated products related to domestic primary productions. New England, due to its relatively meager agricultural endowment, became adept at the uses of its rich timber resources, concentrating on shipbuiliding and fitting, fishing and whaling, provision of shipping services, and small-shop manufacturing of all sorts.

Mercantilism Again

Such patterns of economic specialization were understandable, especially given trading opportunities between the colonies and overseas. A colony could gain from specialization and trade more than it could from self-sufficient production of everything. Comparative advantage and trade were like technological improvement: Each unit of labor could gain more from efficient production and trade than if that labor had been spent on less efficient enterprises. It paid to trade rice for the wines of Portugal, even though wine grapes could have been grown in Virginia and the wine made there.

The fly in the ointment was the set of (hundreds of) laws that Parliament had produced over the decades to govern economic life in Britain and the colonies. If it is true that the object of those laws was to restrict colonial economic life to patterns complementary to the British home economy, then we would suppose that those laws would apply most stringently to New England and to the Middle colonies since their products were most similar to domestic British production. Yet, from the beginning, the list of commodities contained Southern products—tobacco, rice, indigo, and other dyewoods—items that were most exotic to English agriculture, and the cost to the Upper South alone of the British regulations was by no means negligible, as Roger Ransom has shown.[2] However, Parliament had forbidden the growing of tobacco in England to protect the Southern planters! So, it is partly misleading to suggest that those laws, "British mercantile policy," were designed to create a strict colony-metropolis relationship—to impoverish, relatively, the overseas dominions for the benefit of domestic British producers and consumers. It was a two-way street.

Nevertheless, free trade and laissez faire was hardly the policy either. The two-way street had twists and turns in it. Over the decades, vested interests in England had managed (as do our own vested interests today) to create distortions in the market by special legislation, creating artificial advantages for themselves and corresponding disadvantages for society at large. When Parliament forbade the working of iron shapes in the colonies (a law flagrantly ignored) or the export of colonial woolen goods, the object was, if not to place the colonies on growth path S in Figure 4.1, panel (b), at least to give favored British industries the advantage. Much has been made of those laws by American writers, but there is little evidence that the colonists found them really burdensome. Besides, some colonial production (pig and bar iron) was favored by such laws. The colonies were favored too by subsidies, bounties, protection from European competition, and *drawbacks*—payments made to colonial producers for goods re-exported from England.

Enumerated Commodities

We saw in the Navigation Act of 1660 the beginning of the list of commodities that could be shipped only from the colonies to England. Tobacco and rice were the main ones. Later on, rice could be shipped from the colonies directly to southern Europe, but the tobacco merchants of England and Scotland continued to be able to divert all colonial tobacco, aside from that lost to smuggling, to themselves, to be resold at higher prices to European markets. Presumably, the Americans would have been better off absorbing the "middleman" profits by selling directly to the world. But how much better off? That turns out to be very difficult to measure in any believable way.

All Costs

To understand how much American tobacco producers (and others) lost by having only indirect access to Europe, via England, involves knowledge that we do not now, and never will, have. We do not know what European demand for tobacco would have been at prices that excluded the cost of transshipment through England. We do not know what the American supply

prices would have been. One reason we cannot know those prices is that, had America not been an English colonial dependency, the cost of maintaining an independent nation (taxes) would have to be added to the supply prices of Americans. We also would need to know how much, if any, American GNP was reduced, per year, by the payments, out of tobacco (and other commodities) receipts, for transport and administrative costs to the British.

We do not have such GNP figures for the colonies. We would need the equivalent information on colonial imports as well. We also would need an aggregate calculation of the overall costs and benefits of being in the British Empire; all of the taxes (T) and costs (C) of the restrictions per year in current prices *minus* the sum of all the subsidies (including protection for colonial enterprises estimated in money terms), bounties, and drawbacks (S), *plus* the difference between British expenditures on administration and defense (E) minus what those would have cost the Americans to do it themselves (A). In any year, at current prices, the aggregate burden of empire membership (B) would be

$$B = (T + C) - [S + (E - A)].$$

Then B/GNP would be the net burden in any year. We do not even know whether the sign of B would be plus or minus. Nevertheless, scholars have attempted these heroic calculations, and their efforts form a sizable literature.

The opening shot of the modern debate can probably be dated to 1935 when Louis M. Hacker baldly asserted that the Americans had been held in "vassalage" by British mercantile policies and that American capitalists would never have gotten control of their own affairs and future if they had stayed in the Empire.

> The interest of colonial enterprises was to be subordinated to every British capitalist group that could gain the ear of Parliament.[3]

To Hacker, the Revolution was fought mainly to remove the British economic yoke from the necks of the colonists. The talk about freedom, inalienable rights, and so forth was just rhetoric to mask the underlying economic realities.

Hacker's thesis was challenged by the historian Lawrence Harper in 1942.[4] He divided "British imperial regulation'' into four parts: (1) transatlantic trade; (2) colonial manufactures; (3) taxes of American trade; and (4) the post-1763 changes in policy. Harper concluded:

1. that Americans suffered a ''heavy'' burden only on their trade with Britain and Europe because of the Navigation Acts; those acts did not reduce trade in the Caribbean or with Africa;
2. that British mercantilism on balance probably did more to ''promote than to hinder colonial industry'';
3. that taxes on sugar, molasses, and rum were ''usually evaded,'' and there is no evidence that trade was distorted by the taxes, in any case;
4. that post-1763 taxes and restrictions were policy disasters since they unleashed an ''avalanche of agitation.''

Overall, Harper concluded, ''It is difficult to understand how British mercantilism discriminated materially against the colonists.'' Even though the requirement that enumerated colonial produce be shipped initially to England was a discrimination against the colonists, they had lived with those rules for more than a century without significant complaint against them. Even in the revolutionary rhetoric of 1776, the enumerated commodities were not mentioned.

Could more precise measurements be made? At the Yale meetings of the Economic History Association in 1965, Robert Thomas made the pioneering attempts, reopening the subject with a far-ranging effort to quantify the extent of the burden placed on the colonists by the enumerated commodities provisions of the Navigation Acts together with the net costs of Empire membership.[5] He found them less burdensome even than did Harper. Others entered the debate to expand upon the work of Thomas.[6] Peter McClelland later criticized Thomas sharply for his assumptions and for oversimplifying the scope of the computational problems. In truth, McClelland's analysis of the problem did point out the appalling problems encountered in quantifying the main relationships. McClelland also emphasized the lack of colonial agitation against the British trade laws that were enacted before 1763:

> The Declaration of Independence, for example, makes no mention of the Acts of Trade, and those hardest hit by

export restraints—Virginia and Maryland—almost never included those restraints in their list of grievances against the mother country.

In his 1971 reprise of the issues, Gary Walton estimated that the gross cost to the colonies of British protectionism and regulation might have been 1 percent of annual income in the 1770s but admitted that the figure would have to be pared down to take into account such factors as British payment for administration, defense, subsidies, and bounties.

Independent America in 1783

The net result of these computations may well be that it paid Americans, in a strictly economic sense, to be in the Empire. Efforts to determine whether this was actually the case were made by Harper and Thomas, based upon American experience of the costs of independent government after 1783. It was clear from those calculations that the net burden may well have been negative, that it paid to be in the Empire and let the British foot the big bills. Americans had to tax themselves far more after the Revolution than the British ever did, and land policy north of the Ohio Valley became one of cash sales, which was more restrictive than had been colonial (British) policies before the Quebec Act itself. Finally, the period after 1783, used both by Harper and by Thomas as a proxy for independence costs to Americans, was the wrong one, and their calculation of the cost of defending against the French without British help was probably wrong, too.

Here we are just ''playing with history,'' imagining what never happened. But surely it would have been more realistic to imagine an independent America in 1763–76 with *England,* and not France, as the enemy to be defended against. It was the British, not the French, who were aggressively enlarging their domains before 1776, and, as we discovered in the Revolution and again in the War of 1812, the British were an expensive enemy.

What the Colonists Said

All that is mere speculation. The American Revolution *was* fought, and the colonists did say why, in the Declaration of Independence. Of King George III, they said:

He has endeavored to prevent the population of these States; for that purpose obstructing the Laws for Naturalization of Foreigners; refusing . . . to encourage their migrations hither, and raising the conditions of new Appropriations of lands.

He has erected a multitude of New Offices, and sent hither swarms of Officers to harass our people, and eat out their substance.

He has combined with others . . .

For cutting off our trade with all parts of the world . . .

For imposing Taxes on us without our Consent.

Complaints on land settlement, population growth, costs and abuses of bureaucracy, restraints of trade, unjust taxation—whether justified or not, that is why the colonists said they wanted to be independent—that, and more. And so they became independent. Fighting started when the Port of Boston was closed under the Act of 1774. By modern standards, closing the port alone would have been more than enough reason to start the shooting.

WAS THERE A MONEY SHORTAGE?

Money is a "fun" topic in colonial history. It is largely a side issue (as we shall see), although some, including Ben Franklin, thought that British incompetence on the colonial money issue contributed to the desire for independence. Also, there are two important facts about colonial money:

1. The Colonists discovered how to use officially engraved pieces of paper as substitutes for coins.
2. In 1781, the Revolutionary Congress chartered a joint-stock, note-issuing bank that was the origin of American commercial banking.

These two precedents were destined to have enormous consequences in American economic history.

Money

Money, conventionally, is any item that performs four jobs:

1. It serves as a medium of exchange.
2. It is a unit of account.

3. It performs as a store of value.
4. It is acceptable as a standard of deferred payment.

It is remarkable how many items in history besides coins have been acceptable as money: animal skins, tobacco, cowry shells, wampum (strings of small shells), rocks with holes bored through them, and engraved bits of paper issued by princes, dictators, republics, and private persons.[7] The only requirement is acceptability, and it need not be voluntary at that. Armies of occupation have long extracted real produce from conquered peoples by issuing paper money that is acceptable—or else. In fact, any money called **legal tender** is coercively circulated; refusal to accept it in payment is a crime—even in modern America.

Specie

Historically, some types of money have tended to be preferred, and *specie payments,* payment in bits of precious metal or larger amounts of it, lead that list.

The British during the colonial period were on a **bimetallic** (two metal) **monetary standard.** The mint, the treasury, and (after 1694) the Bank of England bought and sold both gold and silver at fixed prices. The buying price of an ounce of gold was £3–17–9½— three pounds, seventeen shillings, nine and a half pence—the price fixed by Sir Isaac Newton as the "right" standard of England. A gold coin known as a *sovereign,* of standard weight and fineness, was worth £1–0–0—one pound sterling. Each pound was divided into 20 silver shillings (there were coins of multiples of shillings and several coins of less than a shilling—the sixpence, the penny, the farthing, and halfpenny, for example). A "Guinea" gold coin was worth 21 shillings because it was a sovereign made of Guinea gold, of greater fineness than the ordinary gold. The original Guinea gold was brought from west Africa during the reign of Charles II in connection with the slave trade.[8]

The English did not allow their coins to be exported legally, even to the colonies, but made no objections to the export or import of foreign coins and bullion (bars) since all could be valued by weight and fineness. Hence **to pay in specie** meant to pay in gold or silver in some form. The two metals were not always equally preferred, a problem with bimetallism: If the world gold supply expanded at a faster rate than did that of silver, it took more gold to buy a given amount of silver, and the gold price of silver rose. Expanded silver

One Shilling.

'Tis *Death* to counterfeit.

BURLINGTON *in* NEW-JERSEY,
Printed by Isaac Collins, 1776.

Colonial paper currencies of Connecticut and New Jersey from 1776.

production relative to gold tended to produce the opposite result.

Other Means of Payment

Payments could be made in other ways. The main method, the *bill of exchange* (a dated order to pay), was well known in colonial times. For example, suppose that A, a Carolina planter, ships rice to B, an English merchant. A draws an order for B to pay, say, £100. (This is exactly what happens today when you write a check on your demand deposit; it is an order from you to your banker to pay a given amount out of the funds you have deposited with the bank.) In the case of a bill of exchange representing sale of commodities, it was standard practice to place a date, such as three months, four months, or even six months, on the bill as the due date. The length of time stated was the bill's maturity. A ''three months bill'' matured three months after it was drawn. The next step was to get the bill "accepted"—affirmation by B, or more likely his agent, C, in Charleston, that B will pay. B (or C) signs the bill, and it now becomes money, if B is a person of good credit.

Several things could then happen. A could hold the bill himself until it matured and then present it for payment to B or his agent, C. A could sell the bill to someone else, D, for cash as soon as it has been accepted, and D would then wait for the due date and collect. If the bill were for three months, A would normally sell it to D for a discount. The amount of the discount could be any mutually agreeable sum, but the basic price would usually be determined by the current short-term rate of interest. Supposing the current rate of interest was 8 percent, the interest on a three months bill of £100 would be £2–0–0: 8 percent times 0.25 (since three months is one fourth of a year) times 100. So D would give to A £98 cash and collect the £100 on the due date, with a £2 profit.

An importer in Charleston might want to pay someone in England. Instead of shipping gold or silver, he could buy the bill from D (or A depending on who was holding it) and send it to his supplier in England in payment for goods shipped to Charleston. The supplier would then receive the bill and present it to B, or his banker, on the due date and receive payment. He also could discount the bill with someone else in England and get cash, and the discounter would then wait for the bill to mature and present it to B.

All persons owning the bill at various points along its path had to endorse it to transfer it to another, and in English law *all* signatories to the bill would be liable for payment if B defaulted when the due date came. The bill of exchange was thus normally an excellent form of "merchant money" and could be used to finance trade in all directions.

The important point is that international transactions could take place *without any shipments of specie*. That is how most transactions were accomplished—by remission of bills of exchange for payment. Such bills were also used for purely domestic trade, too. There were many variants of the basic form we have discussed. The point to remember is that bills of exchange fit our definition of money, and therefore, so long as they were current (not in default), they *were* money. Their amount at any time depended not upon banks or mints but upon merchant credit.[9]

The Bank of England (founded in 1694) in colonial times did not issue its own paper as current money. Nor, so far as we know, did any other English bank issue such small denomination promissory notes. The "paper pound," the first paper money issued by the Bank of England, appeared in 1791 when the Bank was forced to suspend specie payments. So far as we know, colonial paper money was the first in the British Empire's history. But other things were "near-moneys." Governments in England and in the colonies issued scraps of engraved paper, evidences of debt, in anticipation of further income (and payment) and promised to pay these off when they matured. They were interest-bearing, and they also, obviously, could be considered "money" if they were transferable and payable to the bearer, except that no one was *forced* to take them in payment (they were not legal tender), and they usually were in denominations too large to be of use as money to the ordinary person. Finally, book credit, like that given by your corner grocer, could be granted by any seller to any buyer. So, when we speak of the colonial "money supply" we are not necessarily speaking of specie. But let us speak of the colonial specie problem explicitly.

The Colonial Specie Problem

One difficult task with any money in the form of specie is knowing how much of it is around. The amount minted into coins is not necessarily the amount available in coins. Gold and silver can be, and were, used for purposes besides money. Coins can be melted down to make jewelry, sword hilts, or other objects. Also, specie is easily hidden (for example, from tax collectors) or exported, and people have a lamentable tendency to be less than honest about how much of it they own, in what forms, or where it is. Given that, there is probably no better known characteristic of colonial money than the much-discussed "shortage" of it. By *money* in this context, colonials meant *specie,* and especially English coins.

The nature of the money shortage may be illustrated by the following. Benjamin Franklin returned to his home in Boston briefly in the spring of 1724 after having spent a short period in Philadelphia. He visited his brother's printing shop, and the journeyman printers there questioned Franklin about Pennsylvania:

. . . asking what kind of money we had there, I produc'd a handful of silver, and spread it before them, which was a kind of raree-show they had not been us'd to, paper being the money of Boston . . . I gave them a piece of eight to drink, and took my leave.[10]

Economic historians have scoffed at colonial complaints about a shortage of money primarily for three reasons. First, interest rates in colonial times remained moderate, and with usury laws in all colonies placing ceilings on interest rates (8 percent in seventeenth-century Massachusetts, 5 percent a century later in Pennsylvania), a real money shortage that inhibited trade would have produced significant evidence of violations of the usury laws. There is no such evidence. People would have found ways around the laws, or violated them, as they did when commodities were smuggled into the colonies in violation of the navigation laws. There would have been a record of such activities. Secondly, the trend of prices in colonial America (Figure 4.4) was upwards, which is not a sign of money shortage. With long-term rising prices and falling nominal interest rates, the *real* rate of interest cannot have been a serious inhibiting factor to borrowers. Finally, the rate of real growth of the colonial economy at rising prices also is not evidence of a money shortage. We have seen that there were many ways to have money, command over real resources, without specie.

The Balance of Payments and Specie

Were the colonists imagining that they suffered from a money shortage? No, not necessarily. The colonists could only obtain major long-term increases in specie supplies by selling more goods and services to the world than they bought. As we saw in the last chapter, they seem to have had a small deficit on current account, at least by the end of the colonial period. There is no reason to suppose there was any earlier period of substantial surpluses. Without mines of gold or silver, net accumulation of coin could occur only through trade or piracy or accumulated indebtedness. You can have your pockets bulging with coins if your banker lends them to you on credit, and this is what the British did—they gave the colonies credit. Meanwhile, there were opportunities to get specie from trade with south-

ern Europe and with the Caribbean, making Spanish, French, Portuguese, and Dutch coins common in circulation. (The Spanish milled dollar of 1728 was so acceptable and useful that it became the standard for the first American dollar of 1794). Year-to-year specie supplies could come from those sources. As we saw, the overwhelming source of bilateral trade deficit was with England, and that was financed by sales of services and by the long-term accumulation of American debt instruments in English hands. The British extended credit, and they also spent large sums, as we have seen, on administration and military operations in the colonies. As Larry Neal has pointed out, a large proportion of that British money landed in American hands.[11] Walton and Shepherd find net American indebtedness growing at a maximum rate of about £40,000 a year in the early 1770s, but the net was no doubt slightly less since some small part of the deficit would have been covered by net specie shipments, the source of the colonial complaint. According to Walton and Shepherd, in 1776 British merchants claimed about £2,516,000 in outstanding debts owed them by Americans.[12] This amount, which translates into about £1 per head of the population at that time, was no doubt a considerable exaggeration.

Devaluation

The colonials tried several monetary tricks to attract coin. The obvious tactic (always a favorite stopgap with financially strapped governments) was **devaluation:** to raise, or attempt to raise, by law, the domestic price of foreign money. In the late seventeenth century, New York, Massachusetts, and Pennsylvania all tried to attract Spanish coins by offering a premium (from one-third to as much as one-half of a percent). In 1704, the British issued a proclamation setting official (lower) rates on foreign coins. These exchange rates, known as "Queen Anne's Money," merely made a confusing situation worse. The system was flexible enough for trade to flourish despite governments, and foreign coins came by way of that trade, attracted by something real—colonial commodities at prices dictated by the market. The Massachusetts mint, in existence from 1652 to 1684, made silver coins of shillings and half and quarter shillings. Given the same name as the standard English coin, they were about 23 percent underweight to prevent their being shipped to England, it is said. They were shipped anyway, by their actual weight.

Payments-in-Kind

As has been noted, many things besides coins served as money. The coin shortage tested colonial creativity.

Country Money.   In the colonial countryside, payment was made in corn, wheat, skins, livestock, and almost anything else that could serve as a substitute for specie. The Massachusetts laws, in recognition of the irregularities that could arise from debts accumulated through such exchange media, contain a wonderful statute from the year 1654:

> All *contracts* and *engagements,* for *money, corn, cattle,* or *fish,* shall be satisfied in kinds according to Covenant, or in default of the very kind contracted for, in one of the said kinds, provided that in such cases, where payment in kind is not made according to Covenant; all just damage shall be satisfied . . . according to bargain.[13]

In modern parlance, such contracts were **indexed**— that is, if the relative values of the kinds of commodities and livestock changed, those who promised to pay at the old ratios were committed to trying to honor the value of the original commitment.

In Virginia, tobacco, of course, quickly came to serve as money. But as Studenski and Krooss wrote, there could be no long-term future for tobacco money in the place where it was grown:

> Since anyone with a modicum of ambition could grow money in his own back yard, the cultivation of tobacco increased so rapidly that its price in terms of silver fell 80 per cent within a few years.[14]

No controls, no matter how stringent, could hold back tobacco planting, and tobacco long served in Virginia and on the frontier as money. Studenski and Krooss also cite early livestock payments for tuition at Harvard College and for the building fund, "a goat 30s plantations of Watertown rate which died."[15] Commodity moneys were thus imperfect and probably made the "shortage" of specie seem worse because of Gresham's law: You hoarded your coins if you could pay off with a sick goat or a pile of your own tobacco leaves.

Wampum.   There also is an excellent example of Gresham's law at work in the colonial annals of wampum money. The Dutch at New Amsterdam, trading with the Indians, accepted and paid out wampum money—shells strung into beads—as the medium of exchange. The Indians, wanting more European goods, "devalued" the currency by offering short strings and unstrung wampum in exchange, thus undervaluing the superior wampum and driving it out of circulation. In reply, Wilhelm Kieft, the wily Dutch governor, ordered a 50-percent increase in the quoted prices of European goods against such inferior moneys. Since strung wampum was no longer undervalued at the Dutch trading posts, it returned to circulation.[16]

The Pilgrims in Massachusetts had first been introduced to wampum money in 1623 by a Dutch visitor from New Amsterdam named De Rasieres. Finding that the Massachusetts Indians would indeed accept wampum for their goods, the Pilgrims tried to go directly "to the mines" by picking up the right shells and stringing their own wampum. They soon discovered that they had the wrong factor combinations for this endeavor ultimately to pay. Wampum was cheaper when acquired in exchange for their own goods than when it was "manufactured." So, comparative advantage took over and the Pilgrims traded goods for wampum, wampum for furs, and furs in England for more European goods. Wampum continued to be strung by Indian women and maintained its career as money whenever and wherever it was mutually acceptable.

Paper Money, Bills of Credit, and Banks

The colonists' truly fateful discovery was paper money. The Chinese had it centuries earlier, so perhaps it was a case of unnecessary originality. Nevertheless, in 1690 the government of Massachusetts issued 7000 one-year notes, yielding 5 percent, redeemable at par, and acceptable at par for taxes. The government had borrowed from merchants in anticipation of revenues as early as 1676, and these notes had been used among merchants like bills of exchange—that is, money. In 1690, the need was to pay off soldiers returning from an unsuccessful campaign against Quebec, but there was no specie to pay out. The soldiers accepted the small-denomination bills of credit, the bill passed current as money and the follies in America of **fiat money** (paper money with no specie backing) had begun. It was a wonderful thing: interest-earning cash. The other colonies noted this phenomenon and quickly followed with issues of their own: South Carolina in 1703; Connecticut, New York, New Hampshire, and New Jersey in 1709; Rhode Island in 1710; North Carolina in 1712; and Pennsylvania in 1723. Apparently, private citizens joined in on an irregular basis with their own issues since Quaker pacifists in Pennsylvania were moved to legislate the death penalty for counterfeiting in 1767, perhaps the most severe penalty for plagiarism in American history.

Money and Colonial Inflation

Inflation in the colonies meant a general rise in the prices of commodities *and* a reduction in the exchange rates between colonial money and specie. Parliament in 1751 prohibited the status of legal tender from being applied to the paper money of New England and in 1764 extended that prohibition to all the colonies. But the bills themselves were not prohibited. There seems to be little doubt that this addition to the money supply contributed to the rising prices of produce. First, there

was a depreciation against specie; how much depended upon circumstances in each colony. It was most severe in New England. In Rhode Island the extreme of depreciation against specie was 26 to 1; in Massachusetts, the paper fell to 7½ to 1 against specie. But in the Middle colonies where the money was better managed and sinking funds were provided, the record was much better. Money issues had even been made in a counter-cyclical way "to steady the rate of business expansion."[17]

If we return to Figure 4.2, we can see the exchange rate of Pennsylvania paper against pounds sterling. While the pound rose strongly at the beginning, after the 1740s, the rate was stable. Fifty-five years after the issues began, there had been no runaway depreciation, and the Pennsylvania currency was only a bit less than one-third depreciated against the pound—against specie. In 1932 in the United States, you could buy an ounce of gold for $20.67; today, it costs more than 16 times as much. By comparison with ours, the colonial Pennsylvania currency was the acme of fiscal conservatism and probity. Secondly, the colonial price trend was indeed upward (Figures 4.3 and 4.4), but again, by modern standards it is difficult to take seriously writers

Figure 4.2   Annual Rate of Exchange in London for Pennsylvania Currency

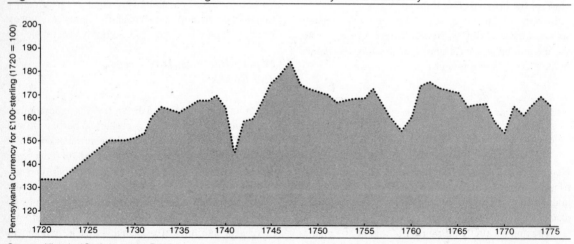

Source: *Historical Statistics*, series Z 585.

The trend of exchange rates between English sterling and Pennsylvania's paper currency shows an irregular upward movement. Over time, it took more Pennsylvania money to buy an English pound, but there were periods when the sterling rate fell.

who overemphasize such a gentle wafting. Wholesale prices in Philadelphia did not double in more than half a century.[18] Some specific prices, such as that of bread, did rise more strongly. Overall, the experience was mixed and seemed to fascinate the English (who would soon enough make abundant use of paper money). Better than any central-bank policy statement in the sub-sequent two centuries was Ben Franklin's summation of the colonial experience in his *A Modest Inquiry into the Nature and Necessity of a Paper Currency:*

> There is a certain proportionate quantity of money requisite to carry on the trade of a country freely and currently; more than which would be of no advantage to trade, and less, if much less, exceedingly detrimental to it.

Figure 4.3   Price of Bread in Philadelphia

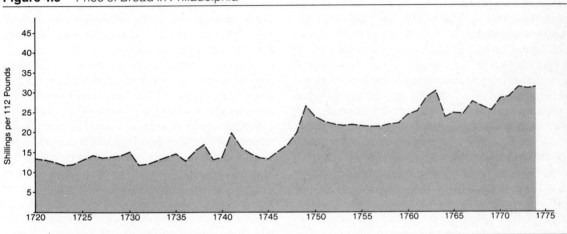

Source: *Historical Statistics,* series Z 562.

The price of bread in Philadelphia rose over time, but only slightly, indicating only a mild long-run inflation.

Figure 4.4   Wholesale Prices, 1720–1775

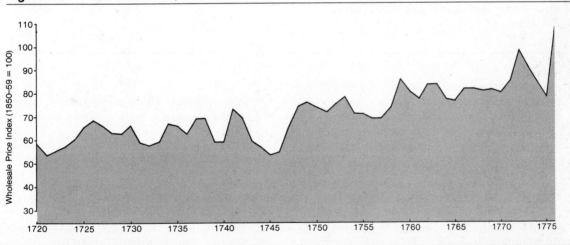

Source: *Historical Statistics,* series Z 557.

The mild long-run inflation of the period shows more clearly in wholesale prices, with a dip just before the Revolution.

That famous Massachusetts land bank of 1740 did alarm the British and some Americans, and it was put down by Parliament a year later by "An Act for Restraining and Preventing Several Unwarrantable Schemes and Undertakings in His Majesty's Colonies and Plantations in America." The "unwarrantable schemes and undertakings" consisted of the formation of a private, joint-stock company issuing its own paper money secured by mortgages on land, a prototype of frontier banking to come. The English prohibited such ventures in England after 1720 by the "Bubble Act," which was prompted by the sensational financial manipulations, company boom, and subsequent panic called the "South Sea Bubble." It was then decided that the government must protect people from themselves, and, in 1741, the Bubble Act was applied to the colonies to protect the colonists as well. However, private banking did exist in all the colonies, if not in joint-stock form. In 1733, a group of Boston merchants issued notes redeemable in silver (which, naturally enough, were hoarded, like the silver they represented). They opposed the land bank, and they had the ear of Parliament. Joint-stock banking would have to wait for 1781 and the power of the Continental Congress to create a banking corporation.

IN CONCLUSION

In a later chapter, we will examine another period of American financial history, from 1789 to 1863, that is known as "financial chaos." Yet, there is no evidence, as we shall see, that the long-term effects of such financial disorder were adverse to economic growth and development. The same must be said of the colonial period. Paper money was a substitute for the elusive coins and the clumsy "country" money of tobacco and goats, and it served variously, as it does today, according to how rapidly it was issued relative to the increase in what it bought. What cannot be said is that economic growth was harmed by it, and as Franklin said, in some circumstances it served well. In fact, he thought a worse problem would be insufficient amounts of money. Modern political leaders all over the world must certainly agree with him.

Inflation in colonial times, as now, eased the problems of debtors against their creditors. Then too, as now, the rich favored fiscal conservation, while those not so wealthy favored liberal money issues. When the Revolution came, Congress issued so much paper money that its value against specie fell drastically, but that Continental currency was redeemed and absorbed by land sales and economic growth. The product of colonial monetary genius, the invention of paper money, must be recognized as one of the greatest legacies the colonists left to their heirs. Writers in the past who were scandalized by the "inflationary" consequences of the colonial moneying need not be taken seriously by persons living in our era. From 1720 to 1775 the annual compound rate of price increase was, on the average, just over 1 percent, less that one tenth the inflation rates of the late 1970s.

Notes

1. This is an extreme assumption made for simplicity's sake. Actually, there *was* technological improvement. Walton and Shepherd, for example, measured significant increases in productivity, achieved through reductions in turnaround time for shipping due to improved docks and wharves. Such technological improvement would be expected in most trades at least. Introduction of successful new crops, like rice and indigo in the South, had the same effect, raising output (the value of it) per man employed. James F. Shepherd and Gary M. Walton, *Shipping, Maritime Trade, and the Economic Development of Colonial North America* (1972), p. 79; and the same authors, *The Economic Rise of Early America* (1979),

ch. 6. Shipping apart, Walton and Shepherd find colonial productivity increases, after the initial years, irregular and not large.

2. Roger Ransom, "British Policy and Colonial Growth: Some Implications of the Burden of the Navigation Acts," *JEH*, September 1968.

3. Louis M. Hacker, "The First American Revolution," reprinted in Gerald D. Nash, *Issues in American Economic History* (New York: Heath, 1972), p. 107.

4. Lawrence A. Harper, "Mercantilism and the American Revolution," reprinted in Gerald D. Nash, *Issues in American Economic History* (1972).

5. Robert Paul Thomas, "A Quantitative Approach to

the Study of the Effects of British Imperial Policy on Colonial Welfare: Some Preliminary Findings," *JEH,* December 1965.

6. Peter D. McClelland, "The Cost to America of British Imperial Policy," *AER,* May 1969 (See also comments there by Jonathan Hughes and Herman Krooss); Gary M. Walton, "The New Economic History and the Burdens of the Navigation Acts," *EHR,* November 1971. McClelland's analysis was subjected to refinement, in turn, by Joseph Reid, "On Navigating the Navigation Acts with Peter D. McClelland: Comment," *AER,* December 1970.

7. For example, the modern Special Drawing Rights of the International Monetary Fund.

8. As the modern American tourist in the United Kingdom soon discovers, items priced in guineas (which haven't circulated for a long, long time) cost 5 percent more than those priced in pounds.

9. Colonial understanding of such finance may be illustrated by the following Massachusetts ordinance of 1647: "Any debt, or debts due upon bill or other specialty assigned to another, shall be as good a debt and estate to the Assignee, as it was to the assigner, at the time of its assignation; and that it shall be lawful for the said Assignee, to sue for, to recover the said debt due upon bills, and so assigned, as fully as the original creditor might have done; provided the said assignment be made upon the backside of the bill or specialitie." [William Whitmore, ed., *The Colonial Laws of Massachusetts* (Boston: Boston City Printers, 1889), p. 125.]

10. Benjamin Franklin, *The Autobiography of Benjamin Franklin,* edited by Charles Eliot, The Harvard Classics, vol. I (New York: P. F. Collier and Son, 1937), p. 30.

11. Larry Neal, "Interpreting Power and Profit in Economic History: A Case Study of the Seven Years' War," *JEH,* March 1970.

12. Shepherd and Walton, *The Economic Rise of Early America,* p. 109.

13. Whitmore, *The Colonial Laws of Massachusetts,* p. 183.

14. Paul Studenski and Herman Krooss, *Financial History of the United States* (1952), p. 13.

15. At a distance in time, the passage might be translated thus: "A goat, valued at 30 colonial shillings, in the accepted rate of exchange then current between colonial and English money at Watertown, Massachusetts, had been contributed to the college. The goat died."

16. John Romeyn Broadhead, *History of New York* (New York: Harper & Bros., 1859), vol. 1, p. 304, for a more extensive discussion of this episode.

17. Richard Lester, "Currency Issues to Overcome Depressions in Pennsylvania, 1723 and 1729," in Ralph Andreano, ed., *New Views on Economic Development* (Cambridge: Schenkman, 1965).

18. The extent to which colonial money issues inflated commodity prices seems to have depended to some extent on how the money was "backed." Sinking funds made people more willing to hold money than more nebulous promises to pay. Bruce D. Smith, "Some Colonial Evidence on Two Theories of Money: Maryland and the Carolinas," *JPE,* December 1985. The role of fiscal and monetary policies in determining the value of money is discussed in Charles Calomiris, "Institutional Failure, Monetary Scarcity, and the Depreciation of the Continental," *JEH,* March 1988.

Suggested Readings

Articles

Burstein, M. L. "Colonial and Contemporary Monetary Theory." *Explorations in Entrepreneurial History,* 2nd series, vol. III, no. 3, Spring 1966.

Calomiris, Charles. "Institutional Failure, Monetary Scarcity, and the Depreciation of the Continental." *Journal of Economic History,* vol. XLVIII, no. 1, March 1988.

Greene, Jack P., and Jellison, Richard M. "The Currency Act of 1764 in Imperial-Colonial Relations, 1764–1776." *William and Mary Quarterly,* 2nd series, vol. XVIII, no. 4, October 1961.

Hacker, Louis M. "The First American Revolution." *Columbia University Quarterly,* part 1, September 1935. Reprinted in Gerald D. Nash, *Issues in American Economic History.* New York: Heath, 1972.

Harper, Lawrence A. "Mercantilism and the American Revolution." *Canadian Historical Review,* March 1942. Reprinted in Gerald D. Nash, *Issues in American Economic History.* New York: Heath, 1972.

Lester, Richard. "Currency Issues to Overcome Depressions in Pennsylvania, 1723 and 1929." Reprinted in Ralph Andreano, ed., *New Views on American Economic Development.* Cambridge: Schenkman, 1965.

McClelland, Peter D. "The Cost to America of British Imperial Policy." *American Economic Review: Papers and Proceedings,* vol. LIX, no. 7, May 1969.

Neal, Larry. "Interpreting Power and Profit in Economic History: A Case Study of the Seven Years' War." *Journal of Economic History,* vol. XXXVII, no. 1, March 1977.

Nettels, Curtis P. "British Policy and Colonial Money Supply." *Economic History Review,* vol. III, no. 2, October 1931.

Ransom, Roger. "British Policy and Colonial Growth: Some Implications of the Burdens of the Navigation Acts." *Journal of Economic History,* vol. XXVII, no. 3, September 1968.

Reid, Joseph D. "On Navigating the Navigation Acts with Peter D. McClelland." *American Economic Review,* vol. LX, no. 5, December 1970.

Smith, Bruce D. "Some Colonial Evidence on Two Theories of Money: Maryland and the Carolinas." *Journal of Political Economy,* vol. 93, no. 6, December 1985.

Thomas, Robert Paul. "A Quantitative Approach to the Study of the Effects of British Imperial Policy on Colonial Welfare: Some Preliminary Findings." *Journal of Economic History,* vol. XXV, no. 4, December 1965.

Ver Steeg, Clarence. "The American Revolutionary Movement Considered as an Economic Movement." *Huntington Library Journal,* vol. 20, August 1957.

Walton, Gary M. "The New Economic History and the Burdens of the Navigation Acts." *Economic History Review,* 2nd series, vol. XXIV, no. 4, November 1971.

Weiss, Roger W. "The Colonial Monetary Standards of Massachusetts." *Economic History Review,* 2nd series, vol. 27, no. 4, November 1974.

Books

Andrews, Charles M. *The Colonial Period of American History,* vol. 4 of *England's Commercial and Colonial Policy.* New Haven: Yale University Press, 1938.

Beer, George L. *British Colonial Policy, 1754–1765.* Gloucester, MA: Peter Smith, 1958.

Dickerson, O. M. *American Colonial Government 1695–1765.* Cleveland: Arthur H. Clark, 1912.

Harper, Lawrence A. *The English Navigation Laws.* New York: Columbia University Press, 1939.

Lester, Richard A. *Monetary Experiments: Early American and Recent Scandinavian.* Princeton: Princeton University Press, 1939.

Miller, John C. *Origins of the American Revolution.* Stanford: Stanford University Press, 1959.

Morgan, Edmund S. *The American Revolution: A Review of Changing Interpretations.* Washington: Service Center for Teachers of History, 1958.

Nettels, Curtis C. *The Money Supply of the American Colonies Before 1720.* Madison: The University of Wisconsin Press, 1934.

Shepherd, James F., and Walton, Gary M. *Shipping, Maritime Trade, and the Economic Development of Colonial North America.* New York: Cambridge University Press, 1972.

———. *The Economic Rise of Early America.* New York: Cambridge University Press, 1979.

Studenski, Paul, and Krooss, Herman. *Financial History of the United States.* New York: McGraw-Hill, 1952.

Ver Steeg, Clarence. *The Formative Years, 1607–1763.* New York: Hill & Wang, 1964.

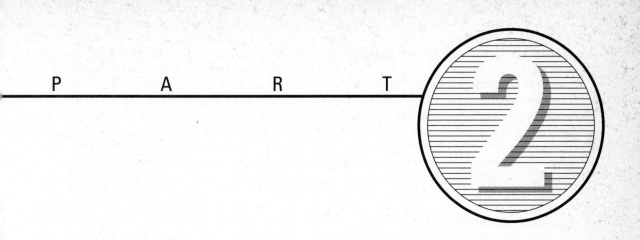

The National Period and Constitutional Crisis: 1781–1861

Main Currents 1781–1861

Until the outbreak of the Civil War in 1861, the national experience was largely dominated by three forces:

1. organization and the development of appropriate governmental institutions;
2. westward expansion and continuing sectionalism;
3. early industrialization and urban growth.

Like most generalizations, this one covers a multitude of sins. But it will prove to be a useful arena within which to consider, in greater detail, the most important forces motivating economic and social development in the first seven decades of independent national life.

Basic constitutional developments—including the great federal document itself, which launched the nation on new legal grounds in 1789—will be our initial concern. We will note especially the establishment of secure property rights for persons and institutions. The Revolution broke our bond with the ancient constitution of England. A new basis was required if there was to be a single national government. The colonies had been largely separate powers even under the Articles of Confederation. Before that they had been unrelated, constitutionally, except via their common English connection. England's constitution was (and is) unwritten—a body of laws and practices with Parliament, after 1688, as the direct amending force.

When we observe what the Americans created, we see a cautious spirit at work. The historian Charles Beard and his followers have labeled this caution **conservatism,** which is a misconception. Professional high divers are very cautious. What they are doing is dangerous. So are representatives trying to create a constitution. The great federal charter of 1789 was developed by representatives of states that already possessed full sovereignty. They, the leaders of the victorious rebel colonies, were now in the king's place. Before surrendering that power to another sovereign, they were likely to examine carefully just what they ought not to give up.

The federal Constitution was an agreement among the states about power: how much should be lodged in a single place and how much might be reserved to those entering into the agreement. We will see decades of adjustments of power in subsequent court decisions, in new state constitutions, and in private law—adjustments made by broad strokes as well as by subtle ones. The Americans, by written agreement, legislation, and judicial interpretation, had to discover a way to live in peace among themselves during a period of massive economic and geographic expansion, even as new sovereign states were being created within the federal frame. Conflict between the new federal power and those rights reserved by the states to themselves would be the object of recurring dispute and adjustment. Sectional interests were partly incompatible with each other, and the traditional rights of private persons were not entirely consistent with the expressed needs of economic growth. In the first decades, a framework of government and law had to be devised that would enable further economic prosperity to emerge peaceably from the shell of colonial agrarianism.

Such problems pressed for solution, especially because of massive westward expansion in the North and South alike, from the Atlantic coast strip of colonial settlement all the way to the Pacific. When the agreements among the states that were framed in 1789 failed in 1861, the nation had spanned the continent. Compromises finally failed to resolve sectional differences rooted, as we have seen, in colonial times. The tragedy of war between the states of the union, when it came, threatened to create two continent-wide nations out of colonial America's descendants to join the other artifacts of that era: Canada and Latin America.

The third force, industrialization, we have already observed in its infancy in the colonial period. By 1860 the United States was second only to England itself in industrial output—but a far second. Industry meant urban growth for the most part, even at primitive levels. Flour mills and water-driven factories could be placed away from centers of population, and sometimes were. But there were powerful locational reasons to set mills and factories near markets and breaks-in-transport, as there were, of course, for other activities to locate near such manufacturing and processing.

The founders of 1789 cannot have imagined that in a mere seven decades the number of urban places with populations in excess of 2500 would grow from 24 to 392 (with two cities in excess of 500,000 inhabitants) and that fully one fifth of the entire population would reside therein. In 1790 only 5 percent of the population had lived in such places after more than 150 years of settlement. The same factors of location and external economies that produced the little colonial towns and cities—specialization of labor and technique, together with breaks-in-transport and trade—would be augmented now by increments of the industrial revolution and would start the United States on the path to becoming an industry state. Thomas Jefferson's dream of an Arcadia was doomed.

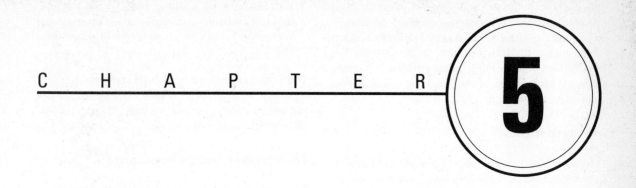

Westward Expansion

In this chapter we will examine the intellectual and geographic dimensions of the new national framework the Americans created for themselves after they had gained independence. We begin with the new system of law, the federal Constitution, and the resulting authority of the states and the common law. We will then see how the genius of Thomas Jefferson and his colleagues produced, in the Land Ordinances of 1785 and 1787, the way for orderly westward expansion. This was an achievement probably as great as the Constitution itself.

THE CONSTITUTIONAL SETTLEMENT OF 1789–91

Articles of Confederation

To fight the War of Independence, the 13 colonies had been tied together loosely by the Articles of Confederation and Perpetual Union. Submitted to the colonial legislatures in 1777, it was finally ratified by all in 1781. The Canadians were invited to join the Confederation but did not. The Confederation was too weak to be entirely effective as a frame of national government.

In particular, the taxing power to pay for the operations of the government of "The United States in Congress Assembled" was left to the individual states. This delegation of responsibility set up crucial free-rider problems and left the new nation buried in debt and inflation when the war ended.

The Constitutional Convention

Virginia, and Maryland in January 1786, took the lead and appointed commissioners to consider the development of a more adequate form of government. They met with delegates of other states (Delaware, New York, New Jersey, and Pennsylvania) at Annapolis and issued a call for a Constitutional Convention. The first meeting was held at Philadelphia on 14 May 1787 with 55 delegates in attendance. James Madison's account of the discussions presents the modern student with a clear picture of that most remarkable assemblage.[1] In slightly more than four months, on 28 September 1787, George Washington, president of the Convention, sent the complete document with a covering letter to the states for ratification. Delaware ratified 7 December 1787 and New York on 26 July 1788. But on 21 June 1788 the crucial ninth favorable note had already been cast by New Hampshire, and the new Constitution had become effective. The Congress declared the Constitution to be in effect as of 4 March 1789. The first ten amendments, the Bill of Rights, fashioned after the Declaration of Rights of Virginia (written by George Mason), were passed by the first Congress and went into effect 15 December 1791.

Reserved Rights

The debates of the Convention, according to Madison's account, were a careful discussion of state interests and different points of view about them conducted by delegates determined to succeed. They seemed to know well enough what they wanted. They drew on the past when it served well (judicial review) and invented new forms when necessary. Where compromise was required, as in the case of slavery, they compromised. The representatives of the individual states (each with virtually sovereign powers) jealously guarded their power and gave up to the new central authority only those rights they believed would be necessary to create a strong central government. To strengthen the reserved rights, the Tenth Amendment was added.

> The powers not delegated to the United States by the Constitution, nor prohibited by it to the States, are reserved to the States respectively, or to the people.

The powers left to the states were the police powers—local rules, laws, and ordinances that, as in colonial times, included licensing, inspection, and the regulation of local business activities (see Chapter 7). In relations among themselves, the people had the common law, the ancient set of rules their ancestors had found congenial for nearly two centuries in America. In 1774 the Continental Congress had claimed in the "Declarations and Resolves" the "common law of England" as the right of all Americans. Several state constitutions explicitly laid claim to the same body of law. It became policy to leave the development and interpretation of that law to the states. In cases of ambiguity, the Supreme Court of the United States, as in *Robinson* v *Campbell* (1818), ordered the state courts to look to England for guidance:

> The remedies in the courts of the United States are to be, at common law or equity, not according to the practice of the state courts, but according to the principles of common law and equity, as distinguished and defined in that country from which we derive our knowledge of those principles.[2]

The Constitution could be as brief and sweeping as it is because it did not have to be a complete code of law and statement of rights and privileges. Much could be taken for granted—and was.

The Federal Constitution in Brief

The document itself is remarkably simple. We can usefully note here those parts of special significance to our study of American economic history. The powers given explicitly to Congress are in Article I, Section 8, and they number 18. They say, in summary, that Congress shall have the power:

1. to tax, with the proviso that federal taxes shall be uniform in and among all the states;
2. to borrow, from anyone, on the credit of the new government;
3. to regulate commerce with foreign countries, among the states, and with the Indian tribes;
4. to make rules regarding naturalization and bankruptcy;
5. to create money, regulate its value, and fix a standard of weights and measures;
6. to provide punishments for counterfeiting;
7. to establish post office and post roads;
8. to create patent and copyright laws;
9. to create courts inferior to the U. S. Supreme Court;
10. to define crimes and felonies committed on the high seas and to provide punishments for the same;
11. to declare war and to make "rules" regarding it;
12. to raise and support armies, but with no single appropriation of money to remain in force for more than two years;
13. to create and maintain a navy;
14. to create martial law for the military services;
15. to provide for militia to "suppress insurrections and repel invasions";
16. to govern the militia employed by the United States, reserving to the states the appointment of officers;

17. to exercise sovereign powers over the site of the federal government's installations;
18. to make necessary laws to "carry into execution" the powers stated above.

The compromise on black slavery is contained in Article I, Section 9, paragraph 1. The Atlantic slave trade could continue for 20 years, but it would be taxed.

> The migration or importation of such persons as any of the States now existing shall think proper to admit, shall not be prohibited by the Congress prior to the year one thousand eight hundred and eight, but a tax or duty may be imposed on such importation, not exceeding ten dollars for each person.

In Section 9 of Article I, paragraph 5, Congress is forbidden the power to lay duties on exports from any state. The next paragraph prohibits Congress from creating regulations under the commerce power (Article I, Section 8, number 3 of the enumerated powers) in a way discriminatory between the states and also forbids interstate duties for vessels clearing a port in one state and entering another.

Such sweeping powers required restrictions upon the sovereignty of the states. These are given in Article I, Section 10. The first paragraph restricts dealings with foreign powers; prohibits creation of state bills of credit (state paper money), legal tender except gold and silver coins, bills of attainder, and ex post facto laws; and includes the famous contract clause: No state shall make a "law impairing the obligation of contracts." Paragraph 2 prohibits restrictions on interstate commerce except as "may be absolutely necessary for executing its inspection laws." The latter was consistent with the reservation of police powers by the states.

Article II sets up the executive branch; Article III sets up the judiciary. Article IV contains the "Full Faith and Credit" provisions, ordering each state to recognize the laws and judicial practices of the others. The citizens of each state have the rights of the citizens of the others. The ancient English doctrine of "hue and cry" (surrender of fugitives from justice) is enshrined in this article in paragraph 2. In paragraph 3 of Article IV the continuation of the colonial practices of servitude and slavery is again recognized.

> No person held to service or labor in one State, under the laws thereof, escaping into another, shall in consequence of any law or regulation therein, be discharged from such service or labor, but shall be delivered up on claim of the party to whom such service or labor may be due.

Application of this rule in the Dred Scott case in 1857 would help launch the American Civil War. Article IV also provides for the entry of new states and the guarantee of a "Republican form of government." Article V provides for amendment. Article VI provides in paragraph 1 for continuation of debt obligations made under the Confederation into the federal era. The second paragraph is the "supremacy clause."

> This constitution, and the laws of the United States . . . shall be the supreme law of the land.

The Fifth Amendment, famous in political history for the lines—

> nor shall any person be subject for the same offense to be twice put in jeopardy of life and limb, nor shall be compelled in any criminal case to be a witness against himself . . . ,

is equally famous in economic history for the next words—

> nor be deprived of life, liberty, or property, without due process of law; nor shall private property be taken for public use without just compensation.

Subsequent Economic Development

The Constitution, this amazingly brief and clear document, has been, as amended and interpreted, the "supreme law of the land" for two centuries now. Along with the settled and reserved rights of the states and citizens with knowledge of the common law and their rights under it, the federal Constitution secured property rights and the rights of persons. A fundamental element of economic development, the reign of calculable law, was to continue. We will see how each clause of the Constitution was used by lawmakers and judges to maintain the orderly growth and development of a massive economy in the decades to come. The process continues. We will be referring again and again to the clauses dealing with commerce, contracts, reserved rights, and due process as our study proceeds.

THE LAND ORDINANCES OF 1785, 1787, AND 1790

Agreement among the states regarding the forms and powers of the federal union had been preceded by agreement about the Western lands. What the colonists got from the British in settlement in 1783 was less than "sea to sea" (the Virginia grant) because of the British settlement of 1763 recognizing French and Spanish claims (and those of the Indian tribes) west of the Mississippi and reserving the old Northwest to Quebec (1774). What had to be settled first was the territory below the Canadian boundary between the Mississippi and the Alleghenies. Who owned it, and how was it to be settled? At stake was the nation's future social and economic structure: From the land and its resources would come income, wealth, cities, and future populations. The nature of the land policy was crucial.

Cessions of Western Lands, 1781

The process of agreement was begun before peace actually was achieved, since after 1781 the British cause was irretrievably lost. Seven of the colonies had claims on the Western lands from their original grants or from dealings with the Indians. Virginia's claim was for everything north of its southern border thereby overlapping the claims of other colonies. As we have seen, before the Revolution settlers were moving into the Western lands without awaiting resolution of the conflicting claims. The Articles of Confederation contained a clause stating that the Western lands should not be taken from the states for the benefit of the national government. Land speculators favored the opposite policy, but some politicians with purer motives also wanted the new government to be endowed with the public lands so that a national policy might evolve in the West.

Maryland (a state with no western lands) would not ratify the Articles until the land question was settled. New York's claims were based upon treaties with the Iroquois nation, and when it gave over those claims to the national government in 1781, Maryland responded by ratifying the Articles. In the same year Virginia offered to contribute its enormous claim, and a national policy was assured. Virginia's gift was accepted in 1784. The Virginians wisely stipulated that their lands were not to be granted by the national government to those who had made private deals for land with the

Indians and whites mix peacefully at Fort Snelling (Minneapolis), as American civilization moves westward.

Indians, speculators with vast claims thus derived in what are now Illinois and Indiana. To enforce such shoddy claims against the resident Indians, the speculators would have needed the backing of federal troops.

Collective Property Rights and the Public Domain

Before we examine the disposal of the public domain, it will be useful to consider briefly the problem in the abstract. The public domain was an enormous collective property. It could easily have been (and was by some) considered a true **public good**—an inexhaustible asset produced by government that private exploitation could never seriously diminish. It was not quite that. It was, however, a true case of community property, one that *paid no single person to conserve* unless the communal rights could somehow be passed on to others by assigning them secure private rights. Why should one person restrain his or her own use of an asset all others could freely exploit or even destroy? Unless private rights could be assigned, free riders could never be excluded, and it would pay each to overuse the communal rights of the rest so long as private profit exceeded the cost of use. A free-for-all would end in violence. It was unthinkable that the public domain would remain in government ownership; we had no Tsar to own it all and no hereditary feudal nobility whose assigned property rights would be paramount over those of the common people (such a development was feared, and the creation of titles of nobility was prohibited in the rules for the public lands).

A way would have to be found to distribute the land. Each piece of land opened to bona fide settlers instantly became a **collective good,** a ripe plum to be expropriated individually by those with the qualifications or money. There was no way in a free society, therefore, to prohibit speculation. That was Problem 1. It was part of the process of assignment of rights. Those who bought the public lands resold them at the highest prices they could get. Problem 2, apparent since colonial times, was the white settlers' intentions to expropriate the public (and Indian) lands individually. The cutting edge were the squatter families, steadily knifing their way into the wilderness. The British could not keep them out, nor, as the white population multiplied, could the Indians. What was needed was a policy that could serve as an overall rule. The public domain was destined to be cut into millions of pieces by private owners. How was it to be done? Only when the best lands were gone and the private costs of expropriation rose sufficiently would occupation of the empty spaces slow down or cease.

Jefferson and the Ordinances of 1785 and 1787

What would the land policy be? Here again the nation is in debt to Thomas Jefferson of Virginia, the guiding spirit behind the great Land Ordinances of 1785 and 1787. Had he been a student of modern theories of property rights, he could scarcely have done better in theory. No one, and certainly no force, could have made the disposal of the public domain more fair than it was. There were too many pressures at work. Jefferson realized that the "donation" (sovereign sources of clear titles) would begin with the national government. The government, now legatee of this power, had inherited control from the king of England through the colonial charters and the surrender of that power by states like Virginia whose claims came from the British Crown.

Jefferson wanted the land (a) to be a one-time source of revenue to the national government, (b) to become the seat of republican government and democratic institutions, and (c) to be a secure property to the private owner. He feared the potential abuse of power by the national government and wanted the land, wherever possible, removed from its grasp. His most important ideas about the land may be summed up as follows:

1. Tenure in the lands acquired by private persons from the national government should not be further subject to that government once titles were secured.
2. The distribution should be orderly, with scientific survey before sale and with boundaries marked by that survey rather than by the "metes and bounds" of colonial times.
3. Populations occupying the public lands would make those territories eligible to become new states, formed on an equal basis with the old.

Thus, the lands of the west would produce a lateral expansion of the American democracy and not become the basis for radical departures in government and social or economic policy or practice.

Jefferson's memorandum on the public lands of 1784 outlined his policy. He was the leading member of a congressional committee charged with formulating a land policy. Essentially, he viewed the national government's own tenure in the public lands to be fee simple, with the rights transferred to the private buyer by sale. The national government then stepped out, and the donor, in the language of Chapter 1, became the present or future state government. The land was to be then "holden of" the state; taxes were due to the state, and the land should, in Jefferson's words, "never after, in any case, revert to the United States."[3] By this single act, the new states would be endowed with a future tax base, and property owners would be subject to their local governments. The danger of the federal government's power increasing over private citizens was much reduced. Following colonial precedent, an initial

attempt was made to reserve one-third of all gold, silver, and other mineral discoveries, together with salt springs, but no settled policy ever developed reserving mineral rights to the government. Holders in fee simple owned their own minerals, a fact of capital importance when the nation began to develop heavy industry on the basis of minerals privately owned.

It was planned that the lands would be surveyed and then sold at auction. In the Ordinance of 1785 Jefferson's original plan of 10-square-mile townships was modified to the New England custom of 6-mile-square townships, each with 36 sections of 640 acres (see Figure 5.1). A half section was 320 acres, and a quarter section, 160 acres. When the Homestead Act became law in 1862, the squatter's 160 acres would be a standard family homestead. Later on, in the arid west, the assignment of irrigation water rights from government

Figure 5.1   System of Land Survey, 1796

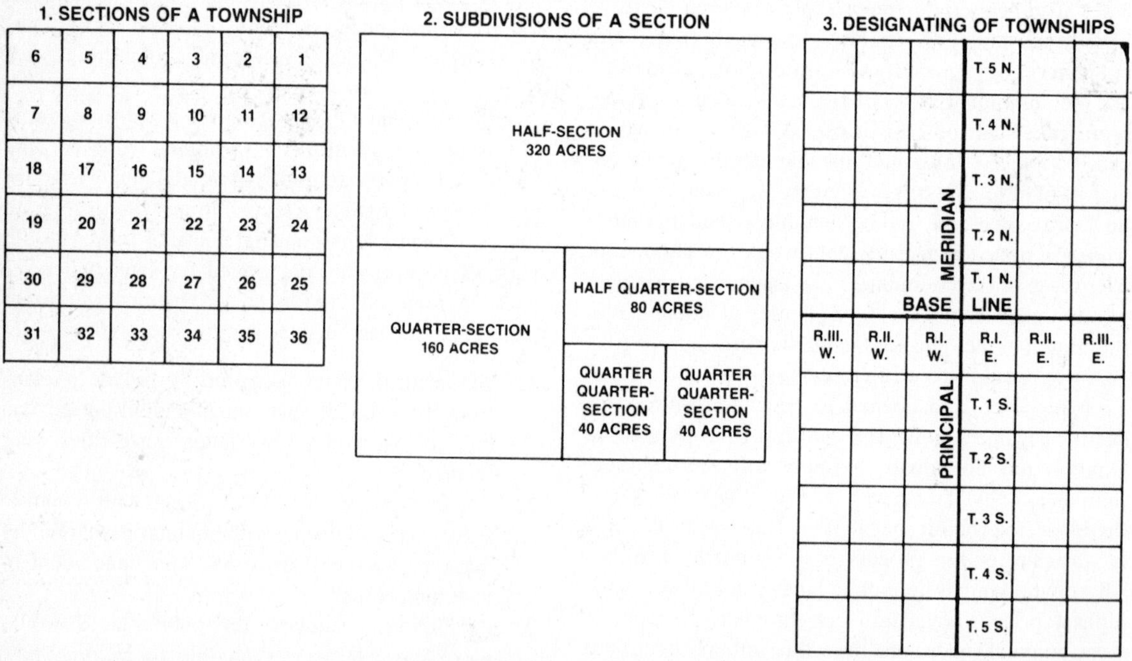

Source: Charles O. Paullin, *Atlas of the Historical Geography of the United States* (Washington, D.C. and New York: Carnegie Institution of Washington and the American Geographical Society of New York, 1932), plate 48.

The basic survey scheme for the public lands under the Land Act of 1796 (which followed the outline of the Northwest Ordinance of 1785) is shown here. Each township is 36 square miles. A section, 1 square mile, contains 640 acres. Divided into four farms, it was the "squatter" 160 acres, which still prevailed as the basic homestead in the Homestead Act of 1862. The base and meridian survey lines are division lines used to number the townships.

projects would be for the same-sized "family farm." One section in each township was to be set aside for the support of public schools (following traditions in Virginia and New England) and four sections for government uses. A proposal to include *glebeland* (see Chapter 1) to support churches, common practice in colonial New England, was defeated, in anticipation, perhaps, of the First Amendment.

The Northwest Ordinance of 1787 embraced Jefferson's plan to divide the western lands into several roughly rectangular areas that would become states in due course. Slavery was to be prohibited in the Northwest Territory. Land grants to war veterans were to be honored (the size to vary according to military rank).[4] Lands, military "reserves," were set aside for this purpose. Since the soldiers could sell their patents to private speculators for cash, most veterans never settled their lands. The land was strictly payment for their services.

Although Jefferson had wanted restrictions on the alienation and inheritance of the military portions of the western lands, in the end the tenure was one of (a) perpetual possession (no time limit in fee simple), (b) direct inheritance, (c) freedom of alienation, (d) right of waste, and (e) inheritance in cases of intestacy (no will) in equal degrees of consanguinity both male and female, without regard to half-blood, together with the right to devise lands by will. Primogeniture and entailment were abandoned. Giving a double portion to the eldest son was also left to the history books—those states that had practiced it dropped the custom by the early nineteenth century.

The western territory below the Ohio River was organized in steps. Virginia consented to statehood for its territory of Kentucky in 1792. North Carolina gave over its claims to Tennessee in 1790, and the latter was organized as a territory along the lines of the Northwest Ordinances, except that slavery was not prohibited and the survey system was not applied there. The southern territory, previously disputed with Spain, was organized as the Mississippi Territory in 1798, Georgia giving over its claim in 1804. The principles again were those of the Northwest Ordinances, save for the clause prohibiting slavery.

Thus, in a single decade after peace in 1783, the entire territory between the Mississippi River and the Alleghenies was organized, in theory, on "American principles," with constitutional rights and forms of government guaranteed and the method devised whereby the land could pass into secure private ownership and development. The foundation of future American capitalism—private ownership and control of productive resources—was thus created. Since most property rights known to most people were the real property rights imbedded in free and common socage, it was natural that rights to other forms of property were derived from the basic form. An ancient English land tenure thus came to lie at the base of American capitalism.

At first, lands in the Northwest territories were to be sold only in sections, then half sections, and, by the 1830s, in parcels as small as 40 acres—the new states were destined to have their lands filled and owned by a nation of family farmers. Of the present 50 states, 31 came into existence under the organizing principles of the Northwest Ordinances—an incredible achievement from the minds and pens of our eighteenth-century politicians.

In theory it was a social mechanism designed to settle a continent on a lawful and orderly basis with secure property rights for individual owners. It was a great gift to the future. The world today is still strewn east to west, from the *taiga* of Russia to the deserts of South Africa, with nations whose political malignancy reflects failure to solve the problems of land ownership with secure titles for individuals. In reality the disposal of the American public domain was not what Jefferson might have dreamed, but, despite a century and more of graft and corruption in the process, his principles prevailed in the final settlement. Those who live west of the Alleghenies do so mostly in the framework of the Northwest Ordinance.[5]

TERRITORIAL GAINS, 1790–1853

Our acquisition of the continental territory came within six decades of the Constitution. In Figure 5.2 we see the acquisitions between 1790 and 1853. By treaty with England, the territory of the original colonies, together with the land up to the Mississippi River, contained nearly 889,000 square miles. By purchase from Napoleon (for a mere $15 million, with only $11.3 million net of U. S. claims against France), the Louisiana Purchase of 1803 nearly doubled the national territory, adding 827,000 square miles. In 1819, by treaty with Spain, another 72,000 square miles were added—

Florida. The Texans revolted against Mexico in 1836, became an independent nation, and then joined with the United States nine years later, adding another 390,000 square miles. In Texas alone, the federal government never claimed possession of empty lands. They belonged then, and now, to the state of Texas. In 1846, the longstanding dispute with Britain over the Oregon border was settled, adding an additional 286,000 square miles. War with Mexico began that year. The settlement with Mexico added what became the states of California, Nevada, and Utah, and parts of Wyoming, Colorado, and New Mexico—an enormous 529,000-square-mile domain. The Gadsden Purchase from Mexico in 1853 added some 27,000 square miles.

By 1853 the land area of the United States was 1.9 billion acres, and as late as the Civil War, fully two-thirds of it was still empty and in the public domain. The national enterprise—until the early twentieth century and, to a large extent, even today—has been filling out this great territory with cultivation and habitation. Russian rights in Alaska were purchased in 1867, adding a massive 586,000 square miles, which are still barely inhabited. Annexation of Hawaii in 1898 and Puerto Rico in 1899 brought the total area now having the status of states of the Union (The Commonwealth of Puerto Rico is an associated state) to some 3,628,000 square miles.

Where the territorial expansion would cease depended upon future history. The Philippines were

Figure 5.2   U.S. Territory by 1853

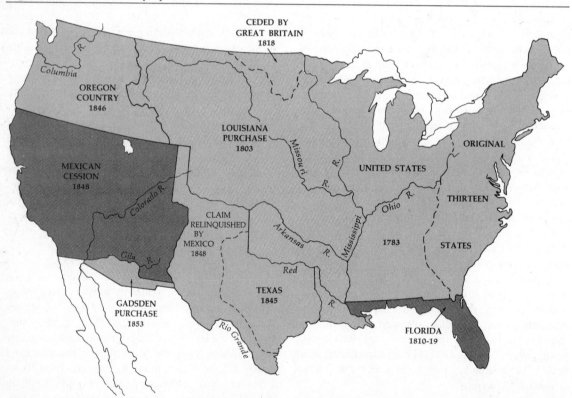

U.S. territorial gains were acquired by various methods. Some—such as Florida, Oregon, the northern section west of the Mississippi, and the Gadsden Purchase—were peaceful transactions; others—such as New Mexico, Arizona, Utah, Nevada, California, and part of Texas—were the result of various military actions. The Louisiana Purchase was, of course, a cash deal.

annexed as a territory in 1898 in our spasmodic phase of imperialism. They were given their independence in 1946. Apart from small holdings, like the Virgin Islands, Guam, and American Samoa, the national surge for territory, which began in Virginia in 1607, seems to have spent itself. In all the places we occupied, the organizational scheme of Jefferson and his colleagues reigned—over land tenure, surveys, support of public schools, sizes of townships, and the rest. The Ordinances of 1785, 1787, and 1790 laid out the ground rules.

DISPOSAL OF THE PUBLIC LANDS

In the actual processes of disposal of land almost nothing went exactly according to plan. Essentially, the government apparatus was too slow off the mark in setting up the system, too cumbersome, and when there were finally sufficient land offices established, too slow again in the recording and granting of titles. Events moved too quickly. It is worth noting that, overall, the federal government seems to have spent more money disposing of the lands than was received in sales revenues. In 1880 expenses had come to about $322 million and revenues to about $201 million, for a loss of $121 million. Those who paid the taxes that supported the government subsidized those who bought the lands from the government.[6] Not even the transactions costs were met by sales revenues.

Speculation

Much has been written of speculation in public lands, as though it were a national disgrace. Such an evaluation might bear some weight, if the system had ever worked as planned. *If* there had been a survey of all the land before settlement, *if* all the lands had been sold at public auction to actual settlers, the orderly plans might have worked. As it was, they didn't have a chance. The government's various **reservation prices** (minimal prices set by Congress below which no bids were accepted) could not encompass differing qualities of land in different areas. As a result, prices were inevitably too high for some lands (which went unclaimed) or too low for others, which resold, often on the spot, at prices that represented actual market demand and supply. Malcolm Rohrbough in his book, *The Land Office Business,* gives an account of sales in Kalama-

zoo, Michigan, in 1836, at the height of the land boom of that period. The office had been closed to catch up on recordkeeping, but the registrar bowed to the demands of the throng on his doorstep and reopened the bidding. He "accepted numerous applications, marked the tracts as sold on the maps of the office, and watched helplessly while the prospective purchasers speculated with the approved applications."[7] In that case, the reservation price was clearly far too low.

Parcel Size

Disposal of public lands by Congress opened with a sale of 1 million acres to the Ohio Company of Associates in 1787 at about 10 cents an acre. Two more sales of similar size were made that year to the Scioto Company and to John Symmes. It was left to these buyers, as in colonial times, to find settlers and resell the lands at prices and on terms the new buyers would accept. This was hardly what Jefferson and his colleagues had anticipated, but it was a portent of things to come. Despite pressures in Congress for sales in parcels affordable by small farmers, until 1800 the minimum-size purchase was set at 640 acres (at a government reservation price of $1.00 per acre until 1786, then $2.00 per acre, changing again in later years). Credit terms were allowed until an act of 1820, and in 1804 a cash discount ($1.64 per acre) was given. In 1800 the minimum size was reduced to 320 acres, in 1804 to 160 acres, in 1820 to 80 acres—all with no maximum set for purchases. Then in 1830 a 160-acre maximum sale was set at the reservation price of $1.25 per acre. Speculation—free market sale—was the method of adapting farm size, price, and location to individual demand. In 1832 the minimum size was reduced to 40 acres, cash only, and a 160-acre limit was placed on lands bought by right of **preemption,** the right to buy, for the minimum price, the land one had already settled. There was no upper limit on lands bought for cash.

It seems clear that the public land auction, which attracted huge throngs of prospective buyers for lands being opened in good years, was seen merely as the *initial* transaction necessary to move land out of the public domain into the free market. It was not uncommon, officials charged, for buyers to agree to submit low bids for reservation prices only at the auctions and then to bid among themselves for the newly released lands at much higher prices. But nothing prevented informed buyers from bidding higher at auction (except threats of violence) for choice lands when there were no preemption claims involved after the General Preemption Act of 1841.

Preemption and Graduation

Settlers in colonial times had commonly "squatted" on lands, as we have seen, and outside of Massachusetts, governments tended to deal generously with them, valuing their pioneering labors. The federal government was far less generous. Troops were sent out to burn farmsteads and villages. But the squatters returned. They saw no legitimacy in the federal government's claims to the land. Demands for preemption were heavy from the beginning and were honored by special preemption acts from time to time (e.g., in 1813 for settlers in Illinois, Missouri, and the Florida Territory). After 1815 the gradual but steady removal of Indian tribes and the nullification of their claims to tribal lands led to a flood of squatters and demands for a general preemption law. The government, while continuing to pass special preemption acts for specific groups in specific places, resisted the demand for general preemption—the opening of all lands to squatters.

As late as 1830, President Jackson was threatening to use troops to clear the lands of squatters. But instead, Congress in that year passed the broadest preemption act yet, to be renewed biennially. It included a proviso that where two squatters' claims overlapped in a single quarter section, the claim would be divided and each would be allowed to find 80 acres "elsewhere in the said land district." Not surprisingly, a vigorous market in these 80-acre "floaters" quickly developed. In 1841 a general preemption act was passed, limiting preemption to 160 acres but allowing cash sales at $1.25 per acre on parcels as small as 40 acres.[8]

Since much land remained unsold, or the titles were never completed, in 1854 Congress passed the Graduation Act, which lowered the reservation price on public land according to the time the land had remained unsold since the district was opened for sale: $1.00 per acre on land ten years unsold, 12.5 cents per acre on land 30 or more years unsold.

The 1862 Homestead Act opened the remaining public domain to settlers on terms of occupation and improvement only, a century after the Proclamation of 1763 had closed the interior. By then, most of the good lands east of the Mississippi were in private hands.

But there is something else to consider here. The return to colonial methods—land grants for settlement and services performed—embodied in the 1862 Homestead Act has always been something of a puzzle. Especially so because the Civil War was raging when a Congressional act was passed diverting populations away from the cockpit of war, away from the east and midwest. Why then? Perhaps there is not such a mystery in it. The homestead lands were in the domain of the plains and mountain Indians. Although those lands had been claimed by the United States since 1781, effective control over them was never established. Homesteaders were, in many respects, an army of occupation, and far cheaper than the one later represented by George Armstrong Custer and Phil Sheridan. Homesteaders paid most of their own way, and tended to drive out the Indians. So the homesteaders were loosed upon the west (as had been the backwoods squatters in colonial times) and a thousand or so battles later (about three decades) the frontier was closed, the Indians were on reservations, and the federal government ruled all. Homesteading after 1862 was a way for a weak (or preoccupied) government to establish its property rights (by supporting those of the homesteaders) in disputed lands. So says Douglas W. Allen, and the argument makes sense.[9]

Questions of Efficiency and Justice

Studies of the General Land Office and its procedures agree that administration was deficient throughout. The staff was too small, and settlers constantly pressed into choice areas faster than the land could be surveyed. It took as long as five years after purchase to gain title. At first, each patent to land had to be signed personally by the president of the United States. In 1832 the General Land Office needed to issue 42,000 patents to keep pace. From December to June, General Jackson had signed 10,000 patents, there were 10,590 awaiting his signature, and the number was climbing. Congress then passed a law allowing a secretary to sign on the president's behalf.

Land officers were commonly corrupt, selling information on lands privately and speculating in the lands themselves to augment their salaries. It is charged that, at least until the General Preemption Act of 1841, the system was designed to line the pockets of the rich (speculators who could pay cash for large blocks of land and then resell parcels to small holders) at the public expense.

Was a system that embraced greater justice and equity possible? No doubt. Any system less corrupt might have been an improvement, but in part, the question is strictly academic. Most of the public domain was taken by force from the English or Mexicans or from the American Indians. For example, what were the American Indians' compensations in the Louisiana Purchase? Treaties were broken, Indian populations were forcibly evicted from their lands—the Indian Removal Act of 1830 had as its object the transfer of *all* Indians to west of the Mississippi River. It was to become a nice problem of ethics to distribute justly lands thus gained. In any case, Congress in 1850 with the Illinois Central Railroad, in 1862 with transcontinental railroads, and in later grants to railroads by the states, proceeded to give away 10 percent of the continental landmass (about 190 million acres) to subsidize railroad construction. The search for justice and equity there would become even more complex.

Considering what was going on—the wholesale "privatization" of communal property—our system had one overriding virtue; as Professor Lance Davis said of it, "At least it was fast."[10] There were curious inconsistencies in the policies. The farmers wanted more and more land, since clearing it gave them a financial gain. According to Lebergott, a farmer in North Central region could clear 10 to 12 acres a year, a gain of from $140 to $200, or more than an adult son could earn in a year as an agricultural laborer. On the other hand, the policy of selling off the public domain undermined this effort since new lands were constantly being added to supply, reducing land prices overall from the levels they might have been otherwise.[11]

In the end, the land was occupied in *form* as specified by the Northwest Ordinances, and that was a great achievement. The *process* as it actually happened was no more a national disgrace than is any modern river and harbor appropriation by Congress. The public lands were in the nineteenth century what the spending power of Congress would become in our own era, the place where private interests were satisfied because no public interest could be agreed upon or even identified. Jefferson would have been appalled then, as he no doubt would be today. Vernon Carstensen quotes with

approval a 1915 statement by Dean Eugene Davenport of the College of Agriculture of Illinois: "But we have these farms, these cities, the railroads, and this civilization to show for it, and they are worth what they cost."[12] We could spend much time amusing ourselves by imagining a system that could have done it better, considering the vastness of the task to be done.

Land Sales Patterns

Westward expansion was a matter of people as well as land. More people were needed as the nation moved westward; thus, time was involved. Until the late 1840s, immigration was not of great significance; natural increase and the migration of native populations moved the nation westward. Consider the data in Table 5.1 on page 96.

By 1840 the flood of people into the East-North-Central region (Ohio, Indiana, Illinois, Michigan, Wisconsin) and into the East-South-Central region (Kentucky, Tennessee, Alabama, Mississippi) had created populations there of nearly 6 million. By 1860 those two regions, together with growth in the West-North-Central region (Minnesota, Iowa, Missouri, North Dakota, South Dakota, Nebraska, Kansas) and in the West-South-Central region (Arkansas, Louisiana, Oklahoma, Texas), meant that nearly half of the U. S. population lived in areas that in 1800 and mainly even in 1820 contained only negligible numbers.

Now, with settled constitutional and legal systems, secure property rights, land settlement laws uniformly applied, no significant internal shocks (wars, revolutions) to the economic system, and population growth mainly based upon natural increase, there would seem to have been conditions for more or less steady westward expansion. *Such was not the case.* The expansion and sales of lands came before 1860 in three "waves" centered on the dates 1818, 1836, and 1854–55. Why was that? Land sales are plotted in Figure 5.3.

Here we meet, for the first time in this book, the phenomenon in American history known as the **business cycle,** the recurrence of upswings and downswings in economic activity. Before 1860 there were three strong peaks—in 1818, 1836, and 1854–55—with monetary crises followed by depressions in 1819, 1837, and 1857. There also were minor cycles before the Civil War that produced no major monetary crises.

Table 5.1 Regional Populations 1800–1860[a]

Colonies	1800	1820	1840	1860
Old Areas				
New England	1.2	1.7	2.2	3.1
Middle Atlantic	1.4	2.7	4.5	7.5
South Atlantic	2.3	3.1	3.9	5.4
Total	4.9	7.5	10.6	16.0
New Areas				
East North Central	0.0	0.8	2.9	6.9
West North Central	0.0	0.0	0.4	2.2
East South Central	0.3	1.2	2.6	4.0
West South Central	0.0	0.2	0.4	1.7
Mountain	—	—	—	0.2
Pacific	—	—	—	0.4
Total	0.3	2.2	6.3	15.4

[a] Population figures are in millions of persons.

Source: *Historical Statistics*, series A 195.

Table 5.2 Land Sales Around Three Peaks[a]

Year	Acreage	Year	Acreage	Year	Acreage
1815	1.3	1833	3.9	1851	2.1
1816	1.7	1834	4.7	1852	0.9
1817	1.9	1835	12.6	1853	3.8
1818	3.5	1836	20.1	1854	12.8
1819	3.0	1837	5.6	1855	12.0
1820	0.8	1838	3.4	1856	5.2
1821	0.8	1839	5.0	1857	4.2

[a] Acreage figures are in millions of acres.

Source: *Historical Statistics*, series J 20.

In 1818, 1836, and 1854–55 the upswings in land sales were dramatic. Note the data in Table 5.2.

Several obvious explanations for this pattern spring to mind. Since the demand for land is to some extent (apart from "land hunger") derived from the prices of its products, one would expect some correlation between movements in food prices and sales of land. Such was the case, as we see in Figure 5.3, in 1836 and 1854 but only in an unconvincing way; the magnitude of increases in land sales was out of all proportion to price changes, and, of course, in 1818 the relationship held not at all.

People need land, but the only source of *variation* in population growth that might be sudden and large (like the increases in land sales) is immigration. Immigration was not important relative to land sales before or after the Irish and Germans came in the late 1840s and early 1850s because these groups stayed mainly in the cities. There is no evidence that their arrival pushed others out onto the public domain. Land availability increased with improved transportation—internal improvements like roads, canals, and railroads—but these improvements were not in the right locations or timed correctly to account for the sudden huge changes in western land sales. Expenditures on canals, roads, and railroads occurred in years when there were no upsurges in land sales; so, even though they no doubt supported the expansions of activity that underlay the booms in land sales, such expenditures could not have been the cause of the booms.[13]

The late Professor Arthur Cole, examining all these phenomena in a famous study published in 1927, concluded that **speculation**—psychological waves of optimism and pessimism (as in modern gyrations in stock-market prices, exchange rates, commodities, gold prices)—was the cause.[14] He noted, using monthly and quarterly data, that increased sales of land *preceded* the boom increases in commodity prices and other evidences of economic activity and that land sales also started their declines *before* the general downturns in economic activity in 1819, 1837, and 1857. Surviving eyewitness accounts of these episodes certainly support Cole's conclusions; whole town sites were laid out in the wilderness overnight, some of which never developed—the streets were thronged with buyers one year and were empty the next. Harriet Martineau was in Chicago in 1836 just as it was rising from the muck at the junction of the Chicago River and Lake Michigan.

> I never saw a busier place than Chicago was at the time of our arrival. . . . The streets were crowded with land speculators, hurrying from one sale to another. A negro dressed up in scarlet, bearing a scarlet flag, and riding a white horse with housings in scarlet, announced the times of sale. . . . As the gentlemen of our party walked the streets, store-keepers hailed them from their doors with offers of farms, and all manner of landlots, advising them to speculate before the price of land rose higher.[15]

One hopes someone in her party seized the opportunity, Chicago real estate being what it is now. But what of Allegan, Michigan, a tract of 20,000 acres on the Kalamazoo River, all laid out in town lots and ready to go? A survivor of that fiasco, George C. Bates, later wrote—

Figure 5.3   Public Land Sales and Farm Products Prices, 1800–1860

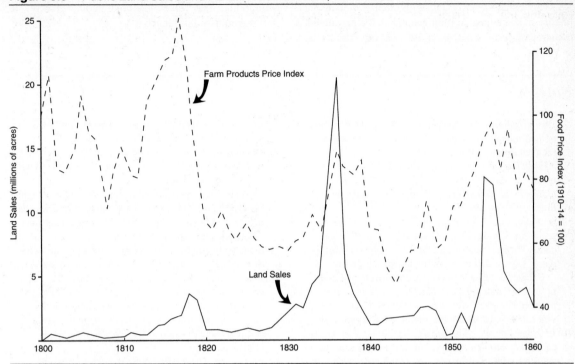

Source: *Historical Statistics,* series E 53, J 20.

There was a (rough) correspondence before 1860 between westward surges of settlement and rising agricultural prices. The correspondence is especially marked in the mid-1830s and mid-1850s by sales of public lands and the index of food prices. Before 1815, westward movement was blocked by disputed claims to the western lands, lack of government land sale surveys and offices, and hostile Indian tribes.

You were not old enough to appreciate the different phases of the inflation, beginning with a gentle breeze in 1834, increasing to a gale in 1835, to a storm in 1836, to a change of wind and an adverse tornado in 1837, leaving wrecks on every hand, succeeded by a dead calm which lasted up to 1844. . . .[16]

The pattern of land sales—borrowing and spending money (debt creation)—was part of the overall cycle in business activity. As we shall see, of the many contributing causes to business cycles, no single force has ever been isolated and agreed upon among economists, except perhaps among the **monetarists,** economists who see money as a remote cause, rather than an instrument of human activity. Nor has the *periodicity,* the timing of business cycles, ever been satisfactorily explained. So, the business cycle is a nuisance, but it happened

and cannot be rubbed out of economic history just because it inconveniently cannot be explained. Observers all agree that economic growth in unregulated capitalist economies occurred in cycles of expansion and contraction around a rising trend.

In conclusion, then, we are left with the fact that although constitutional, legal, and demographic factors laid the groundwork for a steady absorption of the public domain into private hands as the nation grew and spread westward, and although actual settlement followed this pattern of slow but constant spread, the pattern of land sales actually was markedly cyclical. We will meet the problem of the business cycle again and again, intertwined in nearly all social, political, and economic issues in the growing economy. In the twentieth century the modern welfare state will develop partly as a defense against this force. It is an interesting historical and social fact that the business cycle appeared so early and with such power in our history in something so fundamental as the private occupation of the public domain. Because our land tenure made land into a commodity, for sale like any other commodity, the forces of commercial growth, in cycles, could and did reach it.

Notes

1. James Madison, *Documents Illustrative of the Formation of the Union of the American States* (Washington: Government Printing Office, 1927).
2. *Robinson v Campbell,* 3 Wheaton 212 (1818).
3. Quoted in Marshall Harris, *Origin of the Land Tenure System in the United States* (Westport, CT: Greenwood Press, 1970), p. 389.
4. A total of some 9.5 million acres of public land was reserved for veterans of the Revolution and their descendants. The last land warrant for the Revolution was taken out in 1886, over a century after independence. Jerry O'Callaghan, "The War Veteran and the Public Lands," in Vernon Carstensen, ed., *The Public Lands: Studies in the History of the Public Domain* (1962), p. 112. The vets could, and did, sell their claims to others for cash.
5. Jonathan Hughes, "The Great Land Ordinances: America's Thumbprint on History," in David C. Klingaman and Richard K. Vedder, eds., *Essays on the Economy of the Old Northwest* (Athens: Ohio University Press, 1987). Exceptions to the strict interpretation of the statute can be found in Louis Cain, "Carving the Northwest Territory into States," in Joel Mokyr, ed., *The Vital One: Essays in Honor of Jonathan R. T. Hughes* (Greenwich, CT: JAI Press, 1991).
6. Carstensen, *The Public Lands,* p. xviii.
7. Malcolm Rohrbough, *The Land Office Business* (1971), pp. 245–46.
8. For a study of the imperfect results of the 1841 act in the hands of speculators in frontier lands who managed to acquire lands far in excess of 160 acres, see Allan G. Bogue, "The Iowa Claim Clubs: Symbol and Sub-

stance," *Mississippi Valley Historical Review,* 1958, reprinted in Carstensen, *The Public Lands.*
9. Douglas W. Allen, "Homesteading and Property Rights: or, 'How the West Was Really Won'," *Journal of Law and Economics,* April 1991.
10. Lance E. Davis, personal communication. Since "equitable distribution" of stolen goods among the thieves is a matter of pure fancy, the country was benefitted by getting quickly past the act.
11. Stanley Lebergott, "The Demand for Land: The United States, 1820–1860," *JEH,* June 1985. Jeremy Atack and Fred Bateman also note this perverse consequence of continuous releases of new land into the market by the government's policy; rents—income from working land—derived from "eastern lands" were reduced accordingly, and transferred west. *To Their Own Soil* (1987), pp. 7–10.
12. Carstensen, *The Public Lands,* p. xxvi.
13. Carter Goodrich, Julius Rubin, Jerome Cranmer, and Harvey Segal, *Canals and American Economic Development* (New York: Columbia University Press, 1961).
14. Arthur Cole, "Cyclical and Sectional Variations in the Sale of Public Lands, 1816–1860," *REStat,* 1927. Reprinted in Carstensen, *The Public Lands.* Also, Paul W. Gates, "The Role of the Land Speculator in Western Development," *Pennsylvania Magazine of History and Biography,* 1942, reprinted in Carstensen, *The Public Lands.* Gates shows the various roles, virtuous and deplorable, of the frontier professional land speculator.
15. Quoted in Rohrbough, *The Land Office Business,* p. 240.
16. Quoted in Rohrbough, p. 243.

Suggested Readings

Articles

Allen, Douglas W. "Homesteading and Property Rights; or, 'How the West Was Really Won'." *Journal of Law and Economics,* vol. XXXIV, no. 4, April 1991.

Billington, Ray A. "The Origin of the Land Speculator as a Frontier Type." *Agricultural History,* vol. XIX, no. 4, October 1945.

Bogue, Allan G. "The Iowa Claim Clubs: Symbol and Substance." *Mississippi Valley Historical Review,* vol. 45, no. 2, September 1958, reprinted in Carstensen, *The Public Lands.*

Brogan, D. W. "The Quarrel over Charles Austin Beard and the American Constitution." *Economic History Review,* 2nd series, vol. XVIII, no. 1, August 1965.

Cain, Louis P. "Carving the Northwest Territory into States." In Joel Mokyr, ed., *The Vital One: Essays in Honor of Jonathan R. T. Hughes.* Greenwich, CT: JAI Press, 1991.

Carstensen, Vernon. "Introduction." In Carstensen, *The Public Lands.*

Cole, Arthur H. "Cyclical and Sectional Variations in the Sale of the Public Lands, 1816–1860." *Review of Economics and Statistics,* vol. 9, no. 1, January 1927, reprinted in Carstensen, *The Public Lands.*

Freund, Rudolf. "Military Bounty Lands and the Origin of the Public Domain." *Agricultural History,* vol. 20, 1946, reprinted in Carstensen, *The Public Lands.*

Gates, Paul W. "The Role of the Land Speculator in Western Development." *Pennsylvania Magazine of History and Biography,* vol. LXVI, 1942, reprinted in Carstensen, *The Public Lands.*

———. "Charts of Public Land Sales and Entries." *Journal of Economic History,* vol. XXIV, no. 1, March 1964.

Hughes, Jonathan. "The Great Land Ordinances: America's Thumbprint on History," in David C. Klingaman and Richard K. Vedder, eds., *Essays on the Economy of the Old Northwest.* Athens: Ohio University Press, 1987.

Lebergott, Stanley. "The Demand for Land: The United States, 1820–1860," *Journal of Economic History,* vol. XLV, no. 2, June 1985.

O'Callaghan, Jerry A. "The War Veteran and the Public Lands." *Agricultural History,* vol. 28, no. 4, October 1954, reprinted in Carstensen, *The Public Lands.*

Treat, Payson Jackson. "Origin of the National Land System under the Confederation." *American Historical Association Report, 1905,* reprinted in Carstensen, *The Public Lands.*

Books

Atack, Jeremy, and Bateman, Fred. *To Their Own Soil: Agriculture in the Antebellum North.* Ames: Iowa State University Press, 1987.

Beard, Charles A. *An Economic Interpretation of the Constitution.* New York: Macmillan Company, 1913.

Carstensen, Vernon, ed. *The Public Lands: Studies in the History of the Public Domain.* Madison: University of Wisconsin Press, 1962.

Gates, Paul W. *History of Public Land Law Development.* Washington: Public Land Law Review Commission, 1968.

Jensen, Merrill. *The New Nation: A History of the United States During the Confederation.* New York: Vintage Books, 1950.

Riegel, Robert E., and Athearn, Robert G. *America Moves West.* New York: H. Holt and Company, 1964.

Rohrbough, Malcolm. *The Land Office Business: The Settlement and Administration of American Public Lands, 1789–1837.* New York: Oxford University Press, 1968.

Turner, Frederick Jackson. *The Frontier in American History.* New York: Holt, Rinehart, Winston, 1921.

Wyman, Walker D., and Kroeber, Clifton B., eds. *The Frontier in Perspective.* Madison: University of Wisconsin Press, 1957.

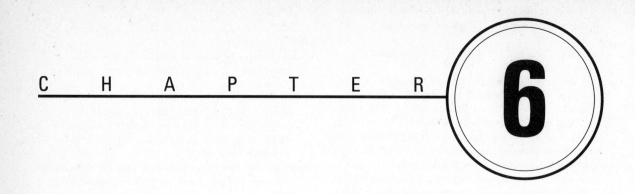

Population and Labor Force

Two major trends and characteristics of American population growth that we saw in colonial times continued from independence to the Civil War: (a) growth was very rapid and (b) populations living in urban places increased, even though this was a period of such extensive settlement of the open country. In addition, a massive change in the sources of immigration occurred. In 1860 there were more than 4 million persons living here who had been born in Europe, a figure nearly equal to the nonwhite population. The proportion of European-born had more than doubled since 1790, and the proportion of nonwhites had fallen by a fourth. This was the inevitable result of ending the legal Atlantic slave trade in 1808 and the expansion of free European immigration. Birth rates were beginning their secular decline in all parts of the population, as was the size of the average family. The processes that would produce major twentieth-century characteristics of population (such as smaller families) were already apparent.

SIZE AND NATURAL INCREASE

Major population data are given by census years in Table 6.1. By 1860 total American population ex-

ceeded that of the United Kingdom, and the white population exceeded that of England and Wales. Of the European countries, only France and Russia had populations larger than ours (German-speaking central Europe was still divided into many small states). The rate of population growth after 1790 continued at about 3.3 percent per annum, compounded, doubling roughly every twenty-three years. This rate was about the same as during the latter part of the colonial era. After the Civil War, however, the rate of population growth

Table 6.1 Basic Population Data 1790–1860

	Count[a]			Percentages	
Year	Total Population	White	Non-white	Non-white	Urban
1790	3.9	3.2	0.7	17.9	5.2
1800	5.3	4.3	1.0	18.9	6.1
1810	7.2	5.9	1.3	18.1	7.3
1820	9.6	7.9	1.7	17.7	7.2
1830	12.9	10.5	2.4	18.6	8.7
1840	17.1	14.2	2.9	17.0	10.8
1850	23.2	19.6	3.6	15.5	15.3
1860	31.4	26.9	4.5	14.3	19.8

[a] Counts are in millions of persons.

Source: *Historical Statistics*, series A2, 57–72, 91–99.

slowed, as we shall see, even though the absolute increases became very large. No European nation sustained such an increase up to 1860. According to Richard Easterlin, one leading scholar of the subject, no European country maintained half our overall population growth rate. Since the evidence indicates that the American death rates up to 1860 were comparable to those in Europe, the cause of the powerful growth of population had to be mainly in fertility—births.[1]

Data on total birth rates before the mid-nineteenth century are still fairly conjectural. Available evidence points to a birth rate of perhaps 55 per 1000 per annum in the early nineteenth century (compared to 30 per 1000 in 1910 and a mere 16.7 per 1000 today). The data indicate a slow but steady decline thereafter, down to 41.4 per 1000 in 1860. The high fertility of the early population is attributed to several causes. First, of course, is the fact that more than half of the population then was in high fertility ages. The median age of the population in 1790 was only 15.9 years, and even in 1860 it was 19.4 years (compared to 33.1 today, the highest in our history). In 1820 when the nation began its westward movement in earnest, the average American was less than 17 years old. In a sense, we were a nation of teenagers, and younger.

Richard Easterlin argues that plentiful land (and the opportunity to own it) also lays at the root of our high fertility.[2] A nation composed mainly of farmers and people planning to farm, in the presence of a vast quantity of empty land, had every reason to create large families. There was the labor of the young while they remained at home and the hope of their settling nearby when they had grown to family-creating ages themselves. Yasukichi Yasuba has shown that between 1800 and 1860 family size was inversely related to population density.[3] While it may seem difficult to credit Americans in the early nineteenth century with such extraordinary sensitivity to spatial existence, this apparently was largely the case.

Data we have on the number of young children tend to verify these findings. In each case in Table 6.2, in each of the years chosen, the number of small children per 1000 women in childbearing years (taken as proxies for birth rates and family size) is significantly smaller in urban areas than in the countryside. Land availability in a time when most of the country was rural (and technological change in agriculture had not yet impressively raised productivity) was no doubt a main basis for expectations about the future.

Available land was prospective family income. Those whose families were "planned" might have reacted favorably to this stimulus. But since urban dwellers were not farmers, why should they have been so sensitized to land availability (or the lack of it, in their case)? The differences in birth rates and family sizes between urban and rural populations are very impressive. There must then have been other factors at work, too. Was it really more difficult to raise a family in a town than in the country? If so, then why were towns growing so rapidly in number and population when so

Table 6.2   Number of Children Under 5 Years of Age per 1000 Women 20–44 Years of Age, 1810 and 1840

Region	1810		1840		Percentage Urban of Rural		1840 as a Percentage of 1810	
	Rural	Urban	Rural	Urban	1810	1840	Rural	Urban
Northeast	1079	845	800	592	78.3	74.0	74.1	70.1
Middle Atlantic	1344	924	1006	711	68.8	70.7	75.7	76.9
East North Central	1706	1256	1291	841	73.6	65.1	75.7	67.0
West North Central	1810	—[a]	1481	705	—	47.6	81.8	—
South Atlantic	1347	936	1185	770	69.5	65.0	88.0	82.3
East South Central	1701	1348	1424	859	79.2	60.3	83.7	63.7
West South Central	1557	727	1495	846	46.7	56.6	96.0	116.4
Total U.S.	1329	900	1134	701	67.7	61.8	85.3	77.9

[a] No data.

Source: Derived from *Historical Statistics,* series B 67–98.

much good and cheap land was available? The answer is that children are **durable goods** (like refrigerators or cars in our time) upon which consumers might spend money. In towns there were more options, more ways to spend money than in the countryside; accordingly, urban families were smaller. The age of females at first marriage was rising throughout the nineteenth century, and this factor would tend to reduce fertility rates, but equally in both the urban and rural areas.[4] Our estimates indicate that birth rates and family sizes declined throughout the United States (except for the increases in urban families in the West-South-Central region).

In aggregate the data, derived from censuses, generally support these arguments, including suspiciously opportune upturns in 1810 and 1860, both (apparently) reflecting recent acquisitions of new territory (see the data in Table 6.3).[5] One should be apprehensive when the data so neatly and easily support a hypothesis. But what else can be said? Sheer accident? Notice that in the Mountain and Pacific regions, where new land had just been acquired after 1848, the numbers rise significantly between 1850 and 1860.[6]

Apart from the Mountain and Pacific regions in 1850 (where there may well have been a short supply of childbearing women or women of any age), it is the case that the older regions (Northeast, Middle Atlantic, and South Atlantic) have more or less consistently lower numbers than the newer regions, both north and south. From these data (Tables 6.2 and 6.3), we can safely say (a) that birth rates and family sizes apparently declined over time from 1800 to 1860, (b) that the data indicate lower fertility in urban than in rural populations, (c) that new frontier areas had higher fertility than was true of older settled regions, and (d) that

New England led all other regions in the development of these trends.[7] After 1860, when better data are available, the same trends continue; birth rates fall (as do death rates), and so do family sizes on average. From what we know, it appears that trends in fertility rates (but not absolute levels) among blacks, both slave and free, were roughly the same as among whites.[8] It is hard to believe that the availability of land and trade-offs between children and other consumer durables counted among the slaves.

Something as important as the long-term fertility decline deserves a believable explanation. Why should the birth rate be in *any* way related to available arable land? Easterlin argues that the negative motivation was bequests: Parents had extra children in order to use their labor in agriculture, and then the parents provided children with farms of their own. This is the "bequest motive." When good farm land became more expensive the price of bequests rose and reduced the demand for extra children. Morton Shapiro found Easterlin's thesis was supported by the evidence.[9] In a recent study Paul David and William Sundstrom offer a "life cycle" explanation. Suppose, they argue, that large families were designed to be old-age insurance for the parents. Then the growing shortage of arable land could be associated with a declining fertility rate. At the beginning of the country's existence the superabundance of arable land meant that land already owned (by the parents) would not rise in price over time sufficient to be a nest egg for old age, and children would, or could, be induced to care for the aged parents. When, later in the nineteenth century, the best lands were growing scarce, then the rent, and therefore the price, of land already owned and settled would increase; it became a nest egg

Table 6.3 Number of Children Under 5 Years of Age per 1000 Women 20–44 Years of Age, 1800–60

Year	Total U.S.	North-east	Middle Atlantic	East North Central	West North Central	South Atlantic	East South Central	West South Central	Mountain	Pacific
1800	1281	1098	1279	1840	—	1345	1799	—	—	—
1810	1290	1052	1289	1702	1810	1325	1700	1383	—	—
1820	1236	930	1183	1608	1685	1280	1631	1418	—	—
1830	1134	812	1036	1467	1678	1174	1519	1359	—	—
1840	1070	752	940	1270	1445	1140	1408	1297	—	—
1850	877	621	763	1022	1114	937	1099	1046	886	901
1860	886	622	767	999	1105	918	1039	1084	1051	1026

Source: See Table 6.2.

due to its capital gain. So you invested in land as a substitute for more children. The scarcer the land, the higher the economic rent, capital gain, and the fewer children needed to provide for the declining years of the parents.[10]

IMMIGRATION BEFORE 1860

A second source of population increase, of course, was immigration. After independence, immigration continued to be unrestricted and remained so until after the Civil War. Scholars in the past twenty years have raised new and intriguing questions about this massive migration of human beings and what it meant to the economic growth and development of the United States.

The Data

First, let us make something clear. We are speaking only of immigrants about whom some quantifiable evidence remains. We shall never know what the unrecorded flow was across the Canadian and Mexican borders, although literary evidence indicates it was considerable. There is also the question of continued slave cargoes landed after the end of legal imports in 1808. That slave imports continued illegally, there is no doubt, but they were apparently very limited in number. The British vigorously suppressed the Atlantic slave trade after 1820, and shipments to the United States, although they continued, were reduced to a trickle. The evidence put together by scholars indicates that imports of slaves after the American Revolution

(nearly all of them before 1808) may have added (counting their American descendants) from a third to a half to the nonwhite population.[11] By 1860 it is estimated that 99 percent of America's black population was native-born and, of course, had *mainly* colonial ancestors. In fact, by 1860 a higher percentage of blacks than of whites was native-born.[12] The contribution of immigration to population increases up to 1860 is shown by decades in Table 6.4.

Before the decade of the 1830s, immigration was a relatively minor source of population increase. It then expanded rapidly, and the increase built up steadily. The annual average number of immigrants in the period 1821–25 was 8000; in 1826–30 it was up to 20,587; in the next five years, 1831–35, it rose to 50,498, then to 69,330 between 1836 and 1840. By the period 1841–45, the expansion had grown to an average of 86,067 per year. At that point in history a series of poor harvests and the failure of the potato crop in northern Europe disrupted European society and produced the first real deluge of immigrants—a portent of things to come. Between 1845 and 1850, 1.4 million came. In the next seven years there was an enormous immigration of 2.2 million from Europe. The major features of this wave of immigration are shown in Table 6.5 on page 104.

The first upsurge came from the British Isles. The British government proved itself utterly incompetent to cope with the famine in Ireland, and Joel Mokyr estimates that more than a million died there in the late 1840s as a result.[13] Those who could fled the Emerald Isle, either to other parts of the United Kingdom or to Canada or the United States. In the ten years 1846–55 inclusive, nearly 1.3 million Irish are known to have immigrated into the United States. Uncounted additional thousands came in across the Canadian border unrecorded. During the same decade, the German-speaking regions of Europe produced nearly 1 million immigrants to the United States. Political upheavals in 1848 contributed some famous names to this flow (e.g., Carl Schurz, later U.S. Senator from Missouri), but most of it was due to harvest failures, as is indicated by the fact that the flow of migrants from Scandinavia and other countries in northern Europe more than doubled before the wave died down at the end of the 1850s.

The main proportions of this flow, by countries of origin, are shown in Table 6.6. They are worth considering at this point because later on, when the

Table 6.4   Net Immigration as a Proportion of Population Increases 1800–60

Years	Percentage of Increase by Decade
1800–10	3.3
1810–20	2.6
1820–30	3.8
1830–40	11.7
1840–50	23.3
1850–60	31.1

Source: Calculated from Richard Easterlin, "Population," Davis et al., *American Economic Growth: An Economist's History of the United States* (New York: Harper & Row, 1972), Table 6.1.

Table 6.5 Immigration 1845–60 by Origin[a]

Year	Total	Great Britain	Ireland	Scandinavia	Other Northwestern Europe	Germany
1845	114.4	19.2	44.8	1.0	9.5	34.4
1846	154.4	22.2	51.8	2.0	12.3	57.6
1847	235.0	23.3	105.5	1.3	24.3	74.3
1848	226.5	35.2	112.9	1.1	9.9	58.5
1849	297.0	55.1	159.4	3.5	7.6	60.2
1850	370.0	51.1	164.0	1.6	11.5	78.9
1851	379.5	51.5	221.3	2.4	20.9	72.5
1852	371.6	40.7	159.5	4.1	11.3	145.9
1853	368.6	37.6	162.6	3.4	14.2	141.9
1854	427.8	58.6	101.6	4.2	23.1	215.0
1855	200.9	47.6	49.6	1.3	14.6	71.9
1856	200.4	44.7	54.3	1.3	12.4	71.0
1857	251.3	58.5	54.4	2.7	6.9	91.8
1858	123.1	29.0	26.9	2.7	4.6	45.3
1859	121.3	26.2	35.2	1.6	3.7	41.8
1860	153.6	29.7	48.6	0.8	5.3	54.5

[a] Counts are in thousands of persons.

Source: *Historical Statistics*, series C 89–119.

Table 6.6 Proportional Immigration 1845–60[a]

	(1) Great Britain	(2) Ireland	(3) Germany	(4) Columns 1 + 2	(5) Columns 1 + 2 + 3	(6) Columns 2 + 3	(7) All Other	(8) Total Columns 5 + 7
Year								
1845	16.8	39.2	30.1	56.0	86.1	69.3	13.9	100.0
1846	14.4	33.5	37.3	47.9	85.2	70.8	14.8	100.0
1847	9.9	44.9	31.6	54.8	86.4	76.5	13.6	100.0
1848	15.5	49.8	25.8	65.3	91.1	75.6	8.9	100.0
1849	18.6	53.7	20.3	72.3	92.6	74.0	7.4	100.0
1850	13.8	44.3	21.3	58.1	79.4	65.6	20.6	100.0
1851	13.6	58.3	19.1	71.9	91.0	77.4	9.0	100.0
1852	11.0	42.9	39.3	53.9	93.2	82.2	6.8	100.0
1853	10.2	44.1	38.5	54.3	92.8	82.6	7.2	100.0
1854	13.7	23.7	50.3	37.4	87.7	74.0	12.3	100.0
1855	23.7	24.7	35.8	48.4	84.2	60.5	15.8	100.0
1856	22.3	27.1	35.4	49.4	84.8	62.5	15.2	100.0
1857	23.3	21.6	36.5	44.9	81.4	58.1	18.6	100.0
1858	23.6	21.9	36.8	45.5	82.3	58.7	17.7	100.0
1859	21.6	29.0	34.5	50.6	85.1	63.5	14.9	100.0
1860	19.3	31.6	35.5	50.9	86.4	67.1	13.6	100.0

[a] Figures are percentages of total immigration, 1845–60.

Source: Table 6.5.

massive immigration from southern and eastern Europe is under way, we will see a growing mood of resistance to free immigration. Note that the United Kingdom's share (column 4) is more than 50 percent of the total in every year save 1846 and 1854. Note also that Ireland and Germany together (column 6) normally accounted for 65–75 percent of total immigration. The ordinary share in these years of just three countries (column 5) was from 79.4 to more than 90 percent. Other northern European nations accounted for most of the remaining immigration.

Based upon what we know of the colonial white population, which was mostly English- and German-speaking peoples (see Chapter 1), these immigrants should have been received congenially in America. But nativism resulted, with the Know-Nothings (members of a secret society whose main goal was to prevent "foreigners" from gaining political power) demanding a twenty-one year residency requirement for naturalization in the 1850s. These immigrants, like the millions that followed, stayed mainly in the urban areas and did not make a proportional contribution to taming the frontier. The impact, therefore, was concentrated, and social frictions increased.

The main bone of contention in the 1850s was religion. Between the Irish and the Catholic Rhineland Germans, the old nonconformist Protestant sects of the United States were about to be swamped by Roman Catholicism. There was talk that the nation would fall to the legions of Rome, to the Grand Army of the Papacy. Later on, when the countries of origin were Italy, Greece, and those of eastern Europe, the talk became straight racism. By then, the children of the Irish and German immigrants had joined the native white Americans in demanding an end to the flow of people from southern and eastern Europe.

Origins of the Atlantic Migration

The data in Table 6.5 record the first great migratory wave from Europe in the nineteenth century. More such waves would come. Between 1815 and 1914 an estimated 50 million persons emigrated out of Europe, and some 35 million were destined to come to the United States. Why? Brinley Thomas, in his great book, *Migration and Economic Growth,* fashioned an elegant explanation based upon European population growth, occupational and class rigidities in Europe

("non-competing groups"), the 18- to 20-year "long wave" cycles in such activities as investment and house-building; and free trade, free migration, and foreign investment.[14] We will treat his thesis in some detail in Chapter 16, but it is worth pausing and considering for a moment now because we have just seen the basic anatomy of the first of his cycles. He measured four major pre-1914 waves of Atlantic migration, with the last one ended by the outbreak of World War I. The dates of the long waves, trough to trough, are 1844–61, 1862–77, 1879–97, and 1898–1914.

Suffice it to say at this point that a combination of "push" from Europe (harvest failures) and "pull" from the United States (an expanding economy—recall the land-sales data for the 1850s) in the presence of continuously growing European population explains the wave of migration between 1844 and 1861. In Europe it meant fewer mouths to feed. What did it mean here in the United States?

The Walker and Uselding-Neal Theses

Again we shall anticipate Chapter 16 for a moment to consider briefly Francis Walker's thesis, the counter-proposals of Paul Uselding and Larry Neal, and the further reservations of Richard Easterlin and Robert Gallman. In the late nineteenth century Francis Walker—economist, statistician, and president of MIT—put forward the thesis that there was some maximum rate of population growth, given American conditions, and that the European migration filled places in that growth that would otherwise have been occupied by native-born Americans. Other things being equal, each European immigrant meant one less native American born into the population. Paul Uselding countered with two proposals: (a) the maximum growth rate never existed and (b) each European immigrant represented a capital transfer from Europe to America equal essentially to the cost of raising the migrant to the age of migration.[15] Since the immigrants were mainly young males ready to enter directly into the labor force, they were Europe's "gift" to American economic growth. We got the benefit without paying the cost. Our resources, therefore, were free to build the capital equipment these immigrants used in their work here.

Uselding traced the idea to the Italian statistician, Augostino De Vita, who argued that the great stock of capital characteristic of the American economy by 1914 was no more than the accumulated cost of rearing, feeding, educating, and transporting the millions of European migrants to the United States. The Atlantic migration had thus "freed" American resources and generated income, enabling the United States to pull ahead of the Europeans economically.

Uselding did not accept De Vita's bold conclusions but pursued the basic idea with several complex econometric models, using the known data concerning the immigration from 1839–1859. He concluded that, by 1859, the additional capital formation due to the immigration was within the range of 5 to 10 percent of the GNP. Professor Larry Neal joined him in the effort, and in 1972 they published a paper carrying the calculations from 1790 to 1912, concluding that the additional capital stock created by immigration fell into the range of 10 to 20 percent of GNP by the end of the period.[16] It was thus true, they argued, that the American economy grew faster than it otherwise would have grown because of the immigration. Robert Gallman, in a critical analysis of the Uselding-Neal work, pointed out various plausibilities, including that, by 1860, probably 35 percent of the adult males in the Northern states were foreign-born (he also noted that half the Union army was foreign-born).[17] A further contribution of immigrants is suggested by William Lazonick and Thomas Brush: The immigrants were more easily "driven" by foremen to greater effort and individual productivity increases than was true of native-born Americans.[18]

Gallman added an additional caveat to the Walker thesis: Since most of the immigrants stayed in the cities, occupying jobs that might have been done by native Americans, their migration to urban areas was less rapid than it would otherwise have been. Thus, *the native American birth rate was higher than it would have been* (urban birth rates being so much lower than rural) if the "places" in urban growth had been filled by native Americans. Easterlin added a number of objections to the Walker thesis but pointed out that the decline in native American birth rates was more likely due to the end of the frontier and the acceleration of urbanization than to any presumed economic competition with European immigrants.

We will return to these issues in Chapter 16 when we have seen the results of the subsequent three "long waves" in European immigration. Up to 1860, however, according to Uselding and Neal, the positive impact of immigration on U.S. economic growth was already strong.

Destinations of Immigrants Up to 1860

Census returns show that most of the pre-1860 European immigration went to the Northern states. In 1860, of a total population of 31.5 million, 3.6 million foreign-born whites lived in the Northeast and East-North-Central states, a mere 391,000 lived in the South, and 144,000 were located in the West, which had 64,000 individuals of "other races"—largely Chinese—by then. Table 6.7 shows the percentages in each region in 1850 and 1860 by nativity. Proportionately, the big increases in the white foreign-born population appeared in the North and the West. In the South, the proportional increase in the white foreign-born population was relatively small. At this time the black population was mainly in the South, in agriculture and in slavery. Was there a connection between the continuation of slavery in the South and the lack of significant European immigration there?

Table 6.7   U.S. Population: Nativity 1850 and 1860[a]

| Population | Northeast | | North Central | | South | | West | |
Segment	1850	1860	1850	1860	1850	1860	1850	1860
Native-born								
White	82.9	79.5	87.1	82.0	60.0	59.7	84.3	70.4
Nonwhite	1.7	1.4	0.9	0.8	37.3	36.8	0.5	0.7
Foreign-born								
White[b]	15.4	19.1	12.0	17.2	2.7	3.5	15.2	28.9

[a] Figures are percentages of regional totals for each census year rounded to the nearest 0.1%.
[b] Less than 0.1% of the foreign-born population was nonwhite.

Source: Calculated from *Historical Statistics*, series A 190–94.

THE END OF WHITE SERVITUDE AND CONTINUATION OF BLACK SLAVERY

The additional contribution of European immigration was to hasten the decline of white indentured servitude inherited from the colonial era. Even by the end of that period, white servitude was declining in competition with the free wage bargain in labor force recruitment. Rising demand for labor drove up the price of *nonfree* white labor compared to that of black slaves. The supply of indentured whites was thus more restricted than that of blacks.[19] Slavery continued to grow as white servitude diminished. David Galenson points out that white skilled workers became able to negotiate wages in the free market that were higher than the comparable real income derived from a contract of indenture.

Servitude and Competition

When the Constitution was being written, in 1787, white servitude still had to be taken into account. It lingered on for some decades as a social institution, used primarily to bind vagrants and orphans into productive employment and to enforce apprenticeships in trades. It finally died off in common usage in the 1820s when judges began to refuse to imprison people for debt. If the contract was not recoverable when breached, the contract lost its value. Negotiated wages were more efficient, especially when they were for long periods (up to a year), and any break by the employee before the time was up released the employer from the obligation to pay wages earned to date.[20] Such a contract was pretty much self-enforcing. Of course, the old ancillary obligations of indenture—such as board, room, clothing, medicine, education in a trade, and payment at the end of the indenture—did not apply with hired labor. The steady, and increasing, flow of free immigrants entering the labor market made white indentures unnecessary, and they slowly vanished.

Apprehension About Slavery

With black slavery, of course, the tide of history ran the other way. Eli Whitney's invention of the cotton gin in 1793 made the short-staple upland cotton grown in the South a new bonanza, and so the South's major agricultural labor form—slavery—evolved with cotton cultivation. We will go more deeply into this topic in

Chapters 10 and 12. For now it will be sufficient to note the consequences in terms of overall population trends. For a country mainly occupied in 1860 by Europeans, the United States was unusual, if not unique, in having some 13 percent of its total population owned in chattel slavery. However, the whole world benefitted economically from that slavery, wherever the cotton cloth of the factories of Europe and America was bought.

The enslavement of Africans in the United States began in 1619 at Jamestown when a Dutch man-of-war sold the colonists twenty African prisoners. Slave codes developed that made the black slaves servants for life and their children born into slavery. By the end of the colonial period the country was faced with a social, political, and human problem that vexed the best thinkers. With more than half a million slaves in 1780, most of them concentrated in the South, the way out was unclear. George Washington said in 1794 of his own situation as a slave owner: "Were it not then, that I am principled against selling . . . [slaves] as you would do cattle in the market, I would not, in twelve months from this date be possessed of one, as a slave."[21]

Before Whitney's gin there was much sentiment in the South against slavery and a belief that it could not last. The decline of the older tobacco-growing regions threatened to produce a surplus of slave labor in those areas. Diversified farming, which used less labor than had tobacco, was spreading. But there also was deep fear of any change. Straightforward emancipation (unless compensated by nonslave owners, as the British would do in 1834) would mean great capital losses to slave owners. There was also the question, unanswered then because it was untried, whether there could be any peaceful future with former slaves settled among their former masters. Jefferson expressed his fears in *Notes on the State of Virginia:*

> Deep rooted prejudice entertained by the whites; ten thousand recollections by the blacks, of the injuries they have sustained; new provocations; the real distinctions which nature has made; and many other circumstances, will divide us into parties, and produce convulsions which will probably never end but in the extermination of the one or the other races. . . .

Even more dramatically, he wrote elsewhere his most frequently quoted dread of slavery's consequences: "I tremble for my country, when I reflect that God is just; that his justice cannot sleep forever.''

It slept a bit longer, though, as Whitney's gin loosed the cotton culture upon the Southern states.

Expansion of Slavery

Cotton did not set fears at rest, but it did make the old South's ''peculiar institution'' marvelously profitable. In 1784 eight bales of American cotton had been seized in Liverpool on grounds of false documentation— everyone knew you couldn't grow commercial quantities of cotton in the United States! In 1792 American cotton exports were 138,000 pounds; in 1794, 1.6 million pounds. By 1800 we exported 18 million pounds, and a new way of life was about to begin. The rush into new cotton lands carried the slave system with it. Alabama, Mississippi, western Georgia, Louisiana, East Texas—all got cotton, and all got slavery as the labor system designed to grow it.

Even though *most Southern whites owned no slaves,* it is surprising how evenly the slave population came to be distributed among the Southern states (see the data in Table 6.8). In the newer areas the increase was most dramatic. Slaves in 1860 were more than 50 percent of the populations of South Carolina and Mississippi and well over 40 percent in Alabama, Georgia, and Louisiana. Widespread as ownership was, proportional ownership within those states actually declined in the 1860s as slave prices rose.[22]

Law and Political Compromise

As a form of labor, American slavery has rarely been acclaimed as a paradigm for others to follow.[23] In Chapter 1 we saw Chancellor Kent's view of it as a legal matter. In law the slaves simply were ''things or property, rather than persons, and are vendible as personal estate.''[24] Black slavery was history's intellectual handicap that scarred the land of Jefferson and Madison.

By 1860 it was mainly a Southern problem, but there had been slavery and slaves in every part of the country earlier. The South simply could not find a way out of it. Modern Americans sometimes find it unreal that just a century and a quarter separates them from slave society. In the North, where slavery had not taken hold so firmly, most slaves were freed by degrees, and the system vanished. In the old Middle colonies the process of freeing the slaves was slow, but it was mainly finished by 1860. Black exclusion laws, forbidding the settlement there of freed slaves, were in force in most Northern states in the hope of avoiding the race problem as more slaves got their freedom in the South.

The courts, following the reservation of powers to the states, continued more or less automatically to enforce slave codes and laws, upholding slavery. In the Dred Scott decision in 1857, the courts returned a black to Southern slavery and in the process did yeoman service to the cause of civil war. The political system had attempted to compromise again and again—in 1820 (the Missouri Compromise), in 1850

Table 6.8 Southern Slave Population, 1790–1860[a]

Year	Virginia	South Carolina	North Carolina	Georgia	Mississippi	Alabama	Louisiana
1790	292.6	107.1	100.8	29.3	—[b]	—	—
1800	345.8	146.2	133.3	59.4	3.5	—	—
1810	392.5	196.4	168.8	105.2	17.1	—	34.7
1820	425.1	258.5	204.9	149.7	32.8	41.9	69.1
1830	469.8	315.4	245.6	217.5	65.7	117.5	109.6
1840	449.0	327.0	245.8	280.9	195.2	253.5	168.5
1850	472.5	385.0	288.5	381.7	309.9	342.8	244.8
1860	490.9	402.4	331.1	462.2	436.6	435.1	331.7

[a] Figures are for thousands of persons, 1790–1860.
[b] No data.

Source: Harold D. Woodman, ed., *Slavery and the Southern Economy: Sources and Readings* (New York: Harcourt, Brace & World, 1966), Table 2, p. 13.

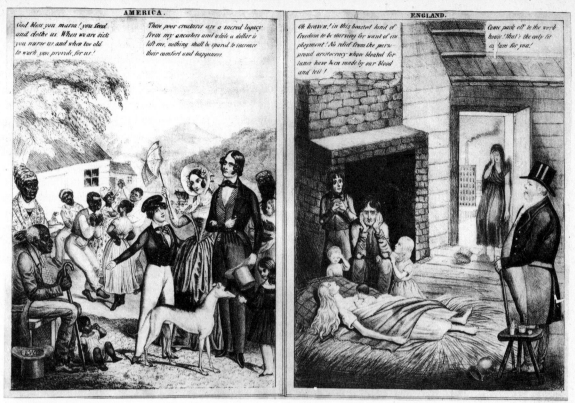

A proslavery cartoon illustrates the advantages of slavery for American blacks compared to working-class life in industrial England.

when California was admitted to the Union, and in the Kansas-Nebraska Act of 1854 (''popular sovereignty''). But in the end, no compromise prevailed. War did.

Slavery and European Immigration

We see the differing fates of colonial America's two unfree systems of labor. One died out as it became uneconomical, while the other thrived precisely because it became so economical. The system of free wage labor in the North flourished as immigrant labor poured into the Northern cities by the tens of thousands, then millions. As we have seen, European immigrants did not seek out the South before 1860, perhaps because it had few cities of any size before that time. Scholars often write that the immigrants shunned competition with slave labor. It is more than likely that, coming into the country relatively poor, they went where they could find jobs with the greatest

ease and least cost. Primarily that was in the cities where they landed or inland along established transport routes.

For the most part, the European immigrants shunned agricultural labor as their ticket to the good life. Few of them had sufficient funds to buy land before 1860. Even in 1910, of the foreign-born stock in the labor force, only 13 percent were in farming; 87 percent had chosen other employments. It may well be true, of course, that immigrants had a distaste for slave labor not shared by native Americans and so shunned places where it existed, but this question is strictly academic. Given the *numbers* of slaves in 1780, the nature of the constitutional settlement, the evolution of law and institutions, and the growth of slave population, it is difficult to imagine that European immigrants could have voluntarily gone south into agricultural labor in numbers sufficient to have made slavery unprofitable. It is not even obvious that slavery would be unprofitable now, if it were not illegal.[25]

LABOR IN AMERICAN SOCIETY BEFORE 1860

By 1860 those in the U.S. labor force, counting all persons over 10 years of age, numbered just over 11 million, about 35 percent of the total population. Roughly 79 percent of these (58 percent free and 21 percent slave) were engaged in agriculture. Within 40 years, the proportion in agriculture would be cut in half. The rise of manufacturing, transportation, construction, and services would account for this change, and it would continue. Today agriculture accounts for a mere 3 percent of total employment, and services and transportation for roughly 66 percent. So far as employment is concerned, modern economic growth consists of rising efficiency in the production of food and goods (including trading for them) at such a pace that most labor and capital are "freed" for other employments. Even by 1860 we are able to see the beginnings of this process.

The Lebergott-Weiss Labor Force Data

It is to Professor Stanley Lebergott's pioneering work on labor force data and to Professor Thomas Weiss' careful reworking of the data that we owe the information in Table 6.9. Note that employment in agriculture grew at a slower rate than did the total labor force; the agricultural labor force has been a declining share of the total. In the 1850s employment in manufacturing grew at a greater rate (42.5 percent) than that in agriculture (28.8 percent), but at only a slightly greater rate than the total labor force (37.8 percent). By contrast, in the 1840s, manufacturing employment grew more rapidly than any other sector (123.2 percent), increasing its share of total employment from 8.9 percent to 14.0 percent. The relative slowdown in the growth of manufacturing employment in the decade of the 1850s probably reflects three forces at work: (a) the renewed land boom in the early part of the decade followed by depression after the panic of 1857; (b) construction, services, and transportation also expanded at comparatively unheard-of rates as millions of new immigrants flooded into the urban labor force; and (c) textile manufacturing growth slowed, while heavy industry had not yet begun its great expansion (which came in the 1870s).

The service sector grew quite rapidly in the 1840s (55.8 percent) and 1850s (62.9 percent). One reason for this is that services include transportation and trade. These two industries accounted for just over one-quarter of the service sector in 1840 and just under one-third in 1860. The other sector is the sum of employment in construction, fishing, and mining. Between 1840 and 1860 the labor force in construction

Table 6.9 Labor Force Distribution 1800–60

Year	Total	Ag	Non-Ag	Mfg	Ser	Other
			(in thousands of employed persons)			
1800	1712	1274	438	—[a]	—	—
1810	2337	1690	647	—	—	—
1820	3150	2249	901	—	—	—
1830	4272	2982	1290	—	—	—
1840	5778	3882	1896	513	1037	346
1850	8192	4889	3303	1145	1616	542
1860	11290	6299	4991	1632	2632	727
			(in percentages)			
1800	100	74.4	25.6	—	—	—
1810	100	72.3	27.7	—	—	—
1820	100	71.4	28.6	—	—	—
1830	100	69.8	30.2	—	—	—
1840	100	67.2	32.8	8.9	17.9	6.0
1850	100	59.7	40.3	14.0	19.7	6.6
1860	100	55.8	44.2	14.5	23.3	6.4

[a] No data.

Source: Derived from Stanley Lebergott, *Manpower in Economic Growth: The American Record Since 1800* (New York: McGraw-Hill, 1964), p. 510; and Thomas Weiss, "U.S. Labor Force Estimates and Economic Growth," in R. Gallman and J. Wallis, editors, *American Economic Growth and Standards of Living Before the Civil War* (Chicago: University of Chicago Press, 1992), pp. 37, 51.

grew by 79.3 percent; fishing, by 29.2 percent; and mining, by 450 percent. The enormous growth in mining is attributable to the growth of iron and coal as inputs in American manufacturing.

Professor Lebergott argues this labor force distribution represents mainly the *domestic demand* for output since, at its peak before 1860, employment in the production of raw cotton (our leading export) accounted for little more than 5 percent of the labor force while exports as a whole (including cotton) probably did not employ more than 10 percent.[26] Unlike most countries experiencing rapid economic growth and development in the nineteenth century, the demand for labor in the United States would be dictated by the domestic economy. This began before the Civil War and would continue to do so for the rest of the century.

Early Organized Labor Activities

Before 1860, those who were not owners of land or other real assets primarily were engaged in selling their labor. They were selling in an expanding market, to be sure, but one in which large-scale immigration meant increasing competition. As was true of other sellers, they sought to create collective goods through labor organization.[27] In this effort, they faced great obstacles.

Labor in colonial America was largely servile. (Remember who worked for others in the colonial economy and who worked for themselves.) The common law and its enforcement was meant primarily for the protection of rights in real property and in chattel goods, although those in skilled trades attained a fairly solid social base. Their skills were many times recognized by special laws protecting entry into their trades, and they enjoyed a fairly widespread system of guilds. But in these guilds, the roles of worker, master (employer), manufacturer, and even merchant were mixed up with each other. One of the most significant developments in the world of laboring people before the Civil War was the emergence of clear differentiations of these roles. This took place in the early textile mills and factories, especially as more goods were made commercially and outside the home. Increasing numbers of urban centers meant more widespread retailing by specialists, who bought from producers and even from wholesale merchants.

One of our first recorded labor strikes, that of the New York bakers in 1741, was the refusal of those who owned the equipment and flour to bake and sell bread at a price set by municipal authority. Employer and employee roles were still intermingled. In the 1805 strike of the Philadelphia cordwainers (tried in 1806), it was the journeymen against the masters in the same guild. The same was true of the strike of the Pittsburgh cordwainers in 1815. In both cases the court held, in accord with the common law, that a formal combination of journeymen against masters was a criminal conspiracy. It was not until the Massachusetts case of *Commonwealth* v *Hunt* (1842) that the criminal conspiracy doctrine was dropped from automatic application in American labor law. Chief Justice Lemual Shaw ruled:

> We think, therefore that associations may be entered into, the object of which is to adopt measures that may have a tendency to impoverish another, that is, to diminish his gains and profits, and yet so far from being criminal or unlawful, the object may be highly meritorious and public-spirited.[28]

An attempt to organize workers on a national scale, the National Trades Union, vanished after the panic of 1837. The early labor organizations were largely a mishmash of secret society hocus-pocus, political agitation, and cooperative economic ventures. By 1860, only about 5000 workers belonged to what are today called *labor unions,* and these unions' powers to improve the lives of their members by collective action were nil, so far as we know. Nevertheless, organizing activity was at times brisk; Philadelphia and New York both had citywide trades union councils. The competitive ethos—"competition is the life of trade"—worked against labor organizations while the nonagricultural labor force was so small. Also, early American unions were not destined to succeed as political organizations in the relatively classless American democracy. It would be a hard-nosed labor organization, devoted to bread-and-butter issues, that finally would succeed in establishing itself; the American Federation of Labor in 1886.

However, the adoption in state after state of mechanic lien laws early in the nineteenth century indicated that property rights in labor that were recognized by law and society at large were possible, despite the colonial background. As Chancellor Kent described *mechanic lien laws* in 1826: "It is now the general rule, that every bailee for hire, who by his labor and skill, has imparted an additional value to the goods, has a lien upon the property for his reasonable charges."[29] Such ideas were fitting in Jacksonian America, and their appearance was an omen of the recognition labor rights were to receive later.

Finally, a national market for labor developed as the country's geographic expansion continued. Laborers (apart from slaves and indentured servants) were free to migrate from low-wage areas to high-wage areas or to the moving frontier, where new settlements were steadily springing up. Transportation improvements (discussed in Chapter 9) hastened this process, but a single wage level for any given grade of labor (the characteristic of a perfect market) was never achieved, not then or now. Labor markets were not perfectly competitive in the early nineteenth century, nor are they today.

Education

According to Albert Fishlow, American efforts to educate their pre-1860 labor force consumed perhaps 1 percent of the GNP (compared to perhaps 8 percent today).[30] Common schools, publicly supported, were relatively widespread in the North by the 1850s, although they still were rare in most of the South. Lebergott estimates that, even by 1870, the average school child in the northern states was in a classroom only three months each year. On the other hand, even as scarce as it was, education seems to have been more readily available in America than it was in Europe. By 1850 the United States actually led the world with an average of 18 percent of its population enrolled in schools of some sort. (Germany was second with 16 percent. The United Kingdom had 12 percent.) In New England the proportion was even higher.

Nathan Rosenberg, in his book *Technology and American Economic Growth,* emphasizes the peculiar effectiveness of this primary education, as far as economic development before the Civil War was concerned.[31] It was technology, not science, that was needed, and the common schools seem to have served—at least better than anything else. Lebergott and Rosenberg both hold, in fact, that the easy adaptability of American workers and mechanics to technical change in the early nineteenth century was due in large part to high literacy and numeracy not connected to preconceived notions of how economic processes

ought to be carried out. Lack of a thorough educational structure beyond the "three Rs" perhaps had its advantages.

POPULATION EXPANSION AND OVERALL ECONOMIC GROWTH

At this point we should consider for a moment the current state of information about the growth of real output per capita of population. The problem is that the data are almost too poor to be accepted with confidence, despite ingenious explorations by a number of gifted scholars.

Sources of Early Growth

We are dealing with a long period (1607–1860) that lacks scope for the development of sources of growth of the kind we later find, such as great new industrial innovations in industries that form the dynamic core of an integrated commercial economy. For most of the period before 1860, we have an economy, apart from the small industrial sector, using techniques known for centuries and spread over a vast area with poor internal transportation. Indeed, as Douglass North argued, there really were three separate economies—Northeast, South, and West.[32] How could economic growth occur in this sort of world? There is no doubt that there was growth of output per capita in the colonial economy and then continued substantial growth before 1860. Since agriculture was still of overwhelming importance until at least the 1850s, the question is a difficult one.

The answer seems to be that growth was the result of a multitude of small local improvements. Better livestock strains, more appropriate field crops adapted to climate and soils, capital accumulation (giving each succeeding generation more productive "tools" to work with), even movement from poor to better land would yield growth, if the process were more or less continuous. Even on the same land, more settlement (if the soil was not exhausted) could, for some period of time, contribute to rising productivity as the trees were felled, rocks were cleared, fields were expanded, ditches and drainage were improved, roads were made more passable, access to water transport was improved, bridges and ferries were built. Improved organization, together with efficient structures (like those enabling improved turnaround times for colonial shipping) could raise output per head. So could external economies, although their effect was slight before the 1820s or so. Even better storage facilities (barns and granaries, for example), reducing losses of stored crops, would raise output per head. The economic history of these early times is filled with such suggested sources of increased overall productivity. There were substantial advances in manufacturing also, but that sector was too small to have real overall impact.

Conflicting and Complementary Views

Obviously growth had to occur after the "starving time" in Virginia and the first terrible years on the Massachusetts shore. In 1964 George Rogers Taylor conjectured that most colonial growth occurred in the eighteenth century and that the seventeenth century was a time of relative stagnation in per capita terms, although, of course, there was aggregate growth to support rapid population growth.[33] Terry Anderson has surveyed later improvements in the data and rejects Taylor's conjecture, arguing that expansion of real wealth per capita (reflecting real income increases) from about 1650 to 1710 was at about 1.6 percent per annum, a respectable rate even by modern standards.[34] Growth then slowed for about eighty years. The slowdown was due to a *decline* in productivity in agriculture. Marc Egnal finds that colonial growth in 1720–75 was perhaps 0.5 percent per annum, and Duane Bell and Gary Walton would reduce that figure to 0.3 percent.[35] Both estimates agree with Anderson's slowdown thesis for eighteenth-century growth. Also, both of the latter estimates fall within the range of overall growth of 0.3–0.5 percent per annum in 1710–1840 postulated by Robert Gallman.[36]

Alan Kulikoff finds a similar poor record of growth in the eighteenth century in the Chesapeake colonies until the 1750s and then some improvement up to 1776.[37] Anderson suggests that the decline in growth in the colonial period after 1710 *had* to be an as-yet unmeasured high cost of "membership in the British empire."[38] One obvious candidate for that cost would be the policies that kept the colonists out of the Ohio Valley and in the poorer regions of the Atlantic Seaboard.

So, what happened after independence and the way west slowly opened? Most scholars agree that the first

decade or so, up to 1790 at least, was a difficult time, with little net growth. Then improvement occurred, but in patterns that are still in dispute among the experts. Paul David comes out for a strong overall annual growth rate in 1790–1860 of perhaps 1.3 percent.[39] By 1840, says David, real product per capita was already 60 percent above that of 1790. But an equally eminent expert, Robert Gallman, considers David's rate of increase too high.[40] Diane Lindstrom, in a study based on the Philadelphia area, finds evidence to support George Rogers Taylor's conjecture for the early nineteenth century that growth came slowly from the late colonial era and then accelerated around 1840.[41] She does not agree with David's studies that show surges of growth in long cycles interspersed with periods of relative secular stagnation.

Apart from the continuing need for better data, the most important issues are (a) the Anderson thesis that a slowdown occurred after the rapid growth between 1650 and 1710 and (b) the question of how the expansion formed itself between 1790 and 1860, whether by slow but accelerating growth or by bursts of economic vigor followed by intervals of lassitude, as David suggests.[42]

INCOME AND WEALTH DISTRIBUTION BY 1860

We have only fragmentary data on the distribution of income and wealth from the end of the colonial period (see Chapter 3) to the Civil War. Foreign visitors in this period remarked on the social and political egalitarianism of antebellum America and assumed that it must have a common basis in a widespread equality of economic condition. And why not? Land was the primary income-earning asset—and, in the North, the major form of wealth—and it was readily available. Rapid economic and spatial expansion provided abundant opportunities in life for new ventures of all kinds. There had been few chances yet for a class of wealth owners to appear that could sustain itself by inheritance alone, outside of the slave-owning South. But even in colonial times, as we already have seen, there was the inevitable bunching of wealth. Equality of economic condition was more apparent in manners and dress than in the realities of probate records. Growth of income was destined to be unequally distributed.

Atack and Bateman have shown that wealth in 1860 in the rural Northern areas was more equally distributed than in the cities, or in the rural South, and more equally distributed than it later would be.[43] They suggest that a large portion of westward migration came from middle-income farm families who, fairly equal in wealth holding even before they migrated westward, tended to perpetuate the Jeffersonian ideal of a sturdy yeomanry without great wealth differentials among themselves. However, even in northern rural areas, there was unequal distribution. The poorer rural families tended to be headed by women, recent immigrants, young people, or the aged. The picture of the ideal rural America of the antebellum period is summed up thusly: "To be wealthy in this egalitarian society of historical tradition was to be a middle-aged, native-born, white, literate, male farmer."[44]

With the rapid growth of population, real income growth *per capita* was substantial enough. As we have seen, Paul David estimated that it grew at about 1.3 percent per annum from 1790 to 1850 (1.77 percent after 1820).[45] After 1850, there seems to have been some acceleration. There were significant regional differences in growth rates. Richard Easterlin's estimates of levels of income by region are shown in Table 6.10.

These data have been variously grouped and interpreted over the years for different purposes.[46] If they are taken seriously at all, they seem to show the following clearly: New England strongly, and the Middle Atlantic and East-North-Central states barely, grew more rapidly than did other regions between 1840 and 1860. Income per capita was higher than the national average

in the West-South-Central states in 1840 and in 1860, but less so in 1860. Moreover, New England and the Middle Atlantic States had higher per capita and more rapidly rising income in 1860 than did the West-South-Central states. The Old South and the newer states of the high plains were the poorer areas in 1840, and they were poorer still, comparatively, in 1860. Some parts of the South, the best cotton-growing areas, were exceptions to this general pattern, and we will deal with them later. The point here is that even regional differences in the pace of economic growth would most likely ensure unequal overall income distribution—the mean-income family in New England would have had a higher money income than the average family in the South Atlantic Region. The evidence we now have indicates that both income and wealth distributions were *more unequal* by 1860 than they had been at the end of the colonial period.

The data for income distribution are very poor in most of the years before the Civil War, but the ingenuity of scholarship has produced valuable inferences from what there is. In particular, Jeffrey Williamson's work on real income goes some distance toward explaining the increased inequality of wealth distribution, for which we have somewhat better data.

Williamson measures implied real incomes of unskilled urban workers and "the rich" from evidence of relative prices of commodities consumer by different income classes between 1820 and 1860. He finds a striking increase in inequality. The reasons seem to be fairly simple: Productivity from machine-made products increased more rapidly than was the case for food and other items traditionally consumed by the poor. Therefore, those in higher income brackets benefitted the most, up to 1860, from productivity increases. Also, secular demand increases for unskilled labor were easily filled by immigrants and those moving to urban areas from agriculture.[47] Even though real and money wages for the unskilled rose, they increased less than did those for skilled workers and others in higher income brackets. The relatively sluggish rise in real wages for the unskilled over several decades would have contributed to a more unequal wealth distribution, other things being equal.

Williamson and Peter Lindert find that the increasing inequality of wealth distribution up to 1860 was marked (strongest from the 1820s to the late 1840s).[48] For example, the top 10 percent of all wealth holders in

Table 6.10   Regional Personal Income per Capita as Percentages of the National Average

Regions	1840	1860
New England	132	143
Middle Atlantic	136	137
East North Central	67	69
West North Central	75	66
South Atlantic	70	65
East South Central	73	68
West South Central	144	115
Total U.S.	100	100

Source: Richard Easterlin, "Regional Income Trends, 1840–1850," *American Economic History,* edited by Seymour Harris (New York: McGraw-Hill, 1961).

1774, according to Alice Jones' figures, held just under 50 percent of total real wealth.[49] Williamson and Lindert find that in 1860, the top 10 percent's share had increased to more than 70 percent. Williamson and Lindert questioned the plausibility of such a large shift in wealth distribution but have found that it is "no mirage." Data errors cannot account for it. Moreover, no single, simple explanation can account for it either. There are several outstanding wealth distribution explanations that they have found unconvincing. We will discuss three of them.

First is the relative-income movement argument, which is implied by Williamson's previous work.[50] Wealth is the sum over time of net saving. Other things being equal, Williamson's data indicate that the unskilled (and, by implication, lower income) families would have had less (proportional) opportunity to accumulate wealth from savings up to 1860 than did those better off financially. Why? Well, for example, as real incomes rise, the proportion spent on food falls. Since the wealthy spent proportionately more of their incomes on machine-made products, whose prices fell relatively, there was in this group a greater possibility for wealth accumulation.[51]

The second explanation is that the increasing age of Americans would have meant simply that a large proportion of the population was old enough by 1860 to have accumulated property (in 1820 the median age of males was 16.6 years; it was 19.8 in 1860). Williamson and Lindert are unimpressed by these possibilities, as they are by our third theory: that urbanization produced a great rise in "rent" as populations concentrated on small amounts of land and that urban land has always been unequally held. Wealth was most unequally distributed in the cities in 1860, followed by the rural South, and then rural areas elsewhere. Farmers on the average were the wealthiest Americans in 1860, and in the South, wealth concentration increased from 1790 to 1860 as a smaller proportion of families acquired more and more of the main form of wealth, slaves. But it must be admitted that none of these explanations appears to be sufficient, especially since increasing concentration ceased after the Civil War.[52] Nor can immigration trends explain it, as Lee Soltow points out.[53]

We seem to be in the presence of a considerable mystery of historiography for now. There is no doubt that unequal wealth and income distribution, as long as there is sufficient wealth at all, is correlated with high economic growth in the early stages of development.[54] So, the trends of income and wealth distribution up to 1860 underpinned the nation's main interest, growth and development. Mrs. Frances Trollope, who didn't like the United States much, made the following observations of the citizens of Cincinnati in 1829:

> Some of the native political economists assert that this rapid conversion of a bear-brake into a prosperous city, is the result of free political institutions . . . a more obvious cause suggested itself to me, in the unceasing goad which necessity applies to industry in this country, and in the absence of all resource for the idle. During nearly two years that I resided in Cincinnati, or its neighborhood, I neither saw a beggar, nor a man of sufficient fortune to permit his ceasing his efforts to increase it; thus every bee in the hive is actively employed in search of that honey . . . vulgarly called money; neither art, science, learning nor pleasure can seduce them from its pursuit.[55]

Growth was what was wanted. With ability being unequally distributed and luck probably dealt at random, unequal rewards are not surprising in a country with few mechanisms for taxing and redistribution. There would appear to be evidence, indirect, in favor of the growing antebellum inequality from a different source: physiological data.

The Evidence of Stature

If all classes of the population had equal access to all kinds of nutrition, and equal information about its effects, then, *ceteris paribus,* one would expect those who were malnourished were so because of income constraints upon outlays for nutrition. That is, populations would not voluntarily impose malnutrition in any degree upon themselves if they had an option—we can assume there were not calorie-deficient diet fads at work among the poor only in the antebellum period. However, the reader should be cautioned about the ambiguities of dietary information. In our own time alcoholics, chainsmokers, lovers of cholesterol-laden fast foods, ruin their nutrition voluntarily. For no greater outlays they could, after all, subsist on raw carrots, milk created from soybeans, and other such healthful foods. Professor Lebergott wrote the following about the dietary data of more recent times.

A major 1965 U.S. Department of Agriculture survey showed that: 14 percent of American families with incomes below $3,000 failed to get enough calories. To this depressing finding, the survey added another: 10 percent of American families with incomes above $10,000 a year also failed to get enough calories. . . . the differences between the two percentages lacking calories . . . is remarkably small. This suggests that something else is at work besides differences in income."[56]

With that much of a caveat, let us now consider the implications of some remarkable new research findings.

The death rate per 1000 had fallen to 23 by 1850 (compared to 40 in 1700).[57] The general rise in well-being in the nation's predominantly rural population had accounted for most of this improvement. Yet new research has shown a decline in heights and a shortening of life-expectancy on the average for those born between 1820 and 1860.[58] There seems to be no doubt that a setback in nutritional standards accounts for this phenomenon. John Komlos' comparison of West Point cadets and the students at Harvard seem to be conclusive on this point.[59] West Point cadets lost about 3.5 centimeters in height between those born in the 1820s and those born in the 1850s. Moreover, the West Point cadets of the mid-century, only about 5'5" tall, were also underweight, many weighing in the range of 100 to 120 pounds. Contemporary Harvard students did not display either characteristic, loss of height or of weight. Komlos notes that food prices rose in the range of from 20 to 40 per cent in the antebellum period. Ordinary families made "inadequate" dietary substitutes, as a result, that parents of Harvard students apparently did not make. One hesitates to ascribe entirely to relative poverty what may have been largely the results of nutritional ignorance. But as Fogel's work shows, by the mid-eighteenth century Americans had already achieved "modern heights," so the early nineteenth century dip in average stature must represent nutritional "insults" that were made up later in the century as per capita income rose, no matter how unequally distributed.[60] On the face of it, this new physiological evidence implies that Lindert and Williamson would seem to have the upper hand in this argument, at least for now.

Notes

1. Robert Fogel, "Nutrition and the Decline in Mortality Since 1700: Some Preliminary Findings," in Stanley L. Engerman and Robert E. Gallman, editors, *Long-Term Factors in American Economic Growth,* NBER *Studies in Income and Wealth,* vol. 51 (Chicago, The University of Chicago Press, 1986), p. 440. Fogel shows that American death rates per 1000 were 40 in 1700 compared to 28 in the UK that year. By 1850 the U.S. death rate was down to 23 compared to 24 in the UK.
2. Richard Easterlin, "Population Change and Farm Settlement in the Northern United States," *JEH,* March 1976.
3. Yasukichi Yasuba, *Birth Rates of the White Population in the United States, 1800–1860: An Economic Study* (1962), pp. 158–59.
4. Michael R, Haines and Barbara A. Anderson, "New Demographic History of the Late 19th-Century United States," *EEH,* October 1988, p. 342.
5. New territory in this period includes the Louisiana Purchase (1803) and the Oregon (1846) and Mexican (1848, 1853) acquisitions. The year 1850, it could be argued, was too close in time to the new land acquisitions to affect vital statistics.
6. For an extended argument along these lines, see Richard Easterlin, "Population Change and Farm Settlement in The Northern United States;" Richard H. Steckel, "Antebellum Southern White Fertility: A Demographic and Economic Analysis," *JEH,* June 1980; or Don R. Leet, "The Determinants of Fertility Transition in Antebellum Ohio," *JEH,* June 1976.
7. Jeremy Atack and Fred Bateman, in *To Their Own Soil* (1987), pp. 49–55, generally underscore these findings comparing the midwest to New England: more children were born to women in the years of highest fertility (16–44) in the midwest than in the northeast, and among all populations, fertility was lowest in New England.
8. Richard Steckel, in work we will be discussing in chapter 12 below, argues that the *absolute* levels of fertility rates among slave women must have been *much* higher (on his evidence, perhaps twice as high), than among contemporary white women, and much higher than we had previously thought.
9. Morton Owen Shapiro, "A Land Availability Model of Fertility Changes in the Rural Northern United States, 1760–1870," *JEH,* September 1982.

10. Paul A. David and William A. Sundstrom, "Bargains, Bequests, and Births: An Essay on Intergenerational Conflict, Reciprocity, and the Demand for Children in Agrarian Societies," Stanford Project on the History of Fertility Control, Working Paper No. 12. We are indebted to the authors for permission to cite this work.

11. Robert E. Gallman, "Human Capital in the First 80 Years of the Republic: How Much Did America Owe the Rest of the World?" *AER,* February 1977.

12. Robert Fogel and Stanley Engerman, *Time on the Cross: The Economics of American Negro Slavery,* vol. 1 (Boston: Little, Brown, 1974), pp. 23–24.

13. Joel Mokyr, "The Deadly Fungus," in J. L. Simon, ed., *Research in Population Economics* (Greenwich, CT: JAI Press, 1980), p. 248.

14. Brinley Thomas, *Migration and Economic Growth* (1954).

15. Paul Uselding, "Conjectural Estimates of Gross Human Capital Inflow to the American Economy," *EEH,* Fall 1971.

16. Larry Neal and Paul Uselding, "Immigration, A Neglected Source of American Economic Growth: 1790–1912," *Oxford Economic Papers,* March 1972.

17. Robert E. Gallman, "Human Capital in the First 80 Years of the Republic," p. 31. The estimate is based on the work of Lee Soltow, *Men and Wealth in the United States, 1850–1870* (1975).

18. William Lazonick and Thomas Brush, "The 'Horndal Effect' and Early US Manufacturing," *EEH,* January 1985.

19. David Galenson, "White Servitude and the Growth of Black Slavery in Colonial America," *JEH,* March 1981.

20. Morton Horwitz, *The Transformation of American Law, 1780–1860* (Cambridge: Harvard University Press, 1977), p. 186.

21. Quoted in Harold D. Woodman, ed., *Slavery and the Southern Economy: Sources and Readings* (New York: Harcourt Brace & World, 1966), p. 3.

22. Gavin Wright, *The Political Economy of the Cotton South: Household, Markets, and Wealth in the Nineteenth Century* (New York: Norton, 1978), pp. 34, 42.

23. See, for example, Stanley Elkins, *Slavery: A Problem in American Intellectual and Institutional Life* (Chicago: University of Chicago Press, 1959), chapter 3, for psychological comparison with World War II Nazi death camps.

24. James Kent, *Commentaries on American Law* (Boston: Little, Brown & Co., 1873), ch. 1, fn. 12.

25. In January 1982, three men who worked as bosses of farm laborers and who had hired from the ranks of illegal immigrants were sentenced to long prison terms for charges that included slavery.

26. Stanley Lebergott, "Labor Force," in Davis et al., *American Economic Growth: An Economist's History of the United States* (New York: Harper & Row, 1972), p. 191.

27. See Mancur Olson, *The Logic of Collective Action: Public Goods and the Theory of Groups* (1971), ch. III, on this characteristic activity of labor organizations.

28. Stephen J. Mueller, *Labor Law and Legislation* (Cincinnati: Southwestern Publishing Co., 1949). p. 42.

29. Kent, *Commentaries on American Law,* vol. 2, p. 914.

30. Albert Fishlow, "Levels of Nineteenth Century American Investment in Education," *JEH,* December 1966.

31. The data are Richard Easterlin's, presented in Nathan Rosenberg's *Technology and American Economic Growth* (1971), Table 1. For his discussion on the effectiveness of the common school education, see chapter II, "The Economic Matrix," in that volume.

32. Douglass C. North, *The Economic Growth of the United States 1790–1860* (1966), ch. IX–XII; Richard Sutch, "Douglass North and the New Economic History," in Roger L. Ransom, Richard Sutch and Gary Walton, eds., *Explorations in the New Economic History: Essays in Honor of Douglass C. North* (1982), ch. 2; Lloyd Mercer, "The Antebellum Regional Trade Hypothesis: A Reexamination of Theory and Evidence," in the same volume, ch. 4.

33. George Rogers Taylor, "American Economic Growth Before 1840: An Exploratory Essay," *JEH,* December 1964.

34. Terry Anderson, "Economic Growth in Colonial New England: Statistical Renaissance," *JEH,* March 1979.

35. Marc Egnal, "The Economic Development of the Thirteen Continental Colonies, 1720 to 1775," *William and Mary Quarterly,* April 1975. Duane Bell and Gary Walton, "Agricultural Productivity Change in Eighteenth Century Pennsylvania," *JEH,* March 1976.

36. Robert Gallman, "The Pace and Pattern of American Economic Growth," in Lance E. Davis et al., *American Economic Growth* (1972).

37. Alan Kulikoff, "The Economic Growth of the Eighteenth-Century Chesapeake Colonies," *JEH,* March 1979.

38. Anderson, "Economic Growth in Colonial New England," p. 256.

39. Paul David, "The Growth of Real Product in the United States Before 1840: New Evidence, Controlled Conjectures," *JEH,* June 1967, p. 155, Table 1.

40. Robert Gallman, "The Statistical Approach," in George Rogers Taylor and Lucius Ellsworth, eds., *Approaches to American Economic History* (Charlottesville: University Press of Virginia, 1971).

41. Diane Lindstrom, "American Economic Growth Before 1840: New Evidence and New Directions," *JEH,* March

1979; also see her *Economic Development in the Philadelphia Region, 1810–1850* (1978).

42. As we noted earlier, Gloria Main does not find evidence of a growth slow-down in the early 18th century in the data on estates. Gloria L. Main, "The Standard of Living in Colonial Massachusetts," *JEH,* March 1983.

43. Jeremy Atack and Fred Bateman, "The 'Egalitarian Ideal' and the Distribution of Wealth in the Northern Agricultural Community: A Backward Look," *REStat,* February 1981. In 1987, they still hold to this finding; *To Their Own Soil,* p. 269.

44. Atack and Bateman, *To Their Own Soil,* p. 129. Donghyu Yang finds that, in the South, the "land owning yeoman farmer class," was "substantially poorer than was its northern counterpart." "Notes on the Wealth Distribution of Farm Households in the United States, 1860: A New Look at Two Manuscript Census Samples," *EEH,* January 1984, p. 99.

45. Estimated from the data in Table 1, p. 155, in David, "The Growth of Real Product in the United States Before 1840."

46. See Fogel and Engerman, *The Reinterpretation of American Economic History* (New York: Harper & Row, 1971), pp. 333–38.

47. Jeffrey Williamson, "American Prices and Urban Inequality Since 1820," *JEH,* June 1979.

48. Jeffrey Williamson and Peter Lindert, "Three Centuries of American Inequality," in Paul Uselding, ed. *REH* (1976), vol. 1, pp. 101–102.

49. Alice Hanson Jones, *Wealth of a Nation To Be: The American Colonies on the Eve of the Revolution* (New York: Colombia University Press, 1980), p. 259, Table 8.1.

50. Williamson, "American Prices and Urban Inequality Since 1820," pp. 313–19.

51. Robert Margo and Georgia Villaflor, "The Growth of Wages in Antebellum America: New Evidence," *JEH,* December 1987, pp. 883–884, 895, argue that their wage data do not support this argument. They show an increase of about 33 percent in skilled wages and about 48 percent in unskilled in the antebellum period.

52. Williamson and Lindert, "Three Centuries of American Inequality," pp. 77, 83.

53. Soltow, *Men and Wealth in the United States, 1850–1870,* pp. 107, 145. After 1860, wealth was slightly more evenly distributed among the foreign-born than it was before 1860. Big immigration by itself did not increase inequality.

54. Simon Kuznets, *Six Lectures on Economic Growth* (New York: The Free Press, 1961), p. 55. As industrialization proceeds, the tendency is for *income* distribution to become more equal. Such also happened in the United States, as we shall see later on.

55. Frances Trollope, *Domestic Manners of Americans,* edited by Donald Smalley (New York: Alfred Knopf, 1949), p. 43.

56. Stanley Lebergott, *Wealth and Want* (Princeton: Princeton University Press, 1975), p.78.

57. Robert W. Fogel, "Nutrition and Mortality Since 1700: Some Preliminary Findings," p. 440.

58. Fogel, p. 466.

59. John Komlos, "The Height and Weight of West Point Cadets: Dietary Change in Antebellum America," *JEH,* December 1987.

60. Fogel, "Nutrition and Mortality," p. 466.

Suggested Readings

Articles

Adams, Donald R. "Earnings and Savings in the Early 19th Century." *Explorations in Economic History,* vol. 17, no. 2, April 1980.

Anderson, Terry L. "Economic Growth in Colonial New England: Statistical Renaissance." *Journal of Economic History,* vol. XXXIX, no. 1, March 1979.

Atack, Jeremy, and Bateman, Fred. "The 'Egalitarian Ideal' and the Distribution of Wealth in the Northern Agricultural Community: A Backward Look." *Review of Economics and Statistics,* vol. LXIII, no. 1, February 1981.

Bell, Duane, and Walton, Gary. "Agricultural Productivity Change in Eighteenth Century Pennsylvania." *Journal of Economic History,* vol. XXXVI, no. 1, March 1976.

Crowther, Simon J. "Urban Growth in the Mid-Atlantic States, 1785–1850." *Journal of Economic History,* vol. XXXVI, no. 3, September 1976.

David, Paul. "The Growth of Real Product in the United States Before 1840: New Evidence, Controlled Conjectures." *Journal of Economic History,* vol. XXVI, no. 2, June 1967.

Easterlin, Richard A. "Influences in European Overseas Emigration Before World War I." *Economic Development and Cultural Change,* vol. 9, no. 3, April 1961.

———. "The American Population." In Lance E. Davis et al., *American Economic Growth: An Economist's History of the United States.* New York: Harper & Row, 1972.

———. "Population Change and Farm Settlement in the Northern United States." *Journal of Economic History,* vol. XXXVI, no. 1, March 1976.

Egnal, Marc. "The Economic Development of the Thirteen Continental Colonies, 1720–1775." *William and Mary Quarterly,* vol. 32, 3rd series, April 1975.

Fishlow, Albert. "The Common School Revival: Fact or Fancy?" In Henry Rosovsky, ed., *Industrialization in Two Systems.* New York: Wiley, 1966.

———. "Levels of Nineteenth-Century American Investment in Education." *Journal of Economic History,* vol. 26, no. 4, December 1966.

Fogel, Robert William, "Nutrition and the Decline in Mortality since 1700: Some Preliminary Findings," in Stanley L. Engerman and Robert E. Gallman, eds., *Long-Term Factors in American Economic Growth,* NBER *Studies in income and Wealth,* vol. 51, Chicago: University of Chicago Press, 1986.

Galenson, David W. "White Servitude and the Growth of Black Slavery in Colonial America." *Journal of Economic History,* vol. XLI, no. 1, March 1981.

Gallman, Robert. "The Statistical Approach." In George Rogers Taylor and Lucius Ellsworth, eds., *Approaches to American Economic History.* Charlottesville: University Press of Virginia, 1971.

———. "The Pace and Pattern of American Economic Growth." In Lance E. Davis et al., *American Economic Growth: The Economist's History of the United States.* New York: Harper & Row, 1972.

———. "Human Capital in the First 80 Years of the Republic: How Much Did America Owe the Rest of the World?" *American Economic Review,* vol. 67, no. 1, February 1977.

Haines, Michael R., and Anderson, Barbara A. "New Demographic History of the Late 19th-Century United States," *Explorations in Economic History,* vol. 25, no. 4, October 1988.

Komlos, John, "The Height and Weight of West Point Cadets: Dietary Change in Antebellum America," *Journal of Economic History,* vol. XLVII, no. 4, December 1987.

Kulikoff, Alan. "The Economic Growth of the Eighteenth Century Chesapeake Colonies." *Journal of Economic History,* vol. XXXIX, no. 1, March 1979.

Lazonick, William, and Brush, Thomas, "The 'Horndal Effect' and Early US Manufacturing," *Explorations in Economic History,* vol. 22, no. 1, January 1985.

Lebergott, Stanley. "Labor Force." In Lance E. Davis et al., *American Economic Growth: An Economist's History of the United States.* New York: Harper & Row, 1972.

Leet, Don R. "The Determinants of the Fertility Transition in Antebellum Ohio." *Journal of Economic History,* vol. XXXVI, no. 2, June 1976.

Lindstrom, Diane. "American Economic Growth Before 1840: New Evidence and New Directions." *Journal of Economic History,* vol. XXXIX, no. 1, March 1979.

Margo, Robert A., and Villaflor, Georgia C., "The Growth of Wages in Antebellum America: New Evidence," *Journal of Economic History,* vol. XLVII, no. 4, December 1987.

Mokyr, Joel. "The Deadly Fungus." In J. L. Simon, ed., *Research in Population Economics.* Greenwich, CT: JAI Press, 1980.

Neal, Larry, and Uselding, Paul. "Immigration, A Neglected Source of American Economic Growth: 1790 to 1912." *Oxford Economic Papers,* 2nd series, vol. 24, March 1972.

Potter, J. "The Growth of Population in America, 1700–1860." In D. V. Glass and D. E. C. Eversley, eds., *Population in History.* New York: Aldine, 1965.

Shapiro, Morton Owen. "A Land Availability Model of Fertility Changes in the Rural Northern United States, 1760–1870," *Journal of Economic History,* vol. XLII, no. 3, September 1982.

Soltow, Lee. "Economic Inequality in the United States in the Period from 1790 to 1860." *Journal of Economic History,* vol. XXXI, no. 4, December 1971.

Steckel, Richard H. "Antebellum Southern White Fertility: A Demographic and Economic Analysis." *Journal of Economic History,* vol. XL, no. 2, June 1980.

Taylor, George Rogers. "American Economic Growth Before 1840: An Exploratory Essay." *Journal of Economic History,* vol. XXIV, no. 4, December 1964.

Uselding, Paul. "Conjectural Estimates of Gross Human Capital Inflow to the American Economy." *Explorations in Economic History,* vol. 9, Fall 1971.

Weiss, Thomas. "U.S. Labor Force Estimates and Economic Growth," in R. Gallman and J. Wallis, eds., *The Standard of Living in Early Nineteenth Century America* (Chicago: University of Chicago Press, 1992).

Williamson, Jeffrey. "American Prices and Urban Inequality Since 1820." *Journal of Economic History,* vol. XXXVI, no. 2, June 1976.

———, and Lindert, Peter. "Three Centuries of American Inequality." In Paul Uselding, ed., *Research in Economic History.* Greenwich, CT: JAI Press, 1976, vol. 1.

Yang, Donghyu. "Notes on the Wealth Distribution of Farm Households in the United States, 1860: A New Look at Two Manuscript Census Samples." *Explorations in Economic History,* vol. 21, no. 1, January 1984.

Books

Atack, Jeremy and Bateman, Fred. *To Their Own Soil: Agriculture in the Antebellum North.* Ames: Iowa State University Press, 1987.

Coale, Ansley J., and Zelnik, Melvin. *New Estimates of Fertility and Population in the United States.* Princeton: Princeton University Press, 1963.

Commons, John R., and Associates. *History of Labour in the United States.* New York: Kelly, 1921.

Elkins, Stanley. *Slavery: A Problem in American Intellectual and Institutional Life.* Chicago: University of Chicago Press, 1959.

Handlin, Oscar. *Boston's Immigrants, 1790–1880.* Cambridge: Harvard University Press, 1959.

Lebergott, Stanley. *Manpower in Economic Growth: The American Record Since 1800.* New York: McGraw-Hill, 1964.

Lindstrom, Diane. *Economic Development in the Philadelphia Region, 1810–1850.* New York: Columbia University Press, 1978.

North, Douglass C. *The Economic Growth of the United States 1790–1860.* New York: Norton, 1966.

Olson, Mancur. *The Logic of Collective Action: Public Goods and the Theory of Groups.* New York: Schocken Books, 1971.

Ransom, Roger L.; Sutch, Richard; and Walton, Gary M., ed. *Explorations in the New Economic History: Essays in Honor of Douglass C. North.* New York: Academic Press, 1982.

Rosenberg, Nathan. *Technology and American Economic Growth.* New York: Harper, 1972.

Soltow, Lee. *Men and Wealth in the United States, 1850–1870.* New Haven: Yale University Press, 1975.

Taueber, Conrad, and Taueber, Irene B. *The Changing Population of the United States.* New York: Wiley, 1958.

Thomas, Brinley. *Migration and Economic Growth.* New York: Cambridge University Press, 1953.

Yasuba, Yasukichi. *Birth Rates of the White Population of the United States, 1800–1860: An Economic Study.* Baltimore: Johns Hopkins University Press, 1962.

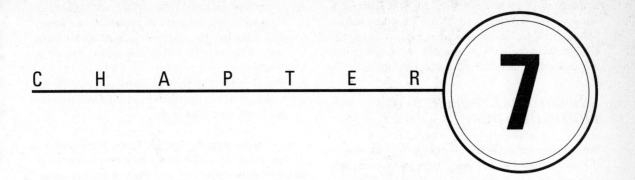

CHAPTER 7

Law and the Rise of Classical American Capitalism

The United States has a written constitution, difficult to amend, against which the laws reflecting political, social, and economic change over time must be measured. This measurement results in tailoring, which is done by the processes of law-making and judicial review, to make the laws "fit." The student of American economic history must come to grips with the major advances, twists, and turns in the relevant parts of our legal history since even major legislation enters the stream of American life through court review. Changes in American society that require a change in the law in order to exist probably will receive definition in the processes of the courts. This is a vast subject, only recently gaining recognition as a tool of historic and economic understanding after a long hiatus. Most economic history texts of the past have scarcely mentioned the contents of this chapter. However, perspectives change, and in recent years the processes of law and public choice have come to the fore. We cannot hope to do more than lay down a basic outline of this subject up to 1860. For further study, we refer you to the references and the Suggested Readings at the end of this chapter—in particular, to the articles of Professor Harry Scheiber, a leading scholar in this line of analy-

sis and pioneer of its use in economic history, and to the book of Professor Herbert Hovenkamp, a legal scholar with insight into economic history.

One of the nineteenth century's economic wonders was the appearance of American capitalism in its classic forms: the giant entrepreneurial business firm, the industrial labor force concentrated in the great manufacturing centers, the complete commercialization of agriculture and extractive industries, and the rise of big-time finance and giant transportation systems.[1] The little world of Madison and Jefferson at the turn of the nineteenth century became, by the end of the century, the world of Pierpont Morgan, John D. Rockefeller, Andrew Carnegie—and also of Samuel Gompers, Eugene V. Debs, the Interstate Commerce Commission, and the Sherman Antitrust Act. Incredible growth was accompanied by incredible change. It is the province of economic history to explain that change.

Even though the full flowering of classical American capitalism came only in the last decades of the nineteenth century, the roots were well developed by 1860. Whether one approves or not of nineteenth-century American capitalism, it must be understood if there is any coherence to be made of what comes after. We live today, institutionally, in its shadow. Most of the language and ideologies—pro and con—of public economics and policymaking to this day have their origins before 1914. In the decades after independence, the changes were made that turned colonial America into the seedbed of classical American capitalism.

THE COLONIAL PROPERTY RIGHTS HERITAGE

We will see that important changes were made within the definitions of the property rights Americans claimed, but that the basic ideas established in the colonial era remained untouched by the Revolution, apart from the abolition of primogeniture and perpetual entailment. It was from those property rights that the modern American economy developed. As Chief Justice Marshall put it in *Dartmouth College* v *Woodward:* "It is too clear to require the support of argument that all contracts, respecting property, remained unchanged by the revolution."[2]

The Revolution was not against the law but against a particular alien authority. The Americans were not going to throw away the common law.

REAL PROPERTY RIGHTS

Even though the tenure in real property had been originally developed in a small rural society of feudal structure, it proved capable of extraordinary flexibility in meeting the changing needs of modern capitalism. Recall from Chapter 1 the basic nature of the real property tenure that was transferred here from England. For the purchaser, or heir in socage (from now on called *fee simple*), there were five vital characteristics of ownership:

1. The maturity of ownership by purchase was perpetual, in theory, as long as incidents (taxes) due the "donor" were met.
2. No extraneous obligations adhered—the "fruits of chivalry," or feudal obligations, were not part of the tenure. The rights of both buyer and seller were "fixed and certain."
3. Land could descend to heirs from earlier generations either by will or inheritance. The latter was direct: The property right did not go back (*escheat*) to the donor to be regranted.

4. Ownership included both surface and subsurface resources, and the right to exploit them (waste) was complete. The reserved rights of the king to a fifth of the precious metals vanished in American practice.
5. Rights were completely alienable—by sale or trade—and reserved rights (minerals) had to be explicit and were limited.

Apart from ungranted public lands, there were no residual rights of government, only the power to tax and the "police powers," and those were held by the state and local (not federal) government. The power of government to take property by eminent domain was mainly a post-Revolutionary American innovation; it was not a reassertion of the donor's rights but of the sovereign power of government to occupy by forced purchase (and sometimes outright expropriation).

This system of ownership was almost ideal as the base for a free-market economy. Rewards from economic activity related to property and its productions were "commodities" in the sense that they were easily bought and sold, with few restrictions that mattered. Being of English origin—property as a "bundle of rights"—the tenure allowed the property to be leased, rented, let out on a sharecropping contract, subdivided, or amalgamated with other properties according to bargain; water and mineral rights could be owned separately. All this freedom was the property right of anyone with the purchase price. It is difficult to imagine a superior tenure for an individual. The only weakness (for the owner) was the donor's right of "reentry" (confiscation of rights) upon nonpayment of taxes. This, on the other hand, ensured American local governments of a solid tax base as development and population increase augmented the demands for public services. In any case, as long as taxes were those imposed by governments popularly elected and were reasonable in amount, such taxes posed no barriers to economic development.

As the nation expanded laterally by farming and land settlement (speculation), the American land tenure was almost the perfect vehicle for economic growth. Once heavy industry began, based upon the extraction of minerals, the tenure gave rewards (which could be of great magnitude) to those fortunate ones who owned or acquired gold, silver, copper, coal, oil, iron ore, and whatever—just as it long had done for farmers, speculators, and timbering interests. Not surprisingly, the wealth and income derived from such exploitation of real property rights was most unevenly distributed because those minerals by nature were not homogeneously present in the soils. Private persons owned the land, controlled it, and exploited it, and that was the basis of American capitalism in its classic form: the unquestioned right of individuals to do with their property whatever they wished and to enjoy the fruits of their enterprise by themselves. It was a system in which self-interest was exalted, and the tenure of real property was ideally designed for that system, even though originally it had served other purposes in medieval England.

BASIC LEGAL DEVELOPMENTS

Constitutions are the basic framework of law. The day-to-day interpretation and application of those fundamental rules, the substantive contents of them, were (and are) matters for legislatures and the courts. We inherited from the English practice of common law a system of judge-made law. To this day, theoretically, legislation is not "law" until it has been interpreted in court tests. For this reason, we are known as a common-law country, even though we operate by positive statute law and written constitutions. The division of American government into three parts, with separate and independent powers bestowed upon the judiciary, is a recognition and reenforcement of common-law principles. Another and related source of authority in economic life is the tradition of police power.

The Police Power

The right of government to maintain settled and peaceable conditions, by force if necessary, is called the **police power.** Application of this power over time has covered everything from weights and measures to sexual behavior. It has been used to order and control business activity since "time out of mind." We already saw many of its uses in colonial America. Even though the police power has been primarily the regulatory power of state and local governments, we will eventually see it elevated to the federal level (e.g., pollution-control regulation). This power is not a trivial one, even at the local level, since by licensing, zoning, and controls over conditions of trade and manufacturing, the police

powers could be, were, and are used by government to control entry into business and, thus, economic structure.

At the beginning of the federal era, the colonial police powers remained in effect in the settled areas. There has been some confusion about this among historians, some of whom incorrectly associated such regulations with "mercantilism" and supposed that they had been overthrown by the Revolution. It was not, after all, against colonial governments that the Revolution was waged, but against the British. The police power regulations were part and parcel of colonial government and the common-law tradition. There was no question of some mythical "break for freedom" into a world of true laissez faire once the Revolution was won. The ideas of laissez faire were not widely known or espoused in colonial times. Regulation was the right of government and its duty. State and local governments did not change when the British were driven out.

In their classic study of Massachusetts from the end of the colonial era to the Civil War, Oscar and Mary Handlin found such continuity for most colonial controls over inns, taverns, public transportation, harbors, and wharves—special franchise monopolies.[3] Massachusetts town governments even "retained the Medieval right to control and organize markets, regulating in great detail the conditions of sale."[4] Manufacturing was controlled, as of old, by inspection. By 1816 "the governor appointed inspectors of pot and pearl ash, or pork and beef, nails, butter and lard, pickled fish, each with a retinue of deputies."[5]

There were, indeed, significant extensions of police powers over economic life. Informers were still used and rewarded by the courts for their support of the controls. Lawyers were in danger of losing their monopoly of knowledge when Joseph Story's treatise on common pleading was published. In true guild fashion, they demanded the creation of a collective good for themselves and were rewarded when the Massachusetts Supreme Court set up formal examinations and required completion of a three-year apprenticeship for entry before the Massachusetts bar.

Louis Hartz, in a similar study of Pennsylvania, found the same continuity for the police powers exercised over economic life in that state.[6] Hartz wrote—

"It is the duty and interest of all governments," asserted a Pennsylvania statute of 1781, "to prevent frauds, and promote the interests of just and useful commerce." The colonial tradition of licensing, inspection, and similar regulations was maintained steadily from the Revolution to the Civil War and was in certain instances appreciably expanded.[7]

Hartz argued that in Pennsylvania these sentiments had been "taken for granted." Licensing, inspection, occasional government price-fixing, all such police-power exercises continued unabated. An act of 1835 set up a very extensive and detailed inspection for all items manufactured for export from the state. There was no questioning of such power. Indeed, we will see the Supreme Court of the United States (in *Hammer* v *Dagenhart,* 1918) uphold this power of the states to regulate manufacturing, and it would continue to do so until 1942.

However, there was also sentiment for greater freedom from control. We saw the beginning of this counterforce developing already in the colonial economy—in the markets for labor, in the abolition of markets overt, and the growing strength of the idea that *caveat emptor* protected the bargain and warranted the legitimate transfer of title where there was no overt fraud. New York State, in its constitutional revision of 1846, abolished outright many of its police-power controls: "All offices for the weighing, gauging, measuring, culling or inspecting any merchandise, produce, manufacture or commodity, whatever, are hereby abolished, and no such office shall hereafter be created by law."[8]

As commerce and manufacturing became more complex before the Civil War and the numbers and kinds of manufacture proliferated in a society without modern recordkeeping and communications technology, the old police-power controls by detailed inspection became increasingly more difficult to maintain. One result was both less and more general regulation. The outstanding exceptions were controls over common carriers (public utility control). These carriers were special franchise monopolies, most of them with eminent domain powers over private-property owners, and there never was any question of their being free of regulation. In fact, the public service commission form of regulation received very extensive development, especially in connection with canals and railroads in the decades before 1860. In other areas, though, free markets increasingly were seen as cheaper methods of

social control than regulation. Hartz suggested that free-market sentiment simply developed "naturally" as business enterprise grew and became less exceptional. Proprietors came to believe that their own property in business establishments ought to be as free as was property in real estate. The Handlins noted the confusion in Massachusetts that had entered by 1860 after extensive economic development:

> It was as if, imperceptibly, all the familiar metes and bounds that marked off one man's estate from another vanished to leave a vast and open space, familiar but with the old landmarks gone. Somewhere, everyone knew, the state could act directly, somewhere it could legislate as arbiter, and somewhere it had no place at all. But where one field ended and another began, no one knew; the master map was not yet drawn . . .[9]

The main point to remember about the police powers is that they are and were unquestioned prerogatives of government. American capitalism *never* knew a time when it was free of these controls. But it did know a time when such controls were not applied by the federal government. The police powers were applied then, as they often are today, by local government to force notions of propriety on business as well as on morals. Like most of our ancient legal background, the police powers were capable of *development.* The precedent was all-important, as we shall see when we examine the great watershed case of state control powers, *Munn* v *Illinois,* in Chapter 17. The federal government today in its regulation of product safety is entirely within the police-power tradition. During the rise of the free-market economy, the police powers continued to be imposed, although sporadically; they were part of the rules of the game. They also had wasteful side effects.

Privilege and Rent-seeking

The police powers could be, and were, used to create privileges that could then be exploited by those to whom the privileges were granted.[10] Suppose only one barber is allowed to cut hair in a town. He or she has a monopoly created by government. At the lowest level of privilege, it is specific individuals who are thus favored. With the lawyers of Massachusetts in 1816, as we have just seen, an organized group received a collective privilege or good from government. They could charge higher fees because entrance to the bar was restricted.

Consider an example from colonial America. The records of Massachusetts contain the following ruling by the colony government in 1641. A certain William Davis "was denied libertie to sell drinke, or ale, or to keep a cookes shopp, because there are others sufficient in the towne of Boston, and his carriage hath been formerly offensive."[11] We see—

1. that to sell drink, ale, or food, permission (a license) was required;
2. that because those already in the business were considered "sufficient," their profits were protected from Davis' competition. His application was denied;
3. that the moral tone of Boston was upheld when Davis was turned away due to his "offensive" behavior on former occasions.

Those already in business gain a **rent**—extra revenue created by regulation—that would not be there without the regulation. In the case of William Davis, this rent would have been lost if Davis' competition had been allowed to increase supply, given Boston's demand for such services. Any kind of business licensing or regulation produces such rents. Thus, it would be difficult indeed for the police power to be economically neutral. Its exercise creates, by definition, circumstances different from those that the free market produces. Otherwise, the regulation would be pointless.

Now clearly, not many of Boston's socially productive resources in 1641 were diverted to create or to gather such rents. Even outright bribery for such privileges cost little in 1641, and the extra price of "drinke," ale, and goodies from the "cookes shops" already existing did not amount to much. Most of Boston's resources were devoted to creating positive new production in other sectors of the economy.

Rent-seeking is a relatively inefficient way for a society to use its resources. To gain such rents, resources are essentially wasted, simply transferred from productive uses. Also, note that the returns to the rent-gainers, which are above the competitive levels, are "transferred" to them from the rest of society *only because of the regulation*. Police-power rents thus tend to be socially wasteful. Society supposedly is compensated

for this social cost by the provision of such things as better health, safety, good order, and higher morals.

In a society mainly agricultural and extractive, a society of small cities and governments with (geographically) limited powers, not many resources were expended on rent-seeking. It was more appropriate to call the receipt of such rents "privilege." Now, as American society grew, there were important changes. No longer were government-created privileges available to a few select persons, as in colonial Boston. Bigger stakes were involved as economic life expanded and organizations became larger. It paid for whole classes of people, organized groups, to agitate for privileges from government, for what Mancur Olson calls **collective goods.**[12] It happened before in land sales. It happened again in the pursuit of special-franchise monopolies to build canals, railroads, and bridges. As it happened, the United States was developing a large rent-seeking sector.

According to Terry Anderson and P. J. Hill, this characteristic becomes important mainly after 1870 with the exercise of *federal* police power.[13] Agitation for collective goods is an economically wasteful byproduct of political authority exercised to control the market. For now, we will be seeing the origins of this rent-seeking sector in the privileges created by the police power. Competitive rent-seeking will produce both waste and corruption. According to E. A. J. Johnson, the first Congressional meeting under the new federal Constitution was alive with competitive rent-seekers.[14] Their first triumphs on a large scale were public land sales to groups of speculators and the protective tariff.

LAW, INCOME, AND WEALTH TRANSFERS

When the existing states elected their first president and launched a new form of government in 1789, they did not seem to recognize that a dynamic interpretation of their new Constitution could make the law an instrument for the redistribution of wealth and income. As Charles Beard pointed out in his *Economic Interpretation of the Constitution*, a reasonable person might see it as a very conservative document intended to preserve the status quo. Of course, such was not to be the case. It was the genius of American jurists that they could stay within the general boundaries of the constitutional settlement and yet modify the substantive content of the law enough to release the powerful forces of change and development that underpinned the expansion of American capitalism within the framework of a growing economy. This freedom to interpret the law, called **judicial instrumentalism,** found its greatest impact in the century between 1780 and 1880.[15] Without it the American economy could never have developed as it did. Judicial instrumentalism gave advantage to some at the expense of others, and thus changed the distribution of wealth and income from that which would otherwise have prevailed.

Property Rights: From Prescriptive Rights to Priority Rights

What judicial instrumentalism amounted to, in the words of Harry Scheiber, was "pragmatic concern to advance productivity and material growth." Since the Constitution was concerned with preventing the redistribution of wealth and income in the interests of order and stability, and since economic growth *meant* dynamic instability, it was left to the courts to encourage entrepreneurial activity by judicial interpretation. So thoroughly was judicial discretion used in this regard that by 1820, as Horwitz puts it in *The Transformation of American Law,* "the legal landscape of America bore only the faintest resemblance to what existed forty years earlier."[16] This change was accomplished in large part by judges placing social weights upon property rights that favored some more than others.

Suppose there were two landowners, existing side by side, with equal amounts of land. In the common law of England each one had "absolute dominion" over his or her property, within tenure rights. Under the common-law doctrine of "ancient lights," one neighbor could not build a structure that would obscure the sunlight already enjoyed by the other. That ancient usage, that enjoyment of the sunlight, was a **prescriptive right,** and it must prevail over the ambition of the neighbor to change it. Scenery, clear air, quiet enjoyment, these were the amenities of real property and the seated property owner. They had real, monetary value and could not be disturbed without compensation. A person could not use his property in such a way as to damage the amenity rights of another without being liable for damages. The same argument would prevail if one neighbor wanted to build a mill dam that flooded the other's meadow. The use of the meadow is a prescriptive right. As William Blackstone, the great English jurist, wrote in 1765 in his *Commentaries on the Laws of England,* any injurious act by one owner against another might be prohibited "for it is incumbent on a neighboring owner to find some other place to do that act, where it will be less offensive."[17]

Now, in such a world you won't build a Gary, Indiana, or a Pittsburgh or a Houston or a Los Angeles. If the country is to grow economically, some property must be commercially developed, even to the detriment of the amenity rights of others. There would be adverse spillovers, or what economists call **negative externalities,** such as smoke, noise, congestion, and all the other unlovely consequences of economic growth. The prospect is expressed by the old English saying, "Where there's muck there's brass." Vested property rights would have to be dislodged. Rights long enjoyed, prescriptive rights, would have to be weakened to make way for other rights, **priority rights,** to grow where there was conflict. Trees had to be cut, streams and rivers dammed up, mines dug, and factories built.

In our own time, with 240 million people, there is great concern about finding ways to adjust and reduce priority rights in the interests of environment and ecology. Between 1780 and 1860, when Americans faced an undeveloped continent, the sentiments were the opposite. The doctrine of ancient lights had to go. Horwitz cites a case in New York State in 1838, *Parker* v *Foote,* in which the judge wrote that the doctrine of ancient lights "cannot be applied in the growing cities and villages of this country without working the most mischievous consequences."[18]

What instrumentalism meant, in fact, was that the entrepreneurial costs of economic development were destined to be subsidized by the public at large. Rivers and lakes might be polluted with industrial wastes, pastoral views obscured, the air made foul, so that there could be cities and jobs. Fortunes would be made by entrepreneurs who were not required to compensate other property owners for damage, *unless negligence could be proved in courts,* which was hard to do. A man had the right to develop his own property commercially if he did so with reasonable care. A stable next door was noisy because horses are noisy; that noise was not negligence. A nuisance might still be abated by lawsuit, but judges became increasingly tolerant about such matters in the interests of economic growth. "You can't stop progress."

These changes in property rights were accomplished by judges in private law cases (see Scheiber and

Horwitz for examples). The content of the law was altered, and not subtly, but no changes were made in the constitutional guarantees of the sanctity of property. Some sanctities became greater than others, in the eyes of the law. The meaning of "rights" changed in accord with the felt needs of nineteenth-century economic development, even though, in theory, eighteenth-century conceptions of property as "absolute dominion" remained. In the twentieth century we continue to change these ideas. In an age of environmental concerns, "progress" is commonly stopped by the courts—despite the old adage—proof that we live in a different era.

An example of the change in attitudes about the social value of material improvements was already noted in the appearance of mechanic lien laws. Another concrete example is the case of *Van Ness* v *Pacard* (1829), in which Justice Story rejected the common-law doctrine that improvements to rental property made by a tenant belonged to the landlord and that the tenant need not be compensated. Nineteenth-century Americans wanted improvements made, just as they valued the frontier squatter's labor when he or she trespassed upon the property of another. The squatter was rewarded for trespass with preemption rights; the tenant must be rewarded as well.

A point to bear in mind is that our ideas of private property rights had been developed in England, then a small, stable, rural society of rigid social-class structure. Americans, with a roughly democratic society, experiencing unheard-of growth on an undeveloped continent, changed the content of the law, strengthening the rights they wanted developed, weakening those they thought were less *economically* efficient. That we might want to change the social weights of these rights again today may be considered entirely reasonable in our circumstances since our needs in present day America do not reflect our ancestors' needs. They wanted factories, not forests.

The Changing Nature of Contracts

Another instrumental change of great consequence concerns contracts. Blackstone wrote of English contract law:

> . . . a contract for any *valuable* consideration, as for marriage, for money, for work done, or for reciprocal contracts, can never be impeached at law; and, if it be of sufficient adequate value, is never set aside in equity.[19]

Who could make a valid contract? Idiots, children, and, in many cases, women were not considered competent to make valid contracts. This ruling was based on the assumption that the contracting parties would be too unequal. Such a contract was void for lack of equity. The notion that a valid contract should be equitable, that the contracting parties should be in some sense equal in contracting ability, was a medieval idea, and it stood in the way of economic development. Could a factory worker make an equitable labor contract with a corporation? One argument used to this day favoring unions and collective bargaining is that it is necessary to equalize the strength on both sides of the bargaining table by combining labor, just as capital is combined. In 1898, in the case of *Holden* v *Hardy* (upholding Utah's right to regulate employment conditions in mines to protect health and safety), the U.S. Supreme Court ruled that:

> . . . the fact that both parties are of full age and competent does not necessarily deprive the state of the power to interfere where the parties do not stand upon an equality, or where the public health demands that one party to the contract shall be protected against himself.[20]

The Court argued that in such cases "self-interest is often an unsafe guide, and the legislature may promptly interpose its authority."[21] Health and safety were involved, but note that the equity argument is added for extra weight. One hears echoes of the "equity" idea even today, for example, in cases of consumer fraud involving minorities.

In the eighteenth century the tradition of equity had prevailed, according to Horwitz, on grounds of "natural justice," and also because so many prices were customary ones. Three changes came quickly:

1. The "meeting of wills" generally ruled against ideas of equity. If two free persons of legal age made a contract without compulsion, it was considered in most cases valid. Factory owners could thus contract with masses of employees for wages, hours, and working conditions if the terms were made known and the laborers agreed to them.

2. Meeting of wills was also important in advancing the rule of *caveat emptor* in the markets. If a vendor *unknowingly* sold defective goods, the buyer's opportunity to inspect the goods before purchase would ensure the vendor's innocence of overt deception.

3. Contracts for sale and purchase made on the basis of current *market* prices ruled. If prices later changed, the original price contracted for still held. This change opened the way for futures trading of all sorts.

These and other changes facilitated free-market determinations of wages and prices, determinations now freed from older "natural rights" ideas of justice. To some, of course, this utter commercialization seemed, and still does seem, immoral. In theory, the new ideas of contracts meant that subsequent changes altering the advantages and disadvantages of the contracting parties became irrelevant to the obligations of the contracting parties. For people in business, the passing of bankruptcy laws brought relief from the rigors of contract. Builders who could not complete their work were allowed by the courts to recover "off the contract" for work done. Workers simply lost their wages if they violated their employment contracts.[22]

Contracts: Employer Liability

Two doctrines developed that relieved employers of liability from the dangers of the workplace and job. First, the courts began to assume that danger was encapsulated in the wage; the greater the danger, other things being equal, the higher the wage. "Normal risk" also was subsumed in the wage, and employees' agreement to the wage contract implied their acceptance of the risks involved. Secondly, the employer's danger of liability for employee injury was reduced by contributory negligence, the negligence of another worker on the job, also known as the "fellow servant doctrine." Injuries in factories (or most other employments) would rarely be free of this element. Since injured workers not compensated by their employers would be thrown upon society at large for their maintenance, these legal doctrines produced yet another public subsidy for business. To this day, workers are not entirely free of the assumption of normal risk or contributory negligence, either by themselves or by another worker on the job.

These changes, like the triumph of priority rights over those of prescription, were what Professor Scheiber calls the "intangible contributions" to economic growth made by the courts in private law cases. They reduced the risks and the costs of business and made

business enterprise more daring (and profitable) than it would otherwise have been.

EMINENT DOMAIN

Other aids to business came from direct government redistribution through eminent domain proceedings. The Fifth and Fourteenth Amendments to the Constitution ensure that private property will not be taken by the federal or state governments without just compensation and due process of law. The technique used to obtain that property present already in colonial times, is **condemnation by right of eminent domain.** The history of the exercise of this governmental power shows that the power itself was ill-defined and irregular but that, gradually, the process of jury awards became standard in cases where the owner of the condemned property refused the government's offer price. What never became clear is the *limit of the use* to which such property may be put by government after it has been sequestered. The power of eminent domain never was, nor is it now, limited to public purposes. Land may be taken for a canal, railroad, grain elevator, toll road, public housing, or slum clearance. Eminent domain has always been a significant rent-seeking sector: Some gain while others lose. The federal government, perhaps honoring Jefferson's desire that it "never after, in any case" regain property sold out of the public domain, did not exercise eminent domain power directly until the 1870s. But states and municipalities did from the beginning.[23] Eminent domain power is the odd case where the costs are concentrated and the benefits, diverse.

INCORPORATION

The privilege of incorporation is the gift of the state to collective business ventures. By special dispensation, an enterprise organized in the corporate form is granted *perpetual life* and diversified ownership, each part of which has *limited liability* for the debts and other liabilities of the firm. A corporation is treated in the law as a legal person; it can sue and be sued in its own name. It is, in Chief Justice Marshall's words, "an artificial being, invisible, intangible and existing only in contemplation of the law." He wrote those words in *Dartmouth College* v. *Woodward* (1819) while upholding that corporation's (the college's) charter, granted by King George III, against an attempt by the state of

New Hampshire to overthrow it. From that point on, the corporation emerges in American history as a vivid reality. It develops, legally and in adaptability, until it, and not the traditional proprietorship, becomes the most important form of business enterprise. It is a being with the rights of a citizen, but with its limited liability and perpetual life, it has superhuman economic powers. It is a center of economic power inside the state, created by the state. As Arthur Selwyn Miller describes corporations, they are "feudal entities within the body politic."[24]

There had long been corporations in Europe and in England. Colonial governments granted the rights to private companies seven times. By 1790 there were 40 American corporations. Between 1790 and 1800 nearly 300 new charters were issued. After that, the volume increased. Each charter was a special act of a state legislature (except in New York and Connecticut). Usually, the charter stated the nature of the business venture: its purpose, its location, the amount of capital it could employ. The charter was a license to do the business in the manner specified. These limitations seemed reasonable at the time, given that the act of incorporation was an extension of the state's sovereign power to a group of private persons.

At first, special franchises were deemed to be grants of monopoly and, therefore, in the province of the sovereign power. The federal government, too, had the power to incorporate enterprises, as it did in the case of the First (1791–1811) and Second (1816–36) Banks of the United States. But in the nineteenth century, and generally until World War I, the federal government was reluctant to use its chartering power. In modern times, of course, federally chartered corporations are commonplace; for example, the Commodity Credit Corporation, was given a federal charter in 1948.

Beginning in 1811, the state of New York allowed general rules of incorporation, without the need of special legislative charters. Connecticut passed a similar law in 1837, but generalized incorporation did not become common in these states until the 1870s (we will discuss why later on). For now, it is sufficient to note that American businesses in the antebellum period had access to incorporation if they wanted it, but the process usually required a special act of legislation, sometimes an expensive, and a corrupt, procedure.

Thousands of special-franchise corporations were produced by the state legislatures between 1790 and 1860, probably half of them in the 1850s. The law re-

garding them was almost uniquely an American product, even though incorporation under English law was known in colonial times. The British Parliament was extremely cautious about allowing limited liability, and from 1720 to 1825, joint-stock enterprises were not allowed in financial business, except for the Bank of England. Since each American state was free to create corporations, it was natural that a good deal of originality would be involved. The great legal historian James Willard Hurst, says of American corporation law that it owed almost nothing to the English.[25]

Development of new laws for incorporation was a necessity because the U.S. Constitution viewed the individual person as the agent of economic life, as an autonomous, self-motivating creature, and, apart from the state government, it made no provisions for groups. Since the corporation is a group of people who have intermingled their capital under a single legal charter, making them a collective person, new thinking was required. From *Dartmouth College* v *Woodward* onward, the law on corporations began to build. We will meet it again shortly.

THE SUPREME COURT AND ECONOMIC GROWTH BEFORE 1860

As we have already noted, the federal Constitution was a general, limited document agreed to by sovereign states that already had law systems of their own. The Constitution was the "supreme law of the land" to be sure, but much was left unsaid. Soon enough constitutional problems arose that required solutions of *national* scope if the new nation was to remain a coherent political entity as it grew and changed. Given an independent judiciary, and that judicial review was provided for, the natural forum for settling disputes of a national character was the Supreme Court of the United States.

Beginning with the reign of Virginian John Marshall as Chief Justice, the Court was not diffident about its powers. In *Marbury* v *Madison* (1803)—the "midnight judges" case—Marshall ruled that the U.S. Supreme Court's review powers extended to actions by the other two branches of the federal government and not merely to the laws of the states. Marshall wrote in ringing words in *McCulloch* v *Maryland* (1819) the classic statement of "implied powers," while upholding the charter of the Second Bank of the United States:

We must never forget that it is a constitution we are expounding—(and it is) . . . intended to endure for ages to come and, consequently, to be adapted to the various crises of human affairs.

Marshall followed a "large policy": that the constitutional power would always be sufficient to meet the need. Since provision was made to amend the Constitution, he could hardly be wrong.

Commerce

By the time of our own era, it became apparent that the broadest power in the federal Constitution is the commerce clause:

The Congress shall have power . . . to regulate commerce with nations, and among the several States, and with the Indian tribes . . . [Article I, Sec. 8, No. 2 of the enumerated powers].

The test case was *Gibbons* v *Ogden* (1824), which overturned New York's grant of a steamboat monopoly on the Hudson River—the river touches both New York and New Jersey. Only Congress could regulate commerce between the states. In *Cooly* v *Board of Wardens* (1851), Chief Justice Roger Taney upheld the powers of the port of Philadelphia to impose controls reflecting its own special needs. But any regulation with national implications, such as of a seaport, was within the regulatory power of Congress. In the case of *Brown* v *Maryland* (1827), the Court had held, in connection with the commerce power, that no state could license and tax importers. Once the commerce power was set, it lay mainly in the background until 1887, when it surfaced again in great boots with the establishment of the Interstate Commerce Commission. For long decades after *Gibbons* v *Ogden,* business enterprises with national or interstate scope were freed of many of the vexations of state police powers. As Harry Scheiber said of *Gibbons* v *Ogden,* it ensured the United States of an internal common market.[26]

In *Gibbons* v *Ogden* (1824) the U.S. Supreme Court secured a single national economy, applying the commerce clause to overturn the steamboat monopoly on the Hudson River that had been granted by New York State to Robert Fulton and his financial backer, Robert Livingston. Shown here is Fulton's first steamboat, the *Clermont,* named after Livingston's estate on the Hudson.

The Contract Clause

The contract clause is contained in Article I, Section 10, of the Constitution and reads (by careful excision):

> No state shall pass any . . . law impairing the obligation of contracts. . . .

The first two cases that came before the Marshall Court concerning contract were *Fletcher* v *Peck* (1810) and *Dartmouth College* v *Woodward* (1819). The first case was a complex one involving two states and American Indian lands. The definitive case was *Dartmouth College*. Great issues were at stake because Dartmouth's claim to legitimacy, a grant from King George III, also involved by implication every land grant held under this authority. If the patent for Dartmouth College could be overturned by a state legislature, what of the rest? The Court held, as already noted, that the charter of Dartmouth College was a valid contract and was subject to the constitutional prohibition.

As we also noted, Marshall wrote that it was "too clear to require the support of argument" that a mere revolution did not upset vested property rights. Associate Justice Story added that it was a "settled principle of the common law that the division of an empire works no forfeiture on previously vested rights of property."[27] He further added that he considered the idea "monstrous" that a successful revolution would upset arrangements already set in place by the government that had been overthrown. Modern revolutionaries must find the American Revolution a fairly odd thing as revolutions go, restricted as it was by the law.

Commercial Law

The rules by which merchants dealt with each other had grown up largely separate from other branches of the law. As we saw in Chapter 1, certain international rules had prevailed by the time of the American colonization, especially the rules of negotiable instruments and shipping derived from the practices of the Hanseatic League. As the U.S. economy grew under the separate commercial experiences of the states, a clumsy variability began to appear. In *Swift* v *Tyson* (1842) Justice Story argued that there must be a general "Law Merchant" in the United States. When the state laws conflicted with each other, the Supreme Court had the obligation to rule for all, so that the right rules could

be found by the Court in the "general principles of commercial law." Again, the national economy felt the unifying force of the Constitution. The Court, until the 1930s, tended to honor states' rights wherever possible, but in matters economic the idea that a single national market must prevail is evident from the beginning.

Business Enterprise

There was also an evident tendency for the Court to favor a competitive national market. In *Charles River Bridge* v *Warren Bridge* (1837), the Court overturned the ancient conception that a state special-franchise charter *implied* a grant of monopoly. The Court held that a state might incorporate competing enterprises if it so wished. This was a vitally important development, especially in transportation. Soon there would be *competing forms of transportation,* with corporate charters, whose efforts "damaged" each other's property rights (profits). Ferries competed with bridges, railroads with canals; later on, airplanes and trucks competed with railroads and each other; wire-transmitted communication systems vied first with wireless and underground cable systems and now with satellite transmissions. It could no longer be, as the common law held, that a franchise was automatically a grant of exclusive right. The *Charles River Bridge* case also involved two other important issues: (a) A prescriptive right, a previously vested property right, was lost. (b) It was argued in the case that the "public good" had to be considered, that it was best served by competition, and that it must be an issue in considering the validity of vested property rights. This issue would loom large in years to come, when the states, and then the federal government, expanded their powers to regulate the private exploitation of private property—the rates, prices, and profits of business enterprises.

Finally, in the case of *Bank of Augusta* v *Earle* (1839), the states were allowed to legislate against out-of-state corporations doing intrastate business but could not restrict the movements of agents of corporations between the states. Each corporate being became a "person," was "domiciled" in the state of its charter, and was free to do business in other states, unless doing so was specifically prohibited by state legislation. The case has always been celebrated for its ambiguity, and the states continue to this day to pass discriminatory legislation whenever possible, thereby suppressing competition by creating in-state rents for their own corporate creatures at the expense of the public. The Court had to genuflect toward the "Full Faith and Credit" clause of the Constitution (Article IV, Sec. 1), but the states' powers to regulate under their police powers had to be respected, too. Chief Justice Taney backed away from defining a corporate person as a *citizen,* however, and the issue of the full rights of the corporate person was thus deferred until 1886. By then the "person" whose property was protected by the Fifth Amendment was a citizen (if born in the United States or naturalized) under the Fourteenth Amendment. The rights of the citizen were protected against state laws. The corporate persons were then called "citizens" and given that protection in *Santa Clara County* v *The Southern Pacific Railroad.* Thus we must consider this issue again later, in connection with railroad regulation.

These cases represent the main trends of judicial review affecting economic development before 1860. Their general tendency was in the same direction as the instrumentalism of the state courts—easing the way for business, economic growth, and the creation of an integrated national market. The Marshall Court was especially robust in the nationalism of its decisions.

However, there is a certain caution, too, as Harry Scheiber emphasized.[28]

Before the 1870s or thereabouts, the powers of the federal government were still seen as circumscribed by the powers reserved to the states—except on the issues of slavery and withdrawal from the federal agreement by the Southern states. Private rights under the common law were still reserved to the states. The big change in this regard begins in 1877, with the Granger cases and their successive legal consequences, which we will treat in due course.

What can be said most generally of the antebellum period is that the law aided the evolution of the main ideas and institutions of developing American capitalism: economic growth based mainly upon private decision-making regarding the exploitation of privately owned productive resources. Behind these developments was the assumption that most economic life was a private matter, with government aiding and supporting private economic power and also relying upon that power to produce growth. Only later will we see the older ideas of governmental restraints, as in colonial times, reemerging, this time at the federal level.

Notes

1. Stuart Bruchey emphasizes that such results were aided and abetted by certain *social* consequences of the Revolution: an established "elite" of landed and commercial wealth that had become ensconced in the colonial era, and whose allegiances were to the crown, was upended, and thousands driven into exile when the war ended. "Economy and Society in an Earlier America," *JEH,* June 1987.
2. 4 Wheaton, 518 (1819) 651.
3. Oscar and Mary Handlin, *Commonwealth, A Study of the Role of Government in the American Economy: Massachusetts 1774–1861* (1947).
4. Handlin and Handlin, pp. 93–94.
5. Handlin and Handlin, p. 70.
6. Louis Hartz, *Economic Policy and Democratic Thought: Pennsylvania, 1776–1860* (1948).
7. Hartz, p. 204.
8. Francis Newton Thorpe, ed., *The Federal and State Constitutions* (Washington: Government Printing Office, 1909), p. 2662.
9. Handlin and Handlin, *Commonwealth,* p. 260.
10. Douglass C. North and Lance E. Davis, *Institutional Change and American Economic Growth* (1971), pp. 74–77.
11. Jonathan Hughes, *Social Control in the Colonial Economy,* (Charlottesville: University Press of Virginia, 1976), p. 139.
12. Mancur Olson, *The Logic of Collective Action: Public Goods and the Theory of Groups* (New York: Schocken Books, 1971), chapter 1.
13. Terry Anderson and P. J. Hill, "Institutional Change Through the Supreme Court and the Rise of Transfer Activity," in Roger L. Ransom, Richard Sutch, and Gary M. Walton, eds., *Explorations in the New Economic History* (New York: Academic Press, 1982).
14. E. A. J. Johnson, *The Foundations of American Economic Freedom* (1973).
15. For two authoritative treatments of this instrumentalism, see Harry Scheiber, "Federalism and the American Economic Order, 1789–1910," *Law and Society,* Fall 1975,

and Morton Horwitz, *The Transformation of American Law, 1780–1860* (1977). Both authors give extensive bibliographies of this literature.

16. Horwitz, p. 30.
17. Quoted in Horwitz, p. 31.
18. Horwitz, p. 46.
19. William Blackstone, *Commentaries on the Laws of England* (Oxford: The Clarendon Press, 1765), book II, p. 443.
20. 169 U.S. 398 (1898).
21. 169 U.S. 398 (1898).
22. For a full discussion of contract changes, see Horwitz, *The Transformation of American Law,* ch. 5.
23. Harry N. Scheiber, "The Road to Munn: Eminent Domain and the Concept of Public Purpose in the State Courts," *Perspectives in American History,* 1971. For a full history, see Errol E. Meidinger's fine survey, "The 'Public Uses' of Eminent Domain: History and Policy," *Environmental Law,* Spring 1980.
24. Arthur Selwyn Miller, *The Supreme Court and American Capitalism* (1972) p. 14.
25. James Willard Hurst, *The Legitimacy of the Business Corporation in the United States* (1970), p. 1.
26. But as Scheiber illustrates in "Federalism and the American Economic Order, 1789–1910," there continued to be cases under the commerce power, and the rule of *Gibbons* was not entirely unambiguous when applied to these cases, especially where police powers were involved.
27. 4 Wheaton, 518, 706–7 (1819).
28. For example, see Scheiber, "Federalism and the American Economic Order, 1789–1910."

Suggested Readings

Articles

Anderson, Terry, and Hill, P. J. "Institutional Change Through the Supreme Court and the Rise of Transfer Activity." In Roger L. Ransom, Richard Sutch, and Gary M. Walton, eds., *Explorations in the New Economic History: Essays in Honor of Douglass C. North.* New York: Academic Press, 1982.

Bruchey, Stuart, "Economy and Society in an Earlier America," *Journal of Economic History,* vol. XLVII, no. 2, June 1987.

Holt, Wythe. "Then and Now: The Uncertain State of Nineteenth Century American Legal History." *Indiana Law Review,* vol. 7, no. 4, 1974.

Horwitz, Morton. "The Transformation in the Concept of Property in American Law, 1780–1860." *University of Chicago Law Review,* vol. 40, no. 2, Winter 1973.

Lively, Robert A. "The American System: A Review Article." *Business History Review,* vol. 29, no. 1, March 1955.

Mann, W. Howard. "The Marshall Court: Nationalization of Private Rights and Personal Liberty from the Authority of the Commerce Clause." *Indiana Law Journal,* vol. 38, no. 2, Winter 1963.

McGuire, Robert A., and Ohsfeldt, Robert L. "Economic Interests and the American Constitution: A Quantitative Rehabilitation of Charles A. Beard," *Journal of Economic History,* vol. XLIV, no. 2, June 1984.

Meidinger, Errol E. "The 'Public Uses' of Eminent Domain: History and Policy." *Environmental Law,* vol. 11, no. 1, Spring 1980.

Scheiber, Harry. "At the Borderlands of Law and Economic History: The Contributions of Willard Hurst." *American Historical Review,* vol. 75, no. 3, February 1970.

———. "The Road to Munn: Eminent Domain and the Concept of Public Purpose in the State Courts." *Perspectives in American History,* vol. 5, 1971.

———. "Property Law, Expropriation and Resource Allocation by Government, 1789–1910," *Journal of Economic History,* vol. XXXIII, no. 1, March 1973.

———. "Instrumentalism and Property Rights." *Wisconsin Law Review,* vol. 1975, no. 1, 1975.

———. "Federalism and the American Economic Order, 1789–1910." *Law and Society,* vol. 10, no. 1, Fall 1975.

———. "Regulation, Property Rights, and Definition of the Market: Law and the American Economy." *Journal of Economic History,* vol. XLI, no. 1, March 1981.

Umbeck, John. "The California Gold: A Study of Emerging Property Rights." *Explorations in Economic History,* vol. 14, no. 3, July 1977.

Books

Bruchey, Stuart. *The Roots of American Economic Growth, 1607–1861.* New York: Harper & Row, 1965.

Coleman, Peter J. *Debtors and Creditors in America: Insolvency, Imprisonment for Debt and Bankruptcy, 1607–1900.* Madison: State Historical Society of Wisconsin, 1974.

Friedman, Lawrence. *A History of American Law.* New York: Simon and Schuster, 1973.

Handlin, Oscar and Mary. *Commonwealth, A Study of Government in the American Economy: Massachusetts 1774–1861*. New York: New York University Press, 1947.

Hartz, Louis. *Economic Policy and Democratic Thought: Pennsylvania, 1776–1860*. Cambridge: Harvard University Press, 1948.

Horwitz, Morton. *The Transformation of American Law, 1780–1860*. Cambridge: Harvard University Press, 1977.

Hovenkamp, Herbert. *Enterprise and American Law, 1836–1937*. Cambridge: Harvard University Press, 1991.

Hughes, Jonathan. *The Governmental Habit Redux*. Princeton: Princeton University Press, 1991.

Hurst, James Willard. *Law and the Conditions of Freedom in the Nineteenth Century United States*. Madison: University of Wisconsin Press, 1956.

———. *Law and Social Process in United States History*. Ann Arbor: University of Michigan Law School, 1960.

———. *The Legitimacy of the Business Corporation in the Law of the United States 1780–1970*. Charlottesville: University Press of Virginia, 1970.

Johnson, E. A. J. *The Foundations of American Freedom*. Minneapolis: University of Minnesota Press, 1973.

Miller, Arthur Selwyn. *The Supreme Court and American Capitalism*. New York: The Free Press, 1972.

North, Douglass C. and Davis, Lance E. *Institutional Change and American Economic Growth*. New York: Cambridge University Press, 1971.

Swisher, Karl Brent. *American Constitutional Development*. Boston: Houghton Mifflin, 1954.

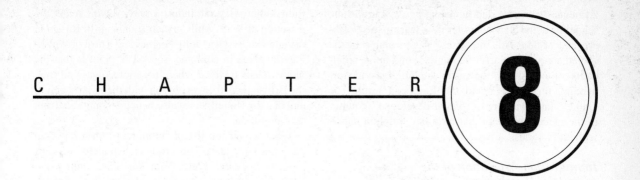

C H A P T E R

8

The Early Industrial Sector

In order fully to appreciate the level American industrial output had reached by 1913—nearly as great as that of all the European nations combined—we must step back in time a moment to consider its small beginnings. In 1790 our manufacturing activity was primitive for the most part. Alexander Hamilton, in his *Report on Manufactures* (1791), estimated that from two-thirds to four-fifths of the population's clothing was homemade at that time. Apparently not a spindle in the country was driven by waterpower. As we have discussed, there were water-powered milling of grain and the basic fabricating activities associated with agriculture, sacking, and cooperage. The towns contained artisans who made tools, shoes, hats, pots, and pans by hand. Lumber mills on the edges of rivers like the Merrimac resembled small factories, as did (according to old prints) the Du Pont powder works on the Brandywine.

THE DIRECTION OF CHANGE IN MANUFACTURING

If America's industrial progress in the nineteenth century had been at the same rate as Europe's, by the early twentieth century America would have been producing no more than 28 percent of Europe's industrial output, perhaps less, considering how agricultural it was in 1790 compared to Europe. In fact, in 1913 it made 31.9 million metric tons of crude steel, compared to 35.5 million for all of western Europe; it mined 517 million metric tons of coal, compared to their 493 million. Over half of world petroleum output was American by 1913, and the same was true of copper output and nearly so of lead production. In 1920 (the first year for such data) American electrical output was 57 billion kilowatt-hours compared to 44 billion for all of western Europe. So, we are looking at the beginnings of an industrial prodigy, and those beginnings will bear careful scrutiny. It has been estimated that by 1914, American industrial productivity was double that of western Europe. In the nineteenth century, the United States astonished the world with its industrial ability, as the Japanese have done since 1945. Let's look at the factors that shaped nineteenth-century American industrial growth.

The Human Element

We can suppose that native Americans in 1790 exhibited an amount of mechanical ability equal to that possessed by western Europeans. They were, by all accounts, as literate and numerate as the Europeans; schooling at the elementary level (at least in the Northern and Middle Atlantic states) was available in the settled areas. In the arts of commerce and in the application of technology, such as in shipbuilding and war-making, they were up to the European level. The United States was not an "under-developed" country in the modern sense of that term but simply a nation without factories.

Immigration-Migration of the Industrial Revolution

The industrial revolution was beginning in Europe and was centered in Great Britain, which had created (and was trying to maintain) the technical lead. Not unlike modern governments attempting to hoard newly developed scientific knowledge, the British tried to achieve technological monopoly. In 1774 and 1781 Parliament passed laws prohibiting the export of the new industrial machinery, imposing a fine of £200 and 12 years' imprisonment for exporting textile machinery. A law of 1782 provided penalties for *labor-pirating,* attempts to lure skilled British mechanics abroad. There was no way for the government to completely succeed in this attempt to control technology. Already in 1775 William Wilkinson, brother of the famed English industrialist, John "Iron Master" Wilkinson, was in France setting up iron works using British machinery and workers—and teaching the French how to use that machinery to bore cannon. On 3 August 1789 Arthur Young, traveling in revolutionary France, had viewed several of Wilkinson's works and wrote of one of them called Montcenis:

> . . . a disagreeable country. . . . It is the seat of one Mons. *Weelkainsong's* establishments for casting and boring cannon. . . . The French say that this active Englishman is brother-in-law to Dr. Priestly, and therefore a friend of mankind: and that he taught them to bore cannon, in order to give liberty to America. The establishment is very considerable; there are from 500 to 600 men employed, besides colliers; five steam engines are erected for giving the blasts, and for boring. . . . I conversed with an Englishman . . . there were once many, but only two are left at present. . . .[1]

In Belgium the beginnings of a manufacturing industry are associated with the name and firm of William Cockerill, another emigré from Britain. In the Ruhr Valley, German industry was growing under the direction of W. T. Mulvany, an Irishman. In Russia in the late 1860s, it was John Hughes and a host of Welshmen involved in coal and iron.[2] The point is that the industrialists traveled where the money was and took the British industrial revolution with them, laws or not, and that the United States also benefitted mightily from that migration.

What would the list of immigrant industrialists in America look like? The brothers Schofield, who arrived in the early 1790s from Yorkshire, built wool-carding machinery driven by waterpower. Notable among others who followed their path was the Scots engineer, Henry Burden, who was responsible for crucial innovations in that "cradle of American technology," the Springfield armory.[3] He followed a policy of bringing over immigrant mechanics to work there. It was David Thomas, a Welsh immigrant, who first introduced anthracite iron smelting into the Pennsylvania iron industry in 1840. Just over three decades later, the Scots immigrant, Andrew Carnegie, would launch the industrial revolution in steel in this country using the English inventor Henry Bessemer's converter, "Bessemer's volcano," where others had tried and failed.

The ideas of industrialization could also be imported by skilled Yankee observers. Francis Cabot Lowell, traveling in England in 1811, was entranced by English weaving machinery and studied it closely. Returning home, he worked with a skilled mechanic named Paul Moody, and by 1814 they had succeeded in making a loom driven by waterpower. The Lowell firm pioneered large-scale weaving factories in this country and significant labor-force innovations, too. In particular, Lowell is famous for the clean and well-supervised dormitories in which he housed the New England farm girls he employed in his factories. Goldin and Sokoloff argue that such factory workers were so prevalent in places like rural New England because their productivity was less in agriculture than in the factories. The labor of young women might have relatively looked "cheap" to Lowell, but his wages were higher than they could have earned by staying home on the farm.[4]

American Innovations

Although we borrowed all we could from Europe, we very early began making peculiar inventions and innovations. The word *peculiar* is used to set apart two characteristics of American industry that became predominant: economy of labor by the use of machines and extravagant use of raw material. Americans were "short" on labor and "long" on raw materials; therefore, they conserved what was scarce and freely used what was plentiful. In short, they practiced good economics.

One measure of the outcome could already be seen in cotton textiles by 1860. The average English integrated spinning and weaving factory contained 17,000 spindles and 276 looms, compared to the equivalent in New England of a mere 7000 spindles and 163 looms. The American cotton textile industry, the nation's largest, with 20 percent of the spindles the British employed and perhaps 25 percent of the workers, consumed 40 percent as much raw cotton.[5] Productivity was higher in the United States than in Britain; by 1860 that already had been the subject of remark and great curiosity. In other parts of industry the high productivity was also noted as well as the fact that none of these industrial technologies began in the United States[6] What was going on?

Philadelphia inventor Oliver Evans in 1784–85 built a flour mill run by gravity, friction, and waterpower that moved the grain from the loading bin throughout the mill's several levels by buckets and leather belts without the intervention of any human effort apart from guiding and regulating. The mill could handle 300 bushels an hour. It was an assembly line more than a century before Henry Ford's Highland Park factory housed the first real automotive assembly line.

Eli Whitney and Simeon North both had contracts from the federal government to make arms. Whitney's was for 10,000 muskets in 1798, and North's for pistols a year later. Both men pursued the idea of interchangeable parts—the use of stamping and cutting machines to make identical parts from a pattern, supplies of which could be assembled into the final product by unskilled workers with a minimum of handfitting (filing).

In the case of the mill, the object was in part the substitution of **capital equipment,** machinery, for unskilled workers. In the case of arms manufacturing, the substitution of technology was for *skilled* workers, armorers, who simply were not available in this country. Whitney said of his years of devising machinery to replace human skills, "I have not only the *Arms* but a large portion of the *Armourers* to make."[7] Oliver Wol-

cott, Secretary of the Treasury, awarded the contracts to Whitney and North. He, at least, had an appreciation for what Whitney was doing. Wolcott wrote to Whitney: "I should consider a real improvement in machinery for manufacturing arms as a great acquisition to the United States."[8] The idea had been tried in France with no known result by a worker named Le Blanc, and Jefferson (in France at the time) had talked with him, hoping to get him to emigrate to the United States. French and English officers to whom Whitney explained his ideas scoffed at them. Whitney completed his contract for the 10,000 muskets in 1809; in 1812 the British, using the old methods, had 200,000 muskets in disrepair and were waiting for armorers to fix each part, one at a time.[9] Because the muskets had been made individually, their parts were not interchangeable.

By the 1830s the ideas of standardization, interchangeability, and division of labor in lengthy production processes were being widely applied in American industry. Their incorporation in the manufacturing sector produced an interesting result that came to characterize much of American economic life: Although skilled labor tended to fetch a higher wage than unskilled, as in Europe, the *ratio* of skilled to unskilled wages was lower than in Europe.[10] The difference in the two ratios, American and British, reflected the relatively higher productivity of unskilled workers in the United States, who were aided in their labor by machinery that substituted for skill.[11] By the 1840s the system was being used for locks, clocks, and watches. In 1846 the sewing machine was patented, and it soon worked its way into the making of boots, shoes, harnesses, and belts as well as into the clothing industry.

At the Great Exhibition in London (1851) American products, not noted for their elegance, were outstanding for their practicality, cheapness and utility.[12] By then what had become known as the "American system of manufacturing"—simplicity of design, standardization, interchangeable manufacture, and large-scale output—had taken over in light consumer goods.[13] Later on, it would work its way into heavy industry, into machine-making (machines to make machines), and, indeed, into nearly the entire economy. By the end of the nineteenth century, American industry contrasted sharply with European and British; the measurement of the contrast was the difference in output per unit of labor. Eventually, the United States would become a nation where an unskilled teenager pumping gasoline at a service station might earn as much as a skilled woodworker and where unskilled assembly-line factory "hands" earn more than bookkeepers, and even school teachers.

The Importance of Factor Proportions

In recent years scholars have made careful studies of the singular pattern of nineteenth-century American industrial innovation to find its remote sources. Did the difference in availability of labor and land account for the path of development taken by the American manufacturing industry? Sir John Habakkuk, in his trailbreaking book, *American and British Technology in the Nineteenth Century: The Search for Labour-Saving Inventions,* argued that the origin of the *need* for labor-cost-reducing (labor-saving) machinery in America was initially the worker's "opportunity cost"—the availability of a viable alternative on the frontier.[14] Cheap land means, said Habakkuk, that wages in manufacturing had to be high enough to keep workers from "going west." The labor market, by implication, was not perfectly competitive. Employers could not hire all the workers they needed at going wages. They had to pay more. Use of machinery by relatively unskilled workers raised their productivity and thus justified the payment of higher wages by profit-maximizing employers. There was, however, a paradoxical result: Labor became even more "scarce"—high priced—and the inducement "to save labor" by raising wages in response was even greater. Thus a rapidly increasing industrial labor force was also a "high-wage" labor force because of rising productivity.[15]

As the system became more general, it also was profitable for American industrialists to pay higher interest rates to buy machinery and hire workers at wages higher than were typically paid in Europe because the machinery was so profitable. In Figure 8.1, if interest rate, r, rises from a_1 to a_2, investment demand falls back from x_1 to x_2. Higher interest rates would restrict investment. But as higher productivity of investment penetrates the economy, investment demand shifts from I_1 to I_2, and the higher interest rate, a_2, now calls forth x_3 of investment. The American economy, because of efficient technology, became one of high wages, high interest rates, high profits, and rapid growth.

Figure 8.1 Outward Shifting Investment Demand Due to the Increasing Profitability of All Investment

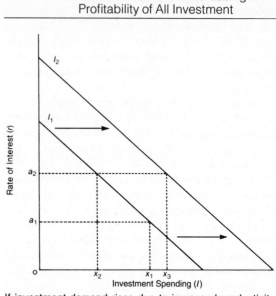

If investment demand rises due to increased productivity, more investment is profitable at every rate of interest.

The pressures in Great Britain to be efficient with machinery were not so great, argued Sir John, in part because the British worker, lacking easy access to a frontier such as America, accepted lower wages for greater skill, thus tempting the British employer to use skilled labor, an abundant resource. As time passed, British industry became a labor-using industry with low wages, while that in America became increasingly a labor-saving industry with higher wages.[16]

The question of choice of technique (actually, the whole range of technical change adopted) must, of course, involve adoption of the technical apparatus *and* development of knowledge, organization of production, labor force, marketing, finance, and much else. Paul David added to the pioneering work of Habakkuk by offering an explanation of why major departures in technological development prove to be self-sustaining.[17] His work was based on both American and British nineteenth-century technology. A shift in technique could begin with changes in the ratio of labor to capital prices that would induce a switch—say, from a labor-intensive to a labor-saving manufacturing process. However, there is a difference between possible technologies and *available* technologies. The latter are fewer than the former, and if the change is to be a fundamental one—for example, from animal to mechanical motive power—other related activities have to adjust to fully exploit the change. Jobs will change; institutions will adapt; major locational consequences involving significant population movements, development of appropriate supporting social infrastructure, and a learning-by-doing process to integrate the technological switch into society at large may occur.

Little by little improvements are made all along the line that commit the economy more steadfastly to the new technology. The older methods and organizations are abandoned as new processes diffuse themselves in a market economy. As time passes, a whole new system evolves; associated economic activities develop in ways congenial to the new technology, making it increasingly productive socially and economically efficient. In a way, the first technical switch sets the tone for subsequent development, *if* the learning-by-doing process is set in train. If factor prices change back toward the old ratios, indicating marginal advantages from a return to older techniques, reswitching most likely will not occur: The economy will not convert back to the old track. Set-up costs, involving abandonment of all recent changes, are too high. It is more profitable to continue making cost-saving improvements in what has become a new, and then a general, way of economic organization.[18]

A fascinating case study of these institutional and technical forces has been published by William H. Lazonick.[19] He adds the reaction of labor and ownership to the background and initial conditions. In the nineteenth-century cotton spinning industry, we might expect to see a uniform technology on both sides of the Atlantic. Yet, although the British industry became labor intensive by using inferior raw material, the American industry adopted a technology that utilized better machinery and higher grades of raw material and conserved labor. British labor organized to protect its jobs and cooperated with management by substituting skill and inferior raw material for new technology. American workers did not unionize; they tended to change jobs and leave the industry for better opportunities elsewhere. The American industry could compensate for this mobility through newer machinery, better grade raw cotton, and less reliance on a stable labor force.

An additional labor-force consideration has recently been advanced by Claudia Goldin and Kenneth Sokoloff. They argue from the established fact that early industrial enterprises depended very largely upon the labor of women and minors. The availability of this input was inversely proportional to its relative productivity in nonindustrial employments. Hence where, for example, farming produced only a poor livelihood, as in New England, women and minors were readily available for industrial employments, and this available labor supply motivated manufacturers to locate there.[20]

Consumption

There was more to it, of course. In both economies demand was rising, but, it is argued, demand itself in America became peculiar. It became demand for mass-produced, standardized products. Edward Ames and Nathan Rosenberg added the element of mass-product demand to the argument.[21] Americans wanted factory-made products instantly to free their own labor for more immediate work in agriculture and extractive industry. If the machine-made tools wore out—and had been profitably used—new ones would be purchased to replace them. Simple designs would suffice. The need was for an immediate availability of the tools. As Ames and Rosenberg asked, "Who used a shotgun in England, and who used one in America?" In England the shotgun, a weapon used to shoot birds by a limited number of people, landowners, was also an item of prestige; in America it was a tool, like the shovel or axe, used by settlers everywhere. The American consumer of durables did not want adornments. In clothing, on the other hand, quality cost money, and clothing could easily be replaced, perhaps in a new style:

> The material, being expected to last for a single season, is purchased in a quality to do that, and no more. The next season the customer supplies himself again . . . This habit of almost constant change in said to run through almost every class of society, and has . . . a great influence upon the character of goods generally in demand which . . . are made more for appearance, and less for actual wear and use, than similar goods are in England.[22]

American consumers would buy tools that worked, no matter what the appearance of those tools, and good-looking, factory-made clothes, no matter whether they wore well or not. In both cases the question was just price and use. Regarding tools, Rosenberg quotes an early twentieth-century British author who noted that Americans allowed machine capability to set their standards:

> . . . where mechanical devices cannot be adjusted to the production of the traditional product, the product must be modified to the demands of the machine. Hence the standard American table-knife is a rigid, metal shape, handle and blade forged in one piece, the whole being finished by electroplating—an implement eminently suited to factory production.[23]

These are examples of consumers getting what they want, *if they intend to use it up and buy something else.* Both sorts of demand are ideal for factory production, and doubtless are the origin of the famous American "throw-away economy" of the twentieth century that has embraced even automobiles and houses.

Resources

An additional element stressed by Rosenberg in his book, *Technology and American Economic Growth,*[24] is the use of raw materials, especially *wood.* It was in abundant supply compared to other materials for houses, tools, furniture, and transport equipment, and Americans used it freely in the nineteenth century, substituting it for metals wherever possible before 1860. In fact, in 1860 the lumber industry was second only to cotton textiles in creation of market value. Rosenberg estimates that in 1860 American per capita wood consumption was five times that of England and Wales.[25] Elaborate woodworking equipment had been invented by Americans in pursuit of a cheap resource (just as, in England, an elaborate social structure had been developed to exploit labor, *their* cheap resource). Europeans were appalled by American wastefulness in wood manufacturing. Rosenberg quotes an English observer (writing in 1872): "Lumber manufacture, from the log to the finished state, is, in America, characterized by a waste that can truly be called criminal. . . ."[26] This is true only if you think that lumber is a scarce resource.

So American manufacturing developed on a labor-saving, resource-using basis, buoyed by consumers who accepted the product of machine manufacturing, later to become the products of machine-moving, assembly-line manufacture. In the twentieth century, Europeans developed the same tastes, especially for automobiles. As Peter Temin points out, the innovation of characteristic American manufacturing techniques proceeded no more rapidly than was profitable.[27] The iron industry stuck to charcoal as long as it was the most profitable fuel, turning to coking coal only when resources and techniques justified the change. By 1860, therefore, the American iron industry might have *appeared* to be technically backward compared to the British since it still depended upon small furnaces and forges run by charcoal, again, a wood product.

Once the industry and a large part of its market moved across the Alleghenies, once transportation to the east coast by rail was developed, and once the right quality of coking coal was discovered, the American iron and steel industry would quickly catch up with and surpass European technical practice. But only when it *paid* to do so. American economic growth was a matter of private profit calculations, not national prestige or planning. The same forces were at work in changing motive power. Even though the steam engine was introduced early in American history and its use was widely diffused, as late as 1869 nearly half of the motive power used in industry was water—so good were the country's millrace streams and rivers.[28]

The Course of Expansion to 1860

Figure 8.2 shows the size distribution of the manufacturing industry in 1860 by *value added* (final sale price less the cost of materials). Of a total manufacturing labor force of 1,530,000 (compared to 5,880,000 in agriculture in 1860), some 1,474,000 were employed in these ten industries alone. Cotton goods production, the largest by value added, was second in order of employment (115,000). Cotton textile manufacturing led off in the growth of American industry, as it had in England, and would in the future in nearly every industrializing country the world over. The machinery was relatively simple, and little or no skill was required of the labor force.

The largest employer of labor in 1860, boots and shoes manufacturing (123,000), was third in order of magnitude by value added. By then the sewing machine was widely adopted in that industry, and factory production was becoming common. The men's clothing industry, by 1860, also had discovered the sewing machine; 115,000 were employed there. Lumbering, second in value added, employed 76,000 men in the exploitation of one of our richest resources and would long remain among our most productive industries. Per worker employed in 1860, though, flour milling and leather goods manufacturing produced the most value added.

Figure 8.2   The Course of Growth by Value Added

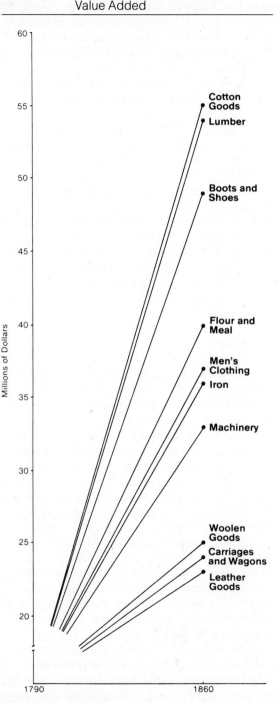

Millions of Dollars

60
55 — Cotton Goods — Lumber
50 — Boots and Shoes
45
40 — Flour and Meal
— Men's Clothing — Iron
35
— Machinery
30
25 — Woolen Goods — Carriages and Wagons — Leather Goods
20

1790   1860

Source: Eighth Census of the U.S., 1860, vol. 3, *Manufactures.*

Machinery production, seventh in value added (with 41,000 employed), in 1860 was already third in value added per worker. As Rosenberg emphasizes, this industry would become the "focusing" industry of future technological change.[29] It would become increasingly more specialized, developing eventually into the machine-tool industry, where machines were designed to make machines. There would also be specialized branches, such as locomotive building and the canning industry.

In another half-century, machine building would become our largest industry by value added. Technical progress would spread through American industry via the machine builders. Americans, already willing to buy standardized products of machine fabrication, increasingly would be paying for the standardization of the machines themselves, then the tools that built them. Standardization was effective when it was most widespread. In World War I, the force of defense spending enhanced the process of standardization because the government, which became the largest buyer, *required* uniform sizes for everything from men's underwear to nuts and bolts—here again we encounter the idea of interchangeability.

The 1860 industrial distribution still shows its close association with agriculture and the forest. In another half-century, we will see more of industries using the products of other manufacturing industries as **inputs.**

ENERGY SOURCES

Manufacturing requires energy, and in early factories the central power source, the prime mover, powerfully influenced industrial location. In the United States in the antebellum period, the variety of energy sources employed was striking.

Animal Energy

We can never know precisely what the amount of animal energy used was. Horses, mules, and oxen could be used for stationary work as well as for traction. Dependable data show that in 1867 there were 6.8 million horses and probably 1 million mules at work in the country. Population then was about 37.5 million, so there were about 5.4 persons per horse. Assuming constant technology for those few years, there must

In 1860, cotton goods, lumber, boots and shoes, and flour milling produced the greatest net industrial income measured by value today.

have been 5.5 million horses at work by 1860, perhaps a million mules, and many, many oxen. How much of the economy's total work was powered by these animals is just unknown. They must have powered most of the traction, and it is estimated that in 1860 they provided an astonishing 63 percent of the total horsepower of prime movers.[30]

Water and Steam

In addition to horse, mules, and oxen, Americans used windmills, waterwheels, and steam engines as prime movers. Scholars have found the official 1838 count of stationary steam engines to be only a partial count. Peter Temin has corrected the official report as far as he feels is possible and has concluded that at least 1616 engines could be identified on that basis.[31] Rosenberg is willing to let that figure drift up to 1800.[32] According to Atack, Bateman and Weiss, the correct figure is 1420.[33] The precise count is not important here. If you can picture 1420 colored pins of a map of the settled regions of the United States in 1838 you can see how abundantly available the steam engine was. In mechanical (nonanimal) energy sources it is clear, though, that waterpower was still predominant over steam.[34] Surviving evidence shows that the 1838 steam engines were built by some 250 firms. Fully 90 percent of the value added by the machinery industry (seventh largest in the country, see Figure 8.1) in 1860 came from the construction of steam engines alone.[35] The builders were primarily small firms engaged in other work. Foreign supply was also present. Despite widespread familiarity with steam-engine design and construction, the evidence shows that Southern users of steam engines had a distinct propensity to import them from England.[36]

Economic Considerations

Waterpower's tenacious hold as a prime mover has several explanations. First, of course, a waterwheel simply was sufficient mechanical power in small grist mills and similar employments. There are also the geographical considerations; industrial sites in New England and generally down the fall line of the Appalachians were generously endowed with fast-moving streams and rivers and good sites for millrace dams. In the South and Midwest, beyond the Appalachians, the use of stationary steam power was predominant quite early

because of the lack of suitable mill sites. Had those areas been endowed with waterpower like the Appalachian fall line, no doubt waterpower would have been more important but not necessarily in the same ways because of differences in the *work to be done*. We will return to this point later in the chapter.

There were other economic reasons for the persistence of waterpower when the steam option was available. As Temin points out, the total life of these early steam engines may have been only five years or so; thus, even though the initial capital cost of waterpower was higher than steam, the life of the installation was much longer, fuel costs were zero, and the longer depreciation period for waterpower made the annual capital cost where there were good water sites somewhat lower than it was for the steam engine.[37] Especially if the raw material, like cotton, could be easily transported to the factory site (the site of the prime mover), steam engines lost one of their advantages over waterpower—flexibility of location. Cotton textiles thus were destined for a long life in New England's water-driven mills.[38]

Location

Because of its locational flexibility, the steam engine had many of the advantages of the modern fractional-horsepower electric motor and internal combustion engine. It could be transported *to the site* of the work to be done. Where raw materials were light and easily transported, this was not a great advantage. Where the raw materials were perishable, as in sugar refining, or where weight reduction was important, as in lumbering, cement, and brick manufacturing, the locational flexibility of the steam engine was of great advantage. Of course, its early adaptation to shipping on the country's vast system of inland waterways as well as on the ocean was the logical extreme of carrying the source of the power *to the job*. Accordingly, the permeation of the steam engine into American manufacturing was most rapid in the Midwest, where appropriate waterpower was scarce and when available, slower than in New England.[39]

In the final analysis, by 1869 steam power predominated over waterpower, just as in the twentieth century internal combustion and electrical power would make the steam engine a rarity. The efficiency of any prime mover is the amount and cost of power delivered relative to the work to be done. Waterpower ultimately

Henry Burden's great waterwheel in Troy, New York, (1850s) was 60 feet in diameter and 22 feet wide. Its speed could be regulated manually with gears to within a second of time.

would be doomed (until it could be generated into electrical energy) by the limitations of the waterwheel itself, no matter how much it was improved. Big factories were difficult to run with waterwheels. Waterpower's last grasp as a direct transmitter of motive force was no doubt the massive waterwheel constructed by the machinery innovator, Henry Burden, to power his machine works in Troy, New York, in 1851.[40] It was an excellent example of the adage that, in technology, old techniques tend to gigantism in their final stages of use.

Finally, steam power, because of its flexibility in location, allowed industry to grow at sites determined by other economic forces, such as markets or transportation advantages, in addition to the considerations we already have discussed.

Low- vs. High-Pressure Steam Engines

Rosenberg's thesis about the American exploitation of abundant resources by the technology adopted plays a part in the history of American steam engines, too. It was somewhat puzzling that the Americans, equally adept at designing and making either low- or high-pressure steam engines (some firms made both, according to demand), for the most part opted for high-pressure engines, while in England, low-pressure engines generally prevailed.[41] The advantages of the high-pressure engine were its cheapness and relatively light weight. The main disadvantage was its extravagant fuel consumption. But fuel was no problem here. As Rosenberg writes:

> These characteristics made such engines attractive in the resource-abundant environment of the U.S., where it was worthwhile, in effect, to "trade off" relative large amounts of natural resource inputs for a reduction in fixed capital costs.[42]

The high-pressure steam engine, appearing almost simultaneously in England and in the United States in 1803–04, was developed in England by Richard

Towns and Cities. In the nineteenth century, America's cities grew rapidly into areas of concentrated economic and cultural activities. Retail stores and numerous street vendors supplied the growing population with their household goods and foodstuffs. City workers took their meals at "eating houses," quenched their thirst at root beer stands, or snacked on oysters on the half-shell after a night at the theater.

Trevithick and in the United States by Oliver Evans. The great advantages of steam over waterpower and animal power were well appreciated by Evans, who pointed out the lack of sufficient water sites for the long run, the problems of freezing in winter, the inconstancy of wind, and the fact that animals were "tedious" and "subject to innumerable accidents." Steam, Evans wrote, "at once presents us with a faithful servant, at command in all places, in all seasons."[43] Ultimately, his view prevailed since electrical power is now generated by burning coal, oil, and nuclear fuels to produce steam. His kind of steam engine was largely replaced by electrical motors and internal combustion engines. Charcoal, wood, coke, coal—all could "raise steam" by combustion and did by 1860. The discovery of commercial quantities of oil in Titusville, Pennsylvania, in 1859 had no effect in the history we have considered. Later on, petroleum produced dramatic changes.

Many Power Sources

That Americans so generally preferred high-pressure over low-pressure engines would have pleased both Trevithick and Evans. That waterpower and animal power would be so long-lasting in the United States might have surprised both. It was a matter of costs and revenues, again, and not technological fashion. Antebellum American industry depended upon many sources of motive and traction power, determined by locational needs and advantages. Since industry grew prodigiously anyhow, there is no evidence that the multiplicity of power sources was any disadvantage to the economy's needs. It is conceivable that modern changes in petroleum prices and availabilities could produce a similar heterogeneous growth of energy sources again. If so, history shows that heterogeneity of power sources is not by itself an economic disadvantage.

INDUSTRIAL LOCATION

In Chapter 2 we discussed the location of initial settlements and towns on a largely unknown and unpopulated territory, breaks-in-transport, and differentiation of productive capabilities in the natural endowment. On that basis, if we were asked in 1790, "Where will the country's future cities be?" we would probably answer that they would be near rivers, lakes, or the oceans, where roads came to such waters, causing the breaks-in-transport. Road locations we would say, would be determined by the needs of the economic activity that would develop in the future. Looking at a modern map of the United States we might be largely satisfied with that answer, except for Denver, Salt Lake City, Spokane, Butte, and some cities in the Southwest, like Amarillo and Lubbock.[44] Can we do any better than this to explain the location of cities and economic activity in general?

In 1955 and 1959, Douglass North published two papers that provide us with a finer focus on the location of economic activity in America throughout its history.[45] These papers combined several ideas we have discussed, together with the analysis of regional development for export only in the initial stages.

The Regional Export Base

First, consider the idea of a region and its export activity. North looked at the development of specializing regions over the course of American history, noting the distinctly *unbalanced* pattern at the beginning, once the problem of subsistence food growing had been solved. Over and over, a territory would open because of the possibility of exploiting some resource—fish, timber, cotton, gold, wheat, coal—that could be exported from the new region to the more settled areas of the country. Population and investment capital would flow in initially to exploit and develop this single resource (or perhaps a linked group, like grains and livestock in the Midwest).

In North's analysis the future of any region after an export activity develops will turn on three factors: (a) the region's natural endowments (at given levels of technology), (b) the "character" of the export industry, and (c) subsequent changes in technology and transport costs.

If the region has a very significant comparative advantage in a single commodity, production will concentrate upon it, and other possibilities will be ignored. The western mining settlements of Telluride, Colorado; Jarbidge, Nevada; and Silver City, Idaho; are examples. When the richest ore veins gave out, the people moved on, leaving ghost towns in their wake. Much later, another change in technology (autos, recreational vehicles) brought in tourists. However, at the time of exploitation of the big export commodity, these regions appeared to be limited in their developmental possibilities.

The "character" of an export industry will influence other important features of a region's subsequent economic development. If the export industry has **increasing returns to scale** (i.e., a large-scale organization has significant competitive advantages over small-scale activities), then income distribution in the region will tend to be relatively unequal, and development will produce only a few urban centers where activities are concentrated on processing and shipping the export commodity. Looking at American history specifically, the North contrasts with both the South and Midwest in this regard. The Southern cotton economy was labor-intensive with scale economies (slavery and large plantations were the most efficient technology), and only a few urban centers devoted mainly to processing and shipping raw cotton were the result. In the Midwest the family-farm agriculture produced a more equal income distribution, and a greater number of possibilities for urban growth as a consequence. (We will return to this point in more detail in a moment.)

The comparative advantage originally established can be altered by some changes in technology and transport costs. In some cases, other (secondary) export industries may develop alongside those that first attracted settlers and investment. These secondary industries, which North calls "residentiary" industries, may even take over the lead in growth or totally supplant the old export sector. The mixture of export and residentiary industries can ultimately give the region the appearance of industrial "balance," *masking the crucial role played initially by exclusively export activities.* Since we mentioned mining towns in the Old West, ski resorts in the modern West made a good example of this point. Transport to ski areas (auto, trains, busses, jets) and the installation of chair and T-bar lifts have brought life back to nearly abandoned mining sites like Ketchum, Alberta; and Aspen, Colorado.

Land Ownership, Social Infrastructure, and Location

North argues that the absence of significant scale economies in nineteenth-century agriculture outside the South produced (a) more equal income distribution, (b) millions of family farms, (c) the need for schools and social services, and (d) more widespread marketing possibilities for manufacturers and sellers. As Rosenberg says, "Nineteenth-century American society was dominated by the tastes of rural households...."[46] These households outside the rural South were rich by European standards, and they were a huge and growing market for all products of urban machine technology. This fact tended to multiply the number of possible sites for cities—sites to be determined less by the needs of a single export commodity than by the needs of millions of families and the opportunities to supply them via urban activities. The multiplication of possible urban sites also meant that clustering or urban-type activities—trades, services, residentiary industries—could be supported in many places. These factors together would multiply demand for investment in *human capital,* for schools and universities. The more equally distributed incomes among a property-owning citizenry with full political rights and responsibilities equally imposed explains the rich social infrastructure of schools, churches, colleges, and the like across the country north of the slave-owning area. To the North, the blessing of the American landownership system was the sturdy communal life in places like Indiana, Ohio, and Iowa. The real cost of slavery to the South, paradoxically *because it was so profitable* to those with the capital to engage in it on a large scale, was the South's lack of such infrastructure west of the tidewater areas. The failure to invest locally in human capital marred Southern society's economic potential well into the twentieth century.

We add now the role of the break-in-transport in determining the location of an urban center. If the surface were homogeneous, then the actual location of such cities would be a curious problem almost entirely solved by transport-cost considerations.[47] But because the continental United States is not a homogeneous surface, nature helps. The continent is carved by rivers and mountain ranges that generally run north and south and are dotted with exploitable natural resources, apart from farmland, in patches—specific locations. Roads, canals, and railroads tend to run east to west, connecting regions to each other where the north-south water transport system has been deemed insufficient to meet the needs of development. Breaks-in-transport between the water and surface routes became the urban sites, locating near export-base regional development. A simplified example is shown in Figure 8.3, where we

Figure 8.3 Hypothetical Determination of Regional Growth and Urban Location

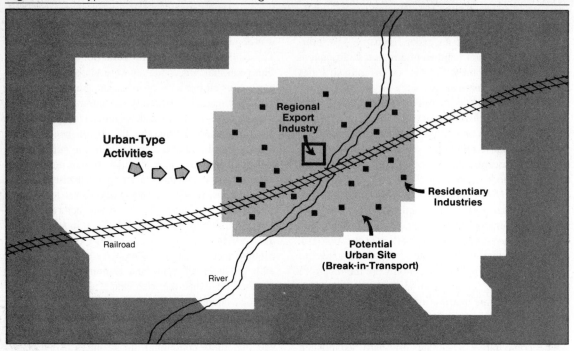

The region's development begins with the exploitation of an export industry. Income from it supports a social infrastructure as well as residentiary industries. The break-in-transport, together with local transport costs and topography, will produce the potential urban site. The external economies of the break-in-transport will pull activities toward the urban site wherever profitable.

have only one export-base industry, a single break-in-transport, and several supporting residentiary activities. Other things being equal, urban location will be where the railroad crosses the river. Inside the region, transport will radiate out from the urban site. External economies at the site will cause residentiary activities to gravitate toward the urban area, where transport costs also are minimized.

The list of American cities resulting from this process as the nation moved west (with Western and Southwestern exceptions already mentioned) is lengthy: Troy, Syracuse, Rochester, Buffalo, Pittsburgh, Wheeling, Youngstown, Cleveland, Akron, Detroit, Chicago, Milwaukee, Minneapolis, Dubuque, Omaha . . .[48] The list continued to grow in the nineteenth century as the nation moved west, and railroads, water, and other natural resources were exploited. In the South there were fewer cities before 1860 as the region exploited its one big export industry in its westward movement. Costs of carrying heavy raw materials

put some cities close to mines or located them in farming areas on water or rail routes. External economies added to export activities caused some cities to grow faster than others, supporting both more residentiary activities and consequential new export industries.

North's theses, added to the break-in-transport analysis, provide a rich background description of regional growth and urbanization, not only up to 1860 but in subsequent decades. Within cities and regions a basically similar locational analysis is relevant but more detailed, with much heavier emphasis upon externalities of transport, markets, and labor force—which need not be pursued here.

CONTRASTS BETWEEN THE NORTH AND SOUTH

North's analysis casts a powerful light on differences between antebellum industrialization in the Southern and Northern regions of the country. By 1860 industrialization in the South was, it is generally held, far below its apparent potential, compared to such achievements in the North. The work of Fred Bateman and Thomas Weiss has underscored this point, but these authors have demonstrated that the differences are more of a puzzle than we had initially assumed because of the accepted tradition of "Southern backwardness" in our historiography.[49] In 1860 manufacturing in the South's major industries like cotton textile production, boots and shoes, clothing, and flour and milling came to only about 20 percent of the national total, and Southern cotton mills were only a third the size of those typically found in New England. Although there were some larger Southern industrial firms, the Southern manufacturing firm typically was smaller than one in New England, or even in the new Western states, and was often found in an isolated rural location. There is no obvious reason why this should have been so. Bateman and Weiss demonstrate that profitability in Southern manufacturing was comparable to that in the North and West, and should have justified a more extensive development than did occur—other things being equal. They offer several possible reasons why it did not:

> Southern investors were exceptionally risk averse, were not knowledgeable about the benefits of diversification, failed to alter their expectations in the light of accumulating evidence on the greater profitability of manufacturing, or attached unagreeably high social costs to industrial diversification.[50]

Jeremy Atack has attempted to explain regional differences through an examination of mainly theoretical possibilities and to contend with those who maintain that the very structure of the antebellum South (low population density, lack of consuming power among slaves and poor whites, preference of the rich for imports and handcrafted luxuries, and so forth) inhibited Southern industrial development.[51] He found that differences in returns to scale and external economies were not sufficient to explain the Southern deficiency in developing industrial potentials. So far as Atack's evidence goes, the scale and extent of industry in the South by 1860 was fully justified by existing technical and other conditions. Southern entrepreneurs were neither lax nor sluggish.

Kenneth Sokoloff adds an interesting analysis to the rise of New England as the premier antebellum manufacturing center. His study of the surviving quantitative evidence shows some scale economies in expansion of shop size from the "artisanal" enterprise to a prefactory specialized workshop employing ten to fifteen workers. New England, with its relatively limited supply of good farmland, its "urbanization," and relatively large supply of competent artisans was subject to these scale economies and so developed a "preindustrial" industry based upon reorganization into specialized workshops. Sokoloff is not certain whether the scale economies came from the greater division of labor and specialization made possible from this reorganization (similar to Adam Smith's famous pin factory described in *The Wealth of Nations*), or the more intensive labor effort per unit of work that shop work with greater supervision and management implies. Similar developments were identified in European industrial history.[52]

We will see in Chapters 10 and 12 that an emphasis upon the expectation of rents in cotton production and capital gains in slave-ownership helps resolve these puzzles. The South did not industrialize as rapidly as the North did before the Civil War for many reasons—some logical, some nonsensical. Virtually all the arguments developed in this chapter about the character of American industrialization could apply equally well in the North and the South, especially once steam power neutralized New England's relative advantage as the owner of more waterpower sites. The South, when it did develop its industrial potential, was typically "American" in its choice of techniques. Before 1860, while there were good, purely business, reasons to invest in manufacturing, those who had capital to invest elected in large measure to stay with slavery and cotton production. The export base in the South supported a sufficient number of residentiary industries as Bateman, Weiss, and Atack show. However, it was only after the expectation of greater returns on dollars invested in slave-based Southern agriculture vanished that capital flowed more readily into Southern manufacturing, flowing in sufficient volume to transform local industrial establishments into part of the new export base that was to come from Southern industrialization.

MANUFACTURING AND THE TARIFF QUESTION

To complete our preliminary survey of American manufacturing origins, we need to consider the tariff,

Exterior and interior views of the Paterson (NJ) Iron Works in 1856.

probably not so much because of its purely economic importance in the nineteenth century, but because of its never-ending political interest. A **tariff** is a tax paid by consumers on goods imported from other countries. It is a transfer from domestic consumers to protected domestic producers. Those who produce goods that are competitive with the imports can raise their own offer prices because the import prices are now higher. The tariff is thus a financial umbrella for high-cost domestic producers, or else it adds an element of pure profit to sales and may induce a higher rate of investment in protected industries than otherwise would be warranted.

Consumers who buy the import-competing goods suffer losses in real income due to the tariff-inspired price increases. Foreigners lose income if Americans do not buy as much of their produce because of the tariff, and, as a result, American exporters (such as Southern cotton growers) lose customers abroad. Who gains from the tariff? The government gets tax revenues. Producers of import-competing goods get more customers or higher prices or both, those who work in such industries may receive higher wages than they might otherwise, and higher prospective returns due to

the tariff may induce investors to put their money into protected industries.

The tariff is, strictly speaking, a subsidy. And like most subsidies, it distorts economic processes away from market solutions. As John James has shown, the antebellum tariff shifted resources from the South to Northern industry, a fact Southerners appreciated early in American history.[53]

Why do we have tariffs? Obviously governments want them for revenues (provided they are not *too* protective, stopping imports and revenues altogether). Rent-seeking producers want them for their extra revenues. Who else?

Tariffs have always been popular with politicians as sure-fire vote-getters. The modern arguments for them usually stress protection of American jobs. If Americans buy foreign cars, American auto workers may get laid off. The argument is absolutely true. The obvious response to it, for those who like Geos, is that American manufacturers should make better, cheaper cars. In earlier times tariffs were needed, it was said, to protect American workers from the products of "cheap foreign labor"—which was mainly a bogus argument. Foreign labor was so cheap then because it was so unproductive. The argument was always good for votes, though, because Americans knew that foreign workers had low standards of living; they feared being driven by competition down to those levels. In recent years this argument is heard less since it is affluent German, Swedish, and Japanese workers who have produced the goods Americans want in such volumes, and those workers are both highly competent and highly paid.

The early "unanswerable" argument for tariffs was the "infant-industry" argument. It was stated in our first tariff act, passed 4 July 1789:

> Whereas it is necessary for the support of the government, for the discharge of the debts of the United States, and the encouragement of manufactures, that duties be laid on goods, wares and merchandise imported. . . .

No question here of consumer welfare, free trade, or economic efficiency. The tariff was to raise money for the government and to protect infant American industry from foreign competition. One rarely hears either argument anymore. Customs duties (tariffs) no longer amount even to 1 percent of federal revenues; in 1790 they were 99.9 percent of total revenues, and in 1860, still 94 percent. In some years high land sales changed the proportions, but generally, up to 1860, the tariff was the mainstay of federal revenues.

The argument for protection is separate since the "perfectly" protective tariff would kill off imports altogether and that would reduce government customs revenues to zero. As for protection, Frank Taussig, studying the lusty infant (still protected) industries nearly a century after the first tariff, doubted that any of them owed their successes in life to the tariff, apart from the ever-anemic American silk industry and cotton manufacturing up to 1824.[54] From the 1790s to 1815, American cotton manufacturers had been protected from foreign competition by incessant European wars. When peace came in 1815, and British manufactured textiles hit American shores in full force, the American manufacturers went to Congress with the infant-industry argument, asking for protection, and got it. Peter Temin shows that Francis Lowell, in the tariff of 1816, went after a flat rate, minimum 25 cents per yard on imported cotton cloth. This was a *high* specific tariff for low-count cloth, the kind Lowell's mills produced. It was designed to cut out low-count cloth from places like India, but did not interfere significantly with the finer cloth imports from places like England.

Southerners were satisfied with this tariff, and it produced a transfer to Lowell, while the Rhode Island mills, which produced higher-count cloth got little protection.[55] Alexander Hamilton, in his *Report on Manufactures,* thought there might be something to the infant-industry argument. In 1816 Lowell seemed to be more "infant" than the fine cloth makers of Rhode Island.

A better argument in our time—tariffs for bargaining with other nations who keep out our goods for their own protectionist reasons—was largely irrelevant during most of the nineteenth century since our main foreign competitor, the United Kingdom, adhered increasingly to a policy of free trade after 1825.

Since the tariff was an income transfer to manufacturing, it was clear at the beginning what part of the country was *not* going to benefit from it. The South sold its products in the international market at international prices and either purchased its manufactured goods from rent-seeking American manufacturers protected by tariffs or else imported the manufactured goods and paid the duties. Because of this, the protective element in the tariff rankled Southern political leaders from the very beginning and was a source of increasing sectional division.

Agitation for greater protection of manufacturers in the North tended to be concentrated in or near cyclical depressions; thus, the main protective tariffs were passed in 1816, 1824, 1828, and 1842. The reasons for this singular correlation are obvious: In depressions prices tend to fall (or did, until recently) and tariffs reduce the extent to which they need to fall to meet foreign competition. The 1828 tariff act, known to fame as "The Tariff of Abominations," raised the average rate on dutiable goods to 61 percent of value and inspired Southern statesmen, led by John C. Calhoun, to seriously reconsider the nature of the constitutional bargain that had been struck in 1789, and whether on this issue the individual states might themselves "nullify" an act of Congress. Underlining, perhaps, the wisdom of John C. Calhoun (without the aid of econometric analysis) Mark Bils concludes that the protective tariff was about the only reason the United States had a cotton textile industry as late as 1833![56] Compromise in 1833, federal surpluses at embarrassingly high levels, and lower tariffs in 1846 and 1857 blunted the force of the anti-tariff feelings in the South in the 1850s.

By 1860 tariff rates had fallen so low that tariff revenue as a percentage of the value of dutiable imports was a mere 19.7 percent, whereas in 1830, when the nullification controversy raged, that figure was 61.7 percent. So, the growth of manufacturing took place in the presence of a declining tariff from 1833 to 1860. Although the tariff declined, it was a political issue of note, and it *did,* after all, gratuitously transfer income from the South and other nonindustrial areas to manufacturers. It is not accidental that when the Confederacy was defeated, rent-seeking manufacturers returned

to drink from the tariff trough. The tariff percentage of dutiable import value rose to nearly 50 percent in 1865 and, with the exception of 1873 and 1874, was never below 40 percent again until the 1920s.[57] The tariff may not have determined the growth of American industry, as Taussig pointed out, but it did generate extra income for manufacturers at the expense of everyone else—a fact that John C. Calhoun had well understood about tariffs to encourage "infant industries."

Notes

1. Quoted in Jonathan Hughes, *Industrialization and Economic History: Theses and Conjectures* (1970), p. 74.
2. For a fuller discussion of entrepreneurial migration and suggested readings on the topic, see Hughes, pp. 71–77.
3. Paul Uselding, "Henry Burden and the Question of Anglo-American Technological Transfer in the Nineteenth Century," *JEH,* June 1970.
4. Claudia Goldin and Kenneth Sokoloff, "The Relative Productivity Hypothesis of Industrialization: The American Case, 1820 to 1950," *QJE,* August 1984.
5. Hughes, *Industrialization and Economic History,* p. 132.
6. For a detailed analysis of this industry, Robert Brooke Zevin, "The Growth of Cotton Textile Production After 1815," in Robert Fogel and Stanley Engerman, eds., *The Reinterpretation of American Economic History* (1971), ch. 10.
7. Jonathan Hughes, *The Vital Few: American Economic Progress and Its Protagonists* (1986), p. 123.
8. Quoted in Hughes, p. 141.
9. Hughes, pp. 141–42.
10. Nathan Rosenberg, "Anglo-American Wage Differences in the 1820's," *JEH,* June 1967.
11. Moreover, the evidence for 1821–1859 shows that unskilled wages rose at an average rate of 1.4 compared to 1.0 for skilled workers in the antebellum period, reenforcing the pattern. Robert A. Margo and Georgia C. Villaflor, "The Growth of Wages in Antebellum America: New Evidence," *JEH,* December 1987. Gerald Friedman's findings show that after the Civil War this pattern was finally reversed, that skilled wages, 85 percent above unskilled in 1903, exceeded unskilled by 80 percent in 1890 and only 61 percent in 1880. The huge influx of unskilled labor in the great Atlantic migration of the late 19th century seemed to overwhelm the historic pattern established in the early industrial period. Gerald Friedman, "Strike Success and Union Ideology: The United States and France, 1880–1914," *JEH,* March 1988.

12. Nathan Rosenberg, *Technology and American Economic Growth* (1972), p. 50.
13. Henry Burden's machines, by 1871, could produce 3600 horseshoes an hour. Uselding, "Henry Burden," p. 331.
14. H. J. Habakkuk, *American and British Technology in the Nineteenth Century: The Search for Labour-Saving Inventions* (1962). For a qualification of the Habakkuk thesis in bold form, Paul Uselding, "Factor Substitution and Labor Productivity Growth in American Manufacturing 1839–1899," *JEH,* September 1972.
15. Habakkuk, ch. III.
16. Stated thus boldly, the essence of the "Habakkuk thesis" is simplicity itself. Underpinning it with relevant wage data has proved to be a most challenging enterprise. Nathan Rosenberg, "Anglo-American Wage Differentials in the 1820's," *JEH,* June 1967; Donald R. Adams, Jr., "Wage Rates in the Early National Period: Philadelphia 1785–1830," *JEH,* September 1968; Jeffrey F. Zabler, "Further Evidence on American Wage Differentials, 1800–1830," *EEH,* Fall 1972; Donald R. Adams, Jr., "Wage Rates in the Iron Industry: A Comment," *EEH,* Fall 1973; Jeffrey F. Zabler, "More on Wage Rates in the Iron Industry: A Reply," *EEH,* Fall 1973.
17. Paul A. David, *Technical Change Innovation and Economic Growth* (New York: Cambridge University Press, 1975). For a critique of David's analysis applied to agriculture, Alan L. Olmstead, "The Mechanization of Reaping and Mowing in American Agriculture, 1833–1870," *JEH,* June 1975. For a critique of Olmstead's critique, Lewis R. Jones, "Comment," *JEH,* June 1977.
18. Technologies abandoned in one economy need not be in another, and a technology can be improved over time in one area even if abandoned elsewhere. An interesting example of this, and a rare case of reswitching, came with the reawakened interest in wood stoves for heating in the late 1970s. These stoves had long been abandoned in favor of cheap (and more convenient) oil in New England. When OPEC fuel oil prices became prohibitive in the

late 1970s, New Englanders were driven back to their inexhaustible (and labor-using) wood supplies. They were surprised and delighted with wood stoves imported from Scandinavia, where they had not been abandoned and had been enormously improved. A technique viewed as outmoded in the 1930s had been improved to an astonishing degree in forty years.

19. William H. Lazonick, "Production Relations, Labor Productivity, and the Choice of Technique: British and U.S. Cotton Spinning," *JEH*, September 1981.

20. Claudia Goldin and Kenneth Sokoloff, "The Relative Productivity Hypothesis of Industrialization : The American Case, 1820 to 1850," *QJE*, August 1984.

21. Edward Ames and Nathan Rosenberg, "Changing Technological Leadership and Industrial Growth," *EJ*, March 1963.

22. Habakkuk, *American and British Technology in the Nineteenth Century*, p. 123.

23. Rosenberg, *Technology and American Economic Growth*, p. 44.

24. Rosenberg, pp. 18–24.

25. Rosenberg, p. 27.

26. Rosenberg, p. 28.

27. Peter Temin, "Manufacturing," in Davis, et al., *American Economic Growth* (1972).

28. Rosenberg, *Technology and American Economic Growth*, pp. 63–64.

29. Nathan Rosenberg, "Technological Change in the Machine Tool Industry, 1840–1910," *JEH*, December 1963.

30. The number of horses in this country peaked at an incredible 21.4 million in 1915, and there still were 4.7 persons per horse, that far into the age of the railroad and the internal combustion engine! The data for animals in this passage are from *Historical Statistics*, series K 564–82; the estimate of total horsepower of all prime movers, from series S 1–14.

31. Peter Temin, "Steam and Water Power in the Early 19th Century," in Fogel and Engerman *The Reinterpretation of American Economic History*, p. 231.

32. Rosenberg, *Technology and American Economic Growth*, p. 64.

33. Jeremy Atack, Fred Bateman, and Thomas Weiss, "The Regional Diffusion and Adoption of The Steam Engine in American Manufacturing," *JEH*, June 1980, p. 285.

34. As noted previously, by 1869, steam had only barely surpassed waterpower as prime movers. Atack, Bateman, and Weiss, p. 282, fn. 10.

35. Temin, "Steam and Water Power," pp. 230–35.

36. Temin, p. 231, Table 1.

37. Temin, p. 197, Table 4.

38. In the New England textile industry, the preferences of industrial lenders also played a part: Lance E. Davis, "Sources of Industrial Finance: The American Textile Industry, A Case Study," *EEH*, 1st series, April 1957 and "The New England Textile Mills and the Capital Markets: A Study of Industrial Borrowing, 1840–1860," *JEH*, March 1960.

39. Temin, "Steam and Water Power," p. 191, Table 1.

40. Uselding, "Henry Burden," pp. 332–33.

41. Temin, "Steam and Water Power," pp. 232–33.

42. Rosenberg, *Technology and American Economic Growth*, p. 65, fn. 6. Also see Harlan I. Halsey, "The Choice Between High-Pressure and Low-Pressure Steam Power in America in the Early Nineteenth Century," *JEH*, December 1981.

43. Quoted in Temin, "Steam and Water Power," p. 228. Rapid innovation in the machine technology did not necessarily mean that American technology was "capital intensive," measured in money terms. For example, in most uses a Geo is more "efficient" than a Rolls Royce, and several Geos may be purchased with the technical improvements "embodied" in each new model, while one Rolls Royce is being fully depreciated. Perhaps such considerations help explain the recent findings of Alexander Field that nineteenth-century British manufacturing seems to have been more "capital intensive" than American manufacturing, measured either as the money value of installed machinery to output or to labor. Alexander Field, "On the Unimportance of Machinery," *EEH*, October 1985.

44. William Dean was the main innovator of the location paradigm just described. It can be used to explain the location of Chicago. Louis P. Cain, "William Dean's Theory of Urban Growth: Chicago's Commerce and Industry, 1854–1871," *JEH*, June 1985.

45. Douglass North, "Location Theory and Regional Economic Growth," *JPE*, June 1955; "Agriculture and Regional Economic Growth," *Proceedings of the American Farm Economics Association*, December 1959. The two analyses are combined in *The Economic Growth of the United States 1790–1860* (1961), ch. 1.

46. Rosenberg, *Technology and American Economic Growth*, p. 48.

47. The problem was worked out long ago by the German economist, August Lösch. Stefan Valavanis, "Lösch on Location," *AER*, September 1955.

48. For applications of location theory to Chicago's siting and growth, see Louis Cain, *Sanitation Strategy for a Lakefront Metropolis: The Case of Chicago* (1979) and "From Mud to Metropolis: Chicago before the Fire," in Paul Uselding, ed., *REH*, (1986), vol. 10.

49. Fred Bateman and Thomas Weiss, "Manufacturing in the Antebellum South," in Paul Uselding, ed., *REH* (1976) vol. 1.

50. Bateman and Weiss, p. 161.

51. Jeremy Atack, "Returns to Scale in Antebellum United States Manufacturing," *EEH,* October 1977.

52. Kenneth Sokoloff, "Was the Transition from the Artisanal Shop to the Nonmechanized Factory Associated with Gains in Efficiency? Evidence from the U.S. Manufacturing Censuses of 1820 and 1850," *EEH,* October 1984. Herbert Kisch, *Die Hausindustriellen Textilgewerbe am Niederhein vor der Industriellen Revolution,* (Göttingen, Vandenhoeck & Ruprecht, 1981) pp. 38–39. Kisch says that the original idea of the "proto-factory" was in Fritz Redlich and Hermann Freudenberger, "The Industrial Development of Europe: Reality, Symbols, Images," *Kyklos,* 1964, p. 381. The generalization of an evolutionary route to industrialization in Europe is set out thusly by Joel Mokyr: ". . . the Industrial Revolution consisted of the emergence of a germinal modern sector, which gradually increased its weight in the economy until it ended up dominating the economy entirely." "Growing-Up and the Industrial Revolution in Europe," *EEH,* October 1976, p. 372. For a survey of the idea of "proto-industrialization" in its complete effulgence, D. C. Coleman, "Proto-Industrialization: A Concept Too Many," *EHR,* August 1983.

53. John James, "The Welfare Effects of the Antebellum Tariff: A General Equilibrium Analysis," *EEH,* July 1978. But there were possible effects that aided Southern cotton producers at various points in time, depending upon the effects on demand for raw cotton produced by the growth of Northern textile manufacturing. Clayne Pope, "The Impact of the Ante-Bellum Tariff on Income Distribution," *EEH,* Summer 1972; Bennett D. Baack and Edward J. Ray, "Tariff Policy and Income Distribution: The Case of the United States 1830–1860," *EEH,* Winter 1973–74.

54. Frank Taussig, *The Tariff History of the United States* (1888). Zevin, "The Growth of Cotton Textile Production After 1815," shows a complex shifting of demand, supply, and technical change accounting for the cotton textile industry's growth, with the major technical innovations coming before 1825. Although it would be difficult to prove that these innovations were the *results* of tariff protection, they certainly would not have harmed investors. Would they have taken place in any case? No doubt, but perhaps with different timing. Zevin thinks the initial impetus of growth in this industry was mainly due to factory production itself, which shifted the industry out of people's homes.

55. Peter Temin, "Product Quality and Vertical Integration in the Early Cotton Textile Industry," *JEH,* December 1988.

56. Mark Bils, "Tariff Protection and Production in the Early U.S. Cotton Textile Industry," *JEH,* December 1984.

57. *Historical Statistics of the United States,* 1960, series U 211–12.

Suggested Readings

Articles

Adams, Donald R., Jr. "Wage Rates in the Early National Period: Philadelphia, 1785–1830." *Journal of Economic History,* vol. XXVIII, no. 3, September 1968.

———. "Wage Rates in the Iron Industry: A Comment." *Explorations in Economic History,* vol. 11, no. 1, Fall 1973.

Ames, Edward, and Rosenberg, Nathan. "Changing Technological Leadership and Industrial Growth." *Economic Journal,* vol. 73, no. 289, March 1963.

Atack, Jeremy. "Returns to Scale in Antebellum United States Manufacturing." *Explorations in Economic History,* vol. 14, no. 4, October 1977.

———. "Fact or Fiction? The Relative Costs of Steam and Water Power: A Simulative Approach." *Explorations in Economic History,* vol. 16, no. 4, October 1979.

———. Bateman, Fred, and Weiss, Thomas. "The Regional Diffusion and Adoption of the Steam Engine in American Manufacturing." *Journal of Economic History,* vol. XL, no. 2, June 1980.

Baack, Bennett P., and Ray, Edward J. "Tariff Policy and Income Distribution: The Case of the U.S., 1830–1860." *Explorations in Economic History,* vol. 11, no. 2, Winter 1973–74.

Bateman, Fred, Faust, James, and Weiss, Thomas. "Profitability in Southern Manufacturing: Estimates for 1860." *Explorations in Economic History,* vol. 12, no. 3, July 1975.

Bateman, Fred, and Weiss, Thomas. "Comparative Regional Development in Antebellum Manufacturing." *Journal of Economic History,* vol. XXXV, no. 1, March 1975.

Brito, D. L., and Williamson, Jeffrey G. "Skilled Labor and Nineteenth Century Anglo-American Managerial Behavior." *Explorations in Economic History,* vol. 10, no. 3, Spring 1973.

Cain, Louis, "William Dean's Theory of Urban Growth: Chicago's Commerce and Industry, 1854–1871," *Journal of Economic History,* vol. XLV, no. 2, June 1985.

———. "From Mud to Metropolis: Chicago before the Fire." In Paul Uselding, ed., *Research in Economic History.* Greenwich, CT: JAI Press, 1986, vol. 10.

David, Paul. "Learning by Doing and Tariff Protection: A Reconsideration of the Case of the Antebellum United States Textile Industry." *Journal of Economic History,* vol. XXX, no. 3, September 1970.

———. "The Horndal Effect in Lowell, 1834–1856: A Short-Run Learning Curve for Integrated Cotton Textile Mills." *Explorations in Economic History,* vol. 10, no. 2, Winter 1973.

Davis, Lance E. "Sources of Industrial Finance: The American Textile Industry, A Case Study." *Explorations in Economic History,* 1st series, vol. LX, no. 4, April 1957.

———. "The New England Textile Mills and the Capital Markets: A Study of Industrial Borrowing, 1840–1860." *Journal of Economic History,* vol. XX, no. 1, March 1960.

Field, Alexander James. "Sectoral Shift in Antebellum Massachusetts: A Reconsideration." *Explorations in Economic History,* vol. 15, no. 2, April, 1978.

Friedman, Gerald, "Strike Success and Union Ideology: The United States and France, 1880–1914," *Journal of Economic History,* vol. XLVIII, no. 1, March 1988.

Goldin, Claudia D. and Lewis, Frank D. "The Role of Exports in American Economic Growth During the Napoleonic Wars, 1793 to 1807." *Explorations in Economic History,* vol. 17, no. 1, January 1980.

Goldin, Claudia, and Sokoloff, Kenneth. "The Relative Productivity Hypothesis of Industrialization; The American Case, 1820 to 1850," *Quarterly Journal of Economics,* vol. LXIX, no. 3, August 1984.

Halsey, Harlan I. "The Choice Between High Pressure and Low Pressure Steam Power in America in the Early Nineteenth Century." *Journal of Economic History,* vol. LXI, no. 4, December 1981.

James, John. "The Welfare Effects of the Ante-Bellum Tariff: A General Equilibrium Analysis." *Explorations in Economic History,* vol. 15, no. 3, July 1978.

Lazonick, William H. "Production Relations, Labor Productivity, and Choice of Technique: British and U.S. Cotton Spinning." *Journal of Economic History,* vol. XLI, no. 3, September 1981.

Livesay, Harold, and Porter, Glen. "The Financial Role of Merchants in the Development of U.S. Manufacturing, 1815–1860." *Explorations in Economic History,* vol. 9, no. 1, Fall 1971.

Margo, Robert A., and Villaflor, Georgia C. "The Growth of Wages in Antebellum America: New Evidence." *Journal of Economic History,* vol. XLVII, no. 4, December 1987.

North, Douglass C. "Location Theory and Regional Economic Growth." *Journal of Political Economy,* vol. LXII, no. 3, June 1955.

———. "Agriculture and Regional Economic Growth." *Proceedings of the American Farm Economic Association,* vol. XLI, no. 5, December 1959.

Passell, Peter, and Schmundt, Maria, "Pre-Civil War Land Policy and The Growth of Manufacturing." *Explorations in Economic History,* vol. 9, no. 1, Fall 1971.

Pope, Clayne. "The Impact of the Antebellum Tariff on Income Distribution." *Explorations in Economic History,* vol. 9, no. 4, Summer 1972.

Rosenberg, Nathan. "Technological Change in the Machine-Tool Industry, 1860-1919." *Journal of Economic History,* vol. XXIII, no. 4, December 1963.

———. "Anglo-American Wage Differences in the 1820's." *Journal of Economic History,* vol. XXVII, no. 2, June, 1967.

———. "Factors Affecting the Diffusion of Technology." *Explorations in Economic History,* vol. 10, no. 1, Fall 1972.

Sokoloff, Kenneth L. "Was the Transition from the Artisanal Shop to the Nonmechanized Factory Associated with Gains in Efficiency? Evidence from the U.S. Manufacturing Censuses of 1820 and 1850." *Explorations in Economic History,* vol. 21, no. 4, October 1984.

Temin, Peter. "Steam and Water Power in the Early 19th Century." *Journal of Economic History,* vol. XXVI, no. 2, June 1966. Reprinted in Robert Fogel and Stanley Engerman, eds., *The Reinterpretation of American Economic History.* New York: Harper & Row, 1971.

———. "Manufacturing." In Lance E. Davis et al., *American Economic Growth: An Economist's History of the United States.* New York: Harper & Row, 1972.

———. "Product Quality and Vertical Integration in the Early Cotton Industry. *Journal of Economic History,* vol. XLVIII, no. 4, December 1988.

Terrill, Tom E. "Eager Hands: Labor for Southern Textiles, 1850–1860." *Journal of Economic History,* vol. XXXVI, no. 1, March 1976.

Uselding, Paul. "Henry Burden and the Question of Anglo-American Technological Transfer in the Nineteenth Century." *Journal of Economic History,* vol. XXX, no. 2, June 1970.

———. "Technical Progress at the Springfield Armory." *Explorations in Economic History,* vol. 9, no. 3, Spring 1972.

———. "Factor Substitution and Labor Productivity Growth in American Manufacturing 1839–1899." *Journal of Economic History,* vol. XXXII, no. 3, September 1972.

————. "A Note on the Inter-Regional Trade in manufactures in 1840." *Journal of Economic History,* vol. XXXV, no. 2, June 1976.

Zabler, Jeffrey F. "Further Evidence on American Wage Differentials, 1800–1830." *Explorations in Economic History,* vol. 10, no. 1, Fall 1972.

————. "More on Wage Rates in the Iron Industry: A Reply." *Explorations in Economic History,* vol. 11, no. 1, Fall 1973.

Zevin, Robert Brooke. "The Growth of Cotton Textile Production After 1815." In Robert Fogel and Stanley Engerman, eds., *The Reinterpretation of American Economic History.* New York: Harper & Row, 1971.

Books

Cain, Louis. *Sanitation Strategy for a Lakefront Metropolis: The Case of Chicago.* DeKalb: Northern Illinois University Press, 1979.

Clark, Victor S. *History of Manufactures in the United States 1607–1860.* Washington: The Carnegie Institution, 1929.

Cole, A.H. *The American Wool Manufacture.* Cambridge: Harvard University Press, 1926.

Davis, Lance E., et al. *American Economic Growth: An Economist's History of the United States.* New York: Harper & Row, 1971.

Fogel, Robert, and Engerman, Stanley. *A Reinterpretation of American Economic History.* New York: Harper & Row, 1971.

Habakkuk, H. J. *American and British Technology in the Nineteenth Century: The Search for Labor Saving Inventions.* New York: Cambridge University Press, 1962.

Hughes, Jonathan. *Industrialization and Economic History: Theses and Conjectures.* New York: McGraw-Hill, 1970.

————. *The Vital Few: American Economic Progress and Its Protagonists.* New York: Oxford University Press, 1986.

North, Douglass C. *The Economic Growth of the United States 1790–1860.* Englewood Cliffs, NJ: Prentice-Hall, 1961.

Rosenberg, Nathan. *Technology and American Economic Growth.* New York: Harper & Row, 1972.

Taussig, Frank W. *The Tariff History of the United States.* New York: Putnam's Sons, 1888.

Temin, Peter. *Iron and Steel in Nineteenth Century America: An Economic Study.* Cambridge: MIT Press, 1964.

Ware, C. F. *The Early New England Cotton Manufacture: A Study of Industrial Beginnings.* Boston: Houghton Mifflin Company, 1931.

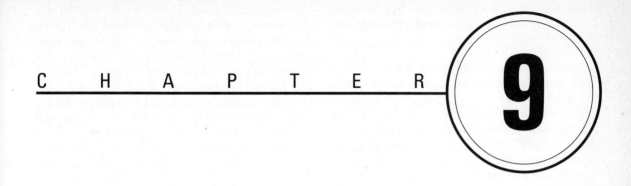

CHAPTER 9

Transportation, Internal Improvements, and Urbanization

As we have seen, in the earliest colonial settlements successful development depended not only upon the establishment of farms and extractive activities but also upon the creation of transportation and communications *nodes* at certain breaks-in-transport. The same process continued, for the same reasons, as economic development spread westward. **Productivity,** output per unit of input, would rise in part as transport and distribution costs were reduced, thus enabling living standards to improve. Americans were aware of this need, and no single collective activity was really more striking in the antebellum period than the nation's energetic pursuit of improvements in transportation and communications.

The way such activities were organized is of special interest. In England canals and railroads were built by private capitalism almost without government participation. But in the United States, overwhelmingly, there was a mixture of enterprise, partly private and partly that of the collective power—government. Whether these mixtures were examples of successful rent-seeking by private operators exploiting the public credit through special privileges extracted from gov-

ernments or whether wily political leaders, who wanted such improvements for reasons of local or national ambition, coaxed private enterprise out into the open by the offer of special advantages, makes a nice historical question. Who co-opted whom? Both arguments have their advocates.

Traditionally it was believed that the sheer size of the investment required for improvements like canals and railroads was beyond the capability of private entrepreneurs acting alone.[1] Because of transaction costs or risk, or both, the theory was that the private sector could not have raised such sums in competition with the other kinds of investment opportunities available. Governmental units—state, local, or even national—could ease this constraint by direct financial contributions or by lending their credit through the issuance of long-term bonds whose proceeds went to pay, in part, for construction.

James Willard Hurst, the legal historian, has advanced a different argument, shifting the initiative from the private sector to government:

> We felt the need to promote a volunteer muster of capital
> for sizable ventures at a time when fluid capital was so

and there were severe practical limits on the government's ability to tax in order to support direct intervention in the economy.[2]

By special franchise incorporation, political leaders could grant privileges and the rights to contract loans, levy tolls, and even (in some cases) print money to support transportation enterprises. For these reasons, state and local governments became vitally involved almost from the beginning. In effect, they delegated the taxing power to private companies along with the other forms of government help that were provided. So, Hurst argues, it is government co-opting private capital that explains the vigor of mixed enterprises. Let us now consider the results in more detail.

THE INTERNAL IMPROVEMENT ERA

Once settlers began pouring into Western lands, the advantages of improved transportation became obvious. At first it was hoped that the new federal government would play a major role, and, indeed, in 1806 work was underway to build a national road from Cumberland, Maryland, westward to Illinois (ultimately, it was hoped, all the way to Missouri). Two proposals for federal aid in canal building had already been before Congress in 1806. The basis for these proposals was that funds from sales of public lands would support such projects.

It often is said that economic planning is somehow foreign to the American scheme of things. Yet, early in the country's independent existence the United States had a full-scale plan for a comprehensive system of internal land and water transport in the Eastern part of the country, the Gallatin Plan. The idea came from the Senate itself. Secretary of the Treasury, Albert Gallatin, was instructed in 1807 to prepare "a plan for the application of such means as are within the power of Congress, to the purposes of opening roads and making ls . . ."[3]

atin delivered his plan to the Senate in April, t he emphasized "the extent of territory com- population," and the lack of sufficient l to exploit potential opportunities. To nvestment, he believed, communica- be set up between areas that could nues. A time would come when

such enterprises would pay, but initially only the federal government, he felt, could command sufficient resources. To give the country a "tidewater inland navigation" from Massachusetts to Georgia, he proposed that canals be cut through Cape Cod, between the Raritan and Delaware rivers, between Delaware Bay and Chesapeake Bay, and between the Chesapeake and Albermarle Sound. In addition, he suggested major east-west links: a northern link from the Hudson River to Lake Champlain, from the Mohawk River to Lake Ontario and Lake Erie, and connecting road links between the Allegheny and the Susquehanna (or Juniata), the Monongahela and the Potomac, the Kanawha and the James, and the Tennessee and the Santee (or the Savannah).[4]

Adding all the canals and road links, the plan would cost, according to Gallatin, $20 million—an outlay of $2 million a year for ten years. He believed that the federal government could bear the expense and that the advantages would be incalculable. Moreover, once the projects generated sufficient revenues, they could be sold to private companies and the proceeds could be used to promote further internal improvements.

The plan, ingenious as it was, was not undertaken by the federal government for a variety of reasons, including doubts about its legality. Presidents Madison and Monroe both favored federal participation in internal improvements projects but considered such federal action within the states unconstitutional. The Constitution had been an agreement between existing sovereignties, and expansion of federal power was viewed with deep suspicion. Monroe had wanted the Constitution amended to allow for such federal action. However, federal intervention in those days of "strict constructionism" faded in 1830, when President Jackson vetoed the Maysville Road bill, calling it "unconstitutional." Between 1824 and 1828, about $2 million of federal funds had been spent on canals.[5] The national road from Maryland to Missouri was never to be completed as originally planned, but, altogether, some $7 million of federal money had been spent on it.

The federal government's failure to implement the Gallatin Plan was offset by private entrepreneurs. Together with state and local governments, they, as the late Carter Goodrich (our leading modern student of this historical episode) showed, completed most of it.[6] Railroads ultimately filled in the gaps. Goodrich argued that politics and sectional rivalries, and not ideology, largely nullified the hope of full-scale federal participation even at these early dates. Tariff votes for the Northeast were traded for internal improvement votes for the Midwest, leaving the South with little to gain from federal expenditures on internal improvements. Gallatin's plan, like Hamilton's *Report on Manufactures,* was indirectly influential in charting the future course of events. It just ended up being done in a different way.

ROADS, CANALS, STEAMBOATS, AND RAILROADS

Turnpikes seemed at first to offer a solution to many surface transport problems. They offered a more dependable road surface (stone, gravel, and later, plank) than did the common roads as well as direct links between well-populated and, therefore, profitable areas. Local roads were adequate for local needs. It hardly paid taxpayers in any location to construct better roads for the advantage of others. However, it was hoped that the offer of superior quality with greater possible speed and dependability would attract sufficient long- and middle-distance traffic to pay a profit to investors in the turnpikes. More than $25 million of private capital was invested by several hundred turnpike companies; turnpike mileage was some 4600 miles in 1810 and about 27,800 miles by 1830.[7] Because most turnpike companies were small and built fairly short roads, a given long-distance route would be served by several such companies, each charging tolls on their own sections. Since tolls were regulated by public officials, and activities of the companies were restricted by their charters to road operations, turnpike profits proved disappointing.

The record of turnpike profitability is, in fact, dismal. Most potential traffic at that time consisted of fairly short journeys, and, for these, common (free) roads were an alternative. Costs per ton mile on the turnpikes were lowest for large loads making long journeys. Unfortunately, most turnpike traffic in those times was not of that nature. Albert Fishlow has estimated that profit rates were only 3 and 4 percent for turnpikes.[8] By the 1830s the turnpikes had been overtaken by canals, and then the railroads, and were subsequently abandoned. Most of the funds invested in turnpikes had been private in origin, even in Pennsylvania, where direct state government investment was

greatest. There it amounted to only 30 percent of the estimated total. In antebellum canal and railroad construction, the proportion of government money to the total was much larger than that.

Canals

The great canal-building era, roughly from 1815 to 1843, had many interesting characteristics that have tantalized modern scholars. (Figure 9.1 shows the canal system.) It was here that the mixed enterprises, combinations of private and (state and local) government money and power, entered American history. American canal-building in the antebellum period was truly on a large scale. According to Professor Harvey Segal, canal investment in 1815–44 was $31 million, of which some 73 percent came from governments.[9] In 1844–60, another $66 million was invested, with about 66 percent being government money. Overall, of the roughly $188 million invested in canals, about 73 percent came from the public sector, and 27 percent from private sources.

Entirely private canals existed but were fairly inconsequential. The Santee Canal, built in 1800 in South Carolina, and the Middlesex, constructed from Boston to Lowell in 1803, were private. But it was the completion of the Erie Canal in 1825 that seemed to point to a great future. As Albert Niemi suggests, some of the effect of the canals was the fostering of a manufacturing sector to serve a regional agriculture made more prosperous by cheaper transport costs. But, as Roger Ransom shows, a major portion of the manufacturing that grew up along the canal routes was for the processing of agricultural output for export out of the regions served by the new canals.[10] In both cases, the canals brought greater economic activity by reducing transport costs.

Hopes for federal aid to build the Erie were dashed in March of 1817 when President Madison vetoed a bill that would have provided $1.5 million. In April, the New York legislature passed the necessary laws to build the canal by state action alone. Funds were to come from earmarked taxes, from borrowing on state credit, and from tolls collected as sections of the canal opened. The canal, which connects the Hudson River with Lake Erie, involved 363 miles of construction and was built for $7 million. Initial issues of Erie bonds were in small denominations and were purchased

Figure 9.1 Principal Canals, 1800–60

In the antebellum period an elaborate canal system was built to exploit the country's internal water-transport possibilities, mainly east of the Mississippi River. The longest canal was the Wabash and Erie, from Evansville, Indiana, to Toledo, Ohio.

mainly by citizens of New York. When the success of the canal became evident, large investors and foreign buyers entered. By 1829, foreigners had purchased half of the canal's debt. The cost of shipping a ton of wheat from Buffalo to New York City fell from $100 a ton to $10. A new era was born in east-west communications in the North. In addition, the connection to Lake Champlain had been finished in 1823, and New York State had constructed feeder canals for the Erie.[11]

Following the Erie's success, a flurry of canal-building began elsewhere. The enterprising citizens of Pennsylvania were early enthusiasts for internal improvements. Already in 1789 they had benefitted from what later was called a "Gallatin Plan for Pennsylvania," produced by a Society for Promoting Improvement of Road and Inland Navigation. The road west, the Pittsburgh Pike, had been completed in 1817. The

state had invested tax funds, which by 1825 amounted to $1.8 million, in fifty-six turnpike and bridge companies, in cooperation with private capitalists. But the Erie presented a new challenge. Philadelphia's preeminence was now threatened, and in 1826 the legislature voted to build the Main Line Canal with state funds.

Because of the Appalachian barrier's height and width between Pittsburgh and the coastal plain, the Main Line was a complicated project involving transfers of cargo to surface transport (later to rail links) at several points. These necessary breaks-in-transport would, from the start, put the Main Line at a competitive disadvantage with the Erie. The Main Line, traversing 359 miles, was completed in 1835 at a construction cost of some $12 million. By then, an additional $6.5 million also had been spent in Pennsylvania on smaller canals. Pennsylvania, as was true of

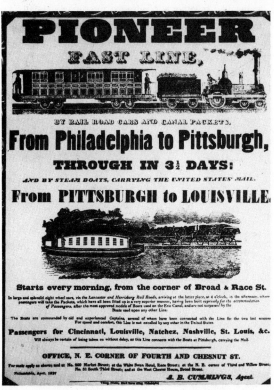

Canals and Railroads. Mixed transport technologies moved westward in the age of internal improvements in the 1830s (above). Canals formed an internal transportation network in the competitive race with railroads in Eastern Pennsylvania (at the left).

several other states, failed in 1842 to meet the interest on the $33 million of state obligations that had accumulated from internal improvements projects but later redeemed the securities. Overall, the Main Line earned only 3 percent on the original investment of $12 million. It was sold to the Pennsylvania Railroad in 1857 for $7.5 million.[12]

Canal-building was also a major state undertaking in parts of the Midwest where natural waterways seemed to offer excellent opportunities for canal improvements. Indiana built the longest waterway, from Evansville on the Ohio River all the way north to Toledo, Ohio. Called the Wabash and Erie Canal, it was 450 miles long. The Wabash and Erie was finished in the 1850s at a cost of some $6.5 million and was abandoned almost at once because of railroad competition. In Ohio, canal-building was extensive. A total of 761 miles of canals were built, connecting Ohio's waterways, at a cost of $16 million. Here, too, railroad competition proved too stiff and most of Ohio's system was quickly abandoned.[13] Illinois had a federal land grant to support the Illinois and Michigan Canal, linking

BOSTON,
Plymouth & Sandwich
MAIL STAGE,

Early Roadways.   Moving people and goods over rutted dirt roads (opposite) which became dangerously muddy and frequently impassable during bad weather discouraged most early travel. Attempts to bridge mud with corduroy roads of logs laid side by side (opposite center left) resulted only in lamed horses and rickety wagons. It was not until roads paved with stone and gravel were built by private companies that travel increased immensely. Fees for use of the roads varied for freight, horsemen, and stages, and were collected at tollgates (top left). By 1811 there were 137 such road companies in New York state alone. Numerous inns and taverns opened along the turnpikes to accommodate the travelers.

Early Waterways. When roadways were implemented by broad, deep rivers that could not be bridged, ferries took the travelers across. Coal, grain, and agricultural products were taken to market on flatboats and rafts, which frequently were sold as well for their lumber. After steamboats were invented, they became the primary mover of goods and people on America's waters.

Lake Michigan to the Mississippi River via the Chicago and Illinois rivers. It, like the Wabash and Erie, cost about $6.5 million in original construction. Some of it is still in use as part of the Chicago Sanitary and Ship Canal.[14] Experience with this canal finally inspired engineers to dredge the Chicago River, reversing its flow and thus making possible the modern Chicago megalopolis. The original canal, however, was a financial failure.

Other canals experienced the same fate. Virginia and Maryland had both supported the Potomac Canal Company with state funds, and George Washington himself had been its first president. The company, which built locks around five falls of the Potomac, ended in bankruptcy. In 1825, a new venture, the Chesapeake and Ohio Canal, was underway with an initial grant of $1 million of federal money and an additional $2 million of state and local funds. Private participation was a minority interest, a mere $600,000. The canal was to extend to Cumberland, Maryland. That goal was finally reached twenty-five years later in 1850 after an expenditure of $10 million, 60 percent of which had been supplied by the State of Maryland alone.

Virginia's efforts with internal improvements were, relatively speaking, immense. Goodrich estimates that at the end of the 1850s, the state had contributed, in all, on the order of $55 million to internal improvements in canals, roads, and railroads. State aid in Virginia was always meant to be a bait to draw private funds into action. Virginia was an explicit example of the Hurst thesis, discussed earlier. As a report of 1815 put it: "The Commonwealth should subscribe so much . . . and on such terms as will suffice to elicit individual wealth for public improvement."[15] Virginians made every effort to open up their interior to commerce by public effort. Apparently, they were not discouraged by the lack of profitability, by private standards, since at the outbreak of the Civil War, Virginia authorized extensive new outlays from the public funds.

The entire canal system made sense, if there had been no railroad competition. But the long-run fate of most canals in the United States—north and south, east and west—was sealed by railroads, which came along in many cases on competitive routes before the canals were even completed. The railroads provided faster, more dependable, year-round service to offset the higher freight charges, and the canals were mainly left in the dust of history.[16]

Steamboats

No account of the country's antebellum growth would be complete without an examination of the innovation of steamboats and their use on the great internal river system—the Missouri, Ohio, and Mississippi rivers—that drains half a continent. Flatboats, keelboats, and the steam-driven paddlewheelers of legend, gave farmers in the vast interior cheap transportation for their crops downriver to New Orleans and the sea, and brought manufactures back from New Orleans into the interior of the country. James Mak and Gary Walton said of this era: "The transformation of these areas, 1815–1860, from unsettled backwoods regions into agricultural heartland was due primarily to improvements in river transportation."[17]

The process began as early as 1811. The supply-side impact of the steamboats is seen in two separate measures: (a) the carrying capacity of the river steamboat fleet as tonnage (tons of water displaced by the vessels) and (b) the productivity of that tonnage. How efficiently was it used? Both factors could increase the available transport supply at every price. Because the entire supply curve of transportation shifted to the right, increases in tonnage, and/or in its efficiency in use, lowered the costs of food transportation and thus the price of food to the consumer.

Erik F. Haites and James Mak considerably refined our ideas of the actual river steamboat fleet and its tonnage on the Western rivers in the antebellum period. They were able to calculate the *net* additions annually to tonnage and number of steamboats by estimating the number and tonnages of boats annually removed from service. The average working life of a river steamboat was only about five and a half years before 1860.[18] Table 9.1 shows the Haites and Mak data for selected years.

By the end of the 1850s a vast fleet of some 800 steamboats serviced the interior rivers of the United States. Freight rates had fallen in real terms by some 90 percent upstream in the period 1815–60 and by nearly 40 percent downstream (where they already were relatively low because of the highly competitive flatboat market for downstream traffic).[19] The heavy loads, crops and raw materials, tended to go downstream, but the lighter and more valuable (per unit) upstream cargoes gained enormously from steamboat technology. Transit and turnaround times were

Table 9.1 Steamboats in Operation on Western Rivers 1811–60

Years	Number	Tonnage
1811	1	371
1815	7	1,516
1820	69	14,208
1825	80	12,527
1830	151	24,574
1835	324	50,123
1840	494	82,626
1845	538	96,155
1850	638	134,566
1855	696	172,695
1860	817	195,022

Source: Erik F. Haites and James Mak, "The Decline of Steamboating on the Ante-Bellum Western Rivers: Some New Evidence and an Alternative Hypothesis," *Explorations in Economic History*, vol. 11, no. 1, Fall, 1973. Derived from their Table A–1.

drastically cut by the steamboats and technology associated with them.

Growth of the river steamboat fleet was not constant, either in construction or in tonnages in service. Haites and Mak found cyclical activity that was roughly in accord with overall economic fluctuations, as did Harvey Segal in his study of canal building.[20] The business cycles were pervasive in their effects upon advances in transport, as we will see shortly in the case of the new railroad system. Construction of steamboats boomed during general expansions, and the construction growth lagged a year or so behind general downturns. Boats under construction tended to be carried through to completion, despite worsening prospects in downturns. On the other hand, since crews could be laid off instantly and the boats docked when trade slumped, tonnage in use did not lag behind cyclical downturns.

As was the case with steamship building more generally, each new expansion of construction embodied the newest improvements; therefore, productivity per ship tended to rise even more than the increases in tonnage indicate.[21] The operating tonnage of the 1850s was far more efficient than that of earlier periods. Mak and Walton measure an increase in per unit productivity of the steamboat fleet by nearly a factor of nine from 1815 to 1860.[22]

Improvements in design (which raised the ratio of net carrying capacity to gross tonnage), together with better engines and improved docking facilities (cutting turnaround times), accounted for most of the productivity increase, and most of that was already achieved as early as the 1840s, according to Mak and Walton.[23] The evidence shows that railroad competition did not cause total steamboat freights to fall before the Civil War.[24] But the disruptions of the river system during the war, together with greater railroad building during and after the war, put an end to the glorious era of antebellum steamboating celebrated by Mark Twain and others.

Mak and Walton emphasize that many factors, each working in its own way, produced the golden age of the river steamboat: Externalities like the "growth of market trade and improvements in commercial organization" contributed to improved turnaround times, while design changes, river improvements, better captains and crews, lowered insurance rates, and a host of other small changes made their contributions. Mak and Walton quote from Louis Hunter's classic work, *Steamboats on the Western Rivers,* which says that "plodding progress" was how it was done.[25] Nevertheless, railroads displaced river steamboats after the Civil War in the legendary "transportation revolution" of the American economy.

Railroads

The railroad long played an heroic and titanic role in American economic history books. No single innovation before, or since, quite gripped the minds of historians, and none seemed to characterize so aptly the adventuresome spirit of the nineteenth century in this country. Apart from the color (in song and story), there were two bases for the railroad's high place in American historiography: (a) The heroic image was one of an empire-builder—a person who "opened the country," building at great risk "ahead of demand," gambling on the future. (b) The titanic image was more complex. The railroads sharply cut down transportation costs, linking the country together in all directions and spurring the nation's growth far in advance of anything that might otherwise have been achieved. Railroad construction even determined in its variations the timing of the nineteenth-century business cycle.[26] Modern scholarship has sharply deflated both of these appraisals.

The work of Albert Fishlow on antebellum railroads pretty well lays to rest the idea that these early railroads were typically built by farseeing geniuses who knew where future development would take place.[27] Fishlow found that the early railroads went mainly into areas already populated and developed, even in Illinois, and that the amount of government money required tended to vary inversely with the profitability of the routes: The lower the profit prospects for private investors, the more government money was needed to attract railroad construction.

Fishlow's findings do not, however, resolve the question raised earlier about who was exploiting whom. Where the proportion of government participation was greatest, Fishlow argues, the motives of local governments to invest tax money were mainly "defensive"—to ensure that certain communities would not be bypassed. Railroad planners sometimes assembled routes based solely on the promise of local public participation: In that case, the evidence supports the traditional view that promoters deceived governments into investing in questionable enterprises. But governments also were willing to make financial offers to attract promoters (as they still do with tax breaks and exemptions), which is evidence that the deception worked both ways. Obviously, in all cases the opportunities were mutually, although not necessarily, equally attractive.

Robert Fogel's work on the social savings created by the railroads for a time threw nearly all historians into a tizzy.[28] The tradition, built up for decades, had placed railroad construction at the very center of explanations of the fantastic economic growth achieved by Americans in the nineteenth century. Instead of recounting once again the truly impressive evidence on American railroad construction in the nineteenth century, Fogel asked an interesting question: How might the country have developed had there never been any railroads? What was the *social saving* of railroads—the difference between the actual cost of shipping commodities and what the cost would have been by the next best alternative mode of transportation (in this case, railroads)?

To the surprise of most, Fogel found that the canal and river systems could very nearly have produced the same results. All but 4 percent of existing agricultural land in 1890 would have been cultivated. The social savings would have been roughly 5 percent of estimated GNP by 1890. Moreover, the weight of common nails consumption in the country in 1849, during a period when railroads supposedly were determining the growth of the iron industry, exceeded that of railroad consumption by more than 100 percent. The "backward linkage" of railroads on the iron industry's growth was not that important, says Fogel, nor was it crucial even before 1860 in the lumbering industry, in coal, or even in transportation equipment.[29]

Fogel was not attempting to eliminate the railroad from American economic history, but rather to broaden our ideas about causality in economic development. Fogel's message is that no single innovation created American economic growth, especially in "take-offs," or great leaps forward. The country's economic growth was indeed magnificent, and the railroad played its proper role, but so did housebuilding as well as the potbellied iron stove. Actually, until 1860 only 40 percent of American rail iron came from domestic sources; the rest was imported from England.

The first operating railroad, the Stockton and Darlington, was in operation in England in 1825. Five years later, in 1830, the railroad era began in this country when the Baltimore and Ohio began operation. Table 9.2 indicates why American publicists were so taken with American railroads.

Although mileage in 1869 was still only a faint beginning of the 260,400 miles of main track (429,883 miles including all yards, switching track, and so forth) that would be operated in the peak year, 1930, already by the Civil War our mileage exceeded that of railroads in the United Kingdom, France, and the German states combined.[30] The regional distribution in 1860 is shown in Table 9.3.

Fishlow estimates that total investment in railroads up to 1860 ran to more than $1 billion, more than five

Table 9.2   Miles of Railroad in Operation 1830–60

Year	Mileage
1830	23
1835	1,098
1840	2,818
1845	4,633
1850	9,021
1855	18,374
1860	30,626

Source: *Historical Statistics*, series Q 321–28.

Table 9.3   Distribution of Railroad Mileage in 1830–60

Region	Mileage	Percentage
New England	3,660	12.1
Middle Atlantic	6,353	21.0
North Central	9,592	31.7
South	8,838	29.2
West of the Mississippi River	1,840	6.0

Source: *Encyclopaedia Britannica*, 1958 ed., vol. 18, p. 918.

times the amount invested in the canals.[31] Government participation was highest in the South, about 50 percent of total investment. There sparse population and competition with river transport reduced initial profit possibilities. In New England and the major midwestern routes, government participation was as little as 10 percent of the total. Chicago, the new Midwest rail center, had some 4000 miles of railroads converging on it by 1860. The state of Ohio had 3000 miles of railroads as well as its canals and river transportation facilities.

Inroads on canal and river traffic made by the railroads were based upon savings in *total* transport costs for shippers. The railroads offered year-round service, whereas the main canals faced ice-bound conditions during the weeks of hard winter. Also, the railroads offered more contact points for producers, thus cutting down the costs of wagon haulage and unloading and reloading. Therefore, even though the railroads could not match the price, per ton mile, of water transport along the whole route from producer to consumer, railroads reduced shipping costs. From their inception, the railroads began cutting into potential canal revenues as well as sharing in the growth of all trade. Because railroads tended to be built along river routes where the terrain was flat (see Figure 9.2), to a large extent they actually ran parallel to available water routes.

Even so, it would be misleading to imply that railroad competition alone was responsible for the financial failures of those canals that were abandoned in the antebellum period. Many of them, such as the Wabash and Erie in Indiana (whose southern part was being abandoned before the northern parts were completed), were fatally compromised by the very element of government support that made them initially possible. Following the commercial crises of 1837 and 1839, a deep depression lasting into the early 1840s so disrupted

state finances that nine states suspended payments on their debts.[32] Included were Illinois, Indiana, Maryland, and Pennsylvania, and their major canals never recovered.

Railroads, too, suffered from that episode, but they were only at the beginning of their great growth experience, and, during the next big expansion, in the 1850s, were able to attract fresh government funds and foreign investment. Also, in 1850 a huge, 3,750,000-acre land grant was made by the federal government to Illinois, Alabama, and Mississippi to finance the building of the Illinois Central Railroad.[33] This was not the first land grant for internal improvements, but it was by far the largest and a harbinger of things to come. The new surge of railroad building that began in the 1850s ultimately would result in tracks that spanned the continent. The details of that growth we will leave to a later chapter. By the time of the Civil War, the waterways, including coastal shipping, still carried far more freight than did the new railroads, but the handwriting was on the wall.

Cycles

The construction of internal improvements very roughly followed the course of the business cycle, with big expansions in construction outlays in the 1830s and the 1850s. Although there is conflict between cycle movements and investment in canals, the data on railroads show a fairly close relationship.[34] It is not believable, however, that railroad construction was the sole cause of business cycle swings and turning points: The amounts involved relative to GNP were too small, and the question of remote cause remains, with conflicts in other areas, including banking and changes in foreign trade and the supply of money.

As Paul Cootner argues, American demand for transport, including railroads, reflected world demand for American commodities.[35] Railroad construction, like the rest of the economy, reacted to changing market conditions in the aggregate. The appearance of a causal force running from railroads to the economy at large is thus merely a result of both moving with the business cycle. Nevertheless, internal improvements and railroads in the 1830s and 1850s no doubt did underpin the expansions of those years and, thus, sped the processes of economic growth in the antebellum period.

Figure 9.2   U. S. Railroads as of 1860

Railroads quickly overtook, and largely displaced, the canal system. By 1860, the major eastern cities were connected, and the country's developed economic regions were no longer so isolated from each other. The railroad network by 1860 was far more dense in the North than it was in the South.

URBANIZATION

As the transportation network spread, the number of possible sites for the establishment of commercial and industrial centers multiplied, and then multiplied again. Every break-in-transport was a possible site, although, as we have seen earlier, other economic factors had to come into play. We would not expect to find a town or city wherever a railroad crossed a river. Nevertheless, if we consider only the U.S. Bureau of Census count of "urban places," those settlements of 2500 persons or more, it would almost seem that the maximum number of towns and cities *was* being established during the antebellum period. From 1790 to 1860, when the population grew by just slightly more than a factor of eight, the number of urban places multiplied by more than a factor of sixteen.

Towns and Cities

In 1790 there were 24 American cities with populations in excess of 2500. By 1830, even before the first real boom in internal improvements, that number had grown to 90. By 1860, the map contained 392 places with populations of more than 2500. The proportion of urban population, a mere 5 percent of the total in 1790, was only 8.7 percent four decades later but was 19.7

percent, nearly one fifth, in 1860. Urbanization was already upon us. The raw data for urban places is shown in Table 9.4 below.

This growth was, of course, a mere token of the urbanization yet to come, but already there were interesting characteristics. Consider Table 9.5, which shows the top ten urban places in 1790 and 1860. The four great urban centers of colonial America still were the largest cities in 1860. New York and Philadelphia had changed positions in the ratings, but the next six colonial urban centers had vanished from the list, to be replaced by new urban places. Newark was growing as a manufacturing and port city. Buffalo was at the head

Table 9.4   Size Distribution of Urban Population in 1790, 1830, and 1860[a]

Urban Size by Population	1790		1830		1860	
	Number of Places	Total Population	Number of Places	Total Population	Number of Places	Total Population
2.5–5	12	44	34	126	163	595
5–10	7	48	33	231	136	976
10–25	3	48	16	240	58	884
25–50	2	62	3	105	19	670
50–100			3	222	7	452
100–250			1	203	6	993
250–500					1	267
500–1,000	—	—	—	—	2	1,379
Totals	24	202	90	1,127	392	6,216
Percentage of Total U.S. Population		5.1		8.8		19.8

[a] Population figures are given in thousands of persons.

Source: Derived from *Historical Statistics*, series A 43–54, 58, 69.

Table 9.5   Top Ten Urban Places in 1800 and 1860

Rank Order	1800	1860	1800 Top Ten in 1860 List	1860 Top Ten Not in 1800 List
1	Philadelphia	New York City	New York City	
2	New York City	Philadelphia	Philadelphia	
3	Baltimore	Baltimore	Baltimore	
4	Boston	Boston	Boston	
5	Charleston	New Orleans		New Orleans
6	Salem	Cincinnati		Cincinnati
7	Providence	St. Louis		St. Louis
8	New Haven	Chicago		Chicago
9	Richmond	Buffalo		Buffalo
10	Portsmouth	Newark		Newark

Source: Lance E. Davis et al., *American Economic History: The Development of a National Economy* (Homewood, Ill.: Irwin, 1969), p. 265.

of navigation on the Great Lakes, connected to the East Coast by canal and railroad. It also was a milling and manufacturing center. The rest of the new top cities were on waterways in the West, and Chicago was already beginning its career as the hub of the country's railroad system. The shift of top urban sites westward reflected the general westward movement of population: The country's population-geographical center by 1860 had shifted from Baltimore to Chillicothe, Ohio.

The Economics of Urbanization

As we noted earlier, external economies are the primary, although not the only, reasons for urbanization. Beyond certain *indivisibilities*—such as minimal sizes for efficient central water, sewerage, and fire protection—there had not yet been sufficient economies internal to city organization itself to sustain growth to the mammoth sizes we now see in our largest urban areas.[36] In general, the actual costs of operating urban apparatuses seem to increase geometrically with expansion, so that the largest cities experience almost insoluble fiscal problems and exist only by revenue-sharing with the federal government.

It is the force of *external* economies that produced most of the urban agglomerations. Each firm or economic agent could capture some advantages by locating in urban areas: The net returns for each exceeded the costs of production, in part because of location alone. This power is evident even before the Civil War. Consider, in Table 9.6, the large proportion of the total urban population concentrated in a few large cities.

In 1790, more than 30 percent of the total urban population resided in Philadelphia and New York City. In 1830, 37.7 percent of the urban population was in just four places: New York, Philadelphia, Baltimore, and Boston. In 1860, when there were 392 urban places, 46 percent of the urban population resided in only 10 percent of them, and the largest two cities alone contained 22 percent of the total.

We observed in our discussion of colonial America that successful growth settlements needed a hinterland to sustain them. That hinterland was a nearby source of commodities and goods to process and transship as well as a market for services and imported goods. As such, each settlement would begin to acquire distinctive regional characteristics because of specialization and division of labor along the most profitable lines. New Orleans would develop services and ancillary trades associated with cotton; Pittsburgh, with iron; Chicago, with livestock, wheat, corn, and railroads; and so forth. Diane L. Lindstrom's study of Philadelphia in 1810–40 shows that the city's growth was dominated by the exchange of its locally produced manufactures and services with its expanding agricultural hinterland. Philadelphia's foreign and interregional trade declined, and it did not become a specialized exporter of any dominant product.[37]

The process developed among smaller regional urban places as well—settlements within a given market area would begin to specialize. As Eugene Smolensky wrote, after a while no town's existence could be understood by its own characteristics considered in isolation since each one, as part of a system, would be

Table 9.6 Size Distribution of Urban Populations

Urban Size by Population	Urban Population					
	1790		1830		1860	
	Number	Percentage	Number	Percentage	Number	Percentage
2.5–5	12	21.7	34	11.2	163	9.6
5.0–10	7	23.8	33	20.5	136	15.7
10–25	3	23.8	16	21.3	58	14.2
25–50	2	30.7	3	9.3	19	10.8
50–100			3	19.7	7	7.3
100–250			1	18.0	6	16.0
250–500					1	4.3
500–1,000	—	——	—	——	2	22.1
Total	24	100.0	90	100.0	392	100.0

Source: Table 9.4.

Figure 9.3   Principal U. S. Cities in 1860

Most of the country's cities were in the North in 1860; the New West was represented by a ring of cities around the Great Lakes that would prove to be the focal points of the new industrialism that came after the Civil War.

specialized within a market area and would depend upon the others for some functions:

> All the towns, villages, and cities taken together form a complete system, each with its place in the hierarchy of urban places serving a region. Furthermore, the towns in a region can be understood only when that region is viewed as a subsystem of an interdependent system of regions.[38]

As the economy developed, with this infrastructure of specialized economic subsystems growing within it, urbanization grew as a natural part of economic expansion. There is, as yet, no end to the process, and by 1860, of course, the main growth of American cities was still to come. The big ones were getting bigger; small ones, larger; and new cities like those to come in the South, Midwest, and Far West were beyond imagination. Figure 9.3 on page 172 shows the main cities by 1860. They all were located at breaks-in-transport produced by the sea, Great Lakes, and main rivers wherever local economic activity was sufficiently intense.

In our own time, advances in transportation and communications have allowed significant decentralization to occur—a topic we will discuss in a later chapter. But until the *diseconomies of size*—typically the disadvantages of excessive taxes, pollution, congestion, and crime—overcome the positive externalities, certain urban places will tend to grow. The most economically advantageous combinations have been those involving transport and communications plus manufacturing. Although it has been shown that industrialization alone does not account for urban growth, even in the antebellum period, in some cases industrialization was dominant.[39] As Lance Davis wrote: "As textile production proved possible in New England, cities literally grew out of the fields (Lowell and Lawrence, for example)."[40] In Southern antebellum cities, commerce was predominant.[41]

Industrialization made factories profitable, especially where a central prime mover was utilized, such as waterpower or steam power before 1860. Factories grew because of internal economies of scale. The location of workers near factories—with attendant services, both to human and mechanical needs, brought nearby for reasons of profit—reduced the real costs to others who contemplated joining them. Towns and cities resulted. We saw this process in Douglass North's model for regional growth around an export base. As Woytinsky and Woytinsky have concluded, "the pattern of urbanization has been determined by a combination of historical, geographical, and economic conditions."[42]

Our list of top cities in 1860 includes no purely commercial, purely transport, or purely industrial centers. Even New Orleans, perhaps the prime candidate as a mainly commercial and transport center in the area, had local industrial activity as well as shipbuilding. In the United States, it was as the great French historian, Paul Mantoux, said of Great Britain: The seed of industry, cast upon the ground, "gave a harvest of cities."[43] What was already evident in 1860 in this country would become overwhelming in another half century.

Thomas Jefferson's hope for a peaceful Arcadia with this huge nation and millions of farmers would never be. Its resources, both human and material, would group around the transportation system and produce an urban society. The system in the United States was still four-fifths rural in 1860, and the South more rural than the North. Internal improvements and the natural system of waterways, even before the appearance of important heavy industry, exerted an urbanizing force.

Notes

1. Carter Goodrich, *Government Promotion of American Canals and Railroads 1800–1890* (1960), ch. 1. The original scholarship on this point was done by Guy Stevens Callender, "The Early Transportation and Banking Enterprises of the States," *QJE*, 1902.

2. James Willard Hurst, *The Legitimacy of the Business Corporation* (1969), p. 23.

3. Goodrich, *Government Promotion of American Canals and Railroads 1800–1890*, p. 27.

4. Goodrich, pp. 27–48.

5. Jonathan Hughes, *The Governmental Habit Redux* (Princeton: Princeton University Press, 1991), pp. 68–76 for this episode.

6. Goodrich, *Government Promotion of American Canals and Railroads 1800–1890,* pp. 34–35.

7. Albert Fishlow, "Internal Transportation," in Davis, et al., *American Economic Growth: An Economist's History of the United States* (New York: Harper & Row, 1972), pp. 472–75.

8. Fishlow, p. 474.

9. Carter Goodrich, Jerome Cranmer, Julius Rubin, and Harvey Segal, *Canals and American Economic Development* (1961), p. 215.

10. Roger Ransom, "Canals and Development: A Discussion of the Issues," *AER,* May 1964; Albert Niemi, "A Further Look at Interregional Lands and Economic Specialization: 1820–1840," *EEH,* Summer 1970; Roger Ransom, "A Closer Look at Canals and Western Manufacturing," *EEH,* Summer 1971; Albert Niemi, "Reply" to Ransom, *EEH,* September 1972.

11. Goodrich, *Government Promotion of American Canals and Railroads 1800–1890,* pp. 53–56; Julius Rubin, "The Erie Canal," in Goodrich, et al., *Canals and American Economic Development.*

12. Julius Rubin, "An Imitative Public Improvement: The Pennsylvania Mainline," in Goodrich et al.

13. Goodrich, *Government Promotion of American Canals and Railroads 1800–1890,* pp. 135–37. Roger Ransom, "Interregional Canals and Economic Specialization in the Antebellum United States," *EEH,* Fall 1967.

14. Louis Cain, *Sanitation Strategy for a Lakefront Metropolis: The Case of Chicago* (1978).

15. Goodrich, *Government Promotion of American Canals and Railroads 1800–1890,* p. 4; also pp. 87–101 for data in preceding paragraph.

16. The Canadians also entered the "transportation revolution" of the antebellum period with canals. Theirs were government financed and financially unsuccessful. Thomas F. McIlwraith, "Freight Capacity and Utilization of the Erie and Great Lakes Canals Before 1850," *JEH,* December 1976.

17. James Mak and Gary Walton, "Steamboats and the Great Productivity Surge in River Transportation," *JEH,* September 1972, p. 620.

18. Erik F. Haites and James Mak, "The Decline of Steamboating on the Ante-Bellum Western Rivers: Some New Evidence and an Alternative Hypothesis," *EEH,* Fall 1973, p. 28.

19. Mak and Walton, "Steamboats and the Great Productivity Surge in River Transportation," p. 625.

20. Haites and Mak, "The Decline of Steamboating on the Ante-Bellum Western Rivers," p. 30. Goodrich, et al., *Canals and American Economic Development,* ch. III, especially Figure 1, p. 173.

21. Jonathan Hughes and S. Reiter, "The First 1945 British Steamships," *JASA,* June 1958, pp. 362–75. As the British steam fleet grew over time, iron screw-driven steamers displaced wooden and paddle-wheel ships.

22. Mak and Walton, "Steamboats and the Great Productivity Surge in River Transportation," p. 637.

23. Mak and Walton, Figure 1, p. 624.

24. Haites and Mak, "The Decline of Steamboating on the Ante-Bellum Western Rivers," pp. 31–33.

25. Mak and Walton, "Steamboats and the Great Productivity Surge in River Transportation," p. 636. Louis Hunter's great work is *Steamboats on the Western Rivers* (1949). For more recent general analyses of the steamboat industry in the Midwest, see Erik F. Haites and James Mak, "Ohio and Mississippi River Transportation, 1810–1860," *EEH,* Winter 1970; and by the same authors, "Steamboating on the Mississippi Before the Civil War: A Comparative Study," *BHR,* Spring 1971.

26. Robert Fogel, *Railroads and American Economic Growth: Essays in Econometric History* (1964), pp. 1–10, for a brief survey of the conventional view. On the business cycle, Joseph Schumpeter, *Business Cycles* (New York: McGraw-Hill, 1939), two vols.; Leland H. Jenks, "Railroads as an Economic Force in American Development," in Frederic C. Lane and Jelle C. Riemersma, *Enterprise and Secular Change* (Homewood, IL: Irwin, 1953).

27. Albert Fishlow, *American Railroads and the Transformation of the Ante-Bellum Economy* (1965). Also, see "Internal Transportation" in Davis, et al. *American Economic Growth.* Lloyd Mercer has shown that the developmental role, "building ahead of demand," cannot be abandoned entirely in the case of railroads financed in large part by government land grants, mainly after the Civil War. Lloyd J. Mercer, "Building Ahead of Demand: Some Evidence for the Land Grant Railroads," *JEH,* June 1974.

28. Fogel, *Railroads and American Economic Growth.* The critical reaction to this book was, at the time, awe-inspiring. See Peter D. McClelland, "Railroads, American Growth, and the New Economic History: A Critique," *JEH,* March 1968.

29. See Fogel, *Railroads and American Economic Growth,* ch. VI, for a summary.

30. In 1860 the U.K. operated 10,410 miles; France, about 5000 miles; and the German states, approximately 7–8000, depending upon which ones are counted.

31. Fishlow's estimates are as follows: 1828–43, $137.1 million; 1844–50, $172.3 million; 1851–60, $737.3 million. The 1850s alone saw nearly double the amount of total

capital investment. "Internal Transportation," Davis, et al., *American Economic Growth*, p. 496.

32. R. C. McGrane, *Foreign Bondholders and American State Debts* (1935).

33. Paul W. Gates, *The Illinois Central Railroad and its Colonization Work* (1934). This superb book contains, in rich detail, samples of all the problems associated with mixed enterprises—federal government, state and local government, foreign investment, financial crises, and political consequence.

34. Jonathan Hughes and Nathan Rosenberg, "The United States Business Cycle Before 1860: Some Problems of Interpretation," *EEH,* August 1963.

35. Paul Cootner, "The Role of the Railroads in United States Economic Growth," *JEH,* December 1963.

36. Solar energy could very well change this radically; for example, a city's population could live beneath an enormous "Superdome" and have all the benefits of solar energy. This would be an indivisibility and would require a city of a certain size and economic characteristics to sustain it.

37. Diane L. Lindstrom, "Demand, Markets, and Eastern Economic Development: Philadelphia, 1815–1840," *JEH,* March 1975, pp. 271–73.

38. Eugene Smolensky, "Industrial Location and Urban Growth," in Davis, et al., *American Economic Growth,* p. 536.

39. Diane Lindstrom and John Sharpless, "Urban Growth and Economic Structure in Antebellum America," in Paul Uselding, ed., *REH* (1978), vol. 3.

40. Lance E. Davis, Jonathan Hughes, and Duncan McDougall, *American Economic History* (Homewood, IL: Irwin, 1969), p. 266.

41. Lindstrom and Sharpless, "Urban Growth and Economic Structure in Antebellum America," p. 169.

42. W. S. Woytinsky and E. S. Woytinsky, *World Population and Production, Trend and Outlook* (New York: The Twentieth Century Fund, 1953), p. 125.

43. Paul Mantoux, *The Industrial Revolution in the Eighteenth Century: An Outline of the Beginnings of the Modern Factory System* (London: Jonathan Cape, 1928), p. 368.

Suggested Readings

Articles

Callender, Guy Stevens. "The Early Transportation and Banking Enterprises of the States." *Quarterly Journal of Economics,* vol. XVII, no. 1, November 1902.

Cootner, Paul. "The Role of the Railroads in the United States Economic Growth." *Journal of Economic History,* vol. XXIII, no. 4, December 1963.

David, Paul. "Transport Innovation and the Economic Growth; Professor Fogel On and Off the Rails." *Economic History Review,* 2nd series, vol. 22, no. 3, December 1969.

Fishlow, Albert. "Internal Transportation." In Lance E. Davis, et al., *American Economic Growth: An Economist's History of the United States.* New York: Harper & Row, 1972, ch. 13.

Fleisig, Heywood. "The Central Pacific Railroad and the Railroad Land Grant Controversy." *Journal of Economic History,* vol. XXXV, no. 3, September 1975.

Haites, Erik F., and Mak, James. "Ohio and Mississippi River Transportation 1810–1860." *Explorations in Economic History,* vol. XIII, no. 2, Winter 1970.

———. "Steamboating on the Mississippi Before the Civil War: A Comparative Study." *Business History Review,* vol. XLV, no. 1, Spring 1971.

———. "The Decline of Steamboating on the Ante-Bellum Western Rivers: Some New Evidence and an Alternative Hypothesis." *Explorations in Economic History,* vol. 11, no. 1, Fall 1973.

Heath, Milton. "Public Railroad Construction and the Development of Private Enterprise in the South Before 1861." *Journal of Economic History, The Tasks of Economic History,* vol. X, 1950.

Hidy, Ralph, and Hidy, Muriel. "Anglo-American Merchant Bankers and the Railroads of the Old Northwest, 1848–1860." *Business History Review,* vol. XXXIV, no. 2, Summer 1960.

Hughes, Jonathan, and Rosenberg, Nathan. "The United States Business Cycle Before 1860: Some Problems of Interpretation." *Economic History Review,* 2nd series, vol. XV, no. 3, August 1963.

Jenks, Leland H. "Railroads as a Force in American Development." In Frederic C. Lane and Jelle Riemersma, eds. *Enterprise and Secular Change.* Homewood, IL: Irwin, 1953.

Lindstrom, Diane L. "Demand, Markets and Eastern Economic Development, Philadelphia, 1815–1840." *Journal of Economic History,* vol. XXXV, no. 1, March 1975.

————, and Sharpless, John. "Urban Growth and Economic Structure in Antebellum America." In Paul Uselding, ed., *Research in Economic History.* Greenwich, CT: JAI Press, 1978, vol. 3.

Mak, James, and Walton, Gary. "Steamboat and the Great Productivity Surge in River Transportation." *Journal of Economic History,* vol. XXXII, no. 3, September 1972.

Mercer, Lloyd J. "Building Ahead of Demand: Some Evidence for the Land Grant Railroads." *Journal of Economic History,* vol. XXXIV, no. 2, June 1974.

McClelland, Peter D. "Railroads, American Growth, and the New Economic History, a Critique." *Journal of Economic History,* vol. XXVIII, no. 1, March 1968.

McIlwraith, Thomas F. "Freight Capacity and Utilization of the Erie and Great Lakes Canals Before 1850." *Journal of Economic History,* vol. XXXVI, no. 4, December 1976.

Niemi, Albert W., Jr. "A Further Look at Regional Canals and Economic Specialization: 1820–1840." *Explorations in Economic History,* vol. 7, no. 4, Summer 1970.

————. "A Closer Look at Canals and Western Manufacturing in the Canal Era: A Reply." *Explorations in Economic History,* vol. 9, no. 4, September 1972.

Ransom, Roger L. "Canals and Development, A Discussion of the Issues." *American Economic Review,* vol. LIV, no. 2, May 1964.

————. "Interregional Canals and Economic Specialization in the Antebellum United States." *Explorations in Economic History,* 2nd series, vol. V, no. 1, Fall 1967.

————. "A Closer Look at Canals and Western Manufacturing in the Canal Era." *Explorations in Economic History,* vol. 8, no. 4, Summer 1971.

Smolensky, Eugene. "Industrial Location and Urban Growth." In Lance E. Davis, et al., *American Economic Growth: An Economist's History of the United States.* New York: Harper & Row, 1972, ch. 15.

Weiss, Thomas. "Demographic Aspects of the Urban Population, 1800–1840." In Peter Kilby, ed., *Quantity and Quiddity: Essays in American Economic History.* Middletown, CT: Wesleyan University Press, 1987.

Williamson, Jeffrey. "Urbanization in the American Northeast." *Journal of Economic History,* vol. XXV, no. 4, December 1965.

Williamson, Jeffrey, and Swanson, Joseph. "The Growth of Cities in the American Northeast, 1820–1870." *Explorations in Entrepreneurial History,* 2nd series, 4 (Supplement), 1966.

Books

Cain, Louis. *Sanitation Strategy for a Lakefront Metropolis: The Case of Chicago.* DeKalb: Northern Illinois University Press, 1978.

Fishlow, Albert. *American Railroads and Transformation of the American Economy.* Cambridge: Harvard University Press, 1965.

Fogel, Robert W. *Railroads and American Economic Growth: Essays in Econometric History.* Baltimore: Johns Hopkins University Press, 1964.

————, and Engerman, Stanley. *The Reinterpretation of American Economic History.* New York: Harper & Row, 1971.

Gates, Paul W. *The Illinois Central Railroad and its Colonization Work.* Cambridge: Harvard University Press, 1934.

Goodrich, Carter. *Government Promotion of American Canals and Railroads, 1800–1890.* New York: Columbia University Press, 1960.

————. *The Government and the Economy, 1783–1861.* Indianapolis: Bobbs-Merrill, 1967.

————; Cranmer, Jerome; Rubin, Julius; and Segal, Harvey. *Canals and American Economic Development.* New York: Columbia University Press, 1961.

Hunter, Louis. *Steamboats on the Western Rivers.* Cambridge: Harvard University Press, 1949.

Hurst, James Willard. *The Legitimacy of the Business Corporation.* Charlottesville: The University Press of Virginia, 1969.

Jenks, Leland H. *The Export of British Capital to 1875.* London: Cape, 1938.

McGrane, R. C. *Foreign Bondholders and American State Debts.* New York: Macmillan Company, 1935.

North, Douglass C. *The Economic Growth of the United States, 1790–1860.* Englewood Cliffs, NJ: Prentice-Hall, 1961.

Taylor, George Rogers. *The Transportation Revolution.* New York: Holt, Rinehart and Winston, 1951.

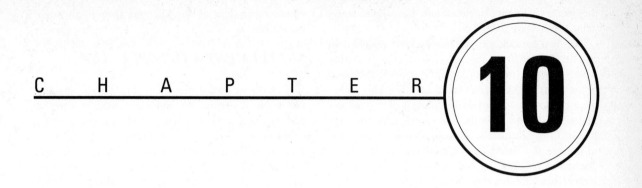
Agricultural Expansion: The Conflict of Two Systems on the Land

A ntebellum America is today a far distant place. No one alive can remember it. It is a land that belongs now entirely to historians, who themselves cannot agree, in some very important respects, about what it was like. We have seen much of this period already, but the heart of the antebellum economy was farms and farmers.

It was the farmers who occupied the continent and brought it into production; whose needs created the demand for industry, towns, cities, finance, and transportation networks; and whose output fed the rising urban masses.[1] By 1850 farmers still numbered 85 percent of the population. They had acquired an empire, but (through their elected representatives) could not agree about one fundamental piece of its organization: whether the labor contract would, or would not, include black slavery. In the end, this issue produced the American Civil War. Was it the sole cause? No. Would there have been a Civil War without the slavery issue? No.[2]

As has been discussed, although slavery was nearly ubiquitous in colonial times, the nature of comparative advantage in regional agriculture had concentrated the slave population in the Southern colonies. In addition,

"history" in a sense had conspired to make slavery continue to expand where it first had become important in agriculture. The drying-up of the indentured servant supply in the late eighteenth century had made slave purchases all the more necessary in the South. After 1725, natural increase provided most of the slave supply in that region; imports from Africa and the Caribbean, the rest. From Pennsylvania north, the heavy, early immigration of whites laid the foundation for a large and growing white population and, consequently, family farming. The passage of time brought an accentuation of the differences in the regional agricultural labor input.

By 1850 nearly 37 percent of the Southern population was slave. In the North by then the number of slaves was negligible. After the invention of Whitney's gin in 1793 and the penetration by Southern planters into Alabama, Louisiana, Arkansas, Mississippi, and east Texas, cotton culture had given the slave South a greatly expandable money crop in addition to sugar production. The expansion of cotton textiles in England, then in New England, and in continental Europe kept cotton demand rising, decade after decade, inducing enormous increases in raw cotton output. Slaves were the necessary labor ingredient. Since cotton was

175

the country's largest single export, the whole nation gained from slave labor.

The two agricultural systems moved westward in parallel fashion from the old colonial area, clashing where they met (in the borderlands geographically and in the courts and Congress intellectually). This movement created the major political themes of the nation's first seven decades after the new Constitution was ratified in 1789. Ultimately, the conflict over slavery was to rupture that agreement. Already in the Northwest Ordinance of 1787 the conflict was on the horizon; slavery was prohibited in the new territories north of the Ohio. The Missouri Compromise (1820), the Compromise of 1850, and the Kansas-Nebraska Act of 1854 were all efforts at the top to find solutions to a problem planted on the land in the colonial era. The issue was one in which financial interests, political philosophies, morals, religion, and politics were all hopelessly embroiled. Whether a solution short of the Civil War was possible is a moot question since in the end, war, and only war, resolved it—leaving the nation scarred and wounded for more than a century after.

The seemingly inexorable conflict between the two systems is neatly projected in a paper by Peter Temin. He poses antebellum American development as two separate solutions to Evsey Domar's well-known "impossibility theorem": It is not possible to have simultaneously (a) free land, (b) free labor, and (c) a land-owning aristocracy.[3] In the south the option taken was slave labor and a land-owning aristocracy. In the North the option was free land, free labor, and no aristocracy. Since the incompatible developments occurred within a single constitutional system, the "solution" was the Civil War. Although Domar's theorem was originally designed for Europe, it does shed considerable light on the dilemma facing Americans before 1861.[4]

SETTLEMENT AND POPULATION

In part, the westward movement of farmers was simply the result of organic phenomena: population growth and the attraction of new land. Young people, growing up on farms in the older settled areas, wanted farms of their own. Once the way west was open, the agricultural populations of the East Coast became the major source of colonizing farmers in the Midwest, and then the Plains. New England people and settlers from Pennsylvania and New York moved into Ohio and Indiana along the rivers. Virginia people moved into Kentucky, Tennessee, and Alabama. Eventually, some of these families or their descendants settled Illinois, Iowa, Mississippi, Arkansas, and Missouri. In 1850 there were 1,449,000 farms by census count, consisting of 293,534,000 acres. A decade later there were 2,044,000 farms, totaling 407,179,000 acres. Older areas might still be more intensively cleared and farmed, but the best lands were taken up long ago. Westward migration was the most attractive course. In the backwoods of New England, the townships began to empty out as farmers headed west. The same was true in Pennsylvania, New York, New Jersey, and the Old South.

The flavor of the Midwest in 1850, which is to some extent evident to this day, may be seen in Table 10.1. If we ignore the proportions of native-born in each state in 1850 for the moment, the external influences take on significance.[5] Note the relatively heavy concentrations of persons from the South in Indiana and Illinois. The "Southern" politics of Indiana and Illinois in the

Table 10.1 Midwest Populations by Place of Birth and Domicile in 1850[a]

Domicile in 1850	Area of Birth						
	New England	Middle States	South	Northwest	Native-Born	Europe	Total
Ohio	3.3	15.0	7.5	—	64.2	10.0	100
Indiana	1.2	8.0	18.5	13.7	52.8	5.8	100
Illinois	4.4	13.2	16.2	12.9	40.4	12.9	100
Michigan	7.8	37.7	1.0	4.5	35.2	13.8	100
Wisconsin	8.9	26.2	1.6	7.5	20.7	35.1	100

[a] Figures given are percentages.

Source: Ray Billington, *Westward Expansion* (New York: Macmillan, 1949), p. 308.

1850s have obvious origins. In Wisconsin, Michigan, and Illinois large portions of the populations were born in Europe, and the old Middle colonies contributed heavy concentrations in the same states. New England people contributed their largest proportions in Michigan and Wisconsin. The effects of western migration were clearly more telling in the dwindling townships of New England than in the lusty new settlements of the Midwest.[6]

Harriet Martineau wrote in the 1830s of a conversation with a Southern legislator who complained of the steady drain of young people to the West:

> He told me of one and another of his intelligent and pleasant young neighbors, who were quitting their homes and civilized life, and carrying their brides "as bondswomen" into the wilderness because fine land was cheap there.[7]

In addition was the ever-present element of land speculation, which we discussed in Chapter 5. Acquiring land, clearing some of it, building a house and barn, then selling it to others and moving on to new land—this was a laborious but profitable frontier enterprise for many farm families.

Comparative population data for sixteen trans-Appalachian states may be seen in Table 10.2.

An area that contained less than 15 percent of the nation's population in 1810 had more than 46 percent by 1850 and in the last decade before the Civil War was still growing in population more rapidly than the rest of the country. In the North, lands that would grow corn and wheat and support animals attracted family farmers. Among the Southern population, family farmers, too, were attracted into the rich cotton-growing lands of the Mississippi drainage basin. Alabama, Mississippi, and the whole southern part of the great gulf plains received them. Where there was good land in the South, there was opportunity for plantation agriculture, and slave owners were quickly attracted. Fogel and Engerman estimated that between 1790 and 1860 an army of some 835,000 slaves moved from the Old South (85 percent from Maryland, Virginia, and the Carolinas). Alabama, Mississippi, Louisiana, and east Texas alone received some 75 percent of this huge black migration.[8]

Looking backward, the trans-Appalachian movement seems logical and obvious. However, certainty from hindsight was not what prompted people to change their addresses. People moved for opportunity, and that was enhanced periodically by rising prices for agricultural produce. Data for cotton, wool, and wheat prices (Figure 10.1), together with land sales, show that both in the South and North the price booms of the antebellum period were closely correlated with big increases in public land sales in 1817–19, 1835–37, and 1852–54. These were big bulges in sales on top of a rising trend. Population was moving westward in any case, but extraordinary opportunities stemming from rising agricultural prices accelerated the movement in both the North and South.

Average Farm Size

About one half of all Southern farms used slave labor by 1860; the proportion was higher than in earlier decades. Conversely, in the North, there was an estimated one hired male worker for every two farms. Northern farms were not labor intensive. They grew grains and fed animals. Considerable improvements had been

Table 10.2   Populations of Trans-Appalachian States[a]

State	1810	1850	1860
Ohio	231	1980	2340
Michigan	5	398	749
Indiana	25	988	1350
Illinois	12	851	1712
Minnesota	—[b]	6	172
Wisconsin	—	305	776
Iowa	—	192	675
Kansas	—	—	107
Kentucky	407	982	1156
Tennessee	262	1003	1110
Alabama	9	772	964
Mississippi	31	607	791
Louisiana	77	518	708
Arkansas	1	210	435
Missouri	20	682	1182
Texas	—	213	604
Total	1,080	9,707	14,831
Total U.S.	7,224	23,261	31,513
Percentage Trans-Appalachia of Total U.S.	15.0	41.7	47.1

[a] Figures given in thousands of persons; excludes Far West and West Coast.
[b] No data.

Source: *Historical Statistics*, derived from series A7, 195.

Figure 10.1   Prices for Cotton, Wool, Wheat, 1815–1816

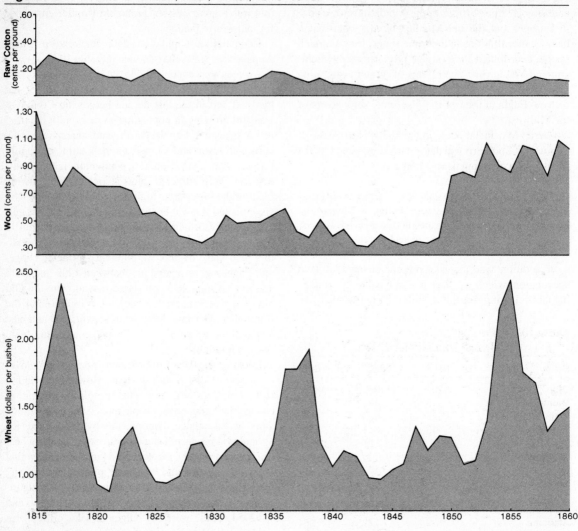

Source: *Historical Statistics*, E123, 126–27.

Commodity Prices fell between 1816 and 1820. Except for a brief surge in the 1830s, they remained on a plateau until the 1850s, when they showed a renewed upward movement.

made in farm machinery and tools, and there was sufficient land so Northern family farms could thrive without a huge supply of hired labor. On the other hand, slave labor in cotton, sugar, and tobacco yielded scale economies. One is not surprised, therefore, that, on average, Southern farms tended to be significantly larger than those in the North. Moreover, one fourth of Southern cotton plantations and farms were *far* larger than any seen in the North except in the rarest cases.

The data in Table 10.3 are only a sample of the important work of Gavin Wright, to which the reader is referred for more detail. Wright analyzed the Cotton South according to soil types.[9] *Piedmont area* refers to the Appalachian foothills of southern Virginia, the Carolinas, Georgia, and Alabama. The *sand hills* are just east of the Appalachian divide in the Carolinas and Georgia. *Western upland* refers to land in Arkansas, Louisiana, and east Texas. *Alluvial lands* are along the

Mississippi and Red rivers in Missouri, Arkansas, and Louisiana.

The more complete data in Wright's work tell substantially the same story as our sample. In the Midwestern states very few farms were larger than 500 acres, although in the Cotton South these accounted for nearly 40 percent of the total. In the Piedmont alone 36 percent of the acreage was in farms of 1000 acres or more. Minnesota and Wisconsin apart (where farming was still in the early stages in 1860), most Midwest farming was on tracts of land in the range of 100–499 acres.

Apart from the newer areas (western upland), Southern farms in the cotton-growing areas showed a distinct bulge at the top of the distribution. Within some relevant ranges there were, apparently, either constant or increasing returns to scale in the use of slaves. The same sorts of limited internal economies exist today on modern farms employing expensive machinery. Enough acres must be employed to cover high fixed costs, and beyond that it pays a farmer to expand only until the marginal costs are *just covered* by additional revenues derived from that expansion.

The evidence indicates that slave labor produced efficiencies—scale economies—in Southern agriculture, but not infinitely so. There were limits to efficient size even in Southern plantations. Costs ultimately rose with plantation size, even if there were scale economies within limits. Significantly, for example, there were no incorporated slave plantations drawing upon widespread sources of capital by the sale of stock—what you would expect if scale economies from slavery were not restricted. At some point the additional costs of size compared to added revenues put a limit on the profitable scale of single plantations.[10] Ideally, with abundant land and a perfectly competitive market in slaves, significant economies of scale would have produced giant plantations.

To give an idea of what this means, let's look at some numbers. In 1969 there were 2,730,000 farms in the United States, one-third more than in 1860, and there were 1,108 million acres under cultivation, or 277 percent more than in 1860. The average-sized farm was 369 acres. Some 60,000 of them exceeded 2000 acres each.[11]

Modern scale economies come from machinery, and they made the use of incorporation profitable. As far as we can tell, problems of management, slave discipline, and communications all played a role in placing limits on scale economies on the cotton plantation. Scale economies were present but constrained. Such is suggested, for example, by the work of Jacob Metzer.[12] In fact, 4.7 percent of all farms in the Deep South were 500 acres or more, compared with a mere 0.1 percent

Table 10.3 Distribution of Improved Acreage by Size Class, Cotton South and Other Farm States, 1860

Region	Percentage of Total Improved Acreage by Improved Acreage Size Class				
	0–49	**50–99**	**100–499**	**500–999**	**≥1000**
South (Town Areas)					
Piedmont	4.1	8.7	36.6	14.5	36.1
Sand Hills	12.0	17.5	40.5	3.6	26.4
Western Upland	15.5	21.7	49.3	10.2	3.2
Alluvine	4.3	4.7	33.0	24.5	33.5
Cotton South (Total)	7.3	11.5	43.5	16.9	20.9
Illinois	8.1	20.7	65.8	4.2	1.3
Iowa	17.8	29.0	52.0	1.0	0.2
Indiana	17.0	28.6	51.5	2.0	0.8
Minnesota	52.0	24.4	23.4	0.2	0.0
Ohio	11.2	28.1	57.8	2.1	0.8
Wisconsin	24.6	27.2	46.7	1.2	0.2

Source: Gavin Wright, "Economic Democracy and the Concentration of Agricultural Wealth in the Cotton South, 1850–1860," in *The Structure of the Cotton Economy of the Antebellum South,* edited by William Parker (Washington, D.C.: The Agricultural History Society, 1970), derived from Table 4, p. 73.

of farms in the Northeastern states—a remarkable difference.[13] Since cotton was a labor-intensive crop, the large growing units in the South were cultivated by a large number of workers, compared to Northern family farms, and the relative efficiency of gang labor in cotton production made the larger Southern farms profitable.

It is clear from Wright's data that the optimal-sized Southern plantation was far larger than the Midwest farm in the antebellum period. Nevertheless, more than half of Southern acreage fell within the boundaries of the family-sized farm, below 500 acres, and half of the farms in the South had no slaves!

The median farm size in the Cotton South in 1860 was 70.6 acres. In the Midwest states median-sized farms were about 70 percent as large, 49.3 acres. But the mean-sized farm in the Cotton South was 135.9 acres, more than twice as large as the mean-sized Midwest farm of 64.5 acres.[14] The difference between the median and mean ratios reflects the bulge at the top in the Cotton South, the extraordinary number of relatively large-sized Southern farms and plantations worked by slave gang labor.

Farm Wealth Comparisons

Heywood Fleisig estimates that the value of farm implements per worker in 1860 was $66 in the free states but only $38 in the slave states. But Fleisig does not include women and children in his calculations of capital per worker in the North as he does in his figures for the slave-worked farms in the South. Since slaves were expensive, too, it should follow that Southern planters used capital to substitute for slaves wherever it was profitable. Slaves, together with land, implements, and buildings, made the market value of a typical slave-state farm $7101 compared to only $3311 in the free states. In the Cotton South, the figure was $8786.[15] What slaves did to differences in wealth holding is described by Wright:

> Slaveholders constituted the wealthiest class in the country by far. The average slaveowner was more than five times as wealthy as the average northerner, more than ten times as wealthy as the average non-slaveholding southern farmer.[16]

The data illustrate the success of slavery as a social mechanism for settlement, hard as that interpretation

might be for modern Americans to accept. Slavery was immoral, but it ensured a labor supply. The hard work of settlement, clearing, plowing, building structures—in an age before the internal combustion engine, when most farm work was handwork—gave the slave system advantages. As the historian Abbot E. Smith wrote of servitude and slavery in colonial America,

> It is a familiar story that mankind, when confronted in America with a vast and trackless wilderness awaiting exploitation, threw off its ancient shackles of cast and privilege and set forth upon the road to freedom. Among the social institutions found most useful in the course of this march were those of African slavery and white servitude.[17]

By the mid-nineteenth century, servitude was gone, but slavery was not.

In Chapter 12 of this section we will consider the economics of slavery in more detail. Our point here, in comparing the two agricultural systems overall, is that slavery and cotton made Southern farming more successful by conventional measures (size of farm and wealth) than Northern farmsteads in the era before extensive mechanization.

COTTON AS A FOREIGN-EXCHANGE EARNER

In the next chapter we will discuss in some detail the balance of international payments between 1790 and 1860; what we sold to the world, what we bought from it, and the pattern of those relationships over time. Here we want to tie agricultural development into the story of domestic growth. Part of its effect is straightforward: the employment of workers and resources in farming and the demand produced by those activities for services and manufacturers. But part of the impact of American agriculture upon the country's growth was indirect, through the balance of payments, and of crucial importance. That impact came from what we now would call *foreign-exchange earnings*.

Paying the Bills

When the United States was growing rapidly, as in the 1830s and 1850s, the economy used more economic resources than it currently produced. The United States

Table 10.4 Structure of Commodity Trade 1851–1860[a]

Commodity	Exports	Imports
Crude materials	61.6	9.6
Crude foodstuffs	6.6	11.7
Manufactured foodstuffs	15.5	15.4
Semimanufactures	4.0	12.5
Finished manufactures	12.3	50.7

[a] Figures are annual averages as a percentage of the total.

Source: *Historical Statistics,* derived from series U214–18, 220–24.

Table 10.5 Average Annual Cotton Exports

Period	Million Pounds	Million Dollars
1815–1820	94	$ 23
1821–1830	204	26
1831–1840	432	53
1841–1850	700	55
1851–1860	1,180	124

Source: *Historical Statistics,* series U275–76.

was forced to borrow the difference. However, borrowed funds bear interest, which is a net drain on the borrower. So, while the loans were timely and enhanced the American economy's growth, the lower the subsequent interest drain (together with repayment of capital), the higher still was the supply of resources available for domestic use in consumption and investment. Hence, exports were of crucial importance. What we imported had to be paid for with something, and exports paid most of the bill. Consider the structure of our commodity trade per annum in the 1850s as presented in Table 10.4.

Our manufacturing sector was not yet able to supply as large a part of our demand as would later be true, so finished and semifinished goods accounted for 63 percent of imports. We exported the products of agriculture and extractive industries; crude materials and food alone accounted for about 84 percent of exports.

Cotton's Export Earnings

In the 1850s exports averaged $211 million, imports averaged $275 million. The difference, $64 million, was made up in part by "invisible" earnings, such as shipping, and the rest by foreign loans, both short-term mercantile credits and longer-term borrowing (like railroad bonds). *More than half* of those export earnings from crude materials came from cotton exports alone. In the earlier years the cotton proportion was even higher.

Cotton, then, was by far the most important single export. This would be true throughout the nineteenth century, although in some later years wheat would run a very close second. Before the Civil War, though, raw cotton earned directly more than half the nation's ability to buy needed goods from abroad. Gold exports,

after the Californian discoveries, became important, too. In 1855, $54 million of gold exports amounted to 61 percent of earnings from cotton. According to Douglass North, earnings from shipping, although rising in absolute amount, were equal to about 10 percent of total export earnings and were actually declining as a proportion of the total.[18]

The expansion of cotton exports in annual value was by a factor of five from the period 1815–1820; the volume increased in the same period by a factor of eleven. The growth of both cotton output and cotton exports was a major event of the antebellum period (see Table 10.5).

In 1860 the earnings from cotton exports totalled $192 billion, nearly four times the revenues of the federal government. It was quite an incredible situation that a single commodity could so dominate the American economy's position in the world. British industry, expanding again and again through the decades, depended upon the American South for 75–80 percent of its raw materials. By 1860, of an employed labor force in England of 10.5 million, nearly half a million were directly employed in cotton textile manufacturing, and the total in cotton textiles in all stages may have come to 1.5 million.[19] If the South felt confident of cotton's economic power in any conflict between the states, it is not surprising.

AGRICULTURAL LABOR: DEPENDENCE ON SLAVERY

Farming depends upon energy. Nearly all farm jobs require lifting, digging, pulling, pushing, cutting, chopping, and carrying. Even with modern equipment farm work is quite astonishingly "hard" compared to nearly any other employment. The human body has limited strength for this kind of work, and the entire history of agricultural invention is the record of innovations designed to lighten and shorten this labor. Any implement, tool, animal, or natural or synthetic force that relieved human beings of this relentless labor has been welcomed. Sharpened sticks, better cutting and hoeing tools, draft animals, pulleys, wheels, levers, wind, water—over the centuries every method has been tried. With slavery, *someone* else (the slave) suffered the exertions of agricultural labor.

One slave can substitute for the labor of one slave owner; many slaves are substitutes for many free workers. Concentration on grain and animal production kept Northern farms to a size that could be managed by single families, as we already have noted. In the Cotton South a competitive market in slaves meant that a labor force was readily available to those who wanted to cultivate beyond the family-farm size and had the money to buy slaves. The problem was to make acquisition of slave labor profitable. Cotton, sugar, and tobacco cultivation would tempt a Southern farmer to purchase the slave capital required. The market for cotton was guaranteed before the Civil War, and there was abundant land for sale. In addition, slave owners could count on a handsome capital gain in the value of their slave property. Plantations, therefore, could be readily established by those who understood the cotton trade. In addition, the widespread use of hired management, white overseers, meant that entry into cotton growing was easily achieved by the wealthy.

Labor-Intensive Slavery

Slaves were substitutes for free labor. Were slaves substitutes for capital equipment, too? Certainly not if that equipment could increase the profitability of Southern agriculture. No sensible plantation owner would deny workers the use of shovels, hoes, and axes. There were no working mechanical cotton pickers before 1860. Until then, there was only slave gang labor. The example of Whitney's cotton gin shows that Southern farmers would quickly innovate productivity-using machinery when it appeared.

The slave gang in the field became extraordinarily efficient by reduction of the work to specialized tasks and by control of its rhythm. As Robert Fogel says: "Once it is recognized that the fundamental form of the exploitation of slave labor was through speed-up rather than through an increase in the number of

clock-time hours per year, certain paradoxes resolve themselves."[20] Those paradoxes include regular rest periods, Sundays off, and probably a shorter work year than that enjoyed by the typical Northern farmer, or Southern free farmer, who still had animals and poultry to tend after the field work was finished. The goal of the slave field gang system was regular *intensive* labor. Cotton production made Southern plantations labor-intensive.

Cotton and the Slave Population

Between 1810 and 1830 cotton production rose from 178,000 bales a year to 732,000 bales, or by 311 percent. By 1860, output was 3,841,000 bales, an increase of another 435 percent.[21] From 1790, of course, the increase was astronomical (see Table 10.6). Moving south and west, the slave labor force under the direction of its white masters created one of the great successes of American economic history.

After Whitney's cotton gin (1793) enabled short-staple cotton varieties to be separated on a competitive commercial basis by mechanical means, American cotton quickly dominated world cotton textile production. For example, three quarters of Britain's massive consumption of raw cotton came from the United States after the 1820s. For decades, world cotton textile development and the expansion of American slave agriculture went hand in hand. Indeed, in a forceful essay Ronald Bailey demonstrates that profits from the international slave trade bolstered a significant part of colonial commercial wealth and provided major capital for early New England industry. Names from the New England pantheon of business history like Cabot, Lowell, Brown, Perkins and even Sam Slater were stained

Table 10.6   Cotton Output

Year	Thousand Bales
1790	3
1800	73
1810	178
1920	335
1830	732
1840	1,348
1850	2,136
1860	3,841

Source: *Historical Statistics*, series K554.

by their connections with slavery. From its inception, the new industrial system, at one remove, exploited slave labor in the United States.[22]

The soils and climate of the cotton-growing areas gave the South an economic rent from cotton—financial returns in excess of alternative competitive uses of resources. From 1820 to 1860, cotton output rose by about a factor of 11.5, and slave population, by only a factor of 2.5. The increase in output of cotton per slave was by a factor of 4.6.

Of course, some cotton was grown by free white farmers, but it probably is fair to say that most of the cotton was grown by slaves. Half of the Southern farms had no slaves, and some 28 percent grew no cotton. The evidence suggests that 86 percent of the cotton was grown on farms of more than 100 acres and that 90 percent of the slaves were owned on these farms.[23] The Cotton South was an astounding agricultural success: cheap land, slave labor, hired management, and a strongly rising demand for cotton all combined to make the slave system profitable for slaveowners.

The Southern population between 1790 and 1860 is shown in Table 10.7. Over the entire period 1790–1860 the slave population increased slightly more rapidly than did that of free whites, and, thus, the proportion of slaves to free whites rose slightly. An interesting feature of the data is that the population of Southern free blacks was growing more than 40 percent more rapidly than either the slave or free white populations. However, by 1860 the free black population was still negligible in absolute numbers or proportion.

Ownership of slaves was becoming more concentrated by the 1850s. According to Wright the percent-age of all Southern families owning slaves declined from 36 in 1830 to 25 by 1860. By that year about 48 percent of Southern farmers owned no slaves at all. The slave owners were the wealthiest, by far. Lee Soltow found that, in both 1850 and 1860, between 90 and 95 percent of all the agricultural wealth in the South was owned by slaveholders.[24] It is clear that as cotton output expanded and slave prices rose, fewer Southern farmers could afford to own this species of property. The game was getting more profitable, but the table stakes were rising sharply. As Wright put it: "The very forces that were strengthening the economic incentives for slaveowners to retain slavery were slowly weakening the political supports for the institution."[25]

Southern Self-Sufficiency Before 1860

It has often been noted that cash crops in Northern agriculture were also subsistence crops: Wheat, corn, oats, hogs, and cattle could be either sold for cash or kept on the farm and consumed there by the grower's own family. The market economy for Northern farmers meant only that they had to extend themselves in activities they would be pursuing in any case.

In the Cotton South the problem was more complex. Hutchinson and Williamson have shown that the South, New Orleans apart, was not necessarily dependent for food upon any other section, despite the importance of the cotton crop.[26] Cotton was not consumed as part of domestic subsistence life. The cotton farmer distributed his resources between growing cotton for cash and growing corn, hogs, cattle, and other

Table 10.7   Southern Population[a]

Year	Free White	Slave	Free Black	Percentage Slave of Free White
1790	1,271	690	33	54
1800	1,704	918	61	54
1810	2,191	1,268	107	58
1820	2,776	1,644	135	60
1830	3,546	2,162	182	61
1840	4,309	2,642	214	61
1850	5,630	3,352	235	60
1860	7,034	4,097	258	58

[a] Figures given are in thousands of persons.

Source: Derived from *Historical Statistics*, 1960, series A114; 1975, series A175–76.

food items to be used, as in the North, for subsistence consumption.

In those early times every farm was in part self-sufficient in foodstuffs, and certain raw materials were processed on the farm: Saw mills, tanneries, blacksmiths' shops, flour mills, dairies, all were located at sites of primary production. Farmers and plantation owners might include one or several of these specialties in conjunction with other farming operations. The problem was, what mix of cash and subsistence crops was most desirable? The mix chosen depended upon relative prices and costs, then as now, but cotton was the main cash crop. Food crops, fodder, and animals could be tended by the slaves, too—by women and children at peak times and by all during slack seasons in the annual cycles of cotton planting, cultivating, and harvesting.

The capacity of any cotton farm or plantation to produce revenues depended upon market prices as well as upon the physical yields of crops. Agricultural prices, then as now, varied considerably from year to year. Given the transportation system of the time and the restricted storage and credit facilities available to Southern farmers, domestic production of basic foodstuffs used spare labor and saved cash for uses other than purchases of food provisions. Grain besides corn *could* be grown in the cotton belt, too.[27] With larger acreage, cotton as an additional cash crop added another dimension. At the most fundamental level, subsistence food growing enabled the farmer or plantation owner to conserve cash in the years of low cotton prices. So, substantial self-sufficiency in food was characteristic of cotton farming. The basic need was labor for picking cotton. Land, the more plentiful factor, could be applied to both food and cotton. Corn was the perfect complement to cotton cultivation.

As it happened, the peak periods of demand for labor in the annual cycles of planting and harvest varied enough so that the same labor force could be kept in steady employment growing *both* cotton and provision crops. Cotton planting began in April, but corn could be planted as early as late February and March, Also, the mature corn could be left in the fields while the cotton crop was brought in between August and December. In the other months there were no peak labor demand periods, and the labor force could be assigned the full range of farm tasks without disrupting essential planting and harvest needs.[28]

Because more labor was available on large plantations in the form of slaves purchased at will, the proportion of land devoted to cotton could be increased according to the marginal product of labor and estimated cotton prices while the basic food and other subsistence needs of the plantations could be covered as well. Hence, the yeoman farmer on a small farm grew relatively little cotton in proportion to other crops, while the slave plantations produced mostly cotton and most of the cotton produced.

The mutually reinforcing link between slave owning and expansion of the cotton economy was strengthened by the practice of achieving substantial self-sufficiency. The more efficient farms, using greater amounts of land, could devote an increasing proportion of their total effort to the cash crop, thus raising the cash-revenue productivity of the slave labor force.

Until 1860 the demand for cotton reinforced the motives for the expansion of slavery, especially among the wealthy who financed the establishment of large-scale plantations. Cotton was cash, and the larger the slave-owning establishment, the greater was the proportion of land used to grow it. Farmers wanted farms, but slave owners wanted *cotton lands*.

WESTERN EXPANSION OF NORTHERN AGRICULTURE

As we saw in Table 10.2, population in the new Northern states beyond the Appalachians actually exceeded that of the new Southern states by 1860. From Ohio to Kansas, farm families took up the new land. The first settlers shunned the open prairies and settled in forested areas and along river bottoms where significant woodlands could be found to provide building materials and fuel.

The Eastern Link

The Erie Canal had first provided a direct east-west link for transportation on a scale beyond oxcarts and poor roads. The result was a rise in the prices farmers received for wheat and other foods grown on the farm and a decline in these prices to consumers in the Eastern markets. Manufactured goods became cheaper for Midwest farmers to buy as the transportation links to the East improved. As a result, Thomas Berry found, farmers by 1860 could buy more than twice as many manufactured goods with a given amount of their products as they could in 1820.[29] Such was the result of the reduction of transportation costs.

These results were augmented by the new canals in Ohio and Indiana and then, very quickly, by direct rail links. By 1853, as we saw in Chapter 9, Chicago was the northern center of a rail network stretching from the Mississippi to the East Coast. Farm products could be shipped quickly and regularly to Eastern and world markets, instead of just seasonally down river to New Orleans, cutting handling and storage costs. More competition for freight, of course, meant alternative buyers for farmers. Connecting railroads like the Illinois Central were in place or under construction by the 1850s, and the Midwestern agricultural cornucopia was near the beginning of its fantastically productive career.

Pioneering

At first, Midwestern land looked like no wonder of nature or humanity. As we mentioned, the early pioneers stayed away from the vast open prairies, where the glaciers had pulverized native limestone into soils of incredible richness and depth. Topsoils were 40 feet deep and awaited the plow. Early settlers preferred lands in or near stands of timber, so that clearing and planting had building materials and fuel production as natural by-products.

The prairies were a puzzle. The deep sod under the natural prairie grasses was a powerful challenge to the traditional wooden plow with its iron-plated moldboard. It took two to three years to get the first full crop of wheat. Initially, the farmer could produce only a "sod crop," cutting the overturned prairie grass roots with an axe to make a slash in which seed was deposited. A year later, with more plowing and working, the soil would begin to yield to regular cultivation as the sod stubble and dry roots decomposed. Danger of prairie fires was constantly present in the summer months, and farms had to be surrounded by plowed strips that served as firebreaks. Also, with 30–40 inches of rainfall a year from the Ohio Valley westward as far as eastern Kansas, the flat prairie lands, when wet, were poorly drained and prolific breeders of mosquitos and malaria.

In the forest areas such as those of Michigan and Wisconsin, it could take a month of backbreaking labor to clear an acre, from five to ten years to make a modest farm. The prairies were also thought at first to be poor soils since they did not seem to be able to support a good growth of hardwoods.[30] Time and experience would change that.

The Cost

Long, hard labor faced Midwest farmers who had to rely primarily on family labor. Progress was slow. Martin Primack estimated that fully a sixth of the Midwest labor force in the 1850s was constantly engaged in the sole task of clearing land.[31] Such activity required capital and was itself capital formation. Indeed, the family opening a new farm must have spent the majority of its work time and effort on activities we would classify as *investment:* clearing land, constructing fences and buildings, feeding and breeding herds and flocks. If all such output could be measured in terms of an abstract *labor unit,* it is clear that the model of frontier economic growth is one in which the ratio of investment must *fall* initially—the opposite of standard ideas about economic growth.[32]

The farm family that devoted 85 percent of its labor effort to activities meant to sustain current consumption and 15 percent to investment in the pioneering stage probably would have failed. In the five to ten years it took to build a modest frontier farm, the ratio of investment to total activity had to be extraordinarily high. Consuming income instead of reinvesting it in the farm was a luxury to be enjoyed only *after* the more rigorous processes of farm formation were carried through.

It was for that reason that so many hardy farmers profited from a sequence of farm "developments," selling out a finished or partly finished farm at a profit and moving on to a new location. The land-sale history we discussed earlier reflected this widespread habit in nineteenth-century America. Primack's estimates show the time spent on land clearing in the Midwest in the 1850s was 18 percent, compared to about 10 percent in the South and only roughly 7 percent in the Northeast.

This labor had to be accompanied by other investment. Clarence Danhof estimated that a hypothetical representative small farm of thirty cleared acres (fifty acres in total) in New York State in the 1820s cost $1145 to establish and stock.[33] Since average wages were less than a third of that figure a year ($325 per year in 1840), it is clear that successful farming was an expensive proposition. According to Donald Adams, a factory worker would have needed from five to ten years of average savings to set himself up in "independent agriculture."[34] Atack and Bateman have now supplied an abundant set of estimates for farm-making in the 1850s.[35] Moving west paid, in general; a typical farm of 80 acres in Ohio in 1860 would cost $2,784 but only $805 in Minnesota.

> A northeastern farmer who sold and moved west to Ohio could purchase a farm perhaps one-eighth larger than that which he vacated, but if he moved instead west or north of Indiana, he could purchase a farm at least twice as large.[36]

Experienced Pioneers

Hence the "old stock" Americans comprised the majority of pioneer farmers moving westward from the old colonies with their farm animals, tools, and equipment. Given promising places to establish farms, they became a remarkable and, indeed, relentless cutting edge of civilization. Penniless immigrants, even those from European farms, went mainly to the cities to do wage labor by necessity. Successful agricultural pioneering required extensive capital, including working family members.

Let's look at two remarkable examples of evidence that have come down. In both cases the data came from the wreckage of wagon trains leaving the Midwest for California. The first is George R. Stewart's gripping account of the Donner party, which came to grief in the snows of the Sierra Nevada in the winter of 1846.[37] There were twenty covered wagons for eighty-seven people. Three families had three wagons each, two with seven yoke of oxen (the number for the third, the "aristocratic" Reed family, is not recorded), milk cows, saddle horses, and beef cattle.

The leading members of the party all had been successful farmers in Illinois. George Donner had grown to adulthood and lived successively in Kentucky, Indiana, and Springfield, Illinois, creating farms and raising in succession three families with three wives.

The equipage of this wagon train seems opulent. Yet there is no evidence that it was more than an average pioneering adventure.

In his masterpiece about the Utah Mormons, *Great Basin Kingdom,* Leonard Arrington quotes from an account of Howard Stansbury in 1849 describing roadside scenes west of Fort Laramie:

> Before halting at noon, we passed eleven wagons that had been broken up, the spokes of the wheels taken to pack-saddles, and the rest burned or otherwise destroyed. The road has been literally strewn with articles that have been thrown away. Bar-iron and steel, large blacksmiths' anvils and bellows, crowbars, drills, augers, gold-washers, chisels, axes, lead trunks, spades, ploughs, large grindstones, baking-ovens, cooking-stoves without number, kegs, barrels, harness, clothing, bacon, and beans, were found along the road in pretty much the order in which they have been here enumerated. . . . In the course of this one day the relics of seventeen wagons and the carcasses of twenty-seven dead oxen have been seen.[38]

Again, there is no reason to suppose that the inventory described came from a wagon train of extraordinary wealth. Pioneering was for generations a way of life. The new farms were made by people who knew how and were equipped to do it. The companies that faced the disasters of the California trail were average American families leaving farms in the Midwest for the Golden State. It remained for successive generations to find ways to turn pioneer farms into what would become the great American breadbasket.

The Importance of Technology

We saw that the cotton economy could expand output by intensive use of slave labor. The Northern family farm had less need for hired labor since the main crops were grain (not labor-intensive) and animals (a 365-day-a-year job). When improved farm machinery came along, the Midwestern family farm became the great "factory on the farm" we know today. Change came slowly but relentlessly—bigger plows, better cultivating and harvesting machinery, steam engines, then the internal combustion engine and with it, tractors and trucks. Therein lay the future of Midwestern agriculture.

In modern times a Midwest family farm rotating soybeans, wheat, and corn commonly contains 500 acres or more and is mostly worked by a single full-time operator disposing of farm machinery worth a small fortune: tractors, seeders, massive discs, spraying equipment, air-conditioned combines, even butane dryers for crops in the storage silos. The origin of this economic wonder of mechanization was the chronic Midwest farm labor shortage in the nineteenth century.

Early Inventions

When the pioneer farmers first approached the Midwest, their technology was remarkably medieval: Ground was broken with a small wooden plow sheathed in iron; seeds were sown by hand; grain was cut by scythe and cradle, bound, shocked by hand, and dried, then separated from the shocks and husks by handheld flail, and winnowed and screened in the wind. Farm implements were mainly improved by small changes impossible to locate in remote origin, but there were several "heroic" improvements we do know something about.

In the Midwest the steel plow was one such improvement. It was lighter and stronger than the old iron-sheathed wooden plows, and the moldboard scoured (cleared itself of mud) more efficiently as it was pulled along. The steel plows, drawn by teams by mules, horses, or oxen, could cut the prairie sod faster and thus extend the practical size of the family farm. By 1857 in Moline, Illinois, the John Deere company's output of steel plows was already 10,000 a year.

The horse-drawn reaper was a similar invention. In 1833, Obed Hussey patented one, and in 1834, Cyrus Hall McCormick patented another. The reaper—consisting of reciprocating cutting blades powered by the wheels as the machine was drawn through the grain by a horse—could eliminate the whole harvest force with scythes. Yet, by 1850, less than 1 percent of American grain was cut by reaper, and only 3400 of the machines had been sold. By 1860, some 80,000 had been sold, and in 1859, about 56,000 of those 80,000 were still in working order. Why the long delay and then the sudden splurge?

Economic historians have had fun trying to find the answer, but it is important to know since the reaper's history is doubtless representative of most large and relatively expensive pieces of agricultural capital equipment. The "traditional view" held simply that the upsurge in wheat prices in the 1850s made the purchase of machinery profitable. That explanation wasn't good enough for Paul David. If the reaper cut production costs, there must have been more to the process of adaptation than just rising prices.

Cost-cutting is profitable at fixed or falling prices, too. David's analysis took into account (a) farm terrain,

(b) wage costs, (c) interest rates, and (d) useful life of the equipment as well as the rising prices of grain in the 1850s. The terrain was important. Obviously, a farmer facing table-flat, stone-free fields in central Illinois would see more hope from such a device than would the long-jawed Vermonter contemplating rock-encrusted hillside fields. As David puts it:

> . . . the efficient use of mechanical reapers required a level, stone-free farm terrain, arranged in large and regularly shaped enclosures—a specific natural resource input that at the mid point of the nineteenth century was obtained much more cheaply (relative to the prices of grain) in the United States than in the British Isles.[39]

So, mechanical reaping would spread as Midwestern agriculture came "on line" in the westward movement. With given labor costs (high), given interest rates, and machine life, a single farm would need to reach a certain threshold size before it paid the farmer to invest in a reaper. Only then would expected production be large enough to cover the lifetime cost of the machine and still yield a profit. To David, that size fell from about forty-six acres in 1849–53 to thirty-five acres in the mid-1850s, and because that threshold matched the average size of a large portion of Midwest farms, reaper investment surged. This account greatly simplifies his elegant argument but contains the gist of it.

Alan Olmstead objected to David's calculations on several grounds: (a) Interest rates in the 1850s were higher than David had conjectured. (b) Reaper life was shorter, thus raising the threshold acreage. (c) Reapers were commonly rented and also jointly owned, so the threshold size in fact was largely irrelevant. It held only for single buyers. Moreover, the reapers were constantly being improved and made more efficient, effectively cheaper, and, hence, more profitable.[40]

Finally, Lewis Jones pointed out that it was not *average* farm sizes that mattered, in any case, but the sizes of those where reapers were used.[41] There were more than enough Midwest farms large enough in the 1850s to meet either David's or Olmstead's thresholds to account for reaper sales. Therefore, increased prices of grain must also have been an important determinant of reaper sales. Small-scale farmers were left with their scythes, or they could rent or invest jointly with others in reapers.

Steam-powered threshing machines became common in the 1850s, eliminating the flail. And these machines were shared out, rented, jointly owned, or

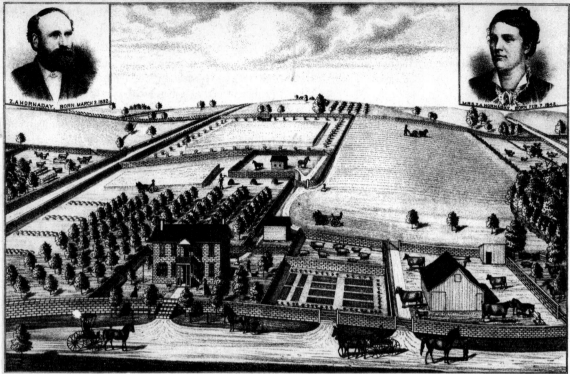

PLEASANT VALLEY FARM.
FARM RESIDENCE OF Z.A.HORNADAY, 3 MILES NORTH EAST OF FT. SCOTT, SCOTT TWP. BOURBON CO. KANSAS.
TP. 25 SEC. 16 R. 25 FARM CONTAINING 440 ACRES.

Two Agriculture Cultures. An artists's conception of an idyllic Northern farm (above) shows how the concentration on grain crops and animals and the use of farm machinery to increase output reduced the need for hired labor. Labor-intensive agriculture of Southern cotton plantations (below) was the primary economy for slavery in the antebellum South.

otherwise acquired. Also, drill seeders became common, as did cultivators, mowing machines, horse-drawn hay rakes, and improved harrows for working the soil just before planting. Even if Midwest farmers could not significantly raise yields per acre (and they could not except with fertilizers) or expand their output by greater labor inputs per farm, machinery allowed them to farm *more acres* and thus to expand their output per farm. They had two expensive factors, labor and capital, and one plentiful factor, land. Adoption of machinery conserved labor, and the addition of plentiful land inputs raised the productivity both of capital and labor. Machinery would become the "slave" of the Northern farmer.

Output

The data one needs at this point in our discussion—outputs of major crops, numbers of animals and fowl, for Midwest farms only—are just the data we do not have before 1860. We have only some rough numbers for the entire country (shown here in Table 10.8).

If we suppose that these numbers are at all representative of the truth, we see bigger decadal rates of increase for two field grains, wheat and barley, in the 1850s than in the 1840s. Reapers were used for these crops but not for corn. However, reapers were used to cut oats, so perhaps that data show (slightly) the increase in wheat and barley prices compared to oats as well as the consequences of the reaper. Of course, other machinery made a difference, too.

How much of the increased output was produced in the Midwest alone? That we cannot say either, although there are some stray numbers that add to the picture. Data for flour and corn exported from the Midwest and Upper South show the expected big increases: flour rose from 800,000 barrels in 1839 to 3 million in

1850 to 5 million in 1860. However, corn exports rose from 1 million bushels in 1839 to 24 million in 1860, and reapers were not used in corn.[42]

The precise impact of mechanization attributed to each individual invention cannot be shown from such data. We can only rely upon common sense. The farmers were buying farm machinery and, in the 1850s, plunged into reapers. They were people who bought farm machinery to use and make a profit. So, the machinery must have been financially desirable. Otherwise, they would have stayed with scythes and "saved money."

THE COMPROMISE FAILS

There is an imaginary line between the wheat-growing northern areas of the trans-Appalachian West and the South in the 1850s that extended east and west from Shelbyville, Illinois. This line of demarcation was at the southern edge of the Wisconsin drift of the last glacier. Above that line lie the flattened prairies, below are the hills and mountains, descending into the alluvial and upland regions of the Cotton South. In the 1850s, in the area between wheat and cotton, lay a mixed farming region in which the main grain crop was corn, eaten by both humans and animals. Professor Merk made an insightful observation about those who lived in that middle ground.

> All the great compromises on the slavery issue came from corn-belt politicians. An Illinois Senator, Jesse B. Thomas, introduced the Missouri Compromise of 1820. A Kentucky senator, Henry Clay, worked out the Compromise of 1850. Another Illinois Senator, Stephen A. Douglas, was the champion of the compromise doctrine of popular sovereignty. A Kentuckian, John J. Crittenden, worked out the Crittenden peace plan of 1860, which failed.[43]

Table 10.8 Output of Major Grains[a]

	Wheat	Corn	Oats	Barley
Decade				
1839	85	378	123	4
1849	100	592	147	5
1859	173	839	173	16
Rate of growth per decade				
1839–49	17.7	56.6	19.5	25.0
1849–59	73.0	41.7	17.7	220.0

[a] Output figures are for grain only and are given in millions of bushels.

Source: *Historical Statistics*, series K503, 507, 512, 515.

As the line extended roughly westward, the compromises gave out. The Kansas-Nebraska Act of 1854 allowed popular sovereignty in Kansas over the issue of slavery, and gunfire was the result when the two systems of agriculture finally came into direct confrontation. Cotton was not going to be grown in Kansas. But in Texas, in Arizona and California—lands that were acquired from Mexico in the 1840s—cotton would eventually be an important crop. Slavery was already into Texas; it was kept out of Arizona and California. Land—who was to own it, how was it to be used, who was to work it—had always been a driving force in American history. As the two systems extended westward in the 1850s, the will to compromise on these issues failed.

As Jennifer Roback emphasizes, to the south the lands beyond the Missouri were a common property resource, to which the southern states had an equal claim by virtue of the contract of 1789—the federal constitution.[44] When Lincoln was elected in 1860, backed by northern groups determined to keep slavery out of the west, the contract was breached, and the South seceded from the Union. Slavery was abolished by fire and sword.

Notes

1. These farmers displaced Native American tribes, in both the North and South on the east side of the Mississippi in the 1820s and 1830s, in episodes like the Black Hawk War and the Cherokee removal that will darken American history forever. Ray Allen Billington, *Westward Expansion: A History of the American Frontier* (1949), chs. XIV, XV, XXXII.

2. For those who would like to see such an opinion "costed out," see Gerald Gunderson, "The Origin of the American Civil War," *JEH,* December 1974.

3. Free land here means not land at zero price, but land freely exchanged at market prices and unencumbered by such restraints as feudal obligations.

4. Peter Temin, "Free Land and Federalism: A Synoptic View of American Economic History," *JIH,* Winter 1991.

5. *Native-born* in this table means a resident in 1850 of a given state who also was born in that state. Richard Steckel advances arguments based upon "human capital," mainly in agriculture, to explain the tendency, strong before the Civil War, for the internal migrations to be predominantly east-west, with relatively little north-south migration. "The Economic Foundations of East-West Migration During the 19th Century," *EEH,* January 1983.

6. Jeremy Atack and Fred Bateman, *To Their Own Soil: Agriculture in the Antebellum North* (1987), ch. 5, "Migration and Immigration," for a detailed examination of the general east-west migration. Although families moved around within regions, they note, that within their sample, ". . . no families . . . made a long-distance move from a state west of Indiana to one east of that state" (p. 75).

7. Harriet Martineau, *Society in America* (1962), p. 181.

8. Robert W. Fogel and Stanley L. Engerman, *Time on the Cross: The Economics of American Negro Slavery* (1974), vol. I, p. 47.

9. Gavin Wright, *The Political Economy of the Cotton South: Households, Markets, and Wealth in the Nineteenth Century* (1978), ch. 2, pp. 15–24 for all soil types.

10. Wright, pp. 74–87.

11. The mean-sized farm in 1990 was 461 acres. *Statistical Abstract of the U.S.* (Washington, D.C.: Government Printing Office, 1992), table 1077.

12. Jacob Metzer, "Rational Management, Modern Business Practices, and Economies of Scale in the Ante-Bellum Southern Plantations," *EEH,* April 1975.

13. Heywood Fleisig, "Slavery, the Supply of Agricultural Labor, and the Industrialization of the South," *JEH,* September 1976, p. 586.

14. Wright, *The Political Economy of the Cotton South,* p. 23.

15. Fleisig, "Slavery, the Supply of Agricultural Labor, and the Industrialization of the South," p. 596. Terry Anderson, in a private communication, has emphasized the element of incomparability in these data. Slaves were "capital equipment" and had a known market value, which is included. But what of the "human capital" embodied in the brains and brawn of Northern farmers? That is not counted. If it were, if its market value (the opportunity cost, measured as income potential from alternate employment) were added into the free state data, the force of this argument would be considerably reduced.

16. Wright, *The Political Economy of the Cotton South,* p. 35.

17. Abbot E. Smith, *Colonists in Bondage: White Servitude and Convict Labor in America, 1607–1776* (Chapel Hill: University of North Carolina Press, 1947), p. 226.

18. Douglass C. North, *The Economic Growth of the United States, 1790 to 1860* (1961), p. 77.

19. Jonathan Hughes, *Fluctuation in Trade, Industry, and Finance: A Study of British Economic Growth 1850–1860* (Oxford: The Clarendon Press, 1960), p. 72.

20. Robert W. Fogel, *Without Consent or Contract: The Rise and Fall of American Slavery* (1989), ch. 3.

21. The 1859 and 1860 crops were extraordinary and, it has been estimated, exceeded 4 million bales. The data in Table 10.6 are census numbers.

22. Ronald Bailey, "The Slave(ry) Trade and the Development of Capitalism in the United States: The Textile Industry in New England," *Social Science History,* Fall 1990.

23. Wright, *The Political Economy of the Cotton South,* Table 2.5, p. 28.

24. Wright, p. 35.

25. Wright, p. 42.

26. William K. Hutchinson and Samuel H. Williamson, "The Self-Sufficiency of the Antebellum South: Estimates of the Food Supply," *JEH,* September 1971.

27. Southern farms were apparently nowhere as efficient in grain production, on the average, as were farms in the Northeast, or North Central U.S. William N. Parker and Judith L. V. Klein, "Productivity Growth in Grain Production in the United States," in Dorothy Brady, ed., *Output, Employment, and Productivity in the United States After 1800,* NBER, *Studies in Income and Wealth* (New York: Columbia University Press, 1966), vol. 30.

28. Wright, *The Political Economy of the Cotton South,* pp. 164–76.

29. Thomas Berry, *Western Prices Before 1861* (1901), Appendix B, Table 19. Reprinted in Douglass C. North, *The Economic Growth of the United States, 1790–1860,* p. 255.

30. Frederick Merk, *History of the Westward Movement* (1978), ch. 21.

31. Martin Primack, "Land Clearing Under 19th Century Techniques," *JEH,* December 1962, p. 492.

32. For example, W. W. Rostow, *The Stages of Economic Growth* (Cambridge: Cambridge University Press, 1961), pp. 7–9, in which the "take-off" into sustained growth occurs as the rate of investment *rises* into the range of 10 percent plus. If American farmers had had such an investment ratio on the frontier, they might have been overtaken by natural reforestation.

33. See Susan Previant Lee and Peter Passell, *A New Economic View of American History* (1979), p. 138.

34. Donald R. Adams, Jr., "Earnings and Savings in the Early 19th Century," *EEH,* April 1980.

35. Atack and Bateman, *To Their Own Soil,* ch. 8, "Relative Costs of Farm Making."

36. Atack and Bateman, pp. 136–137.

37. George R. Stewart, *Ordeal by Hunger: The Story of the Donner Party* (Boston: Houghton Mifflin, 1936), ch. II.

38. Leonard Arrington, *Great Basin Kingdom: An Economic History of the Latter-Day Saints 1830–1900* (Cambridge: Harvard University Press, 1958), p. 70.

39. Paul A. David, *Technical Choice, Innovation and Economic Growth: Essays on American and British Experience in the Nineteenth Century* (1975), p. 89.

40. Alan Olmstead, "The Mechanization of Reaping and Mowing in American Agriculture 1833–70," *JEH,* June 1975.

41. Lewis Jones, "A Comment," *JEH,* March 1977.

42. Diane Lindstrom, "Southern Dependence Upon Interregional Grain Supplies: A Review of the Trade Flows, 1840–1860," Table 7, printed in William Parker, ed., *The Structure of the Cotton Economy in the Antebellum South* (1970).

43. Merk, *History of the Westward Movement,* p. 179.

44. Jennifer Roback, "A Public Choice Perspective on the Coming of the Civil War," MS, by permission.

Suggested Readings

Articles

Adams, Donald R., Jr. "Earnings and Savings in the Early 19th Century." *Explorations in Economic History,* vol. 17, no. 2, April 1980.

Atack, Jeremy, and Bateman, Fred. "Egalitarianism, Inequality, and Age: The Rural North in 1860." *Journal of Economic History,* vol. XLI, no. 1, March 1981.

Bailey, Ronald, "The Slave(ry) Trade and the Development of Capitalism in the United States: The Textile Industry in New England." *Social Science History,* vol. 14, no. 3, Fall 1990.

Bogue, Allan G. "Farming in the Prairie Peninsula 1830–1890." *Journal of Economic History,* vol. I, no. 1, March 1947.

Danhof, Clarence. "Farm Making Costs and the Safety Valve; 1855–60." In Vernon Carstensen, ed., *The Public Lands.* Madison: University of Wisconsin Press, 1963.

Fleisig, Heywood. "Slavery, the Supply of Agricultural Labor, and the Industrialization of the South." *Journal of Economic History,* vol. XXXVI, no. 3, September 1976.

Gunderson, Gerald. "Southern Ante-Bellum Income Reconsidered." *Explorations in Economic History,* vol. 10, no. 2, Winter 1973.

———. "The Origins of the American Civil War." *Journal of Economic History,* vol. XXXIV, no. 4, December 1974.

Hutchinson, W. K., and Williamson, Samuel H. "The Self-Sufficiency of the Ante-Bellum South; Estimates of the Food Supply." *Journal of Economic History,* vol. XXXI, no. 3, September 1971.

Jones, Lewis. "The Mechanization of Reaping and Mowing in American Agriculture: A Comment." *Journal of Economic History,* vol. XXXVII, no. 2, June 1977.

Metzer, Jacob. "Rational Management, Modern Business Practice, and Economies of Scale in the Antebellum Plantations." *Explorations in Economic History,* vol. 12, no. 2, April 1975.

Olmstead, Alan. "The Mechanization of Reaping and Mowing in American Agriculture 1833–70." *Journal of Economic History,* vol. XXXV, no. 2, June 1975.

Parker, William. "Agriculture." In Lance E. Davis, et al., *American Economic Growth: An Economist's History of the United States.* New York: Harper & Row, 1972, ch. 11.

Parker, William, and Klein, Judith. "Productivity Growth in Grain Production in the United States." In Dorothy Brady, ed., *Output, Employment and Productivity in the United States After 1800.* National Bureau of Economic Research, *Studies in Income and Wealth.* New York: Columbia University Press, 1966, vol. 30.

Passell, Peter. "The Impact of Cotton Land Distribution on the Ante-Bellum Economy." *Journal of Economic History,* vol. XXXI, no. 4, December 1971.

Primack, Martin. "Land Clearing Under 19th Century Techniques." *Journal of Economic History,* vol. XXII, no. 4, December 1962.

Ransom, Roger L., and Sutch, Richard. "Growth and Welfare in the American South in the Nineteenth Century." *Explorations in Economic History,* vol. 16, no. 2, April 1979.

Schmitz, Mark D. "Economies of Scale and Farm Size in the Ante-Bellum Sugar Sector." *Journal of Economic History,* vol. XXXVII, no. 4, December 1977.

———, and Schaefer, Donald. "Paradox Lost: Westward Expansion and Slave Prices Before the Civil War." *Journal of Economic History,* vol. XLI, no. 2, June 1981.

Steckel, Richard. "The Economic Foundations of East-West Migration During the 19th Century." *Explorations in Economic History,* vol. 20, no. 1, January 1983.

Temin, Peter. "Free Land and Federalism: A Synoptic View of American Economic History." *Journal of Interdisciplinary History,* vol. 21, no. 3, Winter 1991.

Books

Atack, Jeremy, and Bateman, Fred. *To Their Own Soil: Agriculture in the Antebellum North.* Ames: Iowa State University Press, 1987.

Berry, Thomas. *Western Prices Before 1861.* Cambridge: Harvard University Press, 1943.

Bidwell, Percy, and Falconer, John. *History of Agriculture in the Northern United States 1620–1860.* Washington: The Carnegie Institution, 1925.

Billington, Ray Allen. *Westward Expansion: A History of the American Frontier.* New York: Macmillan, 1949.

Bogue, Allan G. *From Prairie to Cornbelt: Farming on the Illinois and Iowa Prairies in the Nineteenth Century.* Chicago: University of Chicago Press, 1963.

Danhof, Clarence. *Change in Agriculture: The Northern United States, 1820–70.* Cambridge: Harvard University Press, 1969.

David, Paul. *Technical Choice, Innovation and Economic Growth: Essays on American and British Experience in the Nineteenth Century.* New York: Cambridge University Press, 1975.

Fogel, Robert W. *Without Consent or Contract: The Rise and Fall of American Slavery.* New York: W. W. Norton, 1989.

———, and Engerman, Stanley. *Time on the Cross: The Economics of American Negro Slavery.* Boston: Little, Brown, 1974.

Lee, Susan Previant, and Passell, Peter. *A New Economic View of American History.* New York: Norton, 1979.

Martineau, Harriet. *Society in America.* Garden City, NY: Doubleday, 1962.

Merk, Frederick. *History of the Westward Movement.* New York: Alfred Knopf, 1978.

North, Douglass C. *The Economic Growth of the United States 1790 to 1860.* Englewood Cliffs, NJ: Prentice-Hall, 1961.

Parker, William, ed. *The Structure of the Cotton Economy of the Antebellum South.* Washington: The Agricultural History Society, 1970.

Rothenberg, Winifred B. *From Market-Places to a Market Economy: The Transformation of Rural Massachusetts, 1750–1850.* Chicago: University of Chicago Press, 1992.

Wright, Gavin. *The Political Economy of the Cotton South: Households, Markets, and Wealth in the Nineteenth Century.* New York: Norton, 1978.

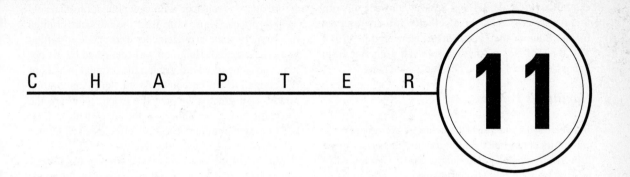

The Financial System and the
International Economy

We now need to retrace our steps to follow the financial system's development during the antebellum period. In finance the Americans relied on their colonial habits and inclinations about paper money, but that money was *privately* issued after 1790. The needs and consequences of the Revolutionary War finance had to be accommodated by new institutions, and stresses developed between the sovereign state powers and the pressures to devise a workable set of national practices and institutions related to banking and money.

CURRENCY AND BANKING DEVELOPMENTS

Financing the Revolution had been a "near thing," as Wellington said of Waterloo. The Americans had barely brought it off. Congress did not have the authority to levy taxes during the Revolution, nor was there any systematic way to raise financial support from the states. From 1776 to 1780, Congress paid bills by printing more paper money. Too much was printed relative to either specie reserves or hope of redemption in specie, and it depreciated badly. A total of $241.6 million

was issued by 1780, driving all specie out of circulation (Gresham's Law again).

In 1780 the states were asked to levy taxes to redeem the Continental currency at a ratio of $40 Continental to $1 silver. The Congress then issued a new currency to redeem the old from the states at a ratio of $20 to $1. The old bills that were not turned in depreciated finally to about $1000 to $1—hence the phrase, "not worth a Continental." From 1776 to 1782, Congress also borrowed domestically about $63.6 million (worth only $7.7 million in specie). From 1780 to 1783, foreign borrowing ($7.8 million, of which $6.4 million came from France alone) and requisitions (honored only in part) on the individual states were the main sources of national finance. After their surrender at Yorktown, the British lost their taste for war with their North American colonies, and there was no need to raise more funds to extend the fighting.

In addition, the states had borrowed and issued paper money of their own, bills of credit and paper money with a nominal value of $209 million. In its efforts to provide financial organization, Congress in 1781 chartered the Bank of North America, a *limited-liability corporation* that handled the government's finances as best it could and in most respects did the chores of a central bank. Studenski and Krooss consider this our first real *central bank,* an appellation usually reserved for the Bank of the United States chartered in 1791.[1] The Bank of North America received a charter from Pennsylvania in 1787 and became a state bank.

Hamilton's Policies

Between 1783 and 1787, the central government's fiscal affairs deteriorated badly; it could not tax, it made little from sales of public lands, and it was forced to borrow from foreign (Dutch) bankers to stay afloat financially. The new Constitution in 1789 established the federal government on a completely different and potentially powerful financial basis, giving it the authority to levy taxes, to borrow, and to issue money and "regulate" its value. These powers were followed by vigorous policies devised by Secretary of the Treasury, Alexander Hamilton.

Only partly achieved (and bitterly opposed by many at the time), Hamilton's policies now have come to be viewed as brilliant in conception, although imperfect in execution. They were (a) establishment of tariffs and other taxes for federal revenue; (b) complete refunding (with arrangements for redemption) of the wartime debts of the Continental Congress; (c) the assumption by the federal government of the states' wartime debts; (d) the establishment of a new central bank; and (e) the creation of a national currency standard based upon newly minted coins.

Beginning with the tariff law of 1789, Hamilton's immediate designs were realized in part. As we saw in Chapter 8, the tariff yielded nearly all federal government revenues. The internal taxes Hamilton wanted yielded much less, and one, the tax on whiskey, provoked the "Whiskey Rebellion" in 1794 among the farmers of western Pennsylvania. On-the-farm whiskey distilleries were a favored technology at the time for "storing" surplus grains. The rebellion was put down by militia.

Hamilton estimated that the national debt in 1790 was about $54 million, and that the outstanding state war debts totaled about $25 million. In 1790 and 1795, provisions were made to refund all this debt with various new issues and then, ultimately to retire it by setting money aside in a *sinking fund.* The debt was never completely retired, although it very nearly vanished in 1835–36 during Andrew Jackson's presidency. Instead,

it rose and was replaced with new obligations that sold at high prices. Those who held the old debt profited handsomely since arrangements were made to refund and prices soared. Hamilton was castigated by his opponents, some of whom wanted the original owners of the obligations to be compensated. Jefferson, among others, also greatly doubted the extent to which the Revolutionary expenditures of the states had, in fact, been in the common cause.[2] Nevertheless, Hamilton's system was more or less adopted.

With their wartime debts taken over by the federal government, the states were placed on a sound financial basis. But they had lost, under the new Constitution, the power to issue their own paper money. The banks they created by acts of incorporation *could* do so, though, and did.

In 1791, a new central bank, The Bank of the United States, was chartered for twenty years, with one-fifth of its stock held by the U.S. Treasury. The rest was held by private persons. Jefferson opposed this bank, as did many others, on the ground that the Constitution provided no such power and that the bank threatened to introduce all sorts of alien practices into the country.

In 1792 the Mint Act provided for a mint in Philadelphia and placed the United States on a bimetallic basis: 15 ounces of silver were equal to 1 ounce of gold. The coins were on a metric basis. There was to be a ten-dollar gold coin (the Eagle), a silver dollar, and fractional coins. There would be no national paper money.

What can be said of the whole system? The tariff was long the mainstay of federal finance, but the internal taxes were less successful. The assumption of Revolutionary debt by the federal government did establish the federal credit, as Hamilton had wished. The First Bank of the United States did by all accounts an excellent job but lost its recharter in 1811 (by one vote). In 1812, the United States went to war without a central bank and suffered accordingly. In 1816, a new one was chartered, the Second Bank of the United States, but its recharter was vetoed by Andrew Jackson in 1832, and the next central bank, the Federal Reserve System, did not come about until 1914.

Little need be said here of the Mint Act. Bimetallism is a poor metallic system to use because the two metals fluctuate in price constantly *against each other* with strange results (thanks to Gresham's Law). In Europe, gold prices rose in terms of silver, and the new gold coins were shipped almost as soon as they appeared in 1796. The silver coins were boxed up and shipped to the Caribbean, where they were exchanged for irregular, tarnished, and heavier Spanish dollars that were brought back to exchange for gold and/or new silver dollars. Americans, thus, for a long time (until the mid-1830s) had no metallic coin of their own in circulation and went back to the colonial practice of using foreign coins, even declaring some of them legal tender.[3] It made little difference, though, because the new state banks provided the currency the people used as a medium of exchange—paper.

Paper Money—State Bank Notes

As we have seen, the states retained the sovereign power to create corporations by special franchise. This power was quickly used to establish state-chartered private banks that issued their own paper money. The paper money was paid out when loans were made, in contrast to the modern practice of establishing a demand deposit against which checks may be written by the borrower. Although the new Constitution forbade the states to issue paper money, their creatures, the state banks, supplied the needed amounts of it.[4]

The notes, unless presented for redemption, circulated at whatever value the market gave them. Guides ("currency detectors") for users of paper money were published commercially to indicate the possible market value of a note, based upon known assets, the characters of proprietors, and so forth. Checks and deposits were not much used before the 1830s. Bank loans thus gave rise to immediate circulation until they were presented for redemption in specie, sometimes long after the issuers had vanished into history. By 1860, 1562 state banks existed, and it is estimated that perhaps 10,000 different kinds of paper money were afloat.

Much was once written about the colorful state banks and their wild "over-moneying," their notes called names like "blue monkey," or "sick Indian." Emphasis was placed by historians upon the restraining influences of the Second Bank of the United States and its measures to "discipline" the state banks before 1836, when its charter expired. As Richard Sylla has pointed out, the critical view of American banking in the antebellum period was mainly a result of disapproval of bank fraud and failure, with widespread consequences.[5]

Critics were puzzled by the tendency of the U.S. economy to grow *despite* its banking system.[6] The paper currency issues of the famous "wildcat banks" (however much undersecured by reserves they were) produced no sustained inflation at all. The banks no doubt did contribute to whatever movement in business sentiment took place, but, in the long run, money issues by state banks were surprisingly conservative. Prices moved generally downward throughout the period 1816–60 with only slight cyclical upswings in the 1830s and the 1850s. Moreover, there is not the slightest evidence that "excess money" was the consequence of such liberal banking laws and the absence of a central bank. The money supply did not even grow as fast as did the population after the demise of the Second Bank of the United States (see Table 11.1). By modern standards this was a most enviable performance, one that the post-World War II Federal Reserve System could not hope to emulate.

Learning New Techniques

As it happens, this time of experimentation in the American economy was paralleled by European developments. Throughout the Western world in the first

Table 11.1   Population, Banking, and Price Data 1836–60

Year	Population (in millions)	Total Bank Deposits (in millions)	Bank Note Circulation (in millions)	Total Bank Assets (in millions)	Wholesale Prices[a]
1836	15.4	$166	$140	$ 622	$114
1860	31.5	310	207	1000	93
Percentage of Change	+ 104.5	+ 86.7	+ 47.9	+ 60.8	− 18.4

[a] Indexed on the basis of 1910–14 = 100.

Source: *Historical Statistics*, series A7, E52, X581, 585–86.

half of the nineteenth century, new financial techniques suitable for industrial economies (given local law and custom) were being tried out. The financial history of that period is strewn with the wreckage of failures, with ideas abandoned,[7] as well as successes celebrated. The American state banks were part of that learning process. The best financial technologies had to be found by trial and error.

The state-chartered banks were also part of the development of a *system* of financial intermediation in the early American economy peculiar to our needs and laws. State chartering created **unit banking,** many small banks, but in the 1830s there were several hundred separate banking companies in England, too. For the future, the difference lay in national amalgamation in England, which never occurred here because of the separate powers of the states. Even now the United States does not have nationwide branch banking, as they do in England and Canada.

As special-franchise corporations before 1838, the state banks represented obvious rent-seeking behavior on the part of their owners as well as the social need for such financial services. But from 1838 to 1863 (the year of the National Banking Act), the spread of competitive "free banking" among the states represented more the need for financial intermediation than mere rent-seeking on the part of would-be local monopolists.

Both ideas later gave way to state banking control by commission as well as to the national banking system. Special franchises for banks and free banking both were experiments, as were the so-called industrial banks—corporations set up for industrial purposes that contained banking powers in their charters. The idea did not work in the United States, but in Europe, banks that did all sorts of commercial banking and were deeply engaged in transportation and industrial activities became commonplace. Americans, like their British cousins, came to prefer that their commercial banks stick to banking and that they lend their funds out primarily for short periods only. As Craig West has recently emphasized, this prejudice underlay, finally, the Federal Reserve legislation in 1913.[8]

The Need for Intermediation

The need for financial intermediation was obvious in colonial times, (a) in the efforts to create banks by charter (which the British stopped when the Bubble

Act was applied to the Massachusetts Land Bank) and (b) in the nonincorporated banking business engaged in by groups of colonial merchants. **Intermediation**—all middleman activity between savers and borrowers—is part of the system of general communication in any society. In its purest form, intermediation is mere brokering. Some persons, businesses, or even regions generate a surplus from current business and household management, while others have need for funds beyond their own current *saving* (free resources not needed for current consumption).

Think, for example, of someone who wishes to build a house. He or she will probably need to borrow funds to do it. The property will be mortgaged to a lender on agreed terms, and the amount of the loan plus interest (the cost of the rent of the money) will be paid back over a fixed term of years. The interest here is a price mutually satisfactory to the lender and the borrower for the use of the money—claims over real resources. The lender, if he or she has in turn borrowed the funds from others (as do bankers when they accept deposits), is the intermediary.

The state banks accepted deposits and paid interest for them. Those who made the deposits earned interest for the use of their deposits. The banks then loaned the money out again at a higher interest charge, completing the circle of intermediation. By this means, the surpluses earned by some were kept "at work" by the industry of others. This was a socially useful function, and it speeded up the pace of economic growth, or at least the possibilities for such growth.

Social Considerations

The intermediary function just described can be considered *mobilization of capital.* One role of intermediation—by banks, life insurance companies, savings and loan associations, the stock markets—is this mobilization. It is necessary, but the *selection* of borrowers is not a socially neutral practice. We will encounter much criticism in United States financial history (as we still do today) of the social consequences of bank lending. The distribution of wealth and income is affected. Those who can pay get the funds, and the potential benefit, and those who cannot, do not.

The state banks, as profit-making institutions, naturally wanted to lend where interest was highest, and that often was where the risks were highest. Because depositors wanted their money back, the safety of the loans became an issue. Since there was no obvious way to combine total safety with highest earnings, even the process of intermediation gave rise to difficulties. If safety (certainty or repayment on schedule) was the first consideration, then farmers likely would have trouble borrowing against the collateral of farm land. If safety was not a requirement, then banks would fail in hard times as their borrowers went broke, depositors would lose their money, and the entire community would suffer.

We will see how these largely incompatible demands upon banking practice created recurrent problems in American banks, repeated efforts at bank "reform," and demands by some elements, notably farmers, for government banks to meet their special requirements—once again, rent-seeking.

Fractional Reserve Banking

Banks, as a group, do not simply intermediate: They can also *create money* in multiples of the amounts of deposits through **fractional reserve banking.**[9] Bankers very early realized that they did not need to keep funds on hand sufficient to repay all deposits at a given moment. Only a fraction of the funds deposited were required to meet any normal day's demand for withdrawals. The rest could be loaned or invested, and banking income from resulting interest payments would be increased. Although no single bank could lend more than was deposited, as a group they could.

Think of the entire banking system as a single bank. If there were only one bank in the whole country, and it kept reserves of 20 percent cash against deposits, then for every $100 deposited in cash, it could create loans (or issue its own notes) in the amount of $500. Of course, this bank could not repay its depositors (or redeem notes held by others) if they all came at once to demand the money due them. *No* system of fractional reserve banking could then or can now. Fractional reserve banking thus was both profitable and potentially dangerous.

The Reserve Ratio

The reserve question, then, centered upon what **reserve ratio** was both safe and profitable for bankers. No one has ever provided an answer. Some reserves were required for daily business, and some extra reserves might be needed in case of emergency. However, cash reserves earned no interest, and bankers had to seek higher-yielding loans to compensate for them.

In large-scale emergencies, no reserve ratio less than 100 percent could suffice, and that was clearly not possible in fractional reserve banking, especially since the promise of redemption was usually given in specie, the legal tender of the country. So, when crises came, the banks would tend to stop paying out specie against their notes and deposits; in the panics of 1819, 1837, and 1857 and in 1860 nearly every bank in the country suspended specie payments. This defensive maneuver continued in later crises, all the way to 1933, when every bank in the nation closed its doors.

Leverage

Creation of bank money by fractional reserve methods can be economic leverage since claims on real resources are being created in excess of those set aside by savers. If the country responds by greater production (the bank money is accepted at current prices for goods and services), the leverage produces real growth. If bidding for resources stemming from the money creation produces no such response, the exchange rate between money and goods and services falls, and **inflation** is the result—more money chasing the same volume of goods. Since bank money usually expanded with business demands, and the big economic expansions were associated with rising prices, the state banks were blamed for excessive money creation when the crash came. But in bad times banks that could not recover all their loans were like other businesses in similar situations, and they had to give up. Widespread bank failures punctuated all nineteenth-century business down-turns.

State Bank Growth

Bank formation boomed between independence and the Civil War. Intermediation was needed, and in most circumstances the leverage worked—people accepted the notes of the state banks as money. As a result, apart from periods of crisis and depression, banking was a desirable business. By 1810 there were 88 state-chartered banks, by 1820, more than 300, and by 1860, despite the multitude of failures, at least 1500 state banks existed. The notes and deposits of the state banks from 1834 to 1860 are shown at intervals in Table 11.2.

What the data in Table 11.2 do not show, nor do the trends mentioned earlier indicate, is the *volatility* (ups and downs) of state bank behavior. It is in this area that the antebellum state banks were subjected to criticism for recklessness. In Table 11.3, we see rough estimates of volatility based upon the available data for bank liabilities compared to wholesale prices.

In the three big price expansions between 1834 and 1860 (1834–37, 1843–47, and 1851–57) for which we have any corresponding bank data, the increase in demand liabilities of bankers—bank money—was far in excess of increases in the wholesale price level in general.[10] Even though there was some inflation, the slower growth of prices relative to bank liabilities suggests successful leverage in real terms.

In all three economic crises that topped these expansions, it was charged that the state banks had contrib-

Table 11.2   State Bank Notes and Deposits

Year	Notes Outstanding	Deposits
1834	95	102
1835	104	122
1840	107	120
1845	90	114
1850	131	146
1855	187	236
1860	207	310

Source: *Historical Statistics*, series X437, 585.

Table 11.3   Volatility of Bank Liabilities[a]

Volatility	Wholesale Prices	Bank Notes Outstanding	Total Deposits
Price Expansions			
1834–37	+25	+54	+ 88
1843–47	+15	+47	+ 42
1851–57	+28	+60	+113
Price Contractions			
1837–43	−40	−90	−112
1847–51	− 7	+49	+ 55
1857–60	−18	− 8	+ 22

[a] Figures represent the percentage of change.

Source: *Historical Statistics*, series E52, X585–86.

uted to the excessive optimism by their "over issues."[11] But one might just as well argue that business optimism gave rise to demand for credit and that the bankers merely responded. As Peter Temin has shown, the expansion of bank money was solidly based upon increased specie reserves in the banking system, and the economy's response was a heightened demand for resources, using a more plentiful money supply.[12] The small size of the price increases compared to those of bank liabilities suggests that either there were significant real production increases to absorb all the bank money, or else bank money was not all that important.

Where prices fell, the record is mixed. The severe depression following the panic of 1837 witnessed sharp declines in notes and deposits (and many bank failures) in excess of the fall in prices. The prostrate condition of the economy was doubtless partly the result of the banking crisis indicated by the data. No other explanation seems plausible. Unfortunately, we cannot be more precise with the data we have from this early period. In the two other periods of falling prices after economic crises, bank note issues continued to increase (although in 1858 they declined in a single year about 15 percent and then made a recovery by 1860). Only between 1857 and 1860 was there a drop in deposits corresponding to declining prices.

Efforts to Regulate

Bank failures created such widespread suffering (for millions of depositors) that efforts were made to force a greater conservatism upon the bankers, partly by private actions and partly by the political system. Since the banks were, by their charters, branches of the state sovereignty, the states were considered partly responsible for the consequences if the public was harmed.

One major private regulatory effort was the famous **Suffolk System** of the Boston banks. As early as 1819, country bank notes, issued against small reserves, circulated in Boston, driving notes from the Suffolk Bank of Boston out of circulation (Gresham's Law again). In retaliation, the Suffolk Bank forced higher reserves on the country banks by regularly presenting their notes to their issuers and demanding redemption in specie. In 1824, six other Boston banks joined the fray. The country banks then agreed to keep reserves in the Boston banks against their note issues if they were not presented by the Boston banks for payment in specie.

The result was higher country bank reserves (hence, lower loan volumes against given deposits) and fewer country bank notes circulating freely again as the exchange rate fell against country notes.

This system was a forerunner of the modern practice of required nonearning deposits for member banks in the Federal Reserve System. The Suffolk System lasted until the 1850s, when a Boston bank clearing house was organized at about the same time that clearing houses were organized in New York, Philadelphia, and other major banking centers. Clearing house rules imposed stricter behavior on individual banks and were a force for banker conservatism.[13]

State power, too, was used to regulate banking practices, which is not surprising when we recall that the state was the origin of the bank charter. **Double liability** (twice the face value of bank stocks) was imposed on bank stock owners in New York in 1827 in an effort to encourage prudence among bankers. The idea spread rapidly.[14]

A notable state regulatory experiment was conducted in New York between 1829 and 1839. This innovation was mandatory deposit insurance paid for by the bankers: the New York **Safety Fund,** a forerunner of the modern Federal Deposit Insurance Corporation (FDIC). Each New York bank receiving a charter (or a recharter) was required to deposit into a fund an amount equal to 3 percent of its capital stock as a reserve against note and deposit repudiation by state banks. The idea was a sound one as long as banks failed at a reasonable rate or in reasonable numbers. But in the panic of 1837, so many banks failed that the fund went broke.

State deposit insurance schemes continued to fail in crises, right up to the 1930s when the FDIC was formed by the federal government with authority to borrow from the U.S. Treasury to pay off depositors. State efforts were doomed because their resources were limited to funds deposited. With the U.S. Treasury behind the FDIC, its funds are potentially limited only by the discretion of government—a very liberal backing.

Efforts to require higher legal reserve ratios produced some successes, most notably, the Forstall System in Louisiana.[15] It was first organized in 1842 after all banks in Louisiana had closed their doors. The **Forstall System** required one-third specie reserves against notes and deposits, and also restricted state

bank loans of deposited funds to commercial paper with maturities of 90 days.

Such conservatism paid off. During the panic of 1857, Louisiana banks continued specie payments when most other banks in the country (all but one in New York, for example) closed their doors. Safety, it seemed, paid for note holders and depositors and bankers, too. High cash reserves became a feature of the national banks after 1863, and the success of the Forstall System probably was the main reason for it.

In 1838 New York led the movement toward competitive **free banking,** a system by which any group of persons could acquire a banking charter by following some general rules to register their group, agreeing to conduct banking business according to state regulations, and, in some states, agreeing to maintain specified reserves. Other states followed New York, and the number of banks multiplied again. It was felt, rightly, that free banking contained less favoritism and temptation to corruption than the old system of special franchise chartering. By 1838, the Safety Fund was dead, and so was the Second Bank of the United States.[16]

The First and Second Banks

There has been a great deal written about the two "central" banks chartered by Congress in 1791 and in 1816.[17] The obvious question to ask is, "Would our economic history have been significantly different without them?" The answer may well be no, since from 1836 to 1914—a period of dramatic change and enormous economic growth—there was no trace of central banking in this country. However, the two banks continue to be of interest in a historical perspective as part of the nation's learning processes about finance, and, of course, there were great personalities involved: Hamilton and Jefferson in the First Bank, and Biddle and Jackson in the Second.

There is no doubt that the Bank of England was the paradigm for both banks; Jefferson charged that Hamilton was simply infatuated by English example in his advocacy of the First Bank of the United States.[18] Like the Bank of England, it was a direct competitor with the commercial banks and was expected to turn a profit. Because both the First and Second Banks were direct competitors with private business, the rest of the banking community was mainly opposed to their recharter.

Some lessons were learned from this. The idea of joint public-private ownership, embodied in both the First and Second Bank charters, was entirely suitable to democratic ideas about the partnership between government and business. But the sale of bank stock to foreigners in both cases raised hostility to these banks. Therefore, when the Federal Reserve System was organized in 1914, stock ownership was limited to member banks, transfer restricted, and government ownership was limited to the headquarters in Washington, D.C. Also, when the Federal Reserve was organized, it was a bank for bankers only and did not compete for business with private bankers.

Why did both the First and Second banks vanish from the scene after a single, 20-year charter? Even though their respective histories are very different, the one thing they did have *in common,* the 20-year federal charter, was fatal. In both cases, politics made survival impossible. The First Bank was tainted in Congress by its Federalist origins. Hamilton's ideas were vigorously opposed by Jefferson, who believed that the First Bank was simply an unconstitutional assumption of powers that were reserved to the states. When it came time to recharter, legislators not favorably disposed, especially if they were of the Jeffersonian persuasion, were urged on by banker competitors.

The First Bank was huge compared to the private banks, and its business was a juicy morsel the private banks longed to gobble, and would if the charter was not renewed. There were 88 private state banks when the recharter was lost in 1811, and 250 of them five years later. In the case of the Second Bank, the recharter attempt was killed in 1832 by a single dose of politics, Andrew Jackson's veto of the recharter legislation, and subsequent withdrawal of federal moneys from the Bank's management.[19]

In all of the First Bank's career, and in most of the Second Bank's life (especially during the reign of Nicholas Biddle as bank president from 1823 on), historians have generally agreed that the *central banking* operations they performed were done well. They conducted most of the federal government's fiscal business with efficiency and provided a brake on the expansionary pace of the state banks by shrewdly sending back state bank notes for redemption in specie when the rate of growth was deemed excessive. But that, in fact, was the rub. Neither bank had been chartered as a *regulatory* agency, and those activities of central bank control

so approved of by modern historians were considered usurpations of power by contemporaries.

Jackson's vigorous veto message was a concentrated attack on the Second Bank's power over the country, but he emphasized also that it was a privileged monopoly, its stock largely owned by foreigners and the "rich." He said he would prefer a government-owned bank, if such a monopoly were needed in the future. He also objected that no one had asked *him* what sort of recharter there should be. Since the Bank of the United States, he said, "is professedly established as an agent of the executive branch of the Government" and its charter was being pushed through four years prior to its expiration without any executive input, the legislation was "dangerous to the Government and country."[20] Jackson began almost immediately to remove federal moneys from the Second Bank, depositing them in favored state banks. The Second Bank of the United States received a Pennsylvania charter after 1836 and expired in 1841, after an unsuccessful attempt to use its funds to corner the market in raw cotton.

As was mentioned, the Second Bank, like the First, was huge compared to the state banks. By using its drafts on its branches as money, it was, in fact, creating a uniform currency, a practice much feared by the private bankers.[21] The Bank's branches were resented as privileged intrusions into local economic life. Monopoly on money is what a central bank *ought* to have, by modern standards. But such was not the prevailing view in the 1830s. As a result, from then until 1914, the United States had no central bank. Instead the Treasury Department tried to conduct its affairs independently of the banking system. The independent Treasury became another experiment left in the dust of history when the country returned to central banking with the Federal Reserve System in 1914. It had also learned from the Second Bank that the regulatory powers should be in the charter, so far as possible, and that was done in 1914 (although they were changed greatly afterward).[22]

The two banks chartered by Congress, modeled after the Bank of England, left one more legacy. The Federal Reserve System has a virtually perpetual charter. The charter can be amended, but the Fed does not come up for recharter every 20 years as did the First and Second Banks of the United States, or no doubt it also would have passed into history along with its ancestors. The present system could, of course, be abolished by Congress if that were the "will of the people."

Other Intermediaries

Other kinds of intermediation were needed to serve other parts of the social system. The state banks were commercial banks, operating, as the term suggests, as intermediaries primarily in the world of business and as instruments of commerce. To borrow long-term moneys and sell equities (shares of ownership), businesses and governments needed organized capital markets. The new transportation companies, and increasingly, the rising manufacturing firms, required a forum. The evolution of capital markets went hand in hand with markets for short-term money. Short-term finance was the lubricant for long-term borrowing and equity sales. New York, Boston, Philadelphia, Baltimore, and New Orleans were early centers.

The New York Stock Exchange Board was formally organized in 1817 after twenty years of less formal existence. It slowly forged ahead of the others as the center of the nation's capital markets—just as New York City itself took the lead in commerce and growth.

Stock exchanges grew up in other cities as well to serve local needs. In time, the major centers were linked by telegraph, with the focus on the New York exchange. Common stocks were sold, as were bonds, from the beginning. In the 1830s *preferred shares* appeared, and later on industrialists followed the lead of governments and began issuing long-term bonds for subscription in the public capital markets.

Such specialized activities appeared wherever there were need and imagination. *Mutual savings banks,* carefully governed depositories for the savings of the poor, appeared early in the American scene. The first one was organized in Philadelphia in 1816. Emphasis was on the *safety* of the loans, even if earnings were deliberately low, and these institutions produced an enviable record of trustworthiness compared to the oft-failing commercial banks. By 1860, there were 278 mutual savings banks in the country, with combined assets of perhaps 15 percent of those of the state banks. According to Lance Davis, the leading expert on the subject, nine of the ten largest businesses in the country by 1860 were savings banks.[23] The idea, imported from England, was to provide the small saver with a secure way to practice thrift and frugality. The huge funds generated by such virtue went into the most secure forms of investment. In England they had been limited to investment in government bonds. Here, the conservative investments of the savings banks freed other funds for more speculative uses.

Life and fire insurance companies were formed in the early nineteenth century, along with burial societies, building societies, and private fire engine companies. All were techniques for mobilizing the funds of a group against disasters that struck individual families. Since fire was not necessarily an individual hazard in towns, municipalities took over the chores of operating fire-fighting equipment in self-defense. The "free rider," not covered by private engine companies, became a real danger. An uninsured house on fire, if not attended to, would ignite insured houses. Private engine companies in towns had to douse the fires of the uninsured as well as those of the prudent (or rich). Nevertheless, insurance against fire losses continued on a private basis.

The list of intermediation attempts is a long one. The point is that experimentation was necessary as new needs developed, and the American economy before 1860 was alive with such experimentation.

THE FINANCIAL LINK: U.S. AND WORLD ECONOMICS

The modern student may well be perplexed by the practice of private banks in the nineteenth century issuing their own promissory notes as "money." To comprehend the history of banking in this period, we must understand that practice. In addition, we must go further into the matter of specie redemption because that promise made by state banks when their notes were issued firmly tied the heterogeneous American monetary system to the international economy. When a state banker in, say, Georgia, paid out gold coin on demand for the return of his own notes, he was paying out international money.[24] If he observed a given reserve ratio, that gold flowing from his vault decreased his ability to lend—*contracted his note issues.*

Bimetallism and the Gold Standard

When the Bank of England suspended gold payments in 1797, England was a bimetallic country, with fixed prices for both gold and silver at the Bank. England was, therefore, on the same monetary standard as the United States. When payments were resumed finally in 1821, only the gold price was fixed at the Bank, and England was on a straight gold standard.[25] Other countries by then—France and the German states, for example—were still bimetallic.

As long as the price of one metal was fixed, stable exchange rates between currencies could exist. The Bank of England's gold price was £3–17–10½ (three pounds, seventeen shillings, ten and one-half pence) per troy ounce. The U.S. mint price was $20.67 for an avoirdupois ounce. Adjusting for differences in ounces and gold quality, the British pound was worth $4.87, each English shilling was worth 24.35 cents, and each English penny worth slightly more than two American cents. Other currency exchange rates could be similarly calculated, once gold prices were fixed.

If an American merchant wanted to remit specie to England in payment for goods, and the English free-market silver price was too low, the merchant could always trade silver for gold, ship it, and receive credit at £3–17–10½ an ounce. The nineteenth-century international financial system was thus based on a *fixed gold price and stable exchange rates.*

Apart from temporary dislocations (like the American suspension of gold payments between 1861 and 1879), stable and fixed exchange rates were the norm during most of the nineteenth century. Even though some countries were bimetallic (or even on a straight silver standard after the California and Australian gold discoveries of 1849–1851 lowered the price of gold in terms of silver), the system has come to be known simply as the **gold standard.**

The Gold Points

As in colonial times, most international payments among merchants in the nineteenth century were not made by shipping specie but by purchasing and remitting bills of exchange. American supplies of sterling (claims on London) came primarily from the export of a single commodity, raw cotton, and from shipping services. The bills of exchange were not themselves fixed in price. What it cost to buy one was determined by its *face value* (the amount payable on the date of maturity), discounted by an interest charge (since it was payable in the *future*), and then by the haggling between seller and buyer.[26] Therefore, what a merchant, say, in Philadelphia, paid for sterling was *to some extent* determined by free-market forces. The qualifier, "to some extent," is there because *shipping specie was always an alternative to purchasing exchange.*

The trouble involved in buying specie and packaging, insuring, and shipping it set a limit on the possible price of exchange. If, for example, the price of sterling bills rose to the point where it was as cheap or cheaper to ship specie in payment, then such shipments occurred, and the bills either were offered cheaper or the owners had the trouble themselves of collecting when they fell due. The upper limit on foreign exchange prices was the *gold export point.* Similarly, if American bills were too expensive in London, gold flowed to the United States. That threshold was the *gold import point.* The two gold points insured the stability of foreign exchange rates under the gold standard. The gold points were the exchange rate extremes, beyond which exchange rates, by definition, did not go.

Because of fixed gold prices and the possibility of gold shipments, nineteenth-century merchants enjoyed an element of stability in their calculations that was most valuable in a time of slow communications. The known limits of the various exchange rates were called the *solidarity* of the gold points. However, since the possibility of gold shipments created that solidarity, there were numerous occasions before the Atlantic cables were laid in the 1860s (allowing fast transfers of bank credit) when exchange rates became unstable because gold was unavailable for shipment for a time.

During monetary crises like the panics of 1837 and 1857, the banks refused specie payments, and gold could only be acquired at a premium. Accordingly, the gold points drifted away from their normally narrow range.[27] This was the free market's way of holding the international financial system together in times of stress, and it meant, really, that the state banks' freedom to pursue their own lending policies was restricted by international conditions—as long as reserve ratios were maintained. The only way to escape the international influence was to abandon specie payments.

When American currency was at the gold export point, usually during times of rapid economic growth when the balance of payments ran into strong deficits (the country was consuming more goods and services than it produced), gold losses from domestic supplies produced tight money, higher interest rates, restricted lending, and a curb upon further immediate expansion. The process was reversed in times of stagnation; gold inflows would encourage greater growth by easing the monetary situation. It is for such reasons that the gold standard was called *self-adjusting*.

Thus it was that the American monetary system and economy were integrated into the world market with a specie standard. It was both an advantage and a disadvantage. The United States benefitted from foreign economic expansions but was set back by foreign economic troubles (except for harvest failures abroad, which always raised demand for American food). The gold standard automatically transmitted monetary shocks, and they reverberated back again via the finan-

cial markets. It became common in London to blame the Americans for monetary troubles and in America, at the same time, to blame the British. The truth is that the gold standard was an *integrated* financial system that transmitted the good and bad with equal efficiency.

Southern Cotton Finance

Before 1860 there was a special element in the U.S. financial system, interesting in itself, that played an important role in antebellum Southern economic expansion. Great Britain was the greatest producer of cotton textiles, and in normal years more than three quarters of its raw cotton was shipped from American

An artist's conception of Wall Street in the 1857 panic.

The California Gold Rush. The discovery of gold brought people from around the world and permanently changed the West. Entire rivers were diverted to wash the gravel for gold (above right) and hydraulically mine the mountains (below). San Francisco's harbor (above) was filled with hundreds of deserted and rotting ships that had brought nearly 40,000 people in just six months. Colorado and Nevada (below right) were the next boom areas. Nevada's Comstock Lode alone yielded over $300,000,000 worth of gold and silver over twenty years.

Southern ports. There was *big money* involved; it was perhaps the antebellum equivalent of financing modern international oil shipments from OPEC nations to the industrial countries.

An intricate system of finance grew up, with agents (factors) of British banks, discount houses, and cotton importers located throughout the cotton-growing and -shipping portions of the South. Finance was thus always available, from international sources as well as Southern cotton growers and shippers. The cotton factor arranged immediate payment in cash to Southern growers. Usually agents "accepted" (endorsed) the bills on behalf of their British principals, and the cotton market was thus instantly infused with British credit.

The cotton was shipped, and the bills of exchange arising from it either were sold to American importers in both the North and South or were purchased by specialized British houses who undertook to wait for payment in England. The cotton bills were discountable in England since they bore British signatures and were the stock in trade of the discount house there. Credit flowed both ways, of course, and the Cotton South was provided with a more efficient financial system before 1860 than it would experience for many decades after 1865.[28]

The Northern economy also benefitted. It was generally in deficit with its trade with England—the largest trading partner by far before 1860—while the South was in surplus. English credit was available to the North, too, and, of course, the North generally had a surplus in its trade with the South. Southern prosperity thus fueled Northern economic growth. As Douglass North has shown in his book, *The Economic Growth of the United States 1790–1860,* the Southern surplus in trade with Europe was largely responsible for Northern industrial and agricultural progress before 1860.[29] The South earned the foreign exchange that the North used for imports of machinery and manufactures. Since the Southern surplus was based upon slavery and the entire system was serviced by British finance, it has not been much celebrated in American history.

American bankers slowly worked their way into the system, too, although it remained primarily a British show before the Civil War. The historical tendrils from the cotton finance were long, and, eventually, were a primary origin of American investment banking. One example will have to suffice. Here we need the detail of personal histories, and our discussion must move from *macro*economic to *micro*economic history.

George Peabody, a Yankee financier from Salem, Massachusetts, had a long and successful career in London. His firm, Peabody & Company, was an "American house" that dealt in cotton finance for the most part. In 1854, he invited a new American partner to London, Junius Spencer Morgan, grandson of the founder (in 1819) of the Aetna Fire Insurance Company of Hartford, Connecticut.

In 1857, J. S. Morgan's son, Pierpont, was at loose ends after a period at Göttingen University studying mathematics. Young Morgan joined his father in London in time to observe the Bank of England's dramatic actions during the panic of 1857 (which included a large loan to Peabody & Company to keep them afloat). After two years' apprenticeship in London, Pierpont Morgan, in the fall of 1859, went to New Orleans with the cotton shipping firm of Duncan Sherman to learn cotton finance from the American side. He immediately got involved in other things and arrived during the Civil War in New York City.

Peabody & Company became J. S. Morgan & Company in 1865. With offices in London and Paris, it became a leading European merchant banking house, financing, among other things, a $50-million loan to the French in 1870 at the time of the Franco-Prussian War. When Junius Morgan died in 1890, his firm was coequal with the Rothschilds and Barings in European finance. His son and heir, Pierpont, became the primary founder of modern American investment banking and was the greatest financier in American history.

Early in his career, Pierpont, together with his father, had helped the young Andrew Carnegie sell Pennsylvania Railroad stocks in London. In 1900 that kindness was repaid when Carnegie turned over his affairs in Carnegie Steel to Morgan for $500 million. The formation of the United States Steel Corporation was underway with that transaction, quarterbacked by Morgan. When he died in 1913, the name J. P. Morgan was already a legend in American financial history and has so remained to this day.[30]

As has been noted, nineteenth-century American finance was a learning experience. We will meet Mr. Morgan and Mr. Carnegie again in later chapters.

THE FINANCIAL SYSTEM AND THE BUSINESS CYCLE

The solidarity of the gold points was very much like a good electrical connection, except that, in the case of the foreign exchanges, the current passing through was made up of *economic* impulses. Because of the South's cotton connection with England, the rhythm of economic fluctuations between the American and British economies was bound to be easily communicated. How deeply into the real economic life of a mainly agricultural nation these variations in the pace of economic growth were felt in the earlier years is difficult to say. Even though money incomes were affected, farming activities continued in the North as well as in the South when prices fell. In fact, it has been a historical pattern, prevailing until quite recently, that farm output was fairly insensitive to price changes.[31] Southern agriculture was perhaps more commercially sensitive than were the mainly self-sufficient farmsteads of the North in the antebellum period, but fixed costs were so relatively high in the slave economy that variations in prices would only affect the scale of output in the most extreme circumstances. Planters would not typically sell off their slaves because of a temporary dip in cotton prices.

Wholesale Price Fluctuations

Figure 11.1 is a chart of annual wholesale prices. These data mask a host of exceptions, and we use them here only as a general guide. In an economy as free to respond to the signals of the market as was the antebellum economy, general price movements indicate changes in the pace of economic life *in a rough way*. The record of prices at the beginning is overshadowed by the sharp variations after 1793, when European wars were in progress and Jefferson's embargo in force—which disrupted the markets on a month-by-month basis.

The small seaboard economy, mainly agricultural and tied closely to international markets, was ex-

After the War of 1812, the downward movement of wholesale prices was interrupted by the cyclical expansions: once in the mid-1830s (ending in the two financial crises of 1837 and 1839), again mainly between 1843 and 1847, and then more strongly beginning in 1851. This last ended in the Panic of 1857.

Figure 11.1 Wholesale Prices, 1790–1860

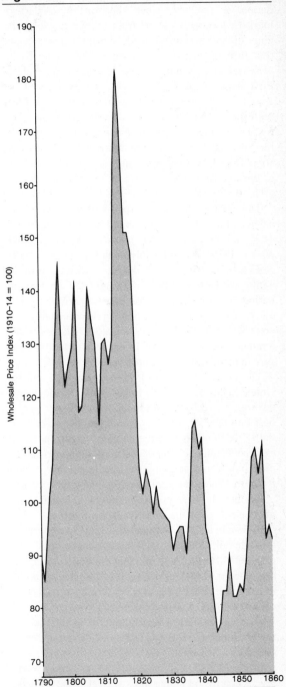

Source: *Historical Statistics*, series E 52.

tremely sensitive to such influences. Next came the inflation of 1812–15, when the wartime American market was largely cut off from European goods, the domestic manufacturing establishment was very small (but thriving in the circumstances), and state banks were free to expand their issues after the demise of the First Bank of the United States. Appearing in 1816 were two general forces that would drive prices down until the 1830s: (a) the return of European manufactured goods to the American market and (b) the gradual recovery of European agriculture, which increased supplies of foodstuffs there and caused farm products to glut the American markets for more than a decade after 1818.[32]

There were three major expansions in activity indicated by these data: (a) the strong expansion ending in 1837 and the panic of that year (followed by a small peak in 1839), (b) a relatively weak expansion between 1843 and 1847, and (c) the double-headed affair of the 1850s, with price peaks in 1855 and 1857. During this period, the British had major monetary crises in 1825, 1837, 1847, and 1857. The first big American financial crisis was in 1819; 1837 was a major crisis, and 1847, a minor one. The panic of 1857 was international, severe in this country and Europe as well.

The crises of 1837 and 1857 in England and the United States were closely linked by the financial connection, but *real* activities in the two countries were at best only vaguely related, economically speaking. In the 1830s the British were pursuing a major industrial expansion, and the Americans, a boom in internal improvements and sales of western lands. We cannot prove that these real activities somehow were coordinated, but all observers agree that the monetary connection detonated the panics in both countries.

In Britain in 1847, the monetary blowup came as the boom in railroad stocks passed its peak and turned into a sell-off. The Bank of England, operating under its new charter (1844), which totally restricted its ability to expand its own note issues except against deposits of specie, very nearly suspended payments.[33] There were other troubles in Britain, too, including bad harvests, the flood of starving Irish, and a sharp decline in railway investment.

In the United States the 1840s had begun with a severe depression (some think it rivaled the 1930s).[34] But war with Mexico in 1846 produced higher expenditures, higher prices. Then, in 1849 came a new surge

in activity related to the California gold discoveries and once again a major westward movement. U.S. gold production of 43,000 ounces in 1847 rose by more than a factor of ten to 484,000 ounces in 1848. That was only the beginning. In 1849 an incredible 1,935,000 ounces were produced, and the figure kept rising until 1853, when production reached 3.1 million troy ounces. It declined after that peak but was still 2.2 million ounces in 1860.

Gold was also discovered in Australia in 1851, and by 1857 the world's supply of monetary gold had been increased by a third, an unheard-of increase for a single decade.[35] The United States became a gold-producing gold exporter, and the new gold, together with rising government expenditures in Europe during the Crimean War (1854–55), gave the early 1850s an aura of renewed prosperity all over the commercial world. As backing for currency, the new gold reserves allowed for a rise in U.S. currency circulation of from $226 million in 1847 to $475 million in 1857. That prices rose only about 50 percent under such a monetary onslaught indicates a great rise in real output in the 1850s.[36]

In the United States the cotton economy was never more prosperous than in the 1850s. American cotton output doubled in a single decade, yet the expansion of world cotton consumption was so great that raw cotton prices continued to rise. In the 1850s it was nearly double those that had ruled a decade earlier. There was a minor new outburst of sales of public lands, but it did not approach the scale of the 1830s. The best lands were gone, and in 1862 the Homestead Act was passed to encourage people to settle in the West on *free* land. An era was ending.

Then, in 1857 came what many scholars have considered the first worldwide economic convulsion.[37] The British blamed the Americans for it, because the banking panic started in late summer in the United States, and the first big failures in England were "American" houses. By November, the panic was raging all over Western Europe. However, research has shown that an economic downturn was clearly underway in Britain, from the spring of 1857 onwards, for complex reasons (partly related to the abrupt ending of government expenditures when the Crimean War ended in 1855) that had little connection with the Anglo-American financial network. Britain began a quick recovery in 1858, based upon renewed textile exports,

The China Trade.   After independence, American merchants were free to trade with China. The first American ships to reach Canton's foreign factories (the Canton waterfront is shown above) carried a cargo of ginseng, woolen garments, cotton, fur skins, and lead. The return cargo was black and green tea, handwoven cotton cloth, silk, cinnamon, and porcelain. Chinese porcelain became so popular that it was soon produced specifically for the export market, as shown in the tea caddy, the plate showing the Salem merchant ship "Friendship," and the vase depicting the signing of the Declaration of Independence.

Figure 11.2   U.S. Balance of Merchandise Trade

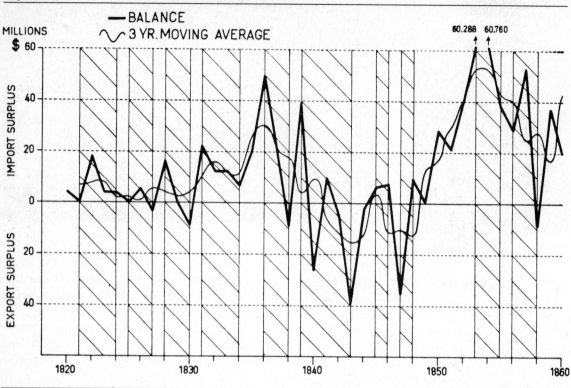

Source: *Historical Statistics*, series U196.

During the antebellum period, the U.S. economy performed in its international transactions much like a modern "Third World" country, using relatively more of the world's goods than it produced itself in expansion. The shaded areas are cyclical contractions. The three-year moving average smooths out the cycles and makes the development features more visible.

and American cotton prices did not fall to pre-1856 levels. Apparently the American economy was still suffering from this financial convulsion when it was overtaken by war in 1861.

Interdependence

Although we could hardly call the international cycles of the antebellum period synchronized, the strongest impulses in the 1830s and 1850s were effectively transmitted by the gold standard mechanism.[38] Such is probably true of the American depression of the early 1840s, too.

It is important to realize that these fluctuations in economic activity, the "business cycle," have never been really understood *as a sequence*. They have perplexed economists for more than a century. Whereas the cycles tend to look alike superficially, each time they have different origins in economic behavior and structural change.[39] The increases in the money supply and prices that occur in each upswing are like a fever, but fevers occur with many illnesses. There is no doubt, though, that a world of growing interdependence, brought about by greater specialization and growing trade on the basis of comparative advantage, that effectively used a single currency—specie within the gold standard mechanism—is one that would necessarily become more vulnerable to the transmission of cyclical disturbances.

THE BALANCE OF PAYMENTS AND THE CYCLE

The growing U.S. economy looked very much like a modern "developing" country in its international

Figure 11.3 Total Federal Receipts and Expenditures

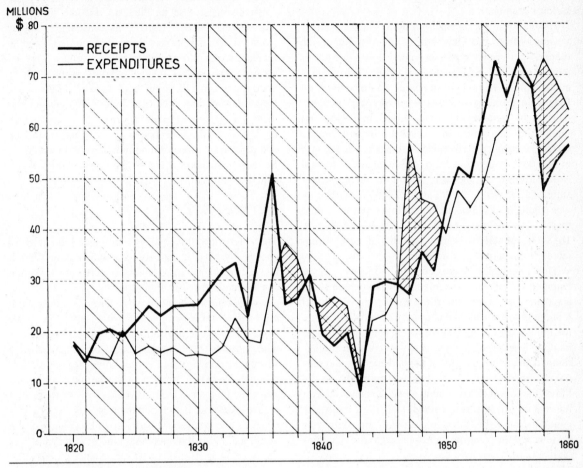

Source: *Historical Statistics*, series Y335–36.

The federal government was accidentally operating a "cyclically balanced budget" from the 1830s until the Civil War: There were deficits (shaded areas) in largely depressed periods and surpluses in the mainly expansionary periods. This "exemplary behavior" occurred in large part because receipts were more income elastic than were expenditures.

relations. During expansions, it used more goods and services than it produced, with trade deficits appearing prominently in the 1830s and 1850s (see Figure 11.2). When growth was sluggish, as in the early 1840s, trade surpluses appeared. The reason for this pattern was the secular growth of the world's demand for U.S. exports, particularly raw cotton, together with the tendency of the U.S. economy to grow in spurts—"booming" periodically and running ahead of the world's growth pace. Foreigners were willing to finance this growth by lending money and by investing in the country. What

would have been a serious specie loss in the 1830s, imposing a correction upon the United States before 1837, was offset, as Peter Temin has shown, by its bimetallism. Mexican silver "filled up" the bimetallic U.S. currency as gold flowed out, enabling the dynamic increase in state-bank note issues we noted earlier.[40]

In the 1850s gold production did slacken a bit, in time to be partly blamed for the U.S. financial debacle of 1857 and for a tightening of monetary conditions in the face of a mounting trade deficit. As always, the banks were blamed for "over issue." Such explanations are not entirely convincing, and that episode, the American side of the 1857 crisis, really needs a closer examination.

An oddity of the antebellum period is the entirely virtuous—from the viewpoint of modern Keynesian theory—performance of the federal government's financial system (see Figure 11.3). The ideal countercyclical policy by modern standards would be to create federal government surpluses in periods of cyclical expansion by withdrawing funds from circulation and moderating the boom. In recessions, federal deficits should be encouraged to moderate the depth and length of the downswing by adding deficit-financed federal expenditures to the spending system. In the big expansions of 1825–46, 1844–46, and 1850–57 the economy was (theoretically) braked by federal surpluses. In the major downswings—1820–21, 1837–43, 1847–49, 1858–60—deficits were run that should have stimulated the underemployed economy.

This enviable macroeconomic record, never equalled by modern governments, was apparently an accident. The federal government was then very small relative to total economic activity. Expenditures were, for the most part, insensitive to changes in domestic income. They went mainly to pay interest on the national debt and the salaries of the bureaucracy and military. After Jackson's veto of the expenditures on the Maysville Road (1830), federal money expenditures on internal improvements remained small. As a result, expenditures more or less kept pace with the country as it grew, and the government responded to provide minimal necessary services.

Revenues, on the other hand, came (as we have seen) mainly from customs receipts. Imports, sensitive to income changes, rose as domestic income increased: These great internal expansions caused government revenues to soar. Since there was no felt need to increase expenditures just because revenues were increasing, the federal budget ran into surplus during good times—just like a textbook case of old-fashioned Keynesian wisdom.[41] Notice, though, that this government behavior would tend to offset the "self-correcting" gold standard mechanism by making expansions and depressions weaker than they otherwise would be. Keynesianism and the classical gold standard were ill-suited to one another.

RETROSPECT

The antebellum financial system was a laboratory of change; by 1860, it scarcely resembled that of 1790. It had been a chaotic episode in large part. One final point can be made that remains a puzzle: *There is no evidence that the financial chaos slowed down the economy's long-term development.* Britain had a far more sophisticated and institutionally "correct" system—with a central bank, amalgamated branch banking, a strict gold standard, and conservative ideas at the Exchequer—yet, U.S. growth in the period simply outstripped that of Great Britain, the world's first industrial nation. If "money matters," as modern Monetarists like to say, our history up to 1860 suggests the question: "Does it matter what kind of money it is?"

Notes

1. Paul Studenski and Herman Krooss, *Financial History of the United States* (1952), p. 31.
2. Richard Hofstadter, editor, *Great Issues in American History from the Revolution to the Civil War 1765–1865* (New York: Vintage Books, 1958), part III, document 3, p. 155.
3. Studenski and Krooss, *Financial History of the United States,* pp. 62–63; David A. Martin, "The Changing Role of Foreign Money in the United States, 1782–1857," *JEH,* December 1977.
4. The view that the states used bank charters to get around the prohibition against printing their own notes has now been buttressed by research showing that the states not only taxed the capital of the banks, but sometimes invested in the banks themselves. It is now estimated that the states in the antebellum period may have raised as much as 20 percent of their finances from bank-chartering. Richard Sylla, John B. Legler, and John J. Wallis, "Banks and State Public Finance in the New Republic: The United States, 1790–1860," *JEH,* June 1987.
5. Richard Sylla, "American Banking and Growth in the Nineteenth Century: A Partial View of the Terrain," *EEH,* Winter 1971–72. Also, Paul B. Trescott, *Financing American Enterprise: The Story of Commercial Banking* (1963), ch. 2.

6. The actual reserve ratios maintained by the antebellum banks seem to have varied widely. Roger H. Hinderliter and Hugh Rockoff, "The Management of Reserves by Antebellum Banks in Eastern Financial Centers," *EEH*, Fall 1973.

7. Examples of unsuccessful systems: in England after the 1837 crisis, the abandonment of the "Palmer Rule" for governing the Bank of England; in France, the failure of bimetallism to stabilize the French currency in the 1850s; also in France, the national development bank, the Credit Mobilier, was founded in 1852—it failed fifteen years later. Jonathan Hughes, *Fluctuations in Trade, Industry and Finance* (Oxford: The Clarendon Press, 1960), chs. 2 and 10.

8. Craig West, *Banking Reform and the Federal Reserve, 1863–1923* (Ithaca, NY: Cornell University Press, 1977), ch. 7. Also, Sylla, "American Banking and Growth," contains a discussion of origins, rationale, and relevant literature on the short-term credit or "real bills" doctrine in American banking.

9. Richard H. Timberlake, Jr., *Money, Banking, and Central Banking* (1965), chs. 5–7.

10. Some of the enthusiastic loan expansion when prices were rising was doubtless due to the insider nature of bank control. Naomi Lamoreaux argued that the New England banks in the federal period were so "closely held" that the records of ownership and loan policies are best studied as a "kinship system." The public made deposits, owner families used them for profit-making investments by their own members. "Banks, Kinship and Economic Development: The New England Case," *JEH*, September 1986.

11. Jonathan Hughes and Nathan Rosenberg, "The United States Business Cycle Before 1860: Some Problems of Interpretation," *EHR*, April 1963.

12. Peter Temin, *The Jacksonian Economy* (1969). See also Hugh Rockoff, "Money, Prices, and Banks in the Jacksonian Era," in Robert Fogel and Stanley Engerman, eds., *The Reinterpretation of American Economic History*, (New York: Harper & Row, 1971), ch. 33.

13. Studenski and Krooss, *Financial History of the United States*, pp. 88–99; Wilfred S. Lake, "The End of The Suffolk System," *JEH*, November 1947.

14. Double liability for stockholders lasted generally until 1933. The Emergency Banking Act of that year removed double liability for new stocks issued by national banks. The national banking law of 1935 enabled national banks to drop this requirement for all their stocks by 1937. State banks followed suit later.

15. George P. Green, "The Louisiana Bank Act of 1842: Policy-Making During Financial Crisis," *EEH*, Summer 1970; Irene D. Neu, "Edmund Jean Forstall and Louisiana Banking," *EEH*, Summer 1970.

16. Studenski and Krooss, *Financial History of the United States*, p. 89; A. Barton Hepburn, *History of Currency in the United States* (1924).

17. John T. Holdsworth and Davis R. Dewey, *The First and Second Banks of the United States* (Washington: Government Printing Office, 1910); Ralph Catterall, *The Second Bank of the United States* (1903); A. H. Schlesinger, Jr., *The Age of Jackson* (1945); Bray Hammond, *Banks and Politics in America from the Revolution to the Civil War* (1957); Bray Hammond, "Jackson, Biddle, and the Bank of the United States," *JEH*, May 1947; Marie Elizabeth Sushka, "The Ante-Bellum Money Market and the Economic Impact of the Bank War," *JEH*, December 1976.

18. Jefferson, in Hofstadter, *Great Issues in American History from the Revolution to the Civil War 1765–1865*, p. 158.

19. George Rogers Taylor, ed., *Jackson and Biddle: The Struggle over the Second Bank of the United States* (1949); see also Schlesinger, *The Age of Jackson*.

20. Jackson in Hofstadter, *Great Issues in American History from the Revolution to the Civil War 1765–1865*, p. 294.

21. Also, according to David A. Martin, the Second Bank was viewed by Jacksonians as a transgressor for not ridding the country of small-note paper currency. "Metallism, Small Notes, and Jackson's War with the B.U.S.," *EEH*, Spring 1974.

22. The Federal Reserve Act became law 23 December 1913, when Woodrow Wilson signed the Act. It has become common practice to say that the Federal Reserve System began in 1914 with the commencement of its operations.

23. Lance E. Davis, et al., *American Economic History* (Homewood, IL: Irwin, 1961), ch. 13.

24. Thomas D. Willett, "International Specie Flows and American Monetary Stability," *JEH*, March 1968.

25. Sir Albert Feavearyear, *The Pound Sterling: A History of English Money* (Oxford: The Clarendon Press, 1963), ch. IX.

26. The interest discount a bill's buyer would desire would be the one equal to his or her "opportunity cost," the return the money would bring from an alternative investment of equal quality. This calculation would depend upon the buyer's options. If a seller wanted to be charged a lower price for cash, he or she would need some alternatives. In Lance E. Davis and J. R. T. Hughes, "A Dollar-Sterling Exchange 1803–95," *EHR*, August 1960, domestic rates were thus used to determine exchange rates implicit in prices of bills purchased in the U.S. For the view and supporting arguments that English rates would better serve the purpose, see Edwin J. Perkins, "Foreign Interest Rates in American Financial Markets: A Revised Series of Dollar-Sterling Exchange

Rates, 1835–1900," *JEH,* June 1978; Lawrence Officer, "Dollar-Sterling Mint Parity and Exchange Rates, 1791–1834," *JEH,* September 1983; Michael Collins,"Sterling Exchange Rates, 1847–80," *JEH,* Winter 1986.

27. Davis and Hughes, Table A-2.
28. N. S. Buck, *The Development of the Organization of Anglo-American Trade, 1800–1850* (1925); R. C. O. Matthews, *A Study in Trade-Cycle History* (1953), ch. V.
29. Douglass North, *The Economic Growth of The United States 1790–1860* (1961); also, a shorter version, Douglass North, "The United States Balance of Payments, 1790–1860," in *Trends in the American Economy in the Nineteenth Century,* NBER, *Studies in Income and Wealth,* (Princeton: Princeton University Press, 1960), vol. 24.
30. Jonathan Hughes, *The Vital Few* (New York: Oxford University Press, 1986), ch. 9.
31. This relationship was discussed by Gardiner C. Means in 1935 in Senate Document No. 13, 74th Congress, 1st session, "Industrial Prices and Their Relative Inflexibility," reprinted and elaborated in Means' book, *The Corporate Revolution in America* (New York: Collier Books, 1964), chs. 4–5.
32. W. B. Smith and A. H. Cole, *Fluctuations in American Business 1790–1860* (1935), section I.
33. On the pattern of British cycles in this period, A. D. Gayer, W. W. Rostow, and A. J. Schwartz, *Growth and Fluctuation of the British Economy 1790–1850* (Oxford:

The Clarendon Press, 1952); W. W. Rostow, *British Economy of the Nineteenth Century* (Oxford: The Clarendon Press, 1952); R. C. O. Matthews, *A Study in Trade-Cycle History;* C. N. Ward-Perkins, "The Commercial Crisis of 1847," *Oxford Economic Papers,* 1950; Jonathan Hughes, "The Commercial Crisis of 1857," *Oxford Economic Papers,* June 1956; Peter Temin, "The Anglo-American Business Cycle, 1820–60," *EHR,* May 1974.
34. Ira Ryner, "On the Crises of 1837, 1847 and 1857," *University of Nebraska Studies,* April 1905; Temin, *The Jacksonian Economy.*
35. Hughes, *Fluctuations in Trade, Industry and Finance,* ch. 1.
36. Gold and currency figures taken from *Historical Statistics,* 1960, series M 268; X 420.
37. Hughes, "The Commercial Crisis of 1857."
38. Temin, "The Anglo-American Business Cycle, 1820–1860."
39. Wesley Clair Mitchell and Arthur Burns, the leading American students of business cycles, attempted to reduce the evidence to those elements common to all cycles. They concluded that business cycles "can be seen through a cloud of witnesses only by the eye of the mind." *Measuring Business Cycles* (New York: National Bureau of Economic Research, 1947), p. 12.
40. Temin, *The Jacksonian Economy,* pp. 80–81.
41. Hughes and Rosenberg, "The United States Business Cycle Before 1860."

Suggested Readings

Articles

Bordo, Michael, and Schwartz, Anna J. "Money and Prices in the Nineteenth Century: An Old Debate Rejoined." *Journal of Economic History,* vol. XL, no. 1, March 1980.

Davis, Lance E., and Hughes, Jonathan. "A Dollar-Sterling Exchange 1803–95," *Economic History Review,* vol. XIII, no. 1, August 1960.

Green, George D. "The Louisiana Bank Act of 1842: Policy Making During Financial Crisis." *Explorations in Economic History,* vol. 7, no. 4, Summer 1970.

Hammond, Bray. "Jackson, Biddle, and the Bank of the United States." *Journal of Economic History,* vol. VI, no. 2, May 1947.

Hinderliter, Roger H., and Rockoff, Hugh. "The Management of Reserves by Banks in Ante-Bellum Eastern Financial Centers." *Explorations in Economic History,* vol. 11, no. 1, Fall 1973.

Hughes, J. R. T., and Rosenberg, Nathan. "The United States Business Cycle Before 1860: Some Problems of Interpretation." *Economic History Review,* vol. XV, no. 3, August 1963.

Lake, Wilfred S. "The End of the Suffolk System." *Journal of Economic History,* vol. VII, no. 2, November 1947.

Lamoreaux, Naomi R., "Banks, Kinship, and Economic Development." *Journal of Economic History,* vol. XLVI, no. 3, September 1986.

Martin, David A. "1853: The End of Bimetallism in the United States." *Journal of Economic History,* vol. XXXIII, no. 4, December 1973.

———. "Metallism, Small Notes, and Jackson's War with the B.U.S." *Explorations in Economic History,* vol. 11, no. 3, Spring 1974.

———. "The Changing Role of Foreign Money in the United States, 1782–1857." *Journal of Economic History,* vol. XXXVII, no. 4, December 1977.

Neu, Irene D. "Edmond Jean Forstall and Louisiana Banking." *Explorations in Economic History,* vol. 7, no. 4, Summer 1970.

North, Douglass C. "The United States Balance of Payments, 1790–1860." *Trends in the American Economy in the Nineteenth Century,* NBER, *Studies in Income & Wealth.* Princeton: Princeton University Press, 1960, vol. 24.

Redlich, Fritz. "American Banking and Growth in the Nineteenth Century: Epistemological Reflections." *Explorations in Economic History,* vol. 10, no. 3, Spring 1973.

Rockoff, Hugh. "Money, Prices and Banks in the Jacksonian Era." In Robert Fogel and Stanley Engerman, eds., *The Reinterpretation of American Economic History.* New York: Harper & Row, 1971, ch. 33.

———. "Varieties of Banking and Regional Economic Development in the United States, 1840–1860." *Journal of Economic History,* vol. XXXV, no. 1, March 1975.

Roll, Richard. "Interest Rates and Price Expectations During the Civil War." *Journal of Economic History,* vol. XXXII, no. 2, June 1972.

Ryner, Ira. "On the Crises of 1837, 1847 and 1857." *The University of Nebraska Studies,* vol. 5, April 1905.

Sushka, Marie Elizabeth, "The Ante-Bellum Money Market and the Economic Impact of the Bank War." *Journal of Economic History,* vol. XXXVI, no. 4, December 1976.

Sylla, Richard. "American Banking and Growth in the Nineteenth Century: A Partial View of the Terrain." *Explorations in Economic History,* vol. 9, no. 2, Winter 1971–72.

———, Legler, John B., and Wallis, John J., "Banks and State Public Finance in the New Republic: The United States, 1790–1860," *Journal of Economic History,* vol. XLLVII, no. 2, June 1987.

Temin, Peter. "The Anglo-American Business Cycle, 1820–1860." *Economic History Review,* 2nd series, vol. XXVII, no. 2, May 1974.

Willett, Thomas D. "International Specie Flows and American Monetary Stability." *Journal of Economic History,* vol. XXVIII, no. 1, March 1968.

Books

Buck, Normal S. *The Development of the Organization of Anglo-American Trade, 1800–1850.* New Haven: Yale University Press, 1925.

Catterall, Ralph. *The Second Bank of the United States.* Chicago: University of Chicago Press, 1903.

Hammond, Bray. *Banks and Politics in America from the Revolution to the Civil War.* Princeton: Princeton University Press, 1957.

Hepburn, A. Barton. *History of Currency in the United States.* New York: Macmillan, 1915.

Matthews, R. C. O. *A Study in Trade-Cycle History.* Cambridge: Cambridge University Press, 1953.

North, Douglass C. *The Economic Growth of the United States 1790–1860.* Englewood Cliffs, NJ: Prentice-Hall, 1961.

Redlich, Fritz. *The Molding of American Banking: Men and Ideas.* New York: Hafner, 1947 and 1951, 2 vols.

Schlesinger, A. H., Jr. *The Age of Jackson.* New York: Mentor Books, 1945.

Smith, Walter Buckingham, and Cole, Arthur H. *Fluctuations in American Business 1790–1860.* Cambridge: Harvard University Press, 1935.

Studenski, Paul, and Krooss, Herman. *Financial History of the United States.* New York: McGraw-Hill, 1952.

Sumner, William Graham. *A History of American Currency.* New York: Putnam's Sons, 1878.

Taylor, George Rogers, ed. *Jackson and Biddle: The Struggle over the Second Bank of the United States.* Boston: D. C. Heath, 1949.

Temin, Peter. *The Jacksonian Economy.* New York: Norton, 1969.

Timberlake, Richard H., Jr. *Money, Banking, and Central Banking.* New York: Harper & Row, 1965.

Trescott, Paul B. *Financing American Enterprise: The Story of Commercial Banking.* New York: Harper & Row, 1963.

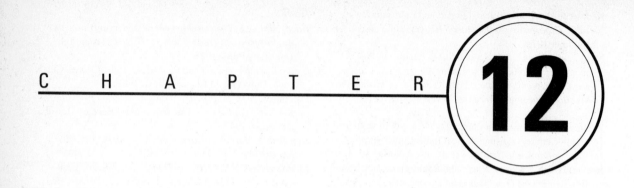

Special Topic: The Debate Over Slavery

W e have discussed antebellum Southern agriculture in previous chapters. This chapter is devoted to a single topic that has engaged the attention of many economic historians: the more controversial aspects of slavery, the main labor input in the cotton crop.

WHY THE CONTROVERSY?

There is probably no topic in American history that can produce deep conflict more readily among historians than slavery. So much of the country's past was molded by that institution, and so many modern Americans are descendants of slave ancestors, that the subject is bound to be of continuing interest. Unrelenting racial discrimination has also kept the slavery issue alive: Black Americans have not been allowed to ignore their slave heritage the way the millions of white descendants of indentured servants in this country have become ignorant of white servitude. While indentured servitude died out peacefully, slavery was ended only by civil war and constitutional amendment.

Especially in the last decade before the Civil War, the slave economy flourished as never before. Why was this? Was slavery "efficient" as a system of production, and did it really have a viable, long-term future that was cut off by the Civil War?

Slavery Was . . .

What was slavery like? Oddly enough, a question that simple is impossible to answer. Partly this is because "what it was like" was determined by the perceptions of all those who lived in it—each with a different experience—and partly because of the innate problems of historical writing. We must first consider the latter reason to understand with any sympathy the contradictions, distortions, misunderstandings, and disagreements among historians regarding slavery.

Slavery and History

The serious study of historical records involves several extremely difficult intellectual problems. The record of the past lies waiting to answer our questions. However, because the historian must choose which questions will be asked, his or her own preconceptions must influence the written history that results. This is why we have all sorts of mutually incompatible interpretations of the same historical subjects. A liberal, a conservative, and a Marxist historian, all studying the same phenomenon, will probably produce three narratives, each based on "the facts," that contradict each other. A neoclassical economist will write a history unrecognizable to these three because the analysis will make sparing use of institutions, individual experience, time, and legal change.

The careful historian, striving for objectivity, will give special attention to three matters. First, an understanding of the *background conditions* of the period is essential. For example, a new dimension can be added to our understanding of American slavery if we remember white servitude. We then see slavery's colonial origins as part of a more general unfree-labor-supply problem *in addition* to slavery's moral repugnance. Secondly, we must consider those recurring processes over time, the *initial conditions,* that continually motivated the institution. A good example would be the secular expansion of demand for raw cotton based upon British, European, and American industrialization. Decade after decade industrialization helped to make rural American slavery profitable because of the international market for raw cotton.

Finally, we must rely upon a *theory* for our understanding, the generalized set of cause-and-effect relationships we think "explain" the subject, given the background and initial conditions. For example, if a slave plantation was a "business," intent upon maximizing profits, it might then occur to the economist that what is rational behavior to a modern businessperson would have been equally rational to a plantation owner. The danger of this view is that it ignores the possibility that racism, ignorance, ingrained irrational custom, or laws designed to maintain the discipline of slavery at the expense of more "rational" behavior would prevail. Theory alone can be a dangerous guide and must be treated with great care.

Now, clearly there is ample room for disagreement about these elements. And plenty of disagreement exists. A great deal of historical writing in recent years has been done on the economics of slavery, and we now know much more about the subject than we did even twenty years ago. But that does not mean that everything is known or that everyone accepts the same explanations. Many questions are still open, and these include some of the most basic.

THE SLAVE FAMILY

Between 1790 and 1860 both the free white and slave populations of the South increased by just more than a factor of 5.5. The slave population, in fact, grew slightly more rapidly than did the white population in the antebellum South.[1] The similarity of the rates of growth largely disposes of two ideas: (a) that, in general, slaves were "bred" at maximum rates because of their value and (b) that living conditions were generally at "inhuman" physical levels among slaves. Slave families, whatever their condition, reproduced the population at a rate only slightly greater than that of whites.

We know that slaves had to have slave mothers, that they had little or no status in courts of law, that their marriages (when there was a ceremony) were not legal (were not binding contracts), that their property was not their own, and that even their own children were not under their control. Slaves were property: They could be sold, willed, or distributed in payment of debts in cases of bankruptcy of the owners. Because there was no legal international slave trade in this country after 1808, the natural increase of slaves was necessary to maintain the system. Slave owners had to depend upon slave mothers to increase the supply. The bases of the system, then, were slave women and their children. Part of our background information is that Americans were governed by a moral code, in part derived from Christianity, that presumably found slave breeding repugnant (despite lurid modern novels and even eyewitness accounts to the contrary). This meant that some sort of pairing off of men and women into families, even though there was no legal marriage, had to occur. What were these slave families like?

Again, a simple question with no ready answer. Whom do you ask? Each slave narrative is only one example out of the millions possible. Besides, it's like trying to describe today's "average" American family. Which family is typical? We could construct an average from census returns. But, in the case of slave families, there is no official census enumeration listing the names of father, mother, and the date of marriage or, lacking that, the amount of time a couple lived together. The birth dates of the children often were not known. Let us consider some alternatives.

In their 1974 study of slavery, *Time on the Cross,*[2] Robert Fogel and Stanley Engerman concluded that, despite the presence of forces that one might suppose would have made stable family formation difficult or impossible, slaves generally *did* hold families together for periods of years. The sale by owners of young children, they say, was not a common practice.

A basic family system is implied for three fundamental reasons: (a) the natural habits of slaves themselves, which made the family unit a stable relationship; (b) the inclinations of slave owners to maintain some approximation of ordinary American sexual conduct among their property; and (c) the fact that families were more efficient economic units than were other arrangements.[3] According to these authors, alternative family life-styles—such as communal living with complete sexual freedom for men and women alike, the pairing of unattached women with a sequence of men, or the grouping of several females with one male as a shared mate, were rejected.[4] Fogel and Engerman concluded on the matter:

> The belief that slave-breeding, sexual exploitation, and promiscuity destroyed the black family is a myth. The family was the basic unit of social organization under slavery. It was to the economic interest of planters to encourage the stability of slave families and most of them did so.[5]

Douglass and Washington: Two Eyewitnesses

Fogel and Engerman's description sounds reasonable enough. Why should anyone have thought otherwise? The reason is that contemporary observers often presented pictures that differed considerably and that abolitionists used effectively in their literature as evidence of sexual exploitation and irregular family life. We are thus left wondering about the matter. Consider the reminiscences of two famous persons who were born into slavery, Frederick Douglass and Booker T. Washington. Douglass described his parentage in an 1845 book that was a widely used piece of abolitionist literature:

> My mother was named Harriet Bailey. She was the daughter of Isaac and Betsey Bailey, both colored and quite dark. My mother was of a darker complexion than either my grandmother or grandfather. My father was a white man. He was admitted to be such by all I ever heard speak of my parentage. The opinion was also whispered that my master was my father. . . .[6]

Of his family life, Douglass wrote:

> My mother and I were separated when I was but an infant. . . . It is common custom, in the part of Maryland from which I ran away, to part children from their mothers at an early age. Frequently, before the child had reached its twelfth month, its mother was taken from it, and hired out on some farm. . . . the child is placed under the care of an old woman, too old for field work.
>
> I never saw my mother, to know her as such, more than four or five times in my life, and each of these times was very short in duration, and at night. . . . She made these journeys (12 miles) to see me in the night, travelling the whole distance on foot, after the performance of her day's work.[7]

In *Up From Slavery,* his autobiography, Booker T. Washington wrote in 1901, more than half a century after the Douglass book:

> I was born near a cross-roads post-office called Hale's Ford, and the year was 1858 or 1859. . . . Of my ancestry I know almost nothing . . . I have been unsuccessful in securing any information that would throw any accurate light upon the history of my family beyond my mother. She, I remember, had a half-brother and a half-sister. . . . Of my father I know even less than of my mother. I do not even know his name. I have heard reports to the effect that he was a white man who lived on one of the nearby plantations.[8]

How was family life?

> The early years of my life, which were spent in the little cabin, were not very different from those of thousands of other slaves. My mother, of course, had little time in which to give attention to the training of her children during the day. She snatched a few moments for our care in the early morning. . . . One of my earliest recollections is that of my mother cooking a chicken late at night, and awakening her children for the purpose of feeding them. How or where she got it I do not know. . . . I cannot remember having slept in a bed until after our family was declared free by the Emancipation Proclamation. Three children—John, my older brother, Amanda, my sister, and myself—had a pallet on the dirt floor . . . we slept in and on a bundle of filthy rags. . . .[9]

It does not seem, on the face of it, to have been much of a family life. However, perhaps it was no worse than family life among the free working poor in the cities.

There are many other accounts of the life of plantation slaves that are in basic agreement with Douglass and Washington. On the other hand, Herbert Gutman's study showed that most slave families after emancipation were found to be "double-headed," a husband and wife living together monogamously.[10] Corroborating evidence on this point comes from findings of Richard Steckel, investigating Civil War pension files. The evidence shows that slave women did not tend to have children as soon as was biologically possible, that slave marriage strongly influenced the birth of the first child, and after that, births were strongly influenced by work patterns of the slave mothers. There is no case of a former slave woman applying for veterans benefits from more than one man.[11] Moreover, the black veterans' wives, although widowed quite early in life, tended not to remarry.

Olmsted: One Plantation

Frederick Law Olmsted wrote in 1860 of a large cotton plantation in Mississippi:

> It was a first-rate plantation. On the highest ground stood a large and handsome mansion, but it had not been occupied for several years, and it was more than two years since the overseer had seen the owner. He lived several hundred miles away. . . . The whole plantation, including the swamp land around it, and owned with it, covered several square miles. There were between thirteen and fourteen hundred acres under cultivation with cotton, corn and other hoed crops, and two hundred hogs running at large in the swamp. . . . There were 135 slaves big and little, of which 67 went to the field regularly. . . . There was a nursery for sucklings at the quarters, and twenty women at this time who left their work four times a day for half an hour, to nurse their young. . . .[12]

Of course, labor demand for field work in agriculture is not so intensive the entire year, and doubtless during the slack winter months there was more time for "family life" than has been indicated by the narratives we have quoted. The problem for the historian trying to generalize from such evidence is that only isolated examples are available, and he or she cannot know if the samples are good random choices or merely outlying cases that happened to be in print.

There is another problem. When we try to move from numbers (natural increase) to an understanding of the living situations that produced those numbers, to an evaluation of the quality of life, we are moving from quantitative to qualitative evidence. There is no natural intellectual transition for such a move. The truth is that most descriptions of life in the slave quarters are bleak. However, populations can and do increase in incredibly difficult and unhappy circumstances—most of humanity throughout history has done so. Given the problems of moving from quantitative to qualitative evidence, it is difficult indeed to argue that a reasonable physical standard of life for slaves (or anyone else, for that matter) implied any degree of contentment among slave families.[13] What we can ask is, "Where are the slave narratives of 'happy days on the old plantation'?"

In the narratives of Douglass and Washington that we have just examined, note the underlying circumstances: (a) There is no male family head of any importance; indeed, Douglass and Washington did not even know who their fathers were. (b) Institutional provision is made for infants so that even nursing mothers can work nearly full time. (c) One mother had little chance to play that role; the other did so only with difficulty. These are standard criticisms of the slave system in agriculture that have their parallels in some modern analyses of the "black family": no steady male head and no home atmosphere provided by the mother because she must be the breadwinner. On the other hand, Gutman agrees with Fogel and Engerman that the typical slave family was headed by an adult couple. Gutman produces a narrative showing, beyond doubt, that normal family ties persisted within slave families.

WAS SLAVERY DOOMED WITHOUT CIVIL WAR?

In recent years scholarly interest in slavery has been continuous and intense, and the major questions have been thrown into sharp relief. Some historians had long held that slavery was a terminally ill institution by 1860 and that it would have died from natural causes without the 1861–65 military intervention. Slavery, these scholars say, was not really profitable enough to continue in the face of better investment opportunities coming down the line with later nineteenth-century industrialization. Historians Charles Sydnor and Ulrich B. Phillips especially were of that conviction.[14] Various "radical" writers found this view congenial because it presented slavery as an anachronism, a precapitalist holdover that could have had no place in an industrializing workers' economy. At least, this is how Marx saw slavery. The American South, with no industrial proletariat, was merely a colonial appendage of capitalist Europe, viewed economically.[15]

It is always convenient to believe that whatever has happened in history has been inevitable. This is the road taken by those historians who believe that the Civil War was merely a tragic waste of lives and resources to erase an institution that was already dying off. Lewis Gray, in his *History of Agriculture in the Southern United States to 1860,* ruled differently, finding evidence that slavery had been perfectly viable before 1861.[16] The issue was thus largely a matter of disagreements among scholars until 1958. Since evidence and argument have seemed to support every view, people have tended to choose their positions on the basis of taste and instinct.

Conrad and Meyer

Then, in 1958, the heavy guns of econometrics (applied mathematical statistical analysis guided by economic theory) were zeroed in on antebellum slavery by Alfred Conrad and John Meyer in their famous paper, "The Economics of Slavery in the Antebellum South."[17] They found that the annual returns to slave agriculture were competitive with the alternatives available to Southern investors and, moreover, that the "whole South" profited from slavery. In the older states it was the sale of slaves from the existing stock to the new cotton-producing areas south and west that created the profits. Cotton production itself was the main underpinning of the system. In important subsequent critical works by Yasukichi Yasuba and Richard Sutch, capital gains from the stock of slaves were factored into the profit equations, and the viability of slavery was reinforced.[18]

The findings of the econometric work seemed to establish the profitability and viability arguments once and for all. They were based upon numbers, and they meant, or seemed to mean, that institutional and cultural analyses of slavery were largely irrelevant. The simple fact was that slavery had been maintained because it paid slave owners as much as or more than they could earn from any other employment of their capital. Historians continued to reassess their own findings, and some, like Kenneth Stampp in *The Peculiar*

Institution, were in substantial agreement with the revisionist view. Slavery was still immoral, repugnant, and sometimes inhuman, but it paid while it lasted.

Time on the Cross: *Theses and Rebuttals*

Then came *Time on the Cross* in 1974. Fogel and Engerman advanced ten major theses about antebellum slavery in a way that produced a virtual avalanche of scholarly criticism. Some of their ideas were not really novel, but they were advanced in so bold a manner, in connection with other more radical findings, that historians were forced to think again of their implications. The "peculiar institution," the critics charged, had never before looked so peculiar. In the end, *Time on the Cross* was subjected to a level of criticism that, in fineness as well as vigor and volume, has rarely been known in the scholarship of economic history.

In brief, the ten major theses of Fogel and Engerman are as follows:[19]

1. Slavery was a rational, profitable way for Southerners who knew their own interests to maximize profits and wealth.
2. Slavery was thriving and growing economically stronger than ever before 1861.
3. Slave owners were not "pessimistic" about slavery's future on the eve of the Civil War.
4. Slave agriculture was more efficient than free agriculture, not only in the South, but when compared to the Northern family farm as well. Scale economies explain much of the difference.
5. The average slave field hand was more hardworking and efficient than his "white counterpart."
6. Demand for slaves was increasing more rapidly in urban areas than in rural, and slaves were competitive with free workers in urban employments.
7. Slave breeding and sexual exploitation were myths. Stable slave families were the norm, and being in the best interests of the slave owners, were encouraged. Most sales of slaves were whole families or else "at an age when it would have been normal for them to have left the family."
8. The material conditions of life for slaves compared favorably with those of free whites employed in Northern factories.

9. The rate of exploitation of slave earnings was only 10 percent: The average field hand received in real income 90 percent of what he produced over a lifetime.

10. The Southern economy was not stagnant; between 1840 and 1860, Southern per capita income increased more rapidly than did Northern and was relatively high in absolute terms compared to that in the North and other countries.

Stated thus baldly, the main theses of *Time on the Cross* were a clear and irresistible target. Moreover, there were supplementary findings that were really inflammatory to many scholars: For example, Fogel and Engerman suggest that force was seldom used and that generally encouragement to productive effort was in the form of positive economic rewards.[20] Further, they conclude that slaves responded to such good treatment by redoubled efforts to be efficient workers.

A heavy bombardment came as soon as the first reviewers recovered from the initial shock. Fogel and Engerman were accused of implying that slavery was a "benign," even progressive, capitalist institution, consisting of diligent well-rewarded workers toiling under the rational and largely benevolent gaze of carefully profit-maximizing Southern entrepreneurs. Their book produced an incredible response. Let us briefly survey, point by point, the major findings on the ten theses. We then will dwell at greater length on some special points of the debate.

Slavery was a rational way for Southerners to maximize profits and wealth. There had been little disagreement before 1974 on this issue. Cotton production produced a rent due to the climate and soils of the South. As Kenneth Stampp emphasizes, only a small minority of scholars by 1974 still clung to the idea that Southern slave owners were operating at losses because they were somehow locked into the system.[21]

Slavery was growing economically stronger before the Civil War. Gavin Wright and others argue that there was an element of illusion here.[22] The market for American cotton was extraordinarily strong during the 1850s because of the significant growth of cotton textile manufactures. That situation could not last much beyond the decade and, indeed, did not. Supplies of raw cotton caught up with demand after the Civil War, and profits in raw cotton production were greatly reduced for years. If the slave system was getting stronger economically in the 1850s, that was no portent of things to come since profitability was rooted in cotton cultivation.

Slave owners were optimistic about slavery's future just before the Civil War. Over the normal slave life cycle, the net return to slave purchases was positive, counting potential capital gains from any sales that might take place. Since slave prices were rising in the 1850s even though, by some estimates, slaves yielded less than the return from alternative investments, it must be assumed that continued slave purchases were evidence of optimism on the part of slave owners about the future of the slave system.[23]

Slave agriculture in the South was more productive than was family farming in the North. There actually is no way to make such a comparison, except to define productive as "revenue-earning."[24] And even that, as we have noted, was based upon extraordinary demand in the 1850s and a spectacular crop in 1860 (the main year of comparison) that sold at high prices. Scale economies, according to Gavin Wright and others, were not overwhelmingly important.[25] On the other hand, it seems clear enough that the use of slaves made slave-worked farms in the South more efficient than free farms there, and, within limits, the dominance of large farms and plantations showed significant scale economies.

Slave field hands were harder working and more efficient than were white agricultural workers. The critics argued that slaves, with no choice in the matter, worked longer hours and more days a year than did free whites. They may have thus produced more revenues from their labors, but this figure tells nothing about output per man hour.[26]

Demand for slaves was increasing more rapidly in urban than in rural areas. Actually, 1976 the work of Claudia Goldin showed the complexity of the situation but supported the conclusion of Fogel and Engerman.[27] Demand for slaves was *price elastic* in urban employment and *inelastic* in agriculture.[28] Higher cotton prices drove up slave prices, and thus urban slave populations declined in 1840–60 as a result.

Slave breeding and sexual exploitation were myths.
The works of Richard Sutch, Herbert Gutman, and others argue that the abolitionists' views on this matter have some merit. The evidence does suggest that slaves were encouraged to raise their birth rates by various means with a view to the sale of the children. The ratio of children to adults on slave plantations rose when the ratio of women to men decreased.[29] However, the long-run decline in birth rates among slaves paralleling the fall in free white birth rates, shows that slave breeding did not successfully defeat other forces determining demographic trends. But, the evidence does not support the thesis that slave sales rarely broke up slave families.

The material condition of slaves compared favorably with free workers.   Sutch points out that the slave data in *Time on the Cross* on this issue compared the largest plantations with the poorest classes of Northern slum dwellers. He also contends that evidence on food, clothing, and medical care is less than supportive of the Fogel and Engerman findings.[30]

Over the course of an entire slave lifetime, the rate of exploitation was only 10 percent for prime field hands.   Paul David and Peter Temin argue that this figure is too low, probably much too low.[31]

The Southern economy was growing more rapidly than that in the North.   The correctness of this statement depends upon which areas are compared. It was true of the Delta region and Louisiana and east Texas but not true of the Old South. Moreover, the per capita income of *most of the Southern population* was below that of the United States as a whole. It is clear that the west-south-central region, where the big cotton-growing expansion took place in 1840–60, did grow remarkably, and faster than any other sector in those years.[32]

These findings amount to a vigorous dissent from the findings of *Time on the Cross,* and here the debate stands. Now let us consider a few of the more interesting parts of the debate in some detail.

From Quantity to Quality

It is understandable that economic historians should try to isolate the purely economic side of slavery. The logic of economic theory allows the economist to make powerful and even definitive deductions from quantitative evidence. However, this can be done only *if* the evidence can be found and *if* it can be analyzed in a world in which the related social facts that produced the evidence *do not matter.* Conrad and Meyer presented evidence mainly on a very general level, and their conclusions produced no great dispute. Subsequent alterations of Conrad and Meyer were also fairly restricted and tied to generally accepted evidence.

Fogel and Engerman were much more ambitious, attempting to illuminate many questions for which the evidence had always been blurred and contested: How much was physical force used to maintain work levels? How well were the slaves fed, clothed, and housed? Was the instability of the slave family responsible for a multitude of social ills that have afflicted the black community ever since? Were those families broken up commonly by slave sales? Were slaves purposely bred like livestock to maximize the capitalized rents? Was infant mortality significantly higher among slaves than among whites? Did approaching urbanization and industrialization inevitably doom slavery in America? Why were there so few slave uprisings?[33] These questions and many more of a very qualitative nature need to be answered if we are really to understand the "peculiar institution" and the hold it had on this country for so long.

In *Time on the Cross* Fogel and Engerman made a bold attempt to face these questions head-on with deductions from primarily quantitative evidence. As we have seen, they met with very heavy criticism. Referring to our earlier discussion of writing history and its intellectual problems, we can now better appreciate the origins of such massive disagreements. To say "what was" and have no dissent is almost impossible. Such is the nature of historical research, and we learn from the resulting "critical fallout."

A fundamental criticism of *Time on the Cross* came from Paul David and Peter Temin.[34] They argued that, on the basis of economics alone, we simply cannot deduce the comparative welfare of the slaves—how "well off" they were compared to any other groups. For example, David and Temin compare two pieces of information, Engel's Law and the slave diet. Engel's Law is an empirical observation that as real income rises, normally a decreasing proportion of it is spent on food. In Fogel and Engerman's data, one result of their suggested high real incomes for slaves is the absence of Engel's Law. The slaves ate more: a calorie-charged diet of carbohydrates.

David and Temin ask, "How poor would a free white family need to be to convert such a high proportion of their income into such a diet?" The point David and Temin are making is that slavery was compulsion, and it is not possible to make comparative judgments about welfare implications from any level of real income if it is produced under compulsion and *consumed the same way.* One might go farther and argue that since slaves had no property rights—in themselves, their earnings, homes, clothing, children, wives, husbands, animals or anything else—it is simply folly to impute *any* amount of satisfaction to them regarding their lives. There is an old antebellum joke still told in Indiana that nicely illustrates the point. A slave escaped from Kentucky and was brought before a Hoosier Justice of the Peace.

Judge: Were you unhappy there?
Slave: Oh no. I had a good life there.
Judge: Were you mistreated?
Slave: No. Old Massa and me was the greatest friends. Fished and hunted together.
Judge: Did you have good food and housing?
Slave: Sho' enuf. Ham and 'taters. Molasses. My little cabin had roses over the door.
Judge: I don't understand. Why did you run away?
Slave: Well yo' Honor, de situation is still open down there if you'd lak to apply for it.

Concerning slave health and diets, even if one accepted the most optimistic conclusions of *Time on the Cross* (nearly all of which are hotly disputed), the well-being of the slaves could no more be imputed from such evidence than could that of present-day prison populations, whose standards of "adequate" clothing, food, and medical and dental care often exceed that of the general run of American citizens. However, there is now further evidence to consider.

Steckel's Findings

Recent papers by Richard Steckel, based on recently discovered data sources, have upended our information about the quality of life of American slaves. Previous evidence (mainly from surviving plantation records) indicated that mortality rates in the antebellum black population were not much different from those of contemporary whites.[35] This appeared to explain the very similar population growth rates of antebellum whites and blacks we noted earlier. But now Professor Steckel has been able to show that the prenatal and postnatal pictures were drastically different.

From new data sources Steckel finds that average birth weights of slave babies were only about 5.5 pounds and that 30 to 35 percent of these babies died. He believes that more than half of all slave conceptions must have been lost either by miscarriages or in very early infancy. The cause of these losses were most probably sheer ignorance on the part of the (presumably profit-maximizing) masters, who pushed slave mothers to work as long before births as they could, and to return to work as soon as possible afterwards.[36] These practices produced malnourished fetuses and newborns—"The adverse consequences of the 'wearied mother' for infant health began at conception."[37]

Considering the rate of natural increase of the overall slave population, Steckel concludes that slave women were far more fertile than has previously been thought. Their losses, from stillbirths and neonatal mortality were in fact 2.5 times as high as similar losses among whites. The difference was made up by new pregnancies. Slave mothers were on average about two years younger than their white counterparts at first conception.[38] The new data on slave children at early ages produce the following conclusion by Steckel.

> At age 3, for example, slave children attained about centile 0.2 of modern height standards, which places them among the poorest populations ever studied by auxologists. Comparative heights suggest that children from the slums of Lagos, Nigeria, and from urban areas of Bangladesh had an environment for growth superior to that of American slave children.[39]

Perhaps more remarkable have been Steckel's discoveries about life-cycle slave nutrition and physical growth. These discoveries are based, as are those regarding birth weights just noted, on 50,606 slave manifests (declarations by shippers), between 1820 and 1860 for individuals transported on coastal and inland waterways. A federal law of 1807 provided for the manifests, and thus the data now available to us. The shipping manifests were made and handed over to the ship's captain at port of origin. The object of the law was to be certain that slaves from the Caribbean or Africa were not being landed as coastwise traffic. The evidence is of disastrous malnutrition of slave children. The survivors, however, caught up in growth and weight once they were old enough to work, and were then given proper diets including meat. A perfectly cold-blooded calculation, had it been consciously made, might have warranted such a feeding policy. The discounted future value of the slave until about age 6 would have justified it, but, it should be noted, Steckel does not argue that such a conscious calculation was why the slave owners starved the children. Slave children before age 6 seemed like dwarfs to observers for good reason: "The stature of slave children would trigger alarm in a modern pediatrician's office."[40] As young children, American slaves were smaller than any of the other populations Steckel examines (European, American, African, Caribbean). Yet by age 16.5 years American male slaves were taller than factory workers and laborers in England, the poor of Italy, students in Habsburg military schools, the middle class of Stuttgart, German peasants, and factory workers in Russia. As adults American male slaves also exceeded in height the aristocrats of Stuttgart.[41] Adequate diet after it paid to feed them—after they could work—allowed the slaves to recover their physical stature.

Steckel then speculates about other problems these data might help explain; for example, the reported docility and lassitude of slaves—the "Sambo" personality (see "The Elkins Explanation" that follows). He speculates that, although stature was recovered, possibly impairment of the brain's functioning from malnutrition was not, and the adverse consequences lasted into adulthood. Steckel speculates that poor black achievement immediately after emancipation could in part be explained by this factor.[42] It is an appalling possibility. But then, American slavery was an appalling institution.

WHY DID SLAVERY PERSIST?

Time on the Cross may be thought of as a scenario designed to explain a historical phenomenon: Black slavery in this country had existed nearly two and a half centuries by 1860 and apparently was never more prosperous than in its final decade. In their pioneering quantitative effort, Fogel and Engerman were attempting to explain such a remarkable set of facts, given the

evidence. Moreover, despite such famous rebels as Nat Turner and Denmark Vesey, millions of slaves lived out their lives in bondage, exhibiting very little resistance besides commonly asserted acts of pretended illness and theft.[43]

In thousands of relatively isolated locations, a handful of whites lived in the midst of black slaves many times their number with little fear. How was this possible? A moment's reflection will show that there is no obvious answer. A well-known antebellum Southern view was that slaves were happy, good-hearted, child-like creatures who responded positively to good treatment and a teaspoonful of chastisement.[44] If this was not the reason why slavery endured, what was?

In *Time on the Cross* we have a model of a world in which slave-operated enterprises paid their labor forces sufficiently with material rewards and occupational mobility to reconcile the slaves to their condition of unfreedom. As Fogel and Engerman put it, the creation of such an overwhelming economic success as the antebellum cotton economy by mainly slave labor was nothing less than "the record of black achievement under adversity."[45] Profit-maximizing slave owners and slaves striving to make the best of their circumstances can explain the high productivity and comparative stability of a gigantic slave economy spread over a third of this country. For this interpretation Fogel and Engerman were scathingly condemned. Kenneth Stampp writes of *Time on the Cross*:

> . . . the book is not a defense of slavery, and its argument is not racist . . . but its highly favorable assessment of life in bondage originates in the traditional proslavery interpretation nonetheless.[46]

and

> *Time on the Cross* replaces the untidy world of reality, in which masters and slaves, with their rational and irrational perceptions and their human passions, survived as best they could, with a model of a tidy, rational world that never was.[47]

The Elkins Explanation

Are there better overall explanations of slavery's persistence in this country? Perhaps, but they also are disputed. Stanley Elkins argues that slavery crushed out individualism, producing the "Sambo" personality—the happy, carefree, clowning slave who loved "Ol' Massa."[48] The slave identified with the master's interests and family, devoting his or her life selflessly to the owner's welfare at the expense of all else, including the slave's own family. The reason, simply put, was that dependence was too great for significant self-interested individualism to develop among the slaves. The result was a docile plantation in circumstances where docility paid more than did any of the alternatives. "Toadying" to figures of power and authority pays where anything else is prohibitively expensive. Low-ranking military personnel, people confined to hospitals, and women in nearly all cultures through the ages have experienced similar phenomena.

Elkins compares American slaves to the inmates of Nazi concentration camps. Arbitrary brutality—together with total dependence, total loss of prior identity, and constant humiliation—produced a similarly docile mass of persons, in that case Europeans, who were almost *unable* to resist excessive work demands and even deprivation of life. The prisoner lost name, language (if he or she were not German), and "culture"—the former life ceased to have any use or meaning. He or she no longer could plan; the future was a blank, the past, meaningless. Survival depended upon instant obedience. All benefits came from the SS guards, whose authority was total. Slowly, the prisoners began to adopt the values of the guards themselves. They began to identify with interests of the guards and even copy them, to some extent. The prisoners tried to please. In the end, they did not seem to hate the SS. Suicide, an individual decision, was rare in those circumstances because it required a degree of independence that had vanished.[49]

The parallels are indeed striking. The slave child's father and mother could not protect him or her; from infancy onward, the child had to depend upon the kindness of the master for whatever good or little favors might come his or her way. The adult slave was conditioned by an entire life's experiences to survive within the system. To disobey was to risk corporal chastisement (beating and whipping, mainly), short rations, perhaps even sale to a slave dealer. Eugene Genovese, in *Roll, Jordan, Roll,* presents a striking account of the slow, almost reluctant way the slaves faced freedom after emancipation, just as the concentration camp prisoners did when liberation came.[50]

The Genovese Thesis

In a later book, Eugene Genovese tries to explain the apparent lack of slave resistance in a more objective way than the Elkins thesis provides.[51] Compared to the Caribbean and South America, slave resistance here was a minor affair in the century before 1860. Why? Genovese, looking at the slave revolts that occurred, narrows down the vital elements to eight factors: (a) the ratio of blacks to whites, (b) the size of slaveholding units, (c) the nature of the surrounding physical terrain, (d) the ratio of African-born slaves to "creoles," (e) the presence of slave owners at the work site, (f) the conflicts within the "ruling class," (g) the poor economic conditions, and (h) the structure of social relationships that allowed black leaders to emerge. Compared to the Caribbean and South America, all these factors weighed against slave resistance in the South, against the prospects of even limited success.

In American circumstances only minor outbreaks were likely to occur. With the prospect so bleak for successful resistance, it paid the individual slave to go along and make the best of it. Except in parts of South Carolina and Mississippi, whites were in the majority. Nearly half of the American slaves were owned in groups of twenty or fewer, making a "critical mass" for an uprising rare. There were few really inaccessible mountains or jungles available to harbor escaped slaves. By the antebellum period the vast majority of American slaves were native born (no longer trained warriors like the Africans) and a large proportion were of partially white ancestry. In fact, since the late seventeenth century, the majority of American slaves alive at any time were native-born.[52]

Slave owners usually lived among or near their slaves on Southern plantations. There was little important conflict over slavery among Southern slaveowners, or between them and non-slaveowning Southerners. Economic conditions were good, starvation among adults (apart from punishment) was unknown. Black leaders were limited to slave preachers of pacifist Christian doctrines for the most part. In view of these data, there was little reason to expect significant slave resistance or revolt in the slave South. A Nat Turner might come along, but no one like the great Haitian revolutionary, Jean-Jacques Dessalines.

In terms, then, of "slave mentality" or of rational rebellion, resistance made no sense. In the world of

Time on the Cross, it made even less. Why would slavery *not* persist? In addition to all else, it was an institution of private property, protected by law and long usage, and profitable to those who owned the slaves.

PROBLEMS OF THE SLAVE "BUSINESS FIRM"

To some critics, one of the most galling aspects of *Time on the Cross* was its analysis of the Southern slave plantation as a small-scale enterprise run on strict maximizing principles, perhaps along the same lines as a modern rural sawmill. The peculiarities of the institution become cost and revenue functions; slave owners are presented as people who know their opportunity costs and act accordingly. Many critics prefer to think of slavery either as a pre-capitalist artifact, lost in time, or as a monstrous perversion. However, if one accepts the neoclassical analysis of *Time on the Cross,* then certain parts of the Fogel and Engerman findings do seem odd and they do seem to lean toward a more humanitarian interpretation. As we noted previously, the authors insist upon three points: (a) Force was used only "optimally."[53] (b) Slave sales were not that common and rarely broke up families. (c) Slave breeding for profit was a myth. The reasons were a mixture of sound economics and Victorian morality.

In a purely neoclassical context where force is a freely available substitute for money or material rewards, it would be employed whenever its marginal product was relatively high. Fogel and Engerman agree and say that it would thus have been used optimally. Others agree, too, but they point out that, according to the evidence, *optimally* did not mean *rarely.*[54] In any case, the threat of the whips could, and probably did, make every hour of slave labor more intensive than free labor would have been. This was especially true of unskilled physical farm work. As Stefano Fenoaltea observes, "Only slaves can be driven with the whip."[55]

Slave Sales

The manager of a modern business firm who discharges workers will typically be unconcerned about their family relationships. Critics of *Time on the Cross* believe that slave families were commonly broken up by sales of children, wives, and husbands. Such critics are more neoclassical than Fogel and Engerman, who

An invoice from an 1835 slave sale.

maintain that efforts were made to hold families together. The issue can be illustrated by a quotation from Olmsted, in which an informant believed a young girl being taken away for sale must have offended her master. What had she done wrong? he asked.

> "Done? Nothing."
> "What are you going to do with her?"
> "I'm taking her down to Richmond, to be sold."
> "Does she belong to you?"
> "No; she belongs to _____; he raised her."
> "Why does he sell her—has she done anything wrong?"
> "Done anything? No. She's no fault, I reckon."
> "Then what does he want to sell her for?"
> "Sell her for! Why shouldn't he sell her? He sells one or two every year; wants the money for 'em, I reckon."[56]

How commonly were slaves sold and with what effects on families? The evidence seems to suggest that slave sales actually were relatively common and that families often were broken up by such sales. Since slave marriages (by whatever authority) had no legal standing and since the children belonged to the master and not to the slave parents, nothing *except* the humanity of slave owners kept the slave families together, at least once the children reached working age. Critics of Fogel and Engerman see common humanity as a much rarer commodity in the Old South than is argued in *Time on the Cross.*

Breeding

What about slave breeding? It was commonly asserted by abolitionists that breeding was the general practice. Consider another quotation from Olmsted:

> A slaveholder writing to me with regard to my cautious statements on this subject, made in the *Daily Times,* says: "In the States of Maryland, Virginia, North Carolina, Kentucky, Tennessee and Missouri, as much attention is paid to the breeding and growth of negroes as to that of horses and mules. Further south, we raise them both for use and for market. Planters command their girls and women (married or unmarried) to have children; and I have known a great many girls to be sold off, because they did not have children. A breeding woman is worth from one-sixth to one-fourth more than one that does not breed."[57]

Richard Sutch, one of the major critics of *Time on the Cross,* describes breeding as any means taken by the owners to increase the fertility of slave women. The profit came from the expected future return from sales over the costs of rearing to the age of sale. By the 1850s, a babe in arms was worth from $150 upwards.[58] The slave stock on any plantation was reproducible, just like livestock. Presumably any profit-maximizing slave owner would consider breeding that stock as an option.

Not so, say Fogel and Engerman, or at least not commonly so, and they unleash a barrage of contrary arguments and evidence.[59] Conrad and Meyer argue that sales and breeding were integral to the system. The Old South, where cotton was not a major crop, supplied slaves to the cotton-growing regions, and the whole South benefitted. Remember also Douglass North's point that the *whole nation* benefitted economically. This had been one of the most powerful abolitionist arguments. Victorian Americans were apparently shocked by such immoral rationality. On this issue Richard Sutch stayed away from the sort of evidence just quoted (which could never be proved typical, or

even common) and instead went after the numbers: census figures of slave ages, sex, and residence. He found

1. that net slave sales from the Old South to the New South were large;
2. that the ratio of children to adults was significantly higher in the selling than in the buying states; and
3. that in the selling states, the ratio of children to adults was actually higher on plantations where the ratio of men to women was lower.

The conclusions seem inescapable. Sutch concluded with no mincing of words:

> Many slaveowners in the American South systematically bred slaves for sale. These slave breeders were concentrated in the border states and in the states along the Atlantic coast. They held disproportionately large numbers of women in the child-bearing age group. They fostered polygamy and promiscuity among their slaves. The products of this breeding operation were sold or transported to the south-western slave states, predominantly as young adults. There is little possibility that this practice was innocent. . . .[60]

We must keep in mind, though, that this conclusion does not show slave breeding as either common or typical in the American South. What it argues is that slave breeding did exist; it was no "myth." Slavery was bad enough without slave breeding, but we cannot ignore the evidence of its presence on at least some Southern farms.

RETROSPECT

This chapter has touched only upon certain vital points of the modern slavery debate. Strictly speaking, many of the most burning issues, like the nature of the slave family, can be only partly a matter of economics. They must be either ignored or analyzed by economic logic in a way that is artificial to many scholars. Those who are interested in gaining more information are urged to read the main literature cited in this chapter. We are far from having settled conclusions on many crucial points, and there may never be general agreement. For example, how much did the "whole South" really gain from slave sales from the East to the West? To what extent did the loss of top-quality slave labor lower the returns to agriculture in the East while raising it in the West? What were the net results? Passell and Wright, followed by Kotlikoff and Pinera, present evidence and arguments that show that the gain in the Old South from sales of slaves to the New South during the westward expansion of cotton cultivation may well have been offset by declining land values in the Old South as the result of so much of the best slave labor moving out.[61] Steckel's work shows that slave owners, systematically malnourishing the slave population at its source, were more ignorant than murderous. If it can be argued, as he demonstrates, that a strict cost-benefit analysis might have justified the huge death rates of the children from a profit-making viewpoint, it is not proof that slaveowners commonly made such analyses of their commissary policies.

Slavery is gone, and so are those who can remember it. Historians, economists, sociologists, and others, picking over the charred remains, will continue their efforts to tell us "how it really was." No doubt the shock waves produced by *Time on the Cross* will be equalled by some future investigation.

Slavery ended more than a century ago. Its ending did not solve all the problems; it merely wove the future of black America into the mainstream on a new basis: American slavery, however much deplored, was one of the prodigies of history. It was in many respects resolutely illogical, and in terms of general (newly-found) European standards of morality by the mid-nineteenth century repugnant. Slavery was prodigiously productive in its main economic applications in Southern agriculture. Discussions of slavery cannot be avoided if American history is to be understood. As a consequence, all the acrimony and dispute, as well as the shame and anger, must be rekindled again and again. Some would prefer American history to be all heroes and purity. However, it was not, and the ownership of human beings was an important part of the story—along with frontier massacres, injustice to minorities of all sorts, corruption in high places, and crime. History is about human beings, and even economic history cannot escape treating the blemishes and imperfections, including the grossest ones.

Notes

1. The slave population actually grew slightly faster than did the Southern white, rising by a factor of 5.8 between 1790 and 1860, compared to 5.5 for whites. The raw numbers were slaves: 1790, 657,327; 1860, 3,838,765; whites: 1790, 1,271,390; 1860, 7,033,973. *Historical Statistics,* 1960, series A 95–122. It should be noted this information was not included in the revised version. Overall slave mortality seems to have been similar to general mortality in the antebellum South. Richard Steckel, "Slave Mortality: Analysis of Evidence from Plantation Records," *Social Science History,* October 1979, p. 110. But Steckel has radically revised his views of infant mortality among the slaves, as we will see below.

2. Robert Fogel and Stanley Engerman, *Time on the Cross: The Economics of American Negro Slavery* (1974), 2 vols.

3. Fogel and Engerman, vol. I, p. 126.

4. For a much-praised, slightly more recent study, see Herbert Gutman, *The Black Family in Slavery and Freedom 1750–1925* (1976). Richard Steckel, "Slave Marriage and the Family," *Journal of Family History,* Winter 1980.

5. Fogel and Engerman, vol. I, p. 5. See Gutman, pp. 418–25, concerning evidence of polygamy and polyandry after the Civil War as black families attempted to sort things out and reestablish themselves. His evidence clearly shows that monogamous families seemed to be the most desired objective, even when sales of slaves had broken up earlier families and multiple husbands and wives had resulted.

6. Frederick Douglass, *Narrative of the Life of Frederick Douglass* (1968), pp. 21–22.

7. Douglass, p. 22.

8. Booker T. Washington, *Up From Slavery* (1963), p. 2.

9. Washington, pp. 2–3.

10. Gutman, *The Black Family in Slavery and Freedom 1750–1925,* ch. 1. For evidence of the existence of the "Plantation Stud," etc., see the footnote on p. 59.

11. Richard Steckel, "Slave Marriage and the Family."

12. Frederick Law Olmsted, *The Slave States* (1959), pp. 200–201.

13. For a modern study of plantation life written from slave narratives, see John Blassingame, *The Slave Community: Plantation Life in the Antebellum South* (1972).

14. Charles Sydnor, *Slavery in Mississippi* (1933), and Ulrich B. Phillips, "The Economic Cost of Slaveholding in the Cotton Belt," *Political Science Quarterly,* June 1905.

15. Karl Marx, *Capital* (London: William Glaisher, 1918), vol. I, p. 790, n. 1.

16. Lewis Gray, *History of Agriculture in the Southern United States to 1860* (1933).

17. Alfred Conrad and John Meyer, "The Economics of Slavery in the Antebellum South," *JPE,* April 1958.

18. Yasukichi Yasuba, "The Profitability and Viability of Plantation Slavery in the United States," *Economic Studies Quarterly,* September 1961; and Richard Sutch, "The Profitability of Antebellum Slavery Revisited," *SEJ,* April 1963.

19. Fogel and Engerman, *Time on the Cross,* vol. I, pp. 4–6.

20. Fogel and Engerman, pp. 144–57.

21. Paul A. David, Herbert G. Gutman, Richard Sutch, Peter Temin, Gavin Wright, "Introduction," by Kenneth Stampp, *Reckoning with Slavery: A Critical Study in the Quantitative History of American Slavery* (1975), pp. 12–13.

22. Gavin Wright, *The Political Economy of the Cotton South* (1978), ch. 6, 118–23; David, et al., pp. 308–12.

23. Fogel and Engerman, *Time on the Cross,* vol. II, pp. 74–83.

24. Paul David and Peter Temin, "Slavery: The Progressive Institution?" in David, et al., *Reckoning with Slavery,* pp. 218–23.

25. Wright, *The Political Economy of the Cotton South,* pp. 44–55. One problem concerning scale economies in slave agriculture lay in the lack of substitutability between slave labor and other inputs. Evidently, slave owners were severely constrained and, to expand output, they added slaves instead of adding capital equipment to augment output from the existing slave labor force, hence, labor intensive agriculture in slavery. Mark D. Schmitz and Donald R. Schaefer, "Slavery, Freedom, and the Elasticity of Substitution," *EEH,* July 1978.

26. David and Temin, in David, et al., *Reckoning with Slavery,* pp. 202–14.

27. Claudia Goldin, *Urban Slavery in the American South* (Chicago: University of Chicago Press, 1978).

28. In the simplest formulation: If the percentage change in quantity demanded divided by the percentage change in price is greater than 1, then demand is price elastic. If the percentage change in quantity demanded divided by percentage change in price is less than 1, then demand is price inelastic.

29. Gutman and Richard Sutch, "Victorians All? The Sexual Mores and Conduct of Slaves and Their Masters," in David, et al., *Reckoning with Slavery,* See pp. 99–133 in that chapter for a discussion of slave sales and pp. 134–62 for one on slave breeding. Also, in a more extended analysis, Richard Sutch, "The Breeding of Slaves for Sale and the Westward Expansion of Slavery, 1850–1860," in Stanley Engerman and Eugene Genovese, editors, *Race and Slavery in the Western Hemisphere: Quantitative Studies* (1975), ch. VIII.

30. Richard Sutch, "The Care and Feeding of Slaves," in David, et al., *Reckoning with Slavery.*

31. David and Temin, in David et al., pp. 187–202. The average rate of exploitation was the proportion of the competitive wage *not* paid to slaves for their labor at any point in time. Fogel and Engerman allow that figure to rise to perhaps 54 percent overall; Richard Vedder sees it as perhaps 65 percent overall, "The Slave Exploitation Rate," *EEH,* October 1975.

32. Richard Easterlin, "Regional Income Trends 1840–1950," in Robert Fogel and Stanley Engerman, editors, *The Reinterpretation of American Economic History* (New York: Harper & Row, 1971), pp. 38–45.

33. Discussions of each of these questions appear in Fogel and Engerman, *Time on the Cross,* vol. I, pp. 144–57.

34. David and Temin, in David, et al., *Reckoning with Slavery,* pp. 183–84 and pp. 223–30.

35. Richard Steckel, "Slave Mortality."

36. Richard Steckel, "Birth Weights and Infant Mortality Among American Slaves," *EEH,* April 1986.

37. Richard Steckel, "A Dreadful Childhood: The Excess Mortality of American Slaves," *Social Science History,* Winter 1986, p. 450.

38. Steckel, pp. 451–52.

39. Steckel, p. 430.

40. Richard Steckel, "A Peculiar Population: The Nutrition, Health, and Mortality of American Slaves from Childhood to Maturity," *JEH,* September 1986, p. 726.

41. Steckel, p. 728.

42. Steckel, "A Dreadful Childhood." This is Steckel's final conclusion in this remarkable paper, but he emphasizes that it must be speculative.

43. Kenneth Stampp argues that such forms of resistance were more important than is commonly assumed and sharply criticizes Fogel and Engerman for downplaying it. In David, et al., *Reckoning with Slavery,* "Introduction," pp. 27–28.

44. Stanley M. Elkins, *Slavery: A Problem of American Institutional and Intellectual Life* (1959), pp. 2–23.

45. Fogel and Engerman, *Time on the Cross,* vol. I, p. 264.

46. Stampp, in David, et al., *Reckoning with Slavery,* p. 18.

47. Stampp, p. 30.

48. Elkins, *Slavery,* ch. III; a discussion of "Sambo" and slave infantilism appears on pp. 82–89.

49. Elkins, pp. 103–33.

50. Eugene Genovese, *Roll, Jordan, Roll: The World the Slaves Made* (1976), "The Moment of Truth," pp. 97–112. The comparison to concentration camps can be found in Elkins, *Slavery,* p. 114.

51. Eugene Genovese, *From Rebellion to Revolution: Afro-American Slave Revolts in the Making of the Modern World* (1979).

52. We are indebted to Professor Thomas Ulen for emphasis on this point.

53. Fogel and Engerman, *Time on the Cross,* vol. I. p. 232. Also force was used *judiciously,* see p. 237.

54. Herbert Gutman and Richard Sutch, "Sambo Makes Good, or Were Slaves Imbued with the Protestant Work Ethic?" in David, et al., *Reckoning with Slavery,* pp. 60–67, 90–93. Also Giorgio Canarella and John A. Tomaske, "The Optimal Utilization of Slaves," *JEH,* September 1975.

55. Stefano Fenoaltea, "The Slavery Debate: A Note from the Sidelines," *EEH,* July 1981, pp. 306–7.

56. Olmsted, *The Slave States,* pp. 49–50.

57. Olmsted, see the footnote on p. 49.

58. Gutman and Sutch, in David, et al., *Reckoning with Slavery,* pp. 159–60.

59. Fogel and Engerman, *Time on the Cross,* vol. I, pp. 78–86.

60. Sutch, "The Breeding of Slaves," in Engerman and Genovese, *Race and Slavery in the Western Hemisphere,* pp. 195, 198.

61. Peter Passell and Gavin Wright, "The Effects of Pre-Civil War Territorial Expansion on the Price of Slaves," *JPE,* December 1972; and Laurence J. Kotlikoff and Sebastian E. Pinera, "The Old South's Stake in the Inter-Regional Movement of Slaves, 1850–1860," *JEH,* June 1977.

Suggested Readings

Articles

Aufhauser, R. Keith. "Slavery and Technological Change." *Journal of Economic History,* vol. XXXIV, no. 1, March 1974.

Canarella, Georgio, and Tomaske, John A. "The Optimal Utilization of Slaves." *Journal of Economic History,* vol. XXXV, no. 3, September 1975.

Fenoaltea, Stefano. "The Slavery Debate: A Note from the Sidelines." *Explorations in Economic History,* vol. 18, no. 3, July 1981.

Fleisig, Heywood. "Slavery, the Supply of Agricultural Labor, and the Industrialization of the South." *Journal of Economic History,* vol. XXXVI, no. 3, September 1976.

Fogel, Robert William. "Three Phases of Cliometric Research on Slavery and Its Aftermath." *American Economic Review,* vol. LXV, no. 2, May 1975.

———, and Engerman, Stanley L. "Explaining the Relative Efficiency of Slave Agriculture in the Antebellum South." *American Economic Review,* vol. 67, no. 3, June 1977.

———. "Explaining the Relative Efficiency of Slave Agriculture in the Antebellum South: A Reply." *American Economic Review,* vol. 70, no. 4, September 1980.

———. "The Relative Efficiency of Slavery: A Comparison of Northern and Southern Agriculture in 1860." *Explorations in Economic History,* vol. 8, no. 3, Spring 1971.

Kotlikoff, Laurence J., and Pinera, Sebastian E. "The Old South's Stake with Inter-Regional Movement of Slaves, 1850–1860." *Journal of Economic History,* vol. XXXVII, no. 2, June 1977.

Phillips, Ulrich B. "The Economic Cost of Slaveholding in the Cotton Belt." *Political Science Quarterly,* vol. XX, no. 2, June 1905.

Schmitz, Mark D., and Schaefer, Donald F. "Slavery, Freedom, and the Elasticity of Substitution." *Explorations in Economic History,* vol. 15, no. 3, July 1978.

Steckel, Richard H. "Slave Height Profiles from Coastwise Manifests." *Explorations in Economic History,* vol. 16, no. 4, October 1979.

———. "Slave Mortality." *Social Science History,* vol. 3, nos. 3 and 4, October 1979.

———. "Slave Marriage and the Family," *Journal of Family History,* vol. V, no. 4, Winter 1980.

———. "Birth Weights and Infant Mortality Among American Slaves," *Explorations in Economic History,* vol. 23, no. 2, April 1986.

———. "A Peculiar Population: The Nutrition, Health, and Mortality of American Slaves from Childhood to Maturity," *Journal of Economic History,* vol. XLVI, no. 3, September 1986.

———. "A Dreadful Childhood: the Excess Mortality of American Slaves," *Social Science History,* vol. 10, no. 4, Winter 1986.

Sutch, Richard. "The Treatment Received by American Slaves: A Critical Review of the Evidence Presented in *Time on the Cross*." *Explorations in Economic History,* vol. 12, no. 4, October 1975.

Thomas, Robert Paul, and Bean, Richard Nelson. "The Fishers of Men: The Profits of the Slave Trade." *Journal of Economic History,* vol. XXXIV, no. 4, December 1974.

Vedder, Richard K. "The Slave Exploitation (Expropriation) Rate." *Explorations in Economic History,* vol. 12, no. 4, October 1975.

Wright, Gavin. "Slavery and the Cotton Boom." *Explorations in Economic History,* vol. 12, no. 4, October 1975.

Zepp, Thomas M. "On Returns to Scale and Input Substitutability in Slave Agriculture." *Explorations in Economic History,* vol. 13, no. 2, April 1976.

Books

Blassingame, John. *The Slave Community: Plantation Life in the Antebellum South.* New York: Oxford University Press, 1972.

David, Paul; Gutman, Herbert; Sutch, Richard; Temin, Peter; and Wright, Gavin. *Reckoning with Slavery: A Critical Study in the Quantitative History of American Slavery.* New York: Oxford University Press, 1978.

Douglass, Frederick. *Narrative of the Life of Frederick Douglass.* New York: New American Library, 1968.

Elkins, Stanley M. *Slavery: A Problem of American Institutional and Intellectual Life.* New York: Grosset & Dunlap, 1959.

Engerman, Stanley, and Genovese, Eugene. *Race and Slavery in the Western Hemisphere: Quantitative Studies.* Princeton: Princeton University Press, 1978.

Fogel, Robert William, and Engerman, Stanley. *Time on the Cross: The Economics of American Negro Slavery.* Boston: Little Brown, 1974, 2 vols.

———. *Without Consent or Contract: The Rise and Fall of American Slavery.* New York: W. W. Norton, 1989.

Genovese, Eugene. *Roll, Jordan, Roll: The World the Slaves Made.* New York: Vintage Books, 1976.

———. *From Rebellion to Revolution: Afro-American Slave Revolts in the Making of the Modern World.* Baton Rouge: Louisiana State University Press, 1979.

Gray, Lewis. *History of Agriculture in the Southern United States to 1860.* Washington: The Carnegie Institution, 1933, 2 vols.

Gutman, Herbert. *The Black Family in Slavery and Freedom.* New York: Pantheon Books, 1976.

Olmsted, Frederick Law. *The Slave States.* New York: Capricorn Books, 1959.

Stampp, Kenneth. *The Peculiar Institution.* New York: Vintage Books, 1964.

Sydnor, Charles. *Slavery in Mississippi.* New York: Appleton Century, 1933.

Washington, Booker T. *Up from Slavery.* New York: Bantam Books, 1963.

Wright, Gavin. *The Political Economy of the Cotton South.* New York: Norton, 1978.

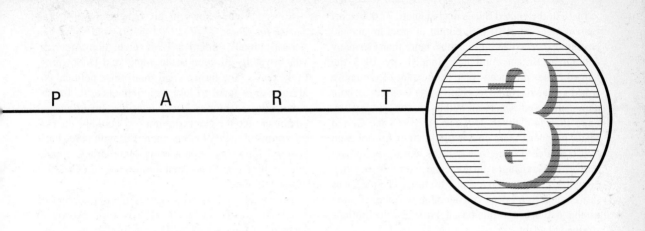

Extended Growth and Development: Achievements and Problems 1861–1914

Main Currents 1861–1941

Even though the Civil War's impact in the country's economic growth was negative, the war's end, in a very imprecise way, was a turning point. The Old South was "gone with the wind," and that region's economic well-being would compare poorly with the rest of the nation for decades to come. Northern agriculture came into its own in terms of production: Wheat exports alone would run raw cotton, the country's leading staple export, a close second by the 1880s. This is also when farming's economic and social dominance was reaching its apex. The next generation of Americans would be the first to live in an industrial nation in which the growth of cities and an urban life and culture really dominated the nation's life and politics. A few figures here will illustrate the nature of the change.

In 1870 we had fourteen cities of 100,000 or more in population, and only 26 percent of the population lived in urban places of 2500 or more. A person born that year would have been 40 years of age in 1910 when there were 50 cities of more than 100,000 in the country and nearly half, 46 percent, of the population lived in urban places. Three cities (New York, Philadelphia, and Chicago) had more than 1 million inhabitants, and five more had populations between 500,000 and 1 million.

In 1870 the United States made a mere 77,000 short tons of steel. In 1910 U.S. output of steel ingots and castings exceeded 28 million tons, more than Germany and Great Britain combined. Indeed, by 1913 the United States produced some 36 percent of the entire world's manufactured goods. In 1860 Great Britain alone surpassed American output of iron and coal by more than four times. However, by 1913 the United States produced more coal than did all of Europe, and it also produced more than half the world's petroleum output. These changes did not come overnight, but they did come easily within a single lifetime. The pace was fast enough to produce considerable social disruption as the nation's agrarian-based laws and institutions strained to adapt.

Although the farmers would make one last heroic stand to achieve their collective aims, in the years after the Civil War the focus would be, appropriately enough, upon the burgeoning powers of the federal government. Control of state governments would no longer be sufficient. An industrial and urban society would be one in which the federal power waxed at the expense of all other. It was the power to redistribute wealth and income, to create rents and disburse them on a political basis.

Robert Wiebe shows in his insightful book, *The Search for Order, 1877–1920,*[1] that the old, unwritten "constitutional settlement" of antebellum America, which was based upon demography and landowning, broke down. The farmers and small-town political coalitions were fated to lose their influence. Railroads, cities, mines, factories, heavy industry, great financial combines, and the giant corporations would be the major origins of the nation's economic growth in the half-century following Appomattox. Immigrants would pour in by the millions, mainly into the cities and industrial regions.

Twenty years after Appomattox the old conflict of free soil versus slavery and westward expansion seemed as long gone as the Puritan forefathers. "Cousin Jonathan's Great Farm," as the English had called antebellum America, had been replaced by the world's major industrial nation, a dynamic volcano of technical and social change. In the entire time span of American history the change was briefly executed. In many respects the period 1870–1914 was truly, as Robert Higgs celebrated it, the transformation of America.[2] Jefferson's ideas and hopes for a land of property-owning yeomen were largely forgotten.

Notes

1. Robert Wiebe, *The Search for Order* (New York: Hill & Wang, 1967).

2. Robert Higgs, *The Transformation of the American Economy 1865–1914: An Essay in Interpretation* (New York: Wiley, 1971).

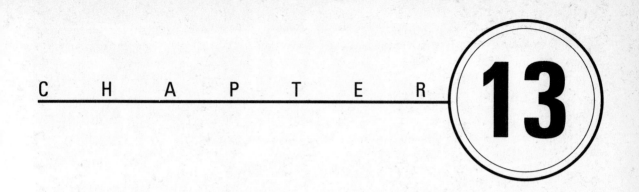

Economic Effects of the Civil War

T he most direct economic consequence of the Civil War was the ending of chattel slavery, in the South, a labor system that had prevailed for nearly 250 years. Southern agriculture, the primary form of the region's enterprise, was organized around forced labor. The "choice of technique" in Southern agriculture had been determined mainly by the supply of slaves in combination with the rents available from the cotton staple. The market values of real estate, of personal wealth, and of specialized tools and equipment were conditioned by the availability of slave labor. A whole society, class structure, system of manners, law, education, and expectations for the future, were rooted in the existence of property rights in human beings.

The Old South as a "going concern"—in an accounting sense—was an economy of compulsion at the fundamental levels of real output. When those slaves were no longer compelled to work, when the capitalized value of their labor ceased to be an article of commerce in which the slave did not share, two and a half centuries of historical development, measured in every conceivable way, were lost. The slaves were free, but a whole new start had to be made by all Southerners, black and white alike.

MEASURES OF THE WAR'S COSTS

What did the war cost? It is not silliness to try to calculate the cost of a war, any war. War has been, and remains, the largest economic enterprise of the modern state. In economics, the cost of things matters. The Civil War wasted men and resources on a vast scale. The attempts that have been made to calculate the cost will seem both cold-blooded and artificial, but we need some figures to answer important questions about the war and about subsequent economic development.

Costing Out the Dead

Some 600,000 men died on both sides. What were their lives worth? If they were valued at the price of a prime field hand in the 1860 market for slaves, say at $2000 apiece, the loss of that "human capital" outright would have been about $1.2 billion. Another 500,000 were wounded. How should the cost of those wounds be measured? Such intellectual calculations are, on the face of it, absurd. What family would have been willing to sell the life of a son or father for $2000 in 1860? (Twenty years' consumption expenditures for each person at 1860 rates—perhaps it is as well that the

The Real Financial Costs of War. Cleaning up the battlefield (above). The hundreds of thousands of young men slaughtered in the Civil War were an "expenditure" of human capital. How does one measure the dollar cost? The loss of physical capital could be measured by replacement cost (below), Richmond, 1865.

question remains rhetorical.) However, any attempt to say what the war cost must begin with such calculations.

Fortunately, Claudia Goldin and Frank Lewis have made the attempt.[1] Taking into account the excess of soldiers' pay over normal earnings as a "risk premium" for the 600,000 dead, they estimate a loss of human capital of $1.06 billion for killed and wounded in the North and $767 million for the South, or about $1.8 billion in human loss for both sides combined. Direct government expenditures were reckoned at $2.3 billion in the North and $1 billion in the South. Physical destruction of property was mostly limited to the South, and it was estimated at $1.5 billion.

The Total Cost

Summing up all their figures, Goldin and Lewis estimate the direct Northern cost at $3.4 billion and the direct Southern cost at $3.3 billion, or perhaps $6.7 billion in all at war's end. What was that cost in some real measure, in prices of 1860? To find such a measure is not easy. But let us try: $6.7 billion was more that *four times* the sum of all federal government expenditures from 1789 to 1860. It was nearly seventeen times the total value of U.S. exports in 1860. It was more than double the sum of total U.S. exports in the eleven years between 1850 and 1860; it was probably double the national income of 1860; it was more than eight times the value added by all U.S. manufacturing enterprises in 1860.

Since we are considering, in strictly economic terms, almost sheer waste of resources, you can easily appreciate the scale of the disaster even by conservative estimates. We have omitted the sum of accumulated costs after 1865—that is, the opportunities and talents forever lost, the accumulated interest charges, and veterans' payments. Lee and Passell note that the war's cost could have purchased all the slaves from their owners at 1860 prices, given each slave family 40 acres and a mule, and still had $3.5 billion left over for "reparations"—back wages.[2]

Goldin and Lewis also estimated the "indirect," long-term, costs. How much did the Civil War alone extract from *future* income? Their total estimates are, of course, much higher than the direct costs alone, and Peter Temin has argued that Goldin and Lewis's figures are overestimated by a factor of four.[3] We cannot re-

solve this dispute. The direct costs alone were a catastrophic misdirection of resources.

Such was the cost of revising American history to exclude slavery. Americans have never known whether it was the price of virtue or the wages of sin. Either way the American Civil War was one of history's long bills that finally came due.

WHO PAID?

In the Civil War, as in all wars, *all* of the money actually paid out in the purchase of material and labor was *received* by someone. So, when we say that the war was a great cost to the participants, we also are saying that it was a great source of income for someone, too. Taxpayers whose taxes rose while they were working a private enterprise selling goods to persons receiving no war-related income, were paying *net* for the war. An army contractor buying beef from farmers and selling it at a handsome profit to Uncle Sam was clearly gaining from the war (his *opportunity costs,* the comparative return from any alternate use of funds, being, no doubt, negative) if his income rose more than his taxes. Destruction of life and property was a dead loss to those who paid. For society as a whole, any gains survivors might have achieved must be subtracted from these losses, as must the external diseconomies of the losses to third parties. The neighboring flour mill was destroyed. The owner lost the mill, and his neighbors had to incur the search, transactions, and transportation costs of finding an alternate mill to grind their wheat.

Financing a war means expropriating resources. Beyond death or wealth taxes, there is very little that can be done to collect money from the past population. The present population can be taxed either directly or indirectly. Finally, a government can raise resources from future populations through increases in net government borrowing, called the *national debt* (and hence taxed in advance if the debt is ever repaid from future taxes).

Taxes and Inflation

Taxes may be either direct levies, such as sales or income taxes, or indirect ones raised by inflation. Money (command over resources) can be taken by governments through direct taxation. Also, governments can create inflation by printing sums of money and circulating them faster than production of goods and services can be increased. Thus, government can buy what it wants and the population must make do with less. The purchasing power of money is decreased; as a result, it takes more and more newly printed money to buy a given bundle of goods. This is inflation. Both the federal and Confederate governments tried this method of taxing as well as nearly all other methods.

Federal Finance

As the Civil War began, both sides grossly underestimated the magnitude of coming events. Neither the federal nor Confederate government contrived tax programs that came anywhere near paying the bills on a current basis. The result was debt and money creation in order to pay for more soldiers and equipment. Inflation and borrowing on the future were necessary. Compare the federal budget results in the two years 1860 and 1865, as presented in Table 13.1.

Even though they imposed taxes on everything imaginable—including a slightly progressive income tax, increased customs, excises, extended federal licensing requirements for merchants, and taxes on whiskey and beer—the federal government by 1865 had only been able to raise tax revenues over 1860 by a factor of 5.9. Expenditures in 1865 were more than 20 times the level of 1860; thus, the deficit had increased by unimaginable proportions, and the gross debt had gone up by a factor of 41 in only five years. It is a wonder that increased financial necessities of such magnitudes could have been coped with at all. Lincoln's Secretary of the Treasury, Salmon P. Chase, has suffered considerable criticism from historians for his programs, including the "farming out" of bond sales to the financier, Jay Cooke; the suspension of specie payments; the printing of federal legal-tender money (U.S. notes, popularly

Table 13.2 Money and Prices

	Index Numbers—Federal Side		
Year	**Money Stock**	**Wholesale Prices**	**Cost of Living**
1860	100	100	100
1865	267	199	167
1869	198	162	156

Source: *Historical Statistics*, derived from series X 420, 585–86; E 52, 183.

called *greenbacks*), and the official harnessing of the private banking system to the war effort in 1864 by the establishment of the national banks and the force-feeding of more of the enormous bond issues into the nation's financial system. Yet, looking back over more than a century (and several wars), Chase and his colleagues really came out fairly well.

The required resources were squeezed from the economy by methods that were necessarily inflationary. With the suspension of specie payments in December 1861, the issue of $415 million in greenbacks in 1864, and an additional issue of $146 million of national bank notes by 1865 (with government bonds as their main security), the money supply had been increased from $442 million in 1860 to $1,180 million in 1865. Prices rose by a less than equal amount.

Consider the data in Table 13.2. In 1860, with the country still suffering some unemployment in the aftermath of the 1857 panic, it was possible for an increase in the money supply to be absorbed by a considerable expansion of real goods and services. However, prices rose when the money stock rose and fell when the money stock fell, even if the proportions were not exactly the same. Also, as Stanley Engerman has shown (to be discussed in a later section), there was a reduction in the growth rate of final demand to offset the

Table 13.1 Federal Government Budgets and Debt[a]

Year	Revenues	Expenditures	Surplus (+) Deficit (−)	Gross Debt
1860	$ 56.1	$ 63.1	$− 7.0	$ 64.8
1865	333.7	1,297.6	− 963.9	2,677.9
1865 data / 1860 data	5.9	20.6	137.7	41.3

[a] Amounts given are in millions of dollars.

Source: *Historical Statistics*, derived from series Y 335–38.

increased demand for specifically military goods and services. So, on the federal side the inflation was surprisingly restrained, especially considering the scale of possible increase in the money supply derived from the debt increase (see Table 13.1). The greenbacks fell against gold on the free market to a maximum of 65 percent, but then recovered by war's end. **Hyperinflation**—which refers to price increases of truly extraordinary amounts, as in Germany in 1923, when prices were billions of times higher than they had been in 1914—did not occur.

The Confederacy

For the South, the financial circumstances were far more difficult, finally ending in a disastrous hyperinflation.[4] Whereas the federal government had been able to raise taxes enough to cover more than 20 percent of the war expenditures, the government in Richmond, its ports cut off by the federal blockade and war raging through its territories, could raise only about 12 percent of its expenditures by taxation. Confederate debt totalled more than $2 billion when the war ended. Prices had risen by a factor of 92. The Confederate monetary officials had neglected to make their notes legal tender—a major management error—and as the South's military fortunes sank, the currency became worthless. According to Eugene Lerner's calculations, the Confederate notes fell to a level of nearly 1/1000 against gold before the war's end.[5] In the South the financial rout was probably worse than the military debacle. Lee negotiated for an army in the field at Appomattox. The same cannot be said for Confederate finances.[6]

Holders of Confederate financial assets were wiped out. The victorious federal Congress did nothing to redeem the "rebel" currency and bonds. Let it be noted that in Germany the Nazis, after 1945, got a better deal from the United States, exchanging the financial assets of the 12-year "Thousand-year Reich" for postwar currency at ratios of 100/1 for bonds and 10/1 for currency.

The Real Burden

Economic historians have puzzled over who paid for the Civil War. The dead, those who owned Confederate financial assets, those whose crops and farm animals were sequestered, and those whose homes and farm buildings were destroyed, of course, paid terrible prices. Slave owners parted with their property without compensation. What of the North? The billions spent became income for some, but not for all or in equal portions.

The decline of greenbacks against gold that we just noted was a measure of the *rise* in foreign exchange prices. Americans, for the most part, paid premium prices for imported goods. Some scholars have considered the resulting decline in purchasing power an important part of the real burden of the war. In Table 13.3 we see the relevant available balance of payments data.

The data in Table 13.3 are five-year averages of Douglass North's estimates for foreign transactions in goods and services. It is clear that the war produced a sharp reduction in exports. Imports also fell, but less. These imports were more expensive because of the decline in greenback prices against gold. The **real terms of trade,** the ratio of exports to imports as measured by volume, turned against the United States. Alchian and Kessel have estimated that as much as 40 percent of the real income lag during the Civil War inflation came from this source.[7] If they are correct, then the foreign transactions of the immediate postwar years must also be considered part of the war burden. Note the huge increase in the deficit figures in the first five peacetime years. U.S. prices fell *immediately* in 1865–66, and foreign prices did not generally decline until 1873. As the gold value of the U.S. dollar rose in the postbellum years, in part because of foreign investment in the renewed expansion in the North and West, the market for U.S. cotton, even at lower domestic prices, must have been adversely affected.[8]

In terms of relative prices and exchange-rate problems, Americans may have been as badly off in 1866–

Table 13.3 U.S. Trade 1856–70, Five Year Averages

| Period | Goods and Services | | |
	Exports	Imports	Balance
1856–60	383.2	396.4	– 13.2
1861–65	294.2	353.4	– 59.2
1866–70	442.4	560.4	–118.0

Source: *Historical Statistics*, series U 1, 8.

70 as they were in 1861–65. The deficit was bigger, exports earned fewer imports, and the real burden of interest rates was higher due to falling domestic prices. The years 1866–70 were distinctly years of recovery and economic expansion. The two sets of data are not incompatible, of course, but they do make the balance-of-payments argument about the real burden of the war far more complex than first seems to be the case.

An older argument, stemming from Wesley Clair Mitchell's early work and given further support by Stephen DeCanio and Joel Mokyr, is that wage earners, suffering declining real earnings as wages lagged behind the inflation, bore a major direct real cost of the war.[9] Fully two-thirds of the decline in real wages resulted from price increases fueled by monetary expansion.

In addition, the U.S. Treasury's conservative postwar policy of reducing the debt (see Table 13.1 on page 240) by applying the proceeds of regressive taxation (taxing the poor to pay the rich) added to the real burden placed upon those who worked and paid taxes. Bonds purchased with inflated greenbacks were paid off in postwar dollars that had considerably higher real value (i.e., purchasing power) in exchange for domestically produced goods. In the South the war had been called "a rich man's war and a poor man's fight."[10] In the North those conscripted could actually pay substitutes, poor men, to go in their places, and many did. As in most wars, those who could not escape the fighting and those who paid taxes picked up the tab. Others did well for themselves on the home front. Those whose income and wealth kept ahead of inflation did especially well.

DID THE WAR AID INDUSTRIALIZATION?

It probably should not be surprising that an older generation of historians saw in the Civil War itself the origin of the great wave of industrialization that came to the United States in the nineteenth century's final quarter. Many of the leading industrialists and financiers of that era, people such as Andrew Carnegie and Pierpont Morgan, had made considerable financial gains during the war (but nothing like the amounts they would make later on). War, it was believed, must have raised enormous demands for the productions of manufacturing industry: all the army shoes, guns, uniforms, wagons, and food.

Historically speaking, agrarian America seemed almost in a flash to have been launched upon the road to industrialization. It happened in a single generation. Muckrakers, like Matthew Josephson, who saw little of virtue or honor in the lives of the late-nineteenth century *nouveau-riche,* those made wealthy in finance and industry, found special motivation in the idea that the American industrial state should have been launched by something so foul and tragic as the Civil War.[11] Even in poetry, such as Stephen Vincent Benét's "John Brown's Body," it was the world of factories and workers that had beaten back the flashing sabers of the Southern cavaliers.

The Tradition and Engerman

Among American historians, the link between the Civil War and industrial expansion is most commonly attributed to Charles A. Beard and Louis Hacker.[12] Sometimes called simply "the Beard-Hacker thesis," it makes a splendid and vulnerable target. Writing in the 1920s and 1930s, with the economic growth of World War I in the immediate background, and arguing along the "industrial North" lines turned to verse by Benét, Beard and Hacker saw the Civil War as a major stimulus to industry, even though they lacked reliable data. The problem was that the war was fought *in the United States,* and it engaged millions of people drawn away from productive labor. For example, the million-odd men under arms in the Union army in 1865 were perhaps 20 percent of the total male population of military age. The war was, in fact, a great drain, and as Stanley Engerman has shown, it stalled U.S. economic, and specifically industrial, development.

Engerman could find few signs of the Civil War gains postulated in the Beard-Hacker thesis. Robert Gallman's total commodity output figures show an increase of 4.6 percent per annum between 1840 and 1860, a decrease to a mere 2 percent between 1860 and 1870, and then a recovery to an annual average of 4.4 percent in the decades 1870–1900.[13] Engerman says of these, "The 1860s were uniquely low for the nineteenth century."[14] It would seem that the war, by these measures, cost the country about five years' growth. Real growth per capita was perhaps 1.5 percent per annum between 1850 and 1860. The war cut that rate sharply. On a per capita basis, the "non-South" grew less than 1 percent per annum in the 1860s.

Output in the South, of course, fell absolutely. Indeed, it is Engerman's opinion that the revived growth rates after the war were, in part, merely "catching up," as in the United States in 1945–50. As for the Confederacy, Engerman writes

> It is in the South that the destructive effects of the war were most severely felt. Per capita commodity output declined by 39 per cent in the Civil War decade, and in 1880 was still 21 per cent below the 1860 level.[15]

He estimates that had the South maintained its prewar per capita income growth, the 1870 level would have been *double* what it actually was. Edwin Frickey's index of industrial production rises a mere 6 percent in the period 1860–65, but from 1865 to 1870 the increase is a stout 47 percent.[16] Data for fixed capital show an annual increase of 8.5 percent in the 1850s and less than half that rate (4.1 percent) in the 1860s.[17]

War Industries Alone

Attempts to narrow the search for benefits down to "war industries" alone show that, woolens (millions of uniforms) apart, the 1860s were slump years. Between 1855 and 1865 the Massachusetts boot and shoe industry showed a decline of some 30 percent in output and about the same in employment. Farm output increased little. The country was well fed when the war broke out. The South suffered badly, but the North, despite rising prices for food, produced apparently little increase in output. For example, wheat flour output, at 41.6 million barrels in 1861, was 42.5 million in 1865.[18] After the 1864 harvest, Cyrus McCormick was carrying an unsold reaper inventory equal to 40 percent of his sales. Iron for guns was in fact a trivial portion of annual iron sales (1 percent) and railroad building, already down from the 1857 commercial crisis, sagged lower (below 1000 miles) in the war years (see Figure 13.1 below).

The South's exit from the national market was, of course, an additional blow. What it did to regional trade can be shown by the change in import quantities of a standard consumer item, coffee. Imports of coffee were 180 million pounds in 1860, about 11 pounds per

capita per annum. In 1862 the figure was, appropriately, nearly cut in half, to 94 million pounds. Coffee was part of a famous front-line swap in which the men in blue traded coffee for the tobacco of the men in grey. By 1870 imports had returned to 272 million pounds, roughly 6.8 pounds per capita per annum, about three-fourths of what it is today.[19] All nonlocal trade must have been severely constrained by loss of the South—the loss of its foreign-exchange earning ability and the loss of its market.

Real Wages and Profits

Engerman disputes the idea that falling real wages must have meant rising real income in other sectors of

Figure 13.1   Miles of Railroad Built, 1850–70

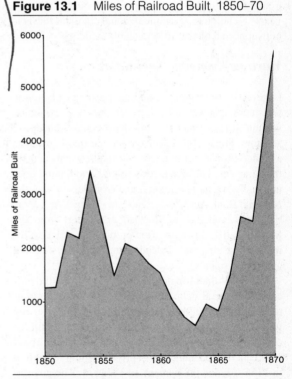

Source: *Historical Statistics*, series Q 329.

Road construction declined after 1854 (although there was a temporary rally in 1857), and then fell even more drastically in the first years of the Civil War. The era of the transcontinentals began after the war, and the statistic, "miles of new railroads built," boomed until the Panic of 1873 played havoc with the economy.

economic life—the **residual claimant hypothesis.**[20] He points out the obvious possibility that no one gained, that income shares remained unchanged, while the real growth of income declined overall.

This is where the Kessel and Alchian argument is most effective. The turning of the terms of trade (export prices/import prices) against the United States during the war simply could have reduced the real level of wages, profits, interest, rents—everything. If the United States traded two bushels of wheat for eight English shirts, and then its export prices (the price of its currency) fell 50 percent against the pound, it would get only four shirts for two bushels of wheat. *Everyone* would share those four fewer shirts per two bushels of wheat, regardless of income distribution. Actually, estimates of income distribution by Edward Budd show a slight rise in labor's income share during the war years.[21] Therefore, even the residual claimant thesis is not supported by the little available evidence.

Wartime Economic Legislation

Engerman also examined the major wartime economic legislation that was not strictly temporary—legislation written in the absence of Southern congressmen and senators. Some historians have seen in that legislation a device to further the interest of industrialists against the agrarians. The explanation sounds good, but it does not really wash. The main legislation passed was the National Bank Act, Homestead Act, Morrill Act, Morrill Tariff, and Pacific Railroad Act. Apart from the Morrill Tariff, this legislation produce no strictly pro-industry results, and, indeed, much of it satisfied old agrarian demands.

Jeffrey Williamson does argue, though, that the outcome of federal debt financing augmented the country's ability to build its real capital structure after the war.[22] Interest payments and debt retirement, paid for out of postwar revenues, he says, made available about 1 percent of GNP annually to private capital formation in 1866–72, and 0.8 percent, in 1872–78. The government, through its fiscal policy, acted as a capital mobilization machine.

From our modern perspective the fact that the Civil War freed the slaves sanctifies its sacrifices. We do not question their necessity. However, because in 1860 Americans did question it, it is worthwhile to consider the economic costs. They are a part of our history, the great past, and they had consequences.[23]

COMPARATIVE RECOVERY: THE NORTH AND THE SOUTH AFTER THE WAR

Between 1860 and 1870 the nation's population grew by 8.4 million, or nearly one-fourth. The East-North-Central and West-North-Central states alone accounted for 3.8 million, or 45 percent, of the increase. The Southern states grew only by 1.1 million persons, contributing a mere 13 percent of the increase. The Midwest raised its population by 42 percent, and the South, only by about 10 percent. Yet before the war, as we have seen, the Southern population had grown about as rapidly as had the Midwest region. The data reflect a host of influences that blighted the South but also measure a sad problem that would vex the country for decades after the Civil War.

The South's agrarian vigor seemed to vanish with slavery, and the South would lag behind the rest of the country for a century to come by almost every measure of social and economic well-being. One caveat is worth considering: Jay Mandle emphasizes that within the South, those states that experienced the least impact of the slave system in the form of cotton plantations showed the best record of growth and development in the postbellum period.[24]

Measures of Physical Growth

Per capita commodity output showed an incredible reduction in the South. In 1860 the South actually had led the non-South by $78 to $75. In 1870 the South trailed by $48 to $82: Even in 1880, when the numbers were $62 and $106, the South had yet to recover to its prewar level, while the rest of the nation had raised its per capita commodity output by 41 percent over the prewar figure. Growth of GNP per capita in the country as a whole ranged between 4.4 and 5.2 percent per annum in 1871–1879, but gross Southern crop output increased by less than 2 percent per annum in the same period.[25] Table 13.4 shows gross commodity output converted to indexes of 1860.

The South's failure to recover by these measures is apparent. Even in 1880, when the non-South had more

Table 13.4   Commodity Output By Region and Industrial Sector

Year	Total	Agriculture	Mining and Manufacturing
Non-South			
1860	100	100	100
1870	140	146	133
1880	232	218	245
South			
1860	100	100	100
1870	75	75	80
1880	118	115	141

Source: Calculated from Robert W. Fogel and Stanley Engerman, "The Economic Impact of the Civil War," reprinted in *The Reinterpretation of American Economic History,* edited by Robert Fogel and Stanley Engerman (New York: Harper & Row, 1971), p. 371.

than doubled its output over 1860 in agriculture and the industrial sector, the South was only 15 percentage points up in agriculture and 41 points up in industrial output. Looking at these numbers, we are studying a failure of giant magnitudes.

Wartime Destruction

The problem of war-related destruction has been considerably illuminated by recent research, some of it producing very surprising conclusions. The common-sense place to look for the origins of the South's post-war backwardness is in the actual wartime destruction of life, wealth, animals, buildings, and the functioning organizational networks for finance, commerce, and the like. These were grievous losses. James Sellers estimated that the money value of total wealth in the South declined by 30 percent as a result of the war. The South lost 20 percent of its sheep, 30 percent of its mules, 32 percent of its horses, 35 percent of its cattle, and 42 percent of its swine. Farm real estate fell in value by 50 percent.[26] These losses were in catastrophic proportions. Except in the most extraordinary circumstances, it would take some years to rebuild the animal herds alone. There was no postwar Marshall Plan to rebuild the South as there was for Europe after World War II.

In addition, the financial structure of the region was wrecked by the fiscal disaster of the Confederacy. Nine-tenths of the state banks of the South, which were

larger than those of the North on average before the war, vanished.[27] The old labor-force organization was, of course, disestablished. How was the land to be farmed? No one knew. With peace came the mighty job of rebuilding, a situation similar to Germany's in 1945.[28] The difference is that by 1950, the West Germans had reestablished real output at 1938 levels. As we have seen, the South had not really recovered 1860 levels of per capita output by 1880. What went wrong?

Cotton

One problem was the long-term decline in raw cotton prices as the South recovered production. At first, cotton prices were very high. Output was the problem. Cotton crops of the size achieved in the late 1850s were only produced again in the late 1870s. By then, the prices were below the 1850s prices and far below those of the war and the immediate postwar years. In 1869, cotton still averaged 16.5 cents per pound (in 1865 it had been 43.2 cents). By the late 1870s, the price was half that and generally stayed at between 8 cents and 9 cents per pound the rest of the century.[29] Roger Ransom and Richard Sutch, in their study of the post–Civil War South, show that cotton prices fell, generally, even more than other prices in a period of generally declining farm prices.[30] To actually gain in such a market, producers would have needed extraordinary increases in efficiency. Such were not forthcoming in the postwar years. As a result, King Cotton was no longer the sure source of prosperity it once had been.

Despite these figures, cotton was still the premier cash crop in the South, and producers redoubled their efforts to raise total output. As Gavin Wright emphasized, the old self-sufficiency of the prewar cotton culture was sacrificed to make more cotton per farm.[31] With prices falling for their cash crop, cotton growers increasingly had to buy food and provisions, and, as we shall see, under onerous conditions. Southern *poverty* associated with cotton now became a fixed feature of the South. Before the war, cotton had meant riches. In 1866, 7.7 million acres were planted in cotton, in 1870 more than 9 million. By 1875, the figure was more than 11 million acres, but the 1875 crop, 4.6 million bales, was possibly smaller than that of 1859.[32] Output per acre had fallen sharply. Why?

Ransom and Sutch and Reconstruction

In their book, *One Kind of Freedom,* Roger Ransom and Richard Sutch trace out the remarkable institutional transformation of the postbellum South. They show how the fundamental elements of economic life, totally disrupted by the war, rearranged themselves into a system of singular economic stagnation. The Southern slave system, rooted in the oppression of black workers, had evolved over two and a half centuries into a powerful engine of economic expansion that was nourished by the market for raw cotton. When that engine was shattered by military defeat and emancipation, there were many possibilities open for the reordering of economic life.[33]

Like iron filings under the force of a magnet, a new pattern formed, and unfortunately that pattern was one of low productivity, poverty, and social backwardness. The magnetic force, argue Ransom and Sutch, was racism. "Keeping the Negro in his place" gave the American economy a huge island of rural backwardness within the larger mold of dynamic American capitalism in the later decades of the nineteenth century. While the Northern and Western states produced the world of U.S. Steel, General Electric, and Standard Oil, a unique phenomenon in world history of financially integrated economic growth and change, the agrarian South was locked into a pattern of static poverty that gripped the region until the boll weevil, a tiny insect, devastated the cotton economy between 1892 and 1922.

Emancipation with No Compensation

Before the war, ideas for "buying out" slavery had focused upon compensating slave owners for the loss of their human property. The war ended that approach. The slaves were freed unconditionally, their rights established by constitutional amendment. Southern slave owners were forced to absorb personally the financial loss, estimated at perhaps $1.6 billion (at 1860 slave prices), or perhaps 40 percent of the total property loss in the South.[34]

Like their owners, slaves also were not compensated—in their case, for the centuries-long oppression of themselves and their ancestors. Ransom and Sutch estimated the rate of exploitation (slave "wages" be-

low the market value of their labor) at about 54 percent.[35] While the entire nation had benefitted from the slaves' labor, no debt was paid. Blacks were left to fend for themselves in the market economy. Without property, without money, without skills (more than 90 percent in 1870 could only labor), without experience in the most ordinary decision-making processes of economic life (bargains for their labor, for example), they were almost uniquely unfitted for the lives they now had to find for themselves.[36] Black males over 20 years of age in 1870 were more than 90 percent illiterate (compared to 20 percent for poor Southern whites in the same age group).[37]

At the end of the war, not one Southern state contained a statewide system of public education. The victorious federal Congress, sunk in corruption and incompetence, did next to nothing to remedy the situation. For the Southern whites, peacetime life began with destruction, poverty, and defeat. For the blacks, peacetime life began in a void. They were free but without property, skill, or education. Their freedom began the process of reaching equality with American whites that would last for generations to come and that, more than a century later, was still largely uncompleted.

Labor and Sharecropping

Initially the problem was determining how to work the land. Defeated or not, the South was still part of the American economy. Because it was mainly rural, farming had to be the basis of the immediate future. The right to use land had to come, as before, from ownership or from some tenure that was a derivative of ownership: lease, rental, or working on shares.

The land still belonged to those whose titles were derived from antebellum ownership. Blacks would need to work for others, initially at least. Various schemes were tried—wages by the month, wages with food and lodging thrown in. A government agency, The Freedman's Bureau, tried to set a minimum wage of $8–$10 a month. (Freedmen had bargained for as low as $2 a month in Georgia in 1865.) No uniform system of wage payment was found, of course. In a free market the wage was competitive on the supply side and determined on the demand side in part by the quality of the land in question, its productivity. Wages would necessarily differ in different locations and circumstances. No general rule was possible.

At this point the South (and some later historians) should have recognized the role *force* had played under slavery. Force meant more hours, and more days, for more people, in common labor than would have been the case in a "free market." Once set free, the former slaves made labor-leisure choices similar to those of whites; they chose to cease "working like niggers," as the old, and half-admiring, antebellum saying had it. Women and children quit the fields, and men opted for more time off, exchanging leisure for money earnings. Here was born the opposite, racist myth that the freedmen were lazy! They no longer would work like slaves once they had the freedom to choose between work and leisure, like anyone else. No one, after all, had ever referred admiringly to someone "working like a redneck" in the South's cotton fields. The extra days, long hours, and extra hard work had been the special contribution of force to slavery's remarkable overall productivity *per head*.

Thus, one immediate result of emancipation was a labor "shortage," although it was an intentional shortage. Since workers withdrew the extra work time that was mandatory under slavery, per capita output fell from antebellum levels and *never recovered* during the rest of the nineteenth century. In 1900 it stood at 69 percent of the 1859 level; in earlier years it had been lower.[38] Ransom and Sutch point out that the withdrawal of about one-third of the available black labor input in fact rendered irrelevant much of the wartime losses of animals, implements, and buildings.[39] With less available labor, these items could hardly have been employed in any case. Ransom and Sutch point out that even by working less, the freedmen raised their real standards of life considerably above anything enjoyed during slave times.[40] One publication quoted by Ransom and Sutch noted with muted outrage in April, 1866: "Most of the field labor is now performed by men, the women regarding it as the duty of their husbands to support them in idleness."[41]

After mixed, and largely unhappy, experiences with attempts to institute work for hire, even efforts to restore gang labor, the South fell back upon alternate methods of putting its lands and people to work: various forms of tenancy and sharecropping. This necessarily meant the atomization of the cotton economy at its basic production level.

Ownership of land was still highly concentrated, but the old plantation lands were now largely subdivided into thousands of family-size farms.[42] Freedmen could not buy, and they had little in the way of stock or equipment to employ at first. After many experiments, the more or less standard agreement for sharecropping was a fifty-fifty split of the crop, the landowner furnishing the farm and buildings, seed and equipment, and provisions for the year. The freedman furnished his own and his family's labor. The contracts were almost universally renewable every year.[43] In 1860, more than 80 percent of all improved lands had been in farms of 100 or more acres. By 1870, nearly 40 percent of the farms were less than 100 acres; 73 percent of the land was owned by the wealthiest 20 percent of the population. In 1860 it had been 75.1 percent.[44] So, the war, whatever it did to individual landowners, did little to "democratize" land ownership. By 1880 in the Cotton South, roughly 70 percent of the farms were operated by whites, and 30 percent by blacks (see Figure 13.2). The average landowner in 1880 who employed tenants employed 4.7 of them. Some of the old plantations had been held together using tenant and hired labor, and in 1880, they still managed to produce about 14 per cent of the cotton grown.[45]

Blacks were half of the Southern population and were probably more than 70 percent of the agricultural labor force. By 1880 they owned 32.1 percent of the 30.5 percent of land occupied by blacks. They owned, therefore, 9.8 percent of the Cotton South's land sown in crops by 1880. Considering conditions in 1865, it seems remarkable that *so much* of the land had come into black possession in ownership by 1880. Not only was land expensive, but resistance, sometimes violent, to any black ownership at all was widespread.[46] Note in Figure 13.2 that, interestingly enough, of the land tenanted, the proportions of the tenanted land rented out and sharecropped were about the same among poor whites and blacks.[47] As Ransom and Sutch point out, sharecropping may well have given poor white farmers their chance too![48]

The sharecropping agreement was a form of labor-force organization and control. Management basically remained with the landowner, who could, by provisioning of the farms, determine what and how much

Figure 13.2   Cotton South in 1880: All Land in Crops and the Tenure

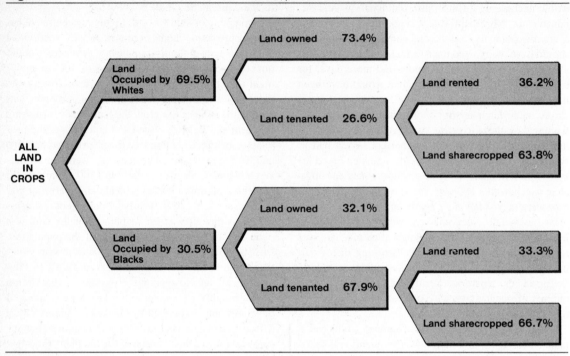

Source: Roger L. Ransom and Richard Sutch, *One Kind of Freedom: The Economic Consequences of Emancipation* (New York: Cambridge University Press, 1977), derived from Table 5.1, p. 84.

Of Southern land tenanted, more than 60 percent of that held by both whites and blacks was sharecropped. Most of the farmland (69.5 percent) was occupied by whites. Of that portion held by whites, 73.4 percent was owner operated. For blacks, the ownership figure was only 32.1 percent (which was less than 10 percent of the total Southern farmland).

could be planted. There has been some considerable debate about the origin in the United States of the sharecropping agreement. Joseph Reid and others have argued that the final form was an optimal outcome of free-agent bargaining.[49] Others have seen different origins. Without presuming to settle the matter, we would add the following regarding the *first* sharecropping agreement in American history, in the Virginia colony:

> After 1618 and until the crown took over in 1625, indentured servants who were farmers and worked the company's land . . . were furnished with a year's provision, tools, and indentured for seven years on condition that they turn half of their product over to the company. At the end of their indentures they received a grant of land. Until then they were sharecroppers.[50]

Since in the above case the sharecropper was actually granted land after seven years, the postbellum agree-

ment, coming 250 years later, actually might be viewed as a step backward! Ransom and Sutch demonstrate that, once set going, the institution of sharecropping spread rapidly throughout the Cotton South. It gave the freed slave and poor white a chance to earn a living and independence from day-to-day supervision, on the job and otherwise in life. Risk of failure was shared by both parties: sharecropper and landlord. The landowners got their property worked and a chance to change tenants in cases of unsatisfactory performance.

It is also argued that it was to no one's benefit to undertake extensive improvements. The tenants were not motivated to make improvements since they might be evicted (with only the uncertain prospect of a lawsuit to realize the value of their improvements). The landlords were also unlikely to make improvements because they would have been trusting their own invested capital into the hands of tenants perhaps indifferent to its long-run value. In any case, the effect of grinding poverty on the South's sharecroppers renders such speculation largely superfluous. Stephen DeCanio, in his study of the South after the Civil War, estimated that mere ownership of land would have doubled share-cropper incomes and that ownership of capital and land both would have tripled it. The failure to compensate the ex-slaves with property for the generations of forced black labor launched the blacks into poverty as well as into freedom.[51] Forty acres and a mule would have made a difference.

Country Finance and Debt Peonage

Probably the most remarkable achievement of Ransom and Sutch is their work on postbellum Southern finance. We can only survey the highlights of it here.

The antebellum cotton economy with its large plantation "management units" had been well served financially by an international network of banking houses and agents representing the cotton spinning industry in this country and abroad. English banks commonly held masses of American paper under discount in import centers such as Liverpool that had originated in the South to move raw cotton. State-chartered banks in the South also granted credit (discounted their paper) to those who had cotton to ship.

At the war's end, there was hardly a trace of the old financial system. The old state banks, filled with Confederate debt, failed utterly. The representatives of cotton-spinning firms had long since left the scene of devastation. It is not entirely clear why the old system did not revive in some form.[52] In fact, Southern banking made a very poor recovery. With the atomization of cotton-growing plantations into family-sized farms (the disappearance of the plantation system) an equally atomized financial system appeared that lasted through the rest of the century. The financial unit was the local provisioning merchant—essentially a country store—which could provide supplies to tenants and sharecroppers. The security taken was a lien against the forthcoming crop.

The postwar Southern banking system, when it did finally appear, was concentrated in urban areas. The national banks needed initial capital of $50,000 to start up, which really limited their appearance except in

those areas. The South, of course, had far fewer urban centers than the North, as we have already seen. Without a system of nationally organized branch banking (as existed in England at the time), it was left to local initiative to produce financial intermediation from the materials at hand. Smaller private and state banks appeared in the smaller towns. However, mortgages on land were no longer primary debt instruments in the South. Loans were made on personal notes and other collateral for those who had sufficient standing. That excluded the mass of sharecroppers and tenant farmers located in isolated country locations.

The South was really bereft of normal banking services and remained largely in that condition. In 1880, when there were 2061 national banks in the country, only 126 were in the twelve states of the old Confederacy, and only 42 in the five cotton-growing states. Unlike in the antebellum period, the Southern banks were now smaller, on the average, than were the banks in the rest of the country. But small or large, there obviously were too few of them for the job at hand.

The vacuum was filled by a more elementary form of financial intermediation, *commodity credit* at excessive markups. Nearly 8000 country stores appeared that gave credit to poor sharecroppers and tenants, at 'normal' mark-ups of from 40 to 70 percent per annum.[53] (Both eyewitnesses and the calculations of Ransom and Sutch produce such estimates.) This phenomenon is one of the stranger examples of market perversion in American history.[54] Poor Southern farmers were paying these effective interest rates while, in cities 50 or 100 miles away, interest rates were one tenth of those levels.[55] An atomized economic system needed an atomized financial underpinning. Decentralized financial management would be created to match the atomization of decision-making units. That is what happened, except that the financial institution was not a deposit bank at all, but a distributor of real commodities. Competitive intermediation between the consumer and commodity source vanished. The result was usury.

What is probably most remarkable about this system of country finance is that it simply "sprang up" in response to changing local needs. The states passed laws establishing crop liens as primary charges on the assets of sharecroppers. Deposits and checks had not been widely used in the South in antebellum times. With state bank notes taxed out of existence and few national banks in the territories of the South circulating their own promissory notes, this primitive and usury-laden system of barter prospered. The merchants themselves spontaneously became shippers of cotton.

The old system, with its large-scale units, had been serviced by traveling "cotton factors," who had issued paper against the movement of cotton. That paper "money" had been discounted at banks in the South, on the East Coast, or even abroad and the South had been provisioned. But because tenancy and sharecropping produced such a vast multiplication of the number of "management units," the system of factors could not be efficiently reestablished. Someone who knew the actual tenants and sharecroppers by sight, name, and reputation had to provide finance. The country storekeeper was that person. As a result this suboptimal form of noncompetitive intermediation appeared and dominated the rural South through the rest of the century. Other changes, especially new ginning and bailing equipment and the burgeoning Southern railway system (12,842 miles in 1860 and 56,786 miles by 1890), cut the cost of bailing cotton and shipping, and multiplied the number of shipping points—any stop on a railroad line—thus helping to localize the postbellum cotton industry.

The basis of the monopoly power was apparently a combination of high transactions costs and rural isolation with poor transportation. As in the location theory of August Lösch that we discussed in Chapter 8, the country stores grew up approximately a half day's journey apart depending on the topography. Any closer and competition might have become possible—the farmer could have "shopped around" for better prices—but only if the farmer were *equally* credit-worthy in more than one locality. The roads were poor, and there was no significant mail-order service (or even enough post offices) until late in the century.

The giver of credit could also supervise the ability of the borrower to pay—that is, tell him or her what to grow. The result of sharecropping and monopoly country finance was what Ransom and Sutch call "debt peonage."[56] Since cotton was the cash crop, credit was given for *cotton growing*. The result was a reduction in the amount of land and resources applied to self-sufficiency in food.[57] Unlike in the antebellum period, the small growing units were now maximizing their cotton acreage. The collateral effect, of course, was increasing dependence upon the country merchant for food—again, on credit. The sharecropper and tenant

sank into continuous indebtedness. Effective economic power slipped into the hands of those who had nothing to gain from "progress." What was needed at the country store was a continually impoverished clientele, as long as it could still grow cotton.[58]

With this new system, the economics of the South had been stood on its head. Cotton was now a poverty crop; the production of it was at the expense of food growing.[59] Finance became small-scale and local. There is nothing else in American economic history quite like this retrograde development over such a vast territory, embracing millions of people. A great opportunity was lost by the nation as a whole in the postbellum American South. It became a region noted for wasting human and natural resources until well into the twentieth century, scarred by backwardness and brutal racism. What the white racist said of the black—"He's lazy, shiftless, and ignorant"—the Northerner and Westerner said of the white Southerner. We had the beginnings of an "underdeveloped country" within the borders of the United States. No economic planner, no matter how demented, could have dreamed up the South's nightmarish fate.

In the twentieth century, the boll weevil, paved roads, autos, and jobs in the industrial cities and in the North finally broke up the postbellum stagnation. Mechanization came to Southern agriculture, and industry arrived at the great ports and commercial centers of the regions. The descendants of the freedmen became primarily urban dwellers and moved not only to the cities, but to the cities of the North. In response, *Jim Crow laws,* which determined where blacks could eat and drink, live, work, and even sit on public transportation, were passed.[60] As Ransom and Sutch write, "Nearly 15 percent of the black population must have left the cotton south between 1910 and 1930. The black exodus was one of the larger migrations in human history." Thousands of poor Southern whites cleared out, too.

In his book *Old South, New South* Gavin Wright argues that the basic problems left over from slavery and the postwar maladjustments were rooted in the continued separateness of the Southern labor market from the North.[61] The South became a low-wage labor market, with Southern entrepreneurship geared to exploit it. Northern and immigrant labor shunned the South. So for seven decades after the Civil War, until the 1930s, there remained a distinctive Southern economy. Southern workers migrated out of it, but high birth rates in the predominantly rural South filled up the labor force with replacements for the emigrants. Wages fell so low in the sugar cane plantations and refineries the hired Chinese laborers abandoned the industry and migrated to the West Coast. Farms in the South actually decreased in average size while the farms were growing steadily larger in the North with the application of successive generations of farm machinery to the land. Under the pressure of abundant rural population Southern farms became actually smaller on average than Northern farms, the reverse of the antebellum situation. Cotton production was labor intensive, was not mechanized, and Southern farming became a fountain of poverty.

Southern manufacturing, also labor intensive, starting from very small beginnings, grew at respectable rates, sometimes faster than growth in comparable industries in the North. But there was far to go. The Southern manufacturing sector in the postbellum years remained too small to be the salvation of the Southern economy. Southern industry developed and perpetuated patterns of racial segregation (whites only in textiles, large numbers of blacks in steel) that can only be understood by employment of social history. Economics alone cannot explain such curiosities.[62] Also, the relative lack of cities and small trading towns (another legacy of slavery), of a financial infrastructure, meant there were few commercial foci for a transformation to a modern economy.

Also, the South was not making the kinds of investment in human capital that characterized the Northern states from Maine to California. The South's lack of an extensive system of public schools was another legacy of slavery. Such schools were irrelevant in slave times and the South resisted establishing them. For decades after the Civil War, according to Wright, such schooling was considered a luxury and a waste in the old South. Education for the poor merely encouraged the beneficiaries to migrate to the North and higher wages.

One result was that the disparity of wages between the North and the South grew, even though within each region the disparities of wages between states tended to narrow, as would be expected from economic theory. Northern investors, according to Wright's account, tended to avoid the South and its poverty. Ransom and Sutch argued that wealthy Southerners, on the other hand, invested generously in Northern industry in the postbellum period. When finally these patterns were reversed after the 1930s the distinctive Southern economy itself vanished from the American scene. Until the 1930s the postbellum South, mainly a world of small farms and labor intensive industry, was a paradigm of economic and social backwardness in the United States.[63]

In the later nineteenth century, given the technology, the culture and traditions, perhaps the old cotton south really had no better alternatives. Stephen DeCanio argues along these lines. He emphasizes that cotton-farming was still the most "productive" activity available for Southern farmers. That they were hardly exploited by being steered into cotton production by the creditors, that cotton farmers were more prosperous, both whites and blacks, than were those who did not grow cotton, whether they were whites or blacks. Sharecropping itself did not *cause* the distribution of income among southern farmers.[64]

CONCLUSION

The Civil War is a never-ending tragedy in American history whose seeds were planted in colonial times. It was the only (to date) breakdown in the constitutional settlement of 1789. The appalling human and economic costs of the war were augmented by the strange perversion of the American market economy that grew up in the ruins of the Old South. To this day, the scars are not erased, and the human and financial costs of the disaster continue.

Notes

1. Claudia Goldin and Frank Lewis, "The Economic Cost of the American Civil War," *JEH*, June 1975.
2. Susan Previant Lee and Peter Passell, *A New Economic View of American History* (1979), pp. 223–26.
3. Peter Temin, "The Post-Bellum Recovery of the South and the Cost of the Civil War," *JEH*, December 1976; Goldin and Lewis and Temin had a further exchange on the war's cost: See *JEH*, June 1978, pp. 487–93.

4. A footnote to Confederate financial history: In 1979, it was reported that surviving Confederate dollars were selling at $1 Confederate to $8 Federal Reserve due, someone quipped, to the conservative money supply policies followed by the Confederate Treasury after 1865.

5. Eugene Lerner, "Money, Wages and Prices in the Confederacy," *JPE,* February 1955.

6. For a concise survey of Civil War finance, see Paul Studenski and Herman Krooss, *Financial History of the United States* (1952), pp. 137–60. The exceptions to the Confederate currency debacle came in *private* wartime note issues in Texas, Louisiana and Arkansas, which depreciated less than did the Confederate currency. Gary Pecquet, "Money in the Trans-Mississippi Confederacy and the Confederate Currency Reform Act of 1864," *EEH,* April 1987.

7. Reuben A. Kessel and Armen Alchian, "Real Wages in the North During the Civil War: Mitchell's Data Reinterpreted," *JLE,* October 1959.

8. Mark Aldrich, "Flexible Exchange Rates, Northern Expansion, and the Market for Southern Cotton: 1866–1879," *JEH,* June 1973.

9. Stephen DeCanio and Joel Mokyr, "Inflation and Wage Lag During the American Civil War," *EEH,* October 1977.

10. Stanley Lebergott shows that Southern cotton planters kept the manpower equivalent of "the entire Confederate army" at home growing cotton and stayed home themselves. "Through the Blockade: The Profitability and Extent of Cotton Smuggling, 1861–1865," *JEH,* December 1981. John James concludes that retiring the debt after the war increased the rate of capital growth in the private sector significantly. Debt retirement policy, in effect, mobilized capital by taking broadly by taxation and transferring narrowly to bondholders. James calls this the "crowding in" effect. The consequences, by increasing productive investment in the private sector (former bondholders now had to invest in the private sector) were to increase the postbellum rate of economic growth. "Public Debt Policy and Nineteenth Century Economic Growth," *EEH,* April 1984, p. 210.

11. Mathew Josephson, *The Robber Barons* (1934).

12. Charles A. Beard and Mary R. Beard, *The Rise of American Civilization* (1930), and Louis Hacker, *The Triumph of American Capitalism* (1940).

13. Stanley Engerman, "The Economic Impact of the Civil War," reprinted in Robert Fogel and Stanley Engerman, eds., *The Reinterpretation of American Economic History* (1971). Gallman's figures are cited p. 371.

14. Engerman, p. 371, note 1.

15. Engerman, p. 373.

16. *Historical Statistics,* series P 17.

17. Engerman, "Economic Impact," p. 374.

18. *Historical Statistics,* series P 231.

19. *Historical Statistics,* series P 227.

20. Engerman, "Economic Impact," p. 376.

21. Cited in Engerman, p. 376.

22. Jeffrey Williamson, "Watersheds and Turning Points: Conjectures on the Long-Term Impact of Civil War Financing," *JEH,* September 1974.

23. A survey of the quantitative research on the economic impact of the Civil War can be found in Patrick O'Brien, *The Economic Effects of the American Civil War* (1988).

24. Jay R. Mandle, "The Plantation States as a Sub-Region of the Post-Bellum South," *JEH,* September 1974. The plantation states are Alabama, Arkansas, Georgia, Louisiana, Mississippi, and South Carolina. Mandle suggests "the possibility that the institutions associated with plantation agriculture might be growth retarding" as a *general* possibility, anywhere in space or time (pp. 737–38).

25. Engerman, "The Economic Impact," pp. 371–72.

26. James L. Sellers, "The Economic Incidence of the Civil War in the South," *Mississippi Valley Historical Review,* September 1927.

27. Roger L. Ransom and Richard Sutch, *One Kind of Freedom: The Economic Consequences of Emancipation* (1977), pp. 108–9.

28. Jonathan Hughes, *Industrialization and Economic History: Theses and Conjectures* (1971), p. 269.

29. Ransom and Sutch, *One Kind of Freedom,* pp. 326–27, n. 30; *Historical Statistics,* series K 555.

30. Ransom and Sutch, p. 192.

31. Gavin Wright, *Political Economy of the Cotton South* (1978). Wright thinks the concentration upon cotton at the expense of other crops resulted from falling prices—an effort to maintain cash income. Ransom and Sutch have a more institutional explanation.

32. *Historical Statistics,* series K 553–54.

33. The student may wish to consider the *entire* contents of the January 1979 issue of *Explorations in Economic History* which has an introduction by William Parker and special papers on the Reconstruction South by Claudia Goldin, Joseph Reid, Peter Temin, Roger Ransom, Richard Sutch and Gavin Wright.

34. Sellers, "The Economic Indigence of the Civil War in the South."

35. Ransom and Sutch, *One Kind of Freedom,* p. 212.

36. Ransom and Sutch, p. 31.

37. Ransom and Sutch, p. 30.

38. Ransom and Sutch, Table F. 2, pp. 258–59.

39. Their estimates range from 28.3 to 37.2 percent as the amount of black labor "withdrawn" from free market. Ransom and Sutch, p. 45; argument about the irrelevance of Southern losses of capital stock, p. 47.

40. Ransom and Sutch, pp. 6–7.
41. Cited in Ransom and Sutch, p. 45.
42. Ransom and Sutch, pp. 78–87.
43. Ransom and Sutch, pp. 89–105, on sharecropping, with examples of agreements.
44. Ransom and Sutch, pp. 71, 79.
45. Nancy Virts, "Estimating the Importance of the Plantation System to Southern Agriculture in 1880," *JEH,* December 1987.
46. Ransom and Sutch, *One Kind of Freedom,* p. 81–87.
47. Gerald David Jaynes provides an interesting interpretation of the emergence of black sharecropping. The slave capital had been transferred to the ex-slave by the emancipation. It was no longer available to the former slave owner as collateral for credit. The black sharecropper, acquiring credit on the promise of his own labor output, was now utilizing that capital as his own collateral. *Branches Without Roots: Genesis of the Black Working Class in the American South* (1986).
48. Ransom and Sutch, *One Kind of Freedom,* p. 104.
49. Joseph Reid, "Sharecropping as an Understandable Market Response: The Postbellum South," *JEH,* March 1973. Robert Higgs, "Race, Tenure and Resource Allocation in Southern Agriculture," *JEH,* March 1973; and "Patterns of Farm Rental in the Georgia Cotton Belt, 1880–1900," *JEH,* June 1974. See Ransom and Sutch, *One Kind of Freedom,* p. 339, note 67, for further discussion.
50. Jonathan Hughes, *Social Control in the Colonial Economy* (1976), p. 57.
51. Stephen DeCanio, "Productivity and Income Distribution in the Post-Bellum South," *JEH,* June 1974.
52. Ransom and Sutch, *One Kind of Freedom,* p. 113, Table 6.4.
53. Ransom and Sutch, p. 129–30.
54. William Brown and Morgan Reynolds, "Debt Peonage Reexamined," *JEH,* December 1973, argue that the rural credit system was not abnormal under the circumstances. They deny the possibility of monopoly power. On a purely theoretical basis, one could doubt Ransom and Sutch and favor Brown and Morgan. One of the present authors, however, has seen a similar institution in action. There is an *intuitive* reason to choose Ransom and Sutch's interpretation.
55. Ransom and Sutch, p. 130. These comparative interest rates are a powerful argument in favor of the territorial monopoly arguments in *One Kind of Freedom.*
56. Ransom and Sutch, ch. 8.
57. Ransom and Sutch, p. 151–59. Wright, and Brown, and Morgan would argue that the force of country finance was not needed. According to them, the South, by growing cotton for cash, was still pursuing comparative advantage. But, if that were so, why the complete turnaround? Before the war, small farmers devoted a relatively small part of their lands to cotton; after the war, a relatively large part. If self-sufficiency paid before 1860, why not afterwards, too? It makes little economic sense to say that Southern farmers became uniquely unable to understand their own self-interest. It was the boll weevil that finally put an end to the system.
58. Why was there no amalgamation? Why not more entry? Why did the local merchants not expand operations? High transactions costs must be the answer. Until communications improved, it paid no one to undertake a business of financial intermediation that required such detailed, strictly local information. Finally, of course, these changes came about. Sufficient banking facilities grew up in rural towns. Farmers could travel to towns, and where there was banking competition, take advantage of it. In part, the phenomenon described so graphically by Ransom and Sutch was a product of three factors: (a) geography, (b) the land tenures adopted to put the postbellum Cotton South under the plough, and (c) the war itself, which destroyed any chance for the antebellum Southern banking system to evolve as the needs of intermediation changed.
59. Suppose one assumed that emphasis shifted to cotton as the expense of food because Southern farmers became more willing to gamble for a good cash-crop year in the competitive economy of postbellum farming. Gavin Wright and Howard Kunreuther, "Cotton, Corn and Risk in the Nineteenth Century," *JEH,* September 1975; Robert McGuire and Robert Higgs, "Cotton, Corn and Risk . . . Another View," *EEH,* April 1977; Wright and Kunreuther, ". . . A Reply," *EEH,* April 1977; Robert McGuire, "A Portfolio Analysis of Crop Diversification and Risk in the Cotton South," *EEH,* October 1980.
60. Robert Higgs, *Competition and Coercion: Blacks in the American Economy, 1865–1914* (1977), for an analysis and survey.
61. Gavin Wright, *Old South, New South: Revolutions in the Southern Economy* (1986).
62. Gavin Wright, "Postbellum Southern Labor Markets," in Peter Kilby, ed., *Quantity and Quiddity: Essays in U.S. Economic History* (1987).
63. For further recent discussion on institutional barriers to progress in the postbellum south and to the 1930s, see Lee Alston and Joseph Ferrie, "Labor Costs, Paternalism, and Loyalty in Southern Agriculture: A Constraint on the Growth of the Welfare State," *JEH,* March 1985; Lee Alston and Joseph Ferrie, "Resisting the Welfare State: Southern Opposition to the Farm Security Administration," *REH,* Supplement 4 (1985); William Phillips, "The Labor Market of Southern Textile Mill Villages:

Some Micro Evidence," *EEH,* April 1986, and Warren C. Whatley, "Southern Agrarian Labor Contracts as Impediments to Cotton Mechanization," *JEH,* March 1987.

64. Stephen DeCanio, *Agriculture in the Postbellum South: The Economics of Production and Supply* (1974), pp. 12–14.

Suggested Readings

Articles

Aldrich, Mark. "Flexible Exchange Rates, Northern Expansion, and the Market for Southern Cotton, 1866–1879." *Journal of Economic History,* vol. XXXIII, no. 2, June 1973.

Alston, Lee J., and Ferrie, Joseph P. "Labor Costs, Paternalism, and Loyalty in Southern Agriculture: A Constraint on the Growth of the Welfare State." *Journal of Economic History,* vol. XLV, no. 1, March 1985.

———. "Resisting the Welfare State: Southern Opposition to the Farm Security Administration." *Research in Economic History,* Supplement 4, (Greenwich, CT: JAI Press 1985).

Brown, William, and Reynolds, Morgan. "Debt Peonage Reconsidered." *Journal of Economic History,* vol. XXXIII, no. 4, December 1973.

Cochran, Thomas. "Did the Civil War Retard Industrialization?" *Mississippi Valley Historical Review,* no. XLVIII, no. 2, September 1961.

DeCanio, Stephen. "Cotton 'Overproduction' and Late Nineteenth-Century Southern Agriculture." *Journal of Economic History,* vol. XXXIII, no. 3, September 1973.

———. "Productivity and Income Distribution in the Post-Bellum South." *Journal of Economic History,* vol. XXXIV, no. 2, June 1974.

———, and Mokyr, Joel. "Inflation and Wage Lag During the American Civil War." *Journal of Economic History,* vol. XXXV, no. 2, June 1975.

Engerman, Stanley. "The Economic Impact of the Civil War." Reprinted in Robert Fogel and Stanley Engerman, eds., *The Reinterpretation of American History.* (New York: Harper & Row, 1971).

Goldin, Claudia, and Lewis, Frank. "The Economic Cost of the American Civil War." *Journal of Economic History,* vol. XXXV, no. 2, June 1975.

Higgs, Robert. "Race, Tenure, and Resource Allocation in Southern Agriculture." *Journal of Economic History,* vol. XXXIII, no. 1, March 1973.

———. "Patterns of Farm Rental in the Georgia Cotton Belt, 1880–1900." *Journal of Economic History,* vol. XXXIV, no. 2, June 1974.

James, John A. "Public Debt Policy and Nineteenth Century Economic Growth." *Explorations in Economic History,* vol. 21, no. 2, April 1984.

Kessel, Reuben, and Alchian, Armen. "Real Wages in the North During the Civil War: Mitchell's Data Reinterpreted." *Journal of Law and Economics,* vol. 2, October 1959.

Lebergott, Stanley. "Through the Blockade: The Profitability and Extent of Cotton Smuggling, 1861–1865." *Journal of Economic History,* vol. XLI, no. 4, December 1981.

Lerner, Eugene. "Money, Wages and Prices in the Confederacy." *Journal of Political Economy,* vol. LXIII, no. 1, February 1955.

Mandle, Jay R. "The Plantation States as a Sub-Region of the Post-Bellum South." *Journal of Economic History,* vol. XXXIV, no. 3, September 1974.

McGuire, Robert A., and Higgs, Robert. "Cotton, Corn, and Risk in the Nineteenth Century: Another View." *Explorations in Economic History,* vol. 14, no. 2, April 1979.

———. "A Portfolio Analysis of Crop Diversification and Risk in the Cotton South." *Explorations in Economic History,* vol. 17, no. 4, October 1980.

Pecquet, Gary M. "Money in the Trans-Mississippi Confederacy and the Confederate Currency Reform Act of 1864." *Explorations in Economic History,* vol. 24, no. 2, April 1987.

Phillips, William H. "The Labor Market of Southern Textile Mill Villages: Some Micro Evidence." *Explorations in Economic History,* vol. 23, no. 2, April 1986.

Ransom, Roger, and Sutch, Richard. "The Impact of the Civil War and of Emancipation on Southern Agriculture." *Explorations in Economic History,* vol. 12, no. 1, January 1975.

Reid, Joseph. "Sharecropping as an Understandable Market Response: The Postbellum South." *Journal of Economic History,* vol. XXXIII, no. 1, March 1973.

Sellers, James L. "The Economic Incidence of the Civil War in the South." *Mississippi Valley Historical Review,* vol. 14, no. 2, September 1927.

Temin, Peter. "The Post-Bellum Recovery of the South and the Cost of the Civil War." *Journal of Economic History,* vol. XXXVI, no. 4, December 1976.

Virts, Nancy. "Estimating the Importance of the Plantation System to Southern Agriculture in 1880." *Journal of Economic History,* vol. XLVII, no. 4, December 1987.

Whatley, Warren C. "Southern Agrarian Labor Contracts as Impediments to Cotton Mechanization." *Journal of Economic History,* vol. XLVII, no. 1, March 1987.

Williamson, Jeffrey. "Watersheds and Turning Points: Conjectures on the Long-Term Impact of Civil War Financing." *Journal of Economic History,* vol. XXXIV, no. 3, September 1974.

Wright, Gavin. "Postbellum Southern Labor Markets." In Peter Kilby, ed. *Quantity and Quiddity: Essays in U.S. Economic History.* Middletown, CT: Wesleyan University Press, 1987.

———, and Kunreuther, Howard. "Cotton, Corn, and Risk in the Nineteenth Century." *Journal of Economic History,* vol. XXXV, no. 3, September 1975.

Books

Andreano, Ralph, ed. *The Economic Impact of the Civil War.* Cambridge, MA: Schenkman, 1964.

Beard, Charles A., and Beard, Mary R. *The Rise of American Civilization.* New York: Macmillan, 1930.

DeCanio, Stephen. *Agriculture in the Postbellum South: The Economics of Production and Supply.* Cambridge: MIT Press, 1974.

Hacker, Louis. *The Triumph of American Capitalism.* New York: Columbia University Press, 1940.

Higgs, Robert. *Competition and Coercion: Blacks in the American Economy, 1865–1914.* New York: Cambridge University Press, 1977.

Jaynes, Gerald David. *Branches Without Roots: Genesis of the Black Working Class in the American South.* New York: Oxford University Press, 1986.

Josephson, Matthew. *The Robber Barons.* New York: Harcourt Brace, 1934.

Lee, Susan Previant, and Passell, Peter. *A New Economic View of American History.* New York: Norton, 1979.

O'Brien, Patrick. *The Economic Effects of the American Civil War.* Atlantic Highlands: Humanities Press International, 1988.

Ransom, Roger L. *Conflict and Compromise: The Political Economy of Slavery, Emancipation, and the American Civil War.* New York: Cambridge University Press, 1989.

———, and Sutch, Richard. *One Kind of Freedom: The Economic Consequences of Emancipation.* New York: Cambridge University Press, 1977.

Stampp, Kenneth. *The Era of Reconstruction, 1865–1877.* New York: Knopf, 1966.

Studenski, Paul, and Krooss, Herman. *Financial History of the United States.* New York: McGraw-Hill, 1952.

Walton, Gary, Sheperd, James, eds. *Explorations in Economic History,* vol 16, no. 1, January 1979.

Woodward, C. Vann. *The Strange Career of Jim Crow.* New York: Oxford University Press, 1966.

Wright, Gavin. *The Political Economy of the Cotton South.* New York: Norton, 1978.

———. *Old South, New South: Revolutions in the Southern Economy.* New York: Basic Books, 1986.

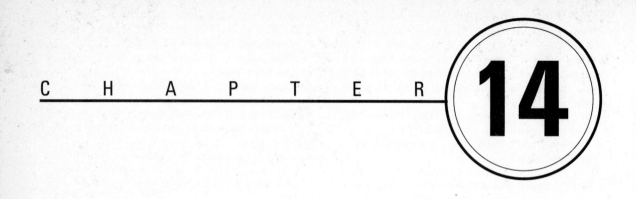

Railroads and Economic Development

We left the building of American railroads in 1860, with a network of rails stretching into the Midwest and South and about 30,000 miles of track in operation, already the most extensive railroad system in any single country. By 1910, the United States had a tremendous 351,767 miles of track on the ground, of which 266,000 miles were main track. It even had far more miles of railroad track than it had of surfaced roads: 204,000 miles.

Constructing the American railroads was such a giant effort that the story of it has become simply overpowering in its influence upon American history. And why indeed not? There had never before been anything like it. A whole continent was bound together by steam engines and bands of steel. The products of farm and factory, thousands of miles apart in their origins, were now easily mixed in the country's new establishments of manufacturing and distribution. Via the railroads, which connected the interior to the ports and docks, the produce of the whole economy could now regularly and conveniently reach the world. Isolation in the United States was almost a thing of the past. The river steamers and canal barges seemed (to many writers)

almost as remote as the era of the pyramids. The railroad had written a new chapter in world history.

In recent years, reexamination of the railroads and American economic growth with quantitative methods has concluded that far too much interpretive weight has been placed on the railroad by economists and historians, to the detriment of our understanding of economic development processes. The purpose of dismantling the legend of the railroad was not debunking for its own sake. It was a necessary next step, once economists and historians had concentrated their attention on the mysteriously different histories of world economic development after World War II.

With the United Nations attempting to spread knowledge of economic development to the world at large, scholars in those countries that had created high per capita incomes, who had largely taken such progress for granted, began to investigate their own records of economic growth. Some countries were (and still are) desperately poor; some relatively rich. Why? Modern technology is available to all. Was there some magical element in the past histories of the industrial nations that explained their success? The rich countries of the West all shared a history of extensive "railroadization" in the nineteenth century that ran parallel to their own industrialization. Was this the answer?

The income effects of the railroad investment—for example, industries of railroad supply and control that were stimulated by railroad expenditures, users of railroad transport that were supplied with regular and dependable communications—all suggested an obvious key. In the histories of the main industrial countries of the West—the United Kingdom, France, the United States—and in eastern Europe, Russia, and Japan, the processes of railroad building seemed to be central explanatory themes, the indispensable factor that led the way to all other forms of modernization. Would a new railway system in east Africa produce the same progressive side effects? And if not, why not?

The importance of such considerations caused the work of Robert Fogel and Albert Fishlow on American railroads to hit the history and economics professions like a bombshell.[1] When the scholarly fallout finally settled, many of their colleagues realized that successful economic development had not been achieved cheaply in the United States by the concentrated development of a single sector or a few "leading" sectors, even one as basic as transportation. In the end, these economists and historians began to worry about "human capital," honest and efficient government, and agriculture—to the great delight of those who had never accepted the railroad story.

COMPLETION OF THE RAIL NETWORK

Looking back at the era of American railroad construction, we are struck by the hurly-burly pace. It is a prime example of the way "waves" of innovation have come to the American economy. Under *free capitalism,* which means that the returns accrue to the entrepreneurs, and with no limit placed by government or other planning agencies on profit levels, high profit prospects in an innovative sector (such as the railroad) attract capital and enterprise. The sector expands until the prospective returns fall back to the competitive level. If there is a government subsidy involved (as in the case of the railroads), the rush to invest is that much greater.

During the period of entrepreneurial exhilaration, when high profits beckon, the innovative sector grows

in a spectacular way. The tobacco culture of the colonial South, the slave-worked cotton culture, the steam engine applied to industry, the westward movement of Northern farmers, the railroads, the application of electricity to industry and households, the automobile culture in the 1920s, television after World War II, electronics, fast-food chains—all are examples of the explosive surges of innovation that have influenced American economic growth.

Somehow, the historian must give credit where it is due without being swept away by the glamour of the great innovative sectors in their time. Some sectors grow, and some decline and vanish, even while spectacular innovations or waves of innovations dominate. The phenomenon of simultaneous growth and decline is well known to scholars. Pioneering studies of it were published half a century ago by Simon Kuznets and Arthur F. Burns.[2] Growth is the algebraic sum of expansions and contractions over time. Joseph Schumpeter's great work on secular growth and the pattern of cycles was powerfully influenced by these great innovative waves.[3] Others followed his lead.[4] Schumpeter argued that the innovative waves were necessary to offset stagnant tendencies among the older and more conservative sectors of the economy. The railroad in the late nineteenth century seemed an indisputably dominating innovative sector.

The Pace and Pattern of Construction

In Table 14.1 we see the growth of the railroads from 1860. The main-track mileage rose until World War I, when the railroads, in precarious financial condition, were taken over by the federal government on national defense grounds. After the war, financial troubles mounted, and the huge system went into a financial decline that continues to the present time. Abandoned lines became a serious problem in the early 1920s; *total* mileage—including main-track, yards, and sidings—reached a peak of 429,883 miles in 1929 (17 times the earth's circumference) and then began to decline as abandonments exceeded new construction. By then, the automobile and truck had cut into railroad growth prospects, and air travel was on the horizon.

Half the main-track mileage existing in 1915 had been built between 1885 and 1915. Professor Fishlow's study of construction patterns within the sector revealed three major waves in the late nineteenth

Table 14.1   Main Track Railroad Mileage
Operated 1860–1915

Year	Mileage[a]	Year	Mileage[b]
1860	30.6	**1890**	166.7
1865	35.1	**1895**	180.7
1870	52.9	**1900**	193.3
1875	74.1	**1905**	218.1
1880	93.3	**1910**	240.3
1885	128.3	**1915**	253.8

[a] Amounts given are in thousands of miles of track.
[b] After 1890, yard tracks and sidings omitted from amount.

Source: *Historical Statistics*, series Q 287, 321.

recovery, railroad construction boomed again. The twentieth-century crises of 1903 and 1907, dramatic as they were, failed to stop the railroad expansion: The downturn of 1929–32 did, but by then new competing forms of transportation were eating into revenues.

The regional construction patterns in the Fishlow postbellum waves are illustrated by Figure 14.1. The railroad is largely a piece of continuous, linear physical capital. Since population and economic activity (the sources of freight earnings) are not homogeneously distributed, the financial prospects and problems of the different lines varied in a bewildering way. Also, the geography of the United States placed practical limits on the routes the roads could take across the continent.

All these considerations had their effects on the financial histories of the different railroad systems, and it is most hazardous to attempt to generalize about them. For example, Figure 14.1 shows that the

century: 1868–73, 1879–83, and 1886–92. Since the railroads were built primarily with borrowed money, it is not surprising that these construction booms were terminated by the major financial crises of 1873, 1882, and 1893. However, each time the economy began a

Figure 14.1   Three Postbellum Railroad Construction Booms by Region

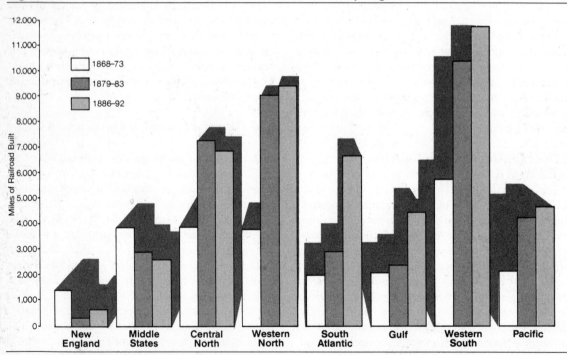

Source: Albert Fishlow, "Internal Transportation," Lance E. Davis, et al., *American Economic Growth* (New York: Harper & Row, 1972), Table 13.12.

Regional figures for miles of railroads built between 1868 and 1892 show that the country's vast midsection—both north and south—the Far West, the Southwest, and the Pacific states dominated. By 1868, the eastern tracks, apart from the South Atlantic region, had been built for the most part.

postbellum railroad construction booms occurred mainly in the southwestern and northwestern regions. In these areas distances were vast, and railroads had to be long to exist at all. Yet, miles of track does not indicate financial success. Fishlow points out that in 1873, measured by earnings, the northeastern region had 60 percent of the nation's effective railroad service.[5] With its concentrated populations and relatively heavy industrialization, the northeastern region generated massive revenues. Because the area was small and compact, and little new construction was needed to earn a dollar compared to, say, western Nebraska, success or failure depended upon management.

James J. Hill's Great Northern railroad never went bankrupt. The Union Pacific, reorganized by Edward Harriman in 1897, went from years of bankruptcy to unexampled financial success. By 1906, its dividend was 10 percent, and Harriman had made a killing. Besides financial reorganization, Harriman had carried out a huge program of physical reconstruction of the old "rusted streak of iron."[6] The Erie, on the other hand, was in continuous bankruptcy for generations, despite its advantageous location. Its early financial management, led by James Fisk and Jay Gould, reigns as one of the most scandalous in U.S. financial history.

Success or failure depended upon a combination of building costs, the character of the financial structure, management, freight returns, and economic development along the lines as well as terminal link-ups with other systems of transport. After the 1893 panic, 153 U.S. railroads were in bankruptcy, each for its own reasons. As we will see, Robert Fogel found that the Union Pacific's freight earnings could easily have justified its great cost of construction, despite the amount of its track that ran through empty deserts.[7] Its bankruptcy in 1895, as Harriman showed, was due to poor management.

Land Grants and Construction

In Chapter 9, we discussed the question of private-sector finance versus government construction aid in railroad building and whether governments cleverly seduced railroad builders with subsidies or railroad builders demanded and got government aid where their own money was at greater risk. The practice (whichever it was!) continued at the national level, with the giant federal land grants after the Civil War. Following the

Illinois Central railroad grants in 1851, Congress gave 100 million acres to the four transcontinental roads alone, 10 percent of the public domain, to encourage railroad construction. Land grants by the federal government to all railroads totaled 131 million acres, and the states added an additional 49 million acres to spur on the railroads. Figure 14.2 shows where that land was located, and there can be little doubt that the object was to tie the country together internally by rail.[8]

The land grants tended to be in areas where the greatest mileage was added (see Figure 14.1 on page 256). The federal subsidy produced railroad *construction,* at least. According to Lloyd Mercer, the railroad grants had the intended effect but may not have been the most efficient kind of subsidy.[9] However, land is what governments had in abundance, and if construction was the object of the land grants, the huge railroad mileage measured the success of policy. In 1869, the first transcontinental link was forged at Promontory Point, Utah, when two heavily subsidized roads, the Central Pacific (building eastward) and the Union Pacific (building westward), met. Other transcontinental roads, north and south, followed in succeeding years. The policy of railroad land grants was both praised and criticized as the crucial government subsidy, or giveaway (depending on your position), without which the transcontinental roads might not have been built.

Despite the appalling financial history of the railroads, the effort has been seen by most historians as praiseworthy. Over much of their routes, the transcontinental roads were built "ahead of demand" by public resources, and the whole country benefitted in subsequent years as the land was settled, bankrupt railroads were reorganized, and freights were increased. That favorable interpretation has occupied American historians ever since.[10] As Stanley Engerman emphasizes, the problems involved in estimating the social gains and costs, compared to the sum of the gain and opportunity costs to both builders and users of railroads, leaves the issues of social profitability and equity involved in the land-grant policies wide open.[11]

RAILROADS AND ECONOMIC GROWTH

Probably no single investigation in economic history since World War II has had a greater impact on the *techniques* of research and analysis than that of Robert

Figure 14.2   Federal Land Grants for Railroads

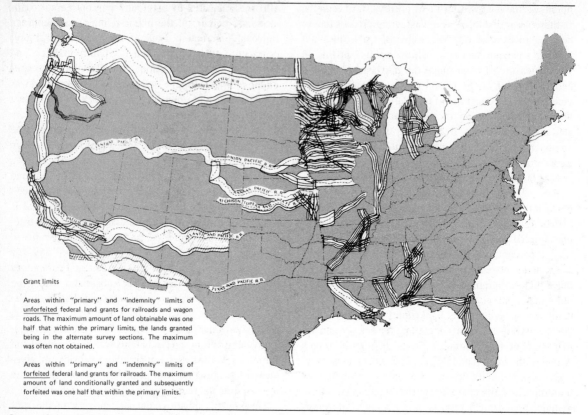

Grant limits

Areas within "primary" and "indemnity" limits of
<u>unforfeited</u> federal land grants for railroads and wagon
roads. The maximum amount of land obtainable was one
half that within the primary limits, the lands granted
being in the alternate survey sections. The maximum
was often not obtained.

Areas within "primary" and "indemnity" limits of
<u>forfeited</u> federal land grants for railroads. The maximum
amount of land conditionally granted and subsequently
forfeited was one half that within the primary limits.

Source: Charles O. Paullin, *Atlas of the Historical Geography of the United States* (Washington, D.C. and New York: Carnegie Institution and
the American Geographical Society of New York, 1932), plate 56D.

Fogel, published in 1964, to estimate the quantitative
importance of nineteenth-century railroads to overall
economic growth. The next year, Albert Fishlow's
book on antebellum railroads appeared. Both studies
downgraded the railroad as *the* overwhelming influence on nineteenth-century U.S. economic growth. The
drama was no doubt heightened because one of Fogel's
main targets was W. W. Rostow, a distinguished economic historian whose own work largely dominated
the writing of economic history in the 1940s and
1950s. Rostow's work was a pioneering effort to employ economic theory to interpret history.

Rostow and Leading Sectors

Fogel's and Fishlow's contributions to our understanding of American economic history are best appreciated
if we consider, first, the work of Professor Rostow and

some of his predecessors and, second, the reasons for
their views. The story really begins with the generally
unsuccessful efforts of earlier generations of economists to explain the causes of the cyclical growth that
characterized the nineteenth-century capitalist nations.
There is a huge, and now largely unread, literature
from these earlier efforts. Expansions and contractions
of the business cycle had been explained by an extraordinary range of causes, running from sunspots and
"manias" to cyclical changes in such "real" factors as
harvests and, of course, the condition of the money
supply and the practices of bankers.[12] Then, the appearance of John Maynard Keynes' *General Theory of
Employment, Interest, and Money* in 1936 riveted attention upon investment and its determinants.

In 1939, the young Paul Samuelson showed that the
cycle could be generated by a simple combination of
two economic phenomena, the *accelerator* and the

multiplier, both of which represented known real phenomena.[13] The **multiplier,** the relationship between changes in initial expenditures and ultimate income, determined by society's consumption and saving habits, had figured centrally in Keynes' *General Theory.* The main expenditure whose variations over time combined the right amount of volatility, cyclical timing, and relations with price and monetary phenomena was private investment. The **accelerator** was a secondary investment effect, induced investment brought about by the using up of excess capacity in expansions. New capacity had to be created, and that was brought about by added investment and more income effects.

Now, *investment,* the value of GNP (or of net national product if capital depletion is taken into account) not utilized as consumption goods or for government expenditure in a given period, is a real thing. To understand the historic role of investment, one must identify the kinds of investments being made—cotton textile machinery and factories in one epoch, railroads or steel mills in another—and why. It was seen that in different cycles over time, different types of real investment came to the fore since technology changed over time and so did consumer tastes.

In a capitalist economy investment is made by private persons. Here Joseph Schumpeter's ideas were crucial. Since the publication of his *Theory of Economic Development* (1914), Schumpeter had emphasized the central role played by the entrepreneur, the individual capitalist who introduced change into the flow of economic life in the form of new commodities, techniques, and ideas in pursuit of his own private gain.[14] The result of all such entrepreneurial activity was the *economic change* that, in fact, occurred. The history of industrial development is filled with great entrepreneurial figures, from James Watt to Henry Ford.

In 1939 Schumpeter had pieced together a lifetime's research in his great two-volume *Business Cycles,* in which the innovative entrepreneur played the central role in determining the direction of investment. The cyclical quantitative results had already been shown by Samuelson. All that was left was the later emphasis upon the net results over time: economic growth.

Subsequent detailed studies of cycles by economists seemed to justify identification of each cyclical upsurge with innovative industries that pulled in resources and produced net growth over time. An influential article by Leland Hamilton Jenks showed a very close identity between the timing of waves of

railroad building and the general business cycle.[15] The inference drawn was that causation ran from the railroads to the cycle, and not that railroad construction passively reflected general movement in the economy. Again, investment was the centerpiece.

Rostow's own *British Economy of the Nineteenth Century* (1948) and his collaborative work with A. D. Gayer and Anna J. Schwartz, *The Growth and Fluctuation of the British Economy 1790–1850* (1953), emphasized the determinants of investment and the time pattern of industrial change produced by those activities.[16] Then, in his *Process of Economic Growth* (1953), Rostow developed his "leading sector" thesis, which suggests that the major growth episodes in cyclical history are motivated by the income effects emanating from the booming innovative sectors.[17] So far, so good.

In 1960 Rostow went a step further and developed a generalized "explanation sketch" of economic development, *The Stages of Economic Growth: A Non-Communist Manifesto.*[18] Central to Rostow's general scheme was the idea of *take-off,* the point at which each economy could sustain a sufficient ratio of investment to income to propel it (via multiplier-accelerator interactions) into the career of secular economic progress that characterized all industrial countries. Innovation and resulting leading sectors continued the process.

Rostow's work integrated decades of progress on the understanding of cycles and growth. He then charted out the main historical outlines of the process in several countries. In the case of the United States, the take-off occurred in the final decades before the Civil War, and investment in railroads was "indispensable" to the process. The railroads consumed iron, labor, and fuel; spun off other innovations; reduced transportation costs; and quickly developed into giant companies with vast resources, thus dominating the era. What was begun before 1860 continued through the rest of the century. For Schumpeter, painting on a huge historical canvas, the long cycle beginning in 1875 was due to the "railroadization of the world." Rostow's "stages" scheme and leading sector idea identified a similar process earlier in the American economy.

Fogel and Fishlow

How big would an indispensable leading sector be? What proportion of the GNP was indeed produced by all railroad activity in the nineteenth century? Providing precise answers to these questions was the ambition of both Fogel and Fishlow in their separate research efforts.

The initial results were a shock, forcing a total reappraisal of our ideas about the country's growth in the nineteenth century. Fogel began his work to demonstrate by econometric methods how right the traditional view of the "railroadization of the world" really was. He wanted to nail down the numbers once and for all. No one was more dismayed that Fogel was at first with the results. No statement was more repeated and less questioned by historians than that railroad construction had played a central role in the growth of the iron and steel industries. The reverse was just axiomatic: Where would the iron industry have been without the iron road? Douglass North, in 1961, had shown that in the year 1860 railroad iron brought the iron industry no more revenues than did sales of iron to make iron stoves.[19] On that basis, could you make any generalizations?

Fogel focused on railroad iron used, taking into account the scrapping and re-rolling of old rails. Of the total pig iron produced between 1840 and 1860, railroad production used less than 5 percent.[20] It seemed that 95 percent of iron output went elsewhere. Economic historians had to think about that one. The weight of iron nails used in building construction, Fogel discovered, was greater than the weight of iron used in the railroads.[21] If the railroads had played as dominant a role in the demand for iron as had been believed by even the most eminent historians, the iron industry would have gotten nowhere.

What about coal? The coal used to make iron for rails was less than 6 percent of total coal output.[22] The wood requirement (all those ties) for the railroads were an almost inconsequential part of total lumber production. As Fogel put it: "The modest position of railroads in the market for lumber products emphasizes the scale of lumber consumption by other sectors of the economy."[23]

In 1859 the value of output of railroad equipment was only a quarter of the market value of all transportation equipment produced. Railroads accounted for a mere 6 percent of the output of machinery. Fogel concluded that in 1859 output generated by the railroads accounted for less than 4 percent of the GNP.[24]

What was the opportunity cost of the railroads? Perhaps they were like imported coffee beans: expensive, but much less so than if they had been grown in Kansas in greenhouses. Perhaps the service provided by the railroad was much cheaper than an equivalent amount of wagon and canal service would have been. Perhaps, then, the *real and indispensable* contribution of the railroad was determined by what it would have cost to haul wagons, build canals, and navigate rivers over the ground covered by the railroad system. The difference between that figure and the actual cost of using the railroads is the **social savings** to the economy of the railroads. Fishlow, in his careful study of the antebellum railroads, estimated the social savings of the railroads at 4 percent of GNP in 1859. There followed the great railroad construction booms. With the huge system of 1890 in place, how much had the picture changed? (Remember, *all* of the economy had grown.) Fogel found that the social savings from railroads in 1890 was less than 5 (actually 4.7) percent of GNP.[25]

Fogel's investigation produced a methodological revolution in the study of economic history. He made elaborate **counterfactual** (plausible, but not factual) expansions of canal, river, and wagon transport to replace the railroads that had actually been built and then studied the differences in costs and benefits. Three-quarters of the farm output of 1890 took place within 40 miles of navigable (or potentially navigable) water, a manageable distance by wagon. So, the epic stories about opening the land with the iron horse on prairie, farm, and mountain valley had to be diluted. It *could* have happened otherwise. Fogel concluded that without the railways, the GNP of 1890 would not have been reached until 1892.[26]

The "greatest" innovation of the nineteenth century, steam traction applied to land transport, was only one piece of the total mosaic of economic growth. The unexampled economic expansion of the nineteenth-century United States was not due to railroads in the way we had believed; they were "indispensable" only if you wanted 1892 GNP as early as 1890. Other scholars, studying comparative railroad productivity, showed that the roads were unremarkable in that regard. This is not surprising, since they were, in the main, a huge application of contemporary technology.[27]

Salvaging the Myth

No one who has studied the nineteenth century, in this country or in other countries, would conclude that the railroads were not in some sense a "leading sector." Neither Fishlow nor Fogel would be willing to relegate them to the dustbin of history, even though they have been lowered drastically in our estimation as growth producers. After all, 5 percent of GNP is a *very large* percent for a single industry. No single industry in this country today accounts for anything like that proportion of total output.

As Alfred Chandler emphasized, the railroads were our first giant enterprises.[28] Their management problems and methods sent all U.S. industrial entrepreneurs to school. Their securities were for some time the dominant commodity traded in the growing U.S. capital markets. Their relentless expansion in good times, for such a long time, helped establish the nineteenth-century American ethos of boundless growth and opportunity. But they were perhaps *too* visible. The growth of an entire economy is a complex phenomenon, involving all the inputs.

However, pursuing angles others ignored, Jeffrey Williamson argues that in various intervals up to 1890 the railroads perhaps could have enhanced the nation's growth by more than is implied by Fogel's calculation of the social savings. Williamson emphasizes that the growth of agricultural products would not have occurred without the construction of the railroads in the West. So, following Williamson, the railroads were more "indispensable" than Fogel would allow.[29]

Oddly enough, the railroads were not even "indispensable" in the evolution of public policy toward big business. It is easily shown that law and practice growing out of the government regulation of the railroads was already extant from past legal history.[30] But, what happened in the area of public policy happened *as it did* largely because of the nation's experience with the railroads. There, without question, the railroads left an indelible mark on U.S. history.

RAILROADS AND THE ATTACK ON BIG BUSINESS

The railroads in the late nineteenth century placed all sorts of dramatic problems on the public table. When those problems were solved, there was really no way that the railroads could go on as ordinary, free capitalistic, business ventures. They had entered that gray area of combined private ownership and government regulation. But, in reality, it is hard to imagine any other fate for them, for several reasons.

1. The railroads were *all* government creatures—they were publicly licensed corporations with the accompanying privileges and liabilities. They were extensions of the sovereign power, having even the right of eminent domain over the property of others. Their government sponsorship, while necessary and profitable, left them singularly vulnerable to changes in, or additions to, public policy—politics.

2. They had been built with government subsidies and land grants in large part and came to be seen as unfairly privileged.

3. Competing, parallel lines and rate wars were loathed by railroad management, yet consolidations and amalgamations tended to establish regional monopolies that were easy targets of public complaint.

4. Their natural oligopolistic tendencies—rate-fixing pools to "stabilize" revenues, rate discriminations and kickbacks, the normal activities of the discriminating monopolist—left their managements very far from common notions of fair play, then and now.

5. Like the modern auto, they went from a novelty to a necessity basis, and their activities came to be seen as the public's business.

There is one other reason why the railroads met the fate they did. Those who built them included a fair share of notorious scoundrels and rough characters whose careers, attitudes, and *nouveau riche* lifestyles got them little public sympathy. In some cases the leading railroad figures had reputations little better than those of common criminals. The railroads were easy targets of public hatred, and when the time came, they became simply puppets of public policy. The problem was that policy had no particular object to it. The great railroad system became a pitiful giant whose future was to be determined by the vagaries of politics and public opinion.

The Monopoly Issue

Strictly speaking, a *monopolist* is a single seller. It is true that along the isolated trunk lines, there was only one railroad. If you bought the railroad's services, you were buying a monopoly service. What would the monopoly price be? For the railroad, with many kinds of services for many kinds of customers, there was the tantalizing prospect of attempting to be the perfectly discriminating monopolist, to provide services at varying prices to all who applied. The old rule-of-thumb in railroad pricing was to "charge what the traffic will bear." How much is that? Theoretically, the *potential revenue* is equal to the area under the railroad's demand curve, if you ignore the problem of the railroad's costs, which we will do for a moment.

In Figure 14.3, the first panel shows a monopolist who has found the point of maximum total revenue in the market if the monopolist charges a single price for service. That price is p_1 for quantity q_1. Total revenue, price times quantity, is the square op_1aq_1. Demand above that price is *elastic:* a price increase will bring a disproportional decrease in the quantity purchased, and total revenue will fall. At any price below p_1, the demand is *inelastic:* a reduction in price will not be compensated for by the increase in the quantity purchased; therefore, total revenue will fall. The demand curve shows *all* prices and quantities wanted by the railroad's customers. If the monopolist takes the maximum revenue at the single price p_1, the monopolist still

"loses" revenues p_1p_2a (upper triangle, those customers all paid p_1, but each would have been willing to pay more) and revenues q_1aq_2 (lower triangle, those customers didn't buy at all).

Now, the thinking monopolist must regret those revenue losses. If the monopolist's variable cost is small for additional service (typical of railroads, an extraordinarily large part of their total costs are fixed), the monopolist may begin to think about picking off those triangles by providing services to all potential customers at prices they are willing to pay, instead of just charging one price, p_1.

Think of modern "deregulated" airline fares. We see surcharges for top service, "supersavers" for cheap seats, and cheaper round-trip fares from New York to Los Angeles than from Chicago to Bozeman, Montana. Ideally, the perfectly discriminating monopolist could pick off every customer at the monopolist's demand price, and total revenue would become op_2q_2 in panel (a), op_1q_1 in panel (b). The perfectly discriminating monopolist serves everyone at his or her demand prices; the price charged is all of "what the traffic will

Figure 14.3   Two Cases of Monopoly Pricing

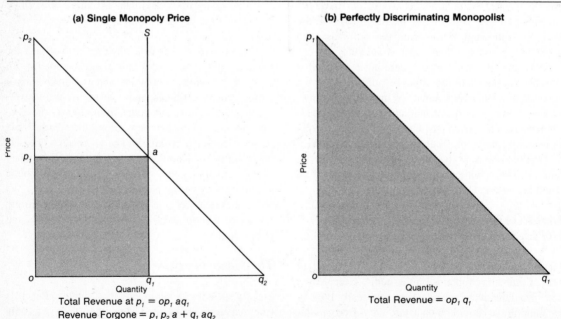

Total Revenue at $p_1 = op_1, aq_1$
Revenue Forgone $= p_1 p_2 a + q_1 aq_2$

Total Revenue $= op_1 q_1$

In panel (a) the single price p_1 produces total revenue op_1aq_1. The triangles p_1p_2a and q_1aq_2 are potential revenues not captured. All prices along the demand schedule could be captured by the perfectly discriminating monopolist, panel (b), who is able to charge every buyer his precise demand price.

bear.'' The railroad creates external economies, and the object of the discriminating monopolist is to internalize these at the expense of his customers.[31]

There is no record of a perfectly discriminating monopolist operating in the real world on the scale of a railroad. Country doctors (knowing their patients' wealth and incomes) who fit their fees to their patients' abilities to pay, would be a close approximation. Charging what the traffic will bear is the nearest thing, in the real world, to perfect monopoly discrimination for the old-time railroads. They charged lower rates in areas where there was competition, higher rates where there was none. Rebates were given to the larger customers, who could go elsewhere for service; higher rates were charged for short hauls than for long ones—the whole bag of tricks.[32] Airlines do it now, and railroads did it then. The resulting outcry from disgruntled shippers and travelers produced government regulation.

To be fair, the railroads tried to solve the problems of pricing their services through mutual consultation and cooperation. Where Mammon got the upper hand, they resorted to conspiracy. Professor Tom Ulen has recently shown us that some price cartels were long-lasting and relatively stable, despite a great temptation for cartel members to cheat, to shave prices below cartel levels.[33] There were many such price-fixing rings among the old railroads.

The economist's rule-of-thumb, that the competitive (and therefore ''fair'') price is always equal to marginal cost, was of no help to the railroads. Imagine two passengers waiting for a train in Wolf City, Wyoming. They buy two tickets to Omaha, Nebraska, and stand on a Union Pacific station platform. The train stops. How much should the first passenger pay? What is the marginal cost of the second ticket? Is it different from that of the first one? Now multiply this problem across all stations, all passengers, and all types of freight, and you can understand why no one—railroad owners, judges, state or Interstate Commerce Commission officials—*ever* figured out what were fair or ''reasonable'' rates for railroad service.

Edward Harriman, our greatest railroad financier by a country mile, once tried to defend his own rate-setting policies by a unique standard, the maximum (presumably) rates that his customers could afford to pay him and still be competitive in their own markets.

It would be suicidal for a railroad to throttle or paralyze the industries along its lines by charging exorbitant rates. Even if there be no direct competition by parallel roads, every industrial plant located along a line of railroad is competing with plants located on other lines, and every railroad is forced to make such low and reasonable rates as will permit the industries in the territory tributary to it to make sales in competitive markets, and thus furnish the traffic from which the railroad company derives its earnings. It is impossible for a railroad company to sever its interests from those of its patrons.[34]

The trouble with this standard, apart from its vagueness and irrelevance for the discriminating monopolist (customers' demand prices already reflect their own competitive positions), is that the customers still knew they were vulnerable to rate-setting agreements among the railroads. These agreements allowed *all* rates or particular classes of rates to be raised in unison, thus transferring income *en masse* from railroad users to railroad owners. Cartels could still work perfectly. Because railroads are necessarily vulnerable to political pressure, the result was public regulation.

The Coming of Regulation

By 1890 we had about 1000 separate railroad companies. Together, they were the railroad system, moving goods and people across the land. Were they really supposed to operate like 1000 corner grocery stores, without mutual evaluation and collaboration? These companies were the survivors of a colorful and chaotic past that had included incredible episodes like the Susquehanna War (in which rival railroad investors hired small armies of toughs to fight it out for physical control of railroad property). They had allegedly bribed judges and individual politicians and ''salted'' whole legislatures. They had purposely built lines parallel to each other to engage in rate wars and takeovers. Despite their collective vigor, many, including huge systems like the Union Pacific, had finally become financial basket cases, ruining thousands of investors in the process. Their discriminatory rate-setting practices had made many enemies.

The Granger Cases

Public antagonism to these new corporate giants was not long in coming.[35] In the 1870s the state legislatures

Railroad Expansion. The railroads engaged the country's resources to expand commerce. From Chinese laborers building the roads (above left) and the business talents of railroad agents (below left), the railroads soon carried western products to eastern markets for consumption and export. The Grangers believed the cost of transportation was too high relative to the value of the products, as shown in this 1873 cartoon "The Grange Awakening the Sleepers" (below right). In the case of *Munn v Illinois*, the Supreme Court confirmed the right of states to regulate commerce because, at the connection between rail and lake transport in Chicago (above right), the grain elevators stood astride the very "gateway of commerce."

passed laws to allow state agencies to control various aspects of railroad operation, including rate setting. The railroads fought this kind of regulation in the courts, and in the fall of 1876 five of these cases reached the U.S. Supreme Court together and became known as the "Granger Cases." They were called such because they were largely the result of farmer discontent, focused by the National Grange leaders of the period. (Granges were local organizations of farmers that were originally established for social and educational purposes. They became political forums and channels for farmer protest—the railroad being a frequent adversary.) The cases were: (a) *Munn* v *Illinois;* (b) *Chicago, Burlington, and Quincy Railroad* v *Iowa;* (c) *Peik* v *Chicago and Northwestern Railroad;* (d) *Chicago, Milwaukee, and St. Paul Railroad* v *Ackley;* and (e) *Winona and St. Peter Railroad* v *Blake.*[36]

The five cases were reported out in March 1877, and, one sees in retrospect, they sealed the fate of the U.S. railroad system. The court covered all five cases in its ruling in *Munn* v *Illinois,* which was actually a case involving a grain elevator. But the rule of *Munn* was then applied by the court across the board to the four railroad cases. Even though *Munn* became inoperative for railroads a decade later (because of *Wabash* v *Illinois,* discussed in the next section), the principle that railroads were unquestionably subject to permanent regulation remained.

We already noted (in Chapter 6) the legal foundations of public control over private property employed in business ventures. The railroads in the Granger decision were seen as private property that had mutated into public property. Chief Justice Waite ruled that any business firm whose property and activities were crucial to the public at large, "clothed in the public interest," was, by ancient tradition, subject to government regulation. The relevant level of government in the *Munn* ruling was state government. By 1886, there were 25 state railroad commissions.

Wabash, Legal Persons, and the ICC

In 1886, a Supreme Court decision involving discriminatory pricing (our discriminating monopolist at work), *Wabash, St. Louis, and Pacific Railroad* v *Illinois,* set the stage for federal regulation. The Supreme Court held that the railroads, being mainly in interstate commerce, were only properly subject to congressional regulation on their interstate business, under the federal Constitution's commerce clause. In the same year, in *Santa Clara County* v *Southern Pacific Railroad,* special local taxes on railroad property were held to be in violation of the Fourteenth Amendment, the protection of the property of "persons" from state power without due process of law.[37] The amendment was meant to protect the property of former slaves, and the Court simply defined the Southern Pacific Corporation as a legal person. The marvelous subtlety of the legal mind in this decision did nothing for the image of the railroads in that Populist era.

The timing was accidental but historically fateful. A year later, in 1887, the Interstate Commerce Commission (ICC) was established by Congress, at first without the power to set railroad rates. The ICC was the first permanent independent federal regulatory agency, and its founding marked the beginning of a kind of federal government power capable of almost infinite expansion. Noted historian Gabriel Kolko, and others, have argued that the railroad operators saw the Commission as an opportunity to coerce the federal power into solving the problems of cartel management.[38] The ICC could provide a national and federally funded forum for the railroad interest. The ICC was, in this view, the first case of the "capture" of a regulatory commission by the regulatees.

In 1898, the case of *Smythe* v *Ames* was seen initially as a solution to the dilemmas of rate setting that had been attempted by the courts. The standard set was that the rates were to be sufficient to provide a "fair" rate of return upon investment.[39] This apparent solution in fact merely shifted the ground, since the question now became valuation of railroad assets: whether original or replacement cost was to form the rate base. In 1906, the power to set maximum rates was given to the ICC by the Hepburn Act.

Martin and the Capture Thesis

How did the "captured" federal control agency act? Were rates raised sufficiently to guarantee profitable operation? Here the work of Professor Albro Martin is crucial evidence. Martin, in *Enterprise Denied,* shows that the ICC, if it was captured by anyone, was captured by the users of the railroads—passengers and shippers.[40] As prices rose after 1896, railroad rates fell behind, first because of rate setting by the courts, then by the ICC. After the Hepburn Act, the ICC refused to grant the rate increases the railroads said they needed. According to Martin, repair and replacement of capital equipment could not be sustained and by 1914, the railroads were financially strapped and physically disabled. This set the stage for the federal takeover in 1917 in the interest of national defense.

The Sherman Act and the Long Future

In the *Northern Securities* case in 1904, the Sherman Antitrust Act was employed to block the formation of a giant holding company uniting the interests of the Union Pacific, Northern Pacific, Great Northern, and Burlington roads.[41] The Court argued that such a combine would tend to reduce competition. In 1913, the 1901 purchase and reorganization of the Southern Pacific railroad by Harriman's Union Pacific was dissolved on similar lines—that Harriman's last masterpiece of organization reduced competition.[42] Railroad amalgamation seemed a natural course for railroads all over the world since economic forces were propelling railroads in all the major countries toward fewer operating units, and finally, state monopoly ownership. Application of the Sherman Act, and after World War I, the lodging of veto power over railroad mergers in the hands of the ICC, meant that railroad amalgamation here would not proceed at the pace it had in Europe.

Use of the Sherman Act in its early years to constrain railroad amalgamation reflected, in those days, an understandable fear of monopoly, even government-regulated monopoly. But this left the railroads dependent upon government initiative for the future, where the scale economies and externalities to be gained by car pooling, terminal sharing, and continuous service were concerned. That initiative was sluggish and only in our own time, through government subsidies, planning, and management, were amalgamation and rationalization finally carried out on the scale that the old-time tycoons had tried in the Northern Securities Trust. Amtrak and other government-sponsored and subsidized systems designed to save the remnants of the great railroad network seem to summon up the ghosts of Harriman, Hill, and Pierpont Morgan for one last cheer. By the 1960s when Amtrak was organized, the American railroad system was mainly an area of financial desperation.[43]

We will never know if the American railroad system could have been anything but what it became because government regulation was imposed so early, and continuously. Some, like Martin, argue that the railroads were never given the chance. On the other hand, Henry Ford, who bought a railroad, ran it on *his* principles, made it profitable, and was forced by the ICC to sell it, argued that *both* the traditional railroad management and the government control agency were utterly incompetent. He may well have been correct. His brief experience as a railroad magnate is the one example we have of a modern railroad run on straight, twentieth-century business principles, without regulation, without collusive arrangements with other roads, and with no unions or work rules. Ford was satisfied with his little railroad, but the ICC was outraged.[44]

We never followed the Populist demands and nationalized the railroad system. To this day, American railroads are privately owned, although management remains largely a creature of regulatory agencies. The main problem with the method we used, private ownership and development on the one hand and government control on the other, is that no one got what they wanted from the great railroad system—not the investors in the railroad companies, not their management, not their users, and not the government since it really never had a policy.

Notes

1. Robert W. Fogel, *Railroads and American Economic Growth: Essays in Econometric History* (1964); Albert Fishlow, *American Railroads and the Transformation of the Ante-Bellum Economy* (1965).
2. Simon Kuznets, "The Retardation of Industrial Growth," *Journal of Economic and Business History,* August 1929; Arthur F. Burns, *Production Trends in the United States Since 1870* (New York: National Bureau of Economic Research, 1934), ch. IV, "Retardation in the Growth of Industries."
3. Joseph Schumpeter, *Business Cycles* (New York: McGraw-Hill, 1939), 2 vols.

4. For example, Thomas Wilson, *Fluctuations in Income and Employment* (New York: Pitman, 1949).

5. Fishlow, "Internal Transportation," in Davis et al, *American Economic Growth: An Economist's History of the United States* (1972), p. 500.

6. Jonathan Hughes, *The Vital Few* (1986), pp. 374–79.

7. Robert W. Fogel, *The Union Pacific Railroad* (1965).

8. Stanley Engerman, "Some Economic Issues Related to Railroad Subsidies and the Evaluation of Land Grants," *JEH,* June 1972, p. 444, n. 2.

9. Lloyd Mercer, "Land Grants to American Railroads: Social Cost or Social Benefit?" *BHR,* Summer 1969.

10. J. Haydon Royd and Gary Walton, "The Social Savings from 19th Century Rail Passenger Services," *EEH,* Spring 1972; Gerald Gunderson, "The Nature of Social Savings," *EHR,* August 1970; E. H. Hunt, "Social Savings in 19th Century America," *AER,* September 1967; Stanley Lebergott, "United States Transport Advance and Externalities," *JEH,* December 1966; Peter D. McClelland, "Railroads, American Growth, and the New Economic History: A Critique," *JEH,* March 1968.

11. Engerman, "Some Economic Issues," p. 463.

12. Gottfried von Haberler, *Prosperity and Depression* (Cambridge: Harvard University Press, 1958).

13. Paul Samuelson, "Interaction of the Multiplier and Accelerator," *Review of Economics and Statistics,* vol. XXI, no. 2, May 1939.

14. Joseph Schumpeter, *Theory of Economic Development,* English edition (Cambridge: Harvard University Press, 1934).

15. Leland Hamilton Jenks, "Railroads as an Economic Force in American Development," in *Views of American Economic Growth* (1966), vol. 2.

16. W. W. Rostow, *British Economy of the Nineteenth Century* (Oxford: Clarendon Press, 1948); and A. D. Gayer, W. W. Rostow, and Anna J. Schwartz, with the assistance of Isaiah Frank, *The Growth and Fluctuation of the British Economy 1790–1850: An Historical, Statistical, and Theoretical Study of Britain's Economic Development* (Oxford: Clarendon Press, 1948).

17. W. W. Rostow, *The Process of Economic Growth* (Oxford: Oxford University Press, 1953).

18. W. W. Rostow, *The Stages of Economic Growth: A Non-Communist Manifesto* (1960). Rostow returned to these themes in his massive work, *The World Economy* (1978).

19. Douglass C. North, *The Economic Growth of the United States: 1790–1860* (New York: W.W. Norton, 1966), p. 164.

20. Fogel's main findings were reported in Robert W. Fogel and Stanley Engerman, eds., *The Reinterpretation of American Economic History* (1971). The iron measurement is on pp. 200–201.

21. Fogel in Fogel and Engerman, p. 201.

22. Fogel in Fogel and Engerman, p. 201.

23. Fogel in Fogel and Engerman, p. 201.

24. Fogel in Fogel and Engerman, p. 202.

25. For Fogel's social savings estimate and commentary on Fishlow, Fogel and Engerman, pp. 194–96.

26. Fogel, *Railroads and American Economic Growth,* p. 92 for a map of his hypothetical canal system.

27. Trevor Dick, "United States Railroad Inventions' Investment Since 1870," *EEH,* Spring 1974. As Dick points out, the dependence of railroads on capital from the money markets for investment funds made them unlikely candidates to lead the rise in productivity. They followed the cycle. Of course, the last word is not in on the nineteenth-century railroads and growth. Bradley Lewis has promised a considerable upward revision of estimated social savings due to the railroads.

28. Alfred Chandler, *The Railroads: The Nation's First Big Business* (1965).

29. Jeffrey Williamson, *Late Nineteenth-Century American Development: A General Equilibrium Approach* (New York: Cambridge University Press, 1974), p. 193. Rostow replied to Fogel's criticism in *The World Economy* (1978), in a long footnote, pp. 748–49, and in Chapters 13 and 14 of his text. Rostow sticks to his leading sector analysis and places the railroads preeminently as a leading sector.

30. Jonathan Hughes, *The Governmental Habit Redux* (1991), pp. 102–09.

31. Engerman, "Some Economic Issues," pp. 446–47.

32. The most famous of these, the "midnight rebates," were paid to Standard Oil by the railroads, who had to deal with John D. Rockefeller, Sr.

33. Thomas Ulen, "Railroad Cartels Before 1887: The Effectiveness of Private Enforcement of Collusion," *REH* (1983).

34. Quoted in Hughes, *The Vital Few,* p. 391.

35. Anne Mayhew, "A Reappraisal of the Causes of Farm Protest in the United States, 1870–1900," *JEH,* June 1972; Robert A. McGuire, "Economic Causes of Late Nineteenth Century Agrarian Unrest," *JEH,* December 1981.

36. Hughes, *The Governmental Habit Redux,* pp. 12–15.

37. 118 U.S. 394 (1886).

38. Gabriel Kolko, *Railroads and Regulation 1877–1916* (1965).

39. 169 U.S. 466 (1898). The famous phrase is "a fair return upon the value of that which it (the company) employs for the public convenience."

40. Albro Martin, *Enterprise Denied* (1971). For an earlier critique of the Kolko theses, Robert Harbeson, "Rail-

roads and Regulation 1877–1916; Conspiracy or Public Interest?" *JEH,* June 1967.

41. 193 U.S. 197 (1904).
42. 226 U.S. 86 (1913).
43. Paul MacAvoy, *The Economic Effects of Regulation* (1965); Thomas McCraw, "Regulation in America,"

BHR, Summer 1975, for surveys of regulation and its long-run consequences.

44. Henry Ford, *My Life and Work* (New York: Doubleday, 1922).

Suggested Readings

Articles

David, Paul. "Transport Innovation and Economic Growth: Professor Fogel On and Off the Rails." *Economic History Review,* second series, vol. 32, no. 3, December 1969.

Dick, Trevor J. O. "United States Railroad Inventions' Investment Since 1870. *Explorations in Economic History,* vol. 11, no. 3, Spring 1974.

Engerman, Stanley L. "Some Economic Issues Relating to Railroad Subsidies and the Evaluation of Land Grants." *Journal of Economic History,* vol. XXXII, no. 2, June 1972.

Fishlow, Albert. "Internal Transportation." In Lance E. Davis, et al., *American Economic Growth.* New York: Harper & Row, 1972.

Fogel, Robert W. "Notes on the Social Savings Controversy." *Journal of Economic History,* vol. XXXIV, no. 1, March 1979.

Gunderson, Gerald. "The Nature of Social Saving." *Economic History Review,* second series, vol. 23, no. 2, August 1970.

Hunt, E. H. "Social Savings in 19th Century America." *American Economic Review,* vol. 57, no. 4, September 1967.

Jenks, Leland Hamilton. "Railroads as an Economic Force in American Development." Reprinted in Thomas Cochran and Thomas Brewer, eds., *Views of American Economic Growth.* New York: McGraw-Hill, 1966, vol. 2.

Lebergott, Stanley. "United States Transport Advance and Externalities." *Journal of Economic History,* vol. XXVI, no. 4, December 1966.

Mayhew, Anne. "A Reappraisal of the Causes of Farm Protest in the United States, 1870–1900." *Journal of Economic History,* vol. XXXII, no. 2, June 1972.

McClelland, Peter D. "Railroads, American Growth, and the new Economic History: A Critique." *Journal of Economic History,* vol. XXVIII, no. 1, March 1968.

McCraw, Thomas. "Regulation in America, A Review Article." *Business History Review,* vol. 49, no. 2, Summer 1975.

McGuire, Robert A. "Economic Causes of Late Nineteenth-Century Agrarian Unrest." *Journal of Economic History,* vol. XLI, no. 4, December 1981.

Mercer, Lloyd. "Land Grants to American Railroads: Social Cost or Social Benefit." *Business History Review,* vol. 43, no. 2, Summer 1969.

———. "Building Ahead of Demand: Some Evidence for the Land Grant Railroads." *Journal of Economic History,* vol. XXXIV, no. 2, June 1974.

Royd, J. Hayden, and Walton, Gary. "The Social Savings from 19th Century Rail Passenger Services." *Explorations in Economic History,* vol. 9, no. 3, Spring 1972.

Ulen, Thomas. "Railroad Cartels Before 1887: The Effectiveness of Private Enforcement of Collusion." *Research in Economic History,* vol. 8. Greenwich, CT: JAI Press, 1983.

Weiss, Thomas. "United States Transport Advance and Externalities: A Comment." *Journal of Economic History,* vol. XXVIII, no. 4, December 1968.

Books

Chandler, Alfred D. *The Railroads: The Nation's First Big Business.* New York: Harcourt, Brace & World, 1965.

Cochran, Thomas C. *Railroad Leaders, 1845–1890, The Business Mind in Action.* Cambridge: Harvard University Press, 1953.

Fishlow, Albert. *American Railroads and the Transformation of the Ante-Bellum Economy.* Cambridge: Harvard University Press, 1965.

Fogel, Robert W. *Railroads and American Economic Growth.* Baltimore: Johns Hopkins University Press, 1962.

———. *The Union Pacific Railroad: A Case of Premature Enterprise.* Baltimore: Johns Hopkins University Press, 1965.

Grodinsky, Julius. *Transcontinental Railway Strategy.* Philadelphia: University of Pennsylvania Press, 1962.

Hughes, Jonathan. *The Vital Few: American Economic Progress and Its Protagonists.* New York: Oxford University Press, 1986.

———. *The Governmental Habit Redux: Economic Controls from Colonial Times to the Present.* Princeton: Princeton University Press, 1991.

Kolko, Gabriel. *Railroads and Regulation, 1877–1916.* Princeton: Princeton University Press, 1965.

Martin, Albro. *Enterprise Denied: Origins of the Decline of American Railroads, 1897–1917.* New York: Columbia University Press, 1971.

———. *James J. Hill and the Opening of the Northwest.* New York: Oxford University Press, 1976.

MacAvoy, Paul. *The Economic Effects of Regulation.* Cambridge: MIT Press, 1965.

Ripley, W. Z. *Railroads: Rates and Regulations.* New York: Longmans, Green, 1912.

Rostow, W. W. *The Stages of Economic Growth: A Non-Communist Manifesto.* New York: Cambridge University Press, 1960.

———. *The World Economy: History and Prospect.* Austin: University of Texas Press, 1978.

Stover, John. *American Railroads.* Chicago: University of Chicago Press, 1961.

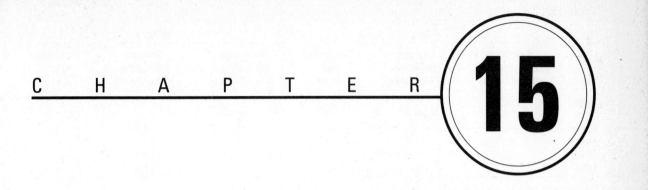

Post–Civil War Agriculture

Our last discussion of American agriculture centered on the parallel westward movements of essentially two agrarian social systems: the family farm of the North and the largely slave-based plantation of the South. The extreme scarcity of hired labor in the North—one laborer for every two farms—already had produced a trend toward relatively capital-intensive agriculture there. Slavery seemed to be creating a remarkably labor-intensive agriculture in the South. In the antebellum period, both "made sense."

The Civil War eliminated the South's slave-based plantation agriculture. For complex reasons the conversion from plantation slavery to sharecropping and a system of hired agricultural labor was relatively unsuccessful, and Southern agriculture became a depressed area in the American economy that was not reformed until well into the twentieth century. In the North, two more great stages of agricultural expansion awaited: one based upon dry-land farming of basic grains and livestock feeding, to be followed in the mid-twentieth century by the great, government-aided water control and irrigation systems that are true engineering marvels of our era.

THE HOMESTEAD AND THE END OF THE FRONTIER ERA

At first, American agriculture grew in the form of continued extensive cultivation, which resulted in a huge expansion of farm output. In the period up to World War I, there was a remarkable phenomenon: The ratio of increases in the acreage of basic crops under cultivation to increases in output was nearly 2 to 1. Consider the data in Table 15.1.

As we can see, the output of wheat per acre increased only by roughly 12 percent in the four decades from the end of the Civil War to 1910, and corn output per acre seems to have declined for at least part of this period. These changes occurred when the level, glacially ground acres of the Midwest were being substituted for the stones and mountainsides of the East Coast in the total mix of farmland.

The farmers continued the westward push into the new lands (recently vacated by the Indians and the great buffalo herds—both suffering near extinction in the process). The Homestead Act of 1862 changed the process of land acquisition, but it was not the utopian dream of previous generations. Most new settlement

271

Table 15.1 Corn and Wheat Acreage and Output 1866–1990

	Corn			Wheat		
Year	Acreage Harvested (in millions)	Output (millions of bushels)	Bushels per Acre	Acreage Harvested (in millions)	Output (millions of bushels)	Bushels per Acre
1866	30	731	24.4	15	170	11.0
1890	75	1650	22.1	37	449	12.2
1910	102	2853	27.9	46	626	13.7
1950	82	3075	37.5	62	1019	16.4
1970	66	4099	61.9	44	1370	31.1
1990	67	7934	118.5	69	2736	39.5

Source: *Historical Statistics*, series K 502, 503, 506–07; *Statistical Abstract*, 1992, Table 1115.

did not come from homesteads. Making a farm was an expensive, risky, and time-consuming proposition. Besides, the lands open to homesteading were mainly beyond the 100th meridian, where rainfall is sharply lower than in the central and eastern parts of the country. New techniques had to be learned to farm these relatively dry regions without irrigation.

The Western railroads had been granted vast amounts of land. They were anxious to sell those lands, and they produced a market in competition with homesteading. The railroads provided financing and helped with problems of settlement. They not only wanted to profit from their land sales but also to promote economic development along their lines in the interest of freight. Even though the homestead land was granted without a money payment, for a long time it was the railroad lands that provided most new farms in the West.

Extensive Growth

The absence of basic chemical and biological improvements to raise output per acre before World War I meant that the ratio of output growth to additional land inputs in American agriculture grew almost in a straight line—a remarkable phenomenon. Roughly measured (see Table 15.1), between 1866 and 1910, the secular increase in land under cultivation produced an increase in the measured physical output of almost equal proportion: An X percent increase in land was matched by about an X percent increase in physical output.

Figure 15.1 is a generalized view of this situation. In this figure we conceptually transform the physical out-put and land input numbers for the other years in Table 15.1 into percentages of 1866, assuming, for the moment, that wheat and corn are representative of all grains. Had the growth rates been exactly equal, the final numbers would have fallen at the tip of a ray

Figure 15.1 Increase of Agricultural Land Inputs and Physical Outputs, 1866–1910, as a Percentage of 1866

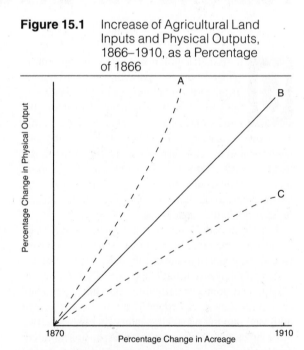

If the percentage increase in acreage were just matched by the percentage increase in output, line *B* would describe the advance in output as the area of cultivation grew. Line *A* shows a set of cases where the percentage increases in output exceed those of the acreage increases. Line *C* is the reverse: Along it, the percentage increase in output is less than the percentage increase in acreage.

drawn from the origin with a slope of 45 degrees (line *B*). It was very nearly so. Had the quality of the new land brought down the average, other things equal, the rate of increase in output should have dropped, say, to curve *C*. Had the land quality improved significantly on average, output may have risen disproportionately, say to curve *A*. It is conceivable that steady substitutions of curve *A* land offset the extensions of grain-farming on curve *C* land, resulting in the growth of outputs and inputs by equal proportions.[1] Later on, the biochemical revolution in agriculture would produce a phenomenon like curve *A*.

From the end of the Civil War until 1910, the great expansion in output of wheat and corn was accompanied by only a small increase in yields per acre. The major source of the increase in total output was simply the increased land input. More land was being planted in corn and wheat. By the mid-twentieth century (see again Table 15.1), the biochemical revolution had occurred in American agriculture. Yields rose phenomenally, and acreage devoted to these basic food crops was actually reduced as output soared. But until 1910 it was increased land input with a fairly constant yield per acre that enabled the great growth of Northern agriculture to occur. In the final thrust westward of the Northern family farm, the *overall* result was almost line *B* in Figure 15.1.

The physical nature of the land suggests that the expansion westward from the old colonies into the Midwest in the antebellum period at least at first shifted total output above the 45-degree line, to something like curve *A*. That change reflects an initial improvement in land quality. Why else abandon Vermont to embrace Iowa? From the Civil War onward, as the system of agriculture spread across prairie and plain, the product of the land alone was constantly increased but in proportion to increased land inputs.

Agricultural Efficiency

Does this mean that efficiency in Northern farming did not improve? *No.* As more land inputs were added, due to increased capacity because of innovations in horse- and mule-drawn implements and machinery, output per worker hour could be raised. Even if the output of the land variable was constant, average costs of output could be reduced by adding other inputs of increasing efficiency. Better plows, steam threshing, more effec-tive reapers, then combined reaper-binders, better cultivating equipment, improved transport—all these things raised total farm productivity and released the Northern farmer from the labor constraint.[2] Therefore, even though output per acre was almost constant, output per worker hour rose and so did the potential for profits in farming. Farming attracted more people, and more investment as a result. Table 15.2 shows the advances made in output per worker hour.

Even in cotton, where fundamental mechanization was slow in coming at the level of actual field work, worker-hour productivity rose. In corn and wheat, it rose markedly. Farmers could hope to become increasingly effective by acquiring more land over which to spread the cost of their draft animals and equipment. Land in farms was truly a variable input in this period of economic history. The land's own fertility was relatively fixed, but changing the proportions of the rest of the input mix could produce rising profits in farming.

The resulting increase of acres in farms and homesteads is shown in Table 15.3 on page 274. Note that the increase in farmland was not mainly due to homesteads. The additional farmland came primarily from cash sales by the government, from railroad grants, and from lands ceded to the states and then sold to individuals. Moreover, three-fourths of the homesteads were taken up after 1890, when the unbroken line of the physical frontier had vanished. The greatest decade of homesteading was, in fact, 1910–20, at a time when high prices for farm products finally returned. Taking up land and making farms, even when the land was free, was a *market decision* because there were costs involved. The other inputs were not free, and the opportunity costs of farm-making were not zero. Homesteading was never a utopian solution to land hunger.

Of all the public lands, homesteads totaled 285 million acres, while cash sales totaled 300 million acres.

Table 15.2 Agriculture: Output per Worker-Hour

	Worker-Hours per 100 Bushels		
Year	Wheat	Corn	Cotton
1840	233	276	438
1880	152	180	303
1900	108	147	284

Source: *Historical Statistics*, series K 449, 454, 459.

Table 15.3   Land in Farm and Homesteads[a]

Year	Land in Farms	Increase per Decade	Final Homestead Entries per Decade
1860	407.2	—	—
1870	407.7	0.5	1.4
1880	536.1	128.4	17.9
1890	623.2	87.1	29.0
1900	841.2	218.0	31.9
1910	881.4	40.2	38.8
1920	958.7	77.3	74.3

[a] Figures for land are in millions of acres.

Source: *Historical Statistics*, series K 5, J 15.

Between 1860 and 1920, land in farms increased by 548.2 million acres, of which homesteads were only 192.3 million acres. From 1860 to the end of the nineteenth century, cash sales, and not homesteads, accounted for the preponderance of new farms.

Patterns of Regional Agricultural Production

One consequence of extensive farming was the creation of the "farm belt," a phenomenon that dominates postbellum American agricultural history. In Figures 15.2 and 15.3 the farm belt is the mass of black dots, each representing 25,000 acres, that runs right across the center of the country from Ohio through the Midwest, thinning out as an east-west finger on the Nebraska-Kansas border to the west, with a separate

Figure 15.2   Improved Land, 1870

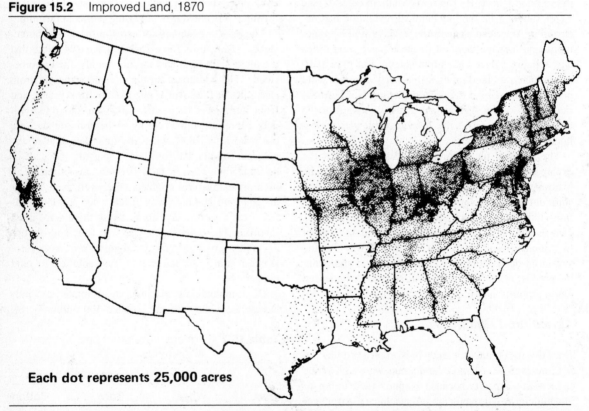

Each dot represents 25,000 acres

Source: Charles O. Paullin, *Atlas of the Historical Geography of the United States* (Washington, D.C. and New York: Carnegie Institution and the American Geographical Society of New York, 1932), plate 144E.

In 1870, improved acreage west of the Mississippi was fairly well restricted to Minnesota, Iowa, Missouri, Arkansas, Louisiana, and east Texas—together with Oregon's Willamette Valley and the Central Valley in California.

Figure 15.3   Improved Land, 1900

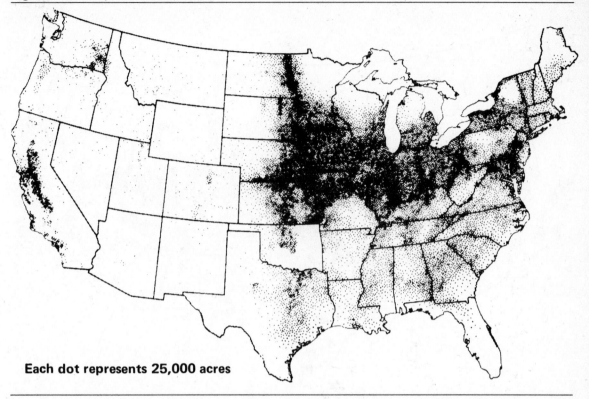

Each dot represents 25,000 acres

Source: Charles O. Paullin, *Atlas of the Historical Geography of the United States* (Washington, D.C. and New York: Carnegie Institution and the American Geographical Society of New York, 1932), plate 144H.

By 1900, although there was more extensive cultivation on the high plains and in the West than was true in 1870, the lack of rainfall from the Cascades and Sierra Nevada ranges eastward to the Midwest farm belt clearly defined those continuing features of dryland and irrigation farming that came to characterize agriculture in the Great Basin, Southwest, and high plains states.

extension running northward into the Red River wheat country of Minnesota and the Dakotas. The basic grains, corn and wheat (and sorghum in the western part), were the root of this great development.

Wheat and corn are used directly for human consumption and are joined by sorghum as livestock feed. They form the base upon which the great Midwestern food industry grew. As we see in Figure 15.4, by 1920 cattle production, ubiquitous in American agriculture (even on the dry ranges of the Western highlands), became concentrated in a Midwestern band running north-eastward from Texas up to Illinois. Chicago, Omaha, and Kansas City became the centers of the great meatpacking industry.

The advance of refrigeration into railroad cars and steamships, beginning in the 1880s, meant that the product of the Midwest grain and livestock industries could come to dominate the markets in the United States and in international trade. Railroads, grain elevators, and river and lake steamers connected the Midwest to the world, and supporting financial services grew up with their center in the Chicago commodities market. These commodities markets, which, in the late nineteenth and early twentieth centuries, were organized by the Chicago Board of Trade, did for food what the New York Stock Exchange had done for securities. The expansion of basic grain output is indicated by Table 15.4 on page 276.

Figure 15.4   Cattle (Excluding Dairy Cows), 1920

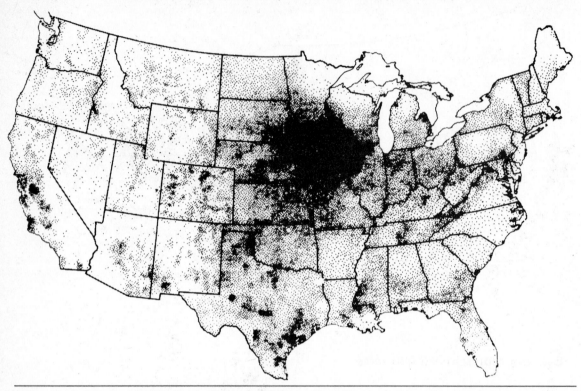

Source: Charles O. Paullin, *Atlas of the Historical Geography of the United States* (Washington, D.C. and New York: Carnegie Institution and the American Geographical Society of New York, 1932), plate 143C.

Cattle production for beef, although very widespread, was dominated in 1920 by feed grains. As a result, cattle production for beef shows a band of concentration from the Texas panhandle north-northeast through the farm belt states. The slaughtering and beef-packing industries also were concentrated in this area—especially in cities like Chicago, Omaha, and Kansas City.

Table 15.4   Output of Basic Grains[a]

Year	Wheat	Corn	Oats	Barley
1859	173	839	173	16
1870	254	1125	268	29
1880	502	1707	418	45
1890	449	1650	609	70
1900	599	2662	945	97
1910	625	2853	1106	142
1914	897	2524	1066	178

[a] Figures are in millions of bushels.

Source: *Historical Statistics,* series K 503, 507, 512, 515.

The Wheat Cycle

Midwest American grain farmers developed remarkable regional specialization in the late nineteenth century that is still followed today: corn in the prairies, sorghum on the high plains, winter wheat in the warmer parts of the midsection, spring wheat in the North. These formed the base of the livestock and poultry industries that were created to exploit the grain output. Other rotations were mixed in later (especially soybeans in the corn belt), but the wheat schedule became basic.[3] Winter wheat was planted in the late fall in Texas, Oklahoma, and Kansas and ripened in late spring, while spring-planted wheat in the northern regions was ready for harvest by August. The great harvesting began in June in the South for the winter wheat and moved north as the hot Midwestern summer advanced. By fall, the harvest was in, and the cycle was ready to begin again.

Grain elevators along the rail routes and in the milling centers made massive storage and shipping possible.[4] Futures trading in grain allowed farmers access to an extended schedule of net receipts. Futures also allowed buyers of grains to contract ahead of need and, to some extent, control the net cost of their purchases. The element of gambling in the futures market, although incidental to the commodities trade, seemed to disrupt it, to the anger of alert political leaders. Abuses and controls of this element appeared early in the history of futures trading as a result.[5] Nevertheless, futures trading attracted nonagricultural money to the financing of grain and livestock as the market increasingly commercialized Midwest agriculture.

Learning-by-doing in agriculture meant experimentation and change. The story of hybrid corn has been much discussed in the literature.[6] As for wheat, in the nineteenth century the Northern grain belt benefitted from the introduction of hard red wheats, which were rich in gluten, for bread. The red wheats came from southern Russia, imported at first by Mennonite farmers who had immigrated from that region. In addition, other drought- and rust-resistant strains were imported that thrived on the Great Plains. Important new strains were developed there by plant geneticists with the Department of Agriculture and Kansas State University. A whole new world of wheat growing was born, and the most ancient approach to agriculture was transformed.

Sorghum corn came in from Africa in the 1870s and was found to thrive in relatively dry, hot areas. With its introduction, ranchers on the high plains could feed cattle in winter off the range with a locally grown row crop. Improved breeding raised cattle and hog slaughter weights in the Midwest. The extraordinary efficiency of the new Midwest grain belt forced farmers in the East and near urban centers to shift into dairying, poultry, vegetables, and fruit.[7] Growing urban populations supported this shift, and since this increased specialization paid (i.e., raised the opportunity costs of grain production outside the Midwest), American agriculture in its entirety became more commercialized and less subsistence-oriented. Other regions benefitted secondarily from Midwest agriculture: New England dairy farmers fed their milk cows with Midwest grains to supplement hay.[8]

In Table 15.5, we see how the north-central states came to absolutely dominate in the production of basic grains and livestock. Even in livestock sales, the potential product of nearly every American farm, the specialization of the Midwest won out. It might be pointed out to the modern student that oats, a primary fuel for horses and mules, was what gasoline became when the internal combustion engine appeared. The adoption of the internal combustion engine liberated millions of acres, formerly in oats, for other uses.

EXPANDING AGRICULTURE AND THE PRICE DILEMMA

If we consider agriculture in physical dimensions alone, the numbers, from the 1870s onward, begin to sound like the basic ingredients of a resounding success story. But the actual history of the United States—dotted with the Greenback, Granger, and Populist movements—shows that the farmers, or a large part of

Table 15.5   Regional Grain and Livestock Production[a]

Product	Northeast		North Central		South		West	
	1880	1900	1880	1900	1880	1900	1880	1900
Corn	91.0	90.7	1,285.3	1,941.2	374.8	629.7	3.5	4.7
Wheat	34.2	33.1	329.6	441.3	52.8	93.8	42.9	90.3
Oats	84.0	87.3	270.2	764.3	43.6	62.3	10.1	29.6
Livestock	286.0	320.5	772.5	1,557.0	392.7	810.8	125.7	367.2

[a] Figures for corn, wheat, and oats are in millions of bushels; those for livestock are in millions of dollars. Totals across the U.S. for corn, wheat, and oats do not agree with totals given in Table 15.5 due to the use of different government sources. Niemi's numbers are from the U.S. Bureau of the Census, selected years.

Source: Albert Niemi, *U.S. Economic History*, 2nd ed. (Chicago: Rand McNally, 1979), Table 13.3.

Figure 15.5   Farm Prices, 1870–1914

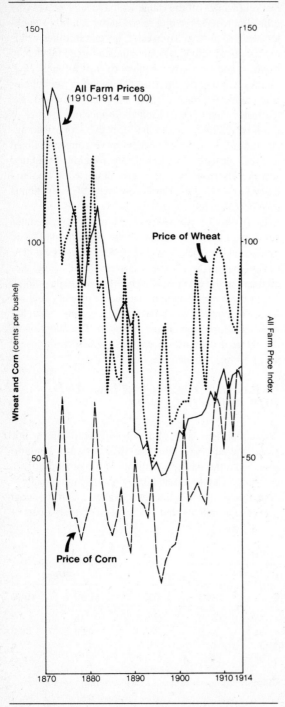

Source: *Historical Statistics,* series E 53; K 504, 508.

them, thought otherwise. In 1860, there had been 2,044,000 farms. By 1890, the number had reached 4,585,000, and the Populist movement was in full cry, demanding basic changes in income and wealth distribution by the federal power. What had gone wrong?

Demand and Supply

Basically, the problem was caused by a slowly increasing demand and a more rapidly increasing supply: The domestic market for food had not grown as rapidly as had output. Prices of farm products generally declined (with only a few years of upward movement here and there) from the end of the Civil War all the way to the late 1890s. Although other prices also fell, farmers believed themselves hardest hit. As a result, farmers' fixed costs—interest and amortization of equipment and livestock—had to be achieved in the face of declining prices. The problem was not, of course, insurmountable. If average cost falls more rapidly than average revenue (prices), increased output can still occur, with increasing profitability. But a lag of (relatively) high fixed costs made that increased output more difficult for the average farmer to achieve. It would have been easier if there had been rising prices, automatic capital gains, and no pressure on the cost side.

What the great American historian Richard Hofstadter called the "paranoid strain" in American politics took over. The farmers, if one is to take seriously the platforms of Populist party contentions, believed themselves the victims of various conspiracies and not just the state of the market. What do the price patterns in Figure 15.5 and the output data in Table 15.4 suggest, if, for the moment, we ignore the various supposed conspiracies? That is the topic of our next section.

Production

We know from the data already presented that, over time, supplies increased and prices fell. Demand was

The trend of farm prices fell off rather sharply from the end of the Civil War to the mid-1890s, followed by a recovery. It was in the era of falling farm prices that the great agrarian political movement of the nineteenth century came into existence.

increasing, too. More and more products were sold at the lower prices.

This situation is depicted for wheat in the abstract in Figure 15.6. At each actual price-quantity combination (shown as a large dot), imagine a supply and demand curve, whose intersection creates a momentary market price. As you can see, supply and demand generally increased, except for the mid-1880s. However, supply increases (moves to the right) in such a way that the intersections of demand and supply produce a downward trend of prices until 1895. That trend is shown by a *long-run supply track,* the hypothetical average over time of the actual prices. Each demand curve *could* have produced *higher* prices had there been less supply in any year. Because that was not the case, the trend of prices was downward for more than two decades. To reverse this trend, as did indeed happen in the late

1890s, demand somehow had to rise more rapidly than did supply.

Even though the American population had risen by a factor of 4.8 between 1850 and 1910, agricultural production outran it. The increased incomes of the larger population were not spent proportionally upon food (remember Engel's law). In addition, increases in productivity may have reduced costs, and thus lowered farmers' offer prices across the board. When prices did turn up in the late 1890s, foreign demand had increased significantly, and, in general, as Jeffrey Williamson argues, the years of price recovery could not have come in any other way.[9]

The rush of farmers into the Midwest and plains after the Civil War meant temporary excess supplies of farm products, even with constant output *per acre.* The export markets became increasingly important, and, in

Figure 15.6   Wheat Markets in the Abstract, 1870–1914

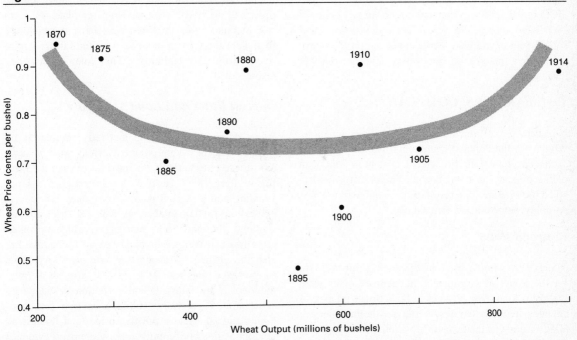

Source: *Historical Statistics,* K 506, 508.

Prices bounded a long-run supply track for agriculture, represented here schematically by wheat, that dipped as output expanded. By 1914, a good recovery in prices had taken place at maximum output levels because demand had finally caught up.

the end, expanding foreign markets pushed up prices. As Williamson put it, "In the long run, grain prices were primarily determined by conditions exogenous to both the Midwest and America."[10] The Populists sought a primarily domestic solution (to be discussed in Chapter 19). They wanted their problems solved by the direct action of the federal government, by measures that were meant mainly to redistribute domestically produced income to the farm sector. Later on, in the 1920s—and to this day—American farmers realized that foreign markets were the best way to sell their excess product. We became the *only one* of the world's giant nations (consider China, India, and Russia) that could not consume all the food product it created.

Had the expansion of output been more profitable for farmers (if there had been, say, rising prices of more rapidly falling average costs), it is conceivable that the great farmer protest movements of the late nineteenth century would not have occurred. But, as we have seen, farm income was rising more slowly than incomes in other sectors, the farmer's share of the GNP was falling, and farm life was hard. Also, it seems clear from the Populist platforms that the farmers simply believed they were losing, did not relish the prospect, and sought rent-creation by government action to relieve them of a market outcome they had created but resented.

THE FARMERS' COMPLAINT

In recent years, much attention has been given by scholars to the Populist complaints. Those complaints produced, in the long run, such a change in American public policy that it has become important to understand their nature. The result of our inquiry is, not surprisingly, something of a mixed bag.[11]

Railroad Rates

Robert Higgs found some justification, prior to 1896, for the Populists' arguments that railroad costs were too high. Analyzing changes in farm prices relative to changes in railroad rates in the postbellum period, Higgs found that the farmers' position did not improve. This finding ran against the grain of conventional modern thought:

> Farmers did not benefit from lower transportation charges over the three decades before 1897. The amounts of cotton, corn, or wheat exchanges for a ton-mile of railroad transportation remained substantially unchanged throughout the Gilded Age. This finding makes the farmers' complaint about "high" railroad freight rates somewhat more comprehensible.[12]

After 1906, the farmers gained from lower *real* freight rates as the politically motivated ICC acquired rate-setting power and the commissioners refused to raise railroad rates as prices soared. The railroads' rates fell behind the rise in their operating costs, and investment in roadbeds and equipment languished. By 1917, when the federal government took over the railroads, their rolling stock (the railroad cars) was a shambles.[13] But the farmers had enjoyed some ten-odd years of favorable freight rates at their expense.

The Terms of Trade for Farmers

Williamson's calculations show that Midwestern farmers' **terms of trade**—changes in the prices of farm products relative to changes in the costs (to them) of manufactured articles—were not adverse, and even improved up to 1890.[14] But, as Higgs emphasizes, farm real income, while growing, was rising more slowly than were incomes in other sectors; the farmers' relative position was declining.[15] They knew it, and they resented it.

Interest Rates and Land Monopoly

Higgs does not view sympathetically complaints by farmers that they were paying usurious rates of interest—those rates actually declined faster than did farm prices after 1870. Despite this decrease, the long-standing belief that all interest on money is immoral existed in fundamentalist, as well as strict Roman Catholic, thought. Short mortgages, which prevailed after the Civil War, meant higher pay-off schedules but also the chance to renegotiate mortgages over time as mortgage rates fell.[16] Charges by farmers of "land monopoly" by railroads and corporations cannot be substantiated generally. While it is true that non-homestead land had a positive price (and homestead land a positive opportunity cost), there is no evidence of any general monopoly element in land prices.[17] There was plenty of land, and, as we have seen, it was rapidly being converted into farms throughout the period from the Civil War to World War I.

On the other hand, the findings of Allan and Margaret Bogue and Robert Swierenga on the profits of land speculation in the Midwest cut both ways.[18] Although "eastern investors" did profit from capital gains in land speculation, so, by the same token, did the farmers who later resold their lands. After all, most of the resale land was sold after initial settlement by the settlers themselves. Robert Fogel and Jack Rutner found *annual capital gains*—the difference between the buying price plus carrying charges over the years owned and the sale price divided by the number of years owned—on Western land, adjusted for losses on mortgages, in excess of 2.3 percent per annum between 1869 and 1889,[19] a respectable figure for capital gains alone at a time of low interest rates. In local situations, of course, individual farmers could, and no doubt were, deceived by moneylenders and monopolists, among others.

The Farm Revolt: Why?

When is dissatisfaction about economic matters justified? There is really no way to answer such a question. *Any* losses may be considered just cause for complaint if they come in a supposedly riskless enterprise (for example, money left in a federally insured demand deposit). But farming has never been a low-risk venture. Moreover, anyone can complain that *any* positive profits are too small, any interest payment excessive. Farmers, like others, did not enjoy paying interest. (Besides, they moralized that hardworking sodbusters were paying idle fat cats for the privilege of working hard.) The Populist position is consistent with the IRS, viewing interest as "unearned income," on this subject. Moreover, the farmers believed they were being denied their just rights in the matter because the national banks, institutions created by federal power, were not allowed to accept farm mortgages as loan collateral. That was discrimination, and the farmers knew it.

There were other financial complaints that can easily be justified.[20] As Robert Wiebe argued, this was a time when the old consensus was breaking up, and among those being brushed aside were the nation's farmers.[21] They objected, even though their predicament was created by their own abundant productivity. Anne Mayhew argues for an umbrella interpretation—that farmers objected to the "commercialization" of their lives as farming became more sensitive to developing market structures.[22] As we already noted, McGuire argues that repeated bouts of income instability fueled farmer discontent, a finding not inconsistent with Mayhew.

It is one of the great paradoxes of American economic history that the tremendous agricultural development of postbellum America ended with political fratricide and social upheaval. The Grangers, the Populists, and their allies declared war on the economics of the Gilded Age, and when, by the end of the New Deal, their major demands had been met, the country had undergone fundamental change. Americans have the Populists to thank for universal public education, women's suffrage, secret ballots, direct election of senators, federal land banks, the Commodity Credit Corporation, the Federal Reserve note, the Export-Import Bank, and a host of other institutions and basic changes in American life created since 1892 by the federal government in the name of reform. What is important, in the end, is not whether their complaints were justified, but what were the practical consequences of their great effort to capture and manipulate the federal power. In 1896, it looked like the Populists were going nowhere: By 1936, they were everywhere.

CLOSING THE FRONTIER: A GLIMPSE OF THE FAR FUTURE

American history in textbooks written in the '30s, '40s, and '50s is a beautiful and inspiring pageant that began in 1607. The binding element is the frontier, ever there, ever moving westward: good, brave people crossing the wilderness in wagons, claiming and clearing the land, then pushing the railroads through it. Finally, at the turn of the century, it ends with the closing of the continuous line of forts and army camps and the Populist revolt.[23] The rest is only an epilogue. Of course, this is a romanticized version of our past. As we have already seen, most of the homesteading occurred after 1890, when the buffalo and the Native American tribes were long gone from the plains and prairies. The greatest expansion of agricultural output came long after the farm population began to decline, and, in fact, wheat and corn output have gone up more in the past thirty years than they did from 1800 to 1910. The drama of American farming was only beginning when the frontier closed.

Mining the Land

At this point it will be useful to consider some possible scenarios for the land and its uses. We noted the relatively constant yields per acre in basic grains from the Civil War to World War I. This potential long-run barrier never became operative, due to the modern revolution in agroscience. The nature of the land input itself was changed. The process actually began with irrigation quite early in the nineteenth century, and, in the development of irrigation schemes linked with conservation policies, the future was radically altered.

What the "closing of the frontier" measured, in part, was simply severely diminishing returns to the purely lateral expansion of traditional American agriculture. Extensive farming methods really meant that the land was being *mined* of its creative power. That process started in colonial Virginia with the migration of tobacco crops from exhausted soils to ever newer fields, and it moved westward for nearly three centuries.

On the prairies and high plains, the problem of obtaining fertilizer meant that specialization in grain rotations was constrained by the need to keep animals for manure. Where rain was irregular or insufficient, crop yields varied widely from year to year. Artificial fertilizer (and machinery to spread it) was needed, and the water supply had to be stabilized. To farm in Illinois, one cut the prairie sod, planted a sod crop, then harrowed, disked, and plowed year after year, depending upon nature's normally abundant rains and sunshine, plus (hopefully) some natural fertilizer to make nutrients for the crops.

To farm in the Snake River Valley of Idaho, or the Imperial Valley of California, a water supply had to be created. Nature had provided almost no water but it did provide plenty of sun. Erosion from wind and water, by the 1930s, was wasting the potential of millions of acres in the semiarid parts of the farm belt. The problem was attacked by a massive government intervention: Reclamation policies would produce the water, and soil conservation practices would check the erosion.

Irrigation and the Sun Belt

The processes of putting surface water where nature did not provide it have now changed the character of farming from the high plains to the Pacific Ocean. The acreage involved is a relatively small part of the total land in farms, about 4 percent (40-odd million acres), but a whole new set of possibilities for American settlement and development have been created.

From the beginning, American economic history has involved the partly coordinated development of urban life in connection with farming. The American land tenure, together with the commercial character of agriculture, has assured that. In the West, a new irrigated agricultural empire produced watered fields and suitable habitat for vast populations of urban dwellers where nature had put only harsh desert. These sun-bathed lands now support huge populations, and, by present judgment, much more of this country's future growth lies in these former deserts than could have been imagined even thirty years ago.

The Beginnings of Irrigation and Water Conservation

The conservation of water by gravity irrigation has been known since antiquity in arid lands such as ancient Sumeria. The Spaniards, entering the desert of Southern California, produced small-scale irrigation in the Los Angeles area. When the Mormons entered the dry basin of the Great Salt Lake in 1847, they planted potatoes immediately and irrigated them with the dammed-up waters of City Creek. They then systematically reorganized their society to allocate property rights (and obligations) in the irrigation systems.[24] From that point, the dry deserts of the country's western third became a challenge, and no longer an insurmountable barrier to development. Here was a problem that could be solved partly by government action and partly by the grant of property rights to private persons.

Early Acts

In 1877 the Desert Land Act was passed by Congress in response to these prospects. Under this law, 640 acres of semiarid and arid public land were sold for $1.25 an acre to anyone who would reclaim by irrigation a third of it within three years. Title passed in this case partly by cash payment and partly by "service" (the reclamation). By 1880, settlers had irrigated a million acres of Western farmland, and by 1890, 3,361,000 acres. The Cary Act of 1894 was meant to speed up the process by granting a million acres to any Western state that agreed to reclaim it by grants for irrigation.

In 1902, the Newlands Reclamation Act was passed, setting up a Reclamation Fund in the U.S. Treasury to receive and allocate funds to assist new irrigation schemes. Procedures were created for the building of storage dams by the federal government. Lands affected were temporarily withdrawn from homestead entry (to prevent speculation), but participants could file for 160-acre homesteads after the basic irrigation works were in place. The settlers organized irrigation districts. They repaid the costs of the works (apart from the storage dams, which the government maintained) and took title to the lands once the majority had repaid their pro-rata shares of the costs.

With such beginnings, by 1919 there were some 19 million acres of land actually under irrigation, and the way was open for joint government-private allocations of property rights to irrigate the land.[25] The dams had to be built, the lands settled, the processes of payment completed, and secure property rights assigned. The whole system then fitted into our standard ways of owning and exploiting the land.

The Future in Brief

What happened lies in the mid-twentieth century and the more distant future. The greatest engineering works in history were developed from those beginnings—giant multipurpose dams for land reclamation, power generation, conservation, and recreation. The deserts and mountains by the 1980s were decorated with huge artificial lakes, and millions of acres of rich, irrigated farmland had been produced. Boulder Dam (now Hoover Dam), finished in 1936, created a lake 150 miles long.[26] As a result, major parts of Arizona and southern California became garden spots, and Phoenix, Las Vegas, Los Angeles, and lesser urban areas grew. By 1941, the Imperial Dam on the Gila River, together with the All American Canal, assured California's Imperial Valley of a controlled water supply. In 1937, Congress appropriated funds to build the fantastic Big Thompson Project in Colorado. Water was pumped up 186 feet from the Colorado River, dropped through a 13-mile-long tunnel under the Rocky Mountains, and routed into storage dams and

farms irrigated on the Big Thompson and South Platte rivers across the continental divide. In 1956, Congress passed the Colorado River Storage Project Act, which created the Glen Canyon and Navajo dams on the San Juan River, Flaming Gorge Dam on the Green River, and Blue Mesa Dam on the Gunnison. The Southwest was flush with water.

The Pacific Northwest, east of the Cascades, contained great tracts of arable lands that were dry-farmed. Grand Coulee Dam on the Columbia River, authorized in 1935, was meant to provide irrigation water to those farms on the surrounding table lands. The distribution of property rights was complex, but by 1948, was under way. Grand Coulee generated power, as did Bonneville Dam, downriver. Smaller dams were also built on the Columbia and its tributaries for power generation. The result, as in the Southwest, has been the creation of an "artificial" world of irrigated agriculture in the formerly desolate (but beautiful) wastes of the Northwest. Also in 1935, the Central Valley Project, a giant storage dam below Mount Shasta intended to generate power and regulate the flow of water from Shasta Lake down the center of the Golden State, was authorized by Congress. The San Joaquin Valley was placed under more extensive irrigation.

In the East, the giant reclamation projects were along the watersheds of the Missouri, Arkansas, and Tennessee rivers. The Tennessee Valley Authority (TVA) was established in 1933 to take over the World War I Dam at Muscle Shoals, Alabama, and its power-generating facilities. Because the TVA's great system of dams (with their power-generating capacity) was created by the federal sovereignty in an already settled part of the country, where established property rights were of relatively ancient lineage (by American standards), great controversy surrounded it, and still does. The TVA created rents, destroyed rents, and made massive changes in the demography, industrial structure, and economic future of the entire area.

Another great reclamation project was the Missouri Valley Project, which set up a system of dams and reservoirs along the course of the Missouri River. Flood control was its basic aim. The Public Works Administration dam at Fort Peck, Montana, was completed in 1937. In subsequent decades, more dams were created by the federal government under the control of a complex, intergovernmental agency called the Missouri

Farm Technology Moves West.   The hand-held cradle, a scythe with fingers to guide the cut wheat, was apparently introduced into America in the 1770s (above left). The later, horse-drawn reaper soon was adapted to mechanized binding (lower left). In the massive farms of the upper great plains and Pacific Northwest, capital intensity was profitable in combined reaping and threshing machines drawn by teams of from twenty to thirty horses (above right). Family farming still required intensive labor when farms were first settled, as shown by a family of ex-slaves seated before a typical Nebraska sod house (below right).

Basic Inter-Agency Committee. By 1973, the system was largely complete, and flooding was nearly ended.

The last major project to be completed to date is the Arkansas River Project, 13 dams and a system of locks making that river navigable from the Mississippi River to central Oklahoma, controlling floods, and providing water supplies to a huge region. The 1965 Water Resources Planning Act opened the way for more river basin commissions to be created by executive order and the process to be repeated wherever future needs arise.

Even with what has been done so far, the applications of this technology are still in the infant stage. The possibilities of water resource planning, conservation, and irrigation are enormous.

The Question of Environment

All these monumental engineering achievements had to be compromises between nature lovers, already vested holders of property rights in the regions affected, and the urge to use federal power to continue the process of creating American civilization from nature's raw materials. Much of this process involved the creation of public goods, some involved the destruction of them (the drowned glories of Glen Canyon). There were free-rider problems, and problems with the distribution of economic rents through the political system at taxpayer expense. Such conflicts produce abundant materials for endless political disputation and fortunes in lawyers' fees as injured persons test the courts. In *Oklahoma* v *Atkinson* (1941), the U.S. Supreme Court opened the way for the federal power to extend into almost any water system via the commerce clause: "Congress may exercise its control over the nonnavigable stretches of river to preserve and promote commerce on the navigable portions."[27]

What will society want to do with its natural endowment now? The energy crisis of the 1970s and 1980s has changed once again ideas about the arid and semi-arid parts of the continental domain. Ubiquitous capture of solar energy is an obvious long-run prospect in these regions. The great dams and irrigation systems greatly extend the possibilities for continued population growth there.[28] Joint government-private enterprise is an old American tradition that is congenial and easily achieved within the constitutional system.

Recall the era of internal improvements in the 1830s. Economic, social, political, and cultural problems are normal outcomes of *any* process of change. After all, the entire westward movement involved three centuries of such conflict. Democratic processes enabled the United States to resolve the conflicts in peace, Indian wars and the American Civil War apart. So, the tale of the closing of the frontier to American agriculture and settlement in the late nineteenth century was really the opening chapter of a new era—the *intensive* use of the land and its resources with the aid of science and engineering. By the 1980s, a century later, Americans were still seeing only glimmerings of the constructive future that was possible.

Remaining Public Land

Finally, there is the question of the remaining public lands that were never sold off. Of the total land area of 2,271 millon acres, about 775 million remain in the public domain, roughly 34 percent of the total land area. Alaska contains an enormous 359-million acres of public land. About 71 million acres are now vested in national park lands, about 53 million acres are in Indian tribal and trust lands. The Forest Service has custody of roughly 188 million acres, and about 30 million acres are assigned to the Pentagon. Other holdings are mainly in the Interior Department's control, including huge areas of grazing lands. These public lands contain vast natural resources, timber, minerals, wildlife, and priceless scenic assets, that can be exploited for settlement, agriculture and grazing. Policies developed on the uses of this vast *common property* can never be free of controversy, threats of corrupt use, or the danger of destruction from overuse—the *inevitable* fate of common property resources if left unregulated. Our knowledge of the economic problems associated with the use of such common property has been greatly enlarged by the work of Gary Libecap.[29]

There are, in addition, the seashores and underwater lands (and their resources—e.g., oil and gas). An increasingly urban nation has changed its attitudes several times in recent decades about the acceptable uses of these common resources. This is fuel for endless controversy. A wilderness area is by definition inaccessible to the automobile-bound general public. Such exclusivity is by its own nature discriminatory and undemocratic—the wilderness cannot be experienced by those who cannot, or will not, enter it on foot, horseback, rubber raft, kayak, horseback, or skis. Turned over to private interests, the common property is a "giveaway." Developed by government it is "socialism." Jefferson wanted the federal government's own-ership of the land extinguished. That is now an impossibility. Many chapters on the public lands remain to be written.[30]

Notes

1. For a further discussion of such hypothetical possibilities, see William Parker, "Agriculture," in Lance E. Davis, et al., *American Economic Growth* (1972), pp. 376–79.
2. Wayne D. Rasmussen, "The Impact of Technological Change on American Agriculture 1862–1962," *JEH,* December 1962.
3. The introduction of nitrogen-fixing soybeans in the twentieth century expanded the rotation to wheat, corn (as sorghum), and soybeans.
4. An excellent discussion of the midwestern grain trade can be found in William Cronon, *Nature's Metropolis* (1991), ch. 3.
5. Jonathan Lurie, *The Chicago Board of Trade, 1859–1905* (1979); Richard Zerbe, "The Chicago Board of Trade Case, 1918," *Research in Law and Economics,* vol. 5 (1983).
6. Zvi Griliches, "Hybrid Corn and the Economics of Innovations," *Science,* vol. 132, 29 July 1960. The analysis developed by Griliches emphasized the role of market forces in spreading scientific advance. Alan Bogue widened our knowledge of this accomplishment by showing the importance of mechanization in the corn belt, which prepared the way for hybrid corn, "Changes in Mechanical and Plant Technology: The Corn Belt, 1910–1940," *JEH,* March 1983.
7. Fred Bateman, "Improvements in American Dairy Farming, 1850–1910: A Quantitative Analysis," *JEH,* June 1968. As Bateman demonstrates, technical improvements were slow in coming in dairying, making the adjustment to changing comparative advantages within agriculture painful.
8. Philip Coelho and James Shepherd, "Differences in Regional Prices: The United States, 1851–1880," *JEH,* September 1974; John D. Bowman and Richard H. Keehn, "Agricultural Terms of Trade in Four Midwestern States, 1870–1900," *JEH,* September 1974. Coelho and Shepherd find consistent price differentials, but they are not systematically against the farm states. Bowman and Keehn find no secular turning of the terms of trade against the Midwest farmers but do find episodes within the period that corresponded to short-term increases of farm-belt unrest associated with the Grangers and Populists.
9. Jeffrey G. Williamson, "Greasing the Wheels of Sputtering Export Engines: Midwestern Grains and American Export Growth," *EEH,* July 1980, p. 200.
10. Williamson, p. 197.
11. Robert A. McGuire, "Economic Causes of Late Nineteenth Century Agrarian Unrest," *JEH,* December 1981, argues that instability of farm income over time correlates most highly with the various episodes of agrarian unrest on the form of political movements.
12. Robert Higgs, *The Transformation of the American Economy, 1865–1914: An Essay in Interpretation* (1971), p. 89.
13. Albro Martin, *Enterprise Denied: Origins of the Decline of American Railroads, 1897–1917* (1971).
14. Williamson, "Greasing the Wheels," p. 200.
15. Higgs, *Transformation,* p. 100.
16. Douglass C. North, *Growth and Welfare in the American Past: A New Economic History* (1974), p. 133.
17. Higgs, *Transformation,* pp. 90–102.
18. Allan Bogue and Margaret Bogue, "Profits and the Frontier Speculator," *JEH,* March, 1957, and Robert Swierenga, *Pioneers and Profits* (1968).
19. Robert W. Fogel and Jack Rutner, "The Efficiency Effects of Federal Land Policy, 1850–1900," in W. O. Aydelotte, A. L. Bogue, and R. W. Fogel, eds., *The Dimensions of Quantitative Research in History* (1972).
20. For a brief round-up of Populist complaints and the consequences, Jonathan Hughes, *The Governmental Habit Redux* (1991), pp. 98–117. The classic is John D. Hicks, *The Populist Revolt* (1961). More recently, Anne Mayhew, "A Reappraisal of the Causes of Farm Protest in the United States, 1870–1900," *JEH,* June 1972.
21. Robert Wiebe, *The Search for Order* (1967).
22. Mayhew, "A Reappraisal of the Causes of Farm Protest," pp. 469–75.
23. Frederick Jackson Turner, *The Frontier in American History* (1921).
24. Leonard Arrington, *Great Basin Kingdom* (1958).
25. Frederick Merk, *History of the Westward Movement* (1978), p. 508.
26. For greater detail and coverage of the entire development of irrigation, reclamation, and conservation, see Merk, ch. 5–7.
27. 313 U.S. 508 (1941) 525.

28. Not without difficulties, of course. The newly husbanded water supplies of the Sun Belt are expensive. They are economic goods with positive prices assembled largely by government expenditures, and their distribution must necessarily be partly political. Since the overall process is mainly unplanned, populations will not necessarily grow where the water is most abundant. One supposes that, in the long run, a specific area could outgrow its water supply. If this happens, population *must* decline.

29. Gary D. Libecap, "Bureaucratic Opposition to the Assignment of Property Rights: Overgrazing on the Western Range," *JEH,* March 1981.

30. There is much excellent material to read about problems of common property resources. Among the best are Garrett Hardin, "The Tragedy of the Commons," *Science,* 13 December 1968, and several papers of Professor Gary Libecap on these issues: "Government Policies on Property Rights to Land: U.S. Implications for Agricultural Development in Mexico, " *Ag. Hist.,* Winter 1986; "Property Rights in Economic History: Implications for Research," *EEH,* July 1986; with George Alter, "Agricultural Productivity, Partible Inheritance, and the Demographic Response to Rural Poverty: An Examination of the Spanish Southwest," *EEH,* April 1982; and with Ronald N. Johnson, "Legislating Commons: The Navajo Tribal Council and the Navajo Range," *Economic Inquiry,* January 1980. Also, on the exhaustion of the California fisheries, see Arthur F. McAvoy, "Public Policy, and Industrialization in the California Fisheries, 1900–1925," *BHR,* Winter 1983.

Suggested Readings

Articles

Bateman, Fred. "Improvements in American Dairy Farming, 1850–1910: A Quantitative Analysis." *Journal of Economic History,* vol. XXIII, no. 2, June 1968.

Bogue, Allan, and Bogue, Margaret. "Profits and the Frontier Speculator." *Journal of Economic History,* vol. XVII, no. 1, March 1957.

———. "Changes in Mechanical and Plant Technology: The Corn Belt, 1910–1940." *The Journal of Economic History,* vol. XLIII, no. 1, March 1983.

Bowman, John. "An Economic Analysis of Midwestern Farm Land Values and Farmland Income, 1890–1900." *Yale Economic Essays,* vol. 5, no. 2, Fall 1965.

———, and Keehn, Richard H. "Agricultural Terms of Trade in Four Midwestern States, 1870–1900." *Journal of Economic History,* vol. XXXIV, no. 3, September 1974.

Coelho, Philip and Shepherd, James. "Differences in Regional Prices: The United States, 1851–1880." *Journal of Economic History,* vol. XXXIV, no. 3, September 1974.

DeCanio, Stephen. "Productivity and Income Distribution in the Post-Bellum South." *Journal of Economic History,* vol. XXXIV, no. 2, June 1974.

Fogel, Robert W., and Rutner, Jack. "The Efficiency Effects of Federal Land Policy: Some Provisional Findings." In Aydelotte, W. O., Bogue, A. L., and Fogel, R. W., eds., *The Dimensions of Quantitative Research in History.* Princeton: Princeton University Press, 1972.

Griliches, Zvi. "Hybrid Corn and the Economics of Innovation." *Science,* vol. 132, 29 July 1960.

Hardin, Garrett. "The Tragedy of the Commons." *Science,* 13 December 1968.

Harley, C. Knick. "Western Settlement and the Price of Wheat, 1872–1913." *Journal of Economic History,* vol. XXXVIII, no. 4, December 1978.

Libecap, Gary D. "Economic Variables and the Development of the Law: The Case of Western Mineral Rights." *Journal of Economic History,* vol. XXXVIII, no. 2, June 1978.

———. "Bureaucratic Opposition to the Assignment of Property Rights: Overgrazing on the Western Range." *Journal of Economic History,* vol. XLI, no. 1, March 1981.

———. "Government Policies on Property Rights to Land: U.S. Implications for Agricultural Development in Mexico." *Agricultural History,* vol. 60, no. 1, Winter 1986.

———. "Property Rights in Economic History: Implications for Research." *Explorations in Economic History,* vol. 23, no. 3, July 1986.

———, and Johnson, Ronald N. "Legislating Commons: The Navajo Tribal Council and the Navajo Range." *Economic Inquiry,* vol. XVII, no. 1, January 1980.

———, and Alter, George. "Agricultural Productivity, Partible Inheritance, and the Demographic Response to Rural Poverty: An Examination of the Spanish Southwest." *Explorations in Economic History,* vol. 19, no. 2, April 1982.

McAvoy, Arthur F. "Law, Public Policy, and Industrialization in the California Fisheries, 1900–1925." *Business History Review,* vol. 57, no. 4, Winter 1983.

Mayhew, Anne. "A Reappraisal of the Causes of Farm Protest in the United States, 1870–1900." *Journal of Economic History,* vol. XXXII, no. 2, June 1972.

McGuire, Robert A. "Economic Causes of Late Nineteenth Century Agrarian Unrest." *Journal of Economic History,* vol. XLI, no. 4, December 1981.

Parker, William. "Agriculture." In Lance E. Davis, et al., *American Economic Growth: An Economist's History of the United States.* New York: Harper & Row, 1972.

Rasmussen, Wayne D. "The Impact of Technological Change on American Agriculture, 1862–1962." *Journal of Economic History,* vol. XXII, no. 2, December 1962.

Williamson, Jeffrey G. "Greasing the Wheels of Sputtering Export Engines: Midwestern Grains and American Export Growth." *Explorations in Economic History,* vol. 17, no. 3, July 1980.

Winters, Donald L. "Tenancy as an Economic Institution: The Growth and Distribution of Agricultural Tenancy in Iowa, 1850–1900." *Journal of Economic History,* vol. XXXVII, no. 2, June 1974.

Zerbe, Richard. "The Chicago Board of Trade Case, 1918." *Research in Law and Economics,* vol. 5. Greenwich, CT: JAI Press, 1983.

Books

Arrington, Leonard. *Great Basin Kingdom.* Cambridge: Harvard University Press, 1958.

Bogue, Allan. *From Prairie to Cornbelt: Farming on the Illinois and Iowa Prairies in the Nineteenth Century.* Chicago: University of Chicago Press, 1963.

Cronon, William. *Nature's Metropolis: Chicago and the Great West.* New York: W. W. Norton, 1991.

Hicks, John D. *The Populist Revolt.* Lincoln: University of Nebraska Press, 1961.

Higgs, Robert. *The Transformation of the American Economy, 1865–1914: An Essay in Interpretation.* New York: John Wiley & Sons, 1971.

Lurie, Jonathan. *The Chicago Board of Trade, 1859–1905.* Urbana: University of Illinois Press, 1979.

Martin, Albro. *Enterprise Denied: Origins of the Decline of American Railroads, 1897–1917.* New York: Columbia University Press, 1971.

Merk, Frederick. *History of the Westward Movement.* New York: Alfred Knopf, 1978.

North, Douglass C. *Growth and Welfare in the American Past: A New Economic History,* second edition. Englewood Cliffs, NJ: Prentice-Hall, 1974.

Shannon, Fred A. *The Farmer's Last Frontier, 1860–1897.* New York: Harper & Row, 1968.

Swierenga, Robert P. *Pioneers and Profits: Land Speculation on the Iowa Frontier.* Ames: Iowa State University Press, 1968.

Turner, Frederick Jackson. *The Frontier in American History.* New York: Henry Holt, 1921.

Wiebe, Robert. *The Search for Order.* New York: Hill & Wang, 1967.

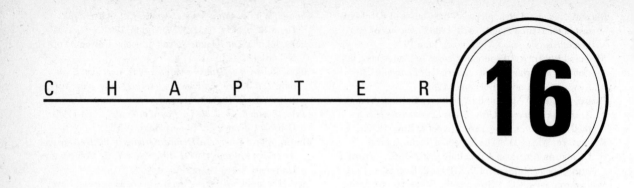

C H A P T E R 16

Population Growth and the Atlantic Migration

Between the Civil War and World War I, the demographic trends already established continued without abatement. But the differing rates of change of the component variables produced, over the long run, important changes in the total profile, in the way the American population was structured.

TRENDS

The established demographic trends had four major effects:

1. They produced a continuing rise in the population living in urban areas.

2. The country continued spreading out geographically, and the East Coast proportion continued to decline. The Midwest, West, and Southwest were producing an internal empire, the promise of which was already extant when the Civil War intervened.
3. The percentage of foreign-born rose, and they were mostly of European origin.
4. The nonwhite portion of the population continued to fall.

These results are shown in aggregate in Table 16.1.

Probably the most surprising conclusion from the numbers in Table 16.1 is that the proportion of those born abroad and still living in 1910 was only a small

Table 16.1 Overall Population Changes

		Percentages of Total					
Year	Total Population[a]	Urban	Rural	White	Nonwhite	Foreign-Born	Residence: East Coast
1860	31,444	19.8	80.2	85.6	14.4	13.2	33.7
1910	91,972	45.7	54.3	88.9	11.1	14.7	28.1

[a] Figures for total population are in thousands of persons.

Source: *Historical Statistics,* series A 57, 69, 92, 99, 105, 112, 195.

percentage increase over the 1860 proportion. Actually, the 1860 number was extraordinarily high because of the influx of Irish and Germans in the late 1840s and the 1850s—nearly 4 million between 1845 and 1860. These immigrants came, as noted in Chapter 6, following the potato blight in northern Europe in the mid-1840s and really were the beginning of mass European immigration. In 1850, the proportion of foreign-born had been only 9 percent. Actually, in 1910, some 40 percent of white Americans were either foreign born or had at least one foreign-born parent. According to Easterlin, half of the American population by 1910 had been the product of the European immigrants who came in after 1790.[1]

Birth Rates and Immigrant Vitality

Immigrants continued to make a major contribution to the total population stock, in part because the vital force of the original colonial stock, both white and black, continued to decline. Their birth rates per 1000 population in the late eighteenth century had been 50 or above. These high birth rates declined steadily (see Table 16.2), all through the nineteenth century. Death rates also declined; they fell from about 22 per 1000 per year to about 16 per 1000 per year between 1870 and 1910 as basic health conditions improved.[2] Population rose, but its high rate of increase required steady infusions from foreign stock.

Also, the rate of increase of the colonial black stock was so similar to that of the colonial white stock that the ratio between the two (their descendants) was about the same in 1920 as it had been in 1790.[3] Both the colonial black and white populations were destined to be enveloped by the nineteenth-century European immigrants and their descendants.

In 1990, the birth rate (16.7) was approximately half what it had been in 1910. Looking back, while that

1910 population appears to be comparatively vital, it is easy to forget the sturdy women of 1800 whose birth rate was nearly four times that of today. The children of these women, as well as the children of immigrants, tended to cut *their* family sizes. The pattern became established in the years between 1860 and 1910.

Population Increase and Economic Growth

During the decades 1860 to 1900, when population nearly tripled, real output grew even more rapidly under the push of rapid industrialization. National product per capita grew at rates varying between 1.4 and 1.6 percent per annum. The growth was not steady—there were serious cyclical problems—but expansion resumed after each downturn. Over time, real output stayed ahead of the rise in population. This is contrary to economist Thomas Malthus' theory that population will increase at high rates to absorb any surplus output until all population exists nearly at the starvation level. The United States, in fact, enjoyed the opposite of the Malthusian nightmare: As population rose, its means to provide increased even faster.[4] It shared this experience with the other major industrial nations. Actually, that is what distinguished these countries from the nations of Asia and Latin America, which were nearly swamped by population increase in the twentieth century.

The data in Table 16.3 on page 292 illustrate these changes in a very simple way. The work force grew faster than did total population, the national income grew faster still, and the workday shortened. The use of power sources, such as steam and then electric power, increased more rapidly than did any other area shown in the table. This increase provides a clue to understanding the rest of the information. Because mechanical power was a substitute for human energy, it was applied so that more people were employed, worked shorter hours, and were better paid for their efforts.

During most of the period, the growth of aggregate real product was extraordinarily high. In fact, of the industrial nations, only Japan maintained as high a growth of GNP in the late nineteenth and early twentieth centuries as the United States did. From the late 1860s until 1900, American GNP grew at about 4 percent per annum, compound, and in 1893–1907, it grew

Table 16.2 Live Births per 1,000 per Annum

Year	Number of Births
1800	55.0
1860	41.4
1880	35.2
1900	30.1
1910	29.2

Source: *Historical Statistics*, series B 6, white only.

Table 16.3 Evidences of Growth: 1910 Data as Multiples of 1860

Area of Growth	1910 Data / 1860 Data
Population	2.93
Employed workers	3.43
Annual hours of work	2.76
National income in 1950 prices	6.00
Horsepower of installed prime movers	8.27

Source: L. E. Davis et al., *American Economic History: The Development of a National Economy* (Homewood, Ill.: Irwin, 1969), p. 388, Table 20.3.

at more than 5 percent. At the latter rate, GNP was doubling every fourteen years. The huge increases in population cut these rates down on a per capita basis,

but the economy maintained sufficient momentum to produce net economic growth, decade after decade.[5]

IMMIGRATION AND GROWTH

In Figure 16.1, the raw immigration data are plotted for each year on an arithmetic scale. These numbers have been so analyzed by economic historians that the nature of the actual achievement tends to be lost within specialized books and papers. Twenty-four million immigrants came here between 1840 and 1914. In the last decade and a half before World War I, we admitted 12,926,000 immigrants, equivalent to the populations of a medium-sized European nation or that of all Scandinavia at the time. In 1905, 1906, 1907, 1910, 1913, and 1914, more than 1 percent a year was added to

Figure 16.1 U.S. Immigration, 1865–1914

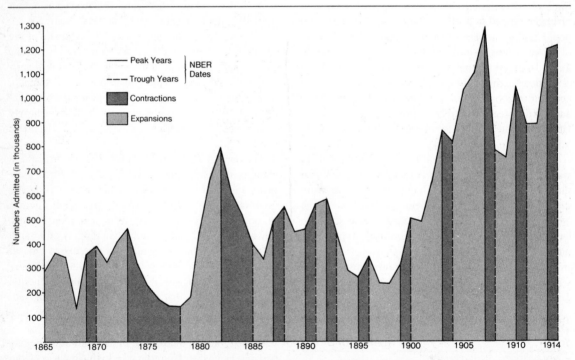

Legend:
— Peak Years (NBER Dates)
--- Trough Years (NBER Dates)
Contractions
Expansions

y-axis: Numbers Admitted (in thousands)

Source: *Historical Statistics*, series C 89; business cycle dates: A. F. Burns and W. C. Mitchell, *Measuring Business Cycles* (New York: NBER, 1947), p. 78.

The great waves of immigration show plainly, even in the raw data. The theories of Brinley Thomas comprise the leading set of explanations of these immigration waves.

population by immigration. It was a magnificent wave unequaled in all of human history. These millions came voluntarily and were voluntarily admitted.

Raw Data and the Cycle

The expanding economy utilized the millions of immigrants. It could have grown without them, of course, but its growth would have been different, and probably not as great as it was.[6] The pattern of the migration has long fascinated economists. We mentioned earlier the first great surge in the late 1840s and in the 1850s, as the millions poured out of Europe following the potato blight. The pace fell to less than 100,000 per year in the initial years of the Civil War, then picked up again. Since the migration was a purely economic phenomenon (backed by no significant governmental policy actions on either side of the Atlantic), one would expect the attraction of the United States to wax and wane somewhat with general business conditions—that is, to fit the changes in the ordinary business cycle.[7] One would think that if an immigrant had the choice, he or she would prefer to migrate to a prosperous land rather than to a depressed country like the United States. Was this generally so?

For the most part, yes. Note in Figure 16.1 the strong peaks in immigration in 1873, 1882, 1892, 1903, 1907, and 1910. These were indeed peaks in business cycle activity, and after each one there was a large downturn in immigration. Letters from earlier immigrants home would warn off younger brothers and sisters, or parents, in bad times. In good times, enthusiastic letters home urged relatives to emigrate. But there were other peaks and downturns without any corresponding turn of the immigration tide. Information lags, extra-strong "push" effects (for example, bad harvests and pogroms or massacres in 1898–1910 in eastern Europe) clearly overwhelmed other influences. What we can say, then, is that there were *some* major correspondences between short-term American business activity and the immigration inflow.

Long Swings

Looking at Figure 16.1, one is impressed by the longer term bulges and slumps, next to which the shorter peaks and troughs appear relatively insignificant, like individual waves moving against changes in the ocean tides. As was mentioned in Chapter 6, these "long swings" came in roughly four cycles, measured trough to trough: 1844–61, 1862–77, 1879–97, 1898–1914. The duration runs from sixteen to eighteen years.

What accounts for these swings? The great economist, Simon Kuznets (after whom these cycles have been named) found corresponding long swings in overall U.S. economic growth and related movements in such fundamental forces as population increase and immigration. He wrote of the underlying processes:

> The long swings in addition to per capita flow of goods to consumers resulted, with some lag, in long swings first in the net immigration balance and then in the natural increase, yielding swings in total population growth. The latter then induced, again with some lag, similar swings in population-sensitive capital formation, which caused inverted long swings in "other" capital goods to consumers. The swing in the net migration balance, and in natural increase, and so on.[8]

Kuznets' study shows that, generally, immigrant waves swelled when the worldwide growth of real incomes was upward and fell back in the secular downswing. Such fundamental forces ruled, even though individual peaks and troughs in domestic economic activity and immigration might not be in strict correspondence. The main attraction, or disattraction, of the United States to potential foreign migrants was the secular trend of U.S. real wages and incomes.

The Thomas Model

In 1954, the noted Welsh economist, Brinley Thomas, published the book, *Migration and Economic Growth,* which may, in the long run, stand as one of the great works of genius in empirical economics.[9] In it, Thomas saw the Atlantic economy (which consisted of all nations near enough to the ocean for their people to reach and cross it) as a single economic unit, with flows of people and capital moving in a self-nourishing rhythm of Kuznets cycles. This migration takes center stage for Thomas, whereas Kuznets was fairly reserved about its importance.

Thomas noted that the immigrant labor force, and its supporting flow of European investment capital, pushed the American economy in its upswings. Cheap labor and demand for food and housing gave the American expansion extra impetus.[10] There was a corresponding lull in the European rate of growth. When the American economy's secular growth rate was subsiding (the Kuznets cycle downswing), there was a corresponding expansion of the European secular growth rate as demand for food and housing rose in Europe—demand from those who now stayed home rather than emigrate. With the free flow of commodities, capital, and *people,* the nineteenth-century Atlantic economy grew in inversely related Kuznets' long cycles, even though the ordinary business cycles were largely synchronized, at least on an annual basis.

International Capital Flows

Thomas emphasizes that individual investors responded as the migrants did. They were all reacting to market conditions, and they all sought the highest return. So, when the American economy was expanding relative to trend, European investment capital flowed copiously into the American economy and helped to employ, feed, clothe, and house the arriving immigrants. There was no "plan" to this, just thousands of persons, rich and poor, reacting to market opportunities. The immigrants poured into the expanding cities of the booming American industrial economy. During these periods, Thomas argues, investment tended to be *labor-using*—more labor per unit of investment was used. Thomas calls this phenomenon the "widening" of capital.

In the reverse circumstances, fewer immigrants came. They worked in Europe and needed food, clothing, and housing there: Wages were lower than they otherwise would have been, and European investment stayed home. In that period American investment tended to be *labor-saving*—machines were substituted for workers. Thomas calls this the "deepening" of capital. Thus, the rhythm of the Atlantic economy's growth was established by the utterly free flow of people and capital, in addition to the normal growth attributes usually credited by economists to the relatively free trade in commodities in the nineteenth century.

It was, in fact, according to Thomas, the disruptive force for freer trade itself that initially launched this pattern of Atlantic migration. Food, raw materials, and some manufactured goods entered the European economy and disrupted the lives of the growing European peasant population by lowering farm incomes just when the European population was entering a phase of rapid growth. European agriculture could not expand in those circumstances, and the new population faced the need to find different employment. Since mobility between social classes and occupations was so limited in European countries, it was more efficient for Europeans to migrate to the relatively open and unrestricted U.S. economy than to try to change occupations and locations within the little national and linguistic cells of the European countries. So, populations dislodged by economic change found the highest net marginal returns to their labor *across the Atlantic Ocean.* The same was true of investors. Improvements in communications and transportation facilitated both forms of "employment search."

Thomas' grand thesis (only briefly outlined here) has withstood well the test of critical examination by scholars for nearly four decades and remains intact.[11] The inverse rhythms of the Kuznets cycle, says Thomas, explain the nineteenth-century Atlantic economy's pattern of growth (and hence the immigration shown in Figure 16.1). The completely open (to Europeans) immigration policies of the Americans, the gold standard (complete currency convertibility—assumed in perpetuity), complete freedom for the movement of investment capital internationally, and the fact that the United States was a "melting pot" society, enabled Europe to adjust to its own population and industrial growth patterns. Europe's unemployed were free to migrate; they had an alternative to conscription into a "reserve army" that might lead a revolution.

Before it was disrupted by World War I, subsequent immigration restrictions, the rise of protectionism in the 1920s, as well as the shattering of the international gold standard and its institutions, the Atlantic was truly a European-American lake. Movement across its surface enabled the economies along its edges to grow and develop at rapid long-term rates. The marginal adjustments made growth easier on both sides of the ocean.

Now, we add the arguments of Larry Neal and Paul Uselding, discussed in Chapter 6, that the immigrants themselves were also a major form of capital transfer from Europe to America—human capital provided cheaply to the Americans—and we begin to see why the United States thrived from its nineteenth century European immigration. Even if it could be argued that the same is true of the millions of Latin Americans (and others) recently coming into the United States, the difference is that this later wave of human capital does not have the force of investment *from* the Latin American countries to help support it. Moreover, American companies have been investing in labor-using factories abroad. Accordingly, Latins have received perhaps a less cordial welcome than might otherwise have been the case.

The Migration's Changing Composition

The cycles of immigration appear in aggregated data as a homogeneous stream from Europe. Actually, that was not so. Internally, the streams' composition changed over time. At first it looked very much like the colonial immigration, being mainly from the British Isles with marginal contributions from northern Europe and little or no immigration from the countries of southern and eastern Europe. Since the northern countries were mainly Protestant (Ireland apart) and the culture of the people congenial to colonial-stock Americans, the immigration aroused little resistance. Indeed, in the first decades after independence, immigrants were generally welcomed, as in colonial times, as necessary and sought-after additions to help conquer and fill up an empty continent.

Beginning with the Irish and Rhineland Germans of the 1840s and 1850s, however, a change occurred. Religion was still a big issue with Americans and so, accordingly, was religious prejudice. Because the Germans were Protestant, their great numbers attracted little resistance; however, between 1845 and 1860, 1.5 million Irish Catholics appeared. The result, as discussed in Chapter 6, was the "Know Nothing" nativist movement.

The anti-immigrant feeling welled up again later in the century. This time Italians, Greeks, and southern Slavs—peoples from the Balkans and Russia—raised the nativist ire. These were the peoples celebrated by Senator Lodge of Massachusetts as "races with which the English-speaking people have never hitherto assimilated and who are most alien to the great body of the People of the United States."[12] Demands increased for restrictions (the Chinese had already been restricted by the Chinese Exclusion Act of 1882).[13] Laborers feared the competition of fresh millions; businesspeople wanted their cheap labor.

By the late 1890s, most of the immigrants were coming from southern and eastern Europe. The 1913 figure, 1,198,000, contained a mere 15 percent from the old immigration area of northwest Europe; about 70 percent, more than 800,000 persons, came from central Europe, Russia, and Italy.

The end of the Atlantic migration was near, in part because the Americans (already safely ashore) wanted no more of such peoples. Seventy-seven percent of American whites could trace their national origins to the British Isles in 1790; by 1920, that figure was down to 41 percent, and more than 30 percent had their origins in central and southern Europe.[14] In 1921 the first law to generally restrict immigration came from Congress, with its "National Origins" quotas designed to halt further innovations in the American racial mix.

What accounted for the change in immigration flow from northwest to southeast Europe was a complicated mixture of rapid population growth—throughout the nineteenth century, from west to east—and spreading industrialization, trade, and other factors that cut death rates. Toward the end, political upheavals added to the forces of "push" from the east. However, France, which had plenty of political upheaval, contributed few American immigrants. France had a very slow population growth and stable agricultural conditions. Presumably the "pull" was of the same force for the French, but there was no significant "push." So, push mattered.

John Tomaske's study refines this analysis.[15] He argues that emigration from various European countries to the United States was *positively* related to the stock of immigrants from a given country already here (who sent information home) and *inversely* related to the ratio of per capita income in any given country at any point in time and per capita income in the United States at the same point in time. Hence information plus opportunity cost affected the patterns of emigration to the United States.

In Table 16.4 we examine the effect of the Kuznets cycle upswing of 1898–1907 by comparing "old" and "new" areas of immigration. We begin with the lull in 1895 at the end of the previous long swing. The pull effects might be expected to have been generally felt in Europe. At first, the "new area" numbers are similar in magnitude to the "old area" data. Then, a great surge in southern and eastern Europe is evident as early as 1899. The numbers quickly become immense.

There was clearly more push at work there than in northern Europe. In Table 16.5 we see the long-run changes in the immigrant origins.

Thomas would not be surprised by this. Nor would Tomaske, since the growth of "new area" population relative to "new area" GNP would have reduced the opportunity cost of emigration. In fact, the opportunity cost was probably *negative*.[16] Kuznets, relying on American expansion to pull the Europeans, might not have expected such a difference between old and new areas. Perhaps push begins the migration from the new area, then pull dominates everything as the new American upswing is underway. The Thomas model embraces the total phenomenon. Political upheaval is something separate from pure economics, so the increase of immigrants from Russia, numbering 25,800 in 1897 and 258,900 in 1907, was no accident.

There is a further point to make here. Thomas argues that U.S. immigration restrictions after 1921 enhanced the rise of totalitarianism in central and eastern Europe. This last part of his book has never been a great favorite among American economists. According to Thomas, the Malthusian wave continued after 1918 in central, southern, and eastern Europe, but now, because there was no open escape route to America, local European governments were forced to make places at home for these rising populations. The results were protectionism, large-scale government intervention in economic life, and, ultimately, totalitarianism. Even if the facts *are* correct, since the United States had no obligation to continue its immigrant inflow, it can hardly be held responsible for European political aberrations. That really is too heavy a load for the American Congress of 1921 to bear.

The important question is why the Americans ended the immigration when they did. If the Atlantic migration was good for American economic growth up to 1914, why was it stopped in the 1920s? The usual

Table 16.4   Annual Combined Immigration from European Areas: 1895–1907[a]

Year	"Old Area" Country (Great Britain, Ireland, Scandinavia, Germany	"New Area" Country (Central Europe,[b] Russia, Italy)
1895	134.2	105.5
1896	129.9	185.3
1897	84.8	122.4
1898	74.4	133.0
1899	84.8	200.9
1900	97.9	305.8
1901	106.4	334.6
1902	128.4	457.7
1903	186.7	572.7
1904	194.1	515.6
1905	238.3	682.1
1906	192.5	753.9
1907	201.3	883.1

[a] Figure for immigrants per year are in thousands of persons.
[b] Includes Czechoslovakia, Yugoslavia, Austria, and Poland.

Source: *Historical Statistics*, series C 91–93, 95, 96, 98, 100.

Table 16.5   Immigrant Origins by Percentage of Total

Year	Europe North & West	Europe East & Central	South	Other American Countries	Asia
1821–1890	82	5	3	8	2
1891–1920	25	39	25	8	3

Source: *Historical Statistics*, series C 89–114.

answer, which may well be the entire truth, was that a combination of nationalism and chauvinism built up during World War I. Fear of European "radicalism" and the resurgence of protectionist sentiment, together with organized labor's resistance to the influx of any new waves of immigrants on the pre-war scale, produced sufficient political support for restriction.[17] Immigration resumed again after World War II, but on a much reduced scale.

Table 16.6 is included to dramatize the astonishing phenomenon of the old Atlantic migration. (We will treat recent immigration, legal and illegal, in a later chapter.) It was a fundamental determinant of this country's historical experience. From 1841 to 1920, the rate of immigration per 1000 of total population was never less than three times the 1951–60 rate.

It is possible to take one final look at the echo of the great migration. The year 1930 was the census year the maximum number of children (25,902,000) of the immigrants were alive, and these children reported their parentage as shown in Table 16.7.

By 1930, Americans with German parents essentially equaled those whose parents had come from the British Isles. Italy, central Europe, and the USSR together accounted for a larger portion than did either the British Isles or Germany. By then, most Americans, particularly those with white or nearly white skins, had little idea of the proportions of their genetic history.[18] In Table 16.7 we see the final traces in the American genetic pool of the great nineteenth-century Atlantic migration, which brought the ancestors of so many millions to these shores.

THE URBAN MAGNET

Even though the European immigrants came primarily from rural areas and small villages, they settled here in cities. By 1890, according to Easterlin, the majority of the nation's urban populations, 53 percent, were foreign born.[19] On the other hand, three-fourths of the native white stock still lived in rural areas, and a mere 8 percent of them lived in cities of more than 100,000.[20]

Political Implications

The foreign-born dominating the cities—and their politics—and the native whites living mainly in rural areas and small towns, would determine the political flavor of the country for decades. After the Civil War, the Republicans were the majority party, and their strength lay in the areas dominated by native white stock. The Democrats, searching for a clientele, catered to the rising urban populations with their foreign-born majorities. Later on in the 1930s, the immigrants and their descendants would give the Democrats huge majorities

Table 16.6   Immigrants per 1,000 Population: 1820–1960

1820–30	1.2
1831–40	3.9
1841–50	8.4
1851–60	9.3
1861–70	6.4
1871–80	6.2
1881–90	9.2
1891–1900	5.3
1901–10	10.4
1911–20	5.7
1921–30	3.5
1931–40	0.4
1941–50	0.7
1951–60	1.5

Source: *Historical Statistics*, series A 7, C 89.

Table 16.7   Native White Population of Foreign or Mixed Parentage by Country of Parents' Origin, 1930

Countries	Number	Percentage of Total
British Isles	5,295,000	20.4
Germany	5,264,000	20.3
Italy	2,756,000	10.6
Central Europe	2,555,000	9.9
Scandinavia	2,247,000	8.7
USSR-Post 1918 territory	1,516,000	5.9
Other Northwestern Europe	701,000	2.7
All Other Europe	252,000	1.0
Asia	152,000	0.6
French Canada	735,000	2.8
Other Canada	1,324,000	5.1
Mexico	583,000	2.3
All Other	2,525,000	9.7
Total	25,905,000	100.0

Source: *Historical Statistics*, series C 195–227. Percentages do not total 100 due to rounding.

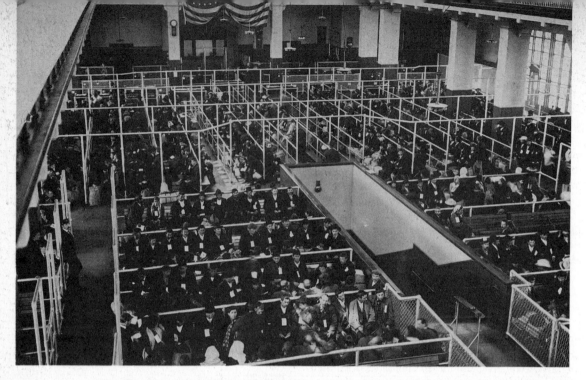

Immigration and the Urban "Magnet." As immigrants began pouring into the expanding economy, New York City was the first stop for most, beginning with "the pens" at Ellis Island for "processing" (above left), then on to tenement life (below left), which, while noisome, was alive with economic activity, as shown by this view of Hester Street (above right). A civilization dependent on horses for transport faced the daily problems of removing the manure and sometimes the beasts themselves (below right).

in national politics, and the GOP, rooted in small town and (dwindling) rural America, would have to struggle for majorities. The pattern lasted far into the twentieth century.

Regional Distribution of the Foreign-Born

The absolute numbers of foreign-born began to dwindle after the census of 1930 because of death rates and the 1920s restrictive immigration legislation. Half of all immigrants remained in the northeastern states after their arrival, near the ports of entry for Europeans, and from 1870 to 1920 the foreign-born made up about one-fifth of the total populations of those states. Table 16.8 shows the patterns of regional settlement.

Although the largest concentrations of immigrants remained in the Northeast, the North Central states, with their huge new industrial cities and fertile agricultural lands, attracted many. In 1880 and 1890, more foreign-born actually were located there than in the Northeast. The more sparse populations of the West also had a relatively high proportion of foreign-born in the total population from the beginning. On the coast—California, Oregon, and Washington—the foreign-born traditionally played leading roles, with whole sections of some cities being mainly of foreign flavor (e.g., San Francisco's Chinatown, Seattle's Ballard). Logging towns and fishing villages attracted large proportions of Swedes, Norwegians, Finns, Portuguese, and Italians.

The South attracted relatively few immigrants before the Civil War, and Appomattox appears to have had no effect on this locational preference. For most of the decades covered in Table 16.8, the proportion of foreign-born residents in the South was less than 6 percent of the total foreign-born population. Of course, the percentage of foreign-born in the Southern population as a whole was minuscule. The South's lack of attraction to European immigrants before 1860 may have had more to do with job opportunities and climate than with slavery, the explanation usually given.

Farming after 1865 was expanding in the Midwest and Great Plains, but it required considerable capital. Many immigrants managed to establish themselves there, as the growth of Minnesota, Wisconsin, and Iowa can well attest. But most immigrants were without capital when they arrived, and their skills (if they had them) could more easily be used in cities. Employment in urban services and in industry were the places where opportunity was greatest, for both the skilled and unskilled, and there the immigrants concentrated.[21] For them the "golden shore" was a town or city, and for about half the entire immigration from Europe, that town or city was located east of the Appalachians.

The once widely circulated idea that the immigrants went to the urban areas because they were incapable of

Table 16.8 Regional Settlement of the Foreign-Born: 1860–1950

Census Year	Total Foreign-Born[a]	Foreign-Born Percentage of Regional Populations				Regional Percentage of Total Foreign-Born Population			
		Northeast	North Central	South	West	Northeast	North Central	South	West
1860	4.0	19.1	17.0	3.5	28.9	50.7	38.7	6.1	4.5
1870	5.6	20.5	18.0	3.3	31.6	45.3	41.9	7.2	5.6
1880	6.7	19.4	16.8	2.7	27.8	42.1	43.7	6.7	7.5
1890	7.8	22.3	18.1	2.6	24.6	50.1	37.6	5.8	6.5
1900	10.3	22.6	15.8	2.3	19.6	46.1	40.2	5.6	8.2
1910	13.5	25.8	15.7	2.5	19.9	49.4	34.7	5.5	10.4
1920	13.7	23.1	13.5	2.6	17.3	50.1	31.9	6.3	11.7
1930	14.2	20.9	11.3	2.2	14.8	50.7	30.7	5.7	12.8
1940	11.6	17.0	8.4	1.5	10.4	52.6	29.0	5.5	12.9
1950	10.3	13.4	6.1	1.6	7.9	51.1	26.2	7.4	15.3

[a] Figures for total foreign-born population are in millions of persons.

Source: *Historical Statistics*, series A 172, 191, 194.

any except unskilled factory labor has long since been abandoned.[22] The nation was industrializing, cities were growing, and the immigrants settled where wages were highest.[23] The urban concentrations may also have represented the attraction of ethnic-group cultures in the cities, but real economic opportunities mattered too. For example, Basque sheepherders went to the wide-open spaces out West. Opportunity for their specialty attracted them there, and they did not settle for factory jobs in the Eastern cities.

Notes

1. Richard Easterlin, "The American Population," in Lance E. Davis, et al., *American Economic Growth* (1972), pp. 124–27. A useful survey of recent research in historical demography is Michael Haines and Barbara Anderson, "New Demographic History of the Late 19th-Century United States," *EEH*, October 1988.

2. Robert Higgs, in an important paper, attributes the decline in rural death rates to a general increasing healthiness of the population due to improvements in nutrition and housing resulting from the growth of real income. "Mortality in Rural America, 1870–1920: Estimates and Conjectures," *EEH*, Winter 1973. The phenomenon of falling death rates in urban areas is more generally attributed to these factors together with improvements in water supplies and urban sanitation. Edward Meeker, "The Improving Health of the United States, 1850–1915," *EEH*, September 1972.

3. Easterlin, "The America Population," p. 127. The same author provides a useful survey of much of the material treated in this chapter in "Population Issues in American Economic History," in *REH*, Supplement 1 (1977).

4. Indeed, it can be argued that strong population growth in the nineteenth century stimulated economic growth (rising incomes per capita) via inventive activity. Allen C. Kelley, "Scale Economies, Inventive Activity, and the Economics of American Population Growth," *EEH*, Fall 1972.

5. Simon Kuznets, "Notes on the Pattern of U.S. Economic Growth," reprinted in Robert Fogel and Stanley Engerman, eds., *The Reinterpretation of American Economic History* (1971), Table 1, pp. 18–19.

6. Jeffrey Williamson, "Migration to the New World: Long-Term Influences and Impact," *EEH*, Summer 1974; similarly, "Immigration and American Growth," chapter 11 in his book, *Late Nineteenth-Century American Development: A General Equilibrium History* (1974).

7. Harry Jerome, *Migration and Business Cycles* (1926).

8. Simon Kuznets, "Long Swings in the Growth of Population and in Related Economic Variables." *Proceedings of the American Philosophical Society*, February 1958, p. 34.

9. Brinley Thomas, *Migration and Economic Growth* (1954).

10. "Cheap labor" means merely that added supplies made wages lower than they otherwise might have been. Some argue that there was also wage discrimination against foreign workers. See Paul F. McGouldrick and Michael B. Tannen, "Did American Manufacturers Discriminate Against Immigrants Before 1914?" *JEH*, September 1977. But other scholars have found little support for the thesis that employers successfully discriminated against immigrants. McGouldrick and Tannen find a "moderately" successful amount of discrimination against newly arrived immigrants from southern and eastern Europe.

11. Richard A. Easterlin, "Economic-Demographic Interactions and Long Swings in Economic Growth," *AER*, December 1966.

12. Quoted in Jonathan Hughes, *The Governmental Habit Redux* (1991), p. 65.

13. The conflicts between Chinese laborers in the western states and Caucasian Americans were extremely complex. In addition to the usual racial problems, Chinese language and customs were incomprehensible to the Caucasians. When they wanted Chinese labor they could not utilize it within their own system of wage labor contracting. Nor could they return to the old system of indentures. Cloud and Galenson argue that indentures could not be re-introduced into the USA economically by the 1860s, and after, because of the cost of enforcing performance. In the case of west coast Chinese, a system developed in which the cost of performance was shifted to a middle-man, the six companies' "tongs." They show a fascinating insight into a labor contracting system of extraordinary eccentricity. In the end racial bias won, and the Chinese Exclusion Act was the result. Their paper is a model of common sense in the face of facts which would make any narrowly theoretical applications extremely artificial. Patricia Cloud and David Galenson, "Chinese Immigration and Contract Labor in the Late Nineteenth Century," *EEH*, January 1987.

14. Easterlin, "Population," Table 5.2, p. 125.

15. John A. Tomaske, "The Determinants of Intercountry Differences in European Emigration, 1881–1900," *JEH,* December 1971.

16. A negative opportunity cost to emigrate from eastern Europe for the Jews in the late nineteenth and early twentieth centuries is the implication of Irving Howe's *World of Our Fathers* (New York: Harcourt, Brace, Jovanovich, 1978). See also, Barry W. Poulson and James Holyfield, "A Note on European Migration to the United States: A Cross Spectral Analysis," *EEH,* Spring 1974.

17. Jeremiah Jenks and Jeff Lauck, *The Immigration Problem* (1926); Edward P. Hutchinson, "Immigration Policy Since World War I," *Annals of the American Academy of Political and Social Science,* vol. 262, March 1949.

18. A fifth-generation American would have had 16 American ancestors; a seventh-generation, 64 ancestors.

19. Easterlin, "Population," p. 136.

20. Native whites, however, were migrating to cities increasingly, and the immigrant decision to locate there reflected the same attractions that were pulling in the native-born: economic opportunities. Lowell Galloway, Richard Vedder, and Vishwa Shukla, "The Distribution of the Immigrant Population in the United States: An Economic Analysis," *EEH,* Spring 1974.

21. David Brody, *Steelworkers in America* (1960), "The Immigrants." For a recent survey of all the tangled issues surrounding the employment of immigrants in the American manufacturing industry, together with a survey of their indicated skill levels, see Albert W. Niemi, *U.S. Economic History: A Survey of the Major Issues* (Chicago: Rand McNally, 1980), second edition, ch. 15. In 1920 immigrants provided roughly 25 percent of the labor force in manufacturing, over 30 percent of the miners, and more than 30 percent of railroad laborers.

22. Lowell E. Galloway and Richard Vedder, "The Increas-ing Urbanization Thesis: Did 'New Immigrants' Have a Particular Fondness for Urban Life?" *EEH,* Spring 1971; and James A. Dunlevy and Henry A. Gemery, "Economic Opportunity and the Responses of 'Old' and 'New' Migrants to the United States." *JEH,* December 1978.

23. Arcadius Kahan, "Economic Opportunities and Some Pilgrims' Progress: Jewish Immigrants from Eastern Europe in the U.S., 1890–1914," *JEH,* March 1978; Gordon W. Kirk and Carolyn T. Kirk, "The Immigrant Economic Opportunity, and Type of Settlement in Nineteenth Century America," *JEH,* March 1978; Robert Higgs, "Landless by Law: Japanese Immigrants in California Agriculture to 1941," *JEH,* March 1978. Higgs makes a vigorous argument against the thesis that immigrants were successfully discriminated against, even in this extreme case. A similar result is reported in the case of immigrant women by Martha Norby Frauendorf, "Relative Earnings of Native and Foreign-Born Women," *EEH,* April 1978. Taking age and skill levels into account, Peter Hill also finds no strong evidence of successful labor-market discrimination against immigrants, "Relative Skill and Income Levels of Naive and Foreign-Born Workers in the United States," *EEH,* January 1975. These findings are at odds with those of McGouldrick and Tannen. Racial discrimination in a competitive market is, by definition, impossible. Labor markets are not, of course, perfect markets. But the force of necessity has a way of wiping out the hope of wage discrimination by employers on the basis of race. For a brilliant demonstration of this, Yuzo Mutayama, "Contractors, Collusion, and Competition: Japanese Immigrant Railroad Laborers in the Pacific Northwest, 1898–1911," *EEH,* July 1984.

Suggested Readings

Articles

Cloud, Patricia, and Galenson, David. "Chinese Immigration and Contract Labor in the Late Nineteenth Century." *Explorations in Economic History,* vol. 24, no. 1, January 1987.

Dunlevy, James A., and Gemery, Henry A. "Economic Opportunity and the Responses of the 'Old' and 'New' Migrants to the United States." *Journal of Economic History,* vol. XXXVIII, no. 4, December 1978.

Easterlin, Richard. "Economic-Demographic Interactions and Long Swings in Economic Growth." *American Economic Review,* vol. 56, no. 5, December 1966.

————. "The American Population." In Lance E. Davis et al., *American Economic Growth: An Economist's History of the United States.* New York: Harper & Row, 1972.

————. "Population Issues in American Economic History: A Survey and Critique." In Robert Gallman, ed., *Recent Developments in the Study of Economic and Business History: Essays in Honor of Herman E. Krooss. Research in Economic History,* Supplement 4. Greenwich, CT: JAI Press, 1977.

Frauendorf, Martha Norby. "Relative Earnings of Native and Foreign-Born Women." *Explorations in Economic History,* vol. 15, no. 2, April 1978.

Galloway, Lowell, and Vedder, Richard. "The Increasing Urbanization Thesis: Did 'New Immigrants' to the United States Have a Particular Fondness for Urban Life?" *Explorations in Economic History,* vol. 8, no. 3, Spring 1971.

———. "Emigration from the United Kingdom to the United States, 1860–1913." *Journal of Economic History,* vol. XXXI, no. 4, December 1971.

———. "Population Transfers and the Post-Bellum Adjustments to Economic Dislocation, 1870–1920." *Journal of Economic History,* vol. XL, no. 1, March 1980.

———, and Shukla, Vishwa. "The Distribution of the Immigrant Population in the United States: An Economic Analysis." *Explorations in Economic History,* vol. 11, no. 3, Spring 1974.

Haines, Michael R., and Anderson, Barbara A. "New Demographic History of the Late 19th-Century United States," *Explorations in Economic History,* vol. 25, no. 4, October 1988.

Higgs, Robert. "Mortality and Rural America, 1870–1920: Estimates and Conjectures." *Explorations in Economic History,* vol. 10, no. 2, Winter 1973.

———. "Landless by Law: Japanese Immigrants in California Agriculture to 1941." *Journal of Economic History,* vol. XXXVIII, no. 1, March 1978.

———. "Cycles and Trends of Mortality in 18 Large American Cities, 1871–1900." *Explorations in Economic History,* vol. 16, no. 4, October 1979.

Hill, Peter J. "Relative Skill and Income Levels of Native and Foreign-Born Workers in the United States." *Explorations in Economic History,* vol. 12, no. 1, January 1975.

Kahan, Arcadius. "Economic Opportunities and Some Pilgrims' Progress: Jewish Immigrants from Eastern Europe in the U.S., 1890–1914." *Journal of Economic History,* vol. XXXVIII, no. 1, March 1978.

Kelley, Allen C. "Scale Economies, Inventive Activity, and the Economics of American Population Growth." *Explorations in Economic Activity,* vol. 10, no. 1, Fall 1972.

Kirk, Gordon W., and Kirk, Carolyn J. "The Immigrant, Economic Opportunity, and Type of Settlement in Nineteenth-Century America," *Journal of Economic History,* vol. XXXVIII, no. 1, March 1978.

Kuznets, Simon. "Long Swings in the Growth of Population and Related Economic Variables." *Proceedings of the American Philosophical Society,* vol. 102, no. 1, February 1958.

———. "Notes on the Pattern of U.S. Economic Growth." In Robert Fogel and Stanley Engerman, eds. *The Reinterpretation of American Economic History.* New York: Harper & Row, 1971.

McGouldrick, Paul F., and Tannen, Michael B. "Did American Manufacturers Discriminate Against Immigrants Before 1914?" *Journal of Economic History,* vol. XXXVII, no. 3, September 1977.

Meeker, Edward. "The Improving Health of the United States, 1850–1914." *Explorations in Economic History,* vol. 9, no. 4, Summer 1972.

Mutayama, Yuzo. "Contractors, Collusion, and Competition: Japanese Immigrant Railroad Laborers in the Pacific Northwest, 1898–1911." *Explorations in Economic History,* vol. 21, no. 3, July 1984.

Neal, Larry, and Uselding, Paul. "Immigration, A Neglected Source of U.S. Economic Growth, 1790–1913." *Oxford Economic Papers,* 2nd series, vol. 24, no. 1, March 1972.

Niemi, Albert W. "The Role of Immigration in United States Commodity Production, 1869–1929." *Social Science Quarterly,* vol. 52, no. 1, June 1971.

Poulson, Barry W., and Holyfield, James, Jr. "A Note on European Migration to the United States: A Cross Spectral Analysis." *Explorations in Economic History,* vol. 11, no. 3, Spring 1974.

Tomaske, John A. "The Determinants of Intercountry Differences in European Emigration, 1881–1900." *Journal of Economic History,* vol. XXXI, no. 4, December 1971.

Williamson, Jeffrey D. "Migration to the New World: Long-Term Influences and Impact." *Explorations in Economic History,* vol. 11, no. 4, Summer 1974.

Books

Brody, David. *Steelworkers in America.* Cambridge: Harvard University Press, 1960.

Easterlin, Richard. *Population, Labor Force, and Long Swings in Economic Growth: The American Experience.* New York: Columbia University Press, 1968.

Erickson, Charlotte. *American Industry and the European Immigrant, 1860–1885.* New York: Russell and Russell, 1967.

Jenks, Jeremiah, and Lauck, Jeff. *The Immigration Problem.* New York: Funk & Wagnalls, 1926.

Jerome, Harry. *Migration and Business Cycles.* New York: National Bureau of Economic Research, 1926.

Kuznets, Simon, and Rubin, Ernest. *Immigration and the Foreign Born.* New York: National Bureau of Economic Research, 1954.

Taylor, Phillip. *The Distant Magnet: European Emigration to the United States.* London: Eyre and Spottiswood, 1971.

Thomas, Brinley. *Migration and Economic Growth.* Cambridge: Cambridge University Press, 1954.

Williamson, Jeffrey G. *Late Nineteenth Century American Development: A General Equilibrium History.* New York: Cambridge University Press, 1974.

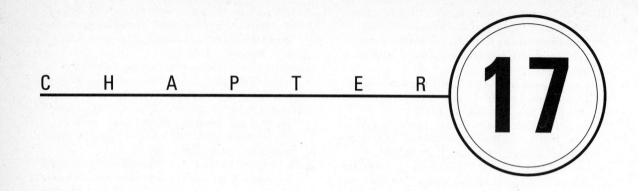

Industrialization and Urban Growth

From the Civil War to World War I, our study of American economic history is, of necessity, concentrated on and colored by industrialization. After the preliminary murmurings, big industry, big business, and the related social and political problems and benefits came to this country in that era. Paraphrasing the superb hyperbole of Lee and Passell: A Rip Van Winkle who slept from 1860 to 1914 would have been astounded to wake up in a country run by Andrew Mellon and Henry Ford.[1] He would have found himself in a nation where cities and groups of factories tended to be largely the same thing.

PRELIMINARY OBSERVATIONS

It will be helpful to consider a few rough generalizations, which nevertheless give useful insights, before we begin. We need a "big picture" to work with, a sort of hypothetical forest for the trees we will examine.[2] What makes the forest—industrializing urban society—grow in that form? Forests are not linear, nor are cities of infinite size. There are shapes, structures, limits. The processes of industrialization in this period of American history were governed by two elementary

economic forces: (a) internal economies, which made production in factories more profitable than scattered small-scale production facilities would have been, and (b) external economies, which made *groupings* of factories more profitable than the same production would have been if conducted in isolated installations.[3]

What made the internal economies? The answer can be broken down into three parts: (a) central power sources, (b) the advantages of labor-force management in the output of standardized products, and (c) the economics of transportation costs.

Power sources are not homogeneously distributed in nature. Those who wanted to use natural power sources had to locate where those activities existed. Buildings and equipment (physical capital) were constructed and attached in order to utilize the power source. Those who had to use those buildings and equipment installations for gainful employment had to go where they were located.

With the development of steam engines (and, later on, electrical engines), the location of power sites was governed more by transportation costs than by Mother Nature. Usually the object was to minimize the cost of moving raw materials and/or fuel. Since the factories were built around a prime mover (in this case, electric power) that was ubiquitous; the factories also could be located near the raw materials. The cost of transporting the lighter, finished products would be less than the cost of transporting bulky and/or heavy raw materials.

If, as was usually the case with nineteenth-century factory production, there then had to be supervision and quality control, the costs of that (management) could be reduced per worker by grouping the workers in a single place. If that place was the location of a single power source, the motivation for grouping people (and the machines and tools they were to use) was re-enforced by management economies. The cost of moving people, equipment, materials, and finished products could be high and also could be minimized by concentration of productive processes in one place—a factory.

What produced external economies? As we noted earlier, industrial locations tend to be grouped, not scattered at random over the continent. Factories tend, other things being equal, to locate near each other, each one gaining from the others' presence, cost reductions stemming from joint use of transportation facilities, labor force concentrations, and social overheads. Historically, the first step was the primary locational activity, usually pinpointed upon a regional export industry. Once that step was taken, a successful industrial nexus tended to develop as export industries and their supporting residentiary industries grew and multiplied.

In modern times, good highways, dependable long-distance communications networks, jets, computers, and satellite communications can relax the power of these forces. But, in the late nineteenth and early twentieth centuries, we are looking at an economy whose industrial locations were strongly influenced by rail and water transport and by what quickly became the major energy source, the burning of bituminous coal to raise steam.

Finally, industrial location and factory clustering minimized transportation costs by locating near markets, if the other locational factors were not dominant. Wheat milling concentrated in the Midwest (the other factors were dominant), but clothing and millinery enterprises sought markets and labor. So, New Yorkers got their flour from Minneapolis, and residents of that city most likely got their clothing from New York. For the most part, the economy at that time was one in which factories *meant* cities. Industrializing America accelerated the processes of urban growth already started, even in colonial times, by commerce, transportation and small-scale fabrication activities. But materials, navigable water, railroads, fuel, and markets would locate most nineteenth-century cities in a few locations.

Concentrations in the old Northeast, at ports, along rivers in the mid-Atlantic states, bordering the Great Lakes, in the Gulf ports, at major river junctions in the Mississippi basin, plus a few inland locations (Dallas, Denver, and Birmingham, Alabama), accounted for most of the population growth in the industrial cities. In proportion to the total land area, very little actual space was changed by the industrialization. Leaving out the twenty or thirty largest industrial locations, by 1914 the country might have seemed to a visitor as rural and unspoiled as it had at the end of the 1820s. Indeed, in places like the backwoods of New England and in Appalachia, the country reverted back to forest as the populations left, heading for urban employment or better farms farther west.

THE RISE OF HEAVY INDUSTRY

Henry Ford was born in 1863, the year of the Battle of Gettysburg. In the model year 1913–14, Ford Motor Company, an 11-year-old endeavor, shipped 248,307 completed automobiles from its plants. Each working day, Ford shipped nearly 800 cars, about 100 cars an hour. Ten years later, the Ford assembly line reached its peak production: a Model T every 15 seconds. The moving assembly line at the Highland Park, Michigan, factory had begun operation in 1913, and with it, the long history of American experimentation with interchangeable manufacture, labor-saving specialization, and capital-intensive and resource-using choices of technology reached fruition. The world of mass-production industry was changed completely. A man born when the country still had slaves had lived through an industrial revolution and would live to fly in airplanes of his own manufacture. But, let it be noted, the great change had occurred *before* the moving assembly line was introduced.

Growth of Industry

If we indexed the basic numbers related to economic growth between the Civil War and World War I on an 1860 base, we would see roughly the outcomes shown

Figure 17.1 Course of Growth by Value Added, 1860–1910

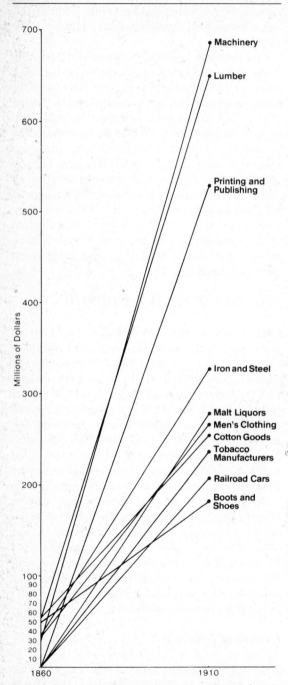

Source: *Census of Manufactures*, 1910.

in Figure 17.1. For example, we would set the 1860 population, 31.5 million, equal to 100. Then the 1914 population, 92.4 million, would be indexed at 293, just less than a threefold increase. The increase of 1914 population over 1860 population was by a factor of 2.93. The 1860 population times 2.93 equals the 1914 population (31.5 × 2.93 ≈ 92.4). The other numbers may be interpreted the same way.

Between 1860 and 1910, food production had grown slightly faster than population. However, textile production grew faster than population by a factor of 3.7; total manufacturing, by a factor of 9; industrial and commercial activities, by a factor of 12.9; iron and steel output, by a factor of 19.9. What Americans had done with cotton textile production before 1860, they now did with the entire known range of industrial and manufacturing commodity production. In the process the mainly agrarian United States had been transformed into an industrial giant.

Factor Inputs

To thus raise production output, the country had to increase the inputs. What can we say about the proportions by which those inputs were increased? Robert Gallman reduced the number of inputs into net national product (NNP) to three. Using his data, the year 1910 as a multiple of 1860 comes out: labor, 3.4; land, 3.7; capital, 10.3; NNP, 6.2.[4] In these numbers, we see the relatively high increase in the use of capital, compared either to land or labor. Substituting capital for scarcer resources, an increase of capital inputs by a factor of 10.3 produced an increase in net national product of slightly more than a factor of 6 in conjunction with the other two inputs.

The *sine qua non* of industrialization is the increased use of "capital"—at first, plant and equipment—to produce final output. Factories had to be built and installed. Where did the capital come from?

It takes the production of output above current consumption to produce investment. Families, businesses, and government must save to release the necessary resources for investment. In economics, an older idea of

By 1910, machinery, lumber, printing and publishing—together with iron and steel production—had taken the lead in value-added among American manufacturing industries. The industrial revolution had moved beyond the predominantly light manufacturing of the antebellum era.

the measurement of growth requirements of this sort was called the *capital-output ratio.* How much capital invested does it take to produce a dollar of final output? If it is 2:1, two dollars of capital to create one dollar of output, it takes a 2 percent increase in investment to create a 1 percent increase in final output. If it is 3:1, it takes a 3 percent increase in investment to produce a 1 percent increase in final output. To measure it, we need a defensible notion of capital. We need to assume that incentives to save exist and that the actual processes of investment will not reduce the average output over time. It is also clear than increasing technical efficiency in investment can *lower* the capital-output ratio.

The late Sumner Slichter measured the amount of *industrial capital* as the replacement values of physical plant equipment—machinery, and unsold inventories. He found an increase in industrial capital per dollar of national income from 41 to 75 percent between 1850 and 1912, depending upon the estimates he used.[5] Had income been fixed, such increases in capital equipment would have called for big increases in the proportion of every dollar of income produced and *not* consumed—that is, invested.

With *growing income,* however, consumption and investment can increase investment simultaneously. Since each family has more income, an increase in the proportion saved (not consumed) does not have to reduce total consumption. For example, assume that income in year T_1 is $100; $80 are consumed, and $20 saved. In year T_2 income grows to $150. Consumption that year is $112.50, and $37.50 is saved. The ratio of savings to income is 20 percent in year T_1 and 25 percent in year T_2, while consumption actually increases from $80 to $112.50.

With a growth of NNP by a factor of 6.2 between 1860 and 1910, it was possible to create a massive amount of capital and still have consumption rise substantially over time. Growing income provided for both increases in investment and consumption.[6] In addition, there were technological factors to consider.

Jeffrey Williamson argues that the increase in the ability to invest came more from reductions in the relative prices of capital goods than from any other single source.[7] Rising productivity of physical capital, itself the result of industrial development, opened the way for the great increase in income, aggregate investment, and savings rates.

Attempts to attribute increases in income to specific factors with pinpoint accuracy are not convincing, even now. For what it is worth at this early period, we have Robert Gallman's own heroic efforts to explain the growth of NNP.[8] He suggests that in 1870–1910 roughly 46 percent of the increase in output came from increased labor inputs, 9 percent from land, 23 percent from the surge in capital usage, and an additional 23 percent from such unmeasurable sources as better education of the labor force, more efficient forms of economic organization, and improvements in design.

Other Measures of Change

Significant technological changes had occurred (which we will discuss later), but the great increase in industrial output was mainly based upon the availability of labor and the exploitation of cheap raw materials. We will now repeat the same operations that produced Figure 17.1, but this time using labor-force inputs (Stanley Lebergott's data) as the basis for comparison. The result is Table 17.1, in which we can get some overall sense of the changes with a bit more precision than we could in Figure 17.1 and without getting lost in detail.

What we are observing in Table 17.1 are the statistical evidences of the shift of resources as America industrialized. Note first that under "Part I: Labor Force," the increase in the agricultural labor force is smaller than that of the total labor force. The agricultural labor force of 11.9 million in 1910 was still roughly double the 1860 figure of 5.9 million, but it had not grown proportionally with the total labor force, which had gone from 11.1 million to 37.5 million in that period.[9] Abstracting for the moment away from changes in technology and productivity, we could say simply: Although the agricultural labor force doubled between 1860 and 1910, its increase was only about 59 percent as great as that of the total labor force. The other data may be interpreted in the same way.

Workers made their way generally into industries experiencing the most rapid growth and demand for labor, producing relatively rapid labor-force expansion. As Victor Clark put it, "the industrial progress of the United States was the result of carrying labor to raw materials."[10] So, even if agriculture's 11.9 million workers in 1910 dominated absolutely mining's 1 million in total numbers, the expansion of labor forces in mining, by a factor of 6.7, indicates that there was an equally extraordinary growth in mining output (and/or profitability). Was there? Observe the expansion numbers for mining activity in "Part II: Physical Output Basis" of Table 17.1 and compare them to total labor force expansion. They are huge. In this period, the country turned to its great store of natural resources to extract the basic materials for industrial expansion.

Apart from food production (Table 17.1, "Part III: Physical Output Manufactured"), the physical output of manufactured products far outstripped the increase in labor force (and population). Even textile output, the oldest manufacturing industry, grew at more than half again the rate of growth of the total labor force (and of the increase in cotton textile workers, Part I). The growth of metals production generally was more than seven times the growth of the labor force.

Rosenberg Again

As we noted earlier, Nathan Rosenberg's improvement of the "choice of technique" argument emphasized that Americans were conserving a relatively scarce factor, labor, by utilizing extensively the most plentiful ones, raw materials. Although most of his discussion was based upon antebellum materials, it is in the late-nineteenth-century industrialization that we see the wisdom of his approach. Americans were still using wood nearly as extravagantly as before (lumber output in 1870–1910 rose by a factor of 3), but they now turned to their (then) superabundant resources of coal and metal ores to produce the great industrialization. More recently, Cain and Paterson have reaffirmed the pervasive biases in American industry toward labor-

saving and material-using technology. Motivations to create giant-sized corporate organizations of business enterprise were justified, according to Alfred Chandler, by both reductions in transportation costs and scale economies emerging from "continuous process production technology." In those industries where such forces prevailed, like tobacco products, steel, and meatpacking, giant corporations appeared between 1870 and 1900. In a separate study Jeremy Atack shows that among such industries, the *average* firm in 1900 was nearly as large as were the very largest plants in 1870. In industries not subject to decisive improvements in transport costs and the appearance of possibilities for such scale economies, the size of individual plants and their management organizations had changed little.[11]

Energy

Such an expansion of output required a similar growth of energy consumption. During 1860–1910, the production of energy from mineral resources rose by a factor of 26.4.[12] The use of bituminous coal for energy production rose by a factor of 43.8, and by 1910, fully 64 percent of all non-animal energy production in the United States came from bituminous coal. Surprisingly, it still produced about 11 percent of its nonanimal energy by burning wood to raise steam. Anthracite coal produced 12.4 percent; oil, 6.1 percent; natural gas, 3.3 percent; and hydroelectric power, 3.3 percent. The coal-burning railroad system had grown from 30,626 miles of track in 1860 to a gigantic 351,767 miles (including yards) in 1910, an expansion by a

Table 17.1 Selected Measures of Industrial Expansion: 1910 Data as Multiples of 1860[a]

Part I: Labor Force		Part II: Basic Physical Output	
Total	3.3	Iron ore	19.8
Agriculture	1.9	Crude petroleum	405.0
Mining	6.7	Bituminous coal	46.1
Construction	3.7	Pennsylvania anthracite	7.7
Total manufacturing	5.8	Cement	70.7
Trade	6.3	Copper Ore	67.5
Railroad	24.3		

[a] All multiples were calculated from the original data.

Sources: Part I: Calculated from Stanley Lebergott, "The American Labor Force," in Davis et al., *American Economic Growth* (New York: Harper & Row, 1972), Table 6.1, p. 187; and Thomas Weiss, "U.S. Labor Force Estimates and Economic Growth," in R. Gallman and J. Wallis, editors, *American Economic Growth and Standards of Living Before the Civil War* (Chicago: University of Chicago Press, 1992), pp. 37, 51. Part II: Calculated from *Historical Statistics*, series M 77–79, 205, 235, 188. Part III: Calculated from Edwin Frickey, *Production in the United States, 1860–1914* (Cambridge: Harvard University Press, 1947), pp. 54, 38–43.

factor of 11.5 with a labor force expansion by a factor of 23.2 (Part I of Table 17.1). Before the diesel engine was applied to railroads in the 1920s, virtually all this mileage was worked by burning coal. An abundant resource, coal was cheap to acquire in money terms (men killed and injured were another matter altogether, of course), and before environmental restrictions, energy for American industrialization was mainly derived from that source. The mere consumption of bituminous coal does not measure a remarkable transformation that was underway in energy use: the generation of electric power using mainly coal (and later) oil-fired central generating plants throughout the country. Ever-cheaper electric power combined with fractional-horsepower motors enabled energy sources to be localized throughout manufacturing plants virtually at will. Plant design and layouts were now freed from the need to conform to shape to the central power source instead of the production processes. By 1909 electric power already accounted for 21 percent of primary horsepower in manufacturing, a figure which would reach 50 percent in 1919, and 75 percent by 1929. As Arthur Woolf shows, electrification would be almost an additional industrial revolution, and its impact was felt even before World War I.[13]

Change in Industrial Income

Table 17.2 on page 312 compares Peter Temin's compilations from the census returns of value added by industry in 1860 and 1910. Here we can see the changes in another measure: how much net income was added to raw materials by manufacturing processes that made the finished products of the economy.

Note that four entirely new industries had moved into the top ten by 1910: printing, malt liquors, tobacco products, and railroad cars. Flour and meal, woolen goods, carriages and wagons, and leather goods, in the top ten in 1860, had dropped to lesser positions. Curiously, these changes mirrored the transformation of society.

The new big industries represented a society with mass communications and transportation, and "higher" consumption standards (for luxuries like alcoholic beverages from identifiable sources, cigars, and cigarettes) than that of 1860. Flour and meal output, exports apart, could not be expected to grow much more rapidly than population, and certainly not as rapidly as income when income per capita was rising (Engel's Law again). Straight woolen goods were less needed with higher incomes because different clothing could be purchased for summer and winter (cottons and linens for summer), improved household and office heating, and the mixing of cotton and woolen yarns to make lighter and more flexible clothing. Also, the Goodyear welt seam, better sewing machines, and a superior distribution raised boots and shoes into the top ten. Mechanization of boot- and shoe-making resulted in factory production.[14] The revolutionary adoption of paper made from wood pulp encouraged the expansion of printing and publishing beyond what was possible with the superior quality paper made from rags.

The machinery industry alone by 1910 created *value-added* (the value of final sales minus all intermediate costs) equal to 85 percent of the top ten industries *together* in 1860. As Rosenberg pointed out, the machine tool industry, which came into its own with automatic and semiautomatic technology by the end of the nineteenth century, served as a focusing and diffusion force in the revolutionary growth of standardized machines.[15] Lumber held its place as the second major income-producing industry. Renewable wood resources were lavish, and Americans continued to use lumber lavishly. It became adaptable to many new uses as cutting and shaping machinery improved. By 1910, steel had become the basic metal of American manufacturing industry.

Finally, these industries were merely the ten largest in 1910. Others were coming down the track with compelling force by the late nineteenth century—

Part III: Physical Output Manufactured	
Total manufacturing output	10.8
Food and kindred products	3.7
Textiles and their products	6.2
Iron, steel, and their products	25.2
Other metals and metal products	26.0

Factories and Mass Production.   Early industrialists attempted to improve living conditions for their workers with model, planned urban living. Lowell's mills in Massachusetts (above) and later workers' houses at Pittsburgh's Homestead Works (below) contained examples of this attempt to stabilize industrial living conditions. Mass production in a simple form may be seen on the floor of a rail mill (at the right, above). In its more complex form, mass production came to the steel industry, as shown at the right, below, at U.S. Steel's Gary plant, where these Bessemer converters were located.

Table 17.2   Ten Largest Industries by Value Added[a]

1860		1910	
Industry	**Value Added**	**Industry**	**Value Added**
Cotton goods	55	Machinery	690
Lumber	54	Lumber	650
Boots and shoes	49	Printing and publishing	540
Flour and meal	40	Iron and steel	330
Men's clothing	37	Malt liquors	280
Iron	36	Men's clothing	270
Machinery	33	Cotton goods	260
Woolen goods	25	Tobacco products	240
Carriages and wagons	24	Railroad cars	210
Leather	23	Boots and shoes	180
All manufacturing	815	**All manufacturing**	8,529

[a] Figures for value added are in millions of dollars.

Source: Peter Temin, "Manufacturing," in Davis et al., *American Economic Growth* (New York: Harper & Row, 1972), pp. 433, 447.

petroleum, chemicals, electricity for lighting and power, the automotive industry (with all its supporting infrastructure, including even highway-building governments)—that soon would disrupt and change the industrial world of 1910 beyond all recognition. They were part of the total onslaught of industrialization, if not yet leaders in sheer size. There was no rest. American industrialization had become a world of constant change, innovation on every hand, with far-reaching social and political consequences.

Technological Change

To achieve manufacturing technology with true interchangeability of parts, great technical progress beyond antebellum industry was necessary.[16] In fact, Paul Uselding doubts that there was true interchangeability anyplace in American manufacturing "at the shop level," even by 1860. Parts still had to be filed and fitted, even in such standardized productions as muskets. Devices for measurements to fine tolerances had to be invented and manufactured. Lathes, milling machines, plug and ring gauges, screw calipers, even accurate flat rules of steel were only commonly available to machinists and manufacturers in the later nineteenth century.

Uselding differentiates between accuracy in "making" machines, one at a time to order, and "manufacturing" them in production batches for all buyers. The

economics is familiar. The Americans become adept at innovating European measurement devices for use in an extensive market. Europeans, Uselding notes, made impressive measuring devices to improve the accuracy of fittings in machine-making. Over and over again, Americans imported these devices, then found ways to incorporate them in machines which could produce interchangeable replicas of various parts. The market dictated the nature of these developments. Americans wanted machines everywhere possible to save labor. Adopting ever finer standards of measurement in machine manufacturing was part of the process.

American society embraced change and improvement in the nineteenth century. As we noted in an earlier chapter, "You can't fight progress" had even infiltrated the courts of law where property rights were concerned—it was priority over prescription. New products and techniques multiplied as the economy grew. A complete catalog of even major late-nineteenth-century technological improvements would be far beyond the ambitions of this chapter. For more detail, see Paul Uselding's masterly survey essay on research in the history of technology.[17]

In iron and steel, the basic changes are both well known and terribly dramatic. First, the expansion of output had been accompanied by developing scale economies that were astounding. According to Temin, a "good" American blast furnace of 1860 produced 7–10 tons of pig iron a day. By 1910, that figure was

500 tons, and it was being made more efficiently by the associated technology of conserving and using the hot gases released, which formerly had been wasted.[18] In steel making, two great innovations, the Bessemer converter and the Siemens open-hearth furnace, came in succession. The Bessemer converter, invented in 1856, had finally been introduced in the United States successfully after the Civil War, and it made the American steel industry the world's largest. But no sooner had Bessemer triumphed than it was left in the dust by the open-hearth technology. The process is illustrated by Table 17.3.

Andrew Carnegie, the greatest steel manufacturer of the era, had come to dominate the industry on the basis of the Bessemer converter. Sir Henry Bessemer himself had convinced the young Carnegie that "Bessemer's volcano" could work with American iron, and Carnegie had come back to Pittsburgh to install his first great Bessemer works in the early 1870s.

In a competitive market, output expands and prices fall, the gains going mainly to the most efficient. Steel rails sold at $120 a ton in 1873 and had fallen as low as $17 a ton in 1898. During that period, Andrew Carnegie had entered the steel industry as a novice and surpassed every steel producer in the world. He had done it by ruthless use of the market, telling his sales force to accept the market price and his managers to meet it profitably. Every time his furnaces were rebuilt, Carnegie demanded improvements in their design.

There was a tariff of $28 a ton on steel rails in the 1890s, and that industry hankered after a price-fixing pool, OPEC-style. Such pools had existed in Pittsburgh traditionally, although after the Sherman Antitrust Act of 1890, joining them was risky. Carnegie knew that his cost-cutting innovations and expansion into open-hearth technology could give him all the sales he wanted. He told a competitor he wanted no more pooling agreements: "The market is mine whenever I want to take it. I see no reason why I should present you with my profits."[19]

Carnegie freely scrapped his massive Bessemer plants to install the Siemens open-hearth furnaces and, in the process, was reported to have opened a board meeting with, "Well, what shall we throw away this year?"[20] Technological change produced rapid obsolescence, and a competitive economy forced new innovations to be adopted.[21] Those who fell behind the pace had to give up.

Andrew Carnegie was the classic nineteenth-century American tycoon, the Schumpeterian entrepreneur, whose competitive methods were characterized by the great economist, Joseph Schumpeter, as "creative destruction." If new inventions are to be introduced into the stream of economic life, less efficient processes must be retired. The innovative economy necessarily leaves a trail of obsolescent junk. In a competitive market, the measure of need is profit. It can be increased by cutting costs, and that is what the new technologies did in the nineteenth century. Steel was perhaps the most dramatic example. Vast quantities of money were involved—thousands of workers, coal, coke, railroads, lake steamers, barge lines—whole communities and cities appeared as the industry grew. Great fortunes were made (and lost) from it, dramatic confrontations in social relations (the famous and violent Homestead strike of 1892, in which the company used the

Table 17.3   Steel Production 1870–1913[a]

Year	Total	Bessemer Converter	Open-Hearth Furnace	Percentage Bessemer Converter	Percentage Open-Hearth Furnace
1870	77	42	2	54.5	2.6
1880	1,397	1,203	113	86.1	8.1
1890	4,779	4,131	566	86.4	11.8
1900	11,227	7,481	3,638	66.6	32.4
1910	28,330	10,478	17,672	37.0	62.4
1913	34,087	10,604	23,340	31.1	68.5

[a] Figures are in thousand short tons unless otherwise indicated.

Source: *Historical Statistics*, series P 265–67.

Scale Economies in The Retailing Revolution.   Mass production presupposed mass consumption and a national market. Wanamakers in Philadelphia (1876, above) was the epitome of the big city department store. But even in the more humble circumstances of a National Tea Company store in Chicago (below), the customer had the advantages of food preparation and standardized packaging.

Pinkerton agency and the National Guard to protect "scab" workers and break the strike, was against Carnegie Steel).

In the 1890s, production of special alloy steels increased, then electric furnaces were introduced. The constant pressure was to reduce the time (and need for reheating) between ingot production, rolling, shaping, and drawing. Progress was steady, competition intense, and the industry continued its cost-reducing expansion.

Reductions in production costs, passed on to buyers, are the private economy's version of *subsidies,* except that no forced transfers of income are involved. Instead, the buyer's real income is increased. Competition forced producers to pass the gains on to their customers. Judge Elbert H. Gary, then head of Illinois Steel, said it all, commenting upon the results of Carnegie's competitive onslaught. It no longer would be possible "to do business on the basis of high profits for comparatively small tonnage."[22] Even when J. P. Morgan bought out Carnegie and put together two-thirds of the industry's ingot capacity as United States Steel, the industry kept expanding.

Improvements in agricultural machinery, steam threshing, and better reapers and harvesters kept agricultural machinery a growing industry as the Midwest wheat and corn economy expanded. The introduction of refrigeration in meat packing, beginning in the 1870s, opened up a national market to packers, and the race for amalgamation produced such names as Swift and Armour. The petroleum industry's John D. Rockefeller was slowed by a successful antitrust prosecution in 1911, and that industry was not monopolized.[23] Discoveries of oil in the Southwest gave it further impetus. In textiles, the latter decades of the century saw the further development of automatic power looms, better sewing machines, and cutting tools reduce the cost of manufacture in clothing. Standard sizes in men's wear had resulted from the experience of making uniforms for the union army, thus increasing the possibilities of mass production, including boots and shoes.

By the last part of the century, standardization and interchangeable parts, an older American tradition, had finally become characteristic of American manufacturing. Production for a national market had been the object of the growth and merger of industrial firms, increasing the drive for standardization of sizes in producer goods, consumer durables, in clothing, and tools. These made mass production possible as the huge American market grew and eased the problems of industrial expansion by simplifying product designs.[24]

EXPANSION OF THE MARKET

Where did all the growth of output go? Since the cost of output is income to the factors used to produce it, the answer is simply that it was sold, in the American market. The incentive to invest and expand output was there because the incomes produced were distributed in such a way that the product found profitable sales. Probably Adam Smith's most-quoted maxim has been, "The division of labor is limited by the extent of the market." In the case of the United States, the market was massively extended.

Between the Civil War and World War I, the population grew, as we have seen, by a factor of 2.93. Net national product in constant prices grew by something like a factor of 6. The average person could thus buy two times as much in 1914 as could his or her counterparts in 1860, and there were nearly three times as many people. Even if there had been no *substitution effects* (one product bought at the expense of another), the expansion of the domestic market would have given splendid scope for new industries, products, and techniques. But, in fact, some products and industries declined as others came to the fore, so there were *product displacement effects* as well. Actually, at current market prices, GNP per capita may well have tripled from 1860 to 1914, and, other things being equal, the resulting increase of per capita incomes was mostly available for the purchase of manufactured goods or services. Engel's law yet again, Americans were already reasonably well fed in 1860.

Gallman's Performance Estimates

Professor Gallman's estimates of real GNP (at prices of 1860) are shown in Table 17.4 in overlapping decades. The estimates show an expansion of roughly the order of 5 to 6 between 1858 and 1903.

With his estimates pushed back to the 1830s Professor Gallman estimates of GNP show that by 1840 US GNP was probably just below the GNP of Britain and of France. *Per capita,* by 1840 the United States was from a quarter to 40 per cent higher than France and somewhere near the British. Gallman concludes:

"Very early in her history the United States was one of the great economic powers."[25]

The rate of growth of GNP was about 48 percent per decade in 1834–43 to 1894–1903, and slowed to 34 percent per decade in 1894–1903—1944–53. With the *rate of growth* of population also decelerating however, per capita growth was about constant, at 16 percent per decade from 1834 to 1953.

In the entire period there was one really striking change; there was a powerful increase in the share of capital formation. Gallman is not certain just exactly when this occurred, but it centered around the era of the Civil War. In pre–Civil War decades, gross capital formation was somewhere about 14–15 percent; after the Civil War it was about 24–28 percent, and that high rate continued into the twentieth century, up to 1914. Gallman notes of this phenomenon that it was ". . . from a high level to an exceptionally high level."[26] The origin of this was almost entirely an increase in domestic savings rates.

As economic growth proceeded it was striking that the supply of manufactured producer durables was mainly made domestically. Americans produced their own machines, for the most part, as they industrialized.

In addition to the domestic market growth, there was a massive expansion of the markets for manufactured and semimanufactured goods abroad.[27] Between 1860 and 1914, exports of manufactured food grew by a factor of 7.5, from $39 million to $293 million; exports of semimanufactured goods expanded from a mere $13 million to $374 million, or by a factor of 28.8. Exports of finished goods grew by an extraordinary factor of 20.1, from $36 million to $725 million. Crude

materials, the antebellum winner in international trade, only increased from $217 million to $800 million in the same period, by a factor of 3.7. The farmers did well enough—crude food exports increased from $12 million to $137 million. By 1914, then, manufactured food, semimanufactures, and finished manufactures together actually earned 49 percent *more* than did crude food and raw materials combined. In 1860, exports of manufactured materials and food had equaled only 12 percent of the combined exports of crude materials and crude food. In that era of fairly free trade, American manufacturers had done well indeed in the foreign economy, while constantly pressing for unnecessary protective tariffs at home!

Simon Kuznets estimated NNP at market prices at an annual average of $6.20 billion in the five years 1869–73 (his earlier published figures) and $34.6 billion in 1912–16.[28] This rise by a factor of 5.6 is on the same order of magnitude, given the differences in dates (and uncorrected prices), as our other estimates. It seems clear enough that every dollar of potential market in 1860 was five to six dollars by 1914. American industrialists faced the prospect of secular rising demand for their product.

Other things being equal, innovations in technology, together with steady labor force increases in a competitive market, can be considered bright market conditions for Adam Smith's extended divisions of labor—investment in new technologies to make new products. There were the great cyclical swings, but as Schumpeter argued, they actually *helped* the processes of growth in a capitalist economy. The massive expansion of American manufacturing seems to have been in the cards toward the end of the nineteenth century, once the country's first "great game," the public domain and its private expropriation, had been attended to in its best parts. Extensive acquisition of the best publicly held resources was nearly over, and it was time for intensive processes of growth to take over, those characterized by the rise of the manufacturing industry.

URBAN GROWTH

That urban places are also industrial places is nearly a truism, since (in Douglas North's terminology) even a Florida city consisting of the retired elderly and winter tourists would grow supporting residentiary

Table 17.4 GNP 1834–1908 (Prices of 1860)

Overlapping Decades	$ Billions
1834–43	1.56
1849–58	3.30
1869–78	6.40
1874–83	8.40
1879–88	10.6
1884–93	12.7
1889–98	14.4
1894–03	17.3
1899–08	21.8

Source: Robert E. Gallman, "Gross National Product in the United States 1834–1909," Dorothy S. Brady, ed., *Studies in Income and Wealth* (New York: N.B.E.R., Columbia University Press, 1966), vol. 30, Table A1.

employment.[29] Given any scale economies at all, some of these employments would produce agglomerations of workers—factory-style grouped employment. Some residentiary industries would then achieve regional and national status as their products penetrated the market. What has been really rare has been industrialization *without* accompanying urban growth. With modern communications, it would seemingly be possible, but it has seldom occurred.

For example, England, during its industrial revolution, experienced a general population growth of 130 percent (1751–1831). London, already a huge and ancient city in the mid-eighteenth century when the process of industrialization accelerated, had grown, by 1831, some 170 percent over the 1750 figure. But, in that same period, populations of the industrial county of Lancashire expanded by a factor of 5. Manchester, its largest city, expanded by more than a factor of 6.7. Leeds grew by a factor of 7; Bolton, by more than a factor of 8. Britain's new industrial cities (mainly in the north and the midlands) were growing at rates similar to that of Los Angeles in the 1940s. All over Europe, once industrialization spread, new cities grouped around factories appeared where formerly only sleepy medieval villages had existed. Mulhouse and Lyon, Namur and Liege, Ruhrort and Essen, Chemnitz, Kharkov, and Yuzovska (Stalino, now Donetsk) were among the new places of industrial urban populations that appeared.[30]

In this country the westward movement of populations and industry produced the same effects: Troy and Buffalo, then Erie, Youngstown, Cleveland, Toledo, Detroit, Gary, Chicago, Milwaukee, and Duluth grew up around the Great Lakes and in the North. Scranton, Allentown, Pittsburgh, Akron, Wheeling, Columbus, Fort Wayne, Indianapolis, Minneapolis, and Cincinnati developed inland along the rivers. Birmingham, Mobile, New Orleans, Shreveport, and Houston appeared in the South and along the Gulf. So, the list of cities of late-nineteenth- and early-twentieth-century America grew as populations flocked to the centers of industrial activity. By 1960, 160 metropolitan areas contained some 90 percent of the American population.[31]

The process is never finished. As technologies change, some older cities decline, while new ones expand. The "energy crisis" of the late 1970s is credited with locating many new manufacturing enterprises in the "Sun Belt" of the American South and West, leaving the grimy old steel and coal towns of the upper Midwest and East to die on the vine. Also, some older industries have proved to be migratory, like machine tools, whose centers have moved many times to follow their customers: leaving Troy, Cincinnati, and then Chicago behind as the population moved to Houston and Los Angeles. Textiles and clothing manufacturing have also proved remarkably mobile.[32] Cotton textiles brought urbanization to the South, dominating Southern industrial life, just as earlier in history, raw cotton dominated Southern rural life.[33]

Table 17.5 shows the outline of urban growth up to 1910. Three cities—New York, Philadelphia, and Chicago—had more than a million in population and contained together very nearly 10 percent of the nation's

Table 17.5 Urban Growth

	Incorporated Places, 2,500 and Over		Incorporated Places, 100,000 and Over		Incorporated Places, 1,000,000 and Over	
	Number	**Percentage of Total Population**	**Number**	**Percentage of Total Population**	**Number**	**Percentage of Total Population**
1790	24	5.4	—[a]	—	—	—
1840	131	10.8	3	3.0	—	—
1860	392	19.8	9	8.4	—	—
1880	939	28.2	20	12.3	1	2.4
1890	1,348	35.0	28	15.4	3	5.8
1900	1,737	39.7	38	18.7	3	8.5
1910	2,262	45.7	50	22.1	3	9.2

[a] No urban areas of this size yet existed.

Source: *Historical Statistics*, derived from Series A 57–69.

Early Urban Mass Transit. Urban public transportation soon enough produced suburbs. The early horse-drawn omnibus (introduced in the 1820s) was succeeded by the horse-drawn trolley on tracks in the 1850s until about 1900. Electricity produced a revolution in public transportation. In 1887, Richmond, Virginia, introduced the country to the first electrified trolley system, which spread

like wildfire by 1890 to nearly every major American city. The picture (above right) of Oak Park, Illinois, in 1890 with its electrified trolley shows open country, which was suburbanized within twenty years. Real estate speculators immediately got the point, as shown (below right) in the advertisement for lots along Chicago's Lincoln Avenue (soon to be served by horse-drawn trolley).

entire population. There were already 50 urban places with populations in excess of 100,000, containing 22 percent of the total population. One of five Americans by 1910 lived in a really large urban place. It might have seemed at the time that the whole country would evolve into a few great cities. But that did not happen, and even in the nineteenth century, the vigor of smaller urban places was partly apparent in the data. Urban places of more than 2500 but smaller than 25,000 managed to hold more than 30 percent of total urban population, even while the big cities were growing most rapidly.[34]

The maximum city size had not yet been tested in the United States. That would come later in the twentieth century when the giants would stop growing and lose populations, and smaller cities would take over the processes of urban growth. Nevertheless, the chronicles of the nineteenth century already revealed the familiar urban problems of crime, congestion, and pollution, the *diseconomies* of urban life. The advantages of urban life prevailed, though, already draining the *increase* of population out of the countryside (in another half century, the countryside would experience absolute decreases in numbers and appear to be largely abandoned).

The significant scale economies of cities included transport, education, medicine, central water and sewerage systems, "culture," communications—all the amenities that attracted people.[35] But, most of all, the cities meant jobs and varieties of opportunity for the growing population of the country. The large tertiary sector—services, trades, and professional employments that service the industrial base—was clearly evident. Lebergott's labor-force data show that by 1914, fully 54 percent of the nonfarm labor force was in basically tertiary employment, and these jobs tended to be concentrated in urban areas. The research of Thomas Weiss on the origin of the increase in tertiary sector employment shows that, in the main, it is the result of the rise in per capita income attendant to the growth of cities and the urban workforce.[36]

By the mid-twentieth century, about two thirds of *all* employment would be in the tertiary fields.[37] Such employments are based upon the productiveness of extractive industries, manufacturing, and primary industry. Essentially, the tertiary sector consists of services traded for food, clothing, shelter, and other services. Notice in Table 17.6 that tertiary employment (either including or excluding transport and utilities) expanded while the proportion in manufacturing *actually declined*. This trend would continue and is, in fact, typical of successful industrialization.[38] Rising productivity frees labor for employments besides making food and goods.

The tertiary employments tend to require specialized education and/or training and, therefore, cluster in cities. Industrial activity attracts them and pays them. They are the creatures of external economies and tend to locate near each other—advertising in New York City, television in Hollywood, for example. So, urban growth created more urban growth. The industrialization of American life sealed American society as an

Table 17.6   Employees in Nonfarm Establishments[a]

Area of Employment	1900		1914
	Number	Percentage	Number
Mining	637	4.2	1,027
Contract construction	1,147	7.6	1,267
Manufacturing	5,468	36.0	8,210
Transport and utilities	2,282	15.0	3,445
Trade	2,502	16.5 ⎤	4,128
Finance	308	2.0 ⎟ 37.2 } 52.2	657
Service	1,740	11.5 ⎟	2,647
Total civilian government	1,094	7.2 ⎦	1,809
Total	15,178	100.0	23,190

[a] Figures that are not percentages are in millions of persons.

Source: Stanley Lebergott, "The American Labor Force," in Davis et al., *American Economic Growth* (New York: Harper & Row, 1972), derived from Table 6.2, p. 192.

urban one. People whose ancestors had cut down the woods and plowed up the prairies would typically be uncertain whether cheese and butter had a common origin. But, it was information they no longer needed for survival.

INDUSTRIAL GROWTH UNDER CAPITALISM

Not the least notable phenomenon in American economic development was the absence during most of our history of any effective centralized economic planning. Governments taxed and spent, on a small scale, passed tariff laws, gave some subsidies, and sold part of the public domain to private owners. Under police powers, certain businesses were regulated or required to have licenses by state and local governments. There was little more that one might call central direction, apart from the spate of internal improvements in the 1830s and 1840s. For the most part, the country's growth and development patterns and structure simply resulted from the sum, over time, of individual reactions to their own desires and opportunities.

Motivation

Economists usually remove from their discussions all except purely economic stimuli to human action. But, of course, reality is far more complex than that. For example, something as noneconomic as the religious instinct generally directed the enterprise of thousands

of people from Plymouth Colony onwards. Individual motivations are complex beyond imagination, and people entered into economic enterprises for the full range of possible reasons. However, in American society, there was always one powerful centralizing force: private rights in property of all sorts, well understood and protected. So, such universal motivations as survival, greed, avarice, and envy as well as more elevated impulses could always be counted upon to focus and produce economic increase in all but the most difficult circumstances.

Wealth and Entrepreneurial Supply

As we have seen from very earliest colonial times, wealth was unequally divided among the population by inheritance, hard work, or blind luck. Because of uneven wealth, and hence uneven opportunity, not everyone undertook extensive entrepreneurial ventures. After all, in every population some are very risk averse, most are cautious, and a small portion always are gamblers and plungers. Other things being equal, any randomly selected population will contain some potential entrepreneurs. If knowledge and opportunity were present, and distributive rights to the profits settled and assured, entrepreneurial activity occurred in American history.

This force in our past was long the dominant power shaping the country's development. It could be counted upon to flourish. But there was far more to it than unequal wealth distribution. One is impressed that, until recent times, when American innovative and entrepreneurial powers seemed to weaken, virtually no comment was made about the effectiveness of our entrepreneurial prowess.[39] It was just there, always, whenever it was needed.

The great entrepreneurs themselves tended to be the focus of popular envy and abuse. As Theodore Roosevelt said of the railroad financier, Edward Harriman, "[He is] a malefactor of great wealth." Since successful entrepreneurs tended to be wealthy, and newly rich at that, they were the butt of acid commentary and ridicule. Today, their descendants, who have done nothing but be born to wealth, are venerated. No one is laughing at the Harrimans, Goulds, and Vanderbilts in the *New York Times* social pages, but those who earned that money have been treated in American history much like common criminals. Only when the

Percentage		Percentage Increase (1914 over 1900)
4.4		61.2
5.5		10.5
35.4		50.1
14.9		51.0
17.8		65.0
2.8	39.8 } 54.7	113.3
11.4		52.1
7.8		65.4
100.0		

Boomtown. Chicago was both the most dramatically growing city of the nineteenth century and representative of the way so many American cities grew. From 50 people in 1830, to 4200 at its incorporation as a city in 1837, to 30,000 in 1850, to 300,000 in 1870, to 600,000 in 1880, to 1,200,000 in 1890, to 2 million just after the turn of the century. Since Chicago was built next to a waterway and was subject to periodic flooding (like so many cities), the city was raised in the 1860s by several feet. All buildings near the Chicago River, including downtown Chicago, were mechanically raised several

inches (above left) which left the city on two levels (below left). Chicago is shown (below right) a year before the great Chicago fire of 1871 which burned a path 4 miles long and a mile wide, leaving 100,000 people homeless. A similar view taken just after the fire (above right) shows the devastation. The Chicago Water Tower is the second tower from the right in the top picture and just to the left of the flagpole in the bottom one.

American steel industry in the 1970s needed a new Carnegie and the automobile industry needed a new Henry Ford—*and no one stepped forward*—did we begin to worry about entrepreneurship, call conferences, make government grants to study the problem, and otherwise sound the alarm.

Schumpeter

As we mentioned in Chapter 14, the leading student of capitalist entrepreneurship was the great economist, Joseph Schumpeter. In three of his books, *The Theory of Economic Development, Business Cycles,* and *Capitalism, Socialism, and Democracy,* as well as in many shorter works, Schumpeter expounded his analysis of the entrepreneurial role in the development of modern capitalism.[40] The end of a chapter on late nineteenth-century industrialization is a good place to pause a moment and consider Schumpeter's thesis in brief outline.

The period from about 1842 to 1897 was really the one that fascinated Schumpeter, the building internationally of what he called, in a nonpejorative sense, the "bourgeois culture." He meant by *bourgeois* the middle class—its values, culture, ideals: the whole package of liberal democracy, representative government, open societies that encouraged social mobility, easy access to education, personal freedom, toleration of diversity, and secure property rights. To Schumpeter, a deep student of history, these were unique creations of nineteenth-century capitalism. No other kind of economic system had created, or could create, this type of society.

Invention and Innovation

What motivated the growth of bourgeois society? To Schumpeter, the driving forces were the innovating capitalist entrepreneurs. They were the risk-takers. Their visions of the future—for themselves, their families, and their associates—created the future, if they succeeded. The weapon they used to force change into the competitive marketplace was innovation—new products, new ideas, new services, new technologies.

Invention and *innovation* were two separate things. Invention was a passive employment of human talent. A "better mousetrap" made no difference to society-at-large or to economic growth if it remained in the workshop. To produce and sell it in the competitive

marketplace took a different kind of talent, entrepreneurial ability. An invention successfully placed into the stream of economic life diverted that stream, changed the allocation of resources, and became an innovation. Those innovating entrepreneurs (some of them, like Bell and Edison, were also inventors) who were able to succeed on a gigantic scale became the "natural" leaders of bourgeois civilization because of their success.

The nineteenth-century industrialization was created by individual business firms, which had been created by individual persons: the entrepreneurs. People started businesses, "conditions" started nothing. Therefore, those who were the "Robber Barons" to critics of bourgeois civilization were to Schumpeter its heroes. Cyrus McCormick and John Deere in farm machinery; Cornelius Vanderbilt in steamships and railroads; Collis Huntington, Leland Stanford, Edward Harriman, James J. Hill, even Jay Gould and Jim Fisk in railroads; Carnegie and Henry Frick in steel; John Pierpont Morgan, August Belmont, Andrew Mellon in finance; John D. Rockefeller in oil—so the list goes of the late-nineteenth-century's Schumpeterian entrepreneurs.

It was a competitive world, not zero-sum, but one in which the inefficient were "driven to the wall"— a necessary result of the capitalist growth process. The disruption caused by the competitive battles was the price of progress. Entrepreneurs reacted to the signals of the marketplace. That was the only "planning" there was. The economy grew in response to consumer demand expressed in dollar votes, either because successful entrepreneurs discovered what consumers wanted or *convinced* consumers, by sales techniques, that the new innovations were essential. Moreover, innovation led to even more innovation by the mechanism of derived demand.[41]

Schumpeterian Growth

The very path of growth was the result of "waves" of innovations, sometimes functionally linked with each other (e.g., steel, chemicals, electricity, autos). The long-term growth path is produced by the algebraic sum of the ups and downs of shorter term business cycles. In expansions, extra entrepreneurial force is released by a wave of optimism, by growing markets, high profits, rising prices, easier access to finance. In cyclical downswings (usually detonated by the financial system's inability to continue the expansion), only the most efficient survive.

Those who have been swept along in the boom, whose ventures are unsound, or whole (older) businesses have become obsolete, are forced to liquidate. The workers and resources they had employed are now free to be bought up (perhaps at cut rates) by the more efficient firms or by the new ones coming on line in the ensuing business upswing. The *recession* itself was thus a critical part of Schumpeterian growth process.[42] Alert operators bought out the losers. That is how Andrew Carnegie bought the Homestead works and Duquesne Steel—in recessions. One of Carnegie's managers said of Carnegie's methods:

> The real time to extend your operations was when no one else was doing it. Whenever there would be a boom in the steel trade most manufacturers would start in and build new steel works. They would have to pay the very highest prices for the materials that entered into these constructions on account of boom times, and about the time they were ready to operate the bloom was off the peach and the works would have to lie idle.[43]

That's when Carnegie made his bid. Other successful entrepreneurs understood when to be "long" in the markets and when to be "short."[44] Those who did not, failed. It was hard and ruthless, and, Schumpeter argues, effective in the creation of economic growth by unimaginable dimensions. The great growth period 1842–96 (trough to trough) was a **Kondratieff cycle** (a long growth cycle of about fifty years). Schumpeter called it "the bourgeois Kondratieff" because it saw vast industrialization all over the commercial world as well as in the United States.

The modern welfare state has been devised in part to take the "sting" out of this kind of growth. That this modern improvement produces stagnation and inflation *simultaneously* has surprised many economists. It would not have surprised Schumpeter. It might be added that Schumpeter himself did not believe that the old system could continue. Americans lost their taste for such a life and voted, in election after election, for something less exciting. This was the final message of his gloomy book, *Capitalism, Socialism and Democracy.*

Notes

1. Susan Previant Lee and Peter Passell, *A New Economic View of American History* (1979), p. 226.
2. For the best short but elegant survey of the period and issues covered in this chapter, see Robert Higgs, *The Transformation of the American Economy 1865–1914* (1971).
3. For a world in which no cities would develop, see Higgs, pp. 59–61. Heterogenous physical features and internal and external economies are sufficient to produce cities in a commercial world.
4. Lance E. Davis et al., *American Economic Growth: An Economist's History of the United States* (New York: Harper & Row, 1972), ch. 2, "The Pace and Pattern of American Economic Growth," calculated from Table 2.9, p. 34.
5. Sumner H. Slichter, *Economic Growth in the United States and Its History Problems and Prospects* (1961), p. 62. His capital-output ratio for industrial capital was 1.63 in 1850 and ranged from 2.3 to 2.9 for 1900.
6. Robert Gallman estimates that savings rates in fact did increase powerfully as industrialization proceeded, as in the example in the text. He estimated savings rose from about 14 percent of NNP in the 1860s to more than 25 percent in the 1880s. "Gross National Product in the United States, 1834–1909," *Studies in Income and Wealth,* N.B.E.R., vol. 30 (1966).
7. Jeffrey Williamson, "Inequality, Accumulation, and Technological Imbalance: A Growth Equity Conflict in American History?" *Economic Development and Cultural Change,* vol. 27, no. 2, January, 1979, p. 249.
8. Robert Gallman, "The Pace and Pattern of American Economic Growth," in Lance E. Davis et al., *American Economic Growth* (1972), pp. 33–39. The calculation for the years 1870–1910 is from Lee and Passell, *A New Economic View of American History* (1979), Table 13.3.
9. Measured in constant dollars, agriculture generated 61 percent of total real output, to industry's 39 percent. By 1909, these numbers were 26 and 74—more than a reversal of roles. Robert E. Gallman and Edward S. Howle, "Trends in the Structure of the American Economy Since 1840," reprinted in Robert Fogel and Stanley

Engerman, eds., *The Reinterpretation of American Economic History* (1971), p. 26.

10. V. S. Clark, *History of Manufactures in the United States* (1929), p. 2.

11. Louis P. Cain and Donald G. Paterson, "Biased Technical Change, Scale, and Factor Substitution in American Industry, 1850–1919," *JEH*, March 1986. In two recent papers, Gavin Wright has emphasized the critical role American natural resources played in late nineteenth century growth: "The Origins of American Industrial Success, 1879–1940," *AER*, September 1990; and "The Rise and Fall of American Technological Leadership: The Postwar Era in Historical Perspective," *JEL*, December 1992.

12. Data from *Historical Statistics*, Series M 83–92. A. D. Chandler, Jr., *The Visible Hand* (1977); and Jeremy Atack, "Industrial Structure and the Emergence of the Modern Industrial Corporation," *EEH*, January 1985.

13. Arthur G. Woolf, "Electricity, Productivity, and Labor Saving: American Manufacturing, 1900–1929," *EEH*, April 1984.

14. William H. Mulligan, Jr., "Mechanization and Work in the American Shoe Industry: Lynn, Massachusetts, 1852–1883," *JEH*, March 1981.

15. Nathan Rosenberg, *Technology and American Economic Growth* (1972).

16. Paul Uselding, "Measuring Techniques and Manufacturing Practice," in Otto Mayr, ed., *The American System of Manufacturing* (1981). The improved quality of American manufactured metal products in the late nineteenth century *and* their competitive prices in the British market is documented by R. C. Floud, "The Adolescence of American Engineering Competition, 1860–1900," *EHR*, February 1974.

17. Paul Uselding, "Studies of Technology in Economic History," in *REH*, supplement 1 (1977).

18. For perhaps the best modern study, Peter Temin, *Iron and Steel in Nineteenth-Century America: An Economic Inquiry* (1963). For an excellent study of blast-furnace technology: Robert C. Allen, "The Peculiar Productivity History of American Blast Furnaces 1840–1913," *JEH*, September 1977.

19. Jonathan Hughes, *The Vital Few* (1986), p. 239.

20. Hughes, p. 259.

21. Americans also took a different view of the purpose of blast-furnace linings. By raising air pressure in the blast, the amount of pig iron per charge could be increased, but the blast furnace linings were worn out more rapidly. The American iron masters raised the pressure, called "hard driving," and their profits, too. British observers were critical of the technique, but the Americans could sell iron cheaper, even at the expense of new blast-

furnace linings. Peter Berck, "Hard Driving and Efficiency: Iron Production in 1890," *JEH*, December 1978.

22. Hughes, *The Vital Few*, p. 238.

23. Joseph A. Pratt, "The Petroleum Industry in Transition: Antitrust and the Decline of Monopoly Control in Oil," *JEH*, December 1980.

24. The new American technological advances were not universally adopted by her trading partners. For example, in clock and watch manufacturing the Swiss copied American techniques, but the British did not. Donald Hoke, *Ingenious Yankees* (1990). The selective international spread of "best practice" technology in these cases remains a mystery. Hoke argues that the savings from this technology were so great as to overwhelm any imaginable differences due to differing factor endowments. There are other and similar puzzles in areas like textiles: Gregory Clark, "Why Isn't the Whole World Developed? Lessons from the Cotton Mills," *JEH*, March 1987; Mira Wilkins, "Efficiency and Management: A Comment on Gregory Clark's 'Why Isn't the World Developed?'," *JEH*, December 1987; and John R. Hanson II, "Why Isn't The Whole World Developed? A Traditional View," *JEH*, September 1988.

25. Robert E. Gallman, "Gross National Product," p. 7.

26. Gallman, p. 14.

27. *Historical Statistics*, series U 214–18.

28. *Historical Statistics*, series F 99.

29. And perhaps even relevant inventions! Irwin Feller found that inventing activity tended to be urban-concentrated, but *not* that inventions in any particular city influenced its growth. "The Urban Location of United States Invention, 1860–1910," *EEH*, Spring 1971.

30. Jonathan Hughes, *Industrialization and Economic History: Theses and Conjectures* (New York: McGraw-Hill, 1970), pp. 60–62.

31. Eugene Smolensky, "Industrial Location and Urban Growth," in Lance E. Davis et al., *American Economic Growth*, p. 582. See also David Meyer, "Midwestern Industrialization and the American Manufacturing Belt in the Nineteenth Century," *JEH*, December 1989.

32. Leonard A. Carlson, "Labor Supply, The Acquisition of Skills, and the Location of Southern Textile Mills, 1880–1900," *JEH*, March 1981.

33. Kenneth Weiher, "The Cotton Industry and Southern Urbanization, 1880–1930," *EEH*, April 1977.

34. From 1860 to 1910, fully 90 percent of the number of urban places continued to be small towns, between 2500 and 25,000 in population. Proportionately, of course, their influence declined: These small towns contained 40 percent of the urban population in 1860 and still contained 32 percent by 1910. *Historical Statistics*, series A 43–67. The growth of cities drew little from the nor-

mal economic activity of rural America and its small towns. John Ermisch and Thomas Weiss, "The Impact of the Rural Market on the Growth of the Urban Workforce, U.S., 1870–1900," *EEH,* Winter 1973–74.

35. K. Celeste Gaspari and Arthur G. Woolf, "Income, Public Works, and Mortality in Early Twentieth-Century American Cities," *JEH,* June 1985.

36. Thomas Weiss, "The Nineteenth Century Origins of the American Service Industry Workforce," *Essays in Economic and Business History* (1984); see also "Urbanization and the Growth of the Service Workforce," *EEH,* Spring 1971; and "The Industrial Distribution of the Urban and Rural Workforces: Estimates for the United States, 1870–1910," *JEH,* December 1972.

37. Jonathan Hughes, "Industrialization. Part I: Economic Aspects," *International Encyclopedia of the Social Sciences,* 1968 edition, vol. 7, pp. 252–63.

38. Hughes, "Industrialization."

39. Times change. Consider the following from a Japanese industrial leader: "Our processing industries are simply better than [those] in the United States. . . . If the United States wants to sell us finished consumer products, they don't have a chance. . . . The Americans are good at inventing new machines, but in the ability to apply those inventions, well, maybe the Japanese have more ability." *Washington Post,* 31 July 1978. So much for the legacy of Carnegie and Ford.

40. Joseph Schumpeter, *The Theory of Economic Development* (1949); *Business Cycles* (1939), 2 vols.; and *Capitalism, Socialism, and Democracy* (1943), ch. 7, "The Process of Creative Destruction." A recent contribution is Israel Kirzner, *Competition and Entrepreneurship* (Chicago: University of Chicago Press, 1973).

41. Ross Thomson, "Learning by Selling and Invention: The Case of the Sewing Machine," *JEH,* June 1987. The phenomenon continued into modern times: Daniel Nelson, "Mass Production and the U.S. Tire Industry," *JEH,* June 1987.

42. The classic critique of Schumpeter's huge system is Simon Kuznets, "Schumpeter's 'Business Cycles,' " reprinted in Simon Kuznets, *Economic Change* (1954). Kuznets noted that Schumpeter's analysis implied that the supply of entrepreneurial talent would not always be forthcoming (p. 112), although Kuznets thought the implication was a cyclical one. Kuznets also doubted that Kondratieff's huge growth cycles had been properly established, in fact *or* theory (p. 118). In 1940, when the review was written, Kuznets was unconvinced by Schumpeter's vision.

43. Hughes, *The Vital Few,* p. 237.

44. See Hughes, *The Vital Few,* pp. 315–17 on Henry Ford in the 1921 recession; pp. 370–74 on Harriman's acquisition of the Union Pacific after the Panic of 1893.

Suggested Readings

Articles

Allen, Robert C. "The Peculiar Productivity History of American Blast Furnaces, 1840–1913," *Journal of Economic History,* vol. XXXVII, no. 3, September 1977.

Asher, Ephraim. "Industrial Efficiency and Biased Technical Change in American and British Manufacturing: The Case of Textiles in the Nineteenth Century." *Journal of Economic History,* vol. XXXII, no. 2, June 1972.

Atack, Jeremy. "Industrial Structure and the Emergence of the Modern Industrial Corporation." *Explorations in Economic History,* vol. 22, no. 1, January 1985.

Berck, Peter. "Hard Driving and Efficiency: Iron Production in 1890." *Journal of Economic History,* vol. XXXVIII, no. 4, December 1978.

Cain, Louis P., and Paterson, Donald G. "Biased Technical Change, Scale, and Factor Substitution in American Industry, 1850–1919." *Journal of Economic History,* vol. XLVI, no. 1, March 1986.

Carlson, Leonard A. "Labor Supply, the Acquisition of Skills, and the Location of Southern Textile Mills, 1880–1900." *Journal of Economic History,* vol. XLI, no. 1, March 1981.

Clark, Gregory, "Why Isn't the Whole World Developed? Lessons from the Cotton Mills," *Journal of Economic History,* vol. XLVII, no. 1, March 1987.

Ermisch, John, and Weiss, Thomas. "The Impact of the Rural Market on the Growth of the Urban Workforce, U.S., 1870–1900." *Explorations in Economic History,* vol. 11, no. 2, Winter 1973–74.

Feller, Irwin. "The Urban Location of United States Invention, 1860–1910." *Explorations in Economic History,* vol. 8, no. 3, Spring 1971.

Floud, R. C. "The Adolescence of American Engineering Competition, 1860–1900." *Economic History Review,* vol. XXXVII, no. 1, February 1974.

Gallman, Robert E., "Gross National Product in the United States, 1834–1909." In Dorothy Brady, ed., *Studies in Income and Wealth,* vol. 30, National Bureau of Economic Research. New York: Columbia University Press, 1966.

———. "Trends in the Structure of the American Economy Since 1840." In Robert Fogel and Stanley Engerman, eds. *The Reinterpretation of American Economic History.* New York: Harper & Row, 1971.

Gaspari, K. Celeste, and Woolf, Arthur G. "Income, Public Works, and Mortality in Early Twentieth-Century American Cities." *Journal of Economic History,* vol. XLV, no. 2, June 1985.

Hanson, John R., II. "Why Isn't the Whole World Developed? A Traditional View." *Journal of Economic History,* vol. XLVIII, no. 3, September 1988.

Hughes, Jonathan. "Industrialization: Economic Aspects." *International Encyclopedia of the Social Sciences,* 1968 edition, vol. 7.

———. "Entrepreneurial Activity and American Economic Progress." *Journal of Libertarian Studies,* vol. III, no. 4, Winter 1979.

Lebergott, Stanley. "The American Labor Force." In L. E. Davis et al., *American Economic Growth.* New York: Harper & Row, 1972.

Meyer, David. "Midwestern Industrialization and the American Manufacturing Belt in the Nineteenth Century." *Journal of Economic History,* vol. XLIX, no. 4, December 1989.

Mulligan, William H., Jr. "Mechanization and Work in the American Shoe Industry: Lynn, Massachusetts, 1852–1883." *Journal of Economic History,* vol. XLI, no. 1, March 1981.

Nelson, Daniel. "Mass Production and the U.S. Tire Industry." *Journal of Economic History,* vol. XLVII, no. 2, June 1987.

Pratt, Joseph A. "The Petroleum Industry in Transition: Antitrust and the Decline of Monopoly Control in Oil." *Journal of Economic History,* vol. XL, no. 14, December 1980.

Rosenberg, Nathan. "American Technology: Imported or Indigenous?" *American Economic Review,* vol. 67, no. 1, February 1977.

Smolensky, Eugene. "Industrialization and Urban Growth." In L. E. Davis et al., *American Economic Growth.* New York: Harper & Row, 1972.

Temin, Peter. "Manufacturing." In L. E. Davis et al., *American Economic Growth.* New York: Harper & Row, 1972.

Thomson, Ross. "Learning by Selling and Invention: The Case of the Sewing Machine." *Journal of Economic History,* vol. XLVII, no. 2, June 1987.

Uselding, Paul. "Studies of Technology in Economic History." In Robert Gallman, ed., *Recent Developments in the Study of Economic and Business History: Essays in Honor of Herman E. Krooss. Research in Economic History,* supplement 1. Greenwich, CT: JAI Press, 1977.

———. "Measuring Techniques and Manufacturing Practice." In Otto Mayr, ed., *The American System of Manufacturing.* Washington: The Smithsonian Institution, 1981.

———, and Juba, Bruce. "Biased Technical Progress in American Manufacturing." *Explorations in Economic History,* vol. 11, no. 1, Fall 1973.

Weiher, Kenneth. "The Cotton Industry and Southern Urbanization, 1880–1930." *Explorations in Economic History,* vol. 14, no. 2, April 1977.

Weiss, Thomas. "Urbanization and the Growth of the Service Workforce." *Explorations in Economic History,* vol. 8, no. 3, Spring 1971.

———. "The Industrial Distribution of the Urban and Rural Workforces: Estimates for the United States, 1870-1910." *Journal of Economic History,* vol. XXXII, no. 4, December 1972.

———. "The Nineteenth Century Origins of the American Service Industry Workforce." *Essays in Economic and Business History,* vol. III (1984).

Wilkins, Mira. "Efficiency and Management: A Comment on Gregory Clark's 'Why Isn't the World Developed?'." *Journal of Economic History,* vol. XLVII, no. 4, December 1987.

Woolf, Arthur G. "Electricity, Productivity, and Labor Savings: American Manufacturing, 1900–1929." *Explorations in Economic History,* vol. 21, no. 2, April 1984.

Wright, Gavin. "The Origins of American Industrial Success, 1879–1940." *American Economic Review,* vol. 80, no. 4, September 1990.

———, and Nelson, Richard R. "The Rise and Fall of American Technological Leadership: The Postwar Era in Historical Perspective." *Journal of Economic Literature,* vol. 30, no. 4, December 1992.

Books

Chandler, Alfred D., Jr. *The Visible Hand: The Managerial Revolution in American Business.* Cambridge: Harvard University Press, 1977.

———. *Scale and Scope: The Dynamics of Industrial Capitalism.* Cambridge: Harvard University Press, 1990.

Clark, V. S. *History of Manufactures in the United States, 1607–1914,* 2 vols. Washington: Carnegie Institution, 1928.

Frickey, Edwin. *Production in the United States, 1860–1914.* Cambridge: Harvard University Press, 1947.

Higgs, Robert. *The Transformation of the American Economy 1865–1914*. New York: Wiley, 1971.

Hoke, Donald R. *Ingenious Yankees: The Rise of the American System of Manufactures in the Private Sector*. New York: Columbia University Press, 1990.

Hounshell, David A. *From the American System to Mass Production, 1800–1932: The Development of Manufacturing Technology in the United States*. Baltimore: Johns Hopkins University Press, 1984.

Hughes, Jonathan. *The Vital Few: American Economic Progress and Its Protagonists*. New York: Oxford University Press, 1986.

Kuznets, Simon. *Economic Change: Selected Essays in Business Cycles, National Income, and Economic Growth*. London: William Heinemann, 1954.

Lee, Susan Previant, and Passell, Peter. *A New Economic View of American History*. New York: Norton, 1979.

Pred, A. R. *The Spatial Dynamics of U.S. Urban-Industrial Growth, 1800–1914*. Cambridge: MIT Press, 1966.

Rosenberg, Nathan. *Technology and American Economic Growth*. New York: Harper & Row, 1972.

Schumpeter, Joseph. *The Theory of Economic Development*. Cambridge: Harvard University Press, 1949.

Slichter, Sumner. *Economic Growth in the United States: Its History, Problems and Prospects*. Baton Rouge: Louisiana State University Press, 1961.

Temin, Peter. *Iron and Steel in Nineteenth-Century America: An Economic Inquiry*. Cambridge: MIT Press, 1964.

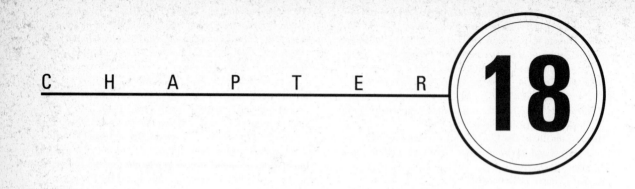

Big Business and Government Intervention

ooking back a little more than a century to the 1880s and the relative positions of private business and the federal government in Washington, D.C., we are struck by a singular realization: There was little federal government control over the daily operations of private economic activity. *None* of the massive modern array of control agencies existed. A scholar would be hard-pressed to locate half a dozen permanent federal agencies a century ago that had any control over business in this country. There were no antitrust laws. There was no federal income tax. The federal government did not license businesses. There were no federally chartered corporations extant. By current standards, one could almost say that there was *no* federal government intervention in the economy.

But we cannot go quite that far. Even by the early 1880s, the federal power was evident. By then, for example:

1. The federal government was in control of the public domain—its resources and its disposition.
2. Through subsidies, the federal government had already produced business configurations that the free market might never have produced.

3. By tariff legislation, the federal government's rules determined the flow of commodities into the country and, consequently, had created extra profitability—rents in domestic productions—that would not otherwise have existed.
4. The federal government reorganized the nation's banking system, thereby producing a pattern of banking different from the one the states and free market had produced. The entire financial structure of the country was profoundly affected by it.
5. The federal government's determination of the monetary standard influenced wages, prices, interest rates, and all else that depended upon them.
6. After the Civil War, the federal government's policies (and lack of them) had undermined the South's recovery. A whole section of the nation was depressed for decades.
7. The federal government's immigration policies actively encouraged a mass migration of Europeans into the country.

So, it was not really true that there was *no* federal influence in the economy. In point of fact, *if the federal government had done none of these things, that too would have been a policy.* And not a neutral one, either, because the classes favored by the existing policies would not have been favored—to the benefit of someone else.

We already know that since the earliest colonial times, governments at some level controlled businesses—regulated them, licensed them, and abolished them. The federal government, though, had been founded in 1789 by other governments, many of them already more than a century old. And as we have already seen, at first the sovereign states were jealous of the powers they surrendered to the new federal establishment. Among the powers withheld were those regulating businesses in small detail. The federal government set the general background—the list of interventions just mentioned—but had neither the precedent, resources, nor inclination to be involved in the regulation of everyday business affairs.

Beginning in the 1880s, this changed, and the intrusive regulatory powers of the states and local governments slowly but surely ascended to the federal level. The modern Occupational Safety and Health Administration, OSHA, is perhaps the ultimate single-agency achievement of this transformation so far. The goal of "deregulation" proclaimed by the previous three federal administrations thus amounts to nothing less than a desire to reverse the direction of a century of American history. Not surprisingly, there is very considerable resistance to deregulation since generations of American business and labor leaders have known little else.

LEGAL CHANGES: CORPORATIONS

Between the Civil War and World War I, two streams of American legal development, priority right and the privileges of incorporation, fused into a mighty current that would mold the future in ways no founder could have imagined. The courts, according to modern scholars, attempted to impose conservatism where there had earlier been pragmatic innovation, but they met with limited success.[1] By 1914, the giant enterprises celebrated by Alfred Chandler simply dominated the American economy.[2] That enterprise was usually a corporation with generalized powers or even a group of corporations locked into pools, cartels, trusts, and other arrangements (by then, in theory illegal) making resource allocations that affected the lives of millions. They were a capital-saving innovation, in the view of

Alexander Field, with corporate management as the efficiency-promoting device: more income from less capital expenditure.[3]

But others believed that monopoly was the game that was afoot, and that the great merger wave of the 1890s, which came *after* passage of the Sherman Antitrust Act, proved it.[4] The giant corporations, called by Arthur Selwyn Miller "feudal entities within the body politic" seemed likely to take over that body.[5] The corporate enterprise became the "agenda setter" of the American economy for many decades to come. In major part, the American economy became what the nation's corporations decided it would be in response, of course, to consumer choice. In the struggle to control the resulting power of "big business," the nation slowly changed again, into the modern regulated economy. Indeed, it is Miller's opinion, baldly stated, that modern "big government" is simply the consequence of government's interaction with big business.[6]

The Size Effect

It is possible to generalize this development from the materials we already have studied regarding the American tradition of **nonmarket control**—the use of government rather than market decisions to allocate resources. As the economy grew, businesses followed the line of settlement westward, or even led it, in cases of regional export industries. The "business society" became familiar in most sections of the country. The police power we studied in Chapter 2 was the common law, and that power to control, forbid, and discriminate existed wherever there were courts and legislatures. However, economies of scale—either in production, organization, or even in collusive action between rivals—made possible business organizations whose affairs simply overlapped many jurisdictions, creating a power potentially above any law, called the *size effect*.[7]

The only way to control this power was with an equally broad political force—federal control. The alternative was giant enterprise uncontrolled. Federal power could cross state lines and move internationally, in response to the organizational genius of American businessowners, whose masterpiece, the huge American corporation, was an economic wonder of the late nineteenth century. The consequences of the size effect were first seen in railroads, and here we can gain perspective from Professor Scheiber:

Organized across nearly half a continent, aggregating millions in capital, and controlling bureaucracies much larger than those of any state government, the giant railroad firms outdistanced the objective capacity of the states . . . to exercise controls over them.[8]

If there were not to be businesses with power beyond that of the political system's control, then the federal government would have to expand. *And it could.*

Recall Chief Justice Marshall's view in *McCulloch v Maryland* (1819) that the Constitution was "intended to endure for ages to come and, consequently, to be adapted to the various crises of human affairs." The federal government's powers, in his view, would always be sufficient to the need at hand.

Privilege, Power, and Suspicion

The states chartered corporations indiscriminately by special franchise, creating a new piece of legislation for each case. It was cumbersome and corrupt. But, as early as 1811, New York had made provision for incorporation by simple registration, adhering to generalized rules. There was no need for an act of legislature for each incorporation. In 1837, Connecticut also provided for general incorporation.

In its 1846 constitution, New York State liberalized the rules further. Restrictions were lifted on the different kinds of business that corporations could do under a single charter, on locations, and on capital requirements. In 1875, New Jersey eliminated capital restrictions and in 1888 allowed its corporations to do all their business outside the state. Delaware followed with similar rules. Gradually, the special privileges of incorporation, once strictly limited and jealously guarded, were becoming available for any business group who sought them.[9]

Another line of legal evolution now came abreast of these developments. The federal Constitution had provided only for relations between *individuals* and the sovereign power. There was no conception of private *collective* economic entities in 1789. In 1819, Marshall, in *Dartmouth College* v *Woodward,* had said that a corporation was in law an intangible "being." It was thus an individual. That squared reality with the abstraction. A series of Supreme Court cases, as we saw in Chapter 7, clarified the position of corporate enterprises with the law.

In 1851, Chief Justice Roger B. Taney had written in *Cooly* v *Board of Wardens of the Port of Philadelphia* that, logically, controls by states and cities could not be extended beyond their own jurisdictions and that the need for greater power would have to be met by Congress. Then in 1886, in *Santa Clara County* v *Southern Pacific Railroad,* the Supreme Court held that the corporate person was protected by the due process clause of the Fourteenth Amendment: State and local governments thus were further limited in their abilities to regulate corporations.

The stage was very nearly set for a reversion to ubiquitous government regulation as in the colonial era, but this time with federal agencies playing the roles of boards of selectmen determining by their own deliberations the "public interest." One may object to the *ways* in which controls were imposed, but it really is inconceivable that no controls would have been imposed.

The big new companies were adept at market manipulations of all sorts—price fixing by pooling agreements, monopoly price, and output controls by cartel agreement. The pooling of the voting stock of competitive firms in trust allowed a more rigorous control, essentially the creation of a single management where there had formerly been competing firms. These devices, in a time of trouble in the agrarian sector, gave rise to really stiff hatred and envy of the corporation itself, as was manifested in the demands of the Populist platforms. The American corporation came to be viewed as alien to the rest of American life.[10]

The general public believed that American industry was being monopolized, that output was restricted, that prices were excessive, and that farmers, laborers, and consumers were being cheated by bloated plutocrats. There *was* a high degree of "concentration" of industrial power. Whether it was exploitive is unknowable. But even by early dates, scale economies were at work, and large firms succeeded. For example, although some 1900 firms made farm implements in 1880, the top four made 65 percent of the industry's whole output. In 1890, the copper industry was dominated by a few giant firms, three-fourths of all copper being produced by the top four. Standard Oil in 1879 refined 90 percent of all domestically pumped crude oil and owned 80 percent of the country's pipelines.[11] The sinister character of John D. Rockefeller, Sr., did nothing to help his firm's public image.

Such signs of private economic power were terrifying to some. It seemed that a new oligarchy would rise up and feudalize Jefferson's Arcadia. President Cleveland said of corporations in 1888 in his message to Congress:

> As we view the achievements of aggregate capital, we discover the existence of trusts, combinations, and monopolies, while the citizen is struggling far in the rear, or is trampled to death beneath an iron heel. Corporations, which should be the carefully restrained creatures of the law and the servants of the people, are fast becoming the people's masters.[12]

As William Vanderbilt had said, "The Public be damned." It would be naive to suppose that the federal government's powers would not be used to intervene. But by 1888, intervention was already coming down the line, and from several different directions.

THE PIVOTAL POINT: MUNN V ILLINOIS

The case of *Munn* v *Illinois* (1877) was ultimately left in the dustbin of history, but to an economic historian, it is of particular interest. On it is focused 270 years of the Anglo-American tradition. It is a pivotal point in regulatory history. In the end, the effort to make the doctrine of *Munn* work as government regulation was a failure, and American history in these matters depended upon subsequent innovations.

The agrarian interest after the Civil War suffered from falling prices and, they believed, discriminatory rate-fixing by the railroads. Where the agrarians had the power, in state legislatures, they took action. The laws they passed came to be identified with the Patrons of Husbandry, a.k.a. the Grange.[13] Laws were passed regulating railroad rates, and Illinois, in its 1871 constitutional revision, provided for the licensing of grain elevators and control of their prices. One Chicago elevator company, Munn and Scott, refused to comply, and the results became the decisive "Granger Case" as we discussed in Chapter 14.

Munn *v* Illinois *and After*

In the majority opinion, many facets are touched but not developed in the *Munn* decision, including the issue of monopoly power. Chief Justice Morrison Waite fell back upon the Anglo-American tradition of police power. He saw nothing novel in the Granger laws, except that they dealt with giant businesses. From "time out of mind," local governments in this country, and the government in England before that, had regulated businesses in the interests of health and safety. The power was unquestioned. It was not so much a matter of "natural monopoly," as some textbooks still argue, as it was the historic basis of public utility regulation. Inns, taverns, carters, draymen, bake shops, brewers, barbers—all had been subject to public regulation. Railroads and grain elevators were no different.

Waite quoted extensively from an essay by Lord Hale, a seventeenth-century English jurist who advanced the doctrine that any private property was subject to government regulation if the public had come to depend on its use. If that property became "affected with a public interest," it lost its private character. There could be no question of this power. As Waite wrote:

> [Such powers had been used] in England from time immemorial, and in this country from its colonization to regulate ferries, common carriers, hackmen, bakers, millers, wharfingers, innkeepers . . . and in so doing to fix a maximum charge to be made for services rendered, accommodations furnished, and articles to be sold. To this day, statutes are to be found in many of the States upon some or all of these subjects; and we think it has never been successfully contended that such legislation came within the constitutional prohibitions against interference with private property.[14]

Professor Harry Scheiber has shown that Chief Justice Waite was not as original as was thought at the time and that American courts had, in fact, utilized Lord Hale's arguments to justify regulation for decades before *Munn*.[15] Contemporaries feared that the doctrine of *Munn* would usher in extreme innovation in government. Associate Justice Field said of it, in a dissenting opinion: "If this be sound law . . . all property and all business in the state are held at the mercy of a majority of its legislature."[16] Quite.

If you recall the character of the original land tenure, free and common socage, you will remember that its incidents *had to be met* for ownership rights to continue. From earliest times, as Waite said, businesses were subject to political controls. Eminent domain proceedings had been regularized over time, but the power of eminent domain was unquestioned. The Constitution's Fifth Amendment prohibited the federal Government from taking property without compensation and due process, and the Fourteenth Amendment had likewise constrained the states. But there was no absolute prohibition against government's ultimate power over the rights of private property.

In the decades that followed 1877, a fascinating blind alley of *Munn* doctrine laws and cases developed.[17] One of them was *Tyson* v *Banton* (1927), a case in which New York State's legislature had passed a law holding that ticket scalping on Broadway was clothed in the public interest and therefore was subject to regulation. Associate Justice Oliver Wendell Holmes, Jr., wrote:

> The notion that a business is clothed with a public interest . . . is little more than a fiction intended to beautify what is disagreeable to the sufferers. The truth seems to me that, subject to compensation when compensation is due, the legislature may forbid or restrict any business when it has a sufficient force of public opinion behind it.[18]

The *Munn* case, to Holmes, was a needless complication.

Seven years later, *Nebbia* v *New York* reached the Supreme Court.[19] The case involved an attempt to hold milk prices artificially high to the apparent benefit of large milk processors. New York State farmers were told that this was to their benefit also. The Court ruled this scheme to be well within the police powers and, agreeing with Holmes, said of *Munn:* "It is clear that there is no closed class or category of business affected with a public interest."[20] Old Justice MacReynolds saw clearly that *Munn* had in fact restricted the spread of government regulation for half a century, and that *Nebbia* would open the floodgates. He wrote in dissent:

> *Munn* v *Illinois* has been much discussed. . . . And always the conclusion was that nothing there sustains the notion that the ordinary business of dealing in commodities is charged with a public interest and subject to legislative control. The contrary has [now] been distinctly announced. To undertake now to attribute a repudiated implication to [*Munn*] is to affirm that it means what this Court had declared again was not intended.[21]

After *Nebbia,* any and all business and control of private property was potentially subject to control wherever governments wanted it. *Munn* had been an affirmation by Chief Justice Waite of a traditional power being legitimately applied to modern business, with Lord Hale dragged in by his hair to set some kind of a limit. Half a century of spreading nonmarket control had been somewhat restricted by that limit. *Munn* was the last gasp of the traditional police powers to counter the size effect of business development. *Nebbia* removed the limit, and the way was open for such phenomena as OSHA and the Commodities Futures Trading Commission.

The ICC

By the 1930s the railroads had already long since escaped the tendrils of *Munn* and had fallen into a different trap, the permanent federal regulatory agency. The first one was the Interstate Commerce Commission (ICC), founded in 1887, which we mentioned earlier.[22] Although the ICC at first had no rate-setting powers, the Hepburn Act changed all that in 1906.

In recent years the creators of the ICC have been given credit for an unlikely amount of rationality. We discussed in an earlier chapter the opinion shared by historian Gabriel Kolko and his followers that Congress knew what it was doing in 1887: that it was giving the railroads a federal agency to act as their cartel manager.[23] Since the ICC has few friends in any political spectrum, Kolko's thesis is usually unquestioned. But in fact, there is plenty of contrary evidence.

Congress had for years, since the Civil War, been attempting to find a way to regulate the railroads and had even imposed financial organization on the Union and Central Pacific Railroads.[24] Secondly, Kolko's conspiracy theory implies that the rustic legislators of the 1880s went along with a scheme to defraud the farmers. What of the cry by Senator Hoar of Massachusetts?

> You give these men power over the business of great towns and great cities and great classes of investments— a power which no Persian satrap or Roman proconsol was ever entrusted with . . .

Or Congressman Oates of Alabama:

> I freely confer, sir, that I am jealous of this eternal tendency to the enlargement and centralization of federal power.[25]

Was this all just an act? Perhaps Hoar and Oates had been left out of the conspiracy? But what of this? Richard Olney, Cleveland's Attorney General, had to explain "capture" to a friend—a railroad president, no less—who also had apparently been left out and wanted the ICC abolished. Olney certainly knew what *he* was talking about:

> The Commission, as its functions have been limited by the courts, is, or can be made, of great use to the railroads. It satisfied the popular clamor for a government supervision of railroads, at the same time that supervision is almost entirely nominal. Further, the older such a commission gets to be, the more inclined it will be found to take the business and railroad view of things. It thus becomes a sort of barrier between the railroad corporations and the people and a sort of protection against hasty and crude legislation hostile to railroad interests. . . . The part of wisdom is not to destroy the Commission, but to utilize it.[26]

But Olney's argument depended upon restrictions imposed by the courts *after* 1887. Moreover, since the ICC was the first case, it was Olney's *wisdom* that led him to believe that the ICC would ultimately be "captured." The fact is that the ICC has only been the worst of many bad examples that followed. Congress no more "knew" what it was doing in 1887 than it does today when it creates a new commission, agency, power, office, or control to conserve energy, stop inflation, boost prices, or whatever.

The regulatory commission is a way to *manage* problems, not solve them. That the commissions get "captured" is not surprising. While there is no way to know the public interest, those who get regulated at least know their own, and they make their interests known in many ways to the agencies. The latter are left with the responsibility for the welfare of those they control. No regulatory agency wants to destroy the industry whose affairs it is to rule.

The ICC never even managed that much. As a "cartel," it was a terrible failure. Albro Martin, in his book, *Enterprise Denied,* demonstrates that by 1914, ICC regulation had reduced the railroads to a shambles.[27] Especially devastating had been the denial of rate increases as prices and wages rose in the early twentieth century. The railroads, Martin argues, could not be maintained. But that was early on. Thomas Ulen has pointed out that the original legislation, trying to in-

clude something for everyone, was hopelessly inconsistent internally, and its subsequent adjustments and amendations seem not to have served *any* interest![28]

The ICC was the granddaddy of all the permanent federal regulatory agencies. Its objectives were never known, or knowable. It has now passed its centennial year and still exists, apparently in perpetuity. There was talk of its abolition early in the Reagan years, but the talk died off. The ICC has special uses in our political system quite apart from its powers of regulation. An "elephants' graveyard of political hacks," it has for years functioned under commissioners who have been largely defeated legislators, saved from a humiliating return to Pocatello or Peoria after their constituents had retired them from elected public service.

The ICC's fate, however ignominious, should not divert us from its origins. Initially, its commissioners were of high intellectual quality. The ICC was part of a parcel of efforts to offset the size effect and to raise to the federal level direct political control over business. After the Supreme Court made one final effort to spread the umbrella of traditional police power over big business in *Munn* v *Illinois,* a fresh attack was needed.

One prong of that attack was the developing army of federal regulatory agencies under the commerce clause. The ICC was the first of these. The second prong was the establishment of organizational and behavioral rules for the new corporations.

THE ANTITRUST ACTS

In 1890 Congress passed the Sherman Antitrust Act, whose famous beginning reads:

> Every contract, combination in the form of trust or otherwise, or conspiracy, in restraint of trade or commerce among the several states or with foreign nations is hereby declared to be illegal. . . .[29]

With that, the federal law courts were launched upon a continuous career of industrial and economic management from which they have never been able to extract themselves. At the very heights of the corporate economy, it became lawyers and judges who decided if the creations of the nation's industrial leaders would live or die. The fact that most lawyers and judges know little or nothing about the management of huge economic enterprises was not considered relevant then, nor is it now. After nine decades, the result, the body of antitrust law, is nonsensical.[30]

The Sherman Act and its subsequent amendments comprise a vast and complex behavioral sumptuary law for business. Just as the Massachusetts Puritans forbade certain classes of people from wearing certain clothing, so the antitrust laws forbade certain organizational behavior. And, just as the Puritan divines never told the lower orders what they *could* wear, the antitrust laws do not say what actions *are* legal. For example, over and over, businesses have been constrained by the courts under the antitrust acts for reducing competition, but there is no act of Congress that says what competition *is*.

Businesses may not engage in activities that reduce something that not only is not mentioned in the Sherman Act, it is unknown outside the ethereal atmosphere of the economics classroom. What is legal under the antitrust laws is simply what has not yet been found to be *illegal*. Since an infinity of collusive action is possible, the antitrust laws produced (in theory) an infinity of court actions. The long shelves of thick books called antitrust law comprise the monument to the Sherman Act and its amendments.

The Purpose of Antitrust Laws

Surprisingly enough, there is no general agreement among scholars about the Sherman Act's precise origins or objects. The agitation in the 1870s and 1880s against trusts, corporations, pools, and cartels we have already noted. Agitation is a political thing that need not represent anything important to be effective; antivivisectionists, prohibitionists, antiflouridation enthusiasts, free silver proponents, anti-Darwinists—all and more have had their moments. What is important in politics is votes, and in this country, almost any cause can be pushed for that purpose.

The big "trust buster" politicians, T. R. Roosevelt and W. H. Taft, arrived in the White House long after the Sherman Act was passed. But Populists and labor leaders had agitated against the new corporations and various business alignments before 1890. Eighteen states had passed their own antitrust laws by 1891. Both major political parties included antitrust planks in their platforms in 1888, and Senator John Sherman (R-Ohio) had introduced antitrust bills in 1888 and 1889 before succeeding in 1890.[31]

Thus, the historian must presume that there was *something* causing all this agitation, even if it did end up as politics. What was it? The answer seems to be fear of economic size and excessive power in private business. F. M. Scherer, one of the leading modern scholars of American industrial development, presents an aggregate of causes for the appearance of our antitrust laws:[32]

1. Growth of large-scale firms was based upon "technical innovations in metallurgy, industrial chemistry, energy generation and utilization, and the use of interchangeable parts." In other words, innovations that produced scale economies in industry existed.
2. Declining transportation costs encouraged growth of optimal plant sizes.
3. Developing financial services in the capital markets made it easier for individual firms to achieve economies of scale.
4. Liberalization of state laws of incorporation encouraged professional management (and plowed-back profits) by separating actual control from the stockholder owners of the firms.
5. Expansion of both domestic and international markets made enlarged plant size profitable. (Recall Adam Smith's dictum about the division of labor and the size of the market.)
6. Depressions in 1873–79 and 1883–86 had produced price wars among manufacturers—unhappy conditions that led to efforts to control markets by collusion or merger when prospects improved.
7. American law, which made cartel agreement unenforceable in the courts (the opposite was widely true in Europe), led to a tendency for firms to merge to achieve control.
8. Merger, the creation of "big business," was more in line with the "expansive frontier spirit" of American entrepreneurs than was quasi-legal participation in pools and cartels.
9. The extravagant lifestyles of the new corporate elite were an affront to the rest of the electorate. Envy made the anti-big-business stance good politics for aspiring candidates.
10. The farmers, who were the majority in many states, were especially harmed by the depressions in the 1870s and 1880s and believed widely that

the growth of big business was against their interest. In the Granger and Populist movements, this political force was an organized one.

Scherer, perhaps wisely, does not attempt to place weights on any one factor. The literature of the time shows little effort by big business leaders to defend their activities on what we now would consider perfectly conventional grounds: job creation and economic growth, for example. Indeed, they may well have believed much of the charge against them, since it came not only from the daily press and the turmoil of politics and economic life but even from the White House itself.

The Sherman Act

William Letwin and others have shown the connections between the Sherman Act and the common law.[33] It was perfectly legal for the king, and later on Parliament, to grant monopoly privileges to an individual person or company. Privately, a single person could gain in trade what we would loosely call "monopoly power" (for instance, the ability to set his or her own prices locally), so long as it was not deemed "unreasonable." What was not admissible was a single person gaining the position of a *single seller* on a wide scale (or even locally, if it were done by agreement with potential competitors) by his or her own action without the sanction of Parliament.[34]

When the possibility of monopoly power occurred due to nature—say a toll bridge over a stream or a ferry site on a river—those situations were regulated, and had been since time out of mind, as "natural" monopolies. The English, and the Americans afterwards, regulated many private businesses, as we have seen, under the police powers for all sorts of reasons, and they also regulated natural monopolies where they occurred. Thomas Jefferson, for instance, wrote of colonial Virginia: "Ferries are admitted only at such places as are appointed by law, and the rates of ferriage are fixed."[35]

So, a federal law passed in 1890 stating that private monopolies, combinations, and other conspiracies in restraint of trade would be henceforth illegal seemed simple enough. This already was the case in common law and had been so since the country was first settled. However, there followed an astounding development called *antitrust law,* which has continued to grow and

develop unabated to our own time. Such had not been the intention. In 1911, William Hornblower wrote, somewhat apologetically, in the *Columbia Law Review* that the Sherman Act had been drafted by the ablest lawyers in the Senate.

> One would have supposed that if ever a statute would prove to be unambiguous, intelligible and enforceable, this would be that statute; yet it is safe to say that no statute ever passed since the foundation of the government has been the subject of more difference of opinion or the cause of more perplexity, both to judges and lawyers than the same statute.[36]

Section 1 of the Act prohibits conspiracies, contracts, or combinations in restraint of trade and provides for penalties (which have since been increased). Section 2 prohibits monopoly or actions tending to monopoly. In Section 4, the attorney general of the United States is authorized to institute lawsuits (in equity) against offenders, and Section 7 allows injured private parties to bring suit for recovery of triple damages against offenders under Sections 1 and 2.[37]

Fine-tuning the Regulation

Experience with the Sherman Act soon made it clear that finer specifications of illegal actions and exemptions, together with more diligent enforcement activity, would be necessary to make a federal antitrust policy effective. In the Clayton Antitrust Act of 1914 (amending the Sherman Act), Section 2 forbids price discrimination that reduces competition. Section 3 outlaws exclusive dealing and tying contracts that reduce competition. Because the Sherman Act had been used against organized labor unions (which either are useless or are successful restraints of trade), Section 6 of the Clayton Act declared grandly (and illogically) that labor "is not a commodity or article of commerce" and that labor unions are not to be considered in law as "illegal combinations or conspiracies in restraint of trade."[38] Section 7 prohibited mergers that would reduce competition, and Section 8 forbids interlocking directorates between firms held to be otherwise competitive (in the same industry).[39]

To police these laws and to intercede by steady surveillance, the Federal Trade Commission was also set

THE BOSSES OF THE SENATE.

The "Billion Dollar Congress" (1889). It was widely believed by Populists and others that big business owned the U.S. Congress and controlled its legislative activities.

up in 1914. Its job was to pursue wrongdoers full time. This is a most curious institution, called by one legal writer a case of "multiple impersonation." It is "complainant, jury, judge and counsel."[40] The FTC commissioners can issue "cease and desist" orders to those whose actions are found repugnant and seek enforcement of their orders in the courts. From 1914 onward, the FTC shared the obligation to enforce the antitrust laws with the attorney general.

The antitrust laws have been much amended since 1914, but not in any ways that have made them more coherent, and the FTC has been given more and more authority to enforce virtue, even to the point of prohibiting misleading advertising. By 1980, the FTC had acquired so many enemies that Congress attempted to clip its wings and give itself the power of legislative veto and the power to override FTC rulings, thus adding to the confusion. In 1983 the Supreme Court had to override Congress on this issue.

Exceptions to the Rule

It is not really apparent what these antitrust laws are, other than lists of problems with which some laws have tried to cope. Simplistically, they oppose monopoly power. Until 1942, the U.S. Supreme Court held that manufacturing was not commerce.[41] Therefore, apparent violations of antitrust law—beginning with the E. C. Knight case (the Sugar Trust) in 1895 in which the business involved could qualify as manufacturing—could not be forbidden.[42]

From the U.S. Steel case in 1920 to the ALCOA aluminum case in 1945, size alone was not considered evidence of monopoly; there had to be "intent" to monopolize.[43] Organized labor was exempted from antitrust laws in 1914. Combines of Americans fixing prices for foreign markets were exempted by the Webb-Pomerene Act of 1918. Farm cooperatives were allowed to fix prices by agreement among themselves by the Caper-Volstead Act of 1922. Gradually, it came to be accepted that industries subject to federal regulatory agencies ought to be exempted from antitrust proceedings: It made little sense for a business to be directed by one regulatory agency into the grip of another, although it has sometimes happened.

Then in 1936 Congress amended the Clayton Act with the Robinson Patman Act, *aimed directly at the consumer* in an attempt to prohibit discounts for large volume purchases by chain stores. Something for everyone. Small business had to be protected from competition by big business. Scherer comments on Robinson-Patman: "There is virtual unanimity among students of the Act that . . . its motivation was desire to limit competition, not to enhance it."[44] In 1937 Congress passed the Miller-Tydings Act exempting resale price maintenance agreements (price-fixing) between manufacturers and retailers.

At first, lawyers objected that the Sherman Act was inconsistent with common law because there was no "rule of reason" in it. In common law, only "unreasonable" restraint was illegal. The Sherman Act said "every" restraint was forbidden, whether reasonable or not. So, in *U.S.* v *Trans-Missouri Freight Association* (1897), the Supreme Court rejected a rule of reason.[45] But in *Standard Oil of New Jersey* v *U.S.* (1911), a rule of reason, whatever the Court should decide was reasonable, was enunciated.[46] *Both* lines of reasoning have been followed by the courts.

All this confusion would be laughable except that companies have been broken up, fines levied, and people imprisoned as a result. Whatever the antitrust acts mean, the courts take them very seriously.

REMARKS ON GOVERNMENT INTERVENTION

The chaos of the antitrust law is not unique. It is characteristic of federal government intervention by nonmarket control methods, and has been since their inception in 1887. The object of this control is to *manage* problems in perpetuity, not to *solve* them. The entire magnificent array established by 1914—the ICC, Sherman Act, Pure Food Act, (1906), Clayton Act, FTC, Federal Reserve System (1914)—was meant to be, and was, ongoing mediation between the agents of the marketplace, the buyers and sellers.

One point must be kept in mind since there would be much less nonsense in American life and history and economics books if it were faced directly: *Nonmarket control means rejection of the market decision* due to someone's successful appeal for a political, or politicized, solution.[47] Usually the object is straightforward enough: One party in the market wished to gain an advantage from government intervention that the market alone will not produce. Otherwise, there is no reason for the control, except the employment of lawyers and bureaucrats.

American capitalism produced in the late nineteenth century giant business firms, usually by way of general laws of incorporation. Americans feared the collective power of these firms, but, at the same time, they wanted:

1. the advantages of large-scale production that only huge firms could provide, and
2. the virtues of the competitive open-market where the consumer interest is protected by the rivalry among sellers.

The two objects conflict with each other.[48] But many desirable things in life are filled with inconsistencies (e.g., careers and families). Americans decided to have it all and have managed it until now. The distrust of the free market is obviously deeply rooted in American society and reaches back to the earliest settlements. On the other hand, the complaints against government regulation are nearly universal and are regularly mouthed by presidential candidates of all parties, and independents, too.

It is a way of life that is characteristic of the American economic system. When the business firms became gigantic, so did the effort made to control them by the political arm of society. The argument was put baldly by the U.S. Supreme Court in 1937 when it held that the Wagner Act—which imposed federally established labor unions on businesses—was constitutional:

> When industries organize themselves on a national scale, making their relation to interstate commerce the dominant factor in their activities, how can it be maintained that their industrial labor relations constitute a forbidden field into which Congress cannot enter . . .[49]

There was to be no area of economic life into which government control could not enter. As we know, this was hardly a new idea, harking all the way back as it did to 1607. But now that government would be the *federal* government. Between 1887 and 1914, that power was raised to the federal level, and there it has remained, grown, flourished, and multiplied. Banking apart, *Munn* v *Illinois* was the end of the ancient system, and the Interstate Commerce Act of 1887, the beginning of the new.

Notes

1. Harry Scheiber, "Federalism and the American Economic Order, 1789–1910," *Law and Society,* Fall 1975; Herbert Hovenkamp, "The Classical Corporation in American Legal Thought," *The Georgetown Law Review,* June 1988; and Morton Horwitz, *The Transformation of American Law 1780–1860* (1977), ch. VIII.

2. Alfred Chandler, *The Visible Hand* (1977) and *Scale and Scope* (1990).

3. Alexander J. Field, "Modern Business Enterprise as a Capital-Saving Innovation," *JEH,* June 1987.

4. The evidence is disputed, but there can be no doubt that monopoly power is a *desideratum* for most business-people, and the data show that in the merger wave of the 1890s, there was much added concentration of power. Anthony Patrick O'Brien, "Factory Size, Economies of Scale, and the Great Merger Wave of 1898–1902," *JEH,* September 1988. However, others have found with Alfred Chandler, that the pursuit of scale economies, and not desire for monopoly power, motivated the great mergers. For example, Jeremy Atack, "Industrial Structure and the Emergence of the Modern Industrial Corporation," *EEH,* January 1985.

5. Arthur Selwyn Miller, *The Supreme Court and American Capitalism* (1972), p. 15.

6. Miller, p. 175.

7. Jonathan Hughes, "Transference and Development of Institutional Constraints upon Economic Activity," in *REH,* vol. 1, 1976, p. 50. The argument is made by Charles McCurdy that even the size effect itself depended upon the courts opening up the national economy to larger scale business operations; "American Law and the Marketing Structure of the Large Corporation," *JEH,* September 1978.

8. Scheiber, "Federalism and the American Economic Order," p. 99.

9. For a general survey, James Willard Hurst, *The Legitimacy of the Business Corporation in the United States, 1780–1970* (1970). Also, Lawrence M. Friedman, *A History of American Law* (1973), ch. VIII. An interesting recent perspective is Christopher Grandy, "New Jersey Corporate Chartermongering, 1875–1929," *JEH,* September 1989.

10. John Moody, *The Truth About the Trusts* (1904); Ida M. Tarbell, *History of the Standard Oil Company* (1925); Matthew Josephson, *The Robber Barons* (1934); Gustavus Myers, *History of Great American Fortunes* (1910). For a more modern view, see Louis Galambos, *The Public Image of Big Business in America, 1880–1940* (1975).

11. Willard L. Thorp and Grace W. Knott, "The History of Concentration in Seven Industries," in *The Structure of Industry* (1941), part IV.

12. Quoted in Jonathan Hughes, *The Governmental Habit Redux* (1991), pp. 112.

13. John D. Hicks, *The Populist Revolt: A History of the Farmers' Alliance and the People's Party* (1931); also, Irwin Unger, *The Greenback Era* (1964).

14. *Munn* v *Illinois,* 94 U.S. 125 (1877).

15. Harry Scheiber, "The Road to *Munn:* Eminent Domain and the Concept of Public Purpose in the State Courts," *Perspectives in American History,* 1971.

16. *Munn,* p. 136.

17. Maurice Finklestein, "From *Munn* v *Illinois* to *Tyson* v *Banton,* A Study in the Judicial Process," *Columbia Law Review,* 1927.

18. *Tyson* v *Banton,* 273 U.S. 261 (1927), Holmes in dissent, p. 446.

19. *Nebbia* v *New York,* 291 U.S. 502 (1934).

20. *Nebbia,* p. 536.

21. *Nebbia,* p. 555.

22. Thomas Gilligan, William Marshall, and Barry Weingast, "Regulation and the Theory of Legislative Choice: The Interstate Commerce Act of 1887," *JLE,* April 1989.

23. Gabriel Kolko, *Railroads and Regulation 1877–1916* (1965).

24. Jonathan Hughes, *The Governmental Habit Redux* (1991), pp. 107–09.

25. Both speeches quoted in Karl Brent Swisher, *American Constitutional Development* (1954), p. 415.

26. L. L. Jaffe, *Judicial Control of Administrative Action* (1965), p. 12.

27. Albro Martin, *Enterprise Denied: Origins of the Decline of American Railroads* (1971).

28. Thomas S. Ulen, "The Market for Regulation: The I.C.C. from 1887 to 1920," *AER,* May 1980.

29. Milton Handler, *Trade Regulation* (1970), p. 1109.

30. For a sympathetic summary: A. D. Neale, *The Antitrust Laws of the United States: A Study of Competition Enforced by Law* (1970). Also, see Lawrence M. Friedman, *A History of American Law,* pp. 405–08.

31. F. M. Scherer, *Industrial Market Structure and Economic Performance,* 1st ed. (Chicago: Rand McNally, 1970), p. 424.

32. Scherer, pp. 422–27.

33. William Letwin, *Law and Economic Policy in America: The Evolution of the Sherman Antitrust Act* (1965). See also Handler, *Trade Regulation,* chs. 1–2; and Hans B.

Thorelli, *The Federal Antitrust Policy: Origination of an American Tradition* (1954).

34. Handler, pp. 105–08.

35. Thomas Jefferson, *Notes on the State of Virginia* (London: John Stockdale, 1788), p. 253.

36. William Hornblower, "Anti-Trust: Legislation and Litigation," *Columbia Law Review,* 1911, p. 702.

37. Handler, *Trade Regulation,* p. 114. Sec. 4 of the Clayton Act superseded Sec. 7 of the Sherman Act.

38. The Pullman strike of 1894 ended with labor leader Eugene V. Debs being jailed for contempt.

39. Gilbert H. Montague, "Anti-Trust Laws and the Federal Trade Commission, 1914–1927," *Columbia Law Review,* 1927, p. 661.

40. Montague, p. 661. For an illuminating study of the FTC's "shakedown cruise," when it first learned the scope and limitations of its power, see Robert M. Aduddell and Louis P. Cain, "Public Policy Toward the 'Greatest Trust in the World,' " *BHR,* Summer 1981.

41. *U.S.* v *Darby,* 312 U.S. 100 (1941).

42. *U.S.* v *E. C. Knight Co.,* 156 U.S. 1 (1895).

43. *U.S.* v *U.S. Steel Corp.,* 251 U.S. 417 (1920) and *Aluminum Co. of America* v *U.S.,* 148 F.2d. 416 (1945).

44. F. M. Scherer and David Ross, *Industrial Market Structure and Economic Performance* (1990), p. 509.

45. *U.S.* v *Trans-Missouri Freight Association,* 166 U.S. 290 (1897).

46. *Standard Oil of New Jersey* v *U.S.,* 221 U.S. 1 (1911).

47. Terry L. Anderson and P. J. Hill, *The Birth of a Transfer Society* (1989).

48. Those conflicts are ably summarized by Alfred Chandler and Louis Galambos in "The Development of Large-Scale Economic Organizations in Modern America," *JEH,* March 1970.

49. *NLRB* v *Jones and Laughlin Steel Corp.,* 301 U.S. a (1937), pp. 41–42.

Suggested Readings

Articles

Aduddell, Robert M., and Cain, Louis P. "Public Policy Toward the 'Greatest Trust in the World.' " *Business History Review,* vol. LV, no. 2, Summer 1981.

Atack, Jeremy. "Industrial Structure and the Emergence of the Modern Industrial Corporation." *Explorations in Economic History,* vol. 22, no. 1, January 1985.

Chandler, Alfred D., and Galambos, Louis. "The Development of Large-Scale Economic Organizations in Modern America." *Journal of Economic History,* vol. XXX, no. 1, March 1970.

Field, Alexander J. "Modern Business Enterprise as a Capital-Saving Innovation." *Journal of Economic History,* vol. XLVII, no. 2, June 1987.

Finklestein, Maurice. "From *Munn* v *Illinois* to *Tyson* v *Banton:* A Study in The Judicial Process." *Columbia Law Review,* vol. 27, no. 7, November 1927.

Gilligan, Thomas W., Marshall, William J., and Weingast, Barry R. "Regulation and the Theory of Legislative Choice: The Interstate Commerce Act of 1887." *Journal of Law and Economics,* vol. 32, no. 1, April 1989.

Grandy, Christopher. "New Jersey Corporate Chartermongering, 1875–1929." *Journal of Economic History,* vol. XLIX, no. 3, September 1989.

Hornblower, William. "Anti-Trust: Legislation and Litigation." *Columbia Law Review,* vol. 11, no. 8, December 1911.

Hovenkamp, Herbert. "The Classical Corporation in American Legal Thought." *The Georgetown Law Review,* vol. 76, no. 5, June 1988.

Hughes, Jonathan. "Transference and Development of Institutional Constraints Upon Economic Activity." In Paul Uselding, ed., *Research in Economic History,* volume 1. Greenwich, CT: JAI Press, 1976.

McCurdy, Charles W. "American Law and the Marketing Structure of the Large Corporation, 1875–1890." *Journal of Economic History,* vol. XXXVIII, no. 3, September 1978.

Montague, Gilbert H. "Anti-Trust Laws and the Federal Trade Commission, 1914–1927." *Columbia Law Review,* vol. 27, no. 6, June 1927.

O'Brien, Anthony Patrick. "Factory Size, Economies of Scale, and the Great Merger Wave of 1898–1902." *Journal of Economic History,* vol. XLVIII, no. 3, September 1988.

Scheiber, Harry. "Federalism and the American Economic Order, 1789–1910." *Law and Society,* vol. 10, no. 1, Fall 1975.

———. "The Road to Munn: Eminent Domain and the Concept of Public Purpose in the State Court." *Perspectives in American History,* vol. 5, 1971.

Thorp, Willard L., and Knott, Grace W. "The History of Concentration in Seven Industries." *The Structure of Industry.* Temporary National Economic Committee,

Monograph No. 23, Washington: United States Government Printing Office, 1941.

Ulen, Thomas. "The Market for Regulation: The I.C.C. from 1887 to 1920." *American Economic Review,* vol. 70, no. 2, May 1980.

Books

Anderson, Terry L., and Hill, P. J. *The Birth of a Transfer Society.* Lanham, MD: University Press of America, 1989.

Chandler, Alfred. *The Visible Hand.* Cambridge: Harvard University Press, 1977.

———. *Scale and Scope: The Dynamics of Industrial Capitalism.* Cambridge: Harvard University Press, 1990.

Friedman, Lawrence M. *A History of American Law.* New York: Simon and Schuster, 1973.

Galambos, Louis. *The Public Image of Big Business in America, 1880–1940.* Baltimore: Johns Hopkins University Press, 1975.

Handler, Milton. *Trade Regulation.* Brooklyn: The Foundation Press, 1960.

Hicks, John D. *The Populist Revolt: A History of the Farmers' Alliance and the People's Party.* Minneapolis: University of Minnesota Press, 1931.

Horwitz, Morton. *The Transformation of American Law, 1780–1860.* Cambridge: Harvard University Press, 1977.

Hughes, Jonathan. *The Governmental Habit Redux: Economic Controls from Colonial Times to the Present.* Princeton: Princeton University Press, 1991.

———. *The Vital Few: American Economic Progress and Its Protagonists.* New York: Oxford University Press, 1986.

Hurst, James Willard. *The Legitimacy of the Business Corporation in the United States, 1780–1970.* Charlottesville: University Press of Virginia, 1970.

Jaffe, L. L. *Judicial Control of Administrative Action.* Boston: Little, Brown, 1965.

Josephson, Matthew. *The Robber Barons: The Great American Capitalists, 1861–1901.* New York: Harcourt Brace, 1934.

Kolko, Gabriel, *Railroads and Regulations, 1887–1916.* Princeton: Princeton University Press, 1965.

Letwin, William. *Law and Economic Policy in America: The Evolution of the Sherman Antitrust Act.* New York: Random House, 1965.

Martin, Albro. *Enterprise Denied: Origins of the Decline of American Railroads.* New York: Columbia University Press, 1971.

Miller, Arthur Selwyn. *The Supreme Court and American Capitalism.* New York: The Free Press, 1972.

Moody, John. *The Truth About the Trusts.* New York: Moody, 1904.

Myers, Gustavus. *History of the Great American Fortunes.* Chicago: Kerr, 1960.

Neale, A. D. *The Antitrust Laws of the U.S.A.: A Study of Competition Enforced by Law.* Cambridge: Cambridge University Press, 1970.

Scherer, F. M., and Ross, David. *Industrial Market Structure and Economic Performance,* 3rd ed. Boston: Houghton Mifflin, 1990.

Sobel, Robert. *The Age of Giant Corporations: A Microeconomic History of American Business 1914–1970.* Westport, CT: Greenwood Press, 1972.

Swisher, Karl Brent. *American Constitutional Development.* Boston: Houghton Mifflin, 1954.

Tarbell, Ida M. *History of the Standard Oil Company.* New York: Macmillan, 1925.

Thorelli, Hans B. *The Federal Antitrust Policy: Origination of an American Tradition.* Stockholm: Akademsk Avhandling, 1954.

Wilcox, Clair, and Shepherd, William G. *Public Policies Toward Business.* Homewood, IL: Irwin, 1975.

Unger, Irwin. *The Greenback Era.* Princeton: Princeton University Press, 1964.

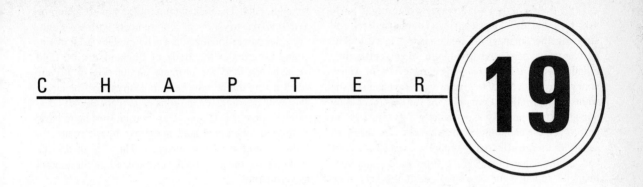

Financial Developments 1863–1914

U ntil the 1863 National Banking Act, banking in the United States was a mixture of (a) licensing by special state charters, (b) banking done by nonchartered private bankers, or under general state rules, and (c) free banking, following New York state's system.[1] Under Civil War legislation, the federal government re-entered American banking for the first time since the charter of the Second Bank of the United States lapsed in 1836, a victim of Jackson's veto.

The national banks created after 1863 were still limited to operations within their state boundaries; and even there, they were forbidden to have branches. What was "national" about them was simply their federal charters. The rival state banking systems continued, thus maintaining the American tradition of confusion in banking. Even in the nationwide **Federal Reserve System,** the central bank of the United States which began operations in 1914 and in which the national banks were forced to participate, the state boundaries prevailed. Branch banking across state lines was not allowed by the National Bank Acts and was prohibited in most states to protect the local monopoly rents derived from the unit-bank charters.

Since the expanding economy required financial intermediation, the financial history of the United States in the period 1863–1914 is essentially the story of creating that intermediation within the constraints of the continuing regime of unit banking. It is an odd, but nevertheless, fascinating tale, as financial history goes.

CREATING FINANCIAL INTERMEDIATION

In 1912, the National Monetary Commission report ripped into the existing American commercial banking system, denouncing it root and branch, and liberally crediting it with a whole multitude of crimes and errors. After a recital of 17 specific points of gross deficiency in the existing system, the report then generalized.

> The methods by which our domestic and international credit operations are now conducted are crude, expensive and unworthy of an intelligent people. . . . The unimportant part which our banks and bankers take in the financing of our foreign trade is disgraceful to a progressive nation. . . . The disabilities from which our producers suffer in our foreign trade also apply largely to domestic transactions.[2]

If all these charges were correct, one might fairly ask, how did the American legislatures, federal and state together, manage to create such a marvel? The answer is that partly they thought it up and partly they blundered into it. It was (and is) characteristic of American government to try to give everyone what he or she wants by legislation. Economic institutions created by our legislative processes are usually only designed in part to achieve economic goals; they are also meant to satisfy the more effectively organized vested interests and, at the same time, garner votes (and sometimes financial support) for those who draft the laws. Not surprisingly, the results of such activity tend to vary remarkably.

The National Bank Acts

As we already know (from Chapter 11), by 1860 there were more than 1500 separate state banks that had survived the various financial crises of the past. They were note-issuing institutions that circulated their own promissory notes, of many denominations, as money. By 1860, there may have been 10,000 different kinds of bank notes in circulation.

The federal government's fiscal position, while not as desperate as the Confederacy's, was nevertheless strained. Efforts to raise money by sales of long-term bonds were only partly successful and borrowing on short-term simply multiplied the problems of federal finance.[3] In 1861, some $189 million of long-term bonds bearing 6 percent interest were sold. In 1862, the financier, Jay Cooke, contracted to sell a huge issue and succeeded, by a door-to-door campaign, in placing $362 million. In that year, the Treasury also sold an additional $150 million worth of bonds. However, also in 1862, the Treasury, desperate for funds, borrowed an additional $682 million on short-term notes and issued $915 million in legal tender notes (a maximum of $447 million outstanding at any time).[4] There were objections to "farming out" any new long-term issues to operators like Cooke.

Because all this was before the pivotal Battle of Gettysburg in 1863, there were several war years yet to be financed, and a new method had to be found to harness the banking system to the federal Treasury's needs. The obvious answer would be somehow to force-feed federal securities into the state banks. The method chosen was the National Bank Act of 1863 and subsequent amendments. The scheme envisaged was to blend the federal Treasury's fiscal requirements with the country's need to rationalize the currency. The Bank of England note under the Bank of England Act of 1844 (which provided for ultimate elimination of private bank notes) might have been an inspiration; the circulation of hundreds of millions of greenbacks was certainly a practical lesson. The thousands of state bank notes could be eliminated at a stroke by the issue of a national uniform bank currency. The way to do this was to have the state banks rechartered by the federal government.[5]

The outbreak of war had removed the Southern legislators temporarily from Congress and thus, the representatives of state banks in half the country. Their absence facilitated the passing of the new banking legislation. The National Bank Act was passed in 1863 but produced only a small response, so, in October 1864, the Act was revised. A new office was established, that of the comptroller of the currency. Under the revised Act, the national banks would have capital requirements according to the size of the cities in which they were located (initially the range was from $200,000 for a city of 50,000 or more down to $50,000 for a city with only 6000 population). By purchasing U.S. bonds equal to at least one-third the required bank capital and then *hypothecating* (depositing) the bonds with the comptroller, each bank would receive back national bank notes (with each bank's name embossed thereupon) equal to 90 percent of the face value of the bonds thus immobilized. This feature was copied from the free banking system of New York.

The national bank notes were to be legal tender for all except customs payments. To make the system seem more sound than the state banking system, legal reserve requirements were imposed upon the national banks and double liability was imposed on the stock of the national banks. These features were supposed to attract deposits to the national system. A small semi-annual tax of ½ percent was placed upon the national bank note circulation, ¼ percent on capital in excess of the government bonds deposited with the comptroller and ¼ percent against deposits. In addition, a tax of 2 percent was levied against state bank notes in June 1864.

Because bankers received the scheme with a singular lack of enthusiasm, in March 1865 the tax on state bank notes was increased from 2 percent to 10 percent.

The high costs of continued state-charter operations now overcame the previous lack of enthusiasm, and membership in the national system soared. By now the war was over, but the new banking system was launched anyhow. It must have seemed at first that the national bank system would finally eliminate the bank-chartering business of the state legislatures. Instead, there now were two systems, adding to the complexity (see Table 19.1).

At first the state system dwindled rapidly, but as early as 1870, once state bankers learned how to earn a profit without issuing notes, it was making a come-back, and its recovery was dramatic. By 1900, the state banking system held considerably more in total assets than did the national. There were far more state than national banks, although the average state bank was only about half the size of the average national bank. There were an astounding 13,000 plus banks in the country then, and the number was still growing by leaps and bounds. What had happened?

Deposits and Checks

In the postwar period the system of checks and deposits became an increasingly common way to make payments. State banks, which could only circulate their own notes with a 10-percent federal tax on them, could loan money in the form of **demand deposits,** accounts against which checks could be written. The checks written against demand deposits are bank money: that is, if the seller is willing to take a check in payment either for goods or services, the check has performed the same function as a gold coin or a bank note.

A check on a demand deposit actually is a *financial bill of exchange,* an order from a principal (one who creates the check) to his or her agent (the bank) to disperse funds to a third party. As we saw in Chapter 1, the financial instrument called the *bill of exchange* had been used by merchants and bankers in western Europe to make payments long before the discovery of America and was apparently known in antiquity. It could become the main financial instrument used by common citizens once other citizens accepted it in payment instead of demanding coins or the promissory notes of bankers. The law relating to checks was already in place in colonial times.

The common use of checks by ordinary citizens was a major innovation, though, since it meant that the need for bank notes and coins could be reduced in daily circulation. All that was needed was that (a) bankers would honor the checks and (b) merchants and others would accept them.

Table 19.1   National and State Banks[a]

Year	Total		National Banks		State Banks		Percentage National Bank Assets of Total
	Number	Assets	Number	Assets	Number	Assets	
1860	1,562	$ 1,000	—[b]	—	—[b]	—	—
1861	1,601	1,016	—	—	—	—	—
1862	1,492	1,012	—	—	—	—	—
1863	1,532	1,209	66	$ 17	1,466	$1,192	0.1
1864	1,556	973	467	252	1,089	721	25.9
1865	1,643	1,358	1,294	1,127	349	231	83.0
1866	1,931	1,673	1,634	1,476	297	197	88.2
1867	1,908	1,674	1,626	1,494	272	180	89.2
1868	1,887	1,736	1,640	1,572	247	164	90.6
1869	1,878	1,736	1,619	1,564	259	171	90.1
1870	1,937	1,781	1,612	1,566	325	215	87.9
1900	13,053	11,388	3,731	4,944	9,322	6,444	43.4

[a] Assets are given in millions of dollars.
[b] No such banks yet in existence.

Source: *Historical Statistics,* derived from series X 580, 581, 634, 635, 656, 657. The data for state banks are for "nonnational" banks and include banks other than commercial banks.

Table 19.2   Mr. Smith and the Demand Deposit System

Old System

Assets	Liabilities
Mr. Smith's personal note + $100	Increase in bank notes in circulation + $100

Demand Deposit System

Assets	Liabilities
Mr. Smith's personal note + $100	Increase in demand deposit + $100

The basis for need (a) was the demand deposit. The principal had to have sufficient bank credit. The basis for need (b) was the *trust* of the third party (the seller of foods or services) in the ability of the principal to make good the amount, either by transfer of bank credit from the principal to the third party (called the *holder-in-due-course*) or by payment in notes or coins by the bank upon whom the check was drawn. Ancillary to the process, of course, was the belief by the seller that the bank itself could pay. The demand deposit upon which the checks were drawn could be created either by a grant of bank credit (e.g., a loan) from the bank to the principal or by the deposit of funds with the bank by the principal. The latter course in the nineteenth century commonly involved the payment of interest by the banker to the depositor.

Common use of checks and deposits meant that the state banks no longer needed to print their own prom-

issory notes to create bank credit—money. The demand deposits, since they served all the functions of notes and coins, were themselves "money." The 10-percent tax levied upon state banknotes in 1865 could thus be avoided without diminution of state bank credit *once the checks and demand deposits became acceptable practice.* That happened within a decade after 1865, and the state bank system grew again.

Just to be certain we understand the process, let's consider the example of Mr. Smith, a borrower. Under the old system, a banker lends Mr. Smith $100 by accepting a personal note from him and then handing over $100 in bank notes. In the new system, the bank notes are replaced by a demand deposit (see Table 19.2). Under the old system, the bank's credit of $100 against a personal note of $100 produced $100 worth of the bank's promissory notes, which Mr. Smith carried in his pocket and spent. Under the new system, Mr. Smith simply carried his checkbook and reduced his deposit by writing checks to cover his purchases. When the checks were taken to the bank by the seller, Mr. Smith's account was reduced in the same way. Under the old system his pocket was lightened when he paid cash. If the seller demanded cash, then Smith's demand deposit fell, and the bank's vault cash was reduced by the same amount.

On the basis of checks and demand deposits, then, the state banks were able to recover the business that formerly had depended upon the issue of their own notes. The resulting growth of the state banks is seen in Table 19.3, along with the growth of the banking system as a whole up to 1914.

Since the number of banks of all kinds, and their assets, more than doubled even in the final decade and

Table 19.3   Commercial Banks 1870–1914[a]

Year	Total Number	Total Assets	National Banks Number	National Banks Assets	State Banks Number	State Banks Assets	Percentage National Bank Assets of Total
1870	1,937	$ 1,781	1,612	$ 1,566	325	$ 215	87.9
1880	3,355	3,399	2,076	2,036	1,279	1,364	59.9
1890	8,201	6,358	3,484	3,062	4,717	3,296	48.2
1900	13,053	11,388	3,731	4,944	9,322	6,444	43.4
1910	25,151	22,922	7,138	9,892	18,013	13,030	43.2
1914	27,864	27,349	7,518	11,477	20,346	15,872	42.0

[a] Assets are given in millions of dollars.

Source: See source note for Table 19.1.

a half before 1914, banking clearly continued to be a growth industry as the economy expanded and became increasingly commercialized in all its aspects. At various points before 1914, efforts were made to reform and control this burgeoning phenomenon. Let's take a look at those attempts.

Currencies and Coins

By the late 1870s, all the state bank notes had vanished from circulation. So had various fractional bank notes issued by the U.S. Treasury in the absence of subsidiary silver coins. The national bank notes were based upon deposits of U.S. government bonds with the comptroller. As interest rates fell—all the way from the Civil War into the 1890s—bond prices rose, and the national bankers were loathe to invest in such low-yielding assets, even to circulate national bank notes with their own names embossed thereupon.[6] Instead, the national banks created demand deposits, too. National bank notes in circulation thus declined (see Table 19.4). The various Secretaries of the Treasury were conservative about any further increases in U.S. notes (greenbacks), and in 1879 the Treasury resumed specie payments after 15 years of inconvertibility.

The currency then expanded, mainly by accretions of gold and silver and the warehouse receipts for them: gold and silver certificates. The U.S. currency circulation filled up with precious metals. Until the turn of the century, the greenbacks and national bank notes remained a stagnant portion of the total means of payment. *After* 1900 there was a large expansion of the national bank note circulation as the numbers of national banks increased (see Table 19.3). With rising interest rates, U.S. bonds were now a better buy for bankers than they had been for a generation, and the cachet "national" over a bank door had come to mean prestige.[7] The national banks had done marginally better than the state banks in surviving the various monetary panics.

Until after 1900, the Civil War national bank "solution" to U.S. currency problems was less than a joke, giving rise to inevitable political movements in favor of other one-shot money solutions to all problems—solid gold, free silver, and commodity money, among others. We will discuss the later nineteenth-century currency controversies in due course. Here, we want

merely to clear the decks for the reappearance of central banking in 1914. According to the arguments of the time, part of the reason was the insufficient "flexibility" of the national bank note supply.

For those who think expansion of currency and coin is sound economics, it was the mining and coining of precious metals, together with those acquired through the balance of payments, that "solved" the country's economic problems until after 1900 (see Table 19.4). By that year the ratio of pure paper money to coins and moneys representing precious metals deposited had been cut by more than 90 percent. Whereas there were $5 of pure paper afloat for every $1 of some metallic kind in 1870, by 1900 there was about 40 cents in paper for every $1 metallic. The largest increases in the circulation came from increased monetary gold supplies together with a (lesser) increase in the uses of monetary silver. When the United States finally adopted the gold standard officially in 1900, the country was well supplied with that metal.

Banking Reforms and the Fed

At first the various comptrollers believed that *upper* limits on the national bank notes might be necessary. That idea was dropped in 1875 since note circulation was already declining. There was no evident way to get national banks (and their notes) spread evenly over the country. Studenski and Krooss report that in 1876 there was a greater national bank note circulation in the town of New Bedford, Massachusetts, than in any Southern *state*. Per capita national bank circulation was $77 in Rhode Island and 13 cents in Arkansas.[8] To encourage the growth of national banks, in 1882 the bond deposit requirement on the smaller banks (those with capital below $150,000) was reduced from one-third to one-fourth of all capital. Reserve requirements were scaled again according to city size. In 1900 national banks were allowed to issue notes equal to the full par value of deposited bonds.

But the national banks were really no system at all. Their check-clearing activities were slow and expensive, and there was no central institution of coordination. In the financial crises of 1873 and 1882 the system was endangered. In the panic of 1893 the national banks were again in deep difficulty, and in the panic of 1907 they came close to universal *suspension of payments*—refusal to return specie in return for bank notes. *Call money rates* (interest charged for loans that could be called in without warning) reached 70 percent in the panic of 1893; in 1907 they hit 125 percent.

When the dust of 1907 settled, reforms were demanded. The 1907 panic once again demonstrated the problems of uncoordinated fractional-reserve banking. As the demand for money increased in times of crisis, its supply was reduced. Small-town bankers counted as reserves their deposits in correspondent banks in the cities. Because of its active call-loan market, New York City especially attracted such deposits. In a crisis, country and small-town bankers withdrew their correspondent deposits, city bankers called in their loans to meet demand, and the credit structure collapsed like a house of cards. Despite efforts of the U.S. Treasury to help by allotting emergency deposits here and there and of the banks themselves by issuing clearing-house certificates to be used as temporary money, there was no way to stop the panics from spreading. They periodically appeared, at the peak of the business cycle, which many believed (and still believe) was caused by the expansions of bank money (deposits).[9]

In 1907 much of the potential damage was averted by adroit and forceful actions in New York City under the direction of the aging Pierpont Morgan.[10] Although it was an extraordinary performance by "Pierpontifex Maximus," the greatest of the old-time financiers, he was not thanked for it. His actions—the pooling of bank funds, rationing of credit, and disciplining of the short interest in the stock market—were, in part, similar to techniques developed by the Bank of England in the decades after 1857, which Morgan knew well. By 1907, he had been spending, for half a century, part of each year in London managing his bank there. What there was to learn about crisis management from the Bank of England he had grasped. He had in fact prepared for similar actions in 1903 when conditions were becoming ominous. His method was central banking without a central bank.

A return to some sort of central banking had been in the wind for years. The supposed transgressions of Nicholas Biddle and the Second Bank of the United States were forgotten in the terror of 1907 and the memories of 1873–1893. Congress in 1908 passed the Aldrich-Vreeland Act, which provided for a temporary emergency currency for the "next time," recommended formation of a National Currency Association of national banks for that purpose, and ordered that a National Monetary Commission be set up to suggest changes in the banking system. For details on the background and genesis of the resulting Federal Reserve System, see Robert Craig West's excellent study.[11]

We will only follow the main outlines here. The Commission's chairman, Senator Nelson Aldrich of Rhode Island, produced a plan in 1911 for a National Reserve Association organized nationwide in 15 districts, to be owned and operated by the private banking interests to be sponsored by federal action. In fact, the senator's plan was similar to other large-scale financial reorganizations prepared in the past by his old friend, Pierpont Morgan.

Table 19.4 Currencies and Coins in Circulation 1870–1914

Year	U.S. Notes	National Bank Notes	Gold Coin	Gold Certificates	Silver Dollars	Silver Certificates	Treasury Notes of 1890	Subsidiary Silver
1870	325.0	288.7	81.2	32.1	—	—	—	9.0
1880	327.9	337.4	225.7	8.0	20.1	5.8	—	48.5
1890	334.7	181.6	374.3	130.8	56.3	297.6	—	54.0
1900	317.7	300.1	610.8	200.7	65.9	408.5	75.3	76.2
1910	334.8	683.7	590.9	802.8	72.4	478.6	3.7	135.6
1914	337.8	715.2	611.5	1026.1	70.3	478.6	2.4	160.0

Source: *Historical Statistics*, series X 424–34.

In 1912 the Commission reported the same proposal. In 1912, however, Woodrow Wilson and the Democrats won the election. They were reform-minded and willing. They took over the congressional work on the legislation and changed it to meet their own standards. The Federal Reserve Act, signed into law by Wilson in December 1913, was the result.

The creation of the Fed was the apparently permanent American contribution to central banking. Much of the Aldrich Plan remained in the final bill, but much was changed, too. Also, an effort was made to politicize the new system by the creation of the Federal Reserve Board, all political appointees with certain executive powers.

The Federal Reserve Act is a curious hybrid, reflecting well its heterogeneous origins. It is a mixture of private interest and political creativity. The Fed's structure and functions were reformed in 1935, and it has now evolved into something that *looks* like "government." But looks can be deceiving.

At first the Federal Reserve System was no more than an empty framework, apart from its purely technical functions of clearing checks and servicing the federal government's financial operations. Central banking with 12 banks was a slight simplification of the Aldrich scheme; the Fed was not meant to be a monolithic central bank like other contemporary institutions: the Bank of England, Bank of France, Reichsbank, or the Swedish Riksbank.

Lessons from the past were embedded in the Federal Reserve Act. Its charter does not expire, so we are spared any more great bank charter crises. The Fed does its business with other banks; it is a bank for bankers. It does not deal with the public directly—that is, it does not *compete* with private bankers as did our earlier central banks. Thus, there is no pressure from the banking sector to abolish it.

Member banks are required to keep non-interest-bearing *cash* reserves in their district banks, a valuable lesson in credit control learned earlier from the Suffolk System. The required reserves (changed many times and now very complex, indeed) were initially copied from those developed under the National Banking System—that is, scaled by city size. Originally there was to have been a deposit insurance scheme in the Federal Reserve Act, but it had to be dropped from the legislation because of opposition from the bankers.[12] After more disaster, between 1929 and 1933, this idea reappears in our history as the Federal Deposit Insurance Corporation (FDIC). The original inspiration was New York's Safety Fund established in 1829.

To please all parties, the ownership and governance of the Federal Reserve System was, from the beginning, a hodge-podge. The national banks, with their federal charters, were forced to belong to the system. They bought the original stock in the district banks. Each national bank was to purchase Federal Reserve stock equal to 6 percent of its capital and surplus (3 percent paid in, the other 3 percent callable in the future). Each district bank was to have nine directors, three in each of three classes: (a) Class A, representing bankers; (b) Class B, representing business, commerce, and agriculture; (c) Class C, representing the "public." Class B directors could not be employees, directors, or officers of any bank. Class C directors bore the same constraints and, in addition, could not own stock in any bank. State banks were invited to join the system, keeping their state charters, or to utilize the Fed's check-clearing facilities without even joining the system.

To glue this all together was the Federal Reserve Board: seven members, originally including the secretary of the Treasury and the comptroller of the currency. The other five members were to be appointed by the president of the United States, with the advice and consent of the Senate. The terms of office were staggered to weaken for future White House occupants the possibility of control over the system through appointments. Top officers of the district banks were appointed subject to approval by the Federal Reserve Board. In

		Sum of	
Minor Coin	Paper Money	Metallic & Metallic Representative	Ratio of Paper to Metallic
—	613.7	122.3	5.0
—	702.1	308.1	2.3
—	516.3	912.9	0.6
26.1	617.9	1463.5	0.4
46.3	1018.5	2130.2	0.5
57.4	1053.0	2406.2	0.4

addition, there was to be a Federal Reserve Board
"agent" in each district bank for liaison purposes. The
district banks, on the other hand, could give advice and
counsel to the Board through the regularly scheduled
meetings of the Federal Advisory Council.

The bankers wanted federal sponsorship without
federal control, and they wanted private ownership.
The Populists in Congress wanted democracy and limited private banking interest at the top. Wilson and the
reformers wanted some sort of central bank. Everyone
got something.

The district banks were to issue their own promissory notes against the commercial paper they purchased, which was supposed to make the currency
"elastic," able to expand when commercial demand
increased. But there was originally a requirement that
the note issues were to be "backed" by gold (originally
the gold holdings were included in the "capital" accounts). That was to placate the sound money interests.
The "note cover" actually lasted until 1968, having
been scaled down by then to 25 percent. Profits of the
district banks in excess of 6 percent were to be split
evenly with the U.S. Treasury, to be used there either
to pay off the national debt or to be a base for further
greenback issues.

The "easy money" interest at first expressed dissatisfaction with the prospects of the new Federal
Reserve notes. They wanted something as easy to
create as the greenbacks had originally been. Just
print them up and pay them out. The Federal Reserve
Act was entitled:

> An act to provide for the establishment of Federal Reserve
> banks, to furnish an elastic currency, to afford means
> of rediscounting commercial paper, to establish a
> more effective supervision of banking, and for other
> purposes....

Many changes in the Fed's structure and functions
were to follow. At the outset, a peculiar sort of genius
obviously was needed to "find the handle," to discover
how to conduct central banking operations from this
strange institution. That man, Benjamin Strong, head
of the New York Federal Reserve Bank, arrived on
history's stage almost instantly. It was he, in the 1920s,
who essentially invented the Open Market Committee
and its operations.[13] By the 1970s the Federal Reserve
notes, based almost exclusively upon purchases of
government securities, would achieve an "elastic

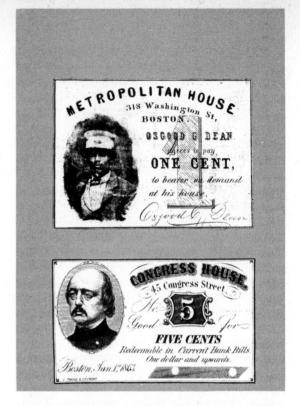

Early in the Civil War, the chaos of the financial system
was made worse by private money issues (above). Below
is a view of the Populist platform of 1892 as seen by a
"regular" Democratic cartoonist.

currency" beyond the wildest fantasies of the greenbackers. If printing more money could have solved economic problems, the Fed would have produced utopia. The year 1914 was only the faint beginning, the return of central banking after eight decades without it.[14]

INVESTMENT BANKING AND THE CAPITAL MARKET

Financial intermediation can take as many forms as there are needs for it to meet, and the varieties of institutions that can be created are almost as numerous. The system the United States finally developed is one of the most complex. In the later decades of the nineteenth century, the growing economy was facile in its ability to create the necessary structures. When the economy was growing on land, speculation, and agricultural commodity trade, the country developed land mortgage companies and merchant banks. When the transportation system and industrialization grew in tandem, the investment bank appeared.

The Davis Thesis

Lance Davis noticed an interesting difference between American and British experience with respect to the linkage between industrial and financial development.[15] In the late nineteenth and early twentieth centuries the English did not characteristically merge industrial firms into large organizations but did amalgamate their commercial banks into a small number of giant, nationwide branch-banking systems. In the United States the opposite was the case. Its industrial firms had a tendency to merge their financial structures, with "giant enterprises" emerging as the characteristic results. The banking structure proliferated by replication—more and more, hundreds, thousands of small banks. By 1900 or so it had huge industrial corporations and a plethora of small commercial banks.

Davis, a student of finance in both countries, noted the crucial link—American investment banking. The investment banker specialized in placing stocks and bonds in the hands of investors, including the thousands of small commercial banks.

British industrialists in a secondary city like, say, Wolverhampton or Sheffield could go to their local branch of Lloyds, Barclays, or the Westminster Bank for all their financial needs. The local branch offices of their banks could draw upon the mobilized capital of a giant system: Their banks were not only national, but international. British industrialists could thus raise expansion capital without surrendering individual firms to amalgamation. Their industrial structure consisted largely of small, family firms.

The American industrial firm in similar circumstances had no such local capital source. To raise the capital, the American firm had to create an intangible asset that could be traded elsewhere, in a major center, for capital funds. It created such intangible assets, stocks and bonds, by merger with its competitors. The American industrialists had access to big money, but not to small. The specialized agencies for such capital-raising industrial reorganizations were the investment banking firms located in the financial center and doing business under names like J. P. Morgan, Brown Brothers, Harriman, Kuhn-Loeb, and Kidder-Peabody.

People like Pierpont Morgan and Jakob Schiff made their careers in investment banking by merging and reorganizing railroads, mining companies, and manufacturers into firms whose prospects were bright enough for their financial paper to be marketable. Transaction costs were reduced by this intermediation. It was widely believed that the result was reduction of competition in industries so organized. The American investment banking industry thus, logically following the Davis thesis, grew up with the American manufacturing industry and the transportation network. Big firms were made by investment bankers, and investment banking grew on the proceeds of organizing big firms. In fact, Pierpont Morgan typically insisted upon placing a "Morgan man" on the board of directors of each of his great financial reorganizations to maintain the ties.

The process can be illustrated with a single man: Carnegie. In the late 1860s Andrew Carnegie, then a Pennsylvania Railroad official, had gone to London to raise money. It could not be done in the United States. In 1900 when Carnegie decided to sell out, he wrote his price, more than $400 million, on a piece of paper, and handed it to his boy-wonder executive, Charles Schwab, who delivered it to Pierpont Morgan. Schwab reported that Morgan merely glanced at the paper and said, "I'll take it." The result was the biggest industrial merger in history to date, United States Steel, which had two-thirds of the industry's ingot capacity, $550 million of common stock, $550 million of preferred stock, and $304 million in bonds. The American capital market, by then centered in Wall Street, had come into its own with investment bankers like Morgan filling the pilot role. It all happened in a single lifetime, in the business career of a single person, such as Carnegie or Morgan. Institutional adaptation, in this case to the remorseless fragmentation of American commercial banking, produced both high finance and big business. So Davis argues, and history seems to support him.

Money and Capital Markets

The institutions of intermediation had to develop. Two fundamental processes were involved: collection and investment. Savers had to find advantages for concentrating their funds in a few collecting institutions, such as banks and insurance companies, before such institutions could become lenders. Borrowers, on the other hand, needed instruments and access to institutional lenders.

All intermediaries are specialized in brokering, borrowing, and lending for various lengths of time. On the short end were the banks, savings institutions, and private bankers like Morgan that took deposits. Then there were houses specializing in commercial paper that borrowed from banks and loaned to merchants. There were nonbank intermediaries, including insurance companies lending at longer term, and houses specializing in the placement of long-term securities, the investment bankers.[16]

Commercial banks, as we already know, had begun shortly after independence. Their growth in numbers and assets was prodigious.

Savings banks began in this country in 1816. They were designed to receive deposits from the poor. The early ones were organized as mutual companies, with the depositors in the role of owners, and investments were restricted to the lowest risk categories. Because their conservative investment policies provided a maximum of safety, the mutual savings banks had a reputation for soundness not shared by commercial banks. Though relatively few in number, they were in fact among the largest companies in the nation. The mutual savings banks, as a result, played a more important role in the nineteenth century as capital mobilizers than they do today. By 1910, the 628 mutual savings banks had combined assets of $3.6 billion, about a third of

those held by the 7000 national banks (as shown in Table 19.2).[17]

Although savings and loan associations were in existence, by 1914 they had not yet begun to play the role they play today. Life-insurance companies also were not yet as critical a part of the capital markets as now, but they were large institutions by the standards of the time. Life insurance had been sold as early as the 1750s in this country by the Presbyterian Minister's Fund of Philadelphia. A century later, sales of insurance policies had expanded to other forms. Sales of a variety of policies added to the appeal of insurance. By 1910 the insurance companies had assets of $3.9 billion, or slightly more than those of the mutual savings banks.[18] Commercial banks, mutual savings banks, and life-insurance companies were the main intermediaries of collection between 1865 and 1914. The funds of all three were available for lending.

Accumulated funds could be loaned to individuals against personal and (except for national banks) real security (mortgages). Although a large portion of any bank's business might be (and is) done in this manner, it is cumbersome compared to the use of standard financial-market instruments—commercial paper, bonds, stocks—all of which have qualified for purchase and sale by specialists. Such specialized evaluation on a steady flow of securities greatly reduced transactions costs for everyone involved.

National banks could not lend against mortgages until 1914, and banks generally were wary of industrial securities until late in the nineteenth century. Organized markets for intermediation were much more efficient. Specialized businesses developed to sort out borrowers for the lenders. **Financial instruments**—such as common stocks, preferred stocks, convertibles, debenture bonds, ordinary bonds—were needed that could be readily classified and placed with buyers and lenders. Investment bankers advised their clients on the best ways to borrow.

Markets for "money" (short-term loans) and "capital" (long-term loans) developed in all the major cities. But New York City, with its port, banks, and proliferation of intermediaries, became the real center of all the nation's money and capital markets by the 1870s. Wall Street centralized and dominated the country's finance.[19]

Professor Davis argues that New York's huge money market was the key. In normal times, funds poured in from country and small-town correspondents to the New York banks. Money brokers in New York were sufficiently specialized even in the eighteenth century to have agreed upon a standard scale of commissions for their services. By the mid-1820s, the New York Stock Exchange Board was in business, and would come to dominate the other domestic money centers.[20] Dealers in long-term debts and stocks were constantly in need of short-term funds, and they formed the basis of the New York call-loan market. Funds could be employed by them on the shortest notice.

At first, few industrial shares were listed in New York. Government bonds, issued by public utility companies and railroads, predominated. Davis credits the huge revenue demands of the federal government during the Civil War with the development of investors' sophistication. Once a taste for portfolio purchases by savers developed, it could be exploited by brokers and investment bankers. By the end of the nineteenth century, industrialists, guided by Wall Street specialists, had easy access to the pooled resources of the country's savers, directly and via the intermediaries of collection. The country had a machine for the mobilization of capital. Expansion of it came through the use of the linked money and capital markets. Davis summarizes it:

> The impressive gains chalked up by the markets in the thirty-five years after Appomattox were the result, in large measure of increasing investor sophistication, the innovation of the new marketing techniques proved during the Civil War, the continued development of the call-loan markets, and the rise of the investment banking house.[21]

THE CURRENCY QUESTION

Success in financial institution building was achieved in the teeth of dysfunctions in the physical supply of the medium of exchange. As we already know, the United States was launched on its career of crankiness in the matter of money when bimetallism was adopted at the beginning of the Republic's independent existence. The experiences of the antebellum period, with thousands of different kinds of bank notes added to the stew, did nothing to simplify matters. Then, during the Civil War, came both greenbacks and national bank notes. From that time essentially until 1933, the posi-

tion was not stabilized. "Money" invaded politics as never before, and more than one presidential campaign was dominated by the question of what kinds of money the country *ought* to have.

What Kinds of Money?

The United States is not alone in its persistent money madness, by the way. The English version of this derangement was the centuries-long campaigns by various reformers to decimalize that wonderfully exotic old money system. Finally, in the 1960s, success came in England, and the decimal currency was fated to become the vehicle for the worst inflation in that country's history. The nineteenth-century debates caused the prime minister, Sir Robert Peel, to observe in the 1840s, "The question of the currency has made more lunatics than love."

With Americans the advantages of decimalization had been enjoyed from the beginning. Once they were able to get things (coins, paper) denominated in dollars, they cut themselves free from English money: guineas, pounds, crowns, half-crowns, florins, shillings, pence, and farthings. Apart from quarters, which made possible continuation of the old two bits, four bits, and six bits, they had 100 pennies in a dollar and divisions thereof. Their problem was deciding what kind of *metal* should be used for the coins. What metal should be the standard?

The Constitution had said that both gold and silver were to be legal tender. That left out copper, lead, and iron. But what about representative moneys like gold and silver certificates? Should they be 100 percent "backed" by deposited precious metal? What about promissory notes of banks? Should they be "backed" by something? By what? Who should issue them? What about the pure fiat issues of the federal government? Who should control those? What parts of all this should be legal tender? What parts not?[22]

To simplify, let us go back a moment to the money question in colonial times (leaving out wampum and deerskins, for example). Debtor classes favored lots of money per capita so that wages would rise. Those who bought and sold commodities (farmers) also favored abundant money supplies since prices might be raised and automatic capital gains accrued. However, those who had money wealth did not want profligate increases in money supplies because interest rates might fall and their incomes from moneylending might be reduced accordingly. So, roughly generalizing, the poor and the farmers wanted increased money supplies per capita, while those who derived income from interest wanted stable or decreased money supplies per capita.[23]

Since gold was the scarcest metal, a gold standard was favored by the wealthy. The most plentiful precious metal was silver, so it found favor among those who gained from rising wages and prices. It follows that the latter groups also favored paper money from whatever source. Bimetallism was a compromise on the metals, reserve requirements were restrictions on paper-money issues by banks. Other limitations were favored on straight fiat issues: in the nineteenth century, greenbacks; today, Federal Reserve notes.

One might add at this point that these conflicts have never been resolved altogether. Today, the "neo-Keynesians" represent the old inflationist interest, while the modern Monetarists represent the "sound money" interest. Now let us examine the fun and games the leaders had with the currency between 1862 and 1914.

Greenbacks and Specie Payments

The issuance of United States bank notes, beginning in 1862 when gold was flowing out of the country, required suspension of specie payments by the banks and the Treasury. The greenbacks were purely fiat money and there was virtually no silver in circulation in 1862, the silver having been undervalued by the Currency Act of 1834. As the issues of greenbacks and national bank notes proceeded, prices zoomed upward (see Figure 19.1). The Civil War inflation set the stage for a half century of further tinkering with the currency. Those who enjoyed increased incomes from the inflation might not have wanted even more inflation, but they surely did not relish what actually happened when peace came. The postwar collapse in prices continued until roughly 1896, with only partial recoveries in a few cyclical episodes. There was, therefore, steady

Although farm and wholesale prices generally did not regain the peaks reached at the end of the Civil War, by the period of 1910–14, a strong recovery had been made from the lows of the 1890s. The rising cost-of-living index mainly represents a rising standard of living with expensive services and rents added to the prices of commodities.

Figure 19.1 Prices, 1860–1914

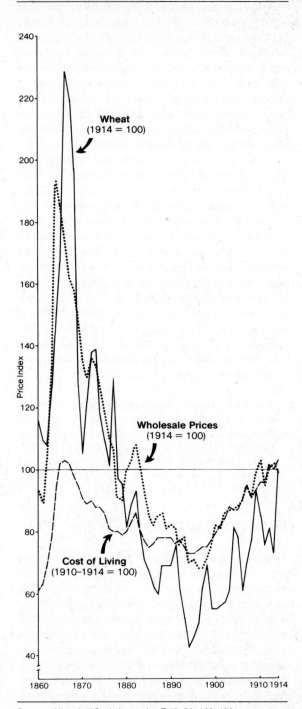

Source: *Historical Statistics*, series E 40, 52, 123, 183.

pressure for 30 years from the inflationists to *do some-thing* to stop the deflation.

The fact that the falling prices reflected rising productivity and produced rising *real* wages and incomes was irrelevant to the inflationists. Those who wanted inflation became enthusiasts for silver and paper money. The "sound-money" interests were for gold, the scarcest metal, and they had every reason to oppose the silver and greenback interests. The recovery of prices from the late 1890s to 1914, while partially placating the forces of cheap money, came more from the increase in the supplies of gold and silver than from paper. As in the late 1840s and early 1850s, increased supplies of metals proved capable at last of raising prices.

The object of successive secretaries of the Treasury, once the war ended, however, was a return to gold payments. Falling prices were necessary to restore the competitiveness of American exports. Therefore, paper money issues had to be constrained. Greenback issues were frozen, then reduced, and, as we have seen, national bank circulation did not expand enough to raise prices. The result was the first "money revolt," the Greenback movement, which advocated expansion of the U.S. note issues to reflate prices.[24] The panic of 1873 produced another sharp fall in prices and more pressure to expand paper money. In 1874, however, Congress placed an upper limit on greenbacks of $382 million and the next year directed the Treasury to resume gold payments in January 1879. This was done, after 15 years of suspension. Provision had also been made in the Funding Act of 1870 to retire greenbacks after 1870 until they reached a level of $360 million.[25] They were to be replaced by a presumed increase in the national bank notes (which did not occur until the twentieth century, in fact, as shown in Table 19.3).

The Crime of '73

Silver had been driven from circulation by the rise in gold supplies in the 1840s and 1850s.[26] The Currency Act of 1834 had set the mint ratio at 16 to 1. The bullion content of each dollar by the early 1870s was $1.0312, so silver did not circulate. It was worth 3 percent more as bullion than as coins. Therefore, in 1873 the Coinage Act omitted any provision for the resumption of the minting of silver dollars. Even by 1861, 15.29 ounces of silver bought an ounce of gold (silver

was $1.352 an ounce). The U.S. Treasury had been forced as a result to print paper money in fractions of one dollar to provide a circulating medium.

When the western silver discoveries occurred, output soared, and by 1874 it took 16.7 ounces of silver to buy an ounce of gold. On the market, silver was down to $1.292 an ounce. The silver producers wanted the subsidy restored. The 1873 Coinage Act, which withdrew the fixed mint silver price, became known as the "Crime of '73," and a new politico-economic force was born, curiously called **free silver,** which saw a restoration of silver's former position. I say curious because taking it off the market was defined as "freedom." It was argued that if the mint bought silver, that would raise the quantity of money and, hence, prices. The inflationists had a new target for legislation: the return of the Treasury silver purchases to the mint par of 1834. President Hayes vetoed legislation in 1877 to restore the subsidy, but in 1878 Congress repassed the legislation over his veto.

The Bland-Allison Act of 1878

The result was the Bland-Allison Act—again, something for everyone. It produced what Studenski and Krooss called the "limping standard," not fully bimetallic, but not anything else either.[27] Under the 1878 Act, the Treasury was to purchase $2–4 million of silver a month but *at the current market price.* On the other hand, the silver was to be coined into dollars weighing 412.5 grains (Troy ounce = 480 grains), 371.25 grains of which were 0.9 fine (pure) silver. This was the silver dollar weight of the old coin under the Act of 1834: $20.67 worth of silver dollars would buy an ounce of gold at the U.S. mint. Moreover, the silver dollars were full legal tender, but if they were exchanged for silver certificates ($10 and up), the certificates were not legal tender for private transactions. Banks, for example, would obviously refuse to accept them.

The cry had gone up before 1878 that silver had been "demonetized" because the Treasury could refuse to buy it beyond the needs for coinage. After the Bland-Allison Act the Treasury was committed to buying silver for coins. The silver flowed in, and the gold flowed out. Prices still fell, and the Treasury was blamed for not buying enough silver at a high enough price. Under Bland-Allison, the price was the market price. By the

1880s, other groups, known collectively as the Populists, came out for restoration of the old price, 16 to 1. They hoped that raising the price of silver might raise the price of other things too, like corn and hogs and cotton.

The Sherman Silver Purchase Act of 1890

Despite the purchase of 291.3 million ounces under the Bland-Allison Act, the price of silver had fallen by 1890 to 93 cents an ounce on the market, and the Treasury had more than $380 million of the white metal in storage. Other prices had not recovered, and the silverites, greenbackers, Populists, and other inflationists were demanding firmer action.

In return for Western votes to support the McKinley tariff (high restrictive duties), the Senate came through with the Sherman Silver Purchase Act of 1890. It doubled the monthly purchase rates—the silver was to be purchased with Treasury notes of 1890, which then could be turned in to the Treasury for gold bullion or coins. So long as silver prices kept falling, it paid to sell silver for Treasury notes, buy gold, use it to buy silver, and then trade it for Treasury notes.

By 1893 when the Sherman Act was repealed because of President Cleveland's urgent appeals to Congress—"Financial distrust and fear have sprung up on every side"—the Treasury's gold reserves were well below the $100-million minimum, dangerously low.[28] Reserves continued declining under balance-of-payments pressures. The government resorted to bond sales. Finally in 1895, President Cleveland went to Wall Street and the investment bankers for aid.[29]

A syndicate was formed by Pierpont Morgan, August Belmont, and others to market U.S. bonds in Europe for gold. The syndicate succeeded temporarily, but a great scandal resulted. Popular opinion considered it disgraceful that the U.S. government should have to turn to private investment bankers for aid. After six months, gold began flowing out again, and Morgan offered to repeat the exercise. President Cleveland instead went back to direct bond sales to the public. The bonds were favorably priced. The public traded in notes for gold and bought the bonds. Had the Treasury refused to give gold for the notes, the silverites would have succeeded in forcing the government away from gold and on to silver.

The balance of payments turned around in late 1896, and gold began flowing back in, relieving the crisis. The Treasury had been through eight years of chaos, several times far below their own minimum gold reserve.

The silver people had demanded a restoration of the silver price to 16 to 1 (1.292 an ounce with gold at $20.67 an ounce). By 1896, silver was down to 69 cents an ounce, or nearly 30 to 1. That summer, William Jennings Bryan won the Democratic nomination, uniting all the inflationists behind his "Cross of Gold" speech. It was a wonderfully effective speech, but McKinley won the election, and the forces of gold, "sound money," were on the march. Under the Bland-Allison and Sherman acts, the Treasury had purchased more than $500 million of silver. Now, with the balance of payments in surplus, gold flowing in again, and prices on the rise with the advance of business prosperity, it was the sound-money people's turn at bat.

The Gold Standard Act of 1900

In 1900, after several abortive attempts, Congress passed the Currency Act, or Gold Standard Act, putting the country legally on the pure gold standard. The dollar was defined as 25.8 grains of 0.9 fine gold. A reserve of $150 million in gold coin was to be set aside for ultimate redemption of the greenbacks and the 1890 Treasury notes. The minimum capital requirements for national banks was reduced to $25,000 in cities of less than 3000 population, and national banks were authorized to issue notes equal to the par value of deposited bonds. The result was a surge in national bank formation.

Gold continued to flow in, and the currency remained mainly metallic. Then came the panic of 1907, the National Monetary Commission, and the formation of the Federal Reserve System with its new Federal Reserve notes, yet another kind of money.

Epilogue: 1933 and Silver Again

Despite all the jiggering and tinkering, the system crashed again between 1929 and 1933, worse than ever before. Among the new "solutions" came one last blast from the Populist silver "crazies." The market price of silver by 1933 was down to 43 cents an ounce, and the government was raising the price of gold by 69 percent to $35 an ounce. To pacify the Populists, President Roosevelt ordered the Treasury to buy silver again. In June the Silver Purchase Act of 1933 was passed, which directed the Treasury to buy silver until its holdings equaled 25 percent of the gold stock, or until the market price reached $1.29 an ounce.

Gold poured into the United States as war clouds threatened in Europe and Asia. By 1939 another billion ounces of silver had been purchased by the U.S. Treasury (draining the world's monetary system of the metal), and the price was still 43 cents an ounce in the market. World War II, photography, electronics (providing a huge industrial use), together with inflation, finally "did something for silver." Monetary stocks disappeared from central banks, and the silver was melted off the coins. By early 1980, silver was at an all-time peak: $50 an ounce. The U.S. Treasury had purchased more than 460,000 *tons* of it between 1792 and 1939, largely in vain. Then came the Hunt brothers.[30]

THE MAJOR CRISES AND THE POOR

Throughout these dramatic monetary struggles, life went on, and the business cycle continued its course. In the great financial crises, banks closed, railroads went bankrupt, factories shut down, and millions lost their jobs. These events gave rise to labor radicalism and to grave dissatisfaction with the free market's way of producing long-run growth by the realignment of the economy, dissatisfaction with the crises and recessions that were produced. The depression of the 1890s was very severe—the bread lines were long—and a great change occurred. People began to say that the *federal*

government had responsibility for the country's economic welfare, and they began to organize on that basis.

The federal government had already launched new regulatory innovations in the form of the Interstate Commerce Act of 1887 and the Sherman Antitrust Act of 1890. In addition, all currency and banking changes since 1862 were overt attempts by the federal government to intervene in the economy. Despite stout disclaimers from the president on down, many had noticed that pensions for soldiers, subsidies to shipbuilders and operators, subsidies and special favors to railroads, and tariffs to protect manufacturers from foreign competition, all federal government money and/or power, could produce economic activity and jobs where the market, if left alone, would not. The arrival of "Coxey's Army" of the unemployed in Washington in April of 1894, with its demands for massive federal expenditures, produced legislative attempts to print money for direct relief. President Cleveland was appalled. But the point was clear: If the federal power could be used to aid railroad magnates and manufacturers, it could be used for the poor as well. In the depression of the 1890s, a *very different* future was beginning to appear.

After the panic of 1907, one last effort was made to solve economic problems exclusively by fooling with the money and reforming the banks. The 1921 recession was too short to test the new forces at play. In 1933 it became clear that "monetary reform" alone would no longer satisfy those who were left destitute by the cyclical downturns, and the New Deal would finally legislate much of the Populist platform into being. True to the great American tradition of jiggering with the money, another kind was created: the Federal Reserve Bank note. It was a sour joke.

Notes

1. Hugh Rockoff, "Varieties of Banking and Regional Economic Development in the United States, 1840–1860," *JEH,* March 1975.
2. *Report of the National Monetary Commission* (Washington, D.C.: United States Government Printing Office, 1912), pp. 28–29.
3. A million dollars borrowed in year T_1 for one year had to be repaid in year T_2, when additional borrowing also was required. Ideally, the Treasury would borrow as far forward as possible, at least shifting the problem of repayment to a period when money would be the only problem.
4. Paul Studenski and Herman Krooss, *Financial History of the United States* (1952), Table 20, p. 156.
5. In *Veazie Bank* v *Fenno* (1869) the scheme was declared constitutional by the Supreme Court.
6. Studenski and Krooss, *Financial History of the United States,* pp. 178–79.

7. From 1863 to 1907, 449 national banks failed; 2000 state banks passed into oblivion in the same period. Of the national bank failures, 80 percent of their debts were satisfied (Studenski and Krooss, p. 248).

8. Studenski and Krooss, pp. 178–81.

9. Some economists also believe that financial crises are the mere epiphenomena of more deep-seated imbalances. The evidence shows no clear tendency toward either monetary or nonmonetary causation alone. It has been a mixed bag. Michael D. Bordo, "The Impact and International Transmission of Financial Crises: Some Historical Evidence, 1870–1933," *Rivista Di Storia Economica,* 1985.

10. Jonathan Hughes, *The Vital Few* (1986), pp. 439–53.

11. Robert Craig West, *Banking Reform and the Federal Reserve 1863–1923* (1977).

12. For an analysis of the Act, Studenski and Krooss, *Financial History of the United States,* pp. 258–62. The standard history is H. Parker Willis, *The Federal Reserve System: Legislation, Organization, and Functions* (1923).

13. Elmus Wicker, *Federal Reserve Policy 1912–1933* (1966); S. V. O. Clarke, *Central Bank Cooperation, 1924–31* (New York: Federal Reserve Bank of New York, 1968).

14. The idea that the Fed was the inexorable outcome of developing corporate capitalism is set out in James Livingston, *Origins of the Federal Reserve System: Money, Class, and Corporate Capitalism* (1986).

15. Lance E. Davis, "Capital Immobilities and Finance Capitalism: A Study of Economic Evolution in the United States," *EEH,* Fall 1963.

16. Margaret C. Myers, *The New York Money Market* (1931), vol. I; John A. James, "The Development of a National Money Market, 1843–1911," *JEH,* December 1976.

17. Lance E. Davis, Duncan McDougall, and Jonathan Hughes, *American Economic History: The Development of a National Economy* (Homewood, IL: Irwin, 1969), 3rd ed., p. 203; Alan L. Olmstead, "Investment Constraints and New York City Mutual Savings Bank Financing of Antebellum Development," *JEH,* December 1972, on the consequences of restrictions on investments by savings banks.

18. Davis et al., p. 203.

19. Robert Sobel, *The Big Board: A History of the New York Stock Market* (1965).

20. Kenneth A. Snowden, "American Stock Market Development and Performance, 1871–1929," *EEH,* October 1987; and "Historical Returns and Security Market Development, 1872–1925," *EEH,* October 1990.

21. Davis et al., *American Economic History,* pp. 215–16. Also, Richard Sylla, "Federal Policy, Banking Market Structure, and Capital Mobilization in the United States, 1863–1913," *JEH,* December 1969. The need for investment banking intermediation was no doubt increased by the lack of interstate branch banking, which helped to maintain regional interest rate differentials. Lance E. Davis, "The Investment Market, 1870–1914: The Evolution of a National Market," *JEH,* September 1965.

22. For two excellent older works covering in detail this material, see A.B. Hepburn, *History of Currency in the United States* (1924), and Davis R. Dewey, *Financial History of the United States* (1934). Hepburn is particularly good on the madcap consequences of the Sherman Silver Purchase Act.

23. One of the Populist demands was for a fixed amount of money ($50) per capita. This idea is still around in current Monetarist thought, although it has been changed to a matching of monetary and population *growth rates.*

24. Irwin Unger, *The Greenback Era* (1964).

25. Numbers in this section from Studenski and Krooss, *Financial History of the United States,* ch. 16.

26. In fact, it can be argued that from the 1850s on, the United States really was no longer on a bimetallic standard. David A. Martin, "1853: The End of Bi-metallism in the United States," *JEH,* December 1973. See also Milton Friedman, "The Crime of 1873," *JPE,* December 1990. Friedman argues most of the decline in prices that characterized the remainder of the nineteenth century could have been avoided had a strict bimetallism been retained.

27. Studenski and Krooss, *Financial History of the United States,* p. 190; see also Milton Friedman and Anna J. Schwartz, *A Monetary History of the United States* (1963), pp. 113–19 on silver and the currency.

28. Studenski and Krooss, p. 219.

29. Matthew Simon, "The Morgan-Belmont Syndicate of 1895 and Intervention in the Foreign-Exchange Market," *BHR,* Winter 1968.

30. By January 1980, silver approached $50 an ounce after a spectacular run-up from $5 an ounce in the previous 12 months. Bunker and Nelson Hunt, the Texas oil millionaires, played a vital role in this boom before it collapsed.

Suggested Readings

Articles

Bordo, Michael D. "The Impact and International Transmission of Financial Crises: Some Historical Evidence, 1870–1933." *Rivista Di Storia Economica,* International issue, 2nd series, vol. 2, 1985.

Davis, Lance E. "Capital Immobilities and Finance Capitalism: A Study of Economic Evolution in the United States." *Explorations in Entrepreneurial History,* vol. 1, no. 1, Fall 1963.

———. "The Investment Market, 1870–1914: The Evolution of a National Market." *Journal of Economic History,* vol. 25, no. 3, September 1965.

Friedman, Milton. "The Crime of 1873." *Journal of Political Economy,* vol. 98, no. 6, December 1990.

James, John A. "The Development of a National Money Market, 1893–1911." *Journal of Economic History,* vol. 33, no. 4, December 1973.

———. "Cost Functions of Post-bellum National Banks." *Explorations in Economic History,* vol. 15, no. 2, April 1978.

———. "Public Debt Management Policy and Nineteenth-Century American Economic Growth." *Explorations in Economic History,* vol. 21, no. 2, April 1984.

Martin, David. "1853: The End of Bimetallism in the United States." *Journal of Economic History,* vol. 33, no. 4, December 1973.

Olmstead, Alan L. "Investment Constraints and New York City Mutual Savings Bank Financing of Antebellum Development." *Journal of Economic History,* vol. 32, no. 4, December 1972.

Rockoff, Hugh. "Varieties of Banking and Regional Economic Development in the United States, 1840–1860." *Journal of Economic History,* vol. XXXV, no. 1, March 1975.

Simon, Matthew. "The Morgan-Belmont Syndicate of 1895 and Intervention in the Foreign Exchange Market." *Business History Review,* vol. 42, no. 4, Winter 1968.

Smiley, Gene. "Interest Rate Movements in the United States, 1888–1913." *Journal of Economic History,* vol. XXXV, no. 3, September 1975.

Snowden, Kenneth A. "American Stock Market Development and Performance, 1871–1929." *Explorations in Economic History,* vol. 24, no. 4, October 1987.

Spencer, Austin H. "Relative Downward Industrial Price Flexibility, 1870–1921." *Explorations in Economic History,* vol. 14, no. 1, January 1977.

Sushka, Marie Elizabeth, and Barrett, W. Brian. "Banking Structure and the National Capital Market, 1869–1914." *Journal of Economic History,* vol. XLIV, no. 2, June 1984.

———. "American Banking and Growth in the Nineteenth Century: A Partial View of the Terrain." *Explorations in Economic History,* vol. 9, no. 2, Winter 1971–72.

Sylla, Richard. "Federal Policy, Banking Market Structure, and Capital Mobilization in the United States, 1863–1913." *Journal of Economic History,* vol. 29, no. 2, December 1969.

Williamson, Jeffrey G. "Watersheds and Turning Points: Conjectures on the Long-Term Impact of Civil War Financing," *Journal of Economic History,* vol. XXXIV, no. 3, September 1974.

Wimmer, Larry T. "The Gold Crisis of 1869: Stabilizing or Destabilizing Speculation Under Floating Exchange Rates?" *Explorations in Economic History,* vol. 12, no. 2, April 1975.

Books

Dewey, Davis R. *Financial History of the United States.* New York: Longmans, Green, 1934.

Friedman, Milton, and Schwartz, Anna J. *A Monetary History of the United States 1867–1960.* Princeton: Princeton University Press, 1963.

Hepburn, A. Barton. *History of Currency in the United States.* New York: Macmillan, 1924.

Hughes, Jonathan. *The Vital Few: American Economic Progress and Its Protagonists.* New York: Oxford University Press, 1986.

James, John. *Money and Capital Markets in Postbellum America.* Princeton: Princeton University Press, 1978.

Livingston, James. *Origins of the Federal Reserve System: Money, Class, and Corporate Capitalism, 1890–1913* (Ithaca: Cornell University Press, 1986).

Myers, Margaret. *The New York Money Market.* New York: Columbia University Press, 1934.

Sobel, Robert. *The Big Board: A History of the New York Stock Market.* New York: Free Press, 1965.

Studenski, Paul, and Krooss, Herman. *Financial History of the United States.* New York: McGraw-Hill, 1952.

Unger, Irwin. *The Greenback Era.* Princeton: Princeton University Press, 1964.

West, Robert Craig. *Banking Reform and the Federal Reserve 1863–1923.* Ithaca: Cornell University Press, 1977.

Wicker, Elmus. *Federal Reserve Policy 1917–1933.* New York: Random House, 1966.

Willis, H. Parker. *The Federal Reserve System: Legislation, Organization and Functions.* New York: Ronald Press, 1923.

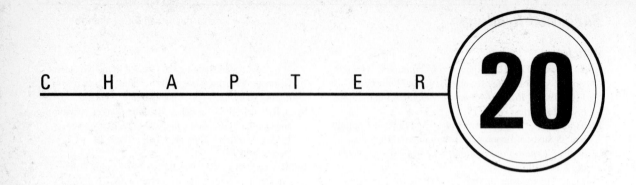

The Giant Economy and
Its International Relations

Unlike the other industrializing nations of the late nineteenth century, America's economic growth was not so heavily dependent upon overseas markets. For example, the European countries commonly relied upon exports for 20–30 percent of the sales of their domestic output, and they imported similar proportions of the goods and commodities used in domestic production and consumption. Comparative advantage thus counted heavily for the Europeans in their efforts to raise living standards by specialization in production. The British had to import textile raw materials, the French, fuel, in order to operate their factories. Proportionately, the United States depended far less on trade.

Throughout the period from the 1820s to the 1920s, U.S. exports were only 6–7 percent of GNP. The proportion slowly declined over time; in colonial times the ratios were far higher, 20–30 percent in the late 1720s and 10–15 percent between 1790 and 1800.[1] Because the raw-material wealth of the interior continental United States was being exploited during the westward movement, Americans needed little beyond exotic (mainly tropical) products and very spe-

cialized manufactured imports overall. However, in certain industries imports and exports figured more prominently: For example, around 20 percent of agricultural output went to the foreign market, and imports of items like diamonds, coffee, tea, spices, and high-grade china and cut glass dominated some parts of domestic trade.

One does not mean to imply, of course, that U.S. foreign trade was unimportant to Americans. Its true value to Americans, since they *did* want to buy foreign wares, was the same as with other marketable goods and services: the *opportunity cost.* If Americans insisted upon drinking tea and coffee and could not import those commodities, the cost to Americans to produce them with American land, labor, and capital would have been very high indeed. Similarly, had American farmers been unable to export 20 percent of their output, their troubles in the postbellum era would have been far worse than they were. Americans had an enhanced standard of life, as did all their trading partners, because of foreign trade. The great difference between the United States and the other industrializing countries was the extent of self-sufficiency.

TRENDS IN TRADE AND PAYMENTS

Each nation, as a result of technological advance and changes in factor proportions, experiences a slow but certain change in comparative advantage over time. Technological change itself, by redefining the factors of production, changes the factor proportions. Even a Caribbean island that grows nothing physical for export but bananas may find itself, because of modern transportation, able to export its climate and scenery in wintertime in the form of a tourist industry. As a result, it will put a smaller proportion of its resources into bananas and more into hotels. The island may end up even *importing bananas,* if it pays all the local labor force to work in hotels and buy bananas from a less fortunate isle.

Changes in U.S. Trade Composition

In Table 20.1 we can see roughly the way the comparative advantage shifted from the early nineteenth century down to the 1920s—away from agriculture in favor of manufacturing. On the export side we see the rise in the proportion of finished manufactures as the country's industrialization proceeded. On the import side the dramatic rise in crude materials and the decline in the proportion of finished manufactured goods comprise the opposite side of that coin. Exports of food as a proportion of the total peaked toward the nineteenth century's end. The increase in agricultural protectionism on the European continent played a role in the relative decline of food exports after that.

Although food imports also slowly declined as a proportion of the total, that decline was not a function of U.S. agricultural protectionism. Americans mainly imported tropical and exotic foods that could not be grown in their own country.[2] Demand for imports of tropical and exotic foods, subject to Engel's Law, soon grew less rapidly than did the demand for other imports.

Expansion

The figures in Table 20.1 reflect the proportions of a rapidly expanding total trade. In value terms we see the numbers in Table 20.2. The growth was extraordinary—exports increased by a factor of 86 and imports by a factor of 68 in one century. But, as we noted already, this actually was slightly *slower* than the economy's rate of growth overall. It was in some ways a peculiarity of the American economy in this epoch that its **marginal propensity to import,** the change in imports relative to the change in GNP, declined. The reason was the long period of relative self-sufficiency of the United States in most raw materials, together with the extraordinary expansion of the economy as industrialization proceeded. The pattern continued until the post-World War II period, when imports of petroleum skyrocketed, and imports of finished manufactures rose again to nineteenth-century proportions. (We will treat this dramatic turn of events in Chapter 31.) For the late nineteenth century and the first half of this century, the demand for foreign goods declined relatively as domestic income expanded, as population soared, and as the competitive economy produced the American industrial revolution.

U.S. Share of World Trade

From the mid-nineteenth century onward, the United States occupied a share of world trade disproportionately large compared to American population. This much would be expected in the case of a rich and growing economy with its doors mainly open to trade. Some relevant data are shown in Table 20.3 on page 364.

Only in the case of imports of manufactures did the U.S. share of world trade rise substantially more than did its share of world population. At first this result might seem paradoxical. After all, it was *exports* of manufactures that rose the most rapidly in the country's trade accounts. But per capita incomes also rose powerfully in the United States as the economy developed.

Manufactured goods are not subject to Engel's Law, and, *because of their variety,* they are not really subject to the tendency toward **diminishing marginal utility** (the reduction of satisfaction derived from the additional use of a given good, substance, or service as its available supply to the user increases). In the classic example, diminishing marginal utility results from the acquisition of additional units of goods the consumer already owns. In the case of an economy with an endless variety of manufactured goods, boredom hardly applies—as today's economy so well demonstrates. Rising imports of manufactures, logically enough,

Table 20.1   Structure of U.S. Trade[a]

Years	Crude Materials		Crude Foodstuffs		Manufactured Foodstuffs	
	Exports	Imports	Exports	Imports	Exports	Imports
1821	60.5	4.5	4.8	11.1	19.5	19.7
1851–60	61.7	9.6	6.6	11.7	15.4	15.4
1881–90	35.9	21.3	18.0	15.4	25.3	17.8
1901–10	31.0	34.0	10.6	11.9	20.1	12.1
1921–30	26.0	37.1	8.5	11.8	11.8	11.4

[a] Figures given are percentages of total U.S. trade.

Source: Lance E. Davis, et al., *American Economic History: The Development of a National Economy* (Homewood, Ill.: Irwin, 1969), Tables 16–3A, B.

Table 20.2   Expansion of Trade[a]

Years	Total		Crude Materials		Crude Foodstuffs		Manufactured Foodstuffs	
	Exports	Imports	Exports	Imports	Exports	Imports	Exports	Imports
1820	$ 52	$ 55	$ 31	$ 3	$ 2	$ 6	$ 10	$ 11
1851–60	232	274	143	27	15	33	36	44
1891–1900	1006	763	296	202	183	129	256	130
1921–30	4499	3742	1165	1387	360	445	528	423

[a] Figures given are mean annual rates in millions of dollars.

Source: Lance E. Davis, et al., *American Economic History: The Development of a National Economy* (Homewood, Ill.: Irwin, 1969), Tables 16–5A, B.

characterize economies with rising per capita incomes. The richest industrially developed countries are the most dynamic markets for manufactured goods. Even though manufactured imports declined as a *proportion* of total U.S. imports, they increased over time and absorbed a growing part of the total world trade in manufacture.

The Direction of U.S. Trade

Throughout the years from the Civil War to the post-World War I era, trade with Europe, both exports and imports, dominated, but there was a steady rise in trade with other parts of the world. By the 1920s, inter-American trade, in aggregate (see Table 20.4 on page 364), accounted for nearly 40 percent of total imports and nearly a third of our exports. Trade with Asia expanded powerfully, especially with Japan, but also with other Asian countries (which were, at that time, mainly European dependencies). Economic development there, as in Canada, Mexico, and Latin America,

created both sources for imports and customers for exports.

As the great Swedish foreign-trade statistician Folke Hilgerdt emphasized, it was economic development, not mere geographical and climatic differences, that created the possibilities of trade.[3] By the 1920s, nearly 90 percent of world trade emanated from the developed countries. Trade *between* the underdeveloped nations was a trivial part of the world total.[4] Producers in various parts of the world that were engaged in foreign trade learned to specialize their outputs to fit the demand of their foreign customers. As incomes rose worldwide, markets expanded, and greater economic development—division of labor—became possible. The U.S. economy benefitted from these changes through its foreign trade.

The Balance of Payments

As we noted earlier, in the antebellum period the U.S. balance of international payments resembled that of

Semimanufactures		Finished Manufactures	
Exports	Imports	Exports	Imports
9.4	7.4	5.7	56.8
4.0	12.5	12.3	40.5
5.2	14.8	15.6	30.8
12.8	17.2	25.6	24.8
13.3	18.2	40.8	21.4

Semimanufactures		Finished Manufactures	
Exports	Imports	Exports	Imports
$ 5	$ 4	$ 3	$ 31
9	36	29	156
82	106	190	197
600	686	1916	801

any developing economy. In expansions Americans used more of the world's output than they produced, creating current-account deficits and increased foreign debt. In periods of economic stagnation the pattern reversed. In the postbellum period, as industrialization expanded, a great change occurred.

The powerful rise in exports of food and materials was spurred on by the growth of wheat, dairy products, and meat as big foreign-exchange earners. Cotton exports, although no longer a source of prosperity for Southern farmers, continued to be produced in large amounts and remained the top foreign-exchange earner. In addition, however, exports of manufactures and semimanufactures grew remarkably as the country's industrialization became more general. As a result, by the late 1870s (Table 20.2) these forces combined to create an overall turnaround in the trend of the trade balance. After 1875, the U.S. balance of merchandise trade went into a long-term surplus position (Table 20.5 on page 365). By the late 1890s the overall current-account balance of payments followed.[5]

The big current-account deficits in the late 1880s and early 1890s reflected a temporary weakening in the trade surplus but also showed the importance of U.S. foreign indebtedness. Americans had borrowed heavily from foreign nations (mainly England), and the payments of interest and dividends—together with net payments for foreign shipping, insurance, and banking—were sufficient to provide one last string of annual deficits. These very nearly drained the U.S. Treasury of gold, as we saw in Chapter 19. After 1895, the current-account balance of payments moved into a long-term surplus position. In World War I the country "repatriated" most of its outstanding long-term debt (the Allies exchanged the stocks and bonds for war supplies) and became, for the first time in its history, a creditor nation on long term.[6]

From the 1890s until the 1950s, the U.S. economy, with its unusual self-sufficiency in food and raw materials, absorbed foreign-exchange credits and gold year after year. We saw in Chapter 19 the initial consequences of the financial system: the "filling up" of the currency and banking system with gold and the formal adoption of the gold standard in 1900. For the country's trading partners, the American current-account surplus became a fact of life for half a century. The U.S. economy's tendency to import so little that there was almost no movement toward a balance-of-payments "equilibrium" (exports − imports = zero), placed the continued agitation for import restrictions—protective tariffs—in an odd light.

THE TARIFF QUESTION AGAIN

We left the tariff question in Chapter 13 with the Morrill Tariff Act of 1861. With Southern legislators temporarily absent from Washington because of the Civil War, resistance to protectionist agitation was weakened. In addition, the Union government hoped both to reduce non-essential imports and to gain revenues from the tariff (a most unlikely outcome). The Morrill Tariff raised tariff levels back to those that had prevailed in the 1830s. In 1860, the average tariff rate on dutiable imports was down to 20 percent; it had been 62 percent in 1830. The 1861 tariff act raised the level to 47 percent, and it stayed above 40 percent from then until the First World War. Baack and Ray, in a survey of American tariff history after the Civil War, conclude that protectionism alone accounts for it.

The fact that tariff cuts were systematically associated with fast growth industries . . . lends support to our contention that tariff rates across industries and tariff changes over time were structured to serve the narrow economic protectionist needs of special interest groups.[7]

A temporary war measure, as so often has happened, became a permanent feature, with the result that the United States became a leader in the world of restrictionist trade policies.

Tariff Revenues

The tariff rates remained high for two reasons: revenues and protectionist sentiments. About the first there were no doubts. The scale of federal government expenditures (revenue needs) rose dramatically during the Civil War. As in the case of all the wars, the postwar expenditures never fell back to prewar levels. The need for additional revenues remained. The average expenditures in the five years 1856–1860 had been $69 million. After the war ended, the armies were disbanded. Wartime expenditures fell, but they got stuck going down. Between 1866 and 1870 average yearly expenditures came to $378 million; the prewar figures were never seen again.[8]

Revenues from sales of public lands were proportionately trivial after the 1862 Homestead Act (although they rose in some years), and federal expenditures had permanently expanded. The Civil War income tax was dropped in 1872, and all efforts to install a new income tax failed until the Sixteenth Amendment of the U.S. Constitution was ratified in 1913. The federal government, from 1872 until 1913,

Table 20.3   U.S. Share of World Trade[a]

Years	Manufactured Articles		Primary Products		U.S. Population as a Percentage of World Population
	Exports	**Imports**	**Exports**	**Imports**	
1876–80	7.4	3.7	15.4	7.1	**(1850)** 2.0
1881–85	9.6	3.8	16.0	8.5	
1886–90	9.1	3.8	14.4	9.5	
1891–95	8.6	4.4	16.1	10.0	
1886–1900	7.0	6.7	16.7	8.0	**(1900)** 4.7
1901–05	7.0	7.7	16.0	8.9	
1906–10	7.2	7.8	14.7	9.6	**(1910)** 5.1
1913	6.4	9.3	14.2	10.0	
1921–25	7.9	13.2 **(1926–29)**	18.9	15.1	**(1920)** 5.7

[a] Figures given are percentages of the totals.

Sources: Trade Data: Folke Hilgerdt, *Industrialization and Foreign Trade* (Geneva: League of Nations, 1945), derived from Tables VII, VIII, IX, XIII. Population: John V. Grauman, "Population Growth," *International Encyclopedia of the Social Sciences* (New York: Macmillan, 1968), vol. 12, p. 379, and *Historical Statistics,* series A2.

Table 20.4   Direction of U.S. Trade 1860–1925[a]

Years	Northern North America		Southern North America		South America	
	Exports	**Imports**	**Exports**	**Imports**	**Exports**	**Imports**
1860	6.9	6.7	8.8	12.5	4.7	9.9
1901–5	8.6	5.4	6.7	13.3	3.2	12.5
1921–5	14.3	11.5	10.1	14.9	6.8	12.2

[a] Figures given are percentages of total U.S. trade.

Source: Lance E. Davis et al., *American Economic History: The Development of a National Economy* (Homewood, Ill.: Irwin, 1969), Tables 16–4A, B.

was dependent almost entirely upon taxes from consumption of goods and services. The tariff, a tax on the consumption of foreign goods, was a mainstay of these regressive taxes. Between 1866 and 1913 the federal government collected just under $21 billion in revenues, and $10 billion, nearly half, came from the customs duties on imports alone. Until the income tax amendment, given the fiscal technology of the time, tariffs were necessary for revenue purposes. It was either that or close down the federal government.

Protectionism

The second reason for high tariffs was the protectionist sentiment in the United States. In Europe, Great Britain's free-trade policies had considerable impact, and the United States had sharply cut the protectionist element in the tariff act in 1857. Then in 1860 Britain and France signed the Cobden-Chevalier Treaty, which committed those two nations and their trading partners to extensive, bilateral, tariff-reducing negotiations. In 1862 the German Customs Union made a bilateral tariff-reducing agreement with France. The United States, engulfed in civil war in 1861, did not respond to European trade liberalization moves. After the Civil War ended, protectionist pressures were intensified.[9] Those who agitated for freer trade were generally unsuccessful. (A slight tariff reduction in 1870 was canceled out by an increase in the rates in 1875.)

In 1882 President Chester Arthur appointed a commission to look into the tariff—the government's budget being then in surplus. The commission recommended cuts, but in 1890 came the McKinley Tariff, followed in 1897 by the Dingley Tariff. In 1879 the Germans had passed protective duties, and in 1881 and 1892 the French passed protectionist measures. By 1914 only the British and the Dutch remained on free trade in Europe.[10] In 1913 President Wilson pushed for a more liberal policy, but World War I intervened. Rates fell in the 1920s to below 20 percent, but the Smoot-Hawley Tariff, a bold protectionist measure passed in 1930, raised the rates to nearly 45 percent, putting them back to late-nineteenth-century levels.

The protectionist sentiment, still pushed in Congress in the 1990s, is based upon a simple fact: A tariff creates a rent, thus providing higher profits for those protected and their suppliers, and higher wages for their employees than would be supported by the competitive market. *All other consumers pay for this.* In the distant past, arguments for the tariff included the **infant in-**

Table 20.5 U.S. Balance of Merchandise Trade and Current Account Balance of Payments Annual Averages 1866–1914[a]

Years	Balance of Trade	Balance of Payments on Current Account
1866–70	$ − 34.8	$ − 118.0
1871–75	− 12.8	− 137.4
1876–80	+ 182.0	+ 131.2
1881–85	+ 114.6	+ 4.4
1886–90	+ 37.8	− 155.2
1891–95	+ 165.2	− 51.4
1896–1900	+ 419.2	+ 394.6
1901–05	+ 505.6	+ 322.6
1906–10	+ 433.0	+ 218.2
1911–14	+ 575.0	+ 240.3

[a] Amounts given are in millions of dollars.

Source: *Historical Statistics*, series U 1, 8, 189.

Europe		Asia		Oceana		Africa	
Exports	Imports	Exports	Imports	Exports	Imports	Exports	Imports
74.8	61.3	2.4	8.3	1.5	0.3	1.0	1.0
72.3	51.3	5.3	15.4	2.0	0.9	1.9	1.1
52.7	30.4	11.3	27.3	3.2	1.6	1.6	2.1

dustry thesis: New industries could achieve success and produce domestic economic growth only if they were shielded initially from foreign competition.[11] This had been Alexander Hamilton's hopeful argument at the Republic's beginning.

Frank Taussig's study of this position indicated that, except for silk and cotton-spinning before 1842, little or no American industry came from infancy to adolescence because of protection.[12] No doubt it can be done. A hothouse banana industry in Maine or Minnesota would work, if tariffs on bananas were high enough. But our politicians apparently kept rates below those that would have strangled trade completely because the government needed the revenues. Legislators did not want to forgo their paychecks.

The main argument used in favor of protection, from the Civil War to the present, has been the *"full lunch-pail"* approach: Tariffs create jobs and prosperity at high American wages. Since this is the solution being pushed these days in defense of American autos, steel, chemicals, textiles, boots, and shoes, it is worth consideration. The argument goes thusly: If products made with cheap foreign labor are admitted into the U.S. economy, then American jobs and prosperity are destroyed. Americans are sacrificing their own welfare for the benefit of foreign producers who employ poor wretches in sweatshops. Every imported BMW is a Buick not bought, causing highly paid union members to face unemployment. This argument, carried to its extreme, would eliminate international trade altogether. But it has always been a powerful vote-getter.

Comparative advantage is not so easily converted into politics. And besides, comparative advantages change over time. Industries like the American steel and auto industries, which once were the world's most efficient and the terror of all foreign competitors, can fall behind in technology and become uncompetitive. If they then fail, men and women are unemployed, factories close, towns decay, and investments are lost. It is little compensation to these people for some professor to point out that resources would be better employed elsewhere—not locked up in factories that cannot produce efficiently by modern world standards. *Total protection,* abolition of all auto imports, solves the problem completely, or so the argument goes. As a result, protectionism remains. Its benefits are concentrated, and its costs widely spread out.

Comparative Advantage Again

Comparative advantage says that you employ your resources where they are most efficiently used. If your resources are not so employed, the alternative output forgone is just wasted. At the two extremes, comparative advantage says:

1. If you are the most efficient producer of everything in the world, it still pays you to deploy your resources in your own most efficient production and trade your output to others for your other needs.
2. If you are incompetent at all production, it still raises your own income to concentrate your production in areas where you are the least incompetent and trade for the rest of your needs.

The great English economist John Stuart Mill (1806–1873) put it very elegantly in 1848:

> We may often, by trading with foreigners, obtain their commodities at a smaller expense of labour and capital than they cost to the foreigners themselves. The bargain is still advantageous to the foreigner, because the commodity which he receives in exchange, though it costs us less, would have cost him more.[13]

It is important to consider carefully what Mill wrote while contemplating the American tariff. Unless a tariff can cause to spring into existence production that is more efficient than those resources could produce in any other application, the tariff redistributes income in favor of those protected *and* makes total income smaller than it otherwise would be.

The issues become more complex when, as today, all nations have tariffs and bargain with each other over their respective heights. Each country exports. So, if a nation whose exports to the United States are constrained by American tariffs counters by placing restrictive duties on American exports, then the two governments must bargain with each other to reduce the *damage to both economies.*[14] If they do not, the harm to both economies is maximized, even though those protected in each economy still gain relative to everyone else in each economy. Since the United States carried out its industrialization after 1866 as one of the world's two most protectionist commercial nations

THE KEEPERS AT THE GATE.

Above, the tariff, guarded by McKinley, enables the greedy monopolist to extract his toll from the honest farmer. McKinley was elected in 1896 as the economy was beginning an expansion phase. By 1900 he could rest on his laurels for reelection. He was for the "full dinner pail" (below).

(Tsarist Russia was the other), one is somewhat taken aback by the thought that it would have done better without tariff restrictions.

Incidence of the Tariff

However, those who were protected at the expense of everyone else would not have done as well as they did. Whereas it is difficult to find any American industry between 1866 and 1914 whose existence depended upon protection, it is obvious that the rents created by the tariffs drew resources into the protected industries that would otherwise have been profitably employed elsewhere.

A calculation by Lance Davis measures roughly the extent of the income transfers over time (see Table 20.6). Agriculture received little in the way of tariff protection; manufactures and semimanufactures received the most. In 1890, for example, manufactures were 29.2 percent of total imports, yet duties on manufactures were 41.8 percent of total import duties. Semimanufactures were 14.8 percent of total imports, but gathered 18.6 percent of total import duties. Agricultural imports, 16.3 percent of the total, yielded only 4.2 percent of the duties. Davis concluded: "Thus it appears that while almost all business received some subsidy (paid for by consumers), manufacturing industry received much more than its proportionate share."[15]

Alternatively, consumers paid far more subsidy—in the form of tariffs—to manufacturing industry than it did to farmers. The farmers were aware of this discrimination and wanted other forms of government subsidies to redress the balance. They failed, for the most part, before 1914. Not surprisingly, the National Association of Manufacturers has been traditionally protectionist.

THE GOLD STANDARD IN 1900

It will be useful at this point to relate our previous discussions of monetary changes to the balance of payments. International transactions benefit from any simplification. We already have noted that payment in commercial bills of exchange facilitated trade in commodities by making credit easily available to growers, shippers, and manufacturers. The bills, when due, were settled either in money or in other bills of exchange. For example, a Liverpool merchant holding maturing American bills payable in England might find it more profitable to take in payment bills payable in the United States and to ship goods to America than to accept payment in cash. Thus did international banking grow in conjunction with the expansion of trade.

Ultimately, such a credit system had to rest upon the expectation of payment in a universally acceptable medium of exchange, and that role was played by specie up to 1914. The declining value of silver in the market

Table 20.6 The Relative Incidence of Tariff Protection, 1860–1920

Year	(1) Manufactured Imports as Percentage of Total Imports	(2) Duties on Manufactured Imports as Percentage of Total Import Duties	(3) Semimanufactured Imports as Percentage of Total Imports	(4) Duties on Semimanufactured Imports as Percentage of Total Import Duties	(5) Total: Column 1 + Column 3
1860	48.7	60.3	9.9	10.2	58.6
1870	39.8	40.8	12.8	12.8	52.6
1880	29.4	40.5	16.6	20.8	46.0
1890	29.2	41.8	14.8	18.6	44.0
1900	23.9	38.6	15.8	18.4	39.7
1910	23.6	37.8	18.3	20.2	41.9
1920	16.6	23.0	15.2	11.8	31.8

Source: Lance E. Davis et al., *American Economic History: The Development of a National Economy* (Homewood, Ill.: Irwin, 1969), Table 16–2.

after the 1870s (as we discussed in Chapter 19) made gold the preferable metal. Although the United States was *de facto* a gold standard country after resumption of Treasury gold payments in 1879, silver continued to play a disturbing role, as we already have seen. Most European countries gave up silver and bimetallism and adopted a purely gold standard in the nineteenth century (Russia, as late as 1893). The United States kept the silver option open at least until 1900, when the pure gold standard was finally adopted.

That move by the United States government placed nearly the entire commercial world on **fixed exchange rates.** Freedom for anyone to buy gold in any form or quantity anywhere in the commercial world and ship it anywhere, at any time, finally produced gold points within a narrow range and assured the stability, the solidarity, of the international monetary system.[16] By nineteenth-century standards, this was the ultimate financial achievement, virtually removing purely monetary uncertainty from international transactions. You knew you could get your money at a fixed rate. The gold standard operated with reserves of gold coin and bullion widely dispersed.[17] The Bank of England at the hub of it guaranteed payment in gold, and gunboats at the fringes of the system collected customs from defaulting third-world nations to ensure their adherence to the major virtues.

The gold standard had many advantages and some major disadvantages. The advantages centered upon the fixed exchange rates and the discipline it imposed on banking systems in all countries, requiring them to control their bank money in such a way as to maintain gold convertibility. Governments, for example, could not (as they now do) print money as they pleased to extract real resources at will from the world economy by inflation. Their two alternatives were to borrow from the public at market rates (as the French did from 1871 to 1873 to pay the German indemnity), or to tax their people to meet financial obligations.[18]

The disadvantages were that losses of gold via the balance of payments required the losing nations to tighten up their financial transactions, usually by curtailing credit, raising central-bank discount rates, and increasing the amount of unemployment and general business distress. This was the harsh "medicine" the gold standard prescribed for nations whose economies expanded too rapidly relative to others. Modern fiscal techniques, based upon unending deficit spending, were not really possible in such a system. Governments had to remain "honest."

A powerful mystique built up around the system that had "rules of the game" to be used by the central banks to enforce sympathetic movements of international trade and payments. Central banks were supposed to *magnify* gold movements in and out by their own lending policies to make the gold standard work.[19] If gold reserves rose, central banks, under the "rules," were supposed to lower their discount rates and increase their loans and investments. If gold reserves fell, central banks were, accordingly, supposed to cut their loans, sell securities, and raise their rates of discount.

It was believed by financial orthodoxy at the turn of the century that the gold standard and its attendant responsible policies (including liberal trade) would create conditions in which balances of payments would automatically tend toward equilibrium and very little actual movement of specie between nations would be required. What had happened to the U.S. balance of trade and payments was not supposed to occur. Add to that a system of competitive internal markets and international free trade. Incomes to the factors of production in traded goods would tend to become equal internationally because of commodity trade alone, with no need for the factors of production themselves, labor and capital, to be traded. In theory, it was practically utopian.

Utopias, of course, don't happen. There were several reasons why this one did not. Millions of people *did*

(6)	(7)	(8)
Total: Column 2 + Column 4	Agricultural Goods Imports as Percentage of Total Imports	Duties on Agricultural Imports as Percentage of Total Import Duties
70.5	12.9	1.3
53.6	12.4	13.0
61.3	15.0	3.2
60.4	16.3	4.2
57.0	11.5	6.1
58.0	9.3	3.9
34.8	10.9	3.0

migrate internationally, and huge capital flows occurred. This was precisely because balances of payments did not tend toward equilibrium and factor prices did not tend to equality, despite the reign of the most liberal system of international trade the world had known. Moreover, the gold standard's monetary adjustment mechanism, far from being the well-oiled machine of theory, regularly clanked to a grinding halt in the great financial crises of the nineteenth and early twentieth centuries. Finally, the central banks, it turned out, honored the "rules of the game" only when it was convenient. They were loathe to create internal disturbances for some hypothetical international adjustment.

It was the free rider problem again. Why should a single central bank disrupt the ongoing processes of its own economy for the benefit of its trading partners? It did not, as Arthur Bloomfield showed for the late nineteenth century and Ragnar Nurkse found in the reconstituted gold-exchange standard of the interwar years.[20] In roughly two-thirds of the relevant cases, central bank reserves moved against the rules of the game in response to balance-of-payments changes. Until 1914 the United States had no central bank, but its balance of payments turned into current-account surpluses every year after 1895, and it accumulated reserves steadily.

We are not arguing that the gold-standard mechanism *could* not work according to theory in the way one hopeful writer described it:

> Comparatively small adjustments in credit policy and small transfers in the ownership of gold to offset temporary changes in international balances of payments were usually sufficient to keep international exchange rates and price levels in close conformity with each other.[21]

The point is that it *did* not. In the real-life circumstances of the nineteenth century, with trading nations' economies growing at different rates, massive international transfers of people and capital were required to make economic progress happen. Net progress occurred, accompanied by the cycle of boom, financial crisis, depression, and unemployment that characterized the old financial system.[22] That cycle was finally ruptured by World War I.

The Bank of England "suspended" the Act of 1844 (the Bank's way of coping with gold-standard break-downs) for the last time in 1914, and the pure gold standard was gone with the wind.[23] Attempts have been made ever since 1918 to bring back some facsimile of the old system since it imposed fiscal probity upon governments and produced something besides permanent inflation. But as of now, all such efforts have failed. Central banks have continued to respond more to domestic economic (and political) pressures than to the requirements of international stability. We will deal with these matters again in later chapters.

After the financial disasters of the 1870s, 1880s, and 1890s, the United States participated as a full gold-standard partner in the old system, but its experience was punctuated by the crises of 1903 and 1907. Even with its new central bank in operation, further major disasters came in 1921 and 1929, and the country finally gave up the gold-standard game in 1933 for good. Partial gold reserves were continued until 1968 but were abandoned just as soon as they were in danger of becoming operative.[24]

The myth of the gold standard is powerful. It never did operate according to theory. The reality was nineteenth-century economic history as it actually occurred: Trade expanded as economies grew, and currencies were pure paper, pure gold, pure silver, or bimetallic as events unfolded. The U.S. economy entered this world as a bimetallic system, slowly left silver, was from 1861 to 1879 inconvertible, then went to a straight gold standard in 1900 with silver dragged along for auld lang syne. By 1914 the country had been accumulating gold for two decades through its balance of payments.[25]

INTERNATIONAL CAPITAL FLOWS

The American current-account surplus after 1895 meant that to balance, it should have been a net lender in international transactions in every year. Net lending counts like positive net investment in the national accounts equation. For example:

$$\text{GNP} = C_p + I_p + G + (\text{exports} - \text{imports})$$

Gross national product equals the sum of expenditures on private consumption (C_p) plus private investment (I_p) plus government expenditures (G) plus the remainder of exports minus imports. The larger the imports figure is, other things being equal, the smaller is the final GNP—what the United States has produced out of total expenditures. Capital imports are added to the payments it makes, negatively. When exports exceed imports, the GNP is greater than domestic consumption, and the country extends credit to its foreign customers to absorb its excess. Thus in the 1890s net exports, exports minus imports, became positive and stayed there.

All trading countries give and receive credits. In periods when the United States had current-account deficits, it simply used more of the world's goods and services than it produced. When it had surpluses on current account, it used less than it produced, and the excess was exported. The resulting credits then were balanced over time, either by net specie shipments to the country—which happened extensively after 1895—or by the debts becoming "funded," as long-term debt instruments of all sorts, together with equities.[26] Thus, even before World War I when evidences of past foreign borrowings were repatriated *en masse,* the current account surpluses slowly were turning the United States around from its traditional international debtor position. It was becoming a creditor nation because of the long-term change in its balance of payments. Before 1895, foreign savings had aided the growth of the American economy by financing its deficits.[27] After that date, its net savings began to finance the growth of foreign economies.

We need to add one caveat to explain data for net capital movements that run counter to expectations for current-account, balance-of-payments data. We have discussed the capital flows as if they were merely passive balancing items. Yet, we know from history that such is not the case. Foreign investors in the United States were interested in investment projects independently of current U.S. balance-of-payments movements. So, when we were in current-account surplus and were automatically lending as a result, we also were recipients of foreign loans and investments in this country. Jeffrey Williamson's recasting of the available data for the nineteenth century reflects these problems. He produces estimates that are in some instances similar and in some not to the data used in Table 20.7. His analysis of the late nineteenth century is, however, more similar to the one developed here.[28]

It is difficult to measure these intangibles. Even today—with computers and platoons of trained specialists in places like the Federal Reserve System, Treasury Department, and Commerce Department—trying to count the value of such capital transactions is largely a guessing game. Commodity trade and many capital and financial transactions can now be counted because of detailed regulation, but from the billions of individual transactions, it is impossible to keep track of everything. Before 1914 the official counting procedures were minimal, and attempting believable statistical reconstructions of the international capital flows associated with balance-of-payments outcomes is a challenge to scholarship.[29]

Table 20.7 shows well-known estimates, summed by decade, of U.S. capital transactions indicated by trade data, fragmentary investment estimates, and so forth. No one claims strict accuracy for these figures.[30] But they do underline our point. Notice that before the 1890s, on a decadal basis, the United States only consumed less than it produced and sold the net to the world during the ragged 1820s, and the (mainly) depressed 1840s. In all other nineteenth-century decades until the 1890s, its economy used more of the world's goods and services than it produced, and there were, in consequence, net capital inflows. Then, beginning in the 1890s, the United States assumed its role as a capital exporter on a larger scale.

The numbers in Table 20.7 estimate net **flows of credit.** The *stock of foreign investment* at any time was the outstanding sum of the flows, less defaults and repayments. Believable estimates of that stock around 1913 were that the American gross holdings of foreign securities came to $3.5 billion. The comparable British

Table 20.7   U.S. Capital Movements Net by Decade[a]

Decade	Net Outflow	Net Inflow
1820–30	$ 14	$
1831–40		186
1841–50	20	
1851–60		160
1861–70		875
1871–80		332
1881–90		1310
1891–1900	393	
1901–14	41	

[a] Amounts given are in millions of dollars.

Source: *Historical Statistics,* series U 18–23.

figure at that time was $19.5 billion, the Germans, somewhere between $5.2 and $5.9 billion, the French, from $8.5 to $9 billion.[31] The United States had become a major foreign investor—not yet caught up to the major European lenders, but the pattern was clear.

Its economic development, so long dependent upon foreign lenders, had finally placed the United States in the position of a major creditor. The disastrous results of World War I would leave the country as the major world creditor nation. But the American effort was smaller before 1914 than the American economy's potential for foreign investment. Its stock of foreign investment in 1913 equalled about 2 percent of its total stock of wealth: The British figure was equal to a quarter of their national wealth; the German figure was about 7 percent of German wealth; the French figure, about 17 percent of French wealth.[32] Americans had found sufficient investment opportunities at home. Their time as a dominant supplier of international capital lay in the future of the giant economy's growth.

Notes

1. Robert Lipsey, "Foreign Trade," in Davis et al., *American Economic Growth* (1972), p. 554.
2. Stanley Lebergott, "The Returns to U.S. Imperialism, 1890–1929," *JEH,* June 1980.
3. Folke Hilgerdt, *Industrialization and Foreign Trade* (1945), pp. 23–25. Also, "the growth of manufacturing, far from rendering the countries concerned independent of foreign-produced manufactured articles, stimulated the importation of such articles" (p. 118).
4. Folke Hilgerdt, *The Network of World Trade* (1942), p. 7.
5. Jeffrey G. Williamson, *American Growth and the Balance of Payments 1820–1913* (1964), Appendix B for yearly data.
6. As a survey in detail of the entire nineteenth century, the classic work is Charles J. Bullock, John H. Williams, and Rufus S. Tucker, "The Balance of Trade of the United States," *REStat,* 1919. For a more recent analysis, see Williamson, *American Growth.* Also, Matthew Simon, "The United States Balance of Payments, 1861–1900," *Studies in Income and Wealth,* vol. 24 (1960).
7. Bennett D. Baack and John Edward Ray, "The Political Economy of Tariff Policy: A Case Study of the United States," *EEH,* January 1983, p. 86.
8. Jonathan Hughes, *The Governmental Habit Redux* (Princeton: Princeton University Press, 1991), p. 189.
9. G. R. Hawke, "The United States Tariff and Industrial Protection in the Late Nineteenth Century," *EHR,* February 1975.
10. S. B. Saul, *Studies in British Overseas Trade 1870–1914* (Liverpool: Liverpool University Press, 1960), ch. VI. For American tariffs, see Frank W. Taussig, *The Tariff History of the United States* (1932).
11. The American iron industry's turn-of-the-century development was deeply influenced by tariff policy changes.

Bennett D. Baack and Edward John Ray, "Tariff Policy and Comparative Advantage in the Iron and Steel Industry," *EEH,* Fall 1973.
12. William K. Hutchinson, "Import Substitution, Structural Change, and Regional Economic Growth in the United States: The Northeast, 1870–1910," *JEH,* June 1985. He generally agrees with Taussig, although he thinks that the wool industry must also be considered a creature of the tariff only.
13. John Stuart Mill, *Principles of Political Economy* (London: Longmans, Green & Co., 1911), 6th ed., p. 348.
14. Gottfried von Haberler, *The Theory of International Trade with Its Applications to Commercial Policy* (1959), pp. 374–90.
15. Lance E. Davis, Jonathan Hughes, and Duncan McDougall, *American Economic History: The Development of a National Economy* (1969), 3rd ed., p. 304.
16. Oskar Morgenstern, *International Financial Transactions and Business Cycles* (1959), ch. V.
17. Arthur I. Bloomfield, *Short-Term Capital Movements Under the Pre-1914 Gold Standard* (1963), pp. 14–19.
18. Haberler, *The Theory of International Trade,* pp. 92–96.
19. Ragnar Nurkse, *International Currency Experience: Lessons of the Interwar Period* (1944), Chapter IV.
20. Bloomfield, *Short-Term Capital Movements Under the Pre-1914 Gold Standard,* p. 19; and Nurkse, pp. 68–88.
21. William Ashworth, *A Short History of the International Economy: 1850–1950* (1952), p. 168.
22. Morgenstern, *International Financial Transactions and Business Cycles,* ch. II.
23. E. Victor Morgan, *Studies in British Financial Policy, 1914–25* (1952), ch. I.
24. That is, in 1968 the legal "gold cover" in the ratio of gold certificates on the Federal Reserve's balance sheets

to its demand liabilities (Federal Reserve notes and demand deposits) was 25 percent. The money supply was rising as the Fed bought government securities to help the Treasury finance the Vietnam War. The gold account had no prospect of rising without a "devaluation" (raising the gold price), so the gold cover was abandoned.

25. R. G. Hawtrey, *The Gold Standard in Theory and Practice* (1939), ch. III.
26. Williamson, "Real Growth," pp. 256–57, shows net specie imports in 1897, 1898, 1899, 1901, 1902, 1904, 1905, 1906, and 1907, after a successive run of net exports from 1889 through 1896.
27. Williamson, pp. 256–57, from 1850 to 1895, 45 years, only the years 1857, 1859, 1861, 1877–79, 1881, and 1893, eight in all, saw net capital outflows.
28. Williamson, ch. 4, pp. 124–88, and Appendix B. Williamson argues (pp. 175–83) that U.S. gold flows did *not*

determine long-term movements in the domestic money stock in strict sympathy to balance-of-payments changes. The conflict between Williamson and others is analyzed in Bijan Aghevli, "The Balance of Payments and the Money Supply Under the Gold Standard Regime: U.S. 1879–1914," *AER,* March 1975.

29. For yearly estimates, see Williamson, Appendix B.
30. For other estimates see Williamson, Appendix B; also, *Historical Statistics,* Series U 15–25.
31. Jonathan Hughes, *Industrialization and Economic History: Theses and Conjectures* (1970), p. 150.
32. Data converted at pre-1914 exchange rates from Herbert Feis, *Europe, The World's Banker 1870–1914* (1965). For a summary discussion, see Hughes, *Industrialization and Economic History* (1970), pp. 150–52.

Suggested Readings

Articles

Aghevli, Bijan B. "The Balance of Payments and Money Supply Under the Gold Standard Regime: U.S. 1879–1914." *American Economic Review,* vol. LXV, no. 1, March 1975.

Baack, Bennett D., and Ray, Edward John. "Tariff Policy and Comparative Advantage in the Iron and Steel Industry, 1870–1929." *Explorations in Economic History,* vol. 11, no. 1, Fall 1973.

———. "The Political Economy of Tariff Policy: A Case Study of the United States." *Explorations in Economic History,* vol. 20, no. 1, January 1983.

Bullock, Charles J., Williams, John H., and Tucker, Rufus S. "The Balance of Trade of the United States." *Review of Economic Statistics,* vol. 1, 1919.

Grauman, John V. "Population Growth." *International Encyclopedia of the Social Sciences.* New York: Macmillan, 1968, vol. 12.

Hawke, G. R. "The United States Tariff and Industrial Protection in the Late Nineteenth Century." *Economic History Review,* vol. XXVIII, no. 1, February 1975.

Hutchinson, William K. "Import Substitution, Structural Change, and Regional Economic Growth in the United States: The Northeast, 1870–1910." *Journal of Economic History,* vol. XLV, no. 2, June 1985.

Lebergott, Stanley. "The Returns to U.S. Imperialism, 1890–1929." *Journal of Economic History,* vol. XL, no. 2, June 1980.

Lipsey, Robert. "Foreign Trade." In Lance E. Davis, et al., *American Economic Growth: An Economist's History of the United States.* New York: Harper & Row, 1972.

Simon, Matthew. "The United States Balance of Payments, 1861–1900." *Studies in Income and Wealth,* vol. 24. National Bureau of Economic Research, Princeton: Princeton University Press, 1960.

Tanner, J. E., and Bonomo, B. "Gold, Capital Flows, and Long Swings in American Business Activity." *Journal of Political Economy,* vol. 76, no. 1, January–February 1968.

Williamson, J. G. "Real Growth, Monetary Disturbances, and the Transfer Process, 1879–1914." *Southern Economic Journal,* vol. 29, no. 3, January 1963.

Books

Ashworth, William. *A Short History of the International Economy 1850–1950.* London: Longmans, Green & Co., 1952.

Bloomfield, Arthur I. *Short-Term Capital Movements Under the Pre-1914 Gold Standard.* Princeton: International Finance Section, Department of Economics, Princeton University, 1963.

Davis, Lance E., Hughes, Jonathan, and McDougall, Duncan. *American Economic History: The Development of a National Economy.* Homewood, IL: Irwin, 1969, 3rd ed.

Feis, Herbert. *Europe, the World's Banker 1870–1914.* New York: Norton, 1965 ed.

Haberler, Gottfried von. *The Theory of International Trade with Its Applications to Commercial Policy.* London: William Hodge, 1959.

Hawtrey, R. B. *The Gold Standard in Theory and Practice.* London: Longmans, Green & Co., 1939.

Hilgerdt, Folke. *Industrialization and Foreign Trade.* Geneva: League of Nations, 1945.

———. *The Network of World Trade.* Geneva: League of Nations, 1942.

Hughes, Jonathan. *Industrialization and Economic History: Theses and Conjectures.* New York: McGraw-Hill, 1970.

Morgan, E. Victor. *Studies in British Financial Policy, 1914–25.* London: Macmillan, 1952.

Morgenstern, Oskar. *International Financial Transactions and Business Cycles.* National Bureau of Economic Research, Princeton: Princeton University Press, 1959.

Nurkse, Ragnar. *International Currency Experience: Lessons of the Interwar Period.* Geneva: League of Nations, 1944.

Taussig, Frank W. *The Tariff History of the United States.* New York: Putnam's Sons, 1932.

Williamson, Jeffrey G. *American Growth and the Balance of Payments.* Chapel Hill: University of North Carolina Press, 1964.

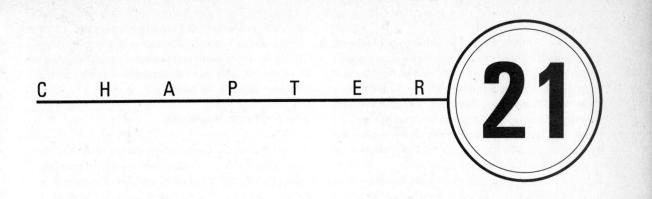

Labor and the Law

T he United States celebrates its working people every year with a major national holiday, Labor Day. It has been a national holiday since 1894. There has been a Department of Labor with a Cabinet officer since 1913.

LABOR'S SOCIAL POSITION

Considering the history of laboring people—the vast majority of whom were indentured servants, chattel slaves, or their descendants in 1790—the succeeding two centuries have witnessed a remarkable improvement in social status. Work, as such, is held in high esteem by Americans. It is a personal accomplishment. "He works hard" or "she works hard" are phrases of respect in this country. The United States has never—yet—had a true leisure class, and it has had no hereditary nobility or aristocracy. As Thorstein Veblen emphasized, it just liked to pretend that it did.[1]

The greatest nineteenth-century family fortunes were accumulated by people who earned the money from scratch, one way or another. Even notorious scoundrels have always gained respect if their money was somehow earned, if they were "self-made." From a log cabin to the White House was supposedly the dream of all red-blooded American boys in the nineteenth century. Americans have never applauded idleness, even for those who had no real need to work for their living. To this day, it is considered scandalous to have no productive occupation, even if one is independently wealthy.[2] The contemporary usage, "flake," applies indifferently to the rich and the poor.

Unionization and the Labor Movement

Attitudes such as admiration of self-made people and disdain of the idle rich are easily understandable in a country such as this one, with its pioneer and frontier traditions. What is also understandable, though, is the widespread parallel hostility toward organized labor, since labor unions represent a threat to the rights of real property employed in business enterprise, another part of the "American tradition." When unions achieve "public good"—changes in job conditions such as increased safety or improved health conditions—there are always employers who resist. They do so because these gains will come out of profits unless they can be passed on to consumers. As a result, labor has been both respected and feared.

The two attitudes seem to be paradoxically related. Even though modern union leaders tend to be staunch conservatives, they have not yet lived down the reputations of their predecessors as radicals: people whose ideas were somehow subversive to right-thinking Americanism. Modern American labor unions are top-heavy with bureaucracy, they rarely change leadership by elections, and they are widely held to be insensitive to their rank-and-file memberships.[3] The unions must fight for social respectability, while the occupations of their members suffer no such disabilities. Although a plumber is a valued member of society, his or her union is looked at with deep suspicion. By now it all seems confusing, but it is easily understood once one considers the history of unions and the labor movement.

The present status of organized labor and the rights of laborers both are the consequences of political change. The unions have been protected, since 1935, by a federal law, the National Labor Relations Act (NLRA), which contains provisions for elections by workers to choose their bargaining agents. These agents must be recognized by employers in interstate commerce for union representation and collective bargaining purposes. Furthermore, the NLRA contains provisions and mechanisms for arbitration. The Fair Labor Standards Act of 1938 contains further protections of the wages and working conditions of labor. More such protection of employees at their jobs is contained in the Social Security Act of 1936, Civil Rights Act of 1964, Age Discrimination Act of 1967, and Occupational Safety and Health Act of 1970. In fact, employees are now surrounded by a veritable cocoon of governmental protection of health, income, and working conditions. (We will discuss the development of this legislation in Chapter 25.)

Modern political concern for labor represents a remarkable reversal of interest in American history. A century ago, one would hardly have argued that American society showed any extraordinary concern for working employees, or for their efforts to combine into unions to negotiate. In legislation, in the law courts, you could indeed argue that society seemed hostile to such interests. The change in attitudes toward the social position of labor commonly has been associated with the success of labor unions as bargaining agents

for workers. The entire history of the struggle for legislation of unions is called the **labor movement.** In the writing of this history, the wider struggle to improve the conditions of labor and the narrower development of organized labor have gotten almost totally mixed together, thanks to the writers.

The Political Dimension

To understand the labor movement we must bear in mind that it has been, in large part, a political phenomenon. Presidential candidates and other aspirants to public office now vie with each other for the support of labor unions. A century ago, such support would almost certainly have been a ticket to political oblivion, at least at the national level. In 1880, of a labor force of some 17.4 million, fewer than 1 percent belonged to labor unions. In 1880 there were more independent entrepreneurs than there were workers in industry. Employees in manufacturing numbered 3.3 million. Fully 72 percent of the total population was still rural. In a total population of 50.3 million, there were nearly 3 million independently owned farms and 750,000 small businesses.

In the presidential election of 1880 there were 9.2 million votes cast. So, perhaps 40 percent of them might have been the votes of independent owners of businesses, who were certainly persons of voting age. The labor vote was smaller—excluding women and those under 21, much smaller—and organized labor's political strength was minuscule. If business people and farmers had believed that their interests were in conflict with those of organized labor, politicians would have been wary of labor's cause.

Today the United States is mainly a nation of employees. The vast majority of businesses are small (86.9 percent have less than 20 employees), but these account for only 26.2 percent of total employees. Factory employment alone is in excess of 17 million, and what the census refers to as "managerial and professional specialty" employment exceeds 31 million. There are about 125 million persons in the labor force, of whom fewer than one-sixth are members of labor unions. In modern presidential elections, the total potential vote is more than 110 million. Smart politicians tailor their appeal to include employees. Even conservative Republican Ronald Reagan sought the support of labor and was actually endorsed by the Teamsters

Union, as was his successor, conservative George Bush.

In the political process changes in voting majorities are crucial. Therefore, it is not surprising that esteem for the rights of labor includes legislation, promises, and politicians supporting those rights. In a political democracy, minorities may be protected and, if well-organized, may achieve successful lobbying, but they cannot *elect*. Owners of independent businesses are now a small minority, and they are unlikely to be served if their ambitions, as a group, conflict with those of labor.

It is interesting to ask whether the interests we call historically "the labor movement" and those of organized labor in the narrower sense are, or ever were, the same thing. The object of unionization is job monopoly, a necessary first step if unions are to achieve their goals by coercion.[4] The historical objectives of the broadly defined labor movement were heterodox and included demands for more job opportunity, a *less* unequal distribution of income and wealth, and broadly focused political and social reforms of all sorts. These objectives made strange bedfellows. But with a great historical shift from a structure dominated by self-employment to a nation of employees, the political alliance proved to be effective, however mismatched.

Equal Rights for Workers

Labor's emergence into an improved status in American society was the outcome of a complex legal evolution. The main benchmarks along the way were

1. a stable and developable political presence;
2. a separate identity within economic life;
3. recognition of a valuable property right in the organization of work; and
4. elimination of ancient legal encumbrances.

Let us consider these briefly.

Political Presence.   In Anglo-American tradition, political rights came with property rights. The English in the seventeenth century allowed no rights to vote except by property qualification. Property ownership qualifications were not entirely removed in this country for free, white, male adults until 1860. And it was another six decades (the Nineteenth Amendment, 1920)

before adult women generally had the vote. The ancient definition of an adult—21 years of age—was not lowered to age 18 until the 1960s. As Claudia Goldin's important book, *Understanding the Gender Gap,* suggests, the lag in political rights had its parallel in a lag in wages and skill acquisition by working women, together with the increasing participation rates of white women in the labor force. The process of linking political and property rights had a parallel development in the achievement by women of marketable property rights as well as their right to vote.[5]

Since those without property qualifications tended to be laborers, their disenfranchisement was a barrier to full participation in American life. Progress was achieved slowly, state by state, beginning in the 1820s in Massachusetts and New York. Some states required tax payments, some allowed non-property owners who paid rents above a certain amount to vote, some required either militia service or payment of a fine. All these requirements were designed to restrict the franchise to those with a permanent, local interest and to exclude laborers. The newer Western states tended to be more liberal with the franchise than the older Eastern ones.

At first it was real property that counted. Since the valuable property of labor was in skill and effort, it required a considerable liberalization of "the public philosophy" for laborers to be counted as equals with other owners of real property. The idea that labor is a property right long remained difficult to fit into the law: In the Clayton Antitrust Act (1914), Congress (illogically) declared that labor, by then recognized as property, was not an article of commerce (which, of course, it is or can be).

Economic Identity.   Who owned such property? The recognition of labor's rights required a clear identification of *who* the laborers were. In early manufacturing processes, the various species of property rights were mingled together. As long as shops were organized in the ancient guild structures (apprentice, journeyman, and master), there was no way to focus separately on labor property. Masters sold the joint product of the entire enterprise.

Early strikes and the withholding of products from the market (usually in opposition to municipal price-fixing) contained no separate definition of employee interest. Indeed, some early trade unions included the

Women and Children in the Labor Force.   Women and children found employment as factory operatives early in American industrial history; later on, the appearance of office machinery placed women *near* management, but not in it.

masters as well as the workers. The reason labor historians have so emphasized the journeymen cordwainers' strike in 1805 in Philadelphia (discussed in Chapter 6) is precisely because *there* the separation of interests became clear. The journeymen were striking against the masters for higher wages. From that time onward, in interests of masters and journeymen in labor, disputes tended toward the standard polarization of employer-employee interests: capital and labor.

By the early 1800s, there were already many masters' associations (forerunners of modern employers' trade associations), which were usually concerned with price-fixing in the markets. The journeymen organized their own associations to claim a piece of the pie by attempting to control wages, hours, and working conditions. By the 1820s, strikes by laborers against their employers seem, from the evidence, to have taken on the form of standoffs between those who owned the means of production and those whose property was in labor only. Once that became increasingly the case, the separate interest of labor could be pursued.

Property Rights in Labor.   The reality and calculable value of labor's own property right was fixed in law by the appearance of mechanic lien laws. If a master went into bankruptcy, the hired workers were allowed to claim their wages against the property of the master's customers.

Mechanic lien laws were an interesting parallel in time and concept to the similar rights of preemption being given to squatters on public lands (a *general* preemption act was passed in 1841, acts specific to various territories were passed earlier) and to recoverable monetary value of improvements made by tenants evicted by their landlords.

Mechanic liens were, after all, an explicit recognition of property rights in labor alone, which essentially created, involuntarily, a third party liability in a two-way business transaction. The acceptance of tenants' rights to recover the value of improvements also paralleled historically the switch we noted in Chapter 7 from prescriptive to priority rights in the state courts when two private property rights were in conflict. All these changes were in the service of economic development. Laborers—like squatters, improving tenants, and entrepreneurial owners—would be encouraged by the courts. They created GNP out of inert property by their own endeavors.

A more difficult and intractable problem was recognition of labor's "corporate" or collective property right in its own organization. It was in some ways similar to the legal recognition of "goodwill" as a valuable property right for ongoing businesses. Insofar as an established labor union *can raise its members' wages above those of the unorganized,* a rent has been created. The rent is an externality of organization that can be internalized only by the union members. The rent is a "collective good" produced by unionization.[6] It is a return to organizational activities above the opportunity cost of those activities applied elsewhere. In this sense it "pays" laborers to unionize. If employers cannot pass this added cost along to their customers, then it must come out of their own returns. There lies the source of what may be a fundamental conflict between employers and their organized workers.

The conflict is over the distribution of a product made jointly by *owned* resources and *hired* labor. The more competitive the industry, the more intense the conflict is likely to be since absence of monopoly power will force the employer to absorb the added cost of union wage increases. This conflict has never been resolved, and it never can be since organization changes a firm's internal revenue distribution in ways adverse to the claims of ownership. The 1935 National Labor Relations Act compelled employers in interstate commerce to accept the extra cost. Much of the bitterness of employer opposition to organized labor has come simply from this elemental conflict of interests.

The Law of Conspiracy.   Among the ancient encumbrances on labor were those associated in common law with the idea of conspiracy: A and B combine to inflict financial damage upon C. Conspiracies by merchants to raise prices had always been unacceptable to common law, and a labor union is nothing if not a conspiracy to achieve collective ends. However, associations of masters in this country had become common by the 1820s. What had to change if unions were to gain legal rights was the law of conspiracy. Some conspiracies had to become legal.

In Chapter 6 we discussed the 1806 cordwainers' case, in which workers were charged with and convicted of two conspiracies: (a) that they had combined to raise wages and (b) that their combination was designed to injure others. Conspiracy cases continued against unions striking for wage increases and union shops. In 1829 the New York State legislature passed a law making a "conspiracy to commit any act injurious to public morals or to trade or commerce" an offense.[7] That seemed a powerful new barrier to labor unions. But in 1842 Chief Justice Lemmuel Shaw of the Massachusetts Supreme Court cut up the criminal conspiracy doctrine in words that permanently changed the position of organized labor in the law. The case was *Commonwealth* v *Hunt,* and the issue was a labor union attempting to exclude non-union workers by a strike. Shaw wrote—

> Supposing the object of the association [the union] to be laudable and lawful, or at least not unlawful, are these means criminal? The case supposes that these persons are not bound by contract, but free to work for whom they please, or not to work, if they so prefer. In this state of things, we can not perceive that it is criminal for men to agree together to exercise their own acknowledged rights, in such a manner as best to subserve their own interest.[8]

Shaw then addressed the issue of damage to others' property resulting from such a strike.

> We think, therefore, that associations may be entered into, the object of which is to adopt measures that may have a tendency to impoverish another, that is, to diminish his gains and profits, and yet so far from being criminal or unlawful, the object may be highly meritorious and public spirited. The legality of such an association will therefore depend upon the means to be used. . . . If it is to be carried into effect by fair or honorable and lawful means, it is, to say the least, innocent; if by falsehood or force, it may be stamped with the character of conspiracy . . .[9]

The remaining issue was, then, what *means* engaged in by labor unions were illegal? Secondary boycotts might be: A and B block access to D's business in order to enforce a work agreement on C, D's supplier. These boycotts have been favorites of the building trades, for obvious reasons. Tertiary boycotts always have been considered illegal.

Court fights continued until 1947, when, in Section 8b of the Taft-Hartley Amendment to the NLRA, secondary boycotts were outlawed. Court tests of that act made exceptions with the doctrines of freedom of speech and unity of interest. Strikes themselves, restricted in various ways over the years, generally came under the doctrine that peaceful picketing was free speech.[10]

Even though the struggle between labor and its employers is a continuing one, at least by the 1840s labor had achieved political power in the franchise, and unions were not considered in law to be *per se* conspiracies and therefore illegal.

THE EMERGENCE OF THE AFL

Because the changing status of labor in the early years involved its political legitimacy (the franchise) and acceptance of organized action to achieve its narrower objects, it is not surprising that labor organizations for decades were indecisive about their goals. They had to choose between achieving broad social ambitions or concentrating upon the pursuit of narrow economic interests—"pure and simple" unionism. In the end, it was pure and simple unionism, embodied in the conservative American Federation of Labor, that won out, and that remains the case today. Until the late 1880s, though, nearly every kind of labor philosophy found an outlet in some sort of labor organization.

Early Unions

The written record of organized labor is found at first in the evidence of strike actions. Few documents remain from the earliest days. As Selig Perlman suggested, the record of a strike may not really be evidence of any effort at permanent organization.[11] It is easier to organize for a strike than it is to establish and maintain a permanent organization. As far as we know, the Philadelphia Journeymen Cordwainers Union, organized in 1794, was the first union to achieve any long-term tenure, although it was preceded by several strikes—some against price-fixing and some to increase pay and shorten the workday.

The Matter of Goals

Early local unions tended to concentrate on bread-and-butter issues, but ideological and utopian elements did influence their activities for awhile, as we saw in Chapter 6. Soon enough, unions turned from Brook Farm and the Oneida Colony, from social issues such as abolishing debtor's prisons and providing public education, to the dream of nationwide organization, One Big Union, with political clout. By the time of the Civil War, ideological factors in the labor movement had achieved successes, and it was not surprising that labor leaders would make a significant move toward national politics.

The National Labor Union

In 1866 the National Labor Union held its first convention. It was an attempt to unite organized labor on a national level to cope politically with the problems of the postwar recession. One of the National's main objectives became the adoption of an eight-hour day in government offices, without wage reductions. A bill was introduced into Congress in 1866 by Senator Gratz Brown of Missouri to achieve that end. Two years later, after a successful lobbying effort by the National Labor Union, President Andrew Johnson signed a federal eight-hour measure into law for government employees. With such successes, the political method must have seemed effective.[12] Eight-hour laws had been passed in several states, and labor leaders realistically might have hoped for a sympathetic response from the private sector.

The National Labor Union then went off the tracks, politically, by advocating *"Greenbackism,"* at its 1867 convention.[13] The idea, much like that actually followed in this country between 1945 and 1951, was to monetize part of the national debt, refunding it on a 3-percent basis and then converting the resulting bonds into legal-tender United States notes at face value. Holders of the debt, realizing an immediate capital gain, could be expected to cash in their bonds for U.S. notes and to lend those notes to worthy borrowers.

The resulting sharp reduction in interest rates would bypass the existing banking system (or, if the funds were deposited there, drive down bank interest rates) and, it was hoped, make investment capital cheaply available to labor cooperatives for expansion of their enterprises. The Greenback movement went nowhere in national politics. But in 1872 the National Labor Union went whole hog—organizing a National Labor and Reform Party, nominating candidates for president and vice-president—and was washed away in the resulting Republican landslide.

The Knights of Labor

In 1873 General Grant's second administration was greeted by a colossal financial panic and an ensuing long and deep depression. By then a new and even more amorphous labor organization, The Noble Order of the Knights of Labor, was on the scene. Organized in 1869 by Uriah Stephens, it was at first a secret order. The post-Civil War years saw a rich development of these groups, in addition to the Ku Klux Klan. In 1878 the Knights went public with a strong, centralized, national organization and a platform as ambitious as anything ever known in the annals of American social organization. The Knights demanded nothing less than a restructuring of society and the abolition of capitalism.[14]

Nearly anyone (except bankers, lawyers, and sellers of alcohol) could join the Knights. They emphasized the uplifting of the unskilled, but with the help of their more fortunate members. As Gerald N. Grob, a recent student of the Knights, phrased it:

> The Order was not an industrial union. It was rather a heterogeneous mass that subordinated the economic functions of labor organizations to the primary goal of reforming society.[15]

During the 1870s and early 1880s, the Knights grew and prospered. Their new leader, Terence V. Powderly, the Grand Master Workman, organized diligently and spread the Knights' gospel of uplift, the elimination of the "wage system" altogether and the reordering of society around cooperative principles. By 1886 the Knights had won some important strikes and face-offs with the most important leaders of the new industrial structure, including a sensational triumph over the "Mephistopheles of Wall Street," Jay Gould.

In 1885 Gould gave in to pressure from the Knights in a strike of workers against his railroads. The result was enormous publicity for the Knights, but then the "Peter Principle" took over.[16] In 1886 Powderly's feckless incompetence as a leader came to the surface in the labor upheavals of that incredible year in American labor history. The country was raked by strikes and violence. It was the year of the Haymarket Massacre, the great strike of the Chicago meat packers, and strikes across the country by railroad coal handlers.

Labor Unrest. Violence was a traditional input in labor relations in the 1877 railroad strike. A hundred were killed, and Pittsburgh's railroad yard (above left) resembled scenes of war. The explosive mixture of immigrants and American laborers (lower left) plus foreign and political radicalism produced events such as the Haymarket Square riot (above right). Together with native American ideas of industrial rebellion (IWW slogans, below right) this kept alive the traditions of violence in American labor relations.

Attention Workingmen!

GREAT

MASS-MEETING

TO-NIGHT, at 7.30 o'clock,

AT THE

HAYMARKET, Randolph St., Bet. Desplaines and Halsted.

Good Speakers will be present to denounce the latest atrocious act of the police, the shooting of our fellow-workmen yesterday afternoon.

Workingmen Arm Yourselves and Appear in Full Force!

THE EXECUTIVE COMMITTEE.

Achtung, Arbeiter!

Große

Maffen-Verfammlung

Heute Abend, ½8 Uhr, auf dem

Heumarkt, Randolph-Straße, zwischen Desplaines- u. Halsted-Str.

Gute Redner werden den neuesten Schurkenstreich der Polizei, indem sie gestern Nachmittag unsere Brüder erschoß, geißeln.

Arbeiter, bewaffnet Euch und erscheint massenhaft!

Das Executiv-Comite.

Economist Henry George was running for mayor of New York on a single-tax platform, and the eight-hour day (from which Powderly tried to disassociate the Knights) was a central issue in the wave of strikes. Utopian novelist Edward Bellamy chose 1886 as the year from which the hero of *Looking Backward* escaped into the year 2000. Powderly called off the strike against the Chicago meat packers after weeks of bitter struggle when a priest told him that wives and children of the strikers were suffering from their actions. Labor quickly fled from his leadership.

The AFL

After 1886 the Knights diminished rapidly, then vanished. Their main antagonists in the business of organizing labor were the skilled craft workers and their trade union. The Knights were inclusive, organized across many occupations, and had a strong central organization aiming at the loftiest goals of moral and social elevation, together with political reform. On the other hand, the craft unions were locally rooted and concerned mainly with the improvement of their own conditions, if necessary at the expense of all others. They were satisfied with creation of a local by organization and negotiation.

Samuel Gompers of the New York union of cigar makers, a founder of the American Federation of Labor (AFL), argued that unions should control the place of employment; stick to wages, hours, and working conditions in their negotiations; build up "in the imitation of capital"; and *win* strikes.[17] His tactics were to keep the membership restricted to craft workers, accumulate large strike funds with high dues requirements, and in politics, "reward our friends and punish our enemies." That was the essence of pure and simple unionism, and it was a far cry from the ethereal objectives of the Knights.

By the fateful year 1886, the two traditions were on a collision course and in open conflict. The soaring Knights were driving to enlist the craft union members into the fold of the One Big Union. A treaty was negotiated between the Knights and the craft unions, but failed, and in December 1886 the AFL was organized. Its object was to maintain craft exclusivity. The Knights faded away, and with them went the mainstream of the long tradition of utopian reformism in the American labor movement. In its conventions in 1930

and 1931 the AFL even rejected compulsory workers compensation insurance.[18] Apart from heretical groups like the Industrial Workers of the World, some reformist unions like the International Lady Garment Workers Union, or some western unions that continued the tradition, such as the Western Federation of Miners, and the International Longshoremen and Warehousemen's Union, craft unionism prevailed for the next half century.[19]

The AFL, rooted in local unions of skilled craft workers and local issues, dominated the labor arena until the movement for industrial unionism began under the leadership of John L. Lewis and the coal miners. In 1935 this culminated in the Committee for Industrial Organization, renamed the Congress of Industrial Organization (CIO), under the protection of the National Labor Relations Act. At first the CIO seemed very politically and socially oriented. But by 1955 it had merged with the AFL and followed that body's tradition of nonaligned political activity.

ANTITRUST LAW AND THE UNIONS

While organized labor struggled to get its own house in order, the country's employers of labor had found a new antistrike weapon in the court injunction and then, in the new Sherman Antitrust Act of 1890. With its appearance, labor faced not only state courts (and state militias used as strike breakers) but the federal government as well.

The Injunction

We saw that after *Commonwealth v Hunt* (1842), employers no longer could count upon a favorable response from the courts in labor disputes. Unions were not illegal conspiracies *per se*, but how they acted *might be* considered illegal. If union actions were illegal, the courts might be brought into labor disputes by the application for injunctive relief.

Injunctions are writs or orders issued in equity proceedings: They are meant to protect property against nuisance or continued trespass. They can be prohibitory or mandatory, either forbidding the performance of a given act or requiring the performance of some act. Failure of an individual so enjoined to adhere places him or her in contempt of court, which is a criminal offense. *Commonwealth* v *Hunt* took labor cases out of criminal courts to the great disadvantage of employers. The use of the injunction brought the element of criminality back into labor disputes to the advantage once again of the employers.

Injunctions began to appear prominently in the late 1880s to halt strikes against railroads. One was issued in Iowa in 1886 to halt a railroad strike. Then in 1888 the federal courts issued an injunction to suspend a strike against the Chicago, Burlington, and Quincy Railroad, appealing to the 1887 Interstate Commerce Act for authority.[20] Two years later, the Sherman Antitrust Act opened more possibilities.

The Sherman Act and Labor

It is astonishing that the framers of the Antitrust Act seem not to have foreseen the antilabor possibilities of its Section 1: "Every contract, combination in the form of trust or otherwise, or conspiracy in restraint of trade or commerce . . . is hereby declared to be illegal." When a union calls a strike, its object is restraint of trade, in a literal sense. But in a legal sense?

The first major application of the Sherman Act was in the Pullman strike of 1894, but it was not a real test. Federal troops were sent to Chicago to move the mails. In the original action Attorney General Olney appealed to the Sherman Act for authority. However, once in court, the government shifted its ground and based its case on the commerce power, and the Court followed that line. Eugene V. Debs, one of the labor leaders, refused to comply with the prohibitory injunction and was sentenced to prison for contempt. He appealed, but the U.S. Supreme Court upheld the contempt conviction.[21]

Fourteen years later, the Sherman Act was used explicitly against labor. An injunction was secured by the Loewe Company of Danbury, Connecticut, to stop a boycott of its product: hats. The resulting case, *Loewe* v *Lawler* (1908) produced an ominously worded Supreme Court ruling:

> The combination [the union] described in the declaration is a combination "in restraint of trade or commerce among the several states" in the sense in which those words are used in the [Sherman] Act.[22]

Labor leaders and sympathizers lobbied Congress for exemption of labor unions from the Sherman Act, and,

as we already noted, this was achieved in 1914 by the Clayton Amendment to the Sherman Act. The Clayton Antitrust Act was hailed as "labor's *Magna Carta.*"

There followed extensive gains by organized labor with government support and sponsorship during World War I, but business interests were not to be so easily beaten, and they renewed their attack upon organized labor (or their defense of their own property rights, depending upon one's viewpoint) and won significant victories. Former President William Howard Taft was appointed Chief Justice in 1921. On labor matters Taft was deeply conservative, as were several other justices. Taft's tenure gave Associate Justice Oliver Wendell Holmes, Jr. plenty of scope for his famous dissenting opinions.

In 1921 the Court, in *Duplex Printing* v *Deering,* ruled that an injunction should be upheld against a printers union, forbidding a boycott by the union and furthermore, that the union involved should pay all the costs of the litigation.[23] In the same year, in *Truax* v *Corrigon,* Chief Justice Taft delivered an opinion that placed, once again, most forms of picketing during strikes under a cloud. Taft wrote that "a single representative at each entrance to the plant" was sufficient. The employer, employees, and those seeking employment must have "free access . . . without obstruction by violence, intimidation, annoyance, importunity, or dogging."[24] He thus overturned a 1913 Arizona antiinjunction statute. Taft's language harbored a scarcely veiled prejudice against all forms of organized labor.

In 1922 came *United Mine Workers of America* v *Coronado Coal Company.*[25] In that decision the court held that the local union organizing a strike was suable even though it was unincorporated. Taft reached all the way across the ocean to the then recent *Taff Vale* decision (1901), in which the English House of Lords held a union financially responsible for damages incurred in a strike. A new suit was brought by the Coronado Coal Company against the United Mine Workers' local, and on the appeal, the Supreme Court held in favor of the company. Other lawsuits for injuries pressed by companies followed and the Supreme Court's view of the Coronado case prevailed. Unions were liable for the damages their actions caused, and they could be enjoined from pursuing those actions if damage threatened.

In 1929, another important turn against organized labor came in *Bedford Cut Stone Co.* v *Journeymen*

Stone Cutters of North America.[26] An injunction against union activities was upheld in an action brought under the antitrust acts: "An act which lawfully might be done by one, may when done by many acting in concert take on the form of a conspiracy and become a public wrong."[27] The central idea was a throwback beyond *Commonwealth* v *Hunt.* The act in question was an attempt to gain union recognition by advertising across the country that the Bedford Company's cut stone was "unfair." Insofar as the advertising reduced demand for Bedford stone, property was illegally being damaged.

In a brilliant article Herbert Hovenkamp argues that labor suffered under the Sherman Act (and *still* under the Clayton Act) because of the Supreme Court's belief that combinations of labor and capital should be treated *equally* as restraints of trade. Labor unions, unincorporated, suffered especially from injunctions, which applied to every individual member, whereas an injunction against a legal-person corporation treated its officers and employees as merely agents of the principal. The officers could arrange a price-fixing scheme internally, among themselves, with perfect safety and be no conspiracy, since the corporation itself would act as a single "person" in the market. Unions refused to incorporate, and thus give state governments power legally to intervene in their internal affairs.

Labor combinations at common law were not *per se* illegal after *Commonwealth* v *Hunt* (1842), and monopoly agreements between businesses were not enforceable at common law. The Sherman Act upset all that. Under the Sherman Act *every* combination in restraint of trade was illegal. Businesses could evade the impact of the Sherman Act in all sorts of ways, price leadership, merger, incorporation. Moreover, they were often protected from competition by high entry costs. But labor, with no scale economies, and perfect entry and exit from their market, were relatively defenseless against market competition, without organization. With organization, combination was obvious, and restraint of trade was obvious. Moreover, economists had developed by the end of the nineteenth century their idea of perfect competition, with each market participant as a mere price taker. Anything less was some degree of monopoly. Since unions aimed precisely to weaken the price-taking aspect of their market, they were anticompetitive by their very nature. The unions' problems with the law seemed to be un-

solvable in the courts. Hence, only the change in governmental philosophy and law embodied in the 1935 Wagner Act could legitimize labor unions and their ways in the American economy. The applications of old-time restraints by the courts against the unions even in the 1920s, just described, neatly illustrate Hovenkamp's thesis.[28]

In addition to such setbacks in the 1920s, even the "yellow dog contract" (an agreement not to join a union made as a condition of employment) was upheld once again by the Supreme Court in *Hitchman Coal and Coke* v *Mitchell.*[29] The gains of the labor movement over decades were wiped away by that case.[30] So far as the U.S. Supreme Court was concerned, therefore, it was perfectly legal for employers to demand abstinence from union membership as a condition of employment. It would take the Wagner Act (NLRA) to unsnarl finally the consequences of *Hitchman.*

So, despite some gains in the nineteenth century, the Clayton Act, and the advances made during World War I, by the end of the 1920s organized labor's place in law was still nebulous. The courts had used the Sherman Act against labor and upheld the yellow dog contract at the highest level; organized labor's primary weapons, the strike and peaceful picketing, were restrained. In addition, other planks in the platform of the labor movement, broadly defined, had been seriously weakened by the courts.

Child Labor and Minimum Wages

The use of children in factory employment had long been the target of liberal reformers.[31] In 1916 Congress passed the Child Labor Act to outlaw once and for all the employment of children in interstate commerce—the one place where Congress could legislate. Right? Wrong.

In the 1895 *E. C. Knight* decision (the "sugar trust" case), the Court found that an apparent monopoly of sugar refining was beyond the reach of the Sherman Act because manufacturing, even if for sale in interstate commerce, was not itself commerce and hence was not subject to congressional restraint.[32] In *Hammer* v *Dagenhart* (1918) the Court was able to apply the *Knight* doctrine to strike down the Child Labor Act.[33] Congress reacted by placing a tax on commodities produced by child labor, and Chief Justice Taft threw that out in his decision in *Bailey* v *Drexel*

Furniture (1922).[34] He cited *Hammer* v *Dagenhart* and ruled that the tax was nothing more than an attempt to force "people of a state to act as Congress wishes them to act."[35]

Whereas municipalities had long legislated maximum wages without encountering legal objections, the idea of minimum wage laws was anathema to business. In September 1918 the District of Columbia passed a law setting the minimum wages for women and children. In 1923, the Supreme Court overturned that law in *Adkins* v *Children's Hospital* on the grounds that the law interfered with freedom of contract and impaired the due process protections of private property in the Fifth and Fourteenth Amendments.[36]

Prelude to the 1930s

These decisions are a mere sample of the Supreme Court's attitudes towards the ambitions and actions of organized labor. Even though they were early twentieth-century decisions, their flavor was of the previous century. They form a prelude to the sharp reversal inflicted by Congress in the 1930s, mainly the Norris-LaGuardia Anti-Injunction Law (1932), the National Labor Relations Act (1935), and the Fair Labor Standards Act (1938).

The question might fairly be asked why leaders of the labor movement were not beaten down by the Court's adverse positions over such a long stretch of history? The answer is, in part, the experience of World War I, which fell in the middle of this history and was a time when organized labor actually realized a moment of full federal support. It became clear that labor's major ambitions could be achieved by friendly politics. That time came in the 1930s. The experience of World War I showed the wisdom of the conservative Gompers approach to politics: Whereas independent labor parties tended to terrify Republicans and Democrats alike, organized labor's support for friendly candidates of the established parties could yield congenial legislation and executive actions. Supreme Court justices did not depend upon votes; elected politicians did.

THE WARTIME GAINS OF LABOR

At the beginning of this chapter we noted the blending of "the labor movement" with the specific ambitions of workers to organize themselves into labor unions.

We noted some of the reasons for this intermingling of interests driven by different economic and social forces: the widespread ambitions for social reform, demographic changes in the population, and the resulting consequences in the political balance. The larger ambitions of the labor movement were to be found in the platforms of all major parties in the late nineteenth and early twentieth centuries, as well as in splinter groups like the Populists. Many political interests were vying for the new labor vote. Progressive Republicans as well as reform-minded Democrats espoused many of the labor movement's causes, for pragmatic vote-getting as well as strictly idealistic motives. In 1912, an activist Democratic administration under Woodrow Wilson's leadership launched the movement for wider government intervention in the economy, and it was inevitable that labor would be included.

The Adamson Act of 1916

A forerunner of federal control of hours and wages made its appearance in the Adamson Act of 1916, which included a federally mandated eight-hour day (with time and a half for overtime) for the railroads under the commerce clause. The Court upheld the act (*Wilson* v *New,* 1917).[37] In 1917, the Court also upheld a state law in Oregon restricting hours (*Bunting* v *Oregon,* 1917).[38] So, there were evidences that more government intervention, at some level, was afoot, even if we ignore the extraordinary, strictly wartime gains made by labor.

The War

War meant a great demand for labor. And that meant a time of strength for wage demands and organizational activities. Total labor stoppages rose from 1204 per year in 1914 to 4450 per year in 1917. Wartime legislation usually gave organized labor an advantageous position. For example, the 1917 Espionage Act imposed punishments for anyone who might attempt to interfere with the production or shipment of war materials, but there was a rider exempting strikes "with the sole and bonafide purpose of securing better wages and conditions of employment."[39] There was a manpower draft into the armed services with deferments only for productive labor. "Work or Fight" was the slogan in the "Age of Preparedness." Some states even passed laws requiring men to work, reminiscent of Queen Elizabeth's *Statute of Artificers and Apprentices.* In World War I, the command economy reappeared after a long absence.

The Lever Food Control Act of 1917, a sweeping emergency measure (which gave birth to the Federal Bureau of Investigation) provided the federal government with the power to take over factories, to allocate materials and products, and to settle labor disputes. These last the government tended to settle by granting union recognition and wage demands, since profits were not in question when the government was both manager and customer. In the railroads, taken over by the federal government in December 1917, wages were immediately raised.

The War Labor Board upheld union representation throughout the government's domain and opposed yellow dog contracts even though the Court had upheld them in *Hitchman.* The War Labor Policies Board was established to coordinate federal government activities in the field of labor. By 1918 the federal government had become the single largest employer of labor in the country.[40] When states passed laws against union solicitation of workers, the Attorney General ordered U.S. attorneys to defend those union organizers so charged. Workers in government employment were given the eight-hour day, and their unions were recognized as a matter of course. The government wanted production; it did not want labor disputes.

When the war ended and the conversion to a peacetime economy was underway, the protective presence of the wartime agencies vanished and with it, the unionized employments of the war period. In railroads, though, a separate peace had to be made. The four old Railway Brotherhoods maintained their gains under the Adamson Act, and in 1926, the Railway Labor Act included a National Mediation Board for railroad labor.[41] Wartime continuity held until 1935 in this area, when the National Labor Relations Board was set up under the NLRA.

It was thus a real-life experience that gave organized labor the hope for future government support. Adverse court decisions and widespread prosperity in the 1920s combined to damp down the energies of unionization. The number of work stoppages was down to a mere 478 per year in 1926, 841 in 1932, and then 4740 in 1937 when the drive to industrialize the mass production industries under the CIO was underway.[42] In the end, the unions were established by government power in interstate commerce; World War I had been a glimpse of the great day coming. To establish labor's rights to organize, the federal power would be needed. That would come in the 1930s.[43]

Notes

1. Thorstein Veblen, *The Theory of the Leisure Class* (1949), ch. 3, "Conspicuous Leisure."
2. Thus our Rockefellers, Kennedys, and Harrimans are noted for public service in the generations succeeding the founding fathers of those family fortunes.
3. Seymour Martin Lipset, "Trade Unionism and the American Social Order," in David Brody, ed., *The American Labor Movement* (1971).
4. Mancur Olson, *The Logic of Collective Action* (1971), pp. 36–43.
5. Claudia Goldin, *Understanding the Gender Gap* (1990).
6. Olson, *The Logic of Collective Action,* especially ch. I and III.
7. Selig Perlman, *A History of Trade Unionism in the United States* (1922), pp. 146–50.
8. Stephen J. Mueller, *Labor Law and Legislation* (1949), pp. 43–44.
9. Mueller, p. 44.
10. Mueller, ch. 6.
11. Perlman, *A History of Trade Unionism in the United States,* ch. 1.
12. Lloyd Ulman, *The Rise of the National Trade Union* (1955).
13. Perlman, *A History of Trade Unionism in the United States,* pp. 51–52. Irwin Unger, *The Greenback Era* (1964).
14. H. A. Millis and Royal E. Montgomery, *Organized Labor* (1945), pp. 59–75.
15. Gerald N. Grob, "Knights of Labor Versus American Federation of Labor," in David Brody, ed., *The American Labor Movement* (1971), p. 41.

16. Each person tends to rise in large organizations to the level of his or her own incompetence.

17. For a careful and classic analysis of the AFL, see Selig Perlman, *A Theory of the Labor Movement* (1949), ch. V. See also Perlman's *A History of Trade Unionism in the United States,* ch. 5.

18. Harold Laski, *The American Democracy* (1949), p. 215.

19. Melvyn Dubofsky, "The Origins of Western Working Class Radicalism," in David Brody, ed., *The American Labor Movement* (1971), pp. 83–100.

20. Perlman, *A History of Trade Unionism in the United States,* pp. 155–56.

21. Quoted in Mueller, *Labor Law and Legislation,* pp. 172–78.

22. Quoted in Millis and Montgomery, *Organized Labor,* p. 569.

23. 254 U.S. 443 (1921). Quoted in Mueller, *Labor Law and Legislation,* pp. 359–70.

24. 257 U.S. 312 (1921). Quoted in Mueller, p. 91.

25. 259 U.S. 344 (1922). A discussion can be found in Millis and Montgomery, *Organized Labor,* pp. 571–75.

26. 274 U.S. 37 (1929).

27. Quoted in Mueller, *Labor Law and Legislation,* p. 374.

28. Herbert Hovenkamp, "Labor Conspiracies in American Law, 1880–1930," *Texas Law Review,* April 1988.

29. 245 U.S. 229 (1900). In 1908, in *Adair v United States,* 208 U.S. 161, the court overturned an act of Congress, the Erdman Act, which had prohibited the yellow dog contract on interstate carriers.

30. Some states (e.g., Indiana in 1891) had passed legislation to outlaw the yellow dog contract.

31. The liberals may well have been more opposed to child labor than were the parents of the children. Goldin and Parsons have found evidence that poor US families essentially "rented out" their children and did not compensate them later for their loss of education. The higher wages of the children were dissipated in higher current consumption expenditures. Claudia Goldin and Donald Parsons, "Parental Altruism and Self-Interest: Child Labor among Late-Nineteenth Century American Families," *Economic Inquiry,* October 1989.

32. *E.C. Knight* v *U.S.,* 156 U.S. 9 (1895).

33. 247 U.S. 251 (1918).

34. 259 U.S. 20 (1922).

35. In *U.S.* v *Darby,* 312 U.S. 100 (1941), the Supreme Court gave up on *Hammer* in a rare comment upon its own follies: "It [*Hammer*] should be and now is overruled," p. 122 of *Darby.*

36. 261 U.S. 525 (1923).

37. 243 U.S. 332 (1917).

38. 243 U.S. 246 (1917).

39. Quoted in Karl Brent Swisher, *American Constitutional Development* (1954), p. 619.

40. Swisher, pp. 596–98.

41. The Transportation Act of 1920 also contained a Railway Labor Board.

42. *Historical Statistics,* series D 970, 977.

43. There are those who believe that even the 1930s assistance by the federal government was essentially halfhearted, and the continued weakness of organized labor in this country as a political and economic force is as much due to government hostility to unions as to any other force. Gerald Friedman, "Strike Success and Union Ideology: The United States and France, 1880–1914," *JEH,* March 1988; and Christopher L. Tomlins, *The State of the Unions: Labor Relations, Law, and the Organized Labor Movement in America, 1880–1960* (1985).

Suggested Readings

Articles

Dubofsky, Melvyn. "The Origins of Western Working Class Radicalism." In David Brody, ed., *The American Labor Movement.* New York: Harper & Row, 1971.

Friedman, Gerald. "Strike Success and Union Ideology: The United States and France, 1880–1914." *Journal of Economic History,* vol. XLVIII, no. 1, March 1988.

Goldin, Claudia, and Parsons, Donald. "Parental Altruism and Self-Interest: Child Labor among Late-Nineteenth Century American Families." *Economic Inquiry,* vol. XXVII, no. 4, October 1989.

Grob, Gerald N. "Knights of Labor Versus American Federation of Labor." In David Brody, ed., *The American Labor Movement.* New York: Harper & Row, 1971.

Gutman, Herbert G. "Work, Culture and Society in Industrializing America, 1815–1919." *American Historical Review,* vol. 78, June 1973.

Hovenkamp, Herbert. "Labor Conspiracies in American Law, 1880–1930." *Texas Law Review,* vol. 66, no. 5, April 1988.

Lebergott, Stanley. "The American Labor Force." In Lance E. Davis, et al., *American Economic Growth.* New York, Harper & Row, 1972.

Lipset, Seymour Martin. "Trade Unionism and the American Social Order." In David Brody, ed., *The American Labor Movement.* New York: Harper & Row, 1971.

McGouldrick, Paul F., and Tannen, Michael B. "Did American Manufacturers Discriminate Against Immigrants Before 1914?" *Journal of Economic History,* vol. XXXVII, no. 3, September 1977.

Pessen, Edward. "The Workingmen's Movement in the Jacksonian Era." *Mississippi Valley Historical Review,* vol. XLIII, no. 3, December 1956.

Books

Brody, David. *The American Labor Movement.* New York: Harper & Row, 1971.

Commons, John R., et al. *History of Labor in the United States.* New York: Augustus Kelley, 1921–35, 4 vols.

Goldin, Claudia. *Understanding the Gender Gap: An Economic History of American Women.* New York: Oxford University Press, 1990.

Laski, Harold. *The American Democracy.* New York: Viking, 1949.

Millis, H.A., and Montgomery, Royal E. *Organized Labor.* New York: McGraw-Hill, 1945.

Mueller, Stephen J. *Labor Law and Legislation.* New York: Southwestern Publishing Co., 1949.

Olson, Mancur. *The Logic of Collective Action.* New York: Schocken Books, 1971.

Perlman, Selig. *A History of Trade Unionism in the United States.* New York: Macmillan, 1922.

———. *A Theory of the Labor Movement.* New York: Augustus Kelley, 1949.

Swisher, Karl Brent. *American Constitutional Development.* Boston: Houghton Mifflin, 1954.

Taft, Phillip. *Organized Labor in American History.* New York: Harper & Row, 1964.

Tomlins, Christopher L. *The State of the Unions: Labor Relations, Law, and the Organized Labor Movement in America, 1880–1960.* New York: Cambridge University Press, 1985.

Ulman, Lloyd. *The Rise of the National Trade Union.* Cambridge: Harvard University Press, 1955.

Unger, Irwin. *The Greenback Era.* Princeton: Princeton University Press, 1964.

Veblen, Thorstein. *Theory of the Leisure Class.* New York: New American Library, 1953.

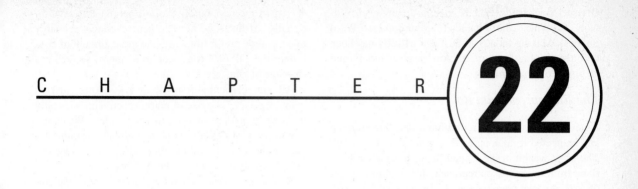

Special Topics: The Post–Civil War Era

There are three subjects in the postbellum period we might usefully reconsider at greater length: (a) the place in American history of the entrepreneurial force; (b) the changing social environment for business; and (c) the deeper meaning of the Populist movement. In retrospect, these three issues were of profound, long-lasting significance in American history, and we are not finished with them yet. They continue to keep the waters of American life swirling.

THE ENTREPRENEURIAL FACTOR

The word *entrepreneur* came into the mainstream of intellectual discourse with the works of Joseph Schumpeter and his followers. James Willard Hurst argued that the greatest change in the nineteenth century wrought by legal reform was the release of entrepreneurial energy that followed the instrumental decisions of the courts favoring economic development at the expense of all other property rights.[1] That energy was motivated by the chance for pure *entrepreneurial profit*, returns to entrepreneurial activity in excess of those possible from any other use of resources.[2]

The definition of entrepreneurship does not change, but its reputation varies with intellectual fashion. For example, by the early 1980s, entrepreneurship was "in" again. In fact, the word appeared in the 1981 inaugural address of President Ronald Reagan: He appealed for *more* entrepreneurship. The same year, George Gilder's book, *Wealth and Poverty,* made the best-seller lists.[3] It is an unabashed plea that the laws and institutions of the United States be changed to liberate the entrepreneurial spirit and thus save the nation from stagnation and inflation.

The Muckraking Tradition

Gilder's enthusiastic reception by the general public must have been a great surprise to him. The mainstream of American writing on the nation's great entrepreneurs had been mainly in the spirit of the muckraking historians of the early twentieth century—deeply hostile.[4] Probably the most influential book ever written on the classical American entrepreneurs was Matthew Josephson's *The Robber Barons,* published in 1934. But other, more important writers who presented very negative (but well-received) reviews of the lives of the entrepreneurs were Thorstein Veblen, Theodore

Dreiser, Sinclair Lewis, J. K. Galbraith, and even William Faulkner (the character, Montgomery Ward Snopes). Making money in business activity has been both the driving force of the American economy and an object of derision.

The Entrepreneurial Role

Americans have always relied upon entrepreneurship and respected it, as long as it was not *too* successful. The great wealth in the United States is nearly all derived from successful entrepreneurship, but the amount of special social position enjoyed by its wealthy entrepreneurs is trivial, except very locally. People such as William Bradford, John Winthrop, William Penn, even Thomas Jefferson and George Washington, played entrepreneurial roles in addition to their other contributions to the country's history. *So did millions of others whose names are not remembered.* The crucial point about entrepreneurship in American history is not who the entrepreneurs were, but that they existed and were able to achieve what they did.[5] *There was no plan for the economic development of the United States.* There was only an original frame of laws and constitutions, which included the developmental rights of property owners. We have already seen how that system evolved.

The property owners were left to achieve their own destinies. Sometimes they did it alone, sometimes with the help of family labor. Hired labor, indentured servants, slaves, and partnerships were also utilized as well as corporations, borrowed money, and plowed-back profits. Sometimes government subsidies (expropriation and distribution of the taxpayers' money by government officials) played critical roles. But always the guiding intelligence—decision making—was left to those who hoped to profit.

Except for the decisions of politicians about taxes, tariffs, subsidies, public construction projects, and the conduct of wars and foreign relations, the nation's economic history is what its people achieved, guided by their own entrepreneurial spirits. That some entrepreneurial spirits were greater than others was always true, as it is today.

Risk-taking and the Entrepreneur

A trip to Atlantic City, Reno, or Las Vegas makes one quickly aware that attitudes toward risk-taking vary widely in the population. Not all people are constitutionally set up to be entrepreneurs.[6] Many, probably most, people prefer life without a great amount of *conscious* risk. If that were not true, there would be a shortage of employees.

All entrepreneurship involves risk-taking, just as gambling does. The rise of entrepreneurship is usually in the open markets of a commercial society. We do not like to think of markets as being similar to gaming tables and slot machines, but there always is an element of luck involved in any market activity.

Risk-averse entrepreneurs will try to reduce the element of pure luck by advertising, by price competition, by higher quality at given prices, but also by collusion, oligopolistic practices, price rigging, and mergers to attain monopoly. American society has tried to limit the extent of much risk-reducing activity among entrepreneurs on the grounds that it is antisocial. Generally, it has preferred that businesses compete openly with each other. The result is the body of antitrust law. Where Americans did not want competition, they usually installed some form of regulation. They also have imposed regulation to reduce the risk *to the population* from any entrepreneurship they have deemed dangerous. And, of course, some forms of entrepreneurship have been outlawed altogether.

Thomas Edison, an inventor/entrepreneur, lost almost as much money as he made because of unsuccessful risk-taking. The U.S. Supreme Court broke up the Northern Trust under the Sherman antitrust law, thus frustrating three of the greatest nineteenth-century entrepreneurs: J. Pierpont Morgan (the all-purpose financier), James J. Hill (of the Great Northern Railroad), and Edward Harriman (of the Illinois Central, Union Pacific, and Southern Pacific railroads).

Entrepreneurship and Virtue

There is no consensus about *whose* entrepreneurship has been beneficial and whose harmful, except the imperfect judgments of the markets, the courts of law, the state legislatures, and the opinions of journalists and historians. Was John David Rockefeller good for the country? How about Howard Hughes or Father Divine? In the case of Alphonse Capone, the courts and the IRS returned a distinctly negative verdict. The markets for illegal alcoholic beverages were of the opposite opinion.

J. PIERPONT MORCAN, UNLIKE ALEXANDER THE GREAT, HAS MORE WORLDS TO CONQUER.
This Stirring American, Having Gained Control of Our Railroads and Steel Business, Is Reaching for the Shipping of the Universe.

The "Gilded Age". Pierpontifex Maximus—J. P. Morgan—attempted unsuccessfully to do for ocean shipping what he already had done for a large part of American railroads: Morganization. With vine leaves in their (thinning) hair, New York bankers in 1900 (below) enjoy a bachelor dinner.

It is the rare entrepreneur who wins universal acclaim for his or her historic role. For example, very few entrepreneurs in the country's history can match the extraordinary life achievement of Brigham Young.[7] But how he was and is viewed depends in large part upon the way nineteenth-century Mormonism is viewed.

Creative Destruction

Schumpeter referred to the entrepreneurial role as "creative destruction," because in the capitalist process of growth, competitive users of resources were driven out of business by more successful entrepreneurs. Henry Ford not only put many worthy makers of carriages into bankruptcy, he also drove hundreds of other automakers out of business. Television went through the weekly and monthly magazine business like the Black Death. Small, fuel-efficient Japanese and European imports very nearly left Detroit a basket case by the early 1980s.

People do not keep everything. New ideas, new products, new techniques are adopted, and the old ones abandoned. Schumpeterian entrepreneurs were the ones who correctly foresaw opportunity and made their moves. The country grew in *a different way* because of their actions. Over time, apart from government-induced constraints, the country's economic growth was the consequence of entrepreneurial decision making. The market always provided choices, but some were taken, and some were not. Equilibrium, as Israel Kirzner points out, was achieved by entrepreneurs who saw their opportunity for pure profit in **price differentials**—the same product selling in two different places, or times, at different prices.[8]

The Classical Entrepreneurs

When Pierpont Morgan died in March 1913, the London *Economist* wrote:

> Mr. Morgan was undoubtedly a man of genius, with strong will power and a commanding personality. He will stand, as a contemporary remarks, with Carnegie the manufacturer, Rockefeller the commercial organizer, Harriman the railway man, as one of the four most original and typical products of modern America.[9]

By 1913 the world had come to recognize in the great American entrepreneurs a social force that had changed the world. The greatest entrepreneurs, or at least those who made the most money, had organized the huge new American industrial economy, root and branch, into vast companies under unified managements that were capable of expansion and diversification. A company like Carnegie Steel was in a dozen different industries: building bridges and skyscrapers, mining and shipping ores by lake steamers, operating railroads. Men such as Pierpont Morgan were the financial organizers and controllers of economic activities that ranged from coal mining to banking.

Wherever you looked in the American economy as it developed from 1865 to 1914, there were individuals who imposed their entrepreneurial vision upon others and became the accepted leaders of their sectors. It was impossible for everyone to be employees; someone had to be the employer. Someone had to have creative ideas, put them to work in the markets, build factories, and organize work forces. These things were not done by "the market" but by people.

"The market" existed outside the United States, too, but other countries did not develop as the United States did in the period 1865–1914. The difference was, in large part, the entrepreneurial role, and that is why even today Americans see the names of the greatest ones—Carnegie, Swift, Armour, Vanderbilt, Rockefeller, Ford, Firestone, and others—all around them. One, or perhaps a handful, of these names dominated each of the new industries as the country grew out of its agrarian beginnings.

Was There Another Way?

The volumes critical of the great entrepreneurs imply that there was some other way, a better way, along which the country should have developed between 1865 and 1914. What might that way have been?

Socialism was not a viable alternative. Whatever the extent of its success in the world since 1917, as a technique for economic development, it was no more than a gauzy dream of theorists and agitators before 1914. Nearly all efforts in the nineteenth century to organize economic life on the basis of "social ownership" of property were failures. Even the communitarian dreams of the Mormon leaders were not successful in competition with the market economy.[10] The techniques for substituting "planning" for the millions of necessary decisions made every day by individuals in the market economy were unknown. Socialism has proved to be a most difficult system to put into practice, no matter how logical it may appear on a planner's desk.

What about perfect competition, the economics professor's dream? In the world of **perfect competition,** no single firm can influence its own price. Each firm in an industry is merely a price taker, like a single farmer selling wheat. The question is, could fifty, or five hundred, steel firms of equal size have grown in the steel industry from 1865 to 1900 and produced the same amount of steel at the same prices? What actually happened was that a handful of firms, finally topped by Carnegie Steel and Federal Steel, fought each other for supremacy and then merged into U.S. Steel, a single giant firm. There are at least two reasons why the first scenario is not likely and the second is—one is economies of scale, and the other is unequal entrepreneurship.

Where there are economies of scale, the first firm to pursue its long-run, downward-sloping average cost curve will be able to expand and undersell all rivals and drive them from the market—as long as the scale economies persist. That situation will lead to domination by a single firm and, under late nineteenth-century conditions, most likely a dominant entrepreneur.[11]

Unequal entrepreneurial ability poses a serious problem for the economic analysis of industry growth. Entrepreneurship is not one of the variables commonly found in the toolbox of microeconomic theory. Yet, in the history of nearly every industry, unequal entrepreneurship has played a dominating role, although it shifts with time. Henry Ford was the terror of the automobile industry until the mid-1920s. By then, in his sixties, he began to lose his lead and was overtaken by people like William Knudsen at General Motors (who had been fired by Ford), Walter Chrysler, and the Dodge brothers. Other automobile firms and entrepreneurs vanished without a trace in the struggle.

Thus, while it is not necessarily true that any one entrepreneur in any industry will produce permanent domination, it is very likely that every new firm in an industry will not be entrepreneured equally well. As the industry expands, some firms will grow dispropor-

tionately as a result of their superior management. In some cases the perpetual life of the (usually) resulting corporation enables firms brought to dominance by great entrepreneurship to survive for decades as leaders, far beyond the lifespans of their founders—General Electric (Thomas Edison and Samuel Insull), Westinghouse (George Westinghouse), Firestone Rubber (Henry Firestone), U.S. Steel (Andrew Carnegie and Pierpont Morgan), Standard Oil (John D. Rockefeller)—are examples.

With the antitrust laws the United States tried to restrain the consequences of uneven firm growth wherever it could be shown that entrepreneuring was succeeding through restraints of trade and monopolistic practices. The history of antitrust law does not argue well that there was another, obvious path for the American economy to take. The great entrepreneurs were clearly survivors in a Darwinian sense. One sees the logic without accepting the justice of the legendary homily given by John D. Rockefeller to his Sunday school class: The American beauty rose can only be produced by nipping off the smaller blossoms as the rose develops. He nipped many a smaller bud to make his great rose, Standard Oil.

Why the Hostility?

One might well wonder why, in a nation so wedded to the idea that great personal achievement is a virtue, would the great entrepreneurs be the targets of so much hostile comment? Why don't Americans honor their memories the way they do those of military heroes such as Napoleon, Lee, or U.S. Grant? Surely it is as honorable to create a firm that employs 10,000 people as it is to kill 10,000 people in battle. If General Grant was a hero to historians, why not John D. Rockefeller?

Partly, the answer lies in a cultural taboo from another time that says that money-making is crass, not noble.[12] Partly, there is the matter of sheer envy; one person rising far above the others in a game, fair or foul, excites emotions more complex than mere applause. (Read about Ted Williams' relations with the Red Sox fans.) Partly, business methods have often enough involved stealth, fraud, deception, lying, and other techniques not usually celebrated as the main Anglo-Saxon virtues. Finally, the great nineteenth-century entrepreneurs were feared and loathed simply because a whole new caste of millionaires was generated almost within two generations after the Civil War.

We had some very rich people before the war—such as Stephen Girard, who made it big in trade in Philadelphia, and John Jacob Astor with his American Fur Company in New York. But such fortunes were rare. Railroads, coal, steel, timber, manufacturing, meat-packing, big-time finance—all these industries appeared ubiquitously between 1865 and 1914. With them came a caste of entrepreneurs, their wives, and children, all living ostentatiously in a world without income taxes. At the same time, millions of European poor were rolling off the immigrant ships and into the factories. Who could admire the "parasitic" entrepreneurs while people of equal or greater innate virtue and promise were working long hours in sweatshops and steel mills and living in fetid slums along the back alleys of industrial America? The answer is, precious few.

There was nothing in the original American dream about yacht-racing at Newport being paid for by the profits of industrial sweatshops. So, the great entrepreneurs and their families became the easy targets of hostile writers. Today, there are just under one million families in the United States with a net worth of $1 million or more, but they are not automatically considered "enemies of the people," like the great tycoons were.[13] That poor press also washed over into the understanding of the role of entrepreneurship in general: It was a scandal. It took a lot of poor people to make one person rich. The nation could do without any more such unruly animal spirits. However, in the period 1865–1914 one factor of production that was not in short supply was entrepreneurship. For two centuries and more, American society and its laws had encouraged the entrepreneur, and the nation had prospered from the consequences.

THE CHANGING SOCIAL ENVIRONMENT

As we know, American business never operated outside a settled form of established legality—except possibly on the remotest edges of frontier settlement, and then only briefly. The social climate for business was the province of the state power from earliest colonial times. The property laws; the common law remedies for injury, fraud, and negligence; and the penchant of American governments to regulate directly meant that entrepreneurs in settled parts of the country lived in a more or less settled legal environment. They knew the law, and their customers and competitors knew it, too.

Just at the time that American business leaders discovered the joys of large-scale organization and proceeded to create the giant manufacturing, transport, and financial combines for which the late nineteenth and early twentieth centuries were famous, popular opinion soured. The very apparatus of the state power seemed to turn against business enterprise.

It became profitable for politicians to oppose "big business," at least during election campaigns. Legislation came to reflect this bias, also. As we already noted, by 1914 the main props for federal control over the nation's business activities were already in place. The important ones were the Interstate Commerce Commission (1887), Sherman Antitrust Act (1890), Pure Food Act (1906), Clayton Antitrust Act (1914), Federal Reserve System (1914), and Federal Trade Commission (1914).[14] For many reasons it is clear that these laws and institutions, and those like them that were soon to follow, were meant to restrain the power of the country's business leadership, to impose political control over it.

Wiebe and North Again

Robert Wiebe argues that during the entire period after the Civil War, the basic social structure of the country was undergoing upheaval: Small-town and rural America were trying to maintain their political power, despite the obvious shift of economic power to the burgeoning new urban areas.[15] The federal imposition of nonmarket control, following Wiebe's line of thought, reflected this basically atavistic force.

Douglass North presents a compatible line of thought.[16] North argues that in a popular democracy the *losers* try to recoup their losses from free-market economic processes through the political system, where their vote counts. Clearly, the rear of the giant new industries and the industrial cities they spawned, together with the relative decline in the fortunes of the farm sector, could have been the source of antibusiness legislation. The labor interest could not yet have mobilized decisive political power, for reasons we have discussed, but labor votes meant something in factory districts. Their representatives could have joined in coalitions to push their interests, minority or not.

In a popular democracy, coalitions of losers can be put together in legislative activities in which voting minority interests are advanced, despite the majoritarian politics that generally prevail.[17] More than one thing can be happening at the same time. Business can get protection from the McKinley Tariff (1890), while at the same time other interests push through the antitrust law.[18] This was as true from 1865 to 1914 for special-interest politics as it is in our own time, and it helps explain why it was in an era of supposedly corrupt Congresses that the first modern moves to impose federal regulation on business were made.

The rise of an antibusiness attitude in government, beginning perhaps with Grover Cleveland and reaching pronounced crescendos with Woodrow Wilson's election in 1912, was clearly good—that is, winning—politics. Both Theodore Roosevelt and William Howard Taft pursued trust-busting rhetoric as the road to election. Farmers' and small-town residents' votes were still a majority in this country, if a shrinking one.

Possible Long-run Cycles?

The change in the country's social environment at the end of the nineteenth century is not well understood by historians. There has been a great deal written about it, and much study of it, but the results are mostly unconvincing arm-waving. Until there is a really satisfactory theory of the state that is relevant to American history and institutions, these giant and fundamental societal changes will remain something of a mystery, which is awkward.

The great change in the social environment of business between 1865 and 1914 lies squarely in the middle of our study of American economic history. Our lack of understanding leaves a bad gap. The problem is similar to that presented by the rise of neoconservatism a century later, in the late 1970s. It has *seemingly* ended a long era of expanding federal intervention in American economic life during nearly half a century of which the federal role was dominant. The country began the turn against free-market determination of economic processes at least as early as the 1870s (the Granger Laws) and *may* have begun reversing the field a century later. If we tried to systematize in an impressionistic way the entire history of regulation and free-market control, we would have something like this:

1. *Period I: Government control dominant, 1607–1776 (169 years).* The expanding frontier of the colonies produced situations in which greater free-market allocation of resources was superior to the tight government restrictions of the early colonial period. Slowly, the grip of government regulation loosened.

2. *Period II: Free market dominant, 1789–1933 (144 years).* In 1776–1783 a whole layer of government regulation, crown and parliament, vanished. There was a change of regime, and at first the new central power, the federal government, had few resources and little power to exert its control of the economy. It was a time when the free market shook itself loose from government control to a large extent. The exceptions are the Civil War emergency and the World War I command economy. During Period II, the dominion of free-market allocation reached its peak and then began to weaken slowly. Regulation (with a hiatus in the 1920s) accelerated to the 1930s, as more and more government controls were imposed.

3. *Period III: Government control dominant, 1933–present (60+ years).* The steady expansion of nonmarket control over allocation from the New Deal forward finally produced a reaction in the Reagan elections. After 1981 there followed across-the-board tax cuts, reductions in federal transfer expenditures, and promises of cuts in federal regulation. Was this the beginning of a long swing toward free-market domination of resource allocation? The Reagan-Bush regime's record of decontrol and deregulation in 1981–1992 was hardly impressive, and the 1992 election of Bill Clinton to the presidency might *suggest* a reversal of the public's approval for a rollback of government intervention.

In this type of interpretation we have the first three turns of a long-run social-control cycle. One hesitates to say so, but a cycle, even of this length, makes more intuitive sense than a deterministic linear course. With a cyclical model, the power shifts back and forth. The losers are compensated, but their identities change. As their numbers increase, they gain the upper hand through coalition-building in the political process and reroute the direction of institutional change for their own benefit.

Invention and Innovation. To Schumpeter, the marriage of invention and innovation, of human talent and entrepreneurial ability, sparked the growth of bourgeois society. The financial risks taken by Thomas Edison, Henry Ford, and the Wright brothers, for example, paid off handsomely in economic profits for them and external benefits for society. A photo taken on a 1918 camping trip shows (upper right, from left to right) Thomas Edison, Harvey Firestone, Jr., Prof. R. DeLoach, John Burroughs, Henry Ford, and Harvey Firestone, Sr. Not all entrepreneurial ventures got their ideas "off the ground." The sixteen-flapping-disc helicopter of Mr. Scott of Chicago failed. Technological progress embraces failure as part of its cost.

Tony Mazzi

Those in colonial times who gained from the trend toward weakening of strict government control were independent spirits, losers in the grip of the big land grantors, the governments of New England who distributed new lands only in townships. They were mainly land-hungry farmers who wanted, and finally gained, access to the land through the free market by revolution (and via the land auctions, beginning under the Northwest Ordinances of 1785 and 1787). They were joined by businesspeople who wanted freedom from the tight nonmarket controls of the colonial towns and cities—freedom from the army of watchers, searchers, viewers, and gaugers of the colonial settlements.

The losers in the second period were again the farmers, now joined by labor and the urban poor, who fell behind urban commercial interests and industrialists in the battle for distributive income shares. They demanded a return to nonmarket controls over business and a systematic transfer of wealth and income. After winning periodic battles, in the 1930s, they won the war.

For nearly half a century what reigned next was the American version of the welfare state, but it was a **transfer society** in which only a very small portion of the wealth was transferred from the rich to the poor.[19] The losers in the Period III system were those who worked and earned and were taxed excessively by both direct income taxes and inflation to create rents that were transferred elsewhere: to government contractors; to those with specially protected incomes; to some extent, to the poor; and to some extent, even to those abroad, as military and nonmilitary government grants to foreign powers. The losers in Period III were joined by business interests who wanted freedom from expanding regulation, and by 1980 they were able to swing the system around through political action.

Admittedly, any idea of a long-term cycle in the nation's life is speculative and, in part, fanciful. Yet, it is a method worth considering as a way of understanding the swing in sentiment against business that became so strong between 1865 and 1914—in the heyday of "free-market capitalism," when the governments were constrained in debt-creation by a specie-backed currency and business seemingly was free to do as it pleased.

Douglass North's argument helps us understand the change. There always are losers. No social system can

eliminate unequal distribution of benefits. Even if all incomes were equal and all taxes were equal, all preferences would have to be homogeneous if none were to be aggrieved. In reality, with unequal incomes and taxes, as well as unequal preferences, a growing economy generates discontents. They find compensation through the political process when they cannot get it in the market.

WHAT DID THE POPULISTS REALLY WANT?

In our hypothetical cyclical framework, the Populist revolt looms very large, especially when one considers, as we did in Chapter 15, the long-run influence of their ideas upon subsequent federal administrations. There is no doubt that the Populists considered themselves to be the losers in late nineteenth-century America. They also had no intentions of waiting for economic evolution to solve their problems. They took their demands straight to the political arena where they could best be met, at the federal level. To the Populists, the national government was not simply the compromise of 1789; it was a source of *power*.[20]

The Political Demands

The Populists were not revolutionaries in the sense that they wanted to overturn the settlement of 1789. They stayed within the bounds of the federal Constitution, but they wanted its substantive content very considerably altered.

For example, the Populists wanted a more direct democracy at the federal level. They demanded that the state legislatures be stripped of their powers to appoint the members of the U.S. Senate. By that reasoning, all government (except the federal courts) would be subject to the forces of direct popular democracy. There was to be no area reserved for an establishment based upon economic power and (local) influence. All must be subject to the ballot at regular elections.

Their demand for a secret ballot reinforced the idea of the greater influence of popular democracy. The corrupt practices of the rising urban political machines would be curbed by their inability to monitor the actual votes cast. It was, no doubt, naive to suppose that a secret ballot cast among competing office-seekers would by itself produce good government; but at least bad governments would be more freely chosen. Events in Poland during 1980–81 might impress one with the importance of a secret ballot in primitive political circumstances. It is a great step forward. When the Poles wanted it, the Communist government intervened with a military crackdown. In the early 1990s, the USSR has undergone a profound transformation, and what are reported to be free elections have produced a bewildering variety of new governments—some progressive, some oppressive. Bad government is more easily acceptable if it can be shown by secret ballot that bad government is what the people prefer.

Women's suffrage was part of the same package—political advantage—which, in addition, would eliminate the obvious disenfranchisement of half the population as things stood. The same could be said of the sympathetic statements in the Populist platforms favoring the cause of labor. The demand for improved public education can probably also be considered basically political. Education was the obvious ladder to success in public service, and in 1890 the proportion of people who graduated from high school was very small (only 7 percent in 1900). Without a broader educational system, the way was barred to all but a small portion of the children of the poor.

These political demands ultimately were met, and if it cannot be shown that the quality of American political life was improved thereby, at least it can be argued that bad politics does not now come from lack of opportunity to vote. Likewise, functionally illiterate, modern high-school graduates are not the product of a public education system that *cannot* matriculate and educate the children of the poor. If it *does not,* that is a different matter.

Broad Economic Demands

The economic demands are a straightforward attempt to use the federal power for income and wealth redistribution. The Populists clearly saw that this already had been accomplished—for industry, by the tariff; for railroads, by subsidies; for corporations, by the courts and legislatures. The Populist rage had thus only in part been generated by the inequitable outcomes in the free market.

The most extreme Populist demands were never met, but they are interesting in their own right:

1. *Abolition of the national banking system.* These banks, chartered by the federal government, were objects of scorn and hatred because they had not expanded their operations (loans) as the country grew, and in any case, they systematically discriminated against agriculture by refusing to make mortgage loans on farm real estate. State bank note issues had been taxed out of existence to assure the success of the national bank issues. The national banks were of little help, and possibly much disadvantage, to the Populists.

2. *Nationalization of the railroads and telegraph system.* Here were prime cases, from the Populist viewpoint, of abuse of privilege. Railroad and telegraph companies had been the beneficiaries of government power: rights of way, eminent domain, special franchise monopolies on routes, subsidies of every kind. These businesses were placed under federal regulation, not nationalized. From the Populist viewpoint, the "private" character of these enterprises was a joke.

3. *Prohibition of subsidies to corporations.* No legislature then or since has been found that could meet this demand. Corporations are groups of people whose capital has been intermingled. It makes no sense for government to grant subsidies to single individuals and not to groups. The U.S. Supreme Court's 1886 decision that corporations were individual persons was one of several reasons why this demand, by the end of the 1880s, was unrealistic. Had it been met at the federal level, the subsequent history of the United States could not have occurred. The Commodity Credit Corporation, COMSAT, and the Chrysler Corporation, not to mention the entire aircraft and defense industries, are all monuments to federal subsidization of corporations.

4. *No alien or corporate ownership of land or natural resources.* This was nativism, atavism, *and* early-day environmentalism. The point was that the land should be reserved for farming and conservation. "The land, including all the natural resources of wealth, is the heritage of the people." There are still rumblings on these two issues, including recent lawsuits in California to restrict the water rights of each farm to the original 160-acre homestead. Foreign owners of American land are widely held to be odious, as in the past.

What ultimately would become the concern of ecologists and environmentalists was not invented for the Populist party platforms. The Desert Land Act of 1877 and the Timber and Stone Act of 1878 were the beginnings of an effort to "put something back" into the environment as part of the settlement process. By 1868 the people of California already had withdrawn Yosemite from private ownership, and Yellowstone Park was set aside by the federal government in 1872. It is easy now, as we shall see shortly, for us to view the Populist movement as a massive forerunner of modern special-interest politics. However, the Populists also professed deep concerns of a general nature that would in time find broad support in the nation's policies. The picture drawn of the Populist as a "dumb hayseed" is an elitist caricature.

Closer to Home

Where the Populists' demands were narrowly concerned with their own economic interests, we find a model of politics to come. The Populist program was camouflaged by a series of charges against the existing order—big monopolistic business, corruption in the courts and in the legislatures, and the accumulation of "colossal fortunes" therefrom. According to the Populists, "from the same prolific womb of governmental injustice we breed two great classes—paupers and millionaires." Such rhetoric was necessary because the Populist demands were couched in the language of reform. For a reform to take place, something has to be improved, and what the Populists proposed to improve was their share of the national income.

There were essentially two kinds of currency demands, both for a "commodity money." The various silver proposals were part of that issue. Prices of farm commodities fell drastically between 1864 and 1896, as we saw in Chapter 15. The Populist campaigns, in the late 1880s and early 1890s, came near the trough of this long-period price decline. The Populists knew that the money stock had to grow as fast as real output, other things being equal, or else prices would fall. The greenback issues were frozen; the national banks had not increased their note issues. The 1878 Silver Purchase Act had been insufficient, and the Populists wanted the Treasury to purchase more silver with new money (they got that one, temporarily, in the Sherman Silver Purchase Act of 1890, which nearly emptied the

U.S. Treasury of gold). Otherwise, the only hope for an increased money supply was gold, which was favored by the Eastern hard-money people but viewed as a dim prospect by the Populists. Hence, they came up with the "sub-Treasury scheme," which would utilize agricultural output to increase the supply of money.

The "sub-Treasury scheme" called for the establishment of regional Treasury offices in farm areas. At harvest time farmers could either sell their crops to the government or use them as collateral for government loans. The Treasury would print new money to be used for these transactions. Crops would thus produce new money. Agricultural prices would no longer be depressed at harvest time, and the farmers' incomes would benefit accordingly. In 1933 the Commodity Credit Corporation would ultimately be innovated to do this job for the farmers, using the more conveniently "elastic" Federal Reserve notes. The scheme didn't solve the farm problem.

The absence of a secure lending source for agricultural mortgages was to be met in the same way, by direct government loans on farm mortgages. This method would bypass the existing banks and mortgage companies and increase the money supply in the bargain. The deed was finally done in 1916 when the Farm Loan Act established the Federal Land Banks to make loans on farm mortgages, the first of many federal efforts to come in this service. By 1981 farm organizations were petitioning the government to stop the land banks from foreclosing defaulted mortgages. Even though the land bank system had helped some farmers enormously, it also had not solved the farm problem.

An interesting forerunner of modern Monetarism was the Populist demand that the currency supply be maintained by the Treasury at $50 per head of population (it is now about $500 per head). The idea was to insure against falling prices, and the Populists were firm "quantity theory" people, if nothing else. They, like the Greenbackers before them and hosts of others later on, knew that rising farm incomes—prices times quantities—could not be guaranteed unless the general level of money demand could be kept abreast of farm output. They supposed that an arbitrary sum of currency per head would be some assurance against a continued decline in farm prices as output soared.

As we saw in Chapter 15, it was not just the decline in farm prices that rankled the Populists but their belief that they were worse off than others; that farm prices had fallen more than other prices; that their terms of trade against industrial goods, transportation costs, and interest rates had worsened. Since this situation was due in part to the farmers' own prodigious energies in production, which they did not intend to cut back, the way out was to use government power to raise demand.

RETROSPECT

The Populists were not the first American special-interest group to seek government rent creation and distribution as a solution to their economic problems. Manufacturers understood that trick in 1789, when the first protective tariff was passed. What was most portentous about the Populist movement—and, of course, the Greenbacker and Granger movements before them—was the use of *national* political power to serve their own interests. They elected some governors and legislators. They backed William Jennings Bryan four times for the presidency. They made themselves heard. For the next century there would be countless efforts by aggrieved groups of "losers" in American society to do the same thing. By the 1970s it would be widely complained that special-interest politics in the nation's capital was sandbagging Congress, keeping it from governing wisely. The Populists were truly people of our time—a century early.

Notes

1. James Willard Hurst, *Law and the Conditions of Freedom in the Nineteenth Century United States* (1964).
2. Israel Kirzner, *Competition and Entrepreneurship* (1973), ch. 1–2.
3. George Gilder, *Wealth and Poverty* (New York: Basic Books, 1981).
4. The best are T. W. Lawson, *Frenzied Finance* (New York: Ridgeway Thayer, 1905); Henry Clews, *Fifty Years in Wall Street)* New York: Irving, 1908); Gustavus Myers, *History of the Great American Fortunes* (Chicago: Charles Kerr, 1910); W. Z. Ripley, *Trusts, Pools and Corporations* (New York: Ginn & Co., 1916); John Moody, *The Masters of Capital* (New Haven, CT: Yale University Press, 1919); Ida M. Tarbell, *History of the Standard Oil Company* (New York: Macmillan, 1925); C. W. Baron, *They Told Baron* (New Yorker: Harper & Bros., 1930); Matthew Josephson, *The Robber Barons* (New York: Harcourt Brace, 1934).
5. Arthur F. Cole, *Business Enterprise in its Social Setting* (1959). For a sympathetic view of American entrepreneurs, see Jonathan Hughes, *The Vital Few* (1986).
6. Much has been written about these differences in people's attitudes toward risk-taking. The student might be interested in the work of Reuven Brenner in this regard: *History—The Human Gamble* (1983); *Betting on Ideas: Wars, Inventions, Inflation* (1985).
7. Hughes, *The Vital Few*, ch. 2.
8. Kirzner, *Competition and Entrepreneurship*, pp. 47–52.
9. Hughes, *The Vital Few*, p. 454.
10. Leonard Arrington, *Great Basin Kingdom* (Cambridge: Harvard University Press, 1956).
11. For evidence of industrial concentration in the late nineteenth century, see F. M. Scherer and David Ross, *Industrial Market Structure and Economic Performance,* 3rd ed. (Boston: Houghton Mifflin, 1990), pp. 153–56.
12. For a long excursion into this idea, Thorstein Veblen, *The Theory of the Leisure Class* (New York: Charles Scribner's Sons, 1904).
13. *Statistical Abstract of the United States,* 1992, Table 736, p. 464.
14. For an account of the continued efforts to impose anti-food contamination laws and the opposition to such laws, from 1879 onward (190 bills introduced into Congress): Mitchell Okun, *Fair Play in the Marketplace: The First Battle for Pure Food and Drugs* (1986). For the view that the Pure Food Act of 1906 was in fact a case of "capture" by design; a legal gadget designed by established firms to keep out the competition: Donna J. Wood, *Uses of Public Policy: Business and Government in the Progressive Era* (1986).
15. Robert Wiebe, *The Search for Order, 1877–1920* (1967).
16. Douglass North, "Structure and Performance: The Task of Economic History," *Journal of Economic Literature,* vol. XVI, no. 3, September 1978.
17. James Buchanan, *The Limits of Liberty: Between Anarchy and Leviathan* (Chicago: University of Chicago Press, 1975), pp. 100–03.
18. For a structuring of American economic history from this viewpoint, see Stanley Reiter and Jonathan Hughes,

"A Preface on Modeling the Regulated United States Economy," *Hofstra Law Review,* vol. 9, no. 5, Summer 1981, especially pp. 1403–21.

19. Alan S. Blinder, "The Level and Distribution of Economic Well-Being," in Martin Feldstein, ed., *The American Economy in Transition* (Chicago: University of Chicago Press, 1980), pp. 443–47. The term is taken from Terry Anderson and P. J. Hill, *The Birth of a Transfer Society* (Lanham, MD: University Press of America, 1989).

20. The following discussion comes from the appendices of John Hicks, *The Populist Revolt* (1931). For further readings on the Populists, refer to the Suggested Readings for Chapters 14, 15, 17, 18, and 19.

Suggested Readings

Articles

Bell, Peter F. "The Direction of Entrepreneurial Research: A Review Article." *Explorations in Economic History,* vol. 5, no. 1, Fall 1967.

Cole, Arthur H. "An Approach to the Study of Entrepreneurship." *Journal of Economic History, The Tasks of Economic History,* vol. 6, supplement 1946.

———. "Meso-Economics: A Contribution From Entrepreneurial History." *Explorations in Economic History.* Boston: Little Brown, 1980.

Hughes, Jonathan. "Entrepreneurship." *Dictionary of Economic History.* Boston: Little Brown, 1980.

Smith, Howard R. "A Model of Entrepreneurial Evolution." *Explorations in Economic History,* vol. 5, no. 2, Winter 1968.

Thomas, Robert Paul. "The Automobile Industry and Its Tycoons." *Explorations in Economic History,* vol. 6, no. 2, Winter 1969.

Books

Aitken, H. G. J. *Explorations in Enterprise.* Cambridge: Harvard University Press, 1965.

Billington, Ray Allen. *Westward Expansion: A History of the American Frontier,* 4th ed. New York: Macmillan, 1974.

Brenner, Reuven. *History—The Human Gamble.* Chicago: University of Chicago Press, 1983.

———. *Betting on Ideas: Wars, Inventions, Inflation.* Chicago: University of Chicago Press, 1985.

Carosso, Vincent P. *The Morgans: Private International Bankers, 1853–1913.* Cambridge: Harvard University Press, 1987.

Cole, Arthur F. *Business Enterprise in its Social Setting.* Cambridge: Harvard University Press, 1959.

Hacker, Louis. *The Triumph of American Capitalism.* New York: Columbia University Press, 1947.

Hicks, John D. *The Populist Revolt.* Minneapolis: The University of Minnesota Press, 1931.

Higgs, Robert. *The Transformation of the American Economy, 1865–1914.* New York: Wiley, 1971.

Hughes, Jonathan R. T. *The Vital Few: The Entrepreneur and American Economic Progress.* New York: Oxford University Press, 1986.

Hurst, James Willard. *Law and the Conditions of Freedom in the Nineteenth Century United States.* Madison: University of Wisconsin Press, 1964.

Josephson, Matthew. *The Robber Barons.* New York: Harcourt Brace, 1934.

Kirzner, Israel. *Competition and Entrepreneurship.* Chicago: University of Chicago Press, 1973.

Myers, Gustavus. *History of the Great American Fortunes.* Chicago: Charles Kerr, 1910.

Okun, Mitchell. *Fair Play in the Marketplace: The First Battle for Pure Food and Drugs.* (DeKalb: Northern Illinois University Press, 1986).

Turner, Frederick Jackson. *The Frontier in American History.* New York: Henry Holt, 1921.

Wiebe, Robert. *The Search for Order, 1877–1920.* New York: Hill & Wang, 1967.

Wood, Donna J. *Uses of Public Policy: Business and Government in the Progressive Era.* (Marshfield: Pitman Publishing, 1986).

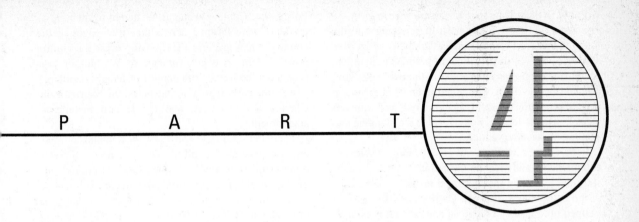

The Climacteric of American Capitalism: Expansion of the Federal Power, 1914–45

Main Currents 1914–45

In the first half of the twentieth century two great changes occurred that had profound effects on America's economic future:

1. The independent power and influence of business leadership were drastically weakened by the long depression of the 1930s.
2. The centralizing and social-control powers of the federal government expanded and came to dominate the course of the economy's development.

It was not until the 1960s and 1970s that the enormous implications (and further development) of these changes became *obvious features* of the nation's economic landscape. However, by studying the economic history of the period 1914–45, their growth path is apparent.

Although to some extent these two changes ran counter to each other, the extent to which they were complementary was most important. Business leaders partly resisted the growth of government, but they also assisted it in crucial ways with their advice and expertise. They wanted the benefit of federal power to organize and stabilize, but they hated the necessary cost—the loss of initiative in the private sector. Modern war, in 1914–18 and again in 1939–45, did push these changes to the fore, but the Great Depression was probably as decisive as either war—its impact brought permanent political, social, and economic change. As in the two wars, government in the 1930s was called upon to intercede in private economic life, and, as in the two wars, the advice of business leaders was critical in the planning and shaping of that intervention.

In Part 3 we saw the rise of great business leaders as entrepreneurs and creators of the industrial and financial transformation that occurred in the United States in the half century after the Civil War. These people stepped onto history's stage as natural (but nonpolitical) leaders who seemed destined, by their great economic achievements, to shape the nation's future from their positions in the factories and the counting houses. However, the great names, from Andrew Carnegie to Henry Ford, those of enormous power and even popular influence, stayed out of the political arena for the most part. Yet it was to be there—in politics, in war and economic crisis—that a wholly new force, great economic power in the hands of the federal government, would come into existence.

Looking back from the late twentieth century, the early symptoms of this coming change can be seen. Between 1875 and 1914, even as the greatest industrial corporations were being born (companies like General Electric, Standard Oil, United States Steel, and the Ford Motor Company) and as the names of their entrepreneurs were flashing across the front pages of the country's newspapers, the transfer of social-control powers from local governments to Washington was producing the initial critical mass of federal regulatory power: the early regulatory agencies, the Sherman and Clayton antitrust acts, and the federal income-tax amendment.

Then, between 1917 and 1919, the demands of modern war generated a full-blown, government-directed "command economy." Business leaders poured into the top levels of the wartime government to "make it work," to produce the armies and weapons that went to France in 1917–18. Economic power in the hands of Woodrow Wilson's second administration seemed to vanish in the peaceful interlude of the 1920s with Harding and Coolidge in the White House. But in 1929, the onset of a great and longlasting economic crisis brought the command economy back to Washington to create new structures for economic control and (it was hoped) greater stability. The Second World War brought renewed total mobilization, supported this time by the pay-as-you-earn income tax and highly graduated tax rates. By 1945, the balance of economic power had been altered for good, away from the primacy of private decision making and into the arena of government and politics. The American "welfare state" had come into being, in large part the child of modern war and economic crisis.

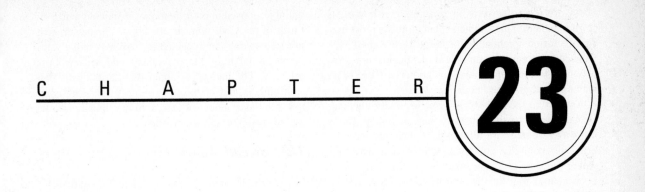

23

The Command Economy Emerges: World War I

World War I was the first in a nearly continuous sequence of crises that engaged the American economy in the twentieth century. The actions then taken and the lessons learned provided a rough blueprint of things to come. It is a curiosity of American economic history that so much of the war's institutional apparatus has been used to cope with crisis after crisis since 1918.[1]

By the 1920s most of the wartime command economy had vanished, and *normalcy* (President Harding's word) reigned. But in the New Deal emergency of the 1930s the techniques of war mobilization reappeared in various guises and have remained the main options for meeting emergencies by federal action ever since. The importance of World War I for institutional evolution has been neglected in most U.S. economic history textbooks, although it is well known among specialists. Murray Rothbard, one of the more unsympathetic critics of the second Wilson administration (1916–20), wrote of the "war collectivism" that it was—

> a totally planned economy run largely by big-business interests through the instrumentality of the central government, which served as the model, the precedent, and the inspiration for state corporate capitalism for the remainder of the twentieth century.[2]

In this chapter we will see how this came about and examine the basis of Rothbard's doleful assessment.

THE INCOME TAX AMENDMENT OF 1913

Federal power, beyond "police power" regulation like the ICC or the Federal Trade Commission, required a greater control over resources than could be achieved by revenues from land sales and customs and excise taxes, the financing provided by the country's founders. These taxes fell mainly, and regressively, upon consumers. What was needed was a tax on general economic activity to give the federal government decisive economic power. A permanent, federal income tax was the answer.

The Background

Taxation in its crudest form is simply forcible seizure of property by a king for his own use. What the king does with the property is his business, not that of its former owners. This simple explanation is a most useful one for comprehending taxation. Unless the king's subjects have equal incomes and identical desires, unless they lose equal amounts of property, there is no way for taxation to be "equal" or "fair."

Any tax in the real world is subjectively unequal. Because we all try to avoid taxes, any tax policy affects the way resources are allocated.[3] Self-interested citizens will naturally attempt to direct their activities where taxes are lowest or nonexistent. Similarly, there is no neutral way for the king to spend his revenues. Taxation thus is always a burden, and expenditures a boon, to some more than to others. If the king invites you to his birthday feast, you gain more from the royal largess than those not on the invitation list. The men who drafted the U.S. Constitution in the hot summer of 1787 in Philadelphia had a lively interest in taxation, and they restricted the new government's taxing power severely. Article I, Section 8, Clause I of the federal Constitution states that all "Duties, Imposts and Excises shall be uniform throughout the United States."

In response to the Civil War emergency, a desperate federal government imposed a progressive income tax. It needed immediate revenues and could worry about lawsuits later on. In 1872, the tax was abolished by Congress. A subsequent Supreme Court ruling in 1881, *Springer* v *U.S.*, actually held that the income tax was not a direct tax; therefore, it had been constitutional.[4] But in 1894 Congress passed an income tax, and the U. S. Supreme Court rejected it on constitutional grounds. In *Pollock* v *Farmers' Loan and Trust Company* (1895), the Court reversed the *Springer* decision and held that an income tax was a direct tax upon land and its products and must be apportioned equally.[5] The only way out for those who wanted incomes taxed would be a constitutional amendment that allowed unequal taxation.

How that was achieved has recently been analyzed by Ben Baack and Edward Ray. The continued growth of government, in its military building programs, foreign interventionism, military pension systems, and expanding regulatory functions required a new and renewable revenue source. The need for an amendment of the Constitution meant that resistance to an income tax had to be bought off in advance by an adroit targeting of expenditures and proposed expenditures to the high-income, industrial eastern states. They had

mainly opposed another income tax, having paid two-thirds of the Civil War income taxes. The newer western states could be expected to harbor Populist sentiments in favor of income taxing and redistribution schemes. The data show about two-thirds of the pension outlays and of the new military spending channeled to those states with a record of opposition to the income tax. The scheme worked.[6]

The Sixteenth Amendment

In 1913 the income tax was ratified and fiscal theorists were free to use this taxing power for whatever purposes sprang to mind, including the narrow one of raising a revenue. The income tax amendment to the federal Constitution was a total abridgement of the limitations in Article I of the original document:

> The Congress shall have power to lay and collect taxes on incomes, from whatever source derived, without apportionment among the several states, and without regard to any census or enumeration.

The immediate result: Of total revenues collected between 1915 and 1919—the fiscal years of the war effort—$6 billion of $11.4 billion, or 53 percent, came from income taxes on individuals and corporations.[7] This was the initial yield of the Sixteenth Amendment. It was the small beginning of a fiscal revolution that would change the American economy beyond the wildest dreams of those who pushed for the Sixteenth Amendment as a needed social reform. In addition, the federal government increased certain excise taxes, laid imposts on the profits of munitions manufacturers, and placed a surtax above the normal income-tax rates that had been provided by Congress.[8]

WORLD WAR I: THE NUMBERS

War both influences the amount of real production and diverts resources. The state requires a different kind of production than it has in peacetime to build and equip massive military forces. This production is required in great amounts, and it is needed immediately. Therefore, a government cannot wage a major war with normal taxation. People are conscripted into military service; resources and labor must be diverted from their normal occupations.

Modern War.   In the World War I Command Economy, organizational leadership came from American industry, where the industrial revolution went into the armaments business (above). To free resources for the war effort, patriotic bond purchasing (below) was used to raise the savings rate.

Table 23.1   Military Expenditures 1914–22[a]

Year[b]	Army	Navy	Total
1914	$ 208	$ 140	$ 348
1915	202	142	344
1916	183	154	337
1917	378	240	618
1918	4,870	1,279	6,149
1919	9,009	2,002	11,011
1920	1,622	736	2,358
1921	1,118	650	1,768
1922	458	477	935

[a] Amounts are in millions of dollars.
[b] These are fiscal years ending 30 June (i.e., 1914 includes half of 1913 and half of 1914).

Source: *Historical Statistics,* series Y 458, 459.

Labor in World War I was diverted by force for the first time since the Civil War. The armed forces of the United States averaged 173,000 in the years 1914–16. In 1917 there were 644,000 men and women under arms, in 1918, 2.9 million. One million had been transported to France by 1918 when the Germans asked for an armistice, and the war ended. By 1922 enlistments had fallen back to 270,000 persons.[9] Military finances to pay, feed, equip, and transport this army rose, as shown in Table 23.1.

General Finances

By fiscal 1919, total war expenditures were about 25 percent of GNP.[10] Most of the increase was directly for the war effort, but it included a general expansion of government-associated outlays. Revenues, even including the new income tax and array of war-emergency excises and surtaxes, could not keep up with the rapid increase in expenditures. As a result, the national debt rose by a factor of 21, some $24 billion, and since the financial system absorbed part of the debt by net money creation, the basic money supply soared. In addition, gold was pouring into the United States from Europe, and by 1916 the gold-standard banking system had absorbed some $2 billion, the largest amount of gold ever held by a single nation.[11] Foreign governments, buying armaments from the United States, liquidated the American debts owned by their citizens. The United States became, almost overnight, a "mature creditor nation," having still been a net debtor on long-term only three years previously. Consider the data in Table 23.2.

The $24-billion debt increase from the 1916 figure to the 1919 figure was achieved by well-organized borrowing. Secretary of the Treasury McAdoo had learned the lessons of Civil War financing, and with a more sophisticated banking system than that of 1861, was able to produce a well-orchestrated diversion of resources without recourse to straightforward government money-printing. More greenbacks would not be required. There were now Federal Reserve notes.

If the public bought the debt directly, then a transfer (temporary diversion) of claims over resources went from the public to the government. If the banking system absorbed the debt, the money supply would increase directly. This resulted from net Federal Reserve purchases, together with massive purchases of government securities by the commercial banks. Changes were made that enabled the gold reserve to support

Table 23.2   Federal Finance and Money Supply 1914–22[a]

Year	Expenditures	Revenues	Deficit (−) Surplus (+)	Gross Federal Debt	M_2
1914	726	725	−1	1,188	16.39
1915	746	683	−63	1,191	17.59
1916	713	761	+48	1,225	20.85
1917	1,954	1,101	−853	2,976	24.37
1918	12,677	3,645	−9,032	12,455	26.73
1919	18,493	5,130	−13,363	25,485	31.01
1920	6,357	6,649	+292	24,299	34.80
1921	5,062	5,571	+509	23,977	32.85
1922	3,189	4,026	+737	22,963	33.72

[a] In billions of dollars

Source: *Historical Statistics,* series Y 335, 336, 493, X 415.

more than twice as much bank money than the 1914 Federal Reserve Act allowed; the gold reserve backing was changed to 40 percent in support of Federal Reserve notes, and in 1917 the reserve requirements of the member banks were cut.[12] The result was, of course, a straightforward money-supply increase of massive proportions: Currency in circulation and demand deposits in 1920 were 100 percent higher than they had been in 1914.

The government could tax (and did), could borrow (and did), and could tax invisibly by inflating the currency. In the latter case the government merely purchased its goods and services at whatever prices were necessary to divert them from other uses to the government. Consumers went without, finding by surprise that they had (forced) savings. If that was an insufficient diversion, the government could also resort to various physical allocation devices and did. But in World War I the government never needed actually to resort to ticket rationing: Inflation, taxes and borrowing, re-enforced by an elaborate system of allocating devices (which we will discuss in the next section), did the job.

Guns and Butter

The economy in 1914 was close to full employment most of the time, but it initially dipped into a recession as the European war spread. By late 1916 output and employment had recovered. Thus, the war effort from that point onward occurred in the presence of full-capacity economic activity. The borrowing, taxing, and inflating would simply reduce peacetime output (butter) to raise the output of wartime goods and services (guns) if there were no net increase in overall productive capacity. This situation is shown in Figure 23.1, panel (a). If more capacity were built [Figure 23.1, panel (b)], it would be possible to have more guns *and* more butter. Such was achieved in the Vietnam War, for example, but apparently not in World War I.

Given the limits of capacity (Production Possibility Curve 1 in panel (a)) to raise production of guns from the (hypothetical) 1914 level to that of 1918, the economy would need to sacrifice "butter" of amount *s–t* on the vertical axis. Taxing, borrowing, and inflating would achieve that. If, however, there were investment in productive capacity for war goods, shifting the

Figure 23.1   Wartime Allocation of Guns and Butter

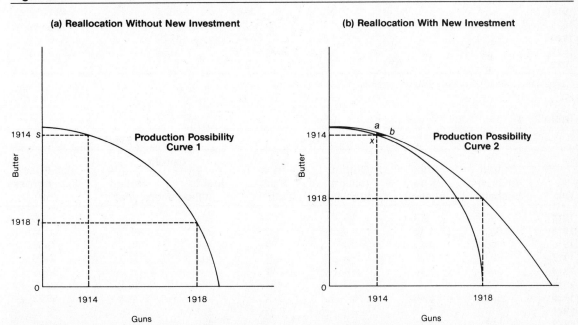

During World War I, the output of war material ("Guns" on the horizontal axis) required some sacrifice of peacetime output ("Butter" on the vertical axis), even with the increase in investment that occurred.

production possibilities to Curve 2 in panel (b), the increase to 1918 levels of guns could be achieved with a smaller sacrifice of butter. The shaded triangle *axb* shows the area within which both more guns and more butter could be achieved. However, that level of guns was not sufficient, so butter was sacrificed to reach 1918 gun production. The great economist, John Maurice Clark, estimated that about 60 percent of the war goods came from consumer retrenchment in World War I and only 40 percent from increased output.[13]

Investment

Clark's results are surprising, considering the data for physical investment.[14] With subsidies, government contracts in hand, and favorable tax treatment, a great rise in investment did occur. Capital outlays on fixed plant and equipment, $600 million in 1915, rose by a factor of 4 to $2.5 billion in 1918, a really astounding increase in just three years. After a slight dip in 1917 (to $2.2 billion), investment outlays hit $3.2 billion in 1920 in response to the inflationary surge. Then the roof fell in, and in a single year investment fell 50 percent (to $1.4 billion).

The Inflation

With such a shift in the production possibilities due to new investment, one can appreciate all the more the sheer force of the monetary stimulus produced by war

Table 23.3   Wholesale and Consumer Prices 1914–22

Year	All Commodities	Foods	Textiles	Metals	Chemicals	Consumer Prices
	1926 = 100 Base					1967 = 100 Base
1914	68.1	64.7	54.6	80.2	81.4	30.1
1915	69.5	65.4	54.1	86.3	112.0	30.4
1916	85.5	75.7	70.4	116.5	160.7	32.7
1917	117.5	104.5	98.7	150.6	165.0	38.4
1918	131.3	119.1	137.2	136.5	182.3	45.1
1919	138.6	129.5	135.3	130.9	157.0	51.8
1920	154.4	137.4	164.8	149.4	164.7	60.0
1921	97.6	90.6	94.5	117.5	115.0	53.6
1922	96.7	87.6	100.2	102.9	100.3	50.2

Source: *Historical Statistics*, series E 52, 54, 56, 58, 60, 135.

Table 23.4   Selected Outputs and Prices 1914–22

	Wheat		Corn		Steel		
					Output		
Year	Output (million bushels)	Price ($ per bushel)	Output (billion bushels)	Price ($ per bushel)	Ingots (million short tons)	Rolled (million short tons)	Rail Prices ($ per gross ton)
1914	897	.94	2.5	.71	25.6	20.6	30.00
1915	1,009	1.29	2.8	.68	35.2	27.3	30.00
1916	635	1.33	2.4	1.14	46.8	36.3	33.33
1917	620	2.30	2.9	1.46	49.8	37.0	40.00
1918	904	2.16	2.4	1.52	49.0	34.9	56.00
1919	952	2.42	2.7	1.51	38.1	28.1	49.26
1920	843	2.46	3.1	0.64	46.2	36.2	53.83
1921	819	1.33	2.9	0.52	21.6	16.5	45.65
1922	847	1.21	2.7	0.73	38.9	29.6	40.69

Source: *Historical Statistics*, series E 123, 130, K 503, 504, 507, M 217, 218, P 265, 270.

financing. *Real* GNP rose some 22 percent in the period 1914–18, yet commodity prices in general more than doubled, and the consumer price index just doubled.[15] The data are shown in Table 23.3.

Once the expenditure program was underway and the diversions away from civilian consumption were beginning to take hold, only increases in physical output proportionate to increased spending could keep prices from rising. Such production increases could, of course, come from existing excess capacity, but that had vanished by 1916. Increased productivity from existing labor and capital, or new capacity, could still reduce the inflationary pressures, and that must have been what occurred, considering the investment data.

In some cases there were significant production increases, but in some cases not, and the inflation in those latter areas was pure, only offset by physical allocation devices. Where such physical allocation occurred, the lapse of controls in 1919 brought forth a surge of prices as pent-up demand hit the markets. Thus, between 1918 and 1920 there was a huge *postwar* inflation in many commodities. The fast reduction of federal expenditures after the war and the appearance of big budget surpluses produced the price collapse of 1921.

Consider some comparisons of specific outputs and prices in Table 23.4. In the cases of wheat and corn, output did not increase sufficiently, and prices soared. Food was needed not only for American forces but for the substantial food assistance given by the United States to its allies and then, in the immediate postwar period, as aid to the hungry millions of war-ravaged Europe, a program administered impressively by Herbert Hoover.

The price collapse in 1921 triggered new demands by the farm interest for a federal solution to the suddenly reappearing problem of farm incomes. Steel ingots, rolled steel output, and pig-iron shipments increased impressively in the war and immediate postwar periods, but so did demand for these products, and prices rose powerfully despite the output increases. Augmented money demand stemming from the great monetary stimulus of the war finance and gold inflow was sufficient to raise nearly all prices, whether output had increased substantially or not.

Hours and Wages

With more people entering the wartime labor force, government enforcement of the eight-hour day in all government employment meant that the average number of hours worked actually declined, while wages, in a labor-short economy, soared.[16] As in previous wars when industrial labor was allocated primarily by the market (and was also massively withdrawn from that market at confiscatorily low rates for military levies), the wartime inflation proved to be a time of temporary prosperity for wage earners. In general, the increase in wages in manufacturing was almost a third more than the rise in the consumer price index, so, on the face of it, the average worker put in fewer hours on the job, and his or her real income could easily have risen by a third in the years 1914–1920.[17] Farm workers did less well than factory workers, but there seems to be little doubt that, on average, real wages rose substantially during the war. Other evidence suggests that income distribution actually shifted away from all other toward labor in World War I and its immediate aftermath. Representative wage and hours data are shown in Table 23.5.

The postwar surge in prices was accompanied by a similar rise in wages. Even with demobilization and the cutbacks in current federal spending (see Table 23.2 on page 412), pent-up demand resulting from induced physical shortages, together with a greatly expanded money supply, provided a base for continued optimism that the coming of peace would extend the prosperity. Then came the sharp setback of 1921. However, wages fell relatively little compared to prices and left labor

Pig Iron	
Shipments (thousand long tons)	Price ($ per long ton)
22.3	12.89
30.4	13.78
39.1	19.87
38.6	39.10
38.1	32.50
30.2	27.49
35.7	42.05
16.0	21.87
24.7	23.98

with net significant gains in real income over the entire course of the war and postwar experience. Indeed, the "normalcy" of the later 1920s, with its aura of great prosperity, was enhanced, many economists believe, by the quick, sharp adjustment of relative prices in 1921, which left employed labor with increased real purchasing power.

War Finance and Income Distribution

The war finance, conducted as it was with massive money creation, inflation, and high wartime income and profit taxes, produced some other unexpected results. The federal income tax was new, and there had not been time to develop the elaborate system of income-tax avoidance that characterizes our own era. As a result, civilian effective demand really was drained off by taxation where the taxes applied. The workers whose wages rose faster than prices gained income shares at the expense of the "rentier classes," those who depended on earnings from investments.

Between 1914 and 1920 prices were rising at compound rates of more than 14 percent a year. Stocks and bonds yielded less than half that rate, in part because of corporate profit taxes actually paid to the Treasury. The "capitalist" who paid taxes and made profits from investments in the capital market instruments came out of the war worse off, compared to others. Interest rates in general were far below inflation rates. It would have been an excellent time to borrow and speculate—and not pay taxes—but a poor time to plod along with AT&T and U.S. Steel. Tales of war profiteering and

Table 23.5   Selected Hours and Earnings 1914–22

Year	Manufacturing Industry Average Weekly Hours	Average Annual Earnings	Agricultural Labor Average Annual Earnings	Railroad Workers Average Full-time Weekly Earnings
1914	55.2	$ 580	$351	$15.36
1915	55.0	568	355	15.78
1916	54.9	651	388	16.62
1917	54.6	774	481	18.84
1918	53.6	980	604	26.40
1919	52.3	1,158	706	27.66
1920	51.0	1,358	810	34.14
1921	50.7	1,180	522	31.14
1922	51.2	1,149	508	30.30

Source: *Historical Statistics*, series D 765, 773, 781, 786.

Table 23.6   The Financial Markets 1914–22[a]

Year	Prime Rate	Corporate Bond Yields	Common Stock Yields Total	Industrials	Railroads	Utilities
1914	5.47	4.44	5.01	5.32	4.64	6.06
1915	4.01	4.62	4.98	4.19	5.21	6.01
1916	3.84	4.49	5.62	6.16	5.13	5.72
1917	5.07	4.79	7.82	9.79	6.12	6.75
1918	6.02	5.23	7.24	7.71	6.32	7.57
1919	5.37	5.29	5.75	5.18	6.26	7.37
1920	7.50	5.81	6.13	5.54	6.81	8.06
1921	6.62	5.57	6.49	5.84	7.08	8.29
1922	4.52	4.85	5.80	5.37	5.95	7.62

[a] Prime rates, corporate bond yields, and common stock yields are given as annual percentage rates.

Source: *Historical Statistics*, series X 445, 476, 479–82, 495–98.

giant fortunes made by the "merchants of death" may well contain their elements of truth, but there was little spillover, apparently, into those financial markets for which we have statistical records.

Consider the data in Table 23.6. In terms of earnings alone, nothing kept up with inflation. Industrial stock prices rose on average 36 percent in the years 1914–17 and 28 percent in the single year 1918–19 as the post-war inflation took hold. Otherwise, the war, financed as it was, proved no friend to the passive capitalist who depended upon the markets for a living. The "widows and orphans," or idle millionaires, who lived off the earnings of the markets could have been better served in real terms with industrial jobs.

Common stocks in railroads and utilities faded slowly in price because their yields could not keep pace with the inflation. Stanley Lebergott found the same results in his study of wealth and income distributions.[18] In fact, it has been the common experience that the wars of this century have tended to reduce income inequality.[19] If, as Marxists and others claim, capitalists start wars to maintain their class interests, they seem to have chosen a poor vehicle.

In the case of World War I the strategy of pursuing mobilization with money creation, inflation, and progressive income taxation was a blueprint for income redistribution favoring the wage-earning population. Since it enabled the Treasury's new debt to be sold at relatively high prices (low interest charges), the policy was well chosen from the viewpoint of debt management. It was, in fact, very clever fiscal policy, and it

was successfully followed in World War II by another massive debt creation at low charges. That the policy succeeded so well was due in large part to the construction of an elaborate system of nonmarket controls, the command economy of World War I.

THE COMMAND ECONOMY

In World War I the federal government was a prolific innovator of nonmarket control devices. The government did not rely simply upon the market's response to its tax and expenditure policies. That course would have left the economy wide-open to free riding. Since expenditures and incomes were soaring, completely rational people would have extracted from the war effort what was best for themselves and left the painful parts to others.

The government wanted rapid mobilization of resources, whether or not the new allocations were desirable to those whose lives were being changed by them. Coercion was necessary, and thus, so was centralized decision making. To achieve this, a bureaucracy of control had to be created to *direct* the economic mobilization. The extreme example, of course, was the draft of labor into the armed forces.

Eligible men were forced to muster to the colors at wages below opportunity costs. Patriotic fervor was encouraged, and prison sentences awaited those eligible for military service who preferred nonmartial lives. In fact, the government got them cheaply by force, and that was in part the rationale for the creation of the wartime bureaucracy of the command economy.

Boards, Offices, and Administrations

World War I began on 4 August 1914. After the failures of the immediate German invasion of Belgium and France and the Russian invasion of Germany, the Europeans found themselves locked into a devastating war of attrition which lasted four long years and from which they never really recovered. Vast armies faced each other across thousands of miles of trenches and fortifications.

The United States at first proclaimed neutrality and played the role of banker to the combatants. Slowly, national support swung behind the allies, and by 1916 the country began preparations to intervene. To do so, it needed ships, armies, weapons, and supplies.

Common Stock Prices (1941–43 = 100 Base)			
Total	Industrials	Railroads	Utilities
80.8	45.0	273.9	181.4
83.1	52.2	263.8	186.5
94.7	66.2	283.5	202.6
85.0	61.5	248.9	182.4
75.4	55.7	224.0	147.0
87.8	71.3	229.4	147.9
79.8	65.0	208.6	133.6
68.6	50.7	201.5	141.8
84.1	63.5	237.1	173.9

Someone had to plan the amounts and the locations of training and production as well as the transport. Since the federal government was in no way able to supply such expertise, leaders from private business were called to Washington to plan and mount the mobilization.[20]

In 1916 the Naval Consulting Board was formed to evaluate the nation's defense needs.[21] It was composed of senior scientific and industrial luminaries, including even Thomas A. Edison, then in his seventies. A spin-off organization, the Committee on Industrial Preparedness, financed by private industry, was formed to actively plan for war. In late 1916 it was, in turn, transformed into the Council for National Defense, a fully government-funded war organization that included cabinet secretaries.

The Council for National Defense was guided by the Advisory Commission, again composed of senior leaders from the private sector. According to Grosvenor Clarkson, the Advisory Commission had decisive influence.[22] It laid plans for food control, industrial allocation, even press censorship. In the prewar phase the defense effort had to rely largely upon private-sector expertise in a semiofficial way. Later, the industrial sector sent its brightest executives to Washington to serve their country in an official capacity for the duration.

Even in 1916 (after the election that Wilson won on the slogan "he kept us out of war"), the writing was on the wall. The National Defense Act of 1916 provided the means for the expansion of the armed forces. The Shipping Act of 1916 organized a formal merchant marine to be controlled by the United States Shipping Board. More appropriations bills followed as the financial scope of the coming war became evident.

The industrialists knew what could be done. Paul Koistinen quotes a letter from Howard Coffin, president of Hudson Motors, to the DuPonts, written in December 1916:

> It is our hope that we may lay the foundation for that closely knit structure, industrial, civil and military, which every thinking American has come to realize is vital to the future life of this country, in peace and in commerce, no less than in possible war.[23]

It truly was a vision of the "military-industrial complex" that so vexed General Eisenhower when he left the White House in 1961.[24]

Carrot and Stick

One piece of legislation, the Lever Food Control Act of August 1917, proved to be the primary control legislation. It provided the power to federally license businesses, requisition commodities, even take over factories directly (it also funded the FBI in its earliest stage). Power was given to establish minimum prices for wheat and other crops. Herbert Hoover was appointed head of the United States Food Administration with primary power under the Lever Act. To gain a patina of legitimacy for such legislation, *Munn v Illinois* was even conscripted: It was written in the Lever bill that food production was "clothed in the public interest."[25] Even in a war emergency, one government eye was focused on the Constitution and the courts.

Fuel supplies could be controlled, outputs determined, and prices set under the Lever Act, and the United States Fuel Administration was established to control output and fix prices of coal. In the summer of 1917 the War Industries Board (WIB) was organized to set production priorities in manufacturing industries, to fix prices, and to coordinate government purchases. It was this board that was headed by the famous financier, Bernard Baruch.

The WIB governed contracts for war production according to its own criteria; there was no competitive bidding. It also launched, through its Conservation Division, a campaign to standardize American industrial sizes of everything from drill bits to clothing.[26] The new army provided an excellent opportunity to reappraise (from the Civil War) the standard physical dimensions of American males! In the 1920s the Commerce Department under Herbert Hoover continued the program for standardization.

In major cases the problem of ownership of war supplies was solved by creation of quasi-public corporations. The United States Grain Corporation, organized under the laws of Delaware, bought food and other commodities to fix prices and store surpluses. The United States Housing Corporation, incorporated under the laws of New York, used government money to supply housing for defense workers. The Emergency Fleet Corporation, chartered in the District of Columbia, faced the immense problem of organizing yards, materials, and labor to build a huge ocean transport fleet. Finally, the War Finance Corporation used federal funds to underwrite bank loans to private industry.

Since the federal government had no tradition of production, or ownership of productive resources beyond the federal armories, these quasi-public corporations turned to another traditional solution for a pattern: They followed the institutional leads of the First and Second Banks of the United States, which were set up in mixed public and private ownership. Although the railroad in the Panama Canal Zone was a wholly government-owned corporation, the main technique was to create corporations that were state-chartered and superficially at least, seemed private. The command economy was approached gingerly, or so it appeared on paper.

Through licensing purchase without competitive bid, emergency regulation, and outright seizure where necessary, the government could, in the short run, extract a desired output that the market, in all probability, would not freely provide. Military labor was conscripted; private labor was largely bribed. Unions were recognized on federal contract jobs; the eight-hour day was enforced. Government lawyers defended people persecuted for labor activity. Labor was placated generally by being granted its reasonable demands or via the War Labor Board forcing settlements by arbitration upon both management and labor.[27] As for the telegraph system and railroads, the federal government had to take them over and impose its own management rules for the duration.

Usually, the price-setting by government authority was aimed at assuring delivery, so prices tended to be minimum prices. As we have seen, though, since output of basic grains scarcely increased at all during the war years, it is entirely probable that food prices would have been inflated without the aid of any policies aimed at that outcome. In other areas, such as steel output, where production did soar, federal price-fixing and price floors may well have been decisive in maintaining and raising prices.[28]

An interesting exception and example was sugar. There were two markets—foreign (mainly Cuban) and domestic. Among the allies an International Sugar Committee was organized as a monopoly buyer in the foreign market to force offshore sellers to deliver at low prices. When the Cubans balked, their food imports from the United States were cut off. They gave in and continued sales at low prices.

American beet-sugar growers, on the other hand, wanted high prices. To meet their demand, the Sugar Equalization Board was established, which sold the cheap Cuban sugar to American refiners at prices high enough to keep a price floor under domestic American growers.[29] Between 1916 and 1918 sugar prices at retail rose only about 21 percent under this system (compared to 60 percent for wheat). But in the two years 1918–20, when the controls lapsed, sugar prices rose strongly. Then the sugar market fell (see Table 23.7).

The Cubans were obviously cut out of the war boom from 1916 until 1918. They gained between 1918 and 1920 when controls were off; but sugar prices fell 80 percent for them in the next two years. Considering that the object of policy was to insure supplies at prices to foreigners below domestic price, the Sugar Equalization Board was a brilliant success. Fortunately, the United States did not need Cuban goodwill at the time.

THE LEGACY OF WARTIME CONTROL

Woodrow Wilson was an enthusiast for the competitive market throughout his political career. He favored policies that limited, he thought, the potential power of big business. During the war, the goodwill and cooperation of giant American firms had been necessary. The Germans would not have been beaten by Ma-and-Pa grocery stores, nor would guns, ships, tanks, airplanes, and munitions be made by small firms gambling on competitive bids. It had been a modern war and a military-industrial complex had been pulled together for the good of the war effort. But when the war ended, Wilson wanted to go back quickly to the previous *status quo*. He ordered the new command economy dissolved, and it began to vanish quickly. The government's wartime support for organized labor was equally short-lived. In the labor unrest of 1919–20, the government pulled back into the role of conciliator, and the labor unions were generally drubbed. Their membership plunged.[30]

Dismantling the Bureaucracy

Many, both inside and outside the government, considered the system of enforced wartime cooperation between firms and industries, together with government direction (and financing), superior to the old dog-eat-dog tendencies of the pre-war competitive economy. But Wilson moved quickly to abolish the command structure. The armistice was 11 November 1918, and on 23 November, not two weeks later, Wilson ordered the WIB to wind up its affairs.[31]

Trying to maintain the "order" of wartime, the Commerce Department bureaucracy set up an Industrial Board early in 1919 of mixed government and private direction. When it became clear that the main object of the Industrial Board was price-fixing, Wilson ordered it dissolved. Baruch and others hoped for some continuation of the war-time system, but the main industrialists temporarily in Washington quickly packed up and headed home, especially when it became clear that the system's basis, the wartime presidential power, was no longer there.[32] In any case, the boom of 1918–20 indicated that no government direction of economic life was required to make the economy prosper.

The U.S. Supreme Court helped push the wartime regime into temporary oblivion by wiping out the 1916 Child Labor Act in *Hammer* v *Dagenhart* (1918) and wage and hour legislation in *Adkins* v *Children's Hospital* (1923) and later finished off state-level wartime controls over prices in *Wolff Packing Company* v *Court of Industrial Relations* (1921). It seemed that World War I was strictly for the history books.

The Legacy

But the lessons learned from World War I would not be forgotten. The WIB would reappear in 1933 as the National Recovery Administration (NRA).[33] The United States Grain Corporation would resurface in the 1930s as the Commodity Credit Corporation. The planning activities of the Food Administration would reappear in the two Agricultural Adjustment Acts. The Emergency Fleet Corporation came back as the National Maritime Administration. The Federal Housing Administration of the 1930s was really born first as the wartime United States Housing Corporation.

The War Labor Board would be continued in part as the Railway Labor Board under the Railway Labor Act of 1926, and then finally, permanently, as the National Labor Relations Board under the Wagner Act in 1935. The Fuel Administration under the Lever Act reemerged in the 1930s as the Bituminous Coal Division in the Interior Department. Senator Joseph Guffey (D, PA), who was instrumental in creating the New Deal laws governing coal and oil output and pricing, had been head of the petroleum division of the WIB.

Table 23.7 U.S. Sugar Prices Paid at Retail and Wholesale and on Average for Imported Sugar[a]

Year	Retail	Wholesale	Imports
1914	.059	.047	.020
1915	.066	.056	.033
1916	.080	.069	.041
$\frac{1916 \text{ price}}{1914 \text{ price}} \times 100$	135.6	146.8	205.0
1917	.093	.077	.045
1918	.097	.078	.047
$\frac{1918 \text{ price}}{1916 \text{ price}} \times 100$	121.3	113.0	114.6
1919	.113	.089	.056
1920	.194	.127	.138
$\frac{1920 \text{ price}}{1918 \text{ price}} \times 100$	200.0	162.8	293.6
1921	.080	.062	.039
1922	.073	.059	.026
$\frac{1922 \text{ price}}{1920 \text{ price}} \times 100$	37.6	46.5	18.8

[a] All prices are in cents per pound.

Source: *Historical Statistics*, series E 125, 202, U 300–01.

The list of World War I institutions that reappeared in the 1930s and/or later in World War II is a long one. The people of the wartime regime also served again, and again. Herbert Hoover himself is the most famous case. But there were many others of note. Gerard Swope, the General Electric executive whose ideas later played crucial background roles in the NRA and the Social Security legislation had worked under Baruch in the WIB. Baruch himself was a tireless planner and enthusiast for the reconstitution of the wartime regime in the crisis of the 1930s. George Peek, a Moline Plow executive, served under Baruch in the war and was appointed by FDR as the first head of the Agricultural Adjustment Administration in 1933. General Hugh S. Johnson, head of the NRA in 1933, also came from Moline Plow and had served under Baruch. New Dealer Leon Henderson, who headed the Office of Price Administration in World War II, had served in 1918 in the WIB Ordnance Division. There were many more.[34]

The lessons of economic mobilization were not lost, and when a new crisis came in the Great Depression of the 1930s, the emergency institutions and the people who understood them were called to history's stage for a rerun.

But for more than a decade after 1918 it seemed that a new, high level of permanent prosperity had been created and that the wartime experience would never be relevant again.

Notes

1. Hugh Rockoff, *Drastic Measures: A History of Wage and Price Controls in the United States* (1984), Ch. 3; Robert Higgs, "Crisis, Bigger Government, and Ideological Change: Two Hypotheses on the Ratchet Phenomenon," *EEH*, January 1985, and *Crisis and Leviathan: Critical Episodes in the Growth of American Government* (1987), ch. 7.

2. Ronald Radosh and Murray N. Rothbard, *A New History of the Leviathan* (1972), p. 66. For specific reference to war mobilization and the New Deal, see William E. Leuchtenberg, "The New Deal and the Analogue of War," in John Braeman et al., *Change and Continuity in Twentieth-Century America* (1967).

3. W. Elliot Brownlee, "Income Taxation and Capital Formation in Wisconsin, 1911–1929," *EEH*, Fall 1970. He argues that Wisconsin's state income tax inadvertently shifted expenditures away from capital formation in manufacturing. Industrialists "voted with their feet," and Wisconsin's development fell behind that of its neighboring states.

4. *Springer* v *U.S.*, 102 U.S. 586 (1881).

5. *Pollack* v *Farmers' Loan and Trust Company,* 157 U.S. 429 and 158 U.S. 601 (1895).

6. Bennett D. Baack and Edward John Ray, "The Political Economy of the Origins of the Military-Industrial Complex in the United States," *JEH*, June 1985.

7. See Paul Studenski and Herman Krooss, *Financial History of the United States* (New York: McGraw-Hill, 1952), Table 42, Ch. 23, for an excellent short study of World War I finance.

8. Rockoff, *Drastic Measures.*

9. *Historical Statistics,* series Y 904.

10. Studenski and Krooss, *Financial History of the United States,* p. 301.

11. Studenski and Krooss, p. 284.

12. Studenski and Krooss, p. 294.

13. Studenski and Krooss, p. 301, n. 16.

14. *Historical Statistics,* series P 107.

15. Studenski and Krooss, *Financial History of the United States,* p. 301.

16. Jonathan Hughes, *The Governmental Habit Redux* (1991), pp. 130–35. The long quest for an eight-hour day for all workers was realized in the years after the war. See Robert Whaples, "Winning the Eight-Hour Day, 1909–1919," *JEH*, June 90. The emergence of a national labor market in the prewar period is discussed in Joshua Rosenbloom, "One Market or Many: Labor Market Integration in the Late 19th Century United States," *JEH*, March 90.

17. Sanford Jacoby points out that, during the war, those manufacturers unable to recruit sufficiently from the "outside" labor market developed their own labor forces, an "inside" market to provide sufficient labor input. This accounts for much of the improvement of wages and working conditions for the manufacturing labor force. "The Development of Internal Labor Markets

in American Manufacturing Firms,'' in Paul Osterman, ed., *Employment Practices in Large Firms* (Cambridge: MIT Press, 1984).

18. Stanley Lebergott, *The American Economy: Income, Wealth and Want* (Princeton: Princeton University Press, 1976), pp. 205–8.

19. Arthur A. Stein, *The Nation at War* (1980), pp. 82–86.

20. See Rockoff's *Drastic Measures* and Higgs' *Crisis and the Leviathan.*

21. See Hughes, *The Governmental Habit Redux,* pp. 126–35; Radosh and Rothbard, *A New History of the Leviathan,* pp. 66–110, for most of the information in the subsequent discussion.

22. Grosvenor Clarkson, *Industrial America in the World War* (1923).

23. Paul Koistinen, ''The Industrial-Military Complex in Historical Perspective: World War I,'' *BHR,* Winter 1967, p. 385.

24. Hughes, *The Governmental Habit Redux,* p. 211.

25. Hughes, p. 131.

26. Radosh and Rothbard, *A New History of the Leviathan,* pp. 75–76.

27. Edwin E. Witte, ''Strikes in Wartime: Experience with Controls,'' *Annals of the American Academy of Political and Social Science,* November 1942.

28. Robert D. Cuff and Melvin I. Urofsky, ''The Steel Industry and Price-Fixing During World War I'' *BHR,* Autumn 1970.

29. Radosh and Rothbard, *A New History of the Leviathan,* pp. 85–88.

30. Edward Berkowitz and Kim McQuaid, *Creating the Welfare State* (1988), p. 59.

31. Robert F. Himmelberg, ''The War Industries Board and the Antitrust Question in 1918,'' *JAH,* June 1965.

32. Berkowitz and McQuaid, *Creating the Welfare State,* p. 58.

33. For these and other examples, see Leuchtenberg, ''The New Deal and the Analogue of War.''

34. Radosh and Rothbard, *A New History of the Leviathan,* pp. 95–97.

Suggested Readings

Articles

Baack, Bennett D., and Ray, Edward John. ''Special Interests and the Adoption of the Income Tax in the U.S.'' *Journal of Economic History,* vol. XLV, no. 3, September 1985.

Brownlee, W. Elliot. ''Income Taxation and Capital Formation in Wisconsin, 1911–1929.'' *Explorations in Economic History,* vol. 8, no. 11, Fall 1970.

Cuff, Robert D., and Urofsky, Melvin I. ''The Steel Industry and Price-Fixing During World War I.'' *Business History Review,* vol. 44, no. 3, Autumn 1970.

Higgs, Robert. ''Crisis, Bigger Government, and Ideological Change: Two Hypotheses on the Ratchet Phenomenon.'' *Explorations in Economic History,* vol. 22, no. 1, January 1985.

Himmelberg, Robert F. ''The War Industries Board and the Antitrust Question in 1918.'' *Journal of American History,* vol. 52, no. 1, June 1965.

Koistinen, Paul A. C. ''The Industrial-Military Complex in Historical Perspective: World War I.'' *Business History Review,* vol. 41, no. 4, Winter 1967.

Leuchtenberg, William E. ''The New Deal and the Analogue of War.'' In John Braeman, et al., *Change and Continuity in Twentieth-Century America.* New York: Harper & Row, 1967.

Rockoff, Hugh. ''Price and Wage Controls in Four Wartime Periods.'' *Journal of Economic History,* vol. XLI, no. 2, June 1981.

Rosenbloom, Joshua. ''One Market or Many: Labor Market Integration in the Late 19th Century United States.'' *Journal of Economic History,* vol. L, no. 1, March 90.

Whaples, Robert. ''Winning the Eight-Hour Day, 1909–1919.'' *Journal of Economic History,* vol. L, no. 2, June 90.

Witte, Edwin E. ''Strikes in Wartime: Experience with Controls.'' *Annals of the American Academy of Political and Social Science,* vol. 224, November 1942.

Books

Berkowitz, Edward, and McQuaid, Kim. *Creating the Welfare State: The Political Economy of Twentieth-Century Reform,* second edition. New York: Praeger, 1988.

Clarkson, Grosvenor B. *Industrial America in the World War.* Boston: Houghton Mifflin, 1923.

Hardach, Gerd. *The First World War, 1914–1918.* Berkeley: University of California Press, 1977.

Higgs, Robert. *Crisis and Leviathan: Critical Episodes in the Growth of American Government.* New York: Oxford University Press, 1987.

Hughes, Jonathan. *The Governmental Habit Redux: Economic Controls from Colonial Times to the Present.* Princeton: Princeton University Press, 1991.

Nelson, L. Keith. *The Impact of War on American Life: The Twentieth Century Experience.* New York: Holt, Rinehart & Winston, 1971.

Radosh, Ronald, and Rothbard, Murray N., eds. *A New History of the Leviathan: Essays on the Rise of the American Corporate State.* New York: Dutton, 1972.

Rockoff, Hugh. *Drastic Measures: A History of Wage and Price Controls in the United States.* New York: Cambridge University Press, 1984.

Stein, Arthur A. *The Nation at War.* Baltimore: The Johns Hopkins University Press, 1980.

Studenski, Paul, and Krooss, Herman. *Financial History of the United States.* New York: McGraw-Hill, 1952.

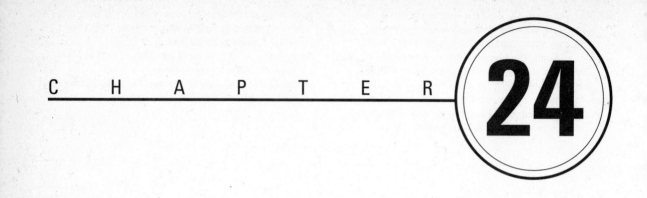

"Normalcy": 1919–30

Between the two world wars, the American economic experience was schizophrenic: a decade of apparently limitless economic advance, followed by a decade of baffling and frustrating depression. Then war once again created the conditions for total economic mobilization.

The interwar period contained many ambiguous elements, and you should be forewarned that economists have been more successful in describing the period than explaining it. That alone is surprising. Oceans of ink have been consumed over these events, and yet, even such a primary question as what caused the 1929 stock-market crash cannot be answered with confidence. There have been many—probably too many—explanations proffered, but there is little consensus.

The period 1919–30 is one of general postwar prosperity. Even the year 1929 was, in most respects, a year of great prosperity, and through most of 1930 there seemed little reason to expect what followed. In 1931 the economy dipped powerfully into depression and was still not fully recovered at the end of 1941 when the Japanese attacked Pearl Harbor. Contemporary politicians could find no way to resolve the mysterious

combination that characterized the depression: high unemployment and low levels of investment. The key to the 1930s disaster may well lie in the boom years of the 1920s. If so, it has never been clearly identified. Let us look at the years of prosperity.

INCOME DISTRIBUTION

The introduction of the income tax and other techniques of wartime finance leveled, to some degree, the country's income and wealth distributions. In the 1920s the process was reversed. Once the war's excess demand for labor passed, the claims of others resumed priority.

According to Robert Lampman, the top 1 percent of adults held 32 percent of the nation's wealth in 1922, and they increased that share to 38 percent by 1929.[1] After that date, a secular decline began. Wealth being the sum of net savings over time, it is not surprising to find that the wealth inequality was in part a reflection of income and savings inequalities. It is easier to save money from a large income than a small one, other things being equal.

In 1922, says Lampman, the top 1 percent of income recipients received 12 percent of all personal income

The New Leisure.   Radio (above) was one of the industries that flourished after World War I. The provision of paved roads by public authorities led eventually to intercity highways and mob scenes on the beaches (below).

and accomplished 49 percent of the country's saving. By 1928, these numbers were 13.7 percent and an astounding 80 percent. In 1929, the income share of the top 1 percent was still 13.6 percent, but savings of that group, after the financial disasters of that year, had fallen to 42 percent.[2]

Inequality of income and wealth was present in colonial times, as you learned in Chapter 3, and, although not fixed in constant shares over time, was a persistent feature of the country's long-term economic growth. According to Williamson and Lindert, up to World War I the line of rising inequality of wealth and income was almost unbroken.[3]

Wartime mobilization raised the shares of income going to labor. But when peace came again, the normal American preference for access to saved resources resumed its course, and so did the enhanced income shares accruing thereto. As Williamson and Lindert point out, this was the normal consequence of rapid growth in a gold-standard setting where there is no easy way to increase the money supply, to increase the command over real resources. Until the onset of the 1930s depression, according to Lampman, the income and wealth structure was a significant feedback mechanism: High incomes led to savings and hence wealth, which produced more income, which produced more wealth.[4] The 1920s saw a resumption of this old pattern.

Whereas the evidence for income received is that inequality increased in the 1920s, the extent of the increase is currently in dispute.[5] Increased income inequality in the 1920s means that consumption expenditures would tend to weaken even though aggregate personal incomes continued to rise. With the 1929 crash and the recession of 1929–32 there was no question about the future of consumption expenditures; they fell. Then came the Great Depression and fundamental changes, including high tax rates on interest incomes, which are discussed in Chapter 25. The trend of both wealth and income distribution, the same since colonial times, was reversed and moved in the direction of greater equality until the 1980s.

THE EXPANSION OF THE 1920s

The "roaring twenties" is the popular phrase that describes the decade: jazz, bootleg booze, gangsters, F. Scott Fitzgerald, H. L. Mencken, Babe Ruth, and the Great Crash of 1929. It remains a legend in our economic and social history.[6] What were its outlines?

Consumer Credit and Consumer Durables

Martha Olney's recent work adds a new dimension to our understanding of the 1920s economy. It was a time when consumers shifted their household demands dramatically into purchases of durable goods on credit. The early decades of the twentieth century saw products based upon the new network of dependable supplies of electric power together with internal combustion engines (and fractional horsepower engines) flooding into the market: Radios, washing machines, electric refrigerators, automobiles, and a host of new electrical household gadgets were creating a bright new world for the ordinary household. To purchase these durable consumer goods Americans waded into installment-plan buying. Instead of saving in interest-earning assets to finance ultimate purchases, a down payment and an installment contract transferred ownership of the assets—with a lien—and consumers *used the assets* while their payments reduced consumption expenditures from other commodities. It was, in effect, a new kind of saving: purchase for future consumption with investment in the asset substituting for other forms of saving.

As a result, consumer durables purchases increased at 8.3 percent per annum, nearly double the increase in GNP and in consumption in the period 1922–1929. By 1925, 75 percent of automobiles, 70 percent of furniture, 75 percent of radios, 90 percent of pianos, 80 percent of phonographs, and 80 percent of household appliances were purchased on installment credit. A permanent new "American way of life" was born, financed by innovation in the country's financial institutions and a desire by consumers to enjoy now and pay later. The consumer-durables revolution added a new flavor to the country's economic life in the 1920s. Even Henry Ford arranged for his cars to be bought on the installment plan.[7]

Output and Prices

By modern standards the extent of monetary expansion in the 1920s was modest. Prices were extraordinarily stable, while manufacturing output very nearly doubled between the 1921 recession and the 1929 crash.

Consider the data in Table 24.1. The expansion falls between two sharp downturns in prices and activity. The 1920–21 recession was short and sharp. In fact, note that prices fell far more between 1920 and 1921 than they did between 1929 and 1930. So also did the money supply. In the 1921 recession little was overtly done by government to compensate, although Elmus Wicker argues that the Federal Reserve System *accidentally* buffered the decline by maintaining high bank liquidity at high rates of interest.[8] Most of the World War I inflation was blown away in the 1921 recession, and when recovery came, there had been a drastic realignment of prices.

From 1921 to 1929 manufacturing output rose with only a small check, the mild recession of 1924, and a leveling from 1926 to 1927. Wholesale and consumer prices were remarkably stable in the face of such a powerful expansion of real output and the slower but still significant money supply increase from the low 1921 level. (When measured from the 1920 level, the money supply increase was much smaller.) A strong boom in real investment and leftover capacity from the war years made real growth without inflation possible. Even though the money supply increased some 25 per-

cent from the 1920 low, prices actually declined. Real wages rose: With prices stable, average industrial wages increased about 17 percent between 1922 and 1929.[9] Even in 1930, after the crash, money supply and price movements scarcely forecast the avalanche that was to come.

GNP and Unemployment

Table 24.2 shows GNP and unemployment figures for the period 1919–30. Leaving out the two recession years (1921 and 1924), the average rate of unemployment was about 4 percent. As in the nineteenth century, the boom years reduced unemployment levels to the rates sustained by frictional and technological job disruptions, together with seasonal unemployment. In 1919, 1923, 1926, and 1929 employment must have been *full* by most definitions of the word.

The high unemployment rates of 1921–22, 1924, and 1930 reflect the natural adjustments believed to be typical of an economy when the federal government makes no attempts at buffering actions. Resources and workers were thrown into unemployment quickly, prices were reduced, wages were reduced—all to be absorbed in more efficient employment in the ensuing expansions. This explanation was believed by orthodox economists and lay at the root of Schumpeter's great

Table 24.1   Money, Prices, and Manufacturing Production

Year	M2[a]	Wholesale Prices	Consumer Prices	Index of Manufacturing Production
			(1967 = 100)	
1919	31.01	71.4	51.8	15
1920	34.80	79.6	60.0	15
1921	32.85	50.3	53.6	12
1922	33.72	49.9	50.2	15
1923	36.60	51.9	51.1	18
1924	38.58	50.5	51.2	17
1925	42.05	53.3	52.5	19
1926	43.68	51.6	53.0	20
1927	44.73	49.3	52.0	20
1928	46.42	50.0	51.3	21
1929	46.60	49.1	51.3	23
1930	45.73	44.6	50.0	19

[a] In billions of dollars.

Source: *Historical Statistics*, series E23, 135, P13, X415.

Table 24.2   Unemployment, GNP, and Federal Finance, 1919–30[a]

Year	Unemployed Percentage of Labor Force	Gross National Product			Federal Receipts	Federal Expenditures	Federal Surplus (+) Deficit (−)
		Current Prices	1958 Prices	1958 Prices per Capita			
1919	1.4	84.0	146.4	1401	5.1	18.5	− 13.4
1920	5.2	91.5	140.0	1315	6.6	6.4	+ 0.2
1921	11.7	69.6	127.8	1177	5.6	5.1	+ 0.5
1922	6.7	74.1	148.0	1345	4.0	3.3	+ 0.7
1923	2.4	85.1	165.9	1482	3.9	3.1	+ 0.8
1924	5.0	84.7	165.5	1450	3.9	2.9	+ 1.0
1925	3.2	93.1	179.4	1549	3.6	2.9	+ 0.7
1926	1.8	97.0	190.0	1619	3.8	2.9	+ 0.9
1927	3.3	94.9	189.8	1594	4.0	2.9	+ 1.1
1928	4.2	97.0	190.9	1584	3.9	3.0	+ 0.9
1929	3.2	103.1	203.6	1671	3.9	3.1	+ 0.8
1930	8.9	90.4	183.5	1490	4.1	3.3	+ 0.8

[a] In billions of dollars unless otherwise noted.

Source: *Historical Statistics,* series F 1, 3, 4, D 9, Y 335, 336.

system of cyclical analysis, discussed in Chapter 17. The 1920s fit perfectly.

Between the 1921 recession and 1929, real GNP (1929 prices) rose 59.3 percent, an average annual rate of 6 percent compound. In real terms it was a vigorous expansion with the added attractions of stable prices, rising real wages, and mainly "full" employment. Even so, as was mentioned earlier, the actual distribution of the gains between the rich and the poor were markedly uneven.

The sharp downturn in 1920–21—with a jump of 6.5 percent in the unemployment rate and a fall of 37 percent in wholesale prices in a single year—was accompanied by a reduction of only 8.7 percent of real GNP.[10] The 1929–30 fall in real GNP was 9.9 percent, nearly 14 percent larger, even though prices declined very little (see Table 24.1). The initial rise in the unemployment rate, nearly tripling the 1929 figure, was still far below that experienced between 1920 and 1921. The supply of money had declined by 3 percent in 1929–30 compared to a whopping 9.3 percent in 1920–21.[11]

At the period's end, by such measures, one might have thought that a recession was at hand, milder than the one of 1920 and 1921, and one would have had every confidence of an ensuing recovery.[12] If one did

not know that the increases in real disposable income were more unequally distributed in the 1920s, the figures for increased per capita GNP might suggest a particular robustness. If rising GNP per capita alone were really indicative of economic health (and it is conventionally measured as such), the increase of 42 percent in the eight years from 1921 to 1929 might suggest an economy of particular strength. Actually, of course, catastrophe was on the way.

The income distribution figures that were discussed at the beginning of this chapter suggest that such considerations are an illusion. Harry Oshima points out that the mechanization of the 1920s associated with fractional horsepower and internal combustion engines reduced demand sharply for nonskilled and even skilled labor. The idea of "technological unemployment" appeared first in the later 1920s. Such factors must have contributed to the change in income distribution in the 1920s.[13]

Fiscal Results

After 1919, the consequences of the federal government's fiscal policy were deflationary. The federal budget outcomes are shown in the last column of Table 24.2, rounded to the nearest tenth of a billion dollars.

There remained a war-related deficit, $13.4 billion, in 1919, but in subsequent years the federal budget was in surplus every year. The net result was mildly deflationary. In 1919, the deficit equaled just under 16 percent of GNP. Purchases of government-issued debt by the banking system had made that a powerful inflationary stimulus. Most of the consequences were blown away by the 1921 recession. Only in 1924 and 1927 were the ensuing surpluses as much as 1 percent of the GNP.

From the Civil War to 1919 federal expenditures never reached $1 billion a year. However, with the new income tax the federal government was funded in 1913 at a new high level. Thus, according to **Parkinson's Third Law,** "expenditures rise to meet income," federal expenditures were never again below $1 billion. World War I, like all American wars of this century, caused a fairly large jump in federal expenditures.

The Farm Sector

Conventional wisdom about the 1920s is that the farm sector was a major contributor to the unprecedented collapse in the 1930s. We know that the farmers themselves believed they were falling behind in the late nineteenth century, and phenomena like the Populist revolt and subsequent reforms were monuments to that agrarian discontent. In the 1920s, the agricultural sector again agitated for special treatment by the federal government. In 1922, farm-bloc lobbyists succeeded, with the Capper-Volstead Act, in lifting the threat of antitrust prosecution from farm cooperatives. This bill paved the way for output restrictions and price-fixing by those organizations.[14]

Efforts were virtually continuous to get federal subsidies for exports of food. Both Presidents Coolidge and Hoover vetoed Haugen-McNary bills that sought such support. The Export-Import Bank of 1933 was the outcome. The farmers wanted outright federal purchases of food to create artificial shortages in the markets. The latter scheme was a favorite of the Populists and had been partly achieved during World War I under the Lever Act.

In 1929 President Hoover caved in to the pressure, and in the Agricultural Market Act and the Federal Farm Board of that year, provisions were made to lend some $500 million to farm co-ops and stabilization groups. By 1930 the Farm Board owned a third of the nation's wheat supply, all in the interest of supporting farm incomes.[15] The farmers clearly felt aggrieved. Why?

In Table 24.3 a shorthand economic history of the 1920s farm problem is supplied. All original data are transformed into index numbers based upon 1920, the peak postwar business-cycle year. In Column 1, notice that the volume of farm output rose only moderately in the period; 1928 was only 7 percent higher than 1920. However, owing to the sharp decline in farm prices, net farm income fell far below that of 1920 and never did recover.[16] Farm prices relative to nonfarm fell sharply from 1919 to 1921 (Column 8, farm net barter terms of trade) but recovered fairly steadily until 1930. The lack of output expansion meant that even though farm income rose from the low of 1921, it never regained the level of 1919, or even that of 1920. As a result, the farm share of national income was more or less steadily eroded (see Column 9 in Table 24.3) throughout the 1920s.

Fixed charges measured against farm income rose disastrously between 1920 and 1925 (Columns 10, 11, 12). Real-estate debt, interest charges, and taxes on real estate pressed against reduced farm income and produced hard times in American agriculture, even though the strict terms of trade of farmers actually improved considerably after the collapse of 1920–21.

The farm disaster of the 1920s did then have strong roots in the 1920s.[17] The high prices occurring between 1899 and 1919 had lent a temporary respite to the problems of the previous generation. But the troubles of the 1920s, tied peculiarly to long-term debt and taxes, prepared the way for the tidal wave of farm foreclosures of the 1930s.

Building Construction

The one indicator nearly every writer has fixed upon as an ominous sign of disaster is the great building boom of the 1920s and its peak from 1925 to 1927, *preceding* the Great Crash. This phenomenon is shown in Table 24.4 on page 432.

Building construction is so ubiquitous that a change in its fortunes affects all communities almost instantly. Building has been subject to long cycles of 18–22 years duration in the American economy, a famous phenomenon among economists. Indeed, A. F. Burns and Wes-

Table 24.3 The Farm Economy, 1919–30: Selected Indicators (1920 = 100 Base)

	(1)	(2)	(3)	(4)	(5)	(6)	(7)
Year	Farm Output	Net Farm Income	Farm Debt Outstanding	Interest Payable on Farm Loans	Real Estate Taxes per Acre	Prices Nonfarm	Prices Farm
1919	94.3	134.9	84.5	82.9	80.4	80.0	104.6
1920	100.0	100.0	100.0	100.0	100.0	100.0	100.0
1921	88.6	55.4	121.0	113.6	105.9	65.0	58.7
1922	97.1	62.5	126.7	118.3	105.9	63.5	62.3
1923	98.6	71.9	127.7	118.3	107.8	64.9	65.5
1924	97.1	75.1	126.2	112.5	107.8	62.0	66.3
1925	100.0	89.6	117.3	106.4	109.8	63.7	72.8
1926	104.3	83.4	115.0	104.2	109.8	62.1	66.5
1927	102.9	82.7	114.3	103.3	111.8	58.3	65.9
1928	107.1	82.2	115.5	102.6	113.7	57.5	70.3
1929	105.7	88.3	115.5	101.2	113.7	56.7	69.5
1930	102.9	63.7	114.0	99.1	111.8	52.7	58.8

Source: *Historical Statistics,* series K 284, 361, 372, 374, 415; E 24, 25; F 125, 127.

ley C. Mitchell concluded in *Measuring Business Cycles* that the building cycle is the most regular and raised total income generated from construction by 80 percent. The value of new construction permits rose by a phenomenal 192 percent between 1919 and 1926.

Then the boom faded. It was not killed by rising building costs, as the composite cost index shows. Costs were stable. Demand simply died off, slowly but remorselessly.[19] A legislated decrease in immigration following World War I slowed the rate of family formation in the early 1920s, a decrease the construction industry did not perceive. By the middle of the 1920s, an excess supply of housing had developed, one which grew worse as incomes fell in the Great Depression.

THE FINANCIAL SECTOR

Weakness in the farm and construction sectors are "old hat" explanations of events in the 1920s.[20] While they may signify some deep underlying unsoundness in the economy, scholars have never been willing to pin the immense turnaround in the 1930s on these sectors alone. What is really frustrating to economists is the conventional view: that basically the economy was sound but that excessive speculation by the public-at-large brought old-time American capitalism to grief. This viewpoint is especially galling to the school of economic thought, centered around Monetarism, that believes the people cannot seriously err if left in control of their own resources. Hence, the efforts in recent years to tag the Federal Reserve System with major responsibility for 1929 and subsequent events.

The Conventional Explanation

Table 24.5 on page 432 presents the basic reasons for the conventional view. For purposes of analysis, again the raw data are converted to index-number relatives based upon 1920. In 1929 GNP in *current prices* stood 7.5 percent below the 1920 level, but prices were nearly 40 percent below 1920. The sum of demand deposits and currency in circulation, M_1, was a mere 12.3 percent above 1920. The Federal Reserve's portfolio of securities, plus its outstanding loans and discounts—the measure of Federal Reserve money-creating activity—stood at only 47.9 percent of 1920. Even if the Fed had been willing, the commercial banking system's conservatism hardly could have been a major expansionary source; demand deposits in 1929

(8) $\frac{\text{Column 7}}{\text{Column 6}} \times 100$ Farm Net Barter Terms of Trade	(9) Farm Output as Percentage of GNP	(10) Farm Debt as Percentage of Farm Income Column 3 Column 2	(11) Interest Payable as Percentage of Farm Income Column 4 Column 2	(12) Real Estate Taxes as Percentage of Farm Income Column 5 Column 2
130.8	13.2	63	61	60
100.0	13.0	100	100	100
90.3	12.6	218	205	191
98.1	12.8	203	191	169
100.9	12.0	178	189	150
106.9	11.1	168	150	144
114.3	11.6	131	119	123
107.1	10.8	138	125	132
113.0	11.0	138	125	135
122.3	10.6	141	125	138
122.6	10.3	131	115	129
111.6	10.6	179	156	176

were a mere 18.1 percent higher than they had been in 1920.

On the other hand, time deposits had risen by 80.3 percent, the single largest element of potential monetary expansion. Even so, entering time deposits into the larger money supply aggregate, M_2, raises it to a mere 33.9 percent above 1920. Since in 1929 the common-stock index had risen by 226 percent over that of 1920, there is something to explain. Wherever the boom in the stock market came from, it is unreasonable to blame it on excess money creation by the banking system. The stock-market price rise of the 1920s stands, as the conventional wisdom always maintained, the great peculiarity of the 1920s.

What could explain stock-market prices? In general, there is a two-part answer:

1. Until 1929, even with those price increases, stocks were apparently sound purchases for those with money to invest.
2. In 1929 a bubble on the boom was the final push to the brink of disaster.

Since the upper-income strata received the lion's share of the increase in income during the 1920s, there was a large stock of saving in search of a return. Because increased stock prices measured increased wealth, playing the market encouraged more investment there. Such a phenomenon is common in gambling casinos, modern real estate, and commodities markets. The elements usually blamed for the rapid increases in 1920s stocks—reckless loans to brokers by bankers and gambling on insufficient margins—surely played a part, as they always do. However, by conventional measures, investments in stocks must have seemed sound enough, until just at the end.

Why buy common stocks? If a person has a certain sum of money to invest, he or she wants a return on it and a certain amount of security. In general, the less secure the investment, the higher will be the potential yield. In normal circumstances, like the 1920s (apart from crisis periods), bonds will, on average, yield less than stocks. While bond prices vary (inversely with interest rates), the coupon payment is definite (a certain percentage of the face value) if the firm does not go bankrupt. Even then, bondholders have the first claim on the assets.

Stock dividends are paid according to the distribution of earnings by a firm's management. Stock prices can rise or fall far more than can those of bonds of solvent firms. So, the risk-averse investor will prefer bonds to stocks in ordinary circumstances. In general, the climate of business will also influence his or her decisions. In good times, in fact, the investor may be willing to "take a flyer" in stocks. In bad times, he or she may shift to government bonds, the surest thing this side of legal tender itself.

Business Conditions Before the Crash

What were business conditions like before the 1929 crash? There had been the cyclical problems, and the ordinary investor was aware of them. He or she also

Table 24.4   Value of Building Construction, 1919–30[a]

Year	Construction Total	Total New	Maintenance and Repair	Permits (1930 = 100)	Cost Index (1967 = 100)
1919	8.9	6.3	2.6	81.9	30
1920	9.7	6.7	3.0	87.6	37
1921	8.9	6.0	2.9	107.6	30
1922	10.6	7.6	2.9	167.6	27
1923	12.5	9.3	3.2	212.7	30
1924	13.8	10.4	3.4	213.3	30
1925	15.0	11.4	3.6	252.3	30
1926	15.8	12.1	3.7	239.6	30
1927	16.0	12.0	4.0	214.4	30
1928	15.6	11.6	4.0	199.1	30
1929	15.0	10.8	4.2	187.3	30
1930	12.6	8.7	3.9	100.0	29

[a] Value of construction figures given in billions of dollars.

Source: *Historical Statistics,* N 1, 61, 111, 118.

Table 24.5   Financial Indexes Based on 1920 = 100

Year	GNP	Wholesale Prices	M_1	Federal Reserve Loans and Securities	Demand Deposits	Time Deposits	M_2	Common Stock Total
1919	91.8	89.7	91.8	95.5	92.3	83.3	89.1	143.2
1920	100.0	100.0	100.0	100.0	100.0	100.0	100.0	100.0
1921	76.1	63.2	90.6	47.1	90.8	102.4	94.4	86.0
1922	81.0	62.7	91.3	41.0	93.4	108.9	96.9	105.4
1923	93.0	65.2	96.6	37.4	98.5	123.5	105.2	107.4
1924	92.6	63.4	99.7	38.6	102.4	134.7	110.9	113.4
1925	101.7	67.0	108.1	43.1	112.7	148.1	120.8	139.7
1926	106.0	64.8	110.3	41.3	115.2	158.1	125.5	157.8
1927	103.7	61.9	110.0	49.2	114.9	168.3	128.5	192.2
1928	106.0	62.8	111.2	55.1	116.8	181.0	133.4	250.0
1929	112.7	61.7	112.3	47.9	118.1	180.3	133.9	326.1
1930	98.8	56.0	108.6	41.8	114.4	180.4	131.4	263.5

Source: *Historical Statistics,* series E 23, F 1, X 412–15, 495, 497.

knew that the economy was growing, and that prices were stable and employment was high.

As can be seen in Table 24.6, the number of business firms rose every year until 1929. People were optimistic enough to start up new firms even though failures were occurring. There was a sharp increase in the failure rate in the recession of 1921 (lingering into 1922), but after that the failure rate was less, although it remained at more than double the 1919–20 rate. Also, the average size of the failures did not rise after 1921. The crisis levels of interest rates of 1920–21 faded, and from 1923 to 1929 the prime rate averaged less than 5 percent. Unlike the wild times in the late 1970s and 1980, the low rates in the 1920s were "positive," higher than actual or expected price increases: 4.3 percent in 1926 was more costly to borrowers than 10 percent was in 1980 when prices were rising even faster.

After 1921, when interest rates fell, yields on common stocks generally were higher than on bonds. Even in 1928, when interest rates fell back, yields on common stocks generally were higher than on bonds. Even in 1928, yields on utilities exceeded those on government bonds in general. A risk-averse investor in 1928 might still have seen stocks as good investments *for their yields alone,* compared to bonds. In addition, the fever for capital gains was building. Stock prices were turning into a new El Dorado, which added to the at-tractions of stocks and tempted some of the less risk-averse investors to shift into stocks. The yields were good, and the capital gains were outstanding.

Consider the data in Table 24.7. Prices of common stocks recovered quickly from the 1921 downturn. They then rose and in general kept rising. By 1928 investors on average had more than doubled their money over 1920 levels, and the economy, by nearly every measure, must have seemed sound. Pessimists could have pointed to housing and agriculture or warned that income distribution was adverse to further growth of mass consumption. However, the signs were mixed.

Auto sales had been down in 1927 due to Henry Ford's conversion to the Model A—from 3,692,000 autos sold in 1926 to 2,936,000 in 1927—but then shot up to 3,775,000 autos sold in 1928.[21] Steel production in 1928 was 67 million tons, up a million tons from the previous high in 1925. Coal production had fallen (501 million tons in 1928; it had peaked at 573 million tons in 1926), but that in part reflected the booming market in the competitive fuel, oil. Crude-oil production, 443 million barrels in 1920, was 764 million barrels in 1925 and 901 million barrels in 1928.[22]

Cheap fuel was available for houses, factories, and the mass of autos now crowding the roads. A buyer of common stocks could look forward to 1929 as a great

Table 24.6 Selected Business Indicators

Year	Number of Business Firms	Failures per 1,000 Firms	Average Liability of Failures (thousands)	Prime Rate	Bond Yields U.S. Govt.	Bond Yields Corporate AA	Stock Yields Industrials	Stock Yields Rails	Stock Yields Utilities
1919	1711	37	17.6	5.37	4.73	5.49	5.18	6.26	7.37
1920	1821	48	33.2	7.50	5.32	6.12	5.54	6.81	8.06
1921	1927	102	31.9	6.62	5.09	5.97	5.84	7.08	8.29
1922	1983	120	26.4	4.52	4.30	5.10	5.37	5.95	7.62
1923	1996	93	28.8	5.07	4.36	5.12	5.40	6.29	7.59
1924	2047	100	26.4	3.98	4.06	5.00	5.25	6.44	7.35
1925	2113	100	20.9	4.02	3.86	4.88	4.75	5.66	6.13
1926	2158	101	18.8	4.34	3.68	4.73	5.24	5.52	5.57
1927	2172	106	22.5	4.11	3.34	4.57	4.72	4.89	4.96
1928	2199	109	20.5	4.85	3.33	4.55	3.82	4.76	4.09
1929	2213	104	21.1	5.85	3.60	4.73	3.65	4.29	2.29
1930	2183	122	25.4	3.59	3.29	4.55	4.45	5.27	3.19

Source: *Historical Statistics,* series V 20, 23, 30, X 445, 474, 477, 480–82.

Table 24.7   Average Annual Prices of Common Stocks Indexed on 1920

Year	Total	Industrials	Rails	Utilities
1919	143.2	109.7	110.0	100.7
1920	100.0	100.0	100.0	100.0
1921	86.0	78.0	96.6	106.1
1922	105.4	97.7	113.7	130.2
1923	107.4	100.6	112.4	135.6
1924	113.4	105.1	119.9	144.8
1925	139.7	133.7	140.0	174.3
1926	157.8	154.5	156.9	180.5
1927	192.2	192.8	183.0	206.8
1928	250.0	260.3	193.7	275.9
1929	326.1	328.5	221.2	444.1
1930	263.5	252.6	190.9	398.5

Source: *Historical Statistics*, series X 495–98.

year for business, and indeed it was, by all our measures, until the fall. Stocks reached remarkable levels.

THE GREAT CRASH

If your tire blew out on Interstate 80 and then the entire automobile fell apart, you would conclude that something besides the tire was defective. Likewise, many economists believe that somehow or other the economy must have been fundamentally unsound in 1929, despite the abundant evidence to the contrary. The stock-market panic was one of the most interesting and puzzling events in American economic history, and one with the most long-lived and far-reaching consequences. It is worth lingering over for a few pages. The tire had failed. That was not unusual. But the auto then fell apart. That *was* unusual. In October 1987 it would happen again, and again apparently without warning. This time, however, the economy bounced back.

Stock-market crashes are interesting phenomena. Does the 1929 crash offer any words of wisdom or warning for the future?

Could They See It Coming?

The previous discussion has been couched in the broadest terms, using very general evidence about the 1920s boom. It is fair to say that if you had not known that 1929 was coming, you would not have expected it in 1928 from the general evidence. A reasonable analyst would have expected a downturn at *some* point. Every expansion in American economic history has come to an end, just as every recession has come to an end. The great crises—all of them—swept away wealth, savings, and jobs, and ruined lives. The one that occurred in the 1920s was no different. Yet a remarkable number of people seemed not to believe that it would happen again.

Such faith is what fuels every boom. Unfortunately, booms are like rubbish burning in an incinerator: *When the flame is highest, the acceleration is exhausted.* Hence, the crisis and sudden collapse. The successful speculator gets out before the collapse, or sees it coming and sells short.

There are two examples of just such a situation in the more recent past. In late December 1980, amid the great precious metals boom of that year—when silver was approaching $50 an ounce, and gold, $850—sober professionals were seeing silver at $75 and gold at $1000 an ounce in "a matter of weeks." Instead, on 21 January 1981, prices crashed: gold fell 20 percent, and silver fell 25 percent in a few days. Then there were weeks of slower decline until silver approached $10 an ounce, and an ounce of gold was below $500. Huge fortunes were lost by the most sophisticated professionals, and others, holding short positions, cleaned up. In October, 1987, the stock-market crash saw about a third of its stock values vanish in a few days. Ronald Reagan, like Herbert Hoover before him, immediately opined that the economy was "fundamentally sound." Yet the crash *had* occurred.

How does one sense the end of a boom? How does one know that there will be a panic sell-off, that yesterday's plungers will be tomorrow's frightened rabbits? How would one have known in 1929 that a great disaster year was at hand, instead of a significant improvement over the splendid results of 1928? Is such prescience possible?

Let us drop back in history another eighty years and cross the Atlantic. On the night of 5 November 1857, Bonamy Dobree, Deputy Governor of the Bank of England, wrote in his diary what one of his fellow directors had found: "Hodgson reports a most unpleasant feeling abroad in Lombard Street, a sort of apprehension of insolvency widespread."[23] On that day, the Bank of England's discount rate had been raised to 9 percent, the highest ever, and the great panic of 1857 was about to let loose in London. A week later the Bank rate was 10 percent, the Bank of England's banking department had been *drained* of its own notes, and application had been made to violate the Bank Charter Act of 1844 and issue more Bank of England notes on the basis of government debt.

The crisis of 1857 was one of the most severe in history, spreading financial ruin worldwide. Yet *The Economist,* even then London's most respected financial journal, had written on 4 July 1857, a few months earlier:

> We have neither excessive trade nor numerous new enterprises, nor is there in the public any great and irregular action threatening future convulsion. Our superfluous energy seems . . . to have blown off in the Russian War.[24]

Late in the summer, bank failures in the United States and British failures of firms connected to the American trade began to disturb the Bank of England's Court of Directors. Fear was there.

Much of this is similar to our case in 1929. The popular conception was one of unlimited good times. President Coolidge, in his farewell State of the Union message in December 1928, had appraised the "tranquility and contentment . . . the highest record of years of prosperity," and had assured the assembled politicians that they could "anticipate the future with optimism."[25] Yet, scholars writing about 1929 report the kinds of preternatural intimations Hodgson had found in Lombard Street. John Kenneth Galbraith quotes Roger Babson's famous address to the Annual National Business Conference 5 September 1929:

> Sooner or later a crash is coming, and it may be terrific . . . factories will shut down . . . men will be thrown out of work . . . the vicious circle will get in full swing. . . .[26]

Galbraith notes that Babson was widely scoffed at for such foresight.

It is in fact Galbraith's *The Great Crash* that contains the best explanation of one curiosity in Table 24.5, the outlandish growth of common stock prices relative to other measures of monetary activity.

The absence of a general monetary expansion would not necessarily weaken the flow of funds into the stock market if alternative methods developed to *divert* funds there from other uses. Other prices would fall, and stock prices would rise. (Galbraith documents the development of such methods after about 1924.)[27] There were two major sources of diversion: (a) direct, nonbank loans to brokers; (b) investment trusts.

Broker's Loans

Business firms that ordinarily used their cash surpluses for internal financing, for short-term, self-liquidating loans, or for securities purchases began lending directly to the stock market through loans to brokers. Because the brokers used such funds to finance their own customers, the loans became a major source of credit—leverage—in the stock market. The loans had maturities at "call," so they were instantly retrievable by nonbank lenders, at least in theory, and the earnings were high.

Such loans must have seemed a godsend to corporate treasurers charged with earning interest on temporary surplus cash flows. By early 1929, according to Galbraith, Standard Oil of New Jersey was diverting an average of $69 million a day into call loans; Electric Bond and Share, more than $100 million. Such nonbanking institutions were pouring more funds into the stock market than was the banking system itself.

End-of-year figures for brokers' loans in the 1920s are shown in Table 24.8. Judging from this evidence, the normal proportion of nonbanking money in such loans in those days (see 1923–25) was less than 30 percent of the total. By 1926, though, a change was evident. Even at the end of 1929, after the panic, the nonbank proportion of the total stood at nearly 60 percent. In early October 1929, when brokers' loans stood at $8.5 billion, $6.6 billion of that figure, or about 78 percent, came from nonbank sources.[28]

Clearly the nonbanking financial world wanted a share of the speculative action in Wall Street, and by 1929, it was providing most of it. Even in 1926, when bank loans to brokers dipped, sources outside the banking system continued to increase their supplies of call loans. In 1932, when the dust had really settled over Wall Street, nonbank sources provided less than 6 percent of the depression-level loans to brokers. If stock prices rose from 1926 to 1929 because of "undue

Location by Automobile. Before the automobile, cities and towns were the economic and social centers for the surrounding countryside. People congregated there on Saturdays and holidays to shop and have fun (above). But the availability of the automobile and government-subsidized highways encouraged the development of outlying areas. Communities were replaced with housing tracts, shopping malls, and highway commercial strips. In an attempt to revitalize their communities, some cities rebuilt their downtowns into mall areas, but that failed to bring back commercial vitality. Suburban and exurban development continues to replace older communities.

Table 24.8 End of Year, Brokers' Loans, Bank and Nonbank 1923–32[a]

Year	Total	New York City Banks	Outside Banks	Nonbank Sources	Percentage Nonbank
1923	1580	720	410	450	28.5
1924	2230	1150	530	550	24.7
1925	3550	1450	1050	1050	29.6
1926	3290	1160	830	1300	39.5
1927	4430	1550	1050	1830	41.3
1928	6440	1640	915	3885	60.3
1929	4110	1200	460	2450	59.6
1930	2105	1280	215	610	29.0
1931	715	540	35	140	19.6
1932	430	335	20	75	17.4

[a] Amounts given are in thousands of dollars unless otherwise indicated.

Source: *Historical Statistics,* series X 547–50.

speculation," and such undue speculation was fueled by loans to stockbrokers, most of the blame lies outside the banking community.

The Investment Trusts

The investment trust was similar to the modern mutual fund. The trust sold its own securities, stocks, and bonds to the public, using the proceeds to purchase other stock. The newly acquired stocks could be those of their investment trusts; one trust could therefore own controlling interest in other trusts. Since stocks then (and now) were commonly purchased on **margin** (the buyer puts up some of his or her own cash, and the broker, the rest) and since the market was rising, investment trusts were, for a short time, a remarkable way to make money.

Galbraith's amusing and carefully researched book describes the affairs of several investment trusts. American Founders Group, started in 1922 with $500, by 1929 grew to thirteen companies with holdings in excess of $1 *billion,* "which may well have been the largest volume of assets ever controlled by an original outlay of $500."[29] In 1928 there were perhaps 186 investment trusts; in 1929 alone, 265 new ones were formed. This rapid growth was one manifestation of the bubble on the boom. In 1927 the investment trusts sold $400 million of securities to the public to finance their operations; in 1929, $3 *billion.* For more history

of the investment trusts in the 1920s, see Galbraith's illuminating Chapter III.

The investment trusts were filled with perhaps more than a fair share of chicanery, but they served as a funnel to divert money into stocks and to exhilarate the market. These two sources of extraordinary diversion, nonbanking money in brokers' loans and investment trusts—added to the amounts put into stocks directly by private investors, banks, and speculators—served to drive an already powerful stock-market upsurge into a roaring boom in prices. By October 1929, of brokers' loans totaling $8.5 billion, only $1.8 billion came from the banking system.

Great as the stock-market boom had been up to 1928, the first nine months of 1929 provided an impressive balloon, from which the air began to escape in September.

Boom and Crash

If one takes July 1926 as a base month, with the monthly stock-market index of prices set at 100, a year later it was 112, and by July 1928, it stood at 148.[30] In two years one could have realized a 48-percent capital gain and could have received dividends as well. Even California real estate in the 1970s was not a better buy than that. But there was more to come. From July 1928, the index rose another 45 points to 193. One would have nearly doubled his or her money in less than three years from the summer of 1926 *and* realized a gain of 30 percent by midsummer.

Apart from veiled warnings about inevitability, the stock market must have looked very good indeed. After all, as we have seen, the economy seemed sound enough. The market churned around the January 1929 level and then took off again. By September 1929 the index stood at 216, up a further 12 percent in a couple of months. The man or woman who bought $1000 worth of those stocks in the summer of 1926 had $2160 by September 1929. In slightly more than three years his or her capital gain alone was 116 percent, and there were dividends as well.

For investment in safe, over-the-counter stocks, the investor's world of 1926–29 must have seemed hard to beat. True, there were signs of weakness in the "real" economy by September, but those signs and portents were only a few months old (auto sales down, industrial production down), were mixed, and had existed in other years.[31] The highest authorities, from the new president (and the outgoing one) down to the Harvard Economic Society, were touting the general soundness of the economy.[32]

There was a short setback in February 1929 after the Federal Reserve (worried about the scale of brokers' loans) publicly warned that it would not support bank loans for stock speculation nor would it stop British gold losses after the Bank of England discount rate was raised 22 percent, from 4.5 to 5.5 in a single step.[33]

On March 26, 1929 there was a paralyzing moment, the largest day (most shares traded) on record, when 8.2 million shares traded *while prices moved down sharply,* and the call loan rate hit 20 percent (an average of 1.7 percent a month—not enough to deter a serious speculator who, on recent history, could expect to earn more). However, the moment passed, and stability was regained. Gold was flowing into the New York banks, exports were strong. In August the Federal Reserve raised its own discount rate to 6 percent, but there was no strong market response to the increase.

Money was tight if you considered such interest rates against commodity prices or the cost of living index. But in the stock market, which had risen nearly 9 percent since January, 6 percent was still a *negative* rate of interest. It still paid to borrow, if you were borrowing from the Fed. For brokers, though, higher interest rates at the peak of the boom no doubt caused some alarm. Galbraith reports that *inside* the Federal

Reserve System, authorities believed by August that a crash was coming but took no further action to offset it. Nor did they probably believe that they should do anything to stop it in those days: A "corrective" in an inflated market was considered a healthy thing.

On 3 September the market reached its all-time high. Two days later, Babson made his celebrated prediction of a crash, and on that day, 5 September there was a bad break in the market. It then began to follow a disturbingly wobbly course, seen in retrospect as a "sure sign" that the boom was over. On Saturday, 19 October, a half-day for trading, the market broke sharply again. On Monday, 21 October, there were more losses. Fear began to build.

Thursday, 24 October, saw 12.9 million shares traded; panic reigned briefly but was stemmed by a flamboyant show of "organized support" from New York financiers. Two more irregular trading days carried U.S. financial history to Monday, 28 October 1929. On that day, more than 9 million shares traded hands, and prices fell in one day more than during the entire previous bad week. Monday was the brink of disaster, which struck the next day.

Raging panic came back on Black Tuesday, 29 October 1929. More than 16 million shares were dumped. The *New York Times* index of stock prices fell 43 points, wiping out in a single day the wealth accumulated in the previous year. Some stocks were down 50 percent from September levels by the end of the day.

Support failed everywhere. **Margin calls** (demands by brokers for more cash from their clients) went out; there were recorded examples of no bids at all for stocks offered for sale. The heavily leveraged firms, the investment trusts, were devastated. Goldman Sachs Trading Corporation, the most glamorous of the investment trusts, was down 42 percent in one day. Tens of thousands of accounts were closed out as margin calls failed, and brokers' loans were called. In U.S. financial history, 29 October 1929 was a day like 7 December 1941 (the attack on Pearl Harbor)—a rare one-day experience that divided one epoch from another.

Partial recoveries came in subsequent weeks, followed by sickening slides. By December, the index (1926 = 100) had fallen to 147, down 32 percent from September. A year later, it was 102, down 53 percent from September 1929. The monthly index found its low of 34 in July 1932, down more than 85 percent from its monthly peak in 1929. An investor who, in

September 1929, had $2116 from a $1000 investment in September 1926, now had $360.

Galbraith gives examples of stocks that declined 100 percent by 1932. By then, general economic depression had overtaken the country, and Franklin Roosevelt and the New Deal were in the wings of American history.

EXPLANATIONS

Was there any believable explanation for the Great Crash of 1929? Galbraith lists five major sources of weakness that laid the groundwork: (a) unequal income distribution; (b) unstable business organization at the corporate level; (c) weak banking structure; (d) international financial troubles; (e) ignorance of financial and economic realities by the nation's leaders.[34] But these factors need not have produced a crash in 1929 or any other time, for that matter. The same may be said of a (similar) list posited by Robert Keller, who also examined technological change and the increasing share of income going to investment capital in the 1920s.[35]

If one studies the history of business cycles and the explanations of earlier financial crises and panics, the explanations for the 1929 crash are not new, not unique, not convincing.[36] It happened under the circumstances of the 1920s, but there were other financial panics: 1825, 1836, 1847, 1857, 1866, 1873, 1882, 1893, 1901, 1903, 1907, 1920–21. They happened under different, but equally compelling, circumstances in the United States and in Europe. Economists have subsequently placed blame on all likely targets for those disasters.

It is frustrating that a single villain cannot be named, once and for all, for 1929 (or any other time). In light of this, it is worthwhile for a moment to consider the opinions of Samuel Jones Loyd (later, Lord Overstone) in 1837, and then ask what has been learned.

There had been a financial panic in London in 1836, blamed then upon unsound trading practices with America. The Bank of England had been inept (it had run out of money), and its governor, J. Horsley Palmer, had written and published an essay on the event, *The Causes and Consequences of the Pressure on the Money Market and the Recent Commercial Distress.* Samuel Jones Loyd, an English banker, was moved to answer Palmer's pamphlet with one of his own, *Reflec-*

tions Suggested by a Perusal of Mr. J. Horsley Palmer's Pamphlet on the Causes and Consequences of the Pressure of the Money Market. In it Loyd set down his impression of the business cycle in words that have never been surpassed for descriptive generalists:

> The history of what we are in the habit of calling the "state of trade" is an instructive lesson. We find it subject to various conditions which are periodically returning; it revolves apparently in an established cycle. First we find it in a state of quiescence,—next improvement,—growing confidence,—prosperity,—excitement,—overtrading,—convulsion,—pressure,—stagnation,—distress,—ending again in quiescence.[37]

The 1929 crash no doubt made investors "feel poor." The losses, sometimes called merely "paper losses," were real enough to those who absorbed them. Even if initially no factory closed because stock prices fell, those who bought stock in such factories following the crash on the basis of secure wealth already accumulated, would come to find they were no longer wealthy. In the future, their ability to invest would be impaired.

In October 1929 alone, the reduction in capital value of the nation's stock portfolio was $15 billion, in a year when GNP was $104.6 billion. October 1929 losses were equal to more than 14 percent of that year's GNP. The 1987 stock market meltdown wiped out "paper" wealth of an even greater proportion of 1987 GNP. Yet 1988 proved to be a reasonably good year, with a small rise in real GNP over 1987. History does not necessarily repeat itself—one hopes. By 1933 the estimated reduction in stock values from the 1929 peak was $85 billion, about 82 percent of the value of 1929 GNP. By 1933 the outcome was an unprecedented economic disaster.

Alexander Field has tied the 1920s stock-market boom to the onset of the Great Depression in a different way. Field argues that the emphasis on the rise in stock prices (334 percent between August 1921 and the September 1929 peak) has overshadowed an even more remarkable expansion in volume (1478 percent over the same period). The greater volume reflected increased public participation in the market (and an anticipation of future participation) and produced a major increase in the transactions demand for money. The Federal Reserve reinforced this increase by raising the discount rate in 1928–29 to slow market speculation.

Since wholesale prices fell by an average of 1 percent a year beginning in 1922, *real* interest rates in 1928–29 reached remarkably high levels, levels that were not seen again until the early 1980s, levels that choked demand in those sectors of the economy dependent on interest financing, new construction, and automobiles. This started an economic downturn, which was reinforced by the stock-market crash in October 1929. Field argues that, had attention been paid to the rise in the transactions demand for money, the Federal Reserve might not have pursued a tight-money policy in 1928–29, and there might then have been a softer landing for the economy. Instead, there was the crash and the long decline in real economic activity that ensued to the very bottom of the depression in 1932.[38]

Decisions to consume and save are supposed by economists to be partly based upon confidence in the future, or lack thereof. The stock-market losses made former investors feel conservative about the future. They saved from current incomes, causing current demand for output of goods and services to slow down. Savings grew, inventories of unsold goods piled up, new orders dropped, factories closed, and men and women were laid off their jobs.

The deeper psychological consequences of 1929 cannot be measured quantitatively. The "New Era" of the 1920s became a bad joke as the economy ground its way down to 1932. It was replaced by the "New Deal," with its implications that the cards would be shuffled and dealt again and that the game of American economic life would be started afresh.

Cultural historians noted the change from the *milieu* of *The Great Gatsby* to the *Grapes of Wrath*. Prosperity was not seen again until World War II, when the economy, its people, and government had been further transformed by the scourge of the Great Depression. Government policy changes at first attempted to correct some of the weaknesses noted by Galbraith but soon had bigger fish to fry: how to get the American economy to grow. Between 1930 and 1940, the economy could not grow enough to employ its own labor force; something almost unknown in American history over so long a period of years.

Notes

1. Robert Lampman, *The Share of Top Wealth-Holders in National Wealth 1922–1956* (1962), p. 228, Table 107.
2. Lampman, p. 236, Table 111.
3. Jeffrey Williamson and Peter Lindert, *American Inequality: A Macroeconomic History* (1981), Ch. 12.
4. Lampman, *The Share of Top Wealth-Holders in National Wealth 1922–1956* (1962), p. 235.
5. Charles Holt, "Who Benefited from the Prosperity of the Twenties?" *EEH,* July 1977, p. 283; and Gene Smiley, "Did Incomes for Most of the Population Fall from 1923 Through 1929?" *JEH,* March 1983.
6. George Soule, *Prosperity Decade* (1947).
7. Martha L. Olney, *Buy Now, Pay Later: Advertising, Credit, and Consumer Durables in the 1920s* (1991).
8. Elmus Wicker, "A Reconsideration of Federal Reserve Monetary Policy During the 1920–21 Depression," *JEH,* June 1966.
9. David Brody, *Workers in Industrial America* (1980), p. 62.
10. The 1920–21 downturn has been attributed by John D. Pilgrim mainly to tight money in, "The Upper Turning Point in 1920: A Reappraisal," *EEH,* Spring 1974. For an argument that supply bottlenecks played a role in capping the postwar expansion, see K. D. Roose, "The Production Ceiling and the Turning Point of 1920," *AER,* June 1958.
11. For an account of this episode and the Fed's policies at the time, see Wicker, "A Reconsideration of Federal Reserve Policy During the 1920–21 Depression."
12. Joseph Swanson and Samuel Williamson, "Estimates of National Product and Income 1919–1941," *EEH,* Fall 1972, show 1922 as the trough year in GNP data, but not in national income, personal income, or unemployment; see Table 3, p. 59.
13. Harry T. Oshima, "The Growth of U.S. Factor Productivity: The Significance of New Technologies in the Early Decades of the Twentieth Century," *JEH,* March 1984.
14. An interesting discussion of the farmers' appeal to the federal government can be found in Elizabeth Hoffman and Gary Libecap, "Institutional Choice and the Development of US Agricultural Policies in the 1920s," *Journal of Economic History,* June 1991.
15. Martin L. Fausold, "President Hoover's Farm Policies 1929–1933," *AgHist,* April 1977.
16. Lee J. Alston, "Farm Foreclosures in the United States During the Interwar Period," *JEH,* December 1983.

17. For a more detailed analysis of the farm problem in the 1920s, see Thomas Johnson, "Postwar Optimism and the Rural Financial Crisis of the 1920s," *EEH,* Winter 1973–74.

18. A. F. Burns and W. C. Mitchell, *Measuring Business Cycles* (1947).

19. Lloyd Mercer and Douglas Morgan, "Housing Surplus in the 1920s: Another Evaluation," *EEH,* Spring 1973.

20. Soule, *Prosperity Decade.*

21. He simply closed down from May 1927 to January 1928, throwing thousands out of work. Ford had been producing a single car, the Model T, since before World War I. Jonathan Hughes, *The Vital Few* (1986), pp. 335–36.

22. All output data from *Historical Statistics,* series Q 148, P 302; and M 93, 138.

23. Jonathan Hughes, *Fluctuations in Trade, Industry and Finance* (Oxford: Clarendon Press, 1960), p. 273.

24. Hughes, p. 20.

25. Quoted, John Kenneth Galbraith, *The Great Crash* (1979), p. 1.

26. Galbraith, pp. 73–74.

27. Galbraith, Chs. II and III.

28. Charles P. Kindleberger, *The World in Depression, 1929–1939* (1973), p. 113.

29. Galbraith, *The Great Crash,* p. 52.

30. Monthly League of Nations data, printed in Kindleberger, *The World in Depression,* p. 111.

31. Lloyd Mercer and Douglas Morgan, "The American Automobile Industry: Investment Demand, Capacity, and Capacity Utilization 1921–40," *JPE,* November-December 1972. The drop in auto sales in the second half of 1929 was not due to market saturation.

32. Galbraith, *The Great Crash,* pp. 127–28.

33. The daily events described here are taken from Galbraith's account, pp. 78–112.

34. Galbraith, pp. 157–65.

35. Robert Keller, "Factor Income Distribution in the United States During the 1920s: A Reexamination of Fact and Theory," *JEH,* March 1973.

36. For example, see Lance E. Davis, Jonathan Hughes, and Duncan McDougall, *American Economic History,* (Homewood, IL: Irwin, 1965), 2nd ed., Ch. 23, for a round-up of explanations. Also see R. C. O. Matthews, *The Business Cycle* (1959) and Gottfried Haberler, *Prosperity and Depression* (Geneva: League of Nations, 1937).

37. Hughes, *Fluctuations,* p. 229.

38. Alexander J. Field, "A New Interpretation of the Onset of the Great Depression," *JEH,* June 1984.

Suggested Readings

Articles

Alston, Lee J. "Farm Foreclosures in the United States During the Interwar Period." *Journal of Economic History,* vol. XLIII, no. 4, December 1983.

Fausold, Martin L. "President Hoover's Farm Policies 1929–1933." *Agricultural History,* vol. 51, no. 2, April 1977.

Hoffman, Elizabeth, and Libecap, Gary. "Institutional Choice and the Development of US Agricultural Policies in the 1920s." *Journal of Economic History,* vol. 51, no. 2, June 1991.

Holt, Charles. "Who Benefited From the Prosperity of the Twenties?" *Explorations in Economic History,* vol. 14, no. 3, July 1977.

Johnson, Thomas. "Postwar Optimism and the Rural Financial Crisis of the 1920s." *Explorations in Economic History,* vol. 11, no. 2, Winter 1973–74.

Keller, Robert. "Factor Income Distribution in the United States During the 1920's: A Reexamination of Fact and Theory." *Journal of Economic History,* vol. XXXIII, no. 1, March 1973.

Mercer, Lloyd, and Morgan, Douglas. "Housing Surplus in the 1920's? Another Evaluation." *Explorations in Economic History,* vol. 10, no. 3, Spring 1973.

———. "The American Automobile Industry: Investment Demand, Capacity, and Capacity Utilization." *Journal of Political Economy,* vol. 80, no. 6, November-December 1972.

Oshima, Harry T. "The Growth of U.S. Factor Productivity: The Significance of New Technologies in the Early Decades of the Twentieth Century." *Journal of Economic History,* vol. XLIV, no. 1, March 1984.

Pilgrim, John D. "The Upper Turning Point of 1920: A Reappraisal." *Explorations in Economic History,* vol. 11, no. 3, Spring 1974.

Roose, K. D. "The Production Ceiling and the Turning Point of 1920." *American Economic Review,* vol. XLVIII, no. 3, June 1958.

Smiley, Gene. "Did Incomes for Most of the Population Fall From 1923 Through 1929?" *Journal of Economic History,* vol. XLII, no. 1, March 1983.

Swanson, Joseph, and Williamson, Samuel. "Estimates of National Product and Income, 1919–1941." *Explorations in Economic History,* vol. 10, no. 1, Fall 1972.

Wicker, Elmus. "A Reconsideration of Federal Reserve Monetary Policy During the 1920–21 Depression." *Journal of Economic History,* vol. XXVI, no. 2, June 1966.

Books

Barber, William J. *From the New Era to the New Deal: Herbert Hoover, The Economists, and American Economic Policy, 1921–1933.* New York: Cambridge University Press, 1985.

Brody, David. *Workers in Industrial America.* New York: Oxford University Press, 1980.

Burns, A. F., and Mitchell, W. C. *Measuring Business Cycles.* New York: National Bureau of Economic Research, 1947.

Galbraith, John Kenneth. *The Great Crash, 1929.* New York: Discus Books, 1979.

Hughes, Jonathan. *The Vital Few.* New York: Oxford University Press, 1986.

Kindleberger, Charles. *The World in Depression, 1929–1939.* Berkeley: University of California Press, 1973.

Lampman, Robert. *The Share of Top Wealth-Holders in National Wealth, 1922–56.* Princeton: Princeton University Press, 1962.

Matthews, R. C. O. *The Business Cycle.* Chicago: University of Chicago Press, 1959.

Olney, Martha L. *Buy Now, Pay Later: Advertising, Credit, and Consumer Durables in the 1920s.* Chapel Hill: University of North Carolina Press, 1991.

Soule, George. *Prosperity Decade.* New York: Holt Rinehart, 1947.

Williamson, Jeffrey, and Lindert, Peter. *American Inequality: A Macroeconomic History.* New York: Academic Press, 1981.

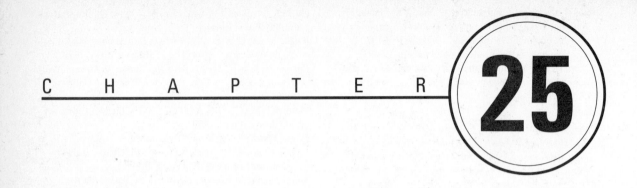

CHAPTER 25

The Great Depression and the New Deal

After the 1929 crash, the economy began a long descent, year after dismal year, to the bleak winter of 1932–33. Nine thousand banks failed. Unemployment rose to a quarter of the labor force when millions could find no work. Bread lines, worn-out clothes, the destitute living in cardboard hovels in Central Park, roads filled with vagabonds—these are the images of that period in our history.

PERSPECTIVE

What number, or set of numbers, can best describe the impact of the Great Depression of the 1930s? What story most vividly evokes the feeling of it? Between 1929 and 1932, manufacturing output fell by half. Railway passenger-car output fell from 2202 units in 1929 to a mere 7 in 1932; automobile production fell 75 percent (from 4.5 million to 1.1 million). The Great Depression was a time when hamburgers were two for 5 cents, and people could not afford to buy them; when people would work for 10 cents an hour, and employers could not profit from their labor; when the (surviving) banks were filled with idle reserves and borrowing did not occur, although interest rates were below 1 percent

per annum; when agricultural produce rotted in the fields, and people went hungry.

Consider Figure 25.1. Marriage rates, birth rates, and even *divorce rates* plunged. The marriage and divorce rates recovered by the mid-1930s; however, because the birth rate was declining in the long run, the recovery was muted. Even so, the low birth rates of 1933 and 1936, 18.4 per 1000 of population per annum, were not reached again until the 1960s (when the long-term decline quickly resumed, aided by legal abortion). The initial shock of the depression sapped the nation at its vital core. It was disaster.[1]

After 1933 the American economy was never the same. The terror of that time was burned into the collective memory, and its results were enshrined in the statute books as social insurance and federal responsibility for the poor and unemployed. The nation turned to the federal government for collective solutions to economic and social problems on a scale not known before, except perhaps in the World War I command economy. Faith in unmixed American capitalism was undermined, apparently for good. Even at the top levels of American industry and finance, hope was lost. Herman Krooss, in his book *Executive Opinion,* recorded the shattered capitalist morale and efforts to

Figure 25.1 Vital Signs, 1929–40

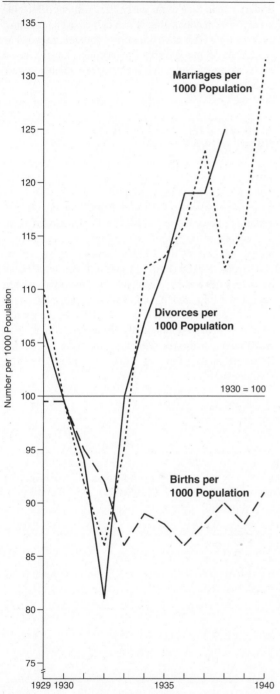

Source: *Historical Statistics*, series B 5, 214, 216.

sustain, with overblown oratory, a faith that was lost for good.[2]

Franklin Delano Roosevelt stayed in the White House for the rest of the 1930s and most of World War II primarily because of the reputation he had gained as the man who "saved the country" from the grip of the depression. We will see in this chapter that the extent of that salvation is ambiguous. What was clear, however, was that the contract of 1789 held; there was no revolution. The economy was changed dramatically, but the political wisdom of the first 150 years held.

The national state constructed by the colonial founders was not destroyed by the economic disaster of the 1930s. This was perhaps the ultimate tribute. And it meant that, however changed by the New Deal, the social contract based upon settled private rights in property and free elections conducted by the calendar would remain the American republic's constitution. It would be tested again and again in succeeding decades, but no test that came in the next half century compared to the one of the 1930s.

There is probably no historical subject that can raise so much heat among economists, even to this day, as the Great Depression. Every part of it is still the subject of controversy. Why did the economy contract for so long (1929 to 1932)?[3] Did government policy help or hinder the recovery attempt? Was the New Deal effort to reorganize the country's economic institutions an admirable act of needed reform or a misguided attempt that derailed the normal processes of adjustment? Was the long depression in employment due to failure of the private sector or a normal response to continuous disruption by government action? Did the New Deal "save" American capitalism or transform it into a permanent **mixed economy** (i.e., dependent upon a strong government role), forever dependent upon the whims of politics?[4]

Real GNP in 1930 was about 10 percent below the 1929 figure; in current prices, the decline was 12.5 percent. As Table 24.2 documented, the 1920–21 decline of nominal GNP was 24 percent, but the *real*

The country's plunging economic fortunes between 1929 and 1933 even cut the divorce rate, as well as those for marriages and live births per 1000 of population. Whereas marriages and divorces soon recovered, live births remained depressed for the rest of the decade as compared to figures for the late 1920s.

decline was much less (in fact, less than 9 percent). There was a very sharp price adjustment in the 1921 recession.

Skilled observers in 1930 no doubt would have noted this difference. But, they might not have drawn the conclusion that the real decline in 1929–30 was more than that of 1920–21 *because* the price decline was less. This is the "Austrian" view, one of several interpretations that will be discussed later.[5] What the observers certainly would not have anticipated was that it would be six years before even the 1930 level of money income would be regained. That kind of experience in this country could not have been anticipated in 1930. It had never been known before.

Instead of suffering in 1930 the temporary setback of a recession, as happened in 1920–21, the American economy teetered on the brink of the Great Depression. The difference was like that between an irrigation ditch and the Grand Canyon. The coming experience was as close to a "collapse" as the American economy would ever come. The terrifying slide to 1933 and the failure to find the means of recovery until the Japanese attacked Pearl Harbor have haunted Americans and their elected representatives ever since. Whatever the troubles of modern **stagflation** (inflation combined with stagnant real output), not even the most radical exponents of deflation have advocated a return to the deflationary experience of the early 1930s. In the 1930s the great forces of expansion, which in the past had seemed ever resilient after each temporary setback, failed. The American people and their government faced a novel problem: an economy that seemed permanently lamed, defective.

1929–41: THE STATISTICAL BARE BONES

What happened in the early 1930s was most extraordinary. Money income, measured as GNP, fell about 46 percent between 1929 and 1933; real income, by about 30 percent (see Table 25.1). Unemployment, 3.2 percent of the labor force in 1929, reached an estimated 25 percent in 1933. Counting those underemployed—locked into agricultural seasonal work between 1929 and 1933 or in jobs that would have been abandoned for better-paying work except for the terror of long-term joblessness—even the 1933 figure for unemployment was undoubtedly an underestimate. The unemployment figures refined by the work of Stanley Lebergott include those on work-relief programs from 1933 onward.[6]

Table 25.1 Unemployment, GNP, and Federal Finance, 1929–41

Year	Unemployed Percentage of Labor Force	Gross National Product Current Prices ($ Billions)	Gross National Product 1958 Prices ($ Billions)	1958 Prices per Capita	Receipts	Federal Expenditures ($ Billions)	Federal Surplus (+) Deficit (−)
1929	3.2	103.1	203.6	$167.1	3.8	2.9	+0.9
1930	8.7	90.4	183.5	149.0	4.0	3.1	+0.9
1931	15.9	75.8	169.3	136.4	3.2	4.1	−1.0
1932	23.6	58.0	144.2	115.4	2.0	4.8	−2.7
1933	24.9	55.6	141.5	112.6	2.1	4.7	−2.6
1934	21.7	65.1	154.3	122.0	3.1	6.5	−3.3
1935	20.1	72.2	169.5	133.1	3.8	6.3	−2.4
1936	16.9	82.5	193.0	150.6	4.2	7.6	−3.5
1937	14.3	90.4	203.2	157.6	5.6	8.4	−2.8
1938	19.0	84.7	192.9	148.4	7.0	7.2	−0.1
1939	17.2	90.5	209.4	159.8	6.6	9.4	−2.9
1940	14.6	99.7	227.2	172.0	6.9	9.6	−2.7
1941	9.9	124.5	263.7	197.7	9.2	14.0	−4.8

Source: *Historical Statistics*, series D 86, F 1, 3, 4, Y 339–41.

Unemployment

It was argued at the time (and still is) that if people had been willing to work for lower wages in the private sector, the federal government's work-relief programs would not have been necessary. At this distance in time, such a point has some interesting theoretical attractions. But by 1933, when the first federal work-relief programs were launched, men and women were desperate. They had been promised that prosperity was "just around the corner" for years. Even with the eventual recovery of output, unemployment stayed high. In real terms (1958 prices), the 1929 level of GNP had been regained by 1937. Real income per capita was nearly at 1929 levels in 1937. But unemployment remained at extraordinary levels. Then came a new recession in 1938, in part engendered by the federal government's own incompetence. In 1940, when real per capita GNP at last *exceeded* that of 1929, unemployment was still more than *four times* the 1929 rate.

Federal Finance and 1938

Federal receipts fell to a low of $2.0 billion in 1932, recovered slowly to 1937, and then leveled off. Expenditures rose until 1937, then dropped 14 percent to the 1938 low. That episode was accompanied by a sharp decline in the deficit because the monetary officials feared an inflationary explosion. John Maynard Keynes, upon hearing of it, said, "They profess to fear that which they dare not hope."

Between 1933 and 1937, money income rose by 63 percent, and real income by more than 43 percent. Prices made some recovery, making fear of inflation perhaps not entirely laughable, except that President Roosevelt had gone to fantastic (and unconstitutional) lengths from 1933 to 1935 to try to *raise prices*. Just as the highest mountain range on earth lies unnoticed at the bottom of the ocean (in the Philippines), that remarkable expansion of GNP between 1933 and 1937 lay submerged beneath the Great Depression and never got the chance to surface. Measured in the crudest Keynesian terms, the potential expansionary impact of the deficit was sharply reduced, which helped plunge the economy into a mid-depression recession in 1938.

Consider the data in Table 25.2. If we take the federal budget deficit as a proportion of total federal expenditures, 1932 and 1933 are the most expansionary

years—they were less financed by tax collections (which merely transfer spending power from individuals and companies to the government) than later years. These expenditures were in large part the doing of the outgoing Hoover administration. FDR had promised to balance the budget if elected. He tried that tactic after the 1936 election when there were signs of a full recovery at hand. The deficits in 1937 and 1938 were sharply reduced (see Table 25.1) and, accordingly, added less to the spending stream. Wholesale prices fell 32 percent between 1929 and 1932, and consumer prices were down 24 percent. They both declined slightly in the 1938 downturn and never recovered the 1929 level before World War II. Manufacturing production fell a catastrophic 48 percent in that period but then recovered by 1937. In 1937 and 1938 the new social-security taxes began flowing to the Treasury, raising federal revenues substantially but reducing consumer expenditures: adding to the forces of contraction.[7] After the sharp setback in 1938, production came back again and by 1940 had surpassed all earlier levels.

Without considering other policies, it is clear that federal spending was (a) not consistently expansionary and (b) never produced a reduction in unemployment to 1929, or even 1930, levels. The depression was a

Table 25.2 Expansion Deficit, Money, Prices, and Industrial Production

	Surplus (+) or Deficit (−)[a]	M_1 ($ billions)	WPI	CDI	IMP[b]
			(1967 = 100)		
1929	+31	26.6	61.9	51.3	23
1930	+29	25.8	56.1	50.0	19
1931	24	24.1	47.4	45.6	15
1932	56	21.1	42.1	40.9	12
1933	55	19.9	42.8	38.8	14
1934	51	21.9	48.7	40.1	15
1935	38	25.9	52.0	41.1	18
1936	46	29.6	52.5	41.5	22
1937	33	30.9	56.1	43.0	23
1938	1	30.5	51.1	42.2	18
1939	31	34.1	50.1	41.6	22
1940	28	39.7	51.1	42.0	25
1941	34	46.5	56.8	44.1	32

[a] Surplus (+) or Deficit (−) as Percentage of Federal Expenditures.
[b] Index of Manufacturing Production.

Source: Table 25.1, *Historical Statistics,* series E 73, 135, P 13, X 414.

The Great Depression. In the 1930s economic depression and natural disasters combined to waste resources on the farm and in the city. Dustbowl farmers (above left, below left) abandoned the land. The cities were overwhelmed with an army of the "ill-housed, ill-fed, and ill-clothed" (Detroit, above right, and Seattle's shantytown, below right).

period of extraordinarily high unemployment throughout. The gyrations of fiscal policy were due in part to sheer ignorance and confusion in policy, as Herbert Stein emphasizes.[8]

We will consider the issues of monetary policy in more detail later. Here we need only note a few important aspects of the money supply data. M_1, the sum of demand deposits plus currency in circulation, declined slightly more than 20 percent between 1929 and 1932. This was less than the decline in wholesale prices and just slightly more than the drop in consumer prices. Questions of policy apart, as Peter Temin argues, the *money supply, M_1* defined as the command over real resources, was arguably as large in 1933 as it was in 1929![9]

Puzzles

Even with such a cursory introduction, it should be clear that understanding the Great Depression is no simple matter. Prices did come back after 1933, and so did manufacturing production. As we have seen in Table 25.2, M_1 rose 46 percent between 1933 and 1937, wholesale prices rose 33 percent, and manufacturing rose 64 percent. Moreover, GNP in current prices went up 63 percent, and real GNP, 43 percent in the same brief period. So, Keynes' jibe to the contrary, by 1937 the economy was showing extraordinary strength. Unemployment had fallen more than 42 percent from its peak in 1933. However, much was lost in the 1938 recession. After that, depression reigned again.

It seems clear that the 1933–37 expansion hardly qualified as a return to the flourishing economy of 1929 and that the bitter criticisms of federal policy suggesting the Great Depression was unnecessarily prolonged may have been justified, at least in part. Don Reading's brilliant paper indicates that the federal government's expenditures may *never* have had aggregate economic growth as a target. What seems clear from his work is that conservation of natural resources and courting of Senate votes may have been more important targets of federal expenditures than industrial advance.[10] Cary Brown's investigation of the New Deal's fiscal policy concluded that attempts to spur economic growth were not even made.[11]

What was tried was a series of policies to "reform" American capitalism so that 1929 would not happen again. These reforms ended American capitalism in its classical form by augmenting greatly the old regulatory techniques and by inventing some new ones to boot.[12]

THE NEW DEAL REFORMS

Franklin D. Roosevelt came to power with the expectation that a new administration would "do something" about the depression. In retrospect it is clear that there was much flailing about (called "experimentation"), giving the appearance, at least, of motion.

Emergency Measures

It is not easy today to catch the flavor of the Roosevelt administration's first 100 days. Most immediately pressing was the banking crisis.[13]

Banking had been a major growth sector, as we saw in Chapter 19. The number of commercial banks had increased from about 13,000 to more than 28,000 between 1900 and 1914. By 1921, there were 31,076 separate commercial banks. That number fell by 16,305 between 1921 and 1934, of which 14,820 were outright failures. In 1929, 659 banks closed their doors. In 1930, the number doubled to 1,352. After the banking crisis of 1930, more failed, and the number of closures in 1931 rose to 2,294.

In 1932, there was a decline in failures to 1,456, but as 1933 opened, a new wave of failures threatened, and state governors began declaring bank holidays *en masse*. People were going into banks and demanding their deposits back. With fractional-reserve banking, then as now, deposits are vastly in excess of the currency in the bank that is used to meet the daily outflow. By 4 March 1933, all banks in 38 states had suspended business. Two days later, Roosevelt finished the job by declaring a nationwide bank holiday, utilizing leftover powers from World War I legislation.[14] When the banks reopened under federal supervision, some 4000 more were found to be insolvent and were liquidated. Ben Bernanke concluded that so severe were the effects of the banking crisis in the early 1930s (especially 1931) that the banking system was simply unable to resume as a competent mechanism of intermediation for the rest of the 1930s.[15]

In the monetary sphere the Roosevelt administration made major changes. An Emergency Bank Act was passed 9 March 1933 which prohibited specie exports. The comptroller of the currency was empowered by executive order to reopen the (solvent) national banks with temporary federal deposit insurance. That stopped the bank runs. Since it was widely believed that "abuses" in Wall Street had created the 1929 stock-market panic and subsequent disasters, an emergency securities act was passed in 1933, placing Wall Street operators under the thumb of the Federal Trade Commission. These changes would be made more permanent in future legislation.

Such temporary measures were preliminary to a devaluation of the dollar. As we know, the United States had been legally a strict gold-standard country since 1900. Now it was believed that many advantages—increased exports, rising commodity prices, a return to full employment—would ensue if the Treasury's gold price were raised.[16] Indeed, "practical people" in this country, as well as theoretical economists, long believed that jiggering with the currency could solve broad social and economic problems. In his recent book, *Golden Fetters,* Barry Eichengreen argues that the operation of the interwar gold standard was a major cause of the severity of the worldwide depression from 1929 to 1933. His explanation lies in the international propagation mechanism, working via the fetters imposed by the gold standard. The "rules of the game" for defending that standard against adverse shocks transformed what otherwise would have been a serious downturn into worldwide depression.[17]

Roosevelt was standing squarely in the mainstream of American tradition on this one. On 5 April 1933, an executive order was issued forbidding gold hoarding. Arrangements were made to "call in" all U.S. monetary gold in circulation, first to the Federal Reserve Banks, then to the Treasury. On 20 April 1933, another executive order halted Treasury sales of gold for export. The United States was off the gold standard. The Reconstruction Finance Corporation then began buying gold at irregularly increasing prices. Of marginal interest is the fact that Roosevelt was receiving some less-than-expert advice on this policy. George Warren, an agricultural economist at Cornell University, was seized by the idea that you could raise all prices by raising the price of gold.[18] Unfortunately, Roosevelt went along with the professor since that advice was also acceptable to most members of Congress.

Apart from these pressing money matters, the primary emergency was the huge unemployment rate. Local unemployment relief funds were largely exhausted.

People looked to the federal government for help, and this introduced the prospect of a departure upon unknown seas. Hoover had not wanted such responsibility to slip to the federal government. Poor relief of nearly all kinds has been, by ancient tradition, a responsibility lodged with state and local authorities. Hoover made federal loan money available to the states for unemployment relief, but he opposed proposals for a permanent federal role that emanated from private business leaders, notably Gerard Swope (president of General Electric). Swope's 1931 plan for federal participation, socializing the problems of unemployment, was characterized by Hoover as "fascist and monopolistic." The "Swope Plan" was destined to reappear, modified, in the Social Security Act of 1935.[19]

Roosevelt rushed in where Hoover had dared not tread. On 20 May 1933, he asked Congress for $500 million as a *grant* to the states for emergency relief. The result, the Federal Emergency Relief Agency (FERA), headed by Harry Hopkins, was the predecessor of more permanent agencies to come. Hopkins immediately put millions of dollars into people's hands through "make-work" projects. He would become famous in the New Deal years for imaginative, work-producing, spending programs.

But these were stopgap measures. Soon enough a structure of federal participation and economic intervention emerged. The experience of the World War I command economy now became a handbook of strategies and tactics.

The First New Deal and the NIRA

The New Deal economic and social programs and institutions are usually treated in two parts, the First and Second New Deals, with a dividing frontier at roughly 1936—or 1935 in the opinions of some scholars. Most of the innovative movement appears before 1936, and a large part of that was declared unconstitutional by the U.S. Supreme Court. The election of 1936 has been considered the dividing line in New Deal history. But, as John Wallis argues, the Wagner Act, Social Security Act, and Emergency Relief Appropriations Act of 1935 were all really part of *renewed* New Deal vigor, and logically, on an economic basis, the Second New Deal really began in 1935.

The National Industrial Recovery Act (NIRA) was the most ambitious part of the First New Deal. It was inspired by the World War I experience, modified by the search for cooperative solutions to business problems that had been pursued by Hoover and others in the 1920s. These people believed that the World War I experience could be made into "industrial self-government" in peacetime, with only a modicum of federal power co-opted. Many economists, business-owners, and labor leaders, as well as government officials and politicians, had come to believe that competition between business firms was damaging, that it raised the levels of risk unnecessarily and made business failure and unemployment more likely (and worse) than they needed to be. By 1932, some American leaders were even looking admiringly at the Italian dictator Mussolini for inspiration, strange as that may seem now.

The NIRA was designed to reduce domestic competition.[20] Industrial self-government required that the threat of antitrust prosecution be lifted so that businesses could openly collude on matters of production, price-setting, and employment. The thinking was that businessowners themselves could plan production and prices that would be profitable, and a stable, full-employment economy would necessarily result. The NIRA would provide the system that, as we saw earlier, President Wilson ordered abandoned at the end of World War I.

One of Bernard Baruch's aides at the old War Industries Board, General Hugh Johnson, was made director of the National Recovery Administration (NRA) to run the program. Businesses were to organize themselves into identifiable industries, each with its own mutually agreed-upon "code of fair practice." The NRA was to have three advisory boards, representing management, labor, and "the public." In Section 7A of the NIRA, workers in NRA firms were given the right to bargain collectively with their employers through agents of their own choosing—unions.

The experiment, although a novel one, was short-lived. It was signed into law 16 June 1933, and within a year 450 codes were written. By May 1935, when the Supreme Court threw out the NIRA (for excessive delegation of power by Congress), 550 industry codes had been adopted.[21] By then, Roosevelt was ready to let it die. The politicians realized that it was an expanding morass of nondirectional regulation. Industrial production made a significant recovery only after the NRA was abolished. About 80 percent of nonagricultural industry was codified, and more than 1000 "unfair" trade practices (i.e., competitive techniques) were identified and prohibited in the codes. The spirit of the NRA was stated by General Johnson, a former cavalry officer:

> The very heart of the New Deal is the principle of concerted action, in industry and agriculture, under government supervision, looking to a balanced economy—as opposed to the murderous doctrine of savage and wolfish competition and rugged individualism . . . dog-eat-dog and devil take the hindmost.[22]

Two parts of the NRA were destined to live, the National Labor Board and the Public Works Administration. There had been a War Labor Board in World War I to arbitrate labor disputes. Many business leaders remembered it fondly and were instrumental in reviving it as part of the NRA. When, in the National Labor Relations Act (Wagner Act) of 1935, Section 7A of the NIRA was rewritten, the Labor Board became the National Labor Relations Board, and it has remained a central force in federal involvement in U.S. labor relations. The PWA, under Harold Ickes, lasted until World War II.

The AAA of 1933

Another early New Deal scheme to solve long-standing problems was the 1933 Agricultural Adjustment Act (AAA). It too was thrown out by the Supreme Court (in 1936), but parts were immortalized in 1938 when the second AAA was written without the offending tax on food processors.[23] A central Populist demand had been that the federal government should provide low-interest loans to farmers on the collateral of stored crops.[24]

People were hungry due to lack of money to buy food, but farm prices actually fell by more than 50 percent between 1929 and 1933. As Roger Ransom points out, the number of farm families did not decline in that short interval, so farm income per capita was reduced by as much as two-thirds.[25] The food growers were desperate for income. Lacking any way to raise demand significantly, Congress opted to authorize a massive reduction in supply in order to raise farm income through hoped-for price increases. By 1933, there was already a year's supply of cotton on hand, and wheat inventories were three times normal. The scheme adopted was to restore farm prices to "parity"—to the levels where the ratio of farm to nonfarm prices recovered the average of those prices in the period 1909–1914. In a famous gesture, 6 million piglets were slaughtered in 1933 to reduce pork supplies.

In the newly created Commodity Credit Corporation (1933) farmers could get loans on stored crops from a quasi-governmental agency—the Populist "sub-Treasury" scheme at long last. Also, the government bought crops outright to remove food from the markets. Farmers were paid not to grow crops, to take land out of production. Restrictions on output, even for on-the-farm use, were agreed upon.[26]

In addition, other government agencies attempted to help farm families, socially as well as financially. The Farm Credit Act launched the Farm Credit Administration (FCA) in 1934, an agency designed to loan farmers money against the collateral of their real property on more liberal terms than had been achieved by the Federal Land Banks. The FCA would live to become one of the largest lending institutions of any kind in the country. Another project was much less successful. One of Mrs. Roosevelt's favorite schemes was the resettlement of the urban unemployed on farms to achieve partial self-sufficiency. It did not work well but was tried by the Farm Security Administration, a New Deal agency headed by Rexford Tugwell, a member of the original Roosevelt "Brain Trust."[27]

An integral part of farm policy was conservation and reclamation, as drought in the 1930s conspired with deficient markets to segment farm misery. The high plains were turned into the "Dust Bowl." The Tennessee Valley Authority, organized around the dam built at Muscle Shoals in 1916 on the Tennessee River, was the center-piece of a nationwide conservation and reclamation effort.[28] In addition, after the Supreme Court's adverse ruling on the first AAA, the Soil Conservation and Domestic Allotment Act passed Congress, a measure which allowed the Department of Agriculture to pay farmers to restrict planting under the guise of conservation.[29]

The Financial Reforms

After the first 100 days and the emergency legislation, the Roosevelt administration dug in. Reforms of older institutions remained high on the agenda, but there were some basic new departures, too.

Reform of the old remained centered on the financial system. In 1933 the Glass-Steagall Act separated commercial banks from most of their securities business.[30] In 1934 the Securities Exchange Act was passed, setting up the Securities and Exchange Commission (SEC) to control the capital markets. A year later, the Public Utilities Holding Company Act placed federal restrictions for the first time on public utility financial structures and practice, and placed them under the SEC's regulation. In 1935 the Federal Deposit Insurance Corporation replaced the temporary arrangements of the 1933 Banking Act.[31] Marriner S. Eccles, a millionaire Utah banker, was the author of the 1935 Bank Act which restructured the Federal Reserve System.[32] The (renamed) Board of Governors was given discretionary controls over bank reserves and margin requirements for loans against securities. The Governors' Committee, innovated by Benjamin Strong in the 1920s, was now moved to Washington; it was renamed the Federal Open Market Committee and had twelve members, seven of whom were to be the governors themselves. The secretary of the Treasury and the comptroller of the currency were removed from government of the Fed. The monetary power was now consolidated at the Federal Reserve System's headquarters in Washington.

The Government as Employer

Direct work relief had been authorized under FERA. In a sense this was a dramatic departure since it was an overt acceptance by the federal government of responsibility for unemployment. Men and women were set to work on government projects *because* they could not find employment in the private sector.

Table 25.3 shows the primary direct employment vehicles of the New Deal. These expenditures were primarily investments in human capital and remain to this day as models of alternatives to unemployment. Twenty percent of New Deal expenditures were for employment. Although *millions* worked in these projects, they never employed enough people to do more than moderate the depression unemployment levels. The New Deal make-work schemes, for all their energy and innovation, were never a real substitute for private-sector employment. In 1938, when expenditures were authorized to employ 4 million, that was still a mere 10 percent of the civilian labor force. The unemployment rate was 19 percent that year. FERA was the first federal agency ever to include blanket relief of all kinds to the needy. The federal programs in Table 25.3 were nearly all matching grant schemes with the states, and involved state-level control of expenditures—to whom, how much. As Professor John Wallis points out, the actual counting of Congressional authorizations, grants made to the states, and total expenditures remains to be done. The numbers in Table 25.3 are the best available estimates. The NYA is included in the table as part of WPA grants and earnings. Of the federal grants to the states of $15.3 billion in 1937–39, only some $10.4 billion (about two-thirds) went directly for work relief. The PWA's constructions did not employ persons who were on relief. It is estimated in another source that from 1933 to 1941 about $15.1 billion in total went directly for work relief.[33]

Labor Law

The Wagner Act and the Social Security Act were lasting social innovations of the First New Deal. The Wagner Act (National Labor Relations Act) of 1935 was a federal effort to cut through the mass of conflicting law and practice that was discussed in Chapter 21. The 1931 Norris-LaGuardia Act had restricted the use of court injunctions to halt strikes. Section 7A of the NIRA had mandated collective bargaining in the code industries. The Wagner Act was a rewriting and expansion of NIRA's Section 7A. It produced a wave of unionization in the mass-production industries and the establishment of the Congress of Industrial Organizations (CIO), while setting the basic structure and rights of organized labor for the next half century. Under its terms, labor had the right to organize, elect (by secret ballot) its own bargaining agents, and bargain collectively. Employers were forbidden to interfere with the process—that is, to discharge or otherwise punish employees for union activity. The National Labor Relations Board was established and given the authority to judge and arbitrate the outcomes.

So much for the Law of Master and Servant. The Wagner Act was the outcome of a history that goes all the way back to earliest colonial laws rooted in the Elizabethan *Statute of Artificers and Apprentices*. The state was always involved in labor relations; compulsion was always there in some form. Belief in the notion that the "wage contract" was ever a free bargain between equals, like any other contract, is either naive or a pretense. For most of American history, law and the state stood on the side of real property in the wage bargain. The slow transformation to 1935 represented democracy at work. When it paid politicians to shift the supreme political instrument, the apparatus of the state, to the side of labor, they did so. Votes made law, indirectly. Organized labor since 1935 has remained secure under the shield of the Wagner Act (as amended). Complaints heard in the 1970s against union power to raise union wages excessively and contribute to inflationary pressures were at root a complaint against the Wagner Act. By the end of the 1980s loss of union power was blamed by the unions on the NLRB's feckless performance during the Reagan regime; either way, the federal power was involved in the wage bargain, apparently for good.

Social Security

The 1935 Social Security Act was a further federal assumption of power and responsibility. As we know, Anglo-American society had long provided a minimal "security net" for its indigent poor. The technique was traditionally a local affair—township- and county-supported almshouses, poor farms, and so forth.[34] The old system was never exceedingly generous; Stanley Lebergott estimates that traditionally such transfer payments made by local governments were from 20 to

Table 25.3   Major New Deal Agencies: Grants to States and Work Relief Earnings 1933–39[a]

National Grants to States		Work Relief Earnings
FERA	3,017	1,238
CCC	2,622	1,734
CWA	807	718
WPA	6,804	6,586
FSA	273	100
PWA	1,791	—
		10,376

[a] Amounts given are in millions of dollars.

Sources: U.S. Office of Government Reports, Vol. 10 (Washington, 1941); *Final Statistical Report of the Federal Emergency Relief Administration* (Washington, 1942), Table 10, p. 38; *Security, Relief, and Relief Policies*, National Resources Planning Board (Washington, 1943), Appendix 10, pp. 560–61. We are indebted to John Wallis for this table.

30 percent of the income earnings of common labor.[35] Workers injured in their employments had to sue their employers for negligence. The Social Security Act of 1935 was an attempt to correct these defects. It provided (a) an income for the aged, (b) a scheme for unemployment compensation funds to be prepaid by the employers of labor, and (c) categorical relief aids to the aged, blind, and dependent children. These ideas followed in part the Swope Plan of 1931.

The Social Security system has never really been "social insurance": It is not a contract.[36] Those who pay into it have no legal claim to any benefits. Moreover, it has never been comprehensive in its coverage. It is inferior to plans set up in the other major industrial countries. Indeed, the United States was the last of the major industrial nations to adopt some form of comprehensive social insurance. The 1935 law was simply a way to get some minimal social protection from an unwilling Congress. Roosevelt, when questioned about the utterly regressive payroll taxes used to launch the system, said, "Those taxes were never a problem of economics. They were politics all the way through."[37]

In subsequent decades the Social Security system was America's main avenue to **socialism**—collective responsibility for human welfare—without requiring public admission by spread-eagled politicians that the country had departed massively from the old ideal of dynamic, rugged individualism. Millions of Americans have benefitted from Social Security payments, which are transfers to them from current wage-earners' payments of their Social Security taxes. Since the Social Security system was never paid for by the general revenues, like the Pentagon was, Social Security has suffered from the exhaustion of its reserve funds as new programs have been loaded onto it and old ones expanded.

Since no one has ever had a legal right to any benefits under the system, it is not surprising that, in 1981, the Reagan administration advocated reducing benefits for the aged, weak, and indigent to keep the excess demand for human welfare from spilling over into those parts of federal expenditures considered to be more central to the national interests. The 1935 Social Security Act was thought to be a great and necessary social improvement, but it was flawed in its beginning. Those flaws have not been corrected, and they have not improved with age.

The Second New Deal and the FLSA

Reforms in the workplace brought about by federal action were almost impossible to achieve before the 1930s except in wartime or in federal employment itself. As we have seen, the 1916 Child Labor Law was thrown out by the Supreme Court in *Hammer* v *Dagenhart* (1918).[38] Efforts to limit hours were overturned in *Adkins* v *Children's Hospital* (1923).[39] In the first instance, the doctrine that manufacturing was not interstate commerce was given its strongest support. In the second, the right to freely bargain for wages and working conditions was held to be jeopardized by the District of Columbia's law placing restrictions upon conditions for hiring women and children. (In those days Congress legislated for the District.)

The Supreme Court allowed greater leeway in the states themselves under the traditional doctrines of the police powers.[40] Resistance to escalation of these powers from the state to the federal level was weakened by *Nebbia* v *New York* (1934), but inadvertently, since that case involved a state price-fixing law.[41] It sabotaged the doctrine of *Munn* v *Illinois* for good, though, leaving only the commerce clause as a barrier to federal regulation. Any business could be regulated, but it must be interstate commerce to be *federally* regulated. After the 1936 elections, the commerce clause became the open highway to federal regulation. The greatest statement was in *NLRB* v *Jones and Laughlin* (1937), which sustained the Wagner Act:

> When industries organize themselves on a national scale, making their relation to interstate commerce the dominant factor in their activities, how can it be maintained that their industrial labor relations constitute a forbidden field into which Congress cannot enter . . .[42]

How indeed? In 1938 Congress passed the Fair Labor Standards Act (FLSA), which placed the federal government's power nationally where the colonial township selectmen had been locally. Federal power to prescribe wages, hours, and working conditions was established. There were exemptions for agricultural laborers (they are still "exempt"), business executives, sailors, and businesses not engaged in interstate commerce of whose labor relations were covered by other federal regulations (e.g., railroad employees). Minimum wages were set with provisions to raise them, while maximum hours were prescribed with provisions to lower them: Overtime pay was set at 1.5 times the regular hourly rate and penalties were laid down for "oppressive child labor." A Wage and Hours Division was established in the Labor Department to enforce all this. What about the sacred division between manufacturing and interstate commerce that had been maintained since *Hammer* v *Dagenhart*? The Court ruled in *U.S.* v *Darby* (1941), the FSLA test case, that *Hammer* v *Dagenhart* "should be and now is overruled."[43] It was as simple as that.

Between the Wagner Act and the FLSA, the New Deal had utterly reversed the traditional position of the state in the wage bargain in this country. In interstate commerce employers *must* negotiate with unionized labor; hours were restricted at their *maximum,* wages at their *minimum.* Old-time capitalists like Henry Ford were stupefied by these changes.[44]

The AAA of 1938

A second Agricultural Adjustment Act was passed in 1938. The crop-control and income-support provisions were even stronger than in the Act of 1933, and this time the U.S. Supreme Court had no objections. It agreed in *Wickard* v *Filburn* (1942), the test case, that farmers participating in acreage-limitation schemes might not grow a bit extra on their unused land to feed their own livestock.[45] Amended over the years, the 1938 AAA, the "Ever-Normal Granary" act, remains the basis of modern farm policy.

Rural Electrification

Although authorized in 1935, the Rural Electrification Administration (REA) brought most of its achievement to fruition after the 1936 elections. By massive organization of rural electric cooperatives, millions of American farms (most of them) were hooked up to central electric power sources for the first time, and a second round of industrialization of American agriculture began, from appliances in the farm kitchen to outlets in the barns and fields. The private sector had not accepted the challenge of electrification of American agriculture. REAs are often criticized by supporters of private utilities, but no one has suggested that "private enterprise" could have done the job better. It did not.

The Reforms in Retrospect

We have touched only upon the main New Deal measures of reform and change. It cannot be denied that New Deal activism produced great changes, some of them permanent. Two generations of American voters have ratified and reratified the permanent New Deal innovations in American society. Most of the New Deal changes were augmentations of lines of government power previously developed in American history, as we know. But there were totally new departures, too. As Charles C. Cox put it:

> Never before [in peacetime] had Federal regulation promoted the interest of labor unions, or set agricultural prices and production or prescribed statutory decentralization of public utilities.[46]

There was, of course, much more. What were the immediate *economic* results? After all, FDR had promised to do something to relieve unemployment and make business prosper again.

THE DEPRESSION LINGERS

As the New Deal has receded into the distant past, studies of it have become slightly more objective than was the case when the politics of the period were still germane. Perspectives have changed.

Unemployment Again

As we saw in Table 25.1, the rate of unemployment remained at extraordinary levels throughout the 1930s. We emphasized earlier in this chapter that the private sector apparently could not employ those out of work. How many remained unemployed if we count *as employed* all those who found jobs in government make-work schemes? We are indebted to Michael Darby for such an estimate. The data in Table 25.4 show the effect of the government's programs on the unemployment rate.

Two conclusions emerge from this exercise. First, the New Deal was, to some extent, effective in reducing the percentage of the jobless work force. Secondly, even with the New Deal's direct federal employment effort, the 1930s constituted a period of disaster-level unemployment.

Urban Growth. In good times and bad the economic attractions of southern California produced explosive urban growth: Wilshire Boulevard in Los Angeles in the 1920s (above) and in the 1960s (below).

Table 25.4   Unemployment Rate Estimates (percentage of labor force)

Year	Lebergott	Darby	Reduction
1933	24.9	20.9	4.0
1934	21.7	16.2	5.5
1935	20.1	14.4	6.0
1936	16.9	10.0	6.9
1937	14.3	9.2	5.1
1938	19.0	12.5	6.5
1939	17.2	11.3	5.9

Source: *Historical Statistics*, series D 86; Michael Darby, "Three and a Half Million U.S. Employees Have Been Mislaid," *JPE*, 2–76, p. 8.

Wages

What about the really hard-nosed view mentioned earlier—that all workers *could* have been employed had they been willing to accept lower wages? In theory, such would have been the case, *must* have been the case, other things being equal (but they rarely are).[47] We can only speculate on this point. It is true that both money *and* real wages of those with jobs did advance after 1933. This *could* indicate that competition over jobs could have been crisper among those without work, although the literary history of the period casts doubt on this purely theoretical proposition.

Again, we have Professor Lebergott to thank for the numbers in Table 25.5. **Real wages,** money earnings before and after unemployment are taken into account, and average hourly earnings all reach their troughs in 1933. Real wages for the employed had fully recovered to the 1929 levels by 1937, and hourly earnings actually had surpassed 1929. Unemployment, together with money wages *times* hours worked, held all other indexes below the 1929 levels throughout the 1930s. With money and real wages rising from 1934 onward, conceivably more people could have left the unemployment rolls at lower wages. Conceivably. As Phillip Cagan put it: "We face in the 1930s experience the need to explain a perplexing combination of large-scale unemployment and substantial increases in wages."[48]

The point will always be argued. Businessowners would not have welcomed further labor trouble. Wage reductions might have produced that. The NRA years had implanted the idea that *rising* money wages were good for the economy. Would more labor have been

Table 25.5   Annual Earnings for Nonfarm Employees: Employed and Adjusted for Unemployment Deductions

Year	Annual Money Earnings		Annual Real Earnings (1914 dollars)		Average Hourly Earnings in Manufacturing (dollars per hour)
	After Deduction for Unemployment	When Employed	After Deduction for Unemployment	When Employed	
1929	1,462	1,534	855	898	.56
1930	1,294	1,494	778	898	.55
1931	1,068	1,406	705	928	.51
1932	807	1,244	593	914	.44
1933	722	1,136	561	882	.44
1934	789	1,146	592	860	.53
1935	851	1,195	623	874	.54
1936	932	1,226	675	888	.55
1937	1,072	1,341	749	937	.62
1938	956	1,303	680	927	.62
1939	1,029	1,346	743	973	.63
1940	1,113	1,392	798	998	.66
1941	1,332	1,561	909	1,066	.73

Source: Stanley Lebergott, "The American Labor Force," in L. E. Davis, et al., *American Economic Growth* (New York: Harper & Row, 1972), p. 213; hourly wages from *Historical Statistics*, series D 802.

employed had it been cheaper once the recovery began from 1933? Evidence shows astounding business conservatism at the time. Business inventories were liquidated from 1929 to 1935. After that, caution reigned in the presence of an antibusiness administration.

Business Conditions

Returning for a moment to Tables 25.1 and 25.2, recall that *real* GNP, output at 1929 prices, had recovered the 1929 peak by 1937 but that real GNP *per capita* only regained the 1929 level in 1940. In current prices, 1929 GNP was not recovered before World War II. The depression lingered on, unmoved by the energetic social reconstruction of the New Deal. It is difficult to measure such a thing as business expectations. But most economists consider them to be of fundamental importance in business planning. There are several series of data that show an extraordinary "down" in business expectations during the New Deal episode. Consider the five entries in Table 25.6.

Expectations

Gross private investment nearly vanished between 1929 and 1932, and, in fact, most estimates of net in-vestment (deducting for current depreciation) show net *dis*investment of the country's capital stock in 1932, 1933, and 1934. The strongest year of the thirties, 1937, was followed by another collapse. Any economic growth that occurs is fueled in part by net investment. Investment in the 1930s was not enough by itself to recover the growth of the 1920s. Year after year, more and more ground was lost. In all the indicators in Table 25.6 the decline to 1933 was catastrophic. Even such a basic activity as invention (or at least applications for patents) was staggered by the slide to 1933. What is equally striking, though, is the failure of business confidence, by these measures, to revive to anything like the levels of 1929 or, in most cases, even back to 1930.

Most businessowners tended to be Republicans and were aligned with Hoover. Business confidence had been flattened in the disastrous Hoover administration. The hero-figure of the 1930s, FDR, and the social and economic activism of his New Deal, may well have been themselves detriments to business hopes. FDR's vigorous characterization of his opponents in the business community as "economic royalists" hardly built confidence. The New Deal prescription for electoral success (usually attributed to Postmaster General

Table 25.6   Investment, Mergers, Patents, Corporate Issues, Stock Prices

Year	Gross Private Domestic Investment ($ billions)	Recorded Mergers	Patents Applied for (thousands)	New Corporate Issues for Capital[a] ($ millions)	Average Prices of Stocks (1941–43 = 100)
1929	16.2	1,245	89.8	8,002	260.2
1930	10.1	799	89.6	4,483	210.3
1931	5.6	464	79.8	1,551	136.6
1932	1.0	203	67.0	325	69.3
1933	1.4	120	56.6	161	89.6
1934	3.3	101	56.6	152(178)	98.4
1935	6.4	130	58.1	(401)	106.0
1936	8.5	126	62.6	(1,062)	154.7
1937	11.8	124	65.3	(1,138)	154.1
1938	6.5	110	66.9	(904)	114.9
1939	9.3	87	64.1	(420)	120.6
1940	13.1	140	60.9	(761)	110.2
1941	17.9	111	52.3	(1,041)	98.2

[a] Series X 367 from 1929–34 is not consistent with series X 502 thereafter.

Source: *Historical Statistics*, series F 52, V 38, W 96, X 495, 502, 511, see also *Historical Statistics*, 1960, series X 367.

Farley), "Tax, tax, tax. Spend, spend, spend. Elect, elect, elect," was scarcely designed to encourage private entrepreneurs or corporate executives to "take a flyer" on the future of American capitalism.

The stock market was also a barometer of private personal expectations. The index shown in Table 25.6 declined 73 percent from 1929 to 1932 and then lingered on at prices half or less than the 1929 levels for the rest of the decade. Business mergers are usually associated in aggregate with periods of economic expansion, periods of big plans and hopes.[49] They fell more than 90 percent in the period 1929–33 and never recovered. New corporate stock issues to raise capital declined 98 percent from the halcyon days of 1929 and lay dead in the water the rest of the decade; the peak of 1937 was about 15 percent of the 1929 level.

Taxation

The flattening of private expectations was due also to real forces, of course. Income taxes had been *raised* in 1932 by major proportions across the board.[50] The reason for such a deflationary move in a deep depression was Hoover's forlorn hope of somehow balancing his budget as revenues fell and expenditures rose. In 1935 federal taxes were raised again, a measure especially aimed at "the rich."[51] Then the new Social Security taxes, utterly regressive in their incidence, were instituted in 1937. They dealt a body blow to private consumption expenditures. During most of the depression, governments at all levels taxed as much as they could. The fiscal consequences we will treat in the next section; here it is enough to note that the psychological problems of business, in dealing with a federal government whose political stock-in-trade was antibusiness rhetoric, were heightened by a hostile tax climate.

Finance

In addition, business conditions simply remained poor, all else aside. Few objective businessowners could have found much reason for optimism between 1929 and 1933 when personal consumption expenditures dropped 40 percent. No need under those conditions for new orders, and, accordingly, there was net liquidation of business inventories for years. The foreign sector was no help; exports fell off in value 75 percent

for the years 1929–33 and then hovered for some years at 50 to 60 percent at the 1929 levels.[52]

The banking system, after surviving the blows of 1929, 1930, and 1933, became extraordinarily cash conscious as interest rates fell to subterranean levels (see Table 25.7). Savers, despite the FDIC, flooded the federal government's Postal Savings System with their hard-earned funds.[53] They did not trust the bankers for more adventures, and the bankers seemed not to trust the public. As we see in Table 25.7, cash reserves as a percentage of deposits had risen in 1936 to 60 percent over the 1929 level, far above any legal requirements, and remained there the rest of the depression years. The interest cost of borrowing money became nearly negligible since business prices (by past and future standards) were generally rising after 1932 (see Table 25.6). Yet, the banks remained stuffed with idle cash.[54] The depression seemed to have an almost unbreakable hold on the private sector. Only after World War II began in Europe, in September 1939, were there sure signs that the glacial conditions might thaw. However, even in 1940, unemployment (not counting make-work jobs) remained at nearly 15 percent of the labor force. The depression had lasted ten long years.

WHY SO LONG?

One might suppose that the economics profession, after two generations, could definitively answer that question. It never has. It is easy to pillory economists for such a failure, but, in fact, the depression of the 1930s was a remarkably complex thing, viewed purely as economics, and economists' models of business-cycle theory have been far too simple to produce satisfactory explanations.

The Money and Real-Forces Arguments

The latest flurry of argument about the depression has concentrated upon its disastrous opening with the stock-market crash of 1929, the banking crisis of 1930, and a powerful two-year crash dive into the pit ending with massive bank failures and the closing of all the banks as 1933 dawned.[55] These arguments depict a monetary beginning, and, if true, helps explain why the depression was so deep and, therefore, longlasting. The Federal Reserve System comes out tarred with the brush of incompetence; it lowered interest rates in

Table 25.7   Personal Consumption, Cash-Deposit Ratios, Interest Rates

Year	Personal Consumption Expenditures ($ billions)	National Bank Ratio of Cash to Deposits	Prime Interest Rate	Rate on 90-Day Commercial Paper
1929	77.2	19.8	5.85	5.03
1930	69.9	23.3	3.59	2.48
1931	60.5	22.5	2.64	1.57
1932	48.6	20.0	2.73	1.28
1933	45.8	24.5	1.73	0.63
1934	51.3	28.6	1.02	0.25
1935	55.7	30.5	0.75	0.13
1936	61.9	32.0	0.75	0.15
1937	66.5	31.3	0.94	0.43
1938	63.9	35.3	0.81	0.44
1939	66.8	37.6	0.59	0.44
1940	70.8	42.0	0.56	0.44
1941	80.6	38.9	0.53	0.44

Source: *Historical Statistics*, series F 48, X 445, 446, 643, 648.

1928, then failed to abort the 1929 stock-market bubble before it burst.[56] The Fed allowed the nominal supply of money to fall, had actually raised its rediscount rate in 1930 for a time, and then sat idly by while thousands of banks failed, to the ruin of their depositors and the desolation of the surrounding economic terrain. Subsequently, the Fed did little to aid recovery.[57] It did, however, pursue policies in 1936–37 that were thought to have contributed to another recession in 1938. This well-documented history has formed the centerpiece of the Monetarist explanation of Milton Friedman and Anna J. Schwartz, later buttressed by Allan Meltzer, Thomas Mayer, and others.[58]

The Monetarist arguments sound convincing. But is there more to be said? Peter Temin was unconvinced by pure Monetarism: The downward *trend* of interest rates after 1929, together with the lack of evidence that the economy was suffering from any *real* shortage of money for business purposes, left him in doubt about the purely monetary explanation. For one thing, as we noted earlier, the *real* money supply by 1932 was about the same as it had been in 1929. Temin found that the one factor that had changed fundamentally and independently of the rest was the drop in personal consumption expenditures (see Table 25.7), which dropped more than 9 percent in 1929–30 (current prices), fell another 12 percent in 1930–31, and another

15.4 percent in 1931–32.[59] Altogether, there was a relentless drop of 41 percent between 1929 and 1933. After the great consumption and stock-market boom of the roaring twenties, Americans by the millions closed their wallets and purses and froze up their spending from current income.

Temin's conclusions made many economists unhappy. They had not ordinarily thought of consumption as such an independent factor. The volatility of private investment had been their customary target in explaining business cycles.[60] Moreover, if Temin were correct, the Great Depression had been almost an act of God in its inscrutability. There is no simple target, no one to blame. Yet, Robert J. Gordon and James Wilcox independently, and perhaps reluctantly, come down on Temin's side:

> The stock market collapse precipitated a drastic decline in consumption spending that interacted with and further aggravated the continuing decline in residential construction.[61]

These factors together gave the depression distinct "nonmonetary" origins. In any case, why not hold back on consumption in those conditions? What a fine investment nonconsumption was! As Joel Mokyr argues, suppose that after the 1929 stock-market panic, risk-averse wealthholders decided just to sit on their cash; suppose they did not put it in a bank? In real terms, measured by the fall in consumer prices to 1933, they earned nearly 25 percent on their idle money. Measured against wholesale prices between 1929 and 1932, they earned nearly 10 percent a year just watching their silver tarnish.

The Austrian View

The pure neoclassical, or "Austrian," view set out years ago by F. A. Hayek and by Lionel Robbins has recently been restated by Murray Rothbard.[62] In this view, the run-up of stock prices to 1929 had its main root in excessive loosening of financial discipline before the crash and then was kept from its normal self-correcting mechanisms by *too much* Federal Reserve effort. Like the Monetarists, the Fed comes out guilty, *but guilty of a different crime.* The Fed expanded its holdings of government securities from $511 million to more than $2.4 billion from 1929 to 1933 in a vain effort to create a greater reserve base for bank loans.[63] Even if the nominal money supply had declined, it had declined too little, according to the Austrians, and not more than prices had. The policy, as far as it succeeded, set back the process of recovery. Had prices fallen far and precipitately, as they did in 1920–21 in connection with a huge drop in the money supply (see Table 23.3 in Chapter 23), the recovery might have begun earlier and sustained a new advance, as it did after 1921, or more viable price-profit ratios. Thus say the Austrians.

Schumpeter and Wicksell

Schumpeter's three-cycle scheme required a realignment of productive resources at new equilibrium price ratios to end a downturn. Efforts to hold prices up, or to raise them in a slump, interfere with the recovery process. Therefore, he would agree with the Austrian view. Schumpeter's explanation for the severity of the 1930s depression was that it was caused by a coalescence of the downswings of several different long-wave cycles.[64]

Followers of the great Swedish monetary theorist, Knut Wicksell (whose ideas faded into almost oblivion as the depression continued) would have been in agreement with the Monetarist position. In Wicksell's scheme, so long as market interest rates lay above the prospective real returns to investment, prices would

fall and the recession would continue. The astoundingly low levels of interest rates in the mid-1930s were still *too high* relative to business expectations.[65]

Stagnation and Excess Capacity

Some explanations of the Great Depression were based more deeply in recent American economic history. Alvin Hansen developed the idea of "secular stagnation."[66] The ending of the frontier, decline in population growth, and drying up of investment opportunities were forces of fundamental depth that had permanently weakened the stimulus of private investment and, hence, American economic growth. The Great Depression was the end of an era.

A similar, long-run analysis, albeit one that was not so pessimistic, was provided by the great British economist, Thomas Wilson, in his *Essays on Income and Employment.*[67] Wilson developed a theoretical and empirical argument that the previous investment boom of the 1920s had produced massive excess productive capacity in American industry that had to be utilized (or abandoned) before a new advance could occur. The depression of the 1930s was the result; new investment was not needed in the basic industries suffering from excess capacity. And, echoing Hansen's beliefs, Wilson said that there were insufficient new innovations, as the depression dragged on, to produce entirely new demand for investment in major product departures. Our series of data on patents (Table 25.6) would tend to support this part of Wilson's thesis.

Of course not all parts of the economy suffered in the same way, by the same amount, in the 1930s depression. Industries such as chemicals, petroleum, food products, and machinery manufacturing expanded their investments, output, and employment. Michael Bernstein has shown recently that much of New Deal policy toward industry was, in fact, aimed at propping up older basic industries, which were saved from innovation by World War II, and again by the Korean War, only to flounder finally in the later decades and require protection from competition. They were the most stagnant industries in the 1930s, and, in fact, were the ones Wilson said were suffering from excess capacity.[68]

Pure Keynes

John Maynard Keynes himself, in the chapter "Notes on the Trade Cycle" in *The General Theory,* attributed business-cycle downturns to psychological "sudden collapse of the marginal efficiency of capital."[69] When discounted future returns of current investment plans were for any reason revised downward, investment fell and the recession began. His followers found the huge surplus cash holdings of the banks as interest rates plunged evidence of the Keynesian *liquidity trap,* cash hoarding that dammed up the demand for securities or other investment.

International Considerations

In addition to these well-known theories are those based upon the United States' place in the international economy. The story—seen from the vantage point of, say, London—is enormously more complex and different from any treated in this text. There the tangled trail goes back to the monetary disruptions of World War I. There are three essential books for those who would like to pursue the subject: *The Network of World Trade,* mainly the work of Folke Hilgerdt; *International Currency Experience: Lessons of the Interwar Period,* mainly the work of Ragnar Nurkse; and Charles Kindleberger's *The World in Depression 1929–1938,* a superb modern treatment.[70] These three are only for openers; Kindleberger's bibliography will lead the way to denser forests.

From the international viewpoint, the American events are only a part (although a crucial one) of a larger pattern. That pattern may run as deeply in history as the *human* losses in Europe in the period 1914–18 due to war and influenza that turned the long-range terms of trade against the world's primary producers; so go the arguments of W. Arthur Lewis.[71] Allied to that is the failure of European industry to modernize after the war. This latter argument, presented by Ingvar Svennilson, is a fascinating view of the world depression and a different explanation of its depth and length than is given here.[72]

There were other theories in vogue at various times, but for various reasons they do not aid our understanding of the 1930s due to the extraordinary length of the depression.

Fiscal Policy

The idea of **compensating fiscal policy,** smoothing out the peaks and valleys of the business cycle through compensating tax and spending programs, was mainly the result of Keynes and the depression.[73] If government deficits were run in downswings and surpluses accumulated in expansions, then the government's budget over the entire course of the cycle might be "in balance," even though it was *not* in any given year. Compensating fiscal policy should then satisfy nearly everyone. The policy not only would produce a more even, long-term pattern of growth but would incidentally ease the problems of debt management: Debt would be accumulated at falling interest rates and could be liquidated when interest rates were rising in an expanding economy.

What was important was to offset the volatility of private investment. Keynes viewed the investment collapse of 1929 through 1933 and the subsequent investment doldrums as a **capital strike.** He argued that investment had to be controlled: "I conceive, therefore, that a somewhat comprehensive socialization of investment will prove the only means of securing an approximation to full employment."[74] There was nothing, Keynes argued, in the economic system that would automatically maintain stable full employment. That was the central message of *The General Theory* and its radical heresy from neoclassical economics.

Many economists considered the (relatively) huge spending programs of the New Deal the first fruits of this wisdom, making the depression less severe than it otherwise would have been while at the same time reforming and saving American capitalism from the consequences of its own follies.

In 1956, a study by Cary Brown gave a rude jolt to this optimistic view of the New Deal. Brown discovered that the increase in federal deficit spending barely offset the decline in other spending, together with the perverse taxing policies by governments at the state and local levels. Brown also noted the possible depressing influence upon private spending of FDR's antibusiness political stance. The result, wrote Brown, was that fiscal policy in the 1930s actually had little expansionary effect. The recovery, such as it was, came primarily from the beleaguered private sector:

> The trend of direct effects of fiscal policy on aggregate full-employment demand is definitely downward throughout the thirties. For recovery to have been achieved in this period, private demand would have had to be higher out of a given private disposable income than it was in 1929. Fiscal policy, then, seems to have been an unsuccessful recovery device in the thirties—not because it did not work, but because it was not tried.[75]

Other economists, notably Alvin Hansen, had earlier suspected the same. The New Deal had not been the Keynesian promised land. Moreover, as a "planned economy" (which people like Rexford Tugwell had wanted), the New Deal was a bust.[76] The planning that did occur was politically motivated, haphazard, and not forcefully pursued. The New Deal did not do what wartime mobilization would do after 1941: end the depression.

A further severe jolt to the New Deal memory came in 1973 from Larry Peppers.[77] He re-estimated Brown's work and found the New Deal even more deficient. By Peppers' calculations of a hypothetical full-employment spending policy, the small federal deficits of the 1930s were actually the equivalents of surpluses at full-employment income levels. The "fiscal drag" noted by Brown was even worse than he had imagined.

Perhaps someone will yet save the New Deal's reputation. But if he or she does, the mystery will only deepen. At least now one can argue that "fiscal policy was no help."

THE DEPRESSION LEGACY

This chapter and the previous one presented two baffling episodes that changed the patterns of economic growth achieved up to 1914. Our world has never been like classical American capitalism since the 1930s, and that is largely because of the reaction to the troubles of that decade. The intellectual and institutional baggage of the interwar period was carried into the future. Even though the New Deal reforms did not end the depression, they were widely approved of and were woven into the fabric of American society. When conditions changed and prosperity returned, the country elected not to return to the old-time mix of public and private control. The technology of enhanced and expanded politicization of economic decision making, so expanded in the 1930s, was altered and amended in later years and would become a new economic way of life.

Notes

1. Studs Terkel's *Hard Times: An Oral History of the Great Depression* (New York: Pantheon Books, 1970), is particularly recommended for its many vivid recollections of the 1930s from the recollections of persons from all walks of life.

2. Herman Krooss, *Executive Opinion: What Business Leaders Said and Thought on Economic Issues 1920s–1960s* (New York: Doubleday, 1970), ch. 5 and 6. Krooss' book is indispensable reading for the student of American business.

3. The scope of disagreement on this issue is made clear in Karl Brunner, editor, *The Great Depression Revisited* (1981) where the "Monetarist" and "real" positions are reasserted and examined.

4. Even staunch Keynesians like Alvin Hansen could see this possibility during the 1930s when Keynesian ideas about fiscal policy were being developed. Alan R. Sweezey, "The Keynesians and Government Policy, 1933–1939," *American Economic Review,* vol. LXII, no. 2, May 1972, especially p. 122.

5. The Austrian view has long been out of fashion. Its latest and most forceful restatement is Murray Rothbard, *America's Great Depression* (1975).

6. Stanley Lebergott, "Annual Estimates of Unemployment in the United States, 1900–1954," in *The Measurement and Behavior of Unemployment,* Princeton: Princeton University Press, 1957.

7. Professor John Wallis has emphasized this point.

8. Herbert Stein, *The Fiscal Revolution in America* (1969), ch. 5–7.

9. Peter Temin, *Did Monetary Forces Cause the Great Depression?* (1976).

10. Don C. Reading, "New Deal Activity and the States, 1933 to 1939," *JEH,* December 1973; and Leonard Arrington, "The New Deal in the West: A Preliminary Statistical Inquiry," *Pacific Historical Review,* August 1969. For a fine-tuning of the issues and analysis, Gavin Wright, "The Political Economy of New Deal Spending: An Econometric Analysis," *REStat,* February 1974.

11. E. Cary Brown, "Fiscal Policy in the Thirties: A Reappraisal," *AER,* December 1956.

12. Jonathan Hughes, *The Governmental Habit Redux* (1991), pp. 159–81. This account of New Deal reforms comes from this source, and Hughes' "Roots of Regulation," in Gary M. Walton, ed., *Regulatory Change in an Atmosphere of Crisis: Current Implications of the*

Roosevelt Years (1979); William Leuchtenburg, *Franklin D. Roosevelt and the New Deal 1932–1940* (1963). For an excellent recent summary: Robert Higgs, *Crisis and Leviathan: Critical Issues in the Emergence of the Mixed Economy* (1986), ch. 8.

13. The best account is still Arthur M. Schlesinger, Jr., *The Age of Roosevelt* (1959), vol. II.

14. A run on the dollar, an increase in the foreign demand for gold as the crisis deepened, was a consequence of the anticipation of the devaluation that came when Roosevelt took office. Barrie A. Wigmore, "Was the Bank Holiday of 1933 Caused by a Run on the Dollar?" *JEH,* September 1981.

15. Ben S. Bernanke, "Nonmonetary Effects of the Financial Crisis in the Propagation of the Great Depression," *AER,* June 1983.

16. An amusing account of the events of 1933 is in John Kenneth Galbraith's *Money, Whence It Came, Where It Went* (1975), ch. XIV.

17. Barry Eichengreen, *Golden Fetters: The Gold Standard and the Great Depression, 1919–1939* (1992). An early version of the argument can be found in Eichengreen and Jeffrey Sachs, "Exchange Rates and Economic Recovery in the 1930s," *JEH,* December 1985. Eichengreen's "The Origins and Nature of the Great Slump Revisited," *EHR,* May 1992, is an excellent review of recent scholarship concerning the depression.

18. Galbraith, pp. 210–12.

19. Edward Berkowitz and Kim McQuaid, *Creating the Welfare State* (1988), pp. 92–95.

20. Michael Weinstein, "Some Macroeconomic Impacts of the National Industrial Recovery Act 1933–35," in Brunner, *The Great Depression Revisited.*

21. *Schechter Poultry Corp* v *U.S.,* 295 U.S. 495 (1935).

22. George D. Green, "The Ideological Origins of the Revolution in American Financial Policies," in Brunner, *The Great Depression Revisited,* p. 224.

23. *Butler* v *U.S.,* 297, U.S. 1 (1936).

24. The federal land banks had been established in 1916 in response to farmers' demands; in the 1920s and 1930s there were fewer foreclosures where those banks were the lending agencies. Lee J. Alston, "Farm Foreclosure Moratorium Legislation: The Lesson of the Past," *AER,* June 1984.

25. Roger Ransom, *Coping with Capitalism* (1981), pp. 559–60.

26. Frederick Merk, *History of the Westward Expansion* (1978), pp. 559–60.

27. Tugwell's views of the New Deal origins are in his *The Brain Trust* (1968). The New Deal safety-net for agriculture was resisted in the south whenever it threatened to raise wages or improve conditions for the poorest. Lee Alston and Joseph Ferrie, "Resisting the Welfare State: Southern Opposition to the Farm Security Administration," *REH,* Supplement 4 (1985); and their "Labor Costs, Paternalism, and Loyalty in Southern Agriculture: A Constraint on the Growth of the Welfare State," *JEH,* March 1985.

28. Merk, *History of the Westward Movement,* ch. 53–56.

29. Randal Rucker and Lee Alston estimate that all of the New Deal measures combined saved from 146,000 to just less than 277,000 farms out of the approximately 6.8 *million* that existed in the 1930s. They wonder, if the effort was worth the price for anyone other than those farm families whose farms were not foreclosed because of the policies, "Farm Failures and Government Intervention: A Case Study of the 1930s," *AER,* September 1987.

30. Fraud and what would now be called "insider trading" was the motivation for this separation of commercial banking and investment banking. Modern research fails to reveal any evidence that the 1929 crash or the ensuing depression had been aggravated by the relationship the Glass-Steagall Act excised from the nation's institutional structure. Eugene Nelson White, "Before the Glass-Steagall Act: An Analysis of the Investment Banking Activities of the National Banks," *EEH,* January 1986.

31. An interesting perspective on this "solution" can be found in Charles Calomiris, "Is Deposit Insurance Necessary? A Historical Perspective," *JEH,* June 1990.

32. Jonathan Hughes, *The Vital Few: The Entrepreneur and American Economic Progress* (1986), pp. 533–39.

33. Hughes, *The Governmental Habit Redux,* p. 161.

34. Joan Underhill Hannon, "Poor Relief Policy in Antebellum New York State: The Rise and Decline of the Poorhouse," *EEH,* July 1985.

35. Stanley Lebergott, *The American Economy: Income, Wealth, and Want* (1976), p. 57.

36. Domenico Gagliardo, *American Social Insurance* (1949).

37. Quoted in Hughes, "The Roots of Regulation," p. 52.

38. *Hammer* v *Dagenhart,* 247 U.S. 251 (1918).

39. *Adkins* v *Children's Hospital,* 261 U.S. 252 (1923).

40. For example, *West Coast Hotel* v *Parrish,* 300 U.S. 379 (1937).

41. *Nebbia* v *New York,* 291 U.S. 502 (1934).

42. *NLRB* v *Jones and Laughlin,* 301 U.S. 1 (1937), pp. 41–42.

43. *U.S.* v *Darby,* 312 U.S. 100 (1941).

44. Jonathan Hughes, *The Vital Few* (1986), pp. 334–51.

45. *Wickard* v *Filburn,* 317 U.S. 111 (1942).

46. Charles C. Cox, "Monopoly Explanations of the Great Depression and Public Policies Toward Business," in Brunner, *The Great Depression Revisited,* p. 189.

47. Joseph Schumpeter, "The Present World Depression: A Tentative Diagnosis," *American Economic Review,* vol. 21, no. 1, Supplement (1931).

48. Phillip Cagan, "Comments," on the Weinstein paper (see note 19) in Brunner, *The Great Depression Revisited.*

49. F. M. Scherer and David Ross, *Industrial Market Structure and Economic Performance,* 3rd ed. (Boston: Houghton Mifflin, 1990), pp. 153–56.

50. Stein, *The Fiscal Revolution in America,* pp. 33–38.

51. Stein, pp. 81–90.

52. In 1929, exports of goods and services stood at $7 billion. This dropped to $2.4 billion in 1933.

53. Maureen O'Hara and David Easley, "The Postal Savings System in the Depression," *JEH,* September 1979.

54. By 1944 these extraordinary levels of cash reserves had vanished; the ratio was back to 24.4.

55. Brunner, *The Great Depression Revisited,* is devoted entirely to the early part of the depression. Brunner's "Introduction" is a summary of the issues. There are outstanding questions about the Federal Reserve's policy in the 1929–32 period regarding its own warrant as a "lender of last resort." From the evidence, it is doubtful the Fed's managers considered saving the thousands of failing banks to be a Federal Reserve obligation. Also, their efforts at "reflation," by purchasing government securities in 1931 and 1932 seem to have been thwarted by the caution of commercial bank lending policies, *even had it been the intention of the Fed* to "force" a recovery, or attempt to, by such methods. Jonathan Hughes, "Stagnation Without 'Flation: The 1930s Again," in Barry Siegal, ed., *Money in Crisis: The Federal Reserve, The Economy, and Monetary Reform* (1984); Gerald Epstein and Thomas Ferguson, "Monetary Policy, Loan Liquidation, and Industrial Conflict: The Federal Reserve and Open Market Operations of 1932," *JEH,* December 1984.

56. A somewhat different impression can be found in David Wheelock, "The Strategy, Effectiveness, and Consistency of Federal Reserve Monetary Policy, 1924–1933," *EEH,* October 1989.

57. If interest rates, which were at 1 percent and less most of the time between 1933 the coming of war in 1939, were at their minima, that is, they could not have been driven lower by monetary policy, then a Keynesian "liquidity trap" existed. If that were true, then there was really little or no scope for monetary policy to contribute to a recovery. Richard Sutch believes the liquidity trap did in fact exist, "Notes on the Ineffectiveness of Monetary Policy During a Keynesian Depression: The Crises of Liquidation in the United States at Certain Dates in 1932," forthcoming. Cited by permission.

58. Chapter 7 of Friedman and Schwartz, *A Monetary History of the United States, 1867–1960* (1963) was published separately as *The Great Contraction 1929–33* (1965). See also Anna Schwartz's defense of it in Brunner, *The Great Depression Revisited,* ch. 1. Brunner contains papers by these other authors defending the Monetarist approach. The Meltzer paper discusses the contractionary consequences of the Smoot-Hawley Tariff of 1931.

59. Temin, *Did Monetary Forces Cause the Great Depression?,* p. 64. See also his defense in Brunner entitled "Notes on the Causes of the Great Depression." A recent exposition of his thoughts on this subject can be found in his *Lessons from the Great Depression* (1989). For a separate defense of Friedman and Schwartz and a critique of Temin's thesis, see Thomas Mayer, "Money and the Great Depression: A Critique of Professor Temin's Thesis," *EEH,* April 1978. Martha Olney's analysis of consumer credit purchases of durable consumer goods support's Temin. Consumers cut new purchases to meet installment payments. Fear of the future also caused them to make fewer new installment contracts as old contracts were paid off. Martha L. Olney, "Consumer Durables in the Interwar Years: New Estimates, New Patterns," *Research in Economic History,* vol. 12 (1990). Christina D. Romer also supports Temin for reasons similar to Olney's, "The Great Crash and the Onset of the Great Depression," *Quarterly Journal of Economics,* vol. 105, no. 3, August 1990.

60. Robert Aaron Gordon, *Economic Instability and Growth: The American Record* (1974).

61. Robert J. Gordon and James Wilcox, "Monetarist Interpretations of the Great Depression: An Evaluation and Critique," in Brunner, *The Great Depression Revisited,* p. 80.

62. F. A. Hayek, *Monetary Theory and the Trade Cycle* (1966); Lionel Robbins, *The Great Depression* (1934); and Rothbard, *America's Great Depression,* ch. 9–11.

63. *Historical Statistics,* series X 800.

64. Joseph Schumpeter, *Business Cycles* (1939).

65. Jonathan Hughes, "Wicksell on the Facts: Prices and Interest Rates 1844–1914," in J. N. Wolfe, editor, *Value, Capital and Growth: Essays in Honour of Sir John Hicks* (Edinburgh: University of Edinburgh Press, 1968).

66. Alvin Hansen stated it in different places and forms, including a book, *Full Recovery or Stagnation* (New York: W. W. Norton, 1939). The shortest statement is his article, "Economic Progress and Declining Population Growth," *AER,* May 1938.

67. Thomas Wilson, *Essays in Income and Employment* (1949).

68. Michael A. Bernstein, *The Great Depression* (1987).

69. John Maynard Keynes, *The General Theory of Employment, Interest, and Money* (1936).

70. *The Network of World Trade* (Geneva: League of Nations, 1942); *International Currency Experience: Lessons of the Interwar Period* (Princeton: League of Nations, 1944); and Kindleberger, *The World in Depression 1929–1938* (1973). See also, Gertrude M. Fremling, "Did the United States Transmit the Great Depression to the Rest of the World?" *AER,* December 1985. Fremling agrees with Kindleberger on the worldwide origins of the 1930s depression.

71. W. Arthur Lewis, *Economic Survey, 1919–1939* (London: Allen and Unwin, 1949).

72. Ingvar Svennilson, *Growth and Stagnation in the European Economy* (Geneva: United Nations, 1954).

73. Stein, *The Fiscal Revolution in America,* pp. 151–68.

74. Keynes, *The General Theory,* p. 378.

75. Brown, "Fiscal Policy in the Thirties," p. 863.

76. Otis L. Graham, Jr., *Toward a Planned Society: From Roosevelt to Nixon* (1976), p. 67.

77. L. C. Peppers, "Full Employment Surplus Analysis and Structural Changes: The 1930s," *EEH,* Winter 1973.

Suggested Readings

Articles

Alston, Lee J. "Farm Foreclosure Moratorium Legislation: The Lesson of the Past." *American Economic Review,* vol. 74, no. 3, June 1984.

———, and Ferrie, Joseph P. "Resisting the Welfare State: Southern Opposition to the Farm Security Administration." *Research in Economic History,* Supplement 4. Greenwich, CT: JAI Press, 1985.

———. "Labor Costs, Paternalism, and Loyalty in Southern Agriculture: A Constraint on the Growth of the Welfare State." *Journal of Economic History,* vol. XLV, no. 1, March 1985.

Arrington, Leonard J. "The New Deal in the West: A Preliminary Statistical Inquiry." *Agricultural History,* vol. 49, no. 4, October 1970.

Bernanke, Ben S. "Nonmonetary Effects of the Financial Crisis in the Propagation of the Great Depression." *American Economic Review,* vol. 73, no. 3, June 1983.

Brown, E. Cary. "Fiscal Policy in the Thirties: A Reappraisal." *American Economic Review,* vol. XLVI, no. 5, December 1956.

Calomiris, Charles. "Is Deposit Insurance Necessary? A Historical Perspective." *Journal of Economic History,* vol. L, no. 2, June 1990.

Cox, Charles C. "Monopoly Explanations of the Great Depression and Public Policies Toward Business." In Karl Brunner, editor, *The Great Depression Revisited.* Boston: Martinus Nijhoff, 1981.

Darby, Michael. "Three and a Half Million U.S. Employees Have Been Mislaid." *Journal of Political Economy,* vol. 84, no. 1, February 1976.

Eichengreen, Barry. "The Origins and Nature of the Great Slump Revisited." *Economic History Review,* vol. XLV, no. 2, May 1992.

———, and Sachs, Jeffrey. "Exchange Rates and Economic Recovery in the 1930s." *Journal of Economic History,* vol. XLV, no. 4, December 1985.

Epstein, Gerald, and Ferguson, Thomas. "Monetary Policy, Loan Liquidation, and Industrial Conflict: The Federal Reserve and Open Market Operations of 1932." *Journal of Economic History,* vol. XLIV, no. 4, December 1984.

Fremling, Gertrude M. "Did the United States Transmit the Great Depression to the Rest of the World?" *American Economic Review,* vol. 75, no. 5, December 1985.

Gordon, Robert J., and Wilcox, James A. "Monetarist Interpretations of the Great Depression: An Evaluation and Critique." In Karl Brunner, editor, *The Great Depression Revisited.* Boston: Martinus Nijhoff, 1981.

Green, George D. "The Ideological Origins of the Revolution in American Financial Policies." In Karl Brunner, editor, *The Great Depression Revisited.* Boston: Martinus Nijhoff, 1981.

Hannon, Joan Underhill. "Poor Relief Policy in Antebellum New York State: The Rise and Decline of the Poorhouse," *Explorations in Economic History,* vol. 22, no. 3, July 1985.

Hansen, Alvin. "Economic Progress and Declining Population Growth." *American Economic Review,* vol. 29, no. 1, May 1938.

Hughes, Jonathan. "The Roots of Regulation." In Gary M. Walton, editor, *Regulatory Change in an Atmosphere of Crisis: Current Implications of the Roosevelt Years.* New York: Academic Press, 1979.

———. "Stagnation Without 'Flation: The 1930s Again." In Barry Siegal, ed., *Money in Crisis, The Federal Reserve, The Economy and Monetary Reform.* Cambridge, MA: Ballinger, 1984.

Hunter, Helen Manning. "The Roles of Business Liquidity During the Great Depression and Afterwards: Differences Between Large and Small Firms." *Journal of Economic History,* vol. XLII, no. 4, December 1982.

Lebergott, Stanley. "The American Labor Force." In L. E. Davis et al., *American Economic Growth.* New York: Harper & Row, 1972.

Mishkin, Frederic S. "The Household Balance Sheet and the Great Depression." *Journal of Economic History,* vol. XXXVIII, no. 4, December 1978.

O'Hara, Maureen, and Easley, David. "The Postal Savings System in the Depression." *Journal of Economic History,* vol. XXXIX, no. 3, September 1979.

Peppers, L. C. "Full Employment Surplus Analysis and Structural Changes: The 1930s." *Explorations in Economic History,* vol. 10, no. 2, Winter 1973.

Reading, Don C. "New Deal Activity and the States, 1933 to 1939." *Journal of Economic History,* vol. XXXIII, no. 4, December 1973.

Temin, Peter. "Notes on the Causes of the Great Depression." In Karl Brunner, editor, *The Great Depression Revisited,* Boston: Martinus Nijhoff, 1981.

Wallis, John Joseph. "Why 1933?: The Origins and Timing of National Government Growth 1933 to 1940." Unpublished.

———, and Benjamin, Daniel K. "Public Relief and Private Employment in the Great Depression." *Journal of Economic History,* vol. XLI, no. 1, March 1981.

Weinstein, Michael M. "Some Macroeconomic Impacts of the National Industrial Recovery Act, 1933–35." In Karl Brunner, editor, *The Great Depression Revisited.* Boston: Martinus Nijhoff, 1981. This is followed by Phillip Cagan's "Comment."

Wheelock, David. "The Strategy, Effectiveness, and Consistency of Federal Reserve Monetary Policy, 1924–1933." *Explorations in Economic History,* vol. 26, no. 4, October 1989.

White, Eugene Nelson. "Before the Glass-Steagall Act: An Analysis of the Investment Banking Activities of the National Banks." *Explorations in Economic History,* vol. 23, no. 1, January 1986.

Wigmore, Barrie A. "Was the Bank Holiday of 1933 Caused by a Run on the Dollar?" *Journal of Economic History,* vol. XLVII, no. 3, September 1981.

Wright, Gavin. "The Political Economy of New Deal Spending: An Econometric Analysis." *Review of Economics and Statistics,* vol. LVI, no. 1, February 1974.

Books

Berkowitz, Edward, and McQuaid, Kim. *Creating the Welfare State: The Political Economy of Twentieth Century Reform,* second edition. New York: Praeger, 1988.

Bernstein, Michael A. *The Great Depression: Delayed Recovery and Economic Change in America, 1929–1939.* New York: Cambridge University Press, 1987.

Brunner, Karl, editor. *The Great Depression Revisited.* Boston: Martinus Nijhoff, 1981.

Chandler, Lester. *America's Greatest Depression: 1929–1941.* New York: Harper & Row, 1970.

Davis, L. E. et al. *American Economic Growth: An Economist's History of the United States.* New York: Harper & Row, 1972.

Friedman, Milton, and Schwartz, Anna J. *A Monetary History of the United States, 1867–1960.* Princeton: Princeton University Press, 1963.

Hayek, F. A. *Monetary Theory and the Trade Cycle.* New York: Kelley, 1966.

Gagliardo, Domenico. *American Social Insurance.* New York: Harper, 1949.

Galbraith, John Kenneth. *Money, Whence It Came, Where It Went.* Boston: Houghton Mifflin, 1975.

Garraty, John A. *The Great Depression: An Inquiry into the Case, Course and Consequences of the Worldwide Depression of the Nineteen-Thirties, As Seen By Contemporaries and in the Light of History.* New York: Harcourt Brace Jovanovitch, 1986.

Gordon, Robert Aaron. *Economic Instability and Growth: The American Record.* New York: Harper & Row, 1974.

Graham, Otis L., Jr. *Toward a Planned Society: From Roosevelt to Nixon.* New York: Oxford University Press, 1976.

Higgs, Robert. *Crisis and Leviathan: Critical Episodes in the Growth of American Government,* New York: Oxford University Press, 1987.

Hughes, Jonathan. *The Governmental Habit Redux.* Princeton: Princeton University Press, 1991.

———. *The Vital Few: The Entrepreneur and American Economic Progress.* New York: Oxford University Press, 1986 (expanded edition).

Keynes, John Maynard. *The General Theory of Employment, Interest and Money.* New York: Harcourt Brace, 1936.

Kindleberger, Charles P. *The World in Depression 1929–1939.* Berkeley: University of California Press, 1973.

Lebergott, Stanley. *The American Economy: Income, Wealth and Want.* Princeton: Princeton University Press, 1976.

Leuchtenburg, William E. *Franklin D. Roosevelt and the New Deal 1932–1940.* New York: Harper Torchbooks, 1963.

Liebhafsky, H. H. *American Government and Business.* New York: Wiley, 1971.

Merk, Frederick. *History of the Westward Movement.* New York: Alfred Knopf, 1978.

Ransom, Roger L. *Coping with Capitalism*. Englewood Cliffs, NJ: Prentice-Hall, 1981.

Robbins, Lionel *The Great Depression*. London: Macmillan, 1934.

Rothbard, Murray. *America's Great Depression*. Kansas City: Sheed & Ward, 1975.

Schlesinger, Arthur M., Jr. *The Age of Roosevelt*. Boston: Houghton Mifflin 1957, 1959, and 1960, 3 vols.

Schumpeter, Joseph. *Business Cycles*. New York: McGraw-Hill, 1939, 2 vols.

Stein, Herbert. *The Fiscal Revolution in America*. Chicago: University of Chicago Press, 1969.

Temin, Peter. *Did Monetary Forces Cause the Great Depression?* New York: Norton, 1976.

———. *Lessons from the Great Depression*. Cambridge: MIT Press, 1989.

Tugwell, Rexford G. *The Brains Trust*. New York: Viking, 1968.

Walton, Gary M., editor. *Regulatory Change in an Atmosphere of Crisis: Current Implications of the Roosevelt Years*. New York: Academic Press, 1979.

Wilson, Thomas. *Essays in Income and Employment*. New York: Pitman, 1949.

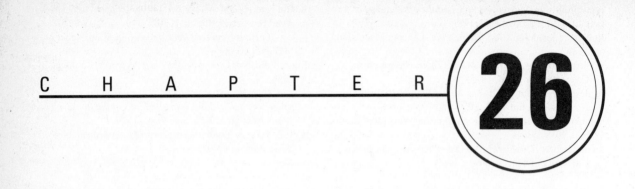

The "Prosperity" of Wartime

As early as 1940, World War II produced demand for the products of American industry. Before the end of that disastrous summer, it was clear that the United States would be drawn into the conflict, at least as a noncombatant supplier of war goods to the beleaguered British once the French sought a truce with the Nazis. Conscription was revived in the United States, and orders for war materials increasingly quickened the pace of industry. Unemployment began to drop as workers moved into industrial work stimulated by war output. Studies by economists within the government showed that war production would push the economy, finally, back to full employment levels.[1]

In January 1941, FDR asked Congress for the means to arm Americans and the British. In March, the Lend-Lease Act passed in Congress, authorizing the Administration to provide supplies to "any country whose defense the President deems vital to the defense of the United States." The financing would come from debt creation. U.S. exports, already up to $325 million in January 1941 were $460 million by August of that year, compared to $250 million in August 1939. By August

1945, the United States was supplying some $50 billion in war materials to its allies under the Lend-Lease Act ($42 billion net, deducting materials they supplied). Lend-Lease deliveries were greater than the *sum* of all federal expenditures from 1933 to 1939.

But Lend-Lease would be almost a sideline compared to the main American wartime expenditures. In December 1941, with Nazi armies deep into the territory of the USSR, the Japanese attacked American forces in the Pacific, and the Germans declared war on the United States. In the process of another full wartime mobilization, the American unemployment problem vanished at last. Other things being equal, it was as Keynes had suggested: Sufficient expenditures by government would stimulate the economy.

Robert Higgs has argued that this view, which he terms the "consensus view," is misleading.[2] After all, the United States was a command economy during the war. Higgs suggests that Simon Kuznets' "peacetime concept" of GNP is a more appropriate measure of the welfare of the average citizen; macroeconomic aggregates that include the war effort are misleading at best. Using Kuznets' measure, the economy during World

War II did not produce increased consumption or investment; it was rigged to produce increased government expenditures.

> It is difficult to understand how working harder, longer, more inconveniently and dangerously in return for a diminished flow of consumer goods with the description that "economically speaking, Americans had never had it so good."[3]

To Higgs, genuine recovery from the Great Depression did not come with the war, but rather with the end of the war. It was caused not by the government expenditures, but by an increase in financial wealth during the war and the expectation that better times were ahead.

Regardless of which view one adopts, it is clear that more Americans earned paychecks during the war, albeit not necessarily in jobs they wanted to hold. They were seldom able to spend those paychecks as they would have liked. When the war ended and these constraints were lifted, and a revitalized economy began postwar economic life, it was at levels and growth rates that made the fabled 1920s look small. The depression never returned, but the memory of it lingered.

THE SCOPE OF WAR MOBILIZATION

Once again war required release of output from peacetime uses as well as expanded output. The control apparatus reappeared.

Apparatus

For a command economy to exist, someone must do the commanding. Experience in World War I as well as during the New Deal had driven that lesson home. When war came, the government could temporarily forget the problems of strict constitutionality that had hamstrung its actions in the NRA and AAA episodes.

The president's "war powers" were extraordinary. Following Woodrow Wilson's precedent in 1916, FDR anticipated the war by bringing planners together to chart out the country's possible mobilization patterns. As a result of agitation and enquiry during the New Deal to reorganize the federal government in the interests of economic planning, the modern Executive Office of the President was established in September 1939, by Executive Order 8248.[4] The president could now expand the executive branch outside the old-line departments and achieve the kind of decisive action war would require. In May 1940, FDR appointed members to the National Defense Advisory Commission (NDAC). It was an umbrella organization under which a large part of the wartime administrative apparatus would be constructed. In June 1940, for example, the National Defense Research Council (NDRC) was set up under the NDAC umbrella to mobilize the country's scientific personnel for war. The war effort resembled the New Deal in this regard, and all of it was indebted to Woodrow Wilson's 1917–18 government for inspiration.[5]

Also under the NDAC umbrella, an institutional framework for the civilian economy was constructed. In 1942, the War Production Board (WPB) commanded operations designed to determine priorities and allocation procedures. That same year, the Office of Price Administration (OPA) was created under control powers set out in the Stabilization Act of 1942.[6] So powerful had the Presidency become, that in February, 1942, he could by mere executive order cause some 115,000 persons with Japanese ancestry living on the west coast to be forcibly interned in concentration camps, and subsequently to be backed up in this action by Congress, and the Supreme Court of the United States.[7] (It was 1988 before the United States apologized to the people who had been interned and Congress agreed to compensate the survivors.)

In 1943, the war effort was intensified by a new bureau, the Office of War Mobilization (OWM), which was set up to coordinate and expedite the efforts of the other agencies.

The complex war effort involved rationing, physical controls, and direct government construction of vast plants and facilities. Leading figures from the New Deal (who had themselves been trained by World War I officials retreaded in the First New Deal) were already available for administrative service in the war effort.[8] In 1943, in any case, Congress canceled out a large part of the New Deal employment-creating bureaucracy; those boards, offices, commissions, and administrations, no longer needed, passed into history. As in World War I and the New Deal, executive talent was recruited from the private sector, and once again these "dollar-a-year" executives (their token government salaries) streamed back to Washington from corporate headquarters, board rooms, and universities across the land. The job at hand was vast, and it was not going to be done by government clerks.

Manpower and Materials

As in our other wars, the need was for an *immediate* requisition of manpower and materials. In many respects the scale of the World War II mobilization was astonishing to all, friend and foe alike. As can be seen in Table 26.1, the armed forces would hold 12,123,000 men and women by 1945. To train, equip, sustain, and transport them between 1941 and 1945, nearly $250 billion were spent directly, more than $80 billion in the single year 1945. That was a sum for military expenditures alone greater in a single year than the entire GNP had been in any year during the period 1931–1935.

In response to such monetary stimuli between 1940 and the peak war effort, the civilian non-agricultural labor force expanded by 30 percent (see Table 26.1), offsetting in part the huge growth of the armed forces. A "worker shortage" existed. The ranks of the unemployed thinned out and then fell to almost meaningless levels, a mere 1.2 percent in 1944. The unemployment levels of the 1930s never returned. In those years, the earnings of teenagers, too young to be drafted, from part-time and summer jobs were commonly more than the annual earnings of their (employed) parents had

been just scant years before. Women, teenagers, the disabled, the aged—all were needed to replace the millions gone to foreign fields if output was to be expanded.

Such unknown economic potential astonished even the most knowledgeable and embittered, those who had suffered through the miseries of the 1930s, when it had been argued that greater expenditure efforts to relieve unemployment would endanger the public and cause government bankruptcy. In real terms (prices of 1929), full employment GNP in 1944 was half again that of 1940, the best New Deal year. In current prices, GNP had doubled in a scant four years under the stimulus of war spending.

Demobilization

War spending, such a huge shot in the nation's economic arm, seemed to revitalize the economy at last. When demobilization came, the new energy remained. As the veterans returned and re-entered the labor force in 1946 and 1947 (and the armed forces and military expenditures shrank accordingly), labor-force expansion picked up again (Table 26.1). Real GNP dipped between 1944 and 1947, but as price controls were lifted, prices rose, and GNP in current prices, down slightly in 1946, rose again. Unemployment resumed the pre-1930s peacetime levels of less than 4 percent. Industrial production in 1943–44 had been about double the 1940 level. Its decline thereafter reflected reconversion shifts into such areas as housing and

Table 26.1   War Expenditures and Manpower Mobilization

Year	Total Military Expenditures ($ billions)	Numbers in Armed Forces (thousands)	GNP Current Prices ($ billions)	GNP 1958 Prices ($ billions)	Index of Manufacturing Output (1967 = 100)
1940	1.8	458	99.7	227.2	25
1941	6.3	1,801	124.5	263.7	32
1942	22.9	3,859	157.9	297.8	38
1943	63.4	9,045	191.6	337.1	47
1944	76.0	11,452	210.1	361.3	51
1945	80.5	12,123	211.9	355.2	43
1946	43.2	3,030	208.5	312.6	35
1947	14.8	1,583	231.3	309.9	39

Source: *Historical Statistics*, series D 86, 127, F 1, 3, P 13, Y 458, 459, 904.

services. Housing would finally (in 1949) regain the 1926 level after the long hiatus. In fact, industrial production would not again see the truly extraordinary 1943 levels until 1953, the last Korean War year, when a new wave of peacetime growth began. Demobilization, because of wartime monetization of the economy and pent-up demand for consumer goods, posed few of the problems economists had feared. The worst pessimists had supposed that the 1930s would be back since by the end of that sorry era, expert opinion held that with "secular stagnation" at hand, the country would never experience growth again.

FINANCING THE WAR

With World War I and the New Deal deficits in the immediate background, World War II caused no peculiar financial problems for government authorities except for the matter of sheer volume. As always, for war purposes the government needed command over resources far in excess of any conceivable taxing power. This necessitated enormous federal deficits. Taxation apart, the impact of war finance on prices was reduced to the extent that funds could be borrowed from the public at large. But, necessarily, bonds had to be sold to the banking system, and that produced money-supply increases with inflationary potential.

First let us consider the financial picture in very broad strokes (see Table 26.2).[9] Expenditures rose to whatever levels were deemed necessary. It was up to Congress and the monetary authorities to find the

means. The problem was to raise expenditures by more than a factor of 10, from $9.6 billion to $95.2 billion, in only five years. Total federal expenditures in 1945 were almost equal to the entire GNP of the fabled year 1929. Taxes had to be raised for this and were. But the maximum revenues of 1945 were only about half of expenditures. As the deficits mounted, so did the debt, rising to a (then) staggering $271 billion.

Bond Sales and Interest Policy

In World War II, as in World War I, celebrities joined in the patriotic effort, and "bond rallies" were held all over the country (the celebrities functioning as cajoling cheerleaders) to influence patriotic income-earners to loan some of their means to Uncle Sam for the duration. Bonds were sold by financial institutions of all sorts, and a total of 6 million agents were involved in the selling. The effort was unprecedented. As a result, $157 billion of bonds were sold directly to the public, more than to the financial institutions. In 1946, individual Americans owned 23 percent of the national debt; banks, 40 percent; and nonbank institutions, 37 percent. These proportions were not significantly different from prewar ones, and maintaining the stable distribution of holdings represented a signal achievement.[10]

The Treasury entered the war when interest rates were at all-time lows, and this circumstance allowed the government a degree of control over the war's deadweight costs, interest charges on the borrowing, that it had not enjoyed in World War I. By close cooperation with the Federal Reserve System, the Treasury in 1945 faced only an average of 1.94 percent on its huge debt, compared to 4.2 percent at the end of World War I.

The Federal Reserve authorities announced in April 1942 that they would buy and sell Treasury bills in unlimited quantities at a 0.38 percent discount of maturity values. This "pegged" the short-term interest on Treasury borrowing at incredibly low rates. Long-term bonds were similarly pegged, at 2.5 percent for the duration as Figure 26.1 reveals. Indeed the stability of government rates is the result of coordinated effort by the Treasury and the Federal Reserve to finance the New Deal and World War II. Commercial banks were allowed to buy bonds with "war-loan" accounts that required neither reserve requirements nor deposit

Nonagricultural Labor Force (millions)	Percentage Unemployed
32.4	14.6
36.6	9.9
40.1	4.7
42.5	1.9
41.9	1.2
40.4	1.9
41.7	3.9
43.9	3.9

Modern War Again.   World War II required a total mobilization of resources. Financial mobilization (above left) was not so radical a wartime innovation as was the opening of industrial employment to women workers (above right). On D-Day (below left and right) Europe began to experience the impact of American industrial power.

Table 26.2 War Finance[a]

	U.S. Government				Money Supply		
Year	Receipts	Expenditures	Surplus (+) Deficit (−)	Gross Federal Debt	Individual Income-Tax Receipts	M_1	M_2	Commercial Bank Holdings of Federal Debt
1940	6.9	9.6	−2.7	50.7	1.1	39.7	55.2	21.9
1941	9.2	14.0	−4.8	57.5	1.6	46.5	62.5	25.9
1942	15.1	34.5	−19.4	79.2	3.2	55.4	71.2	36.5
1943	25.1	78.9	−53.8	142.6	6.5	72.2	89.9	69.3
1944	47.8	94.0	−46.1	204.1	20.2	85.3	106.8	94.6
1945	50.2	95.2	−45.0	260.1	18.4	99.2	126.6	118.0
1946	43.5	61.7	−18.2	271.0	16.1	106.5	138.7	119.3
1947	43.5	36.9	6.6	257.1	17.9	111.8	146.0	105.3

[a] In billions of dollars

Source: *Historical Statistics*, series Y 339–42, 445, X 414–15, 594.

insurance. This was interest-bearing money. The banks, like the population at large, bought bonds. The combined portfolios (see Table 26.2) rose from $21.9 billion in 1940 to $119 billion by 1946. The banks were stuffed with bonds.[11]

Money Supply

The policy of a cheap-money war meant, of course, that the money supply was grossly inflated, and quickly. Since the country entered the war with vast unemployed resources and capital equipment, the inflationary consequences of the first infusions of money were not greatly feared. After all, the New Deal had wanted nothing more fervently than inflation. Even though production of autos and other consumer durables ceased altogether as plants were shifted to war output, production of nondurables rose. A nation starved for consumer goods for a decade surged into the markets to buy what *was* available as incomes rose. Retailers' inventories of old goods evaporated. Price controls—together with ticket-rationing of such items as gasoline, meat, and sugar—ensured some facsimile of "fair shares" as the war progressed. To save cloth, cuffs came off men's trousers; woolens became scarce, and nylon stockings for the ladies vanished. Natural crepe soles on men's shoes disappeared. The buying public got used to substitute fabrics and strange com-

binations of meat and meal. There was plenty, but it was necessarily of different composition.[12]

Taxes

The federal government tried to tax away much of the war-inflated income. Taxes divert command over resources to the government. But the United States was still a democracy, and legislators were constrained in their patriotic fervor by the need to be reelected. So, taxation was at politically viable levels rather than at the technical maxima to finance the war. It can be seen in Table 26.2 that, in fact, federal revenues grew by nearly a factor of 7 in the years 1940–45, compared to the tenfold increase of expenditures. It was not a shabby taxing performance, given the electoral constraints.

Excise taxes were raised, and special war taxes were levied upon luxuries (taxes that, typically, remained for decades after the war ended). The key to success was the pay-as-you-earn individual income tax of 1943. Governments have always had their taxing ambitions restrained by the costs of collection. For example, marauding soldiers stealing grain from peasants is an inefficient mode. The costs are too high, and, anyhow, the peasants may well refrain from planting so much the next season. Since most of the nation's income is earned by the nonrich, the problem of seizing part of the incomes of ordinary working people is constrained

Figure 26.1   Interest Rates (1925–1959)

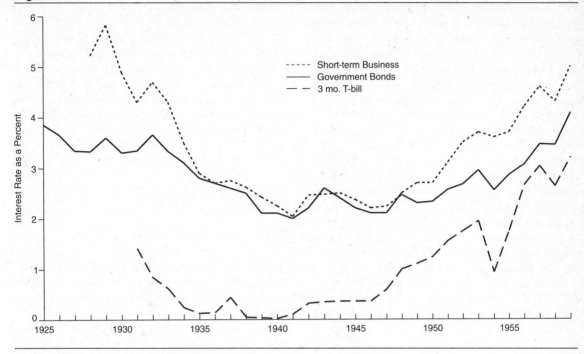

Source: *Historical Statistics,* series X 450, 466, 474.

by the costs of sustaining an army of tax collectors. Already in 1942, the federal government had commandeered the more readily available incomes from visible sources.[13] Employers under the new plan would gather the income taxes from their own employees concurrently with the earning of those incomes. The funds would then be turned over to the Internal Revenue Service. Policing the taxpayers was made easier by this system.

The Social Security taxes of 1937 showed the way. The pay-as-you-earn income tax has been the heart of federal taxation ever since. The tax rates were steeply graduated in the interest of patriotism. Why should individuals at home get rich while "our boys" fought abroad? Naturally, the wartime rates never came back down to peacetime levels.

Individual income taxes, less than 20 percent of the federal government's tax haul in 1940, grew to 37 percent of revenues by 1945 (see Table 26.2).[14] The pay-as-you-earn income tax gave the federal government an automatic "skim" of the personal income of

the entire nation. The New Dealers, living before the Revenue Act of 1943, could never have fantasized such fiscal powers.

In summary, 46.5 percent of the huge war costs were paid for by current taxation. The same figure for World War I had been only 33 percent.[15] Less than perfect, fraught with peril for the future, the tax system of World War II was nevertheless a prodigious achievement. Scaling it down afterward would prove to be a far greater problem than building it had been in the fervor of wartime patriotism.

Monetary Consequences

As Table 26.2 shows, the money supply aggregates necessarily were grossly distended. Excess capacity at the beginning allowed output and employment to expand without full inflationary consequences. Nevertheless, the nation was filled with an overhang of potentially inflationary liquidity. But when the war ended, that liquidity, representing both pent-up demand for consumer goods (especially durables, such as new cars and refrigerators) caused by the war and the long depression that preceded it, was met by a burst of physical output. The nation's manufacturing establishment went to work making goods to capture as profits the war-inflated spending power of the public. The results no one predicted. Some economists feared a return of the 1930s; others, runaway inflation. What actually happened looks obvious only in retrospect.

Consider the data in Table 26.3. They have been indexed on the year 1940 to simplify comparison. By the war's end, M_1 had grown 150 percent, but wholesale prices were up a mere 35 percent over 1940. By the standard of price inflation alone, the war's management had been a triumph; wholesale prices had doubled in World War I (see Table 23.3).

When price controls were removed in 1946, prices rose powerfully, up 50 percent by 1950 over 1945 levels. The money supply also rose, as part of wartime debt holdings were either cashed in or sold to the Fed. These funds helped finance postwar expansion. But the money supply increase in the period 1945–50 was only an additional 15 percent. By the end of the postwar period, the increased money supply was still far greater than increased prices compared to 1940. Now, the money supply was buying power in the public's hands, prices were the cost of spending it. Not surprisingly, Americans still look back to the war and postwar five years fondly: the great prosperity that followed the anguish of the 1930s.[16]

Table 26.3   Wholesale Prices and M_1 1940–50 (indexed on 1940)

Year	Wholesale Prices	Money Supply M_1
1940	100.0	100.0
1941	112.3	117.3
1942	125.6	139.6
1943	131.1	182.2
1944	132.3	215.2
1945	134.6	250.3
1946	154.0	268.5
1947	188.6	281.9
1948	204.3	283.3
1949	194.1	280.4
1950	201.8	287.9

Source: Calculated from data given in *Historical Statistics*, series E 73, X 414.

THE WAR, LABOR, AND FAMILY INCOME

The war expenditures boosted family incomes decisively, and spending incomes earned from war work provided increased demand for most other goods and services. The Keynesian message had been that, if all other factors remained unchanged, large government expenditures financed by new money creation would lay the foundation for a broad advance. Mean family income, $2209 in 1941, was up nearly 64 percent in just three years; in current prices it was $3614 in 1944. Real GNP per capita (1929 prices) rose in those years 45 percent. It was an abrupt change from the futility of the 1930s.

Labor Force Participation

As Table 26.1 helps make clear, the depression-era unemployment rates fell dramatically as the war effort gained pace. There quickly developed a labor shortage. With millions under arms, the labor force needed new recruits from those not normally employed. The 1944 labor force was nearly 10 million larger than that of 1940. For the most part, unused sources were tapped for this increase.

Some of the most striking aspects of this development are shown in Table 26.4. The upward draft of expenditures produced extraordinary employment opportunities and pulled into the labor force unusual numbers from the 14–19 years age group. The increase of labor-force participation among teenage females was 80 percent, and for males, 57 percent. Half the nation's males over 65 were in gainful employment, as were a large portion of the females. Retirement at 65 had gone out of fashion, momentarily. There was even a 10-percent increase of females entering the labor force in the prime family-formation years, aged 20–24 years. The total female participation rate rose by 30 percent.

When the war ended, all participation rates declined, as did the labor force itself. The wartime participation rates demonstrated that our conception of "full employment" depends heavily upon assumptions about what are normal participation rates. Obviously, compared to 1944 participation rates, the unemployment levels of the 1930s were far worse than the actual data show. In the 1970s, female participation rates would rise to more than 50 percent under the stress of inflation's effect on family living standards. World War II, with its image of "Rosie the Riveter," women doing "men's work," presaged things to come a generation later.

As Claudia Goldin has noted, the war proved to a be a boon for older (45–64 years old), married women who had previously been excluded from the labor force. Firms that continued to place restrictions on married women workers, the "marriage bar," put a severe constraint on their ability to acquire labor. This had not been true before the war. Nor did the war benefit other cohorts of women in the same way. Both the oldest and youngest (14–19) groups of women workers showed large increases in employment during the war. The census of 1950, however, documented that, for the youngest cohort, while wartime employment was 200 percent of that reported in 1940, peacetime employment in 1950 showed no difference from 1940. On the other hand, for the older cohort, the difference was maintained—and even widened. For those in the 20–24 year-old cohort, employment in 1950 was less than it had been in 1940.

"Rosie the Riveter" reputedly lost her job when the men returned. If she were young, the chances are that was true. Goldin reports there is still disagreement whether the young Rosies wanted to continue riveting after the war, but it appears neither their old nor an alternative position was an available option. For the older Rosies, alternative employment became available, and they took it.[17]

Wages

The war's extraordinary demand for the output of manufacturing industry meant demand for factory hands. The nonagricultural labor force rose by nearly one-third between the initial buildup in 1940 and 1944, the peak year of defense employment. Employees in manufacturing, which totaled 10.8 million in 1940, numbered more than 17 million in 1944, an increase of nearly 60 percent. Average weekly earnings in manufacturing rose from $25.20 in 1940 to $46.08 in 1944, a gain of more than 80 percent.[18] Even the nation's farmers (now dwindling in numbers) at last shared in the bonanza. Their prices soared, demand for their output was unprecedented, and the rationing system gave them priority for fuel. The extent of mechanization in the late 1930s helped them raise output even as employment in their industry actually declined. Table 26.5 shows what happened to employee earnings.

Table 26.4   Labor Force and Participation

Year	Total Labor Force (in millions)	Percentage Participation Rates						
		Males				Females		
		Total	16–19 Years	20–24 Years	65+ Years	Total	16–19 Years	20–24 Years
1940	56.2	82.5	— 66.4	—	66.9[a]	27.9	— 34.7	—
1944	66.0	88.2	72.2	96.4	49.4	36.3	41.1	55.6
1947	61.8	86.8	67.0	84.9	47.8	31.8	41.1	44.9

[a] The rate for 1940 is for 55+ years.

Source: *Historical Statistics*, series D 1, 30–38.

Table 26.5   Average Annual Earnings per Full-Time Employee

Year	All Industries	Agriculture Fishing Forestry	Mining	Contract Construction	Manufacturing	Services
1940	$1,299	$ 407	$1,388	$1,330	$1,432	$ 953
1944	2,109	1,021	2,499	2,602	2,517	1,538
1947	2,589	1,276	3,113	2,829	2,793	1,996

Source: *Historical Statistics*, series D 722, 739–41, 745, 755.

In all cases the advance motivated by the war continued in the postwar expansion. Earnings in agriculture, although still low absolutely as well as relatively, actually experienced the greatest wartime increase proportionally. America's perennial surplus of food, as in World War I, now became a core necessity, and the farmers found themselves heroes again. All else depended upon food production. Remember that prices had only gone up by about one-third in the war years, so wage earners in nearly all industries experienced very considerable gains in real income.

Distribution

As was the case in World War I, the income distribution was made more equal by war expenditures in a mobilized economy. With a great rise in labor-force participation and priorities placed upon labor for physical production, the poorest families shared in the good times. The change toward greater equality was not as dramatic as one might suppose, but it was real and a part of the modern trend in this country toward greater equality of income distribution.

Table 26.6   Income Distribution

Percentage Distribution of Aggregate Family Personal Income	1935–36	1946
Lowest fifth	4.1	5.0
Second fifth	9.2	11.1
Third fifth	14.1	16.0
Fourth fifth	20.9	21.8
Highest fifth	51.7	46.1
Top 5 percent	26.5	21.3

Source: *Historical Statistics*, series G 319–24.

As in Table 26.6, the lower 40 percent of families increased their shares slightly, and the shares going to the income earners fell. However, the top 5 percent still received far more income than did the lower 40 percent in 1946. The war had made some better off than others. At least, by 1946 the lower 80 percent together received slightly more than did the top 20 percent. That had not been true before the war.

CONSUMPTION AND INVESTMENT

The behavior of personal consumption expenditures during the period contained one small curiosity worthy of note: the rise in the *proportion* spent on food. In addition, the war's impact on consumers' earnings prepared the way for the postwar investment boom.

Increase in Food Consumption

According to Engel's Law, as real income rises, the proportion spent on food declines. Americans were already well fed by 1941. But Engel's Law assumes some sort of normal distribution of consumption alternatives. When the boom in family incomes came in World War II, expensive new consumer durables, such as autos, household machines and gadgets, were not being produced. Having already sufficient savings rates, consumers bought more food and drink (in restaurants as well as for home consumption). It was a curious reversal of form, but probably was not due to anything more fundamental than forced saving, the lack of alternatives. Note the changes in Table 26.7.

When the war ended and consumers' durables became available again, the consumer expenditure on food declined as purchases of durables increased. The

Table 26.7   Personal Consumption Patterns

Year	Total Personal Consumption Expenditures[a]	Food and Drink[a]	Household Durables[a]	Percentage Food and Drink of Total	Percentage Household Durables of Total
1940	$ 70.8	$20.2	$ 4.9	28.5	6.9
1944	108.3	36.7	6.1	33.9	5.6
1945	119.7	40.6	6.9	33.9	5.8
1947	160.7	52.3	13.6	32.5	8.5

[a] Amounts are in billions of dollars.

Source: *Historical Statistics*, series G 416, 419, 434.

huge postwar demand for durables, in turn, fueled the investment boom of the later 1940s.

Investment

Conventional wisdom held that the unexampled out-pouring of commodities from the wartime economy merely showed dramatically the waste of the 1930s—the unemployment of people and resources, the output and working lives lost forever—and that the slack in the American economy in 1941 had made possible such an expansion of output for war uses with so (relatively) little inflationary pressure.

The data in Table 26.8 for private investment show, in fact, a sharp decline during the war years. The comparison with personal saving is particularly interesting. Note the sharp rise in personal savings during the war—from $3.8 billion in 1940 to almost ten times that amount, $37.3 billion in 1944. Then savings declined precipitately once things to buy entered the market in 1946–47. Americans apparently preferred to buy goods but would save if they had no alternatives.

The data for gross private domestic investment, on the other hand, fell nearly by half in 1942, once the war was on. By 1943, private investment was only $5.7 billion, a mere 31 percent of the 1941 level. When the war ended and with it the end of investment priorities, private investment surged to levels never known before, and the great postwar boom was on. But how was the increased output of World War II achieved in the presence of such a sharp decline in private investment?

As Robert J. Gordon points out in a famous essay, a more interesting and unconventional wisdom was concealed in the record of federal wartime expenditures.[19] The Reconstruction Finance Corporation (itself the descendant of World War I's War Finance Corporation) built and equipped industrial buildings largely through its subsidiary, the Defense Plant Corporation. These buildings were made available to private war contractors on favorable terms.[20] After the war, some of the more spectacular installations, like Utah's mammoth Geneva Steel plant at Provo, were sold to private operators. Other buildings and equipment were simply turned over to the wartime users.

Some of the plants used for the atomic bomb project were kept as government property. Others, for example, air bases in the Western deserts were, like the mothballed fleets of ships and airplanes, of no immediate use and were slowly dismantled, scrapped, or put to imaginative peacetime uses (Camp Stoneman, California, for example, is now an industrial park). Naval supply ships were turned into floating fish canneries; surplus jeeps and trucks lingered for years on farms. Army camps were turned over to private municipalities. The miserable barracks buildings and Quonset huts even found further life moved to peacetime locations such as college campuses, where they housed student families.

In any case, nothing could be further from the narrow truth than the conventional wisdom that the underemployed depression economy suddenly rose like a phoenix to make the planes and tanks needed by wartime America. Just as the labor force had to be expanded by increased participation rates, so the country's industrial plant was enlarged by direct government construction. There was, to be sure, excess capacity in 1941, but it was not the sole source of the great output expansion of the war years.

THE KEYNESIAN LESSON

The war gave economists and politicians everywhere an object lesson in a form of Keynesianism that was not forgotten.[21] Keynes had sketched out the main ideas in his 1941 pamphlet, *How to Pay for the War*. It was a powerful application of the analysis developed in his *General Theory of Employment, Interest and*

Table 26.8   Personal Savings and Private Investment[a]

Year	Personal Saving	Gross Private Domestic Investment
1940	$ 3.8	$13.1
1941	11.0	17.9
1942	27.6	9.8
1943	33.4	5.7
1944	37.3	7.1
1945	29.6	10.6
1946	15.2	30.6
1947	7.3	34.0

[a] Amounts given are in billions of dollars.

Source: *Historical Statistics*, series F 162, 564.

Money. Government-directed expenditures would produce the output necessary to create the material goods for war *and* for civilian consumption and investment. Full use of the economy's productive capacity put a lid on what was possible. Since the money cost of the war goods became spendable income in the economy at large and the war products did not enter that economy to absorb those expenditures, taxation, bond sales, postwar credits (interest-earning deposits made by workers and frozen for the duration) must absorb the excess income or else inflation would result. *How to Pay for the War* was also a blueprint for the "national budgets" and planning techniques that became popular in western Europe after the war, but not here.[22]

Thus the war was, in a sense, the full Keynesian message illustrated: Government expenditures, utilizing deficit spending, could and did wipe away the unemployment associated with the depression. But in its full application, monetary measures of a direct nature had to be applied along with physical rationing and other controls to stem the tide of inflation.[23]

American politicians, even the most impeccably conservative ones, could not deny the evidence of their senses: The war had solved the riddle of lingering stagnation and unemployment that had defeated all New Deal efforts. Beginning in the summer of 1941, Americans and their British allies began planning for the postwar world. They embarked upon the grand scheme of world economic recovery and expansion embedded ultimately in the United Nations and the Bretton Woods financial institutions (see Chapter 28). Part of the new international order was, necessarily, the direct assumption by the federal government of the power to control aggregate demand and promote full-employment policies inside the American economy. A new international order would be pointless if the 1930s were going to reappear, as many feared. The war proved, it was argued, that the disaster need not recur. Legislation ultimately appeared (the Employment Act of 1946) which seemed to be justified by the wartime experience—certainly the New Deal itself could not have produced any great confidence in the effectiveness of federal power to produce the full-employment economy.[24]

Whatever the war lesson was, the Employment Act of 1946 was a real revolution in American economic history. Never before had the federal government, the creation of the compromise between the states in the summer of 1787, asserted in law its power and assumed the obligation to "manage" the economy.

Notes

1. Byrd L. Jones, "The Role of Keynesians in Wartime Policy and Postwar Planning, 1940–1946," *AER,* May 1972. Christina Romer has argued that whatever recovery the United States experienced before 1942 was due largely to an inflow of gold which began in the mid- to late-1930s, "What Ended the Great Depression," *JEH,* December 1992.
2. Robert Higgs, "Wartime Prosperity? A Reassessment of the U.S. Economy in the 1940s," *JEH,* March 1992.
3. Higgs, p. 53. Higgs is quoting Seymour Melman, *The Permanent War Economy,* New York: Simon and Schuster, 1985, p. 15.
4. Otis Graham, Jr., *Toward a Planned Society: From Roosevelt to Nixon* (1976).
5. Jonathan Hughes, *The Governmental Habit Redux* (1991), pp. 197–99. Hugh Rockoff, *Drastic Measures: Wage and Price Controls in the United States* (1984), ch. 4; Robert Higgs, *Crisis and Leviathan: Critical Episodes in the Growth of American Government* (1987), ch. 9.
6. Hugh Rockoff, "The Response of the Giant Corporations to Wage and Price Controls in World War II," *JEH,* March 1981. See also Rockoff and Geofrey Mills, "Compliance with Price Controls in the United States and the United Kingdom During World War II," *JEH,* March 1987.
7. Executive Order 9066, 19 February 1942. *Personal Justice Denied: Report of the Commission on Wartime Relocation and Internment of Civilians* (Washington: Government Printing Office,1982); Peter Irons, *Justice At War* (New York: Oxford University Press, 1983).
8. John Kenneth Galbraith, *A Life in Our Times* (1981), contains his reminiscences of the World War II command economy. His *A Theory of Price Control* (1952) discusses the results of the wartime regime of price and wage controls. In two articles shortly after the war, he laid out his beliefs about price controls, their general superiority as a technique of allocation, and his finding that control of prices was easiest in oligopoly markets which he found to be fairly general in American business:

"Reflections on Price Control," *QJE,* August 1946; and "The Disequilibrium System" *AER,* June 1947. A recent study of direct controls in World War II is Hugh Rockoff, *Drastic Measures,* chs. 4–5.

9. This discussion of war financing is largely derived from Paul Studenski and Herman Krooss *Financial History of the United States* (New York: McGraw-Hill, 1952), ch. 30. For a new and critical evaluation of the processes of organizing the World War II command economy, see Robert Higgs, *Crisis and Leviathan,* ch. 9.

10. In 1940 individuals held 20 percent of all government bonds; commercial banks, 39 percent; and nonbank holders, 44 percent. Nonbank holdings declined as business institutions used their resources to finance new capital outlays. Studenski and Krooss, pp. 454–55.

11. For an account of wartime collaboration between the Fed and the Treasury, see L. V. Chandler, "Federal Reserve Policy and Federal Debt," *American Economic Review,* vol. XXXIX, no. 2, March 1949.

12. The issue of wartime quality deterioration was raised in connection with wage controls. Hugh Rockoff, "Indirect Price Increases and Real Wages During World War II," *EEH,* October 1978.

13. It should not be construed from the discussion in this section that our modern member of Congress has lost the kind of deep and considered understanding of taxation principles that ruled in 1943. The tax measure *then,* as now, was an outcome of hearings and debates that had little coherence in them. E. D. Allen, "Treasury Tax Policies in 1943," *AER,* December 1944; also Mabel Newcomer, "Congressional Tax Policies in 1943," *AER,* December 1944.

14. Studenski and Krooss, *Financial History of the United States,* p. 445.

15. Studenski and Krooss, pp. 295–99.

16. Did price controls really slow inflation down, or merely postpone inflation? See Hugh Rockoff, *Drastic Measures,* ch. 4. Rockoff argues that the price controls of World War II actually reduced the amount of inflation we had from, say, 1940–1950.

17. Claudia Goldin, *Understanding the Gender Gap* (1990), pp. 152–54, 175–76.

18. Due to overtime, the increase in earnings was larger than the increase in hourly wage *rates,* which were controlled. D. M. Keezer, "The National War Labor Board," *AER,* June 1946; and Harry Henig and S. H. Unterberger, "Wage Control in Wartime and Transition," *AER,* June 1945.

19. Robert J. Gordon, "$45 Billion of U.S. Private Investment Has Been Mislaid," *AER,* June 1969.

20. Louis Cain and George Neumann, "Planning for Peace: The Surplus Property Act of 1944," *JEH,* March 1981.

21. For a modern summary, see Herbert Stein, *The Fiscal Revolution in America* (1969), ch. 8.

22. Jacob Mosak, "National Budgets and National Policy," *AER,* March 1946.

23. "Disguised" inflation during the war is a further reason why Higgs questions the Keynesian view of wartime prosperity. Higgs, "Wartime Prosperity?" p. 51.

24. For a study of this legislation's misadventures from its earlier version as a "full-employment" act, see S. K. Bailey, *Congress Makes a Law* (1950).

Suggested Readings

Articles

Allen, E. D. "Treasury Tax Policies in 1943." *American Economic Review,* vol. XXXIV, no. 4, December 1944.

Cain, Louis, and Neumann, George. "Planning for Peace: The Surplus Property Act of 1944." *Journal of Economic History,* vol. XLI, no. 1, March 1981.

Galbraith, John Kenneth. "Reflections on Price Control." *Quarterly Journal of Economics,* vol. LX, no. 4, August 1946.

———. "The Disequilibrium System." *American Economic Review,* vol. XXXVII, no. 3, June 1947.

Gordon, Robert J. "$45 Billion of U.S. Private Investment Has Been Mislaid." *American Economic Review,* vol. LIX, no. 3, June 1969.

Henig, Harry, and Unterberger, S. H. "Wage Control in Wartime and Transition." *American Economic Review,* vol. XXXV, no. 3, June 1945.

Higgs, Robert. "Wartime Prosperity? A Reassessment of the U.S. Economy in the 1940s." *Journal of Economic History,* vol. 52, no. 1, March 1992.

Jones, Byrd L. "The Role of Keynesians in Wartime Policy and Postwar Planning 1940–1946." *American Economic Review,* vol. LXII, no. 2, May 1972.

Keezer, D. M. "The National War Labor Board." *American Economic Review,* vol. XXXVI, no. 3, June 1946.

Mosak, Jacob. "National Budgets and National Policy." *American Economic Review,* vol. XXXVI, no. 1, March 1946.

Newcomer, Mabel. "Congressional Tax Policies in 1943." *American Economic Review,* vol. XXXIV, no. 4, December 1944.

Rockoff, Hugh. "Indirect Price Increases and Real Wages During World War II." *Explorations in Economic History,* vol. 15, no. 4, October 1978.

———. "The Response of the Giant Corporations to Wage and Price Controls in World War II." *Journal of Economic History,* vol. XLI, no. 1, March 1981.

———, and Mills, Geofrey. "Compliance with Price Controls in the United States and the United Kingdom During World War II." *Journal of Economic History,* vol. XLVII, no. 1, March 1987.

Romer, Christina. "What Ended the Great Depression?" *Journal of Economic History,* vol. 52, no. 4, December 1992.

Books

Bailey, S. K. *Congress Makes a Law.* New York: Columbia University Press, 1950.

Galbraith, J. K. *A Theory of Price Control.* Cambridge: Harvard University Press, 1952.

———. *A Life in Our Times.* Boston: Houghton Mifflin, 1981.

Goldin, Claudia D. *Understanding the Gender Gap: An Economic History of American Women.* New York: Oxford University Press, 1990.

Graham, Otis, Jr. *Toward a Planned Society: From Roosevelt to Nixon.* New York: Oxford University Press, 1976.

Higgs, Robert. *Crisis and Leviathan: Critical Issues in the Emergence of the Mixed Economy.* New York: Oxford University Press, 1986.

Hughes, Jonathan. *The Governmental Habit Redux: Economic Controls from Colonial Times to the Present.* Princeton: Princeton University Press, 1991.

Krooss, Herman, and Studenski, Paul. *Financial History of the United States.* New York: McGraw-Hill, 1952.

Rockoff, Hugh. *Drastic Measures: A History of Wage and Price Controls in the United States.* New York: Cambridge University Press, 1984.

Stein, Herbert. *The Fiscal Revolution in America.* Chicago: University of Chicago Press, 1961.

Vatter, Harold G. *The U.S. Economy in World War II.* New York: Columbia University Press, 1985.

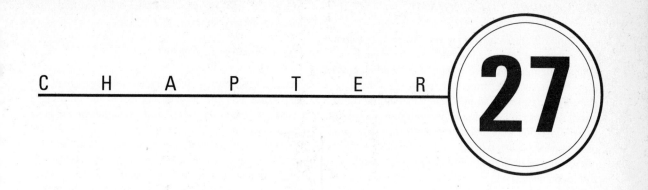

CHAPTER 27

Special Topic: The New Deal at a Distance

Apart from wartime emergencies, we have really made only three attempts to use the federal government to effect, fairly quickly, great objects of economic and social change. All three efforts were in part failures. In the 1930s, the object of federal government policy was "recovery." In the 1960s, it was elimination of "poverty" and discrimination of all kinds. In the 1970s, the main policy target was full employment without inflation. More narrowly, and ignoring the 1960s for the moment, in the 1930s, the problem was unemployment coupled with *deflation;* in the 1970s, it was unemployment coupled with *inflation.* Both times the solutions lay beyond our grasp.

Ronald Reagan's "supply-side revolution" of the 1980s drowned in a sea of federal government budget deficits. What deregulation there was came from legislation and plans going back as far as the Carter and Ford administrations. Just as one cannot make bricks without straw, so one cannot make revolutions out of false hopes alone.

The indifferent record of successes and failures of our three serious reform efforts is worth considering. It is fruitless to simply condemn them all out of hand, unless one is opposed altogether to any federal effort to cope with perceived social and economic ills. What seems clear is that Americans have not yet learned *in practice* to get the sorts of economic results from federal policy that they desire. It is unlikely that people will give up trying, so hopefully they will learn from past experiences, however unsatisfactory they were.

The 1930s make an interesting laboratory for the study of this problem. At first, between 1933 and 1936, the president had the support in Congress to do pretty much as he pleased by way of legislation. There was one great flurry of programs in 1933 and another outburst of legislation in 1935. Much of the 1933 legislation was thrown out by the Supreme Court. Apart from the Fair Labor Standards Act of 1938, the New Deal innovations really ceased. The depression was renewed in 1938 as President Franklin Delano Roosevelt tried to balance the budget by raising taxes and lasted until the all-out war effort came.

Two questions might well be considered at some length in this chapter:

1. From the evidence, what was the object of the New Deal?
2. Was the New Deal in any way a "social revolution"?

WHAT WERE THEY DOING?

In Chapter 23, we saw that, in the World War I command economy, the needs of defense were combined with an attempt to achieve certain long-standing ambitions of the social reformers: The introduction of the eight-hour day, recognition of union bargaining rights, prohibition of child labor, and generation of minimum wage legislation were among those reforms. The same phenomenon occurred in the 1930s. The idea of recovery was mixed up with ambitions for extensive reforms and fundamental changes in the concepts of proper federal responsibility.

NIRA AND TNEC

The policy of the federal government was inconsistent. For example, in the National Industrial Recovery Act (NIRA), Congress had granted business freedom from antitrust prosecution in the hope that business "self-government," cartelization through the NRA codes, might produce profitable prices and larger outputs that would put the unemployed back to work. In 1938, scarcely four years later, the federal government launched a renewed antitrust drive under Thurmon Arnold, and the Temporary National Economic Committee (TNEC) was organized to study the "concentration of economic power" in the American economy with a view to doing something about it. If business confidence was thought important to recovery, such policy perambulations as these can have been of little help.

Moral Reform

The attack on business leadership was prime political currency from the beginning of the New Deal—indeed, from well before the New Deal; it was present in several election campaigns before 1914. The Pecora Committee had already conducted sensational anti-business hearings exposing linkages between banking and the stock market before FDR entered the White House. By 1936, he was castigating the country's business leadership for being "economic royalists" and won the election by a huge landslide. It may well be true that Roosevelt and his colleagues believed the nation's business leadership could benefit from a vigorous purge. It is not clear, though, how they imagined that a sound scourging, however morally beneficial

to the executive ranks themselves, would aid the processes of recovery.

The Securities Industry

Consider the securities industry, commonly blamed for the 1929 crash, and its contribution to the unfolding miseries of the Great Depression. Whether that industry was reformed or not, it contributed little enough to a business recovery after attempts were made to improve it (refer to Table 25.6 in Chapter 25). Roosevelt talked grandly of "an end to speculation with other people's money." The money changers had "fled from their high seats in the temple of our civilization." The Truth in Securities Act of May 1933 and the Securities Exchange Commission in 1934 were meant somehow to take the risk out of the securities industry and encourage virtue. They did not yield a recovery in the capital markets.

The Board of Governors

Moving the Federal Reserve's Open Market Committee to Washington and giving the politically appointed members of the Federal Reserve Board an automatic majority in the 1935 Banking Act may or may not have been economically wise, but its object was to politicize the Federal Reserve System, to weaken the power of the private sector in the determination of monetary policy. The same was true of the board's new powers to alter at will the required reserves of the member banks. Marriner Eccles, who wrote the 1935 Bank Act, believed that control of the nation's monetary system *should* be politicized in our democracy and control taken away from the New York bankers. He thought their prior domination to have been both undemocratic and incompetent.

Policy and Ambiguity

The Export-Import Bank was designed to underwrite the American exports but also was meant to shift the impact of American foreign policy. At first the "Ex-Im" was used to facilitate trade with the Soviet Union, whom the United States had refused to "recognize" until 1933 and who could not, in any case, get ordinary credits from the commercial world for obvious reasons. Later on, while the United States was officially neutral, the "Ex-Im" aided China in its war against Japan (in 1938, $25 million was loaned to build the Burma Road). The country also subsidized trade with assorted and favored foreign governments in other parts of the world. The "Ex-Im" was used then, as it still is, dualistically: to subsidize American exports and to facilitate U.S. foreign policy, whatever it is at the moment. The first function ensures continued support from Congress, the second comes in handy to succeeding administrations.

The NIRA was similarly ambiguous in purpose: It was an effort to allow "industrial self-government," its contribution to recovery, but it was also a way to lift the antitrust laws in the manufacturing industries and, at the same time, to encourage the development of organized labor in those industries favored by the industrial codes of the NRA.

Agricultural policies were fashioned from the same sort of mixed motives. In the original Agricultural Adjustment Act, the tax on processors was an attempt to force the "middle man" to pay the cost of loans against stored crops, subsidize the retirement of land from production, and buy farm surpluses outright. The tone of the legislation was antibusiness. Part of the AAA's object was to raise farm incomes by raising farm prices, but other motives were mixed in. The efforts to reduce supplies by subsidies were offset by other efforts to raise output efficiency on farms through mechanization, financial assistance, improved plowing and cultivation techniques, better fertilizers, improved genetic strains—even to make farm life more pleasant through agricultural extension services. More farming? Less? More output? Less? Higher prices? Lower? All were mixed outcomes implied in the various policies.

Public Power

The New Deal did a good job increasing the nation's production and use of electric power. In the Tennessee Valley Authority (TVA) system, the great multipurpose dams of the Northwest, the irrigation and power systems created in the plains states (discussed in Chapter 15), the organization of Rural Electrification Administration (REA) co-ops to bring power to the country's farms—the New Deal motivated a massive increase in energy use. The power, apart from the REA systems, was largely distributed by private power companies. They, however, were now hobbled by the Pub-

lic Utilities Holding Companies Act of 1935, which had placed them under the control of the Securities and Exchange Commission, restricting their own efforts to be reorganized and prohibiting (profitable) kinds of diversification.

The privately owned utilities had not, in fact, undertaken to provide power sufficiently on a strictly private basis in most rural areas. As a result, the government went ahead with the project, allowing the utilities to participate as junior partners. Only 10 percent of American farms had regular electrical service in 1933, less than was commonly the case in advanced western European countries at the time. This situation was viewed as a case of **market failure.** The country produced a huge new enterprise in this public- and government-sponsored electric industry but purposely restricted the private power sector's growth capacity, at the same time pushing the growth of the public power sector.

The results were ambiguous. Was policy designed to encourage growth of the electric power industry in general, or merely to create a new public-sector industry? Would a greater growth have occurred by a full public-private partnership as in the internal improvements era of the 1830s and 1840s? Without all the antibusiness rhetoric? We will never know.

That such efforts by the federal administration were the product of distinctly mixed motives is no condemnation of the policies. It would be unreasonable to suppose that such great changes in the concept of government responsibility and the implementation of the resulting policies and programs would or could be done without substantial changes in those parts of the economy directly affected. Economically, such changes are the equivalent of technological change in private industry. It is not simply a matter of additional application of the same input combinations. Instead, the production function shifts, and all costs, revenues, and benefits change accordingly. When a Fort Peck or Grand Coulee dam was built, the economic spillovers into the surrounding communities were immense and not really calculable in advance.

Employment and the Prevailing Wage

The Civilian Conservation Corps (CCC) and the Works Progress Administration (WPA) produced similar consequences. The economy derived benefits from

crowding out.

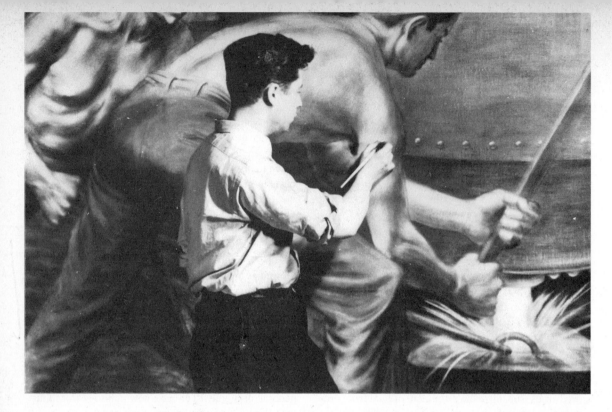

The New Deal Out of Doors. Activism by the federal government was the hallmark of the New Deal. Artists (above left), writers, actors, and musicians all gained from federal projects. On the land, conservation projects (below left) restored nature's bounty. Planned cities like this one in Maryland in 1938 (above right) seemed the coming thing. Perhaps the greatest monuments to federal expenditure were such water conservation projects as Grand Coulee on the Columbia River (below right).

those efforts in conservation, from new sewer and water systems, sidewalks, and roads. Unemployed or underemployed people, to whom society would otherwise have been providing relief support, were put to work in those vast enterprises. Once they were assigned to work on public projects, they were employed at useful labor, *and* society gained the output as a benefit.

The CCC lasted from 1933 to 1940, employing 2.5 million people. In the desperate conditions of 1933, Harry Hopkins put 4 million people to work on Civil Works Administration (CWA) projects *in two months.* The Public Works Administration (PWA), under Secretary of the Interior Harold Ickes, had been designed under Title II of the NIRA to produce significant public-sector input into the construction industry. Billions were ultimately spent by the PWA, but the employment effects were deemed insufficient. So, in 1935 Congress created the famous WPA under Harry Hopkins to spend money on employment under the Emergency Relief Appropriations Act. Hopkins originally had about $4.9 billion to disperse. By 1941, he had employed 8 million people on WPA projects, an estimated 16 percent of the labor force, at a cost of $11.4 billion.

That these measures "put people to work," cannot be denied. But at this distance in time, it is not sacrilege to question the net effects. The federal works projects employed people at modest enough wages—supposedly at the "prevailing wage" in the districts where the projects were located. It was no secret, however, that WPA "security" wages, being regular and actually *paid* in cash, were an improvement for the unskilled, even if they were already employed elsewhere.

In 1936, government employment was made more attractive as a result of the Walsh-Healy Act, which fixed standards for hours, wages, and working conditions in all government employments. Some economists at that time (and since) argued that unemployment was kept unusually high throughout the 1930s because *real* wages were kept from falling. In the private sector, firms cut hours and jobs before they reduced the nominal wage; it was "sticky." In the public sector, the federal employment, through its insistence on the prevailing wage, helped wages in general remain above the *equilibrium*, or full-employment, level. According to the deflationist argument, had wages fallen as freely as prices, full employment *must* have resulted. In addition there might even have been

an advance in real wages, as was true for those people who were able to maintain their employment. Following the logic of the argument, the heroic efforts of the federal government were really counterproductive: The public enterprises consumed labor and materials at prices beyond the reach of the private sector. Hence, the private sector remained in a depressed state even though there was a vast expansion of the public enterprise. Whether or not this argument is wholly fantasy, we cannot say.

Failure of the Multiplier?

Another view holds that the New Deal, in its vast scope, was, in effect, the construction of a permanent depression, given the institutional nature of the American economy. Most of the employment and output relied upon the private sector, and the private sector was held back by all sorts of government policies (e.g., the surtax on incomes in 1935; the drive for a balanced budget in 1937, together with the borrowing of reserves from the commercial banks to demonetize gold flowing into the country and the raising of the required reserve ratios of the commercial banks) which, it is charged, produced an unambiguous return to depression in 1938. The list of possibly counterproductive policies is long. The Wagner Act alone, which installed quite suddenly a whole new system of labor relations in the manufacturing industries, may have frightened potential manufacturers off.

According to basic macroeconomic theory, the multiplier effect of the public sector should have spilled over into the private sector via consumption expenditures and should have provided the means for recovery. However, according to the arguments of Cary Brown and Larry Peppers (discussed in Chapter 25), the New Deal expenditures were insufficient to create the hoped-for income effects via the multiplier process. As Keynesianism, the New Deal was worse than nothing, macroeconomically speaking.

In retrospect, the New Deal was much like an auto with its wheels spinning, sinking inexorably into the mud. The "reforms" of American capitalism via regulation, like the Public Utilities Holding Company Act and the new public-sector departures like TVA and REA, were merely substitutes for normal private sector activity that now did not occur *because,* in part at least, of the reforms themselves. The great make-work projects of the PWA, CWA, and WPA at "prevailing wages" kept wages too high, given the price level, for employers and prospective employers to hire workers. Agriculture policies to raise prices and farm incomes also raised output, in part canceling the other actions out.

THE NEW DEAL: A SOCIAL REVOLUTION?

Whether it is viewed as savior or destructor, the New Deal must be viewed as very innovative in its time. Very little that is *entirely* new in the way of social policy has been achieved since then. The scope of government has been vastly expanded, but always along lines that were to some extent developed by 1940. Even the federal assumption of responsibility for prices, income, employment, and economic growth (in addition to other objectives) in the Employment Act of 1946 was a formalization of activities and ambitions developing in Washington, D. C., before the depression ended. Indeed, the public perception that the federal power *ought* to be used to pursue such policies we saw developing in the late nineteenth century, for example, in the Populist demands.

What Was New?

The pursuit, in peacetime, of policies by the federal government to support any given levels of income, employment, or prices was new. The problem faced by policymakers was partly ideological. Gaston Rimlinger observed that American ideals of individualism formed a "formidable ideological obstacle" to such ideas, even to social insurance.[1] It was not new to utilize the federal power to encourage some industries at the expense of others: Rent creation by government power, as we know, goes back in Federalist America to the first tariff; in colonial America, to the first settlements. But, the tradition of private-sector employment, income, wages, and prices was that, police powers apart, these matters were left to free contracting by private parties. President Hoover had resisted the idea that direct federal responsibilities might be extended to such matters, and so, at first, did FDR.

The use of federal power to set up social insurance schemes for nongovernment employees was new. As we saw, the idea originated in large part (e.g., the Swope Plan) in the private sector.[2] In the 1935 Social Security Act, however, a new beginning was made. For employees, participation was mandatory. That removed all the taint of charity from it. Social Security numbers replaced proper names as a means of identification. The system was very minimal at first: contributory old-age and retirement benefits for certain classes of employees, inducements for states to liberalize and standardize workers' compensation, and the provision of employer-paid state unemployment compensation funds.

Later expansions of Social Security benefits, which have produced a funding crisis for the entire system, were not foreseen. There are now huge benefit payments for medical assistance, under Medicare and Medicaid, that were not envisaged in the original scheme. Social Security now is a program of add-ons and adjustments that has never existed as a well-thought-out whole.

As Berkowitz and Wolff show, the entire program never recovered from its jerry-built institutional origins.[3] Senator Wagner sponsored a national health-insurance plan in 1938 that got nowhere in Congress. Harry Truman tried it in his Fair Deal, and that also failed. Every attempt since then has continued to fail because Congress is a creature of special interests, and there are big special interests opposed to national health insurance. That Social Security got through Congress at all was probably due to its minimal coverage. The taxes to pay for it are among our most regressive, and, as was noted in Chapter 25, FDR admitted that the taxes were pure politics "all the way through."[4]

The year 1935 was a big one for New Deal legislation. Roosevelt was probably at the height of his power over Congress. Three or four years later a Social Security bill might not have passed the national legislature at all.[5]

Federal sponsorship of organized labor in the Wagner Act was only partly new, since there already had been federal sponsorship in the Railway Labor Act of 1926. The Norris-LaGuardia anti-injunction act of 1931 was a further federal move in support of organized labor. The Wagner Act was in fact the culmination of labor ambitions for federal support that had seen already two false dawns, one in the World War I command economy and another in the NIRA.

Outright and overt federal sponsorship of industrial cartelization in peacetime under the NRA was new, but failed. The idea was old. In World War I the government assisted anticompetitive industrial processes in the interests of maximum defense production. When the war ended, President Wilson ordered the connected governmental structures abolished. After the NRA failed to pass the Supreme Court, apart from a revitalization of the Antitrust Division, there really was no continued federal policy of an innovative nature toward the manufacturing industry. There were the beginnings of a policy on natural resources and on manpower, but nothing came of them. There was the National Planning Association, which encouraged parallel regional and state planning organizations.[6] Impressive studies were published, and it appeared that a start toward real economic planning might be made, but all that vanished in World War II, and nothing quite like the planning associations was ever seen again.

There also was a primitive national labor policy beginning to evolve out of the Civilian Conservation Corps, the National Youth Administration, and the WPA. War and conscription took care of all that, and nothing of even that scope ever reappeared. These were movements toward a long-run creative role for the federal power in the country's future beyond mere industry-agency regulation or the random vagaries of monetary and fiscal policies. Planning was based on the assumption that the depression economy was a portent of things to come and that there was an impending need for a greatly expanded federal role if prosperity were ever to be seen again in the land. World War II wiped away all these fears.

What Was Old?

Police-power regulation by the federal government was greatly expanded during the New Deal, as part of the general growth of government activism. But in principle it was not new at the federal level, not since 1887. The number of regulatory agencies was so multiplied that it might have seemed to be a "revolutionary" development when it was not. Regularly scheduled air service was something new; to regulate it was not. Two new federal agencies, the Federal Aeronautics Administration and the Civil Aeronautics Board, were applications of time-tested industry-agency regulation. The ICC was the beginning of all that.

The creation of government corporations and agencies of all sorts to expand federal financial participation in housing, transportation, and agriculture was a technique already perfected in the World War I command economy. The proliferation of such devices of federal influence and control was fairly stupefying to some observers during the New Deal, and a great many of these agencies, offices, boards, and administrations continue to this day. But they were not net institutional innovations of the New Deal.

Was It a Social Revolution?

If by the word *revolution* one means a radical realignment of social classes or a basic change in the ownership of the means of production, the New Deal was no revolution. Also, one can easily dispute the claim that the New Deal "saved" American capitalism, since it has hardly seemed capable of life independent of government aid and management since the 1930s.

There was no radical change. When the New Deal ended, all constitutions remained. The ownership of property was perhaps subject to more federal regulation than had been true, but that property had not been basically altered. Ben Franklin would have recognized our land tenure in 1940, and so would Governor Bradford. Apart from higher taxes, production by private capital was still designed to yield a profit to be distributed as a reward for private ownership.[7] Industry was still managed by private managers. Higher education, medicine, food, clothing, shelter—all were almost entirely private matters in 1940, as had been true in 1929. Economic activity, apart from direct government purchases and police-power regulation, was still almost entirely directed by the "dollar vote" cast by consumers.

Then what was (is) all the excitement about? Why can the New Deal still raise the volume of sound in polite discussion so easily? Why should FDR and the New Deal be so much more a part of the modern consciousness than Herbert Hoover and the New Era, or even Lyndon Johnson and the Great Society?

The answer really does seem to be commonplace. Some new departures were made. In particular, the idea of "community" responsibility for a minimal safety net against personal disaster, always there from colonial times at the local level, was raised to the federal level for the first time and remained there. Not only federal sponsorship of social insurance but the assumption by the federal government, via fiscal and monetary policy, of the responsibility for prosperity in the aggregate, left the New Deal wearing an aura of bold innovation in history.

Secondly, governmental activism itself got a powerful send-off in the New Deal days with the multiplicity of institutions formed to identify, define, and act upon "social problems." Even though hosts of the New Deal boards, managements, offices, and administrations vanished, others survived, and the idea of a self-starting bureaucracy caught on. Before the 1930s, initiatives for basic social and economic change rarely came from within the permanent federal bureaucracy. During and since the New Deal, such initiatives have become commonplace. The federal bureaucracy was traditionally a body of civil servants whose activities were defined and directed by the elected government. Shifting the power *to set agendas* for national policy from Congress and the executive and private sectors to the permanent government was mainly an achievement of the New Deal: John Wallis points out that this rise in the importance of the federal establishment was mainly at the expense of *local* government finances and initiatives. The state governments managed to sustain their expenditures because so great a part of the New Deal expenditures consisted of grants, or grants-in-aid to the state governments. The state governments distributed and administered federal expenditures in large part.[8]

As much as these new departures, the sheer volume of expanded government participation and intervention in the economy coming out of the New Deal created a feeling of "revolution," fundamental change, in the quality of everyday life. The federal government was into most people's lives by 1940. That was different. It was not new to have the federal government subsidize building construction. It *was* new to have the finance become a permanent feature of the country's housing industry, supported by a huge network of federal mortgage institutions. Quantity, in the end, appeared to transform quality, and to some extent, that was true. The police-power controls, regulations and regulatory agencies proliferated in the New Deal, and that prolif-

eration continued for decades, despite promises by succeeding presidential candidates to "get the government off people's backs."

As for income and wealth distribution—the alteration of the traditional "class" relations—there has been some narrowing of the range of inequality in the past fifty years (as we will see in Chapter 31), but it remains unclear what the New Deal's real contribution was to this long-run development.

Finally, the number of really new departures in social and economic policy since the New Deal has been so small that the New Deal looks terribly bold in retrospect. Millions of workers receive relatively few benefits from the social insurance programs they pay taxes to support. There was never any national standardization of workers' compensation or unemployment compensation. We have never developed even a national system of subsidized higher education based upon *merit*. In spite of years of discussion, the United States does not yet have universal national health insurance. In other words, its welfare state, expensive as it is, has never been very extensive compared to those of other economically advanced countries. Apart from some huge extensions of particular programs (like the explosion of Aid to Families with Dependent Children expenditures after 1965), the 1930s remains the great era of general innovation. In truth, the permeation of New Deal intervention into the private economy was astonishing.

It is for these reasons that we refer to the New Deal as the one great modern social revolution in the United States. Compared to the civil rights movement of the 1960s and 1970s, the New Deal looms as a moment when elemental forces seemed to have been unleashed. Partly that is an illusion. Partly modern reform movements have concerned themselves with fairly narrow sections of population: those defined as official minorities or the official poor. In these terms, the New Deal was comparatively broad in its reach into American society. That the New Deal *seemed* to embrace the vast majority of Americans was also an achievement. In the panorama of American history, the position (whether positive or negative) of the New Deal and Franklin Delano Roosevelt seems to grow with time.

Notes

1. Gaston Rimlinger, "The Historical Analysis of National Welfare Systems," in Roger Ransom et al., *Explorations in the New Economic History: Essays in Honor of Douglass C. North* (New York: Academic Press, 1982), p. 163.
2. Edward Berkowitz and Kim McQuaid, *Creating the Welfare State* (1988).
3. Edward Berkowitz, and Wendy Wolff, "Disability Insurance and the Limits of American History," *The Public Historian,* Spring 1986.
4. A. M. Schlesinger, Jr., *The Age of Roosevelt: The Coming of the New Deal* (1959), p. 308.
5. Certainly this view is supported by Carolyn Weaver's conclusions that normal progress toward private-sector provision of old-age and survivors' insurance was disrupted by the shock of the 1929–33 recession, and that the New Deal then stepped in, for various reasons, to fill the void. Carolyn L. Weaver, "On the Lack of a Political Market for Compulsory Old-Age Insurance Prior to the Great Depression: Insights from Economic Theories of Government," *EEH,* July 1983.

6. Otis L. Graham, Jr., *Toward a Planned Society: From Roosevelt to Nixon* (New York: Oxford University Press, 1976).
7. The research of Thomas Renaghan leads one to accept even the much-touted "class welfare" interpretation of New Deal taxation with a large dose of salt, "Distributional Effects of Federal Tax Policy, 1929–1939," *EEH,* January 1984.
8. John Wallis, "The Birth of the Old Federalism: Financing the New Deal, 1932–1940," *JEH,* March 1984; see also Jonathan Hughes, "Roots of Regulation: The New Deal," in Gary M. Walton, editor, *Regulatory Change in an Atmosphere of Crisis* (1979).

Suggested Readings

Articles

Berkowitz, Edward, and Wolff, Wendy. "Disability Insurance and the Limits of American History." *The Public Historian,* vol. 8, no. 2, Spring 1986.

Renaghan, Thomas M. "Distributional Effects of Federal Tax Policy, 1929–1939." *Explorations in Economic History,* vol. 21, no. 1, January 1984.

Wallis, John J. "The Birth of the Old Federalism: Financing the New Deal, 1932–1940." *Journal of Economic History,* vol. LXIV, no. 1, March, 1984.

Weaver, Carolyn L. "On the Lack of a Political Market for Compulsory Old-Age Insurance Prior to the Great Depression: Insights from Economic Theories of Government." *Explorations in Economic History,* vol. 20, no. 3, July, 1983.

Books

Achenbaum, W. Andrew. *Social Security: Visions and Revisions.* New York, Holmes & Meier, 1986.

Berkowitz, Edward, and McQuaid, Kim. *Creating the Welfare State: The Political Economy of Twentieth Century Reform,* second edition. New York: Praeger, 1988.

Chandler, Lester. *America's Greatest Depression.* New York: Harper & Row, 1970.

Dyson, Lowell K. *Red Harvest: The Communist Party and American Farmers.* Lincoln: The University of Nebraska Press, 1982.

Leuchtenburg, William E. *Franklin D. Roosevelt and the New Deal 1932–1940.* New York: Harper Torchbooks, 1963.

Moley, Raymond. *After Seven Years.* New York: Harper, 1939.

Schlesinger, Arthur M., Jr. *The Age of Roosevelt,* 3 vols. Boston: Houghton Mifflin, 1957, 1959, 1960.

Shannon, David A. *The Great Depression.* Englewood Cliffs, NJ: Prentice-Hall, 1960.

Sherwood, Robert E. *Roosevelt and Hopkins,* 2 vols. New York: Harper, 1948.

Walton, Gary, ed. *Regulatory Change in an Atmosphere of Crisis: Current Implications of the Roosevelt Years.* New York: Academic Press, 1979.

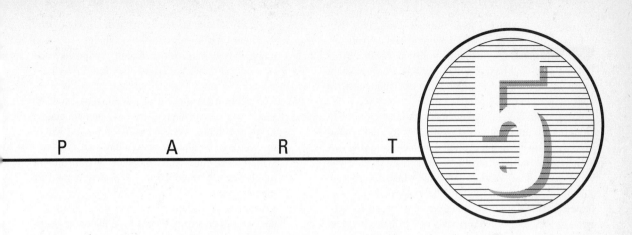

P A R T

Brave New World?

Main Currents 1945–85

For Americans, World War II ended in August 1945. The Japanese surrender ended a national collective effort not seen, probably, since the end of the American Civil War in 1865. The possibilities seemed boundless in the still air of that wonderful late summer. The Depression and the war—altogether sixteen long unremitting years—were at last in the dust of history. Americans could breathe again. They were, it seemed then, masters of their own fates. The United States had emerged from the long ordeal as the economic colossus of the entire world, and there was no close second. Its industry, science, agriculture, and affluence gave its people a heady feeling of superiority. The Constitution had held, the rule of law prevailed, and elections occurred at their appointed intervals. People still spoke of the United States as "young and free." Americans were, in a phrase of the time, on the threshold of "The American Century."

In point of fact, Americans were only about three years from the Berlin Blockade and five from the Korean War and the beginning of the Cold War—never-ending war, never-ending emergency, never-ending peril for what became known as the "national security." That luminous, fragile episode that began in August 1945, less than five years of peace, vanished without trace. And, indeed, remembering the harsh political campaign of 1948, it may well have been an illusion. Perhaps there really was no peace at all, merely an interlude between wars.

After 1950, U.S. economic history became locked in a fateful mixture, the new "welfare state" descended from the New Deal, intermingled with continuous, vast military and national security expenditures at home and abroad. The wartime tax rates remained for the most part, and soon enough, the federal deficits resumed—at first small, then larger and larger. Economists in 1945–50 talked seriously of "full employment and price stability" as the legitimate—and achievable—objects of fiscal and monetary policy. By 1980, with double-digit peacetime inflation, 6 to 7 percent unemployment, and huge deficits at the highest interest rates in American history, sober economists spoke of government expenditures as being "out of control" and predicted the end of home ownership for the average American family under the weight of 15-percent mortgages. What happened? A popular song in 1945 was "Let the Good Times Roll." Where did they go?[1]

The post-World War II economic history of the United States was dominated by perhaps ten themes:

1. American involvement in international trade and finance helped produce a healthier international economy than anything known since 1914, but with powerful, partly adverse consequences inside the U.S. economy itself.

2. The Cold War and vast expenditures for military and quasimilitary hardware, labor, foreign aid, and foreign military operations clouded the prospect and wasted resources.

3. A slowing down in the rates of investment and saving from current income starved the economy of housing and plant capital that, by the 1970s, might have helped regenerate the economy's growth.

4. The resulting decline in the rate of growth, increasing obsolescence of American plants and equipment, and the inability to compete in international markets in many areas of traditional American strength (e.g., steel and automobiles) helped produce balance-of-payments problems and currency crises.

5. A steady rise of tertiary employments compared to direct employment in the production of food and goods has moved increasing proportions of new entrants into the labor force into lower paying jobs.

6. The continuous growth of government expenditures as a share of GNP after 1947 and expansion of the regulatory system finally embraced nearly the whole of legal, private economic activity connected to commerce. Opponents of government involvement blamed relative U.S. decline on this phenomenon.

7. Chronic federal deficits, in both good times and bad, produced steady increases in the money supply and the national debt.

8. The result was inflationary pressure in basic goods and services.

9. Crises in state and local finance, developed as old-fashioned property-tax systems, failed to meet the challenges of inflation, resulting in a decline of civic services.

10. There was an increased concern over debilitating externalities, with the focus on the "energy crisis," pollution, the environment, the "quality of life."

Now, these were problems, and not necessarily catastrophes (the language of media politics). Until the late 1970s, the trend of per capita income had continued to rise, but the United States was no longer the leading nation in that regard. It appeared that, as the industries of other nations made the effort to catch up, they began to develop superior techniques of production and distribution, techniques which American industries either could not or would not adopt.

In the 1980 presidential election, the conservative Republican victory promised a reversal of the "welfare state" trends of nearly half a century, but those entitlement expenditures continued. By 1988 the objective of neoconservatism was no longer mentioned, and in 1992 a liberal Democrat with a plurality of the popular vote started his administration with a strong majority in the opinion polls supporting his pledge to balance the budget and enhance welfare, particularly in the area of health. The American techniques and habits of government participation and control in the economy are deeply rooted and of ancient lineage.

Notes

1. For a clear, if skeletal, summary of events, policy, and
opinions of economists, see Robert J. Gordon, ''Postwar
Macroeconomics: The Evolution of Events and Ideas,'' in
The American Economy in Transition, edited by Martin
Feldstein (Chicago: University of Chicago Press, 1980),
ch. 2. Also see the comments of Arthur Okun and Herbert
Stein immediately following Gordon's article.

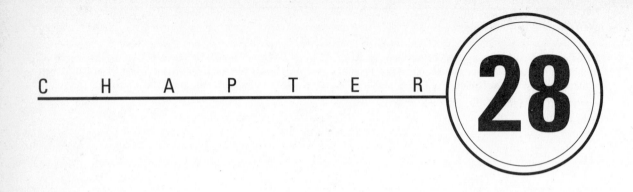

28

From World War II to the New Frontier

rom World War II until the sixties, American economic progress was the envy of the world. By 1960 the American economy had been transformed. The postwar conversion was far behind and had been even surpassed by economic activity in the 1950s. The problems of conversion to peacetime production had been far less difficult than many had imagined they would be. Those who had feared runaway inflation once price controls were removed also were surprised. By 1950 consumer prices were only a third or so above the 1945 level, and real income per capita had nearly regained the 1945 position while total real GNP had surpassed it. The economy had stumbled slightly in 1949 but had resumed its expansion afterward.

Then in June, 1950, the Korean War broke out. Korea had been divided by the Russians and the Americans into Communist North and non-Communist South Korean governments. After much hostility between the two governments, a North Korean tank army burst across the border in June 1950, captured the southern capital, Seoul, and headed south, threatening to take the entire peninsula.

American ground forces were committed by the president, Harry S. Truman, who called for and re-

ceived United Nations support. General Douglas MacArthur pulled off the last brilliant amphibious landing of his career at Inchon and the U.N. forces drove the Communists north to the Chinese border. Communist China then committed an army, and the war continued. For three years, the battles raged, finally coming to a halt by truce at approximately the original frontiers of the two Koreas.

The Korean War was the occasion for a renewed surge of U.S. economic expansion, which lasted, with small cyclical disruptions in 1954 and 1958, until 1960. By then, overall U.S. industrial output was half again the size of the wartime level of 1945. GNP had more than doubled, and real GNP had risen nearly two-thirds over the 1945 level. Following eight years of the conservative Eisenhower administration, a Democrat, John F. Kennedy, was elected in 1960 and a more active redistributive federal social policy was begun. The era of "fine tuning" of fiscal and monetary policy combined with tax and expenditure programs to encourage stable economic growth—the New Frontier—was aborted by JFK's assassination in 1963. His successor, Lyndon Johnson, began with a pledge to continue the New Frontier. Instead, he and his advisers committed American armed forces *en masse* to shore up the South

Vietnamese government, and the U.S. economy was again diverted to war, this time with really disastrous consequences from which, more than three decades later, there still are echoes. The war in Vietnam in curious ways led to disastrous consequences for the economy. The "American Century" ended shortly after it began with the "short peace," the conversion and recovery of 1945–50.

THE SHORT PEACE

The American consumer and producer both embraced peace in 1945 with a desire to prosper, and they acted accordingly. The economy did not return to the depressed condition of the previous years as many had feared.

Output, Employment, and Investment

Because of postwar inflation, nominal GNP rose far more than did real GNP as you can see in Table 28.1. However, the reduced output of military goods meant that there would now be a flood of civilian goods; therefore, a smaller real GNP in 1947 than in 1945 was, to the consumer, a bonanza. In this era, for the first time since the 1920s, Americans could indulge their purchasing whims. Unlike the war years, consumers now could find something to own: new cars, refrigerators, soft goods. The country went off on a well-earned spending binge. As the data in Table 28.1 show, consumption expenditures in 1950 were 60 percent higher than those of 1945.

Even though the labor-force participation rate remained higher after the war than before it (see Table 26.4), the unemployment rates only returned to normal peacetime levels. Unemployment in 1950 was more than double the "overfull-employment" unemployment rate of 1945, but 5 percent was no memento of the 1930s. Private investment, operating under the same forces as consumer expenditures, rose to unheard-of-levels, and in 1950 was in fact equal to nearly 19 percent of the GNP (see Table 28.1). Such a high level of private investment was extraordinary, and it produced a healthy, viable level of economic growth. Private investment was greater in 1950 than federal government expenditures (see Table 28.2), unlike today when private investment is typically about one-half the level of federal expenditures.

Balanced Expansion with Declining Government Expenditures

Table 28.2 indicates that postwar growth was a wide advance on all fronts of the private sector, while the government sector of the national income accounts was actually declining. Starved for fifteen years of goods and equipment, the country built and bought. Building construction led the pace of the advance, standing at 277 percent of the 1945 figure by 1950, nearly as high at least as the 1926 figure (refer to Table 24.4 in Chapter 24). New houses, factories, roads, parks—all were represented in the burst of building construction. This was the period when decisive suburbanization began, with shopping centers being built away from the central cities to accommodate the expanding suburbs. The flight to the Greenbelt began and would continue for decades. Manufacturing production was actually half again the 1945 level by 1950, and it was by then virtually all civilian goods.

Table 28.1   Selected Postwar Economic Indicators[a]

Year	GNP Total Current Prices	GNP Total 1958 Prices	GNP Per Capita Current Prices	GNP Per Capita 1958 Prices	Civilian Labor Force (in millions)	Percentage Unemployed	Private Consumption	Gross Private Domestic Investment
1945	$211.9	$355.2	$1515	$2538	53.9	1.9	$119.7	$10.6
1947	231.3	309.9	1605	2150	60.2	3.9	160.7	34.0
1950	284.8	355.3	1877	2342	59.3	5.3	191.0	54.1

[a] Amounts are in billions of dollars unless otherwise indicated.

Source: *Historical Statistics,* series F 1–4, 82, D 4, 14, 86, G 416.

Table 28.2   National Income by Industrial Origin[a]

Year	Total	Agriculture and Forestry	Manufacturing	Wholesale and Retail Trade	Contract Construction
1945	181.5	15.2	52.2	28.0	4.3
1950	241.1	17.6	76.2	40.9	11.9
$\frac{1950\ data}{1945\ data} \times 100$	132.8	115.8	146.0	146.1	276.7

[a] Amounts are in billions of dollars.

Source: *Historical Statistics*, series F 226–37.

Table 28.3   Government, Prices, and Money[a]

Year	Federal Government Receipts	Federal Government Expenditures	Surplus (+) Deficit (−)	Prices Wholesale (1967 = 100)	Prices Consumer (1967 = 100)	M_1	M_2	Prime Commercial Paper Rate
1945	$50.2	$95.2	$−45.0	54.6	53.9	$49.2	$126.6	0.44
1946	43.5	61.7	−18.2	62.5	58.5	106.5	138.7	0.61
1947	43.5	36.9	+ 6.6	76.5	66.9	111.8	146.0	0.87
1948	45.4	36.5	+ 8.9	82.8	72.1	112.3	148.1	1.11
1949	41.6	40.6	+ 1.0	78.7	71.4	111.2	147.5	1.13
1950	40.9	43.1	− 2.2	81.8	72.1	114.1	150.8	1.15

[a] Federal government budget, M_1 and M_2 figures are in billions of dollars.

Source: *Historical Statistics*, series E 73, 135, X 414, 415, 449, Y 339–41.

The postwar recovery, in retrospect, was one of health and vigor, *and* it was basically unsupported by government expenditure, except for the transfer payments provided by the (still new) Social Security legislation, together with the costs of normal government services. Much of the Truman administration's "Fair Deal" social program had been defeated in Congress, and the New Deal activism in the federal service had not yet been reconstituted. Federal expenditures dropped and stayed down. Tax revenues were reduced by perhaps 20 percent, but the lower expenditure levels actually produced federal surpluses, largely by accident.

Government, Prices, and Money

The United States reduced its military forces to skeletal proportions almost immediately in 1945. The war expenditures fell as contracts were completed, but there were still large leftover expenditures for demobilization and purchases of food and supplies for foreign

relief. In the summer of 1947, Secretary of State George Marshall announced a plan for European recovery and cooperation, to be known as the "Marshall Plan," and U.S. involvement in European reconstruction was underway.

Despite the Marshall Plan, federal expenditures fell more than 55 percent below the 1945 level by 1950 (see Table 28.3). The results, with only minor tax reductions, were annual budget surpluses in 1947 and 1948. Because these surpluses lowered the federal government's financing needs, M_1 (currency plus demand deposits) actually *declined* in 1948 and 1949; a rare event.

The economy, having been filled with government securities during the war, suffered no money shortages. The banking system began the process of lending again to private borrowers by selling government securities in the market and to the Federal Reserve System. The rise in interest rates exerted a slightly depressing effect upon bond prices, but that did not hinder the process: Potential profits from private lending far exceeded the

Services	Government	Other
14.1	36.8	30.9
21.8	23.6	49.6
154.6	64.1	158.9

capital losses of government bonds. Because it was Federal Reserve and Treasury policy to hold down interest rates to ease the problems of debt management, the Fed purchased the bank-held securities and produced small net money supply increases. Response on the production side minimized the inflationary impact of the economy's enormous liquidity so that increases in consumer and wholesale prices were really minimal (see Table 28.3).

Thus, during the "short peace," the economy, by conventional measures, made the transition from its wartime mobilization to peacetime production with impressive stability. The postwar depression so confidently predicted by many economists never came, nor did the inflationary explosion that was supposed to follow the lifting of price controls. After the exhilaration of 1942–45, contemporaries, remembering 1918–21, doubted that a smooth transition could be made. Fear of a return of unemployment motivated the presidential campaigns of both Harry Truman and third-party candidate Henry A. Wallace in 1948. Yet, in 1950, with (a) greatly expanded output and investment, (b) prices really stable from 1948 onward, (c) low interest rates and unemployment at 3 percent with a stable level of federal spending and taxing, optimists could hardly be blamed for hopes of an optimistic future. This vision was disrupted by the outbreak of war in Korea.

THE POSTWAR INTERNATIONAL REORGANIZATION

By 1950, the international financial system was still recovering from the debacle of the early 1930s. The recovery was due to an extraordinary episode of international politics. World War II gave the British and Americans an opportunity to try again to reconstruct an international financial order after the follies and disasters of the interwar years.

Fixed Exchange Rates

It was traditionally believed that the pre-1914 gold standard, by fixing the mint price of gold among the commercial nations and thus fixing the rates of exchange between currencies, had contributed stability to the old financial system. Whatever the normal risks and hazards of trade were, they were not compounded by fluctuating exchange rates. It was held that international capital movements in particular had been facilitated by the absence of exchange-rate risk. In the interwar period, the Gold Exchange Standard had maintained fixed gold prices, but central-bank cover laws were changed to admit gold-backed foreign exchange assets as reserves against central-bank note issues. The collapse of that system in 1929–33 had produced a period of disorder, competitive devaluations, and trading chaos that was only partly stabilized by the Tripartite Agreement of 1936 between the United States, Britain, and France.

The ensuing war, World War II, had disrupted all this and had ended with the United States holding two-thirds of all the world's monetary gold reserves. The problem was to devise a new system of international monetary agreements with fixed exchange rates, given the extraordinarily lopsided holdings of gold—the ultimate reserve in the thinking of the time. The solution of that problem, at least at first, was the use of gold-backed dollar assets as reserves against postwar expansions of central-bank liabilities—money.

The 1946 Employment Act

Here our tale takes a slightly bizarre but necessary detour for a moment. The Employment Act of 1946 is usually considered in this country to be a "New Deal" device. It was not. There was an origin much more fundamental than the pure wisdom of Congress. As Richard Gardner explained in his masterpiece, *Sterling-Dollar Diplomacy,* the real origin of the 1946 act was an American reaction to British demands in monetary negotiations during World War II.[1] If the U.S.

Prosperity Again.   In the post-World War II era money supply expansion fueled explosive economic growth in all directions. The GI Bill of Rights brought many new students to campus; tents provided additional classrooms at one California college (above left). Urban growth absorbed prime cropland (below left) and led to moving-day problems that could only have happened in America (above right). One national magazine attempted to depict the American dream circa 1950 (below right).

dollar was to become the legal reserve currency of a new international financial order, the United States must break its laissez-faire tradition about controlling aggregate economic activity *in order to control its balance of payments.*

As has been discussed, American imports as a proportion of GNP had steadily fallen since the late nineteenth century. Historically, in cyclical slowdowns in the U.S. economy, there was the additional tendency for the U.S. current-account balance of payments to turn even more strongly positive (higher than usual surpluses), thus draining the world of its holdings of U.S. dollar assets. Normal offsets to this problem, foreign lending by Americans, had failed in the 1930s. The British demanded some kind of guarantee that the U.S. economy would be kept, by federal action if necessary, from slipping back into depression.

If the U.S. dollar was to become the main, official "reserve currency" of a new international order, there must be some steady supply of it available—the *United States had to maintain stable imports so that others could earn dollars.* If that did not occur, the United States would "export depression" to the rest of the world by constraining foreign ability to earn dollars and *thus* maintain their own dollar-backed currencies. The 1946 Employment Act was a gesture of good faith in response to these reasonable demands. It seems doubtful that such a commitment would have been made *in law* by the U.S. Congress under other circumstances. Federal assumption of responsibility for controlling unemployment was abhorrent, even to FDR. It was one thing to dole out federal aid; it was another to assume the obligation to use the federal power perpetually to intervene in the interests of some given level of employment. As it was, Congress so watered down the act as to make it barely intelligible. If you cut out all the "ifs," "ands," and "buts," it reads:

> The Congress hereby declares that it is the continuing policy and responsibility of the Federal Government . . . to promote maximum employment, production and purchasing power.

Even ignoring the problem of questionable constitutionality, there is the record of the U.S. economy since 1946, which adequately illuminates the causes of congressional hesitation. It was a pretense to assume that the promise of the 1946 Employment Act could be met. The Act launched us into unknown water. Meanwhile, though, the new international currency agreements went into effect under the International Monetary Fund.

At first there was no difficulty with employment and economic expansion, but government policy, apart from its absence, had little to do with that. The dollar-starved world had to receive temporary transfusions *directly* from the U.S. Treasury to sustain itself. The Marshall Plan was the beginning of that process. Decades later, the agreement went sour when "Keynesianism" failed: The United States could not maintain full employment by federal expenditure and maintain stable prices, too. It began "exporting inflation" instead—the opposite of the original British fears. The French, seeing the writing on the wall, pulled out of the agreement and began cashing in their dollars in 1965—just as they did in the late 1920s, to the detriment of the Gold Exchange Standard. General De-Gaulle treated the world this time to a homily on the virtues of pure gold bullion. The U.S. balance of payments was in heavy deficit by then, hemorrhaging dollars into the world spending stream, and in August 1971 President Richard Nixon, facing the approach of a run on our gold hoard (now greatly reduced), reneged on the agreement by refusing any longer to sell U.S. gold for U.S. dollars at the fixed "official" price (which already had been raised from $35 an ounce to $42 an ounce in central-bank clearings).

At that point, the postwar system, known as the **Bretton Woods System,** was dead as far as gold and dollars were concerned. The System had done good service, lasting nearly twenty-six years—a triumph as these things go. However, even it could not stand the effusive "gold discoveries" of the time—namely, the huge expansion of Federal Reserve demand liabilities, "high-powered" money, and by 1980 the price of gold reached $850 an ounce. That price was a massive world vote of no confidence in the U.S. dollar. Gold prices then collapsed as the speculation against the dollar ended. Interest was once more raised, during the Reagan administration, in a return to some kind of gold standard with (once again) fixed exchange rates.

The Bretton Woods Institutions

Even before the entry of the United States into World War II, the reordering of the world by Britain and the United States had begun. In August 1941, Churchill and Roosevelt met on board ship in Placentia Bay, Newfoundland, and issued the Atlantic Charter, a wide-ranging statement of principles and aims that included sections on a reordering of the international system of trade and payments on an expansionist basis—equal access to the world's raw materials, freer (i.e., multilateral, not completely free) trade, and the elimination of trading blocs. In the 1942 Mutual Aid Agreement (Lend-Lease) the principles were restated. All countries "of like mind" were invited to participate in policies directed to:

> . . . the expansion by appropriate international and domestic measures, of production, employment and exchange and consumption of goods . . . to the elimination of all forms of discriminatory treatment in international commerce, and to the reduction of tariffs and other trade barriers.

In July 1944, the United Nations was being planned, and a meeting of financial experts, including Keynes (who had designed the original blueprint) for Britain and Harry Dexter White for the United States, was held at an old tourist hotel in Bretton Woods, New Hampshire. The details of all that can be found in Richard Gardner's book and in Sir Roy Harrod's *Life of Keynes,* to which the interested student is directed.[2] The problem was to find the means to facilitate three objects of policy:

1. to create fixed exchange rates and easy short-term capital movements;
2. to provide a method of releasing and augmenting the flow of long-term capital from the restrictions of the 1931–45 era; and
3. to create a framework for the lowering of tariffs and the elimination of direct barriers to trade.

The solutions were as follows:

1. The International Monetary Fund (IMF), which would set a new schedule of international exchange rates and manage that schedule with the aid of short-term credits backed by gold deposits, or *subscriptions,* taken out by each country at the IMF. Payments of the subscriptions were prorated, the United States being the largest subscriber.

Since credit was based on subscription, the IMF has always been known as a "rich man's club."
2. The International Bank for Reconstruction and Development (the World Bank), which would lend at long-term and in other ways assist capital movements by guaranteeing long-term lending from nongovernment sources. The World Bank was undercapitalized and had to devise methods of achieving its ends without impressive resources of its own.
3. The International Trade Organization (ITO), which, as a U.N. institution, would assume powers (to be surrendered to it by treaty) to regulate world tariffs.

The IMF and the World Bank still exist and have played mighty roles in world economic development. The British and Americans had a hard time finding compromises on these two institutions that could get through both Parliament and Congress. Too many vested interests on both sides of the Atlantic were involved for Keynes's original ideas to be adopted. The final formulation was (is), as Keynes quipped at the time: "The Bank is a fund, and the Fund is a bank." The ITO died when the U.S. Senate refused to ratify its charter. But in 1947 the United States did enter into the General Agreement on Tariffs and Trade (GATT), and that has been ever since the substitute for ITO in the international economic order.

When the United States abandoned its obligation to sell gold internationally at a fixed price in 1971, the basis of the IMF exchange-rate system, the result was called the "collapse" of the Bretton Woods System, but that was a great exaggeration. The IMF, the World Bank, and the new institutions and practices spawned by them to continually ease the problems of trade and payments still flourish to the great benefit of the world economic system. They were the foundation blocks upon which all else rested during the post-World War II decades.

Origins of the European Common Market

By 1947, it was clear that war-devastated Europe (and Japan) faced recovery problems beyond the reach of normal economic processes. The United States offered the Marshall Plan, a straightforward grant of resources in return for a coordinated plan of recovery created by the Europeans themselves—including the defeated Germans and Italians—to use the resources efficiently. It is incidental, but worthy of note, that the United States also offered to include the Communist nations of the Soviet sphere in the arrangement, an offer the Soviets declined on Stalin's orders.

The Committee on European Economic Cooperation (first CEED; then OEEC, when *Committee* was changed to *Organization;* now OEDC, Organization for Economic Development and Cooperation, to which the United States belongs) was a fantastic success story. For a mere $12 billion of direct aid, western European recovery was quickly achieved. By 1951, all OEEC countries had surpassed in industrial production their best interwar years.[3] Then began that stunning economic growth that in a single generation would make the most efficient western European nations equal or superior to the United States itself in per capita GNP. The Marshall Plan remains one of the signal achievements of intelligent international economic cooperation. It also directly inspired the ensuing tradition of foreign aid given every year by the United States and by its U.N. partners.

Part of the Marshall Plan included arrangements among the Europeans to grant central-bank credits mutually to facilitate payments: to *automatically* supply domestic currencies so that exporting firms and individuals in every participating country could be immediately paid. These *swing credits* were much like the operation of the Interdistrict Settlement Fund within the American Federal Reserve System, which eases the problems of transfers within the U.S. economy. In 1950, these arrangements were formalized by the establishment of the European Payments Union (EPU). The United States made gold available to the Bank for International Settlements (BIS) in Basel, Switzerland (a leftover institution from World War I reparations payments) to fund the EPU credit transfers. Trade among the EPU members boomed with these new arrangements.

Meanwhile, the Europeans themselves wanted to seize the opportunity, while national barriers within Europe were temporarily down, to produce their own version of European integration. Leaders like Robert Schumann of France (an Alsatian who had served both as a German soldier in World War I and in the French army in World War II) and Paul Henri Spaak of Bel-

gium deeply felt the terrible cost of nationalism in Europe. But they also were mindful of other European traditions, the various customs unions, the intra-German *Zollverein* of 1834, the great low-countries customs union, BENELUX, and the amount of international cooperation involved in running the old European steel cartel. They began European Coal-Steel Community (ECSC) in 1953, directly reorganizing these basic industries on a supranational basis and establishing the necessary political and social institutions to make the resulting damages to inefficient national firms adjustable.

To make a long story short, in 1958 the ECSC partners signed the Treaty of Rome, the EPU lapsed, and the European Economic Community (ECC)—the famous European Common Market—began its life. By the early 1970s, those countries like the United Kingdom, which had not joined, did, and the beginning of European economic integration was solidified.

All this was the outcome of enlightened U.S. economic policy in and immediately after World War II, and it would in the end benefit all who had participated. The United States had produced its own "competition" in the world economy, in Europe and Japan, but what an improvement over the past! It now had trading partners in a sense that had rarely been experienced before, and American life was enriched by the use in common everyday activities of the products of those countries. American firms that could not compete generally vanished. GATT held, against the resulting resurgence of protectionist sentiment, at least until the early 1990s.

THE KOREAN WAR AND EISENHOWER'S ERA OF STABILITY

Harry Truman was halfway through his second (but first elected) term of office when the war in Korea began. Korea was something new, a limited war that involved only a partial mobilization of resources. Unlike the two world wars, the Korean War produced no significant shortages of materials or manpower. The military mobilization took only a small portion of those who were eligible. The federal deficits were on a small scale, resulting in only a slight money supply increase, and prices remained almost unchanged. Unemployment fell, and business was lively. It was guns *and* butter at home and a horrible little war with no decisive results. But at least it did not produce many distortions in the economy. Economic growth continued apace, literally on a peacetime basis, while the war continued.

Growth with Price Stability

During the years 1950–62, from the Korean War to JFK's last full year, the U.S. economy had the ability to grow without significant inflation. It is laughable today that economists and politicians considered inflation rates of 2.5 and 3.0 percent a year as signs of excess. Consider the data in Table 28.4.

In retrospect, the real drama of those years was the *absence* of drama in the economy. There was the usual political hubbub throughout, of course; according to politicians and the media, the republic was in constant danger. There was McCarthyism, the "Vicuna coat scandal," two presidential heart attacks, and the U2 incident at the end of the Eisenhower administration. So placid was the economic climate that Professor Galbraith was able, in 1958, to send the stock market into a momentary tailspin by reminding a sleepy congressional committee of the events of 1929. Galbraith had just finished his book, *The Great Crash, 1929,* and was invited to testify. A Harvard professor's findings on a piece of economic history was BIG NEWS. No one was more surprised than Galbraith himself.[4]

Look again at Table 28.4. What it shows is the remarkable stability of the time. The recovery after World War II was continued with only small setbacks. The amount of growth of GNP and industrial production with so little inflation over so long a period was remarkable. Year-by-year there was a bit more drama

than is indicated. In 1954 and 1958, for example, the Republican administration received small frights from the sudden appearance of cyclical setbacks. Unemployment, a mere 2.5 percent in 1953 while the Korean War expenditures were still flowing in deficit financing, doubled to 5 percent in 1954 when the deficit fell. In 1958, a serious cyclical recession was apparently stemmed, according to Geoffrey Moore, by the "automatic stabilizers" built into the economy by progressive income taxes and unemployment compensation.[5] As incomes fell, a disproportionate decline in tax revenues gave President Eisenhower, to his chagrin, a sudden deficit of $12.1 billion, the largest since the $20.7 billion of 1946.

In the twelve years 1950–62, the money supply grew by less than a third, about 2.5 percent a year on average, far less than the increase in real production measured by real GNP or industrial production (see Table 28.4). The Federal Reserve System, freed from its automatic support of the federal bond market as the result of a 1951 agreement between the U.S. Treasury and the Federal Reserve System, now managed the money market, coaxing here, restraining there. The "supply side" response was an increase of real income of about 50 percent, industrial production rose by 58 percent, and real income *per capita* (population had risen by about 20 percent) stood at $1602 in 1962 compared to $1233 in 1950, a rise of just under 30 percent.

However, the unemployment rate generally stood at about 5 percent, nothing like the 1930s but apparently about one-fourth or so higher than had been the case in the 1920s, the last comparable years. Why should that have been? A 5 percent unemployment rate was nearly

Table 28.4   Growth with Price Stability[a]

Year	GNP Current Prices	GNP 1958 Prices	Percentage Unemployed	M_1	Industrial Production (1967 = 100)	Prices Wholesale (1967 = 100)	Prices Consumers (1967 = 100)
1950	$284.8	$355.3	5.3	$114.1	45	81.8	72.1
1955	398.0	438.0	4.4	134.4	58	87.8	80.2
1960	503.7	487.7	5.5	141.6	65	94.9	88.7
1962	560.3	529.8	5.5	147.0	71	94.8	90.6
$\frac{1962\ data}{1950\ data} \times 100$	196.7	149.1	—	128.8	157.8	115.9	125.7

[a] Figures for GNP and M_1 are in billions of dollars.

Source: *Historical Statistics*, series D 86, E 73, 135, F 1, 3, P 13, X 414.

double the economists' notions at *that* time of the "full employment" level of unemployment, somewhere in the neighborhood of 2.5 percent. The 5-percent level gave rise to talk of "structural" unemployment: something new that needed to be coped with by federal action, such as new programs to put the long-term unemployed back into jobs. In fact, the 2.5 percent level, known only in the most extraordinary years after 1929 (and never in the absence of some kind of war effort) was rarely seen again after 1953.

Economists now refer to the "natural" level of unemployment as being at least 5 percent.[6] One reason for the change might be utterly mechanical. With unemployment a less disastrous personal experience by the 1950s than it had been in the days before unemployment compensation, there was, not surprisingly, more of it. Also, the steady growth of an urban population and the availability of unemployment compensation made unemployment visible where it had not been before. The doubling of the "natural" level of unemployment may well have been a statistical mirage.[7]

As has been mentioned, prices, by the standards both before and after, were remarkably stable. There was, to be sure, a gentle updraft in the trend, but few economists either expected or advocated a general *deflation* as a corrective to anything. The experience of 1929–33 had cured most of them of any desire to see "equilibrium" conditions produced by downward adjustments of prices and wages.

Government in the Early Welfare State

Compared to earlier times, in the 1950s and early 1960s the United States drifted into a new fiscal state of affairs that seemed to be a temporary aberration then but now can be seen as more serious. Even with conservative management, government expenditures tended to exceed revenues in most years. The sturdy little string of budget surpluses of the 1920s now seemed perverse. In the first place, the "fiscal policy" argument, as it stood then, was for a compensatory policy: surpluses in expansions, deficits in contractions.[8] In fact, that would occur almost automatically, as the 1958 recession showed.

Consider the Eisenhower years alone (in Table 28.5). In 1953 the Republican conservatives faced the prospect of a recession just as they had settled into the White House for the first time in a generation. By August 1953, the signs of a recession were ominously present. Stung by campaign after campaign in which they had been blamed for the Great Depression, these Republicans were understandably nervous. They, in turn, blamed the Democrats for endless deficit spending. Unfortunately, in the face of a recession, budget balancing, Eisenhower's great campaign issue, was out of the question.

Revenues fell in both 1954 and 1955, even though expenditures also fell. The revenues fell in part because of a previously scheduled cut in income taxes in January 1954, which the Eisenhower government could not

Table 28.5   The Eisenhower Budget Years[a]

Year	Federal Receipts	Federal Expenditures	Surplus (+) Deficit (−)	Gross Federal Debt
1953[b]	$71.5	$76.8	$− 2.8	$266.0
1954	69.7	70.9	− 1.2	270.8
1955	65.5	68.5	− 3.0	274.4
1956	74.5	70.5	+ 4.1	272.8
1957	80.0	76.7	+ 3.2	272.4
1958	79.6	82.6	− 2.9	279.7
1959	79.2	92.1	−12.9	287.8
1960	92.5	92.2	+ 0.3	290.9
1961	94.4	97.8	− 3.4	292.9

[a] Figures are in billions of dollars.
[b] Figures for 1953 mainly constitute the outcome of the Truman budget.

Source: *Historical Statistics,* series Y 339–42.

stop. Also, war excise taxes were cut. However, since a tax cut to offset a recession was considered by the enlightenment to be compensatory policy, the economists applauded the results Eisenhower and George Humphrey, his super-conservative Secretary of the Treasury did not want. In 1956–57, with the economy expanding, both revenues and expenditures rose. But the General's conservatism—"no new starts"—held back the growth of expenditures, and two small surpluses resulted. The Republicans were triumphant. They had gotten through a recession without having 1932 again and had then produced budget surpluses.

The 1958 recession produced deficits again. Eisenhower deplored them in any stage of the business cycle, but economists applauded and hoped for a tax cut. Expenditures had risen. All this was properly compensatory. In 1959, an increase in revenues and another reduction in expenditures yielded a further surplus in the 1960 figures. But by 1960, the economy was slowing down, unemployment was rising; expenditures rose again, while revenues fell slightly. The result was another deficit in the 1961 figures, but, again, it had been properly compensatory.

Thus if one knew nothing of the Eisenhower government except the numbers in Table 28.5, one might consider them well-trained, "modern" fiscal theorists. In fact there was nothing, or nearly nothing, in the results that illustrated motives. The Eisenhower people were fiscal conservatives: They wanted balanced budgets and no inflation. They got little enough inflation. The algebraic sum of deficits and surpluses between 1954 and 1961 is − $15.8 billion, and the gross federal debt increased by about $22.1 billion during their tenure. That was almost as much as the increase during the period 1933–41, but at higher prices. Compared to what was coming, though, Eisenhower looks like the rock of "fiscal probity."

That the Eisenhower conservatives feared inflation might seem surprising to us now. *Nothing* experienced during the entire 1945–62 period would seem particularly inflationary to those who lived through the 1970s. But to understand the motives of policymakers historically, one must attempt to see the world through *their* eyes; otherwise, all is incomprehensible. Eisenhower's speeches on inflation, or on the evils of a growing national debt, might seem absurd to us. Similarly, 5-percent interest rates seemed crushingly high to the policymakers of the 1950s.

When the Republicans came into office in 1953, it was after a long absence. They had been successfully tagged by the Democrats with the blame for the Depression and had retaliated by heaping upon the Democrats the responsibility for wars and inflation. In response, the Republicans promised peace and price stability, together with economic growth. But they also feared another depression. The Democrats had succeeded brilliantly with their characterization of Herbert Hoover as the man who had fiddled while the nation sank into the 1930s depression. To combat it, the Republicans backed off their anti-inflationary stance in both 1954 and 1958 when the problem became the threat of recession. In addition, expenditures were more difficult to reduce than were revenues. It was hard *not* to have deficits during recessions. After all, by that measure Herbert Hoover had been utterly "Keynesian" in the 1930–33 fiscal years. His was a predominantly deficit administration, and so was Eisenhower's. But Hoover's White House years were all before arguments had been developed by some economists that perhaps there should be deficits whenever the actual GNP was below the full capacity level.[9]

General Considerations: 1945–62

The period 1945–62, apart from the Korean War, was the first chance since 1929 for anything resembling normal economic processes to be decisive in the American economy's growth. The international economy had been set going again, and there was worldwide growth, helped along by aid programs. The United States did not have to face a stagnating market for its exports, and although no evidence has been presented on the international balance, suffice it to say for now that merchandise exports, $9.5 billion in 1946 (the first peacetime year), were $21.4 billion in 1962, a rise that more than equalled the expansion of domestic GNP.

Internally, domestic private investment, so long in the doldrums, rose powerfully, from $10.4 billion in 1945 to $72 billion by 1959, and stood at $78.8 billion in 1962. During the years from the end of World War II to the New Frontier, no source of growth had been stronger. Millions of new homes and factories—together with the supporting infrastructure of highways, roads, water and sewage treatment works, shopping centers, schools and public buildings—had transformed the domestic aspect of America. All this had been achieved with a most moderate general price increase, and, real income per capita had grown strongly apace. This is not to say there were *no* social or economic problems, but they seemed manageable, given the flourishing economic activity on all sides. Surely there were grounds for self-satisfied optimism at the end of the 1950s. It was a plodding kind of prosperity, of course. The nation responded by only the narrowest victory margin to John F. Kennedy's call to "get this country moving again"—for the simple reason that for the first time in the memory of most adults, it *had* moved forward in semi-peacetime conditions.

When General Eisenhower left the presidency, he was still worried about inflation and the national debt, but those were strictly *ritual* worries. In fact, the ratio of the debt to GNP had been grossly reduced, as can be seen in Table 28.6.[10] The General worried also about the **military-industrial complex,** the tendency of weapons producers to influence policy and expenditures, to link excessively the overall prosperity of critical regions of the country with that of a continuous cold war. That problem has never ended. It would have seemed incredible in 1960 that anyone would look back to the 1950s with nostalgia for the "good times." But in 1960, the future was unknown.

Table 28.6   Percentage Gross Federal Debt of GNP[a]

Year	GNP	Gross Federal Debt	Percentage $\left(\dfrac{GFD}{GNP}\right)$
1945	$213.6	$260.1	122.5
1960	502.4	290.9	57.9

[a] Dollar amounts are in billions of dollars.

Source: Statistical Abstract, 1992, Table 491.

Notes

1. Richard Gardner, *Sterling-Dollar Diplomacy,* (1956).
2. Roy Harrod, *Life of Keynes* (London: Macmillan, 1951).
3. Jonathan Hughes, *Industrialization and Economic History* (New York: McGraw-Hill, 1970), pp. 268–70.
4. John Kenneth Galbraith, *A Life in Our Times* (1981), pp. 309–10.
5. Geoffrey H. Moore, "The 1957–58 Business Contraction: New Model or Old?" *American Economic Review,* vol. XLIX, no. 2, May 1959, p. 305.
6. It still is unemployment, though, and a worrisome phenomenon when connected with declining labor productivity. Richard B. Freeman, "The Evolution of the American Labor Market, 1948–80," in Martin Feldstein, editor, *The American Economy in Transition,* (1980), pp. 385–90, and Figure 24.c, p. 153.
7. That is to say, when those unemployed in the more rural economy of the 1930s did not seek work, an illusion of employment existed where there was in fact a lack of it.
8. Herbert Stein, *The Fiscal Revolution in America* (1969), ch. 9–14, for the Truman-Eisenhower years.
9. Stein, pp. 443–44, on the development of this view in the mid-1960s. On the other hand, Robert J. Gordon found the government in the postwar period to have been the most destabilizing influence in the years 1947–57. "Postwar Macroeconomics: The Evolution of Events and Ideas," in Feldstein, *The American Economy in Transition,* pp. 121–23.
10. In 1990 both the debt and GNP were approximately ten times the levels of 1960, but the ratio of debt to GNP had risen back to the level of 1960 from a low of 38.3 percent in 1981.

Suggested Readings

Articles

Bonomo, Vittorio. "International Capital Movements and Economic Activity: The United States Experience, 1870–1968." *Explorations in Economic History,* vol. 8, no. 3, Spring 1971.

Cain, Louis, and Neumann, George. "Planning for Peace: The Surplus Property Act of 1944." *Journal of Economic History,* vol. XLI, no. 1, March 1981.

Darby, Michael R. "Postwar U.S. Consumption, Consumer Expenditures, and Savings." *American Economic Review,* vol. LXV, no. 2, May 1975.

Gordon, Robert J. "Postwar Macroeconomies: The Evolution of Events and Ideas." In Martin Feldstein, editor, *The American Economy in Transition.* Chicago: University of Chicago Press, 1980.

Jacobs, R. L., and Jones, R. A. "Price Expectations in the United States, 1947–1975." *American Economic Review,* vol. 70, no. 3, June 1980.

Books

Feldstein, Martin, ed. *The American Economy in Transition.* Chicago: University of Chicago Press, 1980.

Freeman, Ralph E., ed. *Postwar Economic Trends in the United States.* New York: Harper, 1960.

Galbraith, John Kenneth. *The Affluent Society.* Boston: Houghton Mifflin, 1958.

———. *A Life in Our Times.* Boston: Houghton Mifflin, 1981.

Gardner, Richard. *Sterling-Dollar Diplomacy.* New York: Oxford University Press, 1956.

Hickman, Bert G. *Growth and Stability of the Post-war Economy.* Washington: Brookings Institution, 1960.

Stein, Herbert. *The Fiscal Revolution in America.* Chicago: University of Chicago Press, 1969.

Vatter, Harold G. *The U.S. Economy in the 1950s.* New York: Norton, 1963.

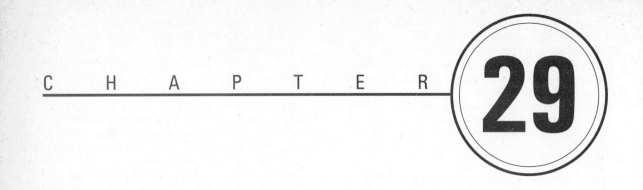

CHAPTER 29

Tertiary Sector and the Labor Force

American economic history, like that of the other advanced economies, has shown that industrialization can be productive enough to spread a prosperous life through virtually all of society. The great eighteenth- and nineteenth-century thinkers in economics left two major legacies, one of which has been largely counterproductive. These two great legacies are (a) the theory of market behavior and (b) the belief in diminishing long-run returns to capital. The first legacy, developed from Adam Smith and David Ricardo through Alfred Marshall, lies securely at the base of most subsequent development of the logic of economics. The second legacy anticipated the development of a massive industrial proletariat, in large part unemployed and receiving a mere subsistence income, as population and labor force grew concomitantly with the industrial structure. Karl Marx is the writer usually associated with the second legacy, but it lay behind the other "classical ideas" of capitalist economic development.[1]

What has actually happened to industrial development has been quite different. Nineteenth-century economists did not clearly foresee the consequences of technological change and the related rise of the **tertiary sector,** professions and services supported by

and nourishing the enormous rise in productivity in the **primary sector** (agriculture, mining, fishing, forestry) and the **secondary sector** (manufacturing, raw-materials processing). The tertiary or service sector consists of teachers, civil servants, hotel workers and others of the leisure industry, nurses and other health-care workers, actors, artists, athletes, and journalists.

As has been discussed in previous chapters, the typical pattern of industrial development among the advanced nations has been characterized by rising productivity that leads to a shrinkage of the *number* of persons employed in the primary sector and a tapering off of the proportion of the labor force employed in the secondary sector. In some sense, these jobs have been replaced by a massive expansion of the tertiary sector. The tertiary sector, crucial in the development of modern economies, is rooted in education, of all kinds. It is concerned with the enhancement of the quality of modern life in professional services—communications, product distribution, education, and the whole host of life-quality-augmenting activities characteristic of advanced economies—and only indirectly with the production of food and goods.

As for the industrial proletariat and the "world revolution," in his little book, *A Theory of Economic*

Facing the Environmental Crisis.   High noon on Liberty Street in Pittsburgh in Indian summer, fall of 1945 (above). Pollution control and cleaning up produced amazing results as attested by the view of the same street in 1951 (below).

History, Sir John Hicks noted that the industrial work forces of the modern economies comprise the solid supports of those systems. The really revolutionary forces in the world today are the poverty-stricken millions of the industrially backward world whose lives are outside modern economic development altogether.[2] In the American economy there is a small example of this: It is not the craftsworkers and assembly-line working men and women who pose the threat of social instability in urban slums, but those who can find no regular employment *anywhere* in the economy.

Hence, reality has refuted the predictions of the nineteenth-century prophets; not a surprising result, since prophecy is a hard trade. The young person entering into economic life today is nearly twice as likely to enter the tertiary sector as the primary and secondary sectors combined. Income from tertiary employment is not directly derived from manufacturing processes but from the marginal returns of planning, distributing, and consuming the products of such processes in the course of providing a service for someone else. The tertiary worker will generally produce a service whose quality is far from the homogeneous product envisaged in simple production theory. The choice of occupation depends upon two factors: social mobility and opportunity cost, the difference between the income earned from the chosen occupation and the potentially higher incomes that might be earned in other employments.

Another way of looking at tertiary sector employments is in terms of **transactions costs.** In a perfectly frictionless economic world relying upon consumer choice and free markets with perfect competition, no government (no taxes or regulation), perfect knowledge, absence of scale economies, and no externalities of any sort, all resources would be allocated according to consumer demand and production costs. Everyone willing to work would be employed at a wage equal to his or her marginal product times its price. Business profits above production costs would just compensate the cost of capital and managerial salaries. There would be no barriers to entry or exit in this world for any employment of economic resources. Obviously there would be no such thing as "market power" in the hands of business firms; they would be nameless production functions competing with each other. Any bargains would be able to be made between any persons

or entities with perfect confidence and at zero cost. The world is not like this. Why not?

In an imperfect world there are positive costs involved in completing business transactions; there are externalities, there are lawyers and accountants, taxes and government, advertising, attempts to limit or monopolize knowledge (information can be *very* expensive, e.g., the Ivan Boesky case). Such costs as these are unknown on the blackboard of the elementary economics classroom, and they are lumped together under the rubric, transactions costs. Much tertiary employment is in the world covered by transaction-cost economics, those costs described by John Wallis and Douglass North as "... the costs of capturing the gains from specialization and division of labor."[3] Wallis and North argue that these costs have risen sharply *as a proportion of GNP:* they were an estimated 22.5 percent in 1870, and 40.8 percent in 1970. They should not be thought of as a drag on GNP growth, but rather, the necessary costs, without which there would be no growth at all. It is more profitable to have half of a dollar than ninety percent of a dime.

RISE OF THE TERTIARY SECTOR

Figure 29.1 depicts the growth of the tertiary sector, according to the census division of occupation, since 1900. The definition of the tertiary sector underlying the data in Figure 29.1 includes only the civilian labor force and excludes all unskilled labor, all transport workers, all construction workers, and the military forces. The tradition of defining the tertiary sector in terms of output, but measuring it in terms of occupations is increasingly problematical inasmuch as vertically integrated firms in the primary and secondary sectors also employ individuals with these occupations. Nonetheless, following tradition, the data in Figure 29.1 yield a tertiary sector slightly smaller than data used to make similar calculations elsewhere.[4]

The census data show that in this century employment in the tertiary sector, thus defined, more than doubled. As real per capita income grew by more than a factor of four from 1900 to 1990, and industrial production and agricultural output rose apace, those workers directly involved in primary and secondary production declined from more than 70 percent to slightly less than 30 percent of the entire labor force. If transport and construction workers are added to the sectors considered to be outside direct participation in primary and secondary production, the tertiary sector

Figure 29.1   Tertiary Sector, Excluding All Unskilled Labor

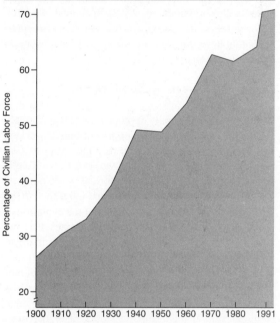

Sources: *Historical Statistics*, series D 15, 183, 193; *Statistical Abstract*, 1980, Table 696; 1992, Table 631.

In this century, the proportion of the labor force employed in activities other than the making of food or goods or in blue-collar employments has steadily grown and now dominates.

makes more than 75 percent of the total labor force. This is a situation far more like that portrayed in Edward Bellamy's *Looking Backward* than anything foreshadowed in the works either of Karl Marx or Arnold Toynbee.

In Table 29.1, the growth of the separate major occupations from 1900 to 1991 is seen in absolute numbers. The decline of employment related to primary production is striking. Also note the failure of the unskilled sectors to increase as the other sectors did. As the economy grew, the numbers of skilled craftsworkers and operatives in industry and transportation increased. However, note the increases in the number of managers and professionals, technicians and sales workers. It is these areas that comprise the tertiary sector. Table 29.1 also shows female and minority participation. The percentage of women employed in the "technical, sales, and administrative support" and "service occupations" categories is greater than average, while the "precision, production, craft, and repair" category is much smaller than the average. A greater than average percentage of minorities can be found in the service, laboring, and farming categories. Minority employment in the managerial and professional category is less than the others.

Women in Tertiary Employment

The importance of employment growth in the tertiary sector is augmented by the consideration that the greatest single change in the composition of the labor force in this century has been in the extent of female participation. There had been possibly a reduction in female

Table 29.1   Labor Force Distribution, 1900–1991

	1900	1991	% Female	% Minority
Managerial and Professional	2,899	31,012	46.3%	10.0%
Technical, Sales, and Administrative Support	2,216	36,086	64.7	15.3
Service Occupations	2,626	15,986	59.8	28.4
Precision Production, Craft, and Repair	3,062	13,162	8.6	16.4
Operators, Fabricators, and Laborers	7,340	17,172	25.2	27.0
Farming, Forestry, and Fishing	10,888	3,459	16.1	21.0
Total	29,031	116,877	45.6	17.6

Sources: *Historical Statistics*, series D 233–682, *Statistical Abstract*, 1992, Table 629.

labor-force participation in the later nineteenth century as wage-work became more common.[5] In 1900, only 18 percent of the *employed* (i.e., wage-earning) labor force was female. By the 1980 census, the female proportion had more than doubled. Since women are underrepresented in two of the growth sectors (precision production-crafts and operatives), the other sectors assume particular significance.

By 1991, more than half of all women over sixteen were in the civilian labor force. Of the entire tertiary sector in 1991, 57 percent of those employed were women, and, of all women in the employed labor force, almost 89 percent were in the tertiary sector. The only nontertiary sector to employ a significant number of women was factory employment, where more than 3 million were employed. As Claudia Goldin shows, the employment of women as factory hands in Massachusetts absorbed a full third of all employed white women, even as early as 1850. Women, history tells us, have traditionally provided a pool of relatively cheap labor in manufacturing. Goldin also shows that the clerical employments provided maximum flexibility for a female labor force increasingly able, over time, to come out of the home during and after the necessary chores of child rearing.[6]

Of the sectors with low female participation, employment in farming, common labor, and the craft sectors is culturally and historically determined in Western countries. The skilled crafts in Western society nearly always have excluded women. American women *can* and *do* farm, but women are involved in farming much more extensively in the rest of the world. The same is true of other unskilled labor. The low participation of women in those areas is due to our "lifestyle," and, as a result, those sectors could not be expected to absorb more women in normal circumstances. "Rosie the Riveter" of World War II was an exception; those older, married women who continued to work following the war were not riveting. The young housewives who went out to help with the harvests in those manpower-short years were also exceptions. In such unskilled areas as migratory farm labor, the participation of women (and children, for that matter) continues to be high.

The managerial and administrative sector has shown remarkable improvement in female participation in the past quarter century; the percentage of women in the managerial and professional category is about the same percent (in fact, a little bit larger) as the percentage of women in the civilian labor force. It had been argued that low female participation here is also cultural— "men don't like taking orders from women," and so forth—but the evidence belies such arguments. Nevertheless it remains the case that some of the sectors growing the most since 1900, in addition to management and professional workers—technical workers, sales workers, and service workers—are also those fields that have the largest portions of female workers *and* are in the tertiary sector.

Demand for Tertiary Employment

Although there is a folk wisdom saying that "supply creates its own demand," the supply of female workers was there far too long without demand for us to take the folk wisdom seriously. The work of Elyce Rotella shows that the rise of female clerical workers, from 2.5 percent of the total clerical work force in 1870 to 52.5 percent by 1930, was the result of the evolution of office machinery.[7] Rotella also emphasizes that the "mechanization" of office work also served initially to separate clerical skills from management functions. Note also that household workers, the traditional employment of women working outside the home, declined between 1900 and 1970. Also by 1970, there were 26 million men, about 52 percent of the male labor force, employed in the tertiary sector. Hence, women, like men, have been drawn into the tertiary sector by the expansion of demand in that sector.

The tertiary sector is not just jobs, but jobs in special locations. The tertiary sector is predominantly urban; it has grown up with the urbanization of the country. Of the 44.3 million employed in that sector by 1970— nearly 20 years ago—37.8 million, or roughly 85 percent, were employed in the central urban areas. Hence, half the men and four-fifths of the women were now in the tertiary sector, and 85 percent of that employment was in cities.

Minorities

In 1991, 64 percent of the black and other minority labor force was employed in the tertiary sector, and 85 percent of that was in the central urban areas. While the tertiary sector has expanded more rapidly than the primary or secondary sectors, it also depends more heavily on some sort of noncraft instruction for advancement, most often formal education, but not necessarily so (e.g., launderers, maintenance workers). It is also a sector where the racial discrimination characteristic of American society has produced dramatic results. In Figure 29.2 the percentage distribution of the black and white labor forces are listed separately.

According to Figure 29.2, since 1960 the power of the tertiary sector to provide jobs has become ever more apparent. White-collar employment has risen for all races, but the proportion of blacks and other minorities in white-collar employment has more than doubled. In all racial categories, the proportions in blue-collar employment and agriculture have declined. The mechanization of agriculture has gone hand in hand with that dramatic change. As can be seen, the proportion of white service workers rose slightly (9.9 to 11.9 percent), while black and minority employment in that category, *as proportions of total black and minority employment,* actually declined sharply, emphasiz-

ing the powerful movement of black and minority workers into white-collar employment in the past two decades. Yet, it should be recalled from Table 29.1 that black and minority workers in 1981 represented 17.6 percent of all workers employed. Such workers are still underrepresented in the white-collar categories. Within the two blue-collar categories, there is a slight underrepresentation in "precision production, craft, and repair" employments, and an overrepresentation among "operators, fabricators, and laborers." The underrepresentation of blacks among the ranks of craftsworkers is apparently fairly straightforward. Until recent years, the craft unions have notoriously discriminated against blacks and other minorities in apprenticeships and memberships.[8] Full representation of blacks and other minorities in this category will, of necessity, take years to achieve, even though the grosser forms of racial discrimination have ended.

To be a competitive farmer today requires a very large capital cost for land, buildings, and equipment.

Figure 29.2   Employed Persons by Occupation and Race, 1960–91

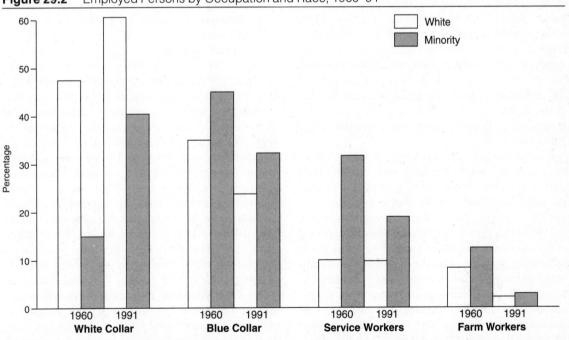

Source: *Statistical Abstract,* 1980, Table 698; 1992, Table 629.

Between 1960 and 1991 black and other minority workers more than doubled the proportions of their total employment in white-collar jobs, while their proportions in service work declined. Among whites, paradoxically, the proportion in service work rose slightly, but the main shift among whites was also to white-collar jobs.

In view of this fact, the overrepresentation of blacks and other minorities in farming suggests, given our economic and social history, they are employed as operators and laborers in the primary sector as well as the secondary sector.

An even greater overrepresentation in "service occupations" suggests a similar explanation—these too are jobs where poor education and racial discrimination traditionally have placed minorities. Despite the decline of blacks in this category between 1960 and 1991 (see Figure 29.2), they still predominated in total employment in a wide range of jobs, everything from sanitation workers to private security personnel. Not surprisingly, these are jobs where educational, language, and skill requirements are minimal and where, in large part, discrimination has not been so important in recent years.

For all workers, and especially white women, expansion of the tertiary sector has provided the majority of net employment opportunities since 1900. Of the net increase of 48.3 million jobs between the census years 1900 and 1970, only a net 6.5 million came outside the tertiary sector. Thus, the tertiary sector accounted for an amazing 89 percent of the overall job increase. The large rise in female labor-force participation in the past decade or so no doubt explains some of the failure of female wage rates to gain on those of men. But real discrimination against women still accounts for some of the difference.[9] In addition, part-time employment is largely associated with increased female labor-force participation.

Claudia Goldin's general survey of female *labor-force* contributions to the economy's growth yield some useful facts in connection our tertiary sector discussion. Goldin shows that the labor force participation rate for females age 15–64 increased from 19.6 percent in 1890 to 59.9 percent in 1980. The female component of the labor force rose from 17 percent to 43 percent in that period. The ratio of female to male full-time earnings increased from 46 percent to 60 percent in that period.[10] The net contribution of female labor she estimates to have been 14 percent—that is, had the female labor force not risen, then GNP would have been 14 percent lower in 1980 than it was. She believes that urbanization added to the rate of increase of female labor force participation, and as should be clear, urban America is where most of the tertiary sector jobs are to be found.[11]

The Paradox of Tertiary Employment

Since it was the tertiary sector that was of little consequence, numerically, a century ago, it is not surprising that social theorists like Karl Marx were completely off the target when they predicted that the growth of an underemployed industrial proletariat would swamp capitalism. The "workers" would rise up. Had it not been for the growth of the tertiary sector, who knows?

Since the tertiary sector eats most of the food and employs the machines and other produce of the primary and secondary sectors, it is *primary and secondary sector productivity* that has largely made possible the growth of the tertiary sector, at least at the relative incomes commonly earned by those in tertiary employment. On the other hand, it is the efficiency of the tertiary sector—its science, planning, and organization—that has made such increased productivity in the other sectors possible. *The tertiary sector is a paradox in the history of capitalism: It has been both the creation and possibly the savior of the primary and secondary sectors as the population has grown and the capacity to create food and goods has multiplied.*

Structural Change

Table 29.2 records the growth of employment in the six major sectors in census years from 1900 to 1991. Across the bottom, the percentage increase from 1900 to 1991 is calculated. The structure of occupations in 1991, compared to 1900, embraced a 7.4 million *decrease* in the numbers of farmers, foresters, and fishermen. In 1900 they were 37.5 percent of the employed labor force; in 1991, a mere 3.0 percent. In 1900, the sum of the first two columns, the occupations normally considered to be white-collar occupations, totaled 5.1 million, or 17.6 percent of the employed civilian labor force. By 1991 their numbers were nearly 67.1 million and 57.4 percent of total employment.

The relative growth in white-collar occupations in Table 29.2 reflects both the growth of the tertiary sector and a corresponding increase in those occupations within the manufacturing sector. There are larger numbers of physicists and chemists employed by universities and by research and development departments of manufacturing corporations. There are more attorneys practicing out of their own firms as well as within corporations. The growth of these occupations

Table 29.2   Occupation Employment 1900–91 in Millions of Workers

	Managerial & Professional Specialty	Technical, Sales, & Administrative Support	Service Occupations	Precision Production, Craft & Repair	Operators, Fabricators & Laborers	Farming, Forestry, & Fishing	Total Civilian Labor Force
1900	2,907	2,208	2,626	3,062	7,340	10,888	29,031
1910	4,167	3,795	3,562	4,315	9,919	11,533	37,291
1920	5,033	5,496	3,312	5,482	11,492	11,390	42,205
1930	6,786	7,534	4,772	6,246	13,026	10,322	48,686
1940	7,461	8,620	6,069	6,203	14,393	8,994	51,740
1950	9,717	11,536	6,016	8,205	15,528	6,858	57,860
1960	11,956	15,072	7,903	9,465	16,009	4,132	64,537
1970	16,807	21,050	10,251	11,082	18,086	2,450	79,726
1980	25,990	24,819	12,958	12,529	18,270	2,703	97,269
1991	31,012	36,086	15,986	13,162	17,172	3,459	116,877
1991/1900	10.7	16.3	6.1	4.3	2.3	0.3	4.0

Sources: *Historical Statistics,* series D 233–682, *Statistical Abstract,* 1992, Table 629.

accomplished a reversal of the employment structure in eight decades (1900–1991). This is why economists and other educational specialists have urged that the national priorities in this country should be shifted. Employment in these occupations does not involve much in the way of real property ownership or apprenticeship-style training. It does require a broad education for success, and indeed, unlike the primary and secondary sectors, the tertiary sector is preeminently the sector of educational attainment.[12]

Do the national spending patterns reflect the change? How do federal expenditures on education compare to subsidies to farming, transport, and manufacturing? Are we really facing up to a world in which unskilled factory work, common labor, and agricultural jobs will be as hard to get as were jobs in the tertiary sector in 1900? Does anyone seriously believe that the much-heralded "reindustrialization" of America will reverse these trends? Is it likely that the United States will return to a labor-intensive factory system? Reindustrialization will no doubt utilize labor-saving methods, such as robots, and, as the labor force continues to increase, newcomers must expect to find work in the tertiary sector.

In general, persons entering the tertiary sector have no great opportunity to find suitable work in the primary and secondary sectors. They choose jobs in competition with others like themselves. Since the amount of income available to all tertiary employment is basically determined by productivity increases in the other two sectors (and through foreign trade, of course), the 1970s and early 1980s were times of relative excess of tertiary workers and laggard demand increases—the result was high unemployment. By the late 1980s, due in part to a declining dollar on the foreign exchanges and a consequent export boom, a general expansion in the economy had dropped unemployment to about 5.5 percent, but a recession was right around the corner to drive it up again.

OPPORTUNITY COST AND THE TERTIARY SECTOR

The market for labor (of all kinds) in the tertiary sector is similar to that arising in physical production processes. Demand for labor is a **derived demand.** It is not directly derived from demand for goods, but is derived from demand for services, some of which (e.g., advertising) are themselves more remotely derived from products.

Factors Affecting Labor Demand

The market for labor in the tertiary sector will thus appear to be theoretically like other labor markets. Demand (Figure 29.3a) will reflect the productivity of

Figure 29.3   Tertiary Labor Market

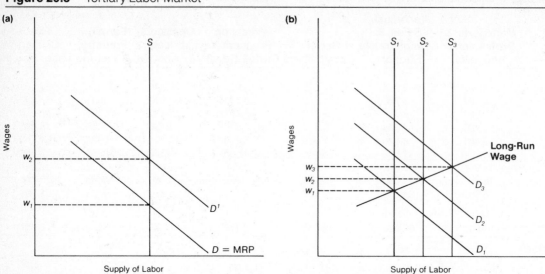

If the increased supply of tertiary labor is in employments that are desired sufficiently by consumers, then wages and incomes will rise despite the increase in supply. For most of the twentieth century, such has been true (that is, real incomes in the tertiary sector have increased).

labor and its price (i.e., the wage rate). This is the demand curve for labor. Demand will increase if either productivity or price, or both, rises.

Other Factors Affecting Demand

There is an additional consideration affecting the demand for tertiary labor. Since the demand for labor is derived, any improvements in the circumstances in which tertiary labor is used raises demand. Hence, the steady growth and development of urban agglomerations in this country, with their attendant facilities—schools, hospitals, public services, communications systems, governing bureaucracies—will raise the demand for tertiary labor.

Similarly, the development of particular capital products that require tertiary labor for their employment (e.g., the whole computer complex with data banks, leased terminal facilities, and so forth) raises demand for the relevant grades of labor. Productivity is also raised by such urban factors as schools and other training facilities, transport systems, and public health. These together can act to increase demand (see Figure 29.3a), raising the wages (w_1 to w_2) of tertiary labor with labor supply given.

Carmel Chiswick finds, on the demand side, a continuation of the nineteenth-century pattern of substitution of capital for high-priced labor: modern technology involves the expanding employment of "high-level" labor associated with capital equipment that displaces relatively high-priced production labor. Imagine technical workers in white laboratory smocks studying computer printouts of robotized manufacturing processes. As before (in the nineteenth century), the wage ratio of this "skilled" (high-level) to "unskilled" (production) labor narrows in the process. Chiswick writes:

> The U.S. economy has been characterized in the twentieth century by dramatic increases in the proportion of the labor force in high-level manpower occupations, together with a decline in their relative wage.

This process over time has produced a

> . . . composition of output favoring industries that make relatively intensive use of high-level manpower.[13]

In these conditions rising labor demand is increasingly for nonproduction—in our terminology, tertiary—employments.

Factors Affecting Labor Supply

Since supplies of tertiary labor require the entire range of special knowledge, from household labor to physicists and other technical people, there are the effects of education on the supply side. In the highly technical parts of the economy, the apparatus of formal education has been of peculiar significance in the creation of supply. In 1989, 35,759 doctorates were conferred; in 1900 there were 382; in 1940, 3,290; in 1957, 8,752. The supply came from the expansion of those university facilities needed for such education. Most of that expansion was tax supported.

Even government is a factor on *both* the demand and supply side. Government hires Ph.D.'s (thus increases demand); it also finances their development (thus helps increase supply). If you were to inquire at your college or university about the number of senior professors whose educations were financed by the G.I. Bill of Rights after World War II or the National Defense Education Act in the 1950s and early 1960s, you would be amazed by the answer.

The historical situation in the tertiary sector is depicted schematically in Figure 29.3b. As has been shown, there was a great increase in the supply of tertiary labor over time (S_1, S_2, and S_3), but personal incomes in that sector have risen steadily. Therefore, increases in demand (D_1, D_2, and D_3) have been marginally greater, with the result that the long-run wage has risen as the sector expanded. As Richard Freeman wrote, these effects slowed down in the 1970s.[14] It is unclear which factors, lagging industrial productivity apart, account for most of the change.

Job Choice

While for the individual such information might be cheering, the choice is different. The individual does not receive the long-run tertiary wage trend for his or her efforts. Instead, he or she receives the wages and benefits available in the particular employment chosen, and today, the choice of employment can become very complicated. For example, a young married woman who has left her position as a bank loan officer to become a full-time mother and household worker faces a major decision once the child reaches, say, age three. She and her husband must evaluate many factors in trying to decide when, or if, she will re-enter the job market, and no small part of their problem is determining the wife's opportunity cost of returning to work outside the home. (**Opportunity cost** is the greatest value that is forgone by choosing an alternative.) They must weigh several new costs against her net salary: the cost of day care and possibly a part-time housekeeper to replace the wife's labor in the home; the possible loss of income from days of work missed due to the child's illnesses, those of the housekeeper, or other needs; and the increased federal income taxes and higher commuting costs incurred by a two-paycheck family. Of course, none of these factors include the sociological implications for the family of having a working mother, which must also be considered by the parents. Goldin's research shows that the mother re-entering the labor force will face lower earnings simply due to lack of time and experience on the job, compared to other workers who did not spend time forming families.[15]

Apparently, many families have chosen to accept the less than ideal opportunity costs created when the wife leaves her position as household worker in favor of the increased income that results—however small the net increase is. By 1984 an astonishing 51 percent of married women had opted to enter the regular labor market. In May, 1984, the government reported that more than half of all adult women were fully employed earning wages or salaries.[16]

Individuals facing the tertiary labor market have two basic kinds of choices to make over their working life (call them "type A" and "type B" choices). Type A choices involve the *kind* of employment their talents, opportunities, luck, preferences, and backgrounds seem to warrant. Then, given all else, type B choices involve the zero opportunity costs of different job locations.

Clearly, the type A choice is crucial to realizing a lifetime stream of earnings. After all, surgeons earn more than truck drivers. Once the decision is made, there are no further trade-offs in most cases. The general information in Figure 29.4 is known to most people. It is also known that very special qualifications, some of them expensive, are necessary to reach top income employments. Although type A decisions are often a matter of luck, most people try to plan for them. Obvious information is relevant: Tone-deaf people avoid musical careers, 90-pound weaklings abjure professional competitive sports, persons who suffer

Figure 29.4 Average Weekly Earnings (Full-Time Work), 1991

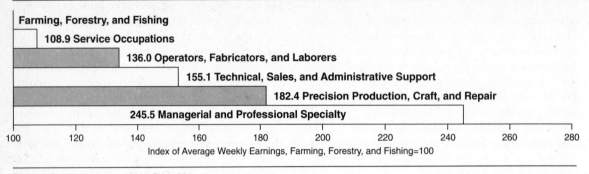

Index of Average Weekly Earnings, Farming, Forestry, and Fishing=100

Source: *Statistical Abstract*, 1992, Table 654.

from "math anxiety" stay away from science. Given opportunities, talents, parental ambitions, or whatever, the labor force equips itself to enter the labor market. Opportunities matter. Money constraints keep people away from medicine and the law and from graduate schools. Union restrictions (on race and sex bases, for example) limit entrance to certain crafts and trades.

The tertiary sector provides a wide range of type A choices. To be entirely rational, earnings potentials must be balanced against preparation costs (training and education). Years in training are measured in part by the cost of forgone earnings in fields with less elaborate background requirements, in addition to the direct costs of training. The prospect of reaching the higher earning levels must be balanced against such considerations.

Figure 29.5 shows the sorts of trade-offs involved. Some fields yield rapidly rising income streams with relatively small initial outlays on education: fields like truck driving or grocery clerking. But marginal annual income yields to additional preparation costs taper off, and little further training occurs after the initial qualification period. Trades, crafts, sales, and clerical work, as well as unskilled jobs, have these characteristics, shown as Occupation 1 in Figure 29.5. Other occupations, such as those involving extensive higher education (neurosurgery, physics) yield little for years as the costs mount, measured both as forgone earnings and current outlays. However, such fields tend to pay off handsomely in the end. They also require steady education of the "refresher" type to maintain the high earnings. The income curve for these is represented by Occupation 2 in Figure 29.5.

Figure 29.5 Income and Preparation Costs: Job Options

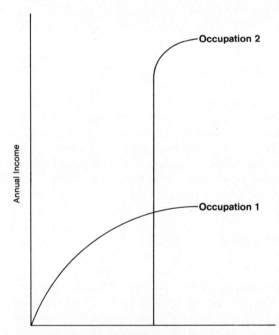

Real Preparation Costs ; Training and Education

Some employments (Occupation 2), such as medicine, science and technology, and liberal arts professions, require long years of preparation, during which they yield little or no income. The payoff comes when education and training end. At that point, incomes rise above those employments that require only on-the-job experience (Occupation 1). Which type of employment offers the highest lifetime earnings depends upon individual circumstances.

TODAYS MONEY MARKET RATES

CERTIFICATES OF DEPOSIT $1,000 MINIMUM	6 MONTH	DAYS	1-2½ YEAR	2½ YEAR	2½ YEAR	4 YEAR	6 YEAR	8 YEAR
	14×0.7				NEW 11.75			NEW

CERTIFICATES OF DEPOSIT ($100,000 and Over)	1 MONTH	2 MONTH	3 MONTH	4 MONTH	5 MONTH	6 MONTH	8 MONTH	9 MONTH	ONE YEAR
	18.0	18.0	18.25	17.5	16.5	16.5	16.5	15.0	15.0

SELECTED COMMERCIAL PAPER — RANGE OF RATES

9 AM GOLD PRICE 614.99%

	15-29 DAYS	30-59 DAYS	60-89 DAYS	90-179 DAYS	180-270 DAYS
$10,000-$25,000	LOW 17.05 HIGH	LOW 17.55 HIGH	LOW 16.75 HIGH	LOW 15.35 HIGH	LOW 13.7 HIGH
$25,000-$100,000	LOW 17.3 HIGH	LOW 18.0 HIGH	LOW 17.2 HIGH	LOW 15.65 HIGH	LOW 14.05 HIGH
$100,000 or More	LOW 17.75 HIGH	LOW 18.3 HIGH	LOW 17.5 HIGH	LOW 16.0 HIGH	LOW 14.5 HIGH

CAPITAL NOTES
12 1/2% TBRU December 31, 19
12% THEREAFTER TO MATURITY

REPURCHASE AGREEMENTS $5,000 MINIMUM	15-29 DAYS	30-59 DAYS	69-89 DAYS
	---	NOT AVAILABLE	---

TREASURY BILLS $10,000 MINIMUM	15-29 DAYS	30-59 DAYS	60-89 DAYS	90-179 DAYS	180-270 DAYS	271 DAYS OR MORE
	15.5	15.5	15.5	14.6	13.7	13.3

The Information Industry. An increasing public sophistication in matters such as finance has accompanied the high-tech revolution. The chalkboards (and high interest rates) of the early 1980s (above) gave way to investment centers (and much lower rates) in the early 1990s (below).

FDIC Insured Deposits — GLENVIEW BANK

Rates as of March 01, 1993

Regular Savings	2.70	
NOW	2.000	
Insured Money Funds		
Individual	2.600	
Corporate	2.600	
Retirement Accounts		
IRA/Keogh Floating Rate	2.600	2.631

Other Certificates of Deposit available as IRA/Keoghs. Please inquire.

Certificates of Deposit under $100,000		
6-month	3.050	3.073
1-year	3.350	3.392
3-year	4.500	4.577
5-year	5.600	5.719

Additional maturities. Please inquire.

Certificates of Deposit $100,000 or over	
30-day	2.700
60-day	2.750
90-day	2.800

Other Investment Offerings — GLENVIEW BANK

Rates as of March 01, 1993

Treasury Bills	
1-month	2.570%
3-month	2.910%
6-month	3.020%
1-year	3.160%

Additional maturities available. Please inquire.

Federated Funds	
Tax-Free Instruments Trust	1.86%
Automated Government Money Trust	2.72%

Gold and Silver
9:00 am Gold Price per Troy Ounce $328.40

Some employments yield only small money-income increases to additional increments of education and training but require considerable educational outlays to enter at all: The classic example of these is teaching in the primary grades of the public schools. (It used to be said that persons employed in such occupations did it for "love.") Other occupations do yield appreciably higher returns to experience or additional training. Management jobs would usually follow that kind of income trajectory.

Once the type A choice is made, either in the tertiary sector or, for fewer people, in the primary or secondary sectors, individual equilibrium depends upon opportunity costs. The individual is still qualified for a certain range of options. A chemist, for example, can work in industry, in a university, or as a private consultant.

Individuals have certain preferences for locational factors—climate, leisure, culture, and family—that can be measured in money terms by the existence of positive opportunity costs and the absence of response to these. A manager in La Jolla, California, may find many nonmonetary reasons to turn down a higher salary in Havre, Montana. She may be surprised by how high the dollar value is, to her, of these "intangible" attributes of La Jolla.

Apart from such implicit valuations of nonpecuniary aspects of employment, the equilibrium of the individual is determined by opportunity costs. Since tertiary employments offer such a range of prospects to the sellers of labor, opportunity cost may be more frequently calculated by the typical individual than is the case in the primary and secondary sectors. This factor may account for the extraordinary mobility of Americans, most of whom are employed in tertiary callings.

Different people prefer different life-styles. The Vermont hippy, roughing it at his or her own pace at the Third World Liberation Whole-Life Commune, will have his or her own preferences, up to the edge of starvation, and great units of potential income (earned at steady employment) will be traded for smaller units of leisure. Your typical shorter haired go-getter, on the other hand, will have the opposite sort of preferences, in which great amounts of leisure are willingly traded for small additional amounts of income. Tertiary employment provides a large range of choices.

TECHNOLOGICAL CHANGE

At this point, our discussion moves toward what used to be the realm of science fiction: What does the future hold for the American economy regarding the tertiary sector? Changes even in this century have already been astonishing and, to someone like Karl Marx, would probably be quite unbelievable. The proportion of the labor force now actually working in factories making foods, processing food, fishing, mining, and cutting timber is only about 20 percent of the total. Adding crafts-workers, supervisors, and nonfarm workers to this total raises it to only 36 percent of the labor force.

These nontertiary employments, as has been noted, declined by half as a proportion of the labor force in this century. As Table 29.2 (p. 521) shows, the number of farmers, foresters, and fishermen—10.3 million as late as 1930 and still 6.9 million in 1950—has fallen to 3.5 million in a further generation, a reduction of one-half since 1950, two-thirds since 1920. Limiting the calculation only to farmers, the reductions are even larger as farms were consolidated, farming was mechanized, and output soared. But farming is so striking because, despite government efforts under the 1938 Agricultural Adjustment Act to maintain price supports, there were no restrictions on entry and exit from the industry. Opportunities in the tertiary sector induced rural people to move out. There was nothing to stop this exodus, and it paid to go. It is widely held that because of union work rules, a similar exodus has thus far been forestalled in other industries. One can find in the newspapers on almost a daily basis warnings that far more labor is now locked into unionized factory employment by contract work rules than could be supported if the latest automated technologies in use elsewhere were introduced.

In fact, there would appear to be a considerable "stockpile" of job-eliminating technology awaiting introduction to American industry in the 1990s. It is wise to consider this subject. From the beginning of this country's industrialization, the emphasis has been upon "labor-saving" technology. Labor has been relatively expensive in American industry, and as has been discussed repeatedly in previous chapters, there is monumental literature documenting this singular characteristic of American economic development.[17]

Historically, conserving scarce factors by substituting more plentiful factors has shifted the production functions upwards and reduced the real costs of output. Labor traditionally has been the scarce factor of manufacturing because of labor's opportunity costs. At first, it was the pull of American agricultural incomes that induced inventors from the time of Eli Whitney (1765–1825) to make a technology that conserved labor. In the twentieth century in this country, the tertiary sector was added with its minimal class structure and relatively easy access to education. Labor unions have attempted to maintain membership, it is often charged, by opposing technical improvements that would reduce their memberships. Featherbedding (requiring more workers than are needed), "bogus" work, soldiering (loafing) on the job, have been the results. Firms, like the Studebaker auto manufacturing company of South Bend, Indiana, collapsed because of their inability to compensate in other ways for such high labor costs.

Just how extensive these practices are in both crafts and unionized manufacturing cannot be estimated overall. It is a matter of looking at every job, every plant. Some say that union contracts are encrusted with work rules forcing redundant labor to be employed in production. It has been more than fifty years since the Wagner Act (1935) was passed and four decades since it was last seriously amended by the Taft-Hartley Act (1947). Complaints by management of labor-wasting practices imbedded in union contracts are routinely denied by union leaders. There is, as a result, a growing array of American industries—steel, aluminum, petrochemicals, automobiles, electronics—that are having problems today even though their productivity a generation ago was legendary.

Union leaders plead for higher tariffs and quotas to protect them from "cheap foreign labor" or, perhaps, from new labor-saving technology. Management imports foreign competing products themselves (steel, autos) or investing in plants abroad, thus "exporting American jobs," as the saying goes. Management argues that it is not the American pay rates that are too high but the amount of boondoggling protected by contract that makes American labor so expensive. Labor leaders have defended themselves by pointing to management's failures. By the 1970s, the massive invasion of American markets by foreign manufacturers indi-

cated that somehow the American industrial house was not in order. These manufacturers, many of them devastated during World War II, given the need to become competitive, adopted new technologies American firms procrastinated adopting. By the 1990s these problems had not been solved.

Restrictive practices by unions are known in European economics as "the English disease." It is widely believed that because of such practices in the face of technological change, English industry may now contain as much as twice the locked-in labor that is warranted by current practice in the Common Market countries.[18] The result is, of course, that the English disease slowly saps the strength of the British economy, and Britain falls steadily behind the other industrial nations in per capita income produced. Efforts to roll back these developments in the 1980s by the Thatcher government produced widespread unemployment in British industrial areas. Americans in the 1970s and 1980s faced factory closings in the old industrial towns of the Midwest and Northeast for similar reasons.

It has been a maxim of economics that labor-saving machinery creates more jobs than it destroys. And, overall, this has certainly been true. The enormous increases in the number of jobs, at secularly rising real wages, in the American economy belie the fear that automation will create net unemployment. Productivity creates markets, and hence, employment. But there is no doubt that specific jobs are eliminated: That is the object! Judging from the history of industrial employment in this century, it is the tertiary sector that will generate the net increase in numbers of jobs and will absorb workers left jobless in industry by rationalization of production.

The scenario this produced for the foreseeable future is reminiscent of Edward Bellamy's world in his book *Looking Backward* in which labor and physical drudgery have been separated.[19] Machines do the distasteful work. Mechanical aids to production of food and goods, centuries in their development, may well end up reducing the industrial proletariat, beloved of Marxist ideologues, to negligible proportions of the employed labor force. Hence, the tertiary options, so many of which are education-intensive, become even more crucial in the future. Hence also, the abandoned folly of those who argue that the labor force in this country is "overeducated." There is obviously no turning back from this, unpleasant as the prospect is for some. An industry that uses inefficient and labor-intensive technology in a competitive world is one that must be subsidized, either directly, by sanctioned monopoly agreements, or by protection from foreign competition, and the American economy already has plenty of these. A nation cannot subsidize *everything,* after all. A sub-sidy transfers wealth from A to B. If there is no third party, then it is impossible to subsidize *both* A and B. So if American industry becomes technologically backward, its exports will be of those items in whose creation it is least incompetent, the exports of goods embodying low-productivity, "cheap" American labor.

Notes

1. William Baumol, *Economic Dynamics* (1951), chs. 3 and 4.
2. Sir John Hicks, *A Theory of Economic History* (1969), pp. 156–59.
3. John Wallis and Douglass North, "Measuring the Transaction Sector in the American Economy, 1870–1970," in Stanley Engerman and Robert Gallman, editors, *Long-Term Factors in American Economic Growth* (Chicago: The University of Chicago Press, 1986).
4. See Jonathan Hughes, "Industrialization: Economic Impact," *International Encyclopedia of the Social Sciences* (1968), vol. 7 and sources cited there.
5. Jane Humphries, " '. . . The Most Free From Objection . . .' The Sexual Division of Labor and Women's Work in Nineteenth Century England," *JEH,* December 1987.
6. Claudia Goldin, *Understanding the Gender Gap* (1990), chapter 2. For more on women in manufacturing jobs, see Alice Kessler-Harris, *Out to Work: A History of Wage-Earning Women in the United States* (1982).
7. Elyce Rotella, "The Transformation of the American Office: Changes in Employment and Technology," *JEH,* March 1981, p. 52.
8. Robert Higgs, "Accumulation of Property by Southern Blacks Before World War I," *American Economic Review,* vol. 72, no. 4, September 1982.
9. Richard B. Freeman, "The Evolution of the American Labor Market, 1948–80," In Martin Feldstein, editor, *The American Economy in Transition* (Chicago: University of Chicago Press, 1980), pp. 356–63.
10. Goldin finds ambiguity in explanations of persisting wage differentials between men and women, differentials usually explained simply as "discrimination," because there seems to be no other explanation. She conjectures that there has been a persistent underinvestment by women in "job-related skills" by successive cohorts whose idea of their own future participation and work experience was primarily based upon that of their mothers. There are other factors though, including continuous job experience, that help account for the persisting differentials. Claudia Goldin, "The Gender Gap in Historical Perspective," in Peter Kilby, ed., *Quantity and Quiddity: Essays in U.S. Economic History* (Middletown, CT: Wesleyan University Press, 1987). See also *Understanding the Gender Gap,* Tables 2.1 and 3.1.
11. Claudia Goldin, "The Female Labor Force and American Economic Growth, 1890–1980," in Engerman and Gallman, eds., *Long-Term Factors in American Economic Growth.* Also see *Understanding the Gender Gap,* pp. 186–89.
12. The bulge in tertiary employment in the 1970s *reduced* the returns to education relatively. (See Freeman, "The Evolution of the American Labor Market," Table 5.7). This is not surprising with a stagnant job market and students graduating in record numbers.
13. Carmel U. Chiswick, "The Elasticity of Substitution Revisited: The Effects of Secular Changes in Labor Force Structure," *Journal of Labor Economics,* Fall 1985, p. 492.
14. Freeman, "The Evolution of the American Labor Market," pp. 382–83, and *New York Times,* 17 June 1984, p. F25.
15. Goldin, *Understanding the Gender Gap.* In particular, see chapter 4 on "The Emergence of 'Wage Discrimination'."
16. Freeman, "The Evolution of the American Labor Market," p. 358.
17. For example, H. J. Habakkuk, *American and British Technology in the 19th Century* (1962); Nathan Rosenberg, *Technology and American Economic Growth* (1972).
18. It is thus not accidental that the United Kingdom joins the U.S. at the bottom of the rankings for productivity increases in the 1960s and 1970s. Belgium, Denmark, France, West Germany, Japan, and the Netherlands all outstripped us by 100 percent between 1967 and 1977 in

manufacturing productivity increases (see Freeman, "The Evolution of the American Labor Market," p. 355, Table 5.3).

19. Edward Bellamy, *Looking Backward: 2000–1887* (Boston: Ticknor, 1888).

Suggested Readings

Articles

Chiswick, Carmel U. "The Elasticity of Substitution Revisited: The Effects of Secular Changes in Labor Force Structure," *Journal of Labor Economics,* vol. 3, no. 4, Fall 1985.

Freeman, Richard B. "The Evolution of the American Labor Market, 1948–80." In Martin Feldstein, editor, *The American Economic in Transition.* Chicago: University of Chicago Press, 1980.

Goldin, Claudia. "The Female Labor Force and American Economic Growth, 1890–1980." In Stanley Engerman and Robert Gallman, editors, *Long-Term Factors in American Economic Growth.* Chicago: The University of Chicago Press, 1986.

Gwartney, James. "Changes in the Nonwhite/White Income Ratio—1939–1967." *American Economic Review,* vol. LX, no. 5, December 1970.

Hughes, Jonathan. "Industrialization: Economic Impact." *International Encyclopedia of the Social Sciences.* New York: Macmillan, 1968, vol. 7.

Humphries, Jane. " '. . . The Most Free From Objection . . .' The Sexual Division of Labor and Women's Work in Nineteenth Century England." *Journal of Economic History,* vol. XLVII, no. 4, December 1987.

Rotella, Elyce J. "Women's Labor Force Participation and the Decline of the Family Economy in the United States." *Explorations in Economic History,* vol. 17, no. 2, April 1980.

———. "The Transformation of the American Office: Changes in Employment and Technology." *Journal of Economic History,* vol. XLI, no. 1, March 1981.

Sexton, Brendon. "The Working Class Experience." *American Economic Review,* vol. LXII, no. 2, May 1972.

Weiss, Thomas. "Urbanization and the Growth of the Service Workforce." *Explorations in Economic History,* vol. 8, no. 3, Spring 1971.

Wallis, John J., and North, Douglass C. "Measuring the Transaction Sector in the American Economy, 1870–1970." In Stanley Engerman and Robert Gallman, editors, *Long-Term Factors in American Economic Growth.* Chicago: The University of Chicago Press, 1986.

Books

Baumol, William. *Economic Dynamics.* New York: Macmillan, 1951.

Benson, Susan Porter. *Counter Cultures: Saleswomen, Managers, and Customers in American Department Stores, 1890–1940,* Champaign: University of Illinois Press, 1986.

Goldin, Claudia. *Understanding the Gender Gap: An Economic History of American Women.* New York: Oxford University Press, 1990.

Habakkuk, H.J. *American and British Technology in the 19th Century.* Cambridge: Cambridge University Press, 1962.

Hicks, Sir John. *A Theory of Economic History.* New York: Oxford University Press, 1969.

Hughes, Jonathan. *The Vital Few.* New York: Oxford University Press, 1986.

Kessler-Harris, Alice. *Out to Work: A History of Wage-Earning Women in the United States.* New York: Oxford University Press, 1982.

Owen, John D., *Working Lives: The American Work Force Since 1920.* Lexington: D.C. Heath, 1986.

Rosenberg, Nathan. *Technology and American Economic Growth.* New York: Harper Torchbooks, 1972.

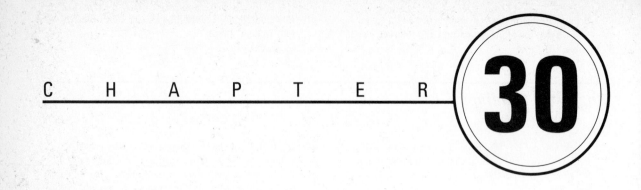

30

Modern Industrial Developments

I t is easy to "cry wolf" about American manufacturing, especially in light of the ongoing crises in steel and autos, which were made worse by the appearance in 1982–83 of the worst recession since World War II, and the uneven recovery afterward. Those two industries will be discussed later in this chapter, following a consideration of overall industrial trends.

MANUFACTURING INDUSTRY AND EMPLOYMENT

As you learned in Chapter 29, most of the expansion of employment opportunities since the Second World War have been in professions and services. Agricultural employment has declined absolutely, and the expansion of employment in manufacturing has been stagnant in absolute terms and was declining proportionally even before the recession.

Some relevant numbers are shown in Table 30.1. There were approximately the same number of production workers in 1991 as there had been in 1947 (12 million). The number had increased to 14 million in the late 1960s and held around 13.5 million for most

of the 1970s. The balance of the economy grew. Consequently, while production workers were more than 20 percent of the labor force in 1947, by 1991 they had fallen below 10 percent. The increase in production was attended by an enormous rise in labor productivity, output per worker.

This is not new, of course. American manufacturing has striven to save on expensive labor costs historically. A labor-saving bias has been a determining factor in the choice of technology from very early in the industrial history of the United States. But the post–World War II record in this regard has really been extraordinary. The Federal Reserve System's Index of Industrial Production (1967 = 100) stood at 58.5 in 1955 and reached 193.6 in 1990, an increase of 231 percent, while total manufacturing employment rose a mere 15 percent in the same period, and the number of production workers decreased by 6.6 percent. Over the entire period, then, physical output in manufacturing industries utterly outstripped the increases in the numbers of workers employed. But the increase was not evenly achieved; some periods saw far higher growth than did others. The issue of the recent slowdown in productivity growth is addressed later in the chapter.

DISTRIBUTION OF EMPLOYMENT AND VALUE ADDED

In what industries are American manufacturing workers to be found in greatest numbers, and what industries contribute most to the national income? Considering the great clamor about steel and autos, the "industrial rust belt" and so forth, Table 30.2 may come as quite a surprise. The table shows the composition of employment and value added in 1990. According to Table 17.2, industrial machinery ranked first in value added in 1910. It still ranks first in employment, although it now ranks fourth in value added. In point of fact, machinery manufacturing alone produces more value added, and employs more workers, *than the steel and automobile industries combined.* In 1990 all steel and iron foundries, blast furnaces, and all motor-vehicle manufacturing employed together 1,096,000 workers (6.2 percent of the total employed in manufacturing) and accounted for $100.1 billion of value added (approximately 7.5 percent of the $1.3 trillion total). The booming electrical and electronics industry also employs more workers and generates more value added than steel and autos combined. In general, Table 30.2 shows that the larger industrial employers are also the larger producers of value added. The greatest exceptions to the rule are apparel and textiles, chemicals, petroleum and coal, and tobacco. The latter three share

the characteristic that their contribution to value added far exceeds their shares of employment. The low-wage manufacturing industries are those in which the opposite is true: The employment percentage far exceeds the proportion of the value added—for example, lumber and wood, textiles, and leather.

STRUCTURE OF RECENT INDUSTRIAL GROWTH

Until the downturn in 1982 there had not been sudden changes in industrial structure for a long time. The recent rates of growth of output for durable and nondurable manufactures are shown in Figures 30.1 and 30.2. In each case the year 1967 is taken as the base year, against which the output reached in 1991 is measured. The indexes are weighted by their contributions to value added in the aggregates (all manufacturing, all durables, all nondurables). Among durable goods shown in Figure 30.1 there are several features of note. First, among the sectors growing slower than the average are primary metals and transportation equipment, two areas from which the cries for protection have been loudest, and where, in the cases of steel and autos, significant protection has been granted (see following). The decline of mining in the United States is also clear. Machinery and electronics are among the largest employment groups and producers of value added, and

Table 30.1 Manufacturing Employment and the Labor Force 1947–90

| Year | Number of Workers, in Millions | | | Percentage of Total Labor Force | |
	Total Civilian Labor Force	Manufacturing Workers	Production Workers	Mfg. Workers	Production Workers
1947	59.4	14.5	11.9	24.4%	20.1%
1950	62.2	14.5	11.8	23.3	18.9
1955	65.0	16.3	13.0	25.1	19.9
1960	69.6	16.2	12.2	23.2	17.5
1965	74.5	17.2	13.1	23.2	17.6
1970	82.7	18.0	13.5	21.7	16.4
1975	95.5	18.3	12.6	19.2	13.2
1980	100.9	20.6	13.9	20.5	13.8
1985	117.2	18.8	12.2	16.0	10.2
1990	126.4	18.8	12.1	14.9	9.6

Sources: *Historical Statistics*, series D 14, P 3, 4, 5; *Statistical Abstract*, 1992, Tables 608, 1243.

Table 30.2   1990 Industrial Distribution of Employment and Value Added in Manufacturing

	Number (000)	Percentage of Total Manufacturing Employment	Percentage of Value Added by Manufacturing
5% of Manufacturing Employment or More			
Industrial machinery	1,877	10.68	9.96
Transportation equipment	1,774	10.09	11.08
Printing and publishing	1,538	8.75	7.78
Electronics; elec. equipment	1,497	8.52	8.07
Food and kindred product	1,470	8.36	10.63
Fabricated metal products	1,439	8.19	6.03
Apparel and other textiles	993	5.65	2.49
Instruments and related products	949	5.40	6.16
Less than 5% of Manufacturing Employment			
Rubber and misc. plastic prod.	870	4.95	3.76
Chemicals and allied products	853	4.85	11.54
Primary metal industries	712	4.05	4.02
Lumber and wood	683	3.89	2.16
Textile mill products	633	3.60	2.00
Paper and allied products	628	3.57	4.51
Stone, clay, and glass products	509	2.90	2.57
Furniture and fixtures	499	2.84	1.63
Miscellaneous mfg. industries	386	2.20	1.52
Leather and leather products	117	0.67	0.35
Petroleum and coal products	112	0.64	2.05
Tobacco products	41	0.23	1.70

Source: *Statistical Abstract*, 1992, Table 1244.

they have also grown the most rapidly. Their growth has exceeded that of durable manufacturing as a whole.

Among nondurable manufactures the modern expansion of rubber and plastics has gone "off the charts" compared to other sectors (and literally, in the case of Figure 30.2). All major nondurable sectors expanded their output between 1967 and 1991. Only the output of leather and leather goods actually declined. Textile mill products has been a relatively slow-growth industry. Like autos and steel, it has encountered significant competition from foreign producers, and, like autos and steel, the leaders of both capital and labor visited Washington, D.C., in search of protection and received it.

THE PRODUCTIVITY ISSUE

Markets are made by productivity, economic growth; increased income per head is the product, by simple multiplication, of rising output per hour worked. If pro-

ductivity slows down, so does economic growth. In a simple model such as the one at the beginning of this book where the amount of grass mown per hour changed with no change in the lawn mower, the measurement of productivity was simple enough. But when whole industries or economies are being considered, productivity measurement becomes an arcane business.

It is widely held that American productivity has been falling in recent years, both absolutely and in comparison to other countries. The Department of Commerce estimates U.S. industrial productivity grew at an annual rate of 3.2 percent in 1948–65, 2.4 percent in 1965–73 (a one-third fall), 1.1 percent in 1973–78 (a 55-percent decline from 1965–73) and, finally, −0.8 percent, an absolute decline, in 1978–80.[1] Such a poor performance would then help to explain the gathering stagflation at the end of the 1970s—higher than trend rates of unemployment, the balance of payments deficit, declining tax revenues. The most widely accepted

Figure 30.1 U.S. Industrial Production Indexes: 1967–91, 1967 = 100 (Durable Goods)

Figure 30.2 U.S. Industrial Production Indexes: 1967–91, 1967 = 100 (Nondurable Goods)

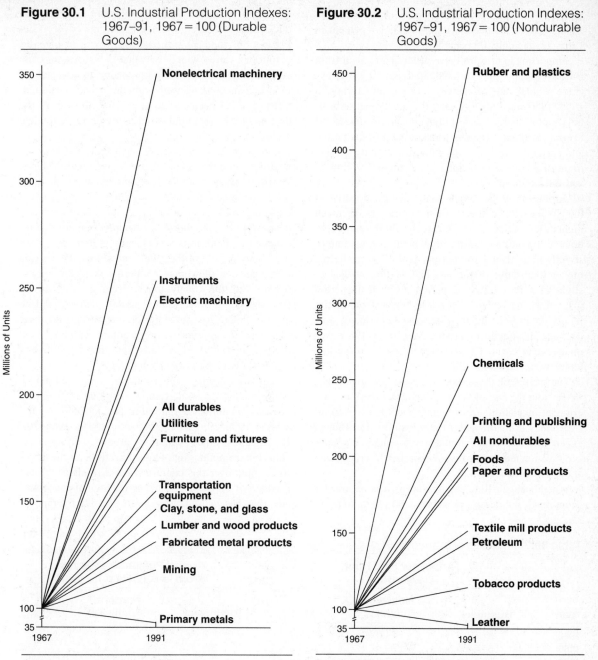

Source: *Statistical Abstract*, 1992, Table 1252.

Source: *Statistical Abstract*, 1992, Table 1252.

estimates for labor productivity are that it rose at an annual rate of 2.6 percent in 1948–65, 1.9 percent in 1965–73, and only .05 percent in 1973–79.[2]

Supporting figures for these patterns are given from Bureau of Labor Statistics data in Table 30.3. The average annual rate of increase for manufacturing in 1975–1980 was only 1.8, only 0.7 for the entire business sector, and 0.6 for nonfarm business. These are lower growth rates than for most of the postwar period and certainly are lower than the productivity growth figures for America's major trading partners in Europe and Asia in those years.[3]

During the 1980s, productivity continued to rise at the slower rates of the 1970s in contrast to the much higher rates of the 1960s. During the 1980s, output per hour in the business sector grew at an average rate of slightly more than 1 percent per year. This is slightly higher than those of the last half of the 1970s, but slightly less than during the period 1973–78, the period just before the "crisis." Nonfarm business productivity peaked in 1978 and then started on a period of slow decline. Manufacturing productivity in the 1980s was greater than in the 1970s; it recovered from the low which was reached in 1982.

The causes of these baleful results are given in a range from the loss of the work ethic to excessive government regulation; from savings rates too low to insufficiency of mathematics in the schools, insufficient expenditures on research and development, Women's Lib—you name it. Expansion experts still crepe-hang about U.S. productivity.

When such startling changes occur it is natural for economists, politicians, preachers, and others to try to explain them. But recall what a range of *different* production experiences these aggregate data cover. As in Figures 30.1 and 30.2, the actual growth of physical output has varied widely between industries, and any statement about something purporting to cover all of industry must be viewed with the greatest caution. Still, there has been a widespread consensus about the decline of American industrial productivity in the late 1970s.

Consider the idea, however, that there has been no decline due to the usual "causes" attributed. Michael Darby proposes a series of reasonable adjustments to the labor force input that leave doubt about the usual explanations. Darby argues that the adjustments for changes in recent labor-force composition are due to: (a) *age* (the labor force has recently gotten younger as the "baby boom" of the 1950s entered it), (b) *sex* (the big expansion of women reentering the labor force), (c) *immigration* (many more recent arrivals are in the labor force than usual), and (d) *education* (the younger, more female, more foreign workers have yet to achieve the appropriate levels of knowledge to boost their productivity). Thus Darby says that the decline in productivity is "statistical myopia."

Once the proper adjustments are made, employee productivity increased at an average rate of 1.52 percent per annum over the entire period 1900–79 and 1.54 in 1900–29, 1.51 in 1929–65, 1.53 in 1965–79.[4] Division into other subperiods produces different results, but the point is that "normalization" of the labor-force input over this century really eliminates the big productivity decline reported by others in the past decade that has caused such a stir. As Darby puts it:

Table 30.3 Indexes of Productivity

Year	Output per Paid Hour (1977 = 100)			Annual Percentage Change (from immediate prior year)		
	Business	**Nonfarm Business**	**Mfg.**	**Business**	**Nonfarm Business**	**Mfg.**
1960	67.6	71.0	62.2	1.7	1.1	—
1965	81.0	83.4	76.6	3.0	2.5	2.2
1970	88.4	89.3	80.8	0.7	0.3	0.8
1975	95.7	96.0	92.9	2.0	1.8	−1.2
1980	99.3	98.8	101.4	−0.3	−0.4	−1.9
1985	106.4	104.8	121.7	1.0	0.5	2.3
1990	110.0	107.5	141.6	0.2	−0.1	2.5

Source: *Statistical Abstract*, 1988, Tables 643, 644; 1992, Table 647.

Thus, it appears that there is no substantial variation in trend private productivity growth over the twentieth century to be explained by variations in regulation growth, oil prices, the failure of American management, labor, or any of the other popular whipping boys.[5]

Observed declines in conventional productivity measures are really due to temporary changes in the quality of a single input. There are still declines in conventionally measured physical output per hour. But not to worry, it will pass.

In the cases of steel and autos, the old-time heart of American industrialization, the results of recent economic history are perhaps more easily explained.

DECLINE OF AMERICAN PRE-EMINENCE IN STEEL AND MOTOR VEHICLES

Beginning in the mid-1970s, the country has been alarmed by successive crises involving manufacturing's supposed decline. The winning candidate in the 1992 election promised to promote the "reindustrialization" of America through government policy. Others who share this goal have urged that laws be passed to prevent existing industrial plants from closing down or relocating to more salubrious climates, that controls be put on American foreign investment to stop jobs from being "exported," that even more stringent tariffs and quotas be imposed to keep foreign products out of the country. Great and famous industrial plants like Dayton, Ohio's Firestone tire plant and U.S. Steel's giant Chicago Southworks have been left by their owners to rust, with thousands of men and women thrown out of work.[6]

It seemed like a strange nightmare. United States Steel bought an oil company (Marathon) and changed its logo to USX (an attempt to exist incognito?); General Motors cut a deal with Japan's Toyota to manufacture autos of Japanese design in California. Moreover, GM itself imported some 200,000 Japanese autos in 1985 to sell under its own logo. Only a generation earlier learned economists had written of the permanent "dollar shortage" brought on by America's invincible industrial superiority, impermeable to any foreign competition. The United States, it was now said, faced inevitable industrial decline, due to superior foreign enterprise. Steel and automobiles, the core industries of the American economy, were in deep trouble.

Since arrangements can be made to manufacture under license to patent holders, to lease and buy patent rights; since internationally traded machinery incorporates new technology, and the world of technical ideas is essentially unified; it is not too much of an exaggeration to say that the entire world *could* employ a uniform technology. No single country necessarily has a lock on any set of production techniques and accompanying machinery. Differences in the technologies actually deployed must be due to such phenomena as relative factor proportions, quality of management and labor force, government policies, availability of relevant financial infrastructure, and access to markets.[7] No seasoned observer who has witnessed the rise of the manufacturing industry in such places as Hungary, Israel, Taiwan, South Korea, Mississippi, and Idaho would bet against the appearance of significant manufacturing establishments in almost any reasonably situated economy—for example, mainland China.[8] To be sure, the world of manufacturing excellence is still concentrated in those countries that were the leaders in, say, 1940, but it is reasonable to expect successful newcomers, and they have appeared. Consider the record of American and world steel output shown in Table 30.4.

Steel had been the metal of twentieth-century industrialization—cheap steel for buildings, machinery, roads, bridges, the triumph of the nineteenth-century's "second industrial revolution," starting with Bessemer's converter in 1856 and ending with the banks of open-hearth furnaces in Pittsburgh and along the Great Lakes in the 1890s. Cheap iron ores, superior and cheap coking coals, a gathered and capable labor force, and huge markets linked by rail and water had made

Table 30.4 World and U.S. Steel Production, 1950–90

| Year | Crude Steel Production | | Percent U.S. of World |
| | World | United States | |
	(Millions of Net Tons)		
1950	207.9	96.8	46.6
1960	379.7	99.3	26.0
1970	654.2	131.5	20.1
1980	790.4	111.0	14.2
1985	792.9	88.3	11.1
1990	849.6	98.9	11.6

Sources: *Historical Statistics*, series P 265; *Statistical Abstract*, 1992, Table 1266.

steel the "natural" basis of American industrial expansion. After the economic disaster of the 1930s depression, the Second World War added another burst of demand which was followed by further expansion in the postwar years. By 1950 nearly 47 percent of world output was made in the United States. Then came another worldwide surge in steel output, and this time American industry did not expand. By the 1980s the American share of world output was about one-tenth of the total, and American industry was under siege from import competition, from Japan, Europe, Canada, and even from Brazil.

A basically similar history may be seen in the record of motor-vehicle production shown in Table 30.5. Between 1960 and 1980 world production of motor vehicles more than doubled in response to the general economic expansion of the 1960s and 1970s. But American industry, the largest in the world in 1960, did not participate in that growth. American auto exports grew, but so did imports.

Motor-vehicle imports, about 5 percent of domestic sales in 1960, reached 25.8 percent by 1990. Iron and steel imports were less than 7 percent of U.S. consumption in 1960 and 13 percent by 1990, despite several protective measures taken to restrict imports. By the end of the 1970s, both steel and automobiles (along with a vast range of related employments) were "in trouble," begging in Washington for protection from foreign competition. Since these two huge industries, dominated by giant firms like United States Steel and General Motors, were to media observers the prime symbols of American industrial power, panic reigned in the media. What happened? Were the industries that had been entrepreneured by those such as Andrew Carnegie and Henry Ford going to vanish from the U.S.

Table 30.5   World and U.S. Motor Vehicle Production, 1960–89

Year	Production World (Million Vehicles)	U.S. (Million Vehicles)	Percentage U.S. of World
1960	16.5	8.0	48.5
1970	29.3	7.9	27.0
1980	38.9	8.0	20.6
1985	43.9	11.7	26.7
1989	49.0	9.8	20.0

Sources: *Statistical Abstract*, 1973, Table 1320; 1982–83, Table 1058; 1988, Tables 990, 1373; 1992, Tables 1000, 1357.

economy or linger on as protected and parasitic lame ducks?

The Modern Technological Revolution in Steel Making

In the 1950s two major innovations in steel making occurred. U.S. producers lagged behind in adoption of both (a) the use of basic oxygen furnaces (BOF) and (b) larger-scale plants with continuous slab or billet casting. The latter replaced ingot production followed by rolling at separate slab, billet, and bloom mills. The American producers were deeply committed to open-hearth technology and to separate rolling operations. Their plants, labor forces (and work-rule contracts), and managements were all the products of the older technology.

Now, an old technology in place is no reason not to tear it down or scrap it if something better comes along—remember Andrew Carnegie's assault on his own Bessemer works in the 1890s when the new open-hearth technology arrived on the scene. To maintain an outdated technology is simply voluntary obsolescence. Carnegie opened one of his directors' meetings in those years with: "Well, what shall we throw away this year?" To him an obsolescent technology was good only for the museum.[9] Such behavior absorbs investment, and, in the short run, reduced profits. According to Magaziner and Reich, two advocates of industrial policy, American steel industry leaders opted for a policy of marginal improvements, adopting new techniques piecemeal, instead of relocation to completely new "greenfield" sites. They reasoned that piecemeal improvement would enable some of the older mills to be kept going to full depreciation, and thus maintain higher short-run profits. Yet piecemeal didn't fit.[10] The policy left some plants with excess capacity, while others were crowded, inefficiently placed, and unable to meet demand. Big Steel's strategy came to be known as the "brownfield" strategy.

American–Japanese Comparisons

Thus Bethlehem Steel's giant Burns Harbor, Indiana, plant, the only "fully integrated large-scale greenfield plant built in the United States since 1952" was held to be unprofitable, as its great capacity could not be fitted into the demands of a multitude of smaller Bethlehem operations.[11] Japanese competitors, meanwhile, scrapped open-hearth and went in for continuous-process mills. By 1978 the Japanese, with a 30–35 percent cost advantage over American producers achieved 51 percent of their raw steel output from continuous casting, compared to a mere 15 percent in this country.[12] The initial American backwardness Magaziner and Reich attribute in large part simply to U.S. management's ideas about world trade. Management argued that ". . . foreign imports were based on cheap labor, dumping, and unfair trade practices, and therefore asked for government protection," which they got.[13]

The Japanese, with no iron ore or coking coal of their own, exporting 40 percent of their steel output (compared to about 3 percent for U.S. producers), *had* to play the international markets and went for the flexibility of low-cost production based on the best-practice technology. That was necessity, and as a result, according to Magaziner and Reich, the Japanese now have ". . . the world's most efficient steel industry." Andrew Carnegie had said, as he tore down his banks of Bessemer converters, "The perfect mill is the way to wealth."

Times had changed in American steel. According to Magaziner and Reich the "bottom line" mentality in the short run was the problem. The Americans went for "rounding out" investments instead of new continuous-casting "green-field" plants in order to maintain short-run profits, and thus missed the boat. By 1977 the Japanese had 25 blast furnaces, each capable of 2 million tons annually: the Americans had none. Eighty-five percent of Japanese production came from steel plants of annual capacity of 4.5 million metric tons or more, compared to 31 percent of American production from plants of such size.[14] American management also believed the Japanese competition was a flash in the pan and that a new era of worldwide steel shortages was (hopefully) dawning. So why take chances?

The American Steel Industry's Modernization

There were, according to Paul Tiffany, other deep-seated problems in American steel related to big government and big labor which led not only to conservative policy regarding plant size, but even to initial refusal to adopt the new BOF technology where it could be done. Tiffany argues that the steel industry's leaders (Big Steel) continuously hoped for a more favorable tax relief and federal subsidy program than they achieved. Their hope was based upon their pivotal position in national defense strategy as the Cold War deepened. During the Korean War, to get expanded steel capacity in a hurry, rapid depreciation allowances were granted the steel producer (five years for a new plant), and the resulting extra after-tax profits could be used to expand old or build new facilities. When the war ended the Eisenhower administration refused to extend the favorable treatment, arguing that such ". . . would be unwarranted public meddling into the workings of a free market economy."[15] A classic case, remembering the public relations homilies of Big Steel spokesmen Roger Blough and Benjamin Fairless, of being "hoist by their own petards." Meanwhile, says Tiffany, labor relations in the steel industry were as sour as ever, with Democrats in Congress backing the wage demands of the United Steel Workers while the Truman, Eisenhower, and Kennedy regimes, in succession, resisted the efforts of the industry to pass through the higher wage costs directly to the consumer.

Truman had once threatened to build federal steel mills and in 1949 seized steel properties in the name of the people (the Supreme Court overturned him). Eisenhower's officials, many of them from big business itself, "jawboned" against higher price rises, and John Kennedy resorted to profanity to describe the Big Steel leaders. It was held that excessive rises in steel prices were inflationary and undermined the economy. Steel prices rose, but more moderately than had been hoped for.

Meanwhile, it was the policy of the federal government throughout the 1950s to extend aid to its European allies and to the Japanese to rebuild their own steel industries. By 1959, for the first time in the twentieth century, the United States imported more steel than it exported,[16] as foreign producers easily undercut the domestic industry in price, quality, and delivery schedules.

Huge investments had been made by Big Steel and it was mostly in out-of-date technology. It is an almost unbelievable record: In the 1950s billions of dollars were sunk into mostly brand-new obsolescence. As two leading students of the industry, Walter Adams and Hans Mueller phrased it:

Most of the melt shops were already obsolescent the moment they were installed.[17]

and

> When the expansion ended in the late 1950s, the U.S. industry found itself in a worse competitive position than at the beginning of the decade.[18]

That had been due in part to the failure to go for greenfield plants; instead, emphasis was on maintaining existing locations, rounding out older plants, and shoehorning the new equipment into sites which had looked choice to Andrew Carnegie and Judge Gary in the nineteenth century.

But an equally serious problem was the failure to adopt BOF for so long. By 1964 when 12 percent of U.S. production came from oxygen furnaces, the Japanese, with their greenfield plants, already were up to 44 percent BOF production, on their way to supremacy. The oxygen converter had been the achievement of a Swiss professor, Robert Durrer, just before the outbreak of World War II. Its first commercial operation was in Austria in 1950. The process was first installed in the United States just four years later by a small producer (McLouth). It took Big Steel another decade to follow suit. Similarly, small American companies began smelting using scrap, with electric furnaces—so-called minimills—in locations far from the production facilities of Big Steel. The commitment to new investments in the old open-hearth technology in the 1950s had been utterly the wrong move by the steel giants.

Consider the data in Table 30.6. Although from 1960 to 1980 net output expanded a third (and then declined) the process composition was a revolution; BOF and electric furnace production very nearly wiped away open-hearth output, and with it, the jobs of thousands of steel workers. Empty plants and decaying economic life in Youngstown, the Pittsburgh area, Wheeling, along the lower reaches of the Great Lakes, and elsewhere are the silent monuments of this revolution. The near disappearance of open-hearth output under pressure from BOF and electric furnaces was even more dramatic than the supersession of Bessemer capacity by the new open-hearth plants eight decades or so earlier (Table 17.3). Despite this revolution, by every measurable criterion U.S. steel production is more costly now than is the international competition: Capital, labor, raw materials, all must be expended in greater amounts to get a ton of steel here than in Japan or western Europe.[19] The huge American industry is the "sick man of steel."

Tiffany says that "the routine" of decision making in American firms accounts for this disaster. But the record made was largely the work of Big Steel, not of all U.S. steel-makers. After all, both BOF and electric minimill technology were entrepreneured early and profitably by "independent" mills, relatively small firms. It was U.S. Steel, Jones and Laughlin, Bethlehem, National, and others, those with most of the steel capacity—the huge, vertically integrated firms—that held back. By 1963 the six largest U.S. companies, operating 50 percent of the American basic steel-making capacity, had not an oxygen furnace among them. Small companies, together operating a mere 7 percent of U.S. basic capacity, made about half of all American BOF output.[20] The technological revolution in steel was here. But not at the top. Why not?

The Power of Inertia

Some blame government for its enterprise-crippling regulations; some blame the unions for their output-crippling work rules and wage demands far in excess

Table 30.6 Raw Steel Production by Process 1950–90

Year	Total	Open Hearth	BOF (Millions of Net Tons)	Electric	Open Hearth	BOF	Electric
						Percentage of Total	
1950	96.8	90.8	—	6.0	93.8	—	6.2
1960	99.3	87.6	3.3	8.4	88.2	3.3	8.5
1970	131.5	48.0	63.3	20.2	36.5	48.1	15.4
1980	118.8	13.0	67.6	31.2	11.7	60.4	27.9
1985	88.3	6.4	51.9	29.9	7.2	58.8	33.9
1990	98.9	3.5	58.5	36.9	3.5	59.2	37.3

Sources: *Historical Statistics,* series P 265–69; *Statistical Abstract,* 1992, Table 1266.

of productivity increases; and some blame management for its shortsighted, short-run, bottom-line mentality. Adams and Mueller see the outcome as the natural consequence of Big Steel's history. There is considerable merit in this view. In retrospect the Big Steel companies have been problem children in American economic development. Once past their earliest stages as dynamic entrepreneurial firms, when the great men of steel made an industry, the corporate descendants became mere bureaucracies, adept at merger, price fixing, and oligopoly behavior. Years ago, in 1950, Nobel Prize-winning economist George Stigler told a Congressional committee

> . . . all the largest steel firms . . . are the product of mergers. Not one steel company has been able to add to its relative size as much as 4 percent of the ingot capacity of the industry in 50 years by attracting customers. Every firm that has gained 4 or more percent of the industry's capacity in this half century has done so by merger.[21]

These giant firms, living decade by decade in a world of oligopoly behavior (and after 1945 of incessant lock-step price increases), protectionism, and periodic bouts both with the huge steel union and its Congressional supporters, became insensitive to competitive changes both within the United States and in the outside world. As Adams and Mueller phrase it:

> Born of multiple mergers, the large steel companies managed to foster a system of coordinated pricing and orderly growth. No unforgiving rivals forced them to remain in the forefront of organizational and technological efficiency.[22]

By the late 1960s foreign competition *inside* the American market (imports were 4.7 percent of U.S. consumption in 1960, 16.7 percent by 1968) frightened the leaders of Big Steel back to Washington for a federal protectionist handout. It was granted. From 1969 to 1975 European and Japanese exporters to the United States were under a voluntary restraint agreement (VRA) that gave them quotas in the American market. The VRA ended in 1975 when a private antitrust suit was brought against the system. However, in 1974 a new trade act not only allowed quotas to be imposed against specialty steel imports but created the Trigger Price Mechanism (TPM) to protect American firms from "dumping"—that is, for charging less for steel in

the U.S. market than at home. The TPM meant that foreign firms could now freely base their offer prices to American customers on high-cost U.S. steel rather than on world-market prices. The consumer was forced to pay the bill. It was a happy outcome for the steel industry, and prices were raised all 'round in celebration.[23] It was admitted, in these circumstances, that the BOF took over within the protected U.S. market more from the pressure of domestic competition—the independents—than from the giant international steel industry growing up overseas.[24] TPM is a case of regulatory capture, with the U.S. government now certifying and publishing the industry's price lists, revised quarterly. When Reagan came in VRA was restored.

The Prospect for Steel

At this juncture the American steel industry's future is anything but predictable. On the average, of course, the data show an industry that cannot compete in the world market—a creature of price fixing and protectionism. Adams and Mueller suggest that it just be put on a straight and open subsidy basis: "You get *x* dollars, on condition that you build *y* plants."[25] What kinds of plants? The data indicate no known technology that would make the American basic steel industry internationally competitive again. That certainly seems to be also the opinion, at least of some industry leaders. Walter Williams, CEO of Bethlehem Steel said in 1988: "You'll never see another integrated steel mill built in the U.S." He did not contemplate any future growth. "There are a lot of things we can do about improving products, but there won't be any growth in steel. . . ." David Roderick, chairman of USX, put it: "Rebuild steel mills to do what? Sit and rust again?"[26]

Due primarily to union pressure, the quotas were imposed to save jobs in the steel mills. The estimated cost of those jobs to everyone else is something to consider. It has been estimated by Arthur Denzau, of the Center for the Study of American Business, that 2800 jobs were "saved" in steel by the price increases that resulted from the quotas, but at the cost of $750,000 per job and 52,000 jobs in steel-using industries wiped out.[27] In 1988 the American steel firms reported profits, but they were still protected by the import quotas and were still pleading for extended quotas.

The reduction in basic American steel output in 1980–85 (Table 30.6) shows the road taken to survive by the American firms. Open hearth production continued to fall as obsolete capacity was junked, while BOF and electric production expanded. By 1990 the industry's capacity was only 75 percent of what it had been in 1980, while, on average, only 164,000 steel workers remained of the 399,000 who labored in 1980. What remained of the American steel industry was profitable (especially the smaller firms), at least before the downturn of the early 1990s.[28]

It is possible that the international steel industry will simply merge with national segments and play the protected markets, like the United States or the European Economic Community, from the inside. In June of 1984 the Justice Department approved the purchase of half of the National Steel Company's stock for $292 million by NKK (Nippon Kabushiki Kaisha), Japan's second largest producer.[29] At home NKK has been a dynamic steel company. A Chicago TV interviewer found that National's American employees, no doubt with vivid memories of the past decade in their industry, welcomed the deal.[30] Hopefully the Japanese steel firm will try to lift its new American acquisition nearer to the average of world technology.

In 1985 Chicago's Inland Steel hired the world's largest steelmaker, Nippon Steel Corporation, to consult on installation of new continuous casting equipment and other improvements. In flat steel production the Japanese experts made more than 700 recommendations for technical improvements worth $100 million a year in savings at the Indiana Harbor plant alone.[31] To remain competitive in basic steel production the American steel firms faced the need by the mid-1980s to acquire a world of technical innovation they had ignored in previous decades. An alternative was just to abandon steel making, in part or altogether. In February, 1986, U.S. Steel stockholders voted to merge their firm with Texas Oil and Gas. A generation earlier U.S. Steel had dominated world steel production. More foreign firms have since bought into the American steel industry, and the international-ownership route now seems the way basic steel is going. It is a worldwide economy, and steel firms are becoming worldwide enterprises.

Automobiles: Market Structure

The steel industry, despite the wooden oligopoly characteristics of Big Steel management, in fact has slowly become less concentrated during the twentieth century.

The automobile industry, on the other hand, has shown no such tendency, apart from the expansion of the range of choice provided by imports. Three companies—General Motors, Ford, and Chrysler—sell virtually all domestically produced automobiles, although foreign companies have begun production within the United States. A fourth U.S. company, American Motors, became part of Chrysler following several years where it was unable to capture more than a negligible share of the market. All other nonspecialized producers vanished from the scene after World War II.[32] American Motors was the residual firm (evolved from the merged firms of Nash and Hudson). Kaiser, Willys, Studebaker, and Packard died off. A small firm, Crosley, attempted to enter the market and produced some thousands of units in the late 1940s and then vanished. New entry is extremely expensive, and, in fact, there have been no successful new entries by American firms for decades. The three remaining American auto firms represent the survivors of more than 1100 automobile companies that existed at one time or another, some 181 of which appear actually to have produced more than a few demonstration models.[33] Ford Motor Company had once been the giant of the industry but was displaced for good by General Motors in the later 1920s.

Despite notorious nonprice competition among the American auto companies, their proliferation of models and options, and the free bargaining between individual buyers and sellers gave the appearance of competitive vigor until the late 1970s. Also, since used cars are competitive with new cars, consumers had plenty of options. Gigantic advertising campaigns attempt to trim consumer tastes to one or the other of the new models each year, but as the Ford Motor Company found out with the Edsel fiasco in 1958, consumer tastes are not so easily manipulated.

Econometric studies show that the auto market is fairly unstable. The price elasticity of demand ranges from -0.5 to -1.5 and the income elasticity from 1.0 to 4.0, so demand will fluctuate considerably with respect to income changes and is sensitive to some extent to price competition.[34] But the industry is characterized by price leadership and the other signs of tight oligopoly behavior, so direct price competition, model by model, is nearly nonexistent. So far as the manufacturers are concerned, GM is the basic price setter, and the other firms follow its lead. The companies watch each other closely; features such as wings and fins,

Table 30.7 U.S. Auto Market Shares 1937–87

Year	General Motors	Ford	Chrysler	Other Domestic	Foreign
		(Percentage of Total)			
1937	41.8	21.4	25.4	11.4	—
1946–50	41.8	21.4	21.6	15.1	0.2
1961–65	49.7	26.2	12.2	6.0	6.1
1966–70	46.2	24.3	15.8	2.8	10.6
1971–75	44.1	24.0	13.4	3.3	15.2
1976–80	46.8	21.1	10.1	1.8	20.1
1987	33.6	17.8	10.7	6.8	31.1

Source: Lawrence J. White, "The Automobile Industry," Walter Adams, ed., *The Structure of American Industry* (New York: Macmillan, 1982, 6th ed.), Table 3, p. 147; *Ward's Automotive Yearbook; Statistical Abstract,* 1992, Table 1002.

square headlamps, double headlamps, even colors tend to appear and disappear more or less simultaneously. In so tightly structured a market any attempt at direct price competition can be quickly countered by the other producers if there are no great differences in the models offered, and there tend not to be. So competition tends to be in styling and product identification through advertising—Image! The price element enters into the individual dealing between buyers and sellers; a market such as real estate, where "haggling" is still the expected norm of behavior. Long dominated by American firms (except for novelties such as luxury cars or sports models), the American automobile industry seemed an unlikely target for a foreign competitor. Table 30.7 shows the market shares from 1937 to 1987.

Imports and Exports

Since World War II the Big Three have dominated domestic production, but imports, less than 1 percent as late as 1955, greatly increased their market share to almost displace American Motors, and to nearly cut in half the share of ill-managed Chrysler Corporation. In 1979 Chrysler nearly went "belly up" with enormous losses and had to get a U.S. Treasury guarantee on its debt—the "Chrysler bailout." In 1981 the Reagan administration acceded to the pleas of the industry and extracted from the Japanese producers a voluntary freeze, a quota, on Japanese imports. Domestic sales then rose, Chrysler repaid its loans, and the auto executives voted themselves enormous bonuses. Also, of course, automobile prices rose dramatically. In 1984 as the recovery continued the auto companies made rec-

ord profits from the domestic economy, free from increases in foreign imports.

As was noted at the beginning of this chapter, the worldwide growth of the automobile industry left the American industry in the dust. Unless the American market were closed off, that vast expansion of world auto output was bound to spill over, even into the land of Henry Ford and Walter Chrysler.

As you can see in Table 30.8, the rise in imports far outstripped the impressive expansion of U.S. exports into that booming international market. In fact, U.S. exports rose in value by a factor of 24.7 from 1965 to 1990, but imports went up by a factor of 71.4 (from $640 million to $45.7 *billion*), leaving the country with a deficit of more than $36 billion in its foreign trade in passenger cars. When the Reagan administration put a lid on imports in 1981, foreign producers held slightly more than a one-third share of the U.S. passenger car market, and the American auto industry was headed for panic. The limits on that trade reduced the foreign

Table 30.8 U.S. Foreign Trade in Autos 1950–90

Year	Value in Millions of Dollars	
	Exports	Imports
1950	179	21
1960	235	513
1965	393	640
1970	822	3,719
1975	2,852	7,483
1980	3,932	16,675
1985	6,027	36,474
1990	9,708	45,716

Source: *Statistical Abstract,* 1992, Table 1000.

Competition Forces Progress.   In modern times, American leadership in basic steel and automobiles has been challenged by foreign competition and has been forced to change to remain competitive. The Chrysler Jefferson assembly plant in Detroit in 1967 (above) gave way to the modern Jefferson North plant in 1992 (below), where an air-operated chain hoist assists the team on the elevated work station.

share to slightly more than one-quarter. Afterward foreign auto makers, established originally in the American market with cheap and efficient small cars, found their staying power in their reputation for quality. They responded to the quantity restriction by exporting more expensive models to the American market, thus maintaining their revenues—and profits.

The Small Car Revolution

For the most part, imports meant subcompacts, a car size not popular with American producers, or consumers, at first. The surge of imports came in the late 1960s.

Observe the data in Table 30.9. By 1970 total imports were almost 20 percent of the sum of U.S. factory sales of passenger cars plus imports. Imports continued to push upward irregularly until the voluntary freeze by the Japanese in 1981 (in that year the Japanese accounted for 61 percent of all imports). Since total motor-vehicle sales include trucks and recreational vehicles, these numbers are not the ones ordinarily quoted; but for the passenger car market, these are the ones that count. In some years the domestic manufacturers did better than is indicated by the numbers in Table 30.9 (for example, factory sales of 9,200,000 in the boom year 1977). Still, the impression given in the table is the right one; beginning in the late 1960s foreign autos, for the first time since the domestic industry's beginning, became a major segment of the American market. They captured a larger share than Ford Motors. Why was that?

Most observers saw a combination of price and size. Recall that the income elasticity of demand for new cars was quite high: from 1.0 to 4.0. As inflation picked up in the late 1960s those whose real incomes lagged behind were willing to pay attention to something besides more expensive, new American cars. The initial volume influx of foreign cars, the VW "bug," the early Toyotas and Nissans, were on the low end of the price scale and offered dependable and economical transportation. In university parking lots, where incomes quickly lagged behind the increase in general prices, foreign cars immediately became common and then became the majority.

Also, the foreign cars were small cars, far smaller than the "standard" American passenger car. This posed a second problem. The American manufacturers were tooled up for and committed to the mass-produced six-passenger sedan. That was the product they made most efficiently and profitably. Small cars were something new and would not be as profitable per unit. The American manufacturers tended to scoff at the idea of a seriously rising demand for cars so small that only two adults and (small) children could ride in them comfortably. Also, since the new car market was already filled with standard production, any new small car offered by the domestic producers was mainly just a threat to *their own* market for standard cars. There was a flurry of smaller models in 1959, but by the 1960s the American product was bigger than ever.

The imported small cars continued to sell, so by 1969 and 1970 Ford and GM were offering domestically made subcompacts. These American cars were of poor quality compared to the foreign competition. The 1969 bloodless coup in Libya and the 1973 renewal of the perpetual Arab-Israeli war brought a sharp increase in gasoline prices by 1974, and a new element entered into the demand spectrum—*mileage.*

The small foreign cars, made in countries with high excise taxes on gasoline, were already relatively fuel

Table 30.9 Factory Sales and Total Imports 1950–90 (Passenger Cars Only)

Year	Factory Sales	Imports (000s)	Total	Percentage Imports of Total
1950	6,666	21	6,687	0.3
1955	7,920	57	7,977	0.7
1960	6,675	499	7,174	7.0
1965	9,306	569	9,875	5.8
1970	6,457	1,280	7,827	16.4
1975	6,713	1,571	8,284	19.0
1980	6,400	2,398	8,798	27.3
1985	8,002	2,838	10,840	26.2
1990	6,050	2,404	8,454	28.4

Sources: *Historical Statistics,* series Q 148; *Statistical Abstract,* 1992, Table 1002.

efficient. The American cars were not. Within a short period of time, the major U.S. auto companies themselves were importing and selling Japanese cars under various model names. Badly managed Chrysler did not introduce a subcompact of its own until 1978 when the third "oil shock" hit (the coup in Iran), producing long before-dawn queues at gasoline pumps, and fisticuffs, knives, even purchases at handgun point. This time most buyers finally became mileage conscious. There was the threat of ticket-coupon gasoline rationing; that the gas-guzzlers simply would not be on the road at all unless the owners could beg, borrow, or steal access to more than their allotted shares. In early 1979 people were trying to trade in new luxury American autos for little Toyotas and Nissans, and were being turned down by hard-nosed small-car dealers. By the end of the 1970s the American companies were producing gasoline-efficient subcompacts in earnest and were "downsizing" the dinosaurs. Even so, a large segment of the American market still hankered after a "full-sized" car. After 1983, as the economy recovered under the cover of protection, and as an international glut of oil had reduced and stabilized gasoline prices, the demand for the traditional product of the American auto industry remained strong.

By the end of the 1970s the imports were no longer "foreign" to American buyers; in the 1980s foreign manufacturers had built assembly plants inside the United States. American Motors had merged with France's Renault, and VW was producing cars in Pennsylvania (an enterprise that failed). Nissan and Honda were both producing parts in this country, and GM and Toyota were engaged in joint U.S. production, as were Chrysler and Mitsubishi. In September, 1988, Ford announced a joint venture with Japan's Nissan Motors to build minivans in Ohio. The limit on increases in Japanese imports employed throughout the Reagan-Bush administrations produced the result predicted by the textbooks—a transfer of consumers' money to protected companies. New car prices soared.

It is conceivable that in the future automobile manufacturers will be international conglomerates, that the era of strictly "national" automobile firms has nearly ended. International conglomeration is the way to get "behind" tariff walls. In the past decade there has been a powerful increase in protectionism, not only in the United States, but in other countries as well; but protectionism only staves off the inevitable. As it is though, the invasion of the U.S. market by foreign producers is the most impressive change in the American automobile industry since the moving assembly line was introduced at Ford's Highland Park plant in 1908.

A NOTE ON INDUSTRIAL RETARDATION

Economists have long been aware that stagnant industries tend to decline and vanish. When factor proportions change, when tastes change and demand flees from a given product, resources move away to seek employments with higher marginal earnings. Over time, as American economic history demonstrates, change in economic structure is inevitable. Nobel Prize-winner Simon Kuznets, in an early study, described the process this way:

> As we observe various industries within a given national economy, we see that the lead in development shifts from one branch to another. A rapidly developing industry does not retain its vigorous growth forever but slackens and is overtaken by others whose period of rapid development is beginning. Within one country we can observe a succession of different branches of activity in the vanguard of the country's economic development, and within each industry we can notice a conspicuous slackening of the rate of increase.[35]

Kuznets found that the early stages of an industry's existence tend to present the greatest range of technical possibilities, and competition for the industry's resources will push the most efficient to the front. Later on, especially if there is no fundamental change in the nature of the final product, technological advance and the industry's physical growth slow down. Lack of sufficient market possibilities will contribute to the power of the forces of decline. A lack of new and cheaper raw materials sources, or of dramatic increases in substitute inputs add to the tendency toward retardation. The rise of significant foreign competition will tend to be an additional retarding factor, on average.

Now, history does not necessarily repeat itself. But if we are to take American economic history seriously at all, Kuznets' findings must be considered, and the modern histories of both the basic steel and auto industries in this country strongly suggest terminal retardation. Notice the shapes of the trend curves for output in steel and autos in Figures 30.3 and 30.4. It is especially ominous in this regard that in neither industry were the major technological advances of the

Figure 30.3   Raw Steel Output, 1920–90

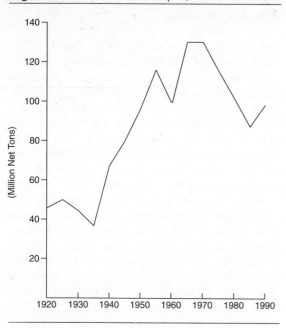

Sources: *Historical Statistics*, Series P 265; *Statistical Abstract*, 1992, Table 1266.

Figure 30.4   New Passenger Car Sales, 1945–90

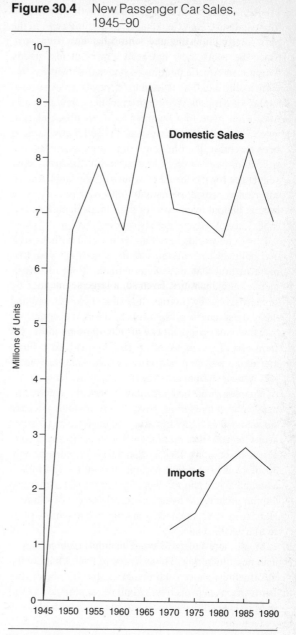

Sources: *Historical Statistics*, Series Q 148; *Statistical Abstract*, 1992, Table 1000.

post–World War II era either discovered or pioneered in this country.

In a similar study in the early 1930s, Arthur F. Burns traced the history of retardation in 104 areas of economic activity in the United States and concluded that retardation almost always led to absolute decline.[36] Burns also argued that such retardation in given industries was healthy, overall, for the entire developing organism as the release of resources from the declining sectors meant an influx into those healthier parts of the economy in expansionary phases. For both Kuznets and Burns the empirical rule was that industrial retardation, in specific industries, was an inevitable part of economic evolution. Possibly the extraordinary record of the two giants of the American economic past, autos and big steel, are manifestations of the Kuznets-Burns rule of industrial retardation. The dynamic, small American steel firms may be the beneficiary of Big Steel's decline.

However, there is one exception to consider, and it is an important one. The very real possibility of internationalization of ownership in both industries is the equivalent of a major new input discovery—in this case, management. Retardation may be overcome.

Internationalization of Industrial Ownership

For some years now foreign investment in American industry has been creating headlines: German, British,

French, Japanese, Korean, Chinese (both Taiwan and the mainland), even Canadian. It is nothing new; in the past foreign investment (ownership) has been vast. Since the 1950s there has been a more or less steady increase in American equities (stocks) owned by foreigners, in addition to bonds, deposits in American banks, or deposits in foreign branches; foreign banks have even gone into business in main financial centers. Similarly, Americans, as is well known, have been extending their holdings of foreign assets (as well as lending vast sums, sometimes with disastrous consequences for the lenders). A number of large American banks seemed in the mid-1980s near the edge of a federal bailout from some of their loans in eastern Europe, Latin America, and elsewhere.

It is "one world," after all. In a world without serious political and military conflicts nothing would be more natural than these international flows of investment capital. National borders are not put in place by economics but by politics. Investment capital, seeking the highest returns given levels of risk and transactions costs, would, in a perfect world, flow to its most efficient uses. Even in today's perilous world, such flows are taking place on a massive scale. American autos and American steel are only the tips of the iceberg.

Japanese direct investment in American manufacturing has been most impressive. It is more than a decade since Matsushita Electric acquired the Quasar TV plant near Chicago. It is more than fifteen years since Sony began assembling TVs in San Diego. Fujitsu bought 30 percent of Amdahl (computers) in 1971. In 1973 Mitsubishi and Nippon Steel bought into the American aluminum industry by acquiring 50 percent of Alumax. Honda, in 1982, opened an automobile assembly plant in Marysville, Ohio.[37]

Much more Japanese investment has entered American manufacturing. Those who still have "nationalistic" feelings about such matters naturally object, but with American firms buying into ownership deals even in Mainland China such objections seem both illogical and antique.

International trade has implied and been associated with direct international investment since at least the end of the Napoleonic Wars. In the past such investment was irregular, coming in long waves, as Brinley Thomas emphasized. We seem to be in another such wave. Insofar as it equalizes management skill and application of technology worldwide, it must be welcomed on grounds of economic efficiency.

Domestic Changes of Industrial Location

The much-publicized "move to the Sun Belt" of American manufacturing industry in the past twenty years is mainly a myth, the result of a few spectacular relocations during a time when the old industrial cities of the Midwest and Northeast were suffering from a multitude of troubles. Indeed, the data suggest a "Sun Belt" effect in the movement of population and the development of industry for most of the twentieth century. Richard McKenzie's recent study of regional industrial development shows that while industrial growth and location have changed, and while manufacturing employment has been rising in the Sun Belt and falling in the Frost Belt, this is *not* primarily due to relocation of plants, functions, and people from Frost Belt industries.[38] That is, it has been a rare event that an old Buffalo or Chicago firm has closed down and moved "bag and baggage" to the South, Southwest, or West. The old Frost Belt industries were located in such places as Rochester, New York, and Gary, Indiana, because those locations made good economic sense *for those industries* in their time. Although some old industries moved with the population to the South and West, the increase in employment is the result of the development of *new* industries—with different needs, technologies, transportation costs, and markets—that have located in the South and West.

The present decline of the old metallurgical and engineering industries that grew up and formed the core of Midwestern economic power in the late nineteenth and early twentieth centuries would not matter so much if new industries were growing up in places such as Rochester, Gary, and Pittsburgh. But they are not and that is an old pattern. James Soltow quotes a 1939 study by Glenn McLaughlin and Ralph Watkins of the old steel industry's capital.

> None of the new important industries which have developed in the United States in the past forty years have taken root in Pittsburgh.[39]

According to Soltow, this perceived economic plateau in the Midwest was masked by the huge demand of World War II and the postwar expansion for cars, tractors, farm equipment, trucks, steel, machines, earth-moving equipment—the bread-and-butter industries of the Midwest. But the plateau was there. While national employment overall rose 52 percent in 1948–1968, and national manufacturing employment rose by more than 26 percent, in the five Great Lakes states those numbers were merely 37 and 15. Even tertiary-sector employment was growing more slowly than the national average.[40] From 1968–1978 manufacturing employment in the Great Lakes states actually declined 1 percent while it managed a 5-percent increase nationally. The old technology would not produce a new expansion of employment in the old locations. Its day has passed. As Soltow puts it:

> In the late nineteenth and early twentieth centuries, the region's economy had been integrated into the national and international economy principally through the creation of the world's most efficient metallurgical-engineering complex.

In the 1960s foreign competition intensified, while domestic demand rose only moderately. New industries based on petrochemicals and high-tech electronics found homes in places like Houston, Phoenix, and Los Angeles—not where water transport, iron ore, and coking coal came together. In New England the declining textile industry was to be replaced by high-tech companies.

The social disaster of the old industrial cities and towns was that minority populations had crowded into them during World War II and afterward just when, in fact, their employment growth had ended, at least temporarily, and just when suburbanization had begun in earnest. As Soltow argues, the perception that relatively high unemployment in the old smokestack cities was due somehow to lack of skills, education, and urban blight produced policies that could not touch the real problem—industrial jobs were being created *elsewhere* in industries that had no advantages awaiting them in the smokestack locations.[41]

Finally, modern legislation designed to freeze industrial location, centered on National Employment Priorities acts that have been introduced in Congress, would seem to be curiously misguided. They would merely dissuade firms from locating anyplace where such legislation applied.[42] This species of legislation is mercantilism, reminiscent of Jean Baptiste Colbert (1619–83), the French "economic planner" who divided France into compartments to locate and "stabilize" economic development.

As this study of American economic history has emphasized, capital mobility is the basis of economic growth, and policies designed to impede mobility will also impede growth. From the study of steel and autos in this chapter it should be obvious that more than laws forbidding plant closures would be needed to make those industries internationally competitive. If they were frozen in place *and* all imports were prohibited, the old jobs could be saved, but at what cost to the overall living standards of the American public at large? Machine tools, now in danger of Japanese competition, had moved from New England and upstate New York to Cincinnati and the Midwest, and are now locating in the Sun Belt. Mobility, domestic and international, is the essence of healthy economic growth. However, states and municipalities in this country have a long history of diverting industrial location through tax breaks, subsidies and other bribes. Questionable as the practice is, it is not new.[43]

ADDENDUM ON MODERN AGRICULTURE

Despite (or possibly because of) more than fifty years of federal intervention and regulation in agriculture and the creation of many institutions to "solve the farm problem," by the early 1980s the agricultural sector seemed to be frozen beyond hope in its myriad difficulties. Farm output and productivity continued to rise, the family incomes of most farmers lagged behind other sectors, surpluses piled up in government storage facilities, and the number of operating farms continued to decline in a wave of farm bankruptcies and sheriffs' sales. Figure 30.5 shows the long-term record of farm population (as a percent of total) from 1820 to 1990 compared to the index of farm output.

Even at the beginning of this century there were still 45.8 million Americans living on farms, but by 1991 this figure had fallen by about a tenth, to 4.6 million, just over 1.8 percent of the total population. As the farm population and the number of individual farms fell, output in agriculture rose relentlessly. By the end of the 1970s farm output per hour was four times the level of 1950. The number of persons fed per farm worker at home rose in that period from 15 to 52. In 1920 6.5 million farms had fed 105.7 million Americans, or 16.3 persons per farm. In 1990 there were more than 116 Americans per farm, and Americans spent, on average, a mere 15 percent of their dispos-

Figure 30.5   Farm Population vs. Farm Output

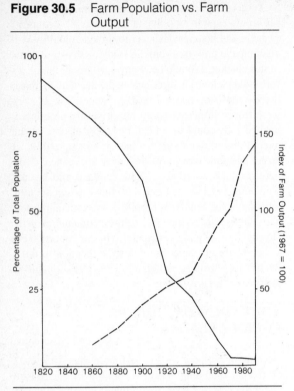

Figure 30.6   Wheat and Corn Output and Labor Hours per Acre

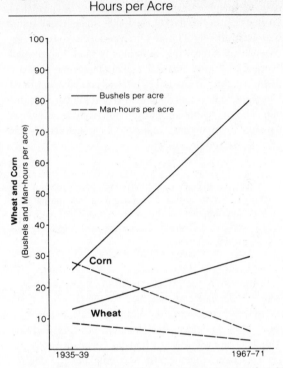

Source: *Historical Statistics*, series A 2, K 1, 414–29; *Statistical Abstract*, 1992, Tables 1073, 1106.

While farm output soared in the past century, the percentage of the total population engaged in farming declined drastically.

Source: *Statistical Abstract*, 1973, Table 1012.

Modern farming technology has produced sharply rising yields of wheat and corn per acre, while reducing the labor input per acre farmed, by extraordinary amounts.

able incomes on food—as late as the 1930s that figure had been 25 percent. In addition, the American farmer was the world's largest exporter of major food crops: 70 percent of world corn (maize) exports, 60 percent of soybean, more than 30 percent of cotton, and between 25 and 30 percent of world wheat exports come from the United States.

This production wonder was one modern outcome of the "industrialization" of American agriculture in recent decades. The application of new fertilizers, herbicides, insecticides, and more efficient machinery had produced an extraordinary increase in labor-hour productivity. The changes wrought by these innovations are illustrated in Figure 30.6.

As farm families left the countryside, farm amalgamations kept the acreage under cultivation high. By 1990 the mean-sized American farm was 461 acres, compared to 147 acres in 1920. By the end of the 1980s farms that were 500 acres and larger, a mere

17.6 percent of the total number of farms, actually contained 76.8 percent of all farmland.

Since American farms are private business ventures, "industrialization" has led to the usual American phenomena of corporate organization, and, to some extent, scale economies. American agriculture is "efficient" in the sense that it is generally not threatened by foreign competition at the most basic levels, say production of wheat, corn, soybeans, peanuts, or raw cotton. But the financing of agriculture, the processing and fabrication of its output, sales both at home and abroad, have for so long been the consequences of mercurial federal policy-making that one would have to be bold indeed to predict its future on the basis of its history, even its recent history. American farming became a technological wonder, and continues now, as in the past, to produce more agricultural output than can be domestically consumed, given the present, or possibly *any* distribution of income. The Populist panaceas of land banks, federal farm mortgages, federal subsidies of exports, domestic food give-away programs, and loans against stored crops have failed to "solve the farm problem." Indeed, in the mid-1980s American farmers faced bankruptcies and foreclosures in record numbers, and yet another appeal was launched for increased federal aid to "save the family farm." The Reagan administration was threatening, once again, to throw the farmers and their troubles into the "free market," but did not. 1986 dawned with yet another farm bill full of price supports and other forms of federal subsidies. By 1988 the entire system of federal farm credit faced bankruptcy, and Congress faced the necessity of a bailout that some feared would approach $100 billion. The prospect of resolving the basic farm problem—that a high agricultural quantity is associated with a low price times quantity—a problem that can be identified in the *Old Testament,* is no brighter today than it was then.

Notes

1. Ira C. Magaziner and Robert B. Reich, *Minding America's Business: The Decline and Rise of the American Economy* (1982), p. 31.
2. M. R. Darby, "The U.S. Productivity Slowdown: A Case of Statistical Myopia," *AER,* June 1984, p. 301.
3. Magaziner and Reich, *Minding America's Business,* p. 36.
4. Darby, "The U.S. Productivity Slowdown," p. 306, Table 4.
5. Darby, p. 306.
6. Barry Bluestone and Bennett Harrison, *The Deindustrialization of America* (1982); Robert Reich, *The Next American Frontier* (1983); Richard B. McKenzie, *Fugitive Industry* (1984).
7. Richard Easterlin, "Why Isn't Everyone Developed?" *JEH,* March 1981.
8. The reader might refer again to Gregory Clark's argument that differences in efficient deployment of labor forces, more than anything else, explain the uneven use of state-of-the-art technology worldwide: "Why Isn't the Whole World Developed? Lessons from the Cotton Mills," *Journal of Economic History,* vol. XLVII, no. 1, March 1987.
9. Jonathan Hughes, *The Vital Few* (New York: Oxford University Press, 1986), p. 259.
10. Magaziner and Reich, *Minding America's Business,* pp. 155–66.
11. Magaziner and Reich, p. 161.
12. Magaziner and Reich, pp. 156–57.
13. Magaziner and Reich, p. 162.
14. Magaziner and Reich, pp. 156–57.
15. Paul A. Tiffany, "The Roots of Decline: Business Government Relations in the American Steel Industry, 1945–1960," *JEH,* June 1984, p. 417.
16. Tiffany, p. 419.
17. Walter Adams and Hans Mueller, "The Steel Industry," in Walter Adams, editor, *The Structure of American Industry,* 6th ed. (1982), p. 76.
18. Adams and Mueller, p. 118.
19. Magaziner and Reich, *Minding America's Business,* p. 167; Adams and Mueller, Tables 11, 14A, 14B. In 1981 the net cost per ton combined of employment, coking coal and iron ore was $303 in the United States, $240 in Western Europe, and $187 in Japan. Because of more efficient plants the costs even of coking coal and iron ore were lower per ton of steel in Japan than in the United States (Table 14B). Japan has no deposits of either. Table 12 of Adams and Mueller shows the U.S. industry to be technologically inferior to the Japanese and the western Europeans in nearly every measurable dimension.
20. Adams and Mueller, p. 111.
21. U.S. Congress, House, *Hearings Before the Subcommittee on Study of Monopoly Power,* 81st Congress, 2nd Session, 1950, pt. 4A, p. 996. Quoted by Adams and Mueller, p. 115.
22. Adams and Mueller, p. 128.
23. Adams and Mueller, pp. 128–33.
24. Adams and Mueller, p. 112, n. 84.
25. Adams and Mueller, p. 133.
26. Rick Wartzman and Carol Hymowitz, "Uneasy Revival: Big Steel Is Back, But Upturn is Costly and May Not Last," *Wall Street Journal,* 4 November 1988.
27. James Powell, "Steel Import Restraints: Flood the Markets with Choice," *New York Times,* 7 August 1988.
28. Rick Wartzman and Carol Hymowitz, "Uneasy Revival."
29. *Boston Globe,* 13 June 1984, p. 51.
30. They knew their old bosses well. U.S. Steel Chairman David Roderick replied to Cardinal Joseph Bernardin's appeal to save the old South Works in Chicago with: "We are not a welfare agency." *Boston Globe,* 13 June 1984, p. 44. Perhaps it was indelicate of His Eminence to ask a welfare recipient, or at least such a large-scale one, to share the loot.
31. *Chicago Tribune,* 10 February 1986, Section 4, p. 5.
32. Robert Thomas, "Style Change and the Automobile

Industry During the Roaring Twenties," in Louis Cain and Paul Uselding, editors, *Business Enterprise and Economic Change* (1973). Two more recent studies are Richard Langlois and Paul Robertson, "Explaining Vertical Integration: Lessons from the American Automobile Industry," *JEH,* June 1989; and Timothy Bresnahan and Daniel Raff, "Intra-Industry Heterogeneity and the Great Depression: The American Motor Vehicles Industry 1929–1935," *JEH,* June 1991.

33. Lawrence J. White, "The Automobile Industry," in Adams, *The Structure of American Industry,* p. 138.

34. White, p. 146.

35. Simon Kuznets, *Economic Change* (1954), p. 254.

36. Arthur F. Burns, *Production Trends in the United States Since 1870* (1934), p. 279.

37. *New York Times,* 6 May 1984, p. F23.

38. McKenzie, *Fugitive Industry,* ch. 2.

39. James H. Soltow, "Management, Entrepreneurship, and the Economic Readjustment of the Middle West," *BEH,* vol. 12, (1984), p. 94.

40. Soltow, p. 95.

41. Soltow, p. 97.

42. McKenzie, *Fugitive Industry,* ch. 4.

43. Harry N. Scheiber, "State Law and 'Industrial Policy' in American Development, 1790–1987," *California Law Review,* January 1987.

Suggested Readings

Articles

Ault, D. "The Continued Deterioration of the Competitive Ability of the U.S. Steel Industry: The Development of Continuous Casting." *Western Economic Journal,* vol. 11, March 1973.

Bresnahan, Timothy, and Raff, Daniel. "Intra-Industry Heterogeneity and the Great Depression: The American Motor Vehicles Industry 1929–1935." *Journal of Economic History,* vol. 51, no. 2, June 1991.

Darby, M.R. "The U.S. Productivity Slowdown: A Case of Statistical Myopia," *American Economic Review,* vol. 74, no. 3, June 1984.

DeVries, Jan. "Is There an Economics Decline?" *Journal of Economic History,* vol. 38, no. 1, March 1978.

Easterlin, Richard. "Why Isn't Everyone Developed?" *Journal of Economic History,* vol. XLI, no. 1, March 1981.

Langlois, Richard, and Robertson, Paul. "Explaining Vertical Integration: Lessons from the American Automobile Industry." *Journal of Economic History,* vol. XLIX, no. 2, June 1989.

Scheiber, Harry N. "State Law and 'Industrial Policy' in American Development, 1790–1987." *California Law Review,* vol. 75, no. 1, January 1987.

Soltow, James H. "Management, Entrepreneurship, and The Economic Readjustment of the Middle West." In Jeremy Atack, editor, *Business and Economic History,* second series, vol. 12 (Urbana: University of Illinois Press, 1984).

Thomas, Robert. "Style Change and the Automobile Industry During the Roaring Twenties." In Louis Cain and Paul Uselding, *Business Enterprise and Economic Change.* Kent, OH: Kent State University Press, 1973.

Tiffany, Paul A. "The Roots of Decline: Business Government Relations in the American Steel Industry, 1945–1960." *Journal of Economic History,* vol. XLIV, no. 2, June 1984.

Vatter, Harold. "The Closure of Entry in the American Automobile Industry," *Oxford Economic Papers,* no. 4, October 1972.

Books

Adams, Walter, ed. *The Structure of American History,* 6th edition. New York: Macmillan, 1982.

Bluestone, Barry, and Harrison, Bennett. *The Deindustrialization of America: Plant Closings, Community Abandonment, and the Dismantling of Basic Industry.* New York: Basic Books, 1982.

Burns, Arthur F. *Production Trends in the United States Since 1870.* New York: National Bureau of Economic Research, 1934.

Crandall, Robert W. *The U.S. Steel Industry in Recurrent Crisis.* Washington: The Brookings Institution, 1981.

Fuchs, Victor. *Changes in the Location of Manufacturing in the United States.* New Haven: Yale University Press, 1962.

Kuznets, Simon. *Economic Change.* London: William Heineman Ltd., 1954.

Magaziner, Ira C., and Reich, Robert B. *Minding America's Business: The Decline and Rise of the American Economy.* New York: Harcourt Brace Jovanovich, 1982.

Maxcy, George. *The Multinational Automobile Industry.* New York: St. Martin's Press, 1981.

McKenzie, Richard B. *Fugitive Industry: The Economics and Politics of Deindustrialization.* San Francisco: Pacific Institute, 1984.

Phillips, Richard, et al. *Auto Industries of Europe, U.S. and Japan.* Cambridge, MA: Abt Books, 1982.

Rae, John B. *The American Automobile Industry.* Boston: Twayne Publishers, 1984.

Reich, Robert. *The Next American Frontier.* New York: Time/Life Books, 1983.

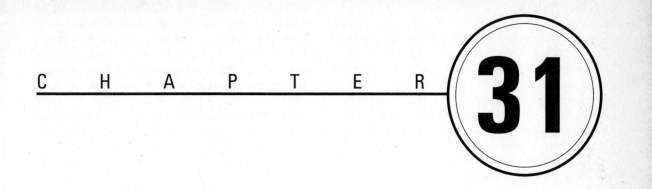

From the New Frontier Past the Supply Side: 1960–90

The three decades between 1960 and 1990, from the election of J. F. Kennedy through the Reagan-Bush years in the White House, witnessed some social and economic changes of extraordinary magnitude. Our discussion of the great issues of 1960–90 takes place against this background of ubiquitous microeconomic change whose larger consequences are yet to be understood in the aggregate.

SOME BACKGROUND CONSIDERATIONS

The core of U.S. economic expansion shifted away from the historic basis in heavy industry that had prevailed from the 1870s to the Second World War. A new life-style based upon a range of new industries—electronics, light metals, new chemical compounds, synthetic materials—and a huge influx of women into the labor force impacted upon American society with elemental force. The benefits to the public of greater safety on the job, cleaner air and water—cleaner than they would otherwise have been—and environmental protection did not enhance the conventional measures of economic growth. Fierce resistance in 1981–83 to a secretary of the interior whose actions many believed threatened to degrade the ecological system seemed to underscore the new American devotion to the "quality of life." Through the 1980s, however, there was increasing environmental degradation of all sorts, including ships (and a famous floating garbage barge) at sea searching for places to dump our wastes. The scorching "greenhouse summer" of 1988 underscored the aching environmental problems within the United States and brought louder demands than ever for fundamental changes as crops wilted and East-Coast beaches were awash in dangerous garbage.

Since the ultimate purpose of economic growth presumably is human welfare, however, and since a democratic society freely voted for changes in government and in the marketplace, it is reasonable to argue that the American people *were* "better off" with the results. They seemed to think they were in 1988 when they elected a presidential candidate who promised to carry on the policies of the Reagan years; four years later they changed their minds.

Heavy Industry

The old basic industries in the Northeast and Midwest slowed down. That meant the end of an epoch in American economic history. It didn't seem to matter who was head of U.S. Steel or General Motors. Apart from various surges of individual firms in "leveraged buy-outs," the "hot" stocks on Wall Street were electronics manufacturing and data-processing firms. Their entrepreneurs were on the television talk shows—well-educated, comparatively young executives with visions of the future that did not involve merely appeals for higher tariffs. The older heavy industries were in entirely different shape. They had become struggling economic cripples, as the examples of the steel and automobile industries discussed in the last chapter attest.

By 1982, auto executives and their associated union leaders had joined the steel lobbyists in Washington pleading for government aid. Chrysler Corporation had a huge loan guarantee to keep it out of bankruptcy, and the auto unions, in an effort to restore the industry's international competitiveness, began offering to "give back" some of their recent monetary gains in exchange for job security. The Reagan administration, despite its hairy-chested homilies about the free market, prevailed upon foreign producers of autos and steel to restrict their exports "voluntarily," and, mainly as a result, U.S. auto makers by 1984 experienced a year of record profits (and bonuses to auto executives). These import restraints lasted throughout the Reagan-Bush administrations, despite the steadfast refusal of both presidents to accede to other forms of protectionism, like tariffs—always a favorite in Congress.

The petroleum industry also went through an upheaval. Domestic crude oil output was about 2 billion barrels in 1950, 2.5 billion barrels in 1960. It rose to 3.5 billion barrels in 1970 and then stagnated during the 1970s until some price controls were removed. Domestic output, down to 3.2 billion barrels in 1972, was still about 3.3 billion barrels fifteen years later in 1988. There were differences, however. OPEC, the oil producers' international cartel which had done so much to create the energy crises of the 1970s by cutting output and raising prices to nearly $40 a barrel, lost its cohesion when faced with new competition from North Sea oil, and, by 1988, oil prices had plunged to less than $14 a barrel, back to a level one would have projected

under the assumption that OPEC had never played the role it did. Half of American consumption was from cheap imported oil. Moreover, significant adjustments had taken place to conserve energy. Higher mileage autos were in vogue, better techniques for heating and cooling homes and offices were innovated, and there were some switches back to coal at electrical generating establishments and greater reliance on natural gas. As a result, there was a growing oil glut by 1982 after a decade of shortages. What was good for consumers was bad indeed for domestic producers, and the 1980s were hard years in the American oil fields. Bankruptcies spread through the "oil patch," the southwestern states.

Economic Growth

Clearly no surge of economic growth could be based on advances in the old-time heavy industries. Yet real disposable income per capita rose by two-thirds between 1960 and 1980; after a temporary decline in the 1982 recession, it resumed its expansion path. Real GNP more than doubled during those twenty years, and by 1990 was almost 30 percent greater than the 1980 level. Despite the energy shortages, more installed power than ever was used. Installed *horsepower* (a unit of power equal to 746 watts) of prime movers (4.9 billion units in 1950) had more than doubled by 1960 (11.0 billion units), doubled again by 1970 (20.4 billion units) and rose another 42 percent by 1980. By 1990 installed horsepower of prime movers was 34.9 billion units. The rate of increase per decade was slowing, but, overall, the total increase far outstripped expansions in other areas of economic activity.

Energy

Between 1960 and 1990, energy used rose by 86 percent, from 43.8 to 81.5 quadrillion British thermal units. This was achieved in part by imports of fuel, both oil and gas. The net proportion of such imported energy sources rose from 9 percent of total energy consumption in 1960 to 24 percent by 1979. Americans had made considerable strides in energy conservation per unit of work in many areas, and by 1985 the net proportion of imported energy sources to total consumption had fallen to 15 percent. Since then, it has risen back to about 23 percent. In terms of real per capita income produced, the U.S. economy was no more efficient in energy consumption in 1990 than it had been in 1960. The modern energy crisis resulted in part from continued economic expansion with a fairly stagnant base of domestic energy supplies. The United States was vulnerable, and the OPEC countries had acted accordingly.

The shift away from coal to oil for environmental purposes had exacerbated the 1970s energy crises. The United States coasted in the 1980s but still imported half of the total oil consumed. It would have been cheaper to fuel its power plants with its own abundant coal resources, but *by law* (e.g., environmental restrictions on sulphur emissions from coal-fired plants) this country chose to burn oil and pay more for the energy, with cleaner air as a positive externality.

Women in the Labor Force

While productivity by conventional measures failed to maintain its historic growth rates in the 1970s, additional inputs propelled increases in total output. The most striking additional labor inputs came from women entering the labor force. The total civilian labor force grew from 72 million persons in 1960 to 105 million in 1980, an increase in 20 years of about 46 percent. More specifically, there were 23 million women in the labor force in 1960 and 45 million in 1980, a more than 90-percent rise. Of the 33-million-worker increase between 1960 and 1980, some 22 million, or two-thirds of the total increase, were women. By 1990 the labor force was nearly 125 million people with slightly fewer than 120 million of them fully employed: 56.6 million workers, slightly more than 45 percent of the total, were female. During the 1980s, the labor force increased by 17.9 million, of which 11.1 million, 62 percent, were women.

Changing Life-styles

Much has been written about the profound consequences upon American life of the two-income family, which was created in large part by the fight against inflation. The demand for equal rights for women, changes in home life, the increasing need for day-care centers, the revolution in the frozen and "fast-food" industries—these issues reflected the higher proportion of women working outside the home.

Aggregate consumption figures also reflected these changes, and, to some extent, their effect was surprising. A *smaller* proportion of consumption expenditures in 1990 went for food than was true in 1960: 15 percent in 1990, compared to 27 percent in 1960, a decline of more than two-fifths. Engel's Law alone did not account for the decline in expenditures on food and drink. More households began relying on prepared foods for weekday dinners, and brisk competition in the fast-food and frozen-food industries kept those prices relatively low.

A surprise to some economists was the *decline* in the proportion of expenditures on clothing between 1960 and 1990, from 9.9 to 5.7 percent. In part, this reflects the failure of clothing prices to keep abreast of inflation. As urban populations continued to increase, and new construction took place at the periphery of the urban area, even with level gas prices and more efficient automobiles, transportation accounted for 18.1 percent of consumer expenditures in 1990.

It all reflected a world in which the two-income family became more and more the norm in response to the bite of inflation. Life was adjusted accordingly.

Population Growth

One other sign of the new life-style was the continuing drop in the birthrate. As late as 1917 there had been 18.4 live births for 1000 of population, but by 1989 that number was down to 16.3, having been below 16 for most of the 1980s. With a death rate of 8.6 per 1000 per annum, the domestic population was barely maintaining its numbers while growing older, on the average. The number of legal abortions, 745,000 in 1973, soared to 1,590,800 in 1988. Further growth of population and labor force was maintained largely by immigration; the immigration rate in 1989 was 4.1 persons per 1000 of population including those given permanent residence under the legalization program approved in 1986. This rate compares to an average rate of only 1.5 for the 1950s, 1.7 for the 60s, 2.1 for the 70s, and about 2.5 for that part of the 1980s before the program went into effect. If it is true, as many believe, that *illegal* immigration was as great as *legal* immigration during the early 1980s, labor-force growth was maintained at vigorous rates, but largely from external sources.

New Industries

In 1980, America was probably still near the beginning of the electronics age. Yet, the growth data were impressive; official estimates of the market value of electronic computers sold in a mere seven years (1970–77) showed more than a 100-percent increase, from $5.7 million to $12.7 million. By 1991 the retail value of the 7.6 *million* personal computers sold came to about $23.7 *billion.*

All signs indicated even more impressive increases to come. Word processors had appeared in offices as if by magic. The applications of silicon chips multiplied daily—desk calculators, lap-top computers, ever more sophisticated stereo equipment, and video games. In the mid-1980s the only industry creating more value added per year than the manufacture of electric and electronic machinery and equipment was telecommunications. The computer was sweeping American business and intellectual life in an irresistible surge.

What are the larger consequences? All that can be directly measured is the cost of production and the value of sales; but what of the satisfaction, the cut in operating costs, the creation of new applications by those who bought this equipment? How much of the "necessities"—food, clothing, shelter, and transportation—would be more efficiently produced by the electronics age in the American economy?

Since it was primarily the free market that ordered this great change, there was no reason to suppose that electronics would not follow the path of older innovations, like steam power, electricity, chemicals, and light metals, in producing higher living standards. The gadgets of the electronic revolution were not adopted for fun only. These things *pay.* By the mid-1980s, Detroit had followed the Japanese auto industry's example of replacing human workers with electronic robots. It is important to recall one of the greatest lessons of economic history: *Resources are defined by technology.*

Some of recent economic history, especially the public-sector disarray with its huge deficits and continued inflation, yields a depressing picture. By the mid-1980s, the fates of the old heavy industries seemed dismal. Yet, growth elsewhere in the economy more than counterbalanced the forces of stagnation, cyclical problems apart. The 1980s had opened with a resounding recession, and then, for the remainder of the 1980s, economic expansion resumed with lower inflation rates than had characterized the late 1970s. A new, brief recession arrived in 1990 and ended in 1991, but the ensuing upswing was extremely slow. So slow that, while the trough was marked in March 1991, the 1992 election campaign focused on the ill health of the economy.

There was a jarring episode in the middle of the upswing, the stock-market "meltdown" of October 19, 1987. It came without warning. After going essentially nowhere in the 1970s and beginning of the 1980s, the stock market "took off" when inflation rates fell after 1983. The Dow-Jones index of 30 industrial stocks, about 880 in 1982, started rising, and reached 2000 by 1986. It then soared and, by August 27, 1987, reached 2746. A slow fade-out began, down to 2640 on October 2. On Monday, October 19, the Dow fell from 2217 an astounding 508 points in a single day. A recovery followed, and the index churned around the 1900 to 2100 range for the next year. An estimated $1 trillion of wealth had been wiped away, more than a fifth of 1987's GNP figure. Economists wondered if 1988 would be like 1930. If a negative "wealth effect" after 1929 had contributed to the Great Depression that followed, would history repeat itself? In 1988, at least, it did not. The index passed through the 3000 barrier in 1991.

OVERVIEW: 1960–80

Let us first survey developments up to 1980, and then bring the discussion up-to-date. From the time of John F. Kennedy's assassination in November 1963, the American republic headed into policies that changed the economy beyond recognition. A modern Rip Van Winkle who went to sleep in 1960 and awoke in 1980 would examine the economy in disbelief. Management, it would seem, had been more than a little careless in the interim.

By 1980 General Eisenhower's legacy of stable growth was but a dim memory. Impressive real economic growth had been achieved, but there was an atmosphere of disorder. Federal deficits were huge and came in every year (there was a single surplus, in 1969). Budget expenditures were described as "out of control." Inflation was double-digit, nearly 14 percent per annum. Short-term interest rates exceeded 20 percent, the highest in American history, either in peace or war.

The money supply (measured as M_1) was three times that of 1960, and so was the national debt; it stood at about $850 billion and was headed for the $1 trillion mark. Real incomes of workers were actually declining by 1980, as was labor-hour productivity.[1] The ratio of private saving to national income was the lowest of any advanced economy. Private investment was stagnating, and, in fact, was less than half the size of the federal budget. It had been five times federal expenditures in 1929, was still greater than federal expenditures as late as 1951, but then started slipping behind it.

In addition, a whole new set of controversial federal controls came into existence that, it was widely charged, were significantly reducing the rate of growth of industrial output.[2] Home-building by 1980 was half the average level of the previous five years, while housing prices were among the most inflated of all. Unemployment exceeded 7 percent of the civilian labor force.

In this period a disastrous war was fought and lost in southeast Asia, one president was assassinated, and one was driven from office. Racial conflict—erupting in rioting, burning, and looting in New York, Detroit, Chicago, Los Angeles, and elsewhere—shook the nation. Crime was rampant, and huge areas in the inner sections of the large cities became burned-out ruins, resembling Hamburg in 1945.

The country had not been invaded by foreign armies or bombed; the Soviet secret police had not been sitting in Congress. The entire debacle had been carefully engineered by Americans themselves. What had happened?

THE LONG PEACETIME INFLATION

Of a time crowded with dramatic events, one great impression remains: inflation. By 1980, it was eating deeply into fixed values of all kinds—into sluggish incomes, old investments, long-term contracts already executed—redistributing wealth and income massively, changing the American way of life. The comment made about inflation during the Napoleonic wars in England applied to this time as well—that it was a time when "debtors pursued creditors relentlessly and repaid them without mercy." It was a time to contract new debt, to gamble on the continued rise of prices; it was not a time for the old virtues of hard work and saving. Loans were readily available, and the money was used to pay off debts contracted at a time when prices and wages were lower, but when the *real* value of money was greater. Oddly enough, though, in the 1980 presidential election the people turned the liberal Democrats out and voted the conservative Republicans into office.

Consumer Prices

The period 1960–80 was one of *general* price inflation for commodities and services, unlike the 1920s when output had advanced with mainly stable prices, as it did during the 1950s. In the 1960s and 1970s output rose, but not as much as prices did. Of course, consumer prices did not all rise equally, but they rose.

From 1960 to 1965 the prices shown in Table 31.1 rose moderately, at 1.3 percent a year; medical care rose twice as fast. Then, in the next five years (1965–70), price increases more than doubled the inflation rate of 1960–65. In five more years, up to 1975, the general level rose by another 50 percent, more than four times the 1960–65 rate. From 1975 to 1980, the rate of increase rose again, to 8.8 percent a year on average; prices more than doubled in a decade. In 1970 the consumer price index was 116.3 (1967 = 100), and it rose to 246.8 in 1980. What was more startling was

Table 31.1   Annual Rates of Change of Consumer Prices 1960–1990

Year	All	Food	Total Housing	Fuel Oil & Coal	Gas & Electric	Apparel	Medical Care	All Commodities
1960–65	1.3	1.4	1.3	1.2	0.2	0.9	2.6	0.9
1965–70	4.2	4.0	6.3	3.1	1.5	4.8	7.0	1.5
1970–75	6.8	8.8	5.7	16.4	9.6	4.5	8.0	7.9
1975–80	8.8	7.7	13.1	18.8	12.2	5.1	11.5	16.9
1980–85	5.5	4.0	6.6	2.3	8.4	2.3	10.3	4.5
1985–90	4.0	4.6	3.6	0.7	0.4	3.4	7.5	3.1

Source: *Statistical Abstract*, 1992, Tables 738, 740.

the impression of *acceleration* that existed by 1980.[3] The hyperinflations of history—Germany in 1923, Hungary in 1945—came back into vogue.

Services, medical costs, home ownership, food, fuel—all had become more expensive, although apparel prices rose more slowly (clothing and shoes flooded in through the import door from southern Europe and Asia). By 1973 the OPEC cartel had raised the price of crude oil by more than a factor of 3. Crude oil prices continued to rise, reaching nearly $40 a barrel in 1980.[4] (The price had been less than $4 a barrel in 1973.) By 1980, all prices except apparel had more than doubled from 1967 levels, and fuel oil and coal prices had more than tripled. The **Consumer Price Index** (CPI), 246.8 (1967 = 100) in 1980, rose 10.3 percent in 1981 to 272.2, and continued to advance in 1982, although at a somewhat slower rate. The Consumer Price Index (see both Table 31.1 and Figure 31.1) stood at 328.1 in 1986, a full 33 percent more than the 1980 figure, despite the recession of 1982. In the early 1990s prices continue to rise at more than

Figure 31.1 Consumer Prices

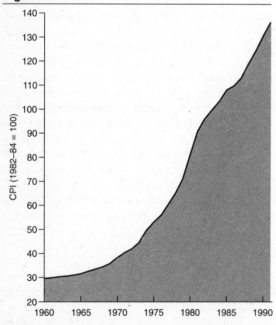

Source: *Statistical Abstract*, 1992, Table 738.

Consumer price increases accelerated in the late 1960s and then zoomed upward in the 1970s, no matter which political party occupied the White House.

4 percent per annum. Finally, even though the inflation of the 1970s had been slowed down, the country remained, by historic peacetime standards, in the grips of inflation (Table 31.1). Where had all this inflation come from?

General Inflation

In the long run, **general inflation,** *ceteris paribus,* requires an increase in the total money supply relative to the output of goods and services; too much money is chasing too few goods. In the seventies and eighties it was fashionable to blame the Arabs for the inflation. After all, they had so grossly raised their oil prices that all other prices rose sympathetically. Not so? *Not so.* Consider the following example.

Suppose that five men sitting around a table, each wearing a necktie, start successive rounds of bidding for each other's ties. Suppose that each man has $1, and only $1, as the trading begins. One man sells his tie for $4. Then, taking his own dollar (he did not bid on his own tie), together with the other four, he offers $5 for a different tie. This is the limit of money demand: $5 for one tie, the other four then are valued at zero.

The prices of the ties can vary against each other at prices of a total of less than $5, but if one tie goes for $5, the others fetch zero. The *only* way to raise total tie demand to more than $5 is to inject more money from an external source. If a sixth dollar is added, then all prices can rise, but a rise in the price of a single tie cannot cause the others to rise without an insertion of more money. Therefore, the Arabs could not have caused all prices to rise simply by raising the price of their oil.[5]

Federal Finance and the Money Supply

The sum of all federal deficits between 1960 and 1980 was more than $400 billion. Of that amount, the Federal Reserve System increased its holding of federal bonds by more than $100 billion. The Fed paid for the securities with its own demand liabilities, "high-powered" money whose increase could be multiplied by the commercial banks in their lending operations by more than $500 billion.[6] From 1960 to 1980, M_1 actually rose by some $282 billion (see Table 31.2), an increase by a factor of 3.2, compared to a general rise

Table 31.2   Securities Prices (Annual Averages of Monthly Averages)

Year	Dow-Jones 30 Industrials	Standard & Poor, 500 Common Stocks (1941–43 = 10)	Bond Yields			M_1 ($ billions)
			U.S. Government Long-Term (10 Year)	Standard & Poor		
				High Grade Municipals	AAA	
1960	618.0	55.9	4.12	3.73	4.41	127
1965	910.9	88.2	4.28	3.27	4.49	171
1970	753.2	83.2	7.35	6.51	8.04	220
1975	802.5	87.2	7.99	6.89	8.83	295
1980	891.4	118.7	11.46	8.51	11.94	409
1985	1328.2	186.8	10.62	9.18	11.37	620
1990	2678.9	334.6	8.55	7.25	9.32	826

Source: *Statistical Abstract,* 1988, Tables 805, 807; 1992, Tables 808, 809.

in prices of a factor of 2.8. Hence, in the crudest possible "Monetarist" terms, the increase in the money supply in response to federal deficit financing was itself sufficient to account for the inflation. As noted, in 1986 the CPI stood at about 33 percent higher than 1980, but M_1 was up 76 percent, so the relation was still an indicator of inflationary trends. It is the economy's ability to expand real output—to sop up some of the money-supply increase—that keeps prices from rising as rapidly as the money-supply increase. The process of money creation accelerated with the huge Reagan deficits, but the rate of inflation has slowed down compared to the late 1970s. The course of federal finance will be examined in more detail later in this chapter.

The Course of the Price Inflation

The course of the inflation is shown in Figure 31.1. The Vietnam War produced the first acceleration; the second began in 1972, after Richard Nixon's ill-fated attempt to impose price controls. By then, the American public had learned to live with inflationary expectations, and the more they succeeded, the worse the inflation became. The idea was to get rid of money in exchange for **real assets,** anything with a market value that might rise faster than the general inflation. Real estate and commodities speculation were special favorites; art objects, jewelry, and precious metals also had their moments.

An interesting sidelight was the failure of the most popular financial instruments to share in the gains. Conventional wisdom *was,* had always been, that com-

mon stock prices would rise in anticipation of inflation, "discounting" it in advance. Professors of economics had lulled generations of students to sleep with that wisdom. Anyone who lived by that wisdom in the 1970s lost his or her shirt. Common stocks fluctuated violently, periodically driving past the magical 1000 mark index on the Dow-Jones average of 30 industrials, then falling back again. The index, however, stayed in the range of 850–1000 for the most part all the way from the mid-1960s to early 1981. The Dow-Jones industrials were sinking toward 800 by early 1982. Then, in the fall of 1982, the Dow-Jones industrials passed the 1000 mark once again on enormous weekly volumes of purchases and peaked at more than 2700 in August 1987, *after* the slowdown in the growth rate of the money supply that began in 1979 and consequently led to the 1982 recession. In the aftermath of the recession, first the inflation rate, and then interest rates, fell.

At the beginning of the 1960s, common-stock prices shared in the new price expansion, but the cost of fighting a war in Vietnam, as well as a domestic "war" on poverty, added to **cost-push** arguments about inflation; there was *no hope.* Unions would relentlessly push wages above productivity increases, and companies would have to try to pass the increased costs along in a competitive market. Such thoughts drove investors into real property and away from traditional financial investments. As inflation proceeded, interest rates rose, too, and average bond prices sank. Had stock prices been favored as much as real estate investments after 1960, the Dow-Jones industrials would have been pushing 2000 by 1982. Instead, they lay dead in the water as late as June 1982, below the 1965 level. Note in Table 31.2 the huge increase in M_1 while stock prices went nowhere. Then recall the later 1920s.

In the end, it turns out that such things as stock-market averages are useless as predictors of the future. In the 1920s it seemed that Americans were overwhelmed with confidence in the American economy's future; the depression of the 1930s followed. In the 1960s and 1970s, as far as the financial markets were concerned, the future seemed dismal. Yet the economy continued to grow overall, even with inflation. After the l982 recession massive federal deficits and money supply increases, together with unprecedented foreign investment in the United States, really bolstered a faltering private economy, and the stock market boomed up to October 1987.

GNP, Real Income, Real Wages

In 1971 the American GNP passed the $1-trillion mark. It had taken 364 years (from the Jamestown settlement) to get there. The $2-trillion level was reached in 1978, seven years later. There were no celebrations because roughly three-quarters of the increase was simple price inflation.

Many, probably most, American income-earners managed to stay ahead of inflation; it was not a constant-sum game. Note in Table 31.3 that total real GNP (in 1982 prices) continued to rise to 1980, and so did disposable personal income per capita.[7] For the average worker earning wages (outside of agriculture), however, real economic advance peaked in the early 1970s; workers could not regain their purchasing power even though their money wages rose nearly by half from 1970 to 1980 (see Table 31.3.).

The rise in wages put workers into (progressively) higher income-tax brackets until rates were indexed in 1985. In addition, prices were soaring. If workers suffered from **money illusion,** large wage increases led them to believe they were getting ahead; this made them happy. But if they wondered where the sirloin steaks had gone, the answer was simple: *Their* wages were not keeping up. Most likely, their spouses were also working to try to help ends meet.

Real GNP rose until 1982, when it fell slightly. Disposable personal income *per capita* in real terms (1982 = 100) continued to increase, but the rate of increase was slowing down. It was rising at about 3.4 percent per annum between 1960 and 1973, and by only 1.6 percent per annum from 1973 to 1978. By 1980, growth had nearly halted. Between 1970 and 1980, real income per capita grew by 17 percent overall (between 1960 and 1970, the increase had been 29 percent). People who were still ahead of the game in 1980 saw their gains being stopped by inflation, and, of course, many were no longer staying ahead by then. Real weekly wages (measured in 1977 prices) declined after 1973. By 1982 average weekly real wages were only about 81 percent of the 1970 level. A slow recovery began in 1983–84, but the recovery could hardly wipe out overnight a decade's losses to inflation. In any case, the recovery in real wages faltered after 1984. *Nominal* weekly wages, of course, rose in every year. There had been real gains for some, but there was fear that the gains would stop as industry after industry ran into trouble with foreign competition and unemployment rose. Table 31.4 shows the unemployment rates for the two decades between 1960 and 1986.

Table 31.3 GNP Income and Wages 1960–1990

Year	Total GNP		Disposable Personal Income per Capita		Average Weekly Wages Nonagricultural	
	Current Prices	1982 Prices	Current Dollars	1987 Dollars	Current Dollars	1977 Dollars
	($ billion)					
1960	515.3	1,651	1,994	7,264	80.7	183.5
1970	1,015.5	2,416	3,521	9,875	119.8	208.0
1975	1,598.4	2,695	5,329	10,906	163.5	214.9
1980	2,732.0	3,187	8,576	12,005	235.1	172.7
1985	4,010.3	3,608	11,872	13,258	299.1	170.4
1990	5,524.5	4,374	16,236	14,154	346.0	163.5

Source: *Statistical Abstract*, 1992, Tables 650, 677, 678.

Table 31.4   Population, Labor Force, Employment, and Unemployment

Year	Total Population (millions)	Total Civilian Labor Force (millions)	Civilian Participation Rate (percentage)	Total Employed (millions)	Total Unemployed (millions)	Unemployment Rate (percentage)
1960	180.7	69.6	59.4	65.8	3.8	5.5
1965	194.3	74.4	58.9	71.1	3.4	4.5
1970	205.1	82.8	60.4	78.7	4.1	4.9
1975	216.0	93.8	61.2	85.8	7.9	8.5
1980	227.8	106.9	63.8	99.3	7.6	7.1
1985	238.2	115.5	64.8	107.2	8.3	7.2
1990	249.9	131.7	66.4	117.9	6.9	5.4

Sources: *Economic Report of the President*, 1985, Table B29; *Statistical Abstract*, 1992, Tables 608–09.

During the Vietnamese War buildup, unemployment rates dipped once more into the full employment range. As Lyndon Johnson told the convention of the AFL-CIO, "You never had it so good." In the 1970s, as growth slowed, the unemployment rate rose, then shot up in the recession of 1975 to more than 8 percent, and by 1980 was again more than 7 percent. Slowing growth, rising unemployment, industrial troubles, accelerating inflation, high interest rates—these and more in a sea of troubles spelled electoral disaster for the Democrats in the 1980 elections. By 1982, the inflation rate, although still positive, had slowed, but interest rates remained high, unemployment had reached an annual rate of nearly 10 percent, and the economy was suffering from a deep recession. Then unemployment fell, and by 1988 was in the neighborhood of 5 percent, *very* low by recent standards.

The relatively high unemployment rates of the late 1970s and early 1980s masked some remarkable changes in the overall U.S. labor picture (Table 31.4). Between 1970 and 1985 population grew by about 16 percent, but the labor force grew more than twice as fast (by about 39.5 percent), and so did employment (about 36 percent). The labor-force participation rate was an amazing 64.8 percent by 1985, actually higher than existed in World War II. The American economy had generated 28.5 million new jobs in those fifteen years, despite all its other troubles. 28.5 million is more than the entire population of Canada or of the Scandinavian countries combined. As the recovery from the 1982 recession continued, the number of new jobs created continued to grow.

Income Distribution

Finally, let us end this brief survey of the entire period with a look at income distribution. It has been an axiom of neoclassical economists that economic growth is a more effective redistributor of income than overt policies of taxation and transfer can ever be.[8] Between 1950 and 1977 there were nearly three decades of fairly well-sustained growth in money terms and in real terms. It ought to be the case, if the growth axiom holds, that evidence of income distribution would show a trend toward greater equality. This has been the case during wartime when there were short bursts of powerful growth. The years 1950–77 constitute a longer period, but still one that is underpinned by actual war and big military expenditures. Indeed, in cold-war conditions it may not be reasonable to look for any periods of "peace." Even if there are no clashing armies, expenditures for military hardware continue as if there were a war.

Even so, there was a recession in 1974–75, then a pickup through 1977. Growth slowed in 1978–80, and in 1982 there was a steep recession. In all, years 1978–83 were years of average stagnation with actual declines in real GNP in 1980 and 1982. It would be expected that the income distribution between 1978 and 1983 would move toward greater inequality; those on the lower end of the distribution being less able to protect their earnings than were those at the top.

The official poverty figures in Table 31.5 suggest this outcome. Standards for "poverty" for various-sized households were established by the Social

Security Administration in 1964 and have been revised since that time. The numbers, imperfect as they are, do show the expected turns in the proportions in poverty as the economy's growth slowed down. The numbers also show, of course, the dramatic reduction in poverty one could expect from 1959 to the mid-1970s when the economy was performing so much better. The numbers also show the disastrously high poverty levels for Hispanic and black families. Poverty increased in 1980–83 as the economy faltered, but in 1984–86 there was a reduction in the proportions of all families below the poverty line as the economy recovered from the 1982 recession.

Other data show that black families slipped back markedly at the end of the 1970s. Black family incomes on average (median) were 54.3 percent of white family incomes in 1950. By 1975 that number had risen to 61.5, but by 1981 it had registered a disastrous fall back to 56.4; more than 96 percent of the gain since 1950 had been lost in just a few years of extremely high inflation. Then it began to rise once again, reaching 59.7 in 1990. Stanley Lebergott's study of income and wealth shows why the United States is unlikely ever to eliminate the hard core of poverty by any conventional policies. Its economy *generates* poverty in the very processes that underlie its economic life.[9]

Table 31.6 shows family incomes divided into quintiles. The distribution for all family incomes in 1990 was such that the top fifth of all families enjoyed more than 44.3 percent of family incomes, compared to a mere 4.6 percent for the lowest fifth. Observe that *among* black families, income is distributed more unequally than it is among white families. One should expect this. Racial discrimination and educational disadvantages tend to act more sharply against minority groups, while the payoffs to economic success tend to be equal to those for whites. (At the upper extreme, for example, white and black brain surgeons and NBA stars can be expected to receive equal remuneration.) The table reveals that the best paid blacks account for a higher percentage of aggregate income among blacks than is true for whites.

Table 31.7 shows family incomes in 1970, 1980, and 1990 grouped by percentages in given income brackets. The proportions of families in the very lowest category rise between 1970 and 1980, then fall to 1990, with the exception of Hispanics who experienced a small increase. Median real incomes generally fell between 1970 and 1980, so the lower categories fill up again as a result. It is also true that the proportions of families in the top categories rose between 1970 and 1980. Overall, Hispanic families fare better in the distribution than do black families, but both have larger portions in the lower, and smaller portions in the upper, parts of the distribution than do white families. In 1990 44.2 percent of white families received $35,000 or more compared to only 28.2 percent for Hispanic families and 25.0 percent for black families. Whites had 12.8 percent of their families below the $10,000 level, while that number for Hispanics was 21.1 and a disastrous 30.8 percent for black families.

For those who want to see greater equality in the distribution of income in this country, these numbers are not encouraging. Over the long haul the distributions seem fairly rigid, although in the 1980s the top incomes ($50,000 and more) gained markedly in all three categories—a greater proportion "rich," but for minorities, especially blacks, a greater proportion

Table 31.5 Families Below the Poverty Level

(In percent in each category)

Year	All	White	Black	Hispanic
1959	18.5	15.2	48.1	n.a.
1960	18.1	14.9	n.a.	n.a.
1965	11.8	9.3	35.5	n.a.
1970	10.1	8.0	29.5	n.a.
1975	9.7	7.7	27.1	25.1
1980	10.3	8.0	28.9	23.2
1985	11.4	9.1	28.7	25.5
1990	10.7	8.1	29.3	25.0

Source: *Statistical Abstract*, 1992, Table 724. Definition of poverty, family of four, 1970, $3,960, changed in 1990 to $13,359.

Table 31.6 Money Incomes of Families, 1990

Percentage Distribution of Aggregate Income

	White	Black	Total
Number	56,803	7,471	66,322
Lowest 20 Percent	5.1%	3.3%	4.6%
Next	11.1	8.6	10.8
Middle 20 Percent	16.6	15.6	16.6
Next	23.6	25.3	23.8
Highest 20 Percent	43.6	47.3	44.3
Top 5 Percent	17.1	17.3	17.4
Total	100.0	100.0	100.0

Source: *Statistical Abstract*, 1992, Table 704.

Table 31.7   Money Incomes of Households in Constant (1990) Dollars

	Number	Under $10[a]	$10–15	$15–25	$25–35	$35–50	$50–75	Over $75	Median Income
All Households									
1970	64,778	15.6	8.7	17.6	18.6	20.0	13.8	5.6	29,421
1980	82,368	16.3	9.7	18.9	16.6	18.6	13.6	6.4	28,091
1990	94,312	14.9	9.5	17.7	15.8	17.5	14.9	9.7	29,943
White									
1970	57,575	14.3	8.2	17.1	18.9	20.8	14.6	6.1	30,644
1980	71,872	14.4	9.3	18.8	16.8	19.4	14.5	6.9	29,636
1990	80,968	12.8	9.2	17.7	16.1	18.0	15.8	10.4	31,231
Black									
1970	6,180	28.0	13.5	22.3	15.6	12.1	7.0	1.5	18,652
1980	8,847	31.8	13.5	20.2	14.5	11.7	6.6	1.7	17,073
1990	10,671	30.8	11.6	19.1	13.5	13.1	8.1	3.8	18,676
Hispanic									
1975	2,948	20.3	13.8	24.2	17.4	15.5	6.9	2.0	21,536
1980	3,906	21.0	13.2	22.9	16.6	14.9	8.6	2.8	21,653
1990	6,220	21.1	12.9	21.1	16.5	14.8	9.1	4.3	22,330

[a] The ranges are in $1000s; the figures are percentages.

Source: *Statistical Abstract*, 1992, Table 695.

poor. As Alan Blinder puts it, "The central stylized fact about income inequality has been its constancy."[10]

Blinder finds a significant impact upon equality produced by the U.S. system of cash transfer payments. The very richest were stripped of some of their funds, and those moneys were given to the poor. The proportion of total family incomes going to the lowest fifth of the distribution in his data (1978) rose about 1.8 percent because of all transfers, cash and in-kind. The proportion of incomes of the highest fifth declined by about the same amount. After all transfers, the lowest fifth in 1978 received 7.21 percent of family income, the highest fifth, 39.35 percent.[11] The richest fifth disposed of 5.5 times as much family income as the lowest fifth, even after the transfers. Judging from the data in Table 31.6, the income distribution after transfers must be about as unequal today as it was more than a decade ago.

THE NEW WAVE OF CONTROLS

The 1960s also seem destined to be remembered for the fiscal policy innovation of the 1964 tax cut and a new departure in federal controls over the economy. The two movements were loosely linked. Beginning with the civil rights movement during the early 1960s,

American social policy at the federal level was reactivated for the first time since the 1930s. Truman had tried with the "Fair Deal," and Congress had defeated him. Influenced in part by John Kenneth Galbraith's *The Affluent Society* (1958), the Kennedy activists brought to Washington a demand that the *quality* of public expenditures as well as the quantity be increased. River and harbor expenditures would not be enough.

The New Breed

There was an unsubtle change in the nature of federal nonmarket controls. New ideas about the quality of life emerged, along with new concerns about human beings in their biological ecology as well as in their inanimate physical environment. The traditional method of nonmarket control, apart from the antitrust laws, was for a given agency to regulate a specific industry or area of economic life. The ICC regulated transportation; the Federal Reserve System regulated banking; the SEC, the securities industry; the CAB, airline routes and fares; the FCC, the communications industry.[12] The great exception was the Sherman Antitrust Act and its amendments, where the Justice Department, together with the Federal Trade

Commission, had power over all infractions of the laws in *whatever* industries those infractions occurred.

Beginning in 1962 with the Food and Drug Amendments (which greatly expanded the Food and Drug Administration's powers) and the Air Pollution Control Act (which laid down national air-pollution standards), a new breed of controls began to appear whose coverage was like the Sherman Act. The regulatory agency involved had its power over *all* violations of the law in whatever areas of economic life they occurred. These new controls have been dubbed *intrusive* because they touch everything, not just specified regulated industries. In fact, *all* industries are regulated by these laws, including those that are subject to other forms of federal regulation as well. Murray Weidenbaum observed in his book, *Business, Government and the Public,* that there is another difference. In the new regulative mode, the federal regulator has no particular responsibility for the economic impact of his or her rulings on those regulated.[13] If a firm goes out of business because of the regulation, the federal agency involved has no liability for that outcome. In the old-time, industry-agency set-ups like the ICC or the Federal Reserve System, the regulator supposedly had some responsibility to allow life to the regulatees. The new controls thus smacked of autocracy in a way the old methods did not.

Between 1962 and 1972, the majority of the intrusive regulatory structure was founded. The year 1964 saw the Civil Rights Act signed into law—a federal prohibition against job discrimination on the basis of race—and the establishment of the Equal Employment Opportunity Commission to monitor the act. In 1965, the Water Quality Act required the states to meet standards for the improvement of water quality. A year later, manufacturers were required by the Fair Packaging and Labeling Act to include an expanded range of consumer information on cans and packages. The same year, 1966, children were protected from dangerous toys by the Child Protection Act. Also, the Traffic Safety Act of 1966 set up the National Highway Safety Administration to upgrade and modernize Detroit's ideas about the necessary safety and health features of its products.

Businesses handling farm products were given a mandatory set of standards in 1967 by the Agricultural Fair Practices Act. In that year, the Flammable Products Act set new standards for fire-resistant textiles that manufacturers had to meet in order to be allowed in the nation's markets. Lenders of all sorts were placed under greater borrower scrutiny by the Truth-in-Lending Act of 1968 and made to spell out in detail and simplicity the conditions of all loans made. Nixon's election in 1968 was not the occasion for any reversal of this expansion of federal nonmarket controls, despite his campaign rhetoric about freedom, *laissez faire,* rugged individualism, and the like. Indeed, the National Environment Act, which required new federally financed building projects to seek federal approval with an environment impact statement, may well prove to be the single most intrusive piece of economic legislation ever passed.

Credit cards in 1970 were endowed with federal control by the Amendment to the Banking Act. The federal government in that year also received permission from Congress to establish general price and wage controls via the Economic Stabilization Act. Securities brokers were required to insure their accounts against loss by the Securities Investors Protection Act. Also in 1970, the National Air Quality Act gave the Environmental Protection Agency authority to administer air-pollution standards. Perhaps the most sensational law of 1970 was the Occupational Health and Safety Act, which created OSHA, one of the most controversial federal regulatory agencies ever created.[14] It was given plenary powers to enforce on-the-job safety standards throughout the economy. In 1972 came the Noise Pollution and Control Act and the Consumer Products Safety Act, whose Consumer Products Safety Commission was placed in charge of the safety features of thousands of manufactured products.

Why All the Regulation?

This burst of regulatory activity introduced a mass of detailed new regulation and regulatory change that was probably unequaled even by the New Deal.[15] Whatever the actual economic impact of these changes (which no one to date had measured with any pretense of accuracy or even basic credibility), the motivation was clear enough: The free market, left to its own devices, either could not or would not produce a quality of life that satisfied lawmakers, so, the force of government was placed at the service of broad reform. Very little was left untouched, to the outrage of all those adversely affected and the delight of those whose lives were improved by the changes. It was primarily legislation of this kind, the drive for instant reform, instant improvement, that characterized the domestic legislation of Lyndon Johnson's "Great Society" and its spillover into the Nixon era.

Moreover, the laws just mentioned are only a sampling, a tip of the iceberg. Public radio and public television, federal funding of the performing arts and the humanities, and change toward broader, "multiple uses" of the federal lands and parks, were all parts of a sudden swing toward improvement in the "quality of life." Whatever else it was, the movement was an example of the American ideal. Expressed in the terminology of the arts, it was described by the American painter Mary Buckley as "a shortcut to a masterpiece."

These changes came suddenly with the civil rights movement, the antiwar movement, the liberation of life-styles and clothing styles—all media events. Time, and politics, will tell whether the quality-of-life movement in this country will stick. The United States can elect to follow the trail blazed by Sweden and followed by the other western European nations: the attempt to reach for social perfection through government authority. The "traditional" American idea of the welfare state has been merely the provision of basic economic security through state action; but if the "good life" is seen to include beauty, comfort, convenience, and culture beyond the amounts supplied through private purchase, interested parties will try to achieve requisite supplies of such items as public goods. All that is required is that the people be willing to be taxed, either directly or via inflation. It may not be good for "economic efficiency" in the narrowed sense, but it has been *good for votes* for politicians.

What Professor Galbraith said in *The Affluent Society* was that the American economy was drowning in private goods and was desperately short of positive and uplifting public goods.[16] E. J. Mishan, in *Technology and Growth: The Price We Pay,* added that "natural amenities," like silence, clear air, and pure water, are prescriptive property rights of all people that the market economy has destroyed, without compensation, for the benefit of private profits.[17] According to Mishan, a restoration is in order. For the followers of Galbraith and Mishan, "the new regulation" is merely a downpayment on the future. For those opposed to government growth, the new regulation is an unwarranted intrusion into private life, including private business life.

Politics will determine the outcome. After the first Reagan administration, which promised massive deregulation, the issue went into deep background. There was little effort at deregulation in his second term. Congress remained less than enthusiastic about dismantling the control system. Nearly all of the old regulatory system remained in place in 1988, and there were demands for "reregulation" in banking and airlines where greater freedom had been followed by results the depositors and flying public found to be suboptimal.

THE FISCAL LEGACY OF CAMELOT

The Kennedy administration's fiscal policy is now mainly remembered for the tax cut of 1964. Such dramatic action was finally decided upon while JFK was still alive, but was put through Congress in a hurry by his successor, Lyndon Johnson. According to Herbert Stein, a careful scholar of modern fiscal history, the tax cut was distinctly *not* the first choice of the Kennedy policymakers.[18] They wanted to raise expenditures. A cyclical downturn had been inherited in 1961 from the Eisenhower administration. The economy remained sluggish in the beginning months of Camelot, and, with unemployment hovering between 6 and 7 percent, the indicated countercyclical policy prescription was for fiscal stimulation. There was fear, however, that a deficit from increased expenditures would be inflationary, which would go against recent Kennedy campaign promises.

Kennedy was himself a fiscal conservative. The famous tax cut, according to Stein, emerged from the idea of fiscal drag:

. . . the main lag in the economy since the fall of 1957 had been a lag in private investment . . . [due to] . . . the high rate of taxation on the return from investment.[19]

But for lack of private investment, the economy might indeed have been producing a surplus at full employment growth. Reduce the taxes, and the deficit would vanish as the economy surged toward full-capacity output, or so the thinking went at the time. The tax cut had to be general and *permanent* if long-term expectations were to be favorably influenced. Opposition within the administration came from the desire to build an activist spending policy and fear that a tax cut would weaken the federal government's long-run taxing power. Nevertheless, the fiscal-drag theorists had their way.

The hoped-for response was to come from the *supply side*—greater production and more employment with the stimulus of an increase in personal disposable incomes. The presumed increase in consumer demand would induce a rise in private investment. Even with reduced tax *rates* the consequent rise in national income would cause *total* tax yields to increase. The best way to increase revenues in an expanding economy is to cut taxes.

The tax cut was made, and the results were as predicted. As can be seen in Table 31.8, revenues increased, and the deficit fell. Prices rose only slightly in 1965 (see Table 31.1), but a sinister cloud was on the horizon: the Vietnam War. It was beginning to escalate, and Camelot and the New Frontier had vanished. Johnson's Great Society had to compete with the war, and it failed. Martin Luther King, Jr., said, prophetically, "The bombs we drop on Vietnam will explode in America's cities." Before Johnson fled Washington for Texas, America's cities burned.

By the end of 1968, expenditures were $179 billion, half again the level of 1964. It was like the trillion-dollar economy. It took 192 years to reach a $118-billion-dollar budget, four years to increase it 50 percent, a mere decade to double it. But once again war had "solved" the problem of high unemployment (see Table 31.4), for the moment. The deficit of 1968, $25 billion, was double the 1958 Eisenhower deficit of

which so much was made by JFK during the 1960 election campaign; but worse was coming, and Lyndon Johnson's administration left its problems to the incoming Nixon administration. The latter experienced a small surplus in 1969, and then the bottom fell out on the fiscal theorists. The "American Century" ended abruptly.

The legacy of the Kennedy administration—the 1964 tax cut, the theory of fiscal drag, the policy of budgeting for a full-employment economy (*compensatory fiscal policy*) even when the economy is underemployed—would have been long forgotten, except that in the 1980 election the idea of a permanent tax cut for fiscal stimulus came back, this time from the conservative Republicans. When "supply-side economics" came in 1981 with the Reagan administration, the Kennedy legacy was a valuable, if ambiguous, memory.

THE DELUGE: 1969–88

With the onset of higher inflation rates in the 1970s, the "national numbers" began to change magnitude in a bewildering way—the problem noted earlier about trillions of dollars in the GNP figures. Was $50,000 a year higher "real" salary in 1979 that $20,000 a year had been in 1960? Were Americans richer or poorer? It is helpful to try to keep the various relationships in some kind of order.

Just as in Chapter 19, consider the ratio of Gross Federal Debt to GNP (see Table 31.9). This percentage had been 121.1 in 1945 and 57 in 1960. So, the wild inflationary binge of the 1970s had not, by this conventional measure, "bankrupted the country." In fact, throughout the huge rise in debt from the 1960s, the

Table 31.8   Federal Fiscal Years 1960–69[a]

Year	Receipts	Expenditures	Surplus (+) Deficit (−)
1960	92.5	92.2	+ 0.3
1961	94.4	97.8	− 3.4
1962	99.7	106.8	− 7.1
1963	106.6	111.3	− 4.8
1964	112.7	118.6	− 5.9
1965	116.8	118.4	− 1.6
1966	130.9	134.7	− 3.6
1967	149.6	158.3	− 8.7
1968	153.7	178.8	−25.2
1969	187.8	184.5	+ 3.2

[a] Figures are in billions of dollars.

Source: *Historical Statistics*, series Y 339–42.

Table 31.9   Gross Federal Debt as a Percentage of GNP

Year	Gross Federal Debt[a]	Percentage
1970	380.9	38.5%
1975	541.9	35.6
1980	908.5	34.0
1985	1,817.0	46.0
1990	3,206.3	58.7

[a] In billions of dollars.

Source: *Statistical Abstract*, 1992, Table 491.

inflation had pushed up wages and prices so that the federal debt was a declining portion of GNP. It was *private* debt that increased dramatically, rising from 82.9 percent of GNP in 1960 to 102.6 percent in 1978.[20] Businesses and individuals who were learning to "live with inflation" increasingly relied on credit, borrowing current dollars knowing they would be repaying their debts with ever "cheaper" dollars. Each year, the money was "worth less" than the year before.

There then developed a "numbers illusion" in reverse. The idea of real income bore less and less relation to money income; interest rates began to be calculated in the media as *real* and *nominal*. How much were interest rates relative to price increases? Ten percent had been a terribly high interest rate in this country historically, but by 1979–80, 10 percent was actually a negative rate of interest. Prices were rising faster than that. It paid to borrow to buy assets on a scale never before known. Real estate in 1979 was a booming market, like the stock market in 1929. It was in the Reagan years of the 1980s that the ratio of federal debt to GNP began rising back toward the levels of the early 1960s.

Nixon and Ford

Richard Nixon's entire reign occurred in the grip of a worsening inflation (see Figure 31.1). The Vietnam War had begun as a "little war." It was assumed that both "guns and butter" would result. Nothing was done to raise taxes to offset war expenditures until the summer of 1968. The Federal Reserve System had embarked upon a policy of tighter money to head off inflation, but it was too little and too late. The Consumer Price Index rose from 100 to 104 in 1967–68, then rose another 5 points in 1969. By 1970, it stood at 116.3, more than a 16-percent increase in a mere three years, and in 1971 it was still rising, ending that year at 121.3.

By conventional ideas at the time, it was a powerful inflation, and serious people wondered how long the republic could survive under such an onslaught. Also, the United States still had an obligation to sell gold to foreign central banks at a special, low, fixed price ($42 an ounce). In 1968, the country had abolished the "gold cover" on Federal Reserve liabilities, and the domestic money supply was entirely *discretionary,* as economists used to say. The domestic monetary use of gold was thus gone, but foreign central banks could and did cash in their dollars at the Fed for gold. As a result, United States holdings of foreign exchange assets were falling alarmingly; they declined by nearly 30 percent between 1968 and 1971.[21] On 15 August 1971, therefore, President Nixon unilaterally repudiated U.S. obligations in this area of international finance. Other countries could no longer automatically redeem dollars at the fixed price. This was the end of the regime of fixed exchange rates installed under the Bretton Woods institutions.

At the same time President Nixon was determined to "do something" about inflation, anything *except* the obvious: Stop deficit spending. Congress had passed the buck to the president in Public Law 91–379, the Economic Stabilization Act of 1970. Further taxes to finance the war would be highly unpopular, and expenditures were soaring. What to do? The new law read: "The President is authorized to issue such orders and regulations as he may deem appropriate to stabilize prices, rents, wages, and salaries. . . ." And what indeed would he deem? What followed were wage and price controls. This was a reprise of old ideas, boards, commissions, powers, and offices going back to the World War I command economy. It didn't work, and lifting the controls produced a worsening inflation rate. The giant oil price-hike imposed by OPEC didn't help matters. In 1972, the Council of Economic Advisers had said that the inflation was nearly over.[22] In 1976, they said it again. The inflation continued onward, just as if such forecasts had not been made by professional authority.

The Fiscal Record and the Balance of Payments

By 1977, both Richard Nixon and Gerald Ford had passed from the Washington scene. Federal expenditures had risen relentlessly, and the deficits were now big ones that came every year, no matter what the state of the economy (see Table 31.10). Gerald Ford's last full year, 1976, yielded a whopping $74 billion federal deficit. A balanced federal budget had come to be viewed as a utopian ideal, no longer really achievable—desirable, yes, but not a practical goal. Admittedly, it was *a* policy in a world where there no longer were identifiable fixed fiscal objectives. By 1982, a new fiscal crisis gripped Washington; the recession coupled with staged tax reductions and higher expenditures threatened the fiscal conservatives of the Reagan administration with a deficit for 1982–83 in excess of $100 billion. The 1983 deficit was $208 billion, and the super deficits peaked in 1986 at $238 billion. Under the new Gramm-Rudman deficit reduction legislation (see following explanation) and a rise in federal revenues in 1987–88, the federal deficit was forced back below $200 billion.

In the United States by 1980, as in all the modern democratic welfare states, inflation was endemic, and no one knew how to stop it or, indeed, if there really was the will to try. As Morris Janowitz argued in *Social Control of the Welfare State,* the deficit-financed inflation was due to competition, not for goods and services but for votes.[23] The result, argued Janowitz, was weak governments that could only perpetuate inflation. Since all political parties were completely in support of extending the welfare state but unwilling to tax its full costs, expenditures ran ahead of revenues and weak coalition government replaced the more ideologically differentiated but stronger governments of former times in the Western democracies. Governments became the helpless puppets of their own pasts. The power to decide, reject, and change course vanished. Expenditures had to rise as more was promised and inflation proceeded apace.

The theory was put to the test in 1981 and 1982 as the Federal Reserve System attempted to hold the line on supplies of money. The ensuing record-high interest rates contributed to a lowering of the inflation rate at the cost of a serious and prolonged recession. In 1983 there was a return to deficits every year, abundant increases in the money supply, renewed inflation (at reduced rates), and a feeling of Keynesian prosperity of the kind that was never enjoyed in the "pinchpenny" reign of Franklin Roosevelt in the 1930s.

Terry Anderson and P. J. Hill, in *The Birth of a Transfer Society,* shifted the emphasis in the analysis of American troubles to the demand side. Federal power was used by special interests to transfer wealth and income from productive activity to nonproductive activity.[24] As time passed, the transfer power came to dominate the American economy. An entire economic sector grew up that was dependent solely upon the transfer power, either by taxing and spending or by inflation. The result, said Anderson and Hill, was that the transfer function dominated government; the clamor for more could only be satisfied by an acceleration of transfers. The infestation of lobbyists and single-issue politicians in Washington reflected an ultimate reality. The U.S. Treasury had become the scene of a modern "gold rush" peopled by rent-seeking beneficiaries of government largesse.

In the 1970s, the United States became vulnerable to its foreign balance for the first time in decades. As the dollar plunged in the foreign exchanges after Nixon's 1971 policy switch, exports earned less per unit, and imports cost more. The inflation-swollen domestic economy demanded more imports to satisfy domestic demand. By 1970 deficits began to appear in the merchandise trade balance, the first since the nineteenth century. Because of positive net earnings on invisibles, including foreign investments, the trade balance deficits were muffled and even offset entirely in the current balance until 1982. Then the current account turned powerfully negative, and by 1988 the sum of the current account deficits had converted the United States,

Table 31.10   Fiscal Magnitudes and the Foreign Balance[a]

Year	Federal Revenues	Expenditures	Sur. (+) Def. (−)	Bal. of Merch. Trade	Current Account Balance of Payments	Gross Federal Debt
1970	192.8	195.6	− 8.7	2.6	2.3	380.9
1975	279.1	332.3	− 55.2	9.0	18.3	541.9
1980	517.1	590.9	− 72.7	− 25.0	1.9	908.5
1985	734.1	946.4	−221.6	− 122.1	−116.4	1,817.0
1990	1,031.3	1,251.8	−220.5	− 108.1	− 69.8	3,206.3

[a] In billions of dollars.

Source: *Statistical Abstract,* 1992, Tables 491, 1315.

in a mere handful of years, from the world's greatest creditor to the world's greatest debtor nation.

It was an added jolt, however, for Americans to discover that not only was the federal government unable to control its own fiscal affairs within the American economy but that the economy no longer enjoyed an unquestioned competitive edge vis-a-vis the rest of the world. Cheaper and superior foreign manufactured goods, from shoes to automobiles, flooded the domestic market. American manufacturers and their unionized labor forces, unable to reduce wages and other costs, once again raised the cry for protection from foreign competition. It seemed a sad comedown from the idea of the "American Century" of the postwar era.

Actually, such arguments were overly pessimistic. Foreign investment was pouring into the American economy throughout the 1970s, virtually balancing the outflow of American funds seeking productive employment abroad. For example, in the period 1971–75, American holdings of foreign assets rose by $124 billion, but foreign holdings of U.S. assets rose by $113 billion in return. In 1978 alone, Americans invested $61 billion abroad, but foreigners invested $64 billion in the United States.[25] *Someone* was keeping faith in America, even if Americans seemed to be losing theirs.[26] Foreign investment continued to pour in, financing the deficits, although by 1988 there were weak knees in American financial circles at the prospect of any potential "loss of confidence" by foreigners and a withdrawal of funds. By late 1988 that catastrophe was still only a fear as foreigners kept up their purchases of the (relatively) cheap American assets for sale.

In a way, the United States was merely rejoining the international economy as a trading partner. It was no longer the master in international economic affairs. This development was viewed with alarm through the media "spectacles" of American politics, but in fact it was the *object* of the postwar international reorganization (discussed earlier). It had just taken three decades for the policies of 1944–47 to come to fruition. It was a new experience for modern Americans to find themselves wanting to buy more from the world's market than that market wanted to buy from the American market, but it was far healthier and viable worldwide than the dependency that countries like Britain, Germany, and Japan had upon the United States in the 1950s. They now could compete with the United States on equal terms, and Americans had to get used to competing with them. Americans even had to admit that *foreigners* were now financing *them*. The worm had turned.

The Carter Years in Brief

It was during the four years of the Carter presidency that the debacle in federal finance reached (then) frightening proportions. There was the feeling that no one was in charge anymore. Between 1976 and 1980 the federal debt rose by 40 percent (see Table 31.10), the money supply (M_1) leapt 30 percent (see Table 31.2), and unemployment increased to more than 7 percent (see Table 31.4) of the labor force and stayed there. The federal deficits (see Table 31.10) seemed huge. Carter's 1976 pledge to balance the federal budget during his administration haunted his presidency with an aura of continuous failure.

By 1980, feelings of impending chaos in the financial world added to the administration's woes. Market interest rates of between 15 and 20 percent brought home-building activity and the real-estate markets to a crawl. The "sure thing" of the 1970s, investment in real estate, became increasingly difficult to negotiate as mortgage rates hit 14 percent. The savings and loan institutions, long the steady bulwark of the real-estate market because of their supply of mortgage money, faced deposit attrition as interest rates surged. They began to fail in droves, and by 1988 a federal bailout in excess of $100 billion was proposed to save the savings and loan industry. Its insurance agency, the FSLIC, was hopelessly overcommitted. The proposed bailout would exceed the sum of the Marshall Plan, and the bailouts of Lockheed, Chrysler, Penn Central, and New York City combined.[27]

The force of international competition by 1980 resulted in locally devastating closings of old heavy-industrial plants in the traditional production centers of the East and Midwest. The growth of business in the Sun Belt was underway, adding to the woes of rising industrial unemployment. In 1980, the huge Chrysler Corporation threatened to go under and joined the ranks of other major firms seeking federal aid to avoid bankruptcy. (The financial markets would no longer accept their paper.) The other auto firms also reported huge losses that year.

From such a sea of troubles, the conventional policy prescriptions seemed to offer no way out. The argument for larger deficits to reduce unemployment was no longer heard. The deficits were already huge, and both unemployment and prices were rising. James Buchanan and Richard Wagner, in *Democracy in Deficit,* underlined the unspoken problem with the conventional, Keynesian, fiscal-policy tradition.[28] In one basic sense, it really was *depression economics.* It assumed that the economy would rise to the bait of money stimulus and expand real output and employment. The huge increases in deficit-financed money demand, however, raised prices more than output, even with unemployed capacity and unemployed workers.

The policy of the 1946 Employment Act now seemed a dead issue altogether. As Buchanan and Wagner argued, it had been a piece of sheer pretense from the beginning:

> This act pledges the government to do something it cannot possibly do, at least so long as our underlying fiscal and monetary institutions are themselves the primary source of instability.[29]

And, said Buchanan and Wagner, if these institutions were stable, there would be no need for the Employment Act.

The old-time liberal Democratic ideal, with such long roots in American history, was stated eloquently by Senator George McGovern in 1980 in his address to Americans for Democratic Action. He argued, according to the *New York Times,* that government was the only "humane" institution in American society:

> Let us insist that Government can and must solve problems, that it can and must eliminate poverty and reduce inflation, that it can and must set goals and define a vision for the nation.[30]

In 1980 he was retired by his constituents, as were other leading liberal Democrats.

Jimmy Carter had been served by economic advice from a profession that did not fully understand his problems.[31] He experienced essentially the same frustration that Herbert Hoover had faced in 1930–32. In Hoover's case, prices were tumbling and unemploy-

ment rose; in Carter's case, prices were soaring and unemployment rose. Economic orthodoxy did not understand the early 1930s, and it did not understand the late 1970s either.

The Supply Side: Reaganomics

Conservative Republicans came back in with Ronald Reagan in 1981. Once again, they pledged to stop the inflation, to reduce government "interference" in economic life, and to adopt policies that would revitalize the American economy. They spoke of *capitalism* and *free markets;* Reagan even used the word *entrepreneur* in his inaugural speech. Reagan brought with him a piece of baggage, **supply-side economics.** The idea was that big, general tax cuts, would induce the entrepreneurial classes to reduce their aversion to taxes and allow a greater portion of their actual income to be taxed, thereby increasing tax receipts. At the same time, workers would be induced to increase their efforts, confident in the knowledge they were taking home more per hour from the identical pretax wage. This additional activity, hopefully, through the Keynesian multiplier process, would put the unemployed and the chronic welfare cases back to work. One piece of evidence cited in support of this theory was the tax cut of 1964, which had been in part supported by these same arguments, as Herbert Stein pointed out. It was a gamble in 1981, just as it had been in 1964.[32] It was a gamble based on three assumptions:

1. The 1981 tax cut assumed that potential profit from new investment could be made more remunerative for individuals and corporations than was tax avoidance and diversification of investment into real estate, commodities speculation, and other areas.
2. The tax cut assumed that since the growth of expenditures would have to be curtailed if gigantic new deficits were to be avoided, Congress would cooperate.
3. It assumed that the American voter would agree with congressional support for a policy of slower growth of government and curtailment of regulation.

All three assumptions were questionable, given the source of the American welfare state—the American

In the early 1980s, it fell to President Ronald Reagan to search for markets for American products in the booming, and protected, Japanese economy.

voter. In any case, the pledge to raise military expenditures even cast doubt on the motives of the new government. It was bad public relations to take milk away from school children in order to buy more military hardware; yet, the new government cut back on subsidies for school lunches even as it began to increase the federal deficit in the name of national defense.

Beginning in 1979, the Federal Reserve System, under the leadership of Chairman Paul Volcker, made a determined, independent effort to crush the inflation rate with high positive interest rates, while the Reagan administration wondered aloud if taxes had been cut too much. By spring of 1982 there was a deepening recession in the land, with unemployment greater than 9 percent. The rate of inflation had fallen, but interest rates were still high, and the markets for housing and durable goods were flat. In addition, projections of federal revenues showed budget deficits in excess of $100 billion coming down the track. Even administra-

tion supporters in Congress were backing away from supply-side economics. The financial markets anticipated the forthcoming strain of funding the huge debt increases, interest remained high, and stock-market values were melting down once more. The cries from members of Congress to reduce the budget deficit by raising tax rates again were hardly the blueprint for a Keynesian solution to unemployment. Once again, as in the Carter administration, the feeling of mindless policy drift was in the air.

By the fall of 1982, the *rate* of inflation was down, interest rates were falling, and stock and bond prices were rising; *but* the rate of unemployment temporarily exceeded 10 percent of the labor force, private investment had not gone up in response to the supply-side tax cuts, and the 1982 recession lingered. Could the American economy back away from the excess cost of its welfare state? If it did, would a viable productivity-raising economic system re-emerge? Was the possibility still there? The supply side said yes, the Reagan administration said yes.

What followed was "predictable" only in retrospect. By the end of 1982 real GNP was down slightly from the annual rate of 1981 (Table 31.3), but unemployment was on average nearly 10 percent (Table 31.4). The rate of inflation had been cut in half (Table 31.1) to less than 4 percent per annum for the first time in years. In terms of unemployment alone the recession was the worst since the 1930s, but by other measures it was relatively mild. The policy mystery of stagflation (how to achieve noninflationary full employment starting out with both high inflation and high unemployment rates) had not been solved. Instead, inflation had been slowed down with an induced recession—the old-fashioned remedy.

The recovery and expansion of 1983–88 then occurred in the presence of hugh deficits in the federal budget—a strictly orthodox Keynesian prescription—and a powerful rise in private investment. The latter represented to a large extent the administration's changes in tax policies designed to encourage private investment. The tax cuts of 1981–82 were not those advocated by the 1980 supply-siders (a one-time, 33-percent cut across the board), but were strung out over three years, which dampened their impact. Not surprisingly the *rate* of private savings did not increase significantly, and the country was spared the predicted "crowding out" effects of the giant increases in federal debt by foreign investors seeking both safety and high interest rates. Billions of dollars of foreign investment poured in. Both the unprecedented federal deficit and the huge balance of payments deficits were "financed" by foreign investors. The unemployment rate sank back to about 7.5 percent in 1984–85, the economy continued to generate net increases in total employment (Table 31.4), and real wages began to rise again along with real disposable income (Table. 31.3). By the end of 1988 the unemployment rate dipped to about 5 percent as the expansion continued.

One extraordinary outcome was the U.S. dollar, freely floating on the foreign exchanges. Instead of collapsing under the weight of its own excess supply, the dollar rose to astounding strength in 1984–85 as foreign investors poured billions of their own savings into the United States, driving the dollar up against all currencies in the foreign exchange markets. Once worth 20.5 percent of a British pound, by the spring of 1985 the dollar had soared to about 95 percent of a pound (£1 ≈ $1.05). The dollar then caved in and declined to the range of $1.80 to the pound in 1988. The huge excess supply of dollars generated by U.S. balance-of-payments deficits finally made its impact felt in the foreign exchanges. A devalued dollar was inflationary inside the United States as import prices soared, but exports, now correspondingly cheaper, soared.

Supporters of "Reaganomics" naturally credited these favorable economic singularities in the whirlwind to "the success of the president's policies." Opponents warned of the dangerous economic threat implied. What if, in the next recession, U.S. interest rates should fall back enough to inspire a mass withdrawal of these hundreds of billions of foreign investment? A recession could be converted into a catastrophic depression. Meanwhile, the federal government could not reduce its spending. President Reagan resisted proposed tax increases as the deficits mounted.

At the end of 1985 Congress passed the Gramm-Rudman bill, an extraordinary piece of legislation designed *automatically* to cut spending in the interest of deficit reduction. By 1988 the bill was given part of the credit, along with the increase in revenues in lowering the deficit. Import quotas remained in steel and autos despite the President's much-declaimed admiration of free trade. Reagan's man, George Bush, won the 1988 election and Ronald Reagan rode into the sunset as if he had balanced the budget, reduced the national debt, and deregulated the economy, just as he said he would back in 1980.

The Reagan years ended with a note of hope. Employment was full, exports were rising, the deficits seemed to be inching downwards. The Canadians agreed to a free-trade agreement. The wave of leveraged buyouts of American firms with "junk bond" financing resumed after a number of Wall Street operators were imprisoned for misuse of insider information. The 1987 stock market crash had not (yet) produced a recession, and a new administration assumed the burden of the federal fiscal chaos, already shackled by campaign promises to balance the budget without raising taxes. Even the defeated Democrats were hoping that President-elect Bush would get lucky. He didn't.

Notes

1. Richard B. Freeman, "The Evolution of the American Labor Market, 1948–80," in Martin Feldstein, editor, *The American Economy in Transition* (1980), pp. 351–560. For a general review with international comparisons of recent productivity trends, see Edwin Mansfield, "Technology and Productivity in the United States," in the same volume.

2. An example is David Packard, chairman of Hewlett-Packard Company, "Productivity and Technical Change," in Feldstein, *The American Economy in Transition,* pp. 604–16. Also, Jonathan Hughes, *The Governmental Habit Redux* (1991), pp. 182–201.

3. Herbert Stein, commenting on economists' ideas of inflation two decades ago put it well: "In our naivete we meant by endless inflation an endless rise of the price level, not an endless increase in the rate of increase of the price level." In Feldstein, *The American Economy in Transition,* p. 174.

4. A glut of crude oil appeared in the markets as a result of such advanced *prices,* and by the summer of 1981, OPEC-posted prices were down to $32 a barrel. In 1982, the oil glut continued, and oil prices declined slowly to around $14 a barrel in the fall of 1988. In early 1993 OPEC is still trying to restrict the output of crude oil in the hope that the higher prices will return.

5. For an analysis of our inflationary adjustment to the "supply shocks" of the 1970s, oil prices and agricultural shortages, see Robert J. Gordon, "Alternative Responses to External Supply Shocks," *Brookings Papers on Economic Activity,* vol. 6, no. 1, 1975.

6. Given average cash reserve requirements of 20 percent or less.

7. The annual rate of growth of real GDP continued throughout the 1970s in the range of 2.5 percent. *Statistical Abstract, 1992,* Table 1372. As Nathan Rosenberg observed to one of the authors, since productivity was barely rising, the growth is mainly attributable to rising labor-force participation rates among women. In *Wealth and Poverty* (1981), George Gilder argues this increased GDP is largely spurious because it depends upon weakening family ties, taking women out of the home where their labor is not counted as GNP, and putting them in a position where it is (pp. 13–16).

8. Vilfredo Pareto, the great Italian economist, believed that economic growth, GNP rising more rapidly than population, was the *only* way income distribution could become more equal. Stanley Lebergott, *The American Economy: Income, Wealth, and Want* (1976), p. 144.

9. Lebergott, *The American Economy,* Part I. Lebergott argues that the U.S. economy *generates* poverty along with economic growth by our social processes. Elderly people living alone, divorce, ineffective public education for the poor—these and other reasons have increased in numbers as income has risen. Basic poverty data for the period 1959–1990 can be found in *Statistical Abstract, 1992,* Table 717.

10. Alan S. Blinder, "The Level and Distribution of Economic Well-Being," in Feldstein, *The American Economy in Transition,* p. 433. Blinder's data show that between 1952 and 1977 the share of the top 5 percent of family incomes fell, but that of the lowest 20 percent rose only slightly.

11. Blinder, p. 446, and Table 6.18, p. 445.

12. The Civil Aeronautics Board is now defunct; it is one of the few major federal agencies to be eliminated in modern times.

13. Murray Weidenbaum, *Business, Government and the Public* (1990).

14. OSHA's code book in 1980 contained some 28,000 regulations. See Packard, "Productivity and Technical Change," in Feldstein, *The American Economy in Transition,* p. 610, for an industrialist's estimate of the consequences. According to Packard, "Government regulations in fact, may be the largest and most important factor in the decline in productivity in the United States."

15. See Hughes, *The Governmental Habit Redux.*

16. John Kenneth Galbraith, *The Affluent Society* (1958).

17. E. J. Mishan, *Technology and Growth: The Price We Pay* (New York: Praeger, 1973).

18. Herbert Stein, *The Fiscal Revolution in America* (1969), ch. 16.

19. Stein, p. 398.

20. Benjamin Friedman, "Postwar Changes in the American Financial Markets," in Feldstein, *The American Economy in Transition,* pp. 16–21.

21. *Statistical Abstract, 1979,* p. 847.

22. Carl F. Christ, "The 1972 Report of the President's Council of Economic Advisers," *AER,* September 1973.

23. Morris Janowitz, *Social Control of the Welfare State* (1976).

24. Terry Anderson and P. J. Hill, *The Birth of a Transfer Society* (1989).

25. *Statistical Abstract, 1979,* p. 847.

26. For a detailed analysis, see William H. Branson, "Trends in United States International Trade and Investment

Since World War II," in Feldstein, *The American Economy in Transition*.

27. *Chicago Tribune,* 1 December 1988. The proposal was from William Seidman, Chairman of the Federal Deposit Insurance Corporation.

28. James Buchanan and Richard Wagner, *Democracy in Deficit* (1977).

29. Buchanan and Wagner, p. 171.

30. *New York Times,* 18 June 1978.

31. See Robert J. Gordon, in Feldstein, *The American Economy in Transition,* p. 157, for the mercurial record of economists' advice to presidents.

32. Stein, *The Fiscal Revolution in America,* pp. 410–11.

Suggested Readings

Articles

Branson, William H. "Trends in United States International Trade and Investment Since World War II." In Martin Feldstein, editor, *The American Economy in Transition*. Chicago: University of Chicago Press, 1980.

Christ, Carl F. "The 1972 Report of the President's Council of Economic Advisers." *American Economic Review,* vol. 63, no. 4, September 1973.

Freeman, Richard B. "The Evolution of the American Labor Market, 1948–1980." In Martin Feldstein, editor, *The American Economy in Transition*. Chicago: University of Chicago Press, 1980.

Friedman, Benjamin. "Postwar Changes in the American Financial Markets." In Martin Feldstein, editor, *The American Economy in Transition*. Chicago: University of Chicago Press, 1980.

Okun, Arthur. "Postwar Macroeconomics Performance." In Martin Feldstein, editor, *The American Economy in Transition*. Chicago: University of Chicago Press, 1980.

Books

Anderson, Terry, and Hill, P. J. *The Birth of a Transfer Society*. Stanford: Hoover Institution Press, 1980.

Buchanan, James, and Wagner, Richard. *Democracy in Deficit*. New York: Academic Press, 1977.

Galbraith, John Kenneth. *The Affluent Society*. Boston: Houghton Mifflin, 1958.

Gilder, George. *Wealth and Poverty*. New York: Basic Books, 1977.

Hughes, Jonathan. *The Governmental Habit Redux*. Princeton: Princeton University Press, 1991.

Janowitz, Morris. *Social Control of the Welfare State*. Chicago: University of Chicago Press, 1976.

Lebergott, Stanley. *The American Economy: Income, Wealth, and Want*. Princeton: Princeton University Press, 1976.

Owen, John D., *Working Lives: The American Work Force Since 1920*. Lexington: D.C. Heath, 1986.

Stein, Herbert. *The Fiscal Revolution in America*. Chicago: University of Chicago Press, 1969.

Weidenbaum, Murray. *Business, Government and the Public,* 4th edition. Englewood Cliffs, NJ: Prentice-Hall, 1990.

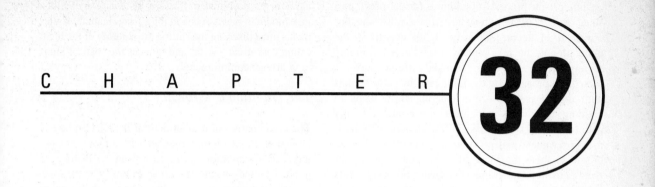

Does This History Have a Future?

It is inconceivable that a society's future could be made without the influence of its past. This book began with a discussion of the influence of England in colonial America and of the influence of colonial laws and institutions in modern America. There is nothing peculiarly American about this continuity.

The power of the "live hand of the past" astonished the world when, in Iran, a twentieth-century royal dictatorship and its modernized economic and social structures were overthrown by a vestige from the distant past. Students of modern Soviet society are amazed by the persistence of ancient Russian forms and traditions, and how quickly many of them resurfaced with the fall of the Communist state. After all the terrible events of the Communist dictatorship in modern Chinese history, Richard Nixon sat down in Peking to a sumptuous dinner of Mandarin delights. The entire cuisine of that ancient culture survived Mao, the Great Leap Forward, and the Cultural Revolution.

Complex human institutions live through time; indeed, institutions are the legacy passed between the generations in any society. It has been so in the United States, and it doubtless will be so in its future. What this means is that a country's recent past cannot be tossed aside. Inasmuch as the malfunctioning American welfare state was created with methods to meet its demands, it will endure. The question, "Who will create the future?" is best answered: "To some extent, those who made the past."

ASSETS

This book has traversed a long route, all the way back to the Virginia colony and even beyond. It will be useful now to summarize those principal elements that sustained the country's economic success, its assets. Similarly, it will be useful, in another part of this chapter, to examine the liabilities in this history, those parts of its history that have raised problems and left its people less well-off than they otherwise might be and that perhaps threaten them with worse in the future.

Secure Property Rights

Even though such developments as modern taxation, eminent domain law, zoning, land-use restrictions, and other regulations have reduced the scope of individual control of private property, so strong was the original property-right endowment that Americans still work to acquire private property of all kinds for their own personal gain. The lure remains. Historically, the endowment of secure property rights energized the population as much as private interest ever did in any society. People were willing to make extreme sacrifices to acquire property rights, to engage in undertakings with distant payoffs—from clearing farm lands to building steel mills—in the hope of personal or family gain from property ownership. In a society with minimal government and no particular centrally directed programs about the shape of its economic future beyond constitutional consensus, secure property rights left the future essentially to the people themselves.

Secure Traditions of Private Contract

All activities founded upon the use of credit, so necessary in any economy dominated by private exchanges of goods and services, require a settled expectation about the security of future commitments. The so-called English legacy was nowhere stronger than in the law of contract and the organization of society to enforce contracts. Americans might well now cringe in horror at the strength of this tradition in earlier times: for example, court enforcement of sales of human beings for life or of their forced labor for terms of years. But such adherence to agreement *in principle* underpinned all private transactions and made the private ownership and control of productive resources all the more powerful as an instrument for economic progress. In the contract clause of the federal Constitution, the power of private contract was even elevated above the legislative powers of the sovereign states themselves: thus, *Dartmouth College* v *Woodward*.

Calculable Law

Americans have been frustrated at times by the very stability of their legal institutions—for example, the "nine old men" (Supreme Court) who killed the first New Deal. It is not easy to achieve basic legal change. Legislatures may pass laws, but the common-law tradition, together with written constitutions against which all legislation is measured, make judicial review a necessity for legislation to become law. The very difficulty of achieving radical change through legislation, however, adds substantial stability to private estimates of future values and adds motivation to all contractual

agreements designed to yield a distant return. Since investment in real assets and long-term financial settlements must discount the future, the stability of the legal framework greatly eases and reduces the costs of planning private commitments.

The Tradition of Growth

The combination of a great natural resource to be exploited at the beginning together with a rapidly growing, *able* population, gave Americans a history of unprecedented overall economic growth. That history, the national experience, produced a built-in optimism about the future that induced decision making in anticipation of further growth. As old J. P. Morgan once put it, anyone who was "bearish" on America's future would surely go broke. Optimism was a self-fulfilling prophecy. The American economy in part succeeded because it had already succeeded. The American people have come to expect economic improvement, and they tend to deal abruptly at election time with those political regimes that fail to deliver it, or at least the politically generated parts of it.

Social Mobility

Many large, extended, American families contain samples of widely different personal incomes, educational achievements, life-styles, and varieties of economic endeavor—a sister who is a physician, an uncle who works in a factory, a great-aunt who still lives on the family farm, and a distant cousin who lives in a commune in northern California. While such varying life-styles add variety and excitement to personal experience, they also reflect a very important reality: the country has no readily identifiable or effective system of class barriers. Money—how much you have, not where you got it or what you do with it—is the main measure of social achievement. While undeniably crass, it is an economically progressive attitude.

The founders forbade "patents of nobility" and thus released the energies of a whole people. The idea was that anybody could be anything. Immigrants still pour across the borders of the United States because of *opportunity*—it is said all over the world that you can be what you achieve in American society. A long string of landed ancestors is of little advantage if the current "bottom line" is financial incompetence. The public educational system that reaches *by law* into every home ensures that, one way or another, every American child can be placed upon the course of personal improvement in a society whose social barriers are fairly porous. Racial and sexual discrimination, legacies of the distant past, have been the major formal barriers to social mobility. For years, reformers have struggled against these anachronisms.

The more social mobility a country has in it, the greater is the chance that talent will not be involuntarily wasted. The more talent is exercised, the nearer the society comes to achieving whatever potential it possesses in its people. While Americans constantly try to increase their social mobility, they already are the "world champions" at this game. It is easier to make it in life if you are born to affluence or are white, more difficult if you are born to poverty or are black; but American society, more than any other, has kept the door to personal achievement open through its social mobility. As Stanley Lebergott has shown, the United States still is a nation of *nouveaux riche.*[1] However gauche, it is a positive force for economic betterment. The top wealth holders now are not the same ones who were in that category two decades ago.

Acceptance of Technological Change

American history is full of conflict produced by the ready acceptance, even *eager* acceptance, of new ideas, new products, new practices—of innovation in general. Whole towns and settled regions are wholly or partly abandoned, populations sent into migration, in the wake of this force. New areas boom, while old ones die. New firms expand, while old ones fail. The recent migrations away from the Snow Belt into the Sun Belt are a contemporary manifestation of this phenomenon.

This love of the new goes deeply into American life, from the kitchen to the factory. It is both a productive and a disruptive force. Businesses fail when their products lose favor, and families are left without financial support. Schumpeter tied the introduction of innovation to the entrepreneurial function in business growth and referred to the outcome as the "process of creative destruction": The realignment of factors of production to embrace both failure and success generates economic growth. As Burton Klein put it, **macroeconomic stability**—growth at something like full employment through technological change—relies

upon **microeconomic instability**—the competitive jostling for markets and control over resources.[2] The dynamic force has been the encouragement and acceptance of innovative technological change. The process maintains a steady element of riskiness in private economic endeavor.

Popular Democracy

The fact that Americans as a people collectively create their own disasters as well as triumphs, from the school board to the White House, adds long-term stability to American economic life. It is quite pointless to advocate violence and upheaval in American life to create social change; the United States *already* has a steady diet of violence and upheaval, together with fundamental social change, and it is all of its own making. Elections come *by the calendar.* Any adult citizen can vote if he or she wants to vote, for whatever candidate, proposal, or political party grabs his or her fancy. Although Winston Churchill once said of democracy that it is an appalling form of government, there is none better. While the United States is faced with carelessness, corruption, abuses of power, and apathy, it has only itself to blame for them.

However dismaying this all seems at any moment of time, in the long run it guarantees the permanence of the forms of the American government. Popular democracy adds to long-term political stability even if it is chaotic at any specific point in time. The system can always be improved, always be reformed; however maddening, it is never hopeless. As a result, the American republic of popular democracy goes on, through good times and bad, war and peace, tranquility and upheaval.

The lack of a serious threat of an irregular change of governmental form adds motivation to investment and to economic growth. Government is not just offices and officeholders; it is a form of collective decision-making. American government is ordered by rules to an astonishing degree. Reflect for a moment on parliamentary procedure. From the student-council meeting to the Senate of the United States, like English-speaking peoples all over the world, Americans live by accepted set of rules. It is not a matter of law; no one requires *Robert's Rules of Order.* Like the rules of language, these rules are simply accepted as the *only* legitimate form. It is a most extraordinary thing. These rules of democratic decision-making prevent both mob rule and dictatorship alike. They also leave the most skilled political demagogues in constant danger of defeat.

Popular democracy is made effective by its settled rules and procedures. In the end, the people can rule themselves because there is a generally accepted machinery with which to do it. *No man, woman, or party could rule in the United States in violation of that machinery.* In American society, parliamentary procedure is the *only* road to legitimate power. Savers and investors can know that radical innovations in the forms of political power cannot come by coup. If the United States were ever to become a "banana republic," it would be by these procedures.

LIABILITIES

The recognition that there is potential for failure forces a consideration of what this history suggests about the methods Americans normally employ that may reduce their potential, that darken their economic future.

Dilution of Property Rights

The classic rights of property are the use, abuse, and fruits of that property. Exploitation of these rights makes ownership desirable, worth struggling to attain. Such rights—and cognate productive motivations—can be weakened in various ways. As the rights weaken, so do the motivations to exploit them.

In recent decades, property rights have been weakened for various reasons. Cumulatively, the dilution of property has been powerful, particularly the taxing of its "fruits," the income generated by that property. In extreme cases, as in some inner-city slums, a peculiarly lethal combination of taxes and regulation has led to actual abandonment of property by its owners. There, arson becomes a profit-making game (through insurance payments). The result is a socially destructive and profitless wasteland. Taxes, jobs, living space, all are lost. The only solution is to condemn property, clear titles, and transfer the property to new owners—a costly procedure. It is rare indeed for a private owner to destroy his or her own property, but the revenue needs and social-control ambitions of government can so dilute the rights of ownership that private development stops. Property taxes placed upon the value of small, private improvements to property are probably the most notorious and wrong-headed example of this effect.

Moreover, widespread property ownership has traditionally "bonded" the American social community together despite economic and political differences between different owners. As Selig Perlman emphasized in his *Theory of the Labor Movement,* the commitment of American labor to peaceable methods and to social stability has always been rooted in accessibility to property ownership, which gave the worker a fixed interest in the established order. For that reason, American labor has adhered to established political parties and has not indulged in extensive support of modern revolutionary movements. In the spirit of reform, the institution of zoning, land-use rules, and building codes as well as outright taxation can dilute ownership to the point where the desire to acquire and control property vanishes, and with it, the social stability associated with it. A drive through any urban slum illustrates the deleterious consequences of property-rights dilution by unwise governments.

Since the late nineteenth century, the dilution of property rights has escalated as governments at all levels have needed revenues and as social reform has created an ever-widening network of restrictions upon the acquisition and uses of property. In the process, the economy has lost some of the improving motives inherent in property ownership. There is a need for greater wisdom than in the past if Americans want to regain and enlarge those motives that are responsible for their present wealth. As long as the whole fabric of American society is rooted in property ownership, it is foolish to weaken it as a mere side effect of other objectives.

Collective Goods and Resistance to Technological Change

Throughout American history, groups have banded together to achieve the economic gains that they could not realize as individuals operating in the free market. Merchant groups, trade organizations, farmer and industrial lobbies, labor unions, all have tried and succeeded in gaining special advantages by collective action. Tariffs and subsidies (given, primarily, to business groups), closed entry to competition by law (given to labor unions since the Wagner Act), special privileges from licensing (given to monopoly groups, from public utilities to doctors, lawyers, and school teachers), protection of farm cooperatives and even Major League Baseball from the antitrust laws—all and more are examples from American economic history of special advantages gained by collective action.

The gains from such organization, called **collective goods** by Mancur Olson in his insightful book, *The Logic of Collective Action: Public Goods and the Theory of Groups,* are greater than competitive profits.[3] It is characteristic of collective goods that the gains from them can only be captured by the relevant special-interest groups. The consumer pays the bill. Resources are attracted to such noncompetitive employments, and a less than optimal allocation results.

There is a further danger from such noncompetitive groupings of economic power—resistance to technological change. Technological change is disruptive, and work is partly distasteful. As Olson points out, where special privilege protected by law makes it possible to resist change and to slack-off work efforts, the result will be technological backwardness and low worker productivity. In a world of international competition where rivals are not "soldiering on the job" or resisting the flow of innovations to an equal extent, protected U.S. industries can fall behind, losing markets abroad and even at home if imports are allowed.

In the 1970s in some parts of the electronics, manufacturing, autos, steel, and chemicals industries, these effects began to be seriously felt. Out-of-date capital equipment matched by nonproductive work rules wiped out the country's competitive edge. Those employers and labor unions more seriously affected went to Washington, D.C., to ask for protection. Since anti-competitive protection was the origin of the trouble, it hardly followed that a further dose of the same medicine would help solve the problems.

Since the American government is a popular democracy where vote-seeking politicians are open to rent-seeking and special-interest pressures, the country's economic future can easily be blighted in what would appear as a perfectly "natural" pattern of responses to economic change. Those who gain collective goods, single-interest groups, are constantly at work seeking the rents derived from special privilege, and the rest of society must be on guard or else be stuck with the bill. Publicity and open debate are the best safeguards.

Big Business, Big Government, and Barriers to Entrepreneurship

Innovation in economic life is the primary cause of advance. Innovation does not just crawl ashore on dark nights like some bizarre mutant. Technological change must be *introduced* by those to whom such innovation is profitable. John Kenneth Galbraith in his book, *The New Industrial State,* makes a useful differentiation between the *entrepreneurial firm* and the bureaucratic ways of present-day giant corporations.[4] Some of the latter were of course once leaders in progressive technological innovation, and, indeed, for that reason became large firms. The major building block in the 1901 merger that created U.S. Steel was Carnegie Steel, of which it can be said that there never was a more revolutionary competitive innovator; but that was long ago. Today's big businesses run by committees of experts, what Galbraith calls the *technostructure,* tend to be stodgy and conservative.

Despite Big Business' current lethargy, any potential competitor still has to face all the financial advantages of a successful past. As a result, the weight of the past has provided a barrier to innovation from entrepreneurial firms. Taxation, which deals equally with all businesses, differentiating only according to reported profits, adds complications. Heavy income taxes have been especially hard upon entrepreneurial firms that must grow from visible taxable income. The efforts by the federal government to reduce those taxes in 1981 were a straightforward admission that the taxes have been excessive.

Entrepreneurial firms cannot easily hide behind a portfolio of tax-exempt investments. To grow, there must be earnings from their major activities, and those earnings are visible and taxable. So, demands for transfers of resources from productive activities to government place limits upon the nation's entrepreneurial resources.

It is a hard problem. Government needs taxes, and entrepreneurial businesses need resources for growth. Judging from past performance, the country's standards in this area of fiscal planning can bear improvement. It is not a problem that has been confronted directly. It first appeared seriously in World War II and must be solved ultimately, or else some other way must be found to produce innovation in the economy. The reliance on private-sector entrepreneurship until the

1930s was a source of strength, but continued reliance upon it during a time when government expenditure came to occupy 40 percent of the GNP has proved to be a source of grievous weakness. Indifference to the problem in an age of Big Government and Big Business has led to a loss of position in the competitive international economy and has slowed down the rate of U.S. economic growth. It is not difficult to be pessimistic about this. Jonathan Hughes' work demonstrated how effortlessly and naturally this country is willing (and able) to resort to government to offset unpopular market outcomes. In recent work, Robert Higgs emphasizes the uses of government in the past century to overcome crises (wars, financial panics, depressions) and the lingering, ''ratchet effects'' of the techniques, either in intellectual or in institutional forms. But when will the crises ever cease?[5]

Racism, Sexism: The Stumbling Blocks

Even though the United States has been called the ''land of opportunity,'' the door opens much more easily for white males than it does for females and minorities. Racial and sexual discrimination continue to plague the country. These prejudices are of ancient and diffuse cultural origins. Only in recent years have concerted, sustained policies based upon new laws (and new interpretations of old laws) at both federal and state levels been implemented in an attempt to suppress and ultimately eliminate their influences from American life.

That distinguished scholars, scientists, writers, artists, jurists, and political and business leaders now flourish in all walks of American life who are women and/or members of racial minorities is proof enough of the sad losses to this nation's intellectual and economic growth that discrimination produced in the past. More than half (women plus minorities) of this nation's distributed ability has been suppressed historically by discrimination. The United States is poorer needlessly in every way as a result. Eliminating systematic discrimination is not a simple matter, however, as should be well-known by now. Progress had been made, but the problem remains.

Since World War II, great strides have been made in the fight to eliminate racial discrimination. Truman did away with segregated military facilities. The Eisen-hower years saw the Supreme Court decision that moved to stop segregated schooling. The Civil Rights Act of 1964 led eventually to the affirmative action quotas of the 1970s. All of this has helped move many American blacks into the American economic mainstream.

The legacy of slavery and the one hundred years of discriminated ''freedom'' following the Civil War, however, left behind a huge black population—found in all American cities and the rural South—unable to cope in a competitive free market. These people's ancestors moved to the cities, especially Northern cities, to seek mostly manufacturing jobs. In most cases, their only qualification was a strong back. Now, these jobs have largely disappeared in the move from an industrial to a service economy. As was discussed in Chapter 29, minimal education requirements now exist for most jobs. At the height of our worst recessions, any Sunday newspaper job section remains full of listings for thousands of unfilled jobs because the minimal education requirements go unmet.

This segment of our black population is falling economically behind the rest of the nation year by year and threatens to become a permanent underbelly. It is a potential time bomb that periodically has exploded in urban riots. If this country does not reach out to these people with some economic incentives or jobs programs, the ability of the U.S. economy to compete in the international arena will be diminished because the welfare costs of supporting the unemployable will become a permanent pressure for budget deficits.

Maintaining the Welfare State

There must be some combination of taxes and transfer payments that is not destructive to the family prospects of the taxpayers and that yet meets the reasonable needs of the aged, ill, infirm, and disabled. Thus far, the American record for discovering that viable combination has been fairly dismal. The social insurance system, the core of which is ''Social Security,'' is the product of half a century of building on the legislation of 1935. It has grown piece by piece, with no overall plan to its pattern of development. Needs were met without correct reckoning of their costs. As a result, the tax rates have steadily increased, with the poorest paying proportionately the most. New higher rates were applied in 1980, and even so, by 1981, HEW officials reported that the system would not be able to meet its commitments by 1982. In that year it was agreed that funds could be borrowed to pay Social Security benefits to retirees. The Reagan administration began what it called "a great reassessment."

The entire apparatus of the American welfare state has become of fundamental importance in the American economy. There is no real possibility that the United States will return to the way of life that existed in the Great Depression. That world has largely vanished. Millions of workers have faithfully paid taxes for decades to support the Social Security system. The country's economic future cannot now be separated from the network of the Social Security system. The rest of society has moved on and adapted to Social Security over the decades. Family life has changed in response to it, individual provision for medical insurance, unemployment protection, retirement in old age, all have changed because of Social Security.

Important as the system is, its own impact upon the population has been a mixed blessing. Parts of the system are known to have perverse effects, (e.g., breaking up families, creating increased dependency and other forms of social incompetence). Moreover, the United States is the only economically advanced nation with no comprehensive national health system. Not only is its welfare inflationary and defective, it is not even as comprehensive as those of western European countries. It must be reworked from "stem to stern," a challenge the Clinton administration has accepted, at least with respect to health. It is a task that will not necessarily be politically rewarding, but a majority of Americans are reported to favor addressing the issue. Whether they will accept the consequences remains to be seen.

Economic Policy and Inflation

Meeting the promise of modern fiscal policy has proved to be far more difficult than economists imagined it would be. The mechanism for a truly "discretionary" policy exists, but the political competence to operate it without the malign side effects of steady inflation vanished in the 1960s. The Federal Reserve link between Treasury expenditures and the monetary system has proved to be lethally inflationary, making hash

of family financial planning and disrupting life-cycle saving and consumption patterns.

The separate existence and autonomy of the American nuclear family has been historically the center of the American social system, producing the sequence of the generation, sustained and educated for productive life; the property and incomes to be taxed; the support of the educational system as well as the children to be educated. All this has been assailed by government-induced inflation. Without a stable base for family life and new family formation, the American economy has no logic to it; yet, the rising divorce rates, low birth rates and population growth, and punitively high housing costs all reflect the callous disregard for family life produced by three decades of pork-barrel federal fiscal operations. Unless the nation moves into a fantasy world of communal life, the undeclared war against the American family being waged from Washington, D.C., must cease. It is not the case that the man or woman who gets up each day and works at productive employment for the welfare of self and family is an "enemy of the people," yet this country's federal income-tax laws daily sabotage these workers' attempts to get ahead of inflation.

Some regard for the taxpayers, either direct or through reduction of inflation, must become an object of fiscal policy (an idea notably absent for some years in Congress), or the people will continue to "vote with their feet," to find ways of living outside the federal fiscal system. Already there is a booming "underground economy" to which Americans are increasingly driven by mindless taxation of productive effort. The IRS has the dubious distinction of having driven the world's most commercial society into extensive barter and massive tax avoidance.

The Regulated Life

Government regulation now reaches everything, from butter to steel. This book has discussed how government regulation has been motivated variously by religion, morals, politics, economics, safety, and public health. The current system, perhaps better called a "nonsystem," from barbershops to nuclear power plants, is totally congenial with American laws and constitutions. It is what *Americans* want. Although technological backwardness through regulation has been imposed purposely at times, that has not usually been the object of regulation, merely a widespread side-effect.[6] The result of regulation is rarely the motive for it. As Bruce Owen and Ron Braeutigam point out in *The Regulation Game: Strategic Use of the Administrative Process,* the process of regulation tends to be its own outcome.[7]

Although *deregulation* is a currently popular political slogan used by ambitious vote-seekers, it is a most unlikely prospect. The regulation of private economic activity by government is as old as government itself on this continent. It is unlikely to vanish because economists and politicians try to wave it away by free-enterprise incantations during election years. It would require a "laissez-faire dictatorship"—a truly crazy idea—to remove regulation of private economic activity from the province of government powers. What can be done is to develop a set of uniform criteria for deregulation based on *some* rational basis. What has been developed in the history of the American economy is a regulatory junk pile that makes no general sense at all. Illogical regulation confounds enterprise and economic progress. A rational motivation is confronted by mandatory nonsense.

Americans have an absolute passion to control economic activity by government, to create social objectives by forcing economic life into regulated patterns, however. It is a most deeply rooted passion and will not likely be eliminated by the processes of popular democracy. Since it now is ubiquitous, it is reasonable to try to seek rational criteria for its reform. One might even begin with the simple question: Which parts of the economy, if any, might better serve the commonwealth by *total exclusion* from government regulation. Is the answer *none*? In that case, the "underground economy" will continue to grow and flourish. Even if it is true that there would be no benefit, the legal economy's future would be brighter if some general criteria for regulation could be agreed upon, because Americans will continue to regulate.

Must the regulation be so destructive of economic progress, as it has been thus far? If so, enthusiasts for regulation would serve the country's future by explaining *why*. **Sunset laws,** which are regulatory self-destruct systems after some fixed period of time, would be a great contribution. If no system of regulation could last longer than, say, ten years without a renewed warrant, there might be a great transformation. It is possible to improve upon the methods of government regulation.[8] A contemporary accounting must ultimately consider our capability to develop further.

NET WORTH

Any balance sheet contains a statement of capital and surplus, the ultimate ownership of any going concern. It usually consists of the capital stock, together with the surplus, which are invested in the assets of the firm. The difference between the assets and liabilities is net worth. Pushing the metaphor for a moment, let's apply it to the United States, and to that part of its capital that is human. What generations of Americans have produced, despite all the errors and disasters, is a population that can live voluntarily, peacefully, and productively within its own stable institutional framework. This simple achievement has been beyond the grasp of most peoples throughout history and remains beyond their grasp today.

Human capital is impossible to measure except for specific tasks at hand. Human capital is the distributed ability to create the material and cultural necessities that are needed to sustain a viable human community and to provide a basis for further development. A wandering desert tribe has sufficient human capital to manage that way of life but not enough to educate doctors, build cities, or launch a space program. Maintaining and enlarging the complicated and productive culture of modern America requires the ability to adapt institutions and technologies to its changing needs. The United States is one of a small minority of human societies that have produced, thus far, the immense productivity of the economically advanced parts of humanity. Americans have been building their society since 1607, sometimes mindlessly, sometimes with great purpose. The measure of the country's ability to continue this process lies within the brains of its living generations. By this measure, the American economy has a very large capital indeed. With luck and sound management, it will continue to grow in the future as it has in the past.

Notes

1. Stanley Lebergott, *The American Economy: Income, Wealth, and Want* (Princeton: Princeton University Press, 1976), p. 161.

2. Burton Klein, *Dynamic Economics* (Cambridge: Harvard University Press, 1977).

3. Mancur Olson, *The Logic of Collective Action: Public Goods and the Theory of Groups* (Cambridge: Harvard University Press, 1971).

4. John Kenneth Galbraith, *The New Industrial State* (Boston: Houghton Mifflin, 1967).

5. Jonathan Hughes, *The Governmental Habit Redux: Economic Controls from Colonial Times to the Present* (Princeton: Princeton University Press, 1991); Robert Higgs, "Crises, Bigger Government and Ideological Change: Two Hypotheses on the Ratchet Phenomenon," *Explorations in Economic History,* vol. 22, no. 1, January 1985.

6. An example is the Alaskan salmon industry. Douglass C. North and Roger LeRoy Miller, *Economics of Public Issues* (New York: Norton, 1971), pp. 104–8.

7. Bruce Owen and Ron Braeutigam, *The Regulation Game: Strategic Use of the Administrative Process* (Cambridge, MA: Ballinger Publishing Co., 1978).

8. A particularly interesting case study can be found in Peter Temin, with Louis Galambos, *The Fall of the Bell System: A Study in Prices and Politics,* New York: Cambridge University Press, 1987, a case in which antitrust was brought to bear on a regulatory problem; AT&T had become "too big to regulate."

aggregate production function a mathematical relationship that shows how the factors of production such as land, labor, and capital are transformed into national income.

---

balance of payments an accounting system for international payments in which the value of all of a country's exports (including foreign reserves) equals the value of its imports.

bill of exchange a dated order to pay (say, 90 days after issuance), conventionally drawn by a seller against a purchaser of goods or commodities delivered. An ordinary bank check on a demand deposit is a financial bill of exchange, an order to pay "at sight" unless it is postdated.

bimetallic monetary standard a currency based upon a fixed price for two precious metals at the mint or the central bank, say for both gold and silver.

break-in transport a place where one mode of transport ends and another begins, a place of loading and unloading (for example, a port where goods are taken off a railroad and put aboard a ship).

Bretton Woods system the post-World War II fixed exchange rate system mediated through the International Monetary Fund.

business cycle oscillations over time in aggregate economic activity. Of the several cycles studied, the most commonly recurring nonseasonal one is 36 to 40 months from trough (low point in production and employment) to trough.

---

call loan the species of loan made by financial institutions with potentially the shortest possible maturity—due for repayment when asked for (i.e.,

"called"). It is a loan most commonly found in money markets like New York or London.

call-money rate the interest rate charged by lending institutions for call loans.

capital the physical instruments of production, conventionally measured as replacement cost for plant, machines, or tools needed for current production. *Capital* is also often used as a financial concept, covering all costs of production except labor and raw materials.

capital equipment the tools, machinery, and physical plant needed for productive activity. For example, an oven is part of the capital equipment of a bakery.

capital gain the net increase in market value of a "capital asset" (e.g., a bond), however conceived, in excess of the purchase cost.

capital-output ratio expressed as a ratio, the amount of "capital" used to produce output in a given period of time. The amount of capital divided by the national income is the capital-output ratio.

cliometrics a neologism created by Stanley Reiter in 1960 to describe work done in the 1950s at Purdue University in economic history that utilized computers, economic theory, and mathematical statistics. It is now used to describe quantitative economic history.

collective good a term developed by Mancur Olson to describe a privilege from government; *see also* public goods.

common law the system of law originating in England based on custom or court decisions.

comparative advantage the technique or activity in which a person, firm, or economy has lower opportunity costs than in any other technique or activity.

compensating fiscal policy   the idea attributable to Keynes that fiscal policy should be countercyclical; it should be expansionary when the economy is contracting and contractionary when the economy is expanding.

conservatism   the name given to the cautious spirit of Americans by Charles Beard.

Consumer Price Index   the weighted average of prices paid by consumers for a representative "market basket" of goods and services. The weights are coefficients that represent the proportion of consumer spending on each item in the index. The CPI is thus different from the Producer Price Index (PPI), which measures prices paid for commodities at the wholesale level.

cost-push inflation   the attribution of inflation-producing powers to individual business firms' abilities to "pass along" increases in their own costs to consumers through administered price increases.

counterfactual   a plausible, but not factual, explanation.

---

deflation   a general decline in prices—the opposite of inflation.

demand deposits   bank deposits which are payable on demand; checking accounts.

depression economics   theories or explanations of economic events that may be adequate in slack periods but will not usefully explain events during full-capacity employment periods, or during inflations. The phrase commonly is applied to Keynesian economics, which was developed during the depression of the 1930s.

deregulation   the process of reducing or abolishing the allocation of resources in accord with the rulings of regulatory government bodies, such as the Interstate Commerce Commission.

derived demand   indirect demand. The demand for auto tires is mainly based upon (derived from) the demand for automobiles. If auto sales (or use) decline, so does the demand for tires. Derived demand is thus the market for intermediate goods and factors that are embodied in goods and services which consumers demand.

devaluation   a reduction in the legally specified metallic content of a country's basic monetary unit.

diminishing marginal utility   the additional satisfaction derived from the consumption of an additional unit of a good, substance, or service which diminishes as the quantity consumed increases.

discretionary policy   action or actions arbitrarily started, stopped, or varied at the will or whim of government, unlike automatic or mandatory policies.

double liability   a liability equal to twice the face value of bank stocks was imposed on bank stock owners in New York in 1827 in an effort to encourage prudence.

dumping   sales of commodities or goods abroad below the cost of production at home.

durable goods   (usually) consumer goods meant to last for repeated use, usually for some years. Automobiles and refrigerators are counted as consumer durable goods unlike food, or even clothing, which vanish relatively quickly in use.

---

economic growth   an increase in real income per capita.

eminent domain   the dominion of the state over all property through which it can condemn private property for public use, but it must pay just compensation to the owner.

entrepôt   a distribution center where goods are warehoused.

equilibrium price   the market price. The price that is produced by the free interplay of demand and supply, with zero leftover (excess) demand or supply. The equilibrium price will remain unchanged unless there is a shift either of demand or supply.

external economies   cost reductions produced outside a given productive process, hence "external" to it. Proximity to a railroad is an external economy to a manufacturer since that proximity lowers the cost of transporting both raw materials and finished goods and yet is not part of the manufacturing process itself.

---

factors of production   the inputs into the production process. There are three basic factors: labor, capital, and natural resources. In some contexts, entrepreneurship is considered to be a factor of production.

Federal Reserve system   the central bank of the United States which was designed as a system of 12 district banks and began operating in 1914.

fee simple   an estate of direct inheritance in land; what Americans came to call their land tenure.

fiat money   currency with no specie backing that is ordered by the issuing government to be full legal tender.

financial instruments   bonds, stocks, mortgages, and all other marketable documents of financial transactions and obligations.

fixed exchange rates   exchange rates which do not fluctuate with market conditions; the exchange rates of the gold standard.

Forstall system   a Louisiana system that required one-third specie reserves against notes and deposits. It also restricted state bank loans of deposited funds to commercial paper with maturities of 90 days.

fractional reserve banking   a system in which banks hold only a fraction of the deposits in reserve in the bank.

free and common socage   the basic land tenure of the United States. Among its characteristics are the following: the land is held in perpetuity; it is directly heritable; all the obligations on it are fixed; the owner has the right of waste; and it is freely alienable.

free banking   a system that originated in New York through which any group of persons could acquire a banking charter by following some general rules to register their group, agreeing to conduct banking business according to state regulations, and, in some states, agreeing to maintain specified reserves.

free rider   a person, or economic agent, that benefits from an expenditure (usually public) without making a contribution. An economic activity analogous to riding a bus without paying. Any publicly provided service *must* produce some free riding since all may utilize the service whether taxed for it or not.

free silver   a movement which sought the free coinage of silver.

free trade   international trade in which there are no barriers (tariffs, quotas, or embargoes) designed to interfere with purchases or sales in order to protect domestic producers from international competition.

full employment   labor market equilibrium in which the number of job seekers is in balance with the number of job vacancies.

full lunchpail   the main argument used in favor of protection; tariffs create jobs and prosperity at high American wages.

general inflation   a generalized increase in the consumer price index caused by excessive money growth—too much money chasing too few goods.

gold standard   an international financial system in which a country's basic monetary unit is defined as a given weight of gold.

greenbackism   the policy platform of the Greenback Party (1875–76), whose object was to repurchase the national debt (redeem it from its holders) through Treasury issues of paper money, United States Notes (''greenbacks''). The object of the policy was to lower taxes and raise farm prices.

Gross National Product   the market value of a country's newly produced goods and services that are not resold in any form during a year; commonly referred to as GNP.

---

human capital   the investment (reckoned at dollar cost) in human skills, education, and health necessary to maintain or increase the output of goods and services.

hyperinflation   inflation rates that are extraordinarily high.

---

increasing returns to scale   the case of falling costs at successively rising input levels. For example, the use of assembly lines in the production of some goods helps provide increasing returns to scale.

indentured servitude   a contract whereby individuals agreed to do certain work for a term of years in return for specified payments—mainly food, clothing, housing—or perhaps some education or training in a craft or skill.

indexed data   information that has been divided by index numbers, thereby showing the relative change between periods.

infant industry   the argument that some form of protection is necessary for new industries until they mature and are internationally competitive.

inflation   an upward movement in the average of all prices of goods and services. During inflation, prices of many individual items rise while others fall and still others see no change. Inflation is usually measured by a general price index, such as the Consumer Price Index.

injunction   in general, a judicial order requiring those to whom it is directed to take or refrain from certain actions. In particular, it was used as a legal tool against organized labor.

inputs the ingredients of output, conventionally measured as the triad of land, labor, and capital in all their forms. For example, flour and yeast are among the inputs used to make the output, bread.

intermediation the financial institutions that transform a flow of savings into a flow of investment.

joint-stock company a partnership in which each partner receives shares of transferable stock equal to the amount of his or her investment. Unlike a corporation, there is no limit on the liability. A suit against (or by) a joint-stock company usually is filed through an officer of the company.

judicial instrumentalism the ability of American jurists to stay within the general boundaries of the constitutional settlement and yet modify the substantive content of the law, the freedom to interpret the law.

Kondratieff cycle the growth cycle in capitalism lasting about 50 years; first proposed by N. D. Kondratieff (1892–1931), a Russian economist who was shot by Stalin. The ''bourgeois Kondratieff'' cycle covered the period of approximately 1846–96, trough to trough.

labor movement the attempt by organized labor to obtain legal recognition of unions and other positions favorable to unions.

labor productivity the amount of production per unit of labor.

labor-saving, labor-using machinery machines used either to displace labor (in case of labor scarcity) or to employ it (in case of labor abundance.)

legal tender money which, under the law, may be tendered (offered) in payment of debts and which may not be refused by the creditor.

long-run supply the movement of effective output (supply) capacity over time at various prices.

macroeconomic stability overall economic activity sustained by investment and technological change sufficient to maintain full employment and adequate economic growth.

Malthusian pressure the case where population increase imposes economic hardship, such as starvation.

margin the amount a customer has deposited with a broker to provide against loss on transactions. Usually expressed as a percentage of the total, it represents the customer's equity in such an account.

marginal propensity to import the change in imports relative to the change in GNP over a given time period.

market decision the allocation of resources by prices determined in market transactions (e.g., by the establishment of market-clearing equilibrium prices).

market failure inability of the price system to produce the socially optimal quantity.

market overt a system of established market days and sites.

mercantilism policies usually attributed to seventeenth- and eighteenth-century European governments designed to bias international trade to ensure steady current-account surpluses and thus to accumulate precious metals.

microeconomic instability an allusion to the competitive battle in the marketplace between business firms. These battles can produce local business upheavals, even bankruptcies and unemployment, but in so doing, ensure the efficient allocation of labor and resources to employment with highest productive returns. Bankruptcies and unemployment ''release'' workers and resources for more productive uses. Although it is instability locally, that instability makes for the most efficient allocation of resources in aggregate.

military-industrial complex the close relationship between the military and the firms that supply goods and services to it.

mixed economy an economy in which there are elements of both capitalism and socialism and elements of federal government regulation and control.

monetarism the school of economic thought that attributes growth of GNP to growth of the stock of money. Monetarists view inflation as a case of money growth exceeding GNP growth.

money illusion the confusion of increased money or nominal income with real income.

negative externalities uncompensated damage inflicted on the neighborhood by economic activity; for example, air pollution.

nominal values   values in terms of the current prices of a time period.

nonmarket social control   the allocation of resources by governments, religious bodies, mob action, or whatever. The opposite of a market decision. Licensing of professions is nonmarket social control.

---

opportunity cost   the maximum income (earnings) forgone as the result of a choice. For example, an account executive in a successful advertising firm has two alternatives—staying on Madison Avenue or chucking it all to raise golden retrievers in upstate New York (his lifelong dream). If he decides to breed dogs, the higher income he gives up is his opportunity cost.

---

perfect competition   a market structure in which there are many buyers and sellers, where access to the market is easy for both buyers and sellers, where no one buyer or seller can influence price, and where price is free to move without restriction.

police power   the right of government to maintain settled and peaceable conditions, by force if necessary.

preemption   the acquisition of a property right by mere occupancy—"squatting." Preemption rights before 1860 usually meant rights to purchase land previously occupied by squatting. Preemption rights also were called *squatters' rights.*

prescriptive right   the inability of one individual to use his or her property in such a way as to damage the amenity rights of another individual without being liable for damages.

price differentials   the difference in price, in different places or times, for the same item.

primary sector   agriculture, mining, fisheries, and forestry. The most basic sources of food, raw materials, and energy.

primogeniture   a system of inheritance in which the first-born son inherits the family estate.

priority rights   rights over and above prescriptive rights.

productivity   the amount of output each input factor (or all factors taken together) produce within a given amount of time.

proprietary colony   large tracts of land granted to specific individuals by the Crown. Citizens of such colonies retained all their English rights, including the right to representative government.

public goods   usually services provided by government, the use of which by a single consumer does not decrease the total supply (e.g., national defense).

---

quit rents   the bundle of fixed incidents combined into a singular periodic payment. These rents eventually became the local property taxes of modern America.

---

real assets   homes, autos, machinery, buildings; unlike financial (sometimes called "intangible") assets such as bonds and stocks.

real terms of trade   the ratio of exports to imports as measured by volume.

real values   real values calculated in constant prices. Nominal income, wages, or GNP may rise over some period, but if the rise is due strictly to inflation, then real income, real wages, or real GNP have not risen.

recession   the decline in aggregate economic activity following the peak of a business-cycle expansion; officially defined as real GNP falling for two consecutive quarters. It is usually associated with rising unemployment of people and resources.

redemptioners   largely non-English immigrants who arranged to repay the cost of passage after arrival in the United States. The repayment was often arranged by indenturing a child.

rent   returns in excess of competitive alternatives to any investment or productive outlay. The income of a concert pianist greater than the income she could earn doing the next best alternative is her rent.

rent-seeking   the allocation of resources to the pursuit of rents.

reservation price   the minimum price at which a seller will agree to sell.

reserve ratio   the percentage of deposits a bank holds in reserve; a tool of Federal Reserve monetary policy.

Residual Claimant hypothesis   the notion that falling real income in one sector of the economy implied rising real income in some other sector or sectors.

royal colony   a colony operated directly by the Crown.

Safety Fund mandatory deposit insurance in New York State that was the forerunner of the modern Federal Deposit Insurance Corporation (FDIC).

scale economies *see* increasing returns to scale.

secondary sector manufacturing and fabrication; second to the primary sector in production of food and goods.

size effect the ability of single business firms, by expanding operations over many legal jurisdictions, to evade localized nonmarket control.

social savings the difference between the actual cost of a particular activity and the opportunity cost of the next best alternative for accomplishing the identical purpose; usually expressed as a percentage of GNP.

Socialism an economic system characterized by central decision making and planning in which the state owns the factors of production.

specie gold, silver, and other metals used as coins.

speculation purchase or contract for sale of commodities, land, or securities in anticipation of price changes, rather than for use or for mere annual yield.

stagflation price inflation accompanied by stagnant real output due to unemployed resources. In recent years, U.S. monetary and fiscal policy has tried unsuccessfully to solve the riddle, "What causes stagflation and how do we get rid of it?"

Statute law law based on legislative enactments.

Suffolk System a plan whereby Suffolk Bank and other Boston banks agreed to accept and pay the notes of those country banks maintaining reserve deposits with the Boston banks.

Sunset laws rules that impose regulation for a fixed period of time. For regulation to continue, the laws must be renewed.

supply-side economics analysis of economic activity that concentrates on the elements of production costs and technological change in the determination of GNP. Used in opposition to "demand-side" economics, which focuses on determinants of consumer, business, and government expenditures.

support price a government purchase-price greater than the market price for any commodity. For example, many agricultural crops have support prices.

swing credits automatic borrowing rights among European countries associated with the Marshall Plan for European economic recovery in 1947–50.

tariff a tax on imported goods (and services) to raise a revenue and/or to prevent or reduce importation of those goods.

technostructure a word invented by John Kenneth Galbraith to describe the secondary layer of skilled personnel, engineers, scientists, production specialists, sales planners, and other skilled workers in the large modern corporation. This layer lies below top management, yet the technostructure of any firm defines its productive and innovative ability. To Galbraith, it is the technostructure, and not top management, that determines a future.

tenure the period or terms of holding property, particularly land.

terms of trade the ratio between the prices which an individual or a nation receives for what is produced and the prices of what they purchase.

tertiary sector services, professions—current economic activity counted as national income that is not directly involved in the production of food, clothing, or shelter; for example, education, restaurant meals, hotel accommodations, health care.

transactions costs the costs associated with bringing buyers and sellers together to complete a transaction.

transfer society a society which transfers wealth from the rich to the poor through government.

unit banking a system in which each bank is a separate business entity unaffiliated with any other bank.

value added the revenue received by a firm minus the cost of its materials.

wealth the sum of net saving over time. Wealth is measured as a *stock* variable, while saving is a *flow* from current income.

zero sum a situation, such as a game, where the total gains or losses are fixed, and the algebraic sum of the gains and losses equal zero. Thus what someone wins, someone else *must* lose.

Figures and Tables

p. 88: Figure 5.1. From Charles O. Paullin, *Atlas of the Historical Geography of the United States.* Copyright 1932 by Carnegie Institution of Washington. Reprinted by permission of Carnegie Institution of Washington.

p. 108: Table 6.9. From *Manpower in Economic Growth: The American Record Since 1800* by Stanley Lebergott. Copyright © 1964 by the McGraw-Hill Book Company, Inc. Reprinted by permission of the McGraw-Hill Book Company, Inc.

p. 112: Table 6.10. "Regional Income Trends, 1840–1850" by Richard Easterlin from *American Economic History* by Seymour E. Harris (ed.). Copyright © 1961 by the McGraw-Hill Book Company, Inc. Reprinted by permission of the McGraw-Hill Book Company, Inc.

p. 164: Table 9.1. From "The Decline of Steamboating on the Ante-bellum Western Rivers: Some New Evidence and an Alternative Hypothesis" by Erik F. Haites and James Mak, from *Explorations in Economic History,* Fall/1973, Vol II, No. 1, p. 35. Reprinted by permission of Academic Press, Inc. and James Mak.

p. 176: Table 10.1. Reprinted with permission of Macmillan Publishing Company from *Westward Expansion,* Fifth Edition by Ray Allen Billington and Martin Ridge. Copyright © 1982 by Macmillan Publishing Company.

p. 258: Figure 14.2. From Charles O. Paullin, *Atlas of the Historical Geography of the United States.* Copyright 1932 by Carnegie Institution of

Washington. Reprinted by permission of Carnegie Institution of Washington.

p. 274: Figure 15.2. From Charles O. Paullin, *Atlas of the Historical Geography of the United States.* Copyright 1932 by Carnegie Institution of Washington. Reprinted by permission of Carnegie Institution of Washington.

p. 275: Figure 15.3. From Charles O. Paullin, *Atlas of the Historical Geography of the United States.* Copyright 1932 by Carnegie Institution of Washington. Reprinted by permission of Carnegie Institution of Washington.

p. 276: Figure 15.4. From Charles O. Paullin, *Atlas of the Historical Geography of the United States.* Copyright 1932 by Carnegie Institution of Washington. Reprinted by permission of Carnegie Institution of Washington.

p. 277: Table 15.15. Adapted from Albert from Albert W. Niemi, Jr., *U.S. Economic History,* Second Edition. Copyright © 1980 Houghton Mifflin Company. Adapted with permission.

p. 318: Table 17.6. From *Manpower in Economic Growth: The American Record Since 1800* by Stanley Lebergott. Copyright © 1964 by the McGraw-Hill Book Company, Inc. Reprinted by permission of the McGraw-Hill Book Company, Inc.

p. 458: Table 25.4. Adapted from *Journal of Political Economy,* Vol. 84, February 1976, p. 8, by Michael R. Darby, by permission of The University of Chicago Press. © 1976 by The University of Chicago. All rights reserved.

p. 458: Table 25.5. From *Manpower in Economic Growth: The American Record Since 1800* by

Photographs

p. 1:   Library of Congress.

p. 13:   Prints Division/New York Public Library, Astor, Lenox and Tilden Foundations.

p. 32:   The New-York Historical Society, New York City.

p. 40t: Walters Art Gallery, Baltimore.

p. 40b: Courtesy of The Newberry Library, Chicago.

p. 41t: Joslyn Art Museum, Omaha, Nebraska.

p. 41b: Missouri Historical Society.

p. 48:   Library of Congress.

p. 70all: National Numismatic Collections/Smithsonian Institution.

p. 80:   The Historic New Orleans Collection.

p. 86:   Minnesota Historical Society.

p. 107:   The New-York Historical Society, New York City.

p. 128:   Library of Congress.

p. 141:   Rensselaer County Historical.

p. 142t: Courtesy American Antiquarian Society.

p. 142b: The Museum of the City of New York.

p. 143bl: The Metropolitan Museum of Art.

p. 143:   The Museum of the City of New York.

p. 147:   Library of Congress.

p. 159t: Library of Congress.

p. 159b: Carnegie Library, Pittsburgh.

p. 160tl: Gift of Mrs. John Sylvester 1936/The Metropolitan Museum of Art.

p. 160tr: Courtesy of the Bostonian Society, Old State House.

p. 160:   Library of Congress.

p. 161cr: Courtesy of The Newberry Library, Chicago.

p. 161all: Library of Congress.

p. 162t: from IU Collections, Indiana University.

p. 162b: Rogers Fund, 1942/The Metropolitan Museum of Art.

p. 188t: from THE ILLUSTRATED HISTORICAL ATLAS OF BOURBON CO., KANSAS, 1878.

p. 188b: Library of Congress.

p. 203:   Gift of the Hon. Irwin Untermyer/The Museum of the City of New York.

p. 204t: National Maritime Museum, San Francisco.

p. 204b: Security First National Bank Historical Collections/Los Angeles Public Library.

p. 205t: California Society Library.

p. 205b: The Bancroft Library, University of California, Berkeley.

p. 209tl: Gift of Mrs. Emily Crane Chadbourne/The Art Institute of Chicago. All Rights Reserved.

p. 209tr: Peabody Essex Museum, Salem.

p. 209bl: Peabody Essex Museum, Salem.

p. 209br: Signing of Declaration of Independence/Courtesy The Henry Francis du Pont Winterthur Museum.

p. 226:   Library of Congress.

p. 232:   Carnegie Library of Pittsburgh.

p. 236t: Chicago Historical Society.

p. 236b: Library of Congress.

p. 264t: The Bancroft Library, University of California, Berkeley.

p. 264b: Courtesy Southern Pacific Railroad.

p. 265t: Chicago Historical Society.

p. 265b: Culver Pictures.

p. 285t: Courtesy, Caterpillar Tractor Company, Peoria.

p. 285b: Solomon D. Butcher Collection/Nebraska State Historical Society.

p. 298all: Library of Congress.

p. 299all: Library of Congress.

p. 311b: Courtesy U.S. Steel Company.

p. 314t: Library of Congress.

p. 314b: Courtesy National Tea Company.

p. 318all: Chicago Historical Society.

p. 319t: Courtesy Oak Park Public Library.

p. 319b: Chicago Historical Society.

p. 322b: Copelin & Melander/Chicago Historical Society.

p. 323all: Chicago Historical Society.

p. 338:   Library of Congress.

p. 350b: Library of Congress.

p. 350t&c: Massachusetts Historical Society.

p. 367t: Culver Pictures.

p. 367b: Brown Brothers.

p. 378t: Lewis W. Hine Photo/George Eastman House.

p. 378b: Courtesy, Metropolitan Life Insurance Co.

p. 382t: From the Stefan Lorant Collection, PITTS-BURGH, THE STORY OF AN AMERICAN CITY (Author's Edition, Lenox, Mass.)

M

N